Skip·Beat!

Shojo Beat

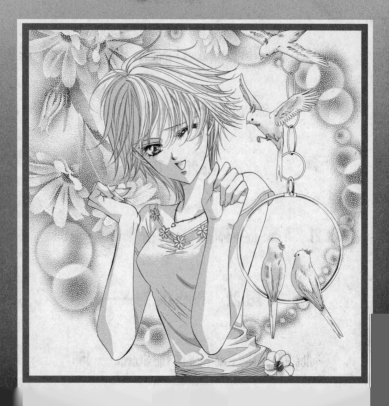

Skip·Beat!

Volume 4

CONTENTS

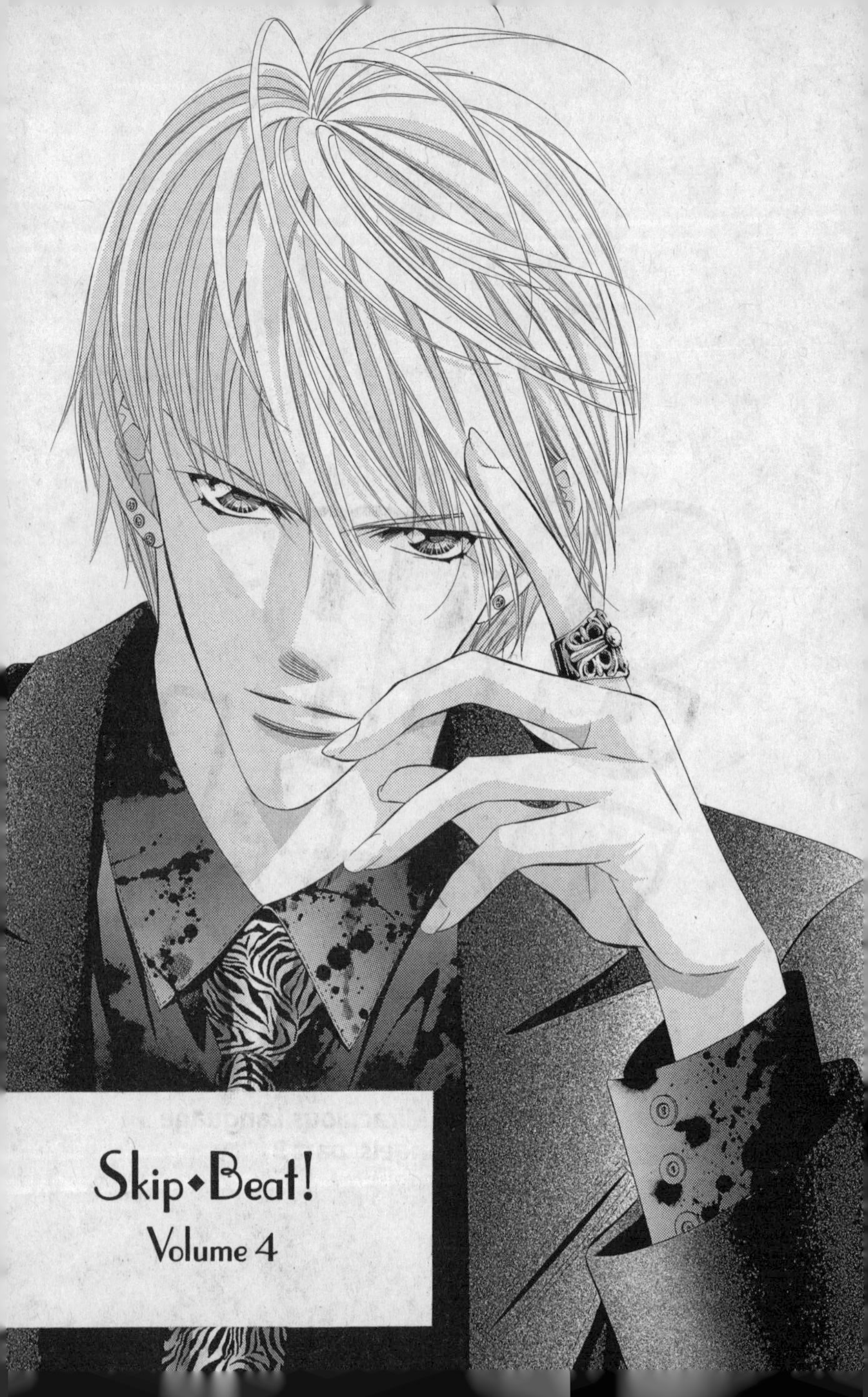
Skip◆Beat!
Volume 4

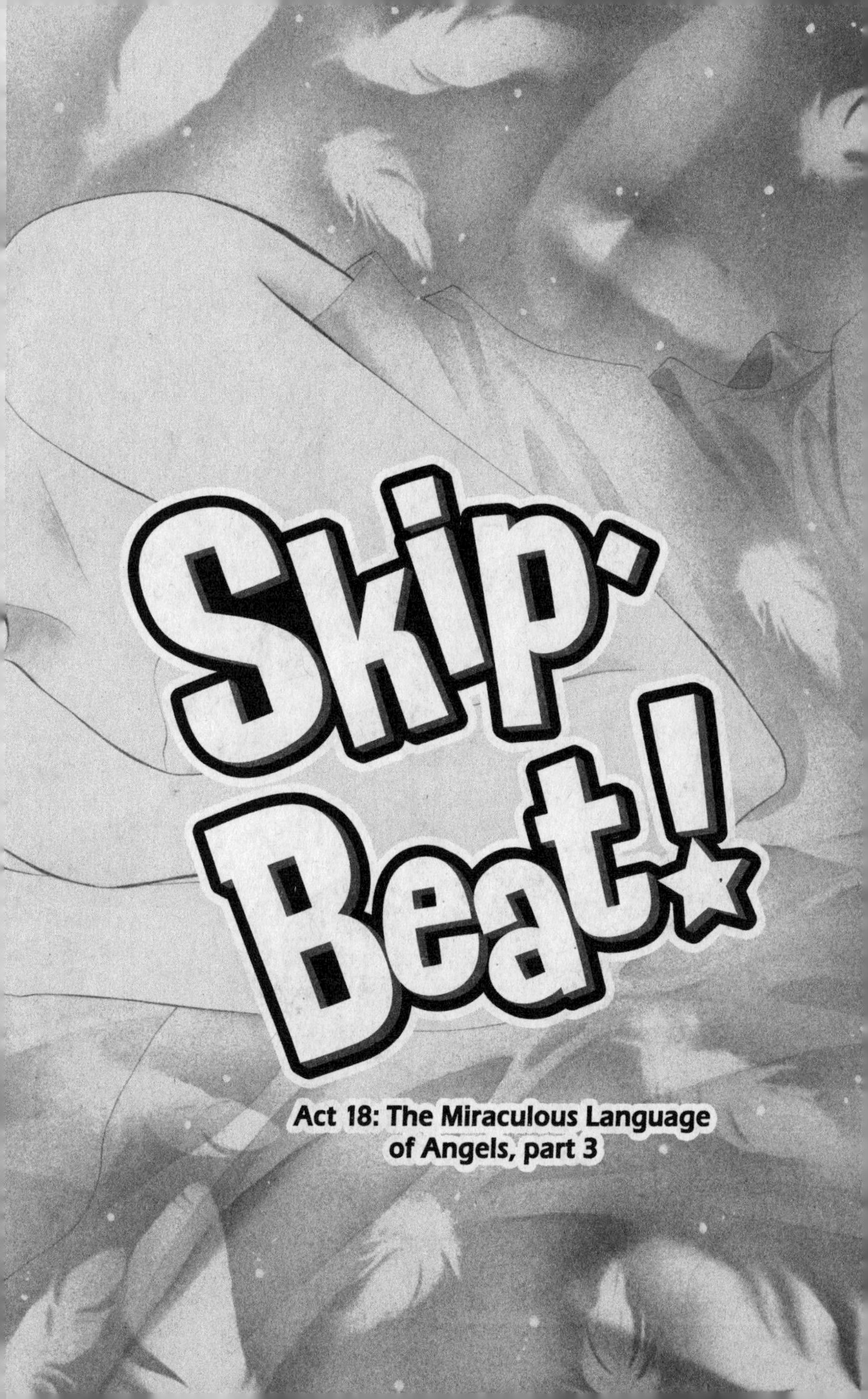
Skip·Beat!
Act 18: The Miraculous Language of Angels, part 3

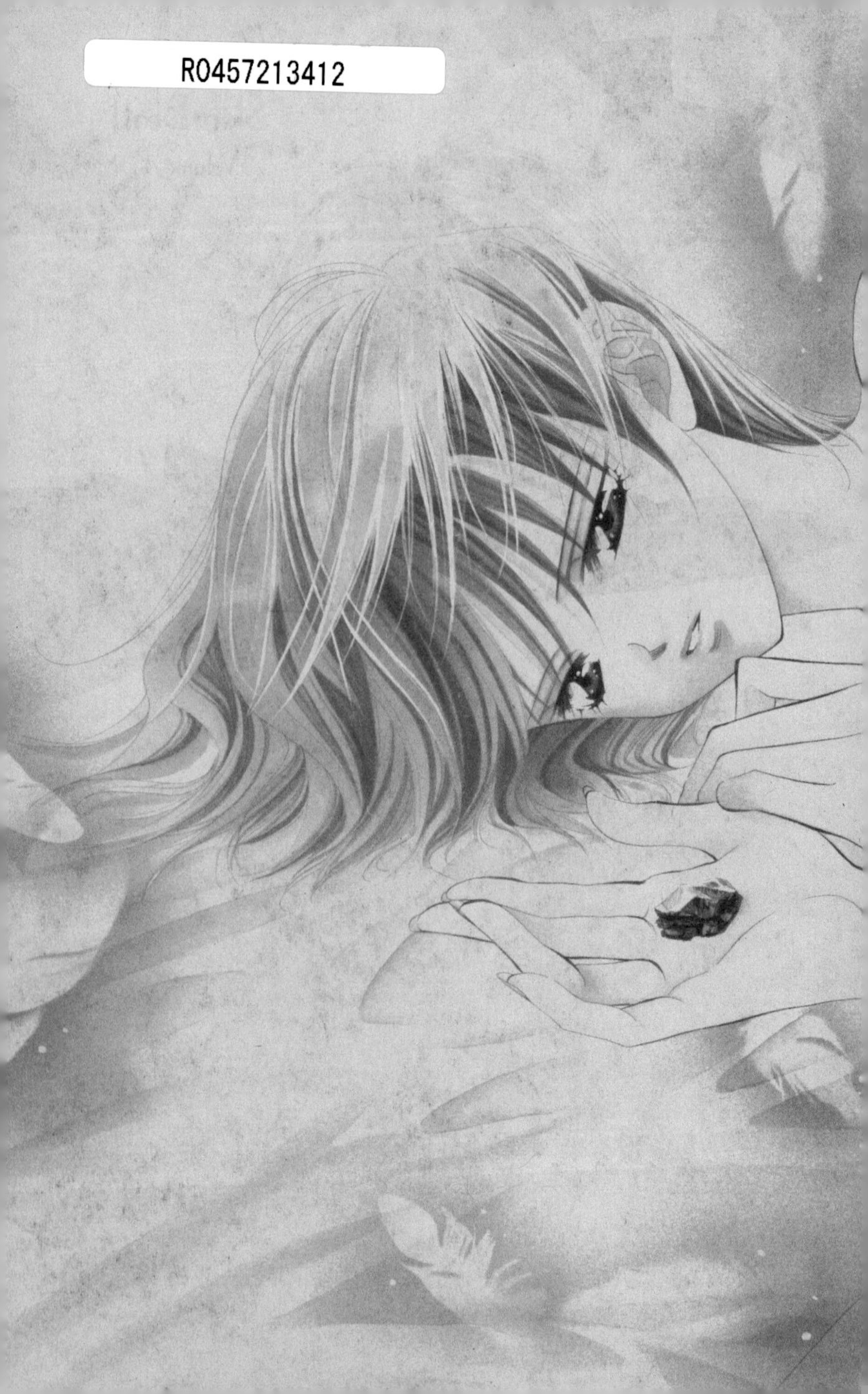

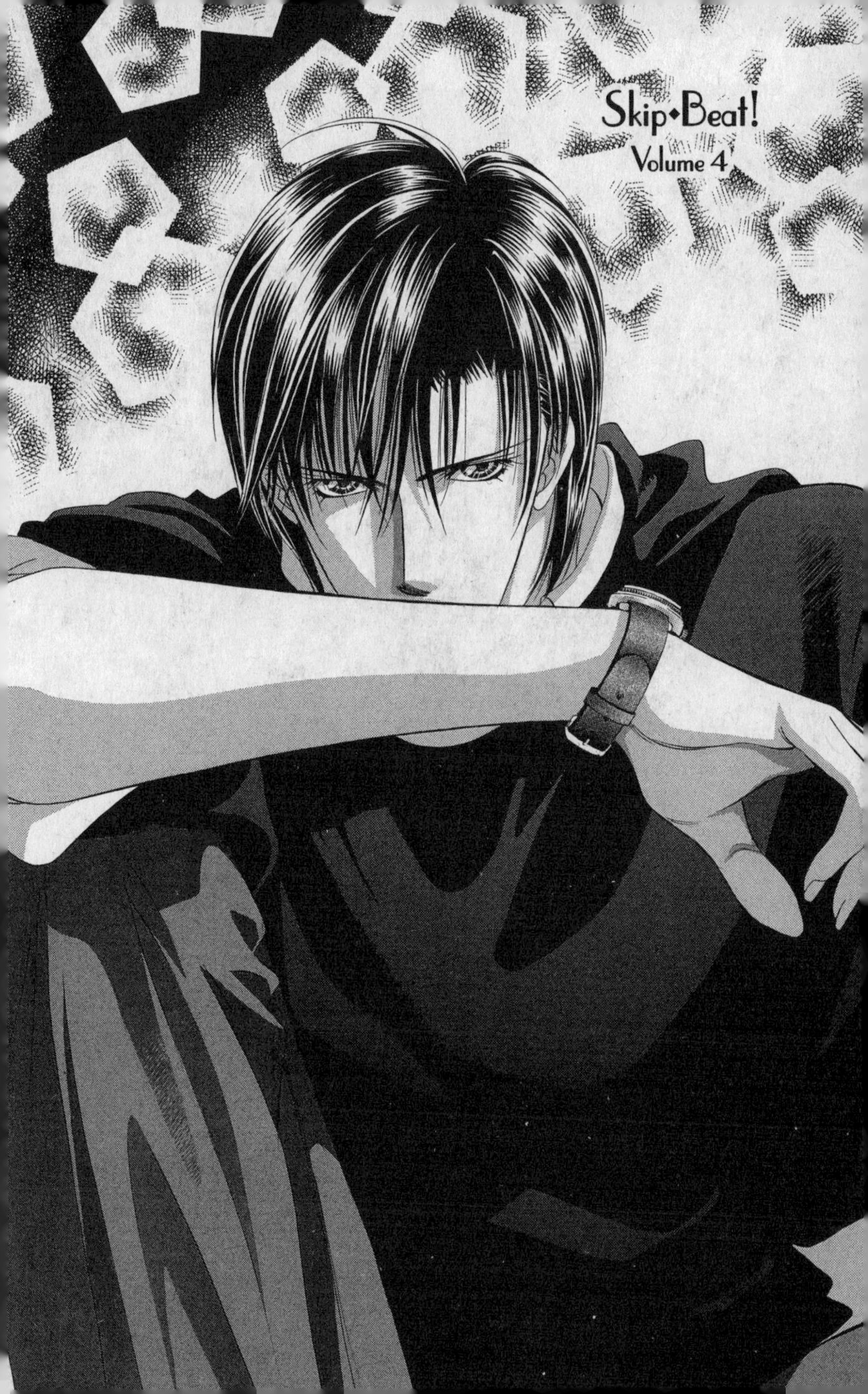
Skip•Beat!
Volume 4

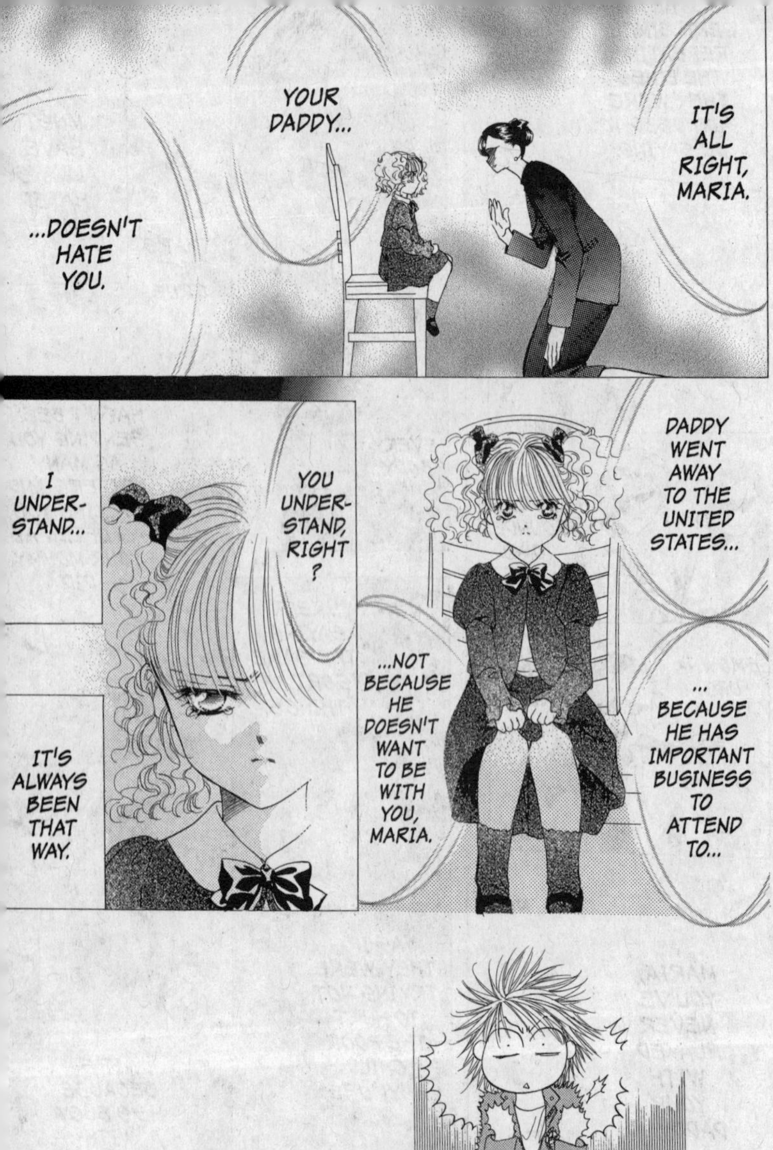
IT'S ALL RIGHT, MARIA.
YOUR DADDY...
...DOESN'T HATE YOU.
DADDY WENT AWAY TO THE UNITED STATES...
...BECAUSE HE HAS IMPORTANT BUSINESS TO ATTEND TO...
...NOT BECAUSE HE DOESN'T WANT TO BE WITH YOU, MARIA.
YOU UNDERSTAND, RIGHT?
I UNDERSTAND...
IT'S ALWAYS BEEN THAT WAY.

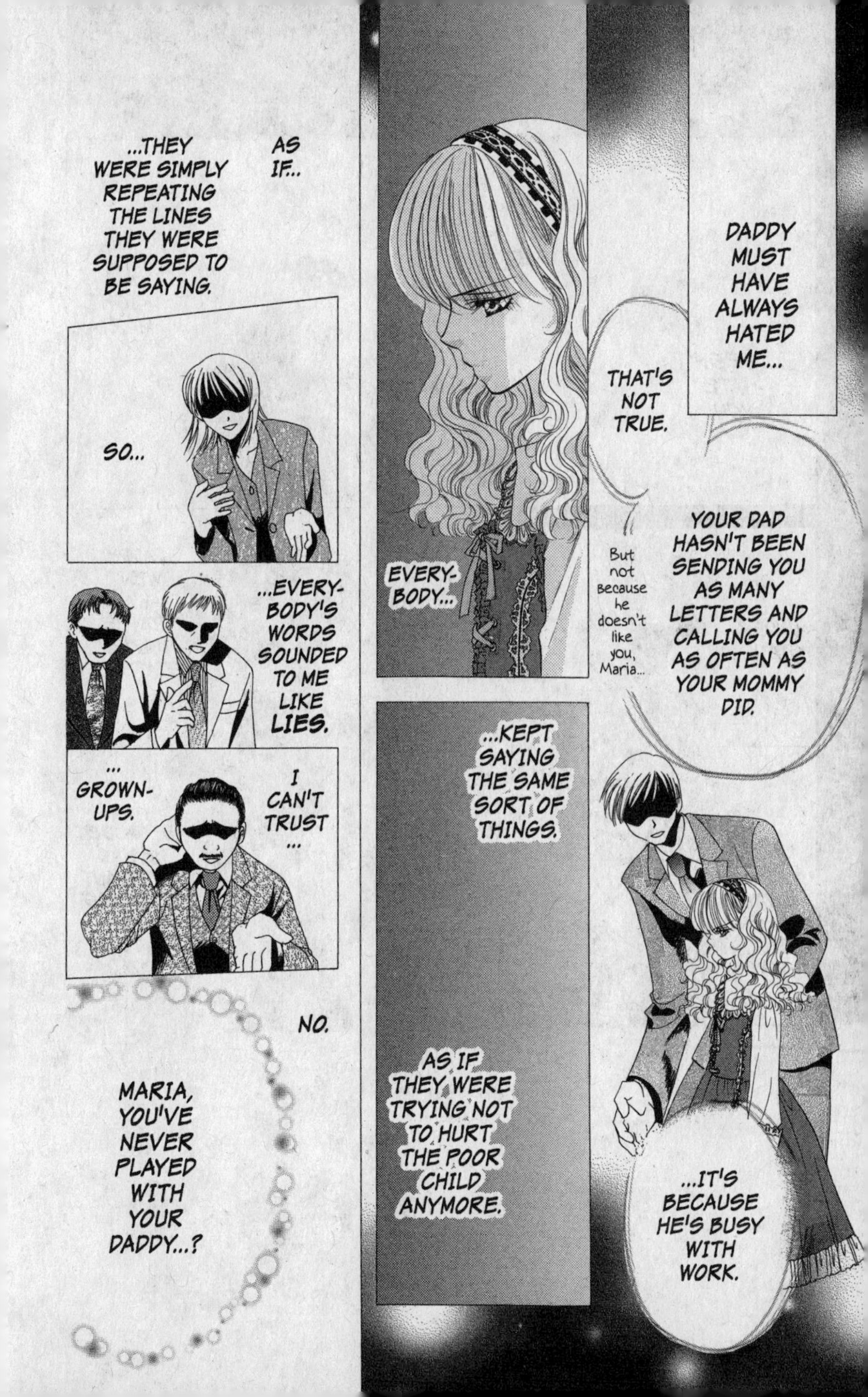
DADDY MUST HAVE ALWAYS HATED ME...
THAT'S NOT TRUE.
YOUR DAD HASN'T BEEN SENDING YOU AS MANY LETTERS AND CALLING YOU AS OFTEN AS YOUR MOMMY DID.
But not because he doesn't like you, Maria...
...IT'S BECAUSE HE'S BUSY WITH WORK.
EVERY-BODY...
...KEPT SAYING THE SAME SORT OF THINGS.
AS IF THEY WERE TRYING NOT TO HURT THE POOR CHILD ANYMORE.
AS IF...
...THEY WERE SIMPLY REPEATING THE LINES THEY WERE SUPPOSED TO BE SAYING.
SO...
...EVERY-BODY'S WORDS SOUNDED TO ME LIKE LIES.
I CAN'T TRUST ...
... GROWN-UPS.
NO.
MARIA, YOU'VE NEVER PLAYED WITH YOUR DADDY...?

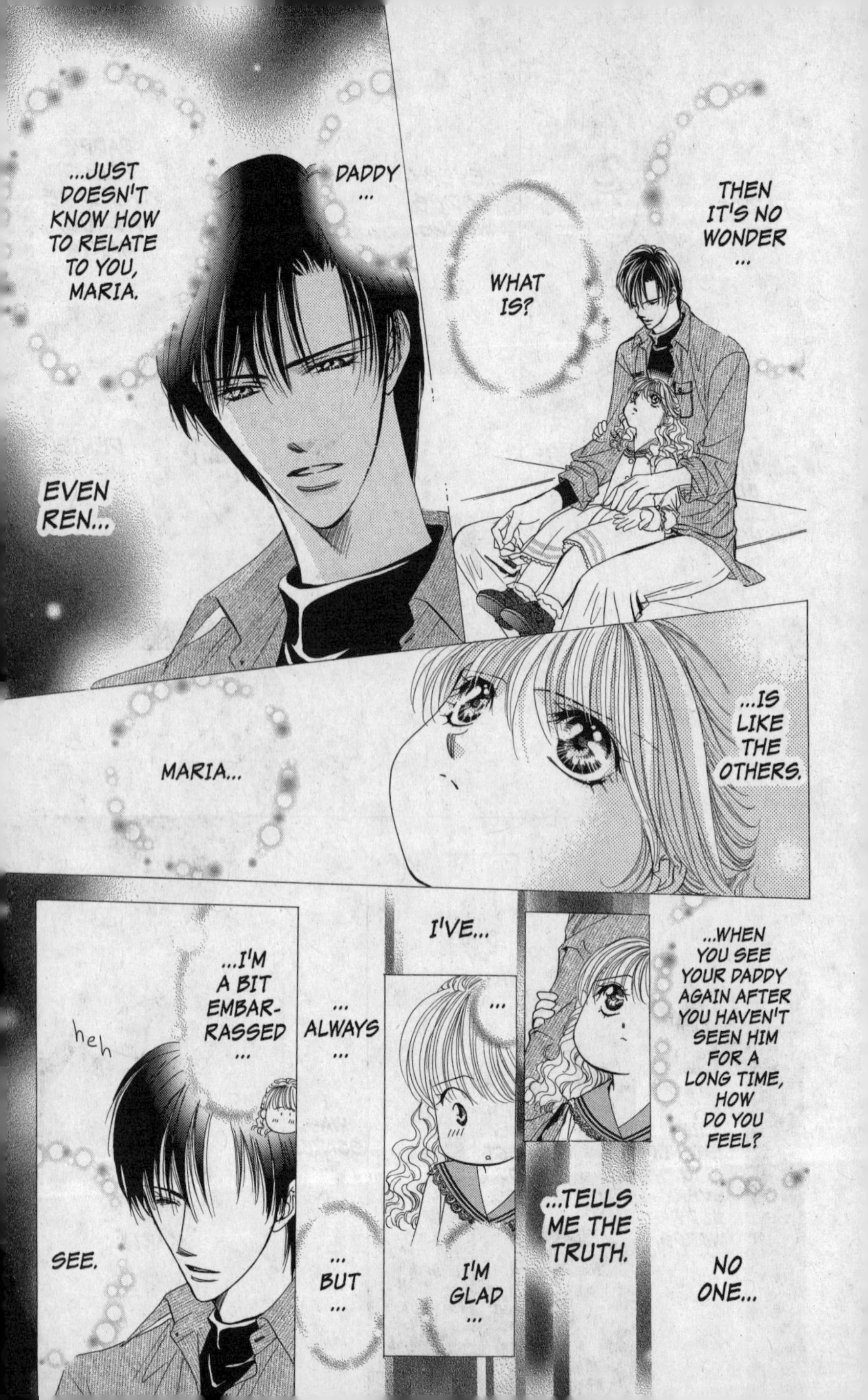
THEN IT'S NO WONDER ...
WHAT IS?
DADDY ...
...JUST DOESN'T KNOW HOW TO RELATE TO YOU, MARIA.
EVEN REN...
...IS LIKE THE OTHERS.
MARIA...
...WHEN YOU SEE YOUR DADDY AGAIN AFTER YOU HAVEN'T SEEN HIM FOR A LONG TIME, HOW DO YOU FEEL?
NO ONE...
...TELLS ME THE TRUTH.
I'VE...
...
... ALWAYS ...
I'M GLAD ...
... BUT ...
...I'M A BIT EMBAR-RASSED ...
heh
SEE.

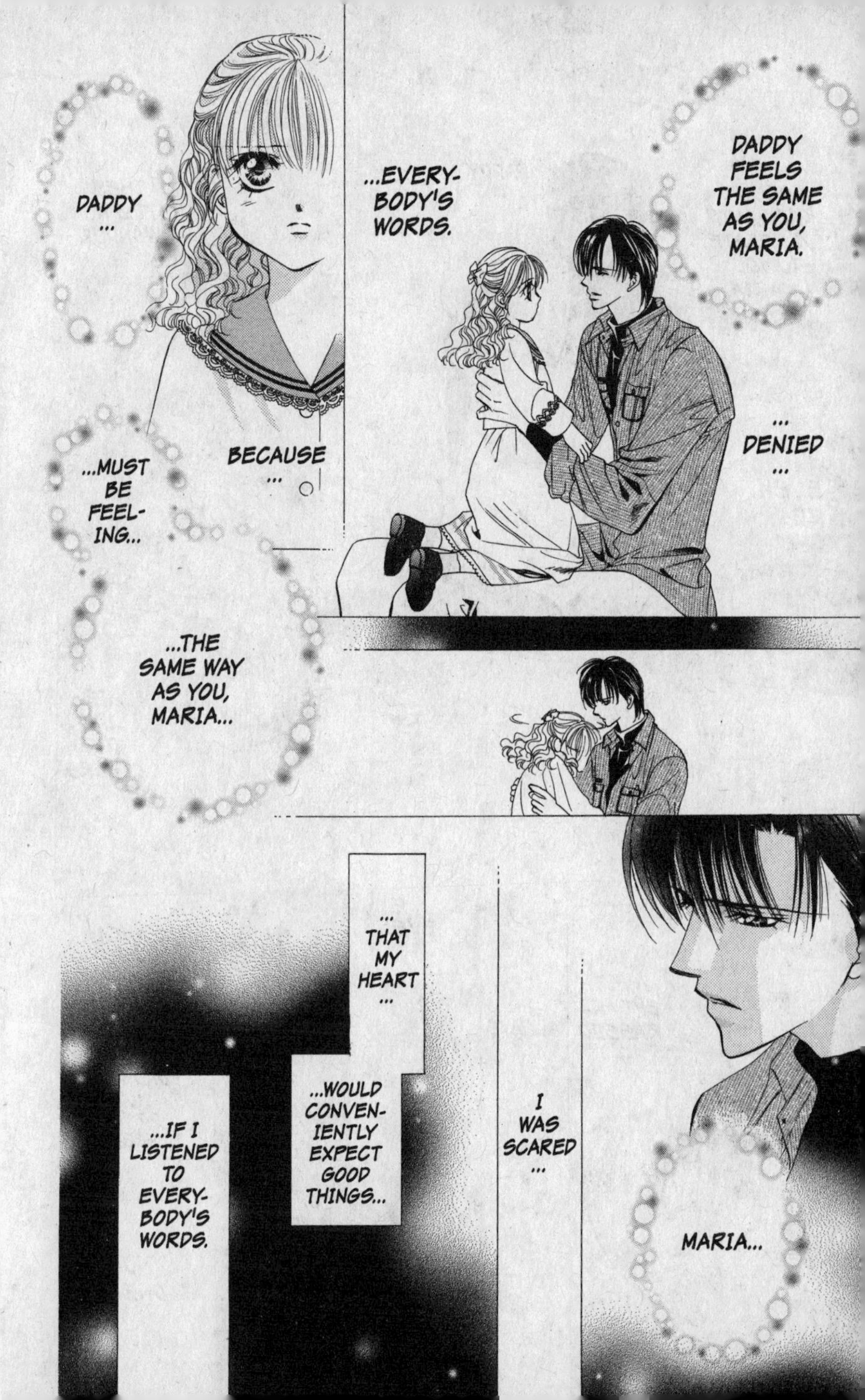
DADDY FEELS THE SAME AS YOU, MARIA.
...DENIED...
...EVERY-BODY'S WORDS.
DADDY...
BECAUSE...
...MUST BE FEEL-ING...
...THE SAME WAY AS YOU, MARIA...
MARIA...
I WAS SCARED...
...THAT MY HEART...
...WOULD CONVEN-IENTLY EXPECT GOOD THINGS...
...IF I LISTENED TO EVERY-BODY'S WORDS.

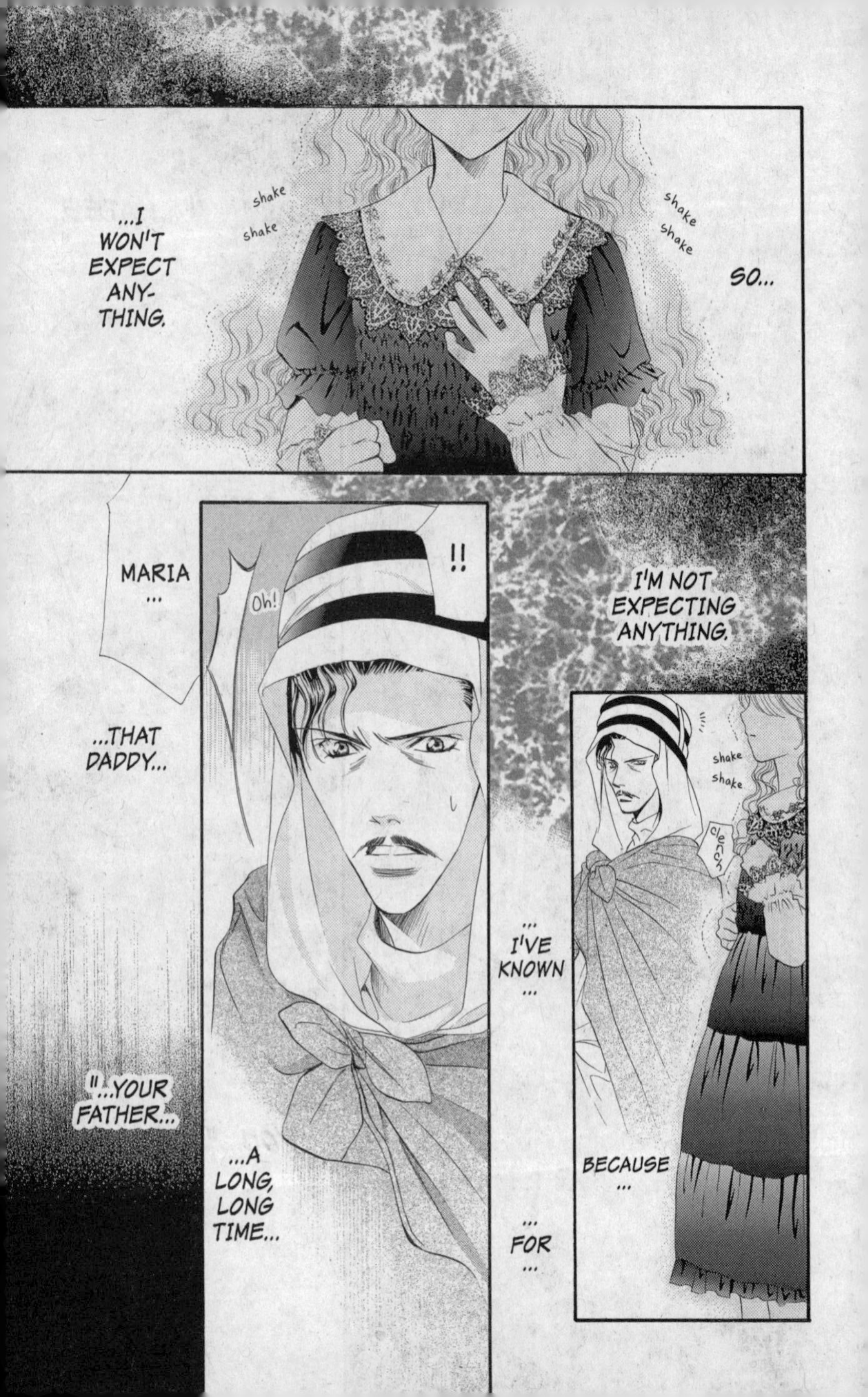
SO...
shake
shake
shake
shake
...I WON'T EXPECT ANY-THING.
I'M NOT EXPECTING ANYTHING.
shake
shake
clench
BECAUSE ...
... I'VE KNOWN ...
... FOR ...
!!
Oh!
...A LONG, LONG TIME...
MARIA ...
...THAT DADDY...
"...YOUR FATHER...

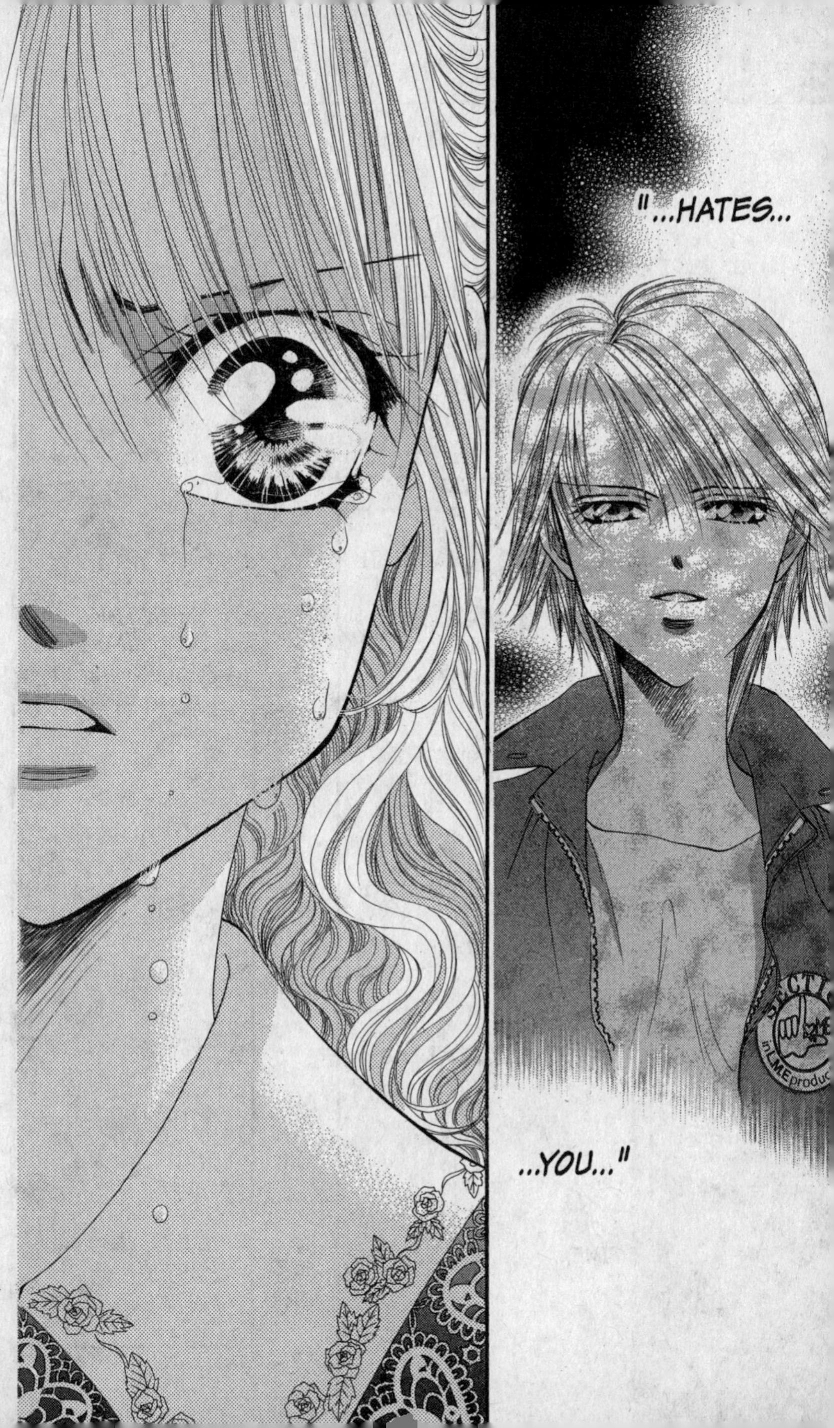
"...HATES...
...YOU..."

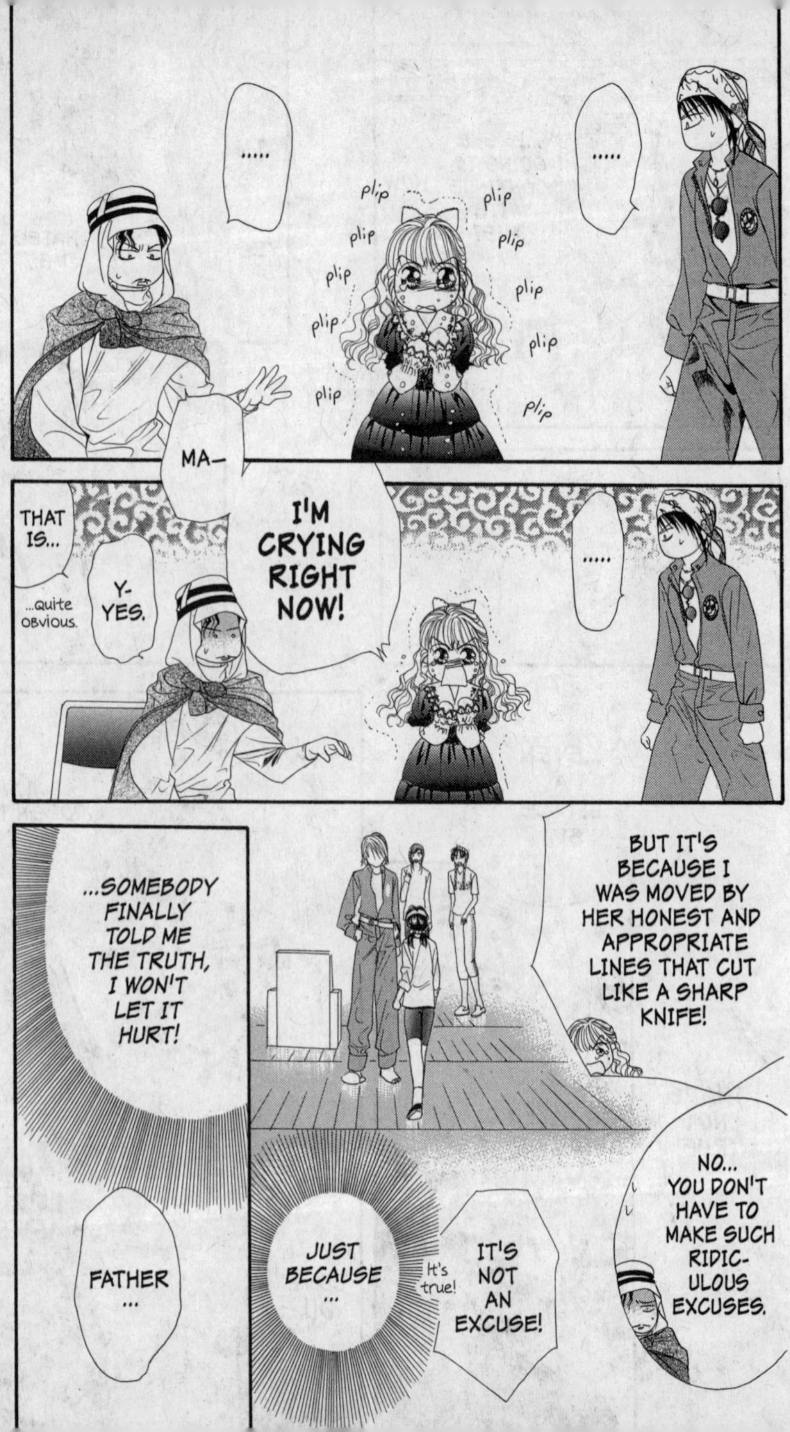
.....
plip plip plip plip plip plip plip plip plip plip
.....
MA—
.....
I'M CRYING RIGHT NOW!
Y-YES.
THAT IS...
...quite obvious.
BUT IT'S BECAUSE I WAS MOVED BY HER HONEST AND APPROPRIATE LINES THAT CUT LIKE A SHARP KNIFE!
NO... YOU DON'T HAVE TO MAKE SUCH RIDIC-ULOUS EXCUSES.
IT'S NOT AN EXCUSE!
It's true!
JUST BECAUSE ...
...SOMEBODY FINALLY TOLD ME THE TRUTH, I WON'T LET IT HURT!
FATHER ...

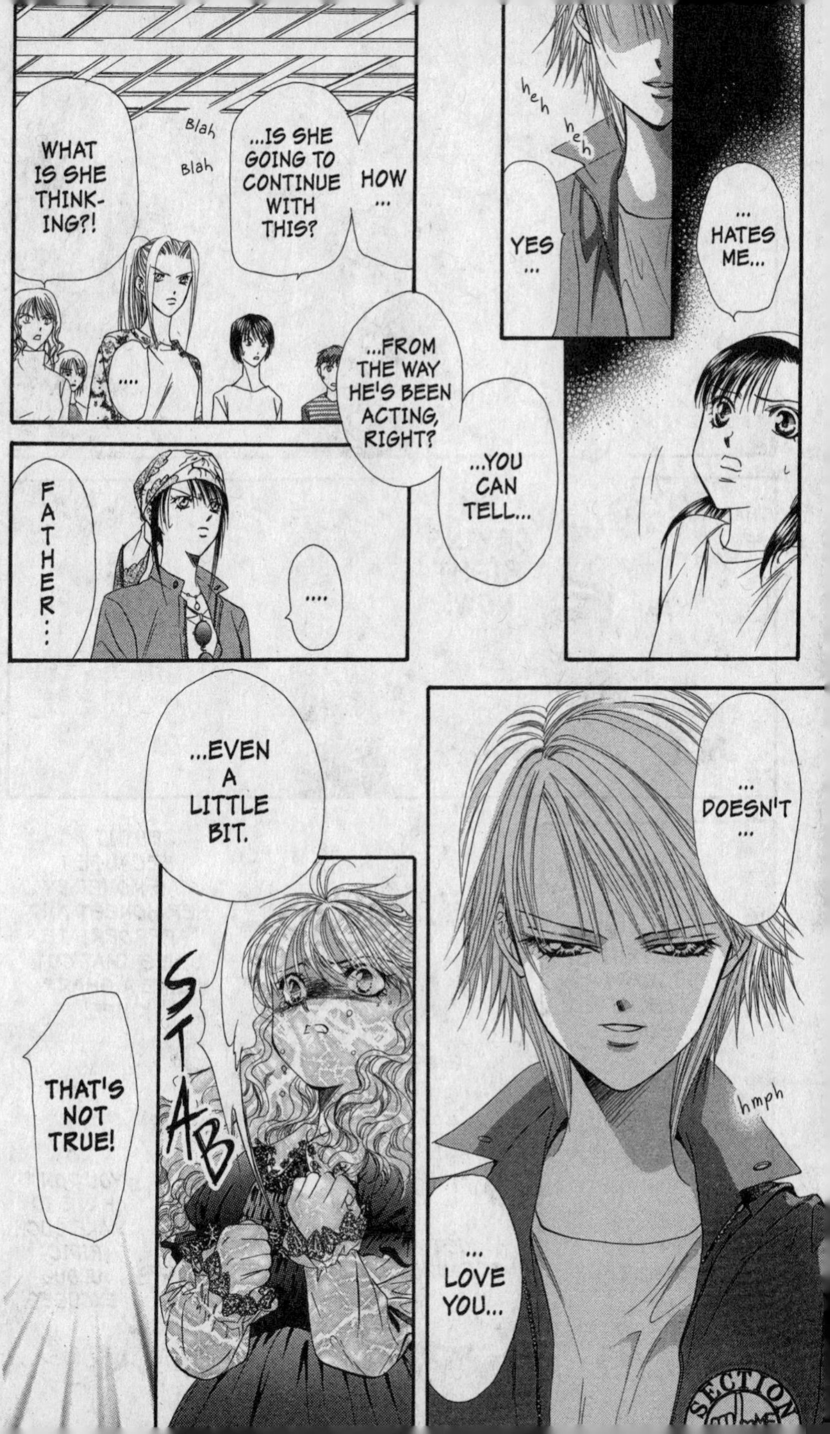
heh heh
YES...
...HATES ME...
...YOU CAN TELL...
...FROM THE WAY HE'S BEEN ACTING, RIGHT?
HOW...
...IS SHE GOING TO CONTINUE WITH THIS?
Blah Blah
WHAT IS SHE THINKING?!
....
FATHER...
....
...DOESN'T...
hmph
...LOVE YOU...
...EVEN A LITTLE BIT.
STAB
THAT'S NOT TRUE!

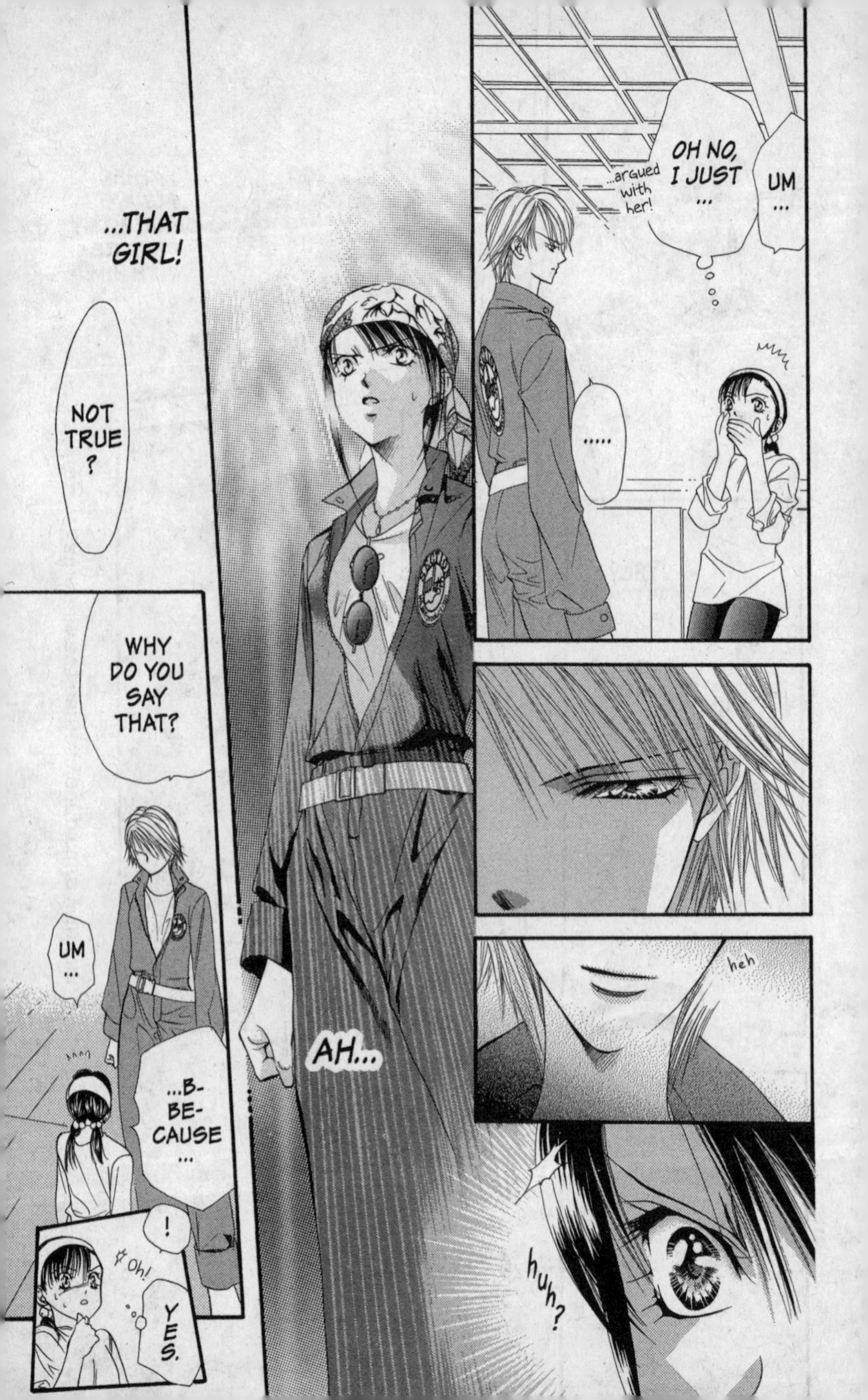
UM ...
OH NO, I JUST ...
...argued with her!
.....
heh
huh?
AH...
...THAT GIRL!
NOT TRUE?
WHY DO YOU SAY THAT?
UM ...
...B-BE-CAUSE ...
!
Oh!
YES.

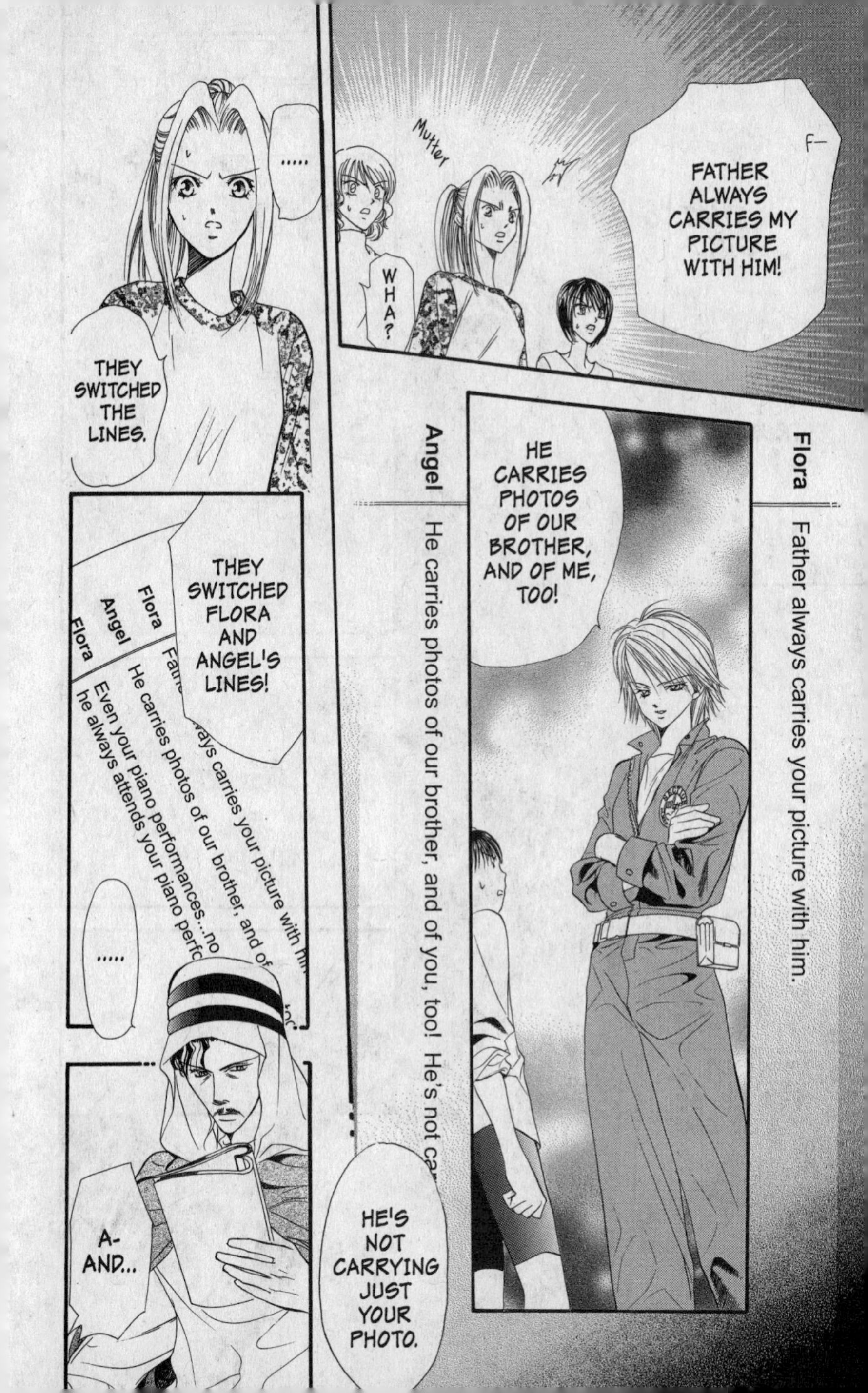
F—
FATHER ALWAYS CARRIES MY PICTURE WITH HIM!
Mutter
WHA?
.....
THEY SWITCHED THE LINES.
Flora
Father always carries your picture with him.
Angel
He carries photos of our brother, and of you, too! He's not ca
HE CARRIES PHOTOS OF OUR BROTHER, AND OF ME, TOO!
HE'S NOT CARRYING JUST YOUR PHOTO.
THEY SWITCHED FLORA AND ANGEL'S LINES!
Flora
Angel
Flora
He carries photos of our brother, and of
Even your piano performances...no
he always attends your piano perfo
.....
A- AND...

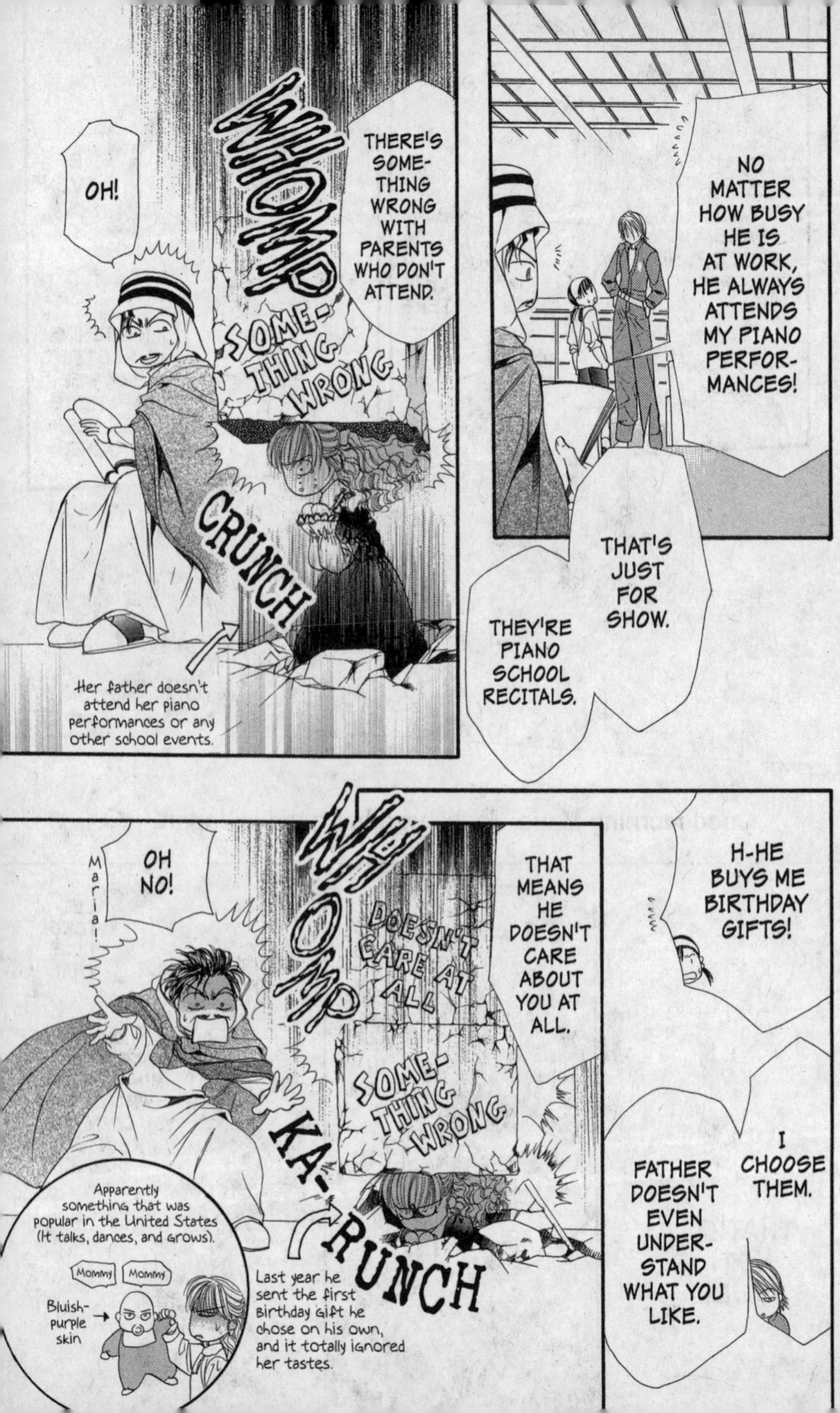
NO MATTER HOW BUSY HE IS AT WORK, HE ALWAYS ATTENDS MY PIANO PERFORMANCES!
THAT'S JUST FOR SHOW.
THEY'RE PIANO SCHOOL RECITALS.
THERE'S SOME-THING WRONG WITH PARENTS WHO DON'T ATTEND.
WHOMP
SOME-THING WRONG
OH!
CRUNCH
Her father doesn't attend her piano performances or any other school events.
H-HE BUYS ME BIRTHDAY GIFTS!
I CHOOSE THEM.
FATHER DOESN'T EVEN UNDER-STAND WHAT YOU LIKE.
THAT MEANS HE DOESN'T CARE ABOUT YOU AT ALL.
WHOMP
DOESN'T CARE AT ALL
SOME-THING WRONG
OH NO!
Maria!
KA-RUNCH
Last year he sent the first birthday gift he chose on his own, and it totally ignored her tastes.
Apparently something that was popular in the United States (It talks, dances, and grows).
Mommy
Mommy
Bluish-purple skin

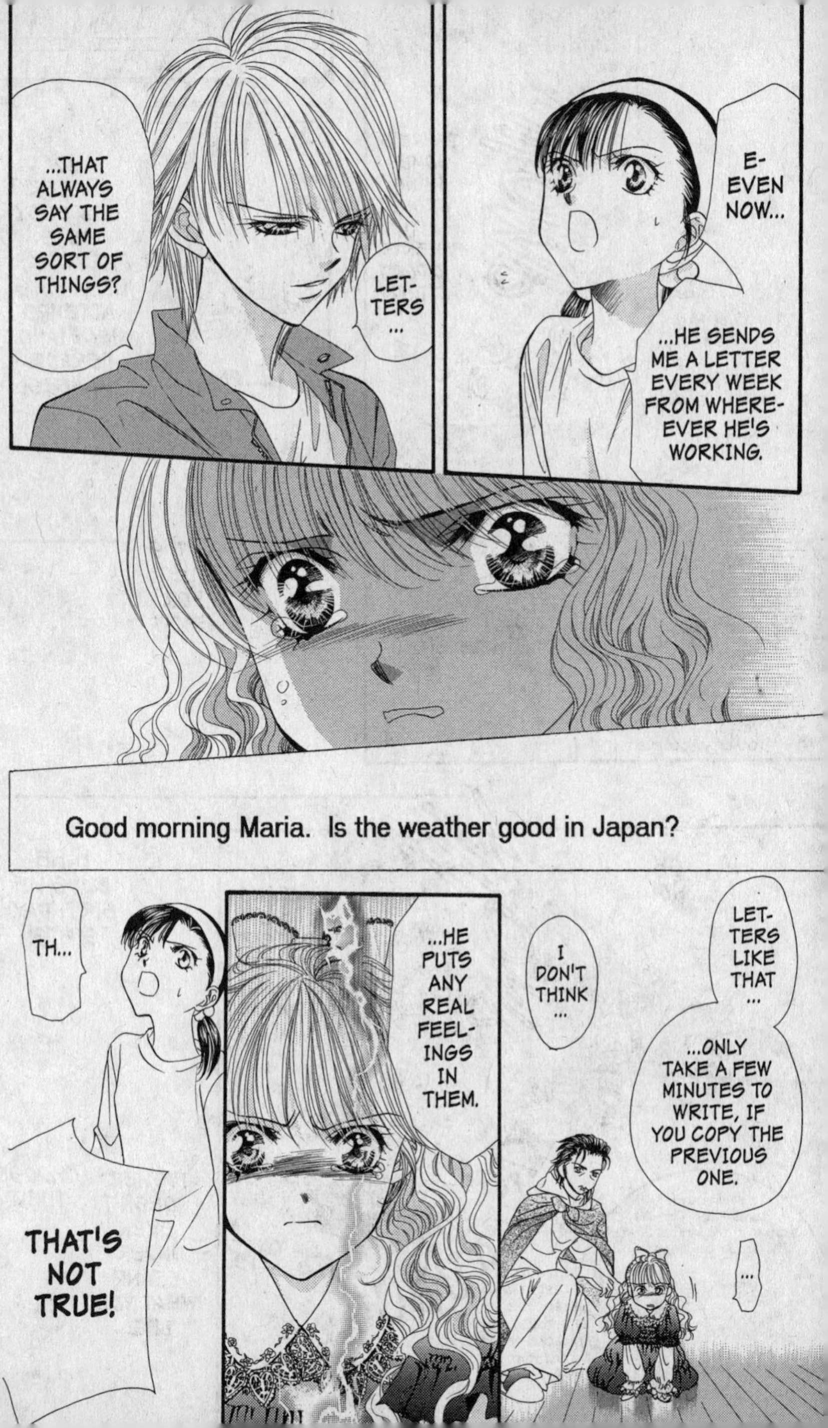
E- EVEN NOW...
...HE SENDS ME A LETTER EVERY WEEK FROM WHEREEVER HE'S WORKING.
LETTERS...
...THAT ALWAYS SAY THE SAME SORT OF THINGS?
Good morning Maria. Is the weather good in Japan?
LETTERS LIKE THAT...
...ONLY TAKE A FEW MINUTES TO WRITE, IF YOU COPY THE PREVIOUS ONE.
...
I DON'T THINK...
...HE PUTS ANY REAL FEELINGS IN THEM.
TH...
THAT'S NOT TRUE!

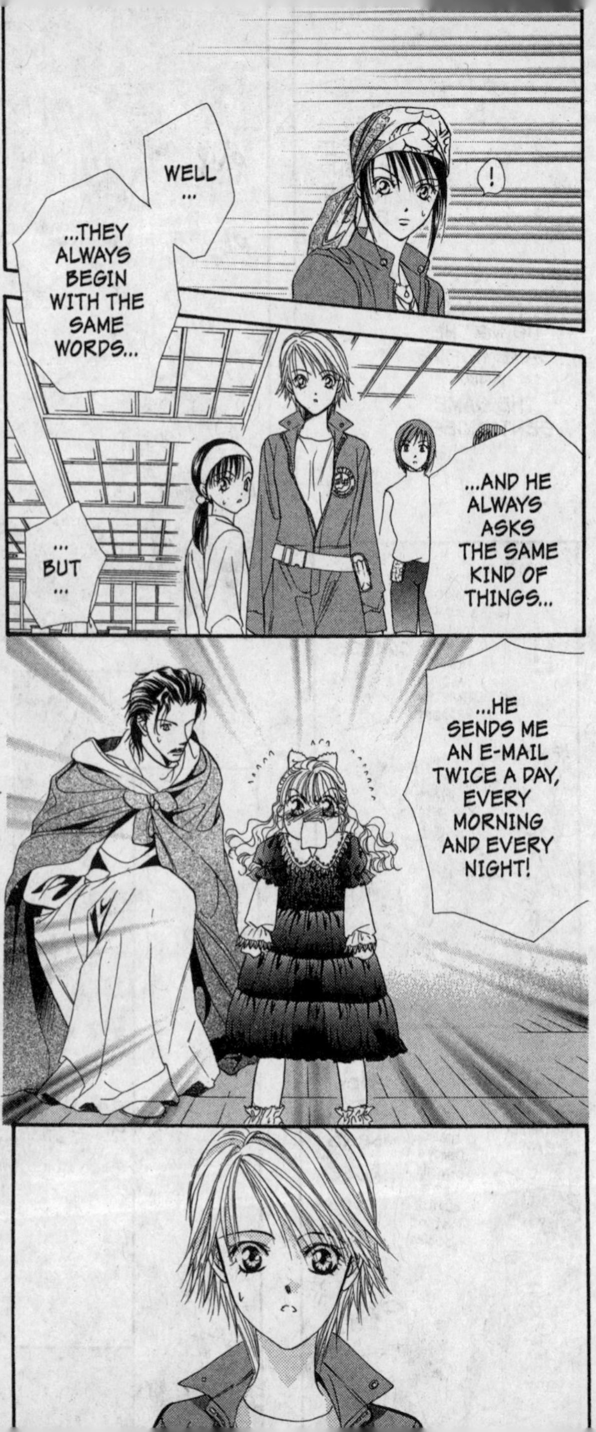

WELL ...
!
...THEY ALWAYS BEGIN WITH THE SAME WORDS...
...AND HE ALWAYS ASKS THE SAME KIND OF THINGS...
... BUT ...
...HE SENDS ME AN E-MAIL TWICE A DAY, EVERY MORNING AND EVERY NIGHT!

Greetings

Hello. I'm Nakamura. Thank you for reading *Skip•Beat!* Vol. 4. This time I was finally able to have Shotaro (who doesn't appear often) and Kyoko interact in the show-biz world. Since Kyoko is just starting out, a super-newcomer, she has no contact with Shotaro, so it's tough... To tell the truth, he hadn't appeared for so long, when I drew him at the end of Act 20, his looks had changed... He looked young, and almost like a girl...

My editor put in "Even if I become a bird, I will not forget that face!" for the copy on that last page. But the moment I read that, I added the snarky comment, "...Yes...even if Kyoko hasn't forgotten, I have..." I'm sorry Haorin...

↑ My editor's nickname

This time I once again redrew lots of stuff, and I suddenly messed up my work schedule... I apologize for not being able to do my work as planned.

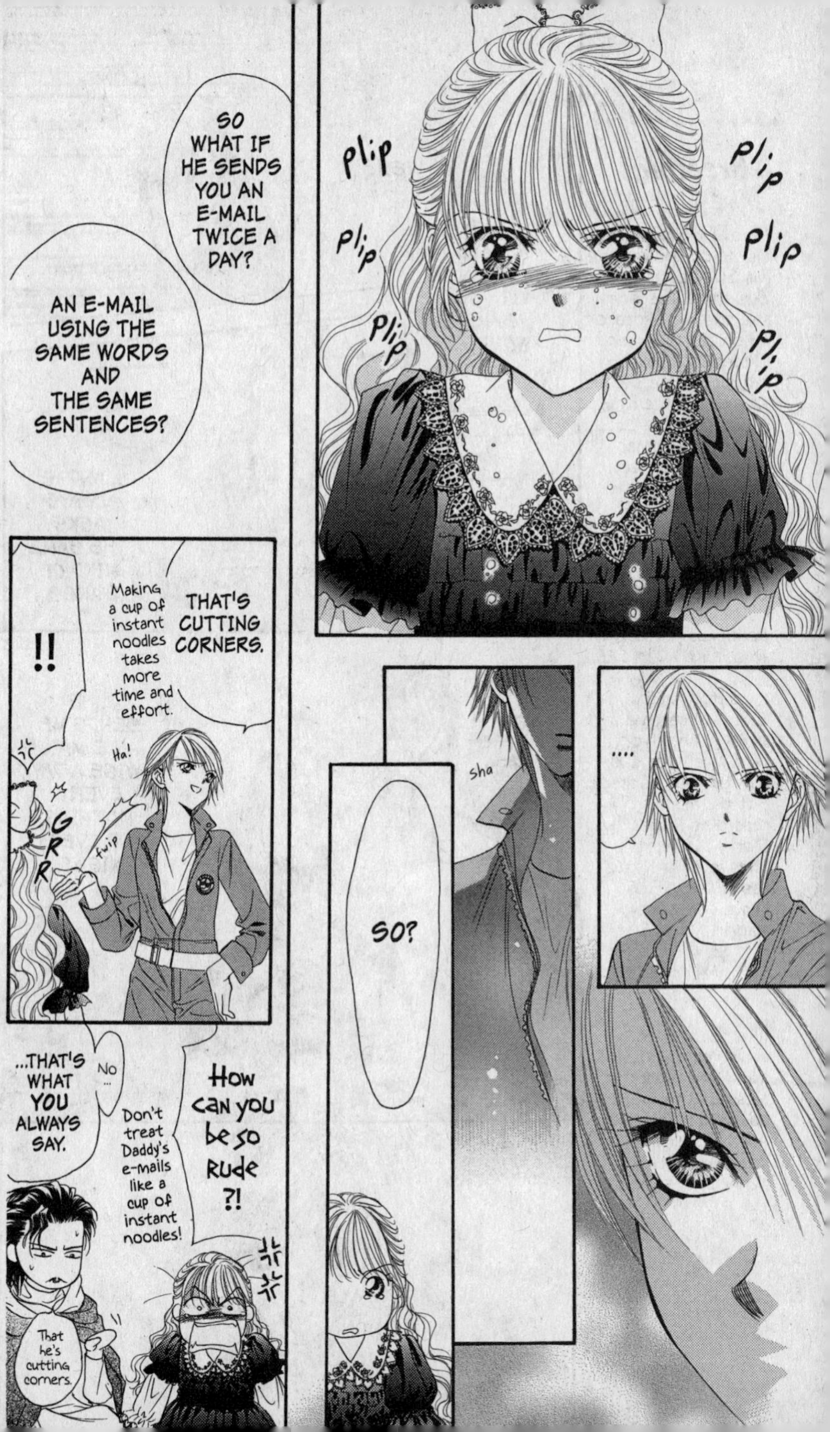
SO WHAT IF HE SENDS YOU AN E-MAIL TWICE A DAY?
AN E-MAIL USING THE SAME WORDS AND THE SAME SENTENCES?
THAT'S CUTTING CORNERS.
Making a cup of instant noodles takes more time and effort.
!!
Ha!
twip
GRR
How can you be so rude?!
Don't treat Daddy's e-mails like a cup of instant noodles!
No...
...THAT'S WHAT YOU ALWAYS SAY.
That he's cutting corners.
plip
plip
plip
plip
plip
plip
....
sha
SO?

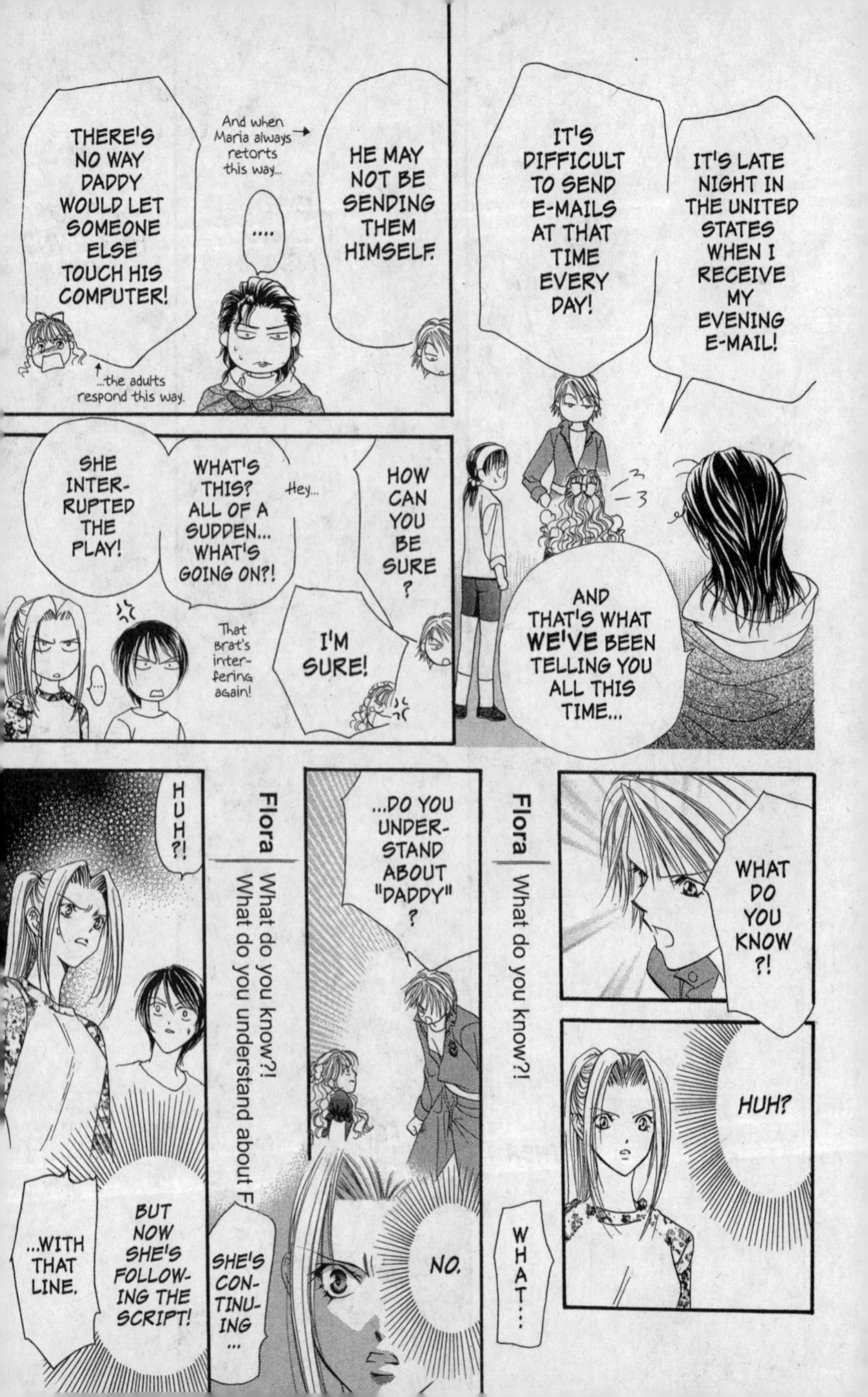
IT'S LATE NIGHT IN THE UNITED STATES WHEN I RECEIVE MY EVENING E-MAIL!
IT'S DIFFICULT TO SEND E-MAILS AT THAT TIME EVERY DAY!
AND THAT'S WHAT **WE'VE** BEEN TELLING YOU ALL THIS TIME...
HE MAY NOT BE SENDING THEM HIMSELF.
And when Maria always retorts this way...
....
THERE'S NO WAY DADDY WOULD LET SOMEONE ELSE TOUCH HIS COMPUTER!
...the adults respond this way.
HOW CAN YOU BE SURE?
I'M SURE!
Hey...
WHAT'S THIS? ALL OF A SUDDEN... WHAT'S GOING ON?!
SHE INTER-RUPTED THE PLAY!
That brat's inter-fering again!
....
WHAT DO YOU KNOW?!
Flora | What do you know?!
HUH?
WHAT...
...DO YOU UNDER-STAND ABOUT "DADDY"?
Flora | What do you know?! What do you understand about F
NO.
SHE'S CON-TINU-ING...
HUH?!
BUT NOW SHE'S FOLLOW-ING THE SCRIPT!
...WITH THAT LINE.

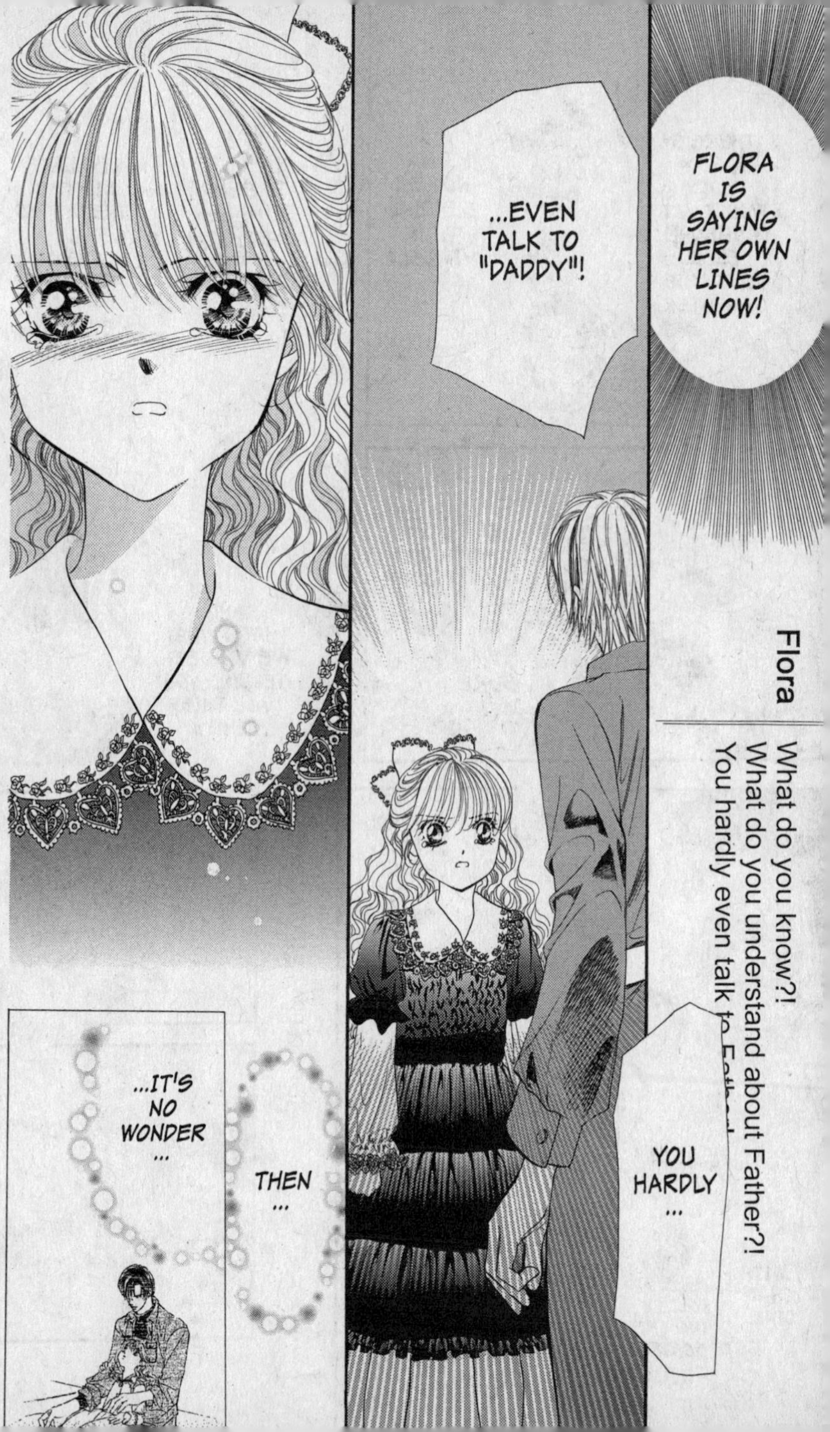

FLORA IS SAYING HER OWN LINES NOW!
Flora
What do you know?!
What do you understand about Father?!
You hardly even talk
YOU HARDLY ...
...EVEN TALK TO "DADDY"!
THEN ...
...IT'S NO WONDER ...

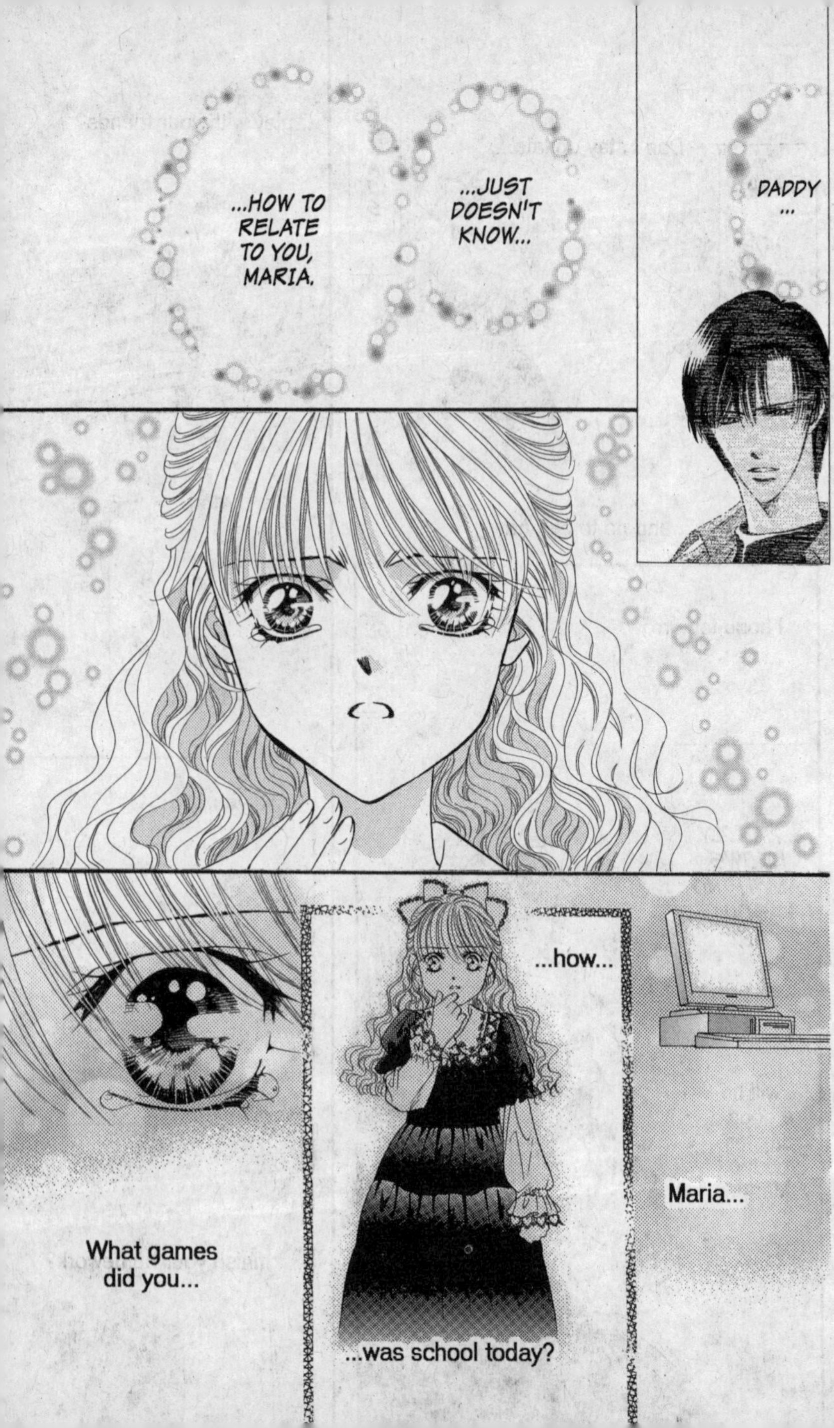
DADDY ...
...JUST DOESN'T KNOW...
...HOW TO RELATE TO YOU, MARIA.
Maria...
...how...
...was school today?
What games did you...

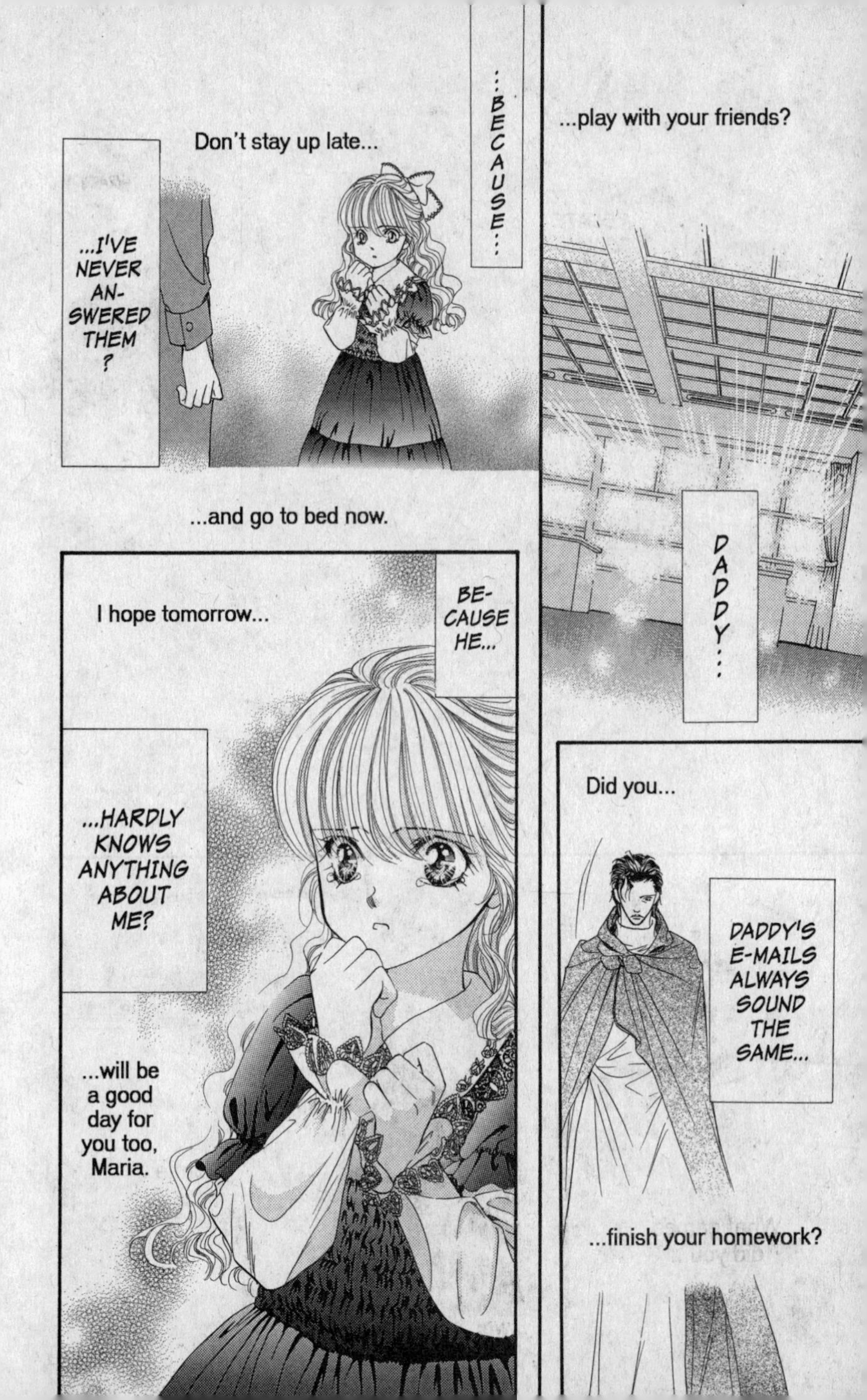
...play with your friends?
DADDY...
Did you...
DADDY'S E-MAILS ALWAYS SOUND THE SAME...
...finish your homework?
...BECAUSE...
Don't stay up late...
...I'VE NEVER AN-SWERED THEM?
...and go to bed now.
BE-CAUSE HE...
I hope tomorrow...
...HARDLY KNOWS ANYTHING ABOUT ME?
...will be a good day for you too, Maria.

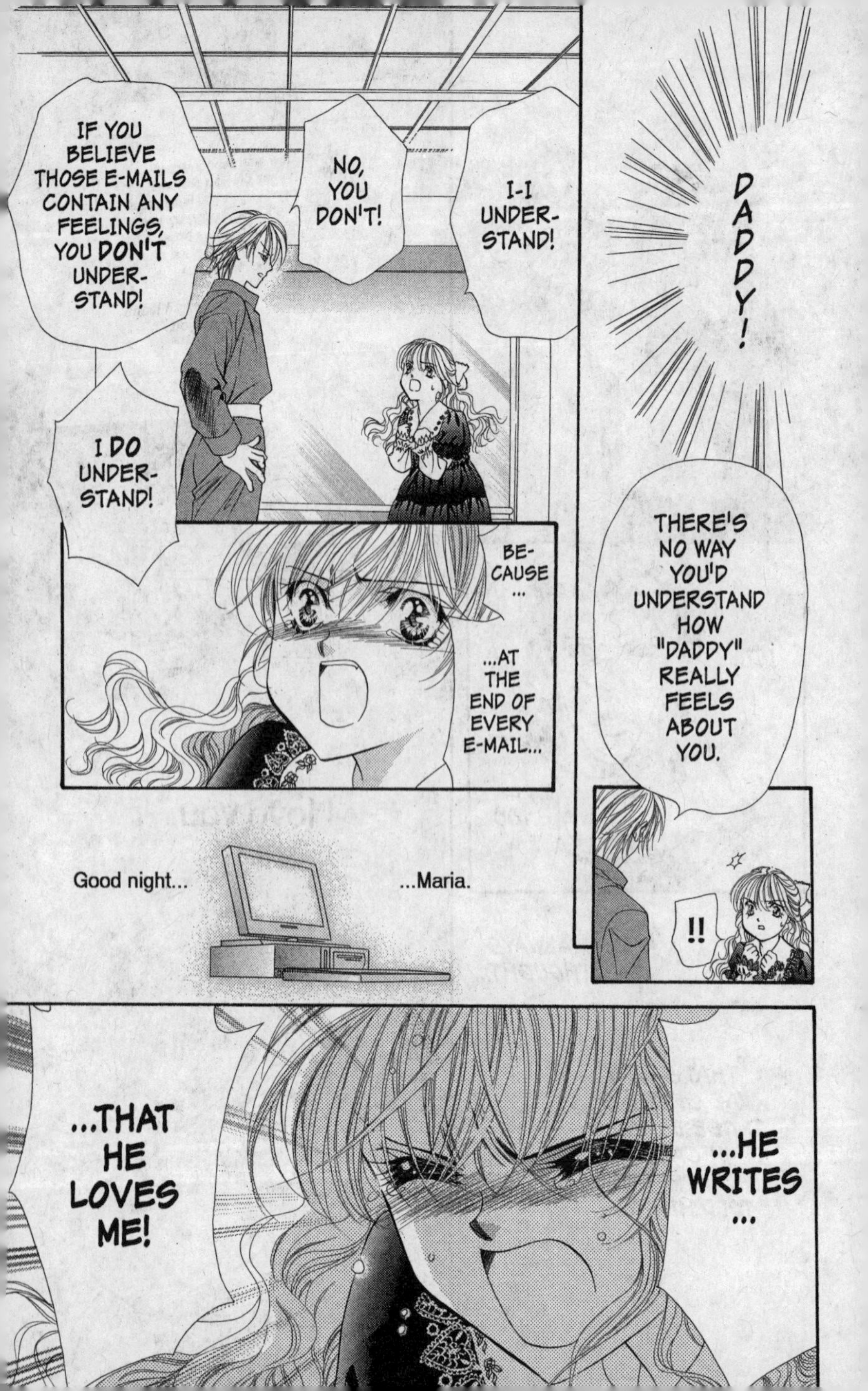
DADDY!
THERE'S NO WAY YOU'D UNDERSTAND HOW "DADDY" REALLY FEELS ABOUT YOU.
!!
I-I UNDER-STAND!
NO, YOU DON'T!
IF YOU BELIEVE THOSE E-MAILS CONTAIN ANY FEELINGS, YOU DON'T UNDER-STAND!
I DO UNDER-STAND!
BE-CAUSE ...
...AT THE END OF EVERY E-MAIL...
Good night...
...Maria.
...HE WRITES ...
...THAT HE LOVES ME!

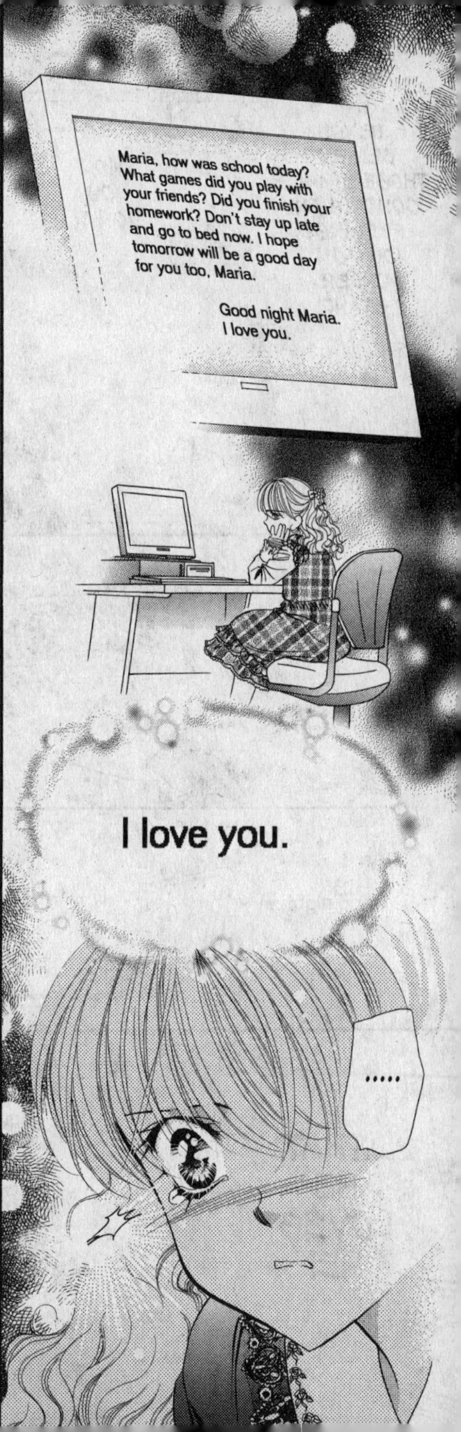
Maria, how was school today? What games did you play with your friends? Did you finish your homework? Don't stay up late and go to bed now. I hope tomorrow will be a good day for you too, Maria.
Good night Maria. I love you.
I love you.
.....

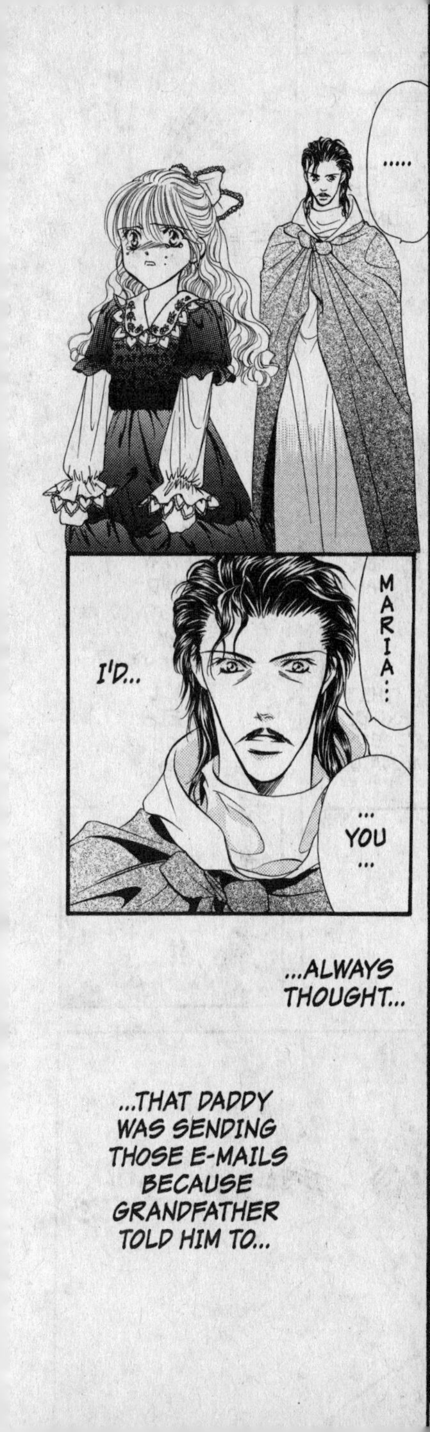
.....
MARIA...
I'D...
...YOU...
...ALWAYS THOUGHT...
...THAT DADDY WAS SENDING THOSE E-MAILS BECAUSE GRANDFATHER TOLD HIM TO...

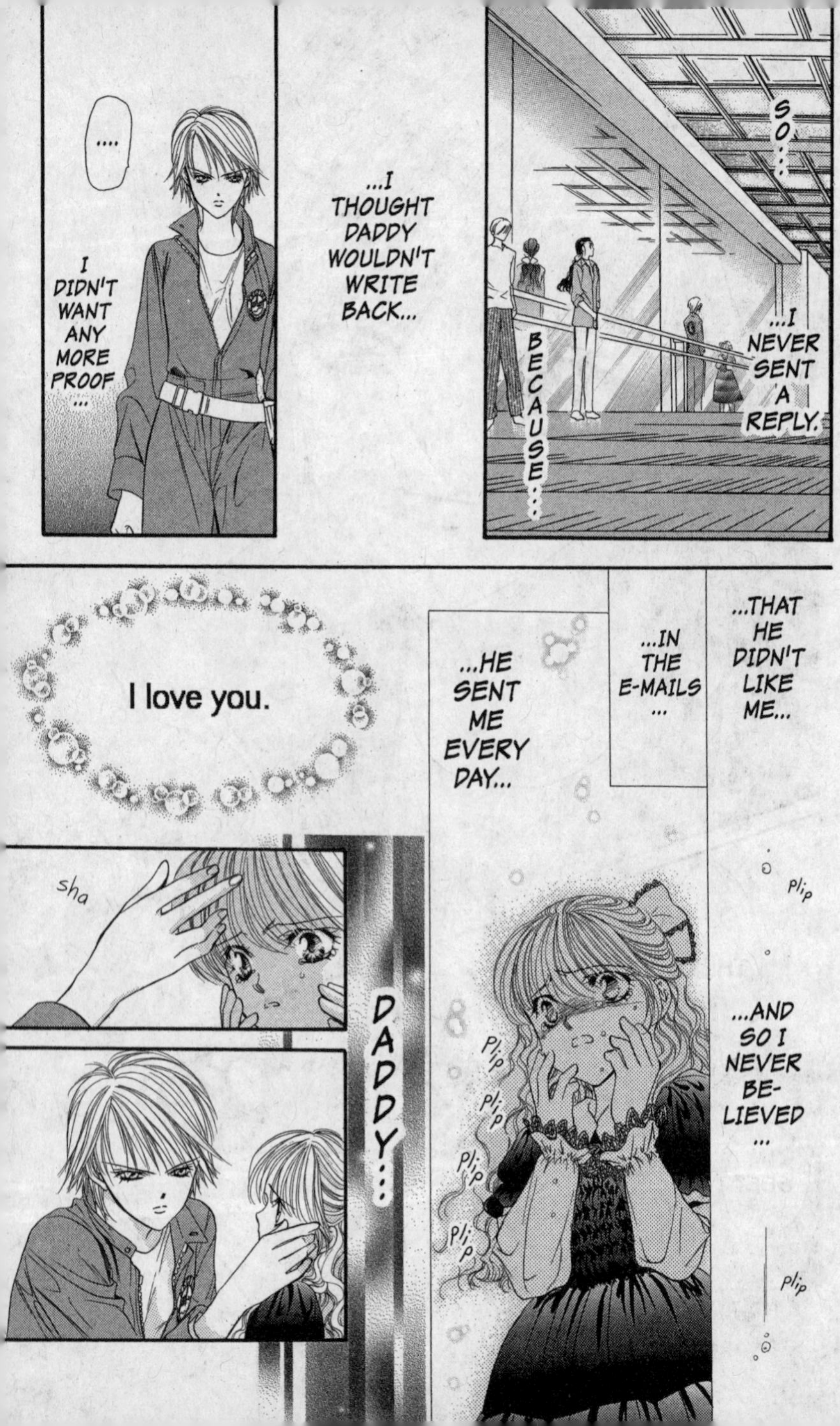
SO...
...I NEVER SENT A REPLY.
BECAUSE...
...I THOUGHT DADDY WOULDN'T WRITE BACK...
....
I DIDN'T WANT ANY MORE PROOF...
...THAT HE DIDN'T LIKE ME...
...IN THE E-MAILS...
...HE SENT ME EVERY DAY...
I love you.
plip
...AND SO I NEVER BE-LIEVED...
plip
plip
plip
plip
plip
sha
DADDY...

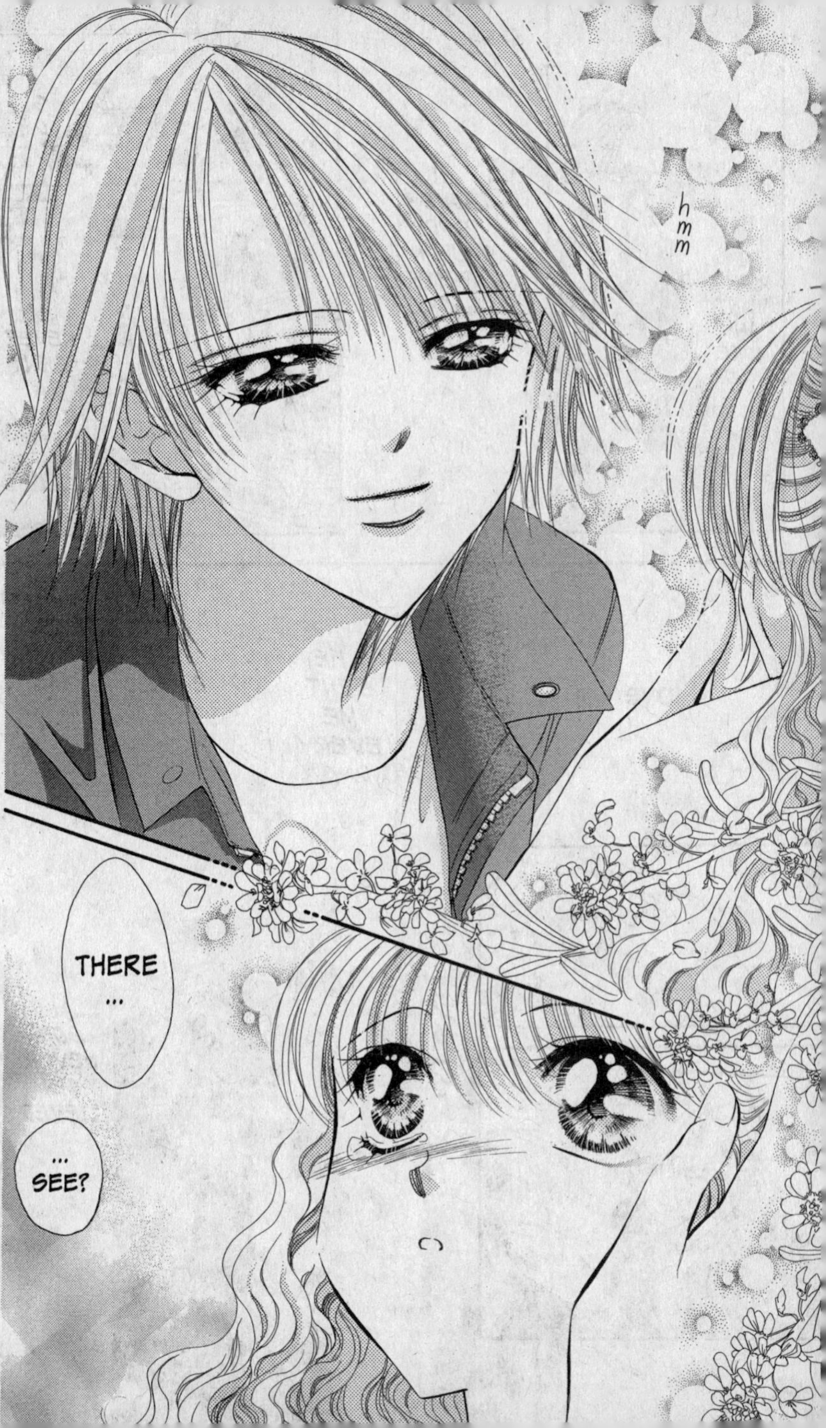
hmm
THERE ...
... SEE?

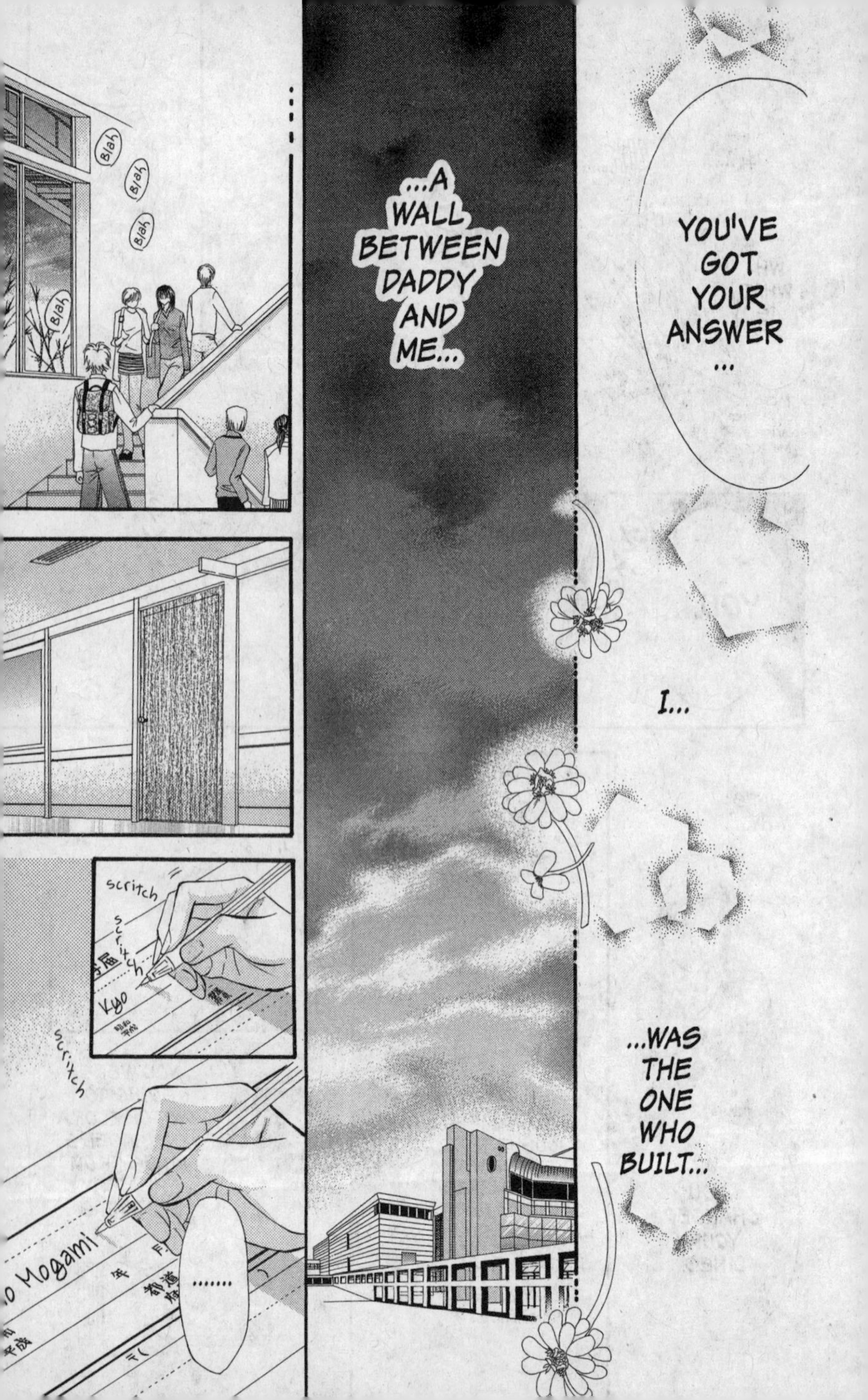
YOU'VE GOT YOUR ANSWER ...
I...
...WAS THE ONE WHO BUILT...
...A WALL BETWEEN DADDY AND ME...
Blah
Blah
Blah
Blah
scritch
scritch
Kyo
scritch
Mogami
....

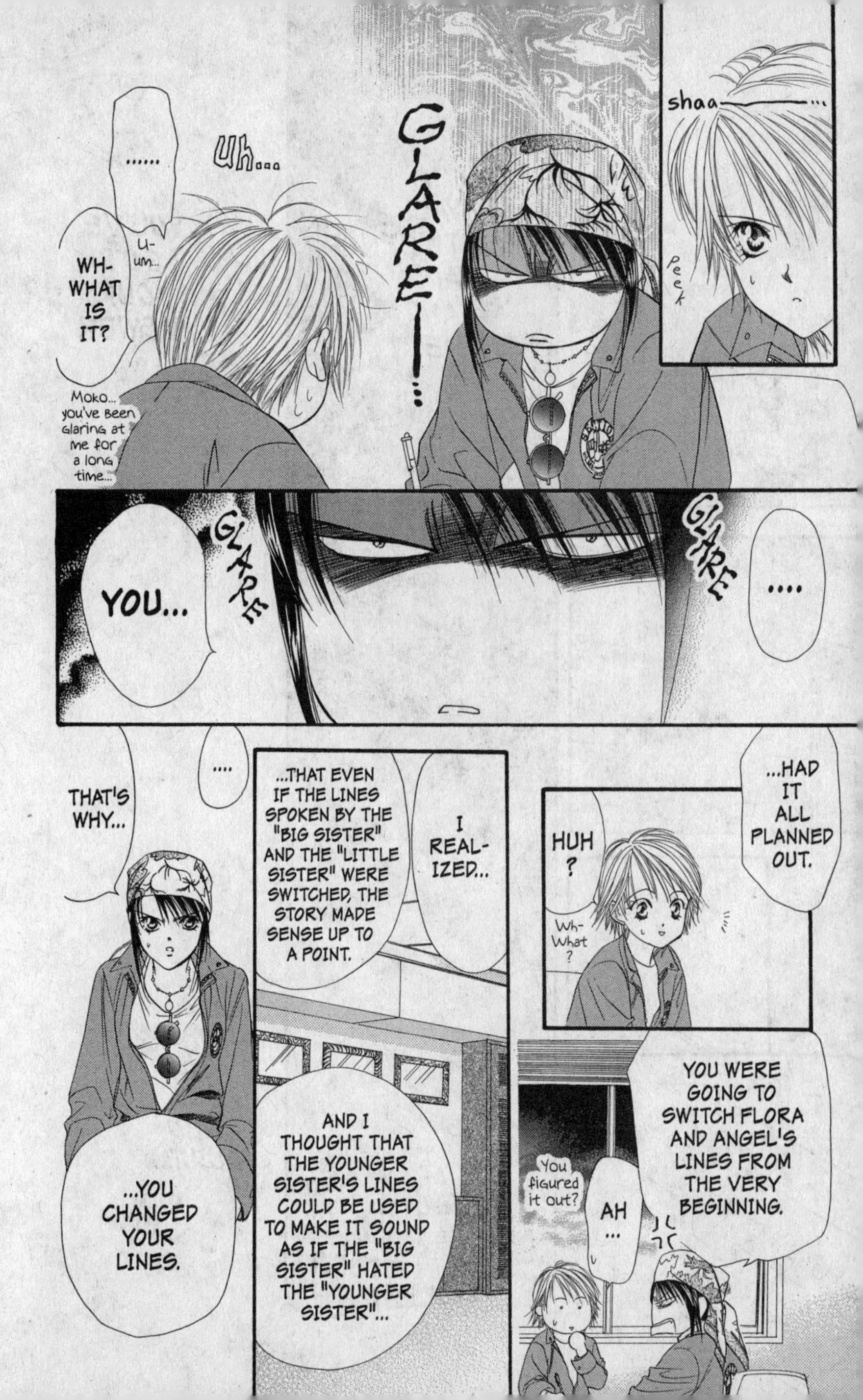

shaa——...
Peek
GLARE...!!
......
Uh...
U-um...
WH-WHAT IS IT?
Moko... you've been glaring at me for a long time...
....
GLARE
GLARE
YOU...
...HAD IT ALL PLANNED OUT.
HUH?
Wh-What?
YOU WERE GOING TO SWITCH FLORA AND ANGEL'S LINES FROM THE VERY BEGINNING.
AH...
You figured it out?
I REALIZED...
...THAT EVEN IF THE LINES SPOKEN BY THE "BIG SISTER" AND THE "LITTLE SISTER" WERE SWITCHED, THE STORY MADE SENSE UP TO A POINT.
AND I THOUGHT THAT THE YOUNGER SISTER'S LINES COULD BE USED TO MAKE IT SOUND AS IF THE "BIG SISTER" HATED THE "YOUNGER SISTER"...
....
THAT'S WHY...
...YOU CHANGED YOUR LINES.

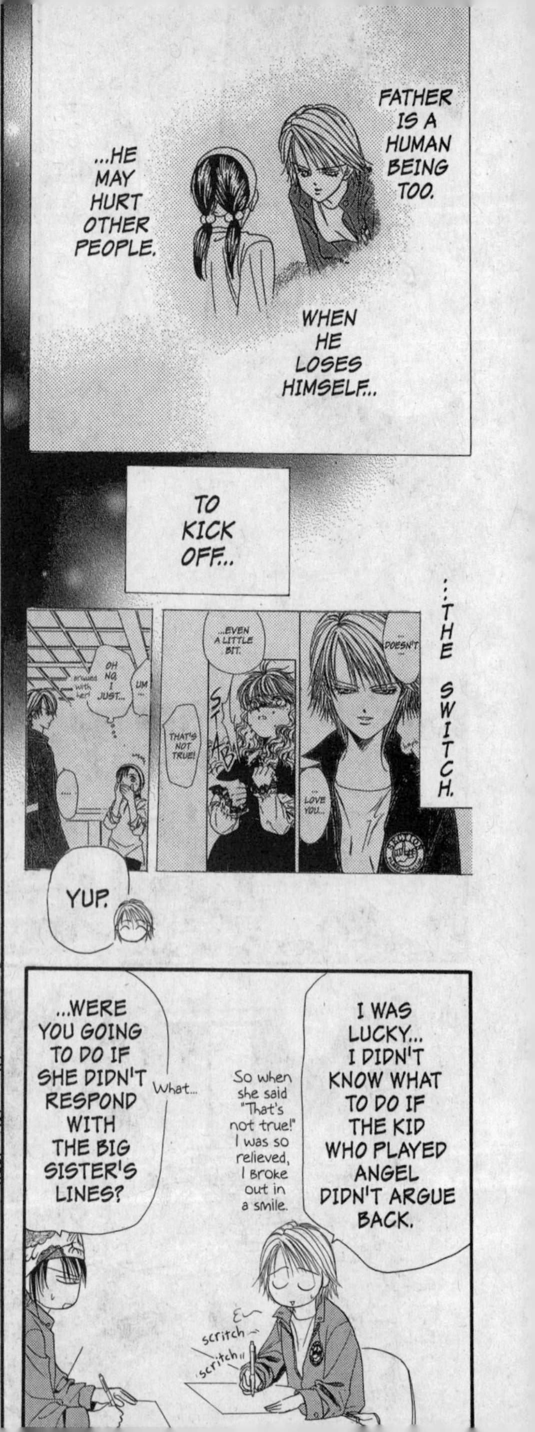
FATHER IS A HUMAN BEING TOO.
...HE MAY HURT OTHER PEOPLE.
WHEN HE LOSES HIMSELF...
TO KICK OFF...
...THE SWITCH.
...DOESN'T
...LOVE YOU...
...EVEN A LITTLE BIT.
THAT'S NOT TRUE!
OH NO, I JUST...
argued with her!
UM...
YUP.
I WAS LUCKY... I DIDN'T KNOW WHAT TO DO IF THE KID WHO PLAYED ANGEL DIDN'T ARGUE BACK.
So when she said "That's not true!" I was so relieved, I broke out in a smile.
...WERE YOU GOING TO DO IF SHE DIDN'T RESPOND WITH THE BIG SISTER'S LINES?
What...
scritch
scritch

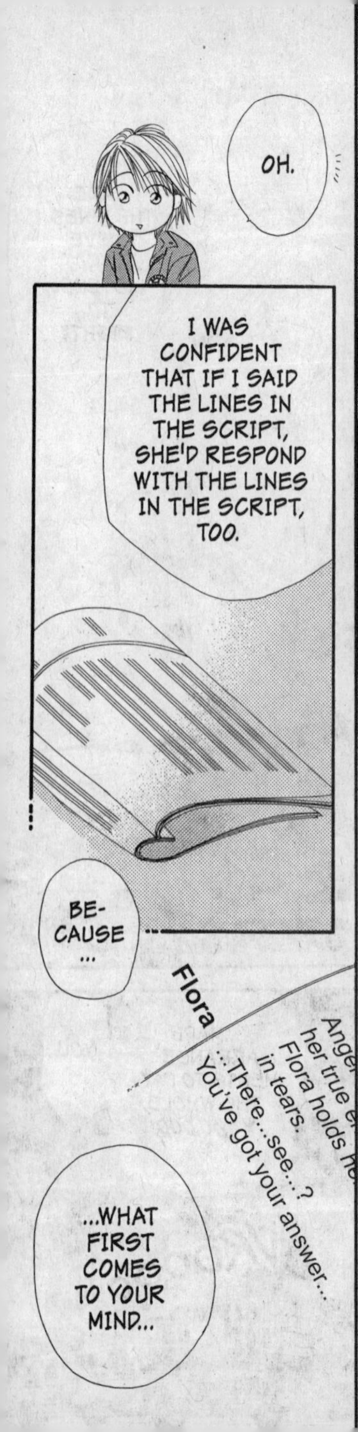
OH.
I WAS CONFIDENT THAT IF I SAID THE LINES IN THE SCRIPT, SHE'D RESPOND WITH THE LINES IN THE SCRIPT, TOO.
BE-CAUSE...
Flora
...There...see...? You've got your answer...
...WHAT FIRST COMES TO YOUR MIND...

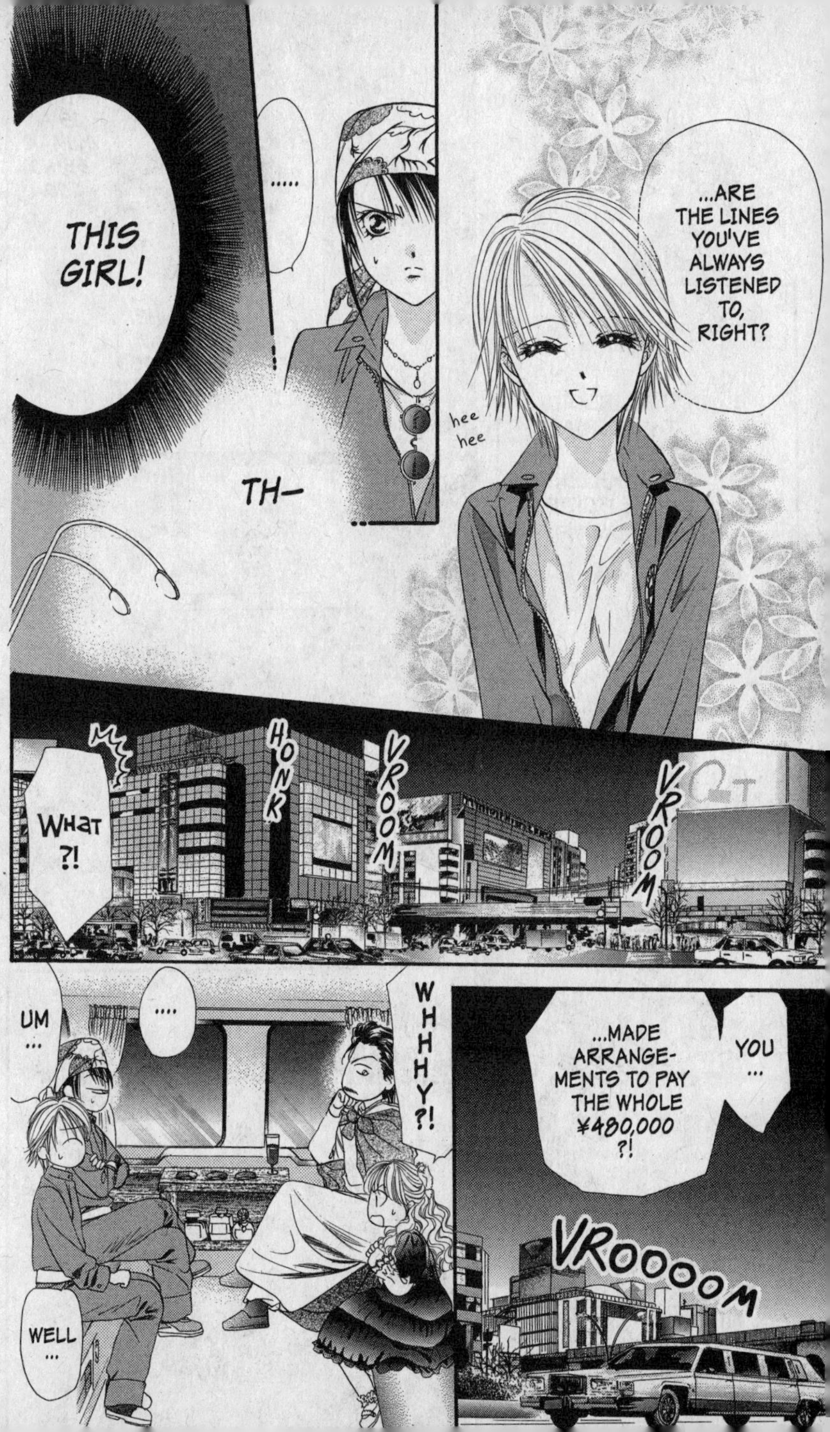
...ARE THE LINES YOU'VE ALWAYS LISTENED TO, RIGHT?
hee hee
.....
TH—
THIS GIRL!
VROOM
VROOM
HONK
WHAT ?!
YOU ...
...MADE ARRANGE-MENTS TO PAY THE WHOLE ¥480,000 ?!
VROOOOM
WHHHY?!
....
UM ...
WELL ...

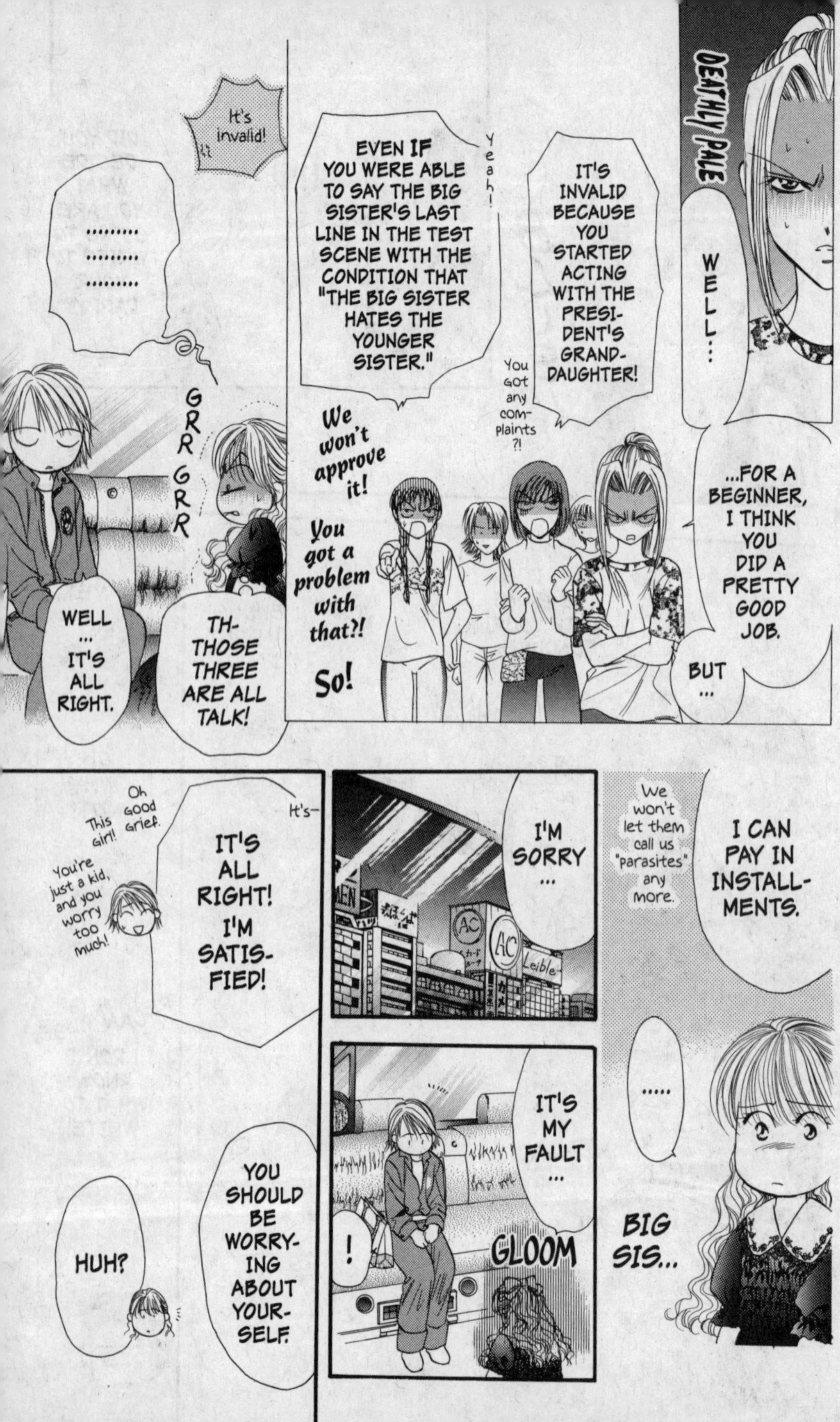
DEATHLY PALE
WELL...
...FOR A BEGINNER, I THINK YOU DID A PRETTY GOOD JOB.
BUT...
IT'S INVALID BECAUSE YOU STARTED ACTING WITH THE PRESIDENT'S GRANDDAUGHTER!
You got any complaints?!
Yeah!
EVEN IF YOU WERE ABLE TO SAY THE BIG SISTER'S LAST LINE IN THE TEST SCENE WITH THE CONDITION THAT "THE BIG SISTER HATES THE YOUNGER SISTER."
We won't approve it!
You got a problem with that?!
So!
It's invalid!
....
....
....
GRR GRR
TH-THOSE THREE ARE ALL TALK!
WELL... IT'S ALL RIGHT.
I CAN PAY IN INSTALLMENTS.
We won't let them call us "parasites" any more.
.....
BIG SIS...
I'M SORRY...
IT'S MY FAULT...
GLOOM
!
It's—
IT'S ALL RIGHT! I'M SATISFIED!
Oh good grief.
This girl!
You're just a kid, and you worry too much!
YOU SHOULD BE WORRYING ABOUT YOURSELF.
HUH?

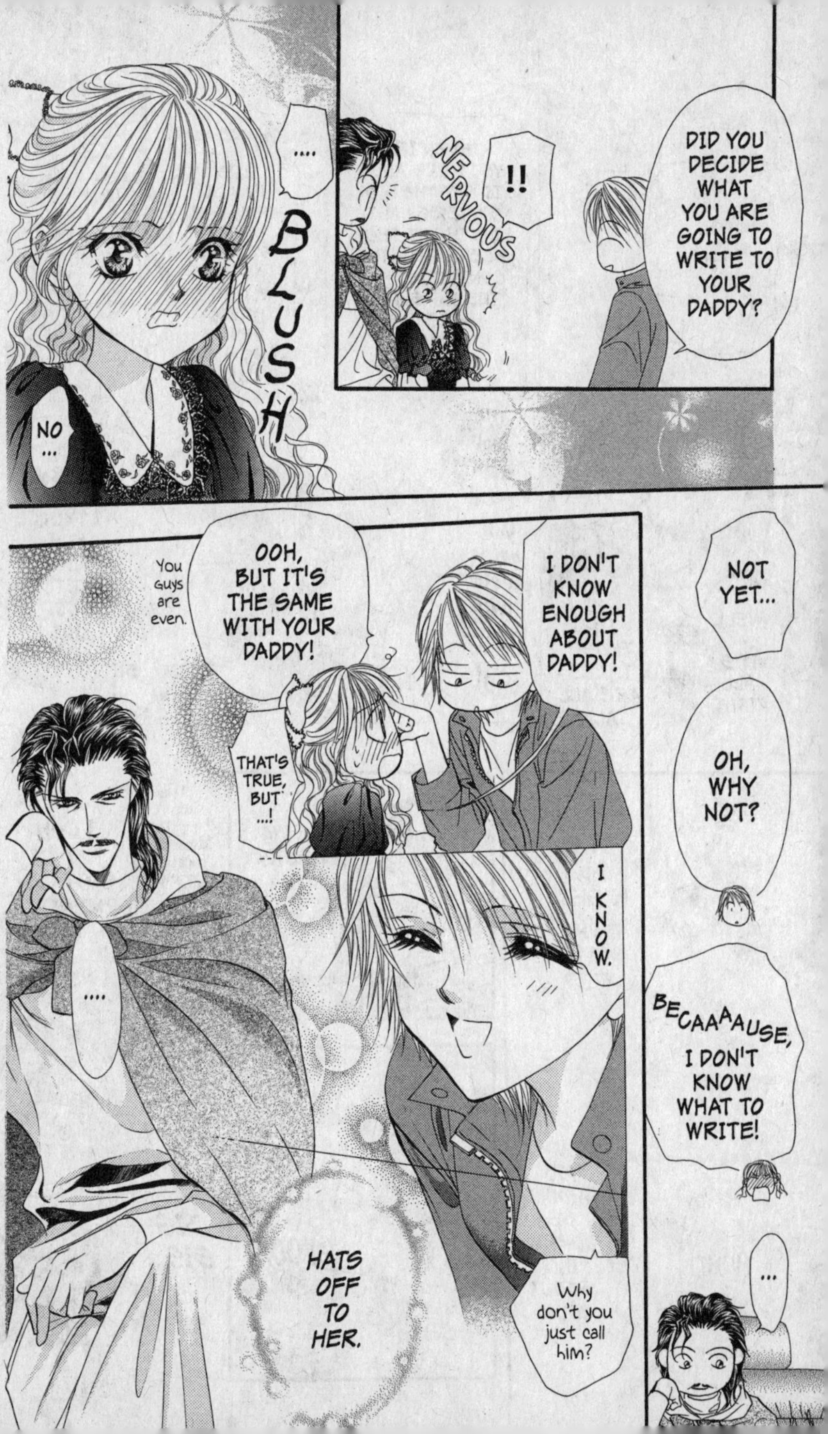
DID YOU DECIDE WHAT YOU ARE GOING TO WRITE TO YOUR DADDY?
!!
NERVOUS
....
BLUSH
NO ...
NOT YET...
OH, WHY NOT?
BECAAAAUSE, I DON'T KNOW WHAT TO WRITE!
...
I DON'T KNOW ENOUGH ABOUT DADDY!
OOH, BUT IT'S THE SAME WITH YOUR DADDY!
You guys are even.
THAT'S TRUE, BUT ...!
I KNOW.
....
Why don't you just call him?
HATS OFF TO HER.

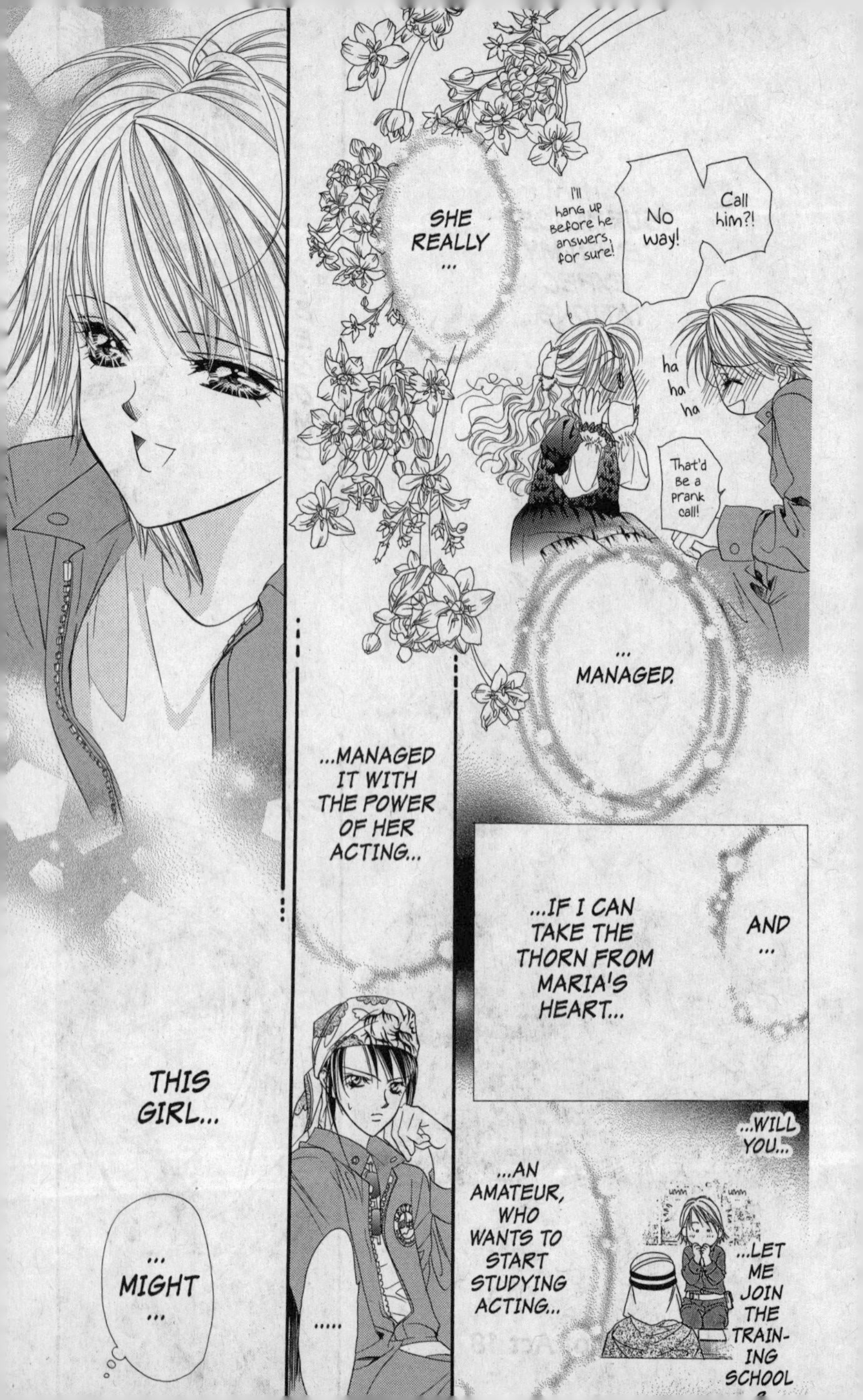
Call him?!
No way!
I'll hang up before he answers, for sure!
ha ha ha
That'd be a prank call!
SHE REALLY ...
... MANAGED.
...MANAGED IT WITH THE POWER OF HER ACTING...
AND ...
...IF I CAN TAKE THE THORN FROM MARIA'S HEART...
...WILL YOU...
...AN AMATEUR, WHO WANTS TO START STUDYING ACTING...
umm umm
...LET ME JOIN THE TRAIN-ING SCHOOL
.....
THIS GIRL...
... MIGHT ...

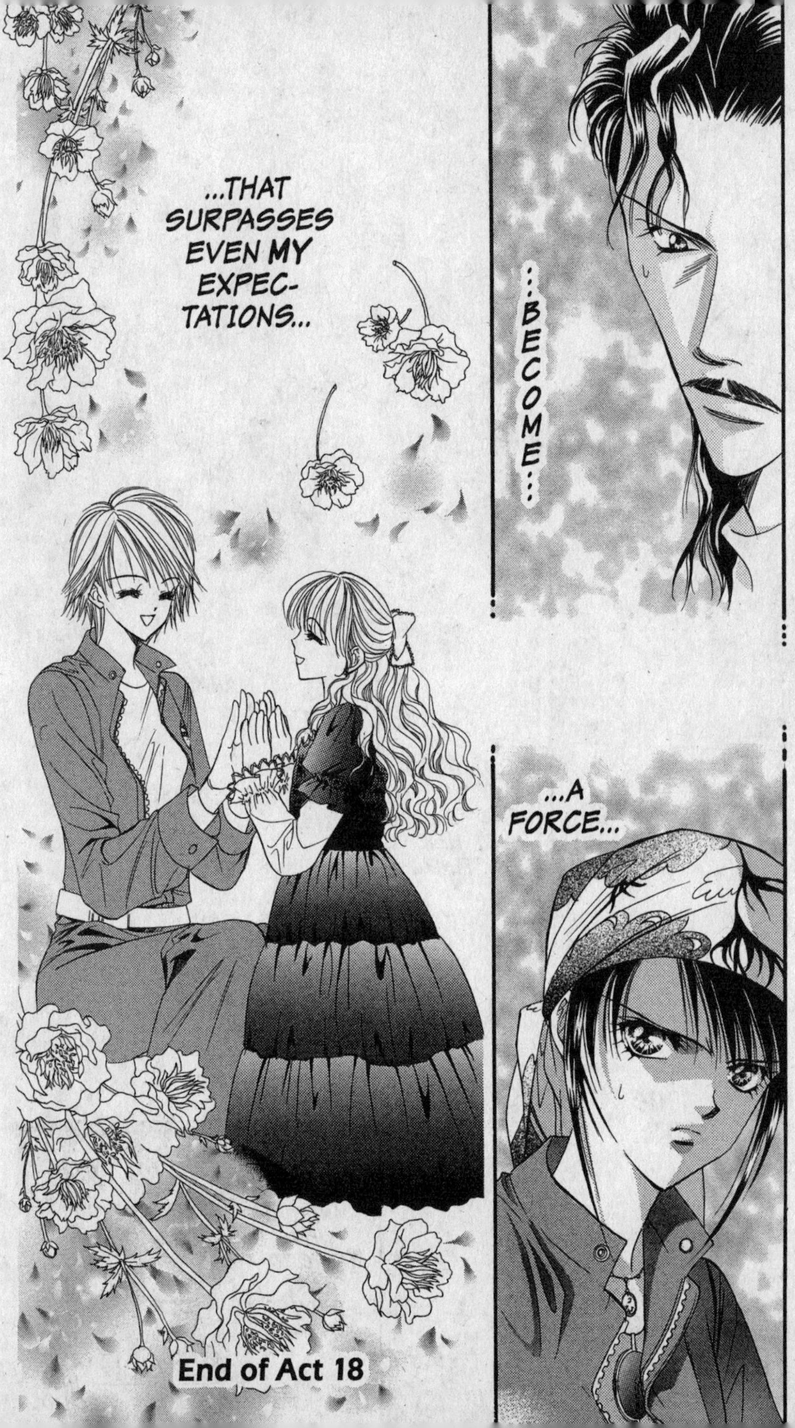
...BECOME...
...A FORCE...
...THAT SURPASSES EVEN MY EXPEC-TATIONS...
End of Act 18

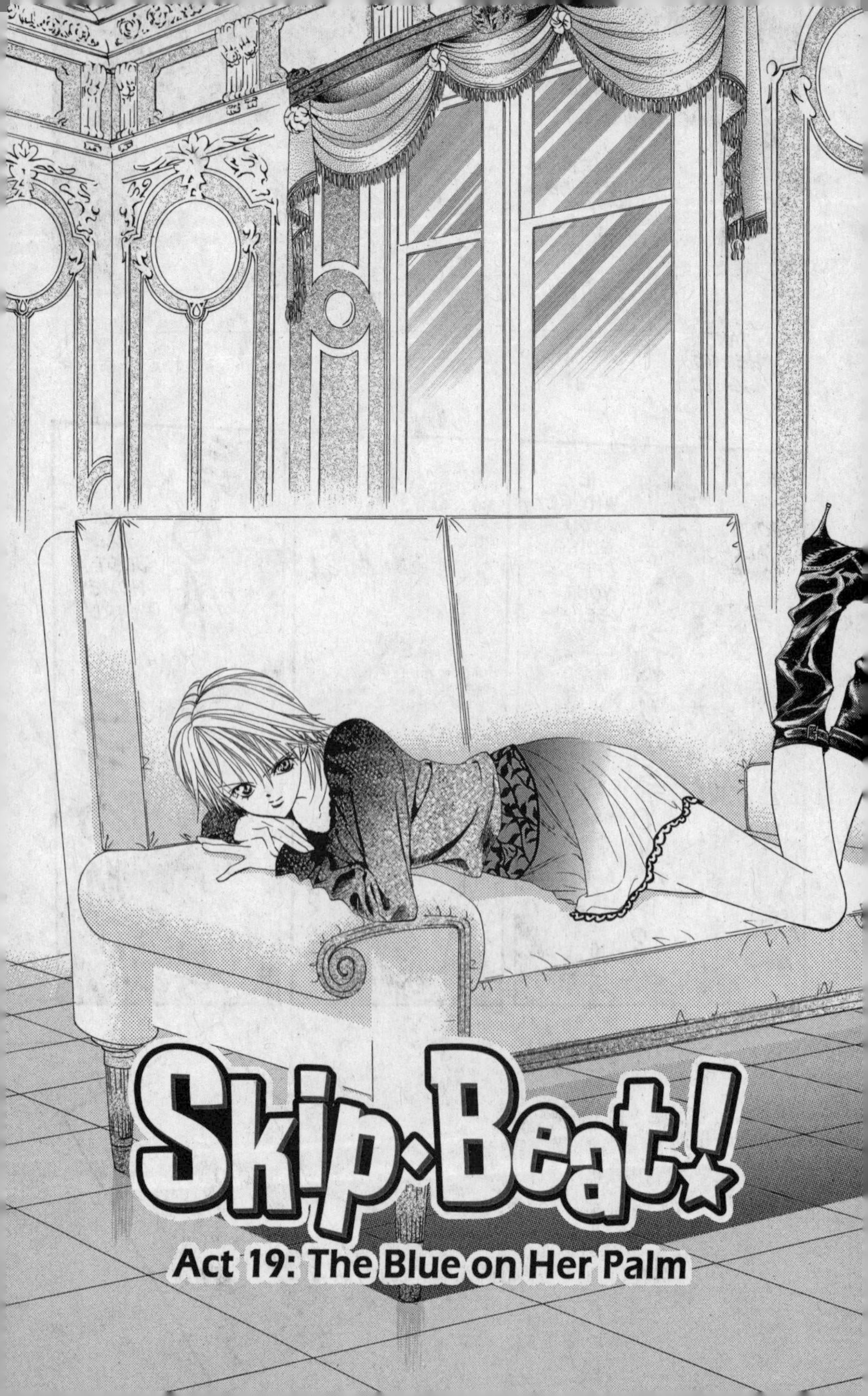
Skip·Beat!
Act 19: The Blue on Her Palm

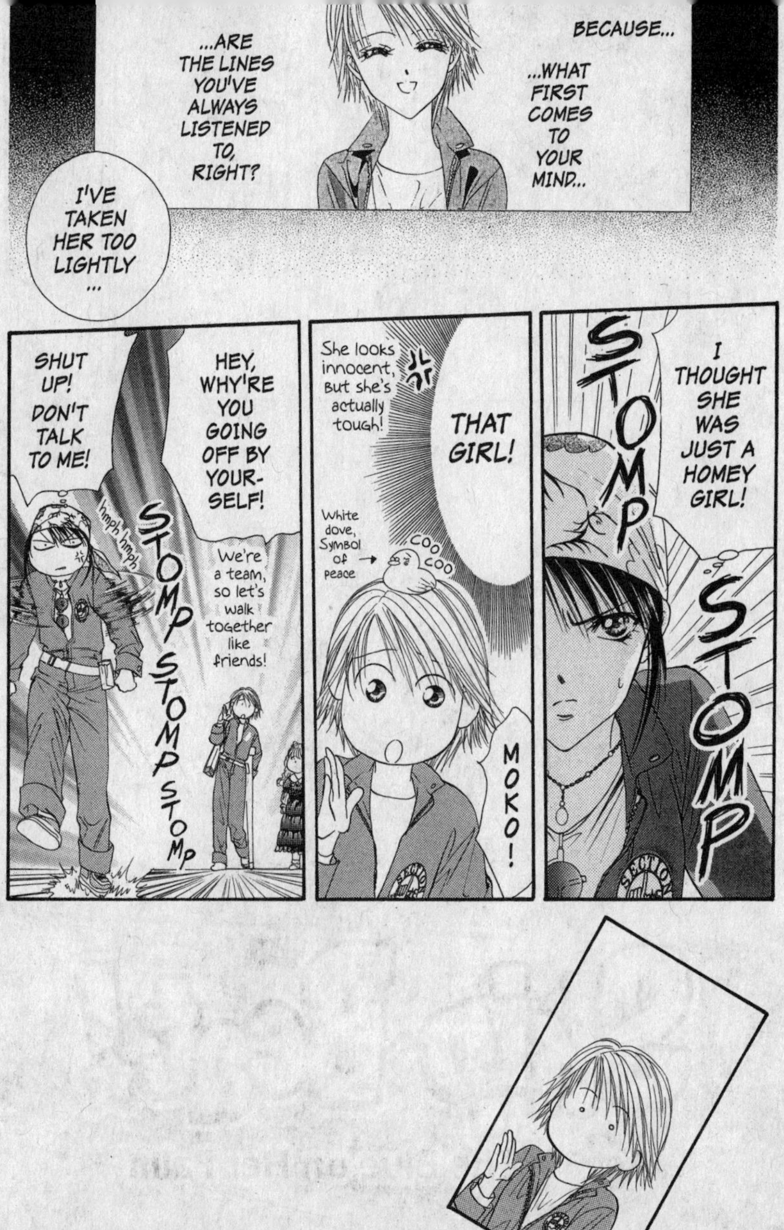
BECAUSE...
...WHAT FIRST COMES TO YOUR MIND...
...ARE THE LINES YOU'VE ALWAYS LISTENED TO, RIGHT?
I'VE TAKEN HER TOO LIGHTLY ...
STOMP
I THOUGHT SHE WAS JUST A HOMEY GIRL!
STOMP
She looks innocent, but she's actually tough!
THAT GIRL!
White dove, Symbol of peace
COO COO
MOKO!
HEY, WHY'RE YOU GOING OFF BY YOURSELF!
SHUT UP! DON'T TALK TO ME!
hmph hmph
STOMP STOMP STOMP
We're a team, so let's walk together like friends!

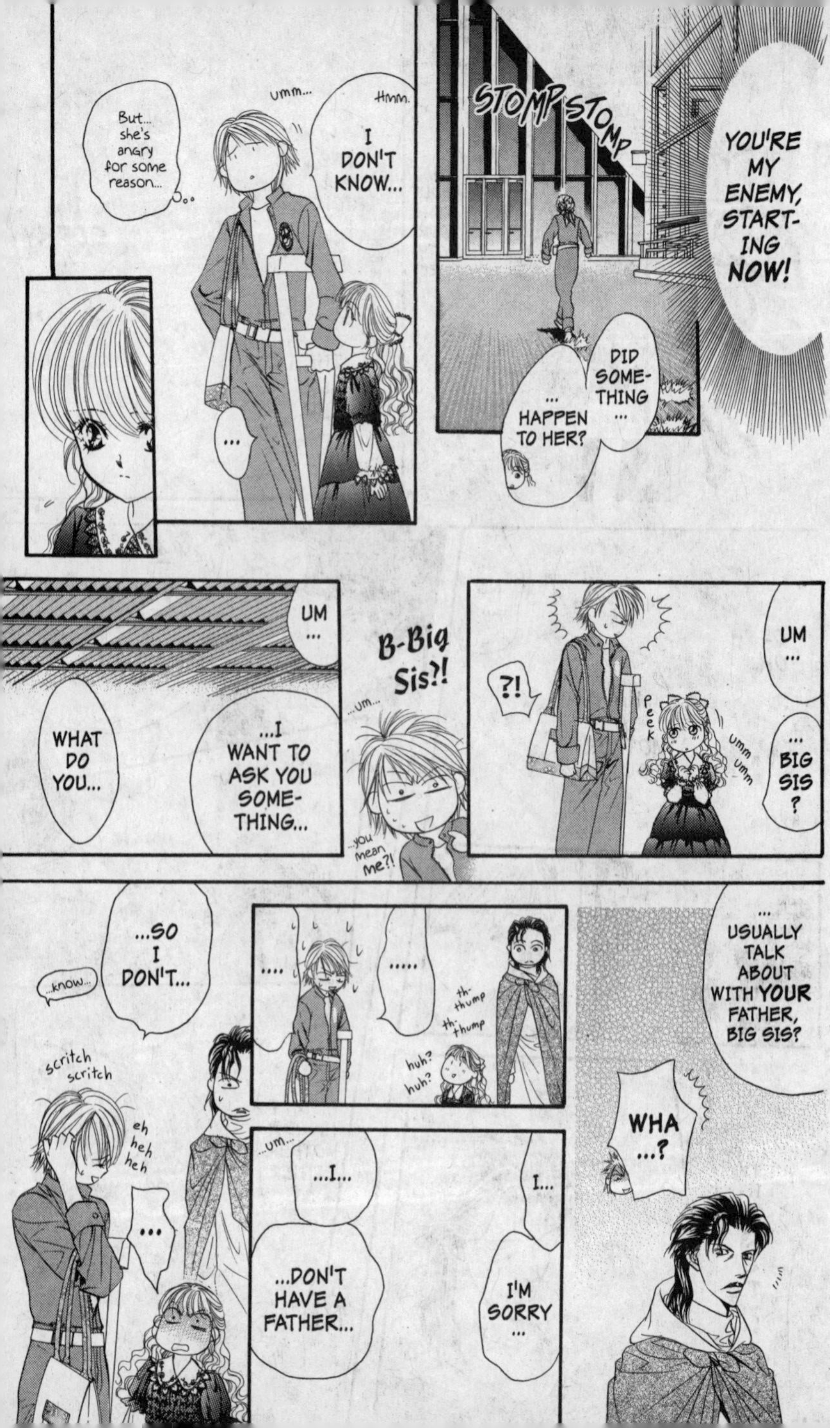
STOMP STOMP
YOU'RE MY ENEMY, START-ING NOW!
DID SOME-THING ...
... HAPPEN TO HER?
Hmm.
I DON'T KNOW...
umm...
But... she's angry for some reason...
...
UM ...
... BIG SIS ?
?!
Peek
Umm Umm
B-Big Sis?!
...um...
...you mean me?!
UM ...
...I WANT TO ASK YOU SOME-THING...
WHAT DO YOU...
... USUALLY TALK ABOUT WITH YOUR FATHER, BIG SIS?
WHA ...?
.....
....
th-thump th-thump
huh? huh?
I...
I'M SORRY ...
...um...
...I...
...DON'T HAVE A FATHER...
...SO I DON'T...
...know...
scritch scritch
eh heh heh
...

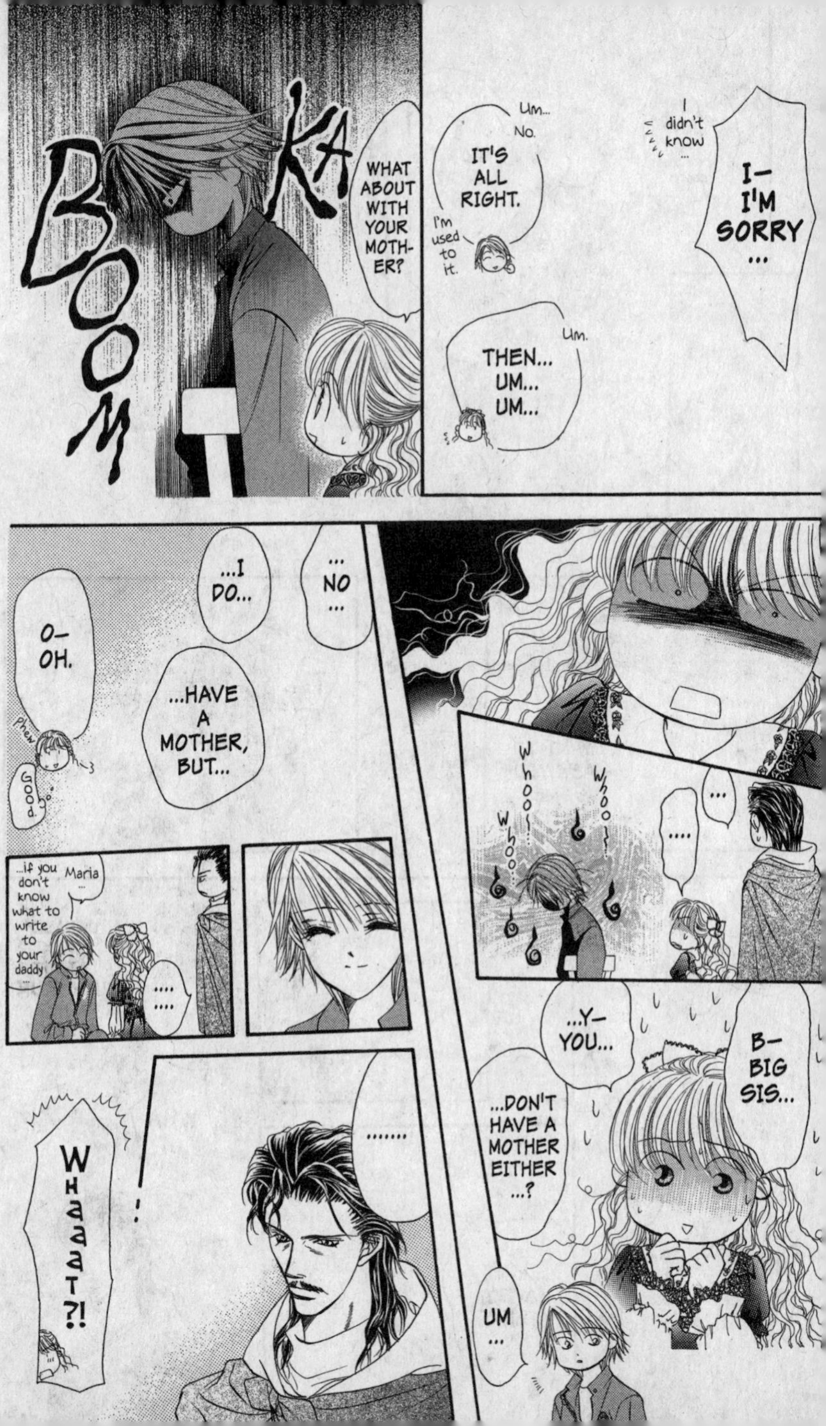
I— I'M SORRY...
I didn't know...
Um... No.
IT'S ALL RIGHT.
I'm used to it.
Um.
THEN... UM... UM...
WHAT ABOUT WITH YOUR MOTHER?
KA BOOM
...
....
Whooo~
Whooo~
Whooo~
B— BIG SIS...
...Y— YOU...
...DON'T HAVE A MOTHER EITHER...?
UM...
...NO...
...I DO...
...HAVE A MOTHER, BUT...
O— OH.
Phew
Good.
Maria...
...if you don't know what to write to your daddy...
....
....
!
Whaaat?!

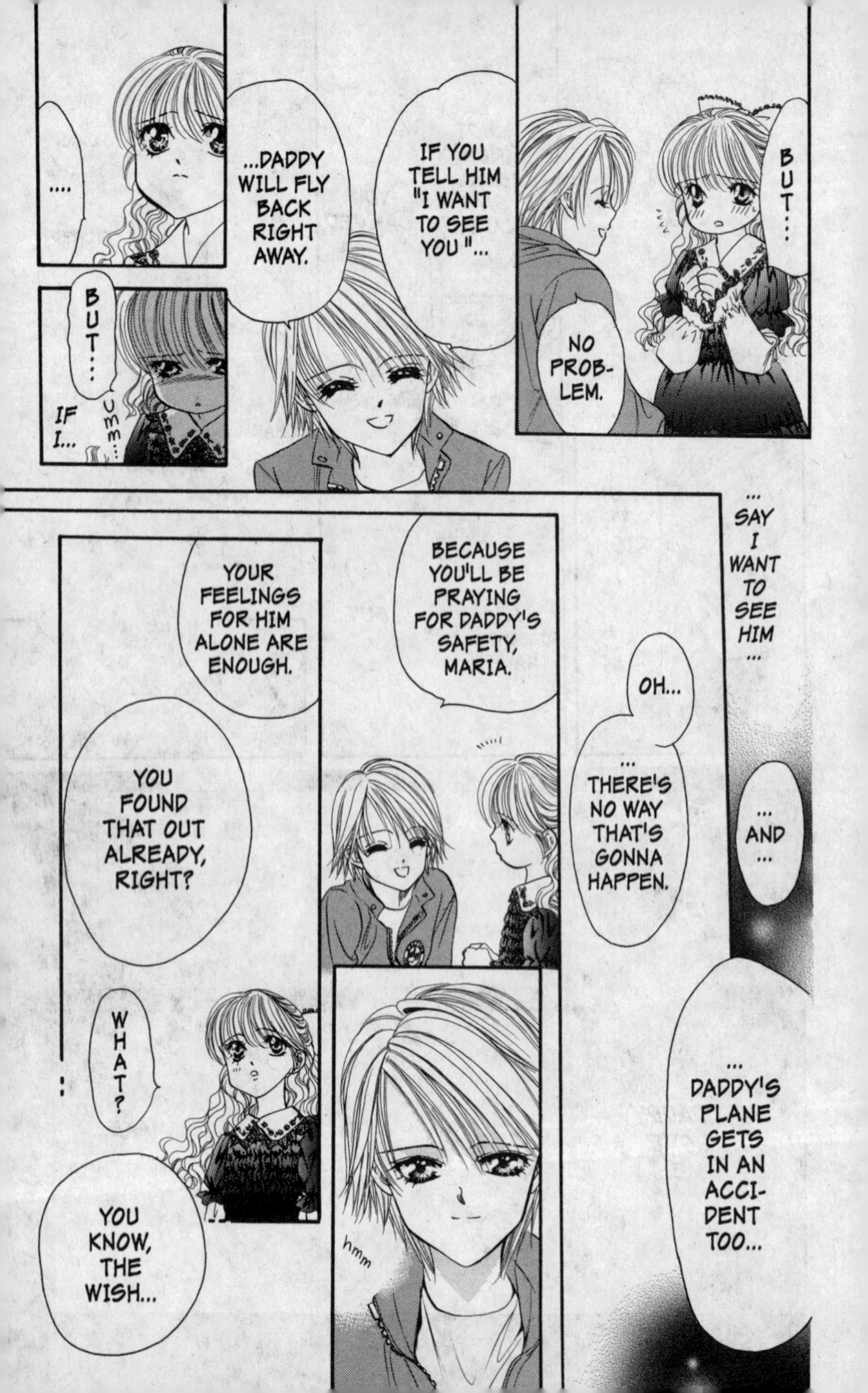
BUT...
NO PROBLEM.
IF YOU TELL HIM "I WANT TO SEE YOU"...
...DADDY WILL FLY BACK RIGHT AWAY.
....
BUT...
UMM...
IF I...
...SAY I WANT TO SEE HIM...
...AND...
...DADDY'S PLANE GETS IN AN ACCIDENT TOO...
OH...
...THERE'S NO WAY THAT'S GONNA HAPPEN.
BECAUSE YOU'LL BE PRAYING FOR DADDY'S SAFETY, MARIA.
YOUR FEELINGS FOR HIM ALONE ARE ENOUGH.
YOU FOUND THAT OUT ALREADY, RIGHT?
hmm
WHAT?
YOU KNOW, THE WISH...

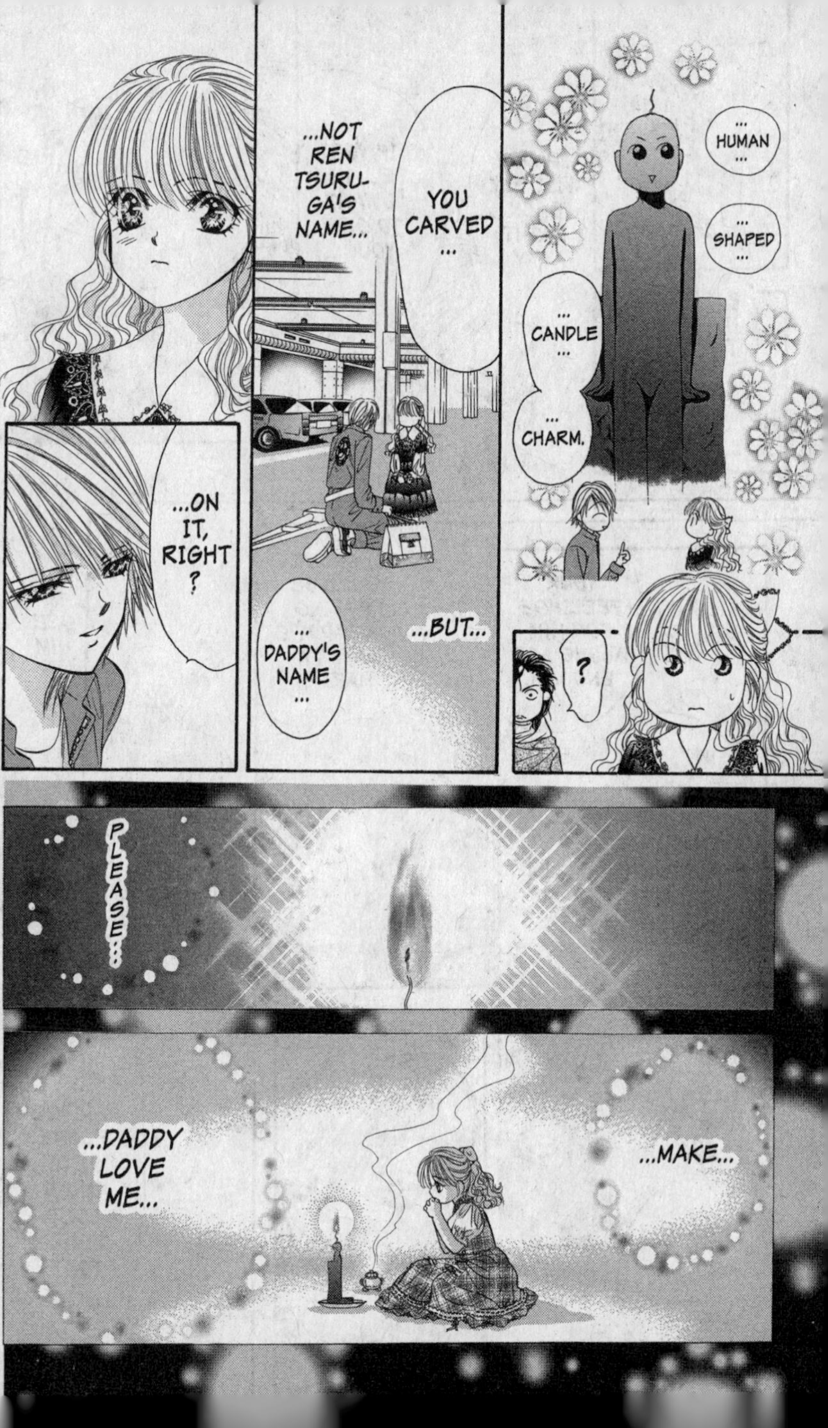
... HUMAN ...
... SHAPED ...
... CANDLE ...
... CHARM.
?
YOU CARVED ...
...NOT REN TSURUGA'S NAME...
...BUT...
... DADDY'S NAME ...
...ON IT, RIGHT ?
PLEASE...
...MAKE...
...DADDY LOVE ME...

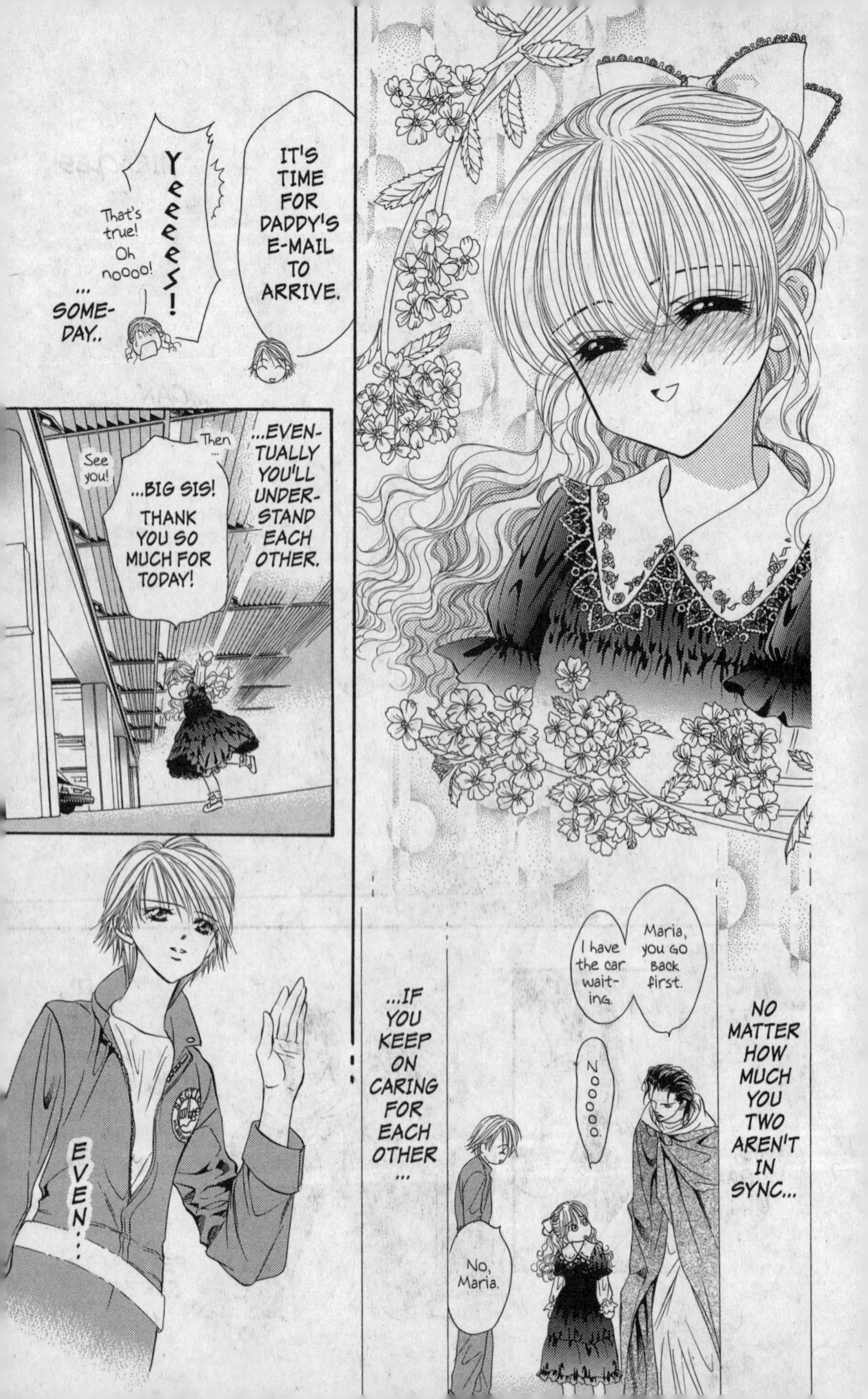
NO MATTER HOW MUCH YOU TWO AREN'T IN SYNC...
Maria, you GO Back first.
I have the car wait-ing.
Nooooo.
No, Maria.
...IF YOU KEEP ON CARING FOR EACH OTHER...
IT'S TIME FOR DADDY'S E-MAIL TO ARRIVE.
Yeeees!
That's true! Oh noooo!
...SOME-DAY..
...EVEN-TUALLY YOU'LL UNDER-STAND EACH OTHER.
Then...
...BIG SIS! THANK YOU SO MUCH FOR TODAY!
See you!
EVEN...

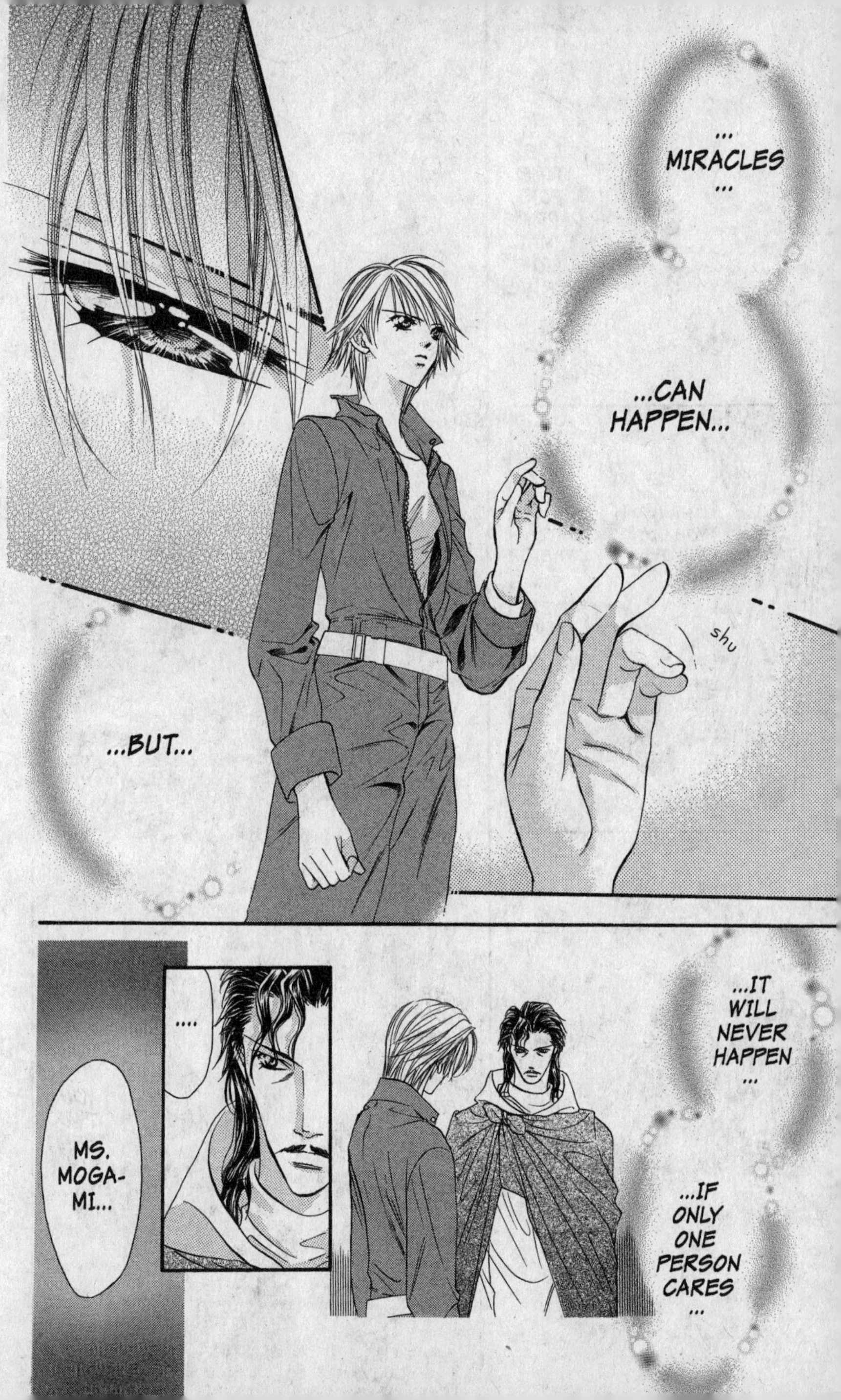
...MIRACLES...
...CAN HAPPEN...
shu
...BUT...
...IT WILL NEVER HAPPEN...
...IF ONLY ONE PERSON CARES...
....
MS. MOGA-MI...

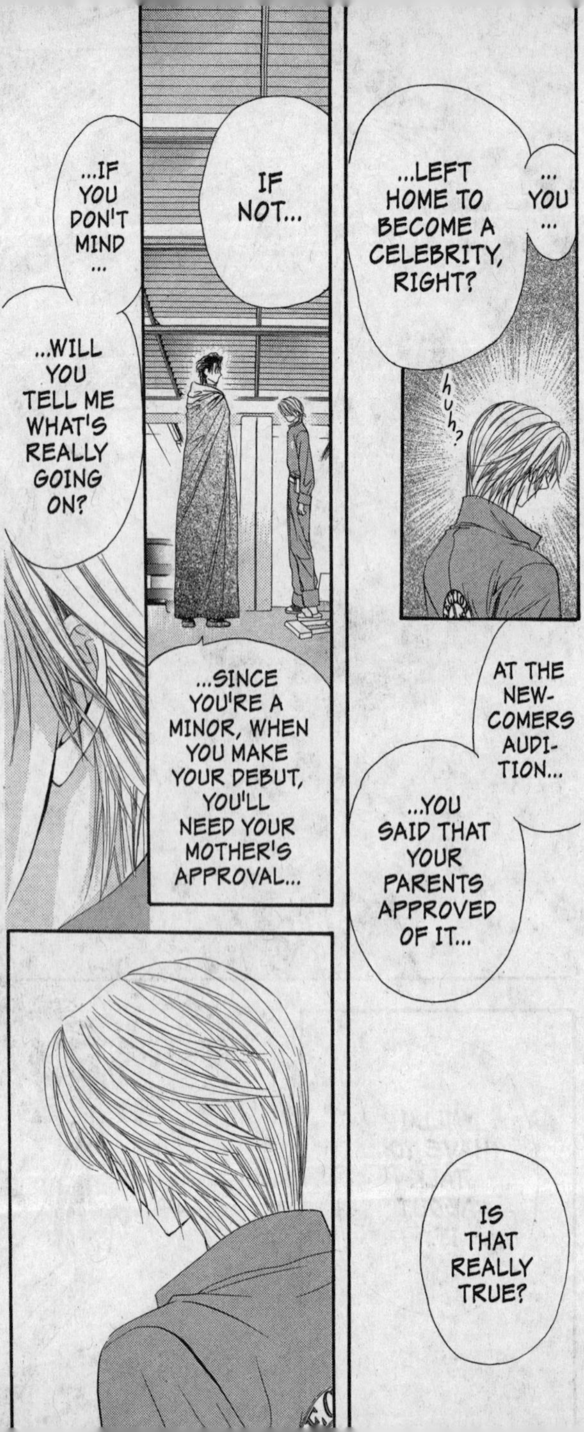
... YOU ...
...LEFT HOME TO BECOME A CELEBRITY, RIGHT?
huh?
IF NOT...
...SINCE YOU'RE A MINOR, WHEN YOU MAKE YOUR DEBUT, YOU'LL NEED YOUR MOTHER'S APPROVAL...
...IF YOU DON'T MIND ...
...WILL YOU TELL ME WHAT'S REALLY GOING ON?
AT THE NEW-COMERS AUDI-TION...
...YOU SAID THAT YOUR PARENTS APPROVED OF IT...
IS THAT REALLY TRUE?

Shoko Aki

Shotaro's manager. I really wasn't thinking anything when I named her Shoko. When I thought about it later...

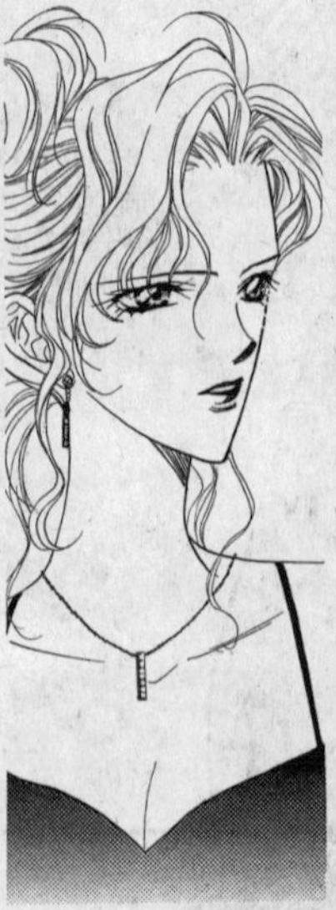

...Sho Fuwa and Shoko becomes a friendly Sho x Sho pair, why...!! And I panicked a little... ...Well actually, they seem to be more friendly than neces-sary. So this woman was carelessly named Shoko, and there are no hidden reasons why.

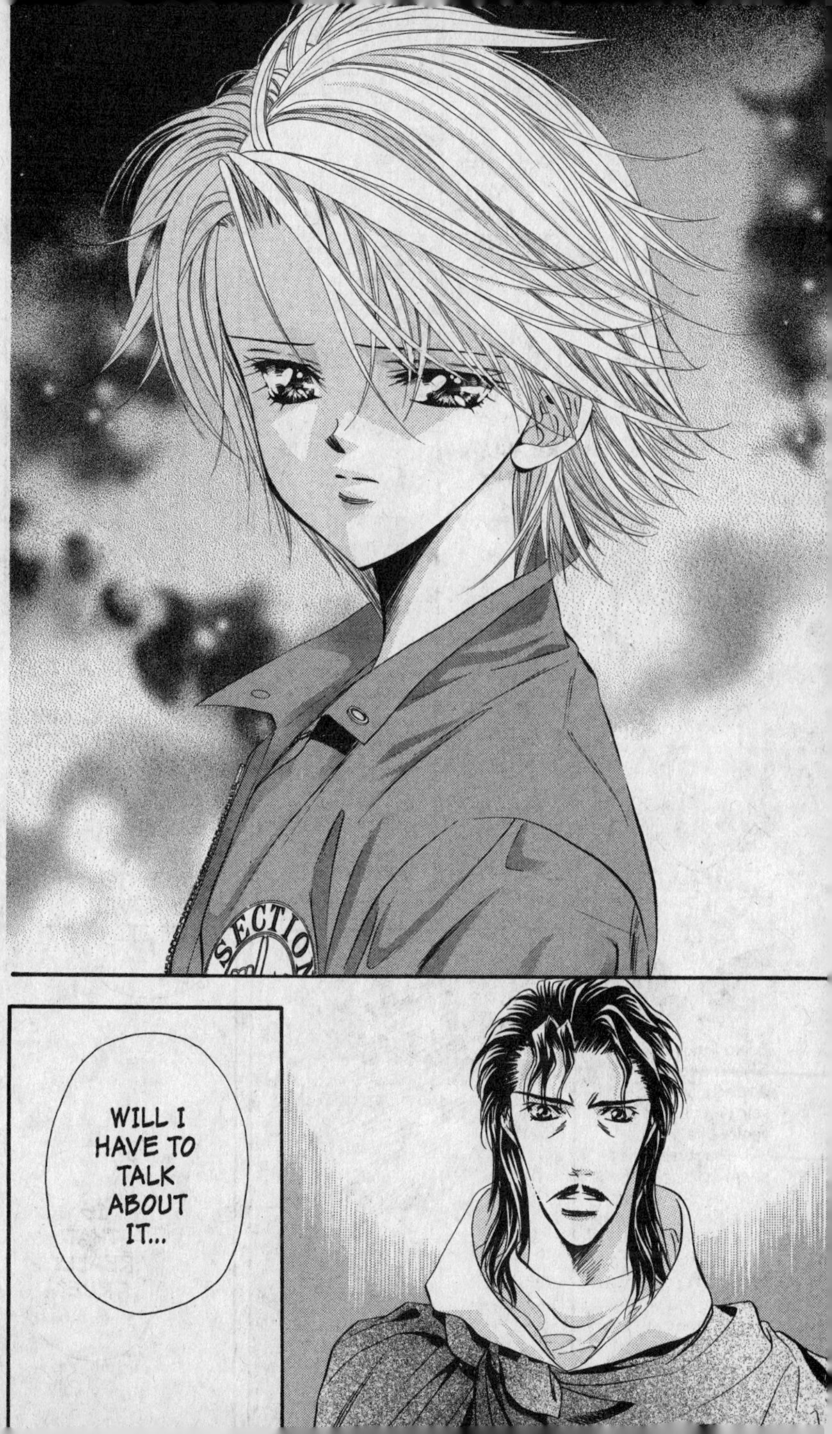
SECTION
WILL I HAVE TO TALK ABOUT IT...

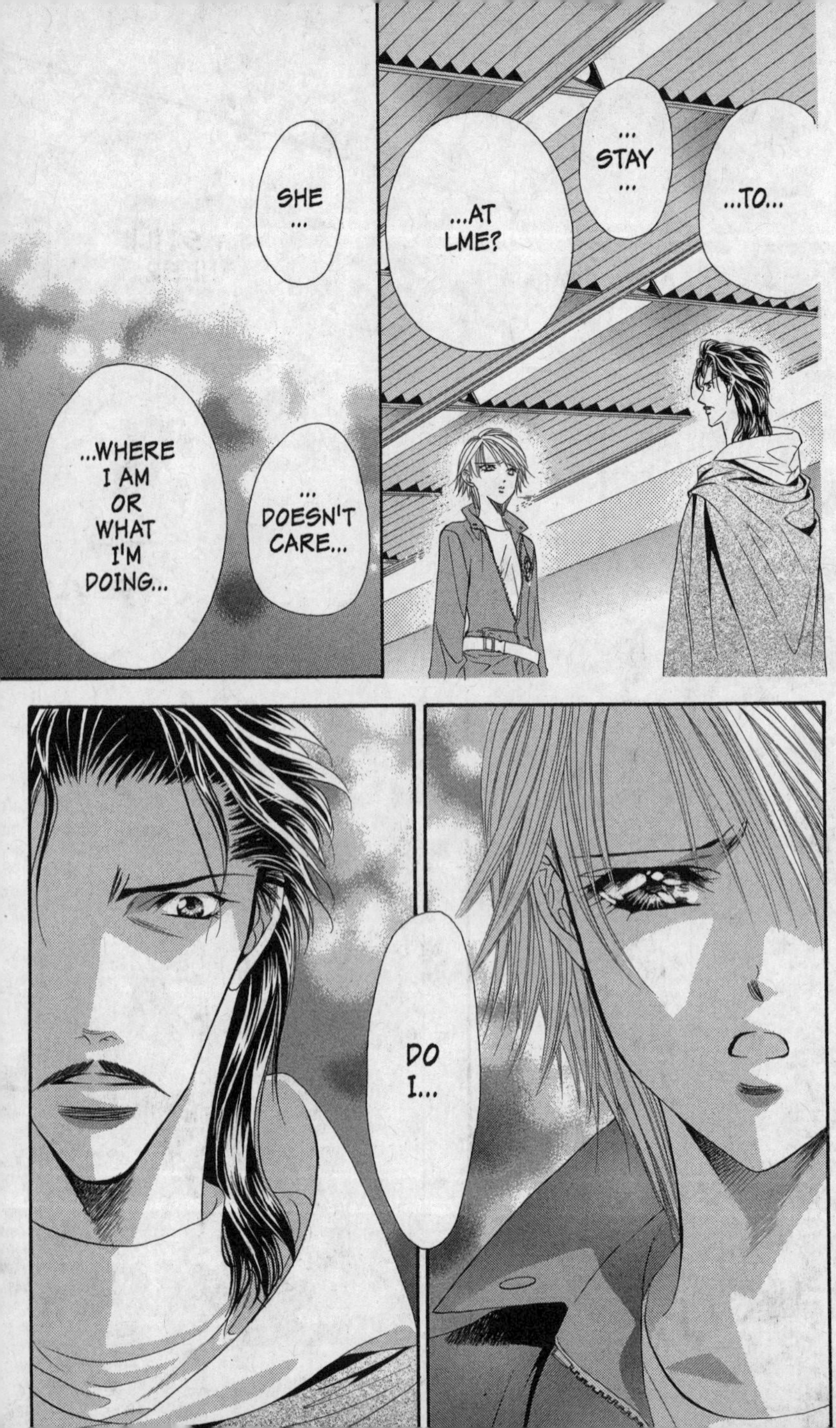
...TO...
...STAY...
...AT LME?
SHE...
...DOESN'T CARE...
...WHERE I AM OR WHAT I'M DOING...
DO I...

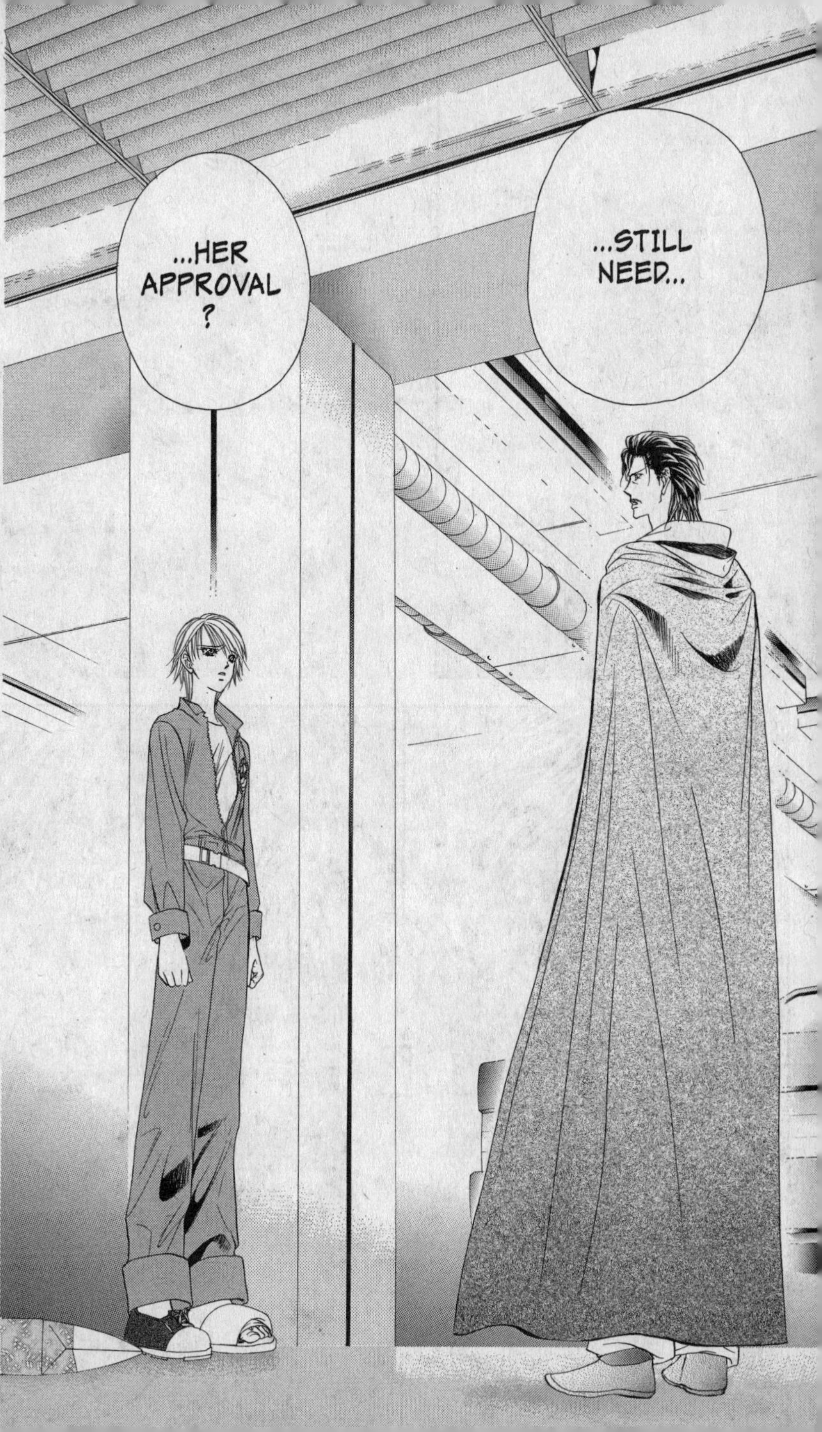
...STILL NEED...
...HER APPROVAL ?

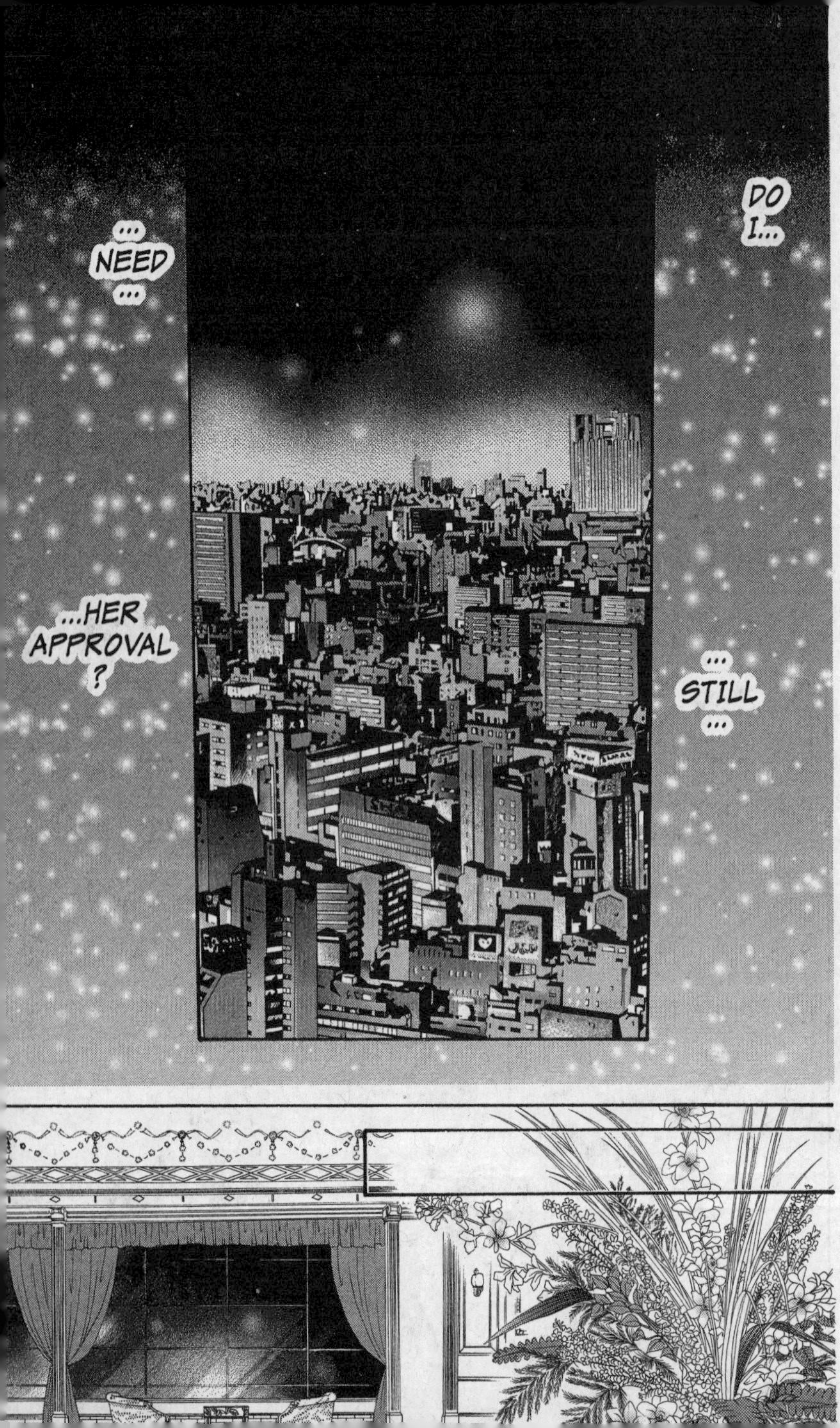
DO I...
...STILL...
...NEED...
...HER APPROVAL ?

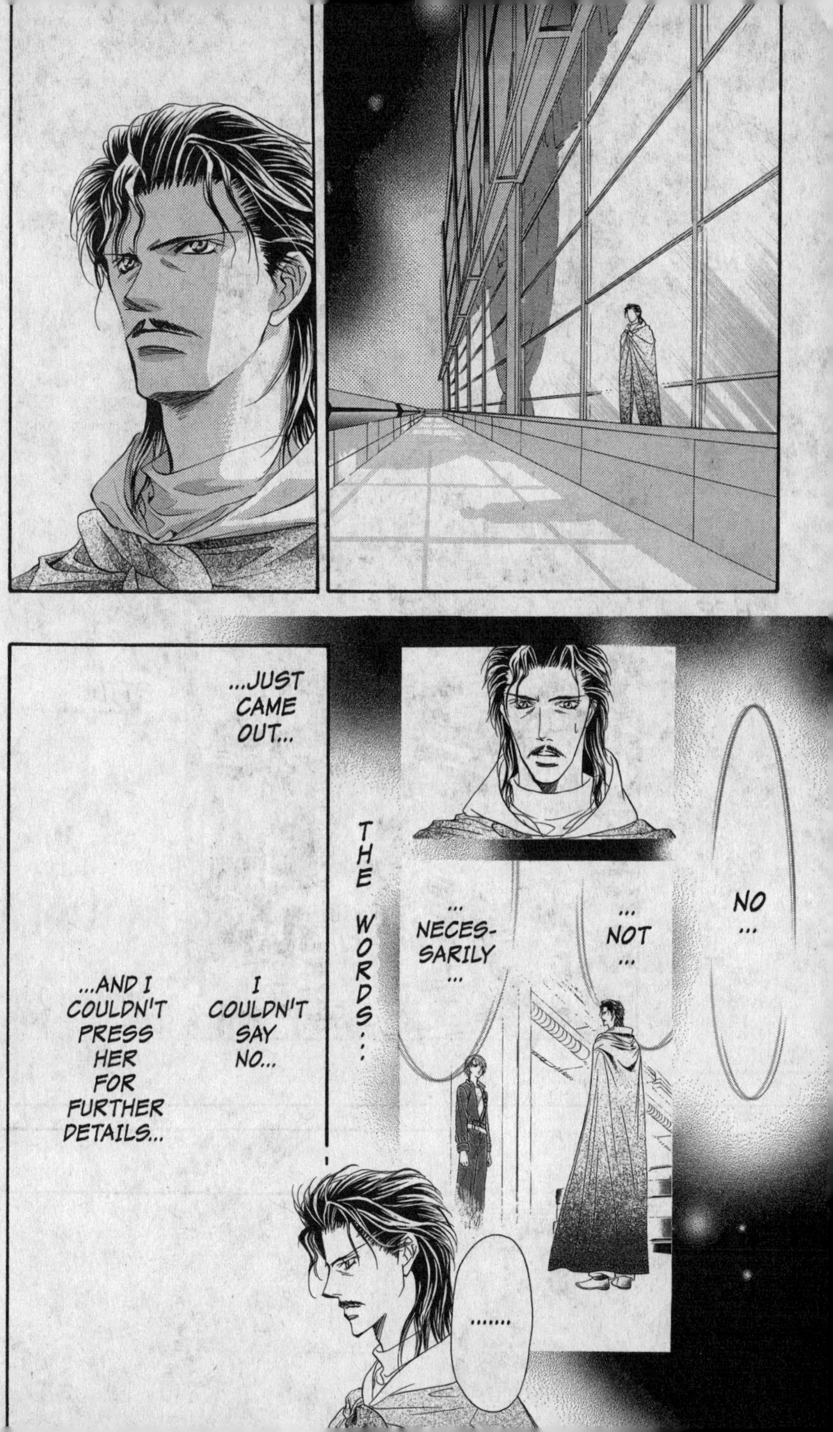
NO...
...NOT...
...NECESSARILY...
THE WORDS...
...JUST CAME OUT...
I COULDN'T SAY NO...
...AND I COULDN'T PRESS HER FOR FURTHER DETAILS...
....

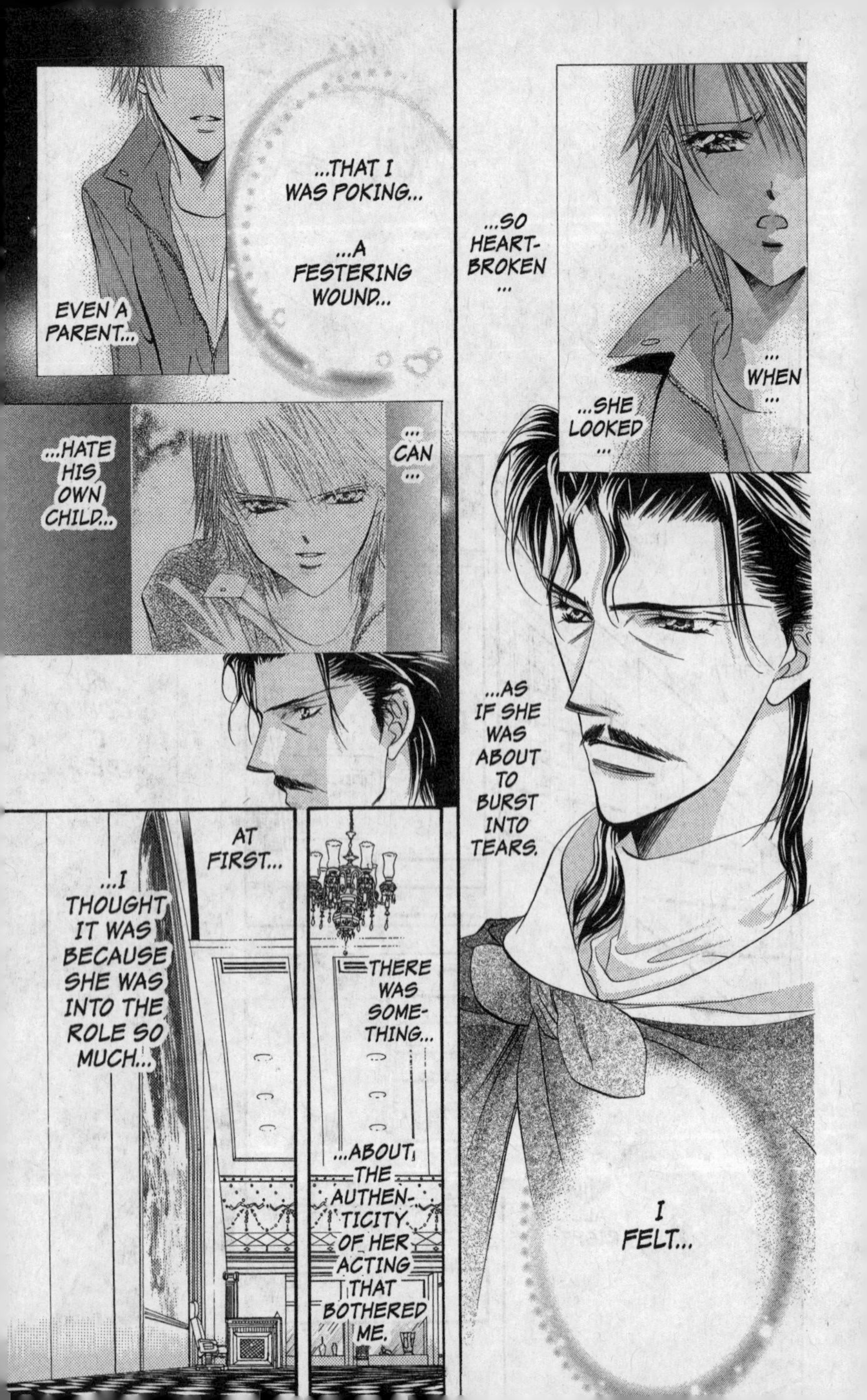
...WHEN...
...SHE LOOKED...
...SO HEART-BROKEN...
...AS IF SHE WAS ABOUT TO BURST INTO TEARS.
I FELT...
...THAT I WAS POKING...
...A FESTERING WOUND...
EVEN A PARENT...
...CAN...
...HATE HIS OWN CHILD...
AT FIRST...
...I THOUGHT IT WAS BECAUSE SHE WAS INTO THE ROLE SO MUCH...
THERE WAS SOME-THING...
...ABOUT THE AUTHEN-TICITY OF HER ACTING THAT BOTHERED ME.

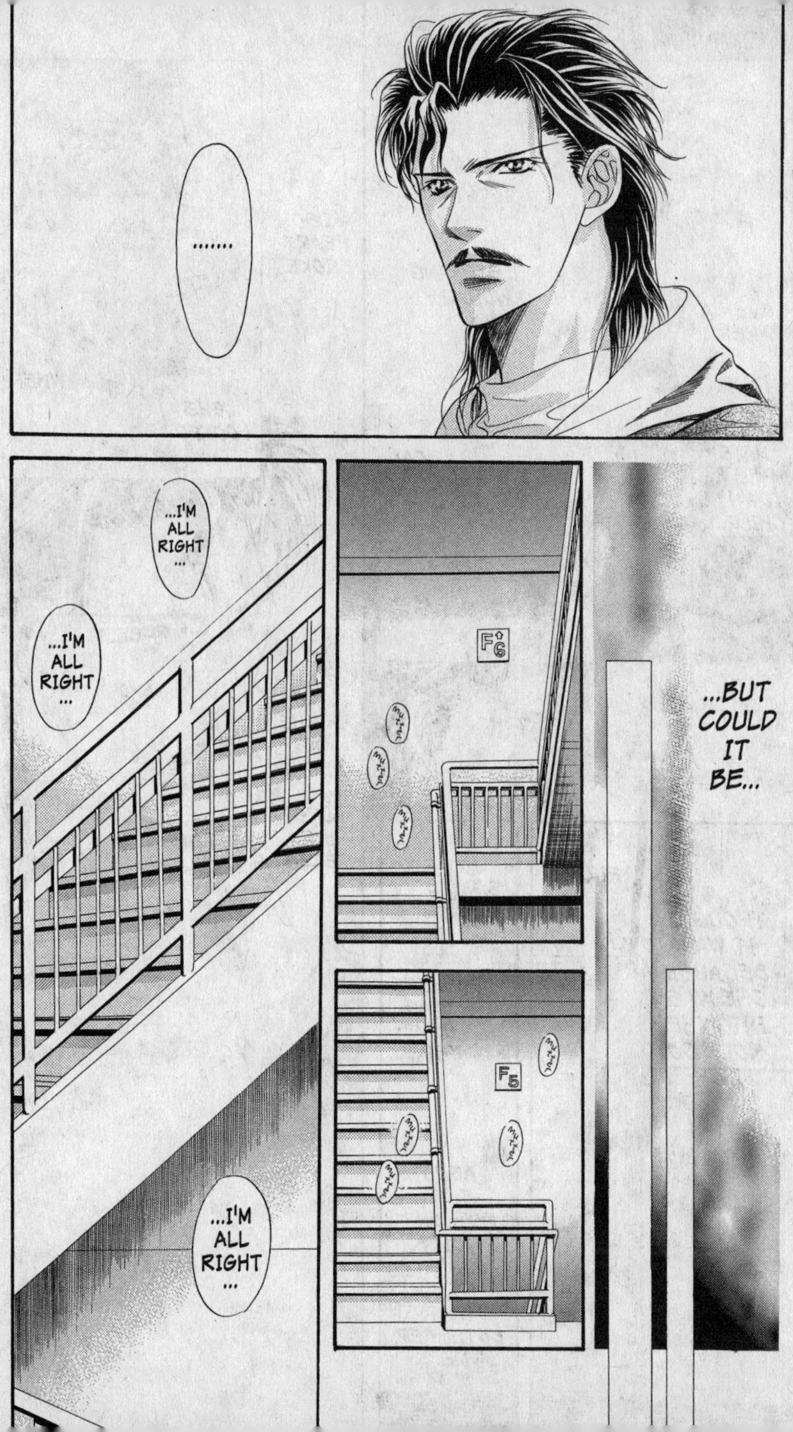
....
...BUT COULD IT BE...
mutter
mutter
mutter
mutter
mutter
mutter
mutter
F6
F5
...I'M ALL RIGHT...
...I'M ALL RIGHT...
...I'M ALL RIGHT...

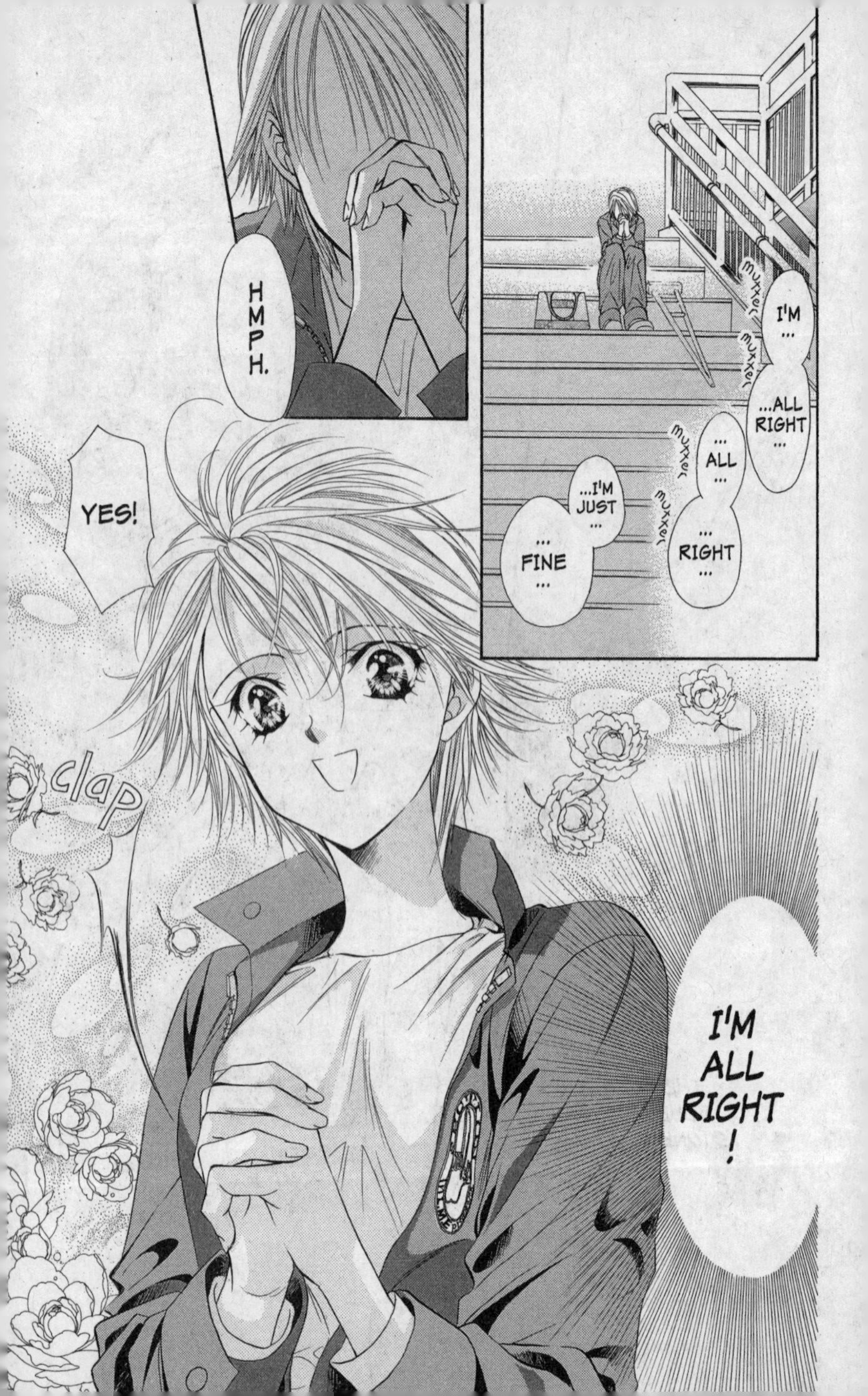
mutter
I'M ...
mutter
...ALL RIGHT ...
mutter
... ALL ...
mutter
... RIGHT ...
...I'M JUST ...
... FINE ...
HMPH.
I'M ALL RIGHT!
YES!
clap

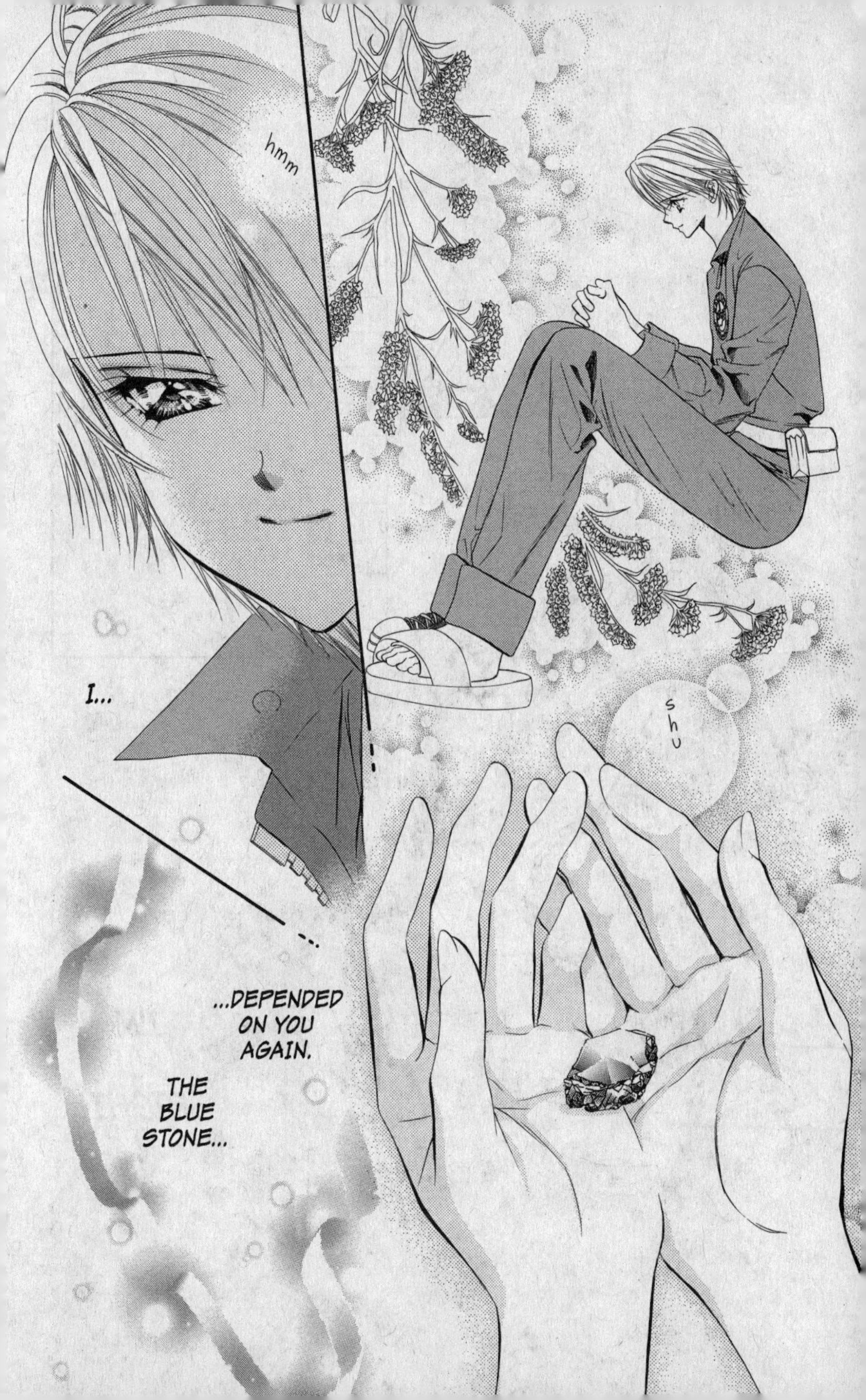
hmm
I...
shu
...DEPENDED ON YOU AGAIN.
THE BLUE STONE...

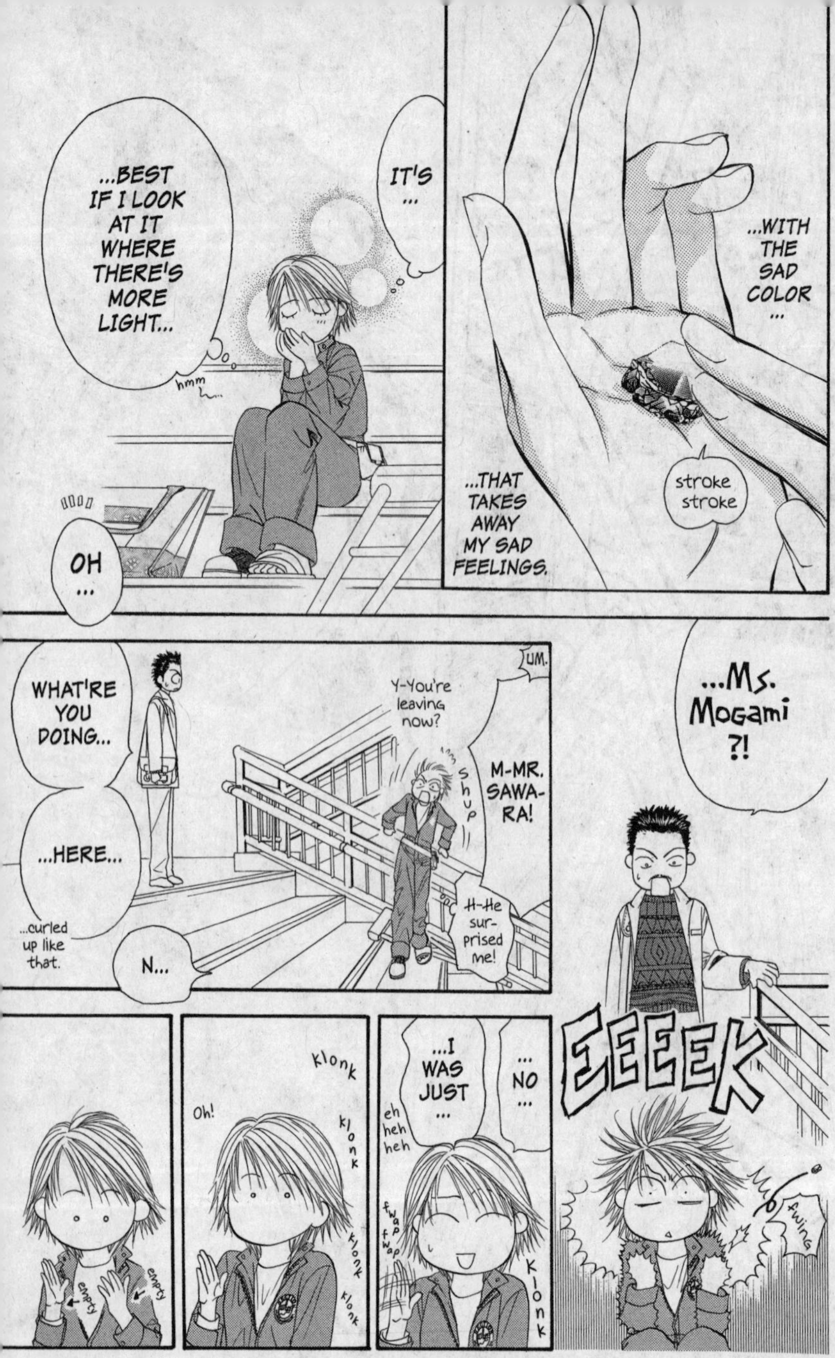
...WITH THE SAD COLOR ...
stroke stroke
...THAT TAKES AWAY MY SAD FEELINGS.
IT'S ...
...BEST IF I LOOK AT IT WHERE THERE'S MORE LIGHT...
hmm
OH ...
...Ms. Mogami ?!
UM.
Y-You're leaving now?
M-MR. SAWARA!
shup
H-He surprised me!
WHAT'RE YOU DOING...
...HERE...
...curled up like that.
N...
EEEEK
fwing
... NO ...
...I WAS JUST ...
eh heh heh
fwap fwap
Klonk
klonk
Oh!
klonk
klonk
klonk
empty
empty

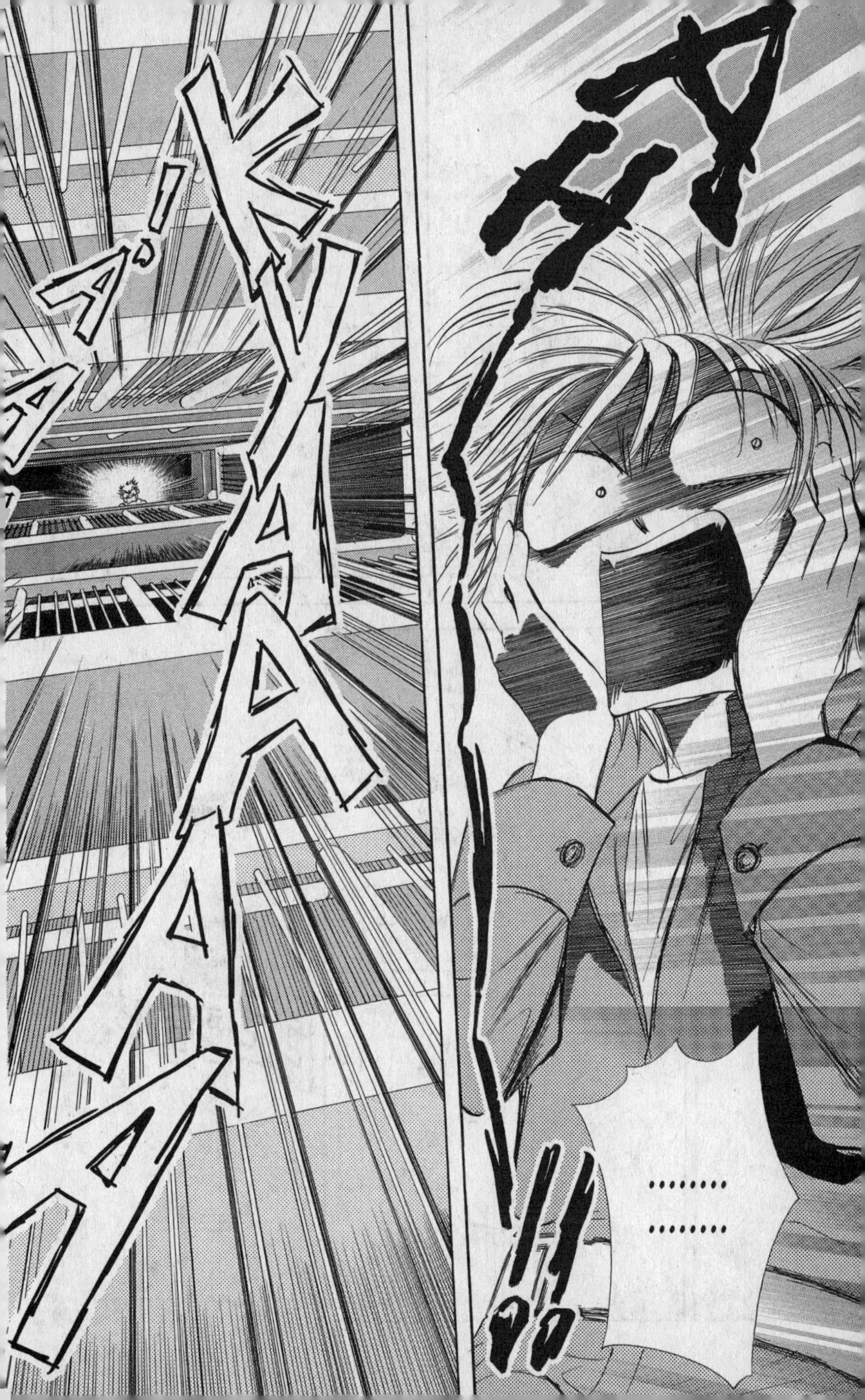
....
....

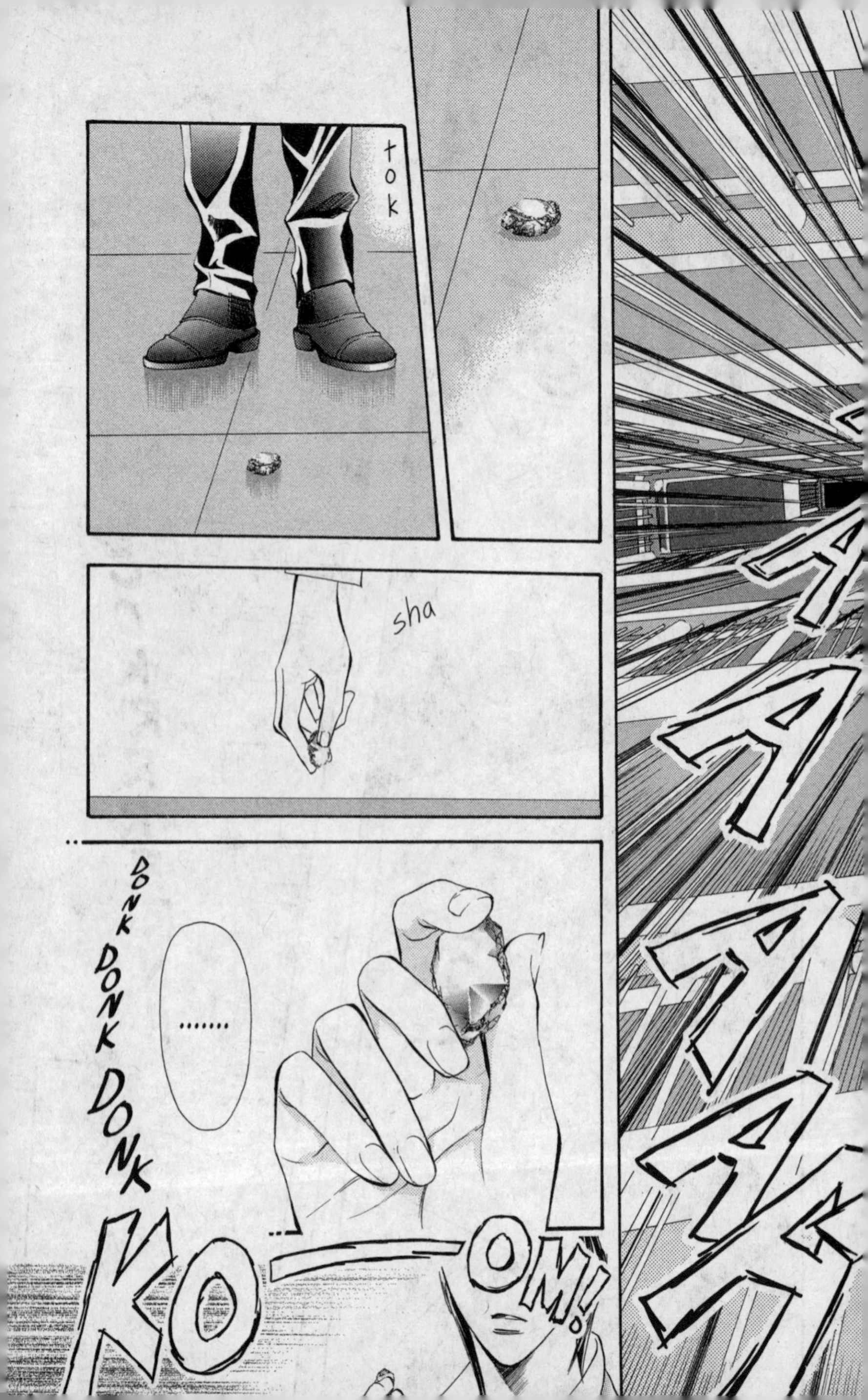

AAAA
tok
sha
......
DONK DONK DONK
KO—OM!

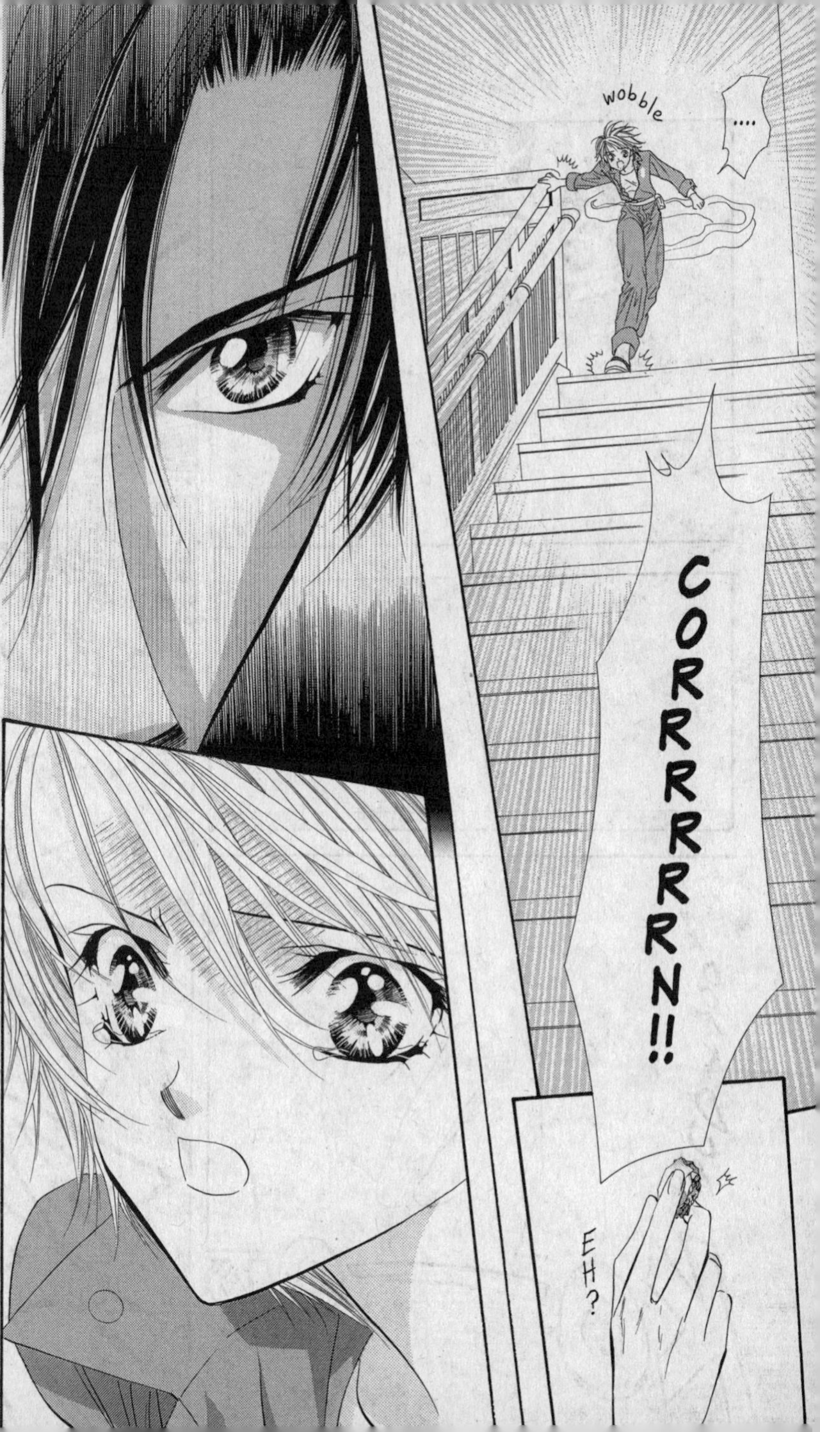
wobble
....
CORRRRRRN!!
EH?

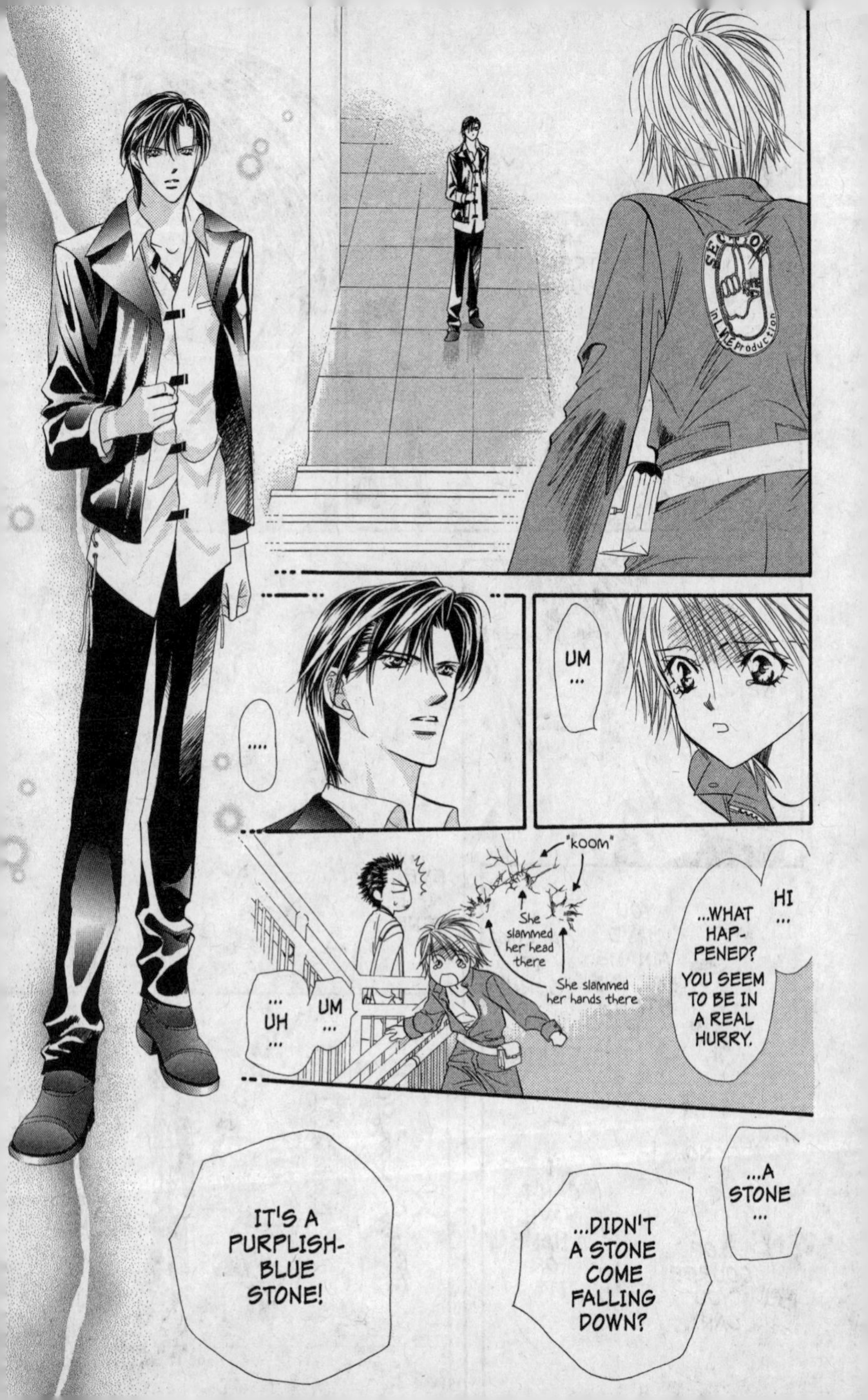
UM ...
.....
HI ...
...WHAT HAP-PENED? YOU SEEM TO BE IN A REAL HURRY.
"KOOM"
She slammed her head there
She slammed her hands there
UM ...
... UH ...
...A STONE ...
...DIDN'T A STONE COME FALLING DOWN?
IT'S A PURPLISH-BLUE STONE!

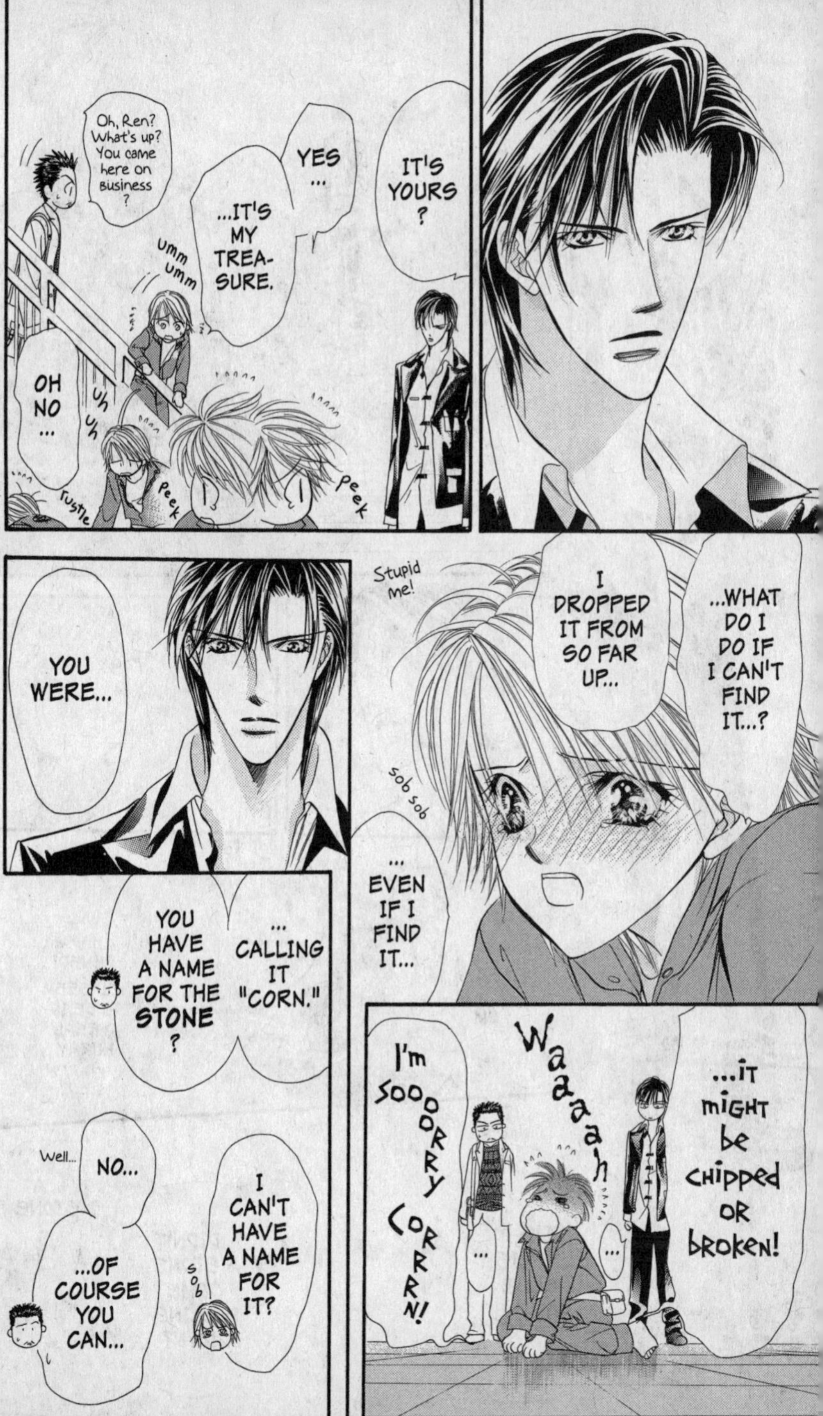
IT'S YOURS?
YES...
...IT'S MY TREASURE.
Oh, Ren? What's up? You came here on business?
umm umm
OH NO...
uh uh
peek
peek
rustle
Stupid me!
...WHAT DO I DO IF I CAN'T FIND IT...?
I DROPPED IT FROM SO FAR UP...
sob sob
...EVEN IF I FIND IT...
YOU WERE...
...CALLING IT "CORN."
YOU HAVE A NAME FOR THE STONE?
I CAN'T HAVE A NAME FOR IT?
sob
Well...
NO...
...OF COURSE YOU CAN...
...it might be chipped or broken!
Waaaah
I'm SOOOORRY CORRRN!
...
...

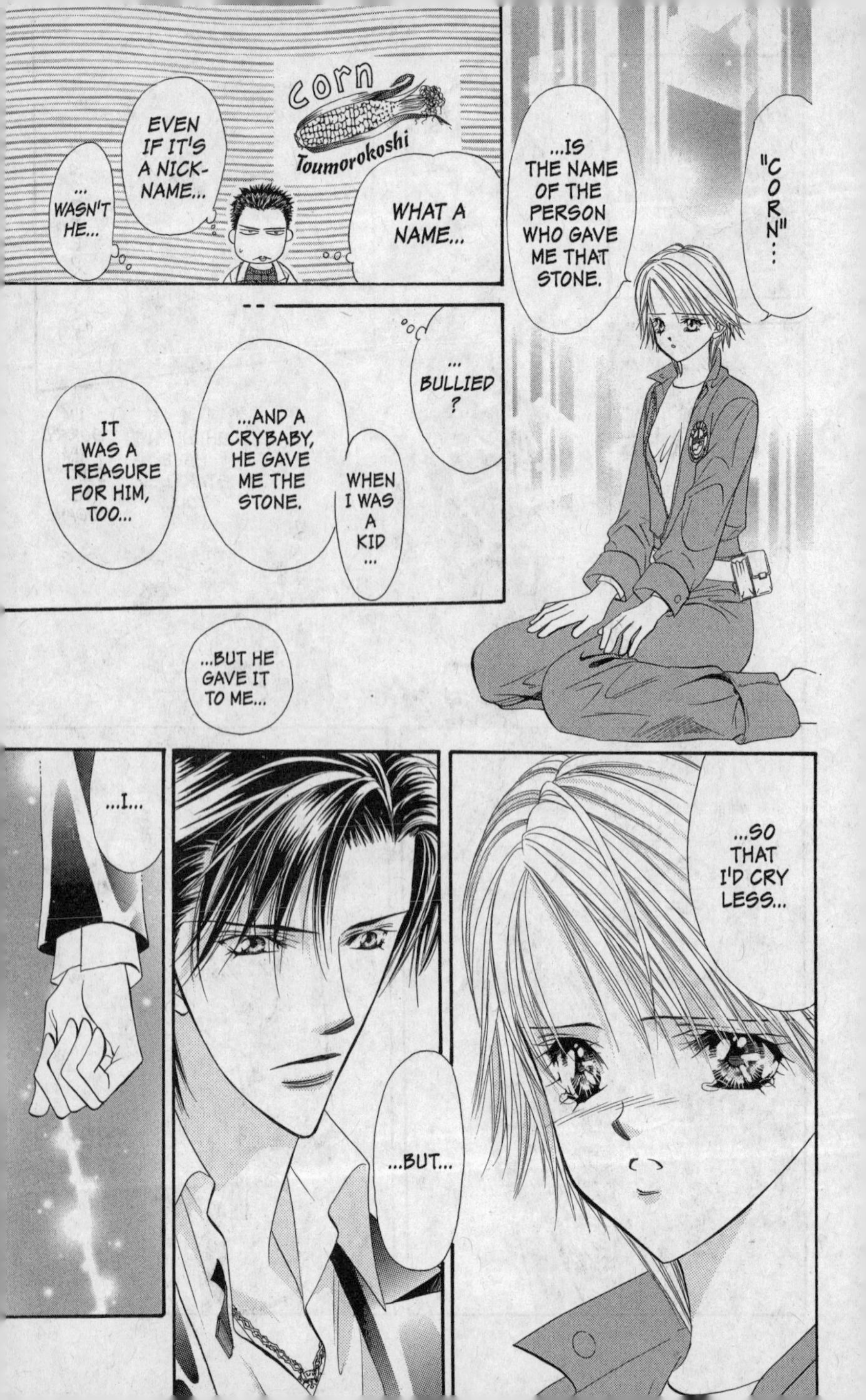
"CORN"...
...IS THE NAME OF THE PERSON WHO GAVE ME THAT STONE.
WHAT A NAME...
Corn
Toumorokoshi
EVEN IF IT'S A NICK-NAME...
...WASN'T HE...
...BULLIED?
WHEN I WAS A KID...
...AND A CRYBABY, HE GAVE ME THE STONE.
IT WAS A TREASURE FOR HIM, TOO...
...BUT HE GAVE IT TO ME...
...SO THAT I'D CRY LESS...
...BUT...
...I...

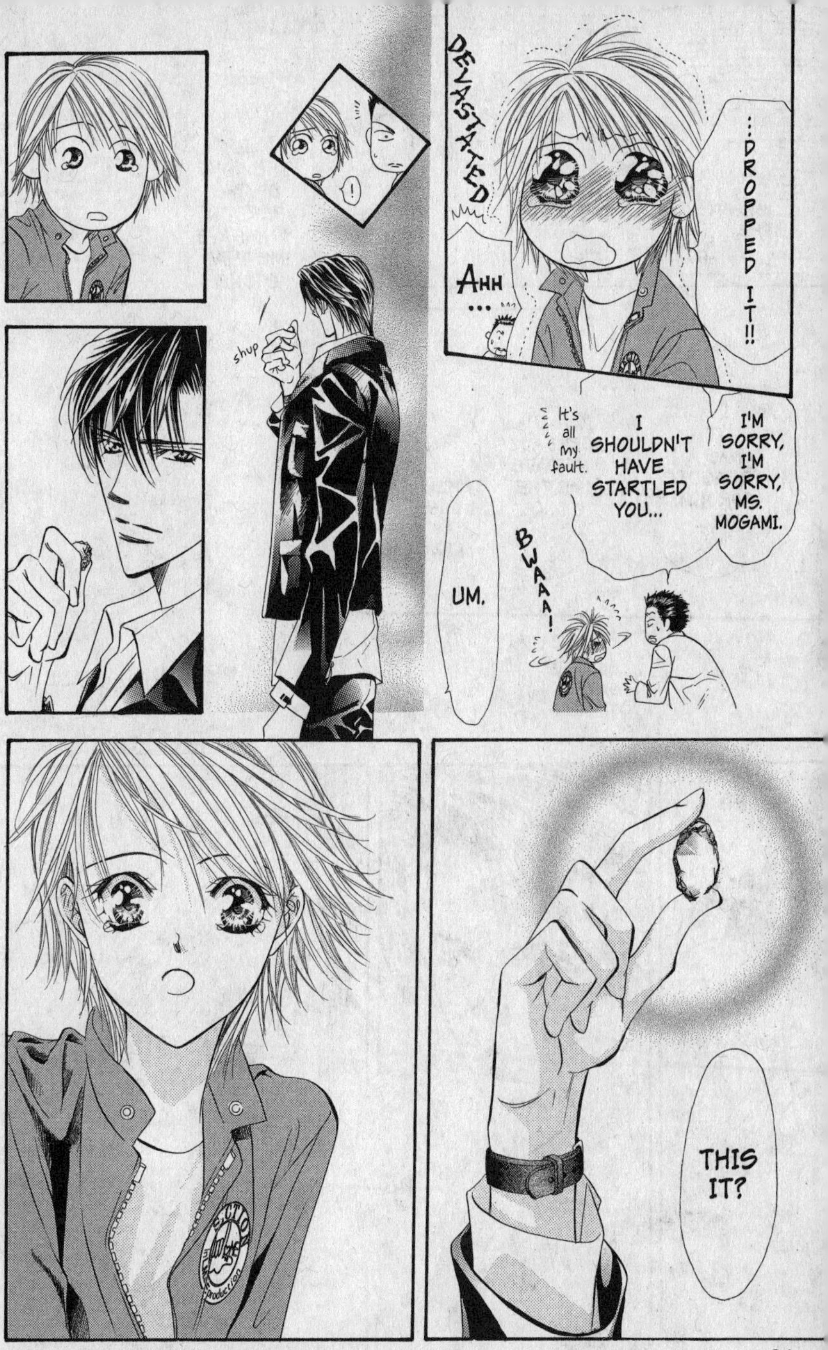
...DROPPED IT!!
DEVASTATED
AHH ...
I'M SORRY, I'M SORRY, MS. MOGAMI.
I SHOULDN'T HAVE STARTLED YOU...
It's all my fault.
BWAAA!
UM.
!
shup
THIS IT?

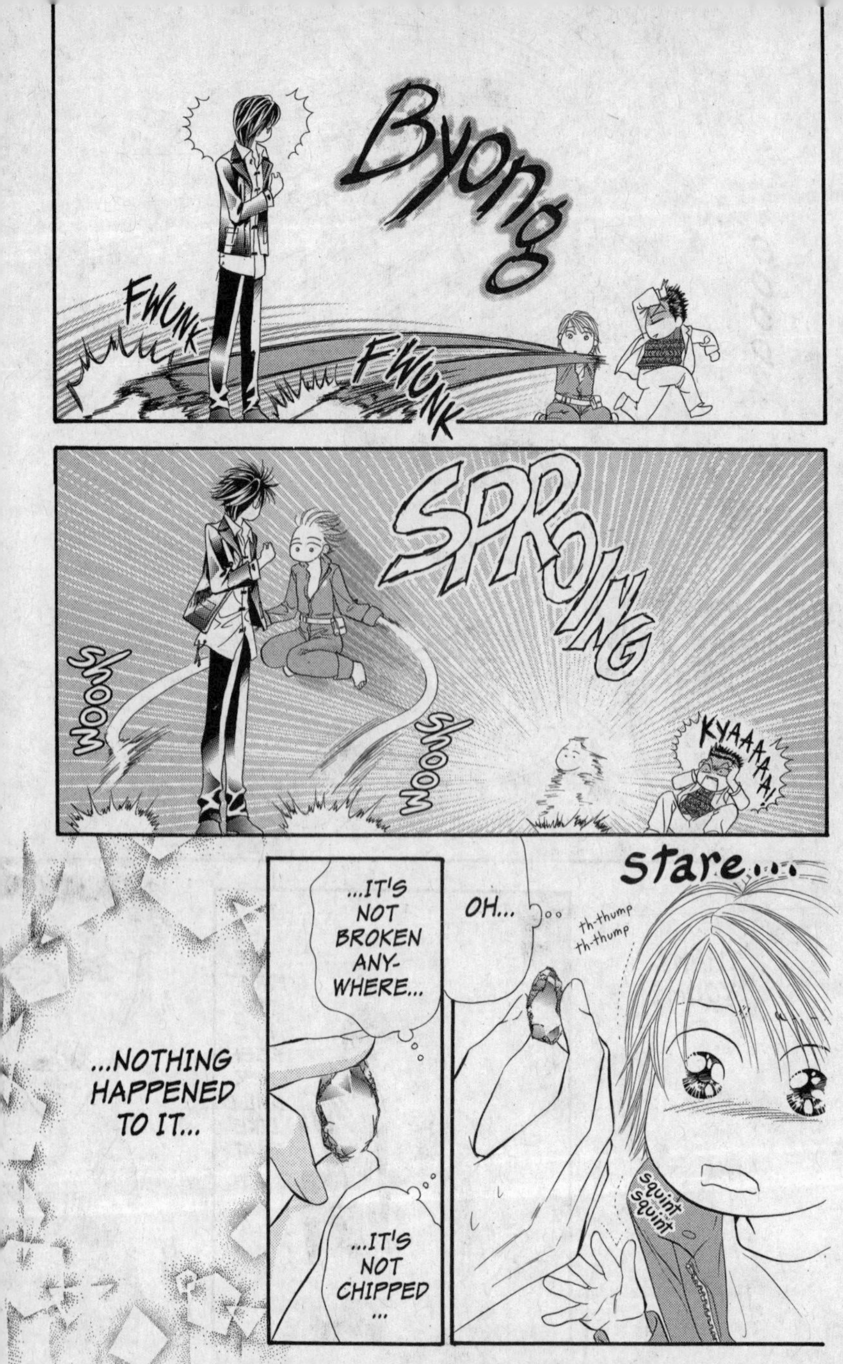
Byong
FWUNK
FWUNK
SPROING
shoom
shoom
KYAAAAAA!
stare....
th-thump th-thump
OH...
squint squint
...IT'S NOT BROKEN ANY-WHERE...
...IT'S NOT CHIPPED ...
...NOTHING HAPPENED TO IT...

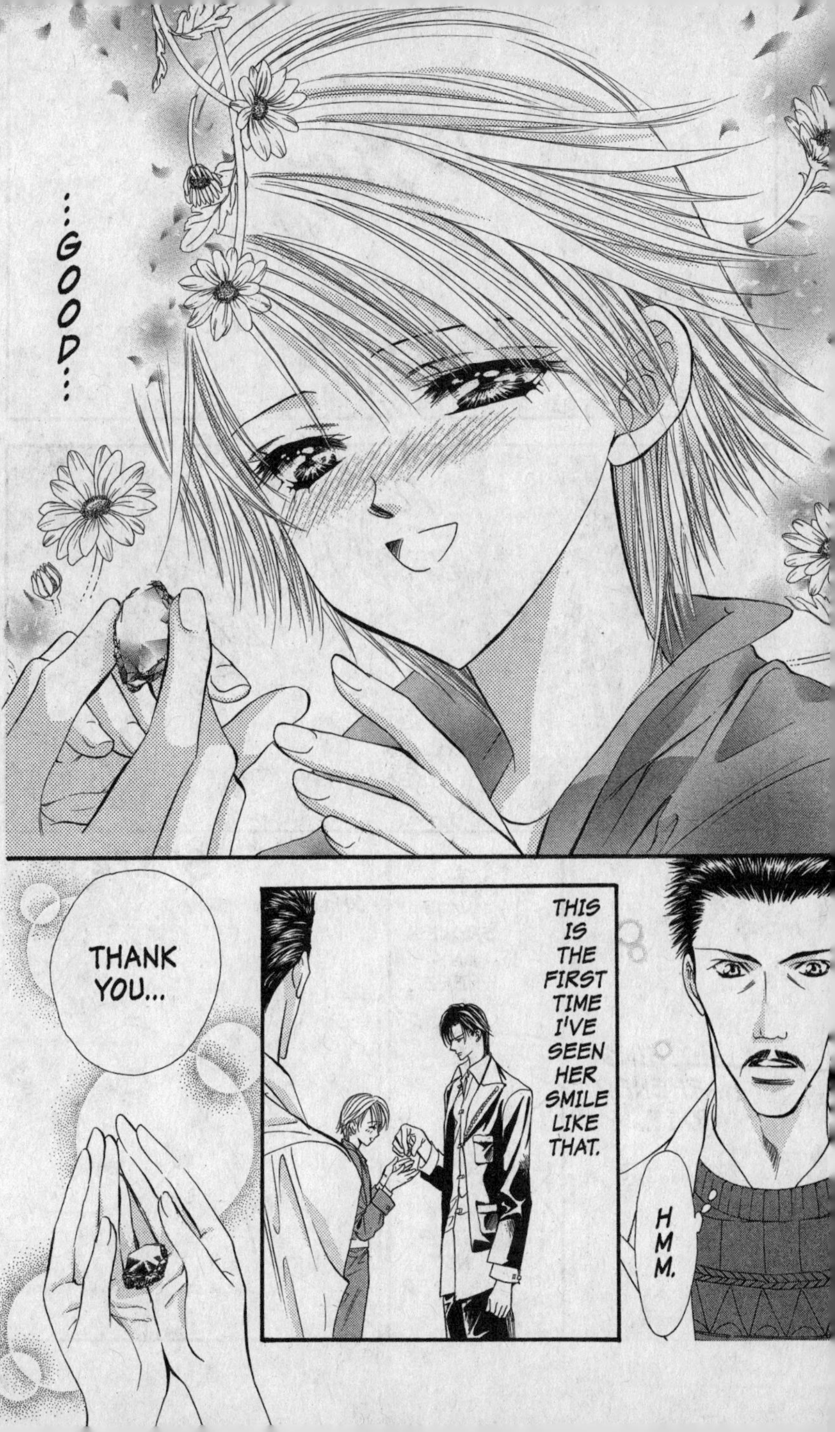
...GOOD...
HMM.
THIS IS THE FIRST TIME I'VE SEEN HER SMILE LIKE THAT.
THANK YOU...

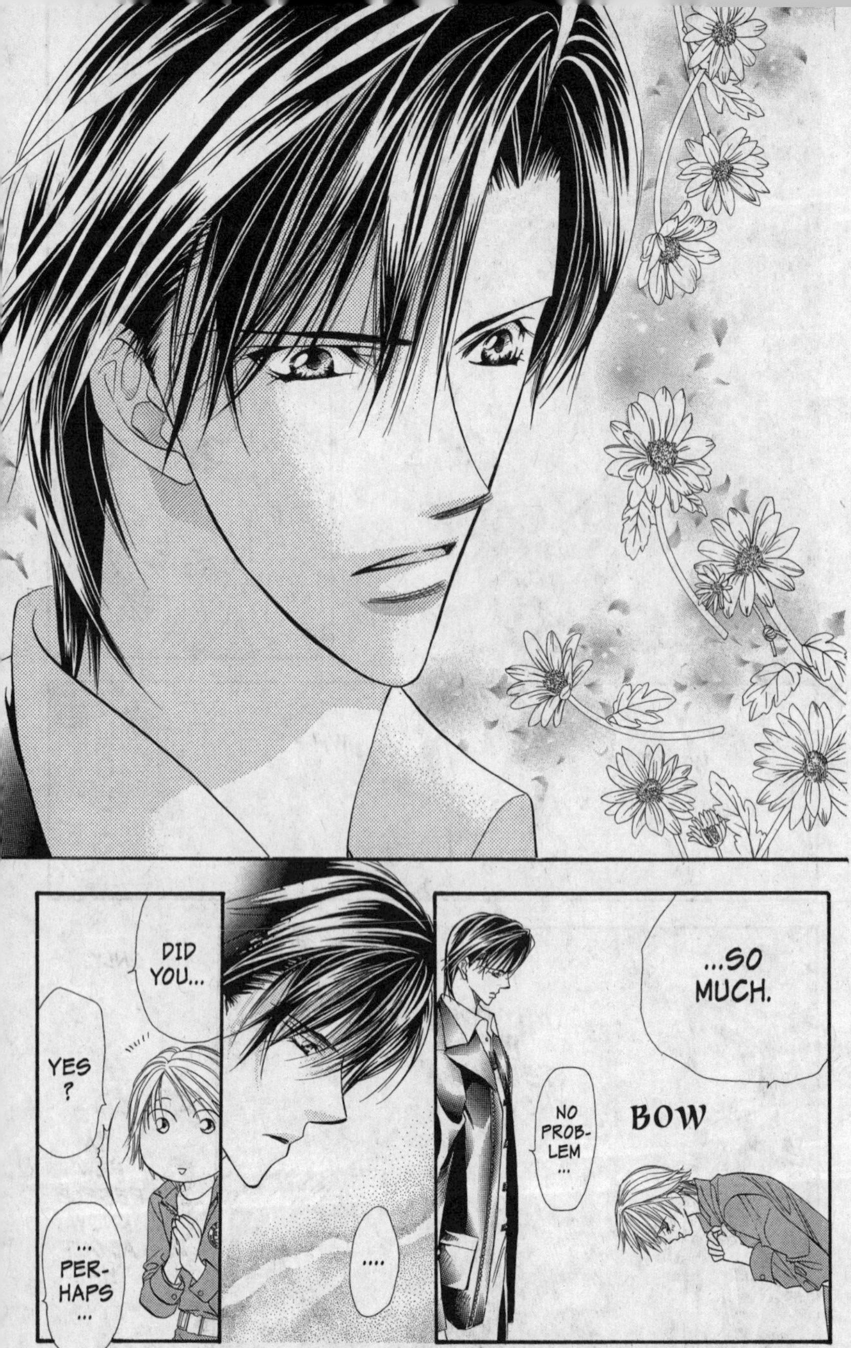
...SO MUCH.
BOW
NO PROB-LEM ...
DID YOU...
YES ?
....
... PER-HAPS ...

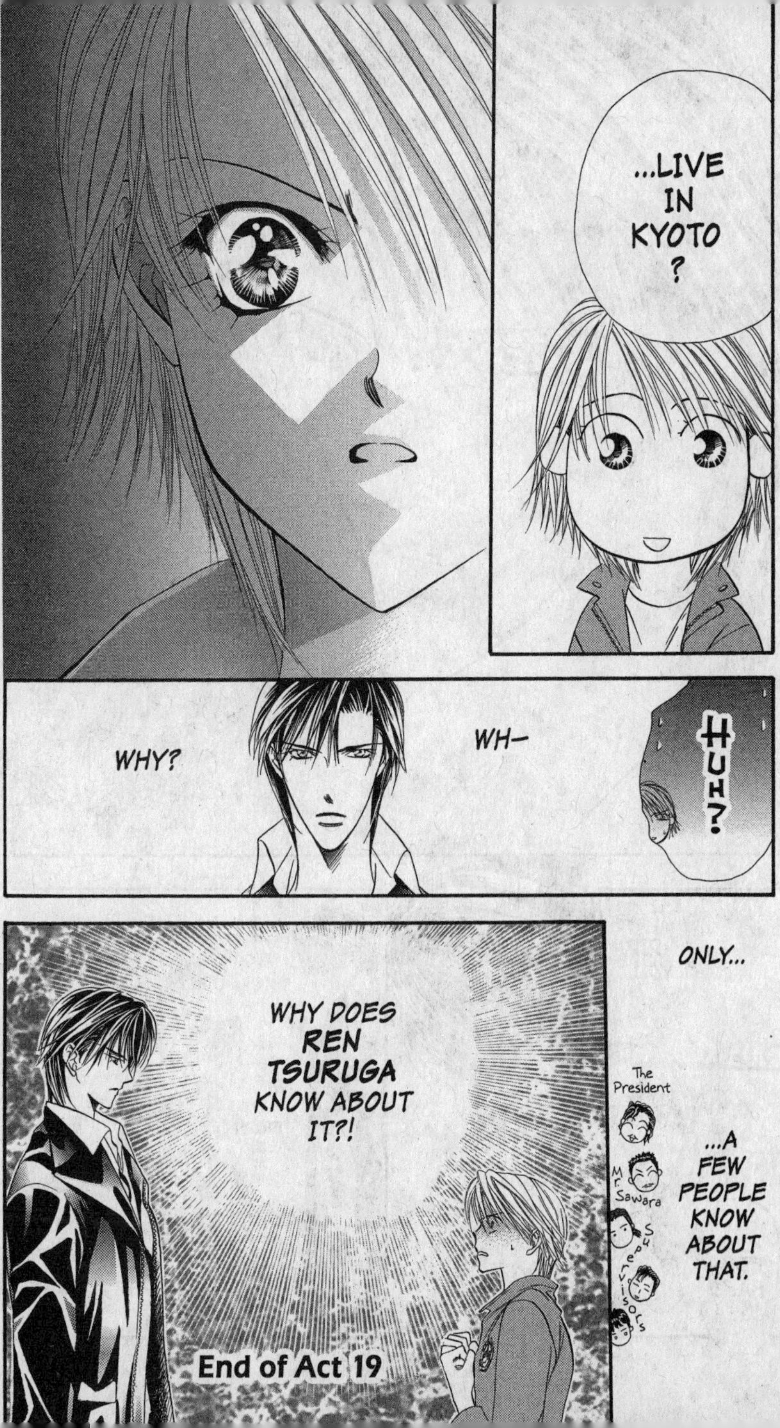
...LIVE IN KYOTO?
HUH?
WH–
WHY?
ONLY...
The President
Mr. Sawara
Supervisors
...A FEW PEOPLE KNOW ABOUT THAT.
WHY DOES REN TSURUGA KNOW ABOUT IT?!
End of Act 19

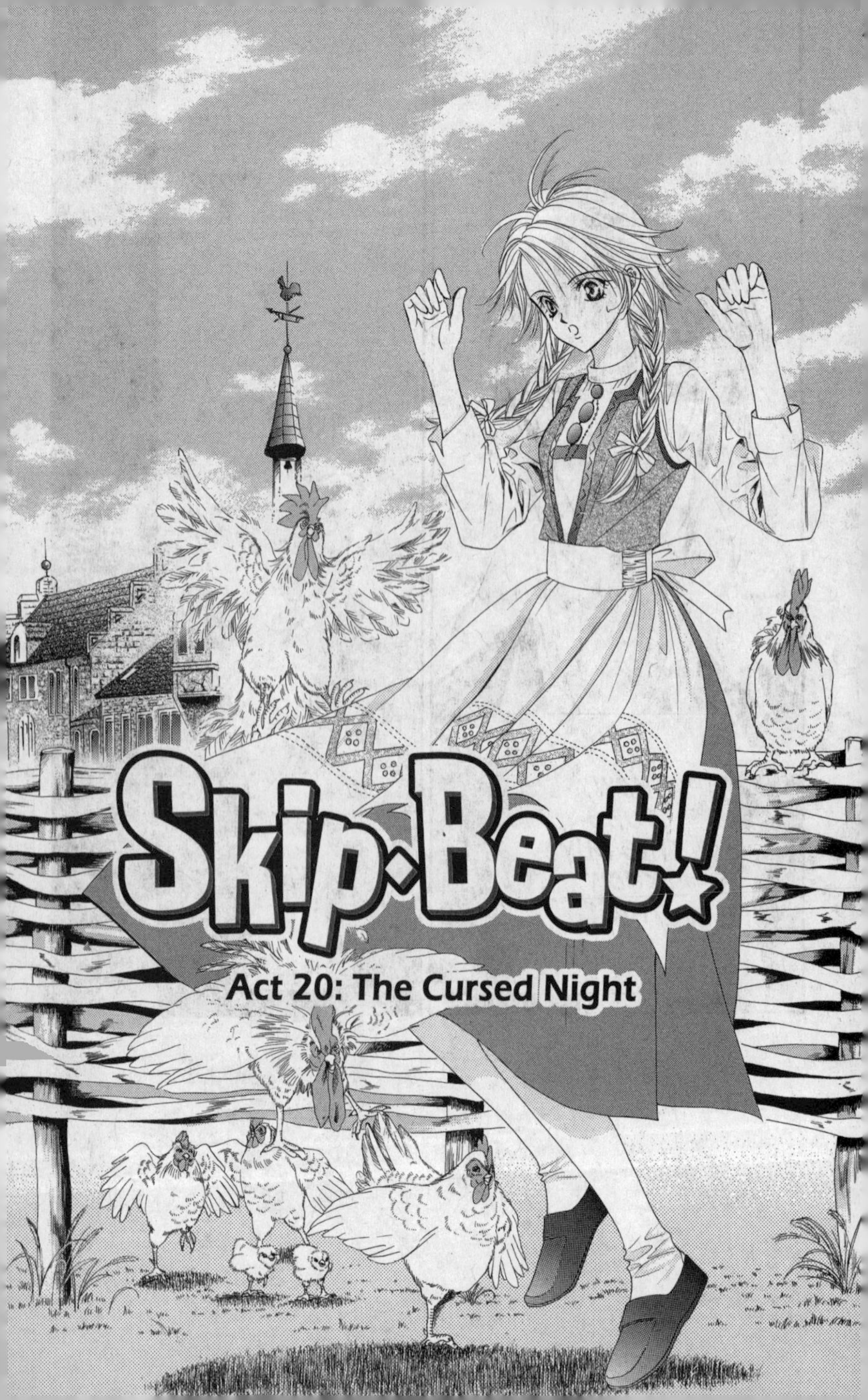
Skip·Beat!
Act 20: The Cursed Night

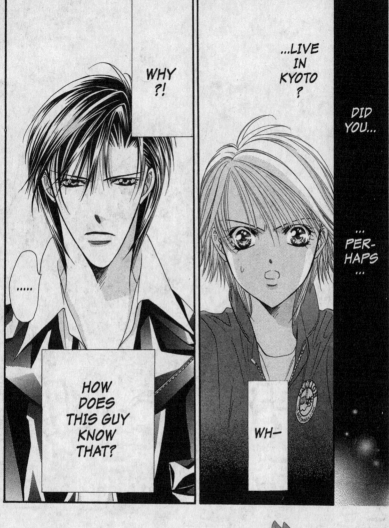

WHY ?!

...LIVE IN KYOTO ?

DID YOU...

...PER-HAPS...

......

HOW DOES THIS GUY KNOW THAT?

WH—

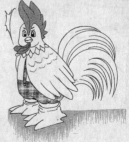

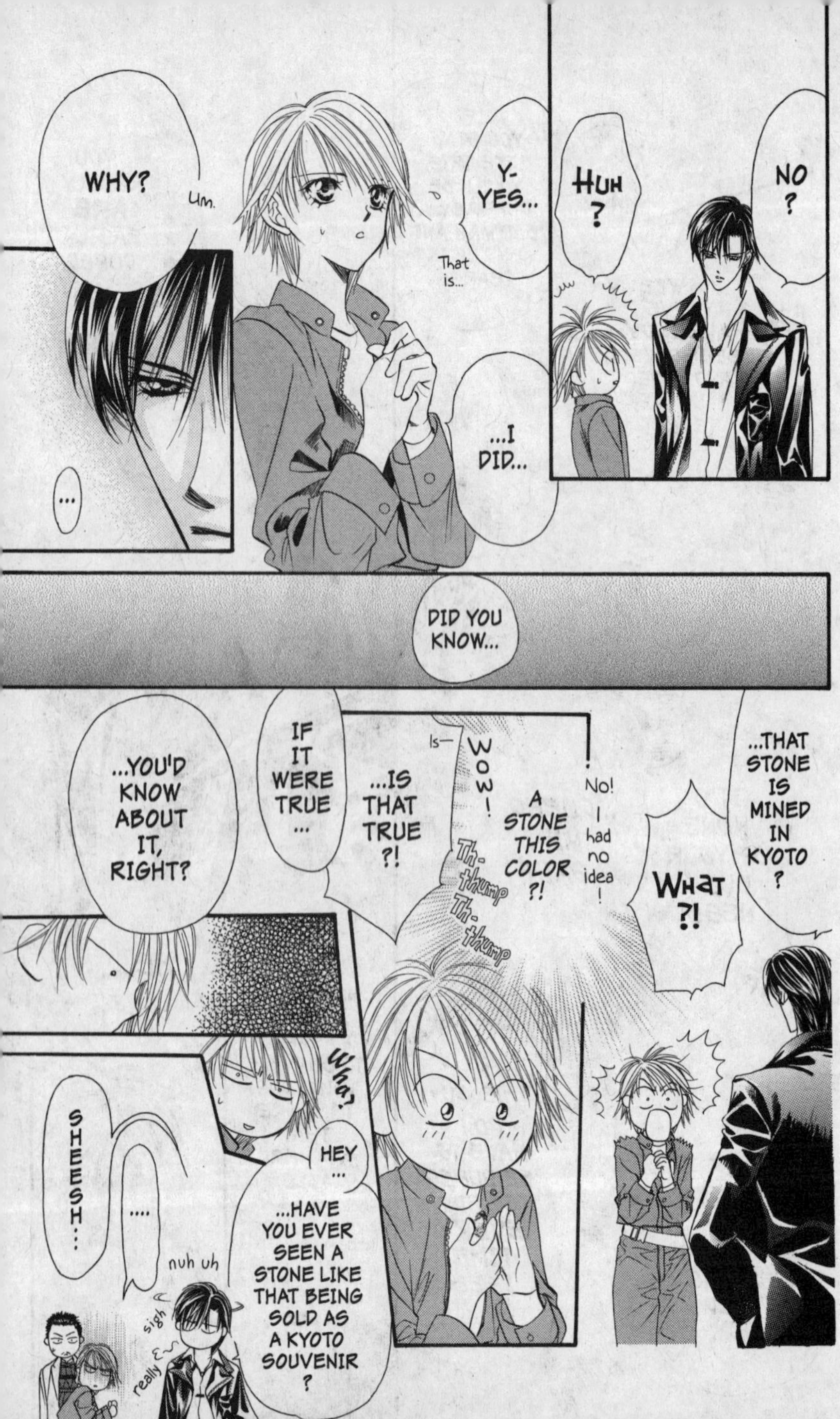
NO?
HUH?
Y-YES...
That is...
...I DID...
WHY?
Um.
...
DID YOU KNOW...
...THAT STONE IS MINED IN KYOTO?
WHAT?!
No! I had no idea!
A STONE THIS COLOR?!
WOW!
Is—
...IS THAT TRUE?!
Th-thump Th-thump
IF IT WERE TRUE...
...YOU'D KNOW ABOUT IT, RIGHT?
Wha?
HEY...
...HAVE YOU EVER SEEN A STONE LIKE THAT BEING SOLD AS A KYOTO SOUVENIR?
....
SHEESH...
nuh uh
sigh
really

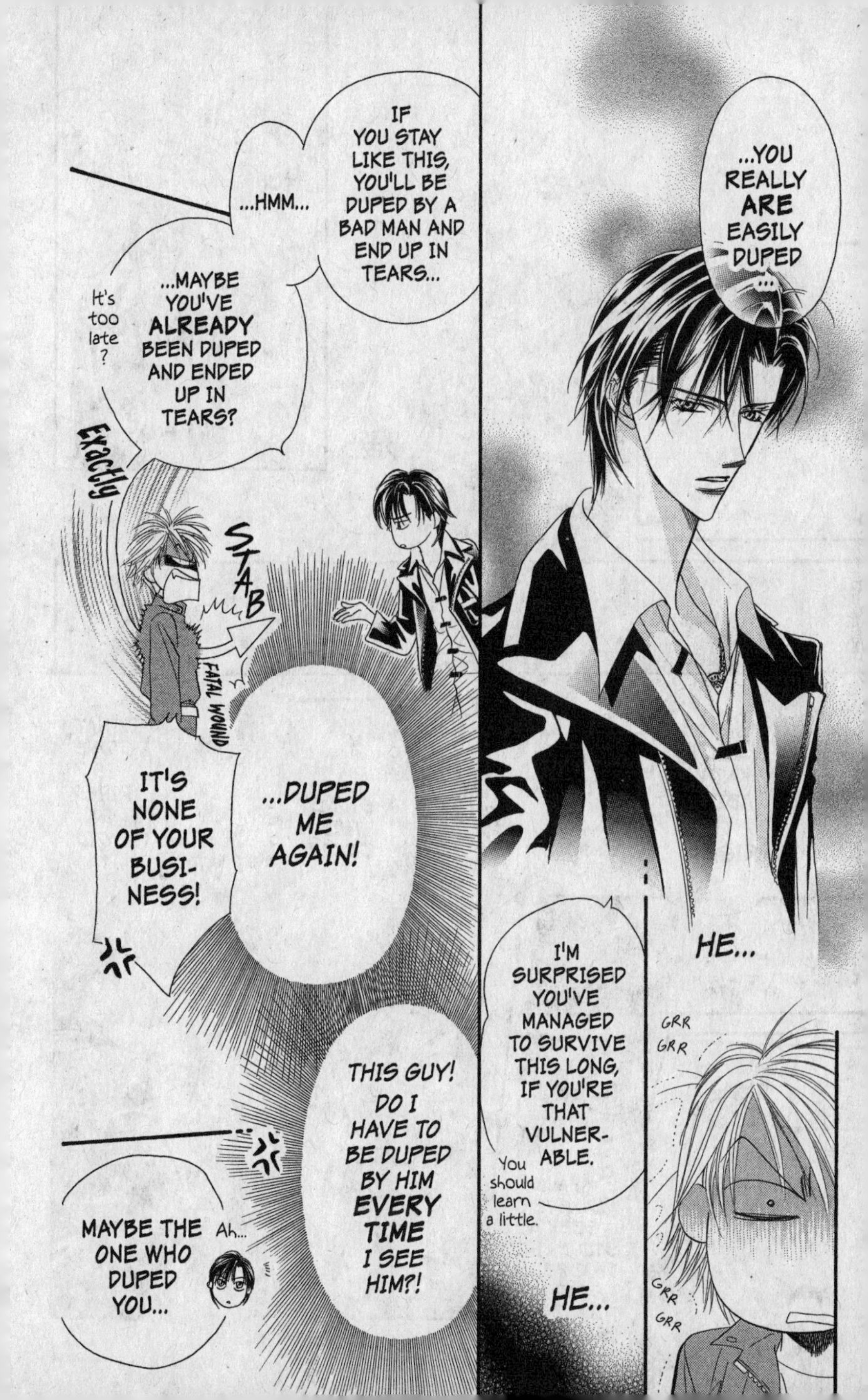
...YOU REALLY ARE EASILY DUPED...
HE...
GRR GRR
GRR GRR
I'M SURPRISED YOU'VE MANAGED TO SURVIVE THIS LONG, IF YOU'RE THAT VULNER-ABLE.
You should learn a little.
HE...
IF YOU STAY LIKE THIS, YOU'LL BE DUPED BY A BAD MAN AND END UP IN TEARS...
...HMM...
...MAYBE YOU'VE ALREADY BEEN DUPED AND ENDED UP IN TEARS?
It's too late?
Exactly
STAB
FATAL WOUND
...DUPED ME AGAIN!
IT'S NONE OF YOUR BUSI-NESS!
THIS GUY! DO I HAVE TO BE DUPED BY HIM EVERY TIME I SEE HIM?!
Ah...
MAYBE THE ONE WHO DUPED YOU...

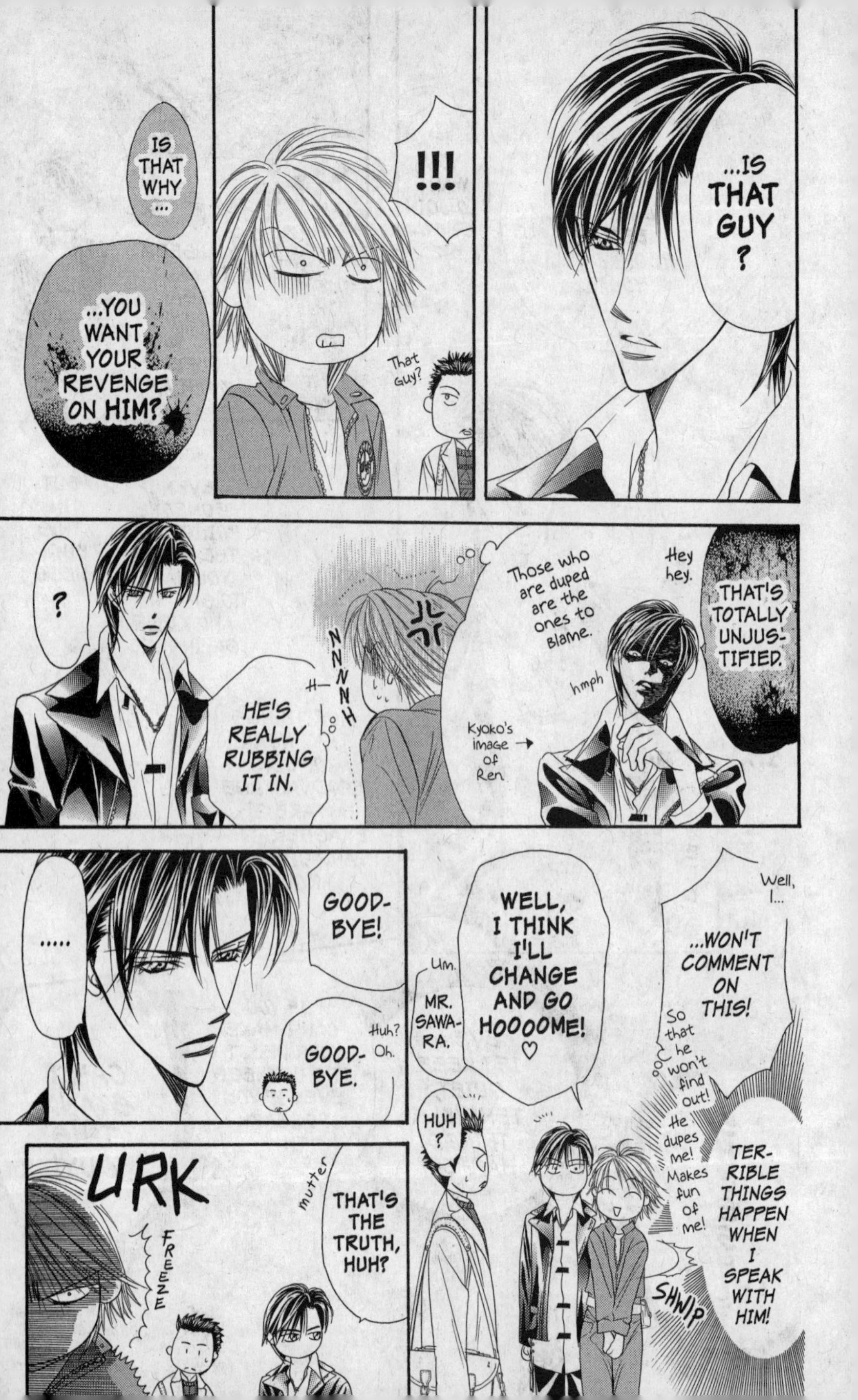
...IS THAT GUY?
!!!
That Guy?
IS THAT WHY...
...YOU WANT YOUR REVENGE ON HIM?
THAT'S TOTALLY UNJUS-TIFIED.
Hey hey.
Those who are duped are the ones to Blame.
hmph
Kyoko's image of Ren →
NNNNH
H—
HE'S REALLY RUBBING IT IN.
?
Well, I...
...WON'T COMMENT ON THIS!
So that he won't find out!
WELL, I THINK I'LL CHANGE AND GO HOOOOME! ♡
Um.
MR. SAWA-RA.
GOOD-BYE!
Huh? Oh.
GOOD-BYE.
.....
TER-RIBLE THINGS HAPPEN WHEN I SPEAK WITH HIM!
He dupes me! Makes fun of me!
SHWIP
HUH?
mutter
THAT'S THE TRUTH, HUH?
URK
FREEZE

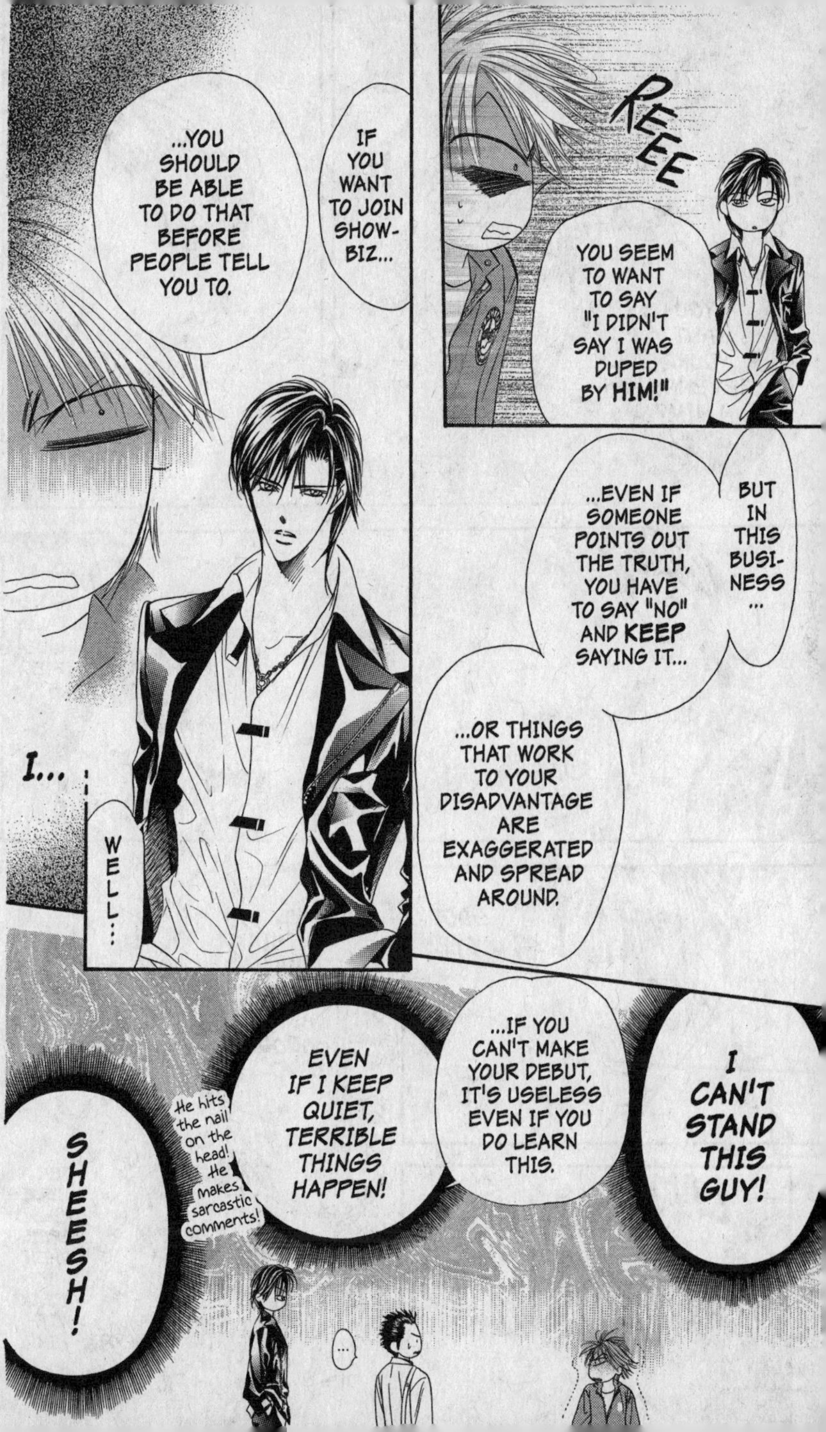
REEE
YOU SEEM TO WANT TO SAY "I DIDN'T SAY I WAS DUPED BY HIM!"
BUT IN THIS BUSINESS...
...EVEN IF SOMEONE POINTS OUT THE TRUTH, YOU HAVE TO SAY "NO" AND KEEP SAYING IT...
...OR THINGS THAT WORK TO YOUR DISADVANTAGE ARE EXAGGERATED AND SPREAD AROUND.
IF YOU WANT TO JOIN SHOW-BIZ...
...YOU SHOULD BE ABLE TO DO THAT BEFORE PEOPLE TELL YOU TO.
I...
WELL...
I CAN'T STAND THIS GUY!
...IF YOU CAN'T MAKE YOUR DEBUT, IT'S USELESS EVEN IF YOU DO LEARN THIS.
EVEN IF I KEEP QUIET, TERRIBLE THINGS HAPPEN!
He hits the nail on the head! He makes sarcastic comments!
SHEESH!
...

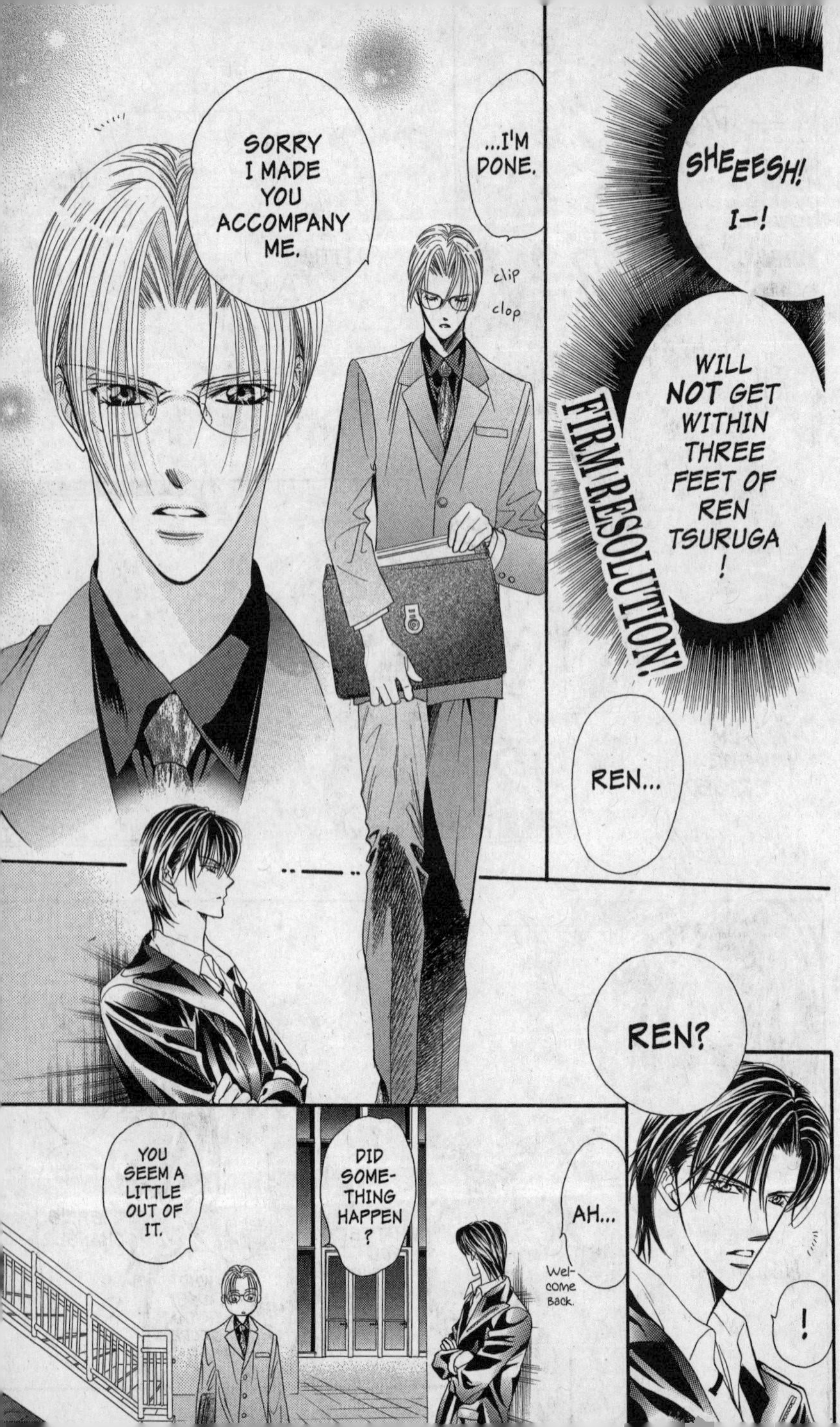
SHEEESH!
I—!
WILL NOT GET WITHIN THREE FEET OF REN TSURUGA!
FIRM RESOLUTION!
REN...
REN?
...I'M DONE.
clip
clop
SORRY I MADE YOU ACCOMPANY ME.
.. —— ..
!
AH...
Wel-come back.
DID SOME-THING HAPPEN?
YOU SEEM A LITTLE OUT OF IT.

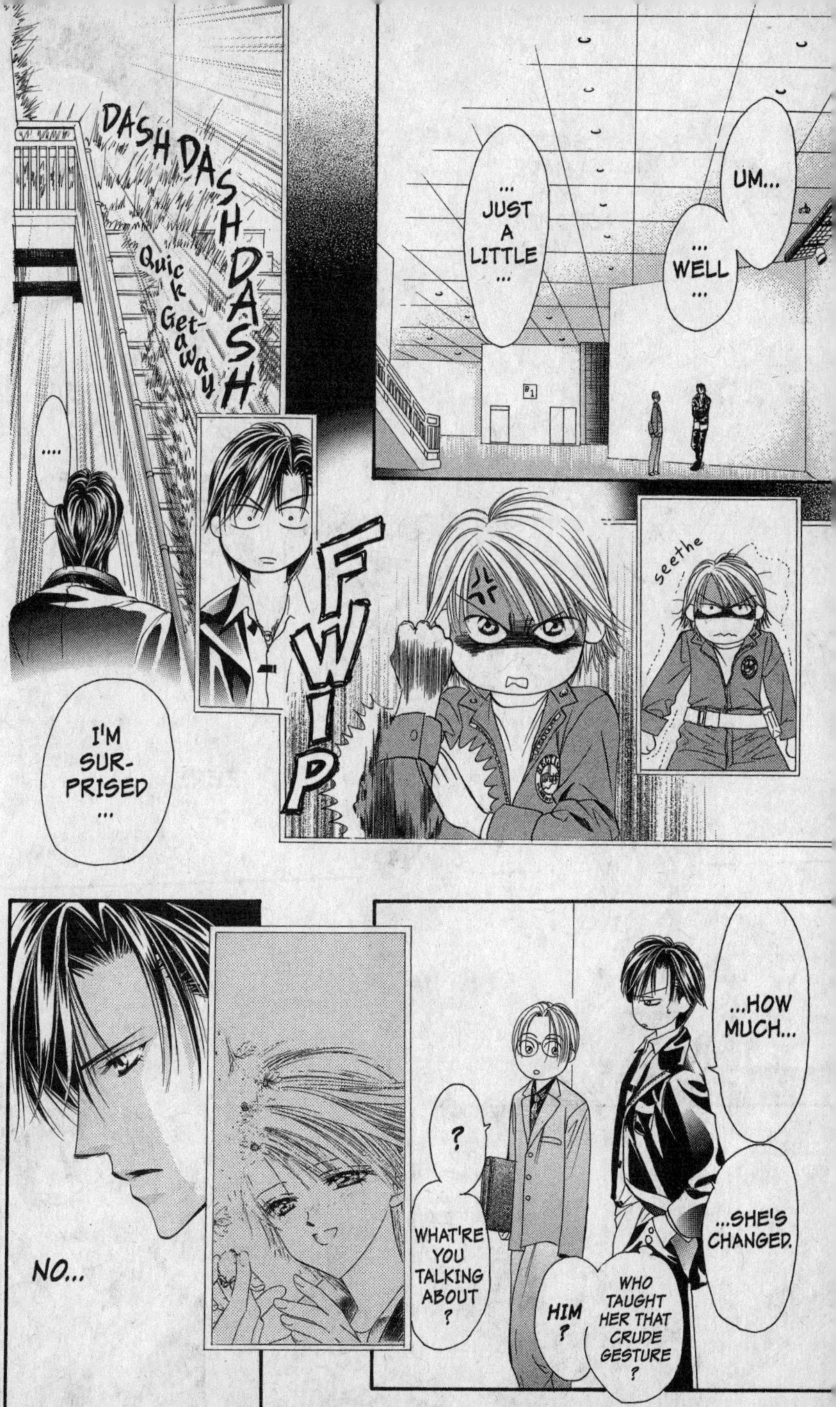
UM...
... WELL ...
... JUST A LITTLE ...
seethe
FWIP
DASH DASH DASH DASH
Quick Get-away
....
I'M SUR-PRISED ...
...HOW MUCH...
...SHE'S CHANGED.
WHO TAUGHT HER THAT CRUDE GESTURE ?
HIM ?
?
WHAT'RE YOU TALKING ABOUT ?
NO...

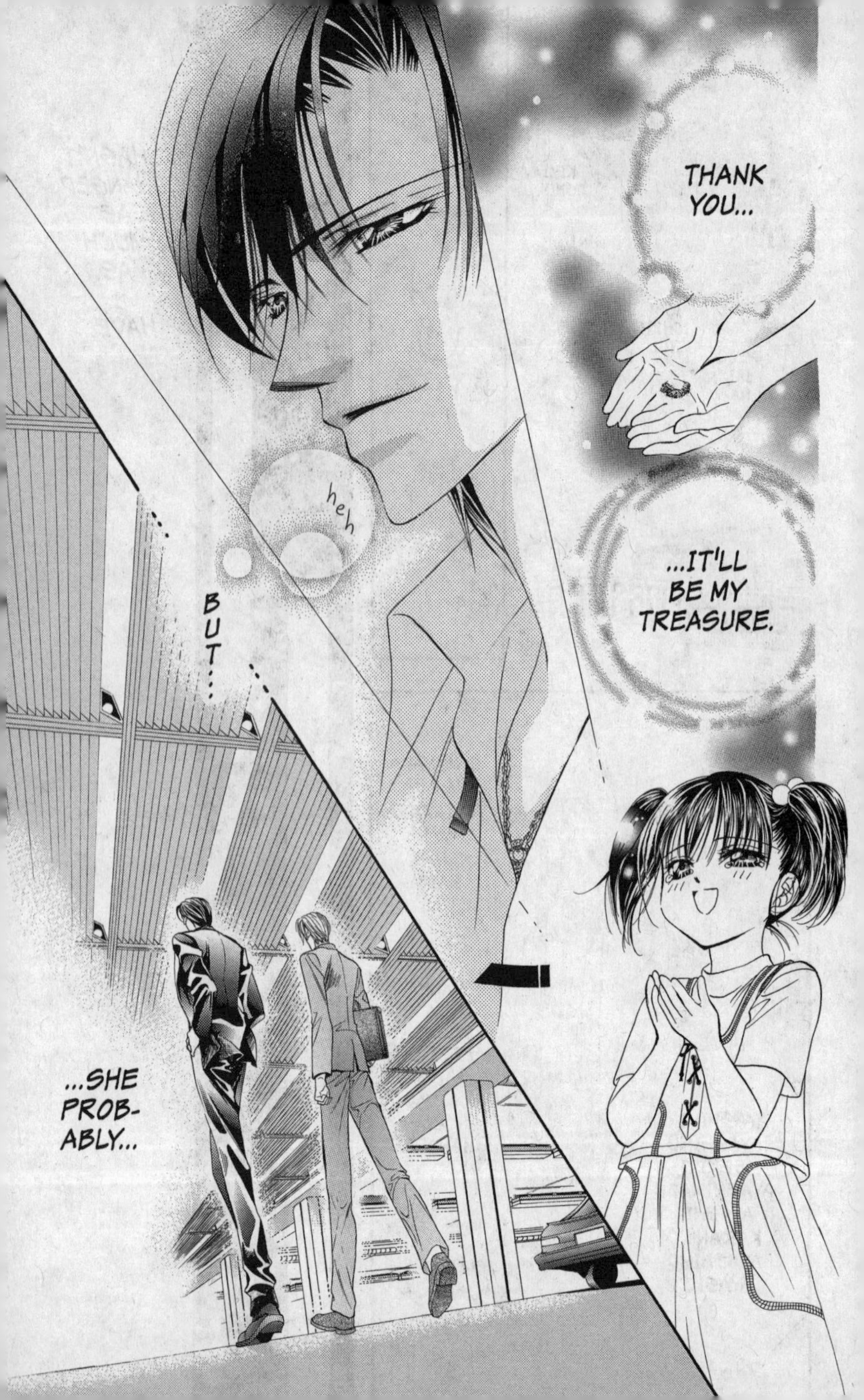
THANK YOU...
...IT'LL BE MY TREASURE.
heh
BUT...
...SHE PROBABLY...

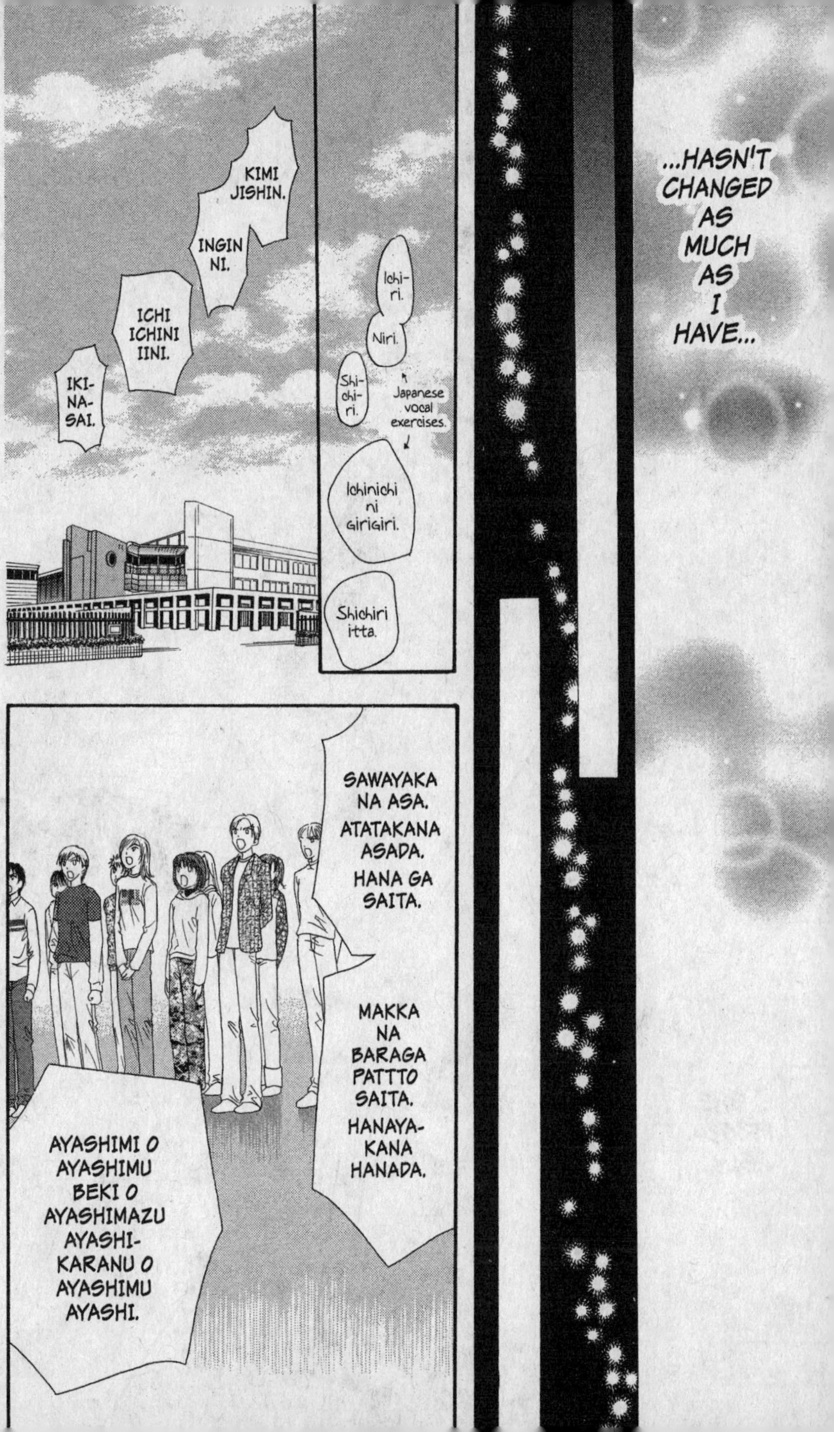
...HASN'T CHANGED AS MUCH AS I HAVE...
Ichi-ri.
Niri.
Shi-chi-ri.
Japanese vocal exercises.
Ichinichi ni girigiri.
Shichiri itta.
KIMI JISHIN.
INGIN NI.
ICHI ICHINI IINI.
IKI-NA-SAI.
SAWAYAKA NA ASA. ATATAKANA ASADA. HANA GA SAITA.
MAKKA NA BARAGA PATTTO SAITA. HANAYA-KANA HANADA.
AYASHIMI O AYASHIMU BEKI O AYASHIMAZU AYASHI-KARANU O AYASHIMU AYASHI.

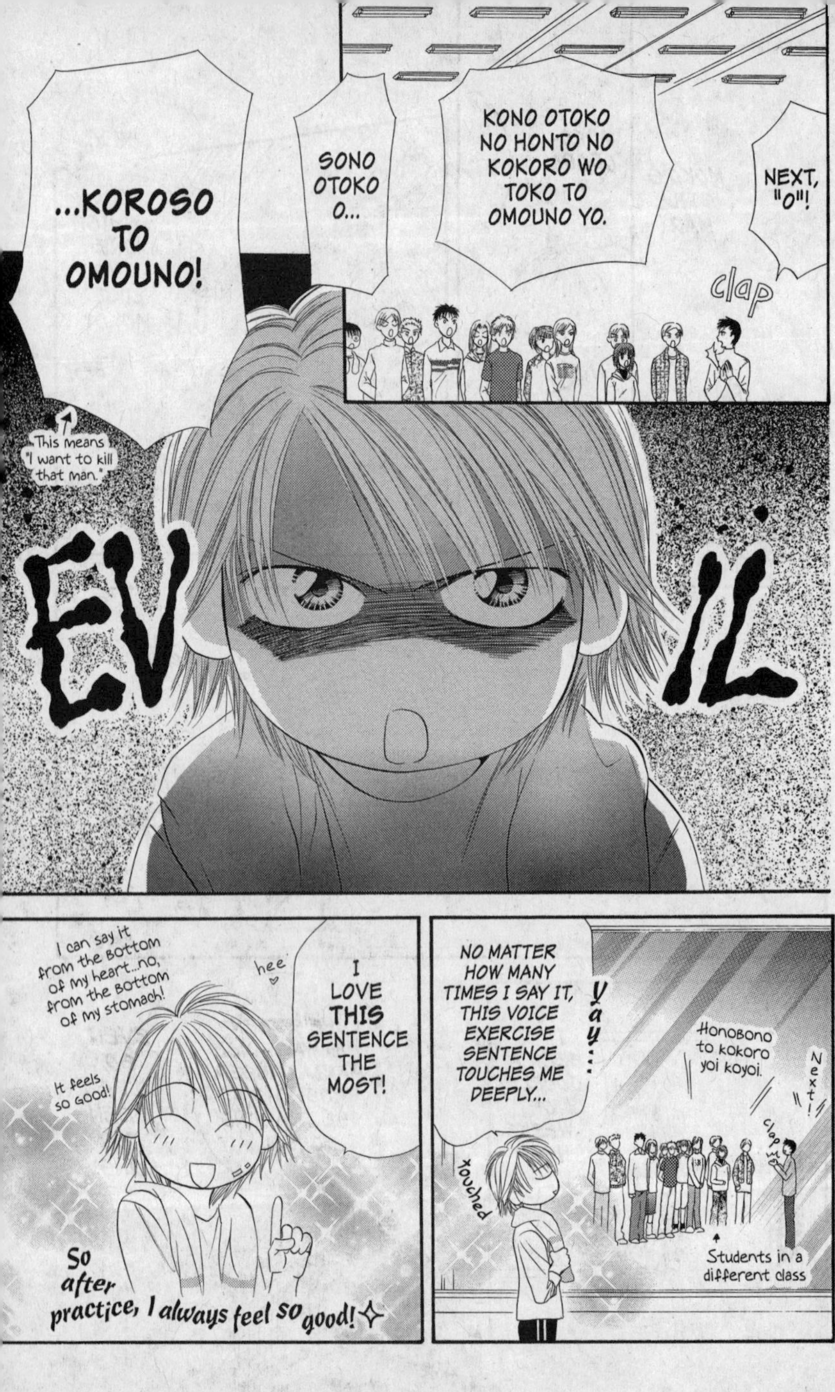
NEXT, "O"!
clap
KONO OTOKO NO HONTO NO KOKORO WO TOKO TO OMOUNO YO.
SONO OTOKO O...
...KOROSO TO OMOUNO!
This means "I want to kill that man."
EVIL
Honobono to kokoro yoi koyoi.
Next!
clap
Students in a different class
NO MATTER HOW MANY TIMES I SAY IT, THIS VOICE EXERCISE SENTENCE TOUCHES ME DEEPLY...
Yay...
touched
I LOVE THIS SENTENCE THE MOST!
hee
I can say it from the bottom of my heart...no, from the bottom of my stomach!
It feels so good!
So after practice, I always feel so good!

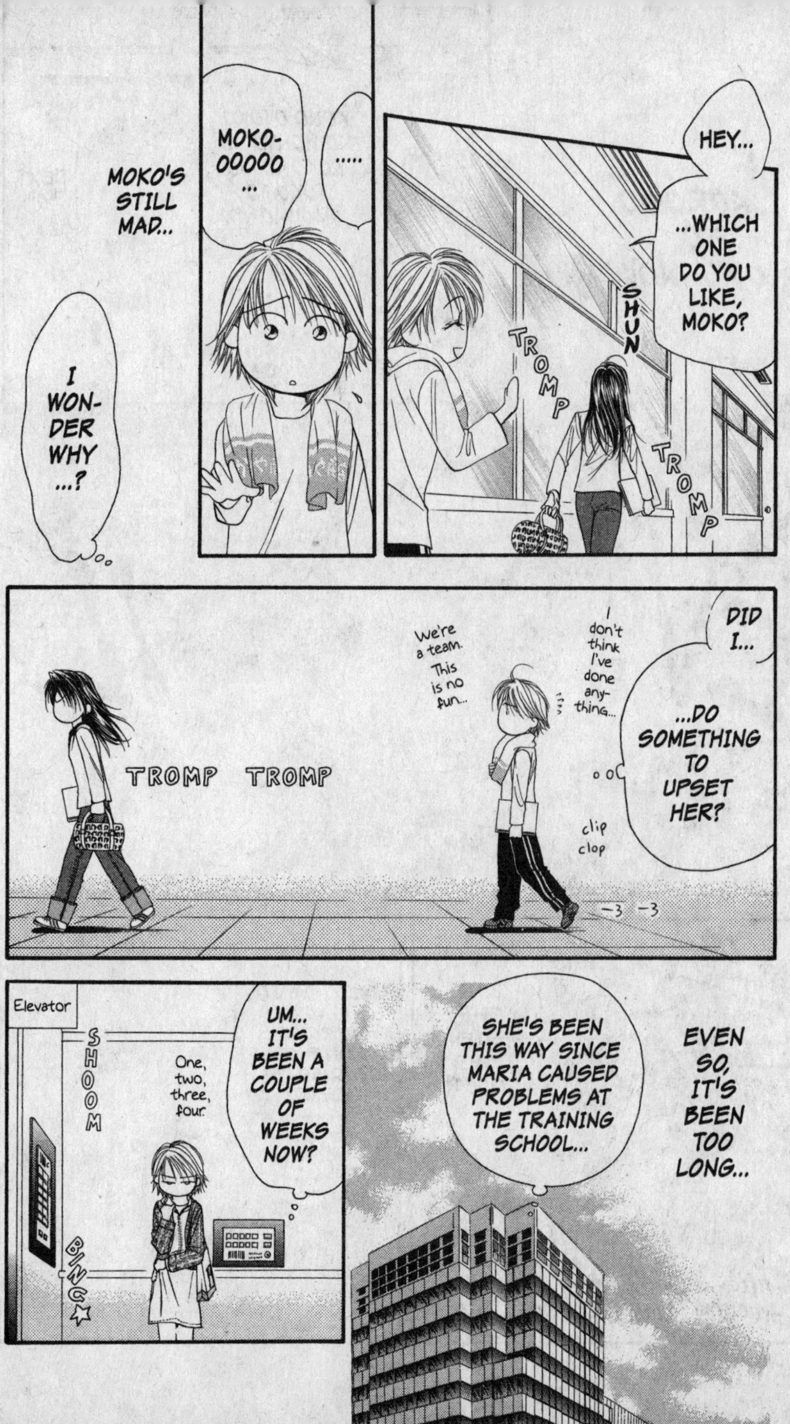
HEY...
...WHICH ONE DO YOU LIKE, MOKO?
SHUN
TROMP
TROMP
.....
MOKO-OOOOO...
MOKO'S STILL MAD...
I WONDER WHY...?
DID I...
...DO SOMETHING TO UPSET HER?
I don't think I've done anything...
We're a team. This is no fun...
clip clop
-3 -3
TROMP TROMP
EVEN SO, IT'S BEEN TOO LONG...
SHE'S BEEN THIS WAY SINCE MARIA CAUSED PROBLEMS AT THE TRAINING SCHOOL...
UM... IT'S BEEN A COUPLE OF WEEKS NOW?
One, two, three, four.
Elevator
SHOOM
BING

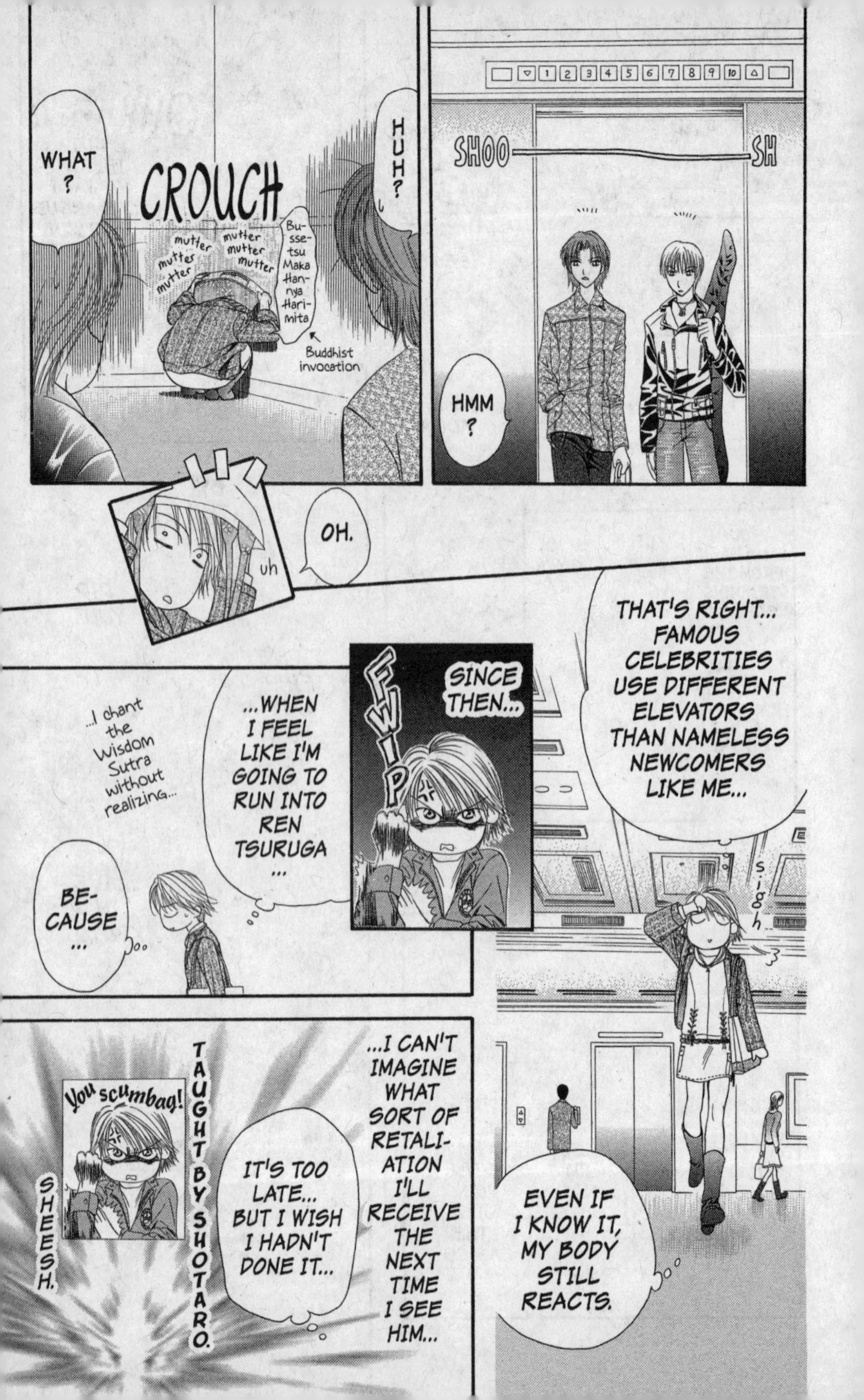
SHOO—SH
HMM?
HUH?
Bussetsu Maka Hannya Harimita
Buddhist invocation
mutter mutter mutter
mutter mutter mutter
CROUCH
WHAT?
OH.
uh
THAT'S RIGHT... FAMOUS CELEBRITIES USE DIFFERENT ELEVATORS THAN NAMELESS NEWCOMERS LIKE ME...
sigh
EVEN IF I KNOW IT, MY BODY STILL REACTS.
SINCE THEN...
FWIP
...WHEN I FEEL LIKE I'M GOING TO RUN INTO REN TSURUGA...
BE-CAUSE...
...I chant the Wisdom Sutra without realizing...
...I CAN'T IMAGINE WHAT SORT OF RETALIATION I'LL RECEIVE THE NEXT TIME I SEE HIM...
IT'S TOO LATE... BUT I WISH I HADN'T DONE IT...
TAUGHT BY SHOTARO.
You scumbag!
SHEESH.

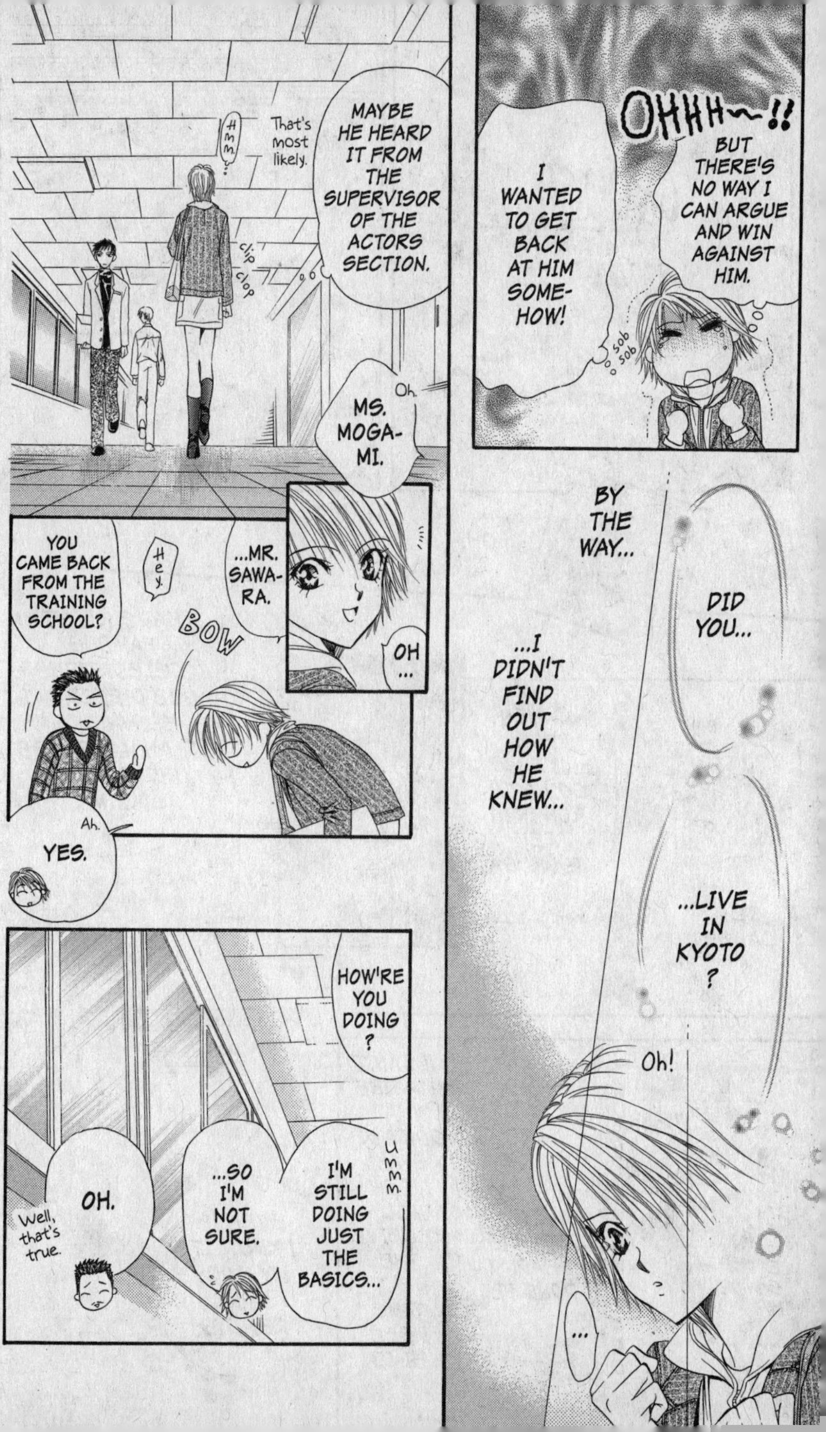
OHHH~!!
BUT THERE'S NO WAY I CAN ARGUE AND WIN AGAINST HIM.
I WANTED TO GET BACK AT HIM SOME-HOW!
sob sob
BY THE WAY...
DID YOU...
...I DIDN'T FIND OUT HOW HE KNEW...
...LIVE IN KYOTO?
Oh!
...
MAYBE HE HEARD IT FROM THE SUPERVISOR OF THE ACTORS SECTION.
That's most likely.
Hmm.
clip clop
Oh.
MS. MOGA-MI.
...MR. SAWA-RA.
OH...
BOW
Hey.
YOU CAME BACK FROM THE TRAINING SCHOOL?
Ah.
YES.
HOW'RE YOU DOING?
Umm.
I'M STILL DOING JUST THE BASICS...
...SO I'M NOT SURE.
OH.
Well, that's true.

Corn

This is the stone that Kyoko secretly treasures. It's not just an ordinary stone. If you cut it and polish it, it becomes a gem. It is called Kinseiseki (cordierite). As the name implies, it is purplish blue, and another name for it is water sapphire.

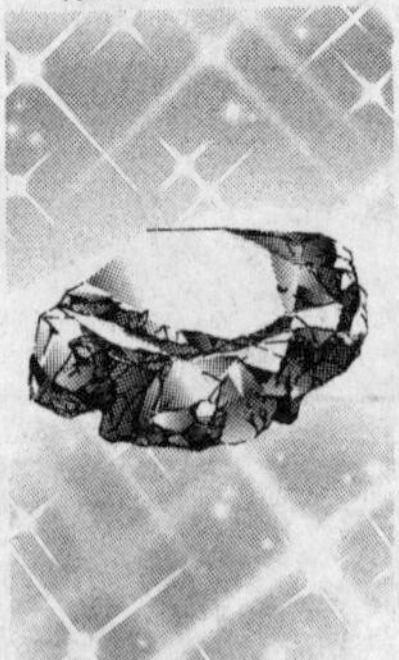

This stone is blue, but if you rotate it about 90 degrees, the blue disappears, and it becomes greenish-yellow, a mysterious(?) stone.

But when this stone is processed as a gem, it is polished so the stone looks blue from the front, and the metal mount hides the sides so that you can't see the greenish-yellow...

That sounds unfortunate, but considering the value of the gem, it is probably better to make it that way...

Reference: From Tanoshii Kobutsu Zukan (The Enjoyable Mineral Encyclopedia)

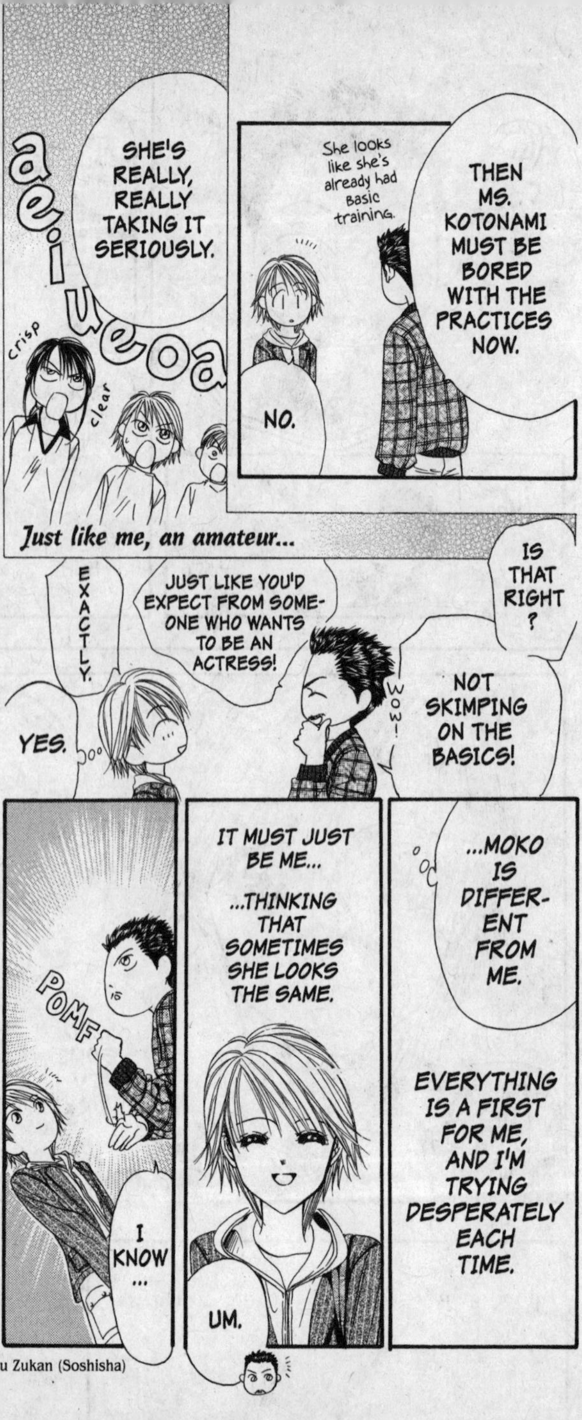
THEN MS. KOTONAMI MUST BE BORED WITH THE PRACTICES NOW.
She looks like she's already had basic training.
NO.
SHE'S REALLY, REALLY TAKING IT SERIOUSLY.
aeiueoa
crisp
clear
Just like me, an amateur...
IS THAT RIGHT?
NOT SKIMPING ON THE BASICS!
WOW!
JUST LIKE YOU'D EXPECT FROM SOMEONE WHO WANTS TO BE AN ACTRESS!
EXACTLY.
YES.
...MOKO IS DIFFERENT FROM ME.
EVERYTHING IS A FIRST FOR ME, AND I'M TRYING DESPERATELY EACH TIME.
IT MUST JUST BE ME...
...THINKING THAT SOMETIMES SHE LOOKS THE SAME.
UM.
POMF
I KNOW...

<Reference> Tanoshii Kobutsu Zukan (Soshisha)

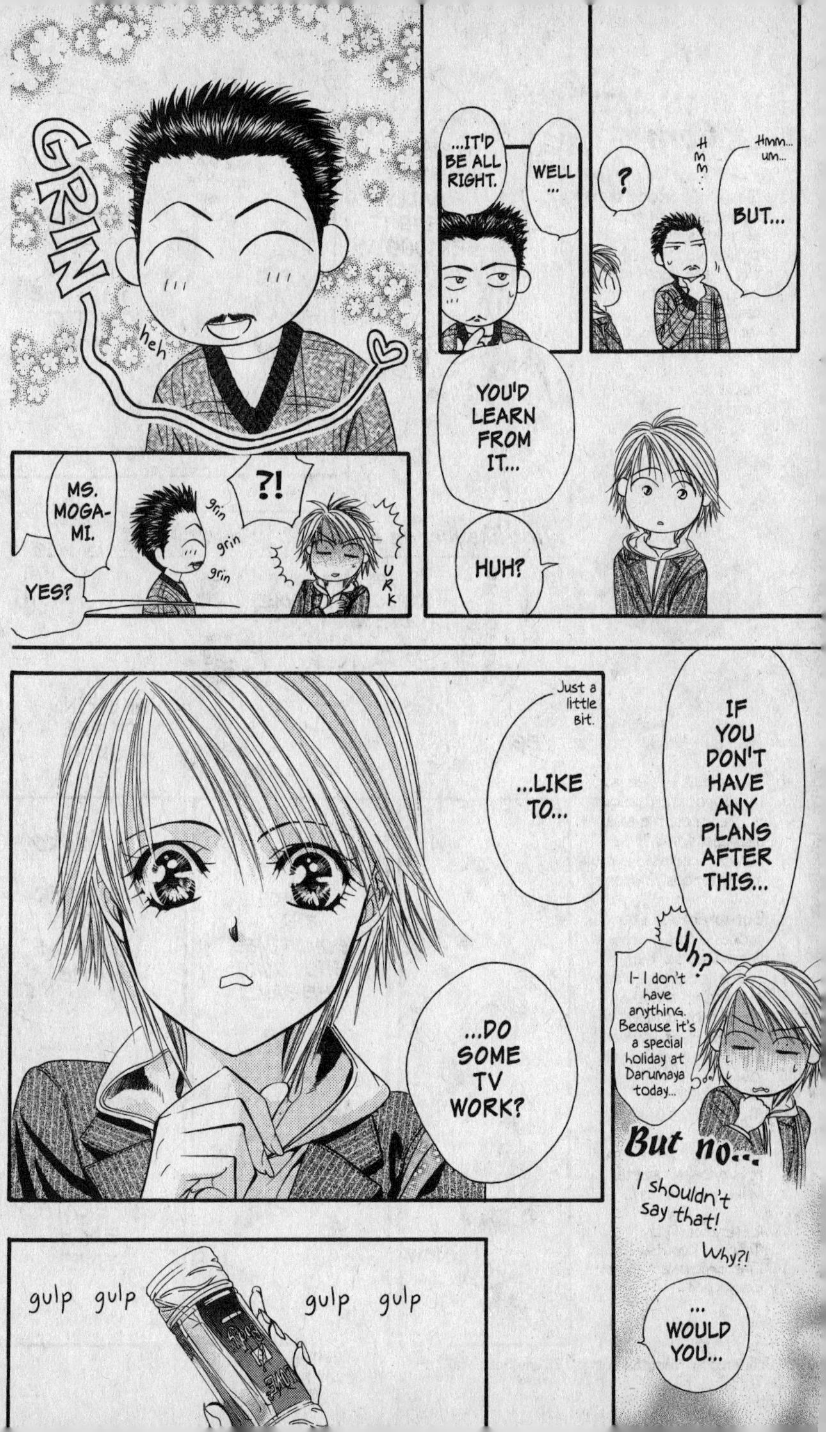
Hmm... um...
BUT...
Hmm...
?
WELL...
...IT'D BE ALL RIGHT.
YOU'D LEARN FROM IT...
HUH?
GRIN
heh
MS. MOGA-MI.
YES?
?!
grin grin grin
URK
IF YOU DON'T HAVE ANY PLANS AFTER THIS...
Uh?
I- I don't have anything. Because it's a special holiday at Darumaya today...
But no...
I shouldn't say that!
Why?!
...WOULD YOU...
...LIKE TO...
Just a little bit.
...DO SOME TV WORK?
gulp gulp gulp gulp

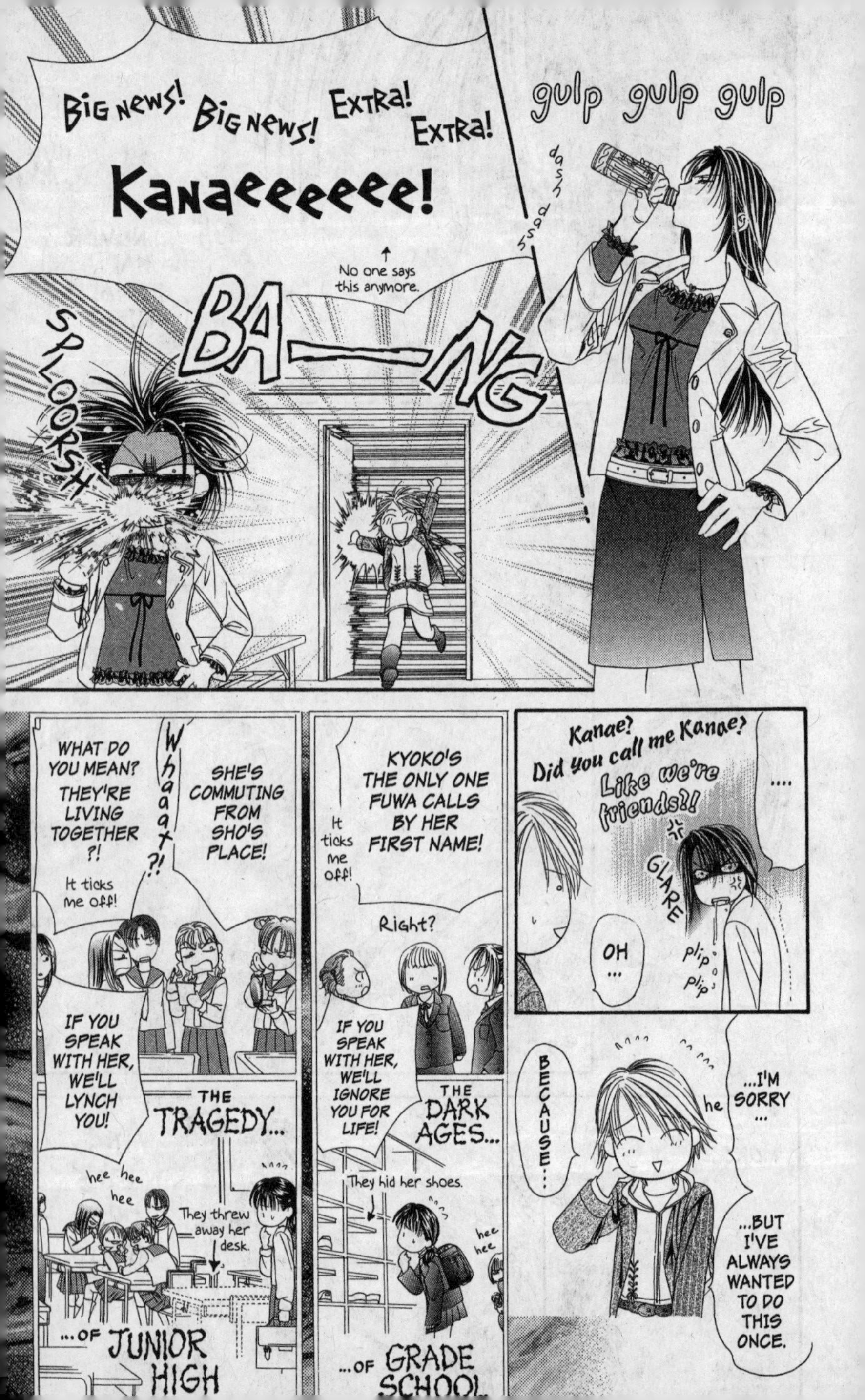

gulp gulp gulp
dash dash
Big news! Big news! Extra! Extra!
Kanaeeeeee!
No one says this anymore.
BA—NG
SPLOORSH
Kanae? Did you call me Kanae?
Like we're friends?!
....
GLARE
OH ...
plip plip
...I'M SORRY ...
he
BECAUSE...
...BUT I'VE ALWAYS WANTED TO DO THIS ONCE.
KYOKO'S THE ONLY ONE FUWA CALLS BY HER FIRST NAME!
It ticks me off!
Right?
IF YOU SPEAK WITH HER, WE'LL IGNORE YOU FOR LIFE!
THE DARK AGES...
They hid her shoes.
hee hee
...OF GRADE SCHOOL
SHE'S COMMUTING FROM SHO'S PLACE!
Whaaat?!
WHAT DO YOU MEAN? THEY'RE LIVING TOGETHER?!
It ticks me off!
IF YOU SPEAK WITH HER, WE'LL LYNCH YOU!
THE TRAGEDY...
hee hee hee
They threw away her desk.
...OF JUNIOR HIGH

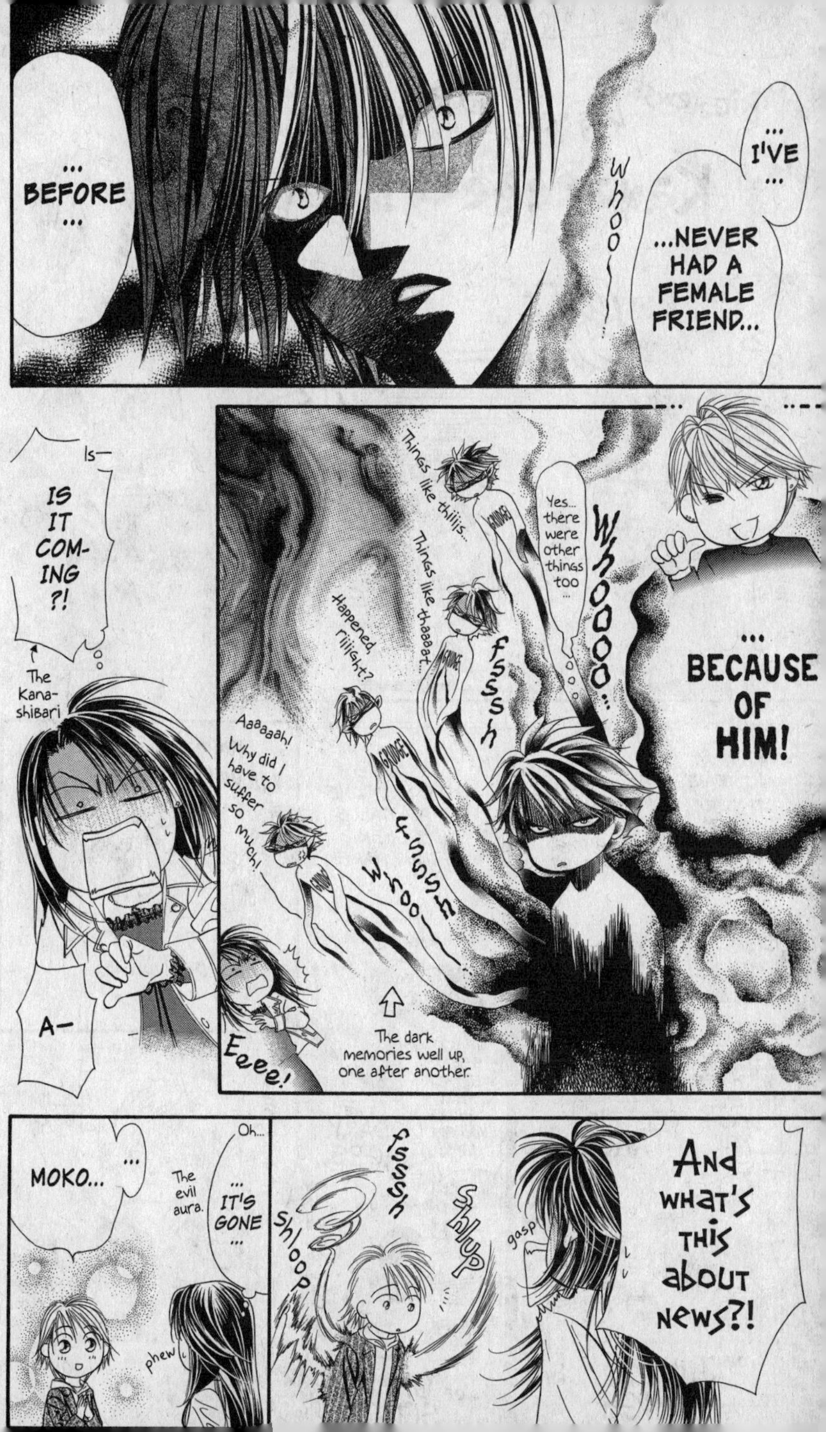
... I'VE ...
...NEVER HAD A FEMALE FRIEND...
Whoo—
... BEFORE ...
... BECAUSE OF HIM!
WHOOOO...
Yes... there were other things too ...
Things like thiiiis...
fsssh
Things like thaaaat...
Happened, riiiiight?
Aaaaaah! Why did I have to suffer so much!
fsssh
W-roo—
The dark memories well up, one after another.
Eeee!
Is—
IS IT COMING?!
The Kana-shibari
A-
And what's this about news?!
gasp
Shlup
fsssh
Shloop
Oh...
... IT'S GONE ...
The evil aura.
... MOKO...
phew

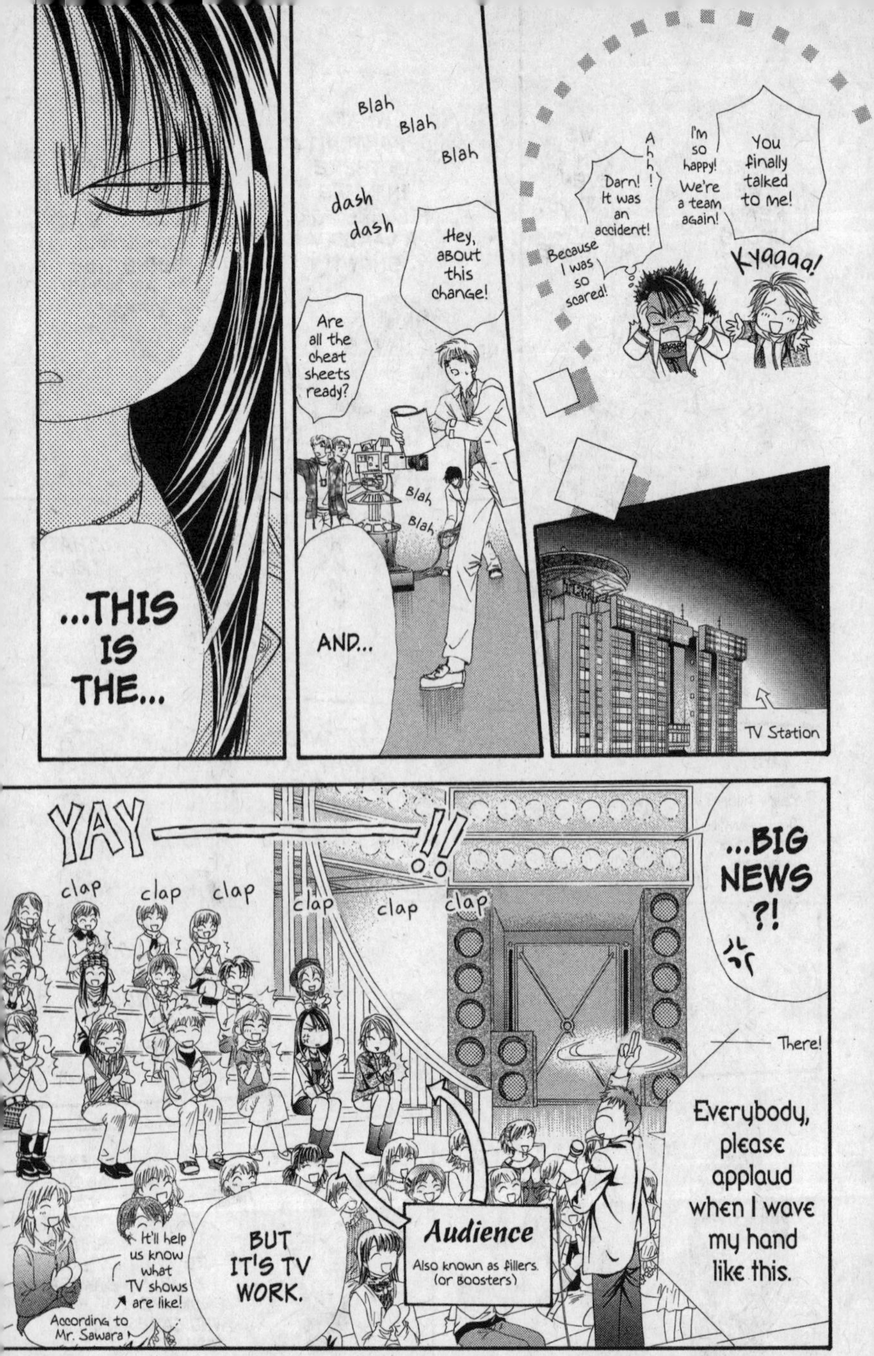
You finally talked to me!
I'm so happy! We're a team again!
Kyaaaa!
Ahh! Darn! It was an accident!
Because I was so scared!
TV Station
Blah Blah Blah
dash dash
Hey, about this change!
Are all the cheat sheets ready?
Blah Blah
AND...
...THIS IS THE...
...BIG NEWS?!
Everybody, please applaud when I wave my hand like this.
There!
YAY——!!
clap clap clap
clap clap clap
Audience
Also known as fillers. (or boosters)
BUT IT'S TV WORK.
It'll help us know what TV shows are like!
According to Mr. Sawara

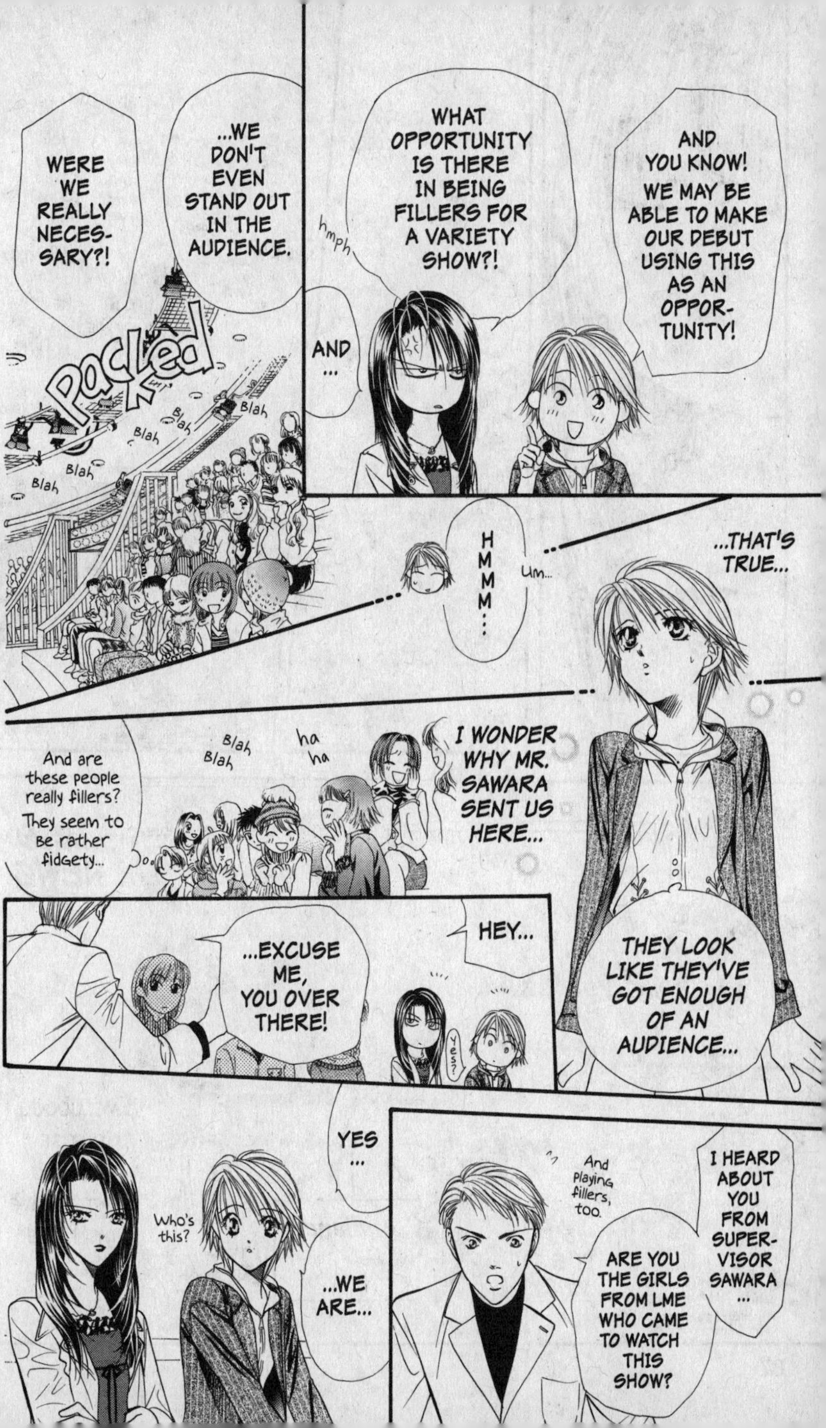
AND YOU KNOW! WE MAY BE ABLE TO MAKE OUR DEBUT USING THIS AS AN OPPOR-TUNITY!
WHAT OPPORTUNITY IS THERE IN BEING FILLERS FOR A VARIETY SHOW?!
hmph
AND ...
...WE DON'T EVEN STAND OUT IN THE AUDIENCE.
WERE WE REALLY NECES-SARY?!
Packed
Blah
Blah
Blah
Blah
...THAT'S TRUE...
Um...
HMMM...
I WONDER WHY MR. SAWARA SENT US HERE...
THEY LOOK LIKE THEY'VE GOT ENOUGH OF AN AUDIENCE...
Blah Blah
ha ha
And are these people really fillers? They seem to be rather fidgety...
HEY...
Yes?
...EXCUSE ME, YOU OVER THERE!
I HEARD ABOUT YOU FROM SUPER-VISOR SAWARA ...
And playing fillers, too.
ARE YOU THE GIRLS FROM LME WHO CAME TO WATCH THIS SHOW?
YES ...
...WE ARE...
Who's this?

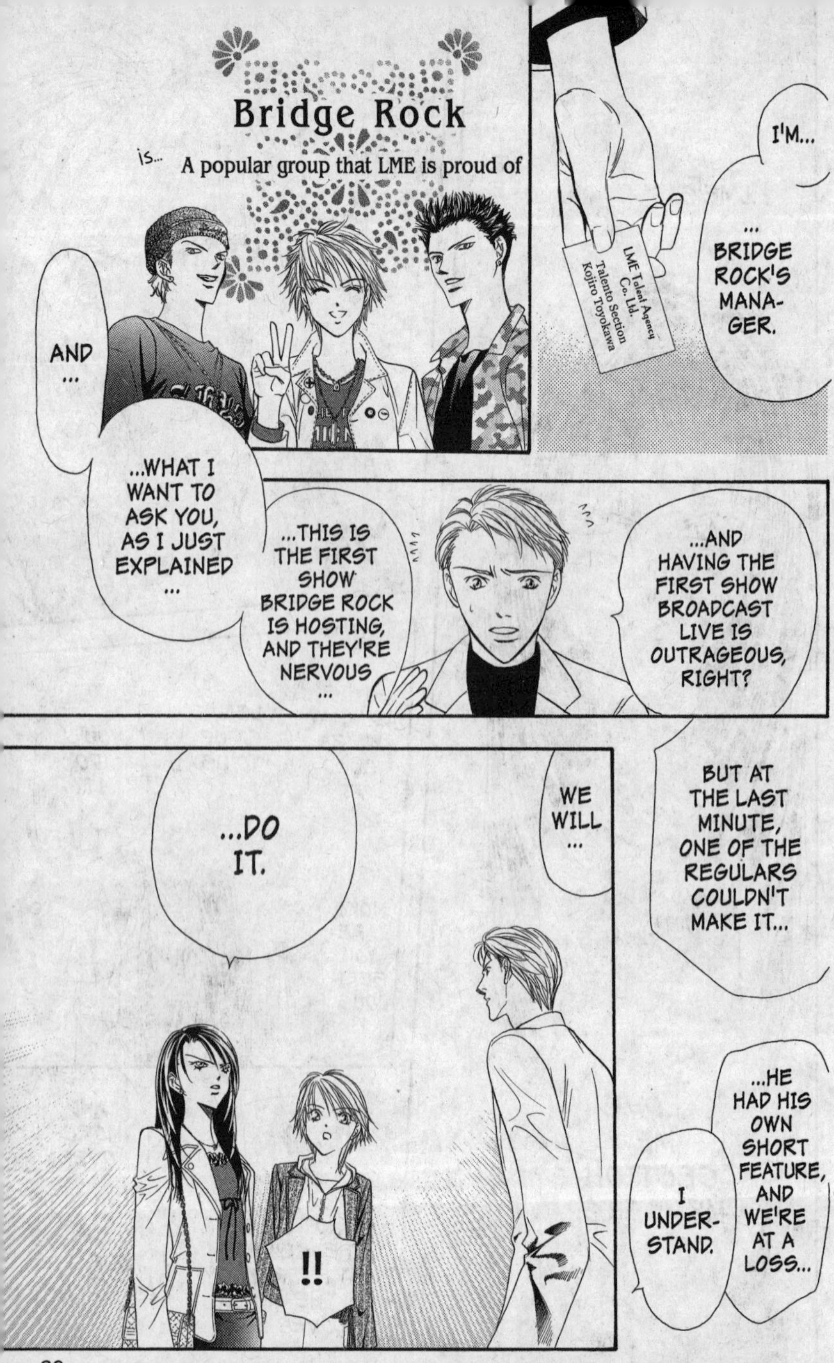
I'M...
...BRIDGE ROCK'S MANAGER.
LME Talent Agency Co. Ltd. Talento Section Kojiro Toyokawa
Bridge Rock
is... A popular group that LME is proud of
AND...
...WHAT I WANT TO ASK YOU, AS I JUST EXPLAINED...
...AND HAVING THE FIRST SHOW BROADCAST LIVE IS OUTRAGEOUS, RIGHT?
...THIS IS THE FIRST SHOW BRIDGE ROCK IS HOSTING, AND THEY'RE NERVOUS...
BUT AT THE LAST MINUTE, ONE OF THE REGULARS COULDN'T MAKE IT...
...HE HAD HIS OWN SHORT FEATURE, AND WE'RE AT A LOSS...
I UNDERSTAND.
WE WILL...
...DO IT.
!!

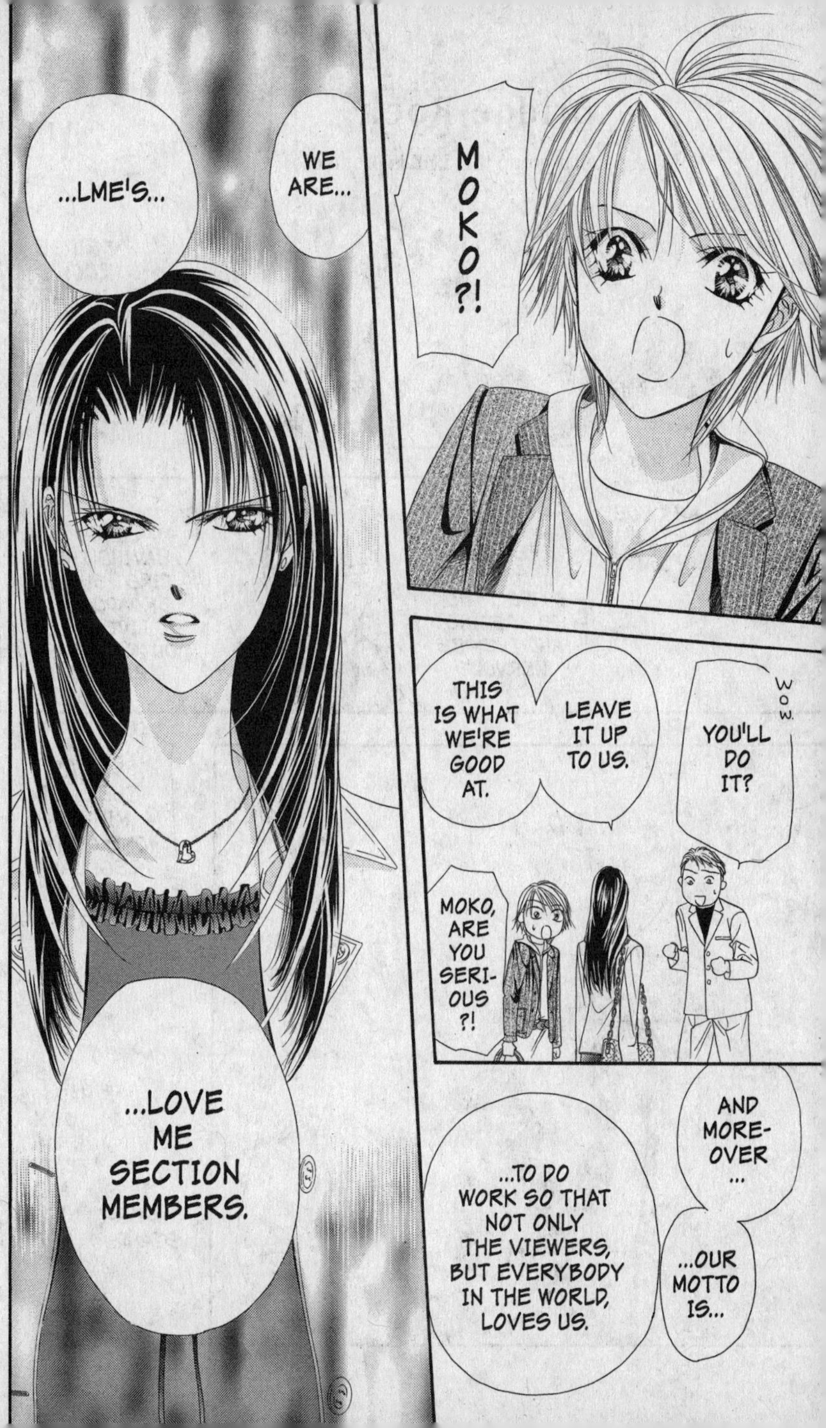
MOKO?!
WOW.
YOU'LL DO IT?
LEAVE IT UP TO US.
THIS IS WHAT WE'RE GOOD AT.
MOKO, ARE YOU SERI-OUS?!
AND MORE-OVER...
...OUR MOTTO IS...
...TO DO WORK SO THAT NOT ONLY THE VIEWERS, BUT EVERYBODY IN THE WORLD, LOVES US.
WE ARE...
...LME'S...
...LOVE ME SECTION MEMBERS.

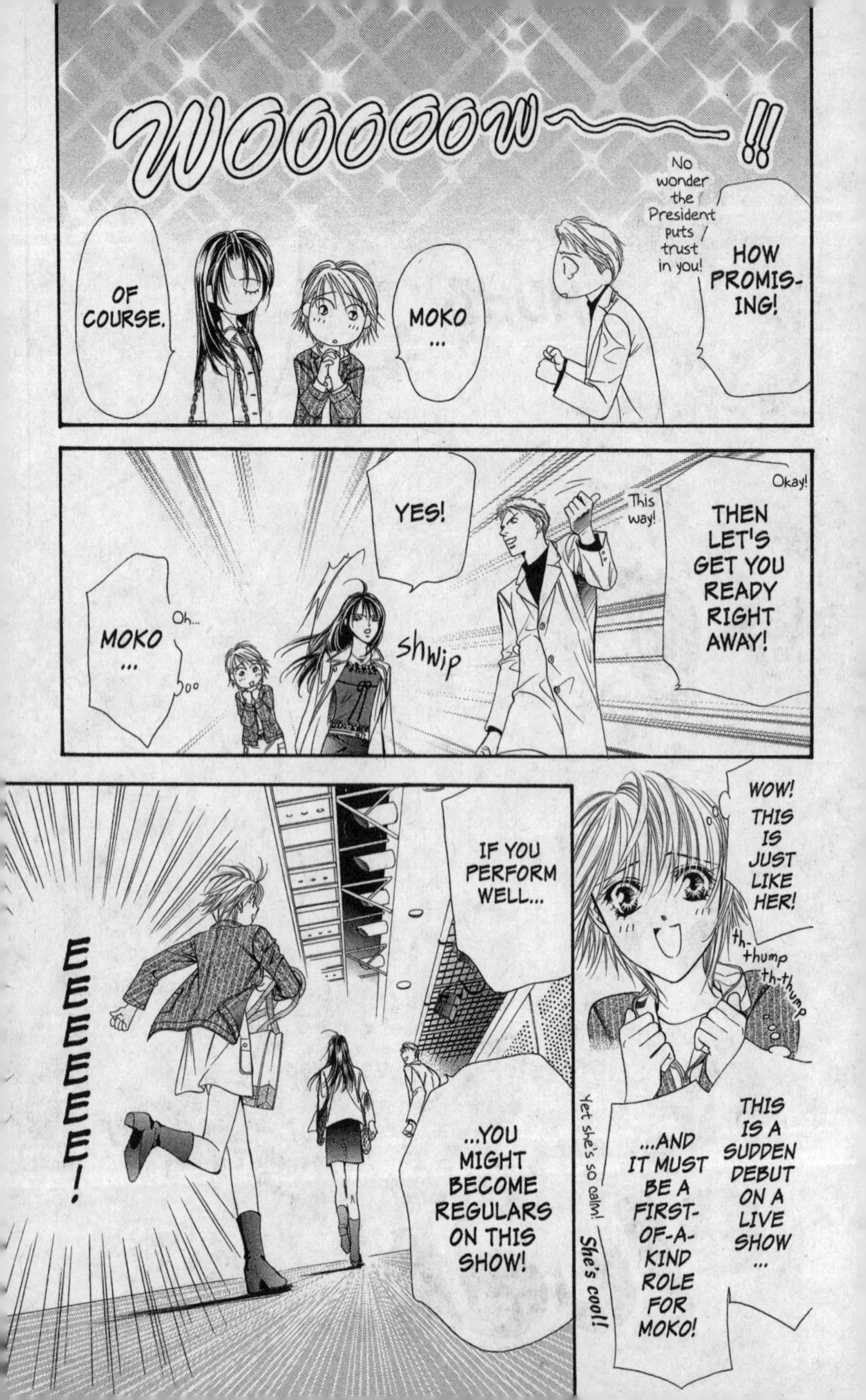
WOOOOOOW~~!!
HOW PROMISING!
No wonder the President puts trust in you!
MOKO...
OF COURSE.
Okay!
THEN LET'S GET YOU READY RIGHT AWAY!
This way!
YES!
shwip
Oh...
MOKO...
WOW! THIS IS JUST LIKE HER!
th-thump th-thump
THIS IS A SUDDEN DEBUT ON A LIVE SHOW...
...AND IT MUST BE A FIRST-OF-A-KIND ROLE FOR MOKO!
Yet she's so calm!
She's cool!
IF YOU PERFORM WELL...
...YOU MIGHT BECOME REGULARS ON THIS SHOW!
EEEEEEE!

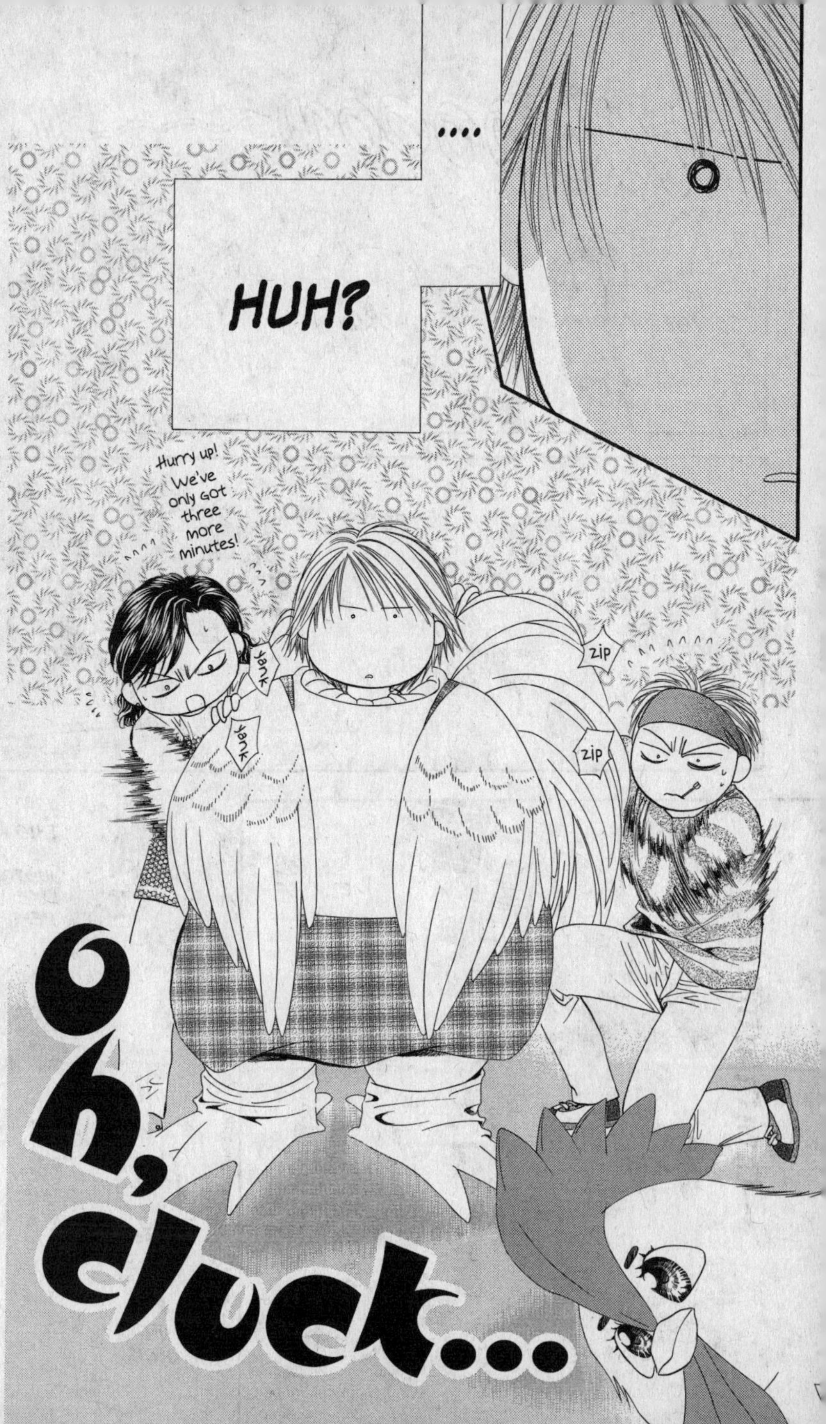
....
HUH?
Hurry up! We've only got three more minutes!
yank
yank
zip
zip
Oh, cluck...

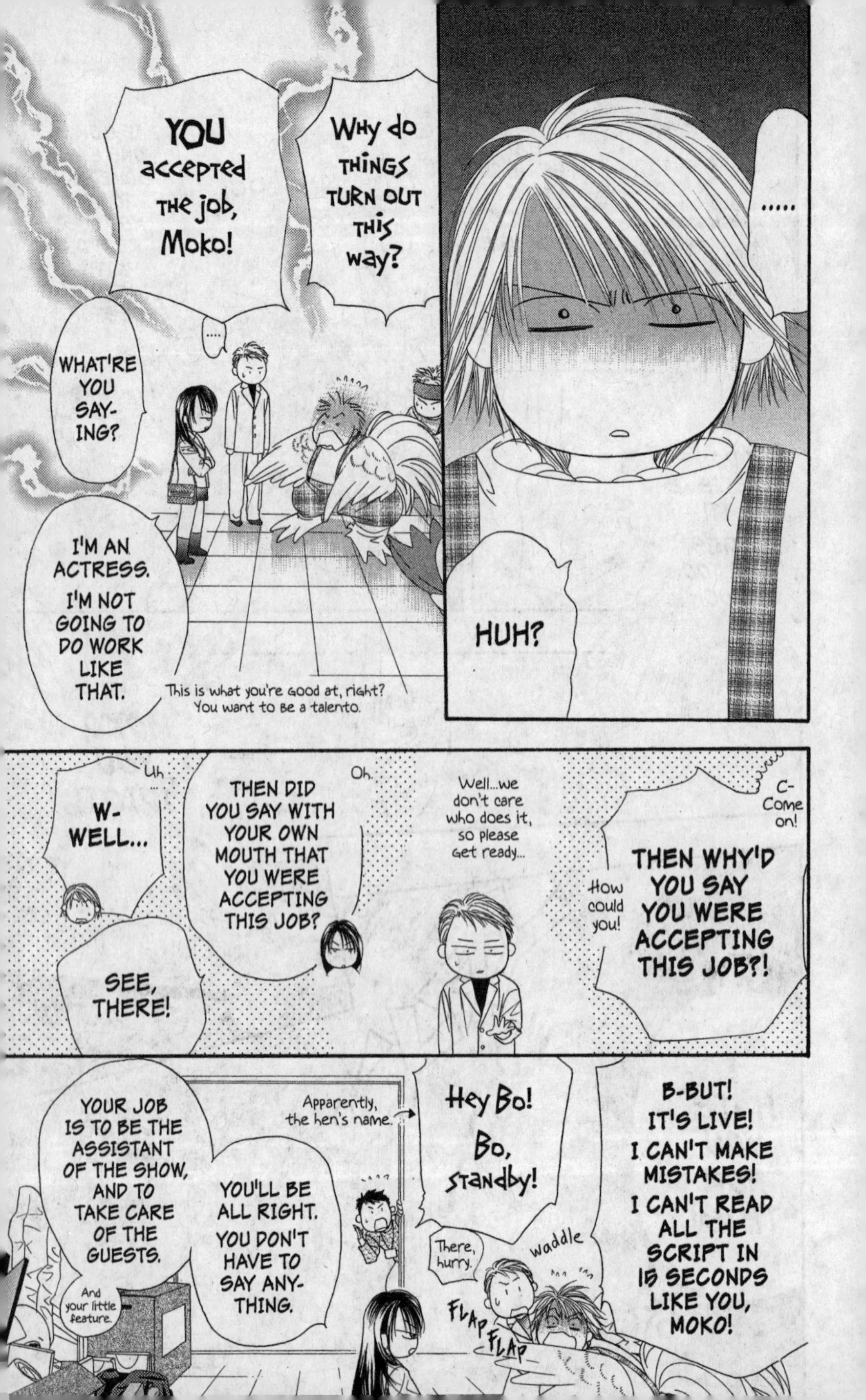
.....
HUH?
Why do things turn out this way?
YOU accepted the job, Moko!
....
WHAT'RE YOU SAY-ING?
I'M AN ACTRESS. I'M NOT GOING TO DO WORK LIKE THAT.
This is what you're good at, right? You want to be a talento.
C-Come on!
THEN WHY'D YOU SAY YOU WERE ACCEPTING THIS JOB?!
How could you!
Well...we don't care who does it, so please get ready...
Oh.
THEN DID YOU SAY WITH YOUR OWN MOUTH THAT YOU WERE ACCEPTING THIS JOB?
Uh...
W-WELL...
SEE, THERE!
B-BUT! IT'S LIVE! I CAN'T MAKE MISTAKES! I CAN'T READ ALL THE SCRIPT IN 15 SECONDS LIKE YOU, MOKO!
Hey Bo! Bo, standby!
Apparently, the hen's name.
There, hurry.
waddle
FLAP FLAP
YOU'LL BE ALL RIGHT. YOU DON'T HAVE TO SAY ANY-THING.
YOUR JOB IS TO BE THE ASSISTANT OF THE SHOW, AND TO TAKE CARE OF THE GUESTS.
And your little feature.

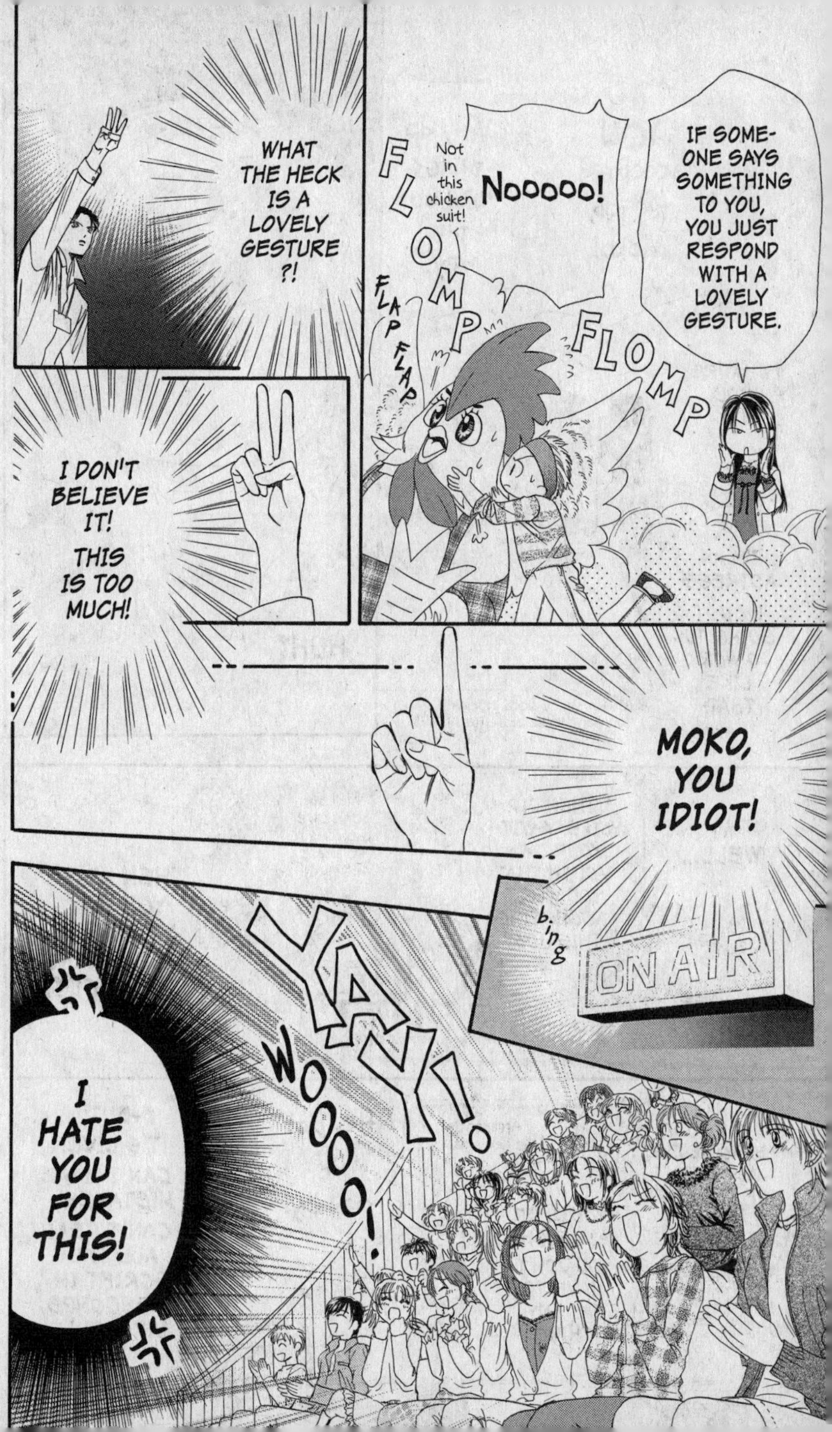
IF SOME-ONE SAYS SOMETHING TO YOU, YOU JUST RESPOND WITH A LOVELY GESTURE.
Noooo!
Not in this chicken suit!
FLOMP
FLOMP
FLAP FLAP
WHAT THE HECK IS A LOVELY GESTURE?!
I DON'T BELIEVE IT!
THIS IS TOO MUCH!
MOKO, YOU IDIOT!
bing
ON AIR
YAY!
WOOOO!
I HATE YOU FOR THIS!

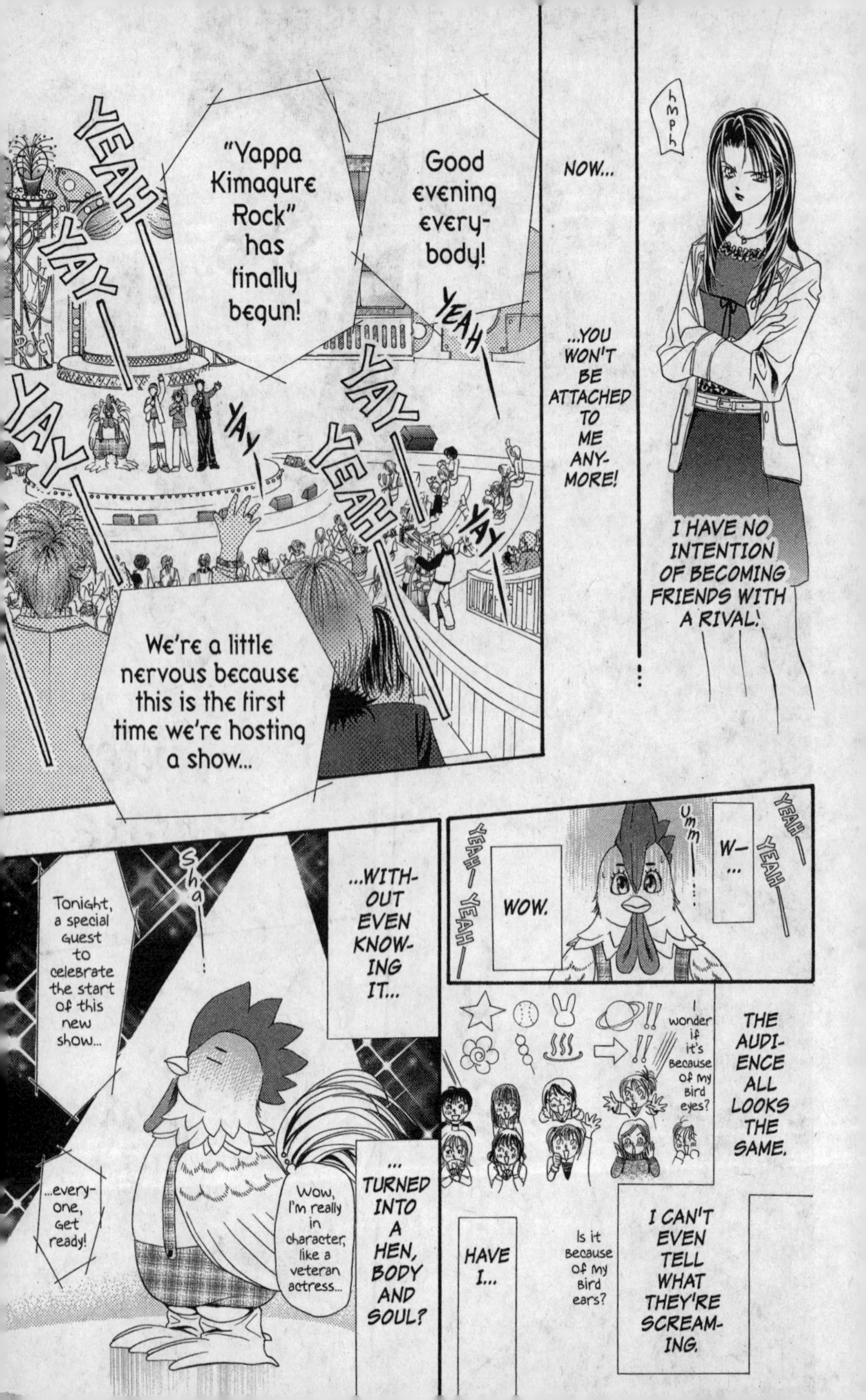
hmph
I HAVE NO INTENTION OF BECOMING FRIENDS WITH A RIVAL.
NOW...
...YOU WON'T BE ATTACHED TO ME ANYMORE!
Good evening every-body!
YEAH
"Yappa Kimagure Rock" has finally begun!
YEAH
YAY
YAY
YEAH
YAY
YAY
We're a little nervous because this is the first time we're hosting a show...
W—...
Umm...
YEAH YEAH
WOW.
YEAH YEAH
THE AUDIENCE ALL LOOKS THE SAME.
I wonder if it's because of my bird eyes?
I CAN'T EVEN TELL WHAT THEY'RE SCREAMING.
Is it because of my bird ears?
HAVE I...
...WITHOUT EVEN KNOWING IT...
sha
Tonight, a special guest to celebrate the start of this new show...
...TURNED INTO A HEN, BODY AND SOUL?
Wow, I'm really in character, like a veteran actress...
...everyone, get ready!

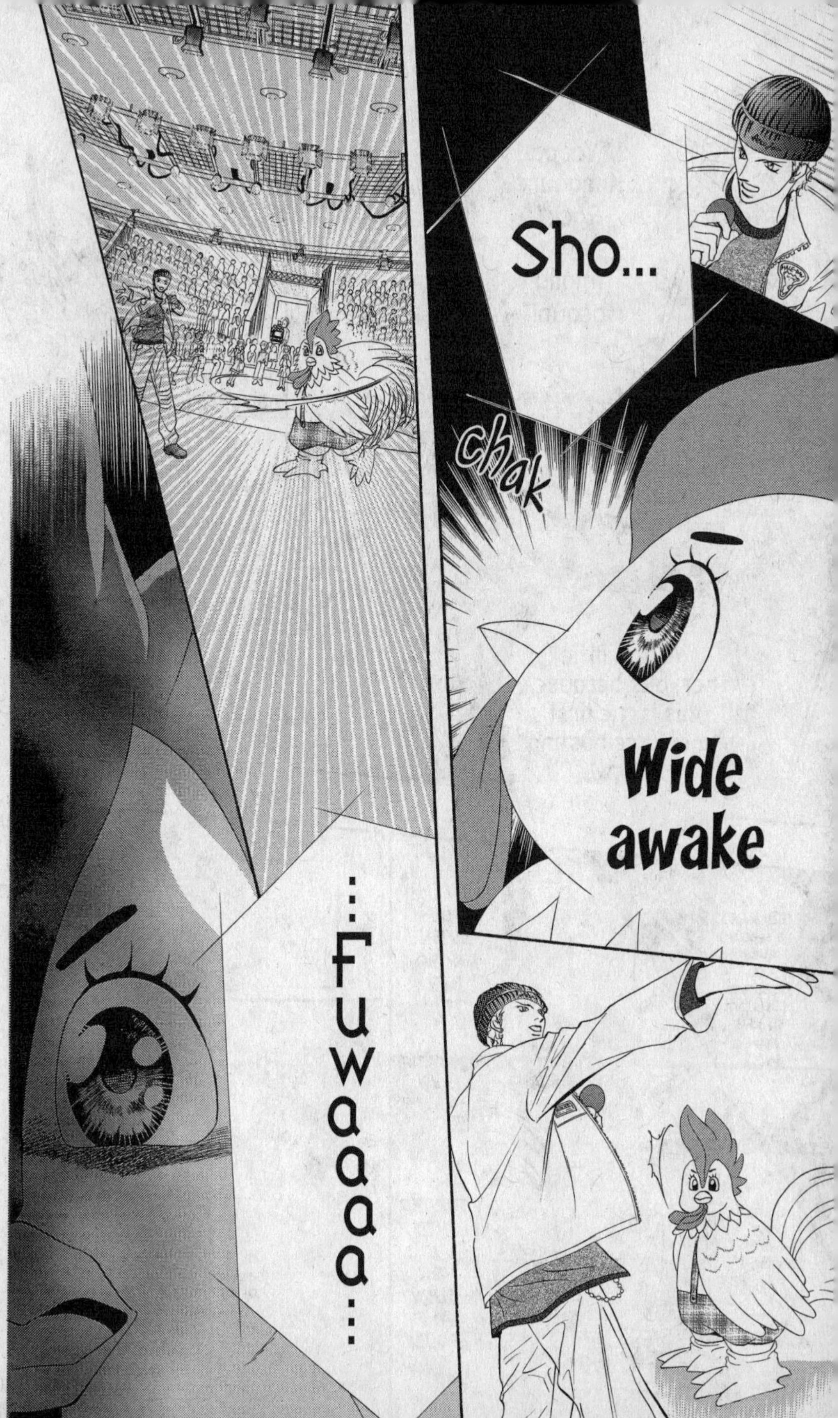
Sho...
chak
Wide awake
...Fuwaaa...

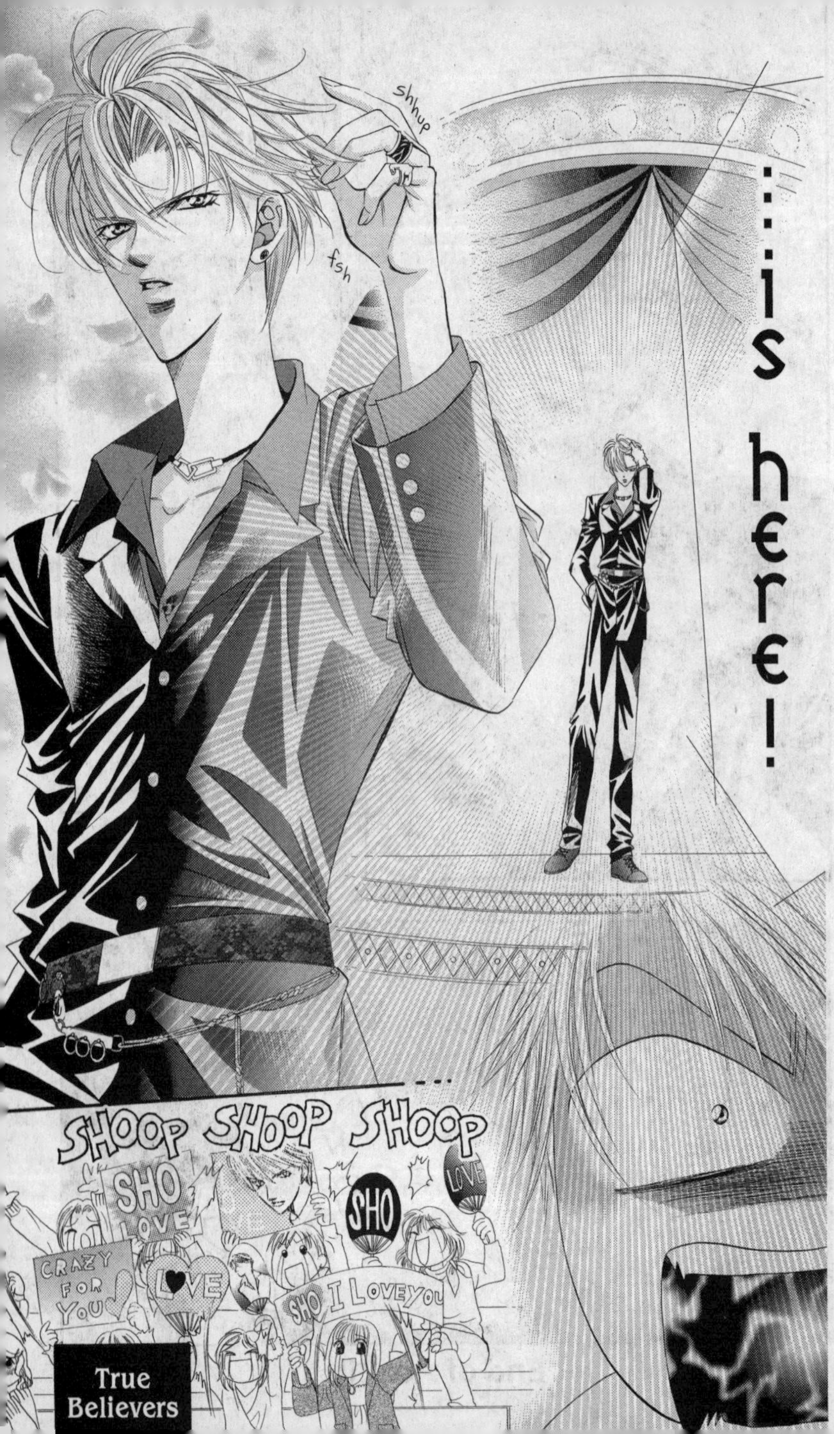
...is here!
shhup
fsh
SHOOP SHOOP SHOOP
SHO LOVE
SHO
LOVE
CRAZY FOR YOU
LOVE
SHO I LOVE YOU
True Believers

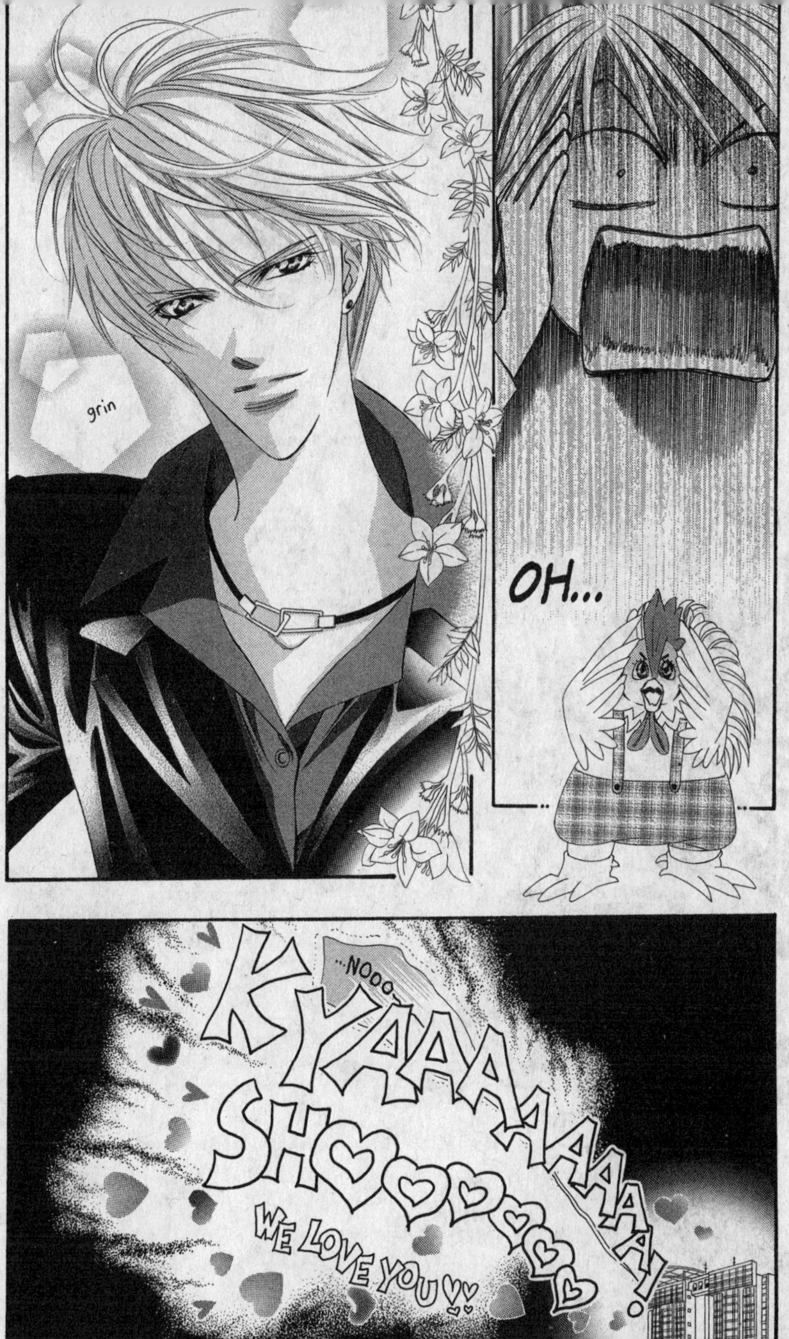
OH...
grin
...NOOO-
KYAAAAAAAAA!
SH♡♡♡♡♡♡
WE LOVE YOU♡!!

End of Act 20

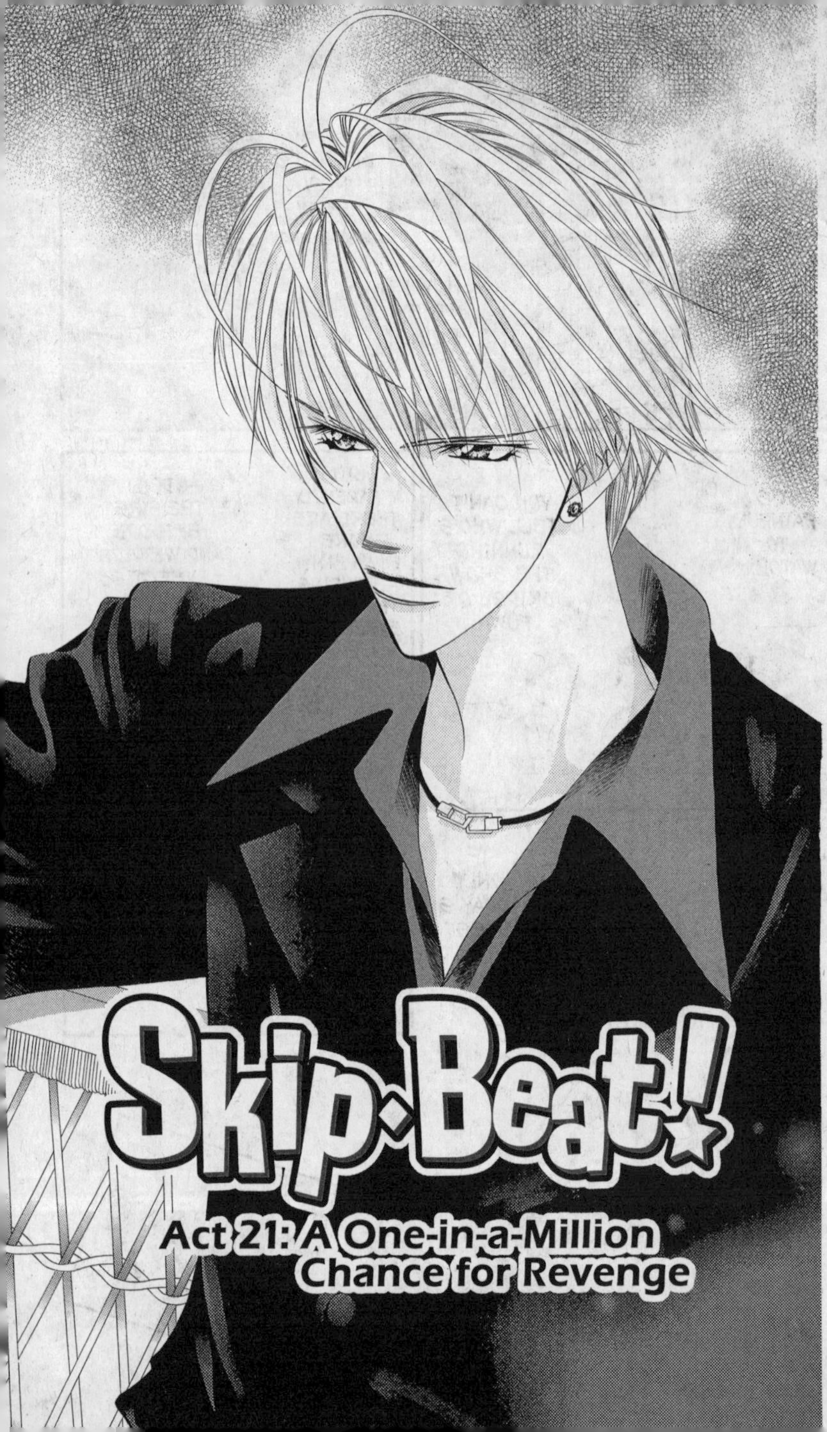
Skip·Beat!
Act 21: A One-in-a-Million Chance for Revenge

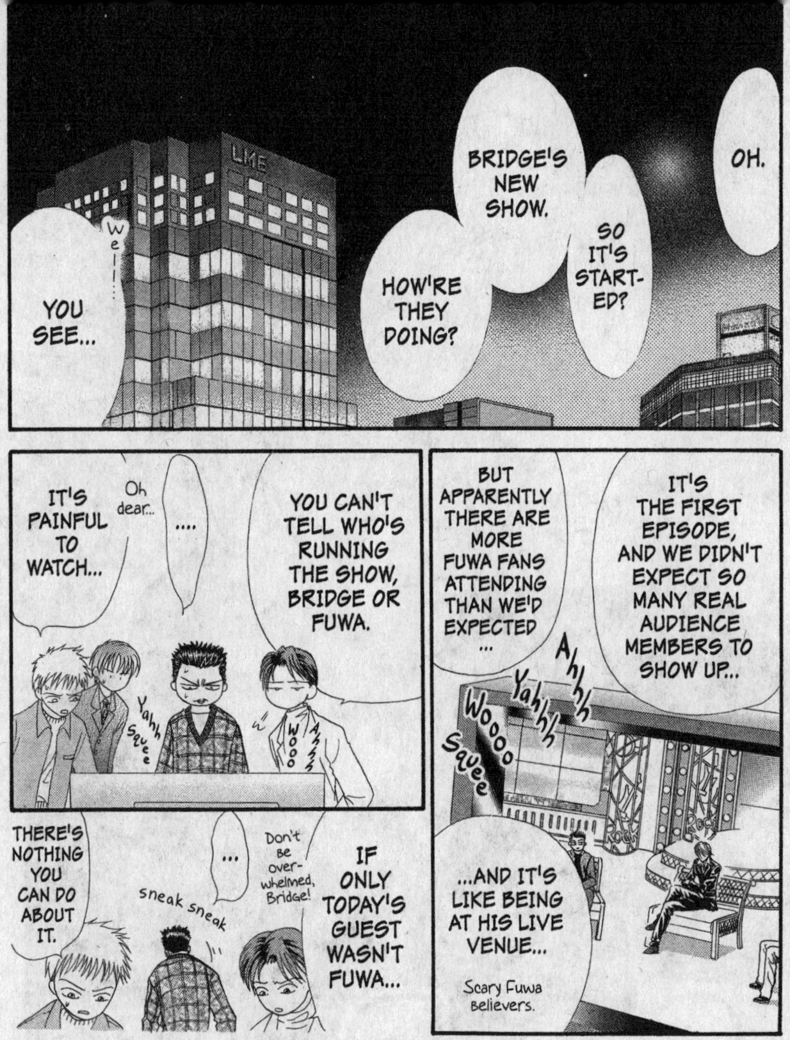
OH.
BRIDGE'S NEW SHOW.
SO IT'S STARTED?
HOW'RE THEY DOING?
Well...
YOU SEE...
IT'S THE FIRST EPISODE, AND WE DIDN'T EXPECT SO MANY REAL AUDIENCE MEMBERS TO SHOW UP...
BUT APPARENTLY THERE ARE MORE FUWA FANS ATTENDING THAN WE'D EXPECTED...
Ahhhh
Yahhhh
Woooo
Squee
...AND IT'S LIKE BEING AT HIS LIVE VENUE...
Scary Fuwa Believers.
YOU CAN'T TELL WHO'S RUNNING THE SHOW, BRIDGE OR FUWA.
....
Oh dear...
IT'S PAINFUL TO WATCH...
Yahh
Squee
Wooo
Ahhhh
IF ONLY TODAY'S GUEST WASN'T FUWA...
Don't be over-whelmed, Bridge!
...
sneak sneak
THERE'S NOTHING YOU CAN DO ABOUT IT.
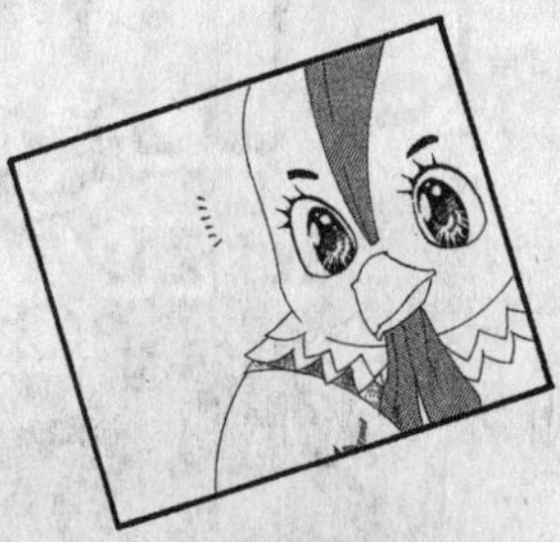

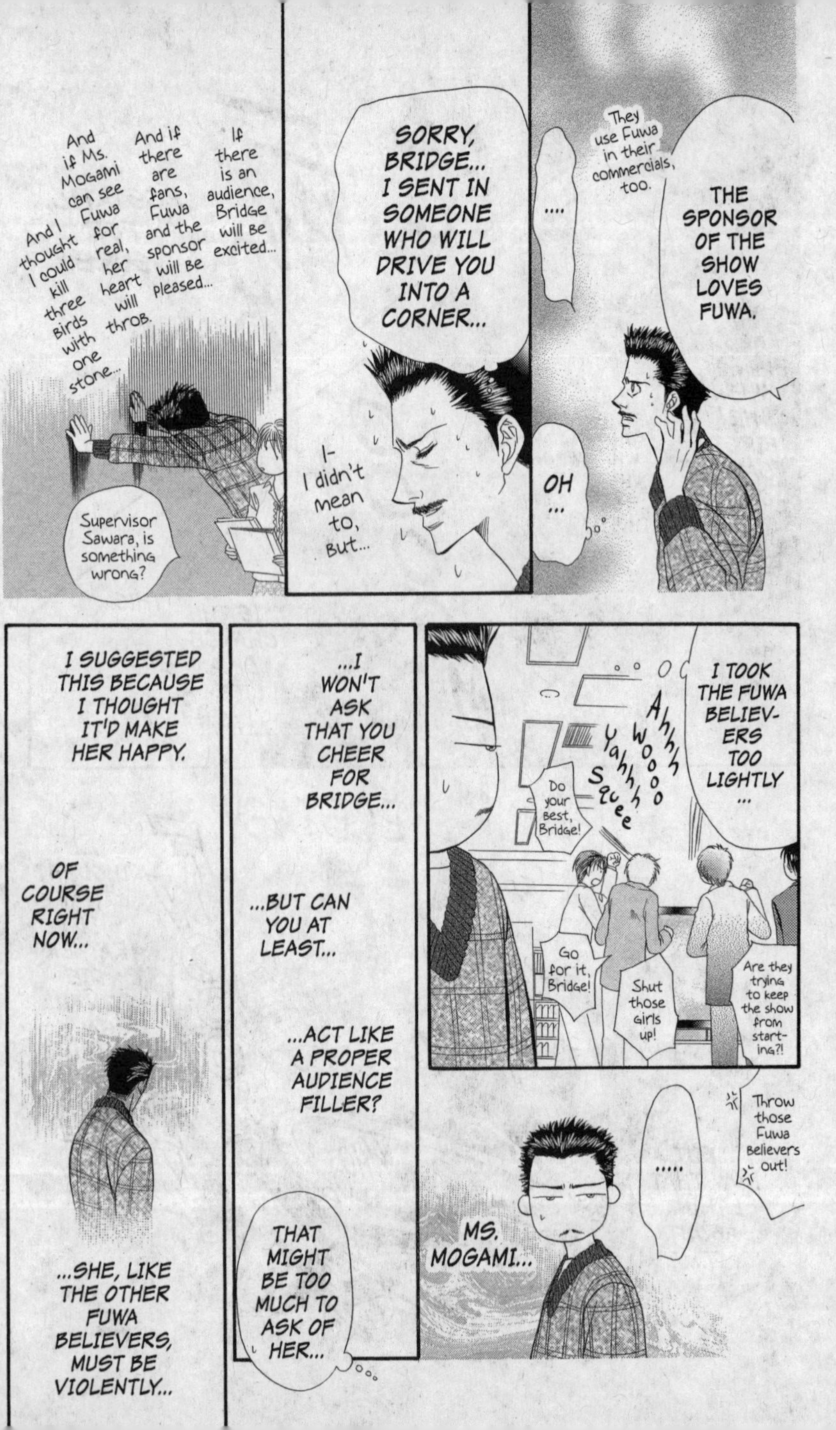

THE SPONSOR OF THE SHOW LOVES FUWA.
They use Fuwa in their commercials, too.
....
OH...
SORRY, BRIDGE... I SENT IN SOMEONE WHO WILL DRIVE YOU INTO A CORNER...
I- I didn't mean to, but...
If there is an audience, Bridge will be excited...
And if there are fans, Fuwa and the sponsor will be pleased...
And if Ms. Mogami can see Fuwa for real, her heart will throb.
And I thought I could kill three birds with one stone...
Supervisor Sawara, is something wrong?
I TOOK THE FUWA BELIEVERS TOO LIGHTLY...
Ahhhh Woooo Yahhh Squee
Do your best, Bridge!
Are they trying to keep the show from starting?!
Shut those girls up!
Go for it, Bridge!
Throw those Fuwa Believers out!
.....
MS. MOGAMI...
...I WON'T ASK THAT YOU CHEER FOR BRIDGE...
...BUT CAN YOU AT LEAST...
...ACT LIKE A PROPER AUDIENCE FILLER?
THAT MIGHT BE TOO MUCH TO ASK OF HER...
I SUGGESTED THIS BECAUSE I THOUGHT IT'D MAKE HER HAPPY.
OF COURSE RIGHT NOW...
...SHE, LIKE THE OTHER FUWA BELIEVERS, MUST BE VIOLENTLY...

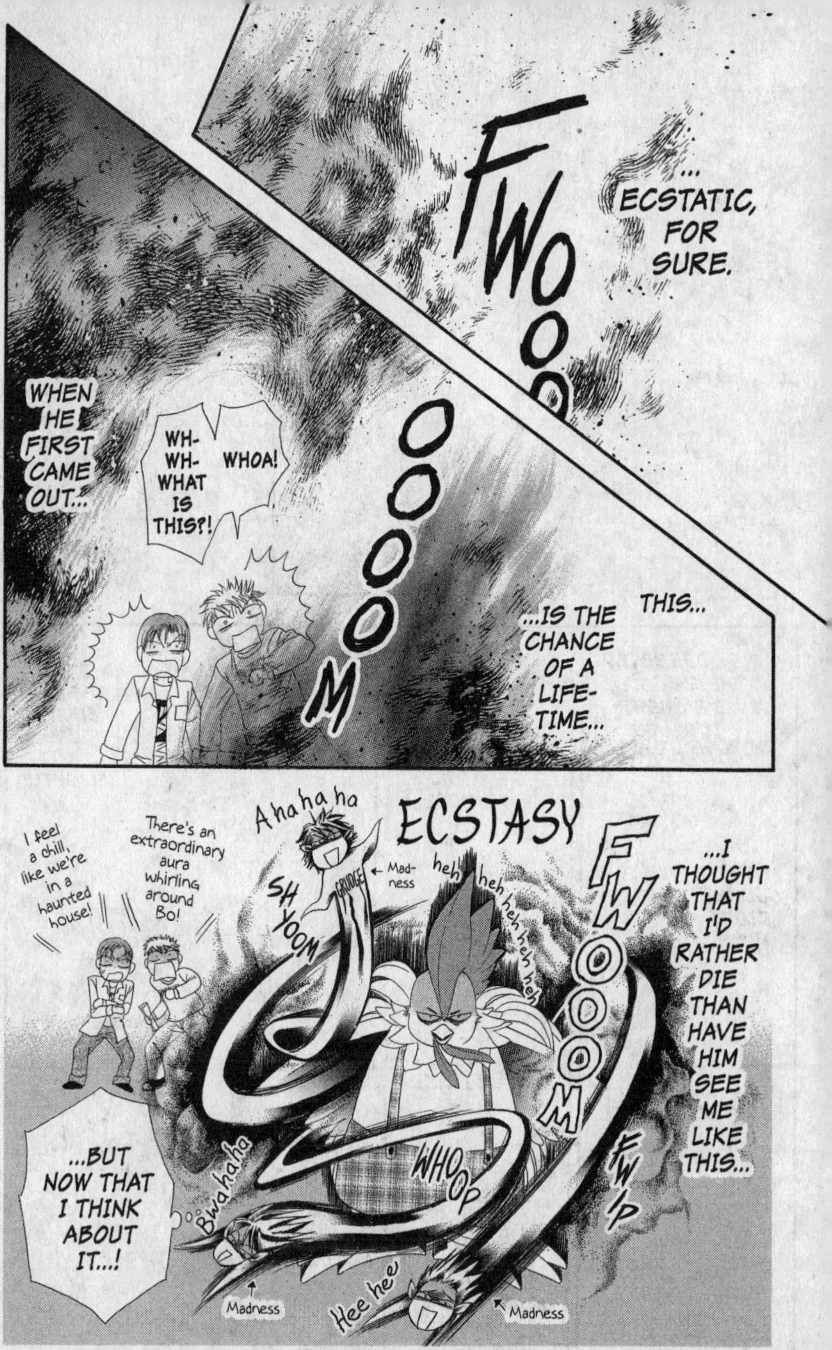
FWOOOOOOOOM
...ECSTATIC, FOR SURE.
THIS...
...IS THE CHANCE OF A LIFE-TIME...
WHOA!
WH-WH-WHAT IS THIS?!
WHEN HE FIRST CAME OUT...
...I THOUGHT THAT I'D RATHER DIE THAN HAVE HIM SEE ME LIKE THIS...
FWOOOOM
FWIP
ECSTASY
heh heh heh heh heh
Ahahaha
Madness
GRUDGE
SHYOOM
There's an extraordinary aura whirling around Bo!
I feel a chill, like we're in a haunted house!
WHOOP
...BUT NOW THAT I THINK ABOUT IT...!
Bwahaha
Madness
Hee hee
Madness

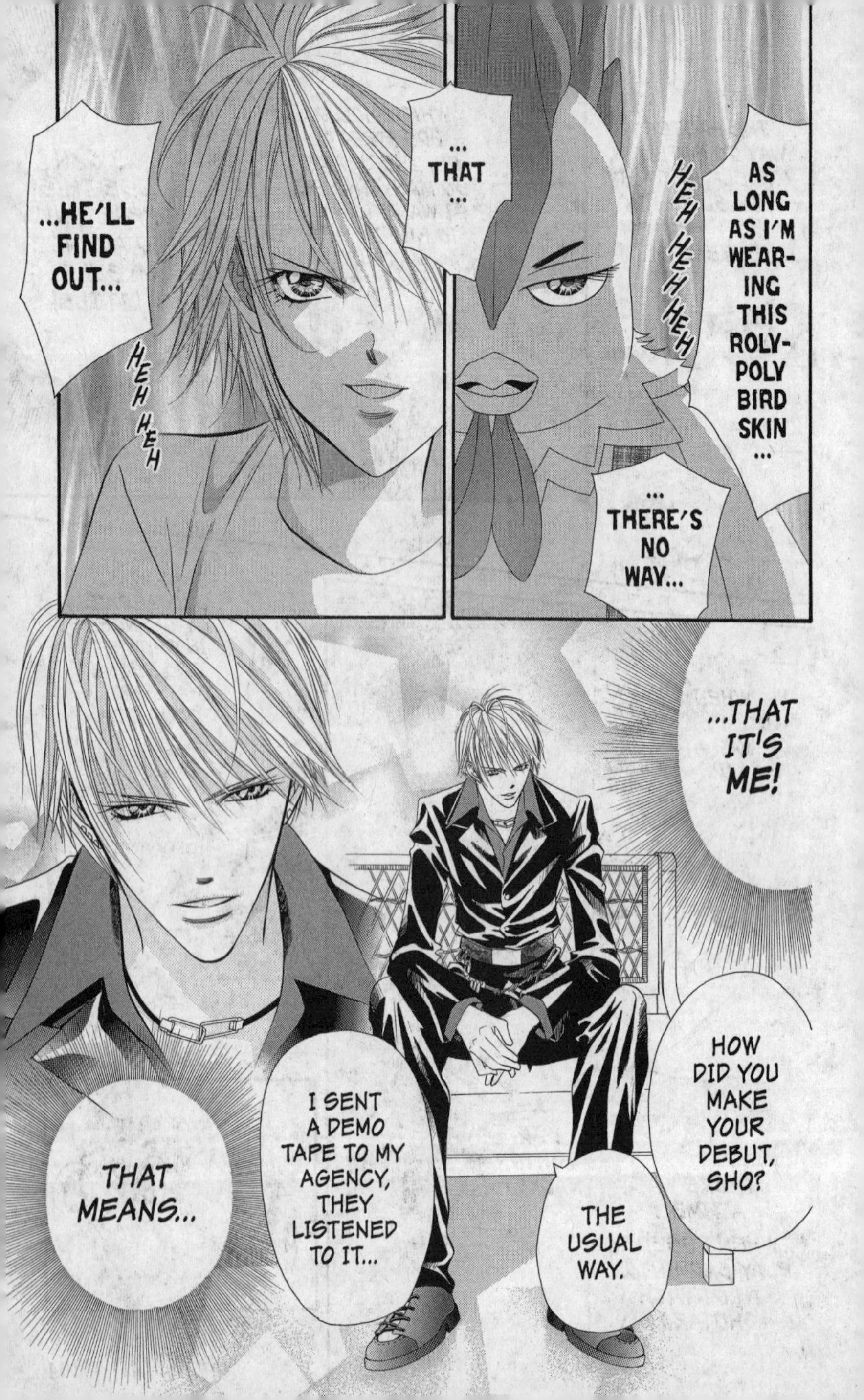
AS LONG AS I'M WEARING THIS ROLY-POLY BIRD SKIN...
HEH HEH HEH HEH
...THERE'S NO WAY...
...THAT...
...HE'LL FIND OUT...
HEH HEH
...THAT IT'S ME!
HOW DID YOU MAKE YOUR DEBUT, SHO?
THE USUAL WAY.
I SENT A DEMO TAPE TO MY AGENCY, THEY LISTENED TO IT...
THAT MEANS...

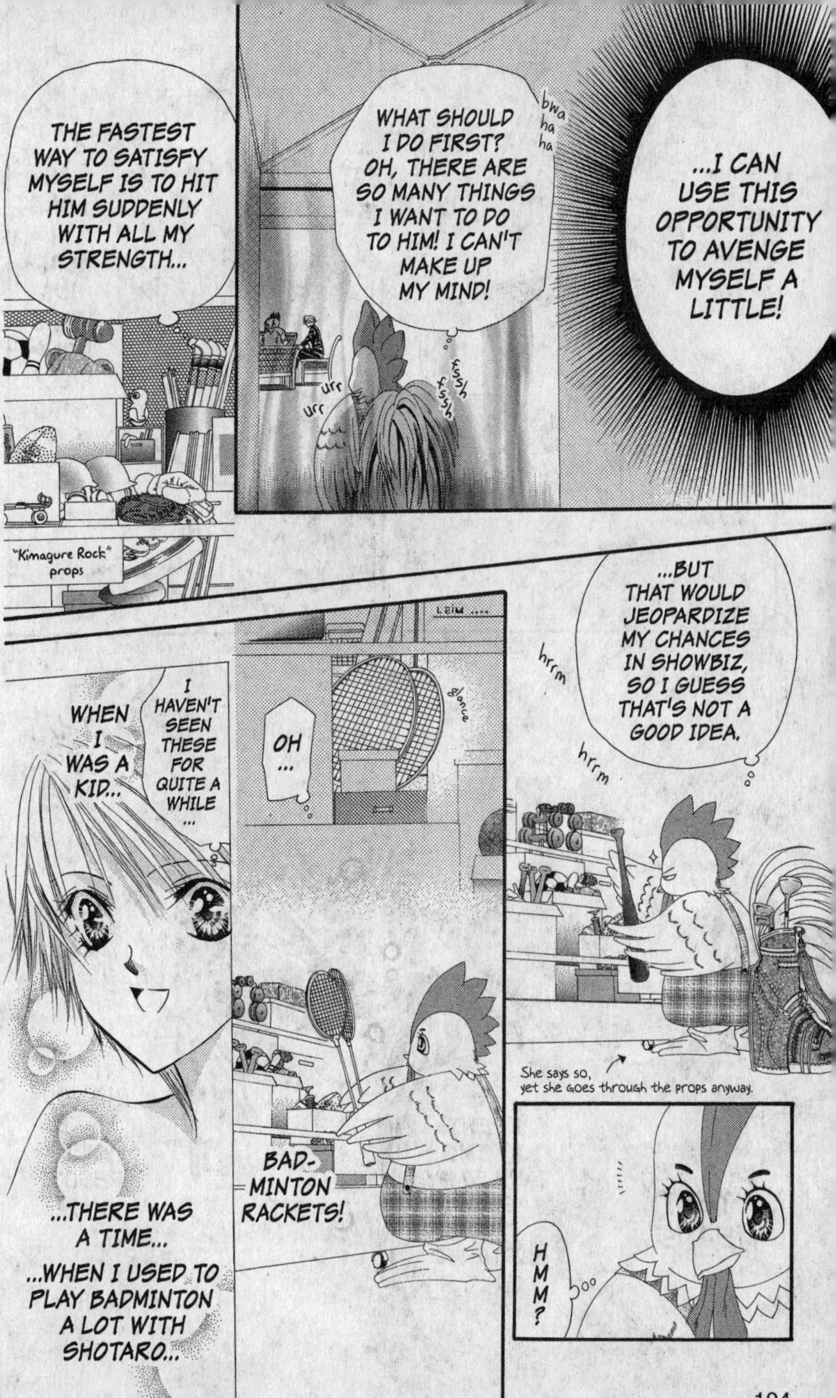
...I CAN USE THIS OPPORTUNITY TO AVENGE MYSELF A LITTLE!
bwa ha ha
WHAT SHOULD I DO FIRST? OH, THERE ARE SO MANY THINGS I WANT TO DO TO HIM! I CAN'T MAKE UP MY MIND!
fssh fssh
urr urr
THE FASTEST WAY TO SATISFY MYSELF IS TO HIT HIM SUDDENLY WITH ALL MY STRENGTH...
"Kimagure Rock" props
...BUT THAT WOULD JEOPARDIZE MY CHANCES IN SHOWBIZ, SO I GUESS THAT'S NOT A GOOD IDEA.
hrrm
hrrm
She says so, yet she goes through the props anyway.
HMM?
OH ...
glance
BAD-MINTON RACKETS!
WHEN I WAS A KID...
I HAVEN'T SEEN THESE FOR QUITE A WHILE ...
...THERE WAS A TIME...
...WHEN I USED TO PLAY BADMINTON A LOT WITH SHOTARO...

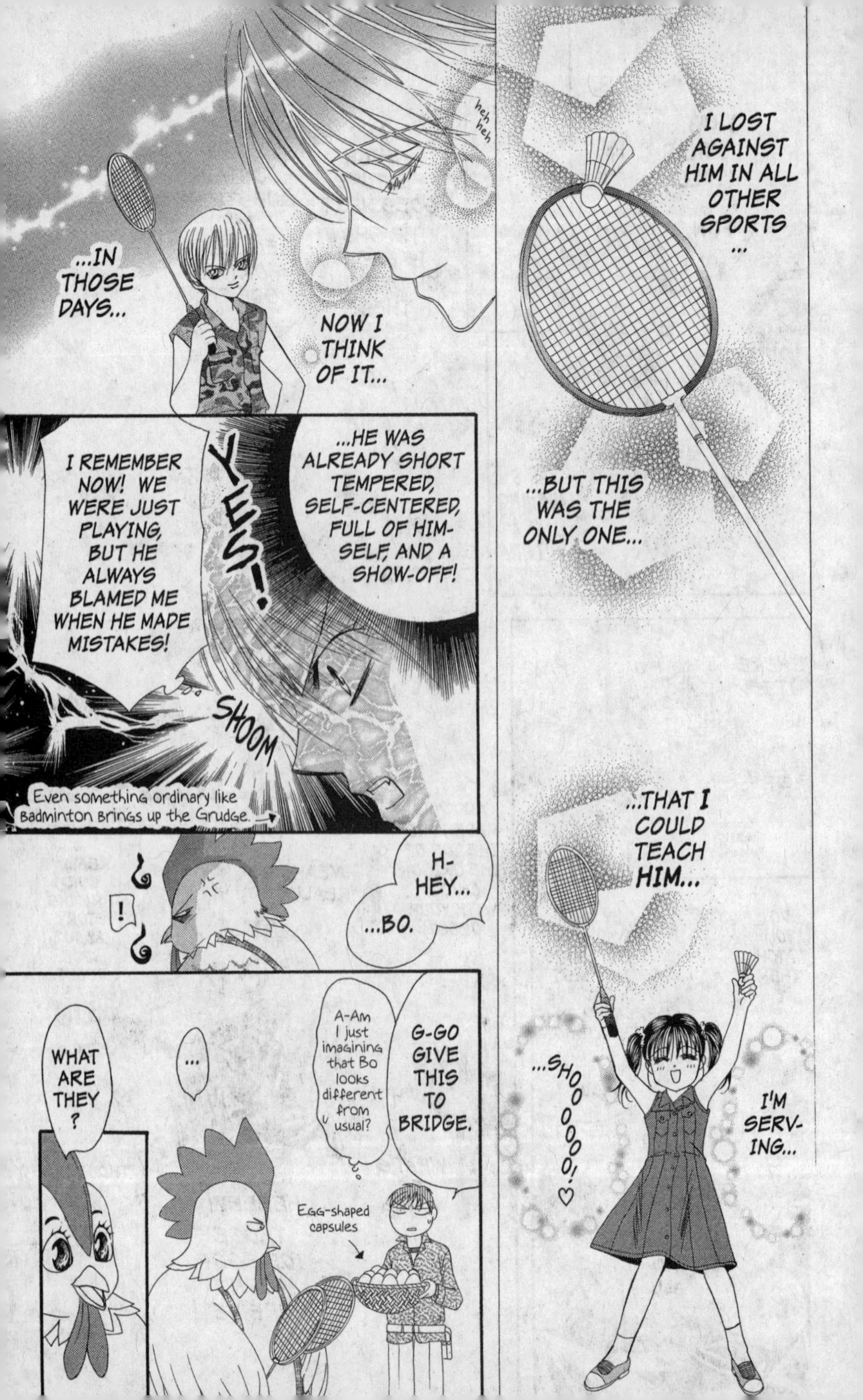
I LOST AGAINST HIM IN ALL OTHER SPORTS ...
...BUT THIS WAS THE ONLY ONE...
...THAT I COULD TEACH HIM...
I'M SERV-ING...
...SHOOOOOOO!♡
heh heh
NOW I THINK OF IT...
...IN THOSE DAYS...
...HE WAS ALREADY SHORT TEMPERED, SELF-CENTERED, FULL OF HIM-SELF, AND A SHOW-OFF!
YES!
I REMEMBER NOW! WE WERE JUST PLAYING, BUT HE ALWAYS BLAMED ME WHEN HE MADE MISTAKES!
SHOOM
Even something ordinary like Badminton brings up the Grudge.
H-HEY...
...BO.
!
G-GO GIVE THIS TO BRIDGE.
A-Am I just imagining that Bo looks different from usual?
...
WHAT ARE THEY ?
Egg-shaped capsules

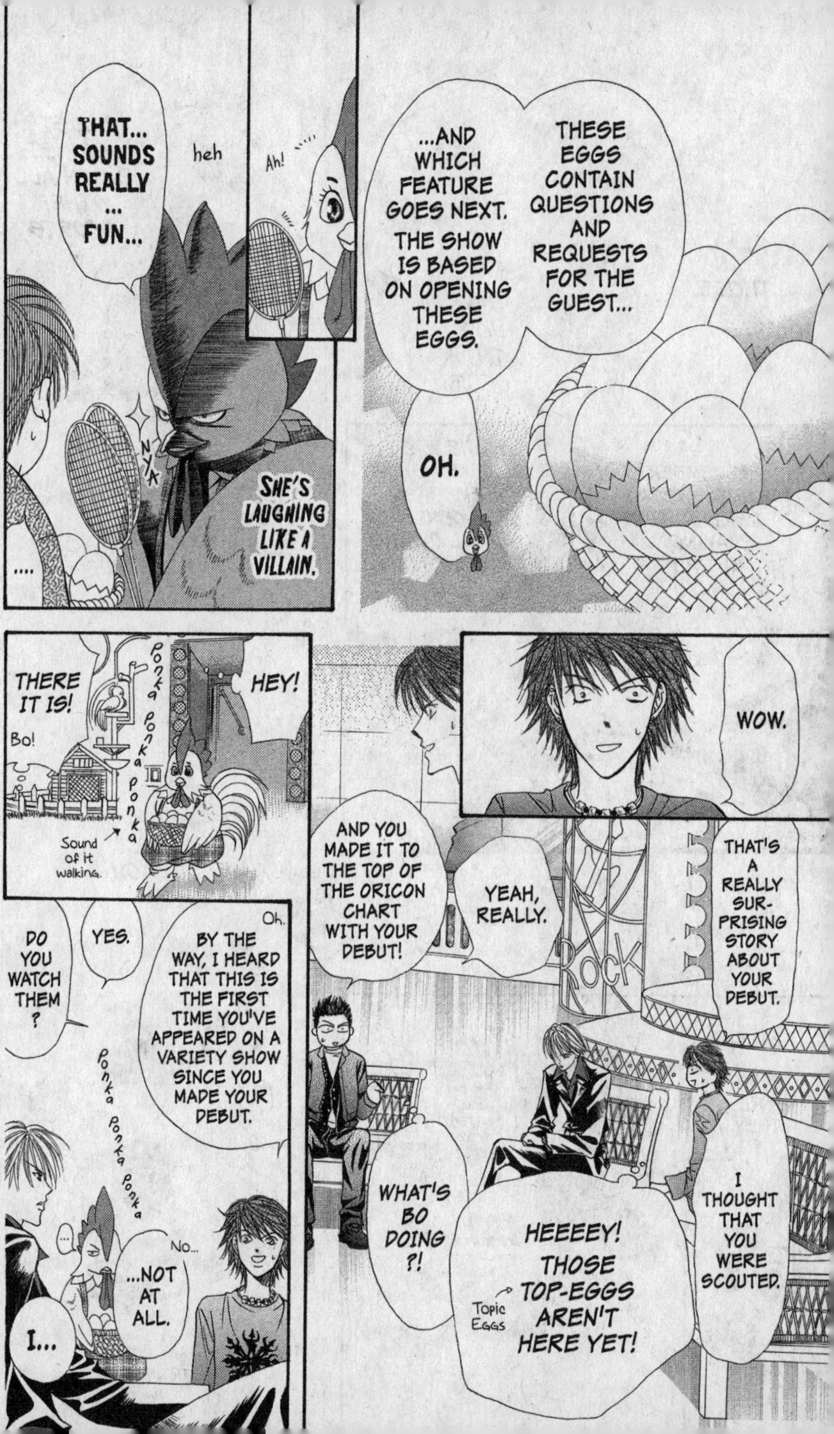
THESE EGGS CONTAIN QUESTIONS AND REQUESTS FOR THE GUEST...
...AND WHICH FEATURE GOES NEXT. THE SHOW IS BASED ON OPENING THESE EGGS.
OH.
Ah!
THAT... SOUNDS REALLY ... FUN...
heh
NYA
SHE'S LAUGHING LIKE A VILLAIN.
....
WOW.
THAT'S A REALLY SUR-PRISING STORY ABOUT YOUR DEBUT.
YEAH, REALLY.
AND YOU MADE IT TO THE TOP OF THE ORICON CHART WITH YOUR DEBUT!
I THOUGHT THAT YOU WERE SCOUTED.
HEEEEY! THOSE TOP-EGGS AREN'T HERE YET!
Topic Eggs
WHAT'S BO DOING ?!
HEY!
THERE IT IS!
Bo!
Ponka Ponka Ponka Ponka
Sound of it walking.
Oh.
BY THE WAY, I HEARD THAT THIS IS THE FIRST TIME YOU'VE APPEARED ON A VARIETY SHOW SINCE YOU MADE YOUR DEBUT.
YES.
DO YOU WATCH THEM ?
Ponka Ponka Ponka Ponka
No...
...NOT AT ALL.
...
I...

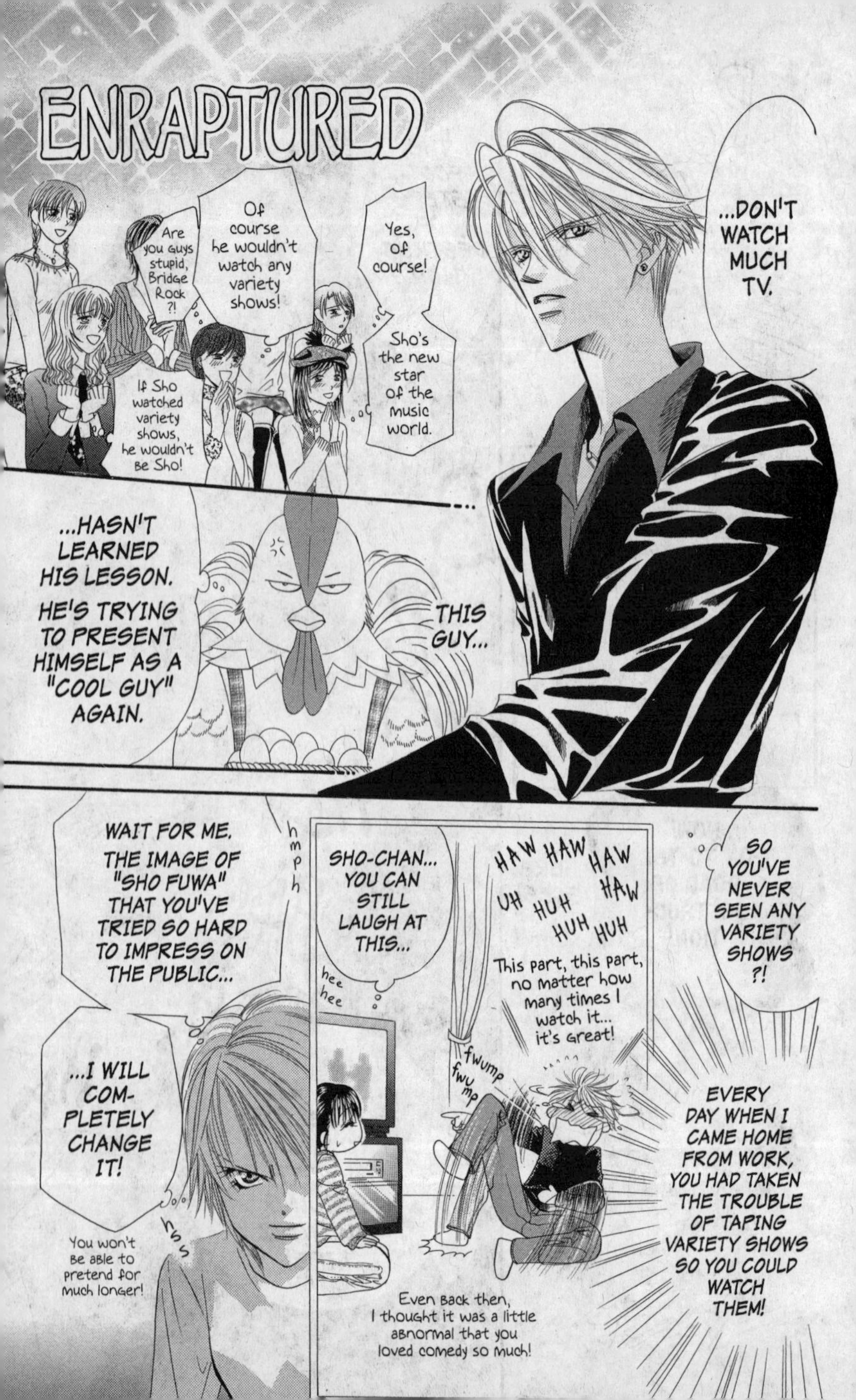
ENRAPTURED
...DON'T WATCH MUCH TV.
Yes, of course!
Sho's the new star of the music world.
Of course he wouldn't watch any variety shows!
Are you guys stupid, Bridge Rock?!
If Sho watched variety shows, he wouldn't be Sho!
THIS GUY...
...HASN'T LEARNED HIS LESSON. HE'S TRYING TO PRESENT HIMSELF AS A "COOL GUY" AGAIN.
SO YOU'VE NEVER SEEN ANY VARIETY SHOWS?!
HAW HAW HAW HAW UH HUH HUH HUH HUH
This part, this part, no matter how many times I watch it... it's great!
SHO-CHAN... YOU CAN STILL LAUGH AT THIS...
hee hee
fwump fwump
EVERY DAY WHEN I CAME HOME FROM WORK, YOU HAD TAKEN THE TROUBLE OF TAPING VARIETY SHOWS SO YOU COULD WATCH THEM!
Even back then, I thought it was a little abnormal that you loved comedy so much!
hmph
WAIT FOR ME. THE IMAGE OF "SHO FUWA" THAT YOU'VE TRIED SO HARD TO IMPRESS ON THE PUBLIC...
...I WILL COM-PLETELY CHANGE IT!
hss
You won't be able to pretend for much longer!

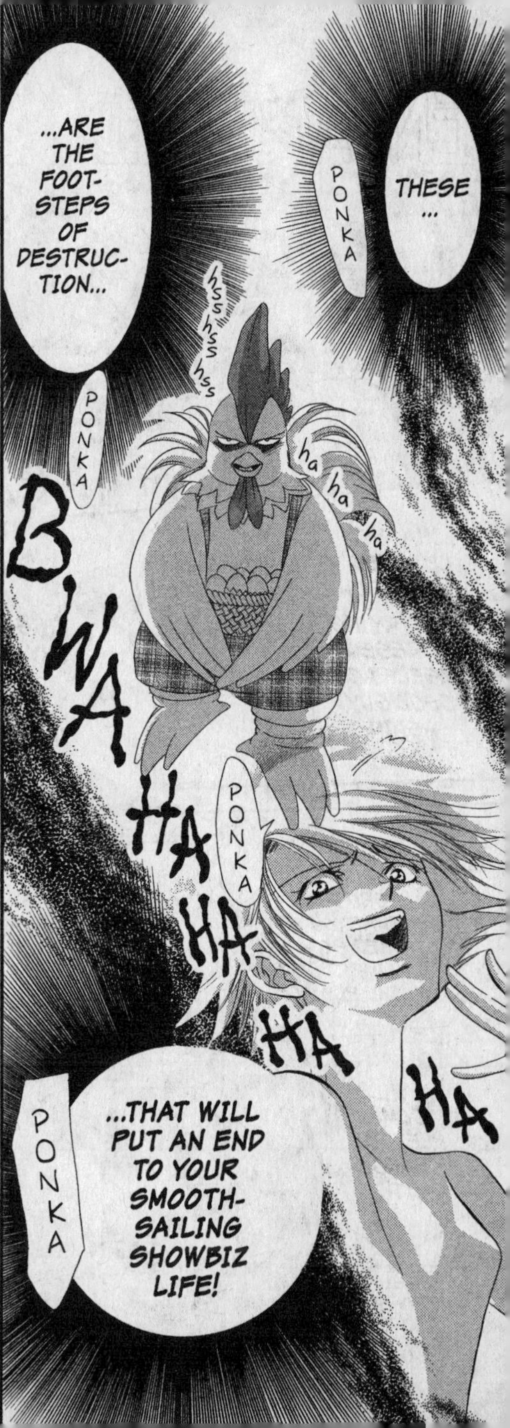
THESE...
PONKA
...ARE THE FOOT-STEPS OF DESTRUC-TION...
hss hss hss
PONKA
BWAHAHAHAHA
ha ha ha
PONKA
...THAT WILL PUT AN END TO YOUR SMOOTH-SAILING SHOWBIZ LIFE!
PONKA

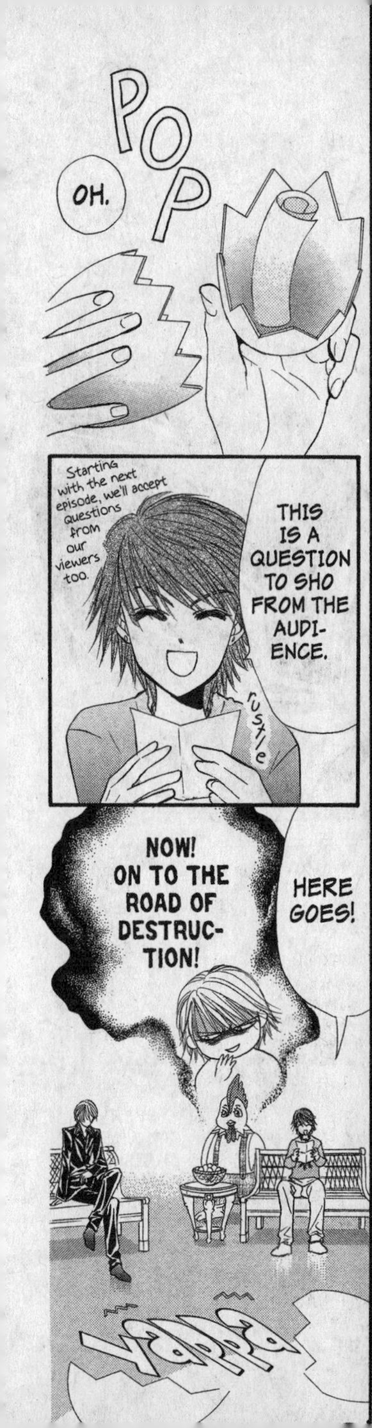
POP
OH.
THIS IS A QUESTION TO SHO FROM THE AUDI-ENCE.
Starting with the next episode, we'll accept questions from our viewers too.
rustle
HERE GOES!
NOW! ON TO THE ROAD OF DESTRUC-TION!

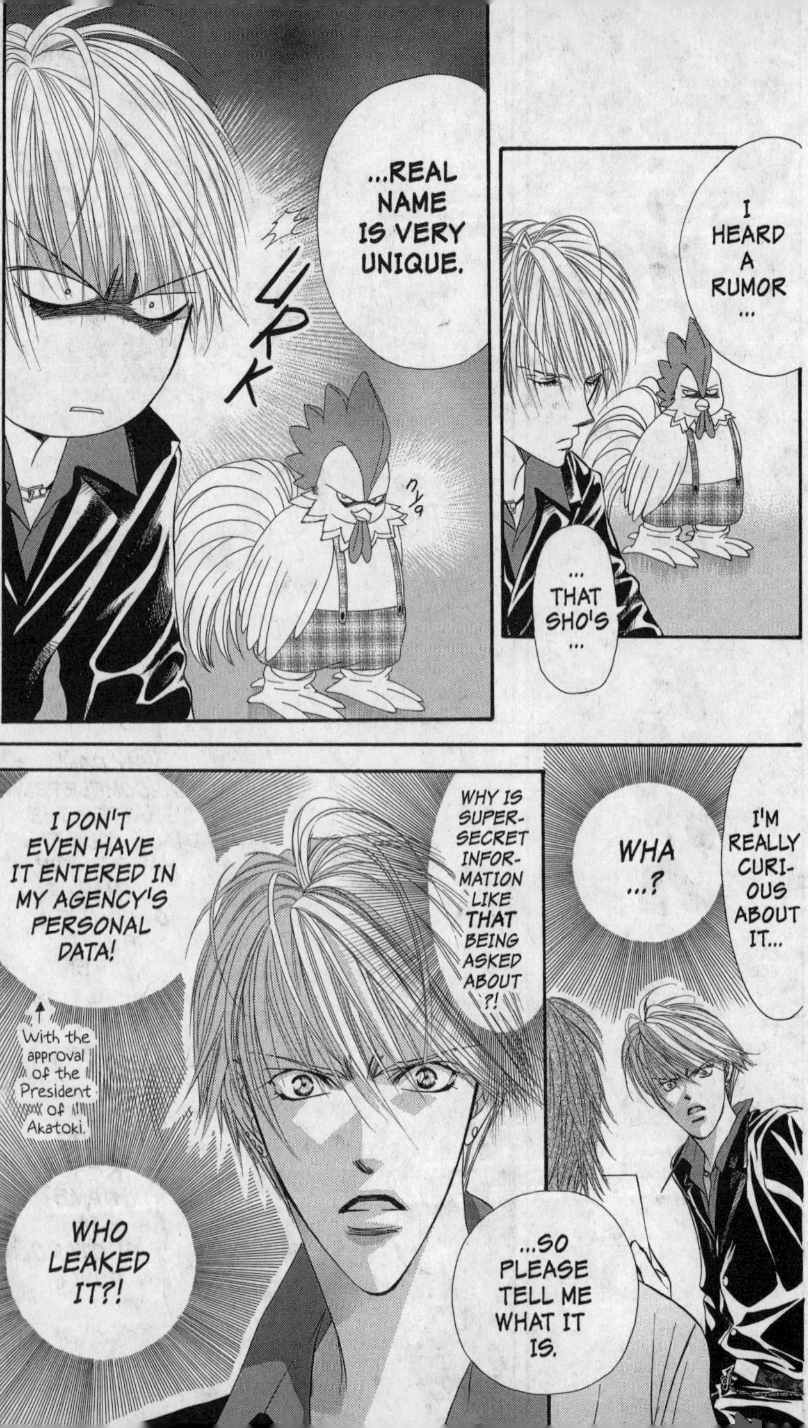
I HEARD A RUMOR...
...THAT SHO'S...
...REAL NAME IS VERY UNIQUE.
URK
I'M REALLY CURIOUS ABOUT IT...
WHA...?
WHY IS SUPER-SECRET INFORMATION LIKE THAT BEING ASKED ABOUT?!
I DON'T EVEN HAVE IT ENTERED IN MY AGENCY'S PERSONAL DATA!
With the approval of the President of Akatoki.
WHO LEAKED IT?!
...SO PLEASE TELL ME WHAT IT IS.

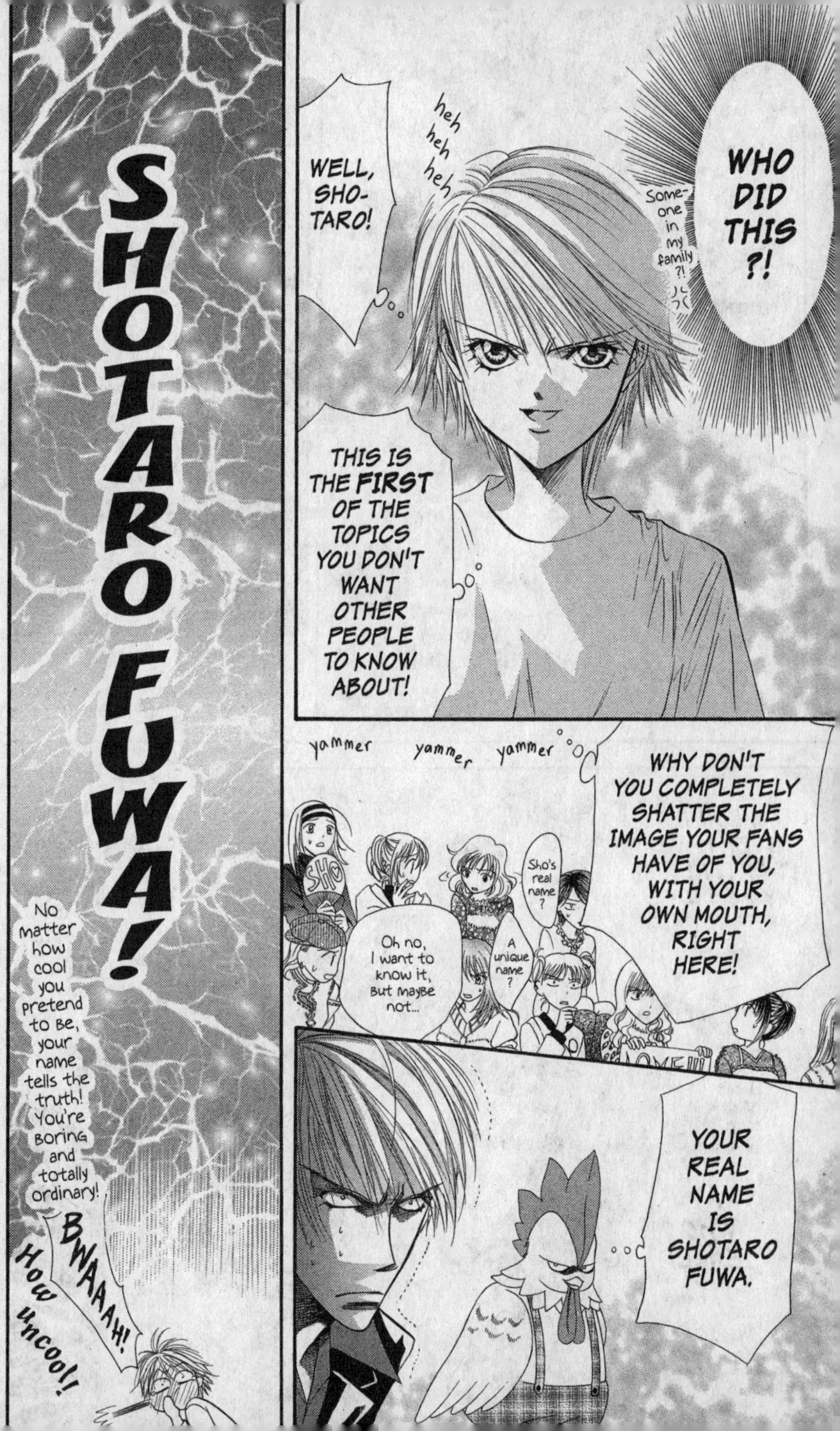
WHO DID THIS?!
Some-one in my family?!
heh heh heh
WELL, SHO-TARO!
THIS IS THE FIRST OF THE TOPICS YOU DON'T WANT OTHER PEOPLE TO KNOW ABOUT!
yammer yammer yammer
WHY DON'T YOU COMPLETELY SHATTER THE IMAGE YOUR FANS HAVE OF YOU, WITH YOUR OWN MOUTH, RIGHT HERE!
Sho's real name?
A unique name?
Oh no, I want to know it, but maybe not...
SHO
YOUR REAL NAME IS SHOTARO FUWA.
SHOTARO FUWA!
No matter how cool you pretend to be, your name tells the truth! You're boring and totally ordinary!
BWAAAH!
How uncool!

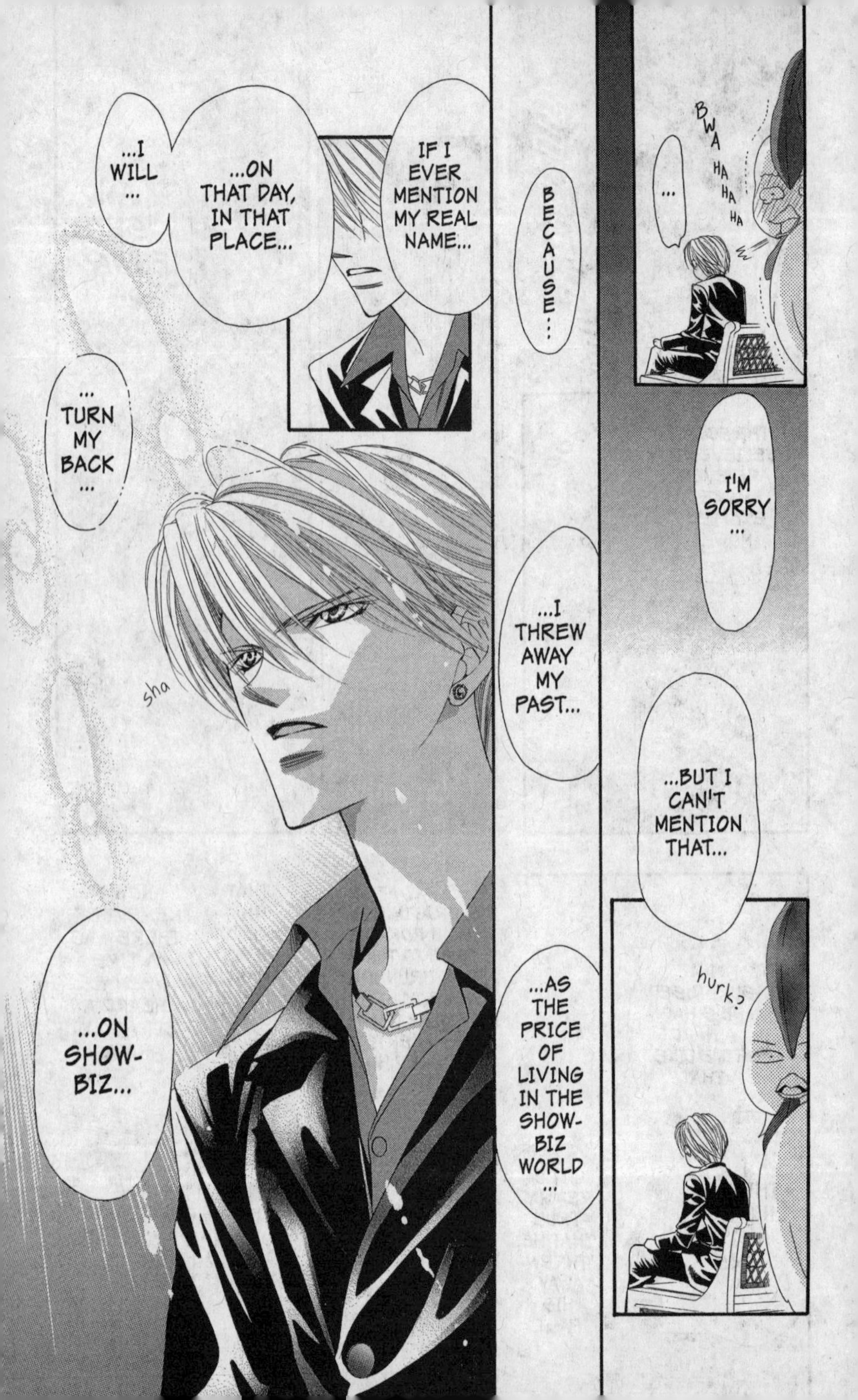
...
BWAHAHAHAHA
I'M SORRY...
...BUT I CAN'T MENTION THAT...
hurk?
BECAUSE...
...I THREW AWAY MY PAST...
...AS THE PRICE OF LIVING IN THE SHOW-BIZ WORLD...
IF I EVER MENTION MY REAL NAME...
...ON THAT DAY, IN THAT PLACE...
...I WILL...
...TURN MY BACK...
sha
...ON SHOW-BIZ...

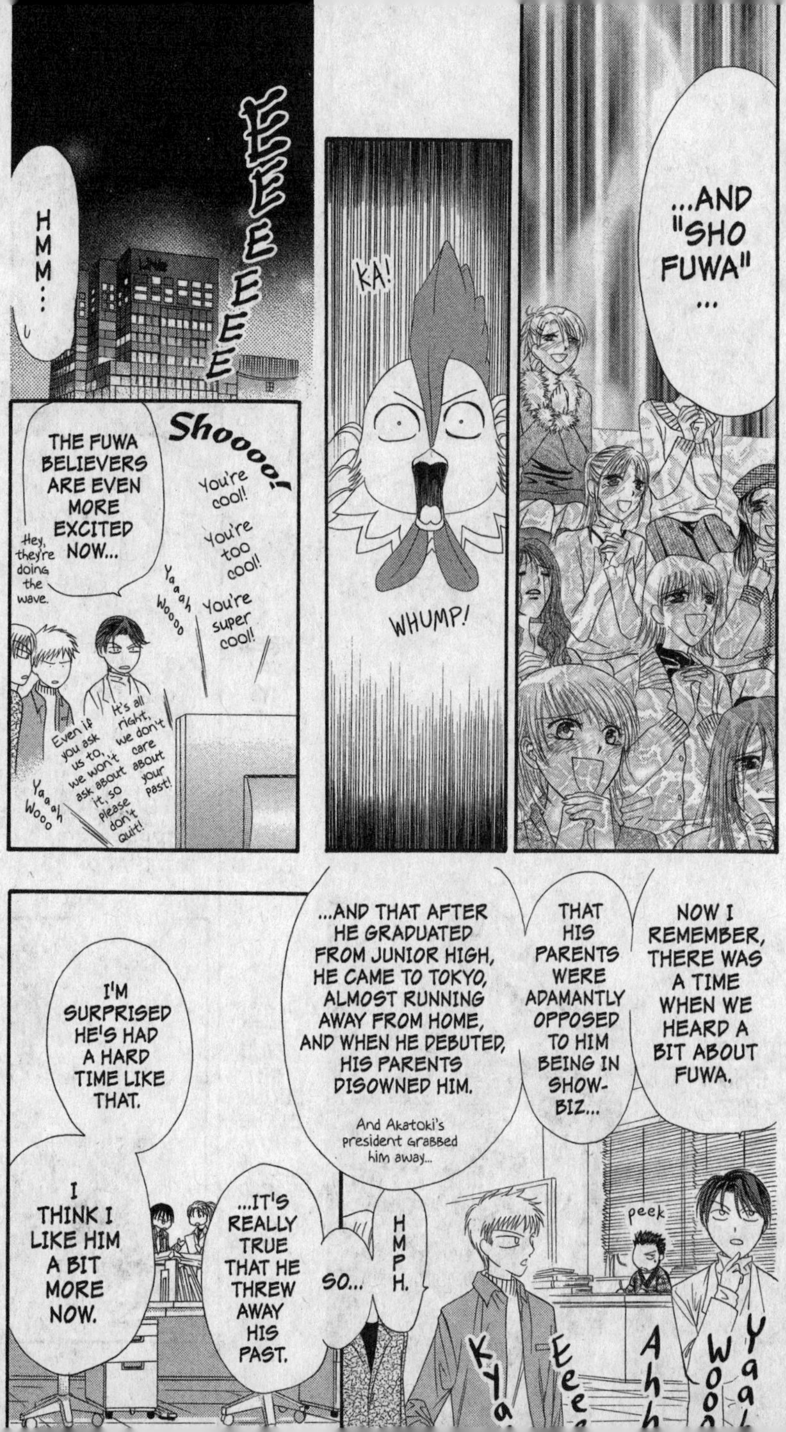
...AND "SHO FUWA" ...
KA!
WHUMP!
EEEEEE
HMM...
Shooooo!
THE FUWA BELIEVERS ARE EVEN MORE EXCITED NOW...
You're cool!
You're too cool!
You're super cool!
Hey, they're doing the wave.
Yaaah Wooo
It's all right, we don't care about your past!
Even if you ask us to, we won't ask about it, so please don't quit!
Yaaah Wooo
NOW I REMEMBER, THERE WAS A TIME WHEN WE HEARD A BIT ABOUT FUWA.
THAT HIS PARENTS WERE ADAMANTLY OPPOSED TO HIM BEING IN SHOW-BIZ...
...AND THAT AFTER HE GRADUATED FROM JUNIOR HIGH, HE CAME TO TOKYO, ALMOST RUNNING AWAY FROM HOME, AND WHEN HE DEBUTED, HIS PARENTS DISOWNED HIM.
And Akatoki's president grabbed him away...
I'M SURPRISED HE'S HAD A HARD TIME LIKE THAT.
peek
HMPH.
SO...
...IT'S REALLY TRUE THAT HE THREW AWAY HIS PAST.
I THINK I LIKE HIM A BIT MORE NOW.
Yaaa
Wooo
Ahh
Eee
Kya

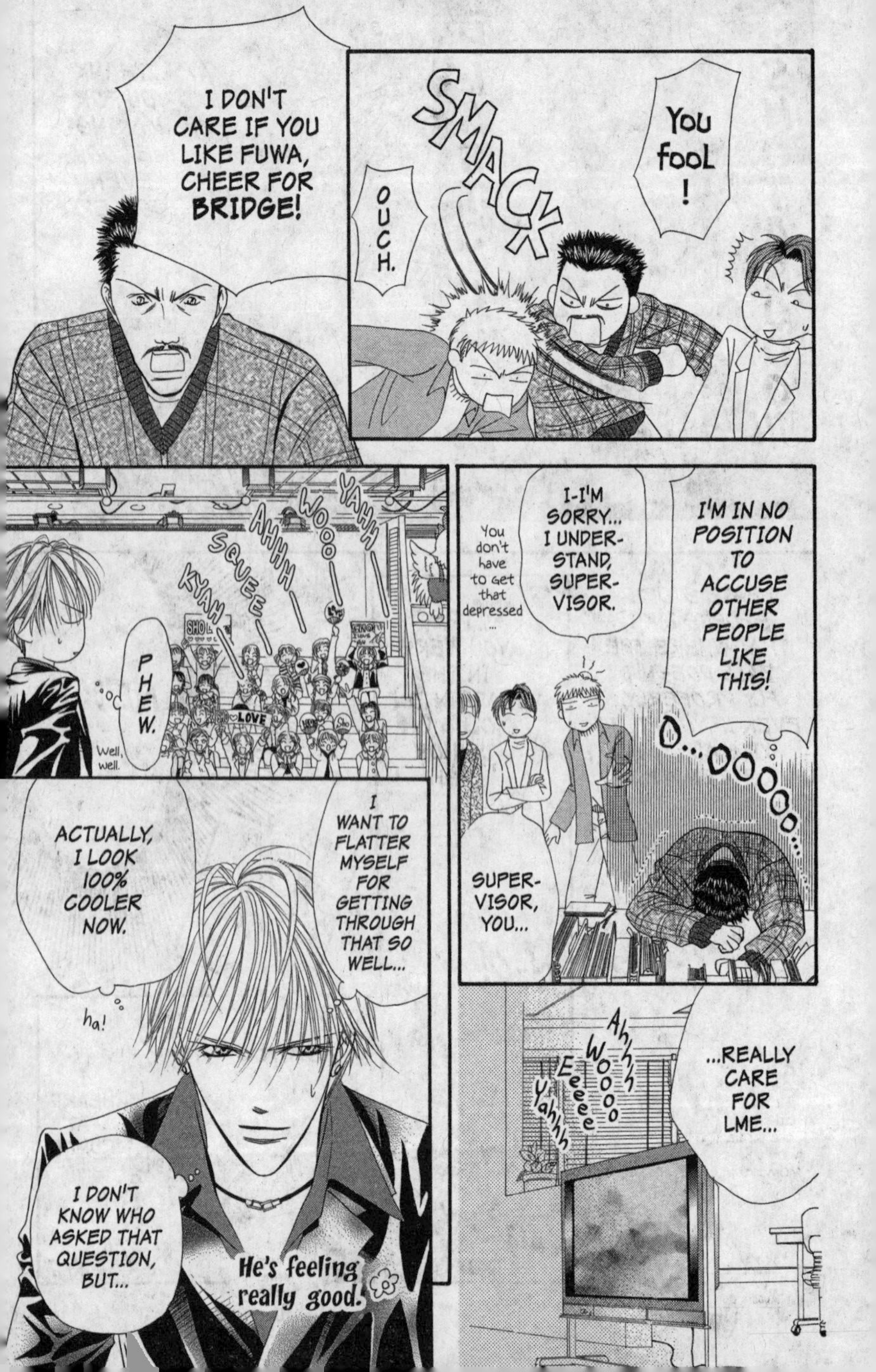
You fool!
SMACK
OUCH.
I DON'T CARE IF YOU LIKE FUWA, CHEER FOR BRIDGE!
I'M IN NO POSITION TO ACCUSE OTHER PEOPLE LIKE THIS!
O...OOOOO...
I-I'M SORRY... I UNDERSTAND, SUPERVISOR.
You don't have to get that depressed...
SUPERVISOR, YOU...
YAHH
WOOO
AHHH
SQUEE
KYAH
SHO
SHO LOVE
PHEW.
Well, well.
...REALLY CARE FOR LME...
Ahhh
Woooo
Eeeee
Yahhh
I WANT TO FLATTER MYSELF FOR GETTING THROUGH THAT SO WELL...
ACTUALLY, I LOOK 100% COOLER NOW.
ha!
I DON'T KNOW WHO ASKED THAT QUESTION, BUT...
He's feeling really good.

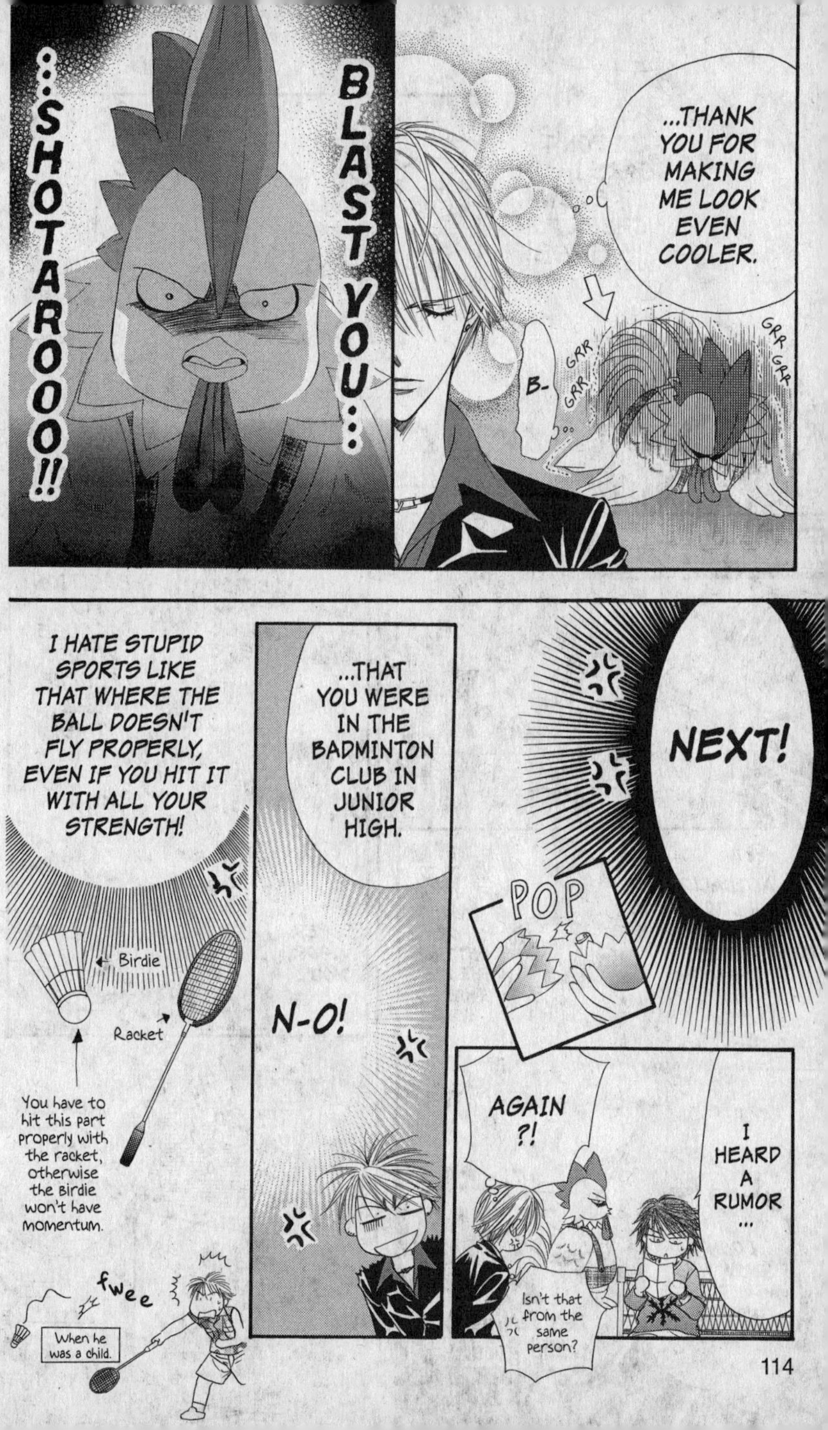
...THANK YOU FOR MAKING ME LOOK EVEN COOLER.
B-
GRR GRR
GRR GRR
BLAST YOU...
...SHOTAROOO!!
NEXT!
POP
I HEARD A RUMOR...
AGAIN?!
Isn't that from the same person?
...THAT YOU WERE IN THE BADMINTON CLUB IN JUNIOR HIGH.
N-O!
I HATE STUPID SPORTS LIKE THAT WHERE THE BALL DOESN'T FLY PROPERLY, EVEN IF YOU HIT IT WITH ALL YOUR STRENGTH!
Birdie
Racket
You have to hit this part properly with the racket, otherwise the birdie won't have momentum.
fwee
When he was a child.

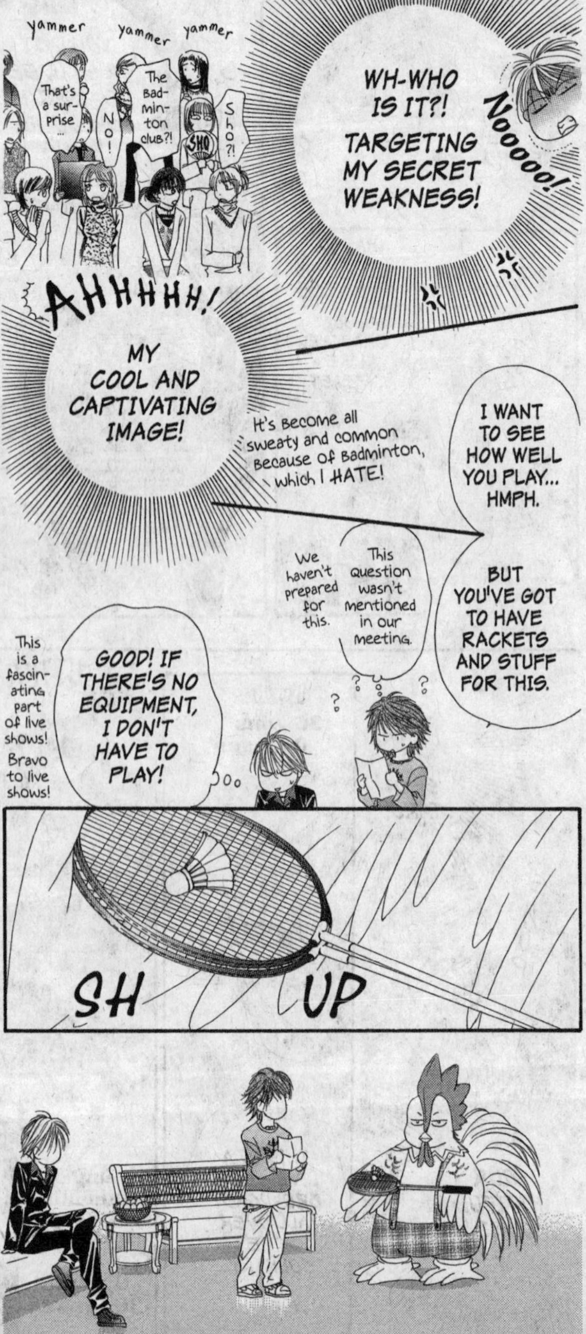
WH-WHO IS IT?! TARGETING MY SECRET WEAKNESS!
Nooooo!
yammer
yammer yammer
Sho?!
SHO
The Bad-min-ton club?!
No!
That's a sur-prise...
AHHHHH!
MY COOL AND CAPTIVATING IMAGE!
It's become all sweaty and common because of Badminton, which I HATE!
I WANT TO SEE HOW WELL YOU PLAY... HMPH.
BUT YOU'VE GOT TO HAVE RACKETS AND STUFF FOR THIS.
This question wasn't mentioned in our meeting.
We haven't prepared for this.
GOOD! IF THERE'S NO EQUIPMENT, I DON'T HAVE TO PLAY!
This is a fascin-ating part of live shows! Bravo to live shows!
SH
UP

Bridge Rock

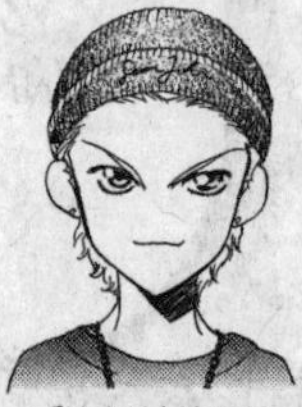

Shinichi Ishibashi
(age 18)

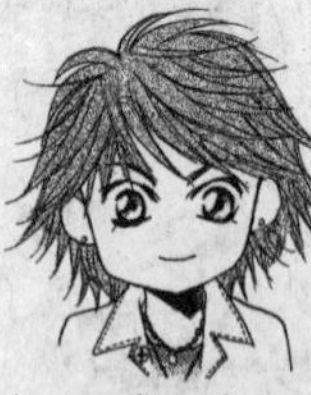

Leader: Hikaru Ishibashi
(age 20)

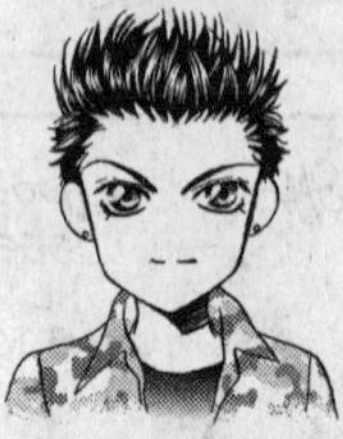

Yusei Ishibashi
(age 18)

The group name comes from their last name...

Ishi (rock) Bashi (bridge)

Flip it to get Bridge Rock... (wry smile)

It's so brainless...

By the way, they all have the same last name, but they aren't related at all...

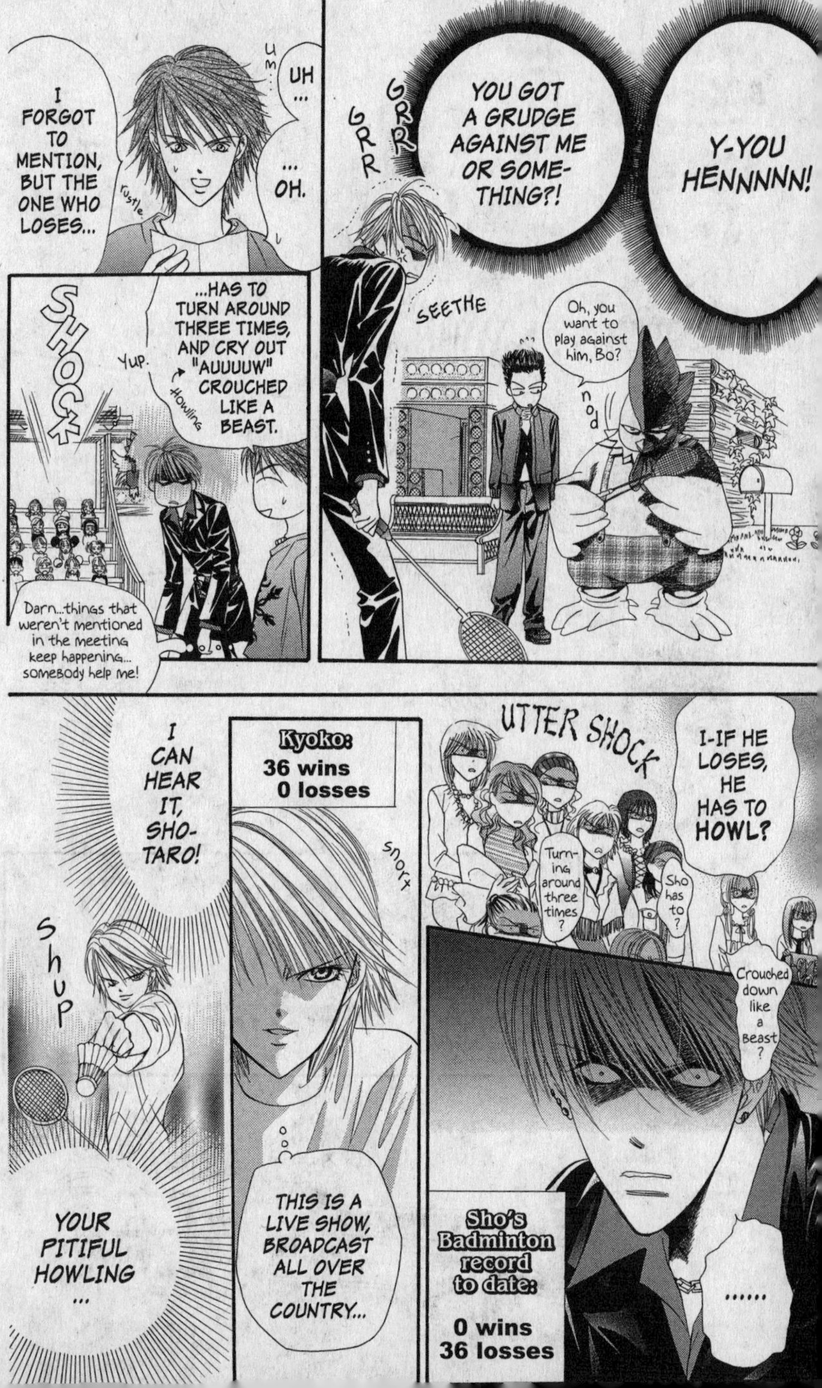
Y-YOU HENNNNN!
YOU GOT A GRUDGE AGAINST ME OR SOME-THING?!
GRRR
GRRR
SEETHE
Oh, you want to play against him, Bo?
nod
UH...
Um...
...OH.
I FORGOT TO MENTION, BUT THE ONE WHO LOSES...
rustle
...HAS TO TURN AROUND THREE TIMES, AND CRY OUT "AUUUUW" CROUCHED LIKE A BEAST.
Howling
Yup.
SHOCK
Darn...things that weren't mentioned in the meeting keep happening... somebody help me!
UTTER SHOCK
I-IF HE LOSES, HE HAS TO HOWL?
Sho has to?
Turning around three times?
Crouched down like a Beast?
......
Sho's Badminton record to date:
0 wins
36 losses
Kyoko:
36 wins
0 losses
snort
THIS IS A LIVE SHOW, BROADCAST ALL OVER THE COUNTRY...
I CAN HEAR IT, SHO-TARO!
SHUP
YOUR PITIFUL HOWLING...

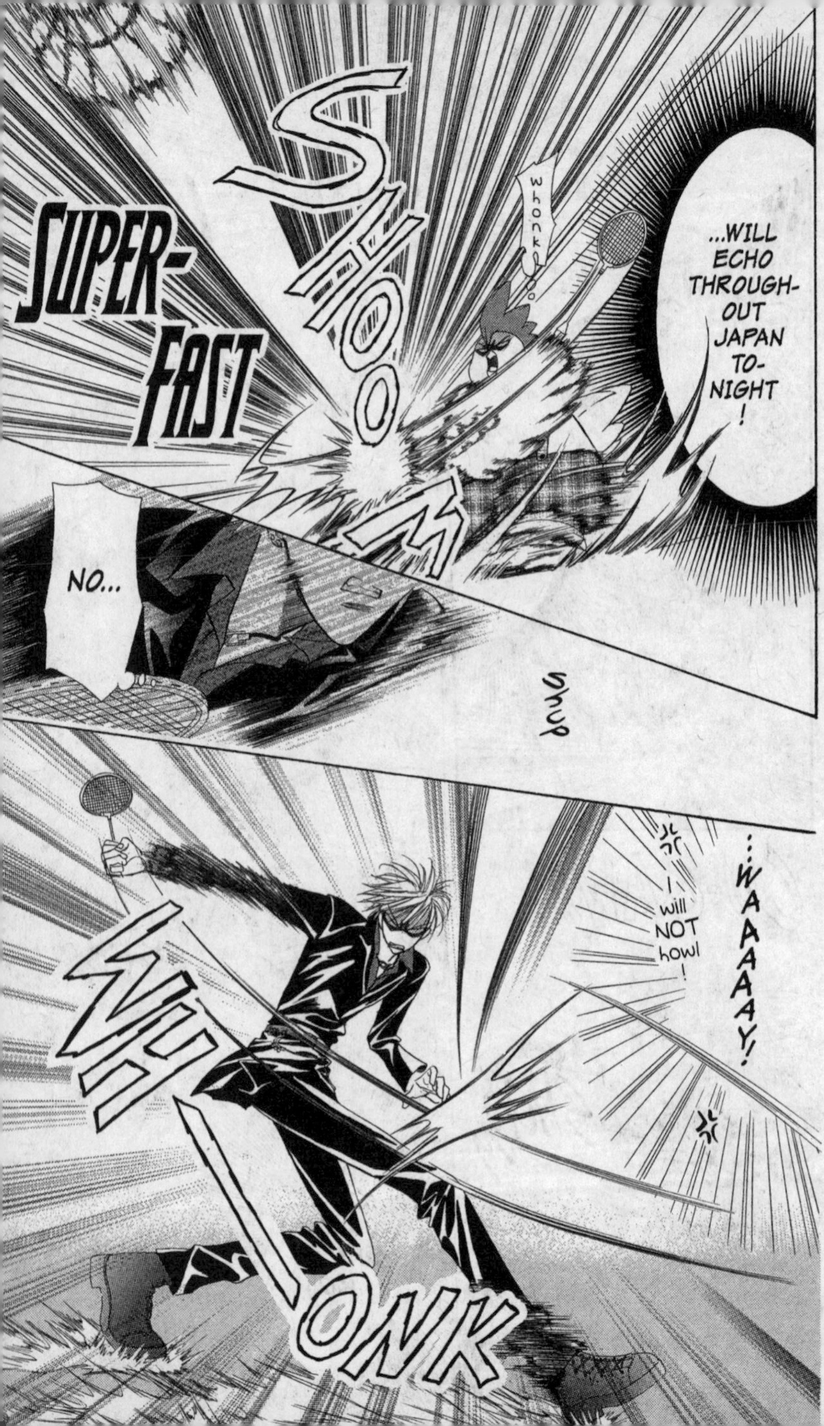
...WILL ECHO THROUGH-OUT JAPAN TO-NIGHT!
whonk
SHOOOM
SUPER-FAST
NO...
...WAAAAAAY!
I will NOT howl!
WHONK

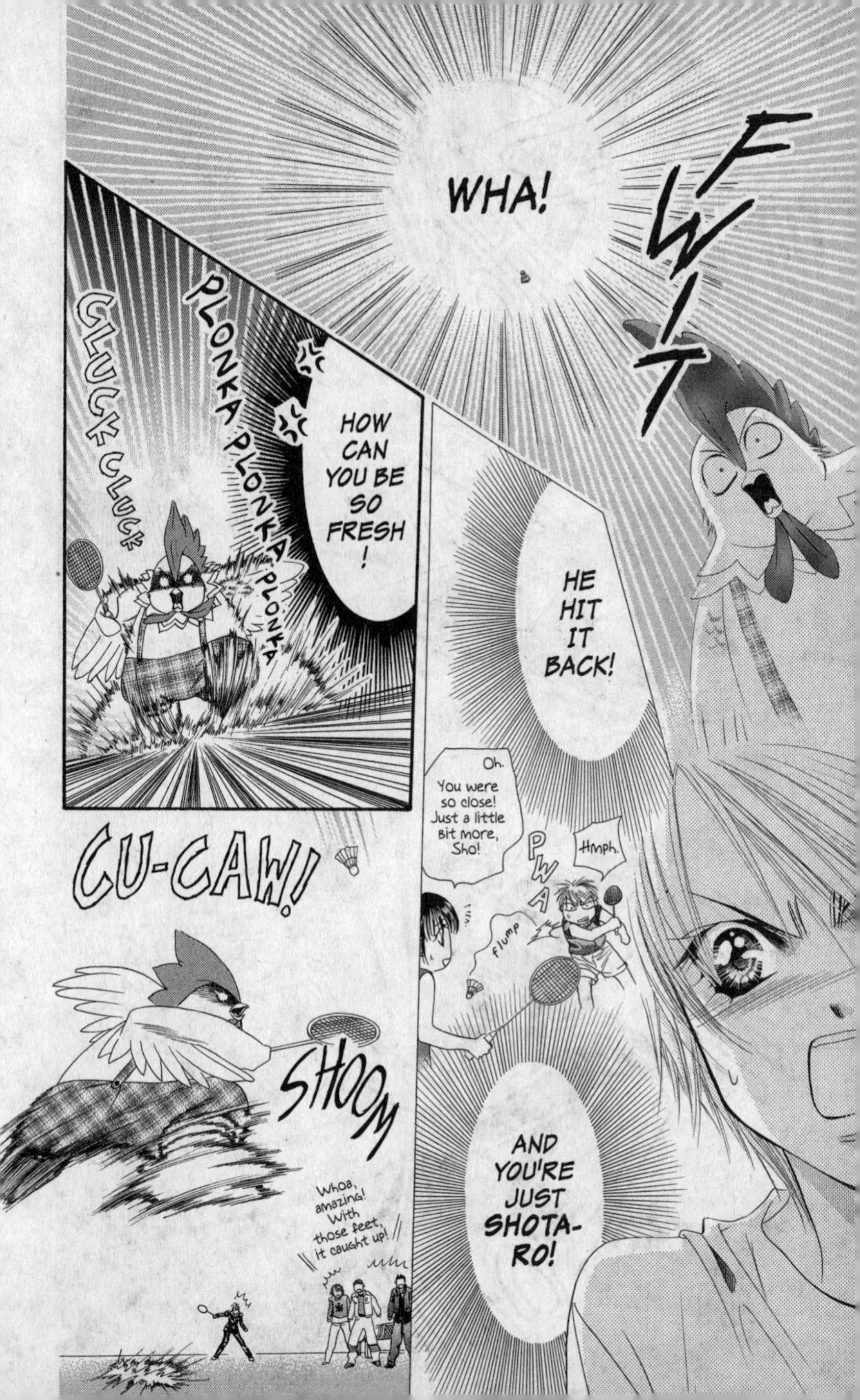
WHA!
FWIT
HE HIT IT BACK!
Oh. You were so close! Just a little bit more, Sho!
Hmph.
PWA
flump
AND YOU'RE JUST SHOTA-RO!
HOW CAN YOU BE SO FRESH!
PLONKA PLONKA PLONKA PLONKA
CLUCK CLUCK CLUCK
CU-CAW!
SHOOM
Whoa, amazing! With those feet, it caught up!

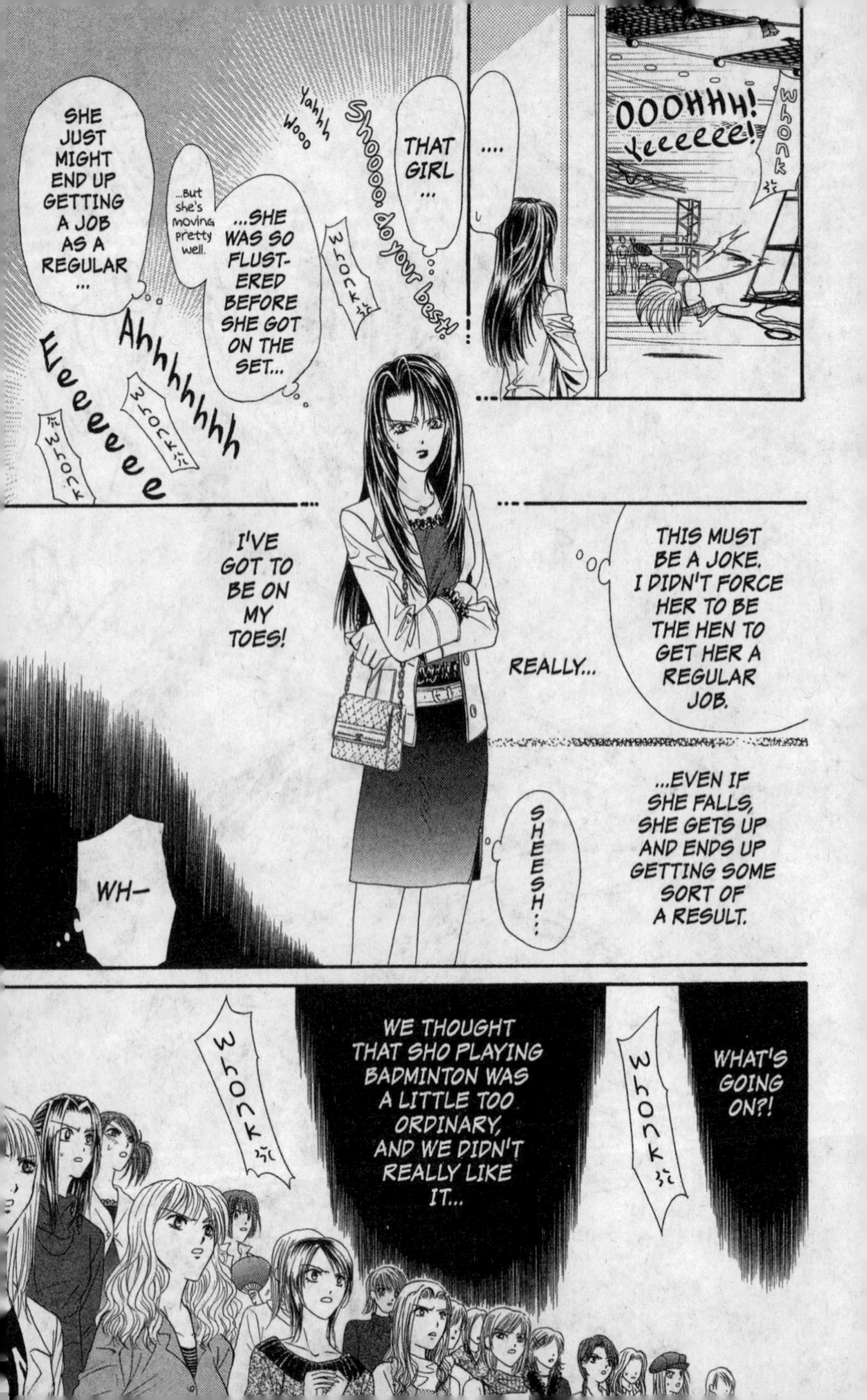
OOOHHH! Yeeeeee!
Whonk
....
THAT GIRL ...
Shoooo do your best!
Yahhh Wooo
...SHE WAS SO FLUST-ERED BEFORE SHE GOT ON THE SET...
...But she's moving pretty well.
Whonk
SHE JUST MIGHT END UP GETTING A JOB AS A REGULAR ...
Ahhhhhhh
Whonk
Eeeeeee
Whonk
THIS MUST BE A JOKE. I DIDN'T FORCE HER TO BE THE HEN TO GET HER A REGULAR JOB.
REALLY...
I'VE GOT TO BE ON MY TOES!
...EVEN IF SHE FALLS, SHE GETS UP AND ENDS UP GETTING SOME SORT OF A RESULT.
SHEESH...
WH-
WHAT'S GOING ON?!
Whonk
WE THOUGHT THAT SHO PLAYING BADMINTON WAS A LITTLE TOO ORDINARY, AND WE DIDN'T REALLY LIKE IT...
Whonk

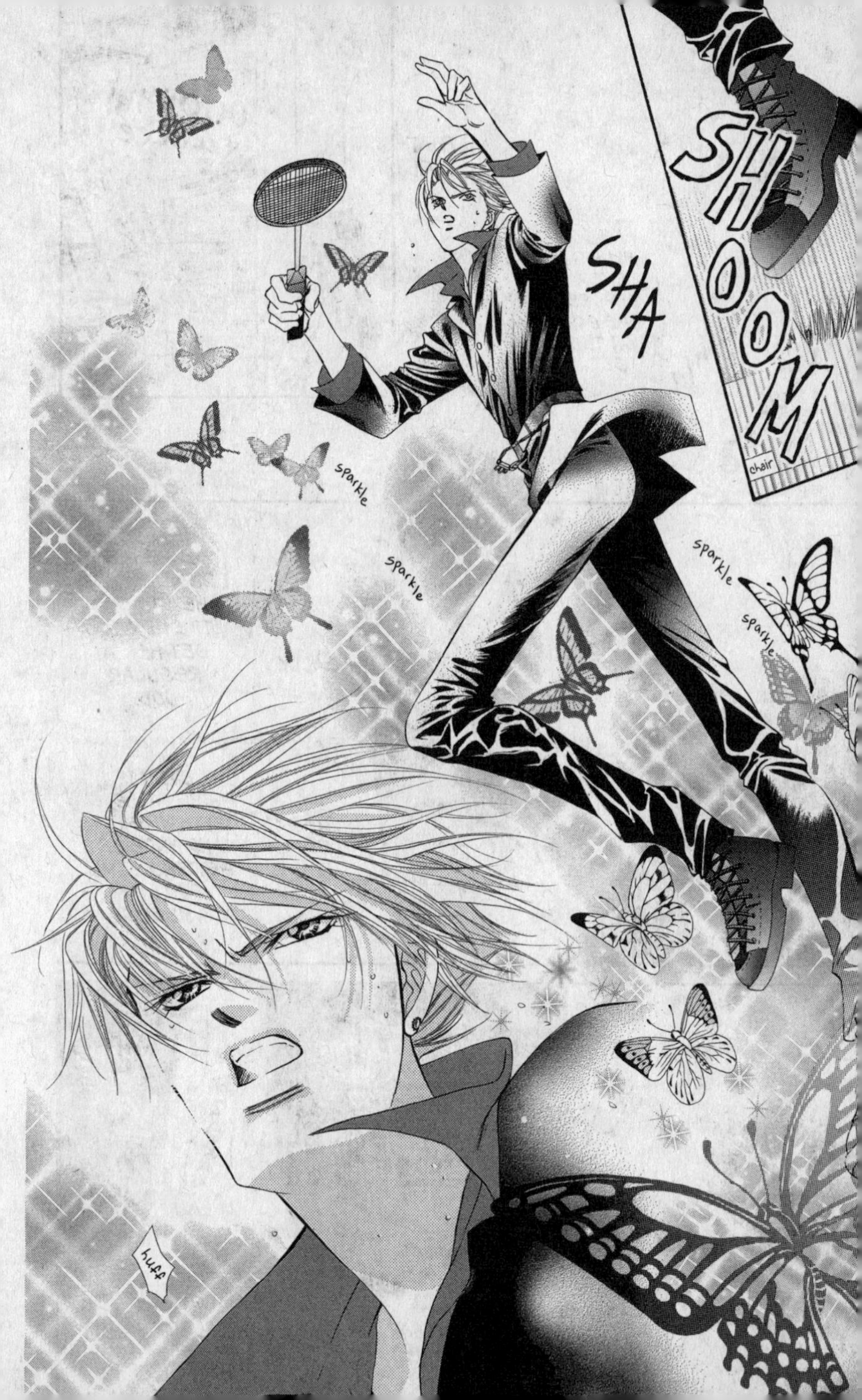
SHOOM
chair
SHA
sparkle
sparkle
sparkle
sparkle
huff

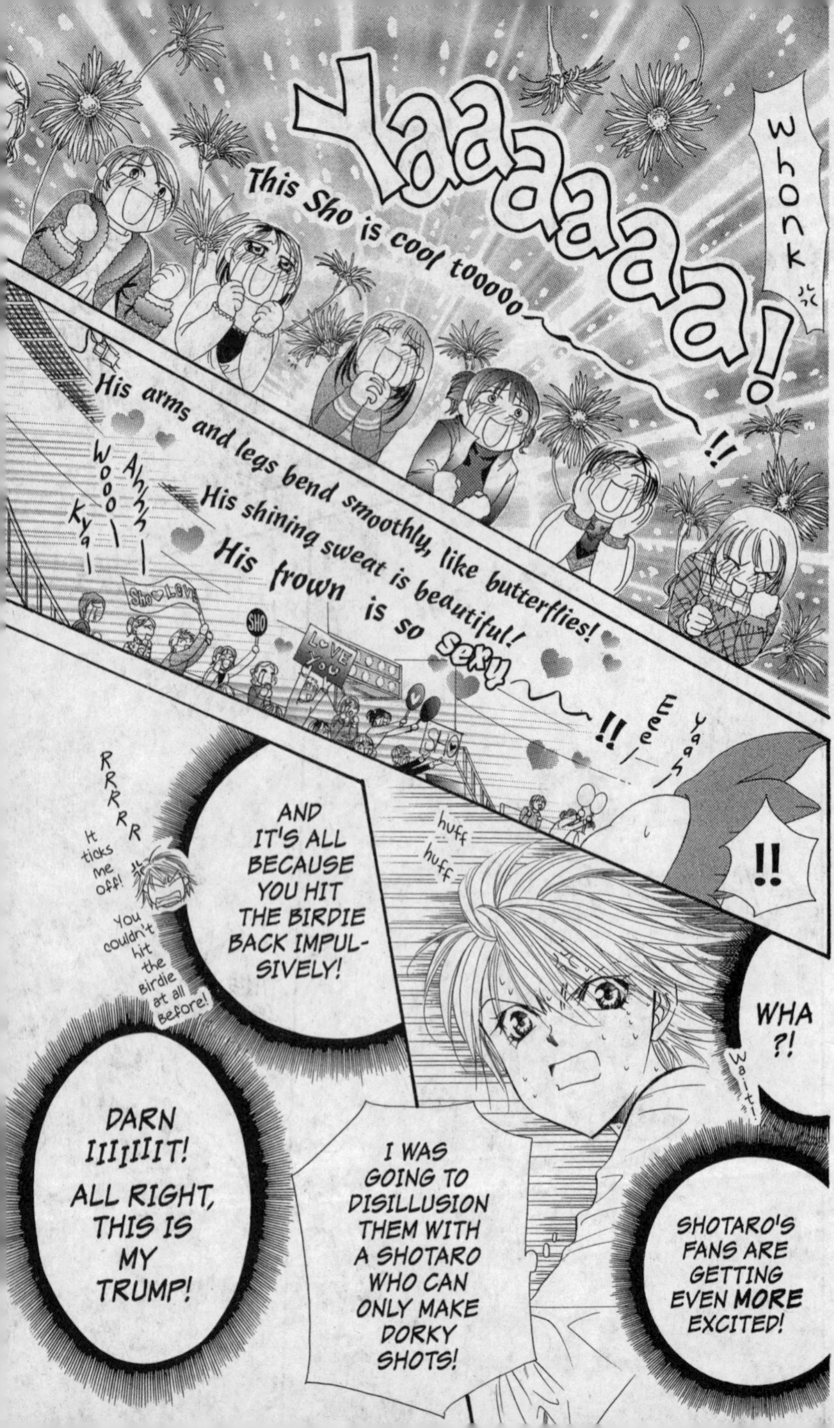

whonk
Yaaaaaaaa!
This Sho is cool tooooo—!!
His arms and legs bend smoothly, like butterflies!
His shining sweat is beautiful!
His frown is so sexy—!!
Ahhh—
Woooo—
Kya—
Sho♥LOVE
SHO
LOVE YOU
SHO
Eeee—
Yaaah—
!!
huff
huff
WHA?!
Wait!
AND IT'S ALL BECAUSE YOU HIT THE BIRDIE BACK IMPULSIVELY!
RRRRR
It ticks me off!
You couldn't hit the birdie at all before!
SHOTARO'S FANS ARE GETTING EVEN MORE EXCITED!
I WAS GOING TO DISILLUSION THEM WITH A SHOTARO WHO CAN ONLY MAKE DORKY SHOTS!
DARN IIIIIIT!
ALL RIGHT, THIS IS MY TRUMP!

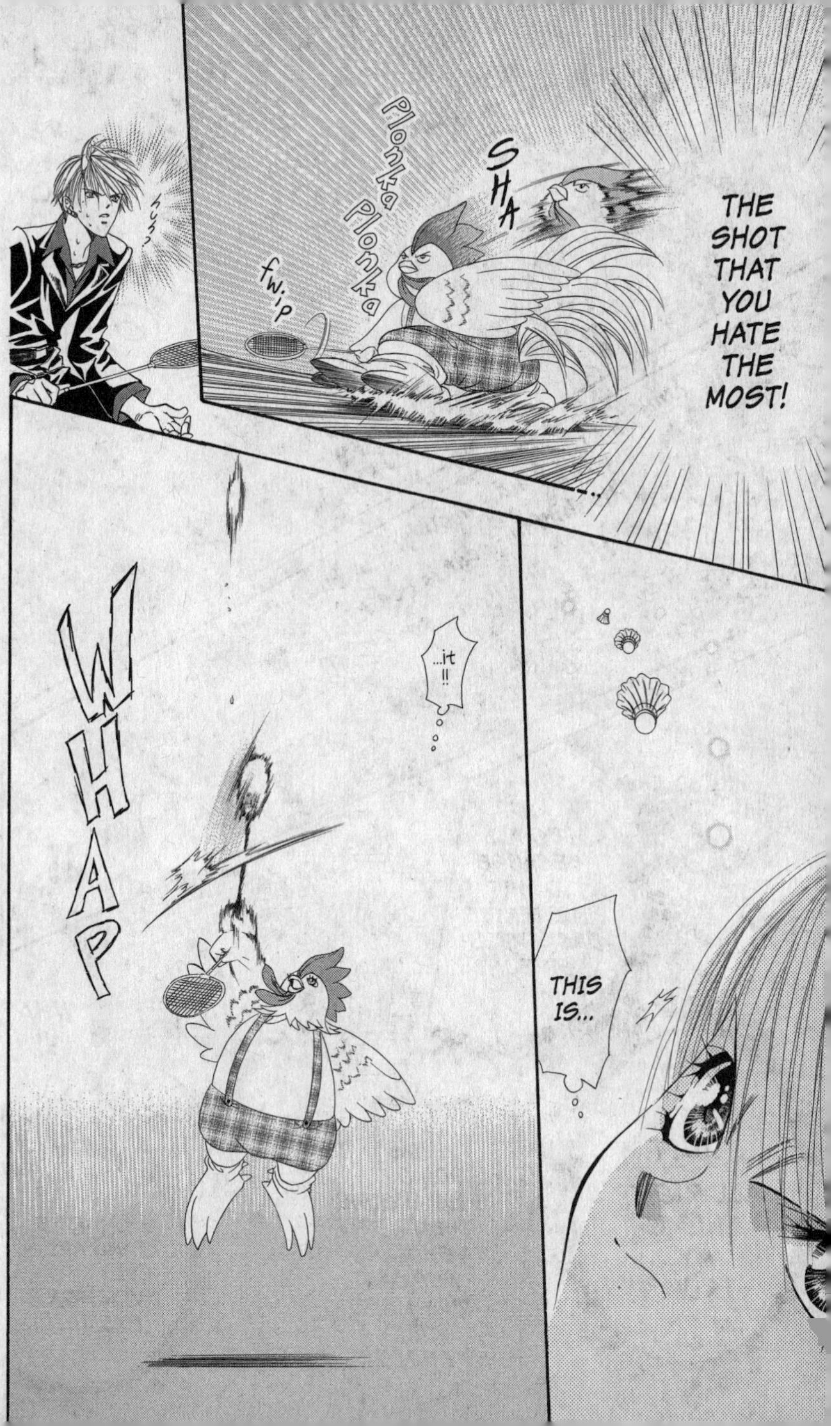
THE SHOT THAT YOU HATE THE MOST!
SHA
Plonka Plonka
fwip
huh?
THIS IS...
WHAP
...it !!

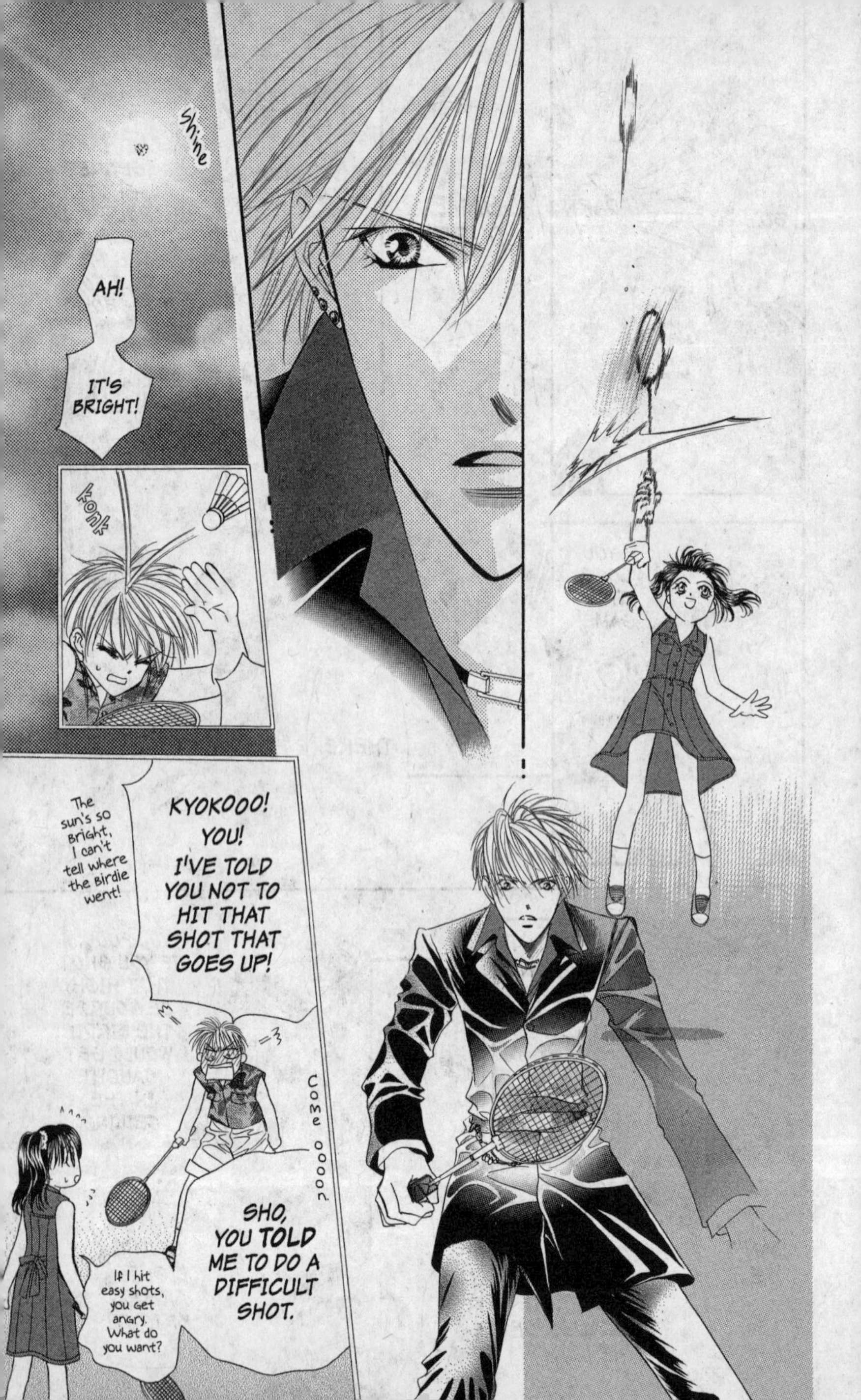
Shine
AH! IT'S BRIGHT!
Kont
KYOKOOO! YOU! I'VE TOLD YOU NOT TO HIT THAT SHOT THAT GOES UP!
The sun's so bright, I can't tell where the birdie went!
Come oooon?
SHO, YOU TOLD ME TO DO A DIFFICULT SHOT.
If I hit easy shots, you get angry. What do you want?

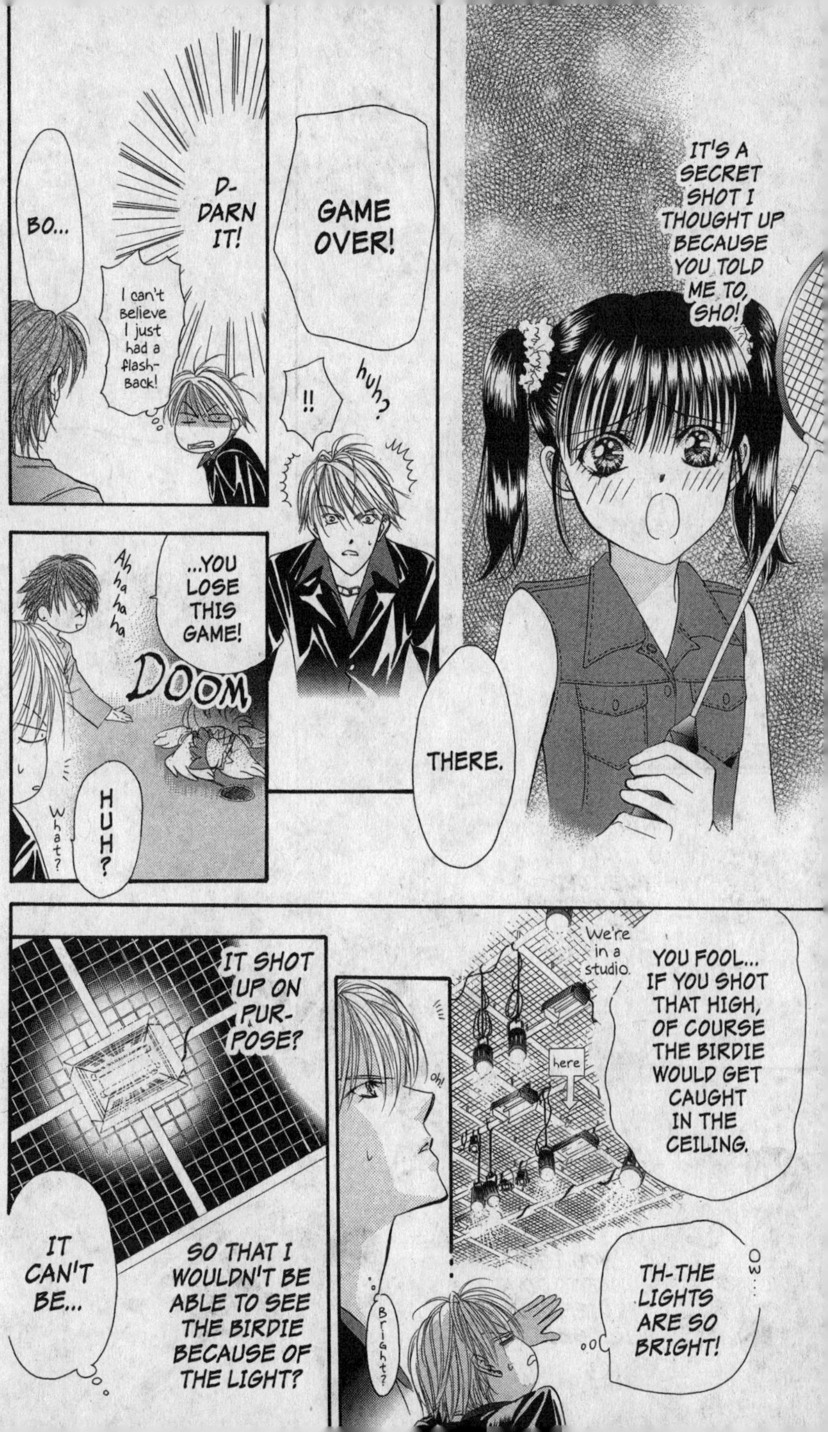

IT'S A SECRET SHOT I THOUGHT UP BECAUSE YOU TOLD ME TO, SHO!
THERE.
GAME OVER!
!!
huh?
D-DARN IT!
I can't believe I just had a flash-back!
BO...
...YOU LOSE THIS GAME!
Ah ha ha ha
DOOM
HUH?
What?
YOU FOOL... IF YOU SHOT THAT HIGH, OF COURSE THE BIRDIE WOULD GET CAUGHT IN THE CEILING.
We're in a studio.
here
TH-THE LIGHTS ARE SO BRIGHT!
Ow...
oh!
Bright?
IT SHOT UP ON PUR-POSE?
SO THAT I WOULDN'T BE ABLE TO SEE THE BIRDIE BECAUSE OF THE LIGHT?
IT CAN'T BE...

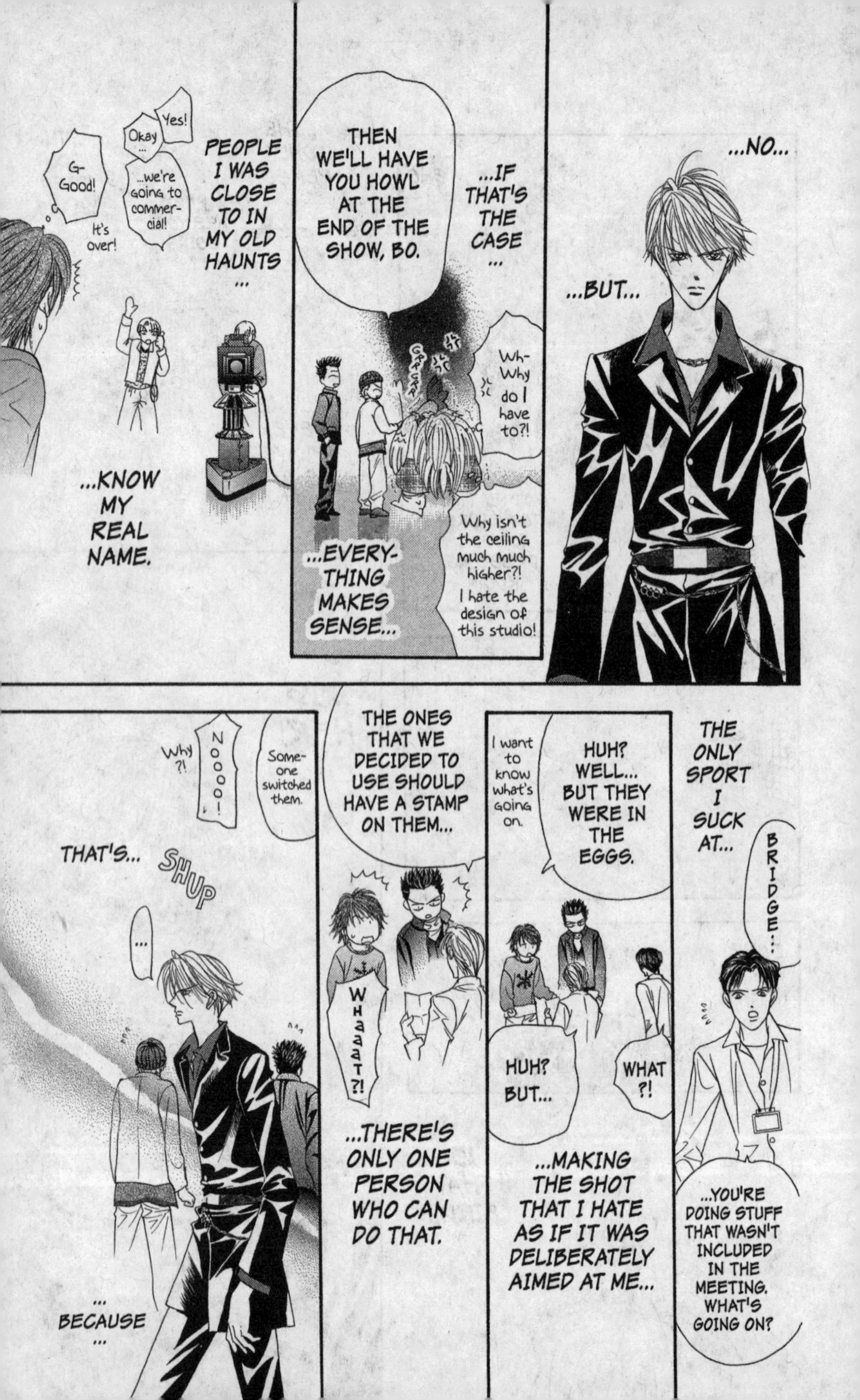

...NO...
...BUT...
...IF THAT'S THE CASE...
THEN WE'LL HAVE YOU HOWL AT THE END OF THE SHOW, BO.
GRRR
Wh-Why do I have to?!
Why isn't the ceiling much much higher?! I hate the design of this studio!
...EVERYTHING MAKES SENSE...
PEOPLE I WAS CLOSE TO IN MY OLD HAUNTS...
Yes!
Okay...
...we're going to commercial!
G-Good!
It's over!
...KNOW MY REAL NAME.
THE ONLY SPORT I SUCK AT...
BRIDGE...
...YOU'RE DOING STUFF THAT WASN'T INCLUDED IN THE MEETING. WHAT'S GOING ON?
HUH? WELL... BUT THEY WERE IN THE EGGS.
I want to know what's going on.
WHAT?!
HUH? BUT...
...MAKING THE SHOT THAT I HATE AS IF IT WAS DELIBERATELY AIMED AT ME...
THE ONES THAT WE DECIDED TO USE SHOULD HAVE A STAMP ON THEM...
Whaaaat?!
...THERE'S ONLY ONE PERSON WHO CAN DO THAT.
Someone switched them.
Noooo!
Why?!
THAT'S...
SHUP
...
...BECAUSE...

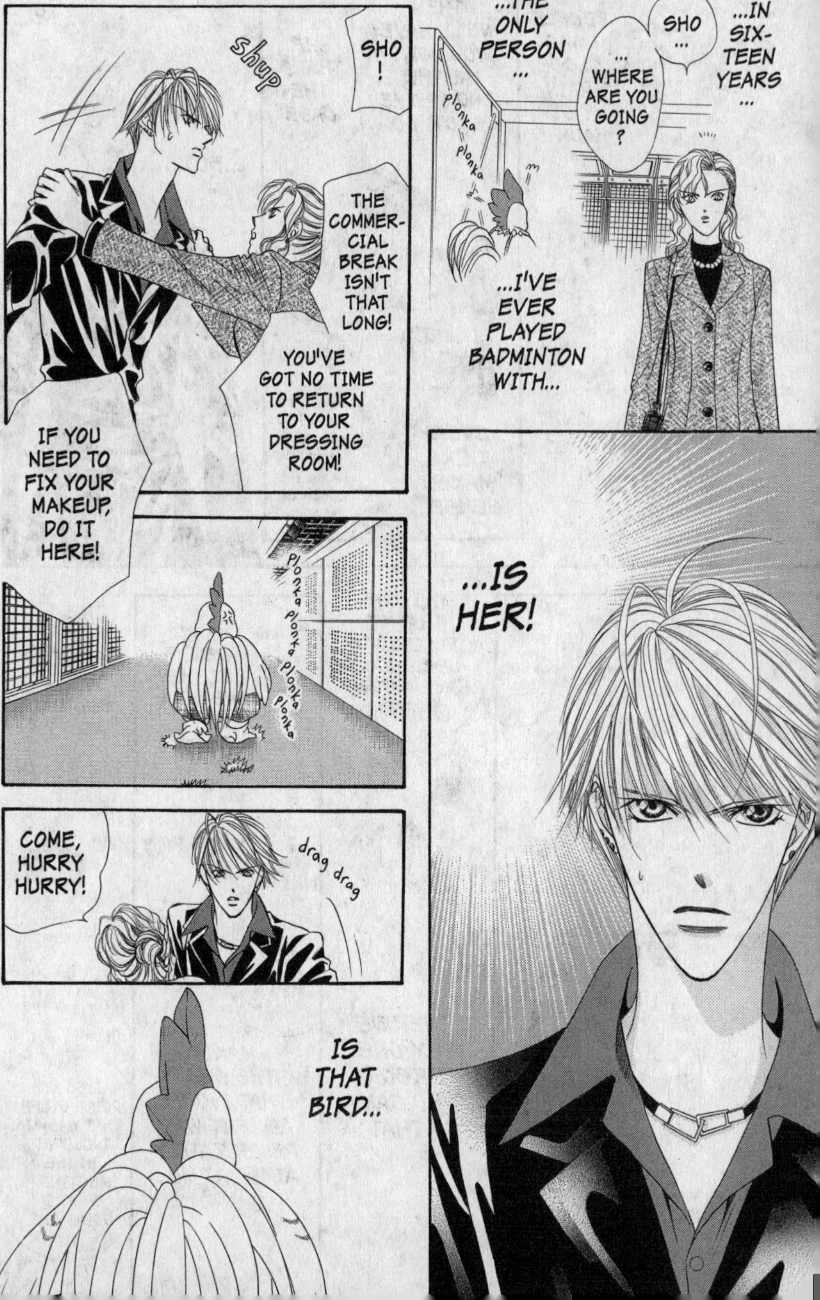
...IN SIXTEEN YEARS...
SHO...
...WHERE ARE YOU GOING?
...THE ONLY PERSON...
plonka plonka
...I'VE EVER PLAYED BADMINTON WITH...
SHO!
shup
THE COMMERCIAL BREAK ISN'T THAT LONG!
YOU'VE GOT NO TIME TO RETURN TO YOUR DRESSING ROOM!
IF YOU NEED TO FIX YOUR MAKEUP, DO IT HERE!
...IS HER!
plonka plonka plonka plonka plonka
COME, HURRY HURRY!
drag drag
IS THAT BIRD...

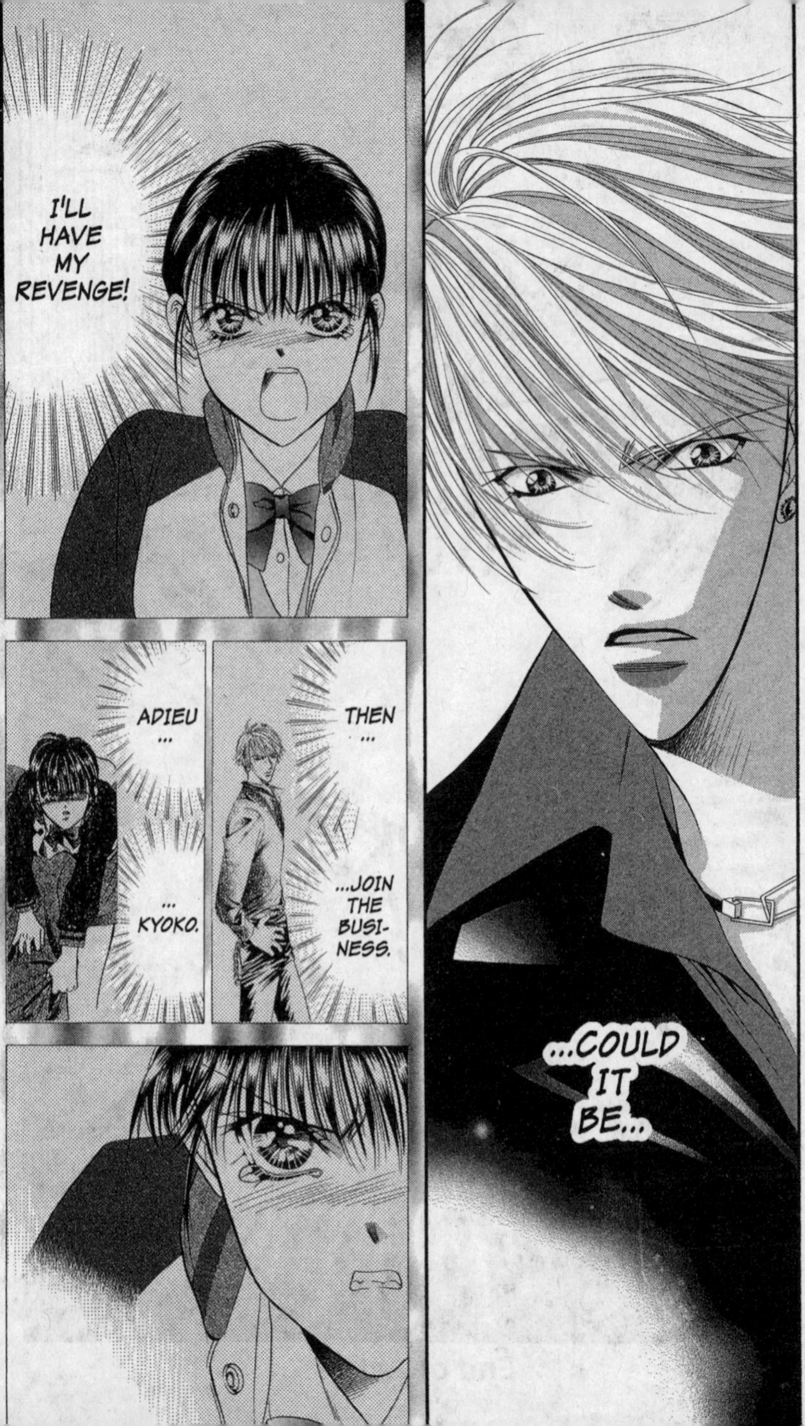
...COULD IT BE...
I'LL HAVE MY REVENGE!
THEN ...
...JOIN THE BUSI-NESS.
ADIEU ...
... KYOKO.

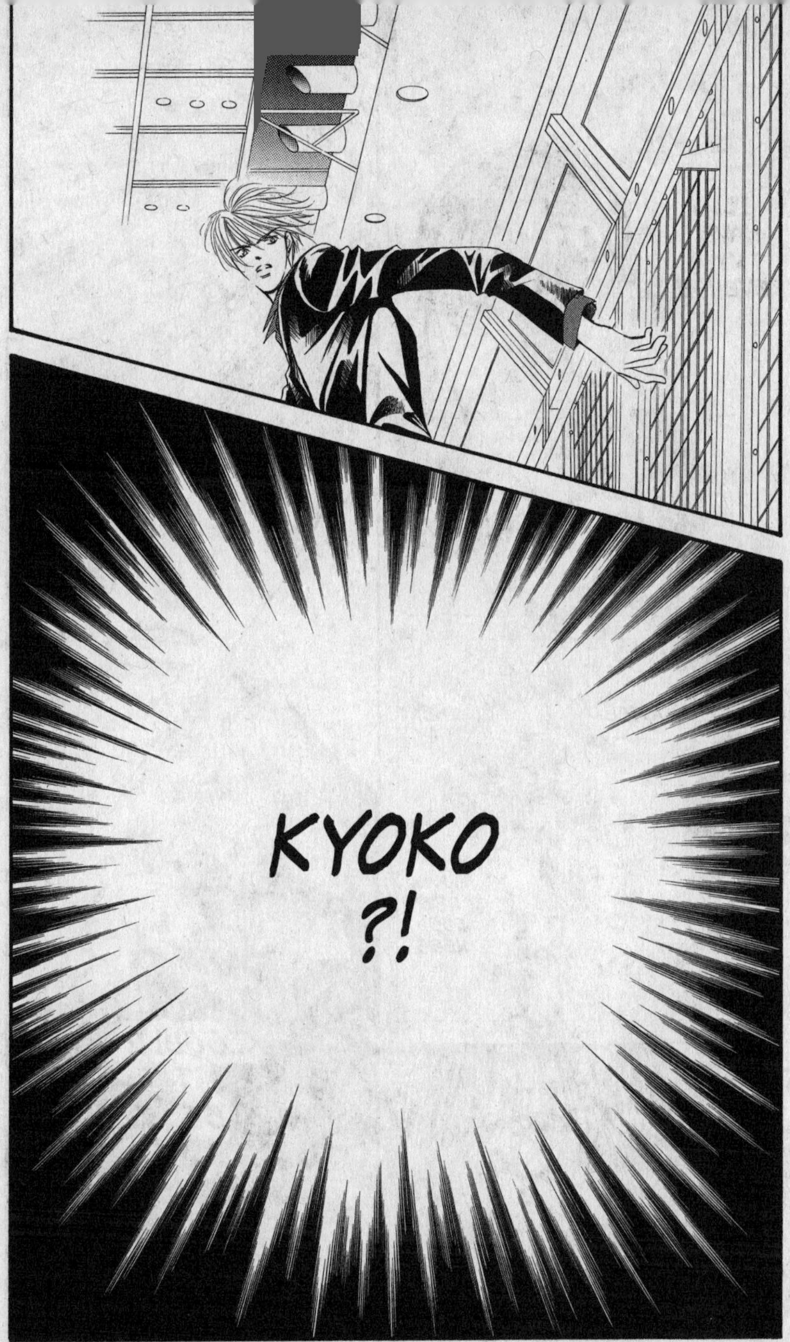
KYOKO ?!

End of Act 21

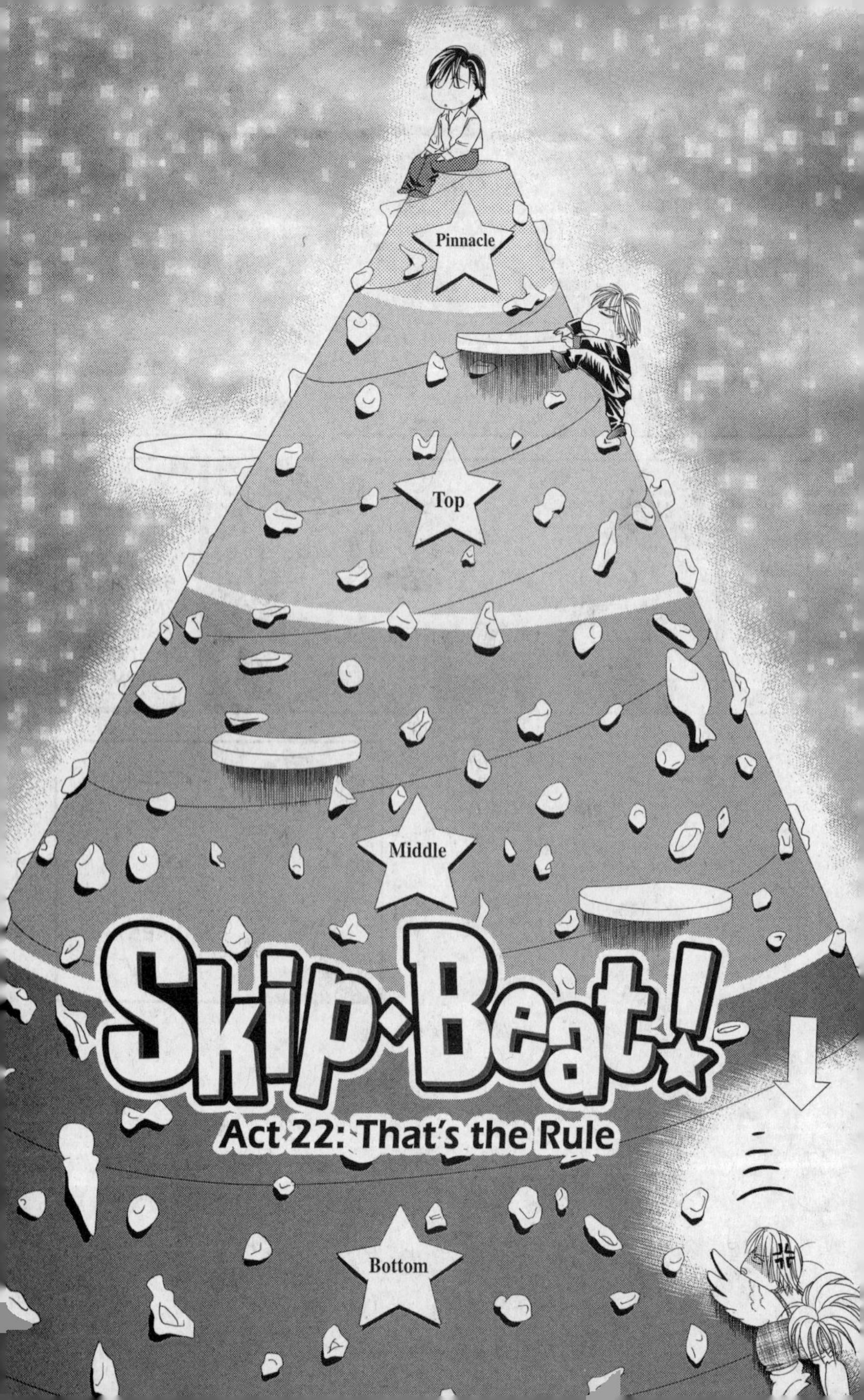
Pinnacle
Top
Middle
Skip·Beat!
Act 22: That's the Rule
Bottom

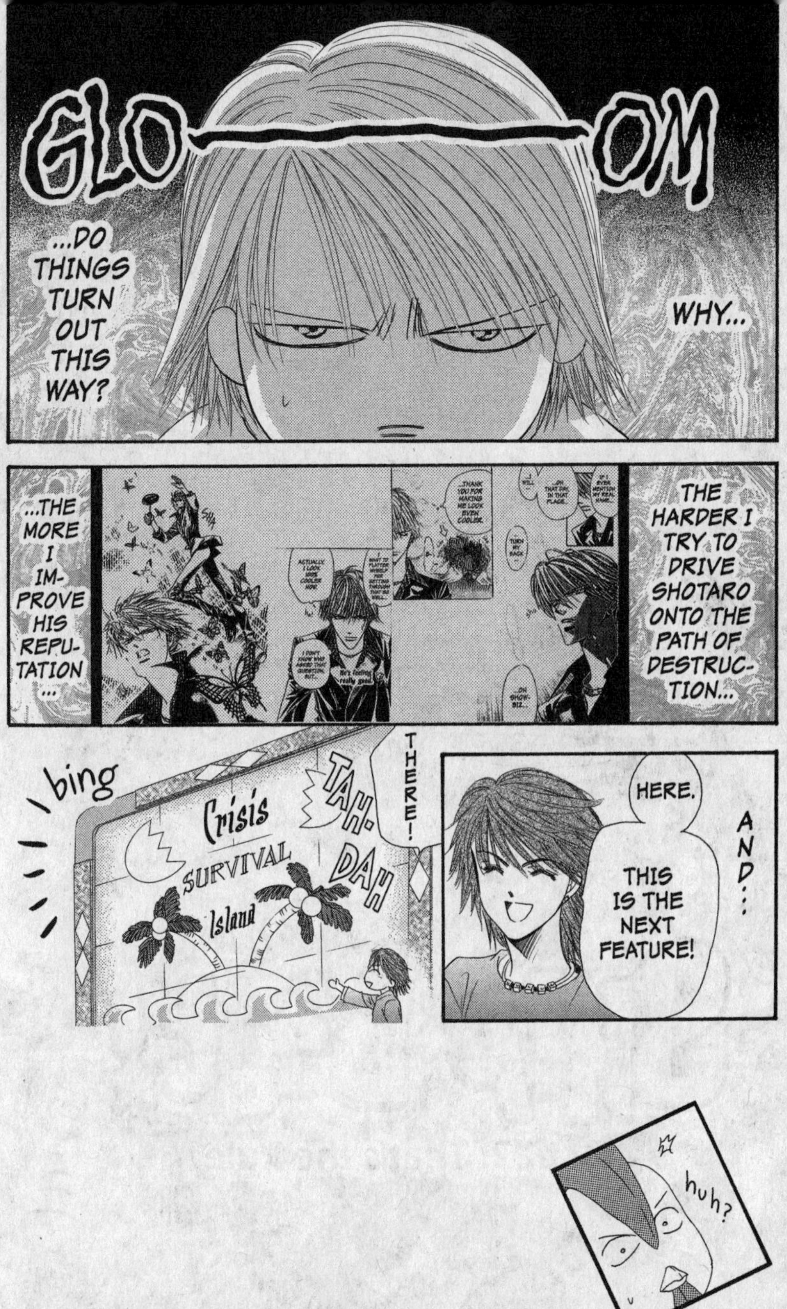
GLO——OM
WHY...
...DO THINGS TURN OUT THIS WAY?
THE HARDER I TRY TO DRIVE SHOTARO ONTO THE PATH OF DESTRUCTION...
IF I EVER MENTION MY REAL NAME...
...ON THAT DAY IN THAT PLACE...
I WILL...
TURN MY BACK...
...ON SHOW-BIZ...
...THANK YOU FOR MAKING ME LOOK EVEN COOLER.
I DON'T KNOW WHO ASKED THAT QUESTION, BUT...
He's feeling really good.
...THE MORE I IMPROVE HIS REPUTATION...
HERE.
AND...
THIS IS THE NEXT FEATURE!
THERE!
TAH-DAH
Crisis SURVIVAL Island
bing
huh?

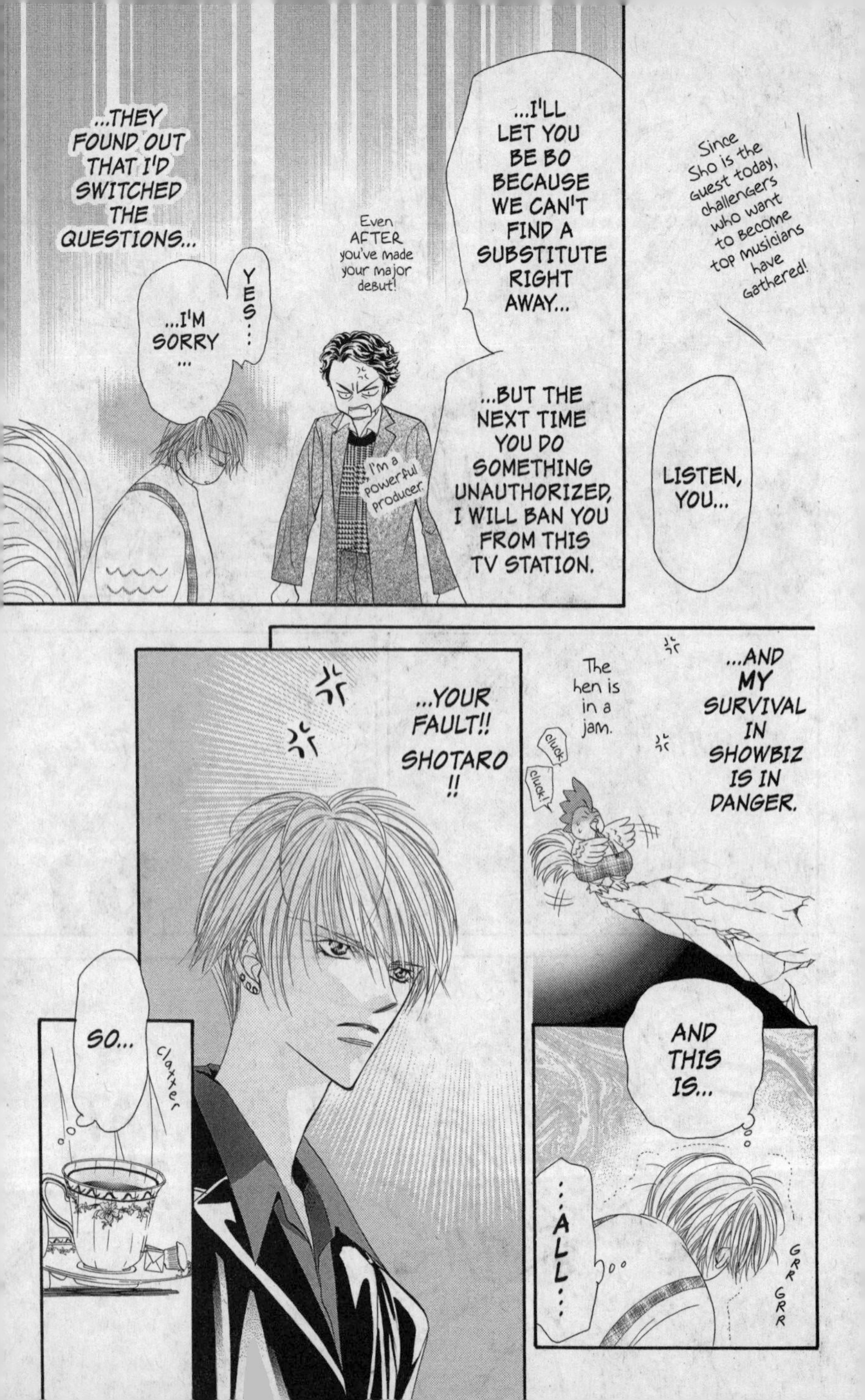
Since Sho is the Guest today, challengers who want to become top musicians have Gathered!
LISTEN, YOU...
...I'LL LET YOU BE BO BECAUSE WE CAN'T FIND A SUBSTITUTE RIGHT AWAY...
...BUT THE NEXT TIME YOU DO SOMETHING UNAUTHORIZED, I WILL BAN YOU FROM THIS TV STATION.
Even AFTER you've made your major debut!
I'm a powerful producer.
YES...
...I'M SORRY...
...THEY FOUND OUT THAT I'D SWITCHED THE QUESTIONS...
...AND MY SURVIVAL IN SHOWBIZ IS IN DANGER.
The hen is in a jam.
cluck
cluck!
AND THIS IS...
...ALL...
GRR GRR
...YOUR FAULT!! SHOTARO!!
SO...
claxxer

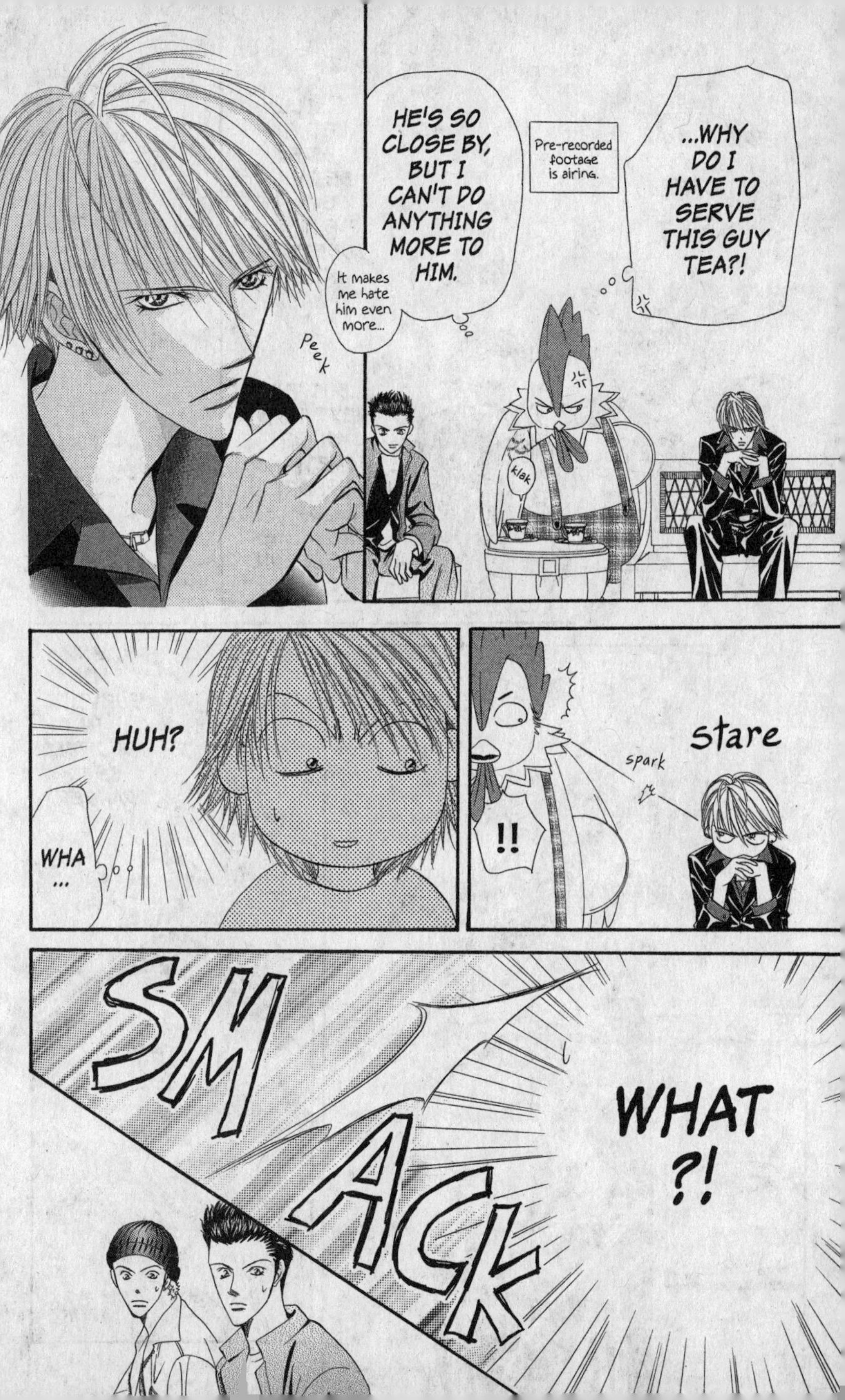
...WHY DO I HAVE TO SERVE THIS GUY TEA?!
Pre-recorded footage is airing.
HE'S SO CLOSE BY, BUT I CAN'T DO ANYTHING MORE TO HIM.
It makes me hate him even more...
klak
Peek
Stare
spark
!!
HUH?
WHA...
WHAT?!
SMACK

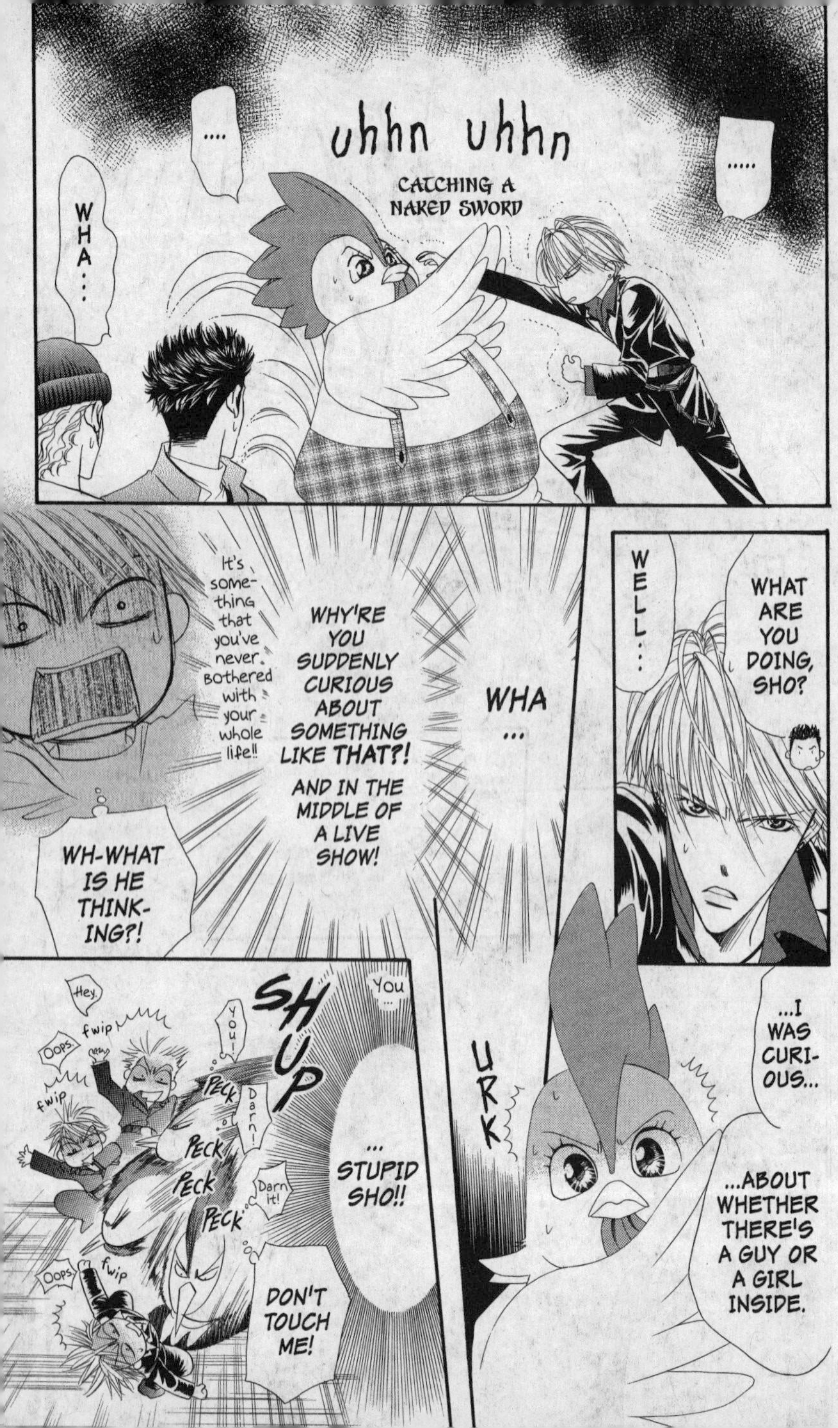
.....
uhhn uhhn
CATCHING A NAKED SWORD
....
WHA...
WHAT ARE YOU DOING, SHO?
WELL...
WHA ...
WHY'RE YOU SUDDENLY CURIOUS ABOUT SOMETHING LIKE THAT?!
AND IN THE MIDDLE OF A LIVE SHOW!
It's something that you've never bothered with your whole life!!
WH-WHAT IS HE THINKING?!
...I WAS CURIOUS...
URK
...ABOUT WHETHER THERE'S A GUY OR A GIRL INSIDE.
You ...
SHUP
... STUPID SHO!!
DON'T TOUCH ME!
Hey.
fwip
You!
Oops.
PECK
Darn!
fwip
PECK
PECK
Darn it!
PECK
fwip
Oops.

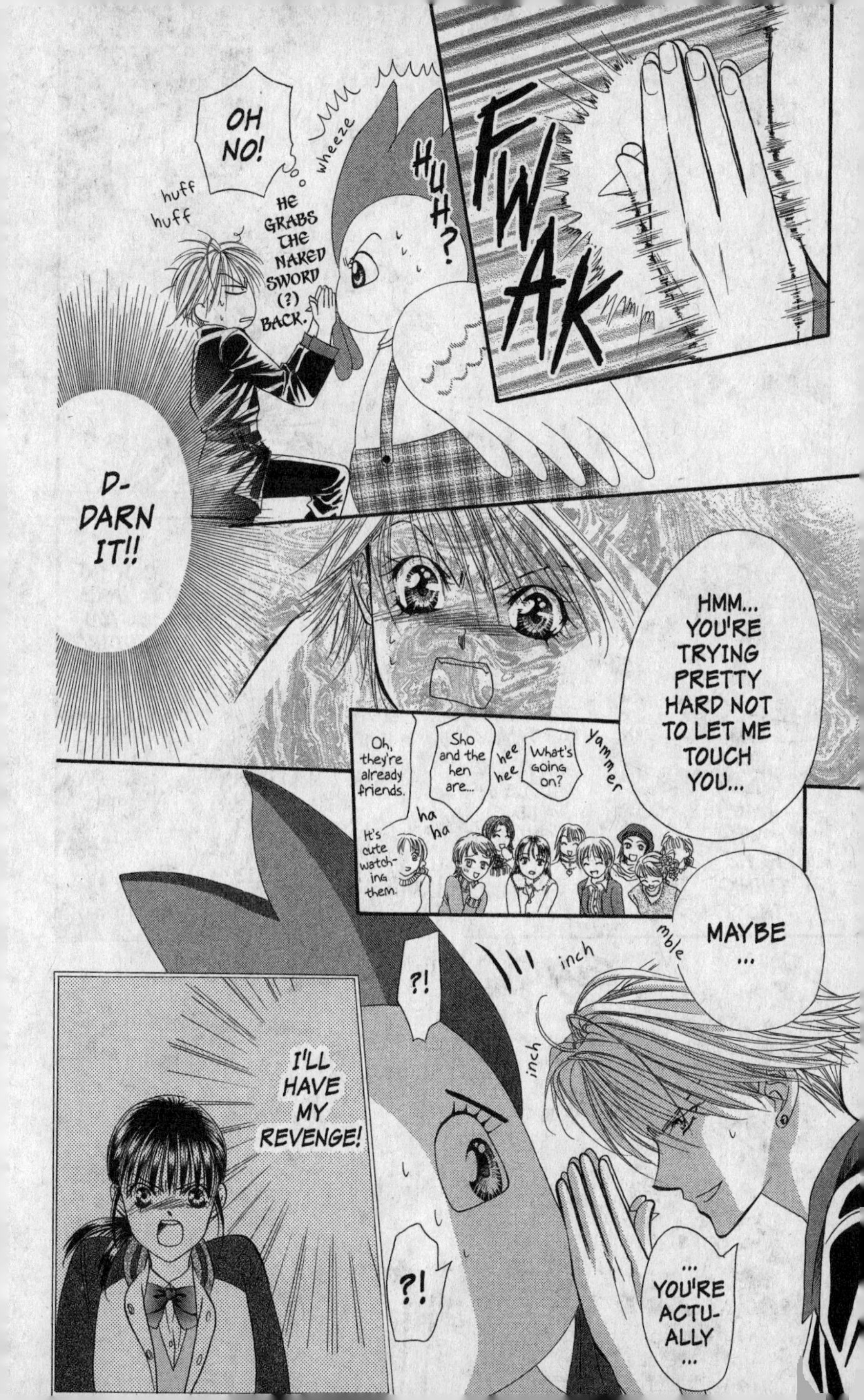
FWAK
HUH?
wheeze
OH NO!
huff huff
HE GRABS THE NAKED SWORD (?) BACK.
D-DARN IT!!
HMM... YOU'RE TRYING PRETTY HARD NOT TO LET ME TOUCH YOU...
yammer
What's going on?
hee hee
Sho and the hen are...
Oh, they're already friends.
ha ha
It's cute watching them.
mble
MAYBE ...
inch
inch
?!
?!
... YOU'RE ACTUALLY ...
I'LL HAVE MY REVENGE!

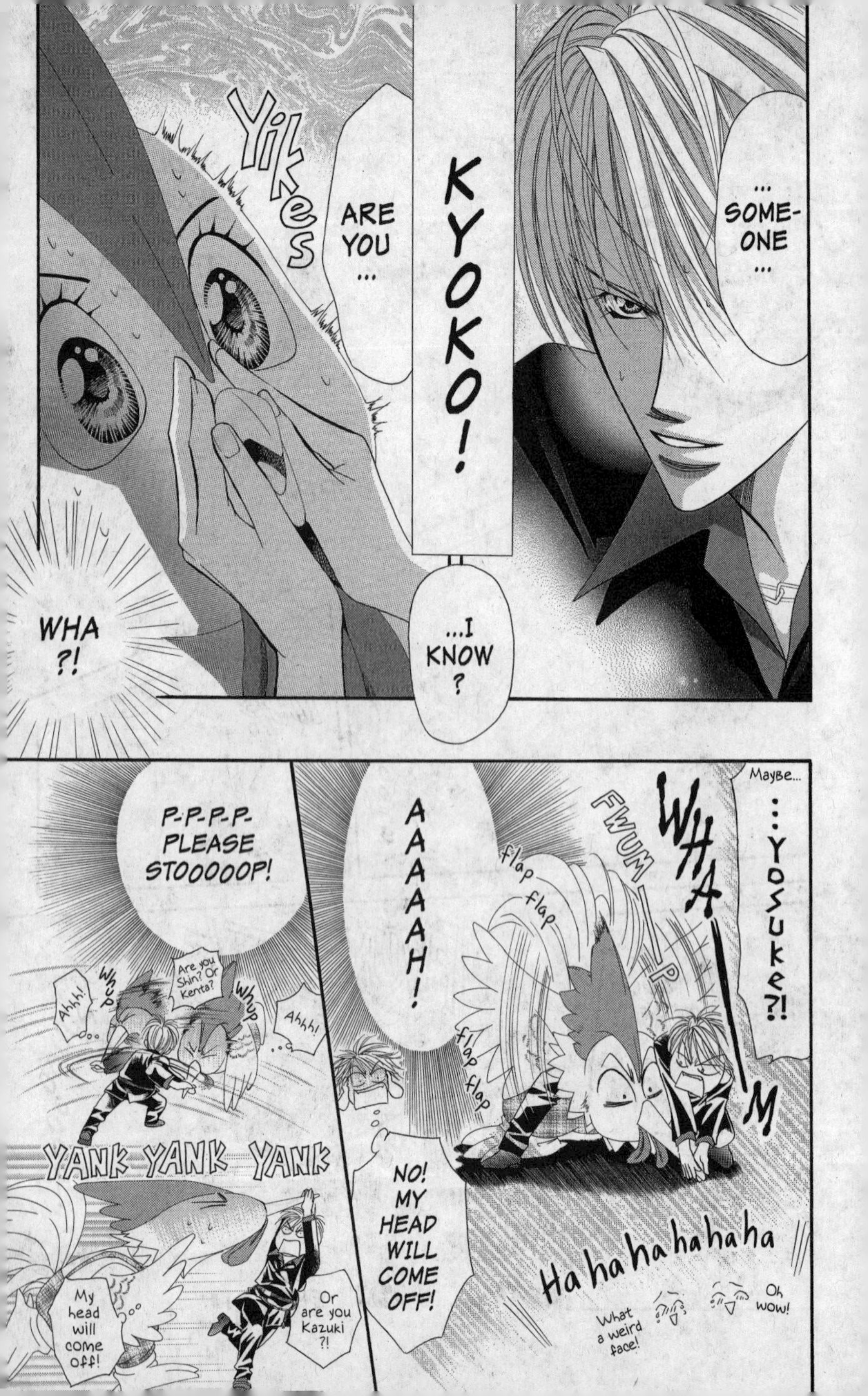

... SOME-ONE ...
KYOKO!
ARE YOU ...
Yikes
...I KNOW?
WHA ?!
Maybe...
...YOSUKE?!
WHA-M
FWUMP
flap flap
flap flap
Ha ha ha ha ha ha ha
Oh wow!
What a weird face!
AAAAAAH!
NO! MY HEAD WILL COME OFF!
P-P-P-P-PLEASE STOOOOOP!
Are you Shin? Or Kenta?
Whup
Ahhh!
Whup
Ahhh!
YANK YANK YANK
Or are you Kazuki?!
My head will come off!

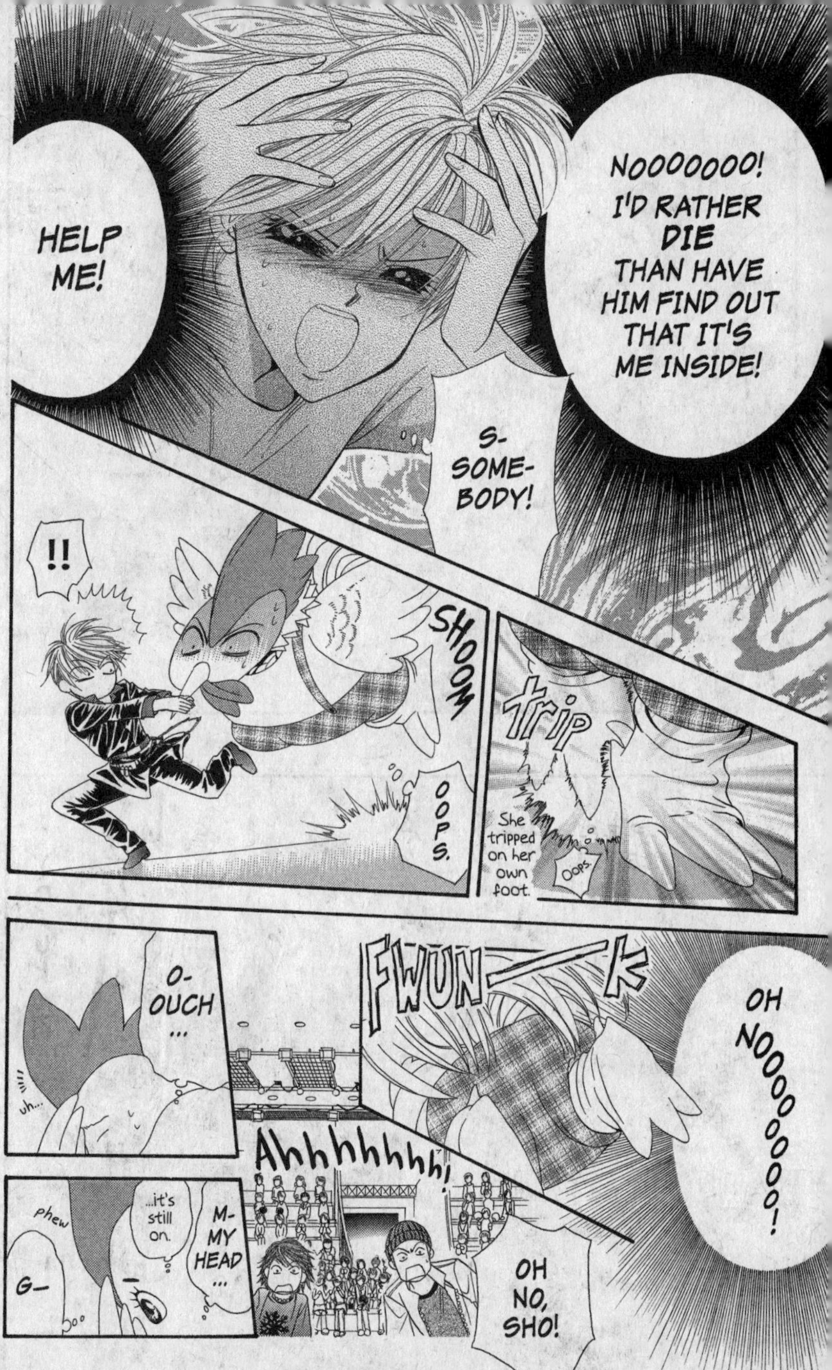
NOOOOOOO! I'D RATHER DIE THAN HAVE HIM FIND OUT THAT IT'S ME INSIDE!
HELP ME!
S- SOME- BODY!
trip
She tripped on her own foot.
OOPS.
!!
SHOOM
OOPS.
FWUN—K
OH NOOOOOOOOOO!
Ahhhhhhhh!
OH NO, SHO!
O- OUCH ...
uh...
M- MY HEAD ...
...it's still on.
phew
G—

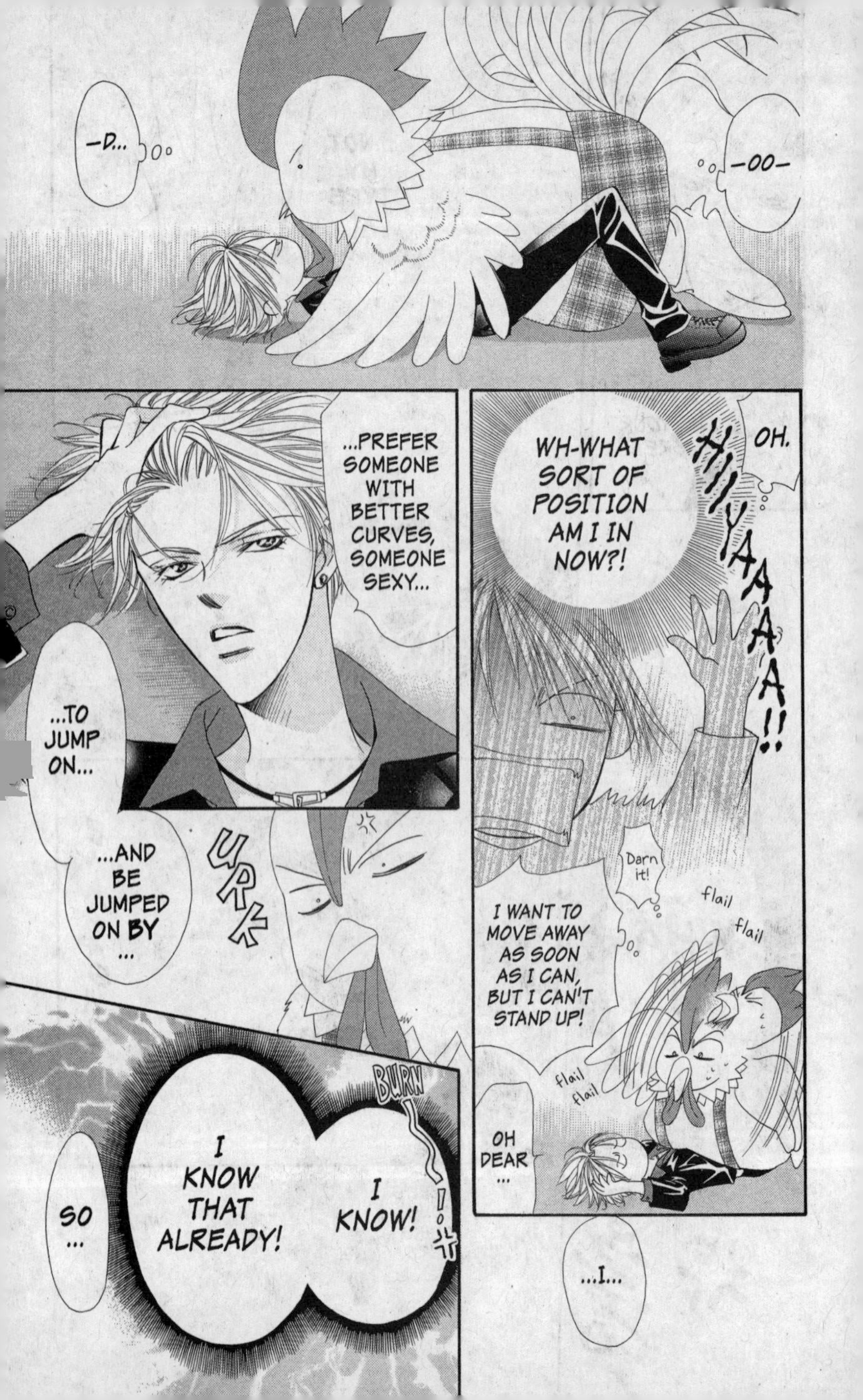
—OO—
—D...
OH.
HIIYAAAAA!!
WH-WHAT SORT OF POSITION AM I IN NOW?!
Darn it!
flail flail
I WANT TO MOVE AWAY AS SOON AS I CAN, BUT I CAN'T STAND UP!
flail flail
OH DEAR ...
...PREFER SOMEONE WITH BETTER CURVES, SOMEONE SEXY...
...TO JUMP ON...
URK
...AND BE JUMPED ON BY ...
...I...
BURN
I KNOW!
I KNOW THAT ALREADY!
SO ...

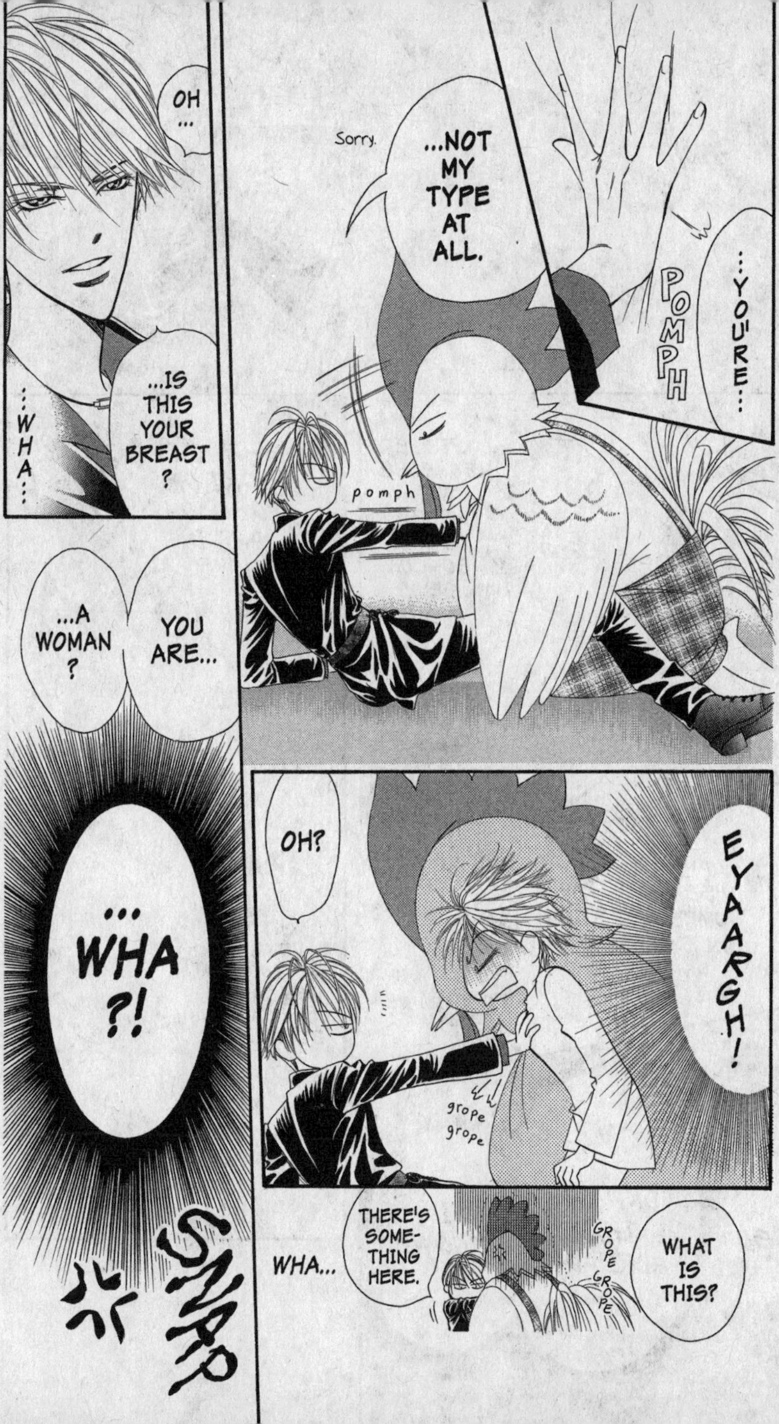
...YOU'RE...
POMPH
...NOT MY TYPE AT ALL.
Sorry.
pomph
EYAARGH!
OH?
grope grope
WHAT IS THIS?
GROPE GROPE
THERE'S SOME-THING HERE.
WHA...
OH...
...IS THIS YOUR BREAST?
...WHA...
YOU ARE...
...A WOMAN?
...WHA?!
SNAP

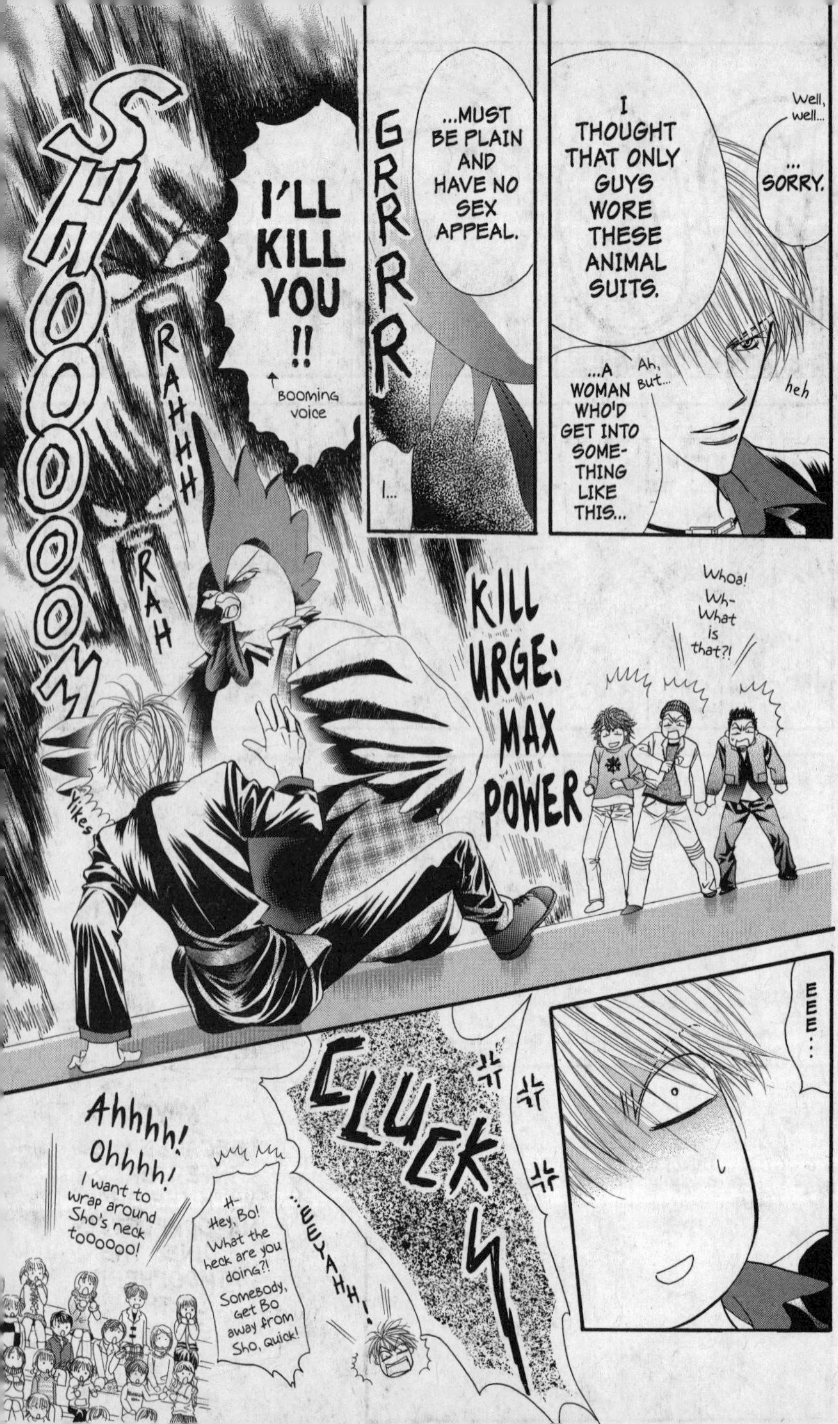
Well, well...
...SORRY.
I THOUGHT THAT ONLY GUYS WORE THESE ANIMAL SUITS.
Ah, But...
heh
...A WOMAN WHO'D GET INTO SOME-THING LIKE THIS...
...MUST BE PLAIN AND HAVE NO SEX APPEAL.
GRRRRR
I...
I'LL KILL YOU!!
BOOMING voice
SHOOOOOOM
RAHHHH
RAH
Whoa! Wh-What is that?!
KILL URGE: MAX POWER
Yikes
EEE...
CLUCK
Ahhhh! Ohhhh! I want to wrap around Sho's neck toooooo!
H-Hey, Bo! What the heck are you doing?! Somebody, Get Bo away from Sho, Quick!
...EEYAHH!

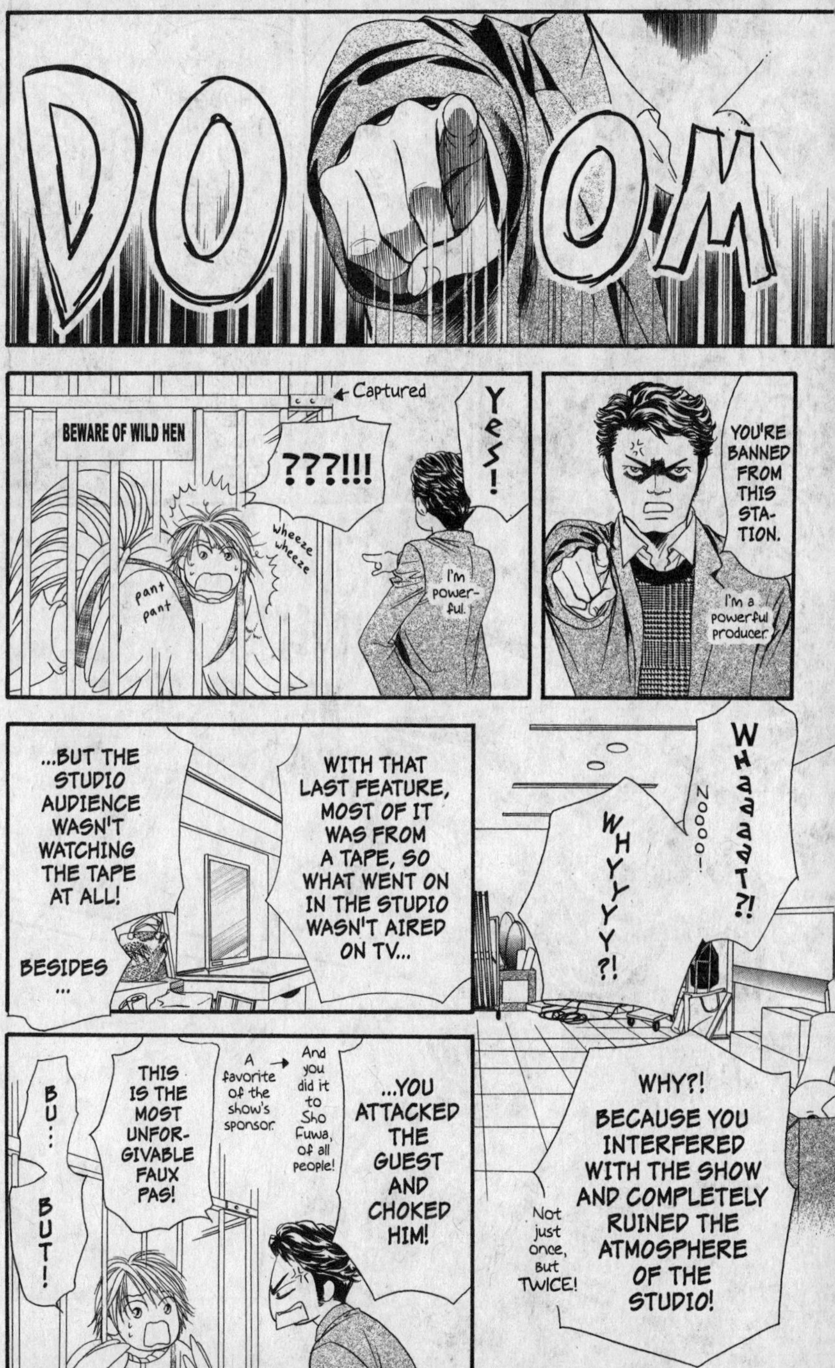
DOOOM
YOU'RE BANNED FROM THIS STATION.
I'm a powerful producer.
Yes!
I'm powerful.
Captured
???!!!
BEWARE OF WILD HEN
wheeze wheeze
pant pant
Whaaaat?!
Noooo!
WHYYYY?!
WHY?! BECAUSE YOU INTERFERED WITH THE SHOW AND COMPLETELY RUINED THE ATMOSPHERE OF THE STUDIO!
Not just once, but TWICE!
WITH THAT LAST FEATURE, MOST OF IT WAS FROM A TAPE, SO WHAT WENT ON IN THE STUDIO WASN'T AIRED ON TV...
...BUT THE STUDIO AUDIENCE WASN'T WATCHING THE TAPE AT ALL!
BESIDES...
...YOU ATTACKED THE GUEST AND CHOKED HIM!
And you did it to Sho Fuwa, of all people!
A favorite of the show's sponsor.
THIS IS THE MOST UNFORGIVABLE FAUX PAS!
BU... BUT!

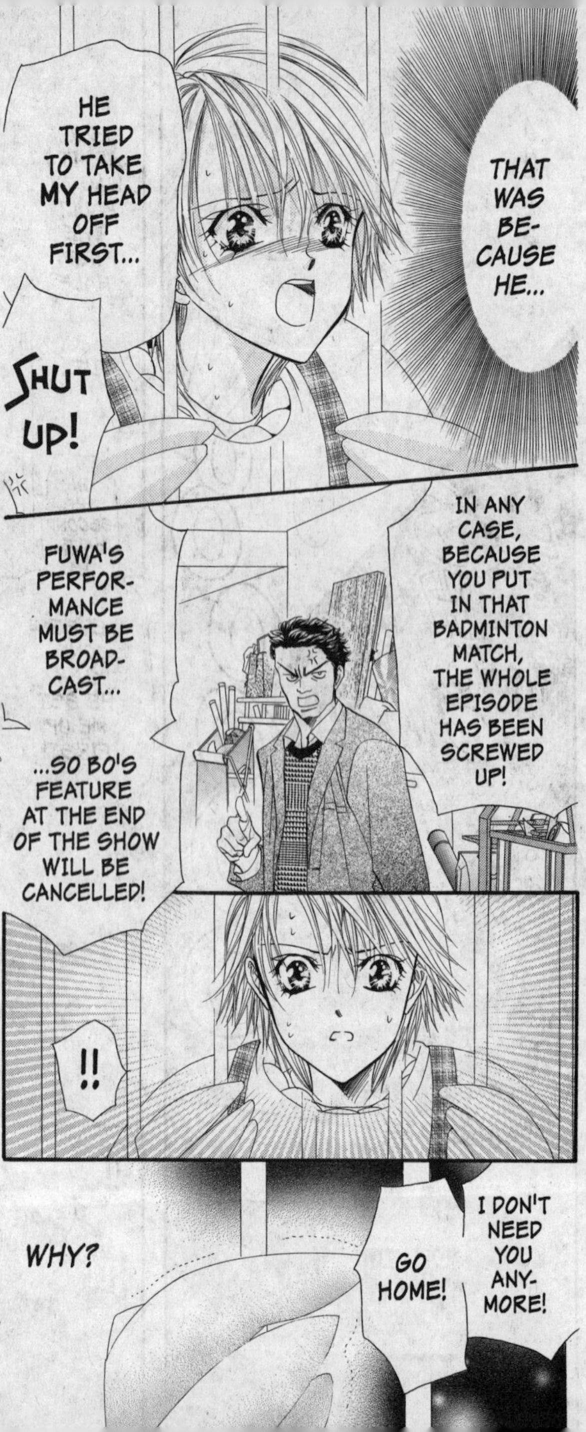
THAT WAS BE-CAUSE HE...
HE TRIED TO TAKE MY HEAD OFF FIRST...
SHUT UP!
IN ANY CASE, BECAUSE YOU PUT IN THAT BADMINTON MATCH, THE WHOLE EPISODE HAS BEEN SCREWED UP!
FUWA'S PERFORMANCE MUST BE BROADCAST...
...SO BO'S FEATURE AT THE END OF THE SHOW WILL BE CANCELLED!
!!
I DON'T NEED YOU ANYMORE!
GO HOME!
WHY?

Bo

From the time I started *Skip·Beat!* I'd told my editor that I wanted to have Kyoko do a job involving animal suits, but I didn't think that animal suit would turn out to be a hen.

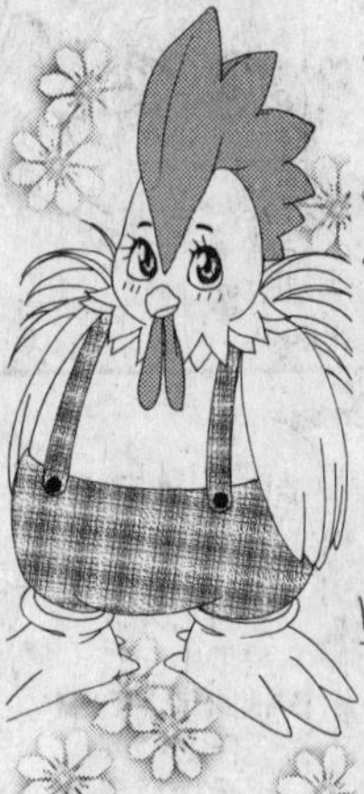

But I had this vague image of an animal suit that would be a mascot character for a talk show or a variety show (Like Manma-chan in Sanma no Manma...)...so...the animal was finally decided by trial and error after the show name "Yappa Kimagure Rock" was chosen.

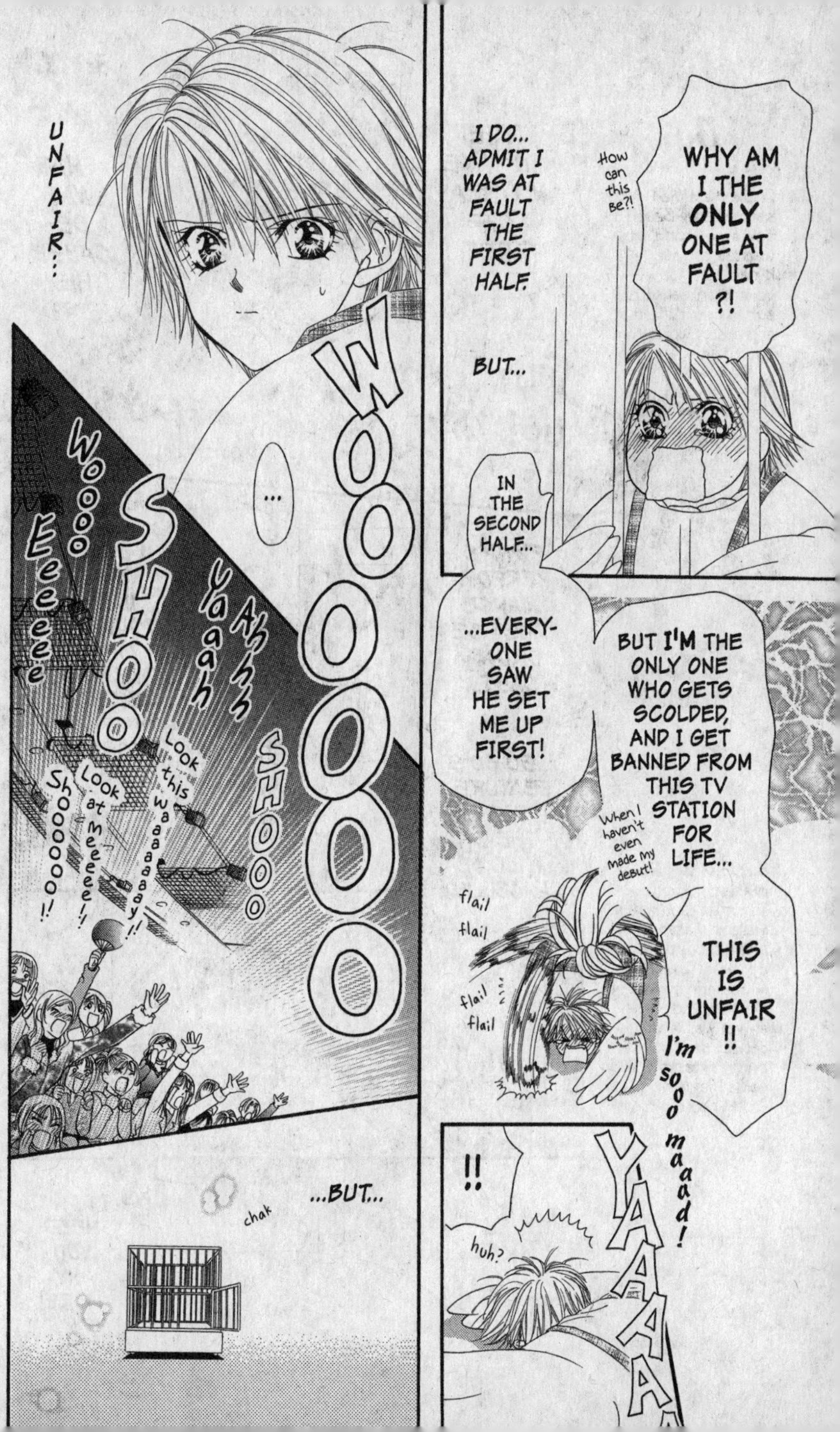
WHY AM I THE ONLY ONE AT FAULT ?!
How can this be?!
I DO... ADMIT I WAS AT FAULT THE FIRST HALF.
BUT...
IN THE SECOND HALF...
...EVERY-ONE SAW HE SET ME UP FIRST!
BUT I'M THE ONLY ONE WHO GETS SCOLDED, AND I GET BANNED FROM THIS TV STATION FOR LIFE...
When I haven't even made my debut!
flail
flail
flail
flail
THIS IS UNFAIR !!
I'm sooo maaad!
YAAAAA
!!
huh?
UNFAIR...
WOOOOOOO
...
SHOOOO
Ahhh
Yaaah
Woooo
Eeeeeee
SHOOO
Look this waaaaaaay!!
Look at Meeeee!!
Shoooooooo!!
...BUT...
chak

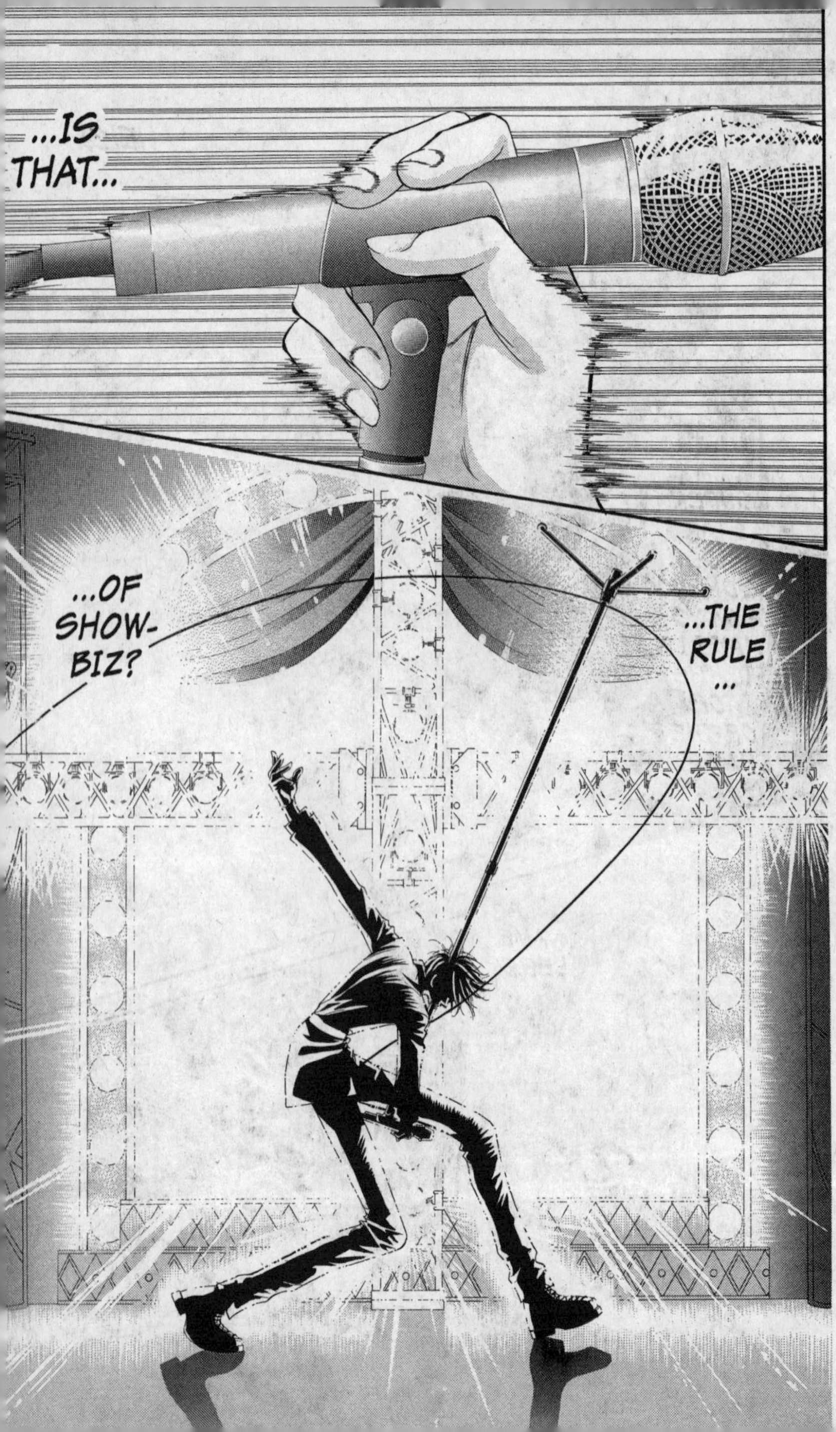
...IS THAT...
...THE RULE ...
...OF SHOW-BIZ?

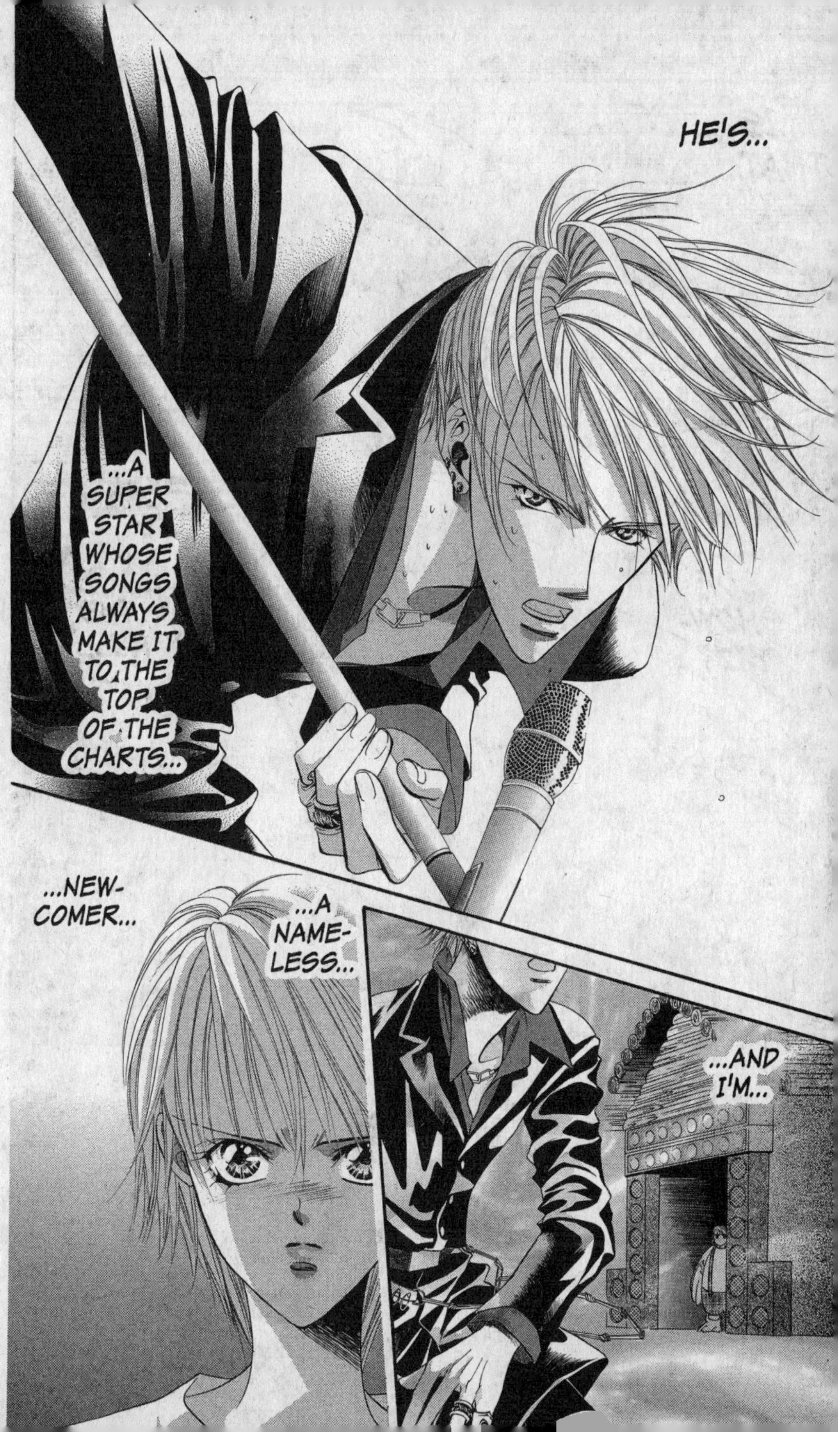
HE'S...
...A SUPER STAR WHOSE SONGS ALWAYS MAKE IT TO THE TOP OF THE CHARTS...
...AND I'M...
...A NAME-LESS...
...NEW-COMER...

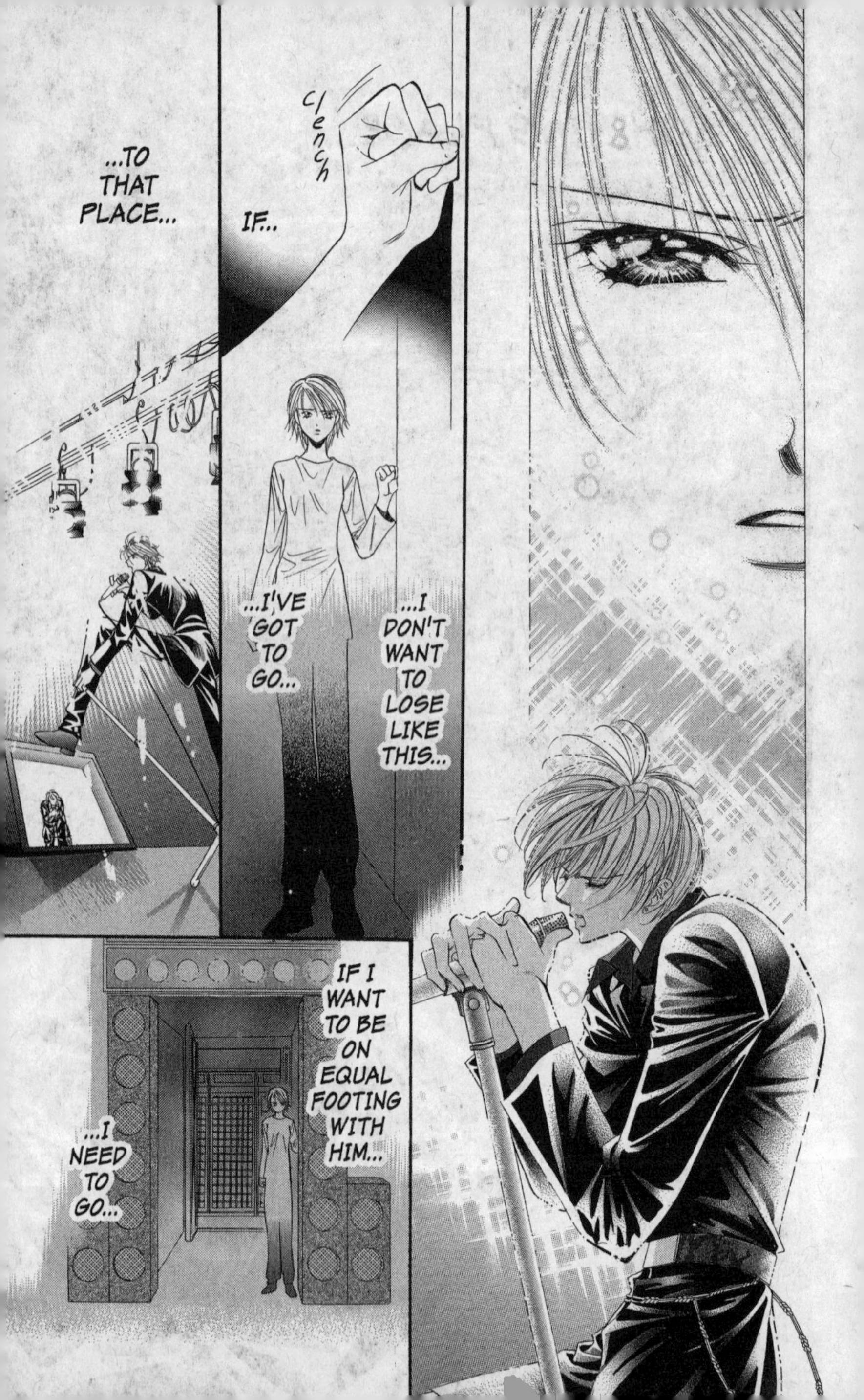
Clench
IF...
...I DON'T WANT TO LOSE LIKE THIS...
...I'VE GOT TO GO...
...TO THAT PLACE...
IF I WANT TO BE ON EQUAL FOOTING WITH HIM...
...I NEED TO GO...

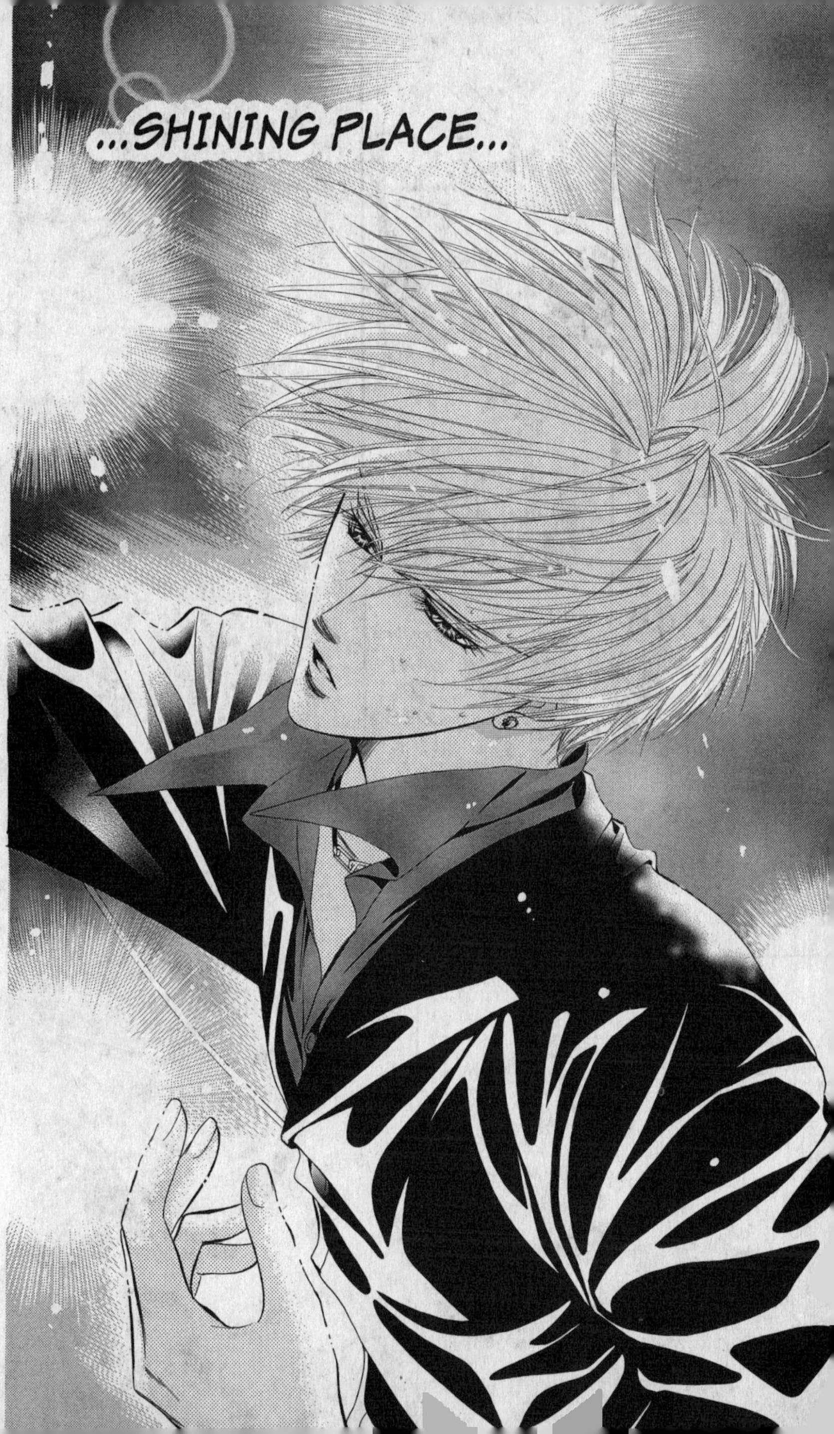
...SHINING PLACE...

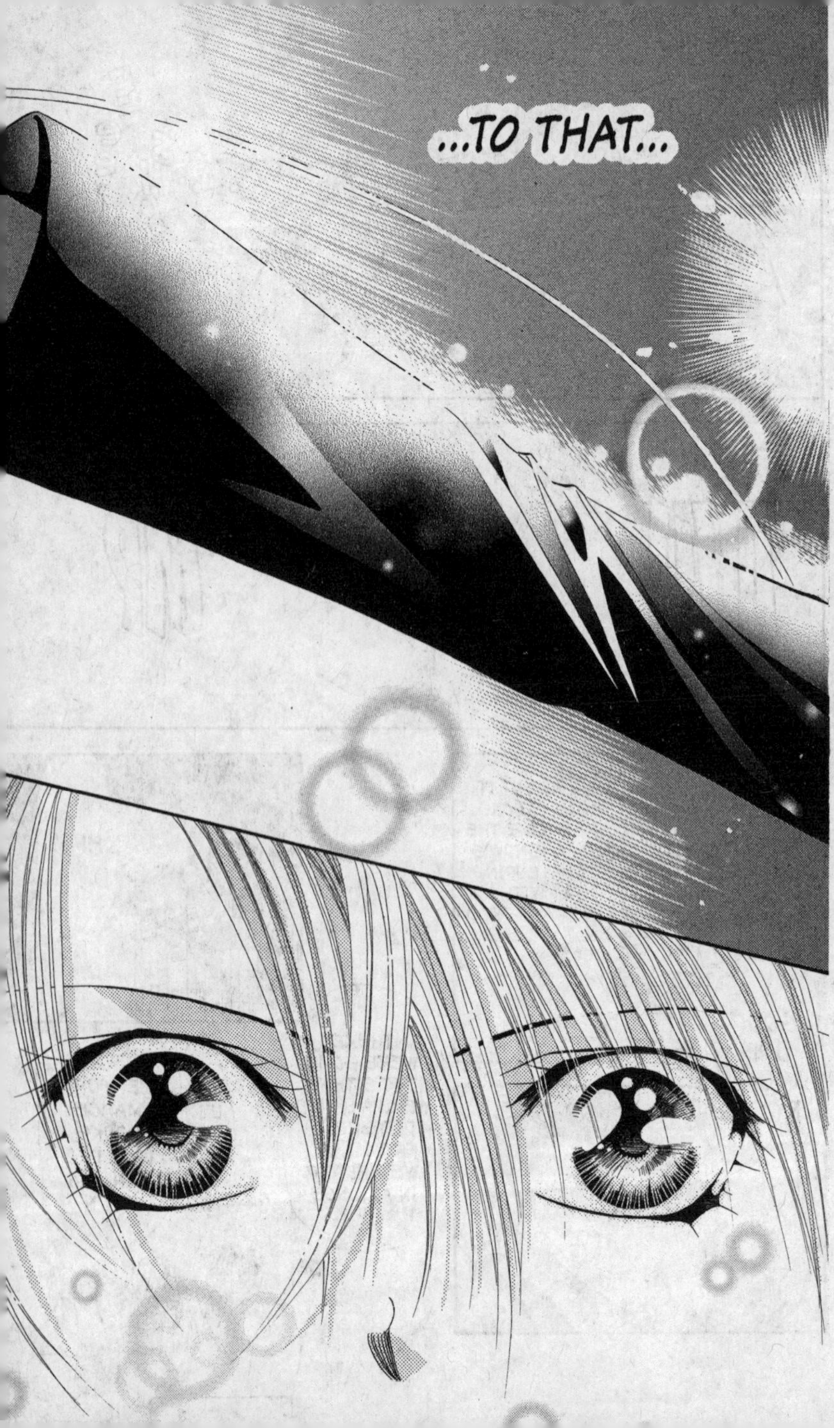
...TO THAT...

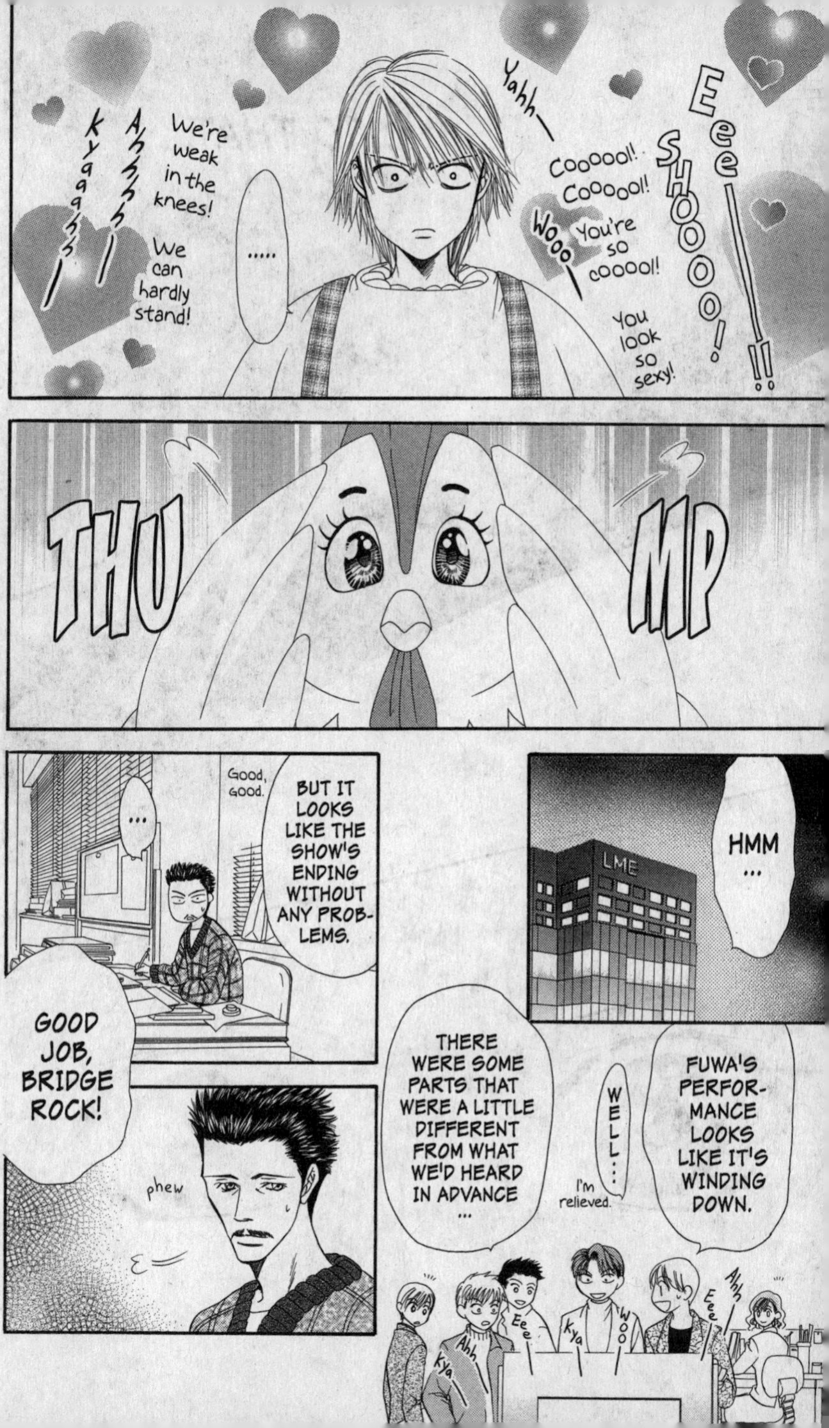
Eee—SHOOOOO—!!
Yahh—
Coooool! Coooool!
Wooo—
You're so cooool!
You look so sexy!
.....
We're weak in the knees!
We can hardly stand!
Ahhhh—
Kyaaahh—
THUMP
HMM...
Good, good.
BUT IT LOOKS LIKE THE SHOW'S ENDING WITHOUT ANY PROBLEMS.
...
FUWA'S PERFORMANCE LOOKS LIKE IT'S WINDING DOWN.
I'm relieved.
WELL...
THERE WERE SOME PARTS THAT WERE A LITTLE DIFFERENT FROM WHAT WE'D HEARD IN ADVANCE...
Ahh
Eee
Woo
Kya
Eee
Ahh
Kya
GOOD JOB, BRIDGE ROCK!
phew

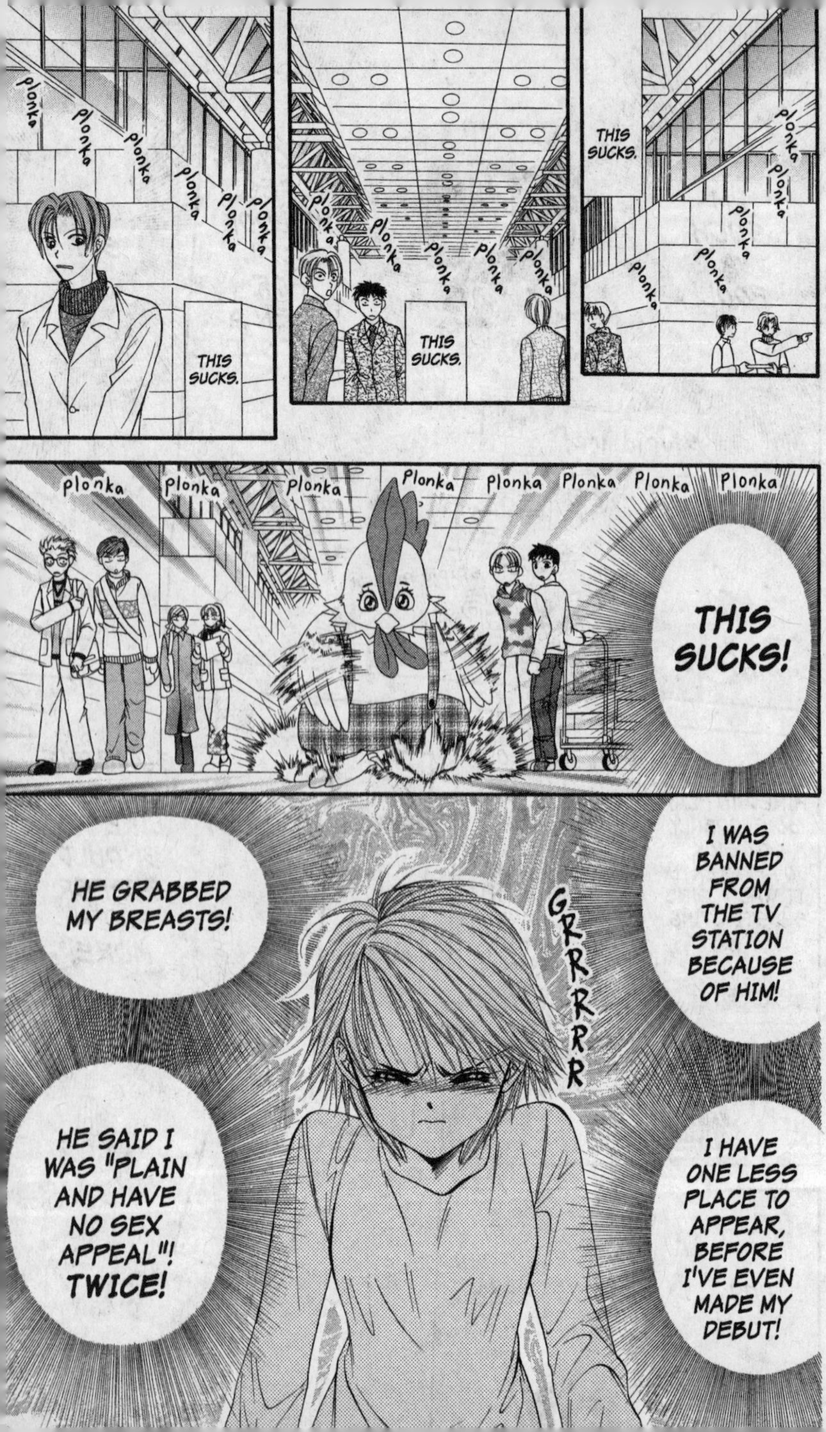
THIS SUCKS.
plonka plonka plonka plonka plonka plonka
plonka plonka plonka plonka plonka plonka plonka
THIS SUCKS.
plonka plonka plonka plonka plonka plonka
THIS SUCKS.
plonka plonka plonka plonka plonka plonka plonka plonka
THIS SUCKS!
I WAS BANNED FROM THE TV STATION BECAUSE OF HIM!
HE GRABBED MY BREASTS!
GRRRRRR
I HAVE ONE LESS PLACE TO APPEAR, BEFORE I'VE EVEN MADE MY DEBUT!
HE SAID I WAS "PLAIN AND HAVE NO SEX APPEAL"! TWICE!

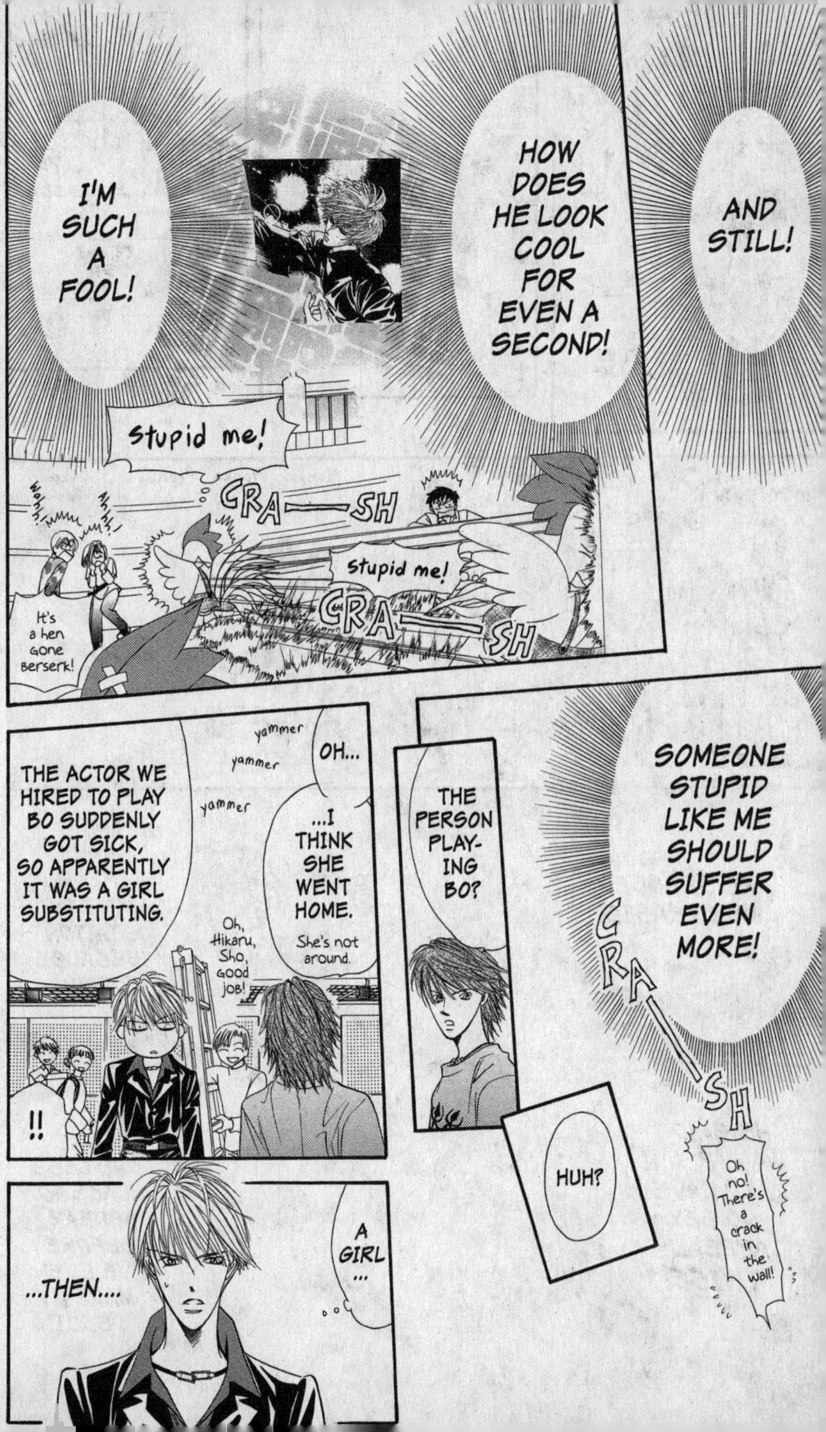
AND STILL!
HOW DOES HE LOOK COOL FOR EVEN A SECOND!
I'M SUCH A FOOL!
Stupid me!
CRA—SH
Stupid me!
CRA—SH
Wohh!?
Ahh!?
It's a hen Gone Berserk!
SOMEONE STUPID LIKE ME SHOULD SUFFER EVEN MORE!
CRA—SH
Oh no! There's a crack in the wall!
THE PERSON PLAY-ING BO?
OH...
...I THINK SHE WENT HOME.
She's not around.
yammer
yammer
yammer
THE ACTOR WE HIRED TO PLAY BO SUDDENLY GOT SICK, SO APPARENTLY IT WAS A GIRL SUBSTITUTING.
Oh, Hikaru, Sho, Good job!
!!
HUH?
A GIRL...
...THEN....

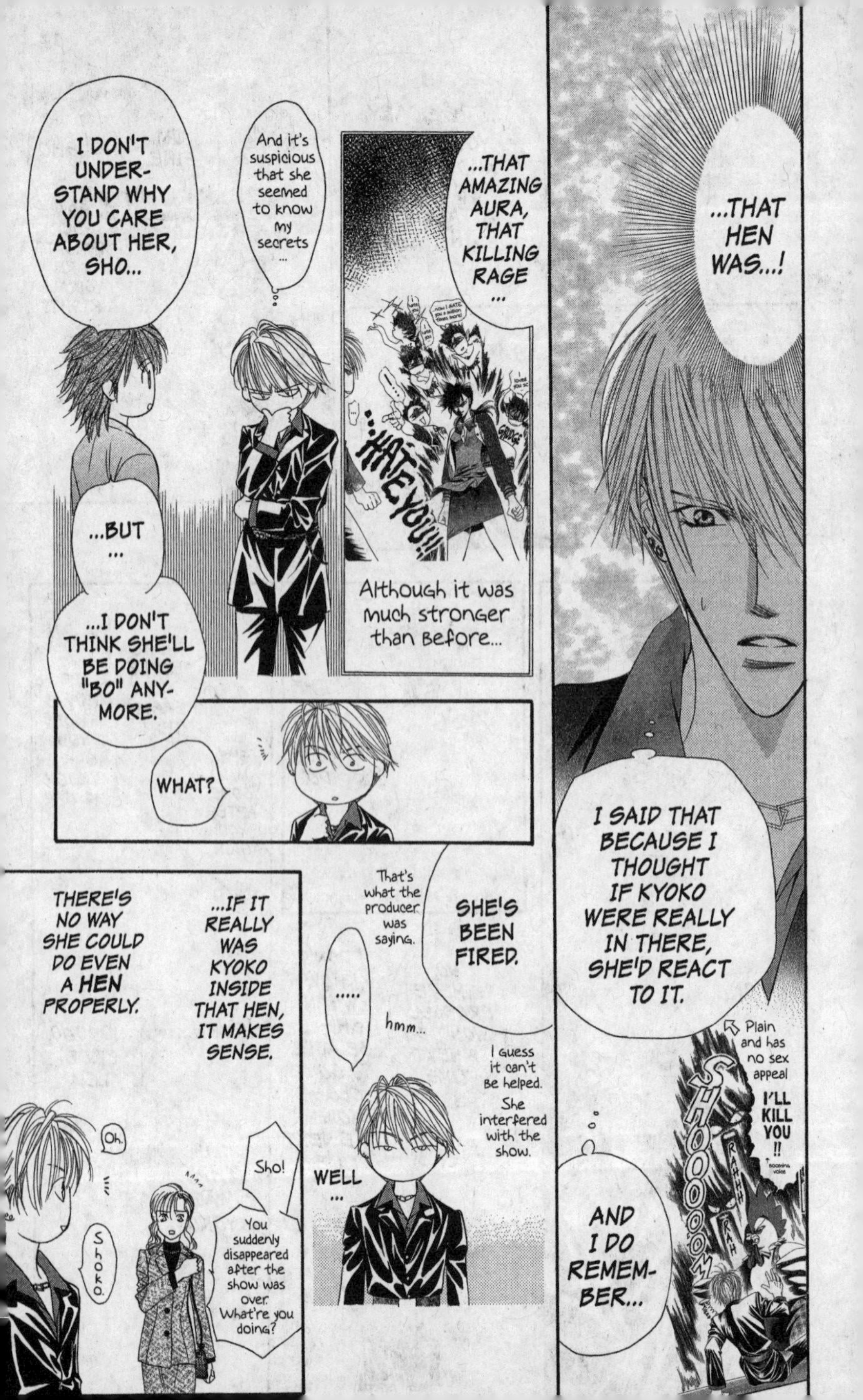
...THAT HEN WAS...!
I SAID THAT BECAUSE I THOUGHT IF KYOKO WERE REALLY IN THERE, SHE'D REACT TO IT.
AND I DO REMEMBER...
Plain and has no sex appeal
I'LL KILL YOU!!
SHOOOOOM
RAHHH
RAH
...THAT AMAZING AURA, THAT KILLING RAGE...
...I HATE YOU!!!
GRUDGE
Although it was much stronger than before...
I DON'T UNDER-STAND WHY YOU CARE ABOUT HER, SHO...
And it's suspicious that she seemed to know my secrets...
...BUT...
...I DON'T THINK SHE'LL BE DOING "BO" ANY-MORE.
WHAT?
SHE'S BEEN FIRED.
That's what the producer was saying.
.....
hmm...
I guess it can't be helped. She interfered with the show.
WELL...
...IF IT REALLY WAS KYOKO INSIDE THAT HEN, IT MAKES SENSE.
THERE'S NO WAY SHE COULD DO EVEN A HEN PROPERLY.
Sho!
You suddenly disappeared after the show was over. What're you doing?
Oh.
Shoko.

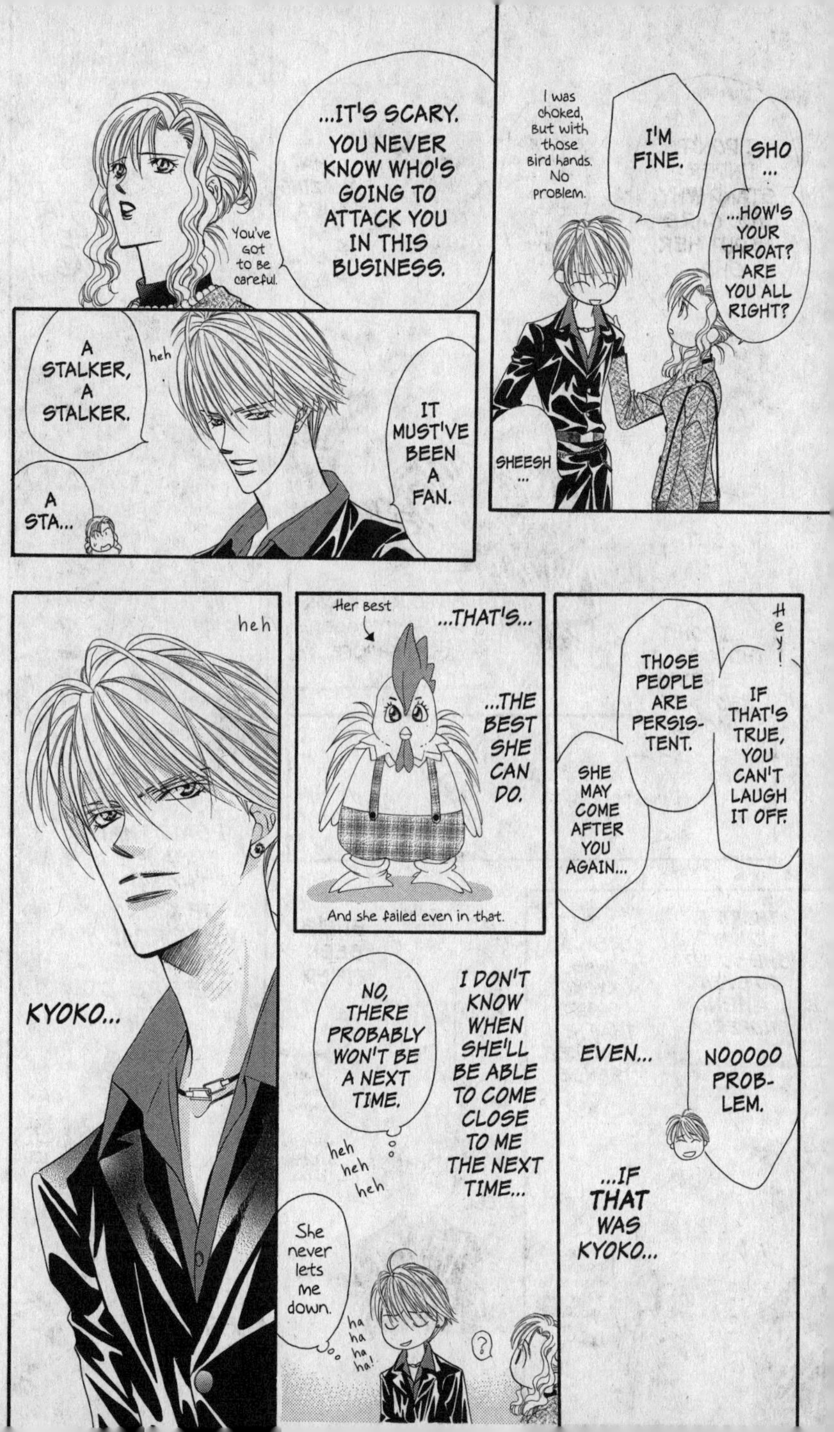
SHO...
...HOW'S YOUR THROAT? ARE YOU ALL RIGHT?
I'M FINE.
I was choked, but with those bird hands. No problem.
SHEESH...
...IT'S SCARY. YOU NEVER KNOW WHO'S GOING TO ATTACK YOU IN THIS BUSINESS.
You've got to be careful.
IT MUST'VE BEEN A FAN.
heh
A STALKER, A STALKER.
A STA...
Hey!
IF THAT'S TRUE, YOU CAN'T LAUGH IT OFF.
THOSE PEOPLE ARE PERSISTENT.
SHE MAY COME AFTER YOU AGAIN...
NOOOOO PROB-LEM.
EVEN...
...IF THAT WAS KYOKO...
...THAT'S...
...THE BEST SHE CAN DO.
Her best
And she failed even in that.
I DON'T KNOW WHEN SHE'LL BE ABLE TO COME CLOSE TO ME THE NEXT TIME...
NO, THERE PROBABLY WON'T BE A NEXT TIME.
heh heh heh
She never lets me down.
ha ha ha ha!
?
heh
KYOKO...

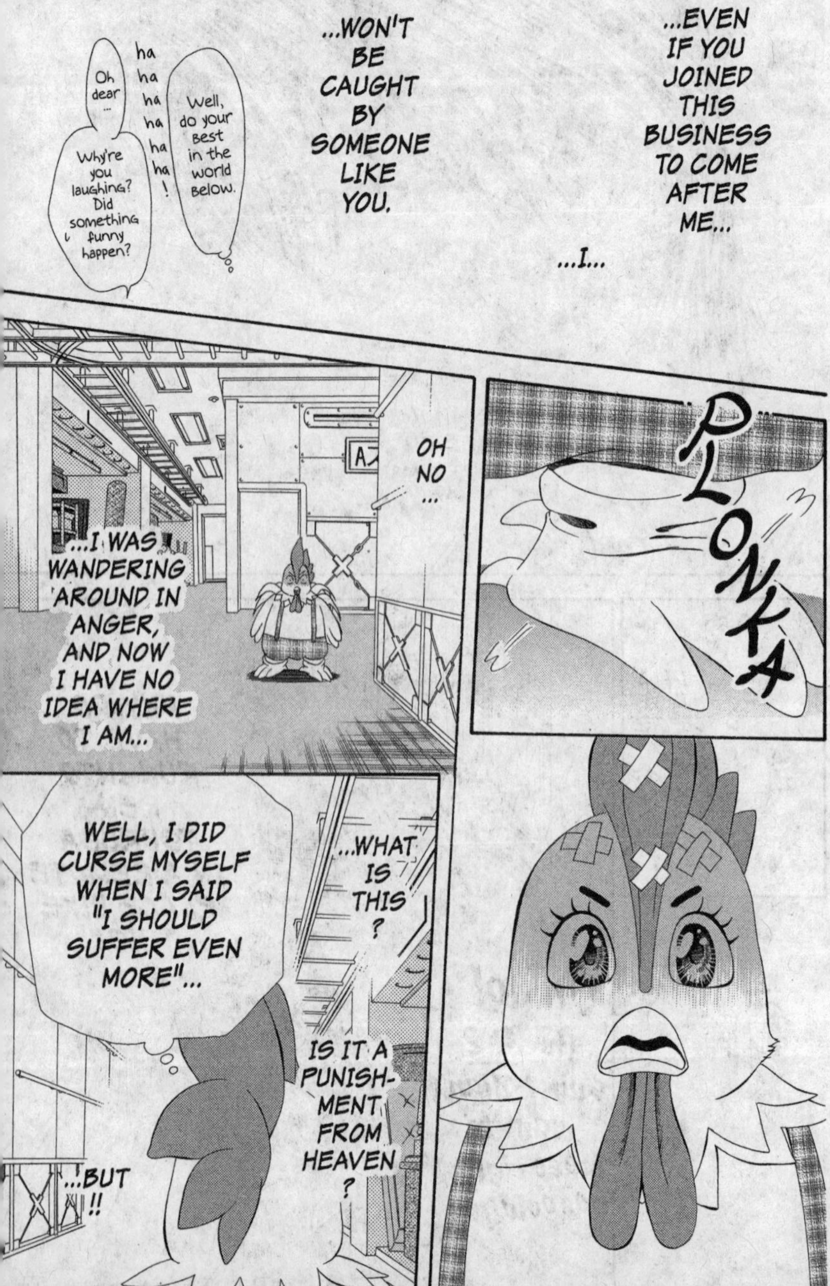
...EVEN IF YOU JOINED THIS BUSINESS TO COME AFTER ME...
...I...
...WON'T BE CAUGHT BY SOMEONE LIKE YOU.
Well, do your best in the world below.
ha ha ha ha ha ha !
Oh dear...
Why're you laughing? Did something funny happen?
PLONKA
OH NO...
...I WAS WANDERING AROUND IN ANGER, AND NOW I HAVE NO IDEA WHERE I AM...
...WHAT IS THIS?
IS IT A PUNISHMENT FROM HEAVEN?
WELL, I DID CURSE MYSELF WHEN I SAID "I SHOULD SUFFER EVEN MORE"...
...BUT!!

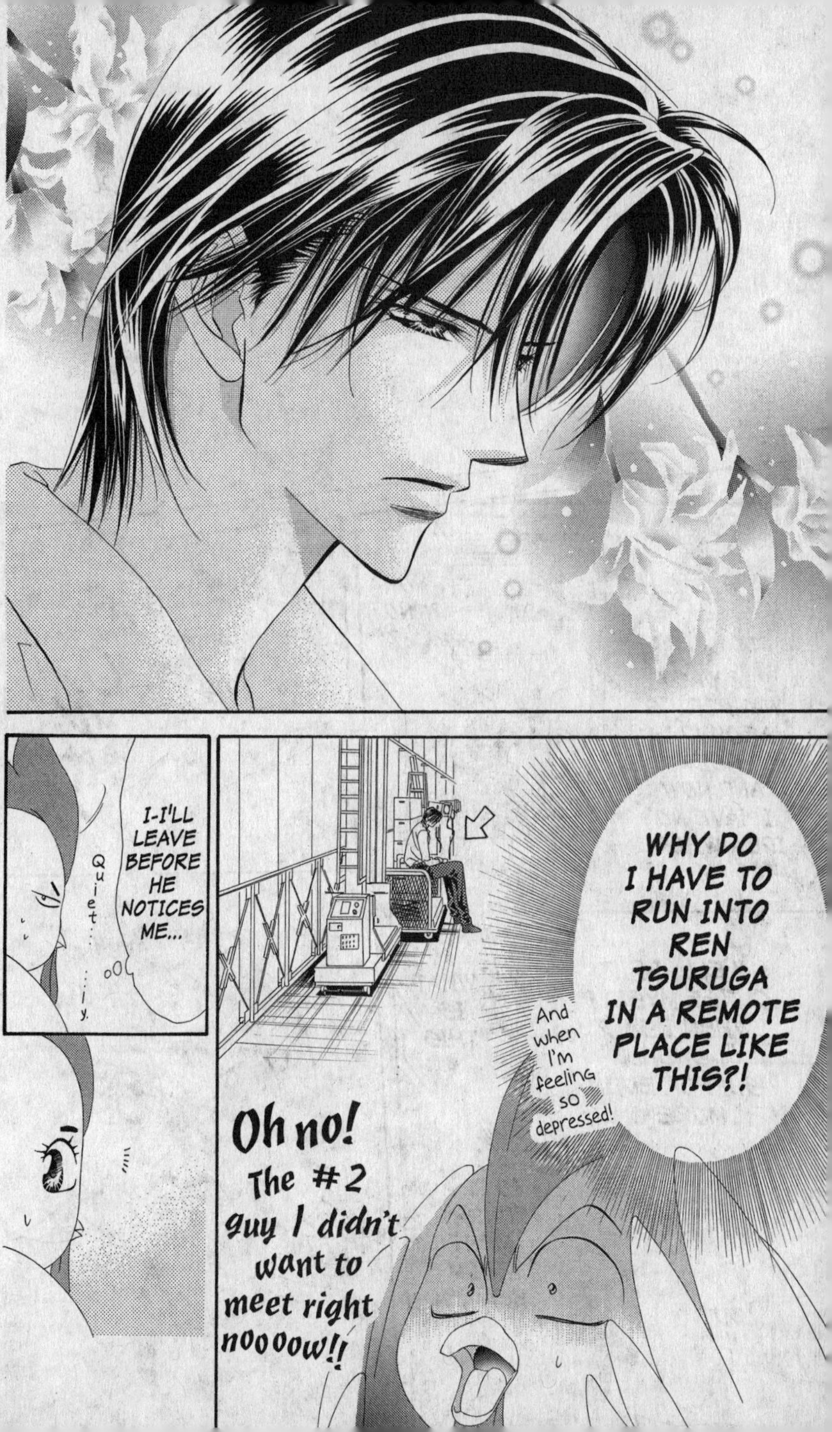
WHY DO I HAVE TO RUN INTO REN TSURUGA IN A REMOTE PLACE LIKE THIS?!
And when I'm feeling so depressed!
Oh no! The #2 guy I didn't want to meet right nooooow!!
I-I'LL LEAVE BEFORE HE NOTICES ME...
Quiet... ...ly.

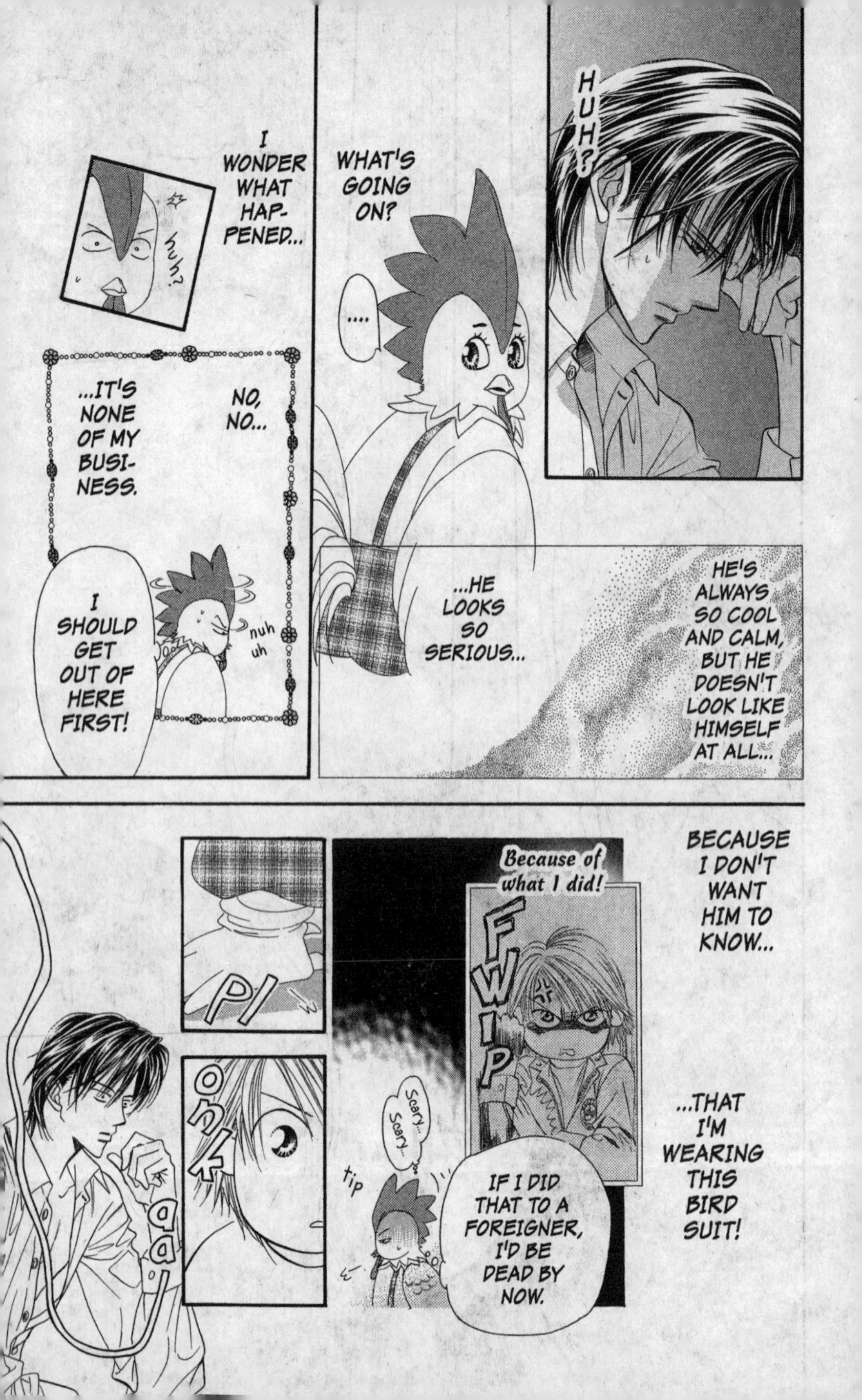
HUH?
WHAT'S GOING ON?
....
I WONDER WHAT HAP-PENED...
huh?
NO, NO...
...IT'S NONE OF MY BUSI-NESS.
HE'S ALWAYS SO COOL AND CALM, BUT HE DOESN'T LOOK LIKE HIMSELF AT ALL...
...HE LOOKS SO SERIOUS...
I SHOULD GET OUT OF HERE FIRST!
nuh uh
BECAUSE I DON'T WANT HIM TO KNOW...
...THAT I'M WEARING THIS BIRD SUIT!
Because of what I did!
FWIP
IF I DID THAT TO A FOREIGNER, I'D BE DEAD BY NOW.
Scary... Scary...
tip
Pl
onk

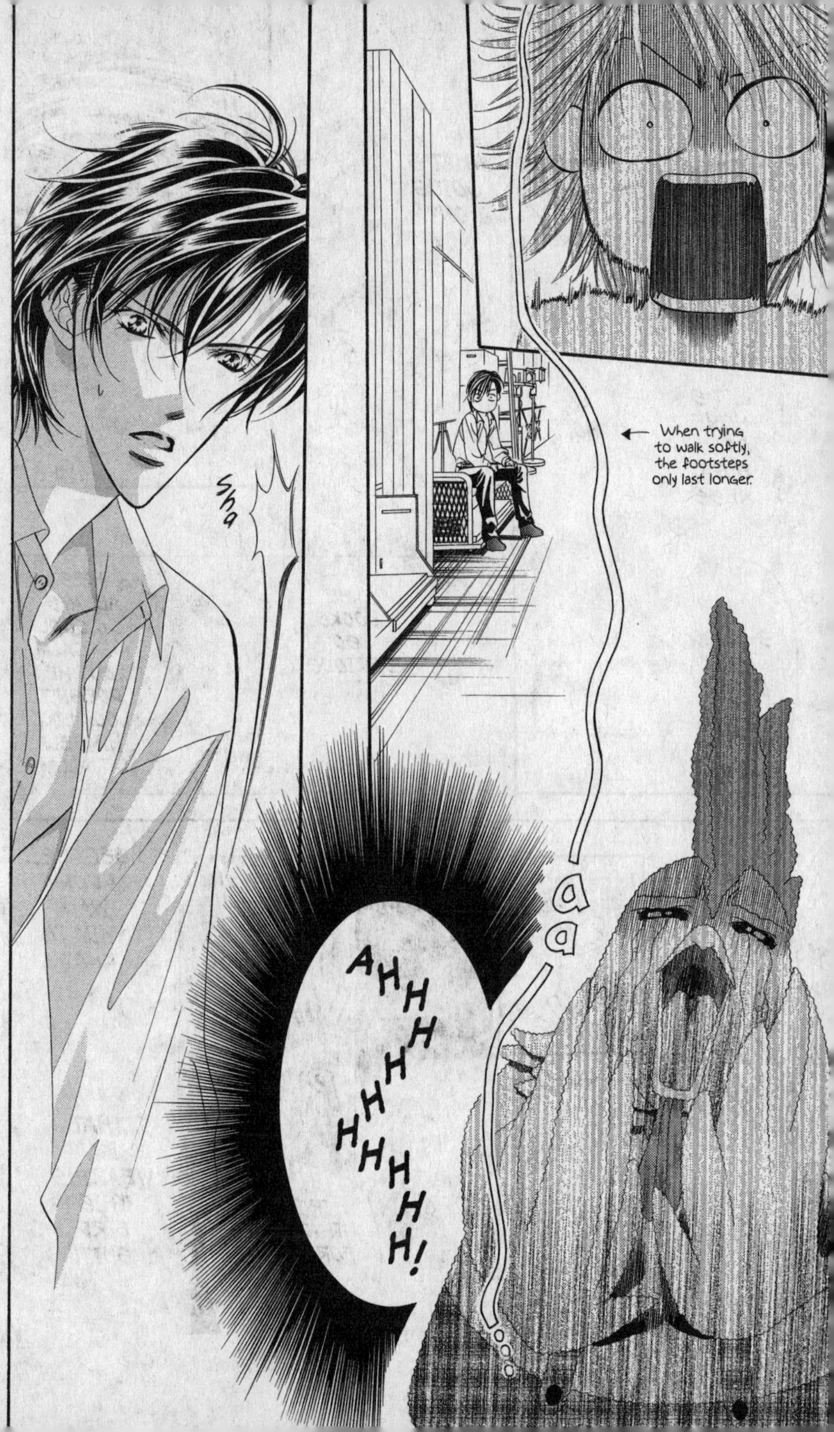
When trying to walk softly, the footsteps only last longer.
Sha
aa...
AHHHHHHHHHHHH!

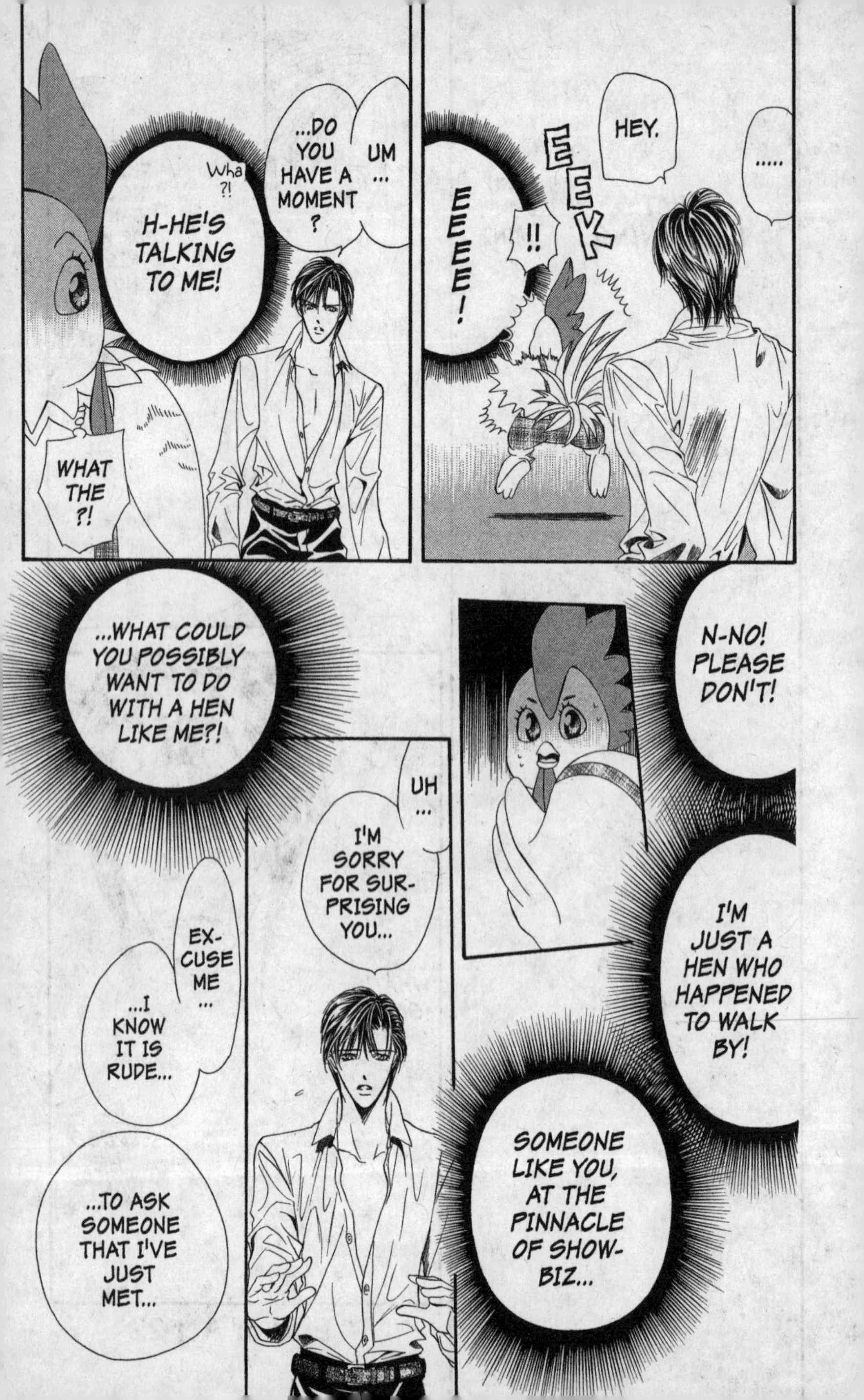
.....
HEY.
EEEK
!!
EEEE!
UM ...
...DO YOU HAVE A MOMENT ?
Wha ?!
H-HE'S TALKING TO ME!
WHAT THE ?!
N-NO! PLEASE DON'T!
I'M JUST A HEN WHO HAPPENED TO WALK BY!
SOMEONE LIKE YOU, AT THE PINNACLE OF SHOW-BIZ...
...WHAT COULD YOU POSSIBLY WANT TO DO WITH A HEN LIKE ME?!
UH ...
I'M SORRY FOR SUR-PRISING YOU...
EX-CUSE ME ...
...I KNOW IT IS RUDE...
...TO ASK SOMEONE THAT I'VE JUST MET...

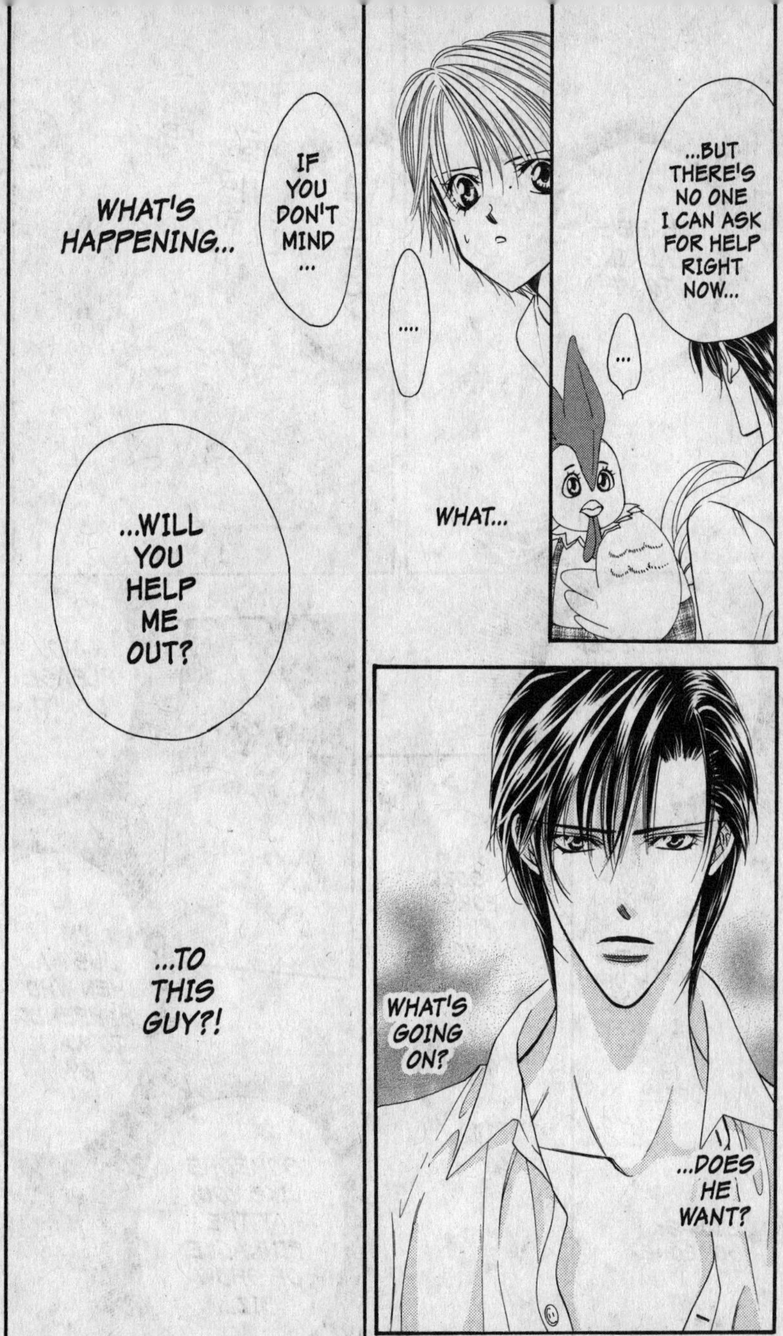
...BUT THERE'S NO ONE I CAN ASK FOR HELP RIGHT NOW...
...
....
WHAT...
WHAT'S GOING ON?
...DOES HE WANT?
IF YOU DON'T MIND ...
WHAT'S HAPPENING...
...WILL YOU HELP ME OUT?
...TO THIS GUY?!

End of Act 22

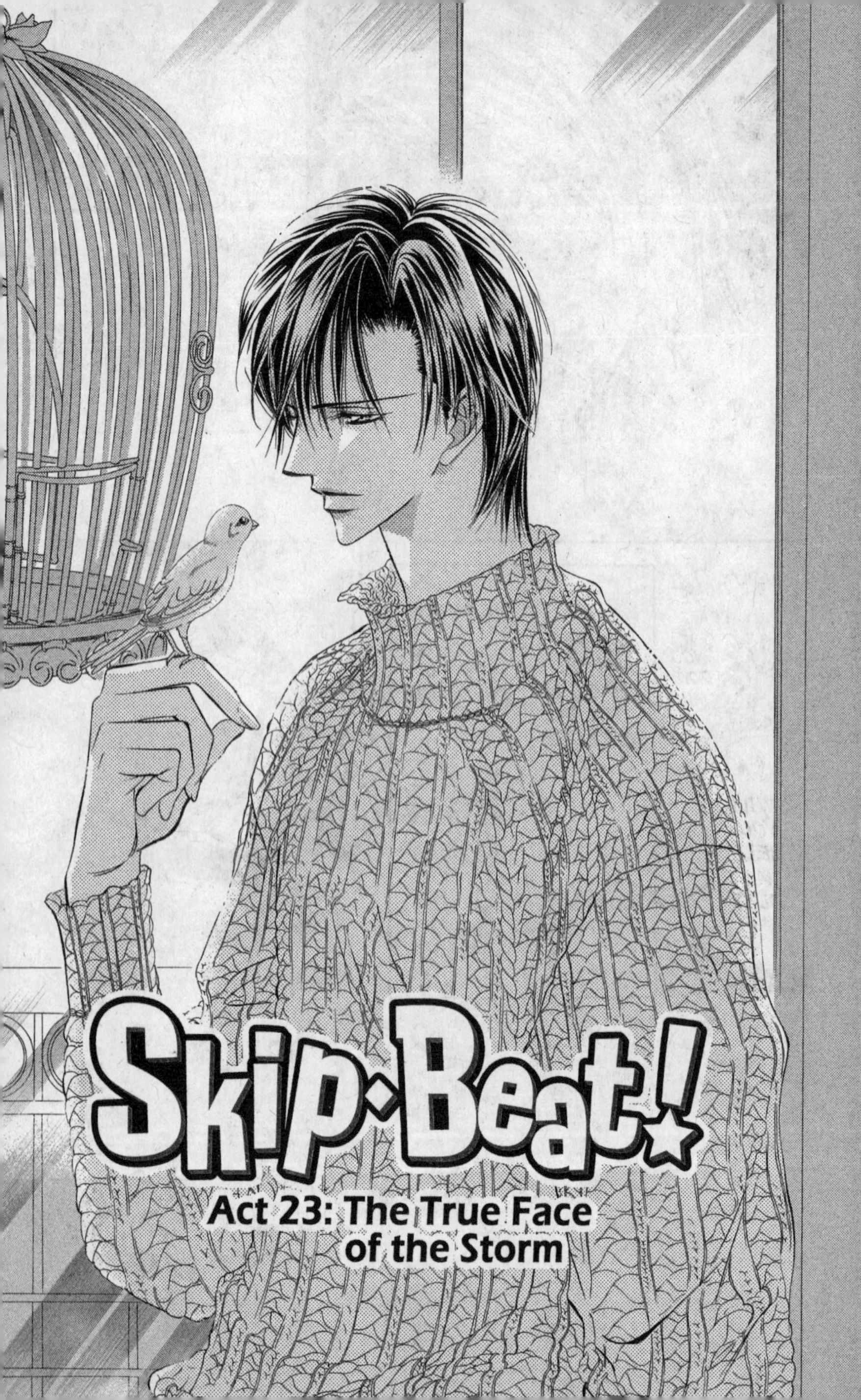
Skip·Beat!
Act 23: The True Face of the Storm

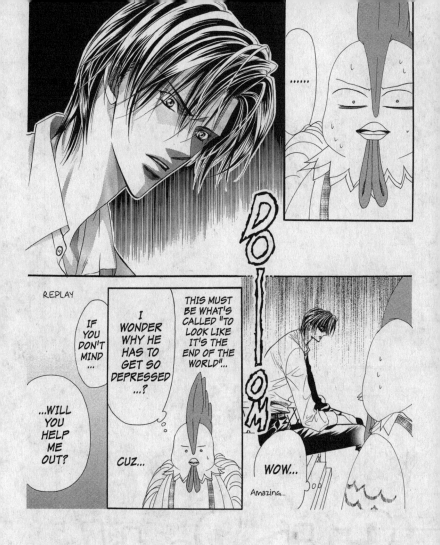

......
DOOM
WOW...
Amazing...
THIS MUST BE WHAT'S CALLED "TO LOOK LIKE IT'S THE END OF THE WORLD"...
I WONDER WHY HE HAS TO GET SO DEPRESSED ...?
CUZ...
REPLAY
IF YOU DON'T MIND ...
...WILL YOU HELP ME OUT?

eep!
eek!
eek!

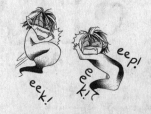

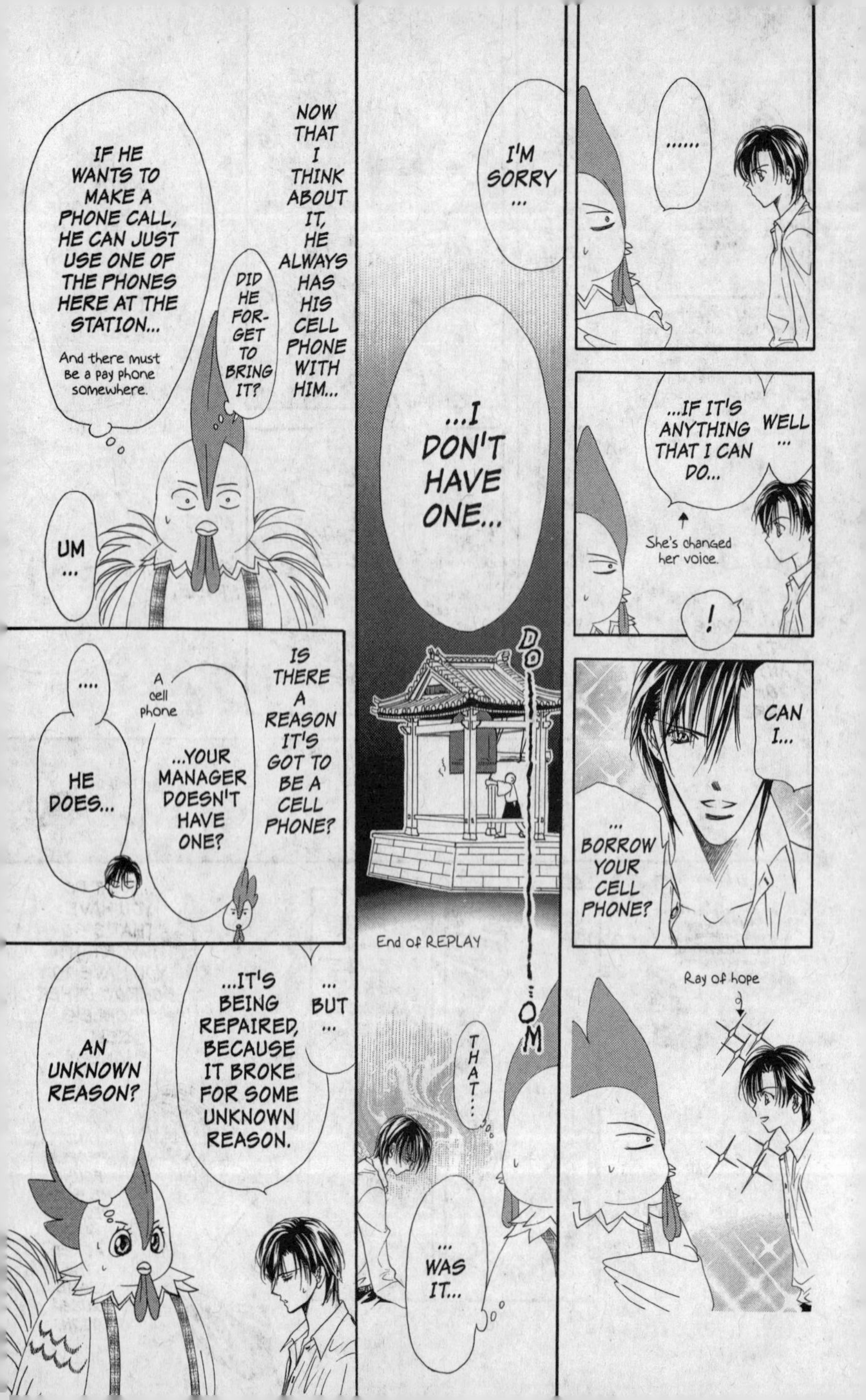
......
WELL ...
...IF IT'S ANYTHING THAT I CAN DO...
She's changed her voice.
!
CAN I...
...BORROW YOUR CELL PHONE?
Ray of hope
I'M SORRY ...
...I DON'T HAVE ONE...
DO..........OM
End of REPLAY
THAT...
...WAS IT...
NOW THAT I THINK ABOUT IT, HE ALWAYS HAS HIS CELL PHONE WITH HIM...
DID HE FOR-GET TO BRING IT?
IF HE WANTS TO MAKE A PHONE CALL, HE CAN JUST USE ONE OF THE PHONES HERE AT THE STATION...
And there must be a pay phone somewhere.
UM ...
IS THERE A REASON IT'S GOT TO BE A CELL PHONE?
A cell phone
...YOUR MANAGER DOESN'T HAVE ONE?
....
HE DOES...
... BUT ...
...IT'S BEING REPAIRED, BECAUSE IT BROKE FOR SOME UNKNOWN REASON.
AN UNKNOWN REASON?

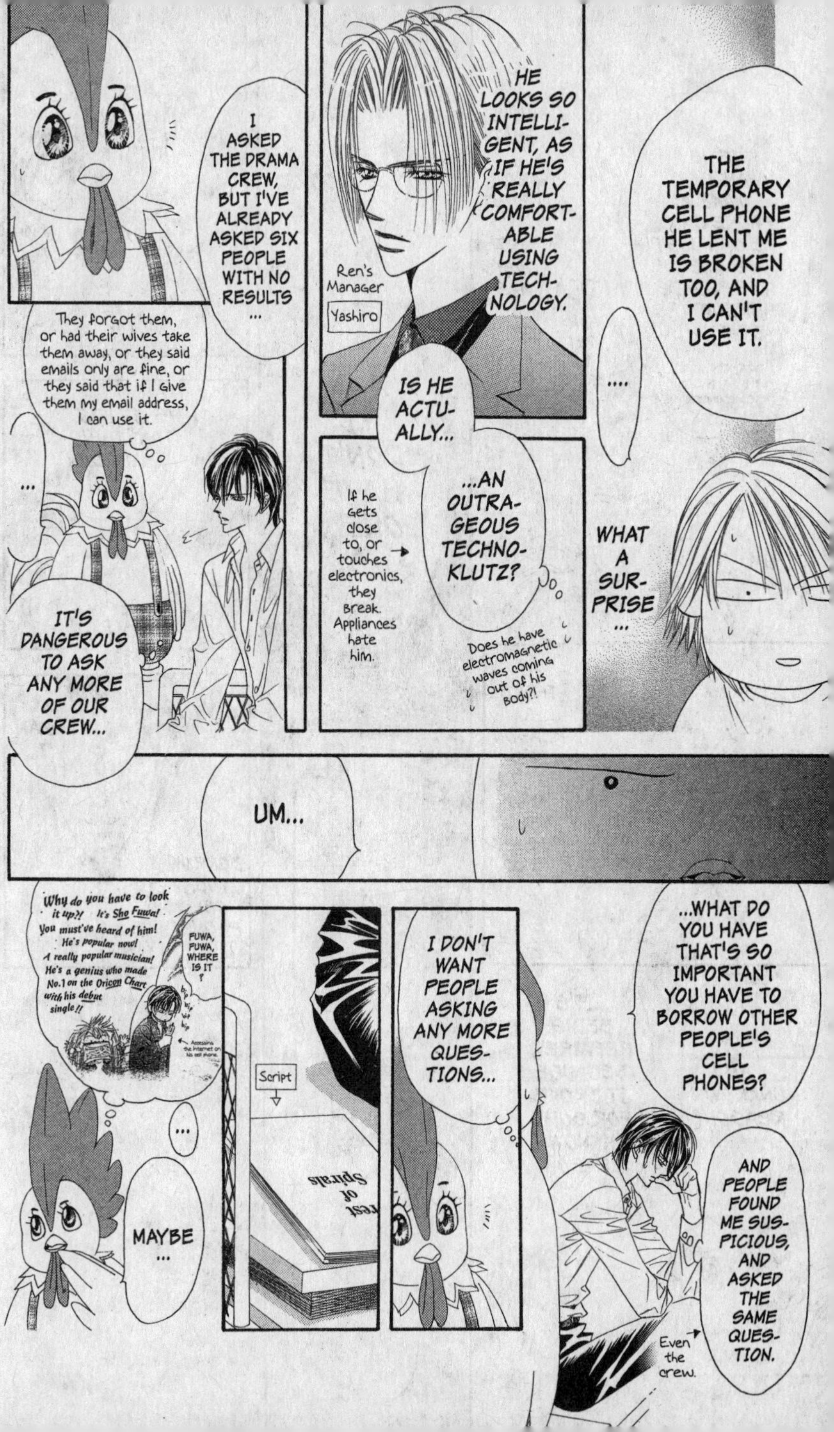

THE TEMPORARY CELL PHONE HE LENT ME IS BROKEN TOO, AND I CAN'T USE IT.
....
WHAT A SURPRISE...
HE LOOKS SO INTELLIGENT, AS IF HE'S REALLY COMFORTABLE USING TECHNOLOGY.
Ren's Manager
Yashiro
IS HE ACTUALLY...
...AN OUTRAGEOUS TECHNO-KLUTZ?
If he gets close to, or touches electronics, they break. Appliances hate him.
Does he have electromagnetic waves coming out of his body?!
I ASKED THE DRAMA CREW, BUT I'VE ALREADY ASKED SIX PEOPLE WITH NO RESULTS...
They forgot them, or had their wives take them away, or they said emails only are fine, or they said that if I give them my email address, I can use it.
...
IT'S DANGEROUS TO ASK ANY MORE OF OUR CREW...
UM...
...WHAT DO YOU HAVE THAT'S SO IMPORTANT YOU HAVE TO BORROW OTHER PEOPLE'S CELL PHONES?
AND PEOPLE FOUND ME SUSPICIOUS, AND ASKED THE SAME QUESTION.
Even the crew.
I DON'T WANT PEOPLE ASKING ANY MORE QUESTIONS...
Script
Why do you have to look it up?! It's Sho Fuwa! You must've heard of him! He's popular now! A really popular musician! He's a genius who made No.1 on the Oricon Chart with his debut single!!
FUWA, FUWA, WHERE IS IT?
...
MAYBE...

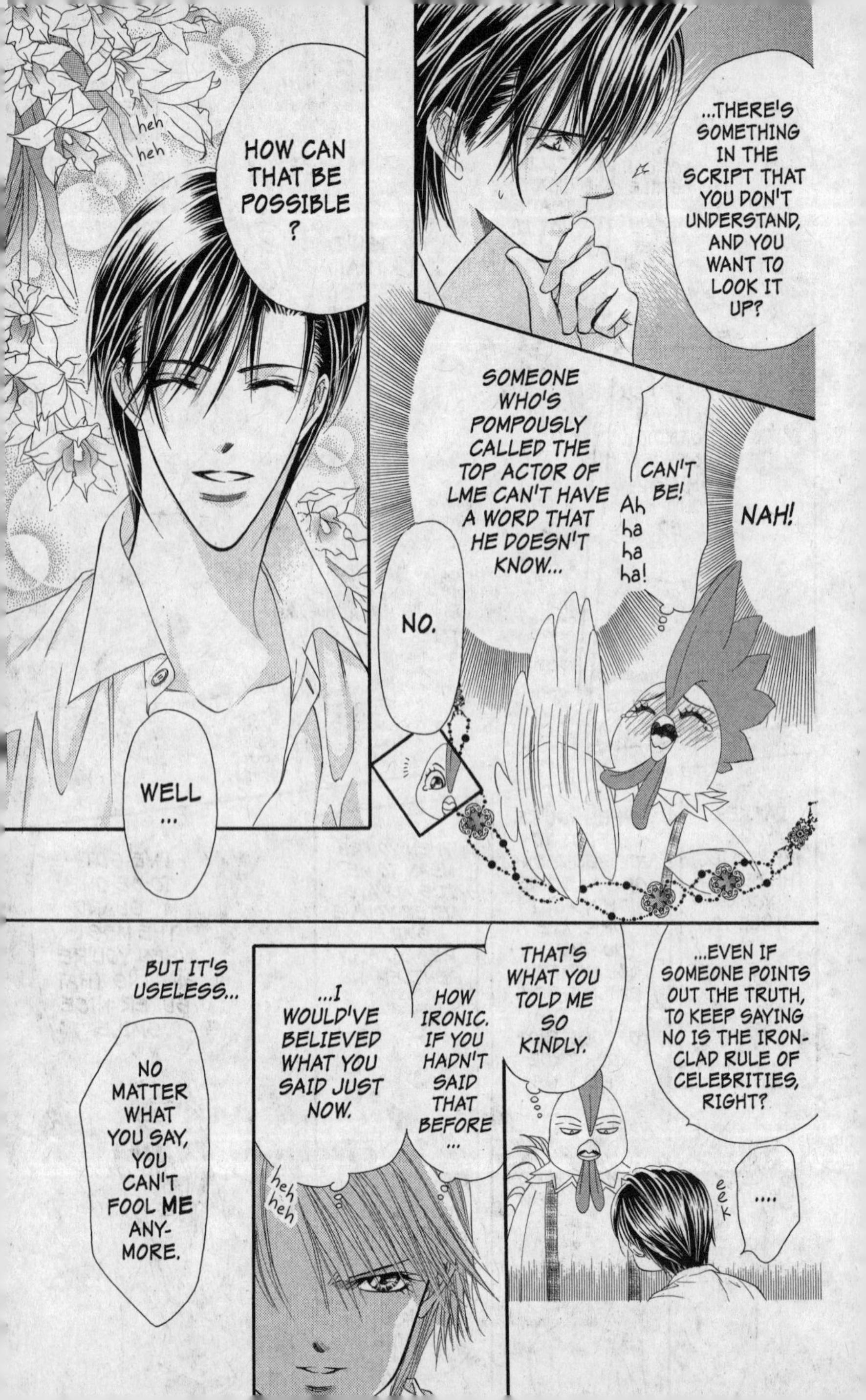
...THERE'S SOMETHING IN THE SCRIPT THAT YOU DON'T UNDERSTAND, AND YOU WANT TO LOOK IT UP?
NAH!
CAN'T BE!
Ah ha ha ha!
SOMEONE WHO'S POMPOUSLY CALLED THE TOP ACTOR OF LME CAN'T HAVE A WORD THAT HE DOESN'T KNOW...
NO.
heh heh
HOW CAN THAT BE POSSIBLE?
WELL...
...EVEN IF SOMEONE POINTS OUT THE TRUTH, TO KEEP SAYING NO IS THE IRON-CLAD RULE OF CELEBRITIES, RIGHT?
THAT'S WHAT YOU TOLD ME SO KINDLY.
eek
....
HOW IRONIC. IF YOU HADN'T SAID THAT BEFORE...
...I WOULD'VE BELIEVED WHAT YOU SAID JUST NOW.
heh heh
BUT IT'S USELESS...
NO MATTER WHAT YOU SAY, YOU CAN'T FOOL ME ANY-MORE.

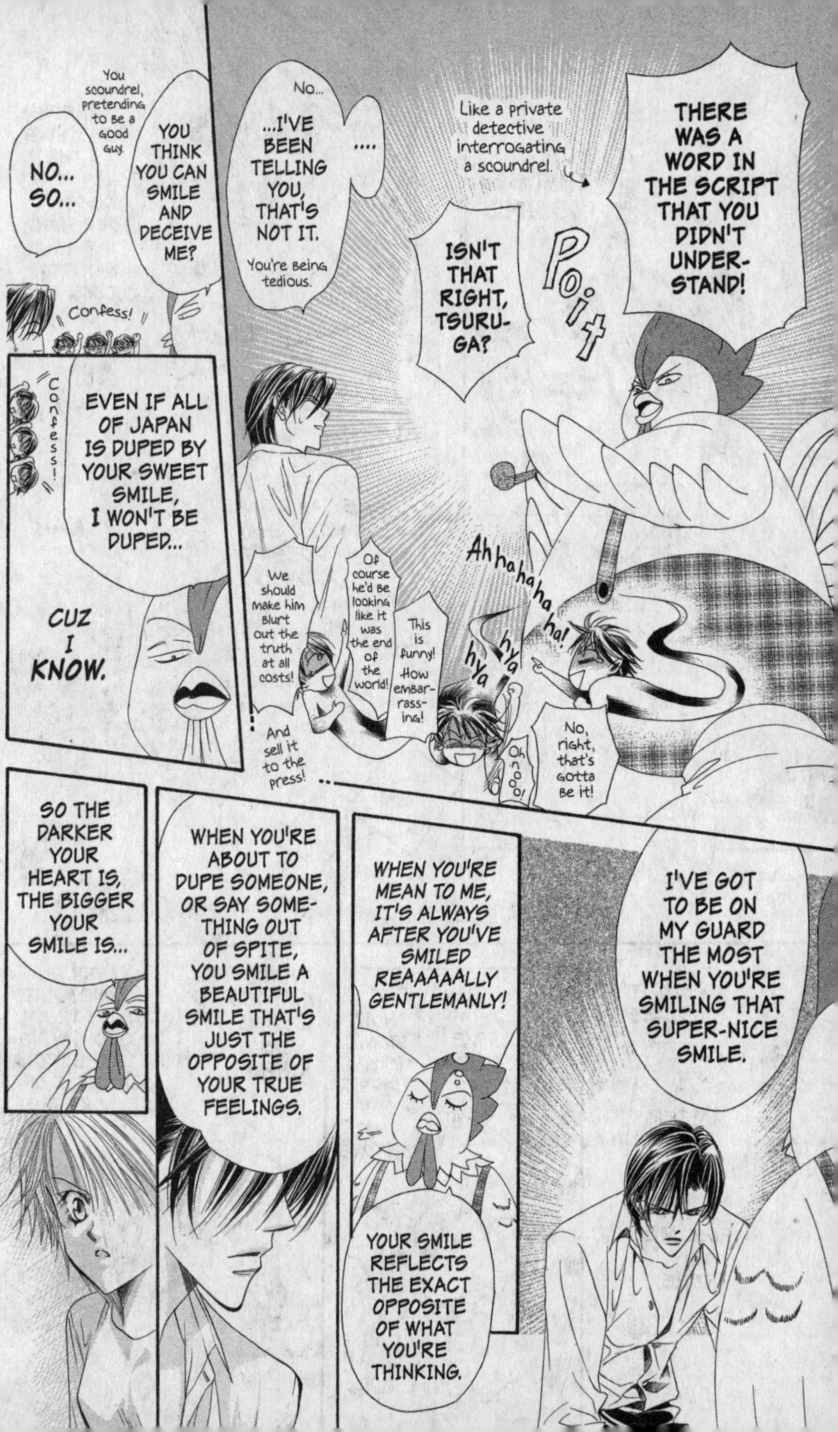
THERE WAS A WORD IN THE SCRIPT THAT YOU DIDN'T UNDER-STAND!
Like a private detective interrogating a scoundrel.
Poit
ISN'T THAT RIGHT, TSURUGA?
....
No...
...I'VE BEEN TELLING YOU, THAT'S NOT IT.
You're being tedious.
Ah ha ha ha ha!
hya hya
No, right, that's gotta be it!
Oh nooo!
This is funny! How embar-rass-ing!
Of course he'd be looking like it was the end of the world!
We should make him blurt out the truth at all costs!
And sell it to the press!
You scoundrel, pretending to be a good guy.
YOU THINK YOU CAN SMILE AND DECEIVE ME?
NO... SO...
Confess!
Confess!
EVEN IF ALL OF JAPAN IS DUPED BY YOUR SWEET SMILE, I WON'T BE DUPED...
CUZ I KNOW.
I'VE GOT TO BE ON MY GUARD THE MOST WHEN YOU'RE SMILING THAT SUPER-NICE SMILE.
WHEN YOU'RE MEAN TO ME, IT'S ALWAYS AFTER YOU'VE SMILED REAAAAALLY GENTLEMANLY!
YOUR SMILE REFLECTS THE EXACT OPPOSITE OF WHAT YOU'RE THINKING.
WHEN YOU'RE ABOUT TO DUPE SOMEONE, OR SAY SOME-THING OUT OF SPITE, YOU SMILE A BEAUTIFUL SMILE THAT'S JUST THE OPPOSITE OF YOUR TRUE FEELINGS.
SO THE DARKER YOUR HEART IS, THE BIGGER YOUR SMILE IS...

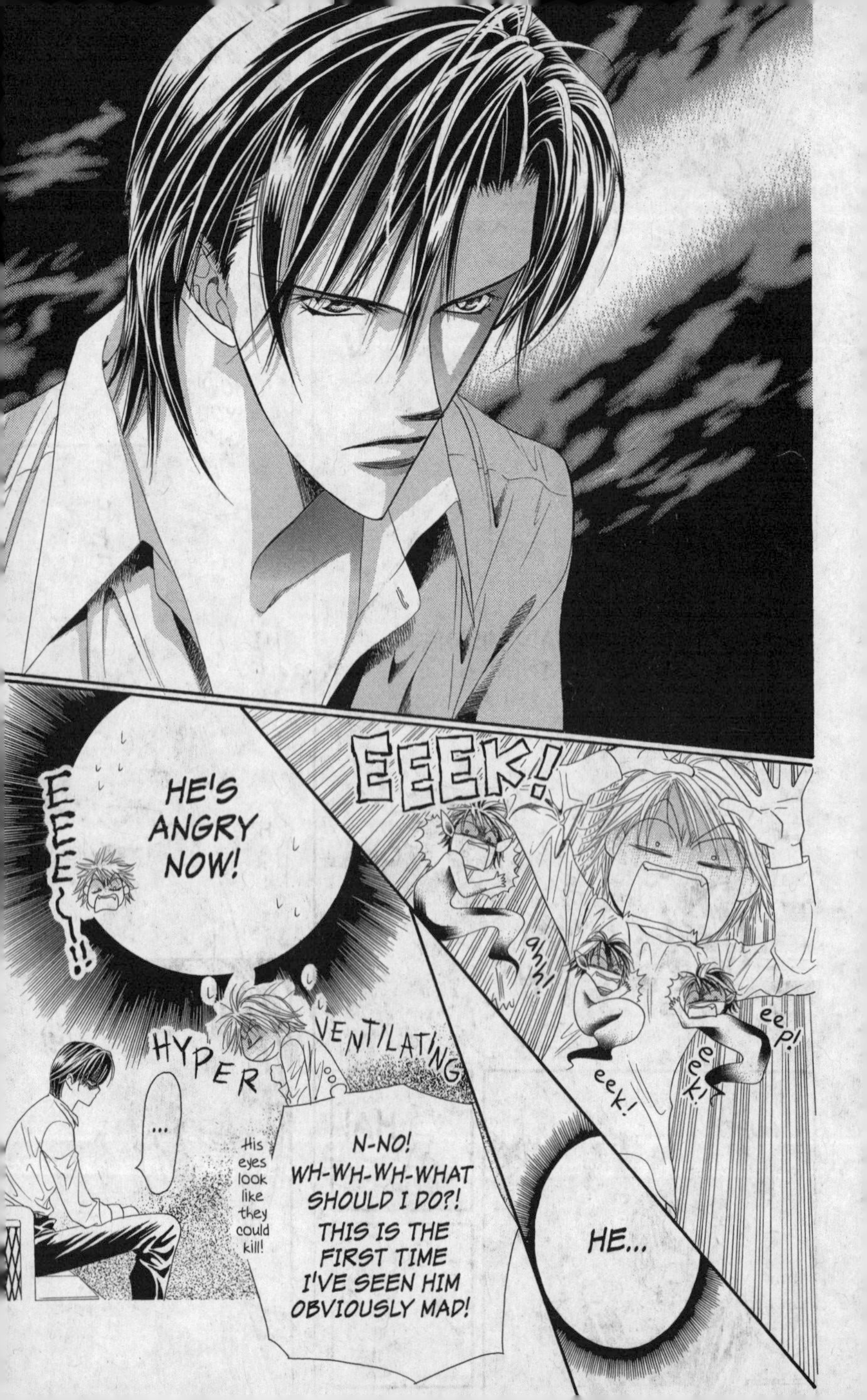
EEEK!
ahh!
eep!
eek!
eek!
HE...
HE'S ANGRY NOW!
EEEE~!!
HYPER VENTILATING
N-NO! WH-WH-WH-WHAT SHOULD I DO?! THIS IS THE FIRST TIME I'VE SEEN HIM OBVIOUSLY MAD!
His eyes look like they could kill!
...

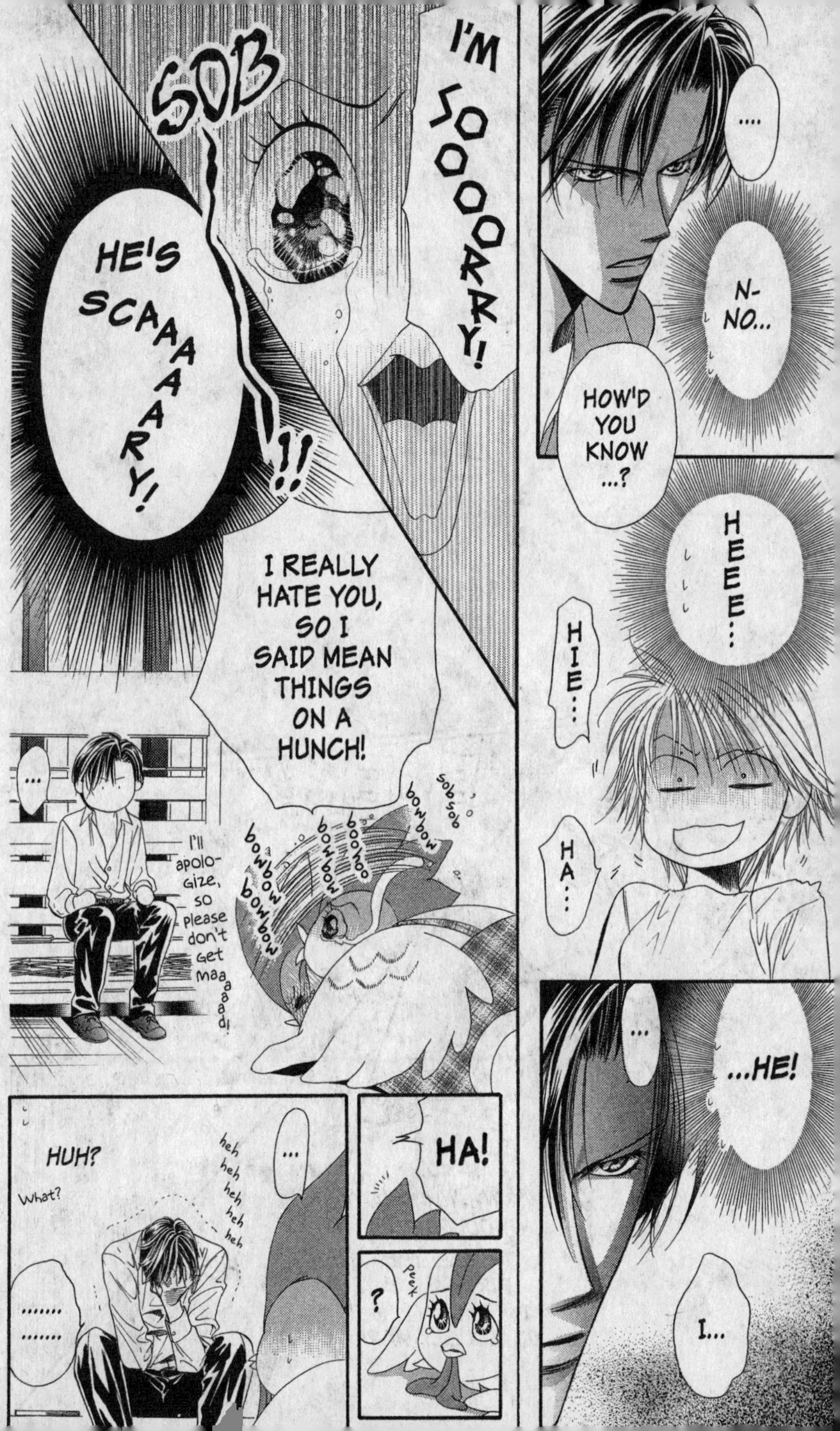
....
N-NO...
HOW'D YOU KNOW ...?
HEEE...
HIE...
HA...
...
...HE!
I...
SOB
I'M SOOOORRY!
HE'S SCAAAAARY!!
I REALLY HATE YOU, SO I SAID MEAN THINGS ON A HUNCH!
sob sob
bowbow boohoo bowbow bowbow bowbow
...
I'll apolo-gize, so please don't get maaaaad!
HA!
...
?
peek
HUH?
What?
heh heh heh heh heh
....
....

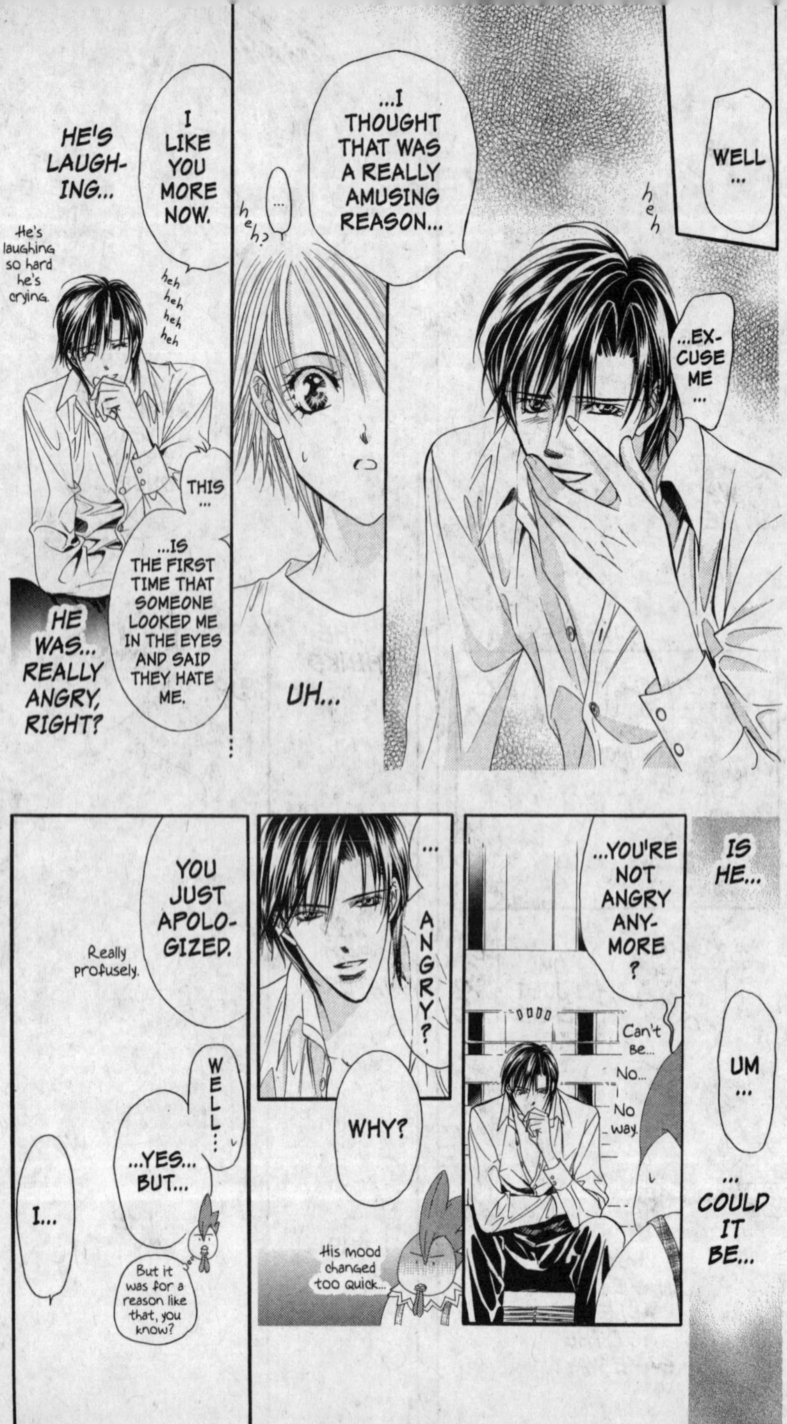
WELL...
heh heh
...EXCUSE ME...
...I THOUGHT THAT WAS A REALLY AMUSING REASON...
...
heh?
UH...
HE'S LAUGHING...
I LIKE YOU MORE NOW.
heh heh heh heh
He's laughing so hard he's crying.
THIS...
...IS THE FIRST TIME THAT SOMEONE LOOKED ME IN THE EYES AND SAID THEY HATE ME.
HE WAS... REALLY ANGRY, RIGHT?
IS HE...
UM...
...COULD IT BE...
...YOU'RE NOT ANGRY ANYMORE?
Can't be... No... No way.
...ANGRY?
WHY?
His mood changed too quick...
YOU JUST APOLOGIZED.
Really profusely.
WELL...
...YES... BUT...
But it was for a reason like that, you know?
I...

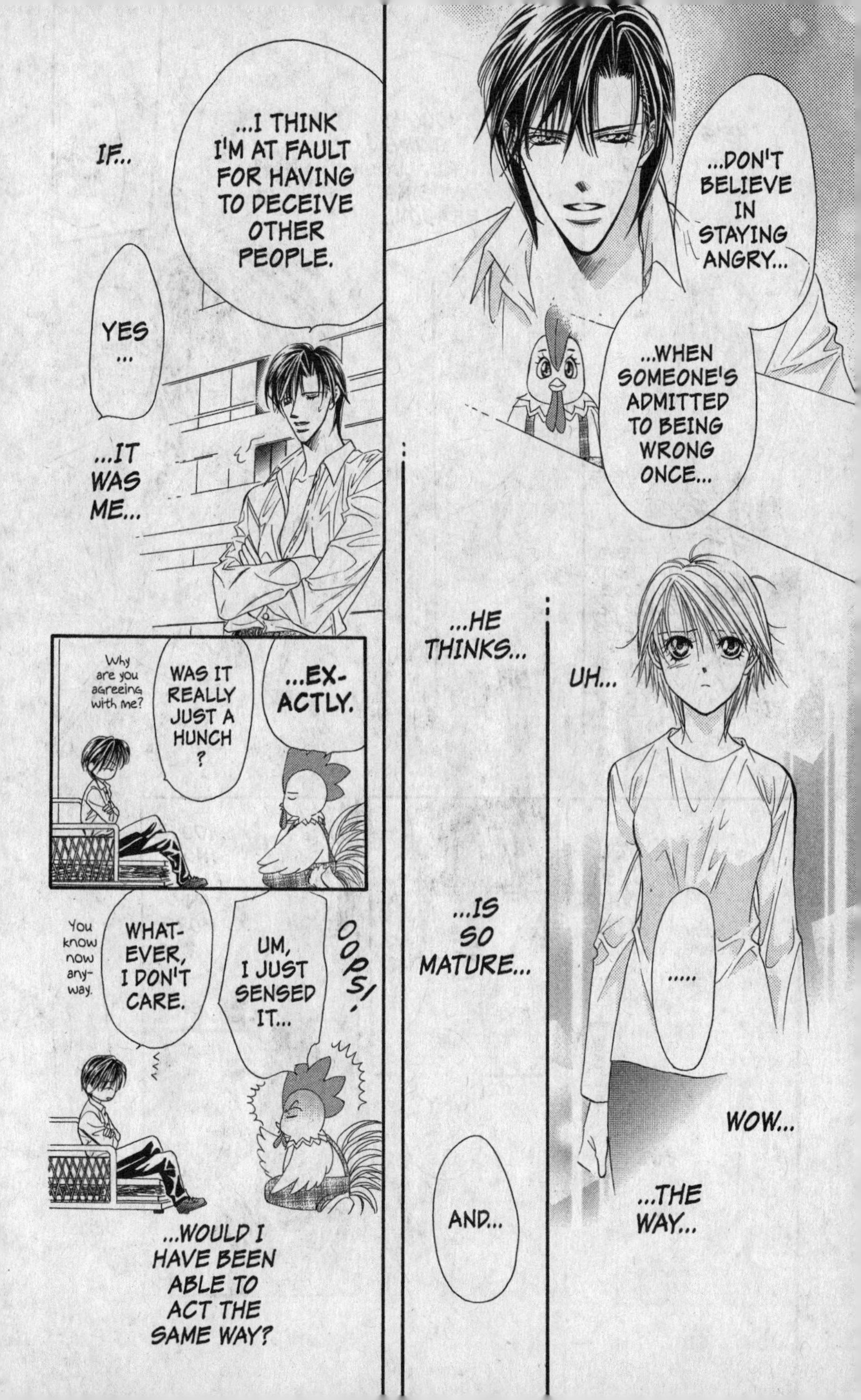
...DON'T BELIEVE IN STAYING ANGRY...
...WHEN SOMEONE'S ADMITTED TO BEING WRONG ONCE...
UH...
...HE THINKS...
.....
WOW...
...THE WAY...
...IS SO MATURE...
AND...
...I THINK I'M AT FAULT FOR HAVING TO DECEIVE OTHER PEOPLE.
IF...
YES...
...IT WAS ME...
...EX-ACTLY.
WAS IT REALLY JUST A HUNCH?
Why are you agreeing with me?
OOPS!
UM, I JUST SENSED IT...
WHATEVER, I DON'T CARE.
You know now anyway.
...WOULD I HAVE BEEN ABLE TO ACT THE SAME WAY?

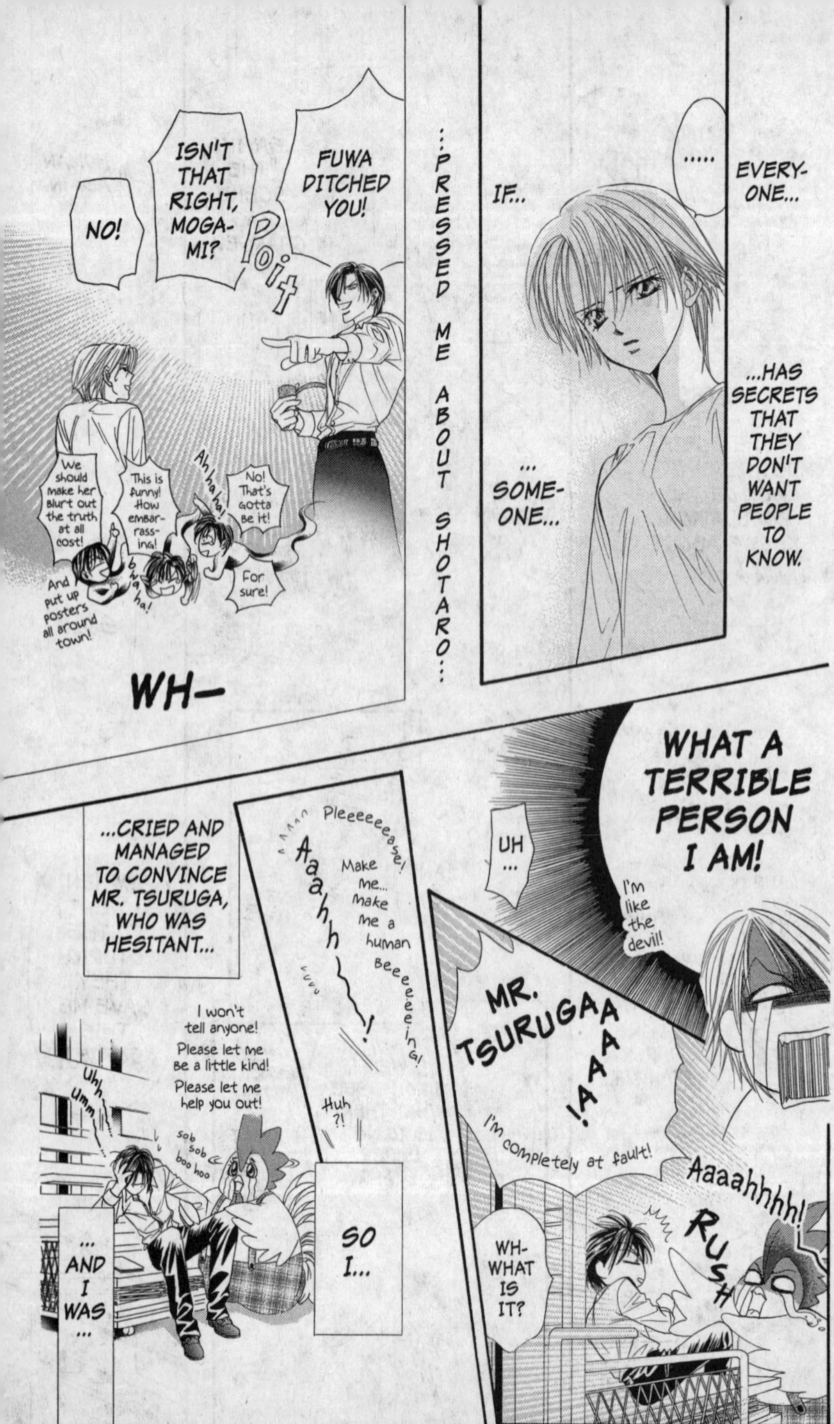
EVERY-ONE...
.....
IF...
...HAS SECRETS THAT THEY DON'T WANT PEOPLE TO KNOW.
...SOME-ONE...
...PRESSED ME ABOUT SHOTARO...
FUWA DITCHED YOU!
ISN'T THAT RIGHT, MOGA-MI?
Poit
NO!
No! That's gotta be it!
Ah ha ha!
For sure!
This is funny! How embar-rass-ing!
bwa ha ha!
We should make her blurt out the truth at all cost!
And put up posters all around town!
WH-
WHAT A TERRIBLE PERSON I AM!
UH...
I'm like the devil!
MR. TSURUGAAAAA!
I'm completely at fault!
Aaaahhhh!
RUSH
WH-WHAT IS IT?
Pleeeeeease!
Aaahh~!
Make me... make me a human beeeeeeing!
Huh?!
...CRIED AND MANAGED TO CONVINCE MR. TSURUGA, WHO WAS HESITANT...
SO I...
I won't tell anyone! Please let me be a little kind! Please let me help you out!
Uhh umm
sob sob boo hoo
...AND I WAS...

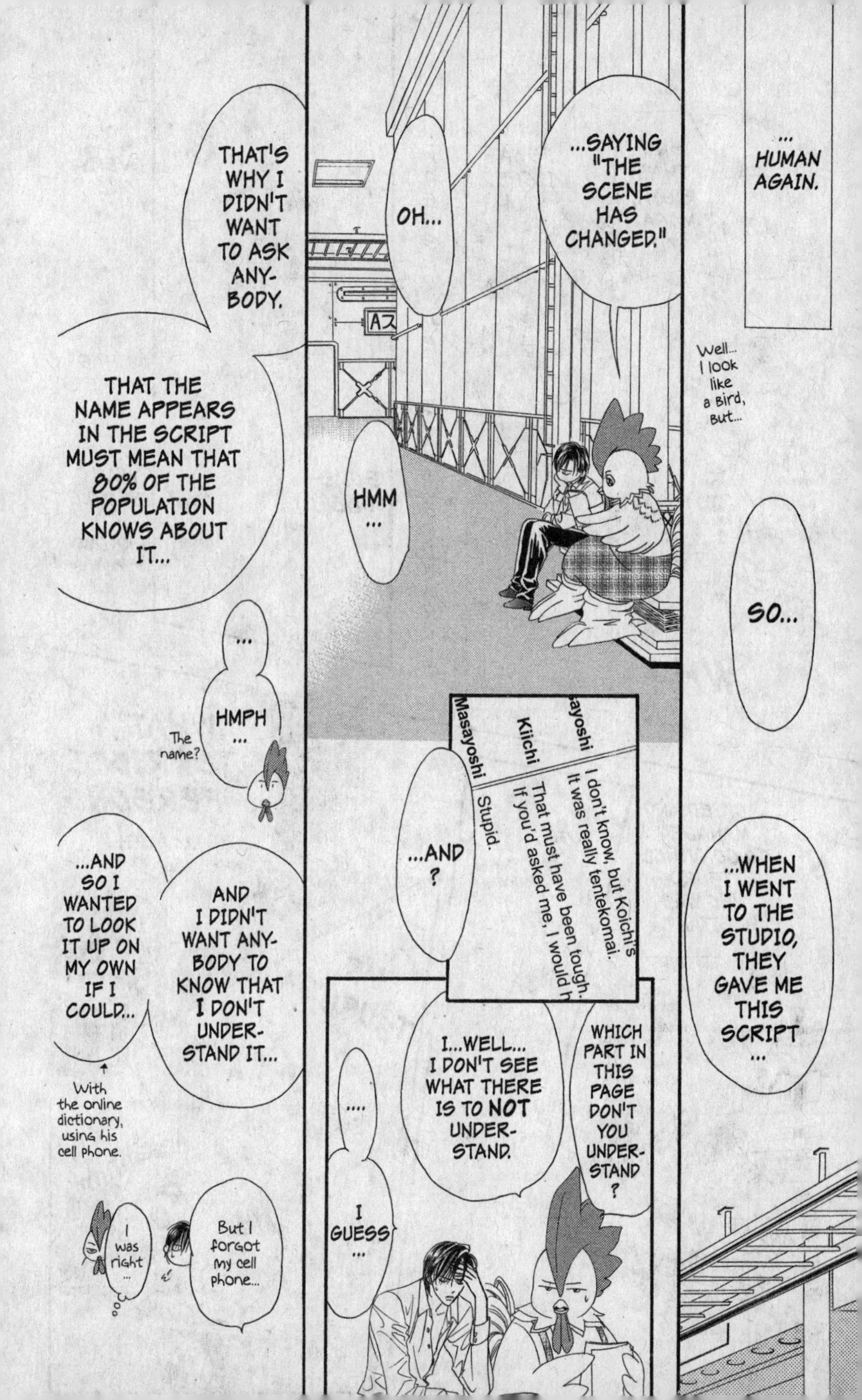
...HUMAN AGAIN.
Well... I look like a Bird, but...
SO...
...WHEN I WENT TO THE STUDIO, THEY GAVE ME THIS SCRIPT...
...SAYING "THE SCENE HAS CHANGED."
OH...
HMM...
sayoshi I don't know, but Koichi's It was really tentekomai.
Kiichi That must have been tough. If you'd asked me, I would h
Masayoshi Stupid.
...AND ?
WHICH PART IN THIS PAGE DON'T YOU UNDERSTAND?
I...WELL... I DON'T SEE WHAT THERE IS TO NOT UNDERSTAND.
....
I GUESS...
THAT'S WHY I DIDN'T WANT TO ASK ANYBODY.
THAT THE NAME APPEARS IN THE SCRIPT MUST MEAN THAT 80% OF THE POPULATION KNOWS ABOUT IT...
...
HMPH...
The name?
AND I DIDN'T WANT ANYBODY TO KNOW THAT I DON'T UNDERSTAND IT...
...AND SO I WANTED TO LOOK IT UP ON MY OWN IF I COULD...
With the online dictionary, using his cell phone.
But I forgot my cell phone...
I was right...

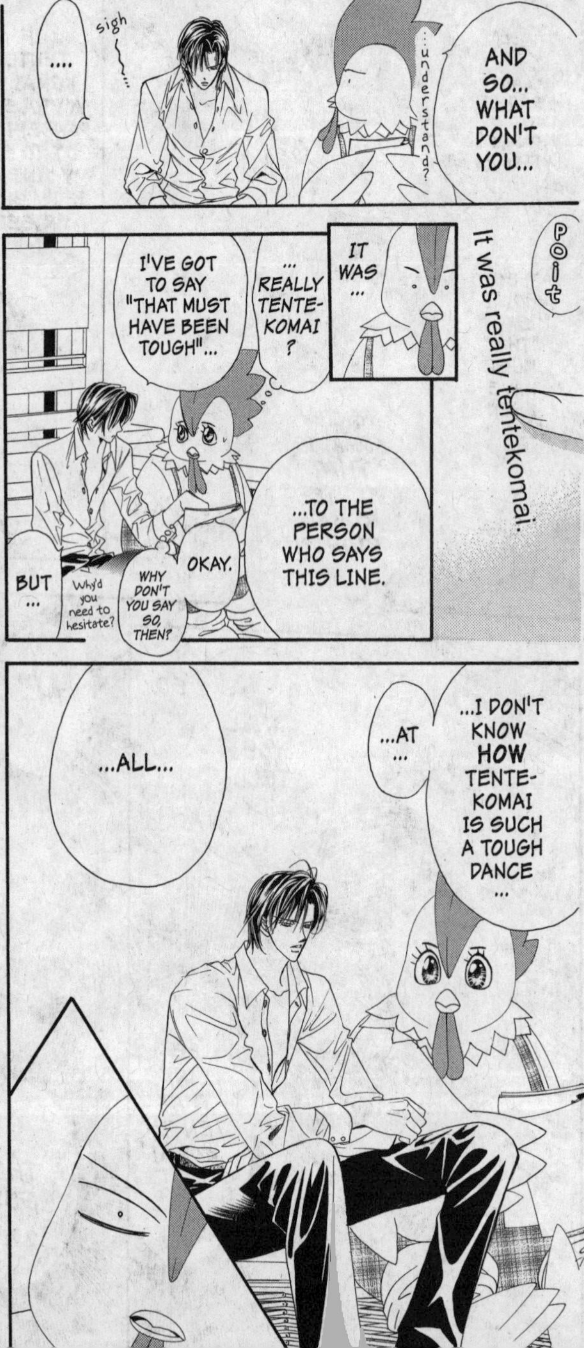
AND SO... WHAT DON'T YOU...
...understand?
sigh
....
Poit
It was really tentekomai.
IT WAS...
...REALLY TENTE-KOMAI?
I'VE GOT TO SAY "THAT MUST HAVE BEEN TOUGH"...
...TO THE PERSON WHO SAYS THIS LINE.
OKAY.
WHY DON'T YOU SAY SO, THEN?
Why'd you need to hesitate?
BUT...
...I DON'T KNOW HOW TENTE-KOMAI IS SUCH A TOUGH DANCE...
...AT...
...ALL...

History

The name is "Bo" by process of association. "Kimagure" of "Kimagure Rock" → Kimagure (Whimsical) → Free and easy → Wanderer → Bo. And for me, gives me this image...

S-Samurai?

No, this is a ronin... a ronin who always has rough-looking eyes...

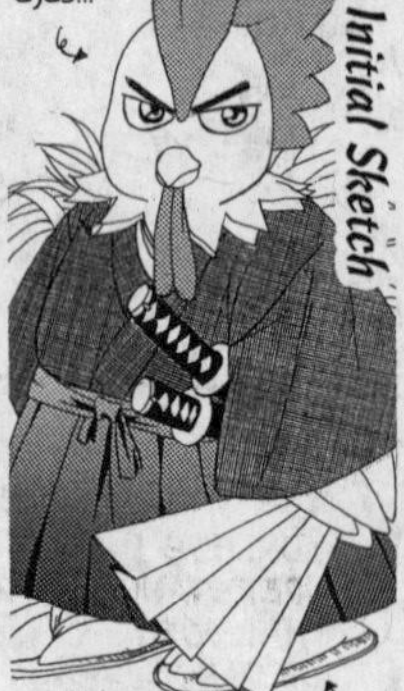

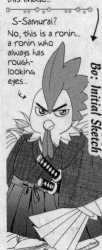

Bo: Initial Sketch

And his own harisen to put a rough punch line in no matter how famous the guest is.

However...this wasn't cute enough to be a mascot of a show, so the visuals changed to the current one...

Bo became a hen in the same way. Wanderer → Wandering in the direction the wind blows → Weathercock → Hen.

So actually, when I was working on my storyboards, the name wasn't "Bo" but "Midori" from the weathercock. But I think "Bo" suits it better now.

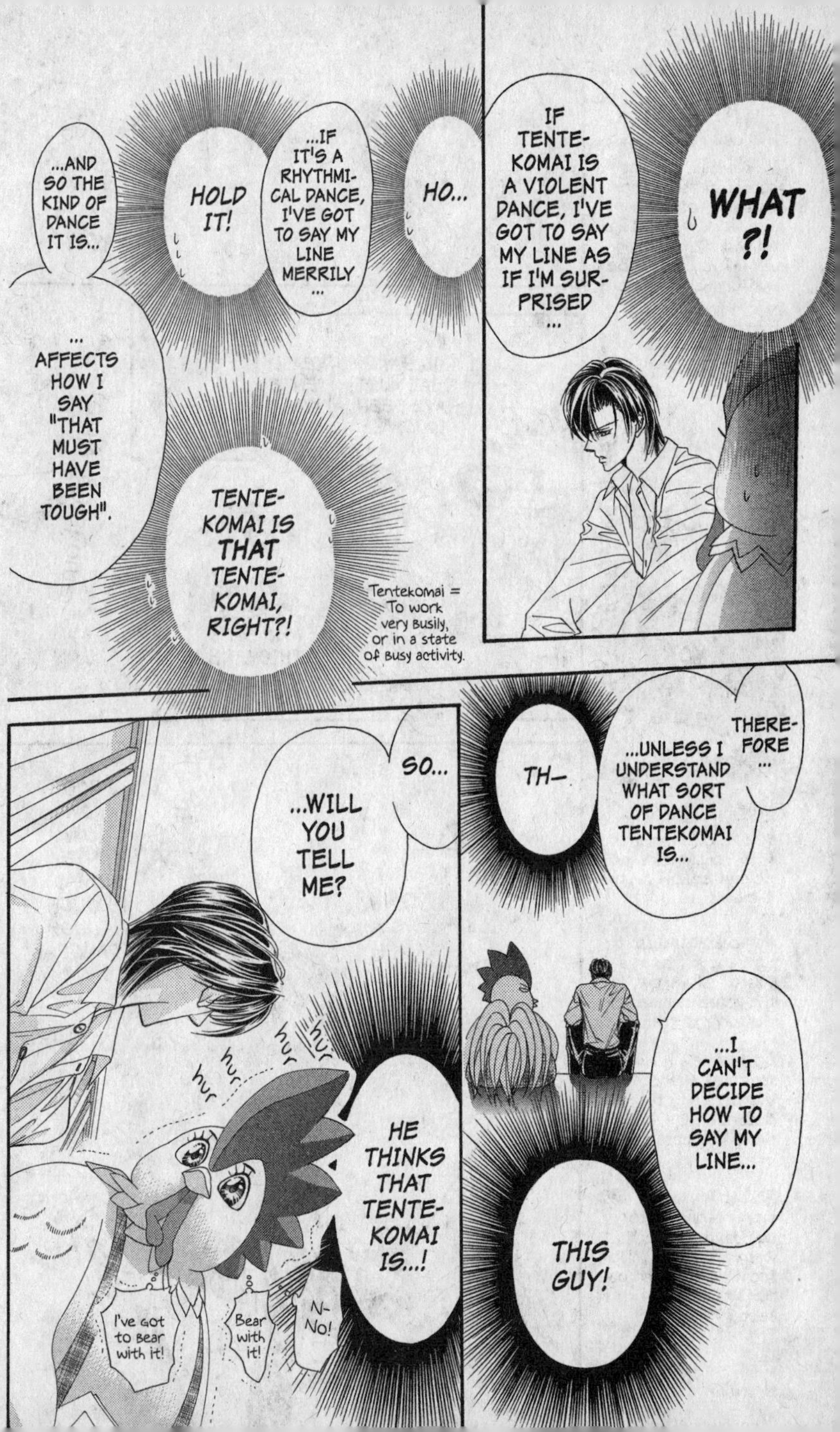
WHAT?!
IF TENTE-KOMAI IS A VIOLENT DANCE, I'VE GOT TO SAY MY LINE AS IF I'M SURPRISED...
HO...
...IF IT'S A RHYTHMICAL DANCE, I'VE GOT TO SAY MY LINE MERRILY...
HOLD IT!
...AND SO THE KIND OF DANCE IT IS...
...AFFECTS HOW I SAY "THAT MUST HAVE BEEN TOUGH".
TENTE-KOMAI IS THAT TENTE-KOMAI, RIGHT?!
Tentekomai = To work very Busily, or in a state of Busy activity.
THEREFORE...
...UNLESS I UNDERSTAND WHAT SORT OF DANCE TENTEKOMAI IS...
TH—
...I CAN'T DECIDE HOW TO SAY MY LINE...
THIS GUY!
SO...
...WILL YOU TELL ME?
hur hur hur hur
HE THINKS THAT TENTE-KOMAI IS...!
N-No!
Bear with it!
I've Got to Bear with it!

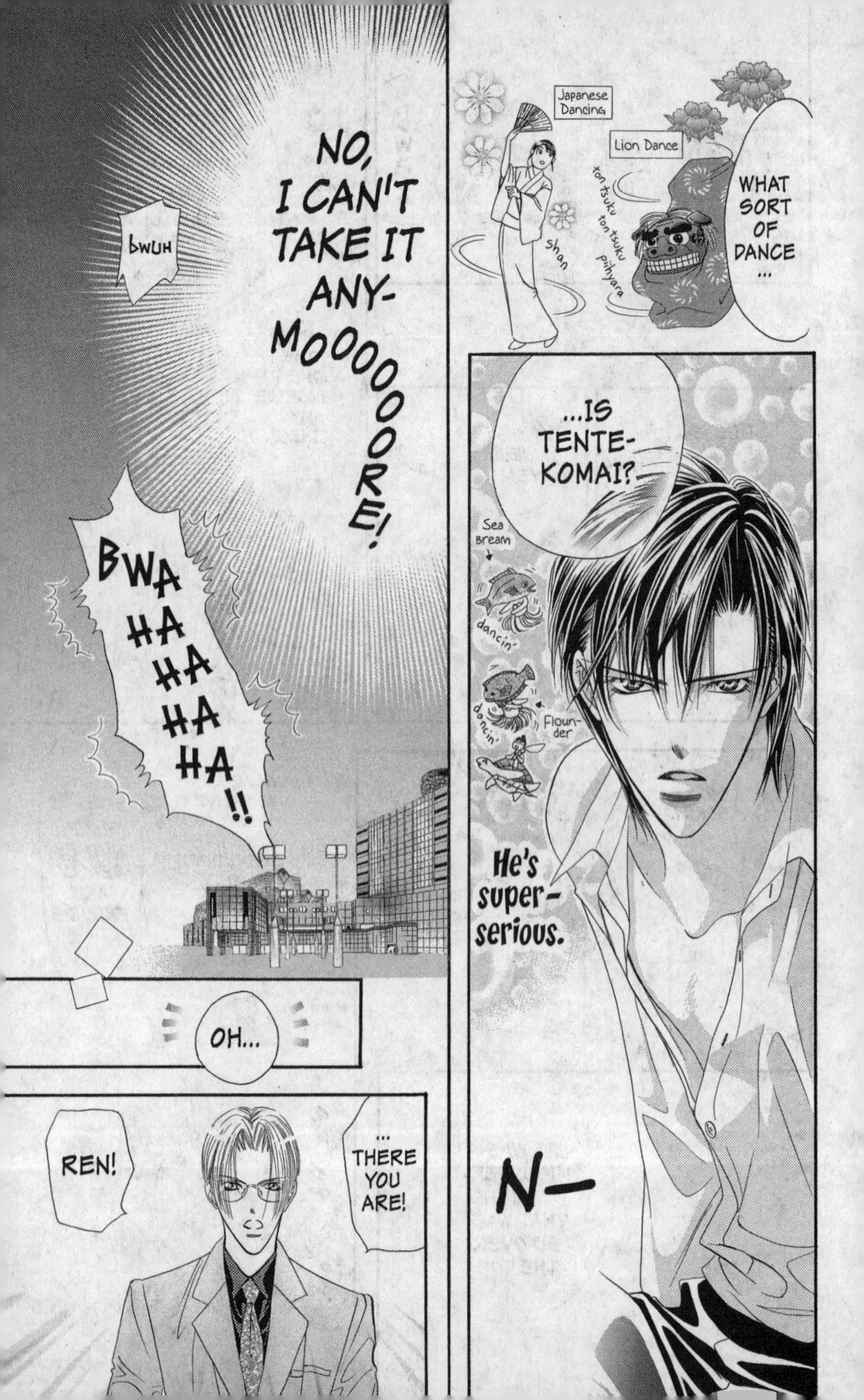
WHAT SORT OF DANCE ...
Lion Dance
ton tsuku ton tsuku piihyara
Japanese Dancing
shan
...IS TENTE-KOMAI?
Sea Bream
dancin'
Flounder
dancin'
He's super-serious.
N—
NO, I CAN'T TAKE IT ANY-MOOOOOOORE!
bwuh
BWAHAHAHAHAHA!!
OH...
... THERE YOU ARE!
REN!

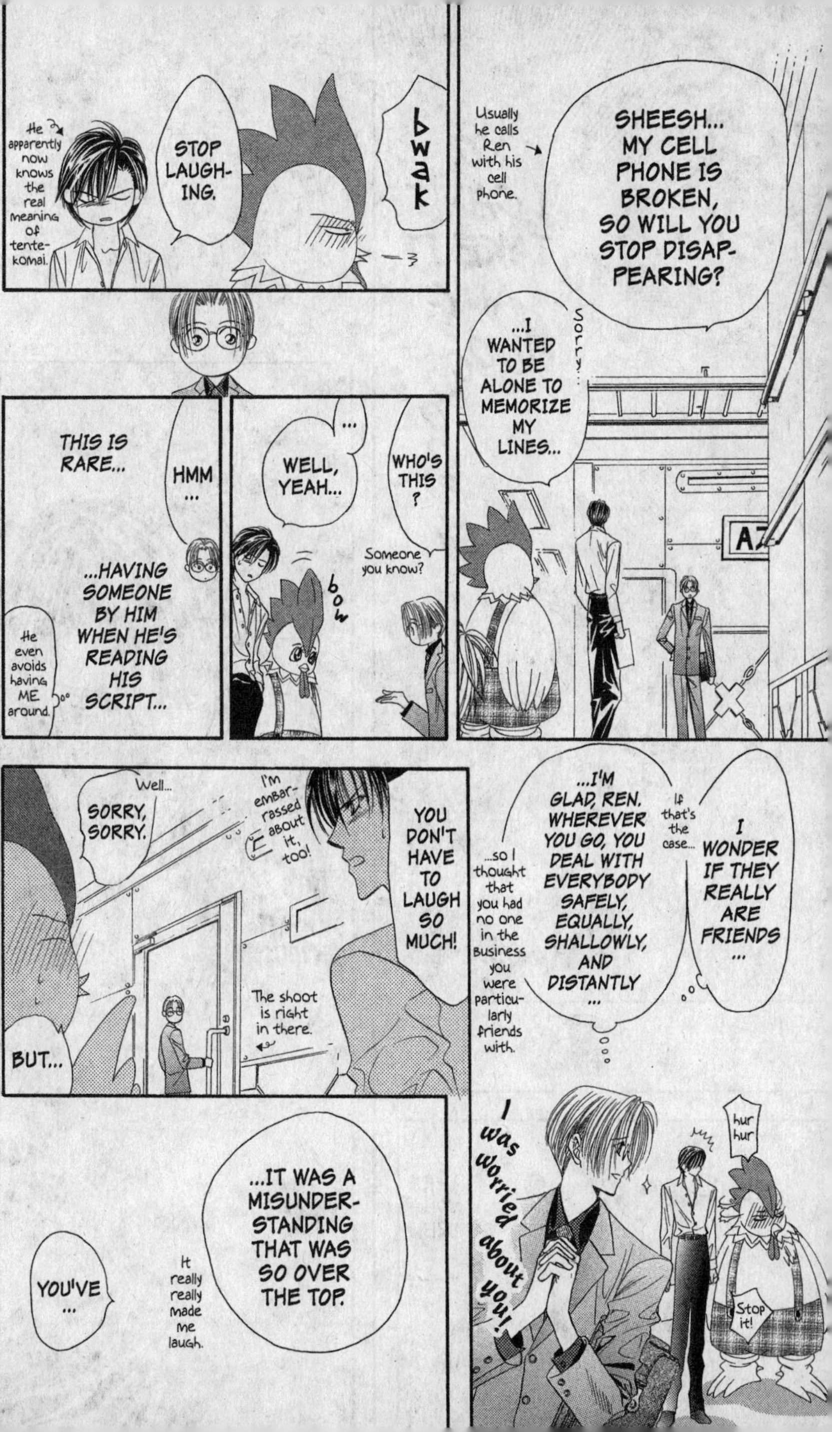
Usually he calls Ren with his cell phone.
SHEESH... MY CELL PHONE IS BROKEN, SO WILL YOU STOP DISAPPEARING?
Sorry...
...I WANTED TO BE ALONE TO MEMORIZE MY LINES...
He apparently now knows the real meaning of tentekomai.
bwak
STOP LAUGHING.
WHO'S THIS?
Someone you know?
...
WELL, YEAH...
bow
HMM...
THIS IS RARE...
...HAVING SOMEONE BY HIM WHEN HE'S READING HIS SCRIPT...
He even avoids having ME around.
I WONDER IF THEY REALLY ARE FRIENDS...
If that's the case...
...I'M GLAD, REN. WHEREVER YOU GO, YOU DEAL WITH EVERYBODY SAFELY, EQUALLY, SHALLOWLY, AND DISTANTLY...
...so I thought that you had no one in the business you were particularly friends with.
YOU DON'T HAVE TO LAUGH SO MUCH!
I'm embarrassed about it, too!
Well...
SORRY, SORRY.
The shoot is right in there.
BUT...
hur hur
Stop it!
I was worried about you!
...IT WAS A MISUNDERSTANDING THAT WAS SO OVER THE TOP.
It really really made me laugh.
YOU'VE...

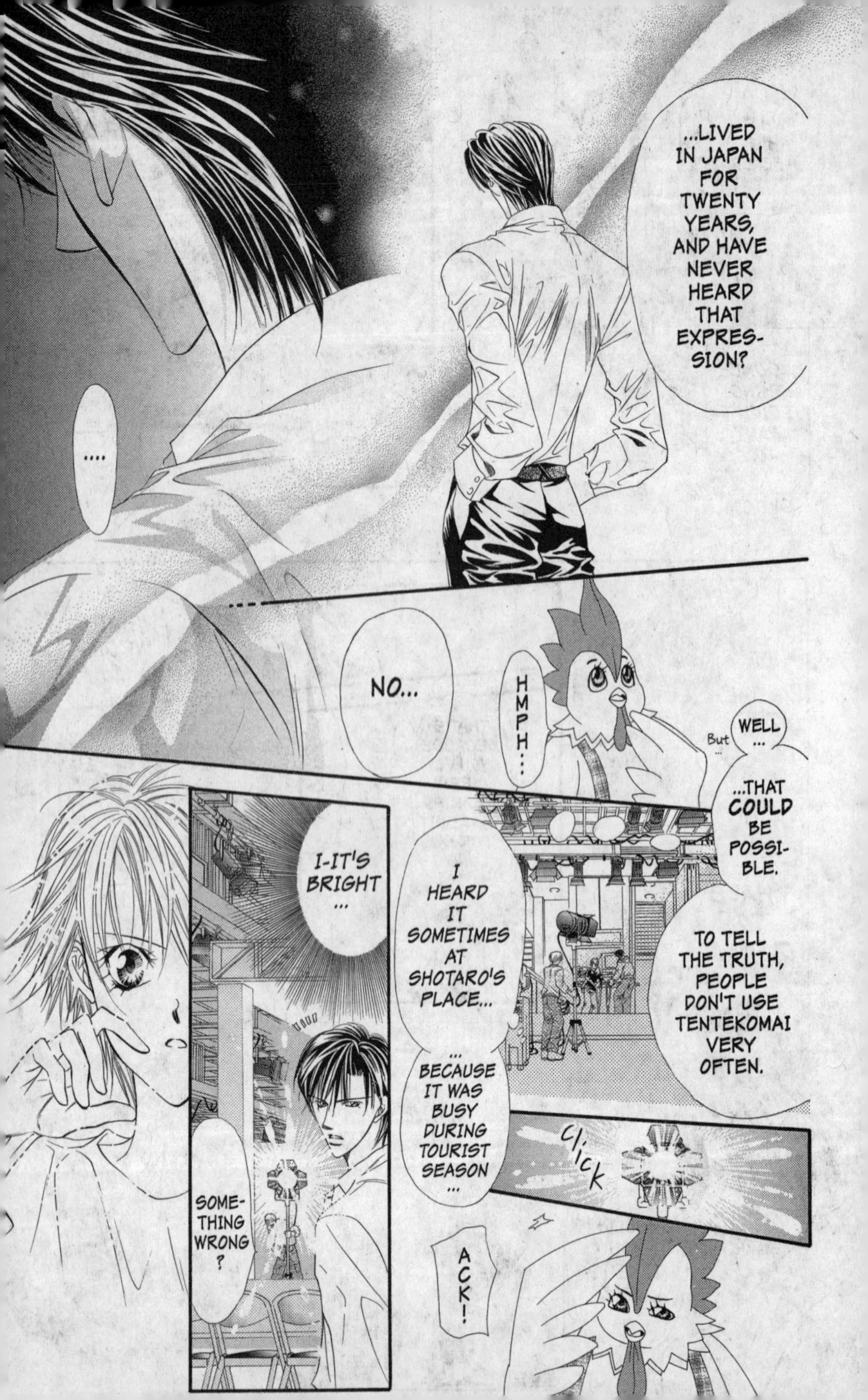
...LIVED IN JAPAN FOR TWENTY YEARS, AND HAVE NEVER HEARD THAT EXPRESSION?
....
NO...
HMPH...
But...
WELL...
...THAT COULD BE POSSIBLE.
TO TELL THE TRUTH, PEOPLE DON'T USE TENTEKOMAI VERY OFTEN.
I HEARD IT SOMETIMES AT SHOTARO'S PLACE...
...BECAUSE IT WAS BUSY DURING TOURIST SEASON...
CLICK
ACK!
I-IT'S BRIGHT...
SOME-THING WRONG?

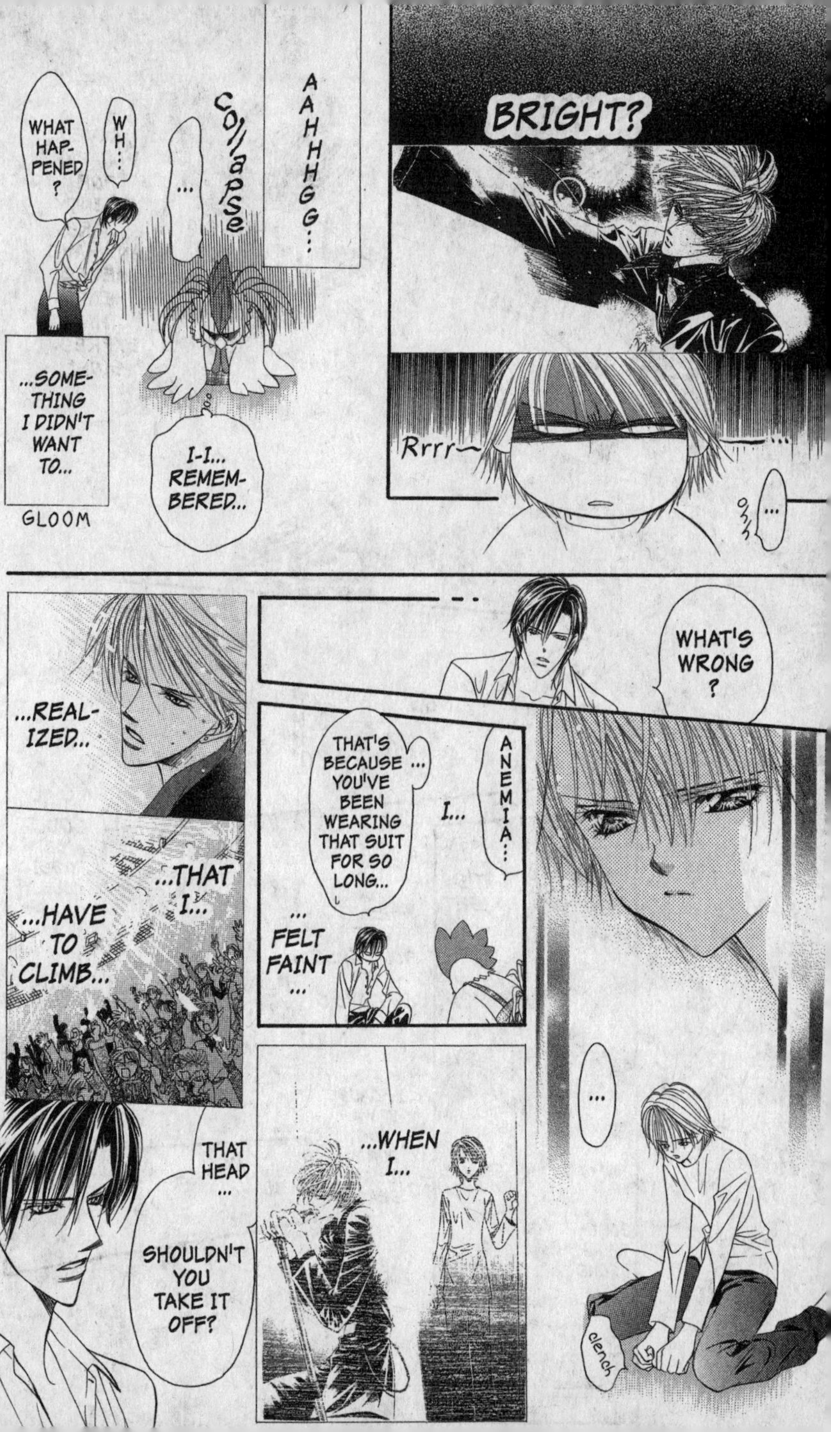
BRIGHT?
Rrrr~
...
AAHHHGG...
Collapse
...
I-I... REMEMBERED...
WH...
WHAT HAPPENED?
...SOMETHING I DIDN'T WANT TO...
GLOOM
WHAT'S WRONG?
...
clench
ANEMIA...
I...
THAT'S BECAUSE YOU'VE BEEN WEARING THAT SUIT FOR SO LONG...
...FELT FAINT...
...WHEN I...
...REALIZED...
...THAT I...
...HAVE TO CLIMB...
THAT HEAD...
SHOULDN'T YOU TAKE IT OFF?

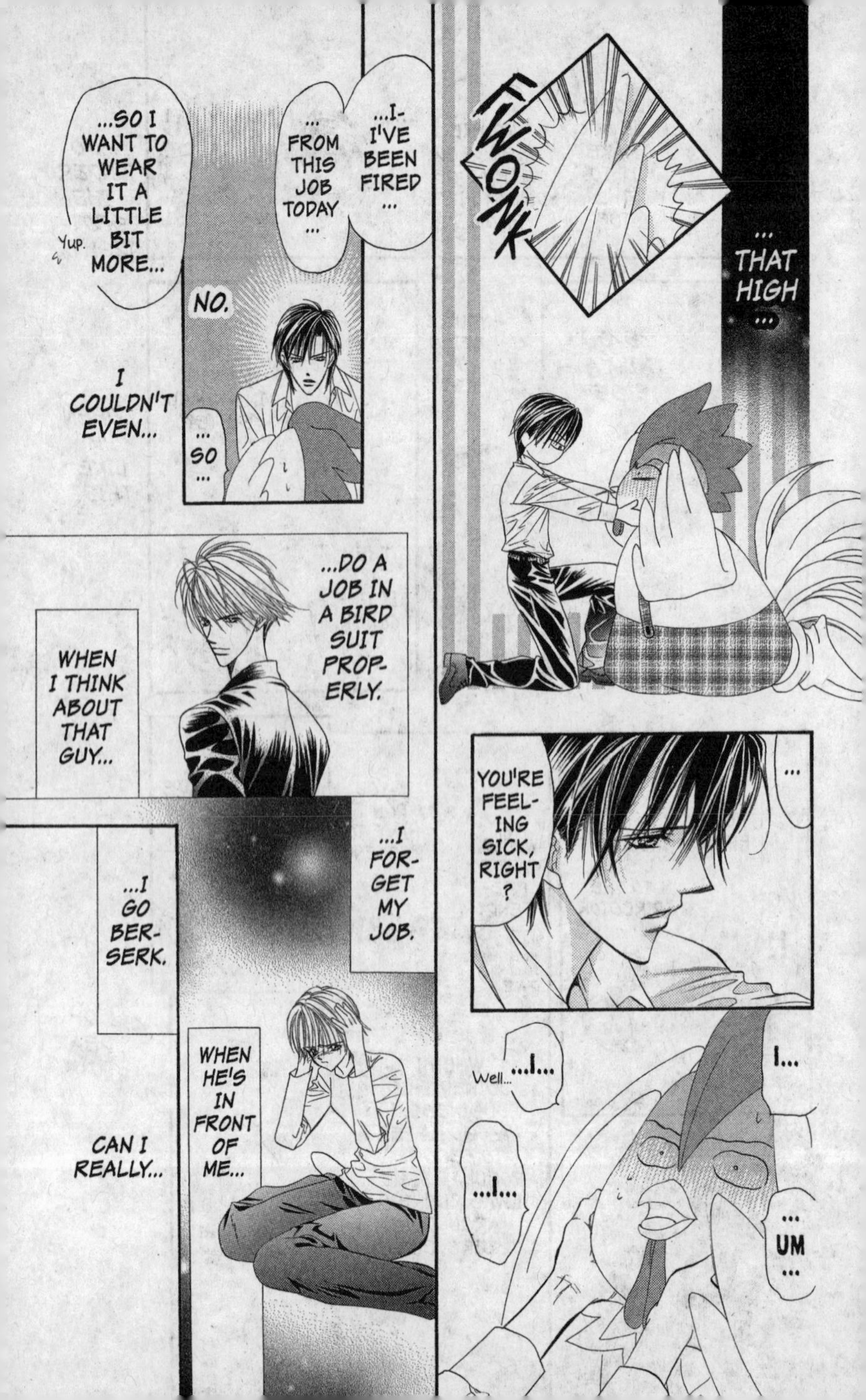
...THAT HIGH...
FWONK
...
YOU'RE FEELING SICK, RIGHT?
I...
Well... ...I...
...I...
...UM...
...I- I'VE BEEN FIRED...
...FROM THIS JOB TODAY...
NO.
...SO...
...SO I WANT TO WEAR IT A LITTLE BIT MORE...
Yup.
I COULDN'T EVEN...
...DO A JOB IN A BIRD SUIT PROPERLY.
WHEN I THINK ABOUT THAT GUY...
...I FORGET MY JOB.
...I GO BERSERK.
WHEN HE'S IN FRONT OF ME...
CAN I REALLY...

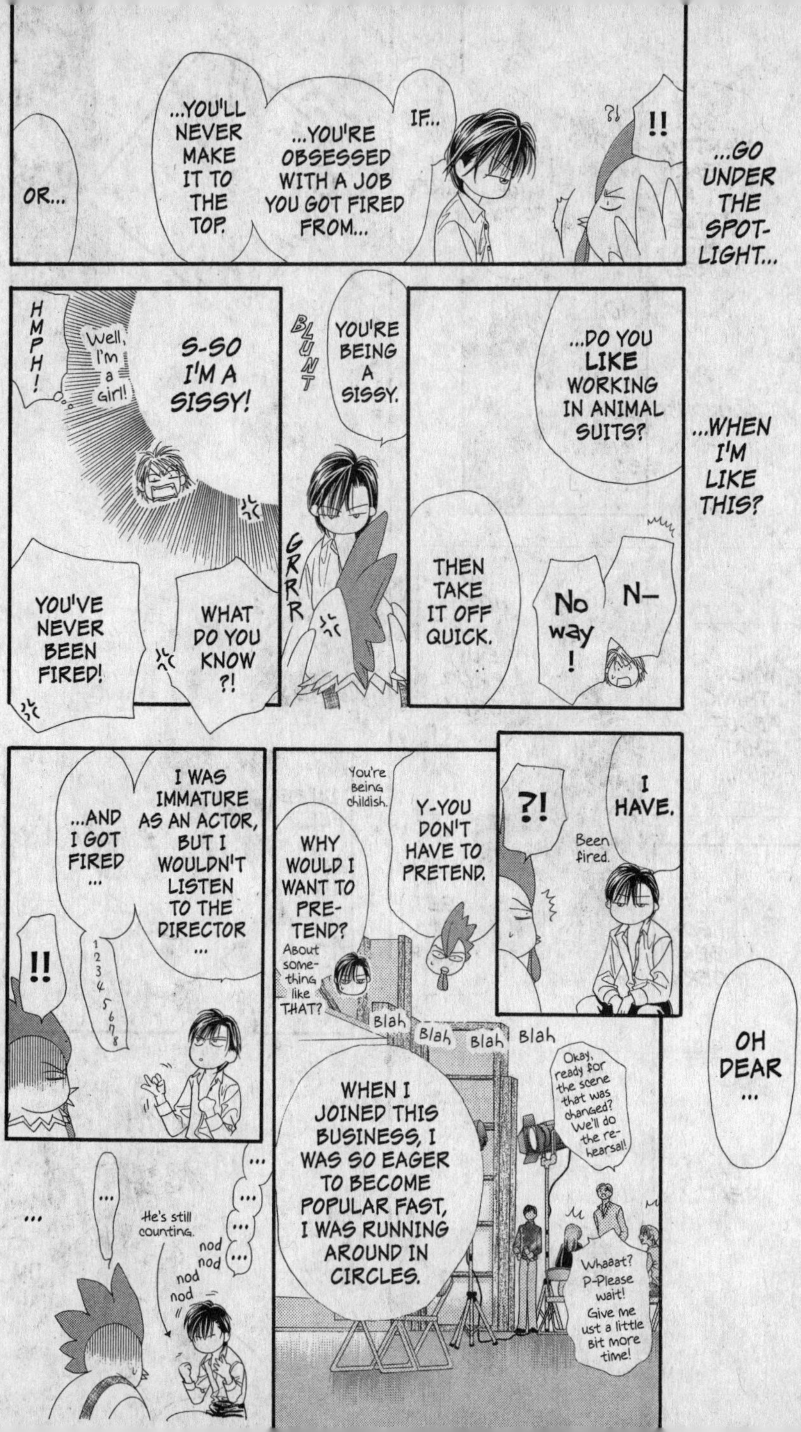
...GO UNDER THE SPOT-LIGHT...
!!
?!
IF...
...YOU'RE OBSESSED WITH A JOB YOU GOT FIRED FROM...
...YOU'LL NEVER MAKE IT TO THE TOP.
OR...
...WHEN I'M LIKE THIS?
...DO YOU LIKE WORKING IN ANIMAL SUITS?
N—
No way!
THEN TAKE IT OFF QUICK.
YOU'RE BEING A SISSY.
BLUNT
GRRR
S-SO I'M A SISSY!
Well, I'm a girl!
HMPH!
WHAT DO YOU KNOW?!
YOU'VE NEVER BEEN FIRED!
I HAVE.
Been fired.
?!
You're being childish.
Y-YOU DON'T HAVE TO PRETEND.
WHY WOULD I WANT TO PRETEND?
About something like THAT?
I WAS IMMATURE AS AN ACTOR, BUT I WOULDN'T LISTEN TO THE DIRECTOR...
...AND I GOT FIRED...
1 2 3 4 5 6 7 8
!!
OH DEAR...
Blah Blah Blah Blah
Okay, ready for the scene that was changed? We'll do the re-hearsal!
Whaaat? P-Please wait! Give me ust a little bit more time!
WHEN I JOINED THIS BUSINESS, I WAS SO EAGER TO BECOME POPULAR FAST, I WAS RUNNING AROUND IN CIRCLES.
...
...
...
...
He's still counting.
nod nod nod nod
...

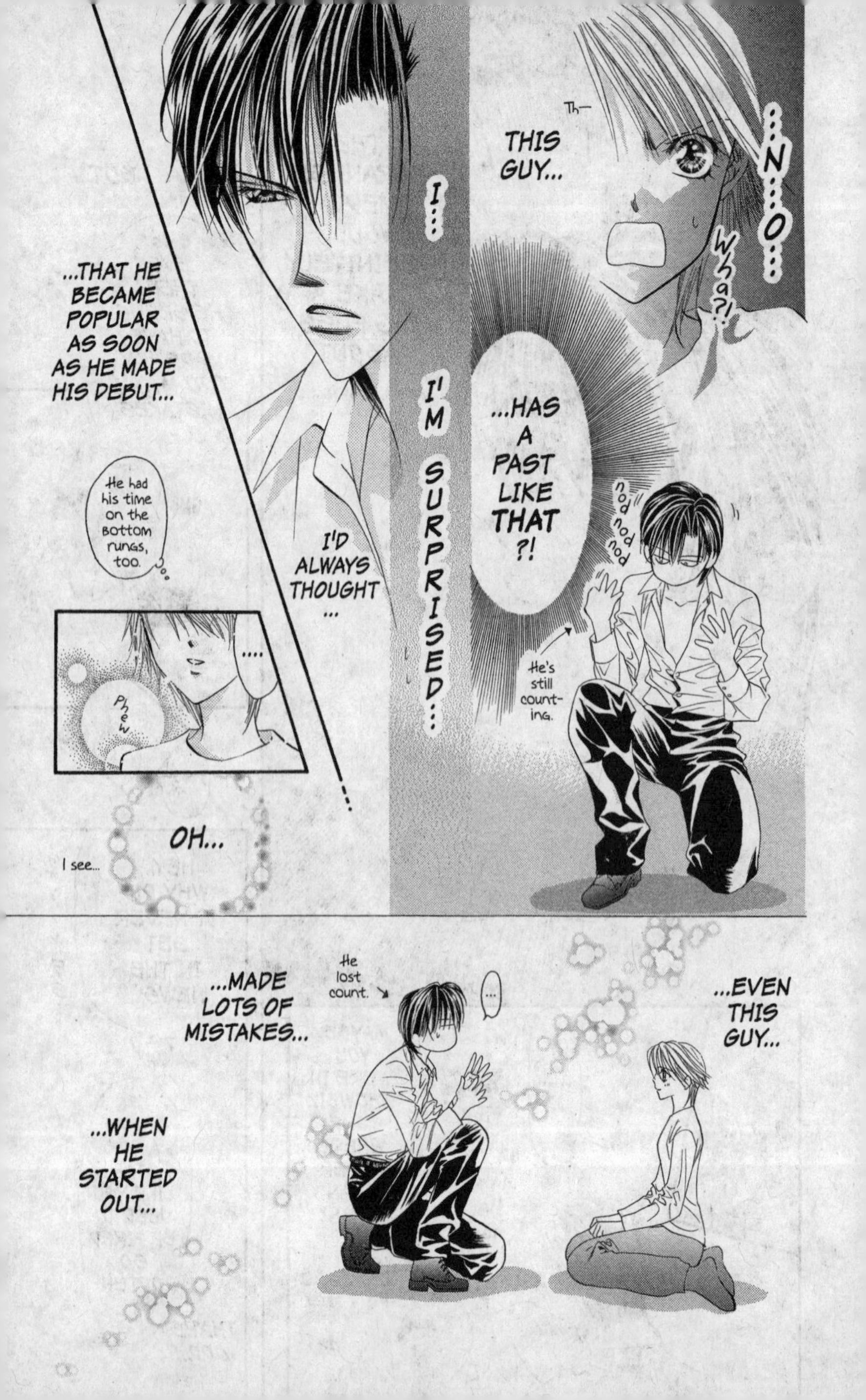
...N...O...
Wha?!
Th—
THIS GUY...
...HAS A PAST LIKE THAT?!
nod nod nod
He's still counting.
I...
I'M SURPRISED...
I'D ALWAYS THOUGHT...
...THAT HE BECAME POPULAR AS SOON AS HE MADE HIS DEBUT...
He had his time on the bottom rungs, too.
....
Phew
OH...
I see...
...EVEN THIS GUY...
...
He lost count.
...MADE LOTS OF MISTAKES...
...WHEN HE STARTED OUT...

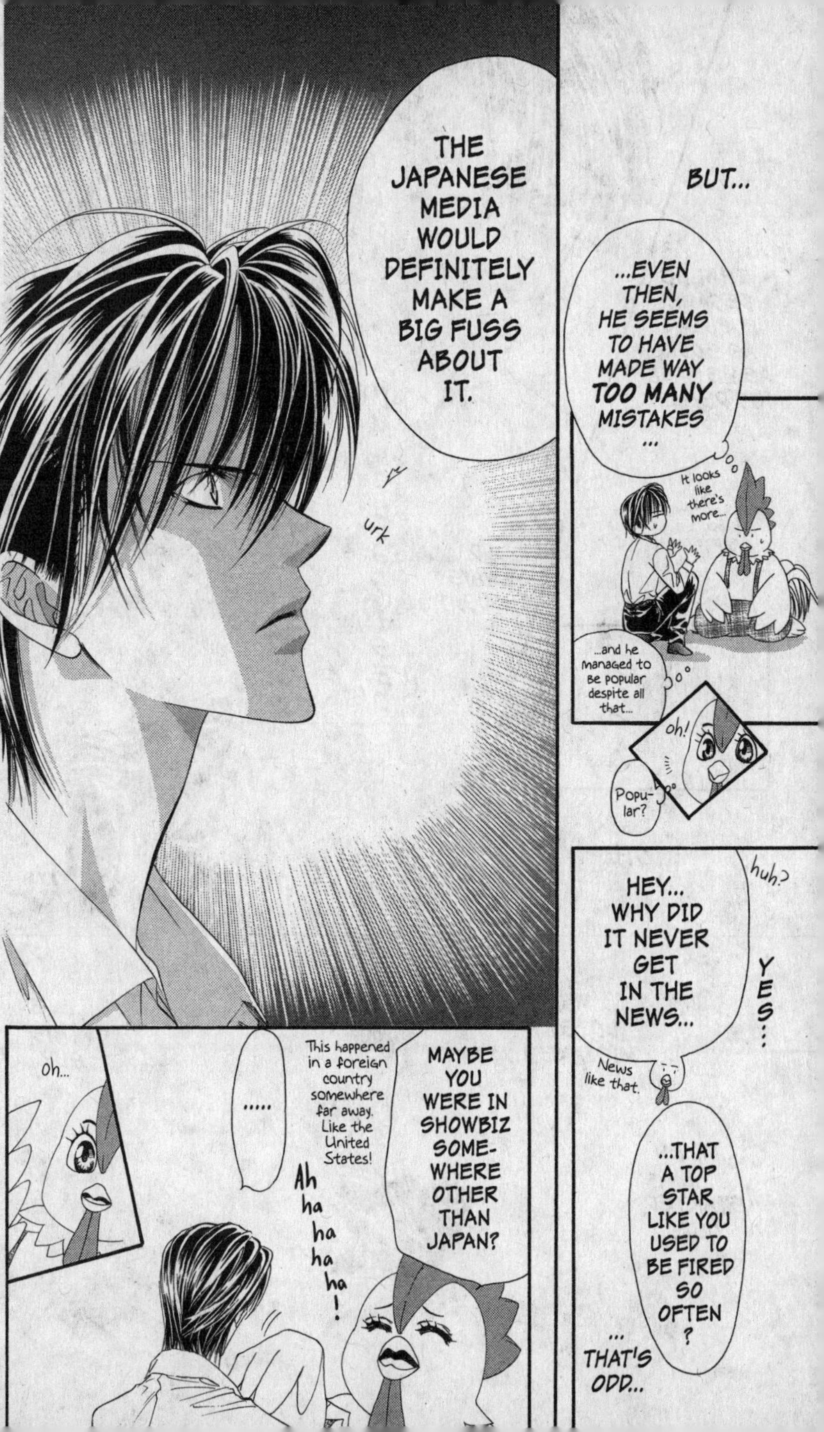
BUT...
...EVEN THEN, HE SEEMS TO HAVE MADE WAY TOO MANY MISTAKES...
It looks like there's more...
...and he managed to be popular despite all that...
oh!
Popu-lar?
huh?
HEY... WHY DID IT NEVER GET IN THE NEWS...
YES...
News like that.
...THAT A TOP STAR LIKE YOU USED TO BE FIRED SO OFTEN?
...THAT'S ODD...
THE JAPANESE MEDIA WOULD DEFINITELY MAKE A BIG FUSS ABOUT IT.
urk
MAYBE YOU WERE IN SHOWBIZ SOMEWHERE OTHER THAN JAPAN?
This happened in a foreign country somewhere far away. Like the United States!
Ah ha ha ha ha!
.....
oh...

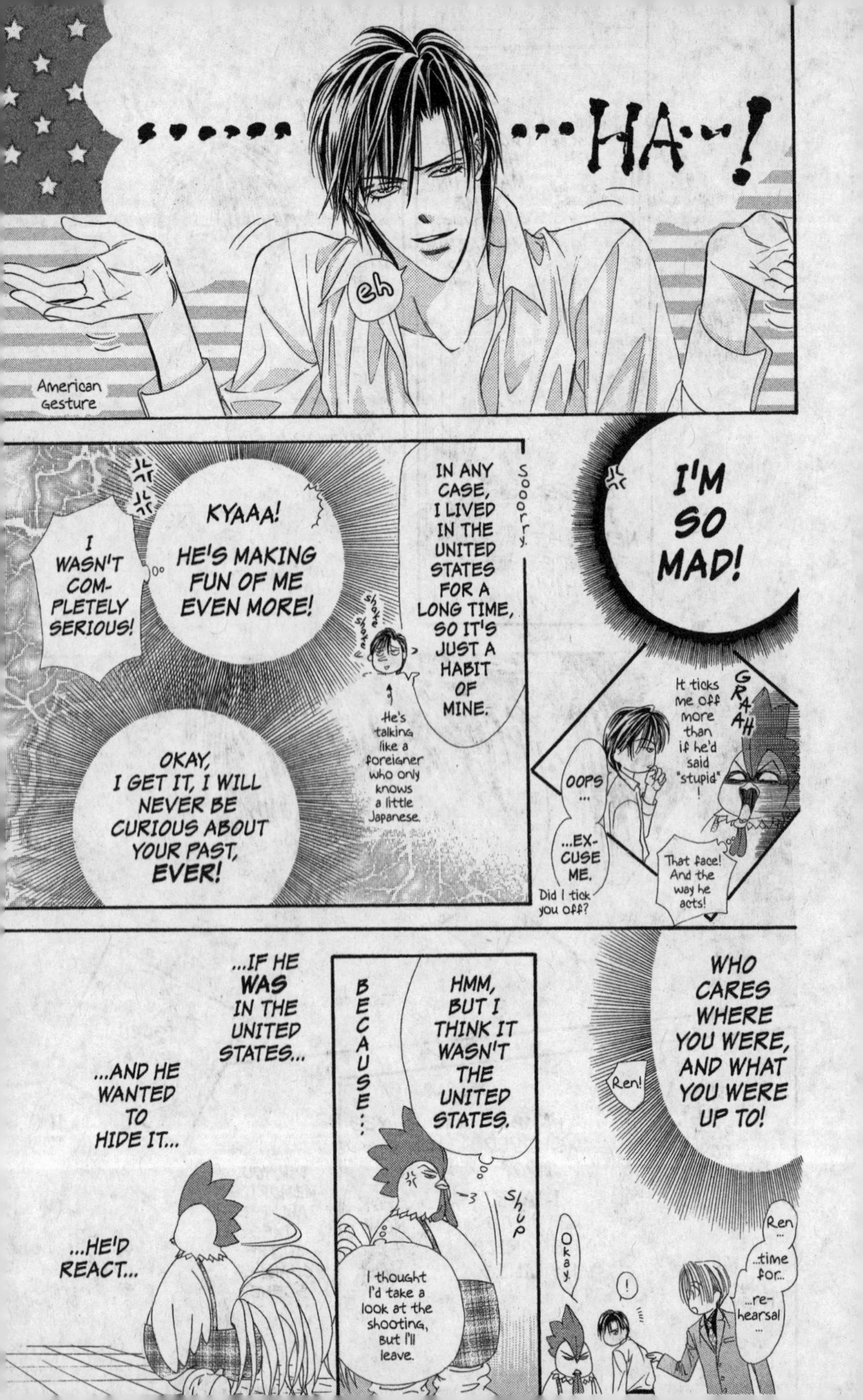

......
...HA~!
eh
American Gesture
I'M SO MAD!
It ticks me off more than if he'd said "stupid"!
GRAAH
OOPS...
...EX-CUSE ME.
Did I tick you off?
That face! And the way he acts!
Sooorry.
IN ANY CASE, I LIVED IN THE UNITED STATES FOR A LONG TIME, SO IT'S JUST A HABIT OF MINE.
shake shake
He's talking like a foreigner who only knows a little Japanese.
KYAAA! HE'S MAKING FUN OF ME EVEN MORE!
I WASN'T COM-PLETELY SERIOUS!
OKAY, I GET IT, I WILL NEVER BE CURIOUS ABOUT YOUR PAST, EVER!
WHO CARES WHERE YOU WERE, AND WHAT YOU WERE UP TO!
Ren!
Ren... ...time for... re-hearsal...
!
Okay.
BECAUSE...
HMM, BUT I THINK IT WASN'T THE UNITED STATES.
Shup
I thought I'd take a look at the shooting, but I'll leave.
...IF HE WAS IN THE UNITED STATES...
...AND HE WANTED TO HIDE IT...
...HE'D REACT...

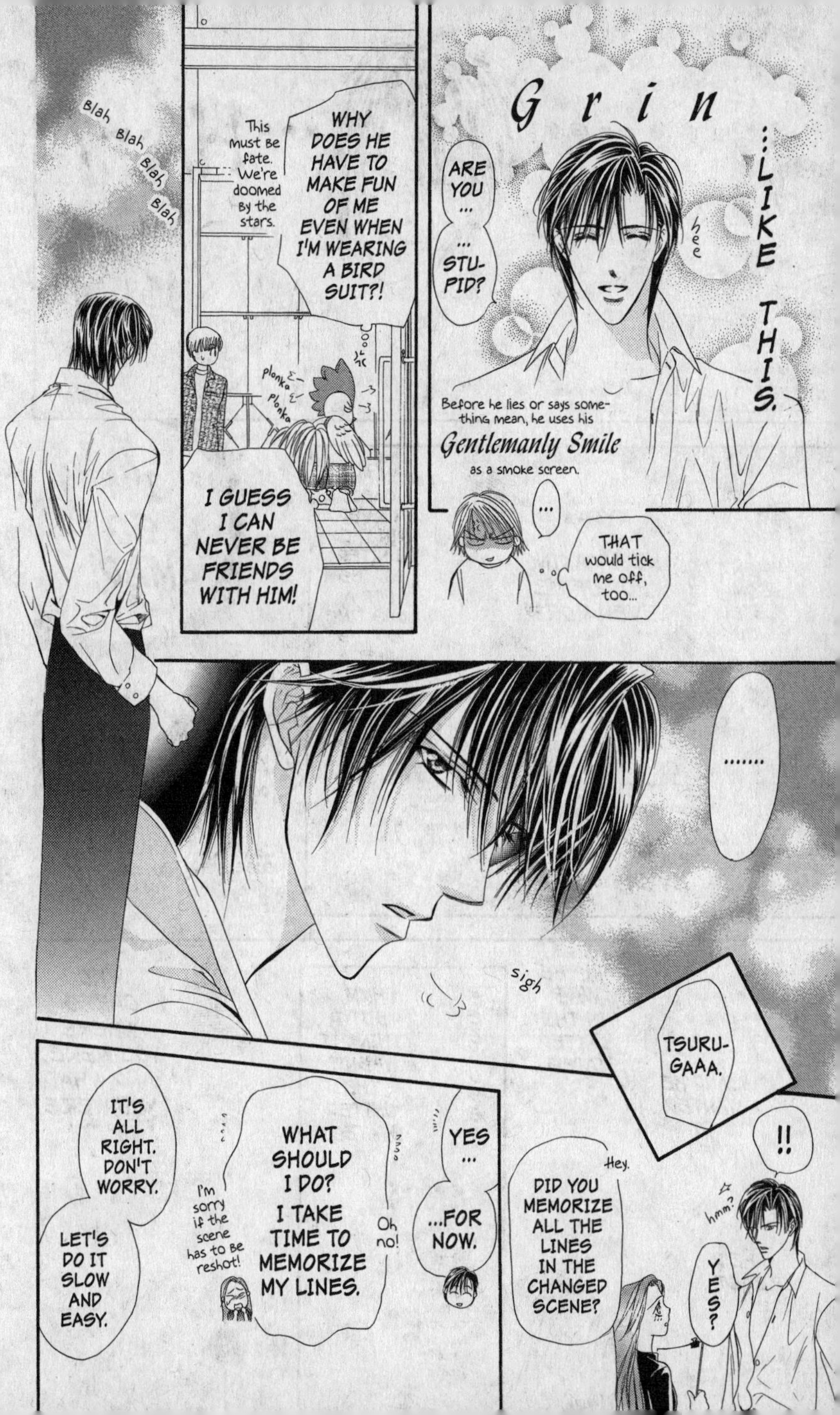
Grin
...LIKE THIS.
hee
ARE YOU ...
... STUPID?
Before he lies or says something mean, he uses his Gentlemanly Smile as a smoke screen.
...
THAT would tick me off, too...
WHY DOES HE HAVE TO MAKE FUN OF ME EVEN WHEN I'M WEARING A BIRD SUIT?!
This must be fate. We're doomed by the stars.
plonka plonka
I GUESS I CAN NEVER BE FRIENDS WITH HIM!
Blah Blah Blah Blah
....
sigh
TSURUGAAA.
!!
hmm?
YES?
Hey.
DID YOU MEMORIZE ALL THE LINES IN THE CHANGED SCENE?
YES ...
...FOR NOW.
WHAT SHOULD I DO? I TAKE TIME TO MEMORIZE MY LINES.
Oh no!
I'm sorry if the scene has to be reshot!
IT'S ALL RIGHT. DON'T WORRY.
LET'S DO IT SLOW AND EASY.

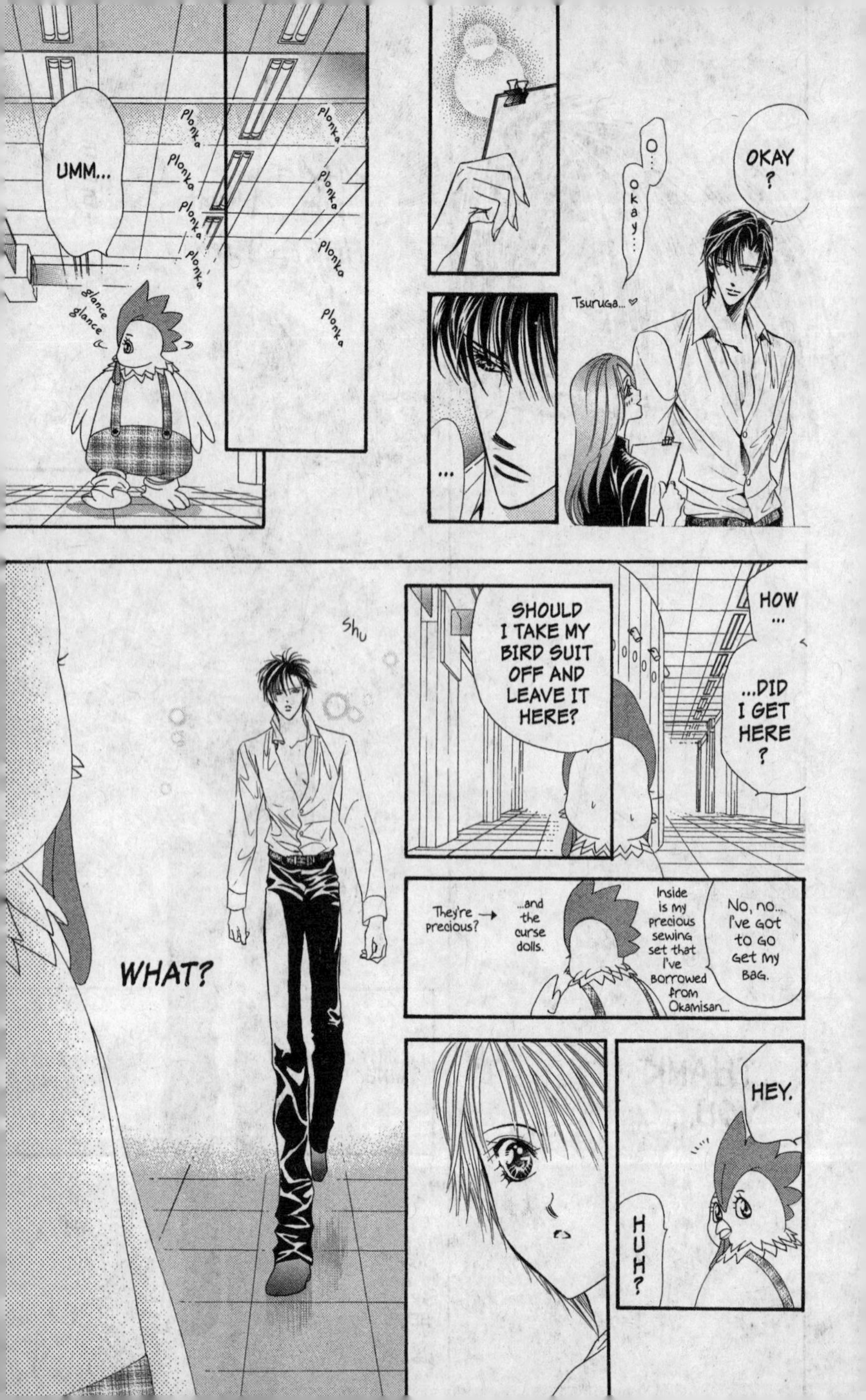
OKAY?
O... Okay...
Tsuruga...♥
...
Plonka plonka plonka plonka plonka plonka plonka plonka
UMM...
glance glance
HOW...
...DID I GET HERE?
SHOULD I TAKE MY BIRD SUIT OFF AND LEAVE IT HERE?
No, no... I've got to go get my bag.
Inside is my precious sewing set that I've borrowed from Okamisan...
...and the curse dolls.
They're precious? →
HEY.
HUH?
Shu
WHAT?

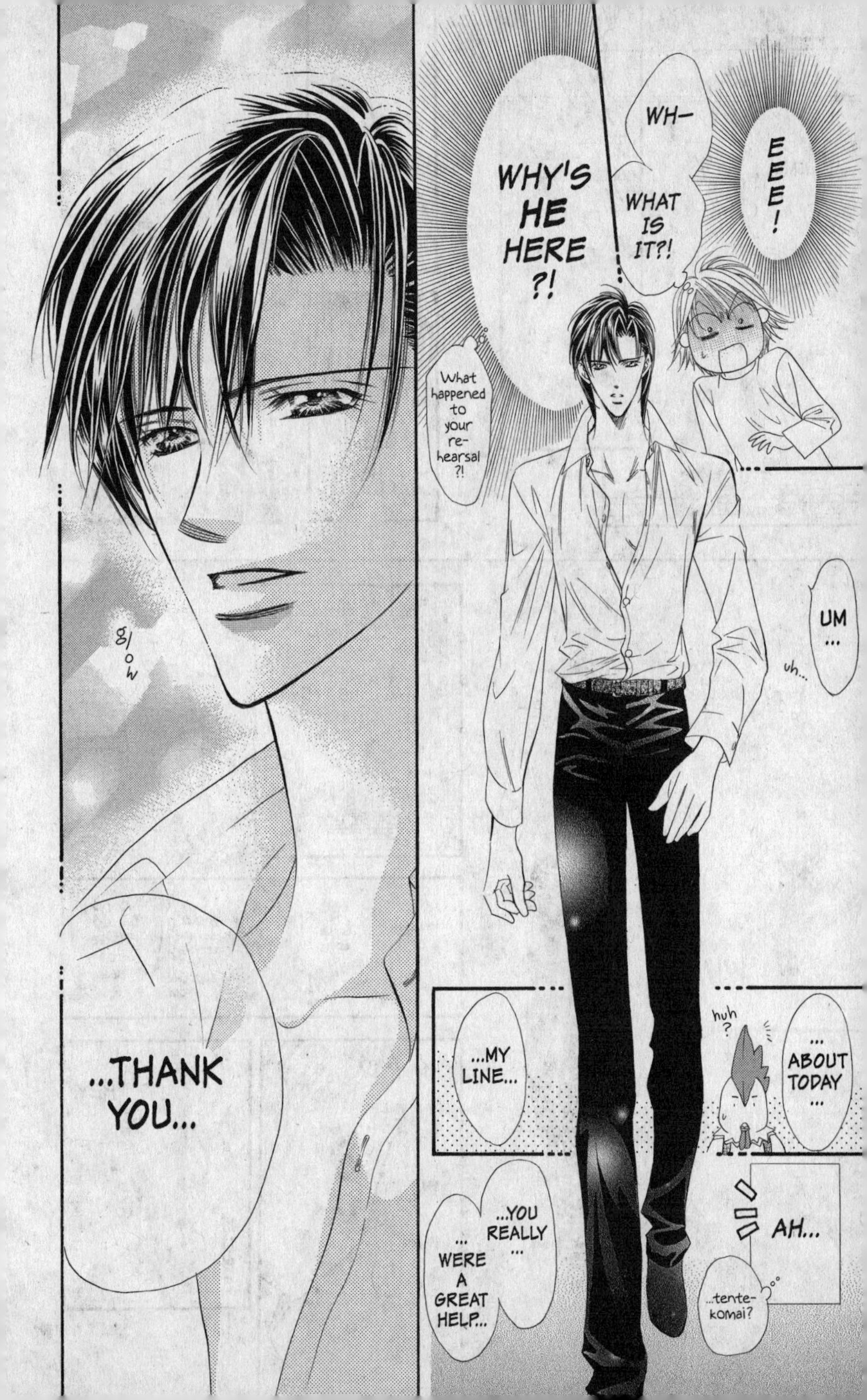
EEE!
WH— WHAT IS IT?!
WHY'S HE HERE?!
What happened to your re-hearsal?!
UM...
uh...
...ABOUT TODAY...
huh?
...MY LINE...
AH...
...tente-komai?
...YOU REALLY...
...WERE A GREAT HELP...
glow
...THANK YOU...

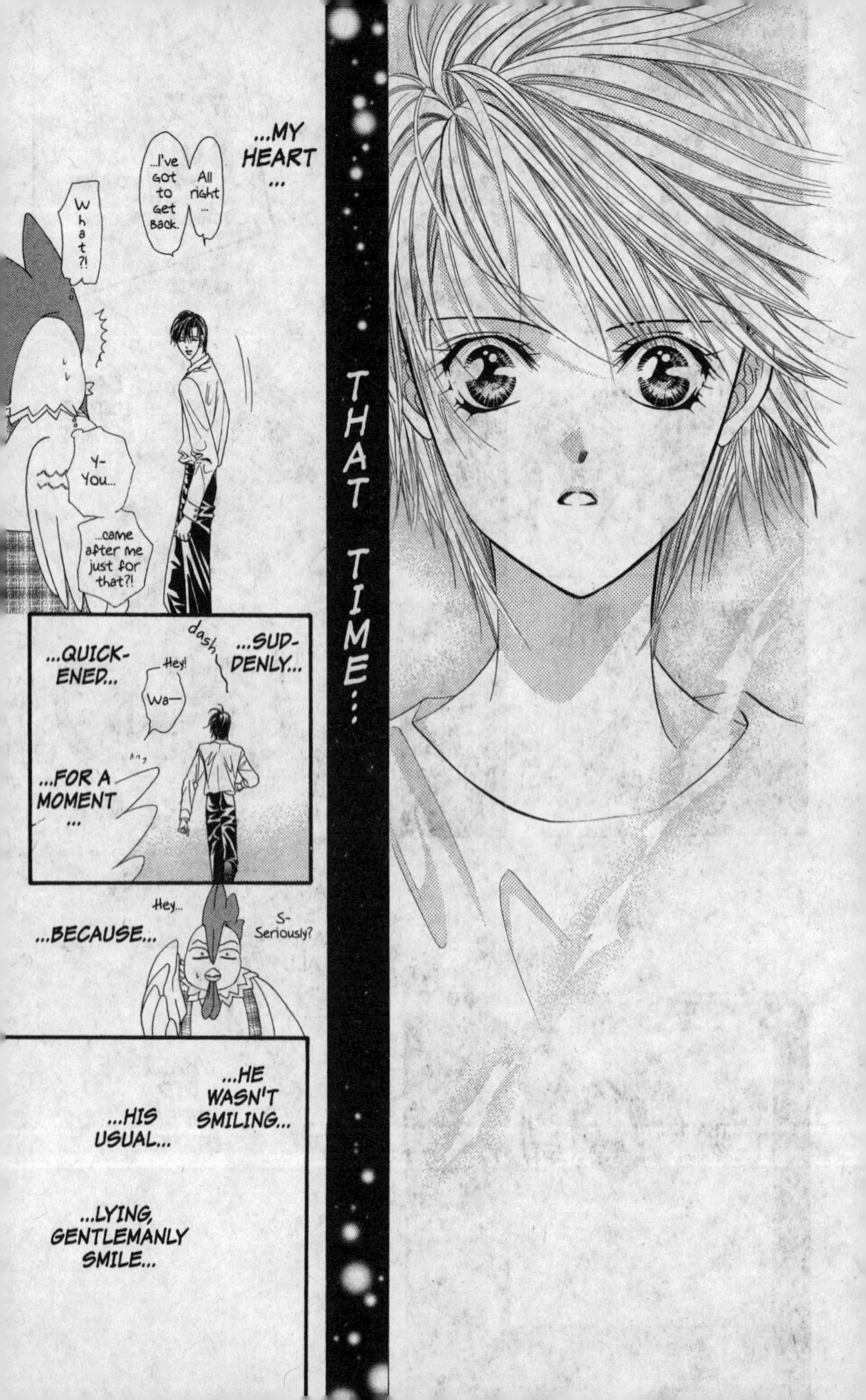
THAT TIME...
...MY HEART ...
All right ...
...I've got to get back.
What?!
Y-You...
...came after me just for that?!
...SUD-DENLY...
dash
Hey!
Wa—
...QUICK-ENED...
...FOR A MOMENT ...
S-Seriously?
Hey...
...BECAUSE...
...HE WASN'T SMILING...
...HIS USUAL...
...LYING, GENTLEMANLY SMILE...

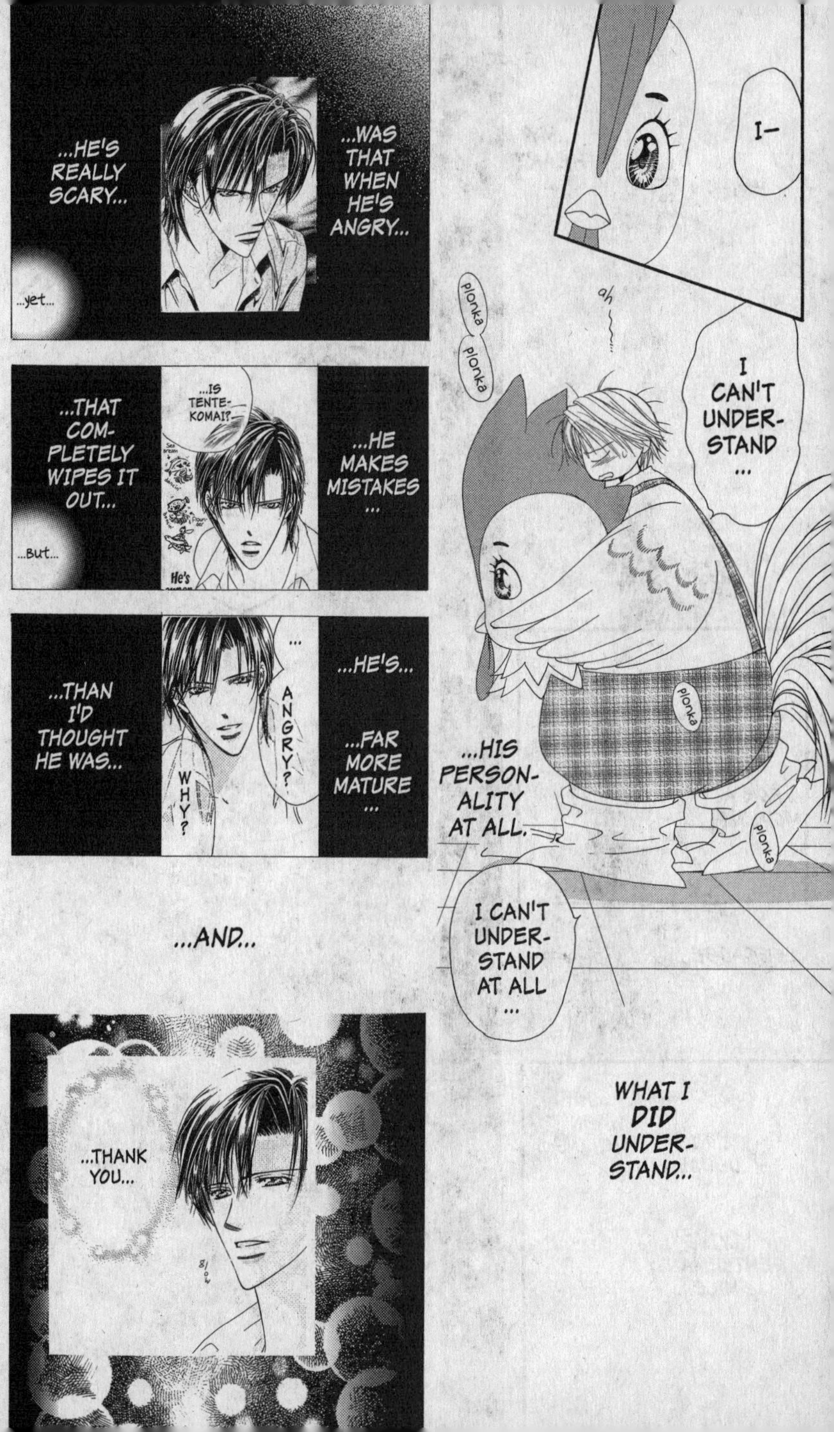
I—
ah~...
plonka
plonka
I CAN'T UNDERSTAND...
plonka
plonka
...HIS PERSONALITY AT ALL.
I CAN'T UNDERSTAND AT ALL...
WHAT I DID UNDERSTAND...
...WAS THAT WHEN HE'S ANGRY...
...HE'S REALLY SCARY...
...yet...
...HE MAKES MISTAKES...
...IS TENTE-KOMAI?
...THAT COMPLETELY WIPES IT OUT...
...but...
...HE'S...
...FAR MORE MATURE...
...
ANGRY?
WHY?
...THAN I'D THOUGHT HE WAS...
...AND...
...THANK YOU...
glow

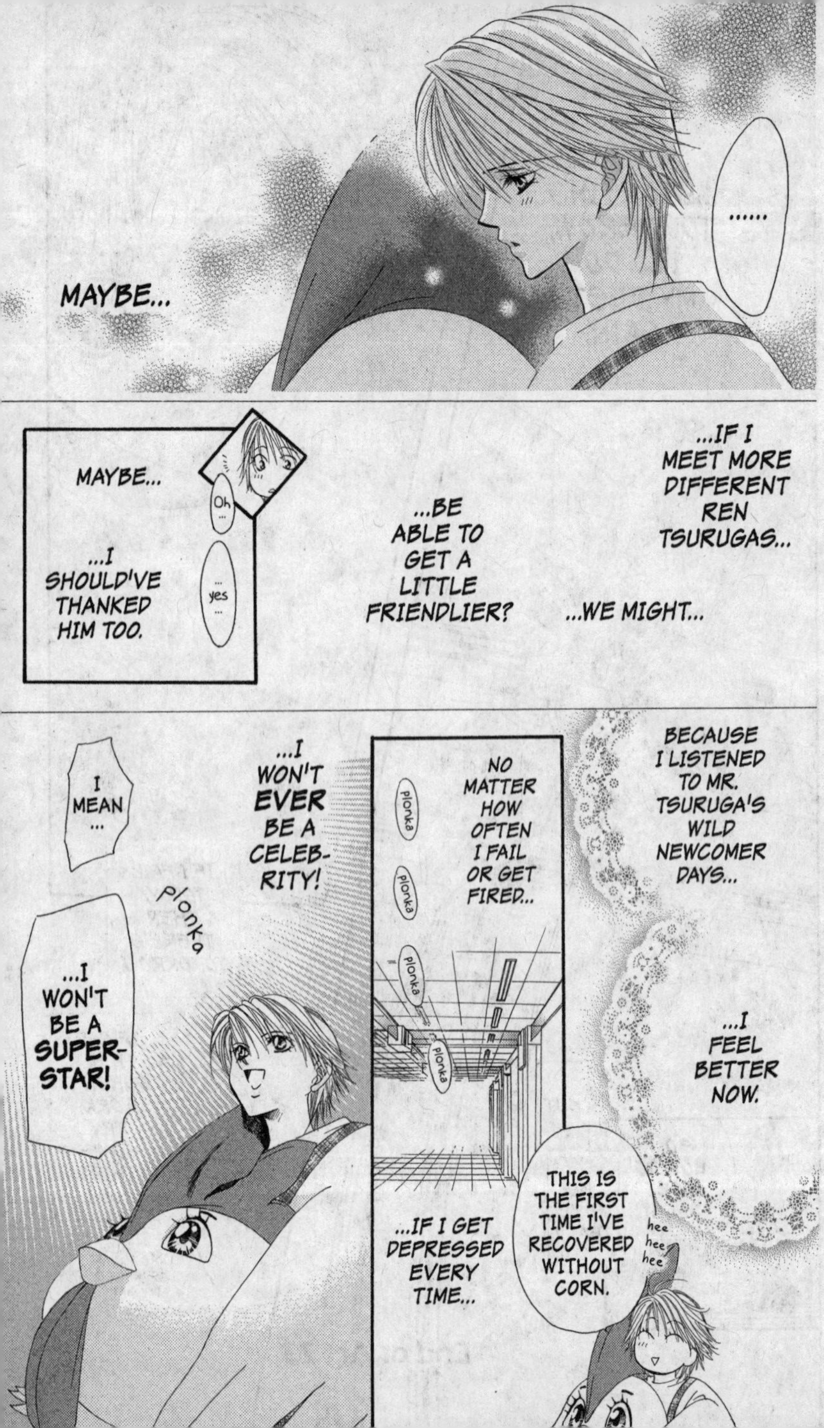
......
MAYBE...
...IF I MEET MORE DIFFERENT REN TSURUGAS...
...WE MIGHT...
...BE ABLE TO GET A LITTLE FRIENDLIER?
Oh...
...yes...
MAYBE...
...I SHOULD'VE THANKED HIM TOO.
BECAUSE I LISTENED TO MR. TSURUGA'S WILD NEWCOMER DAYS...
...I FEEL BETTER NOW.
THIS IS THE FIRST TIME I'VE RECOVERED WITHOUT CORN.
hee hee hee
NO MATTER HOW OFTEN I FAIL OR GET FIRED...
plonka
plonka
plonka
plonka
...IF I GET DEPRESSED EVERY TIME...
...I WON'T EVER BE A CELEBRITY!
I MEAN...
plonka
...I WON'T BE A SUPERSTAR!

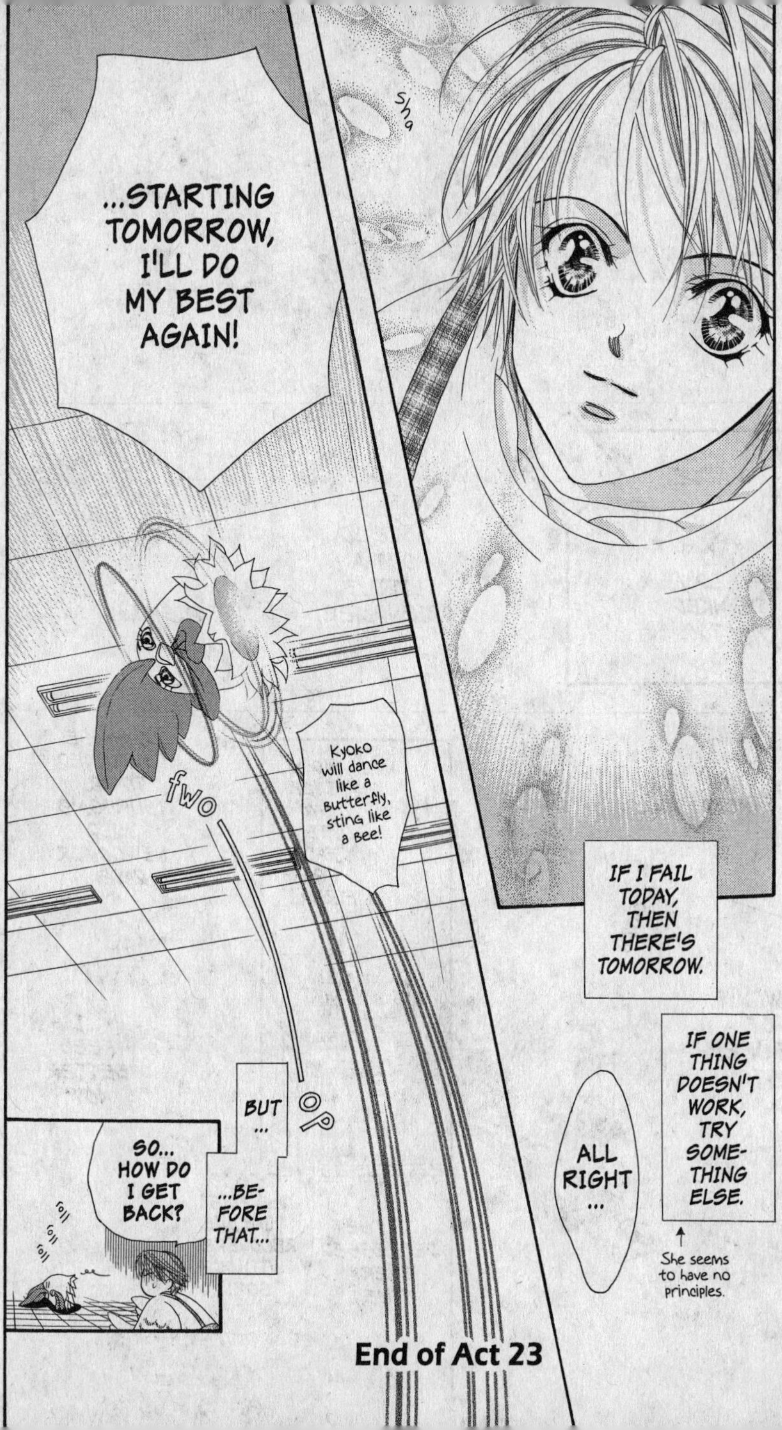
Sha
IF I FAIL TODAY, THEN THERE'S TOMORROW.
IF ONE THING DOESN'T WORK, TRY SOME-THING ELSE.
She seems to have no principles.
ALL RIGHT...
...STARTING TOMORROW, I'LL DO MY BEST AGAIN!
Kyoko will dance like a Butterfly, sting like a Bee!
fwoop
BUT...
...BE-FORE THAT...
SO... HOW DO I GET BACK?
roll roll roll

End of Act 23

Skip-Beat! End Notes
Everyone knows how to be a fan, but sometimes cool things
from other cultures need a little help crossing the language barrier.

Page 78-79: Ichiri. Niri. Shichiri...
This is a Japanese vocal exercise that stresses pronunciation. The translation is
"One *ri*. Two *ri*. Seven *ri*. I barely managed to go seven *ri* in one day. You go
by yourself to say all that politely. A fresh morning. It's a warm morning. A
flower bloomed. A bright red rose bloomed suddenly. It is a gorgeous flower.
The strange one who doesn't suspect the one he should suspect, but suspects
the one who is innocent. I think I will try to figure out what he's really thinking. I'm thinking of killing that guy!"

Page 81, panel 2: Wisdom Sutras
Also called The Heart of the Great Wisdom Sutra, or *Hannya Shingyo*. It is a
summary or essential distillation of the longer Great Wisdom Sutra, and ex-
plains the Buddhist concept of *ku*, or emptiness. It is the shortest of all Sutras.

Page 83, sidebar: Kinseiseki
In the Japanese spelling, the character for *Kin* means "violet" and the character for *sei* means "blue." Cordierite is a mineral popular with collectors for its
unusual blue-violet color and its color-changing ability (known as *pleocro-
ism*). The gemstone variety is called *iolite*.

Page 86, panel 3: Kanashibari
Kanae's typical response to Kyoko's demons. Also known as sleep paralysis,
it is believed to happen when a ghost sits on your chest as you are waking up
and tries to strangle you.

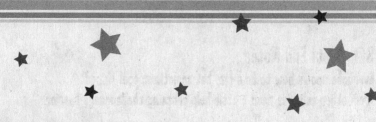

Page 95, panel 3: Yappa Kimagure Rock
The name of this variety show means "It's Gotta Be Whimsical Rock."

Page 106, panel 5: Topeggs
The original Japanese is *netamago,* or *Neta Tamago. Neta* means "topic" and *tamago* means "egg."

Page 110, panel 4: Shotaro
The kanji for *Sho* means "pine" and *taro* is a traditional name for a firstborn son. This is a very traditional, staid, uncool name. The kanji Sho uses for his stage name means "value," which better fits the way he thinks about himself.

Page 141, sidebar: Manma-chan
The dog mascot of the talk show "Sanma no Manma" by comedian Sanma Akashiya. The show is especially popular in Osaka.

Page 171, panel 5: Tentekomai
The kanji used for *mai* in this word could be interpreted as "dance," which is what has confused Ren.

Page 171, sidebar: Harisen
The big folded fan. It makes a lot of noise when you hit someone with it, but doesn't hurt much at all. It's used in Kansai comedy pair routines. The straight man (*tsukkomi*) uses it to punctuate the punch line.

Page 171, sidebar: Midori
The Japanese word for weathercock is *kazamidori.*

Shojo Beat

Skip·Beat!

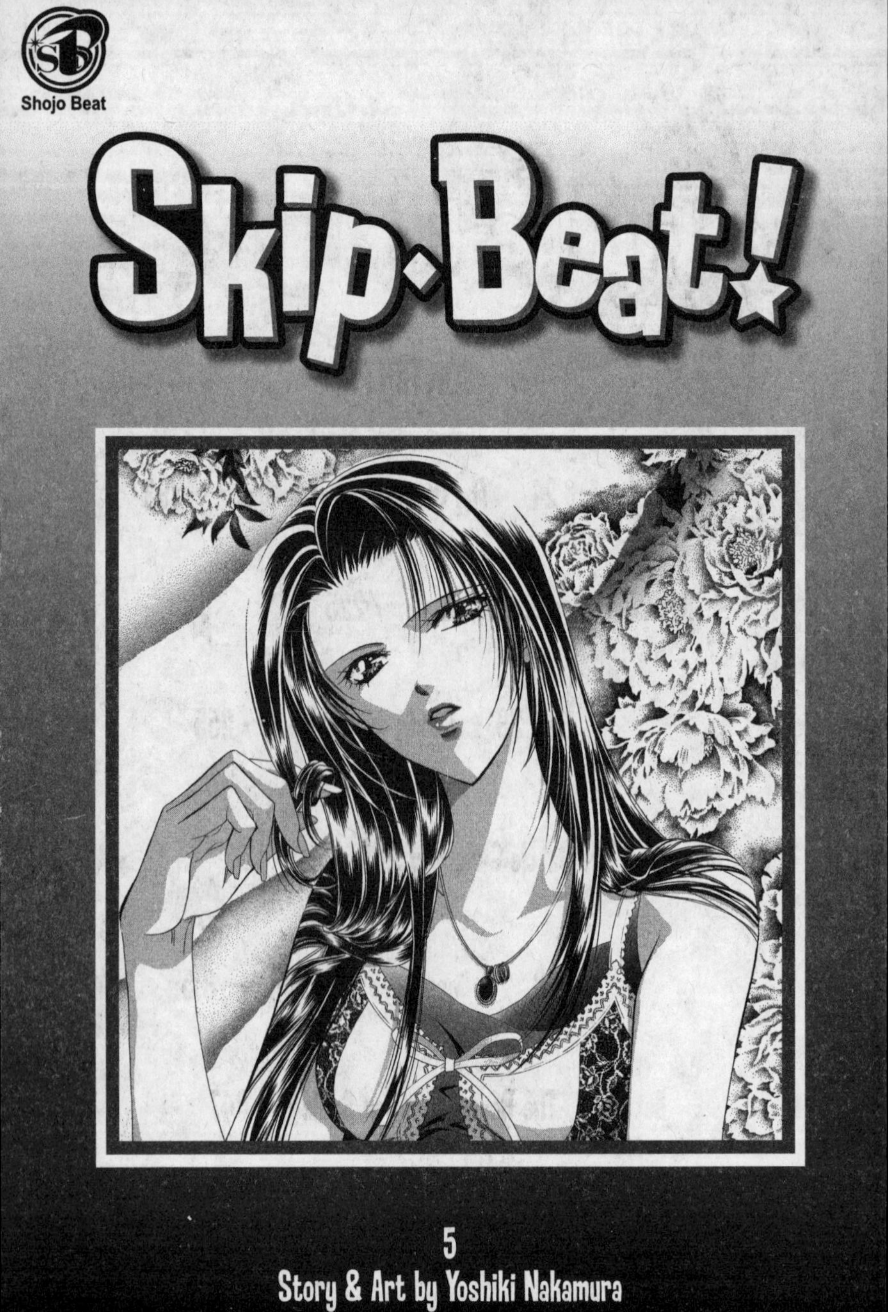

5

Story & Art by Yoshiki Nakamura

Skip·Beat!
Volume 5

CONTENTS

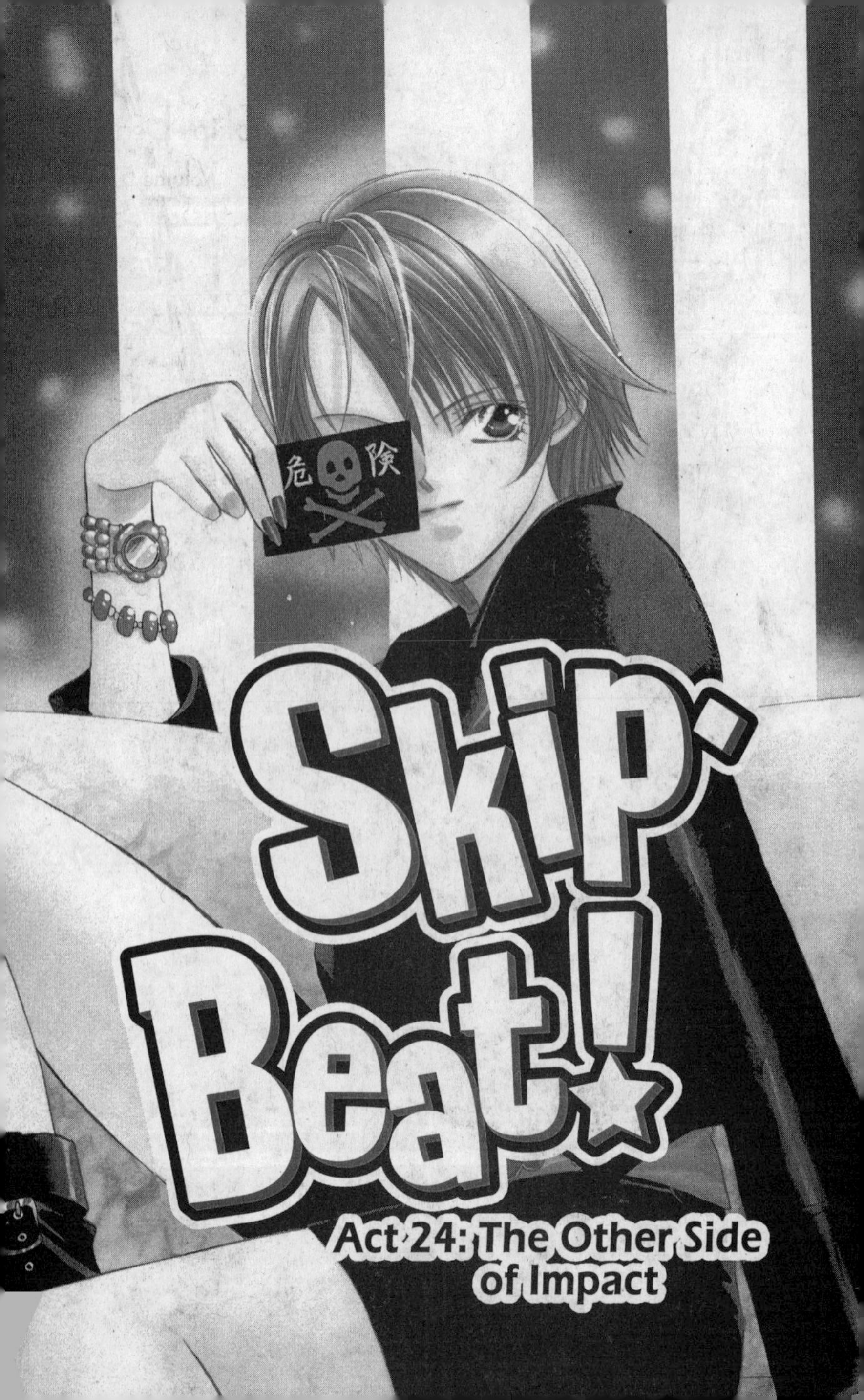
危険
Skip Beat!
Act 24: The Other Side of Impact

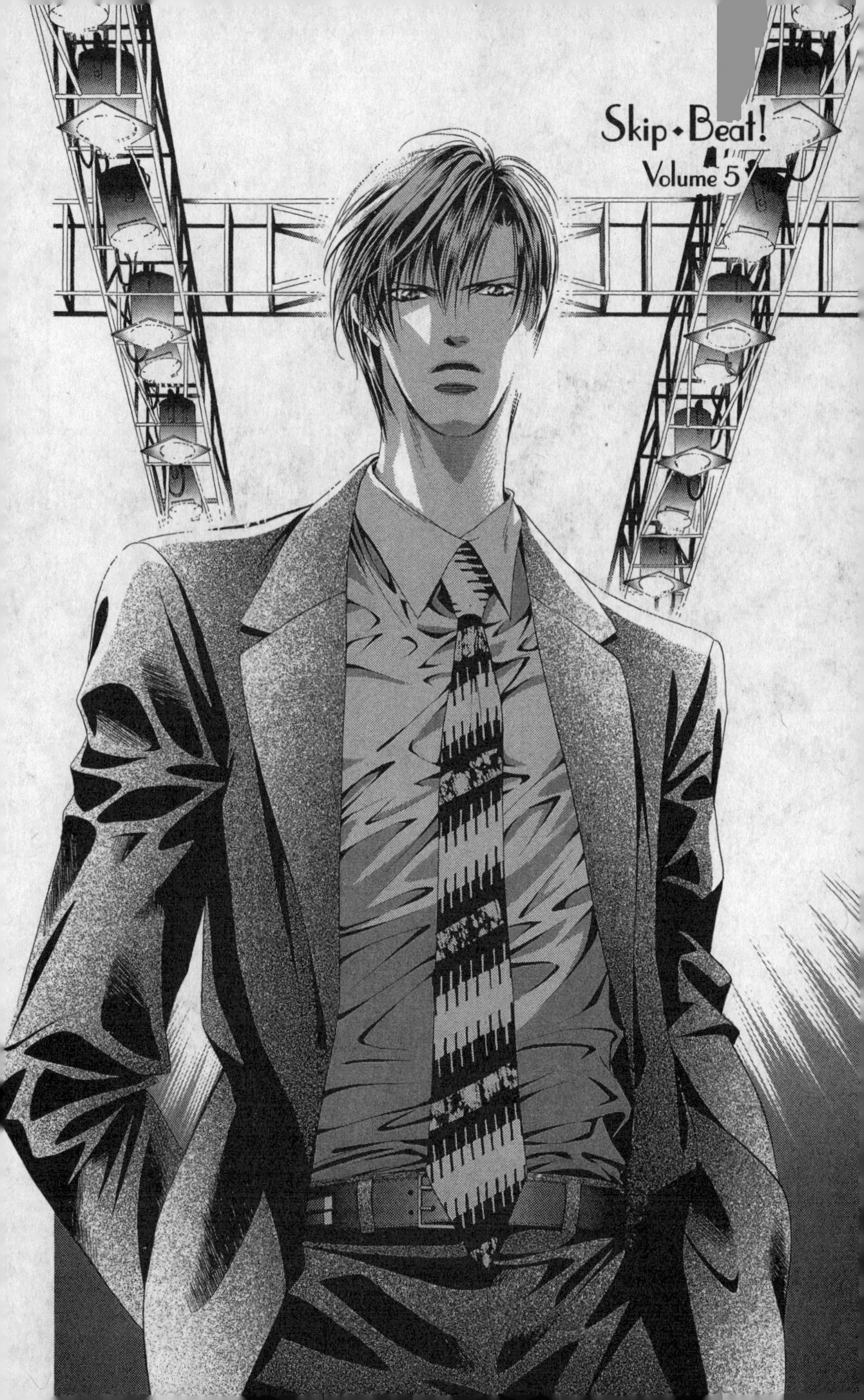
Skip・Beat!
Volume 5

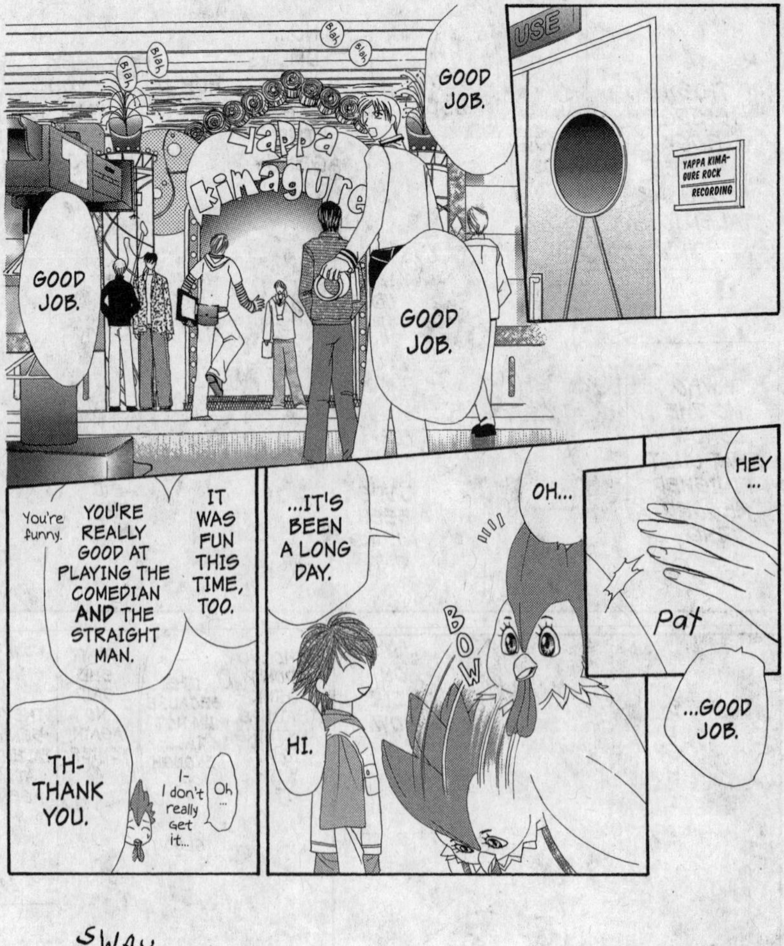
USE
YAPPA KIMAGURE ROCK
RECORDING
GOOD JOB.
Blah
Blah
Blah
Blah
Yappa kimagure
GOOD JOB.
GOOD JOB.
HEY...
pat
...GOOD JOB.
OH...
BOW
...IT'S BEEN A LONG DAY.
HI.
IT WAS FUN THIS TIME, TOO.
YOU'RE REALLY GOOD AT PLAYING THE COMEDIAN AND THE STRAIGHT MAN.
You're funny.
TH- THANK YOU.
Oh...
I- I don't really get it...
SWAY

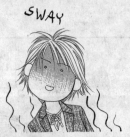

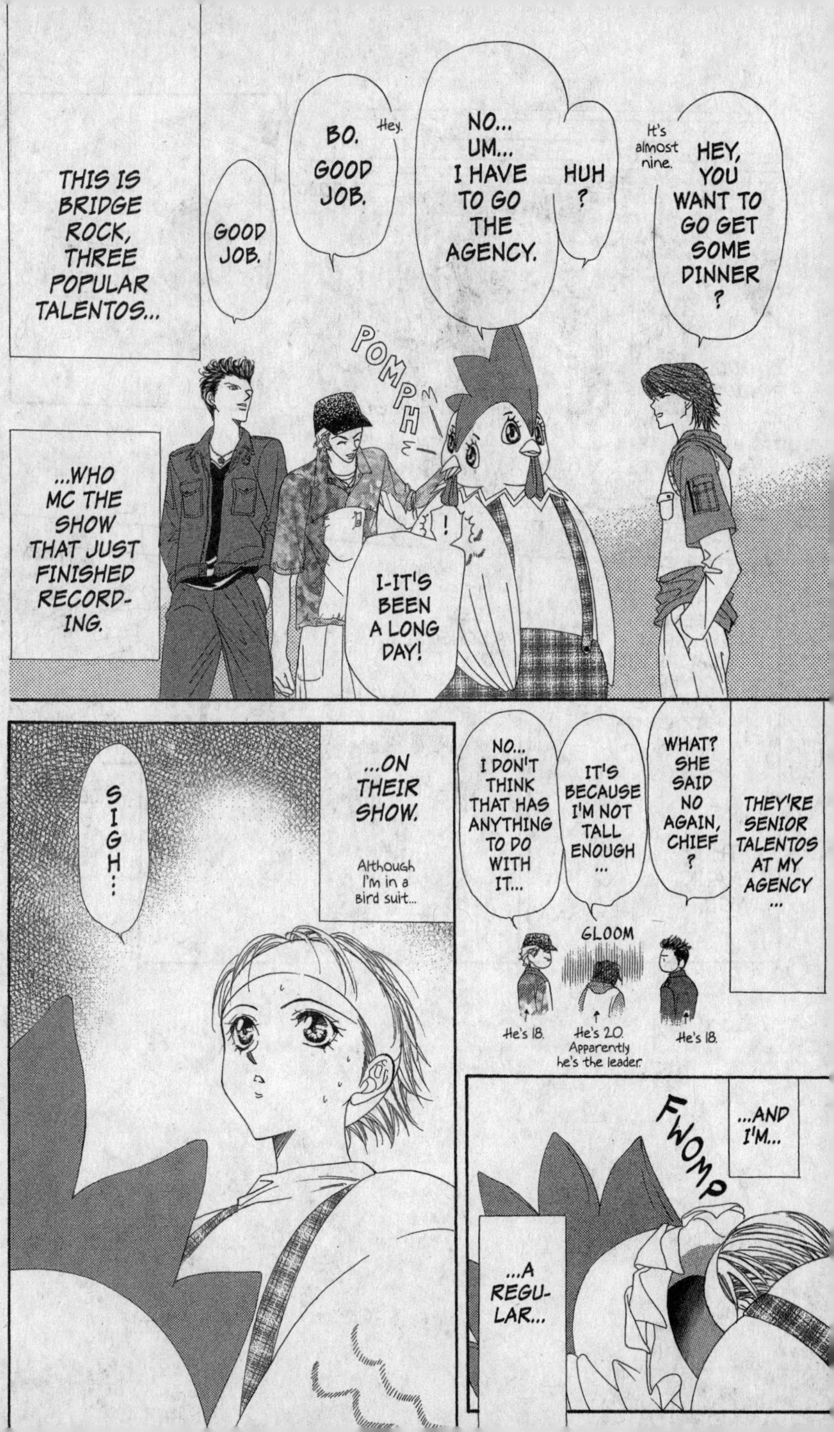
HEY, YOU WANT TO GO GET SOME DINNER?
It's almost nine.
HUH?
NO... UM... I HAVE TO GO THE AGENCY.
BO. GOOD JOB.
Hey.
GOOD JOB.
THIS IS BRIDGE ROCK, THREE POPULAR TALENTOS...
POMPH
...WHO MC THE SHOW THAT JUST FINISHED RECORDING.
!
I-IT'S BEEN A LONG DAY!
THEY'RE SENIOR TALENTOS AT MY AGENCY...
WHAT? SHE SAID NO AGAIN, CHIEF?
IT'S BECAUSE I'M NOT TALL ENOUGH...
NO... I DON'T THINK THAT HAS ANYTHING TO DO WITH IT...
GLOOM
He's 18.
He's 20. Apparently he's the leader.
He's 18.
...AND I'M...
FWOMP
...A REGULAR...
...ON THEIR SHOW.
Although I'm in a bird suit...
SIGH...

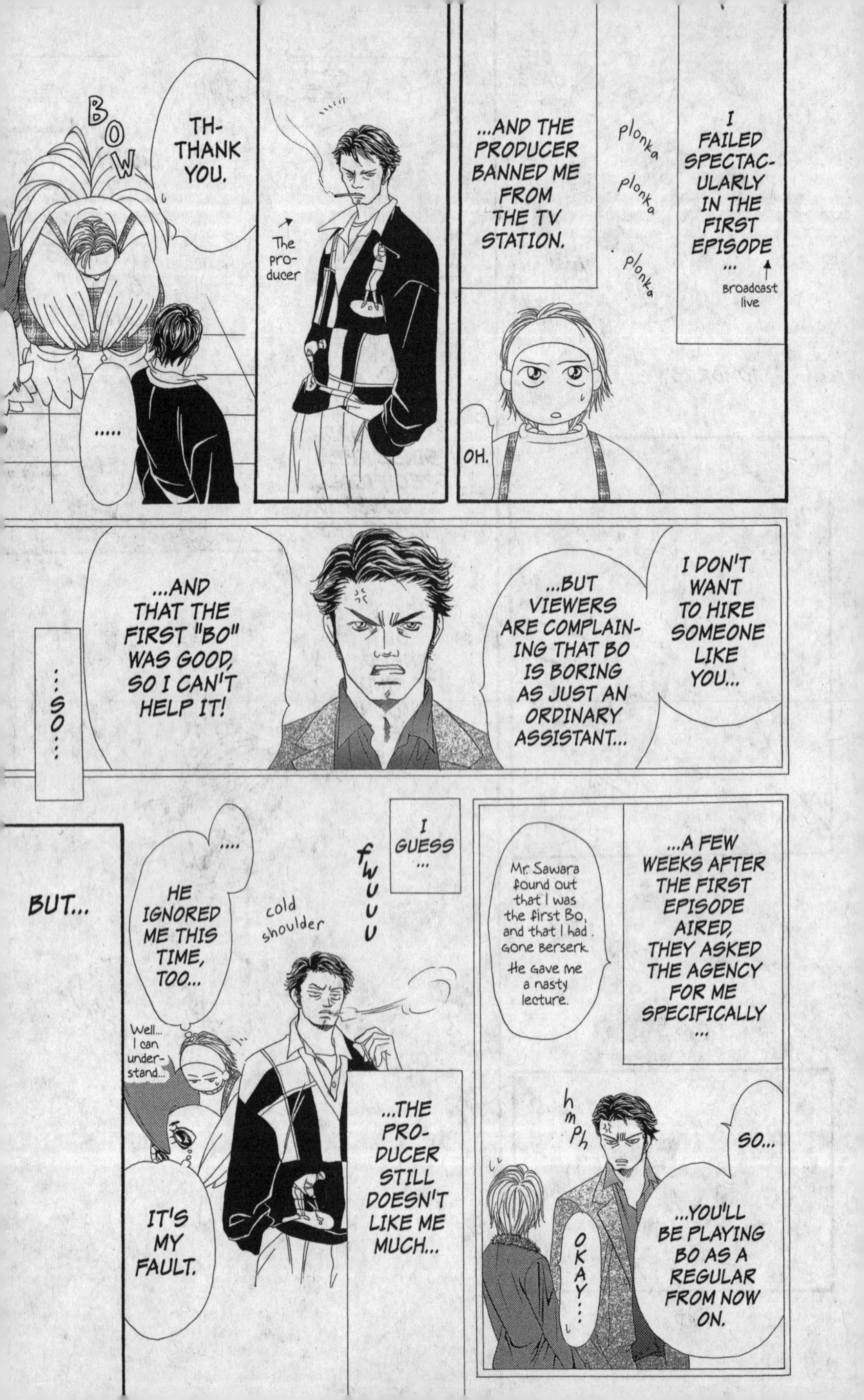

I FAILED SPECTACULARLY IN THE FIRST EPISODE...
Broadcast live
...AND THE PRODUCER BANNED ME FROM THE TV STATION.
plonka
plonka
plonka
OH.
The producer
TH-THANK YOU.
BOW
.....
I DON'T WANT TO HIRE SOMEONE LIKE YOU...
...BUT VIEWERS ARE COMPLAINING THAT BO IS BORING AS JUST AN ORDINARY ASSISTANT...
...AND THAT THE FIRST "BO" WAS GOOD, SO I CAN'T HELP IT!
...SO...
...A FEW WEEKS AFTER THE FIRST EPISODE AIRED, THEY ASKED THE AGENCY FOR ME SPECIFICALLY...
Mr. Sawara found out that I was the first Bo, and that I had gone berserk.
He gave me a nasty lecture.
SO...
...YOU'LL BE PLAYING BO AS A REGULAR FROM NOW ON.
hmph
OKAY...
I GUESS...
FWUUU
cold shoulder
...THE PRODUCER STILL DOESN'T LIKE ME MUCH...
....
HE IGNORED ME THIS TIME, TOO...
Well... I can understand...
IT'S MY FAULT.
BUT...

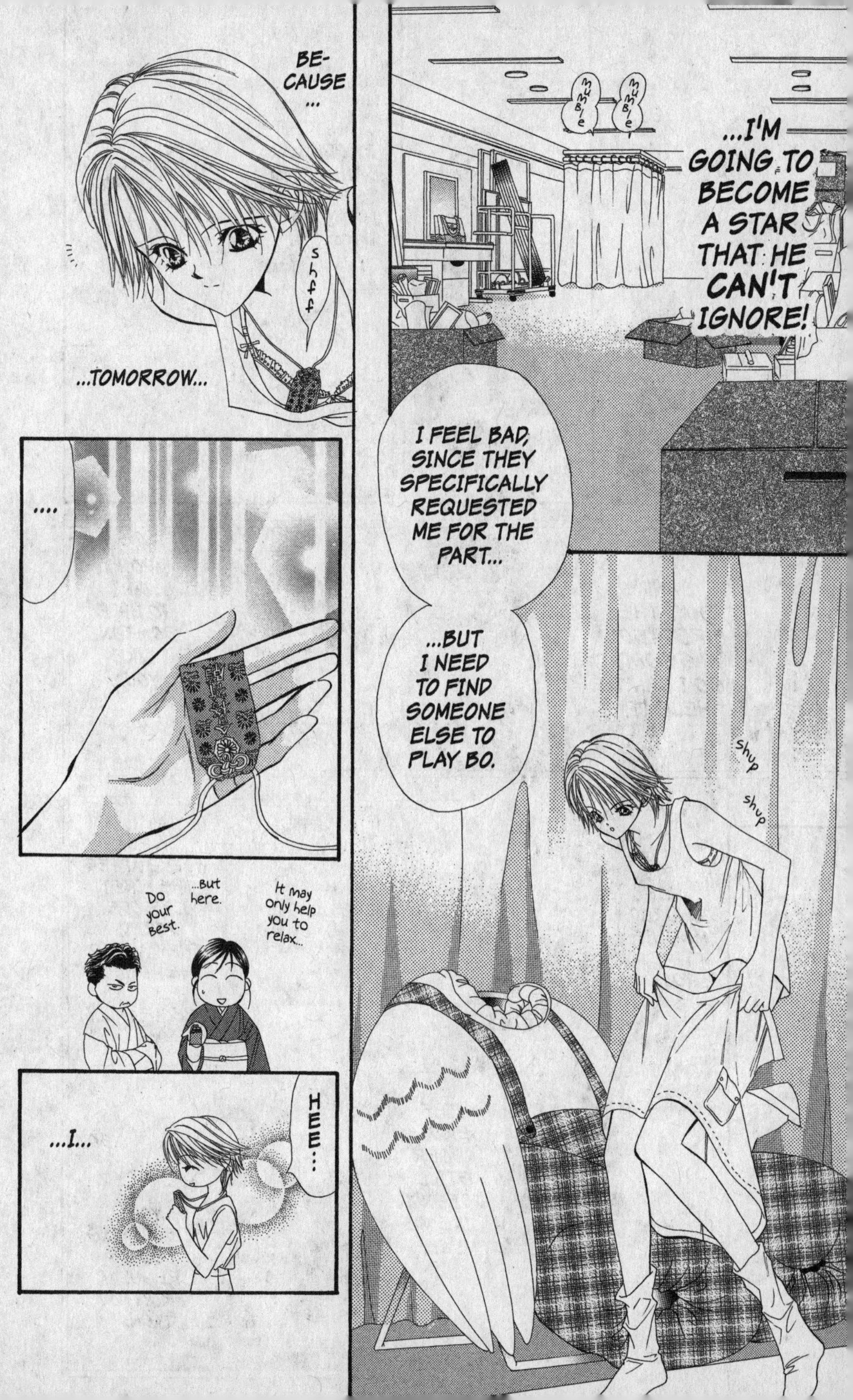
BE-CAUSE...
shff
...TOMORROW...
....
It may only help you to relax...
...but here.
Do your best.
HEE...
...I...
...I'M GOING TO BECOME A STAR THAT HE CAN'T IGNORE!
mumble
mumble
I FEEL BAD, SINCE THEY SPECIFICALLY REQUESTED ME FOR THE PART...
...BUT I NEED TO FIND SOMEONE ELSE TO PLAY BO.
shup
shup

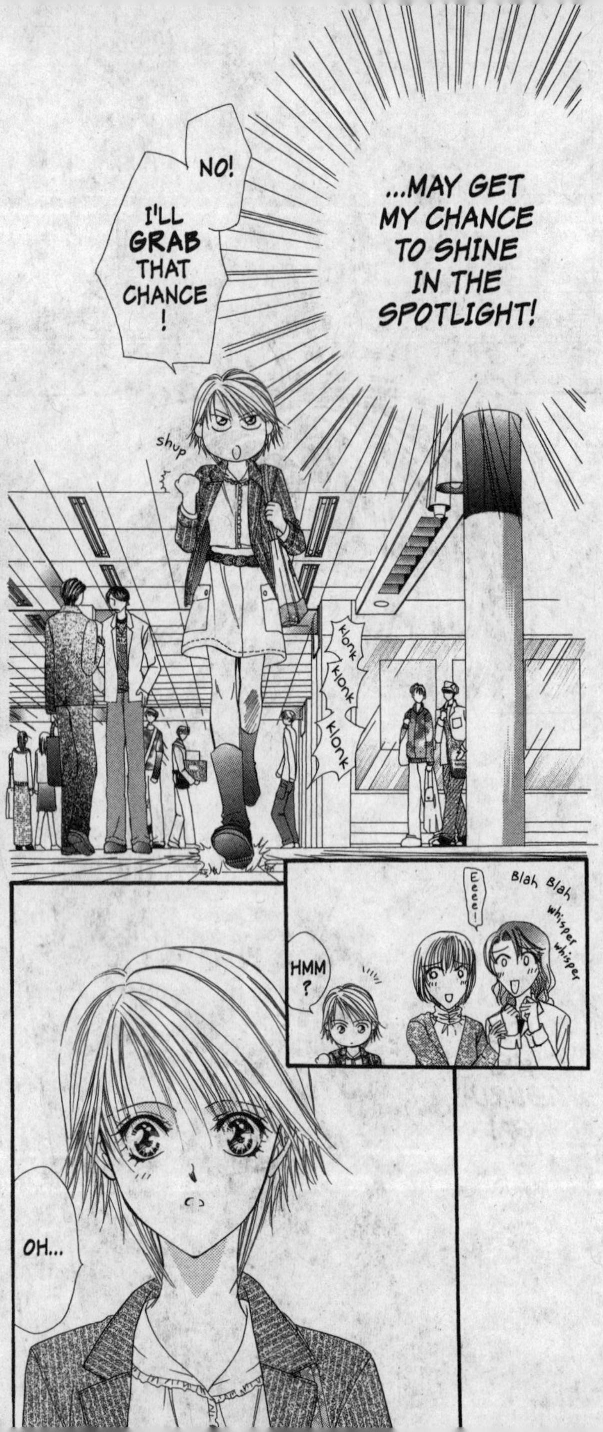
...MAY GET MY CHANCE TO SHINE IN THE SPOTLIGHT!
NO!
I'LL GRAB THAT CHANCE!
shup
klonk klonk klonk
Blah Blah
whisper whisper
Eeee!
HMM?
OH...

Nao and Kazumi

These two were created solely to make Kyoko think "Best friends are nice..." ♡ Therefore in the beginning, they were supposed to be really lovey-dovey girls who make you want to say "You girls, there's something a little wrong with you"...

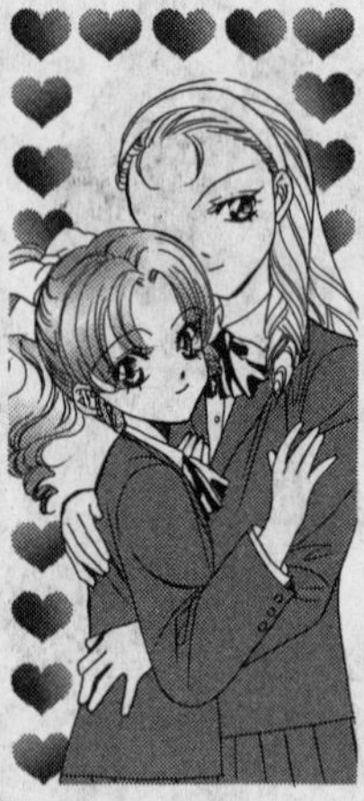

But somehow, when the audition began, they split wonderfully. I was thinking as I was drawing that in reality, people like them could exist. It became fun drawing these two, who only appeared occasionally. However, I was really surprised that Nao became important enough to get long shots in some panels (as Erika's partner)... ...an amazing promotion... they were just supporting players...

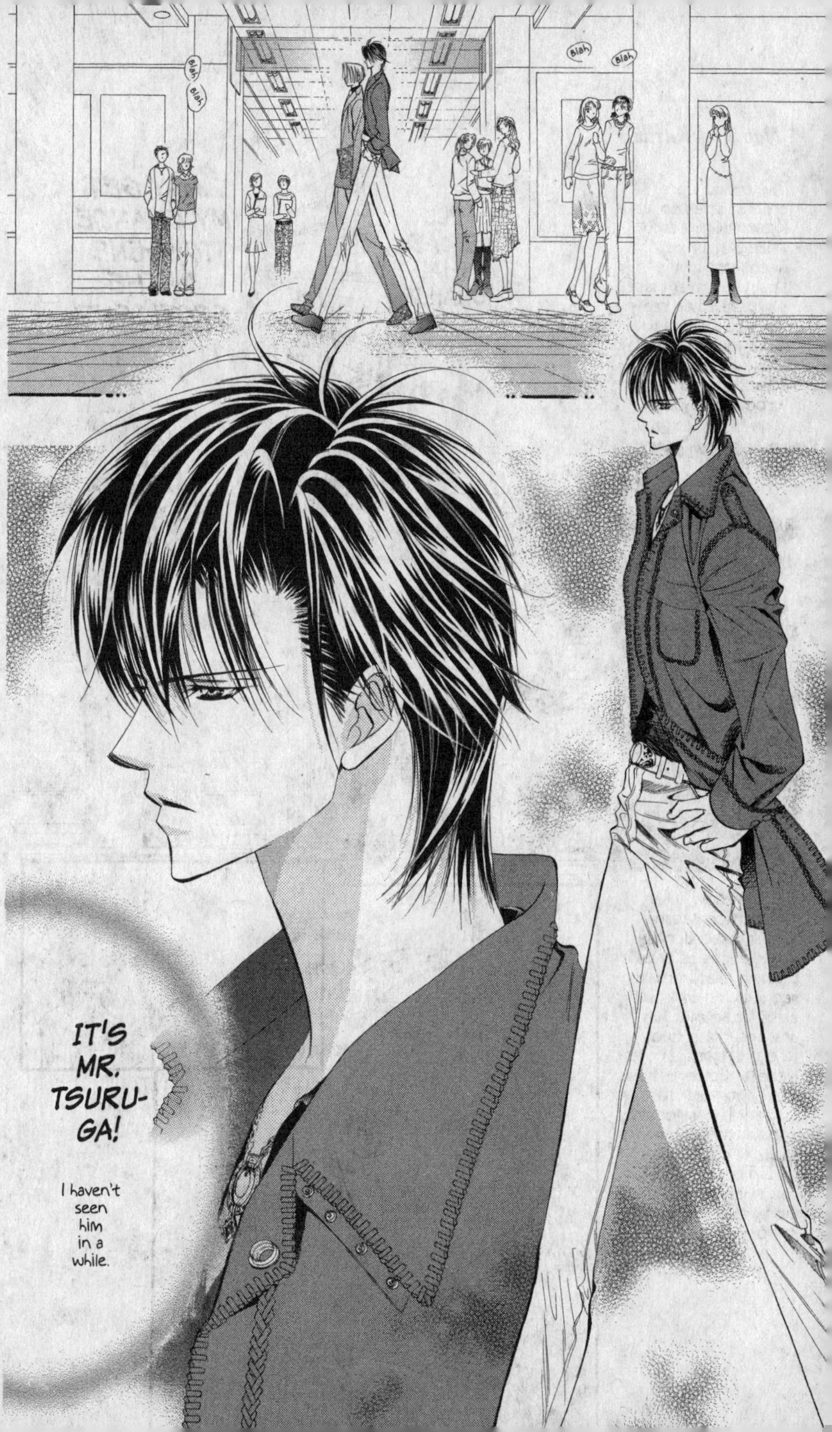
Blah
Blah
Blah
Blah
IT'S MR. TSURU-GA!
I haven't seen him in a while.

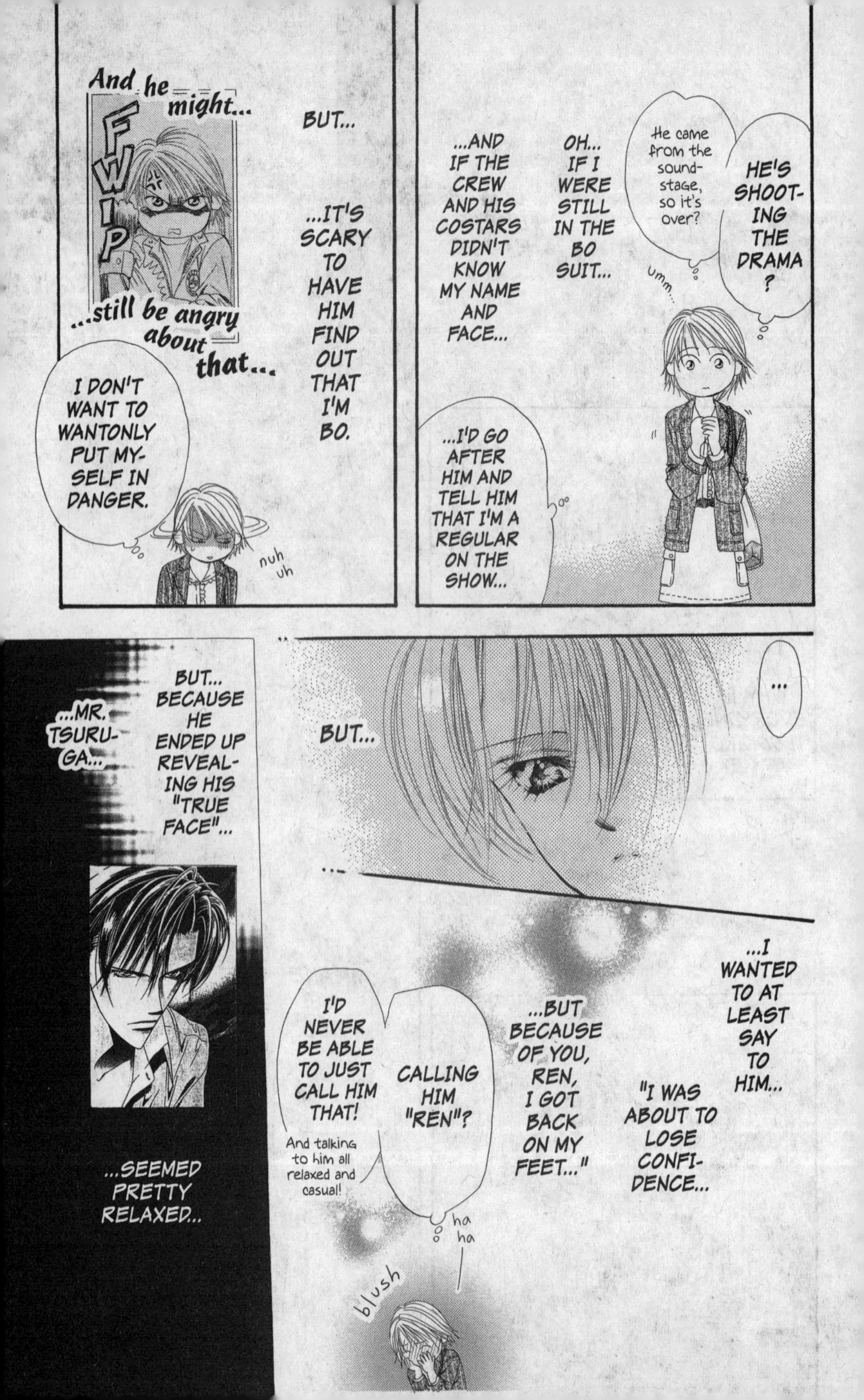
HE'S SHOOTING THE DRAMA?
He came from the soundstage, so it's over?
umm...
OH... IF I WERE STILL IN THE BO SUIT...
...AND IF THE CREW AND HIS COSTARS DIDN'T KNOW MY NAME AND FACE...
...I'D GO AFTER HIM AND TELL HIM THAT I'M A REGULAR ON THE SHOW...
BUT...
...IT'S SCARY TO HAVE HIM FIND OUT THAT I'M BO.
And he might...
FWIP
...still be angry about that...
I DON'T WANT TO WANTONLY PUT MYSELF IN DANGER.
nuh uh
...
BUT...
..
...
...I WANTED TO AT LEAST SAY TO HIM...
"I WAS ABOUT TO LOSE CONFIDENCE...
...BUT BECAUSE OF YOU, REN, I GOT BACK ON MY FEET..."
CALLING HIM "REN"?
I'D NEVER BE ABLE TO JUST CALL HIM THAT!
And talking to him all relaxed and casual!
ha ha
blush
BUT... BECAUSE HE ENDED UP REVEALING HIS "TRUE FACE"...
...MR. TSURUGA...
...SEEMED PRETTY RELAXED...

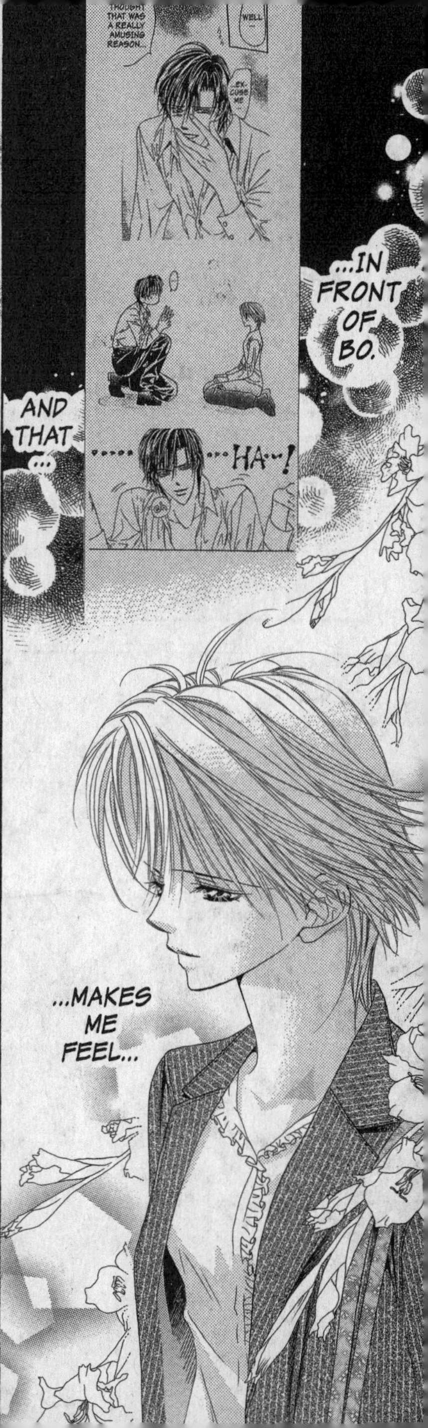
WELL...
THOUGHT THAT WAS A REALLY AMUSING REASON...
...EX-CUSE ME
...HA...!
...IN FRONT OF BO.
AND THAT...
...MAKES ME FEEL...

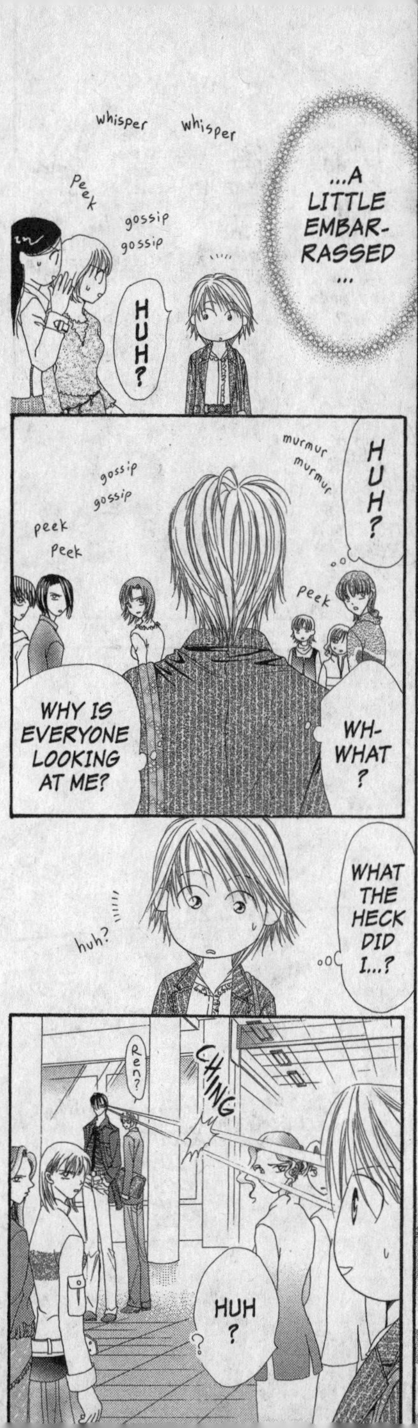
...A LITTLE EMBAR-RASSED...
whisper whisper
HUH?
Peek
gossip gossip
HUH?
murmur murmur
gossip gossip
peek peek
peek
WH-WHAT?
WHY IS EVERYONE LOOKING AT ME?
WHAT THE HECK DID I...?
huh?
Ren?
CHING
HUH?

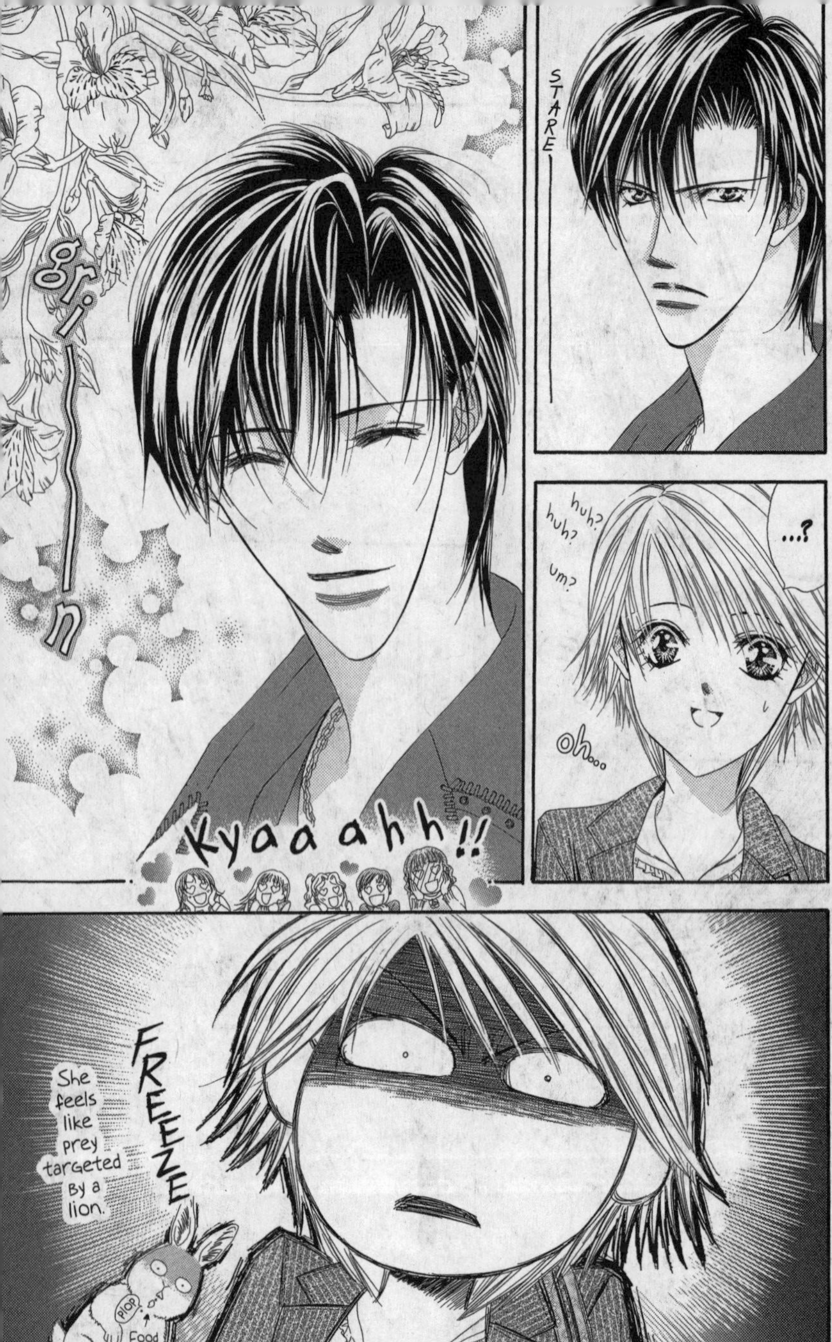
STARE
huh? huh? um?
...?
oh...
gri—n
Kyaaahh!!
She feels like prey targeted by a lion.
FREEZE
PLOP
Food

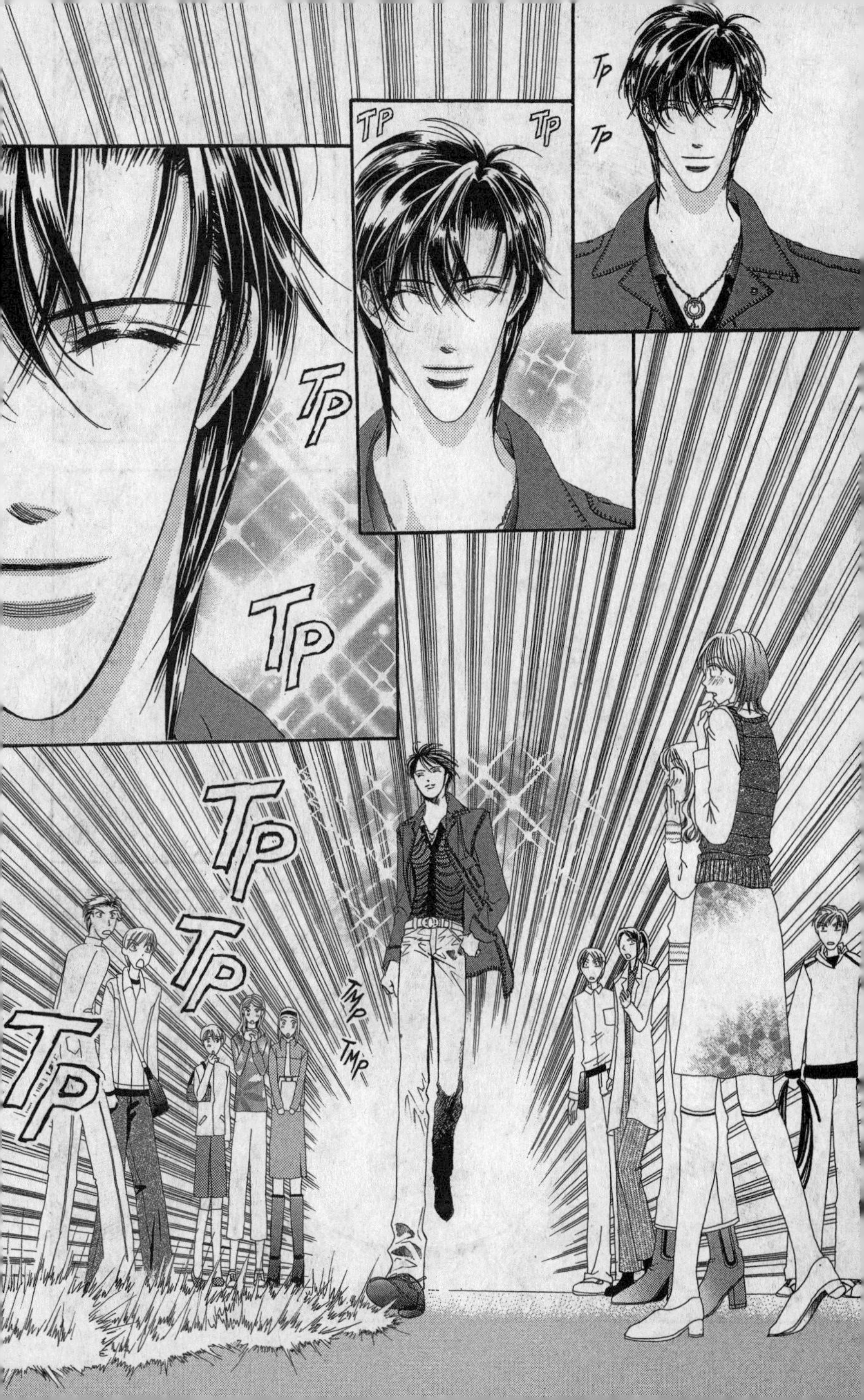
TP
TP
TP
TP
TP
TP
TP
TP
TP
TMP
TMP

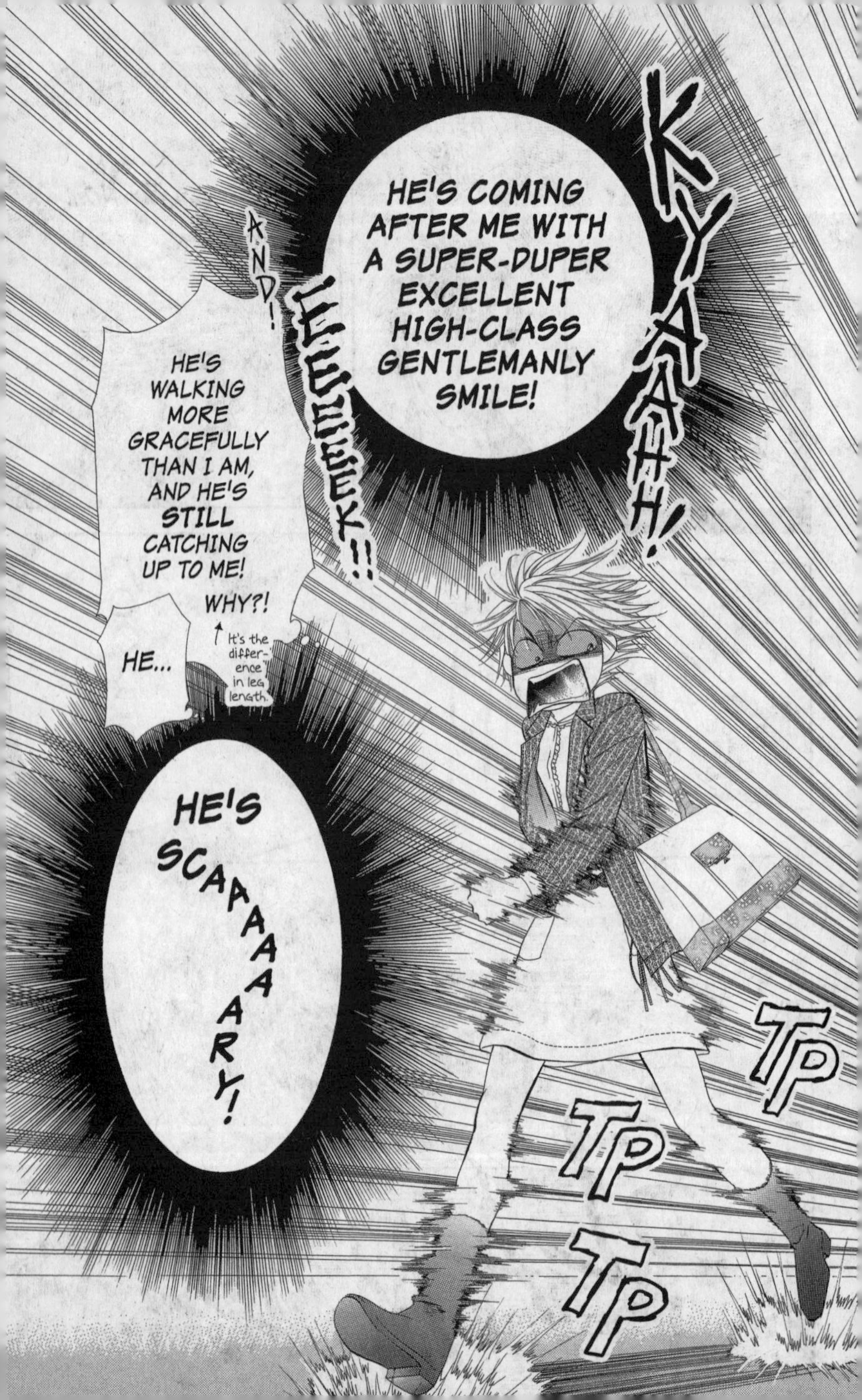
KYAAAHH!
HE'S COMING AFTER ME WITH A SUPER-DUPER EXCELLENT HIGH-CLASS GENTLEMANLY SMILE!
EEEEEEK!!
AND!
HE'S WALKING MORE GRACEFULLY THAN I AM, AND HE'S STILL CATCHING UP TO ME!
WHY?!
It's the difference in leg length.
HE...
HE'S SCAAAAAARY!
Tp
Tp
Tp
Tp

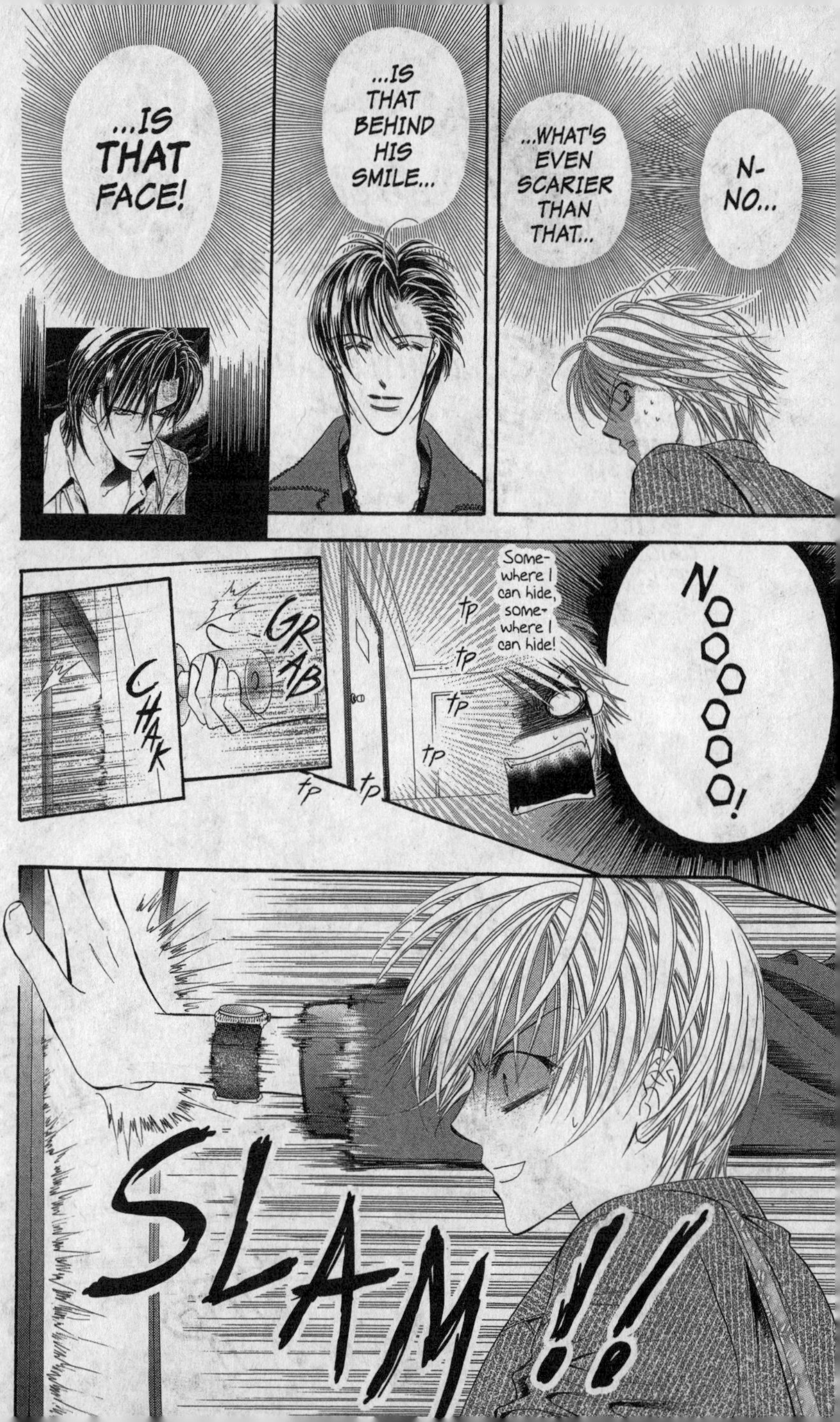
N-NO...
...WHAT'S EVEN SCARIER THAN THAT...
...IS THAT BEHIND HIS SMILE...
...IS **THAT** FACE!
NOOOOOO!
Somewhere I can hide, somewhere I can hide!
tp
tp
tp
tp
tp
tp
GRAB
CHAK
SLAM!!

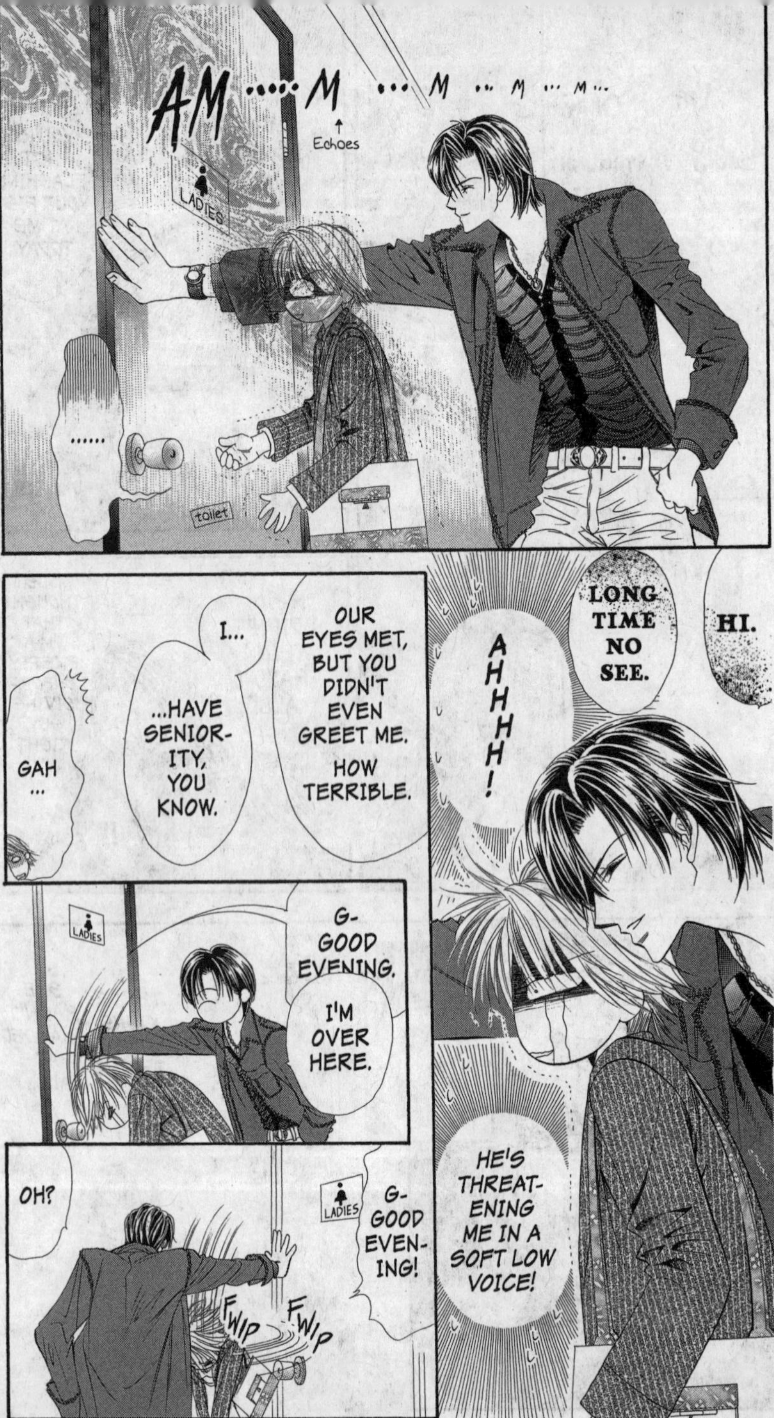
AM.....M ... M ... M ... M...
Echoes
LADIES
......
toilet
HI.
LONG TIME NO SEE.
AHHHH!
HE'S THREATENING ME IN A SOFT LOW VOICE!
OUR EYES MET, BUT YOU DIDN'T EVEN GREET ME.
HOW TERRIBLE.
I...
...HAVE SENIORITY, YOU KNOW.
GAH...
G-GOOD EVENING.
I'M OVER HERE.
LADIES
G-GOOD EVENING!
OH?
LADIES
FWIP
FWIP

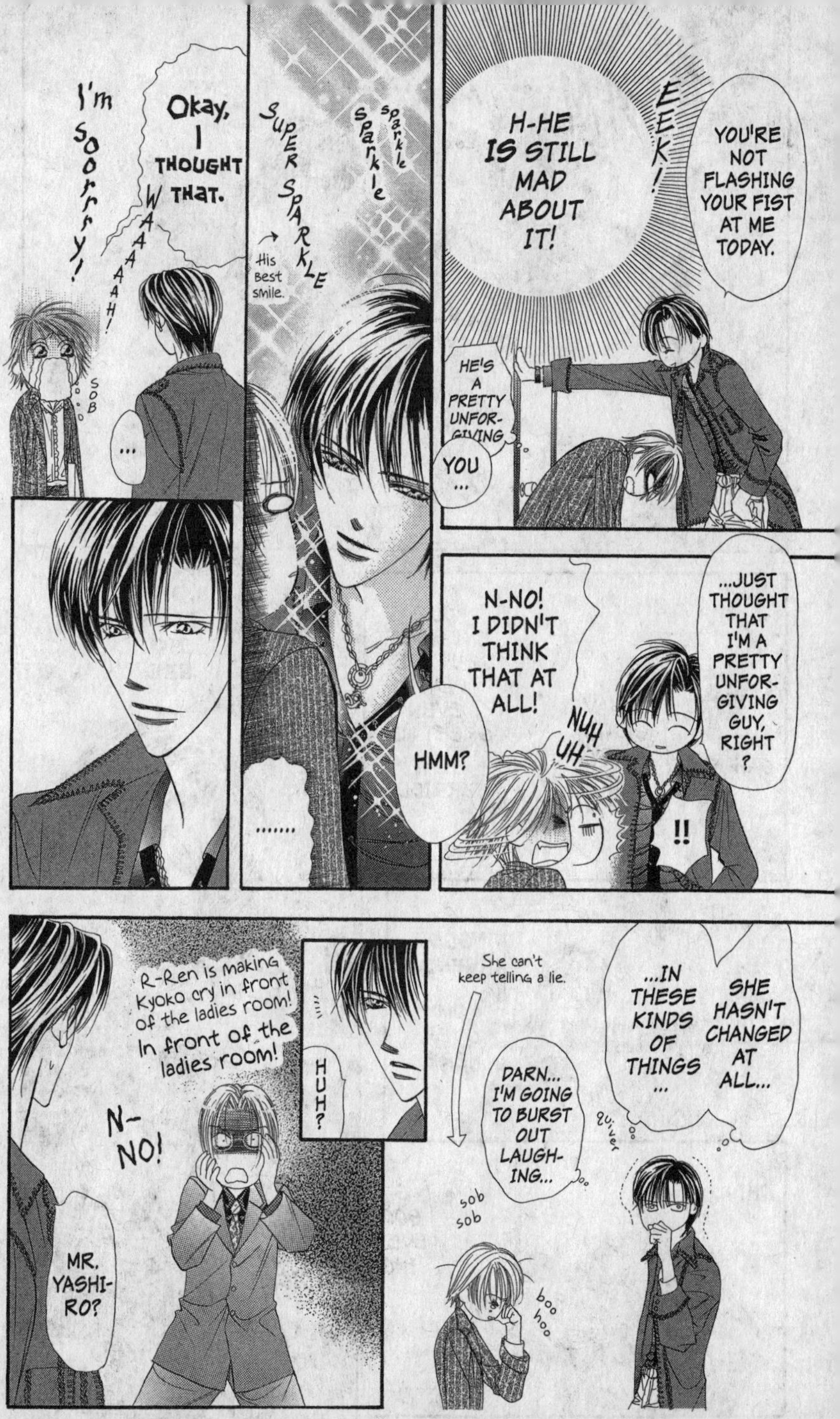
YOU'RE NOT FLASHING YOUR FIST AT ME TODAY.
EEK!
H-HE IS STILL MAD ABOUT IT!
HE'S A PRETTY UNFORGIVING
YOU...
...JUST THOUGHT THAT I'M A PRETTY UNFORGIVING GUY, RIGHT?
!!
N-NO! I DIDN'T THINK THAT AT ALL!
NUH UH
HMM?
sparkle sparkle
SUPER SPARKLE
His Best smile.
....
Okay, I THOUGHT THAT.
WAAAAAAH!
I'm sooorrry!
SOB
...
SHE HASN'T CHANGED AT ALL...
...IN THESE KINDS OF THINGS...
quiver
DARN... I'M GOING TO BURST OUT LAUGHING...
She can't keep telling a lie.
sob sob
boo hoo
HUH?
R-Ren is making Kyoko cry in front of the ladies room! In front of the ladies room!
N-NO!
MR. YASHIRO?

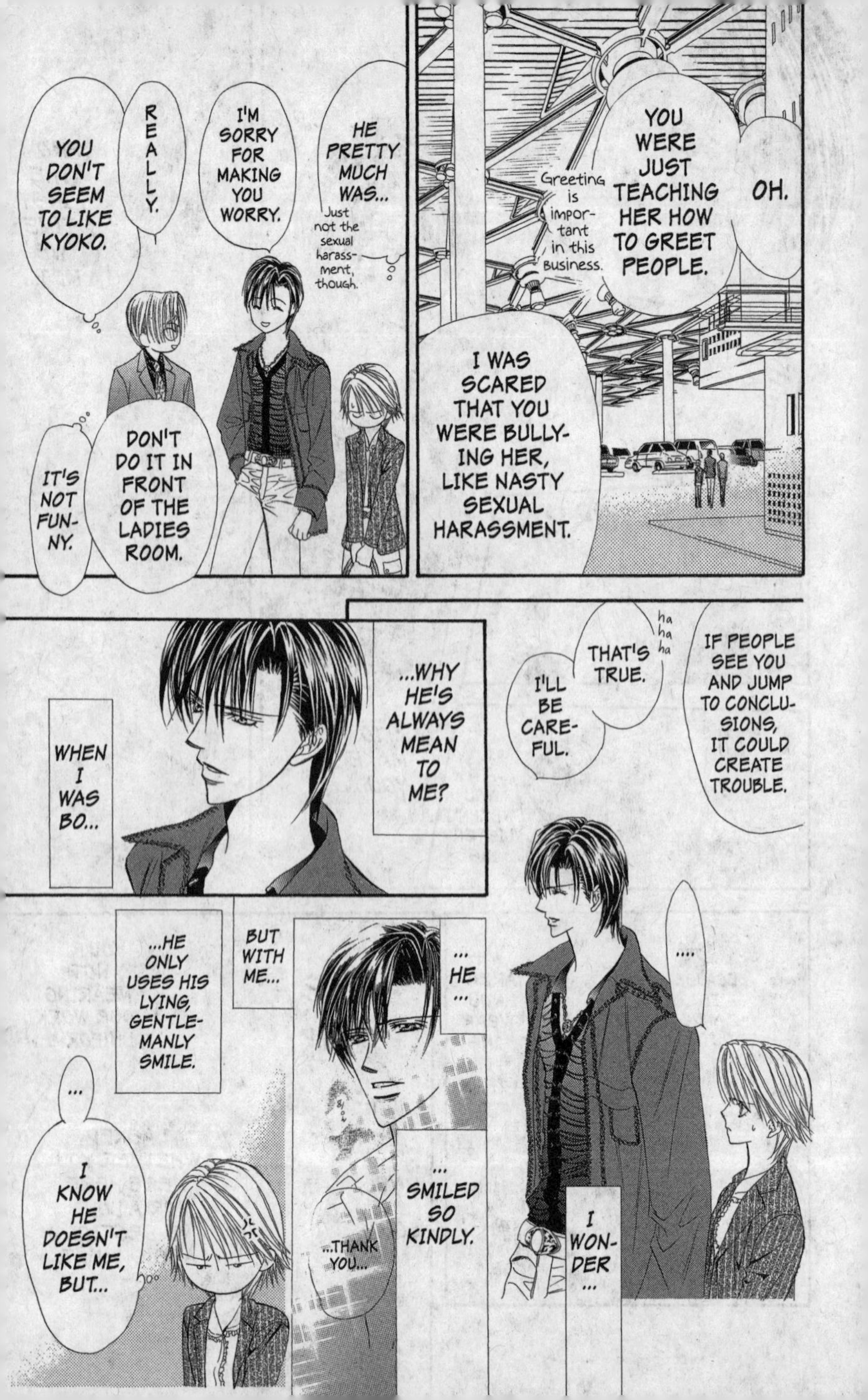
OH.
YOU WERE JUST TEACHING HER HOW TO GREET PEOPLE.
Greeting is important in this business.
I WAS SCARED THAT YOU WERE BULLYING HER, LIKE NASTY SEXUAL HARASSMENT.
HE PRETTY MUCH WAS...
Just not the sexual harassment, though.
I'M SORRY FOR MAKING YOU WORRY.
REALLY.
YOU DON'T SEEM TO LIKE KYOKO.
DON'T DO IT IN FRONT OF THE LADIES ROOM.
IT'S NOT FUNNY.
IF PEOPLE SEE YOU AND JUMP TO CONCLUSIONS, IT COULD CREATE TROUBLE.
ha ha ha
THAT'S TRUE.
I'LL BE CAREFUL.
...WHY HE'S ALWAYS MEAN TO ME?
WHEN I WAS BO...
....
I WONDER...
...HE...
...SMILED SO KINDLY.
...THANK YOU...
BUT WITH ME...
...HE ONLY USES HIS LYING, GENTLEMANLY SMILE.
...
I KNOW HE DOESN'T LIKE ME, BUT...

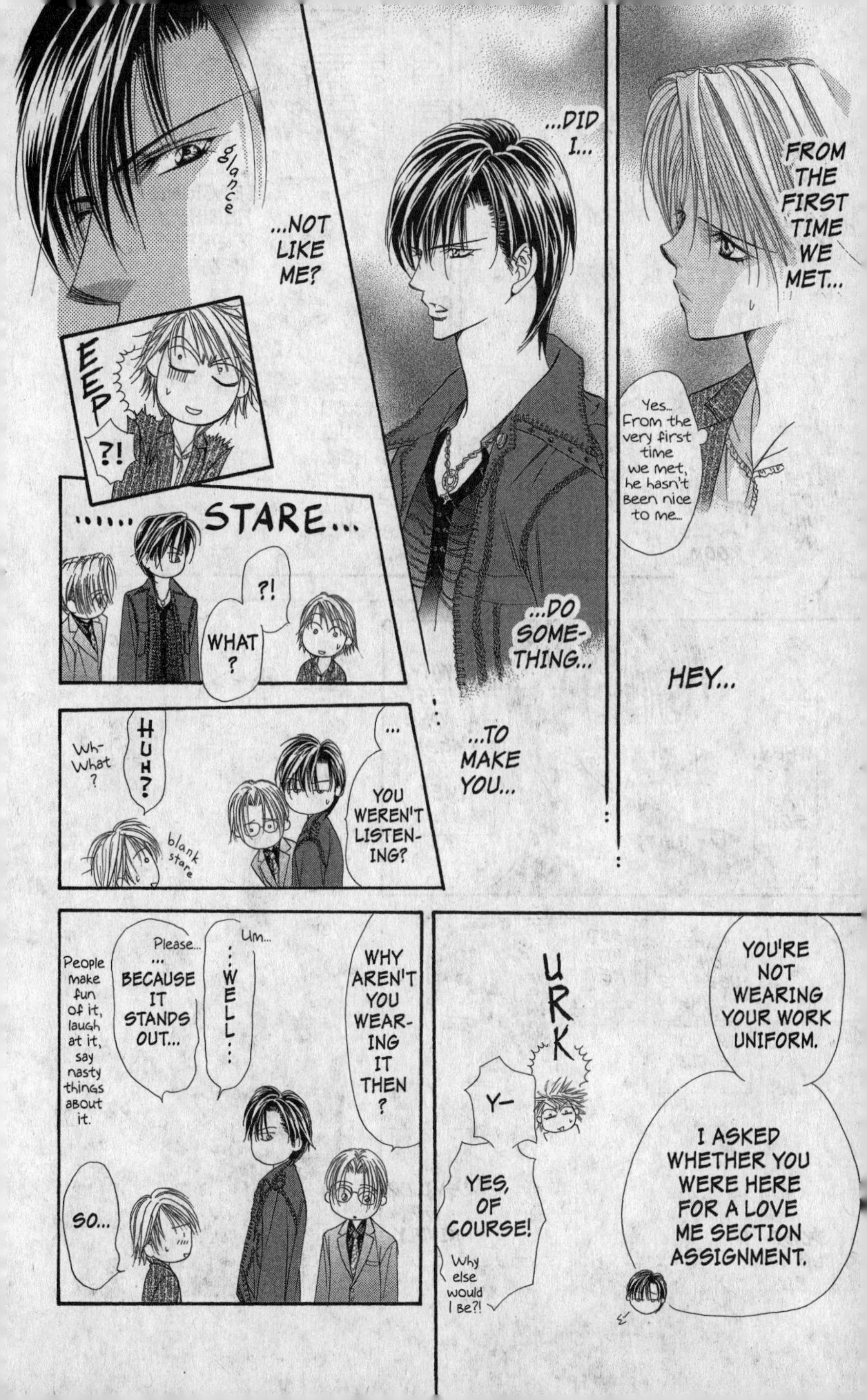
FROM THE FIRST TIME WE MET...
Yes... From the very first time we met, he hasn't been nice to me...
HEY...
...DID I...
...DO SOMETHING...
...TO MAKE YOU...
glance
...NOT LIKE ME?
EEP
?!
...... STARE...
?!
WHAT?
...
YOU WEREN'T LISTENING?
HUH?
Wh-What?
blank stare
YOU'RE NOT WEARING YOUR WORK UNIFORM.
I ASKED WHETHER YOU WERE HERE FOR A LOVE ME SECTION ASSIGNMENT.
URK
Y-
YES, OF COURSE!
Why else would I be?!
WHY AREN'T YOU WEARING IT THEN?
Um... ...WELL...
Please... ...BECAUSE IT STANDS OUT...
People make fun of it, laugh at it, say nasty things about it.
SO...

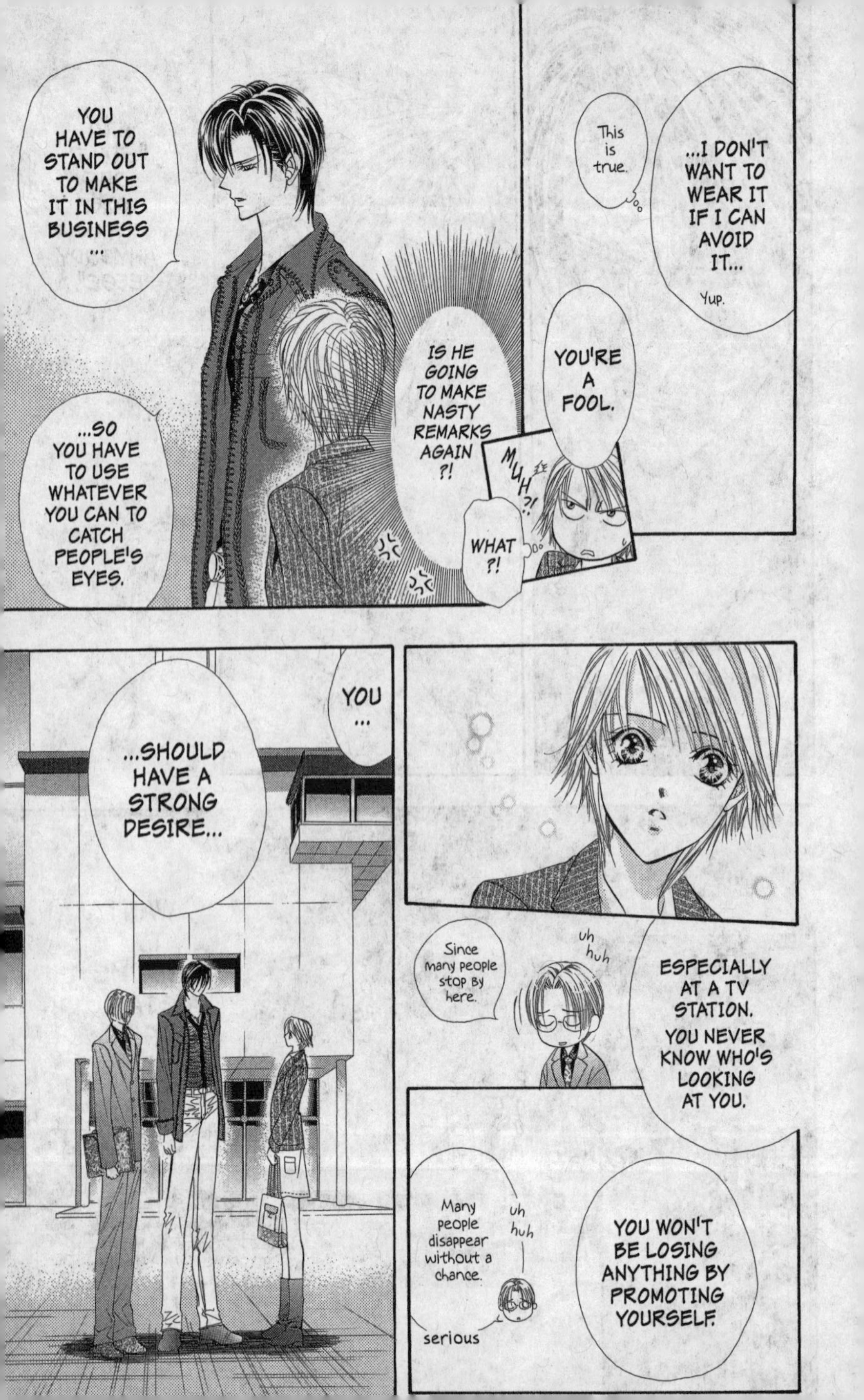
...I DON'T WANT TO WEAR IT IF I CAN AVOID IT...
This is true.
Yup.
YOU'RE A FOOL.
MUH ?!
WHAT ?!
IS HE GOING TO MAKE NASTY REMARKS AGAIN ?!
YOU HAVE TO STAND OUT TO MAKE IT IN THIS BUSINESS ...
...SO YOU HAVE TO USE WHATEVER YOU CAN TO CATCH PEOPLE'S EYES.
ESPECIALLY AT A TV STATION. YOU NEVER KNOW WHO'S LOOKING AT YOU.
uh huh
Since many people stop by here.
YOU WON'T BE LOSING ANYTHING BY PROMOTING YOURSELF.
uh huh
Many people disappear without a chance.
serious
YOU ...
...SHOULD HAVE A STRONG DESIRE...

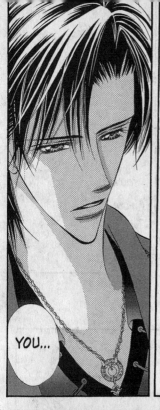

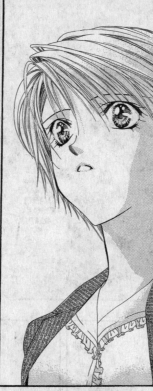

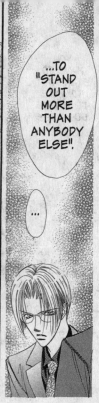

..."TO "STAND OUT MORE THAN ANYBODY ELSE".

...

YOU...

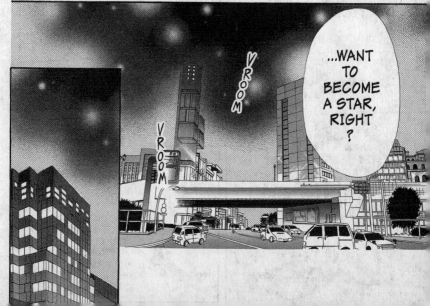

...WANT TO BECOME A STAR, RIGHT ?

VROOM

VROOM

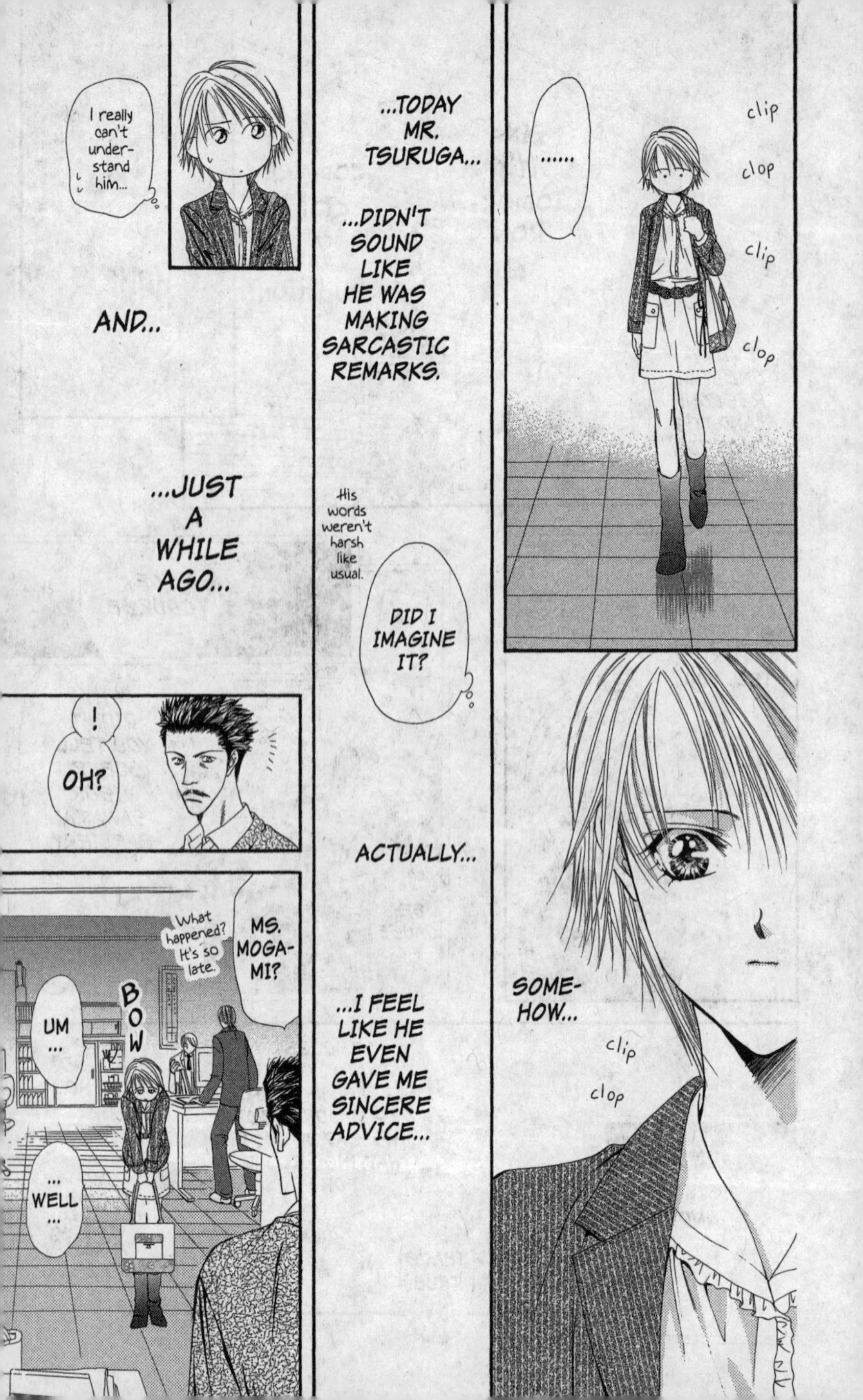

......
clip
clop
clip
clop
SOME-HOW...
clip
clop
...TODAY MR. TSURUGA...
...DIDN'T SOUND LIKE HE WAS MAKING SARCASTIC REMARKS.
His words weren't harsh like usual.
DID I IMAGINE IT?
ACTUALLY...
...I FEEL LIKE HE EVEN GAVE ME SINCERE ADVICE...
I really can't under-stand him...
AND...
...JUST A WHILE AGO...
!
OH?
MS. MOGA-MI?
What happened? It's so late.
BOW
UM...
...WELL...

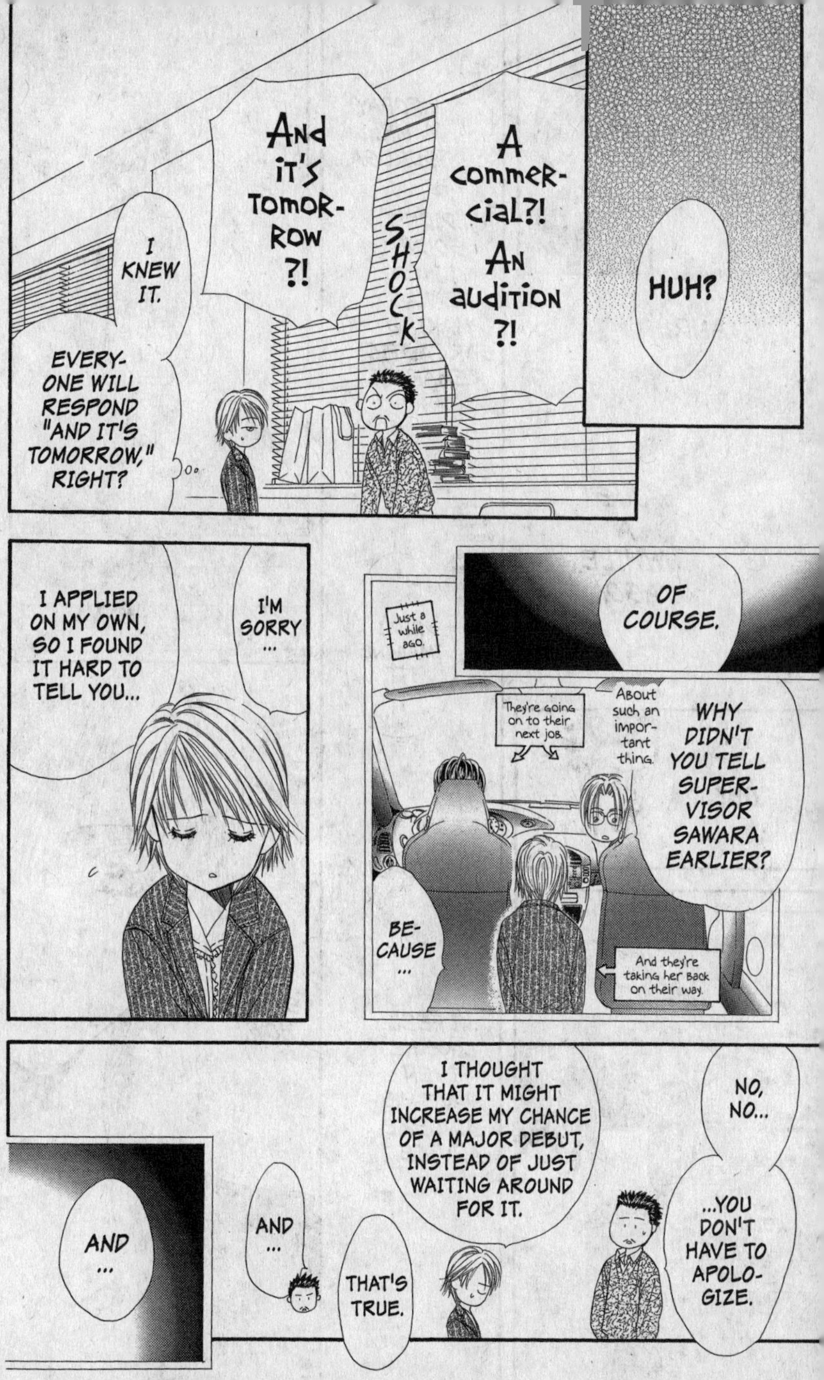
HUH?
A commercial?! An audition?!
SHOCK
And it's tomorrow?!
I KNEW IT.
EVERYONE WILL RESPOND "AND IT'S TOMORROW," RIGHT?
OF COURSE.
Just a while ago.
WHY DIDN'T YOU TELL SUPERVISOR SAWARA EARLIER?
About such an important thing.
They're going on to their next job.
And they're taking her back on their way.
BECAUSE...
I'M SORRY...
I APPLIED ON MY OWN, SO I FOUND IT HARD TO TELL YOU...
NO, NO...
...YOU DON'T HAVE TO APOLOGIZE.
I THOUGHT THAT IT MIGHT INCREASE MY CHANCE OF A MAJOR DEBUT, INSTEAD OF JUST WAITING AROUND FOR IT.
THAT'S TRUE.
AND...
AND...

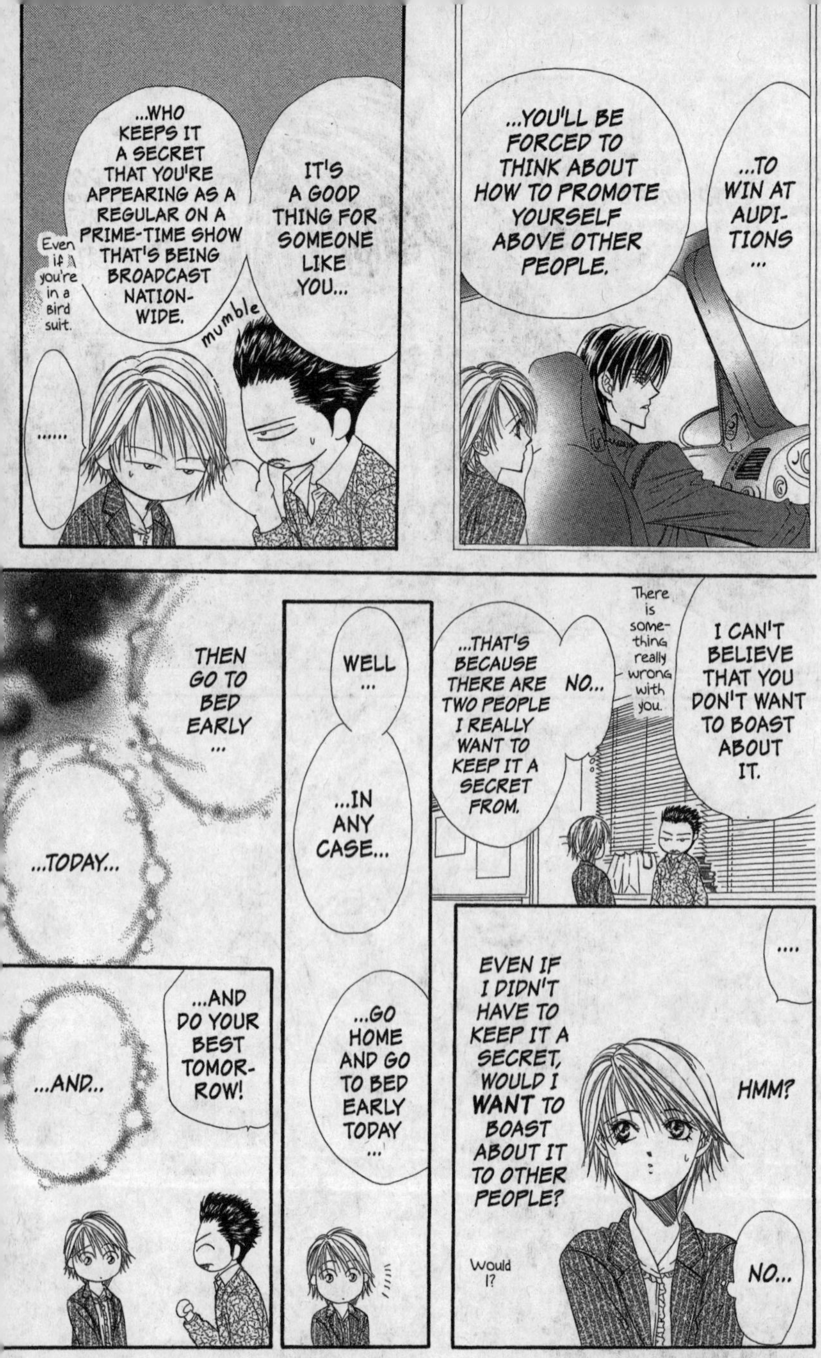
...TO WIN AT AUDITIONS...
...YOU'LL BE FORCED TO THINK ABOUT HOW TO PROMOTE YOURSELF ABOVE OTHER PEOPLE.
IT'S A GOOD THING FOR SOMEONE LIKE YOU...
...WHO KEEPS IT A SECRET THAT YOU'RE APPEARING AS A REGULAR ON A PRIME-TIME SHOW THAT'S BEING BROADCAST NATION-WIDE.
Even if you're in a bird suit.
mumble
......
I CAN'T BELIEVE THAT YOU DON'T WANT TO BOAST ABOUT IT.
There is some-thing really wrong with you.
NO...
...THAT'S BECAUSE THERE ARE TWO PEOPLE I REALLY WANT TO KEEP IT A SECRET FROM.
....
HMM?
EVEN IF I DIDN'T HAVE TO KEEP IT A SECRET, WOULD I **WANT** TO BOAST ABOUT IT TO OTHER PEOPLE?
NO...
Would I?
WELL...
...IN ANY CASE...
...GO HOME AND GO TO BED EARLY TODAY...
THEN GO TO BED EARLY...
...TODAY...
...AND DO YOUR BEST TOMOR-ROW!
...AND...

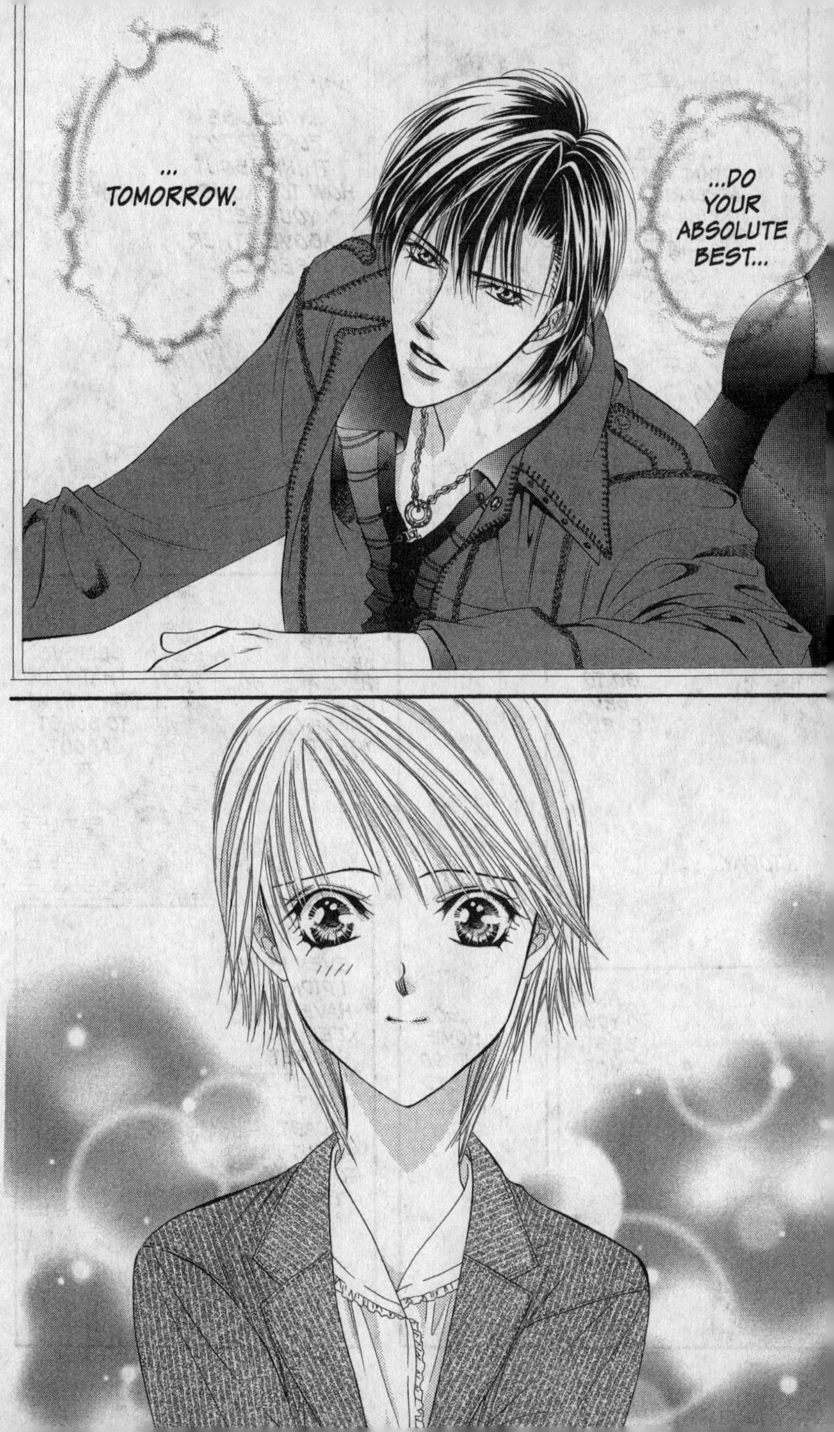
...DO YOUR ABSOLUTE BEST...
... TOMORROW.

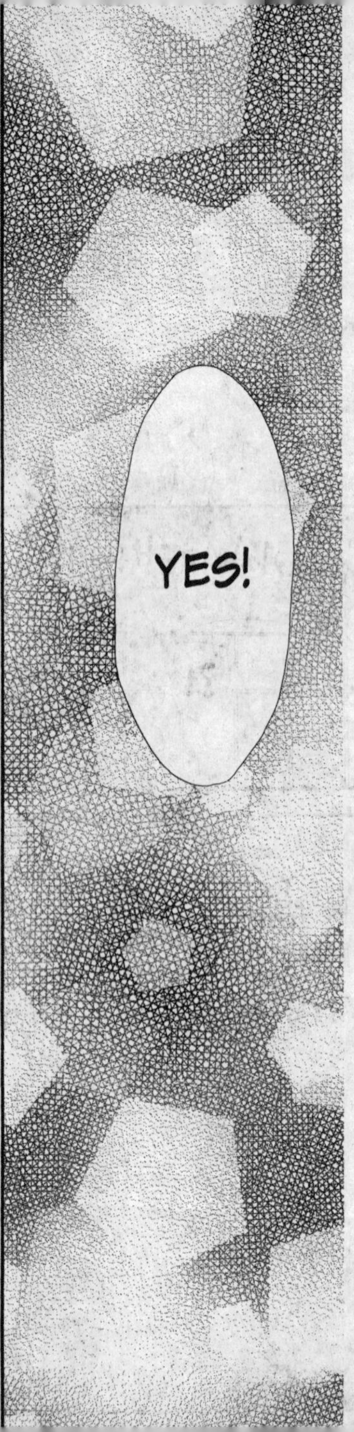
YES!

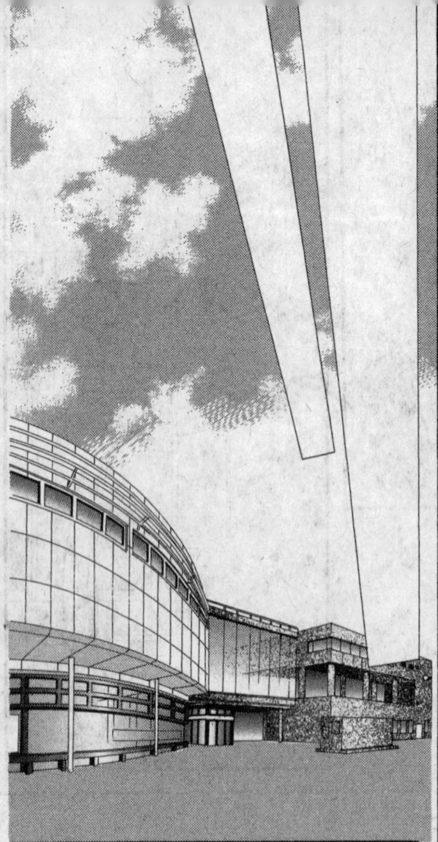

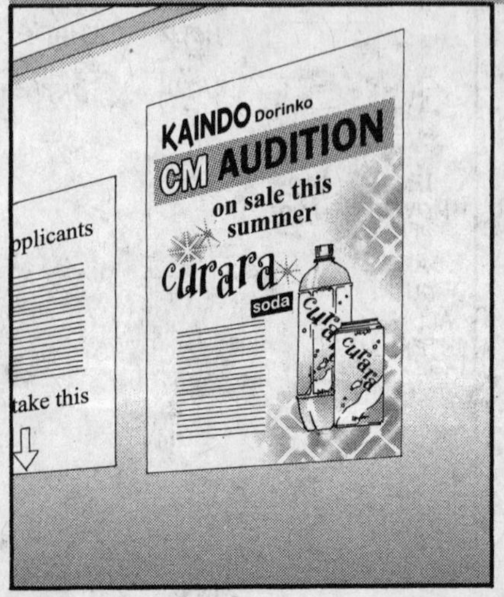
pplicants
take this
KAINDO Dorinko
CM AUDITION
on sale this summer
curara
soda
curara
curara

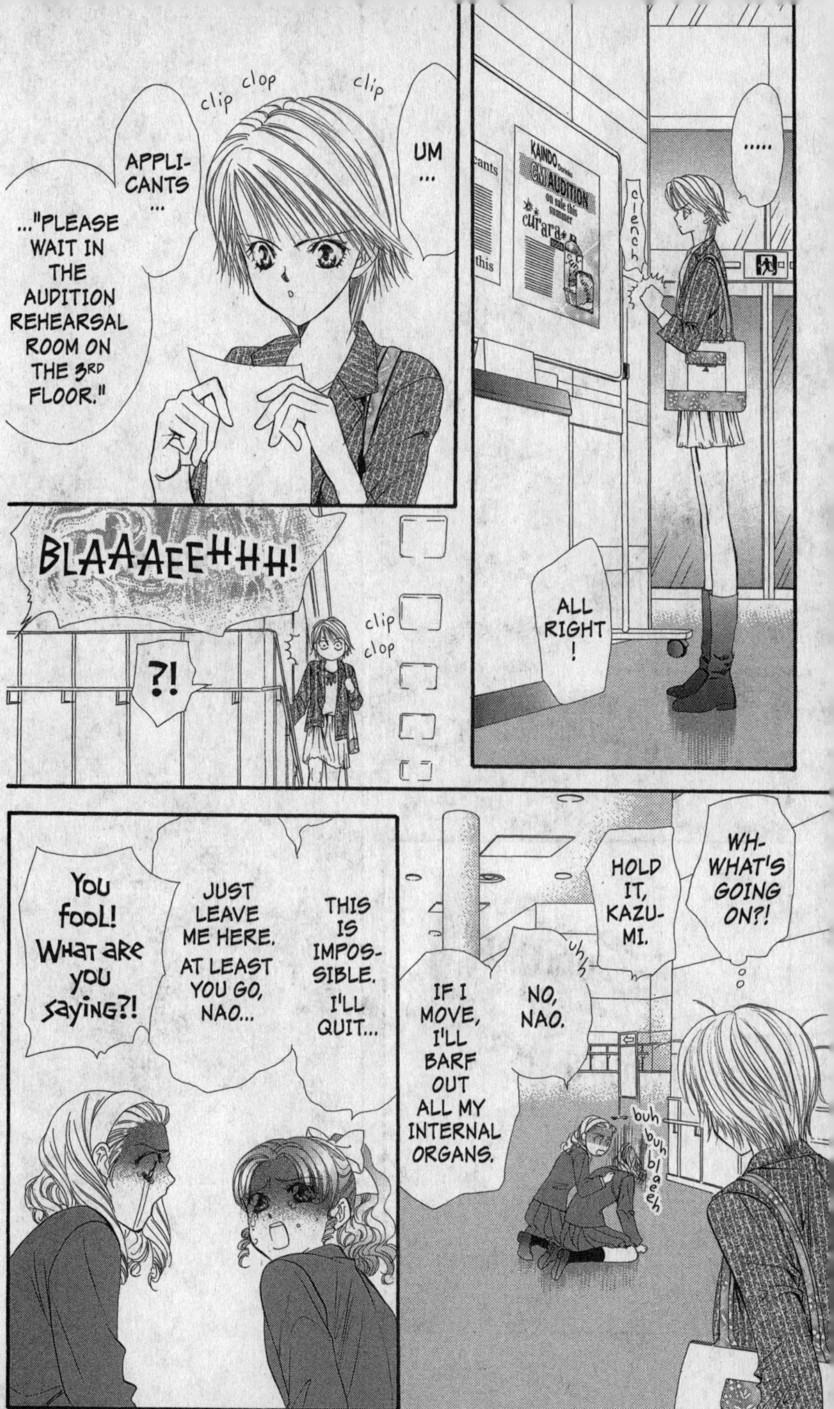
.....
KAINDO
CM AUDITION
on sale this summer
curara
clench
ALL RIGHT!
clip clop clip
UM...
APPLICANTS...
..."PLEASE WAIT IN THE AUDITION REHEARSAL ROOM ON THE 3RD FLOOR."
BLAAAEEHHH!
?!
clip clop
WH-WHAT'S GOING ON?!
HOLD IT, KAZUMI.
uhh
NO, NAO.
IF I MOVE, I'LL BARF OUT ALL MY INTERNAL ORGANS.
buh buh blaeeh
THIS IS IMPOSSIBLE. I'LL QUIT...
JUST LEAVE ME HERE. AT LEAST YOU GO, NAO...
You fool! What are you saying?!

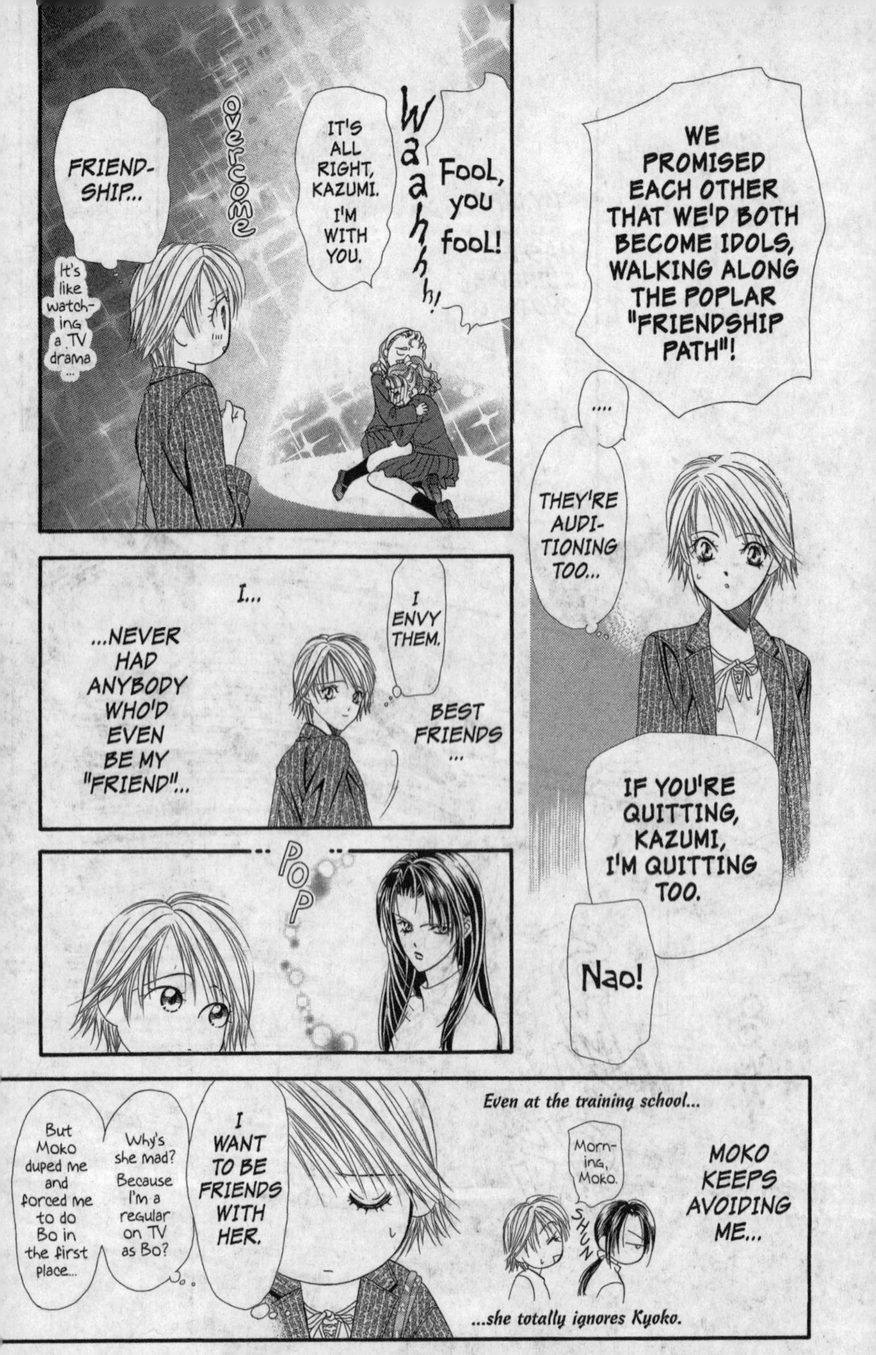

WE PROMISED EACH OTHER THAT WE'D BOTH BECOME IDOLS, WALKING ALONG THE POPLAR "FRIENDSHIP PATH"!
....
THEY'RE AUDITIONING TOO...
IF YOU'RE QUITTING, KAZUMI, I'M QUITTING TOO.
Nao!
Fool, you fool!
Wahhhh!
IT'S ALL RIGHT, KAZUMI. I'M WITH YOU.
overcome
FRIENDSHIP...
It's like watching a TV drama...
I ENVY THEM.
BEST FRIENDS...
I...
...NEVER HAD ANYBODY WHO'D EVEN BE MY "FRIEND"...
POP
Even at the training school...
MOKO KEEPS AVOIDING ME...
Morning, Moko.
SHUN
...she totally ignores Kyoko.
I WANT TO BE FRIENDS WITH HER.
Why's she mad? Because I'm a regular on TV as Bo?
But Moko duped me and forced me to do Bo in the first place...

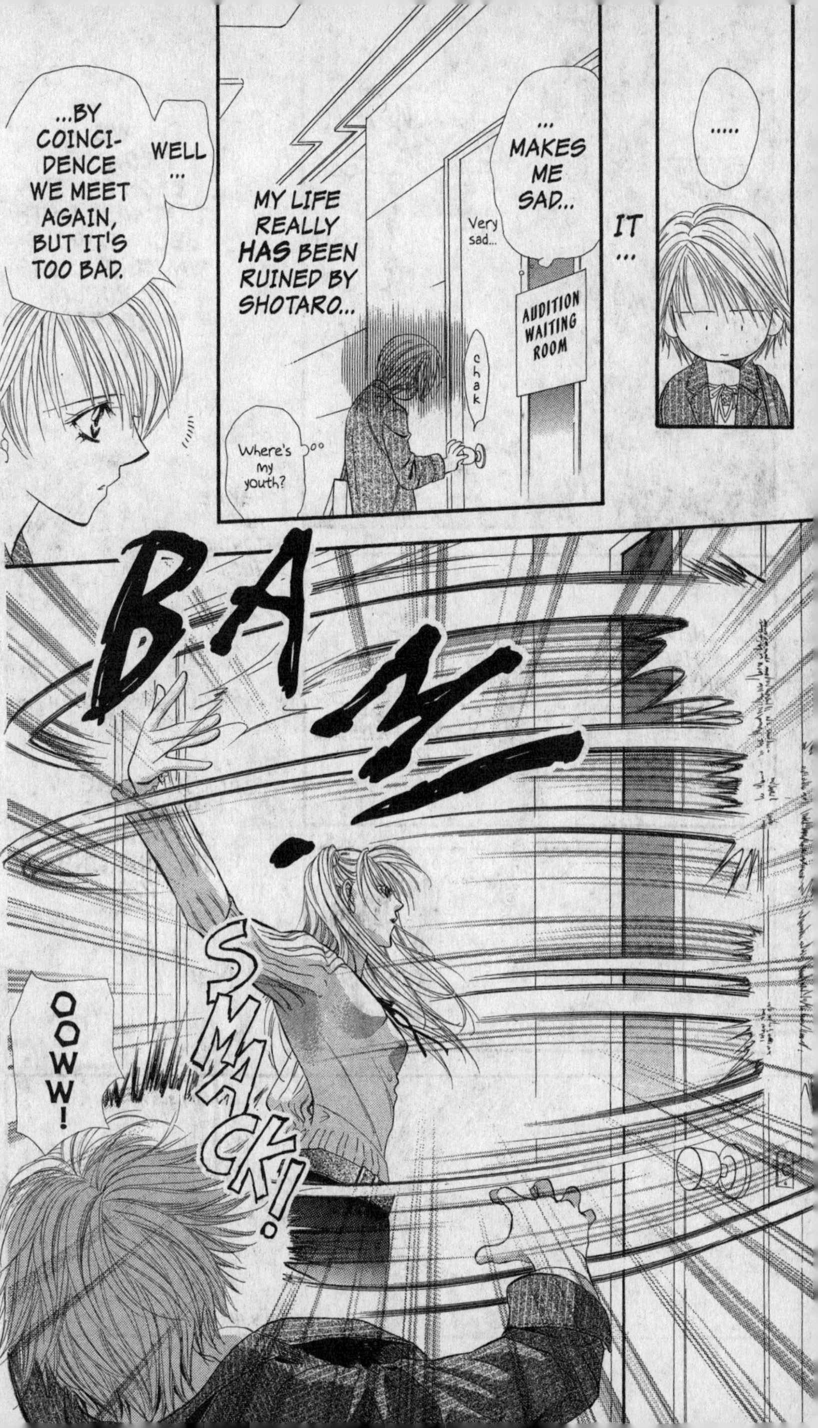
.....
IT ...
... MAKES ME SAD...
Very sad...
AUDITION WAITING ROOM
MY LIFE REALLY HAS BEEN RUINED BY SHOTARO...
chak
Where's my youth?
WELL ...
...BY COINCI-DENCE WE MEET AGAIN, BUT IT'S TOO BAD.
BAM
SMACK!
OOWW!

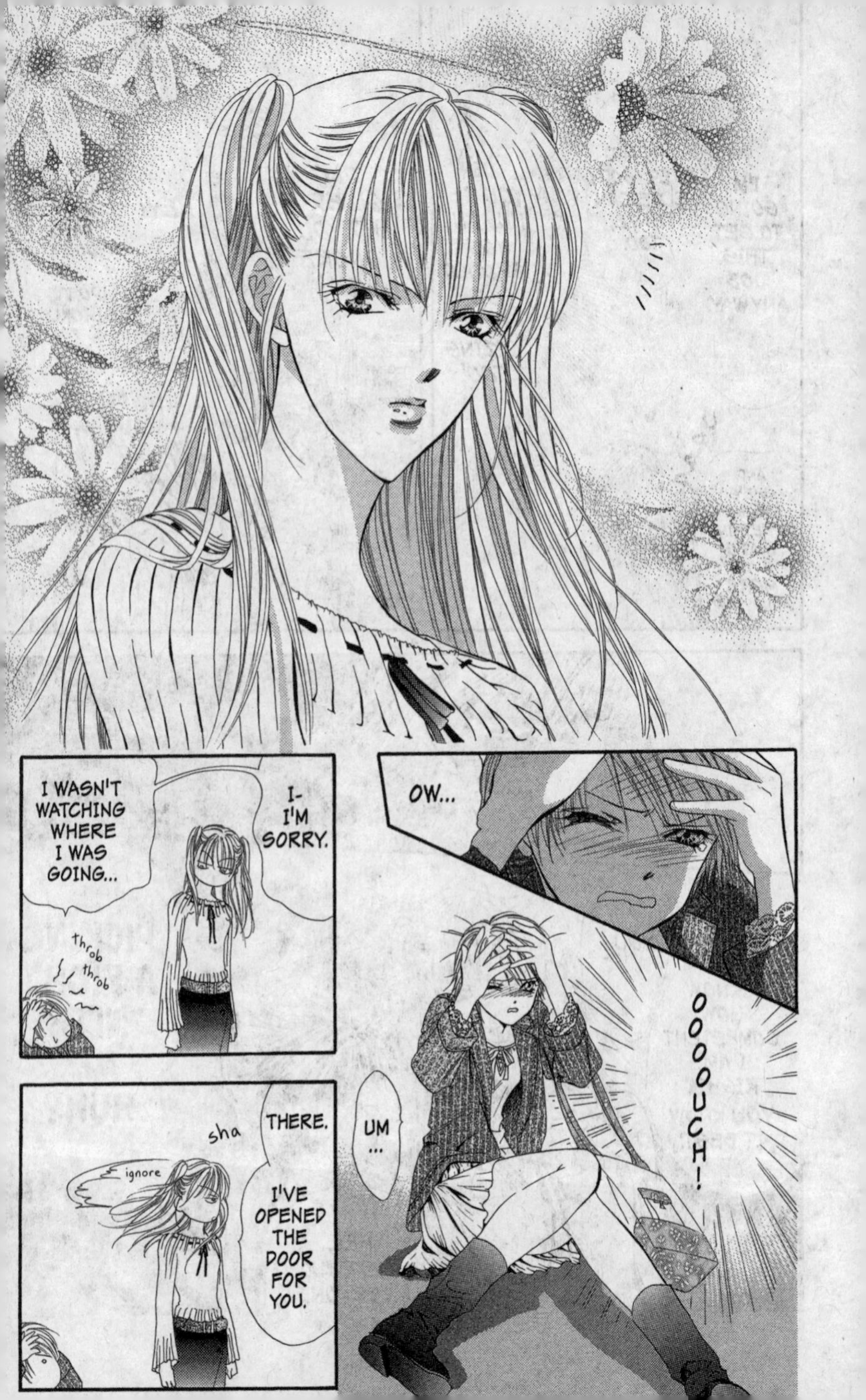
OW...
OOOOUCH!
UM ...
I- I'M SORRY.
I WASN'T WATCHING WHERE I WAS GOING...
throb throb
THERE.
I'VE OPENED THE DOOR FOR YOU.
sha
ignore

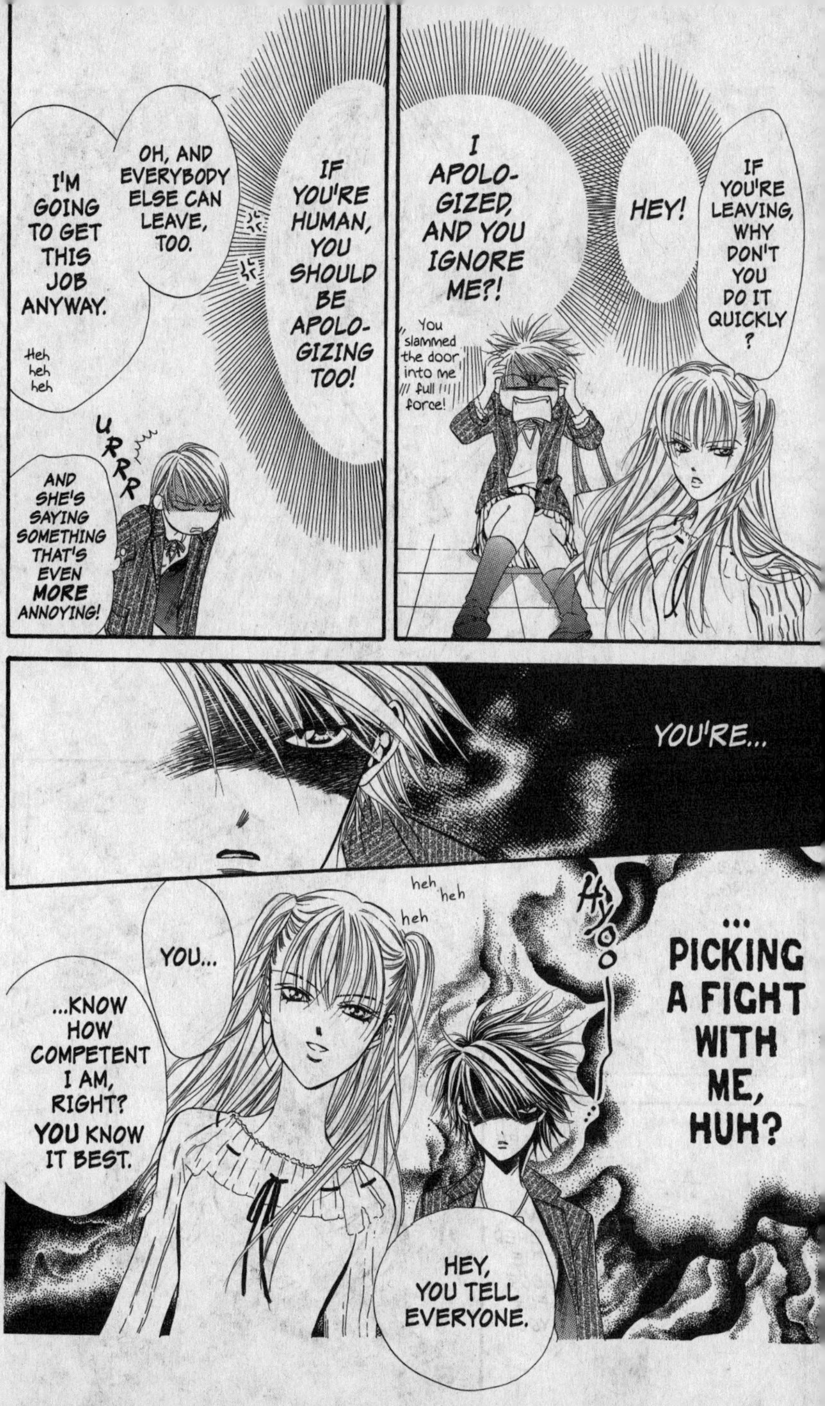
IF YOU'RE LEAVING, WHY DON'T YOU DO IT QUICKLY?
HEY!
I APOLOGIZED, AND YOU IGNORE ME?!
You slammed the door into me full force!
IF YOU'RE HUMAN, YOU SHOULD BE APOLOGIZING TOO!
OH, AND EVERYBODY ELSE CAN LEAVE, TOO.
I'M GOING TO GET THIS JOB ANYWAY.
Heh heh heh
URRR
AND SHE'S SAYING SOMETHING THAT'S EVEN MORE ANNOYING!
YOU'RE...
...PICKING A FIGHT WITH ME, HUH?
Hyoo
heh heh heh
YOU...
...KNOW HOW COMPETENT I AM, RIGHT? YOU KNOW IT BEST.
HEY, YOU TELL EVERYONE.

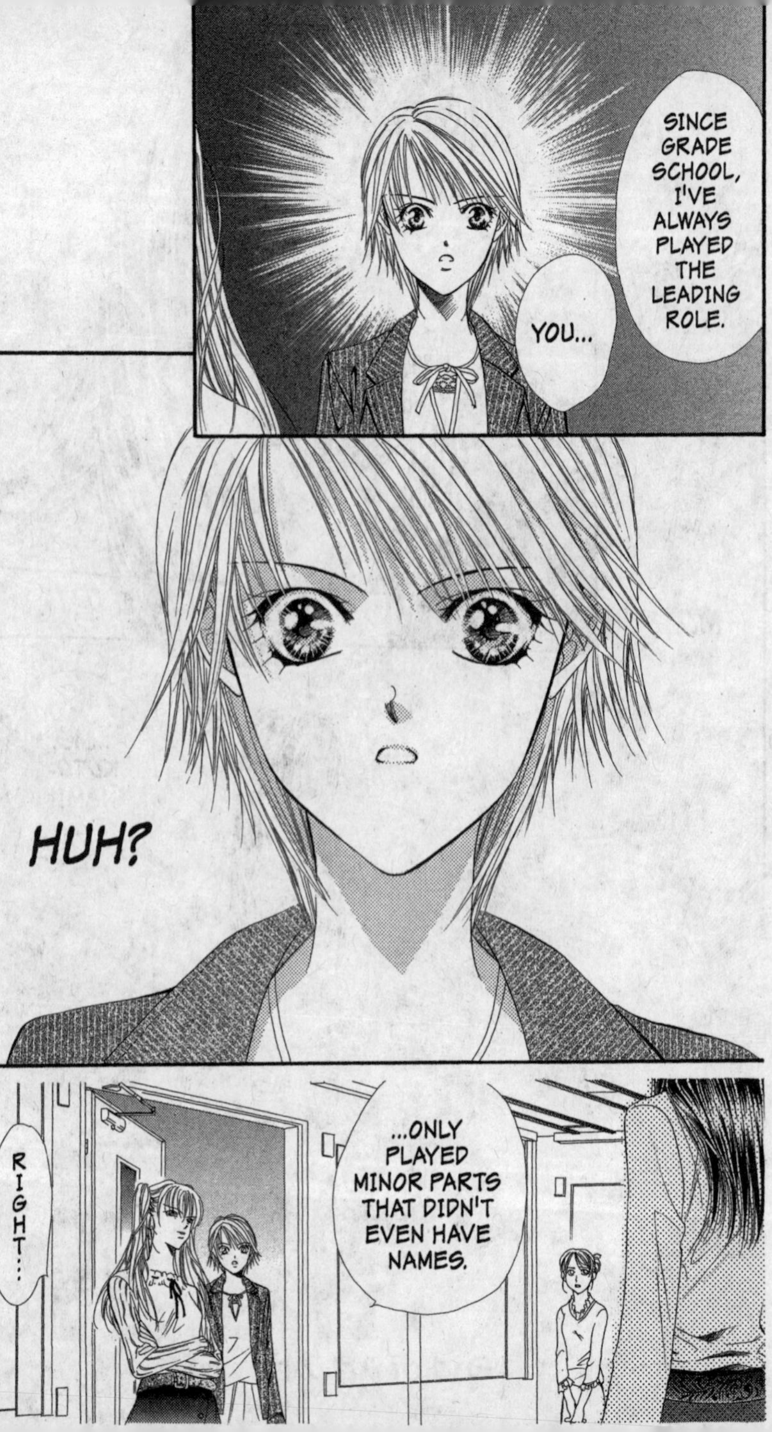
SINCE GRADE SCHOOL, I'VE ALWAYS PLAYED THE LEADING ROLE.
YOU...
HUH?
...ONLY PLAYED MINOR PARTS THAT DIDN'T EVEN HAVE NAMES.
RIGHT...

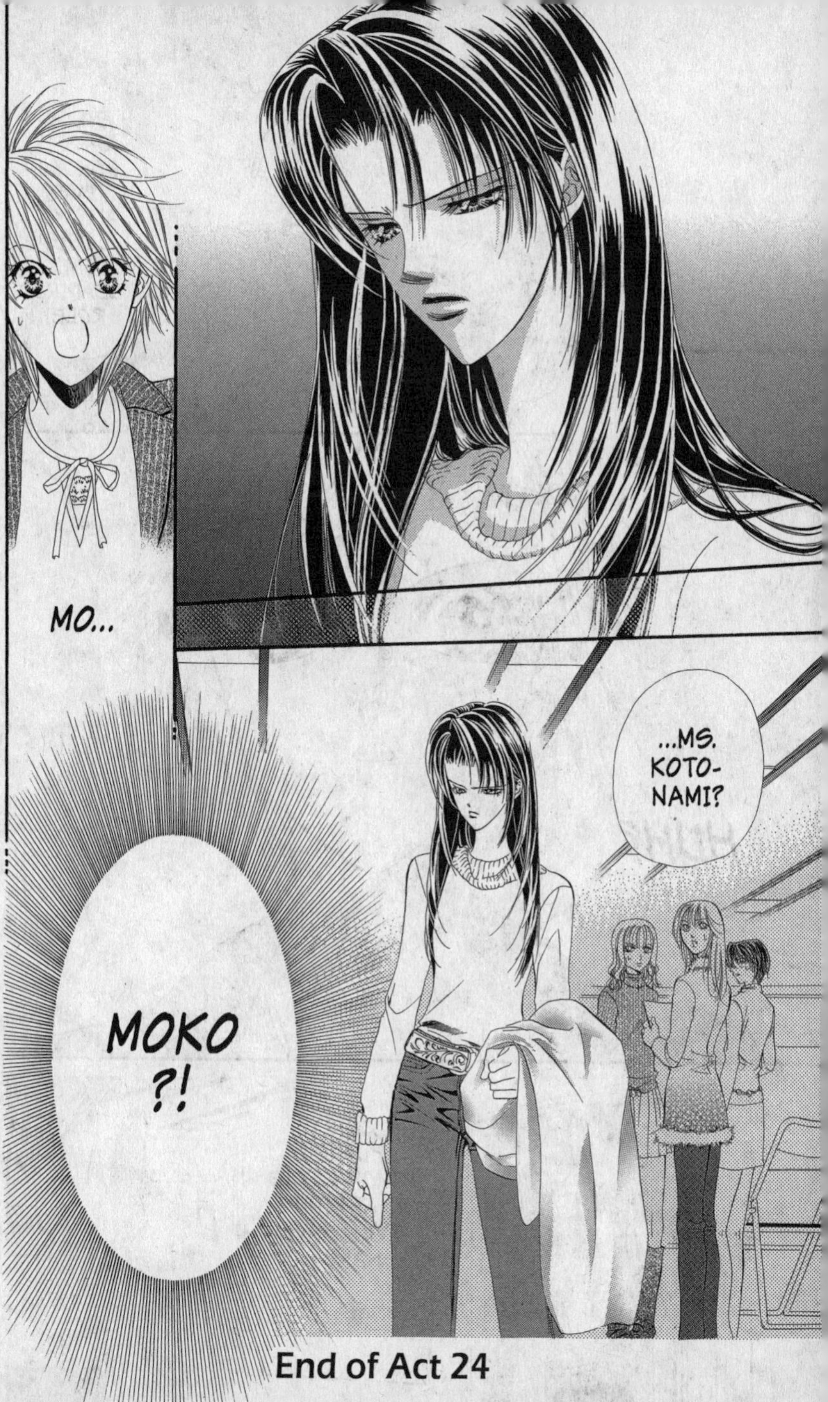
...MS. KOTO-NAMI?
MO...
MOKO ?!

End of Act 24

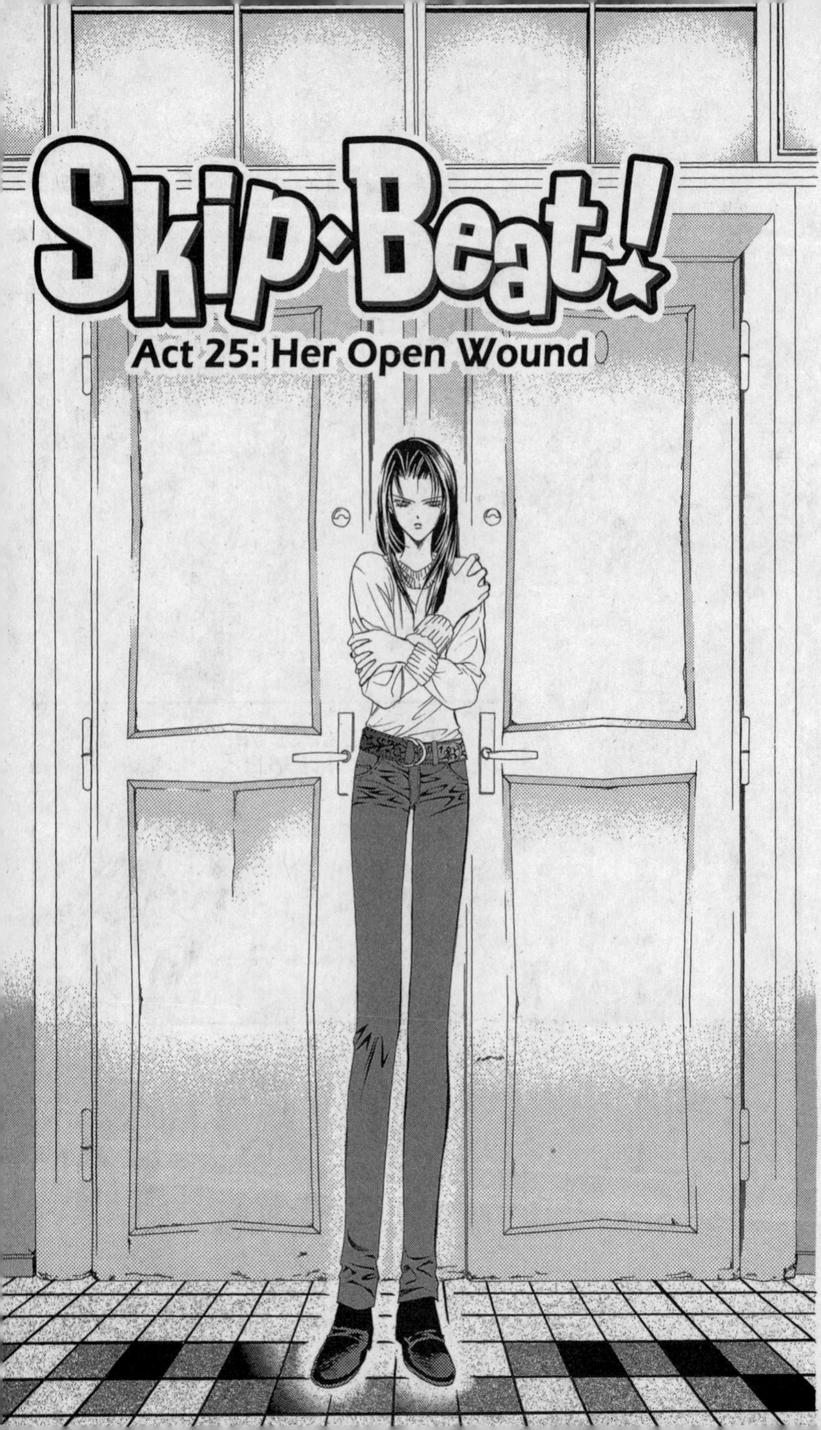
Skip·Beat!
Act 25: Her Open Wound

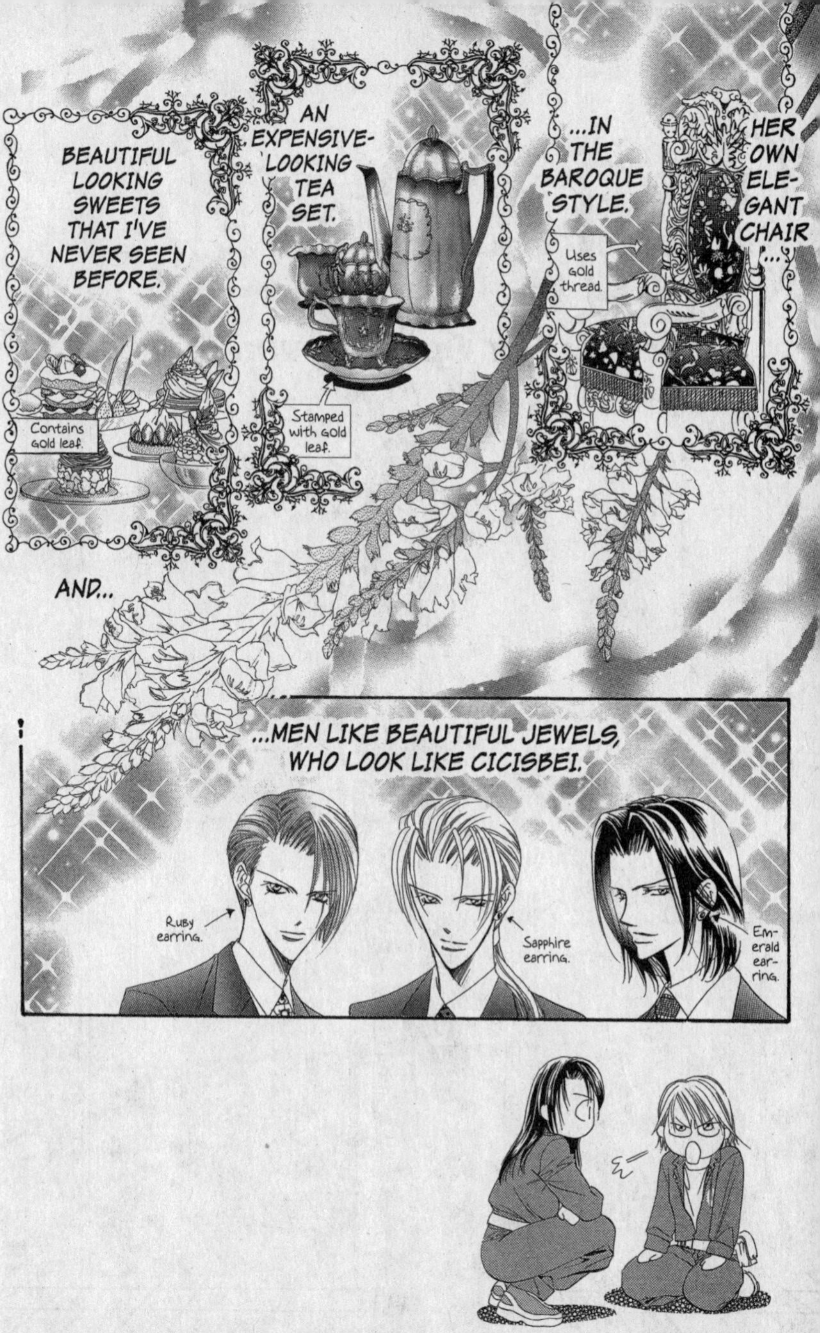
HER OWN ELEGANT CHAIR...
...IN THE BAROQUE STYLE.
Uses gold thread.
AN EXPENSIVE-LOOKING TEA SET.
Stamped with gold leaf.
BEAUTIFUL LOOKING SWEETS THAT I'VE NEVER SEEN BEFORE.
Contains gold leaf.
AND...
...MEN LIKE BEAUTIFUL JEWELS, WHO LOOK LIKE CICISBEI.
Emerald earring.
Sapphire earring.
Ruby earring.

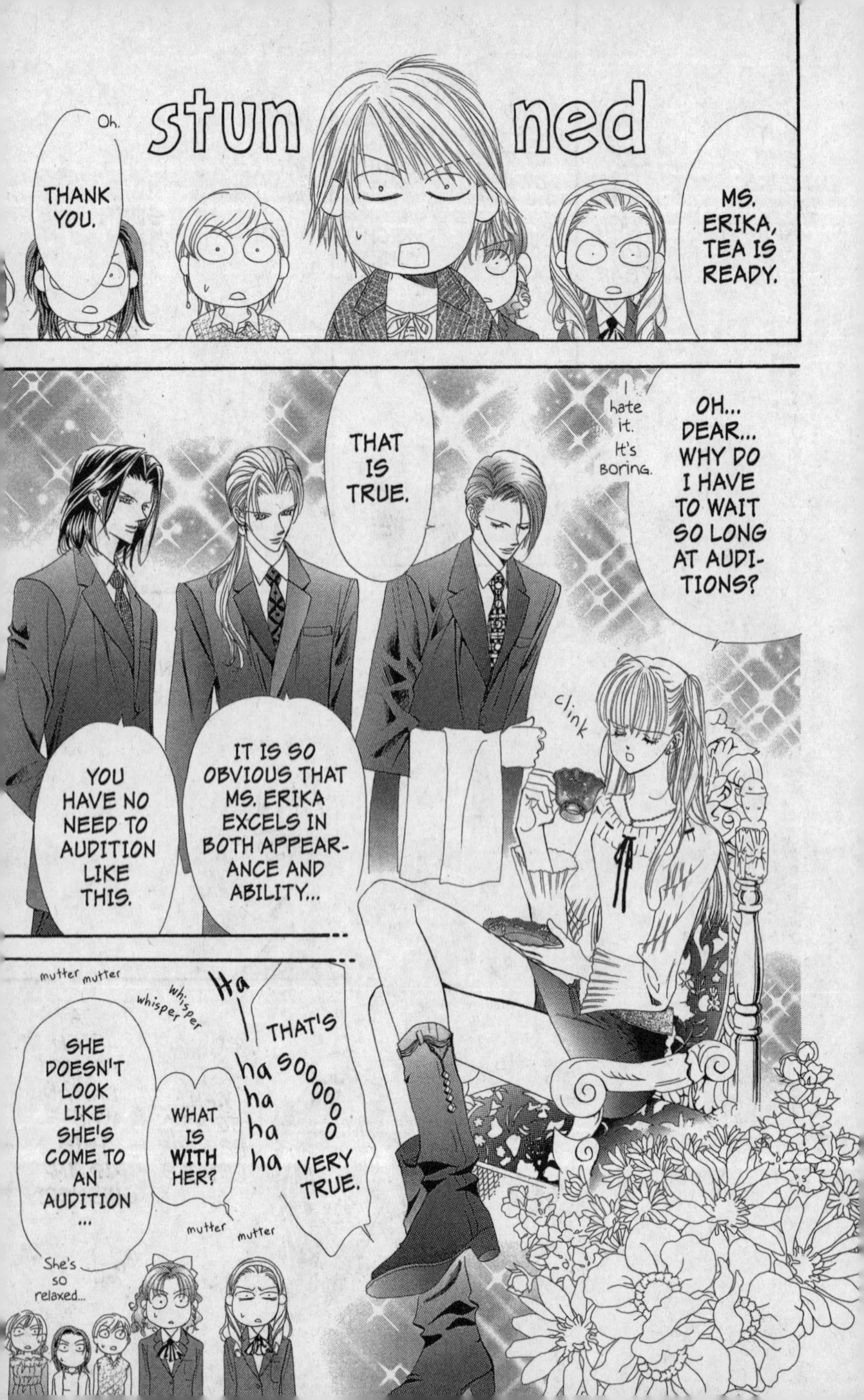
MS. ERIKA, TEA IS READY.
stunned
Oh.
THANK YOU.
OH... DEAR... WHY DO I HAVE TO WAIT SO LONG AT AUDITIONS?
I hate it. It's boring.
THAT IS TRUE.
clink
IT IS SO OBVIOUS THAT MS. ERIKA EXCELS IN BOTH APPEARANCE AND ABILITY...
YOU HAVE NO NEED TO AUDITION LIKE THIS.
Ha ha ha ha ha
THAT'S SOOOOOOO VERY TRUE.
mutter mutter
whisper whisper
WHAT IS WITH HER?
SHE DOESN'T LOOK LIKE SHE'S COME TO AN AUDITION...
mutter mutter
She's so relaxed...

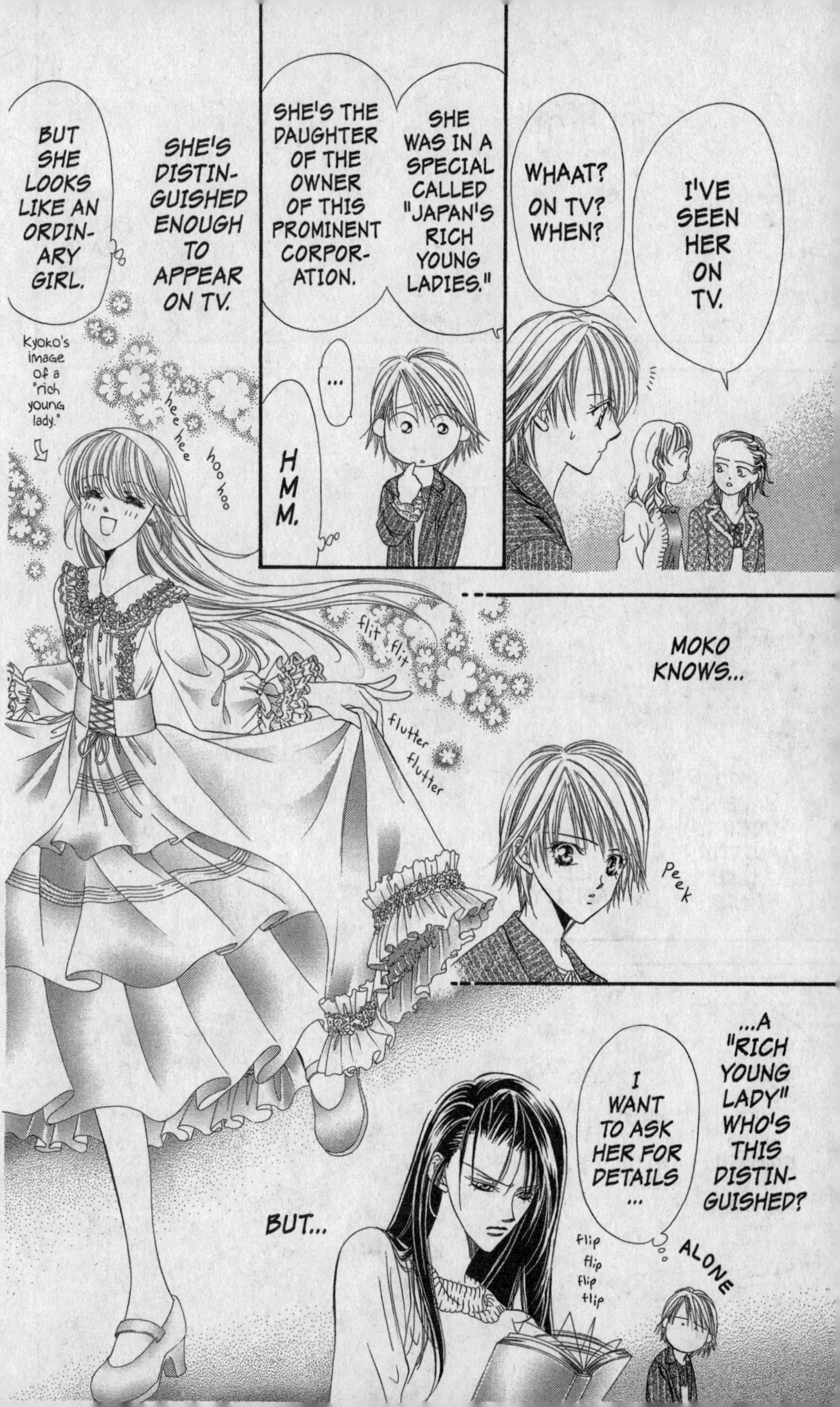

I'VE SEEN HER ON TV.
WHAAT? ON TV? WHEN?
SHE WAS IN A SPECIAL CALLED "JAPAN'S RICH YOUNG LADIES."
SHE'S THE DAUGHTER OF THE OWNER OF THIS PROMINENT CORPORATION.
...
HMM.
SHE'S DISTINGUISHED ENOUGH TO APPEAR ON TV.
BUT SHE LOOKS LIKE AN ORDINARY GIRL.
Kyoko's image of a "rich young lady."
hee hee
hoo hoo
flit flit
flutter flutter
MOKO KNOWS...
Peek
...A "RICH YOUNG LADY" WHO'S THIS DISTINGUISHED?
I WANT TO ASK HER FOR DETAILS...
BUT...
flip flip flip flip
ALONE

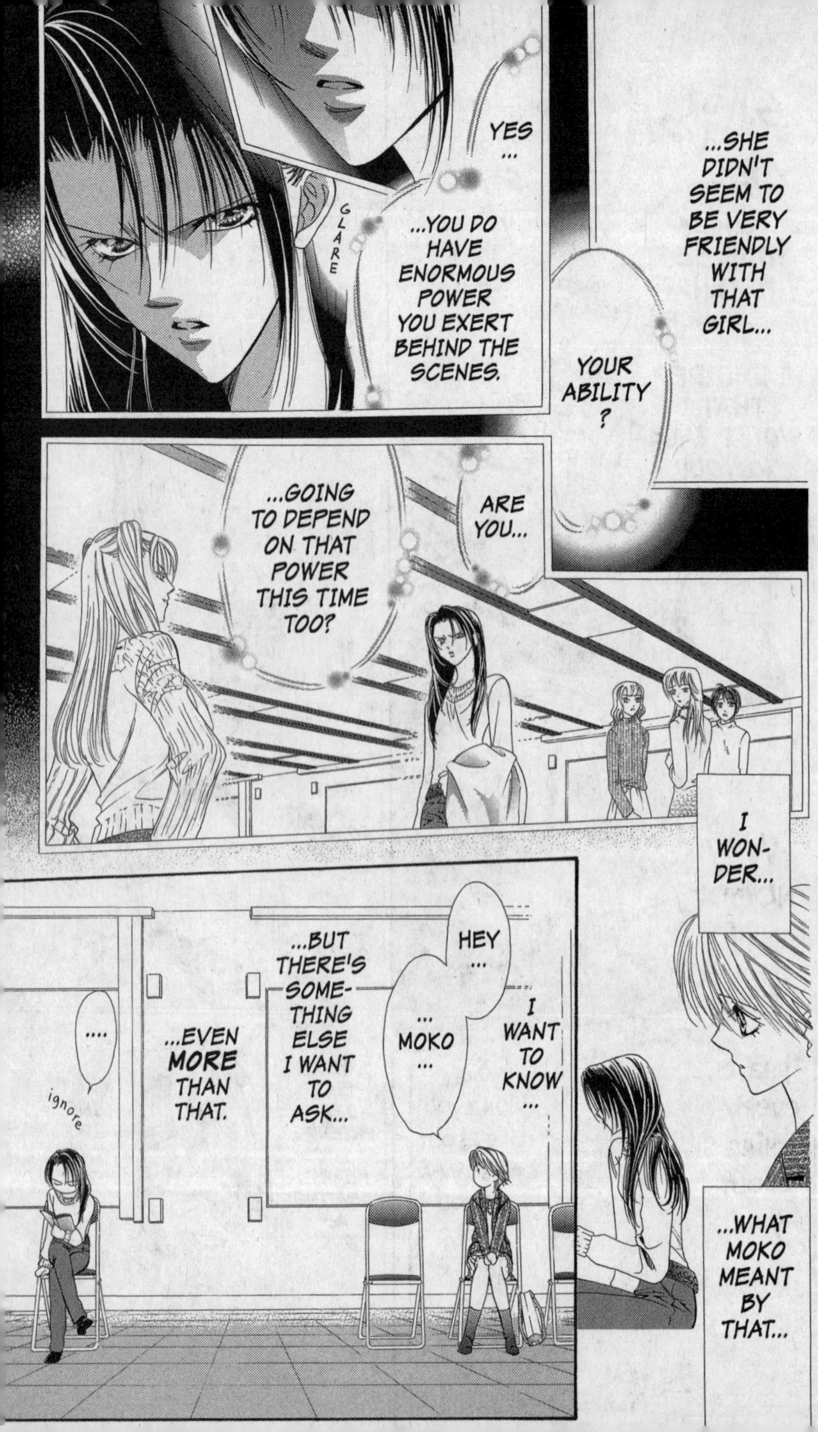

...SHE DIDN'T SEEM TO BE VERY FRIENDLY WITH THAT GIRL...
YOUR ABILITY?
YES...
...YOU DO HAVE ENORMOUS POWER YOU EXERT BEHIND THE SCENES.
GLARE
ARE YOU...
...GOING TO DEPEND ON THAT POWER THIS TIME TOO?
I WONDER...
...WHAT MOKO MEANT BY THAT...
HEY... ...MOKO...
I WANT TO KNOW...
...BUT THERE'S SOMETHING ELSE I WANT TO ASK...
...EVEN MORE THAN THAT.
....
ignore

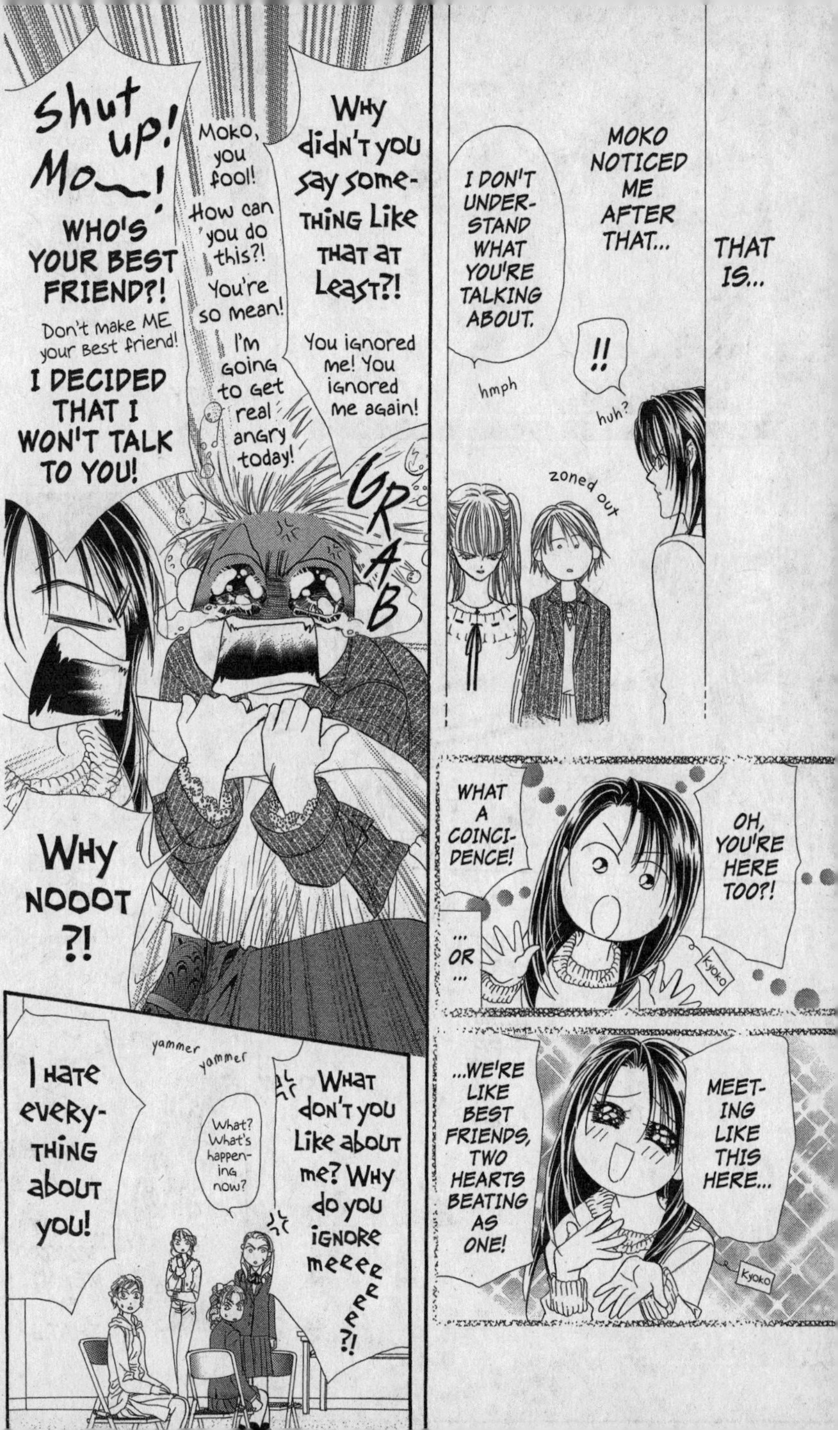
THAT IS...
MOKO NOTICED ME AFTER THAT...
!!
huh?
I DON'T UNDERSTAND WHAT YOU'RE TALKING ABOUT.
hmph
zoned out
OH, YOU'RE HERE TOO?!
WHAT A COINCIDENCE!
...OR...
Kyoko
MEETING LIKE THIS HERE...
...WE'RE LIKE BEST FRIENDS, TWO HEARTS BEATING AS ONE!
Kyoko
WHY didn't you say something like that at least?!
You ignored me! You ignored me again!
Moko, you fool!
How can you do this?!
You're so mean!
I'm going to get real angry today!
Shut up! Mo~!
WHO'S YOUR BEST FRIEND?!
Don't make ME your best friend!
I DECIDED THAT I WON'T TALK TO YOU!
GRAB
WHY NOOOT?!
WHAT don't you like about me? Why do you ignore meeeeeeee?!
What? What's happening now?
yammer yammer
I hate everything about you!

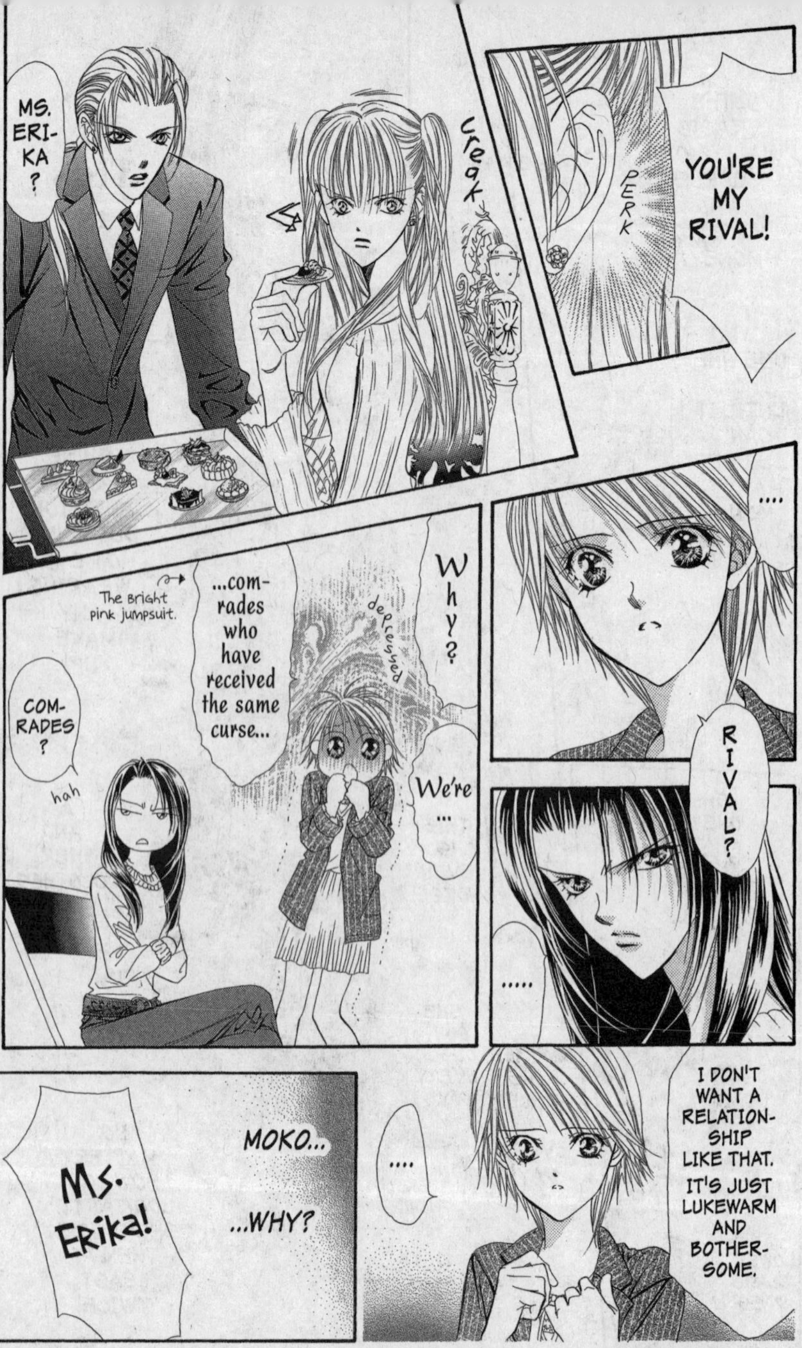
PERK
YOU'RE MY RIVAL!
creak
MS. ERIKA?
....
RIVAL?
.....
Why?
depressed
We're...
...comrades who have received the same curse...
The bright pink jumpsuit.
COMRADES?
hah
I DON'T WANT A RELATIONSHIP LIKE THAT.
IT'S JUST LUKEWARM AND BOTHERSOME.
....
MOKO...
...WHY?
Ms. Erika!

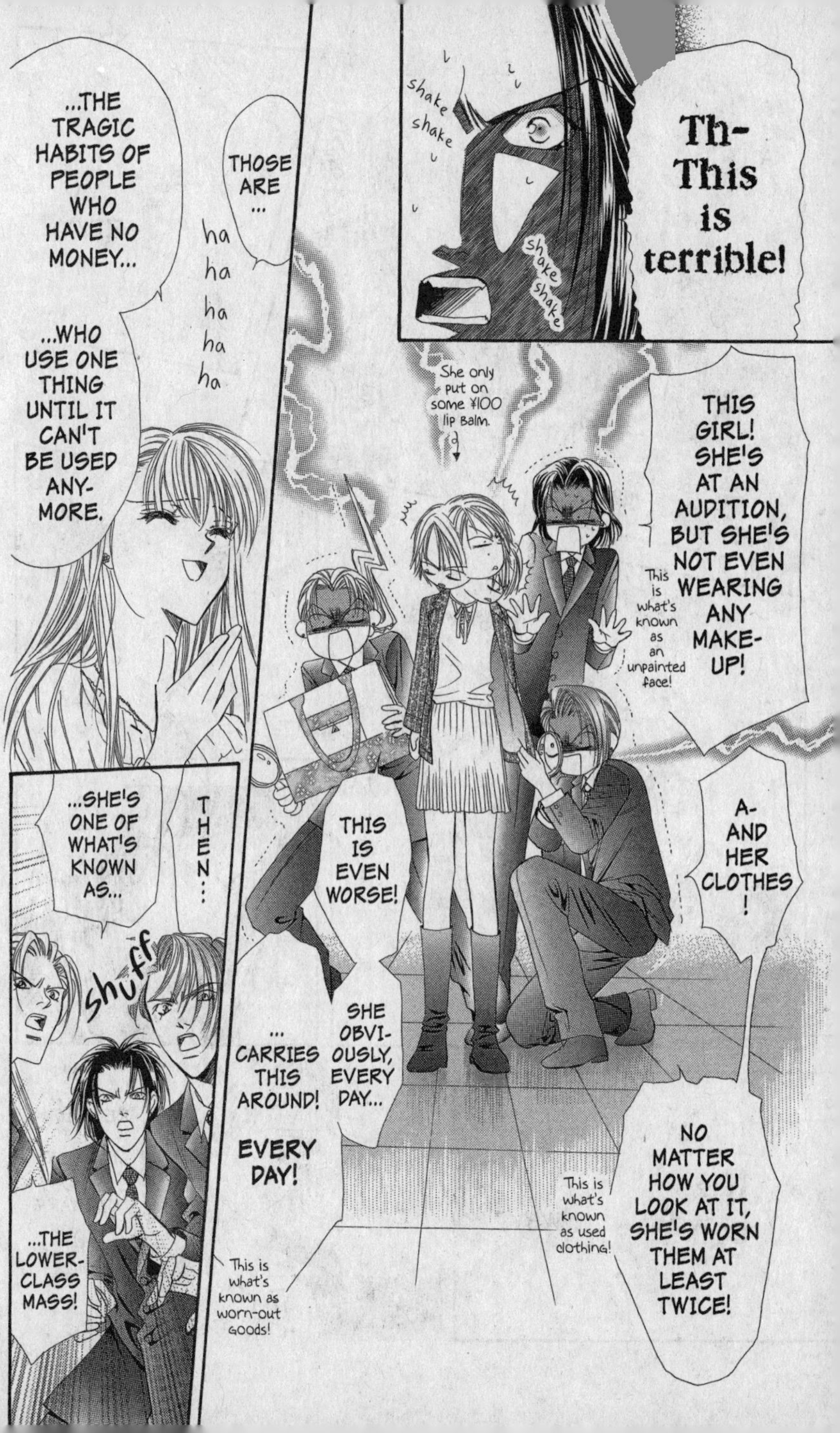
shake shake
Th-This is terrible!
shake shake
THIS GIRL! SHE'S AT AN AUDITION, BUT SHE'S NOT EVEN WEARING ANY MAKE-UP!
This is what's known as an unpainted face!
She only put on some ¥100 lip balm.
A-AND HER CLOTHES!
NO MATTER HOW YOU LOOK AT IT, SHE'S WORN THEM AT LEAST TWICE!
This is what's known as used clothing!
THIS IS EVEN WORSE!
SHE OBVIOUSLY, EVERY DAY...
...CARRIES THIS AROUND!
EVERY DAY!
This is what's known as worn-out goods!
THOSE ARE...
ha ha ha ha ha
...THE TRAGIC HABITS OF PEOPLE WHO HAVE NO MONEY...
...WHO USE ONE THING UNTIL IT CAN'T BE USED ANYMORE.
THEN...
...SHE'S ONE OF WHAT'S KNOWN AS...
shuff
...THE LOWER-CLASS MASS!

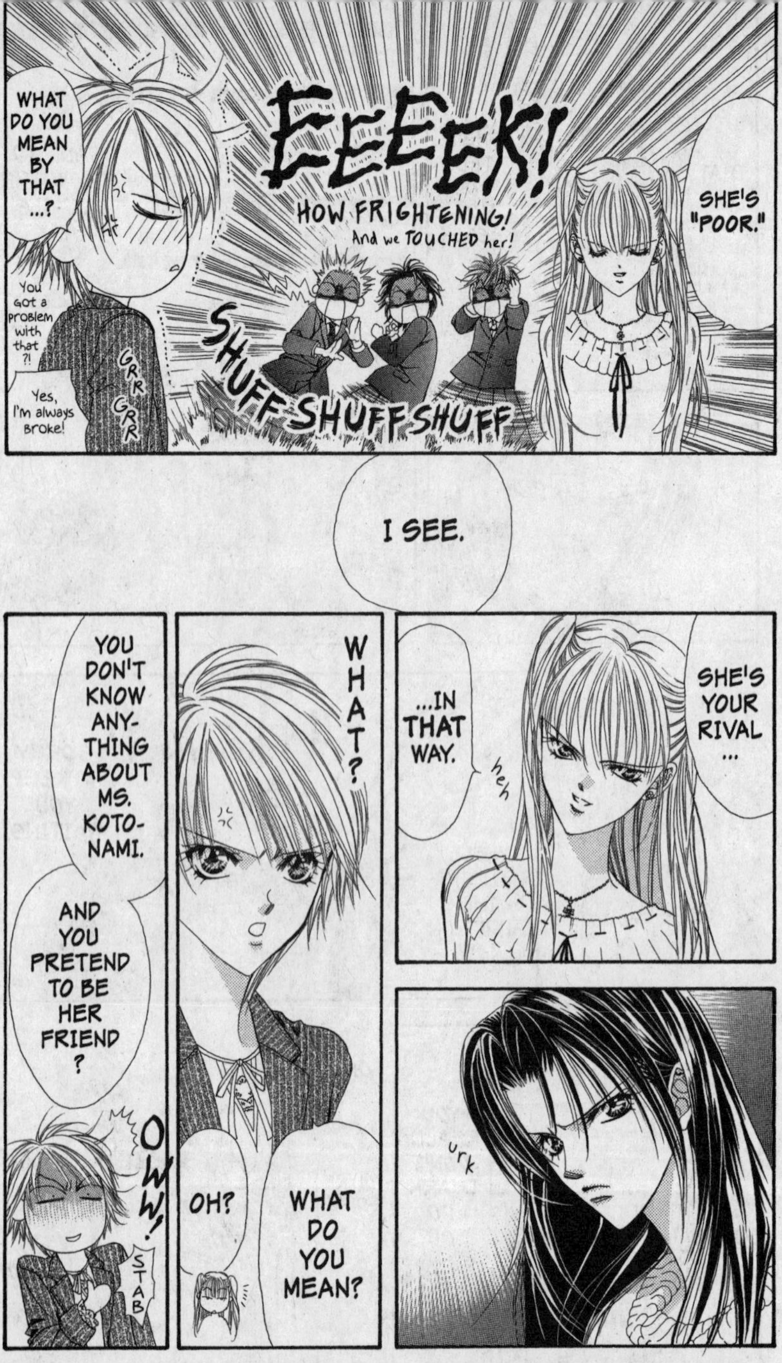
SHE'S "POOR."
EEEEK!
HOW FRIGHTENING!
And we TOUCHED her!
SHUFF SHUFF SHUFF
WHAT DO YOU MEAN BY THAT ...?
GRR GRR
You got a problem with that?!
Yes, I'm always Broke!
I SEE.
SHE'S YOUR RIVAL ...
heh
...IN THAT WAY.
urk
WHAT?
WHAT DO YOU MEAN?
OH?
YOU DON'T KNOW ANYTHING ABOUT MS. KOTONAMI.
AND YOU PRETEND TO BE HER FRIEND?
OWW!
STAB

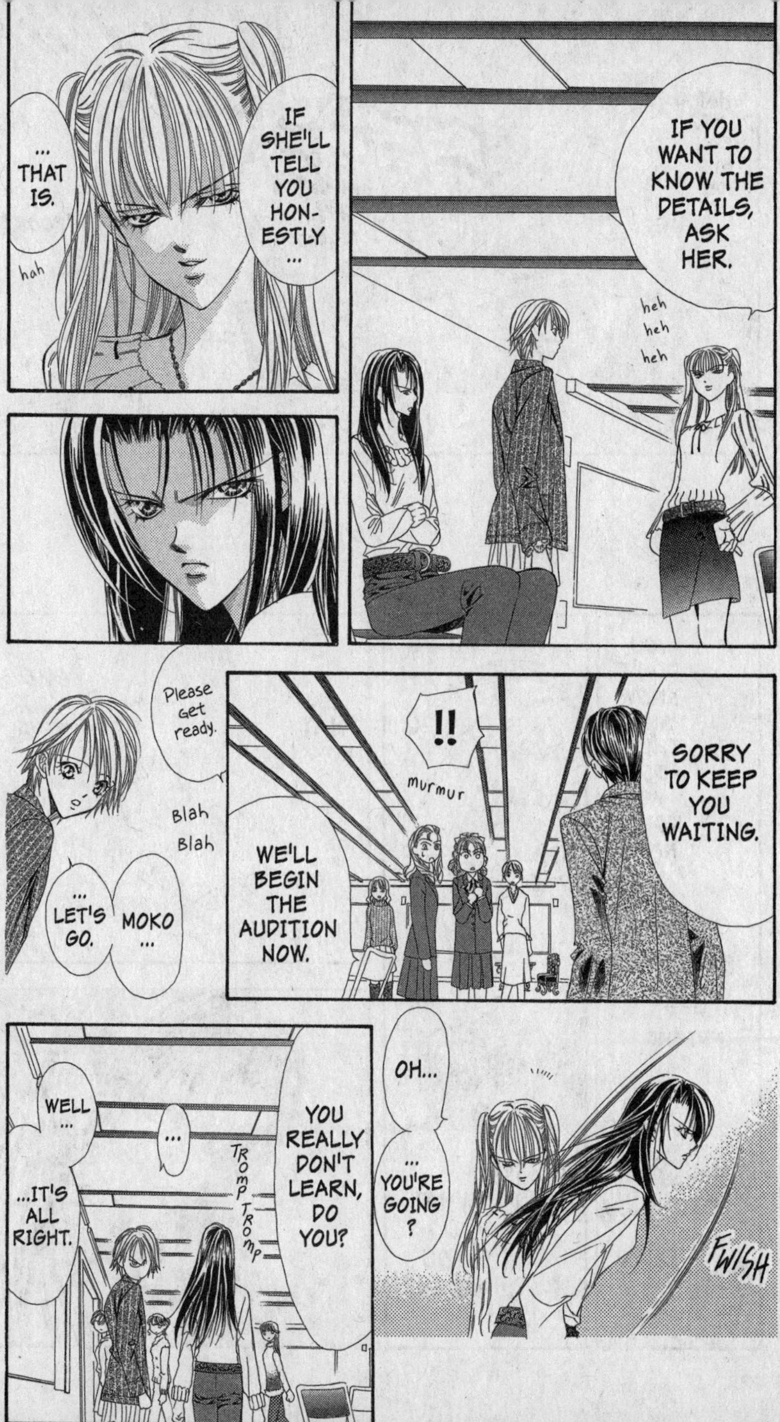
IF YOU WANT TO KNOW THE DETAILS, ASK HER.
heh heh heh
IF SHE'LL TELL YOU HON-ESTLY...
...THAT IS.
hah
SORRY TO KEEP YOU WAITING.
!!
murmur
WE'LL BEGIN THE AUDITION NOW.
Please get ready.
Blah Blah
MOKO...
...LET'S GO.
OH...
...YOU'RE GOING?
FWISH
YOU REALLY DON'T LEARN, DO YOU?
TROMP TROMP
...
WELL...
...IT'S ALL RIGHT.

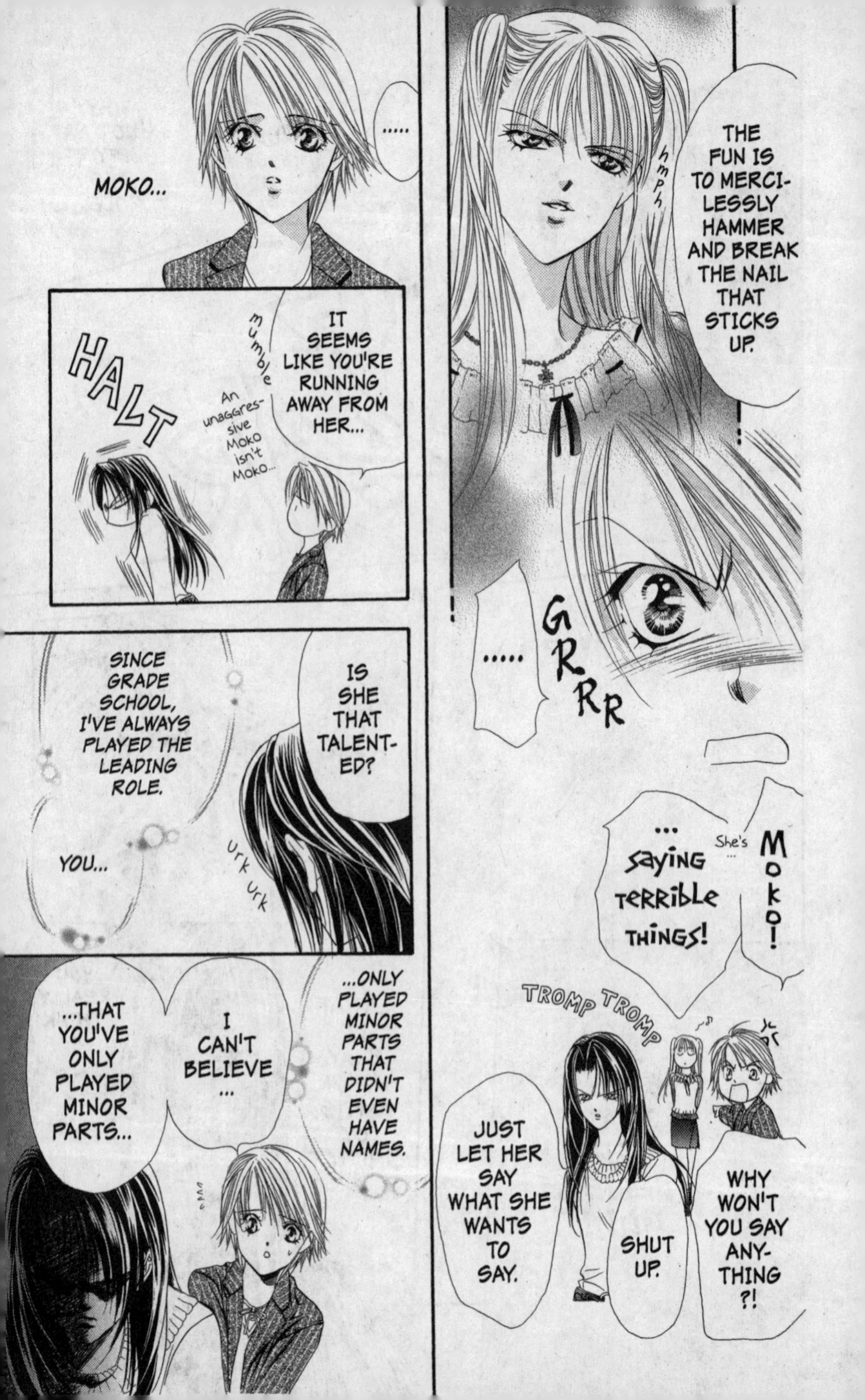
hmph
THE FUN IS TO MERCILESSLY HAMMER AND BREAK THE NAIL THAT STICKS UP.
.....
GRRR
MOKO!
She's...
...SAYING TERRIBLE THINGS!
TROMP TROMP
WHY WON'T YOU SAY ANYTHING?!
SHUT UP.
JUST LET HER SAY WHAT SHE WANTS TO SAY.
.....
MOKO...
IT SEEMS LIKE YOU'RE RUNNING AWAY FROM HER...
mumble
An unaggressive Moko isn't Moko...
HALT
IS SHE THAT TALENTED?
Urk urk
SINCE GRADE SCHOOL, I'VE ALWAYS PLAYED THE LEADING ROLE.
YOU...
...ONLY PLAYED MINOR PARTS THAT DIDN'T EVEN HAVE NAMES.
I CAN'T BELIEVE...
...THAT YOU'VE ONLY PLAYED MINOR PARTS...

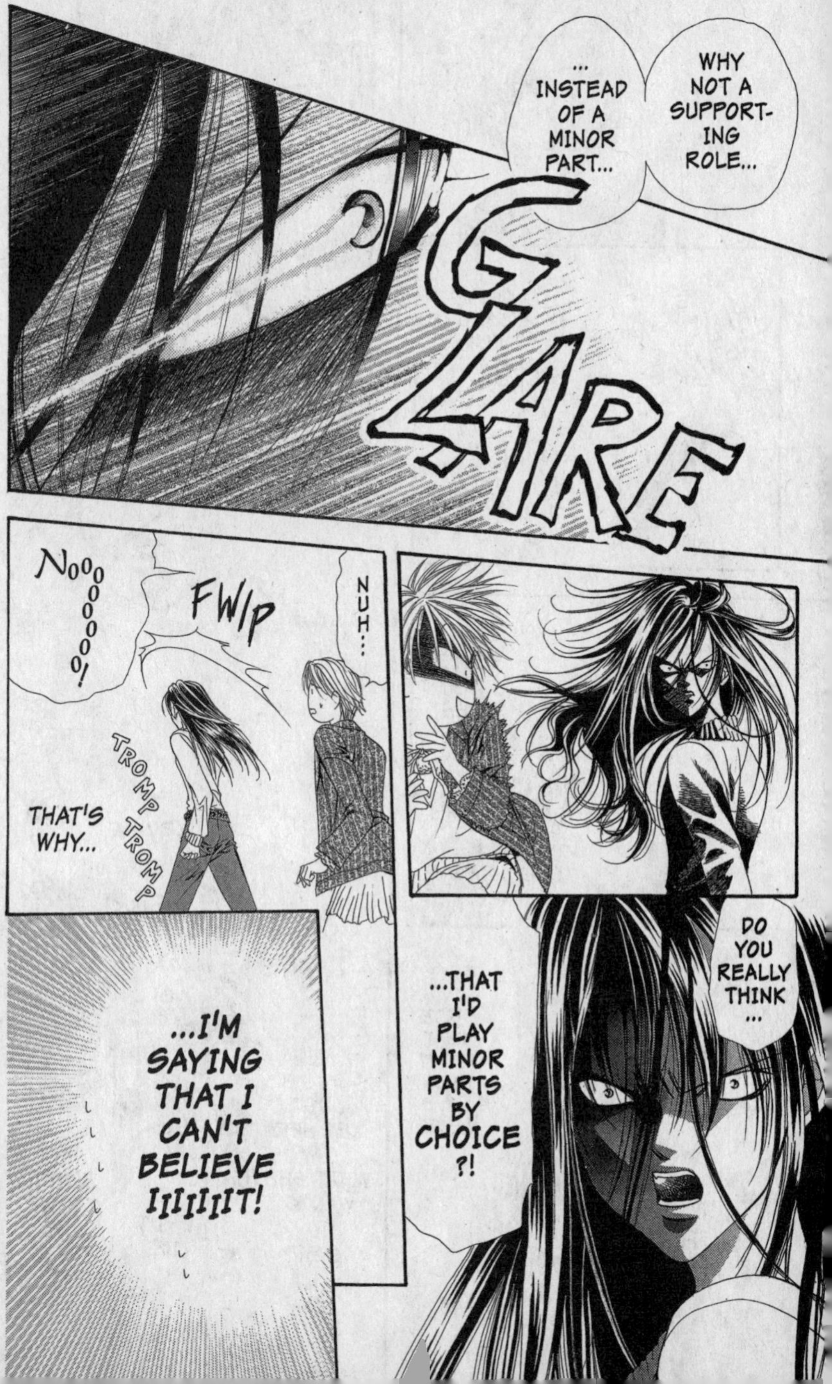
WHY NOT A SUPPORTING ROLE...
...INSTEAD OF A MINOR PART...
GLARE
NUH...
FWIP
Nooooooooo!
TROMP TROMP
THAT'S WHY...
DO YOU REALLY THINK...
...THAT I'D PLAY MINOR PARTS BY CHOICE?!
...I'M SAYING THAT I CAN'T BELIEVE IIIIIIT!

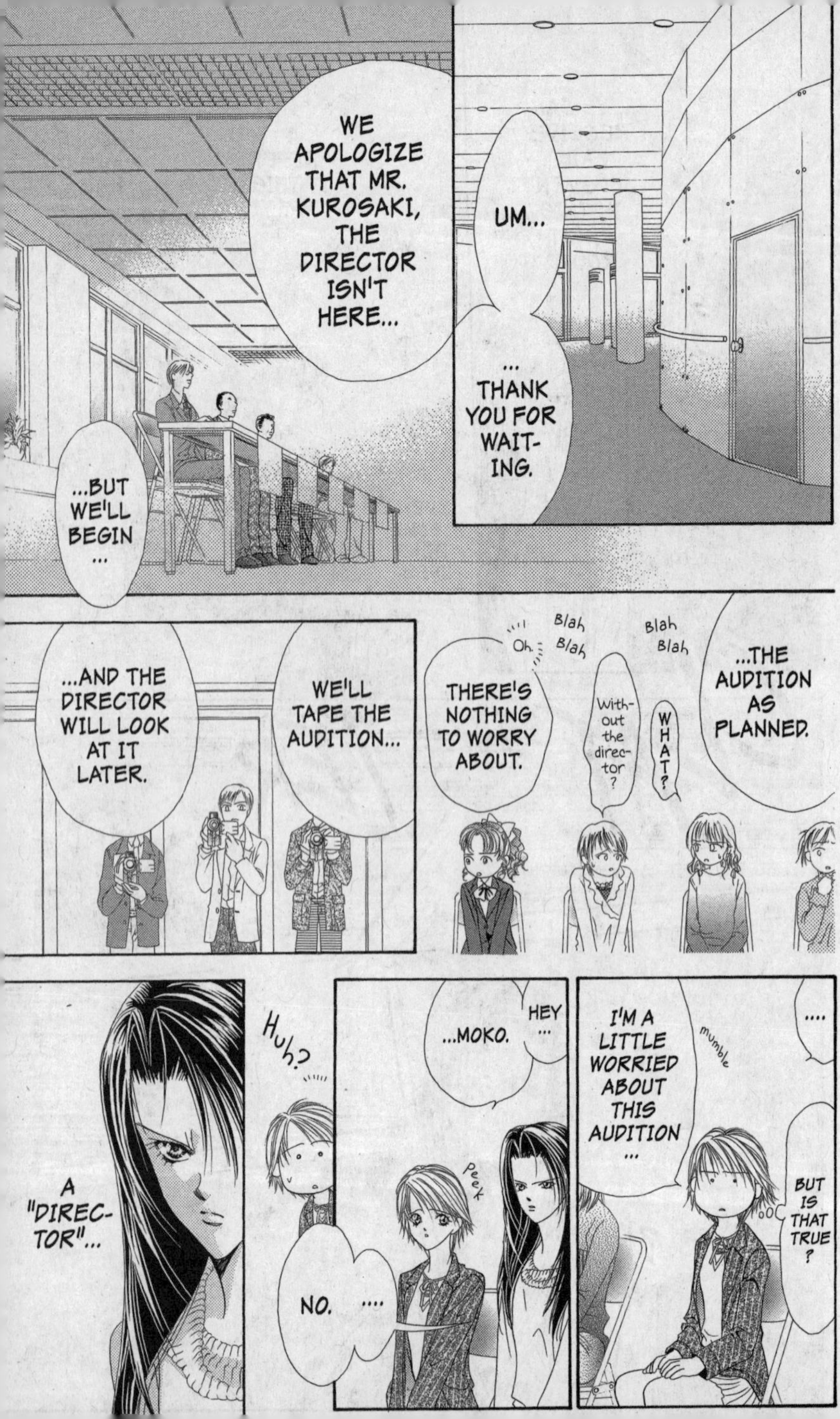
UM...
...THANK YOU FOR WAIT-ING.
WE APOLOGIZE THAT MR. KUROSAKI, THE DIRECTOR ISN'T HERE...
...BUT WE'LL BEGIN...
...THE AUDITION AS PLANNED.
Blah Blah
Blah Blah
WHAT?
With-out the direc-tor?
Oh.
THERE'S NOTHING TO WORRY ABOUT.
WE'LL TAPE THE AUDITION...
...AND THE DIRECTOR WILL LOOK AT IT LATER.
....
I'M A LITTLE WORRIED ABOUT THIS AUDITION...
mumble
BUT IS THAT TRUE?
HEY...
...MOKO.
Peek
NO. ....
Huh?
A "DIREC-TOR"...

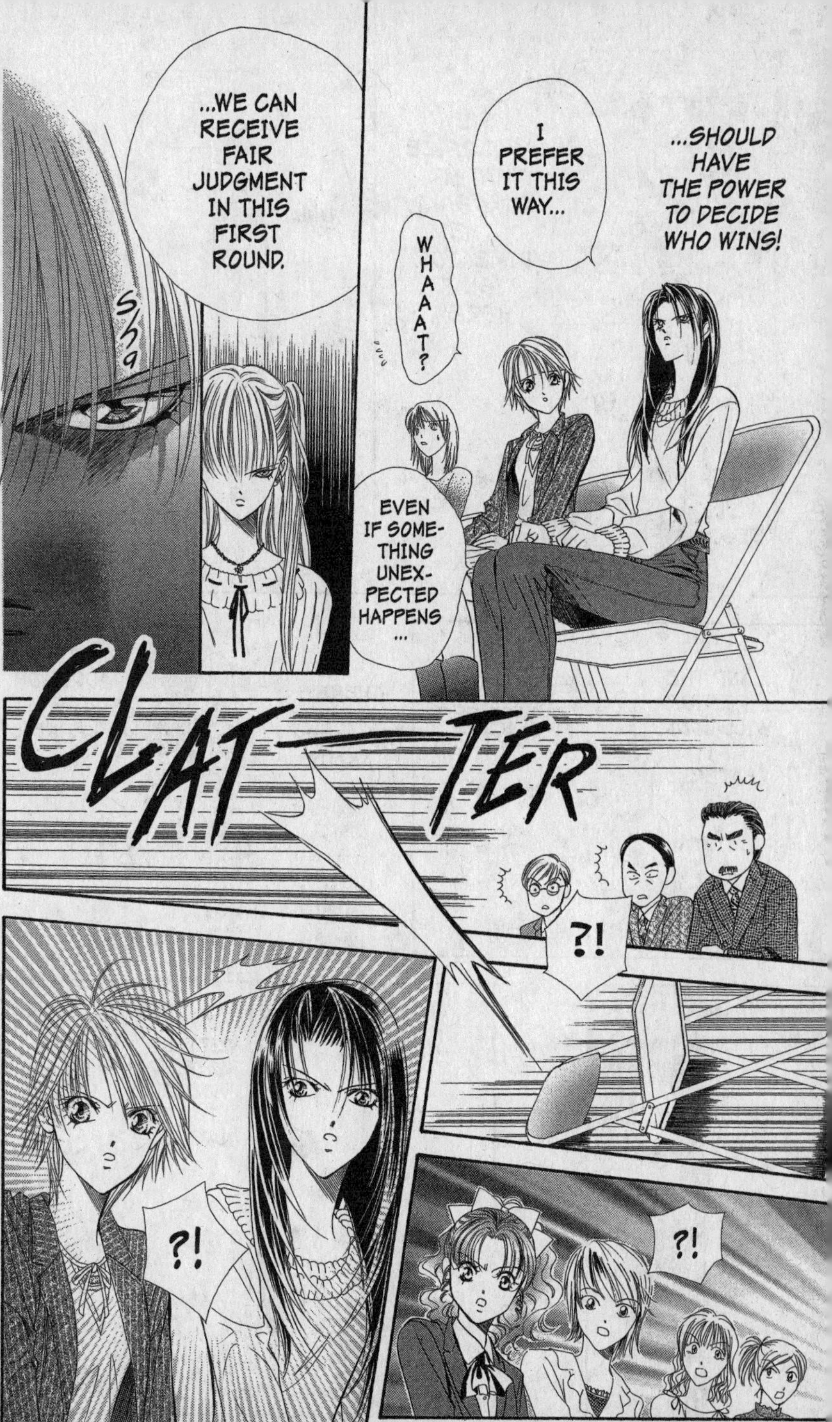
...SHOULD HAVE THE POWER TO DECIDE WHO WINS!
I PREFER IT THIS WAY...
WHAAAT?
EVEN IF SOMETHING UNEXPECTED HAPPENS...
...WE CAN RECEIVE FAIR JUDGMENT IN THIS FIRST ROUND.
CLAT—TER
?!
?!
?!

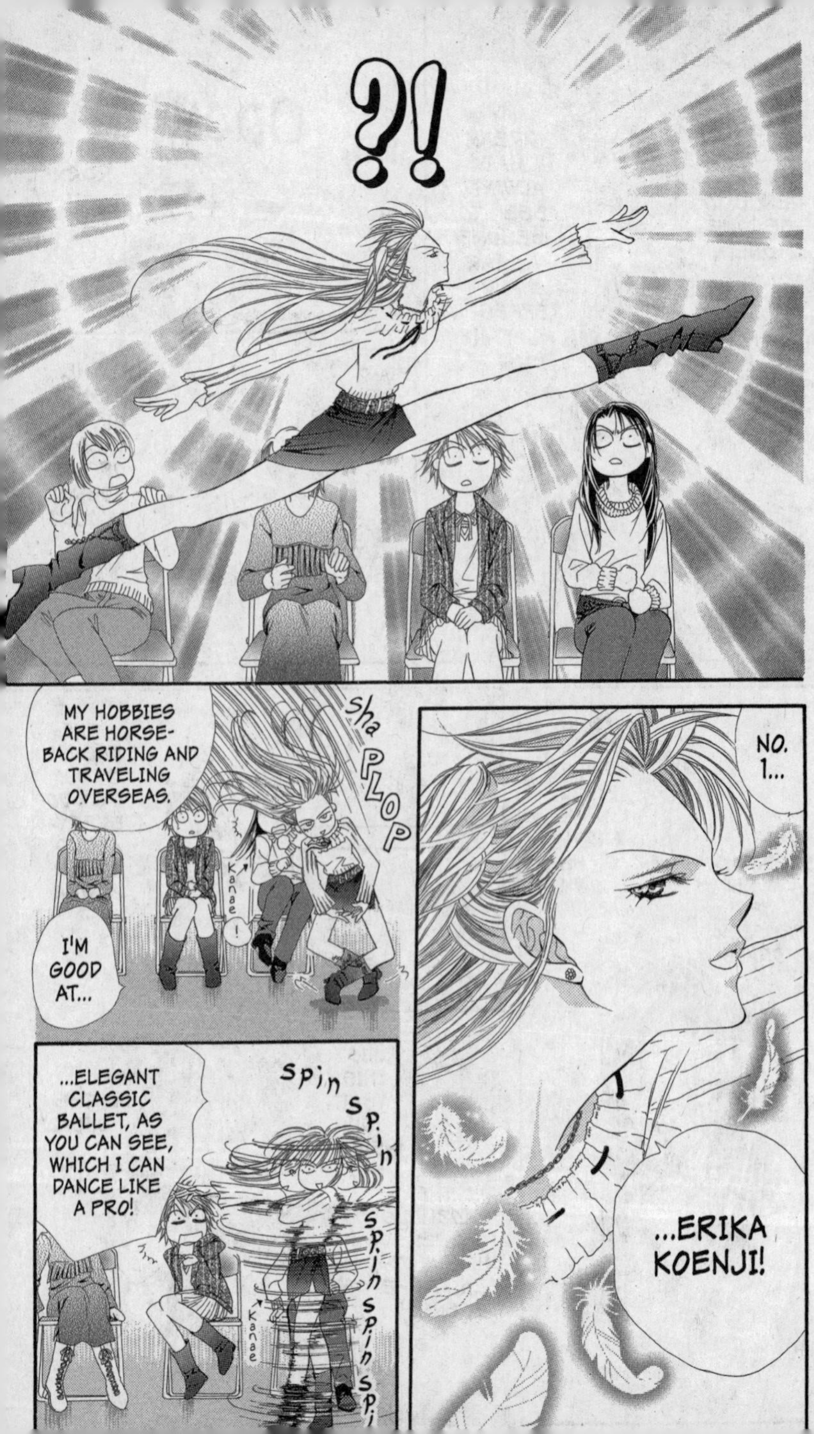
?!
NO. 1...
...ERIKA KOENJI!
MY HOBBIES ARE HORSE-BACK RIDING AND TRAVELING OVERSEAS.
Sha PLOP
Kanae
!
I'M GOOD AT...
...ELEGANT CLASSIC BALLET, AS YOU CAN SEE, WHICH I CAN DANCE LIKE A PRO!
spin spin
spin spin spin spi
Kanae

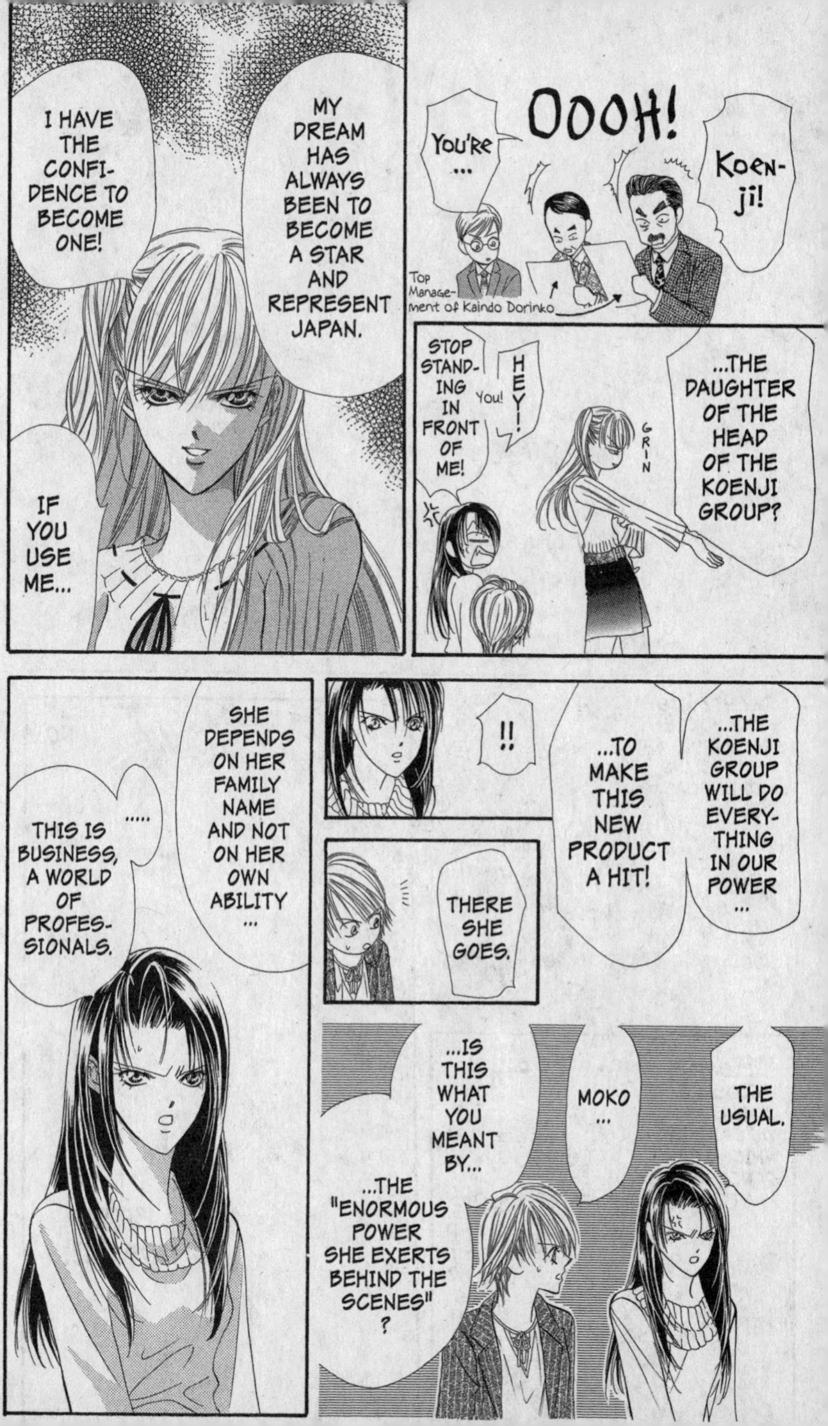
Koen-ji!
OOOH!
You're ...
Top Management of Kaindo Dorinko
...THE DAUGHTER OF THE HEAD OF THE KOENJI GROUP?
GRIN
HEY!
You!
STOP STANDING IN FRONT OF ME!
MY DREAM HAS ALWAYS BEEN TO BECOME A STAR AND REPRESENT JAPAN.
I HAVE THE CONFIDENCE TO BECOME ONE!
IF YOU USE ME...
...THE KOENJI GROUP WILL DO EVERYTHING IN OUR POWER ...
...TO MAKE THIS NEW PRODUCT A HIT!
!!
THERE SHE GOES.
THE USUAL.
MOKO ...
...IS THIS WHAT YOU MEANT BY...
...THE "ENORMOUS POWER SHE EXERTS BEHIND THE SCENES"?
SHE DEPENDS ON HER FAMILY NAME AND NOT ON HER OWN ABILITY ...
.....
THIS IS BUSINESS, A WORLD OF PROFESSIONALS.

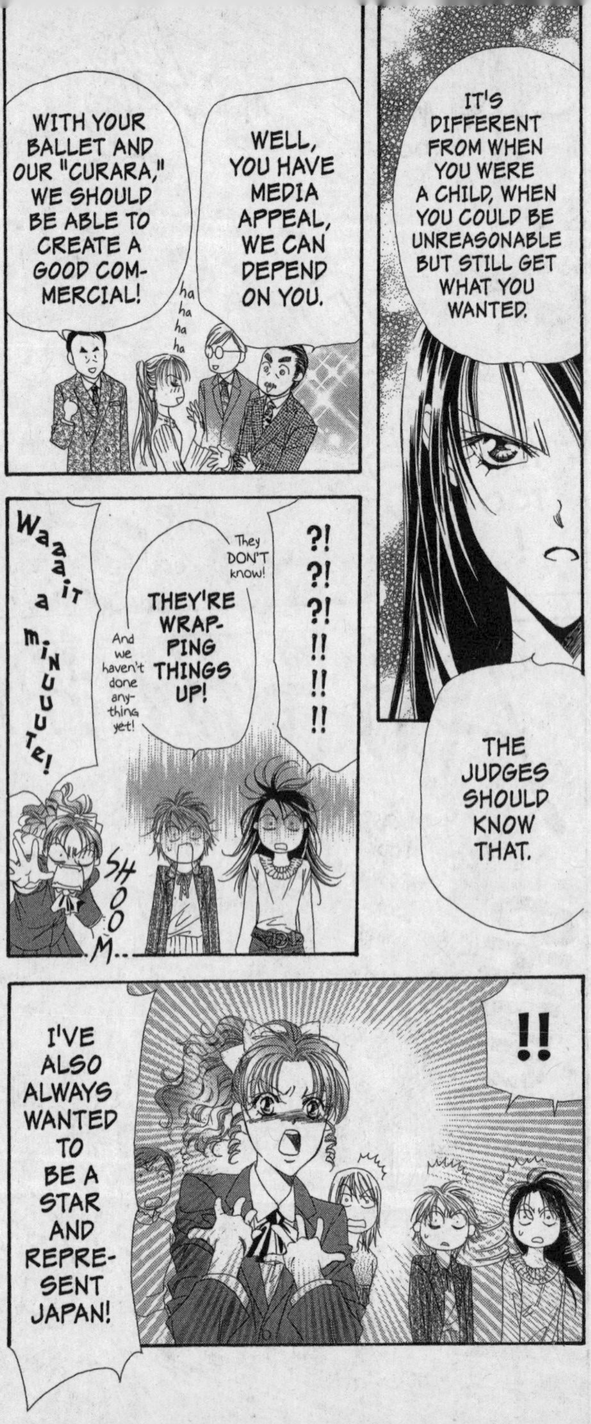
IT'S DIFFERENT FROM WHEN YOU WERE A CHILD, WHEN YOU COULD BE UNREASONABLE BUT STILL GET WHAT YOU WANTED.
THE JUDGES SHOULD KNOW THAT.
WELL, YOU HAVE MEDIA APPEAL, WE CAN DEPEND ON YOU.
WITH YOUR BALLET AND OUR "CURARA," WE SHOULD BE ABLE TO CREATE A GOOD COMMERCIAL!
ha ha ha ha
?! ?! ?! !! !! !!
They DON'T know!
THEY'RE WRAPPING THINGS UP!
And we haven't done anything yet!
Waaait a minuuuute!
SHOOOM...
!!
I'VE ALSO ALWAYS WANTED TO BE A STAR AND REPRESENT JAPAN!

Erika Koenji

Stubborn middle-age guys and rich young ladies are a must in Nakamura's manga now...I myself think "What is this...?" But they are easy to handle, so I can't help it... A rich young lady for a rival is really easy to deal with... sigh...

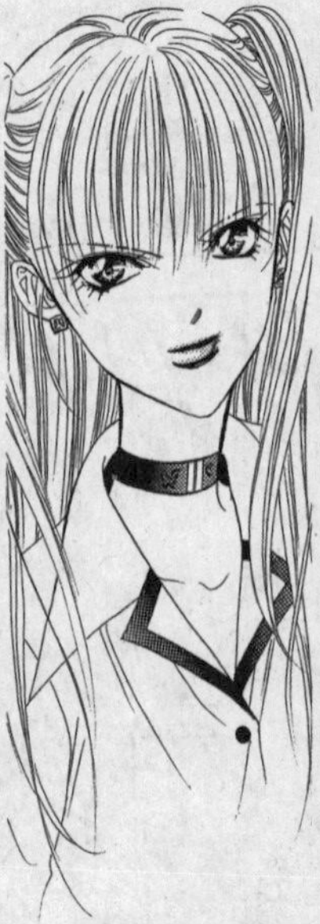

This girl's obsession with Kanae is kind of like love... ...well...you know...in this world, the line between love and hate is a fine one... Kyoko is just like that. She hates Shotaro more than anybody or anything, but that is why she can't get him out of her head... Um... Skip•Beat! is a really negative manga... All of the characters...

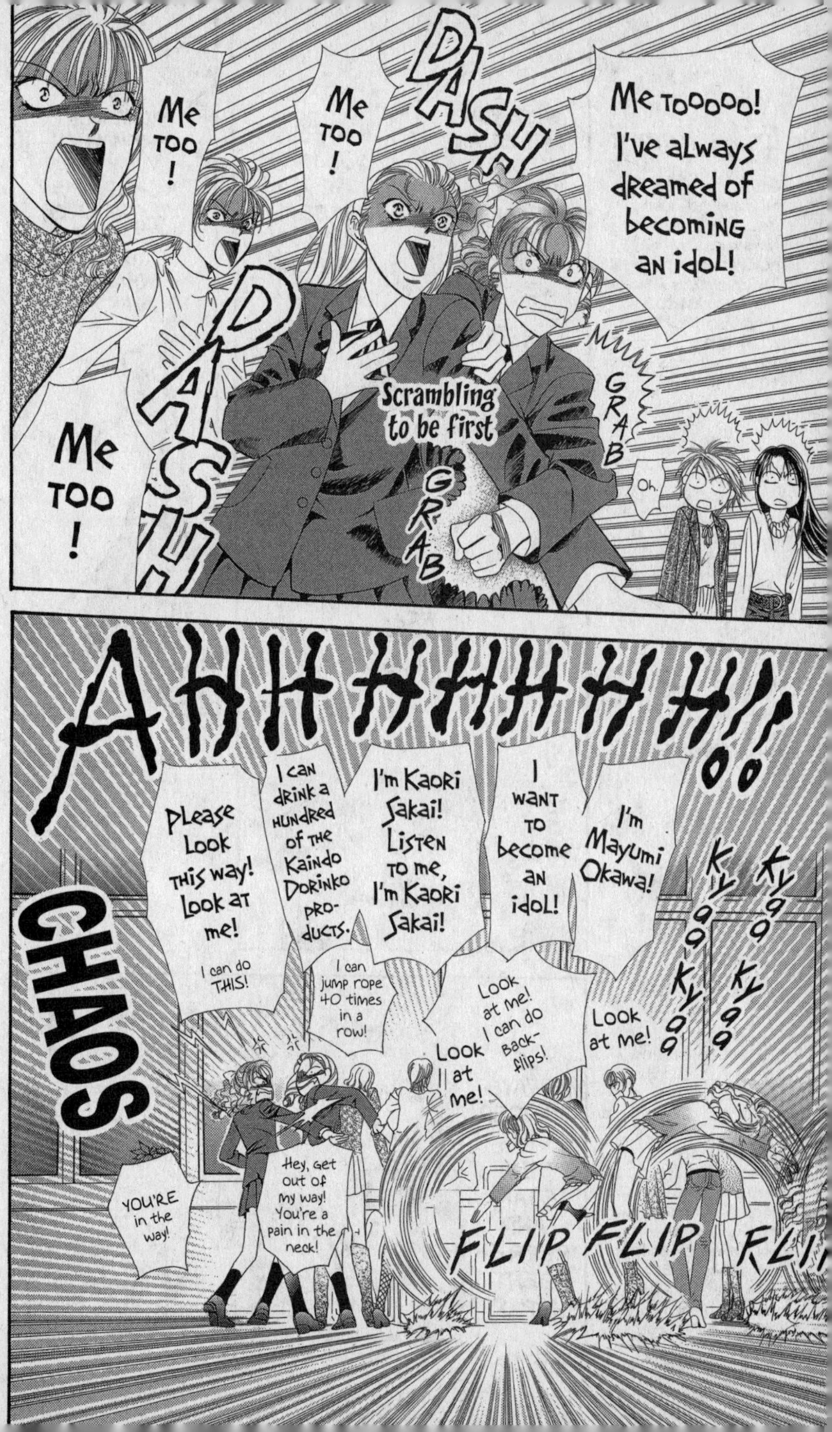
Me TOOOOO! I've always dreamed of becoming an idoL!
DASH
Me TOO!
Me TOO!
MU GRAB
Oh.
Scrambling to be first
GRAB
DASH
Me TOO!
AHHHHHHH!!
Kyaa Kyaa
Kyaa Kyaa Kyaa
I'm Mayumi Okawa!
I want to become an idoL!
I'm Kaori Sakai! Listen to me, I'm Kaori Sakai!
I can drink a hundred of the Kaindo Dorinko pro-ducts.
Please Look this way! Look at me!
Look at me!
Look at me! I can do back-flips!
Look at me!
I can jump rope 40 times in a row!
I can do THIS!
CHAOS
FLIP FLIP FLI
Hey, Get out of my way! You're a pain in the neck!
YOU'RE in the way!

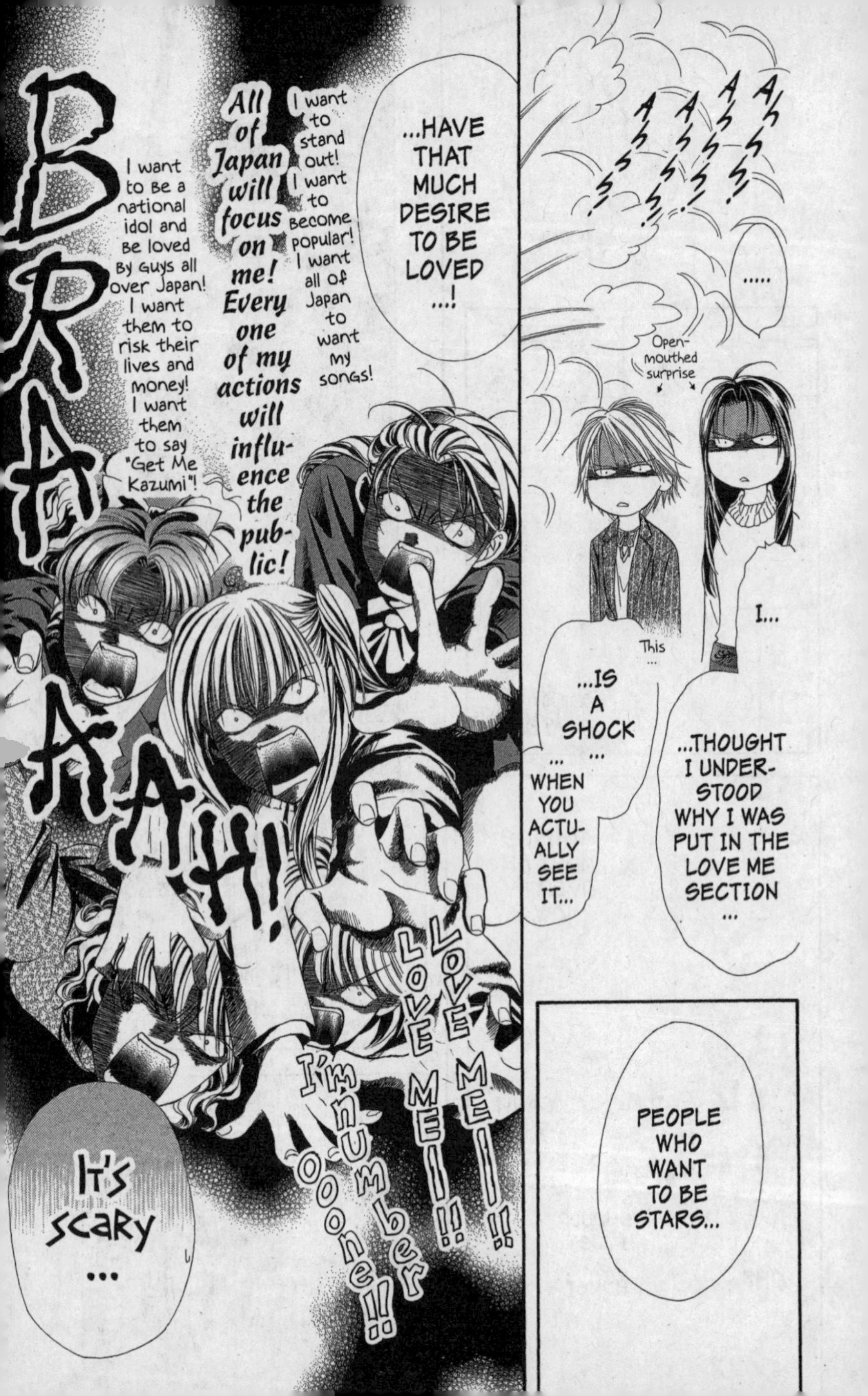

Ahhhh!
Ahhhh!
Ahhhh!
Ahhhh!
.....
Open-mouthed surprise
I...
...THOUGHT I UNDERSTOOD WHY I WAS PUT IN THE LOVE ME SECTION...
This...
...IS A SHOCK... ...WHEN YOU ACTUALLY SEE IT...
PEOPLE WHO WANT TO BE STARS...
...HAVE THAT MUCH DESIRE TO BE LOVED...!
I want to stand out! I want to become popular! I want all of Japan to want my songs!
All of Japan will focus on me! Every one of my actions will influence the public!
I want to be a national idol and be loved by guys all over Japan! I want them to risk their lives and money! I want them to say "Get Me Kazumi"!
BRAAAAH!
LOVE ME!!
LOVE ME!!
I'm number ooone!!
It's scary...

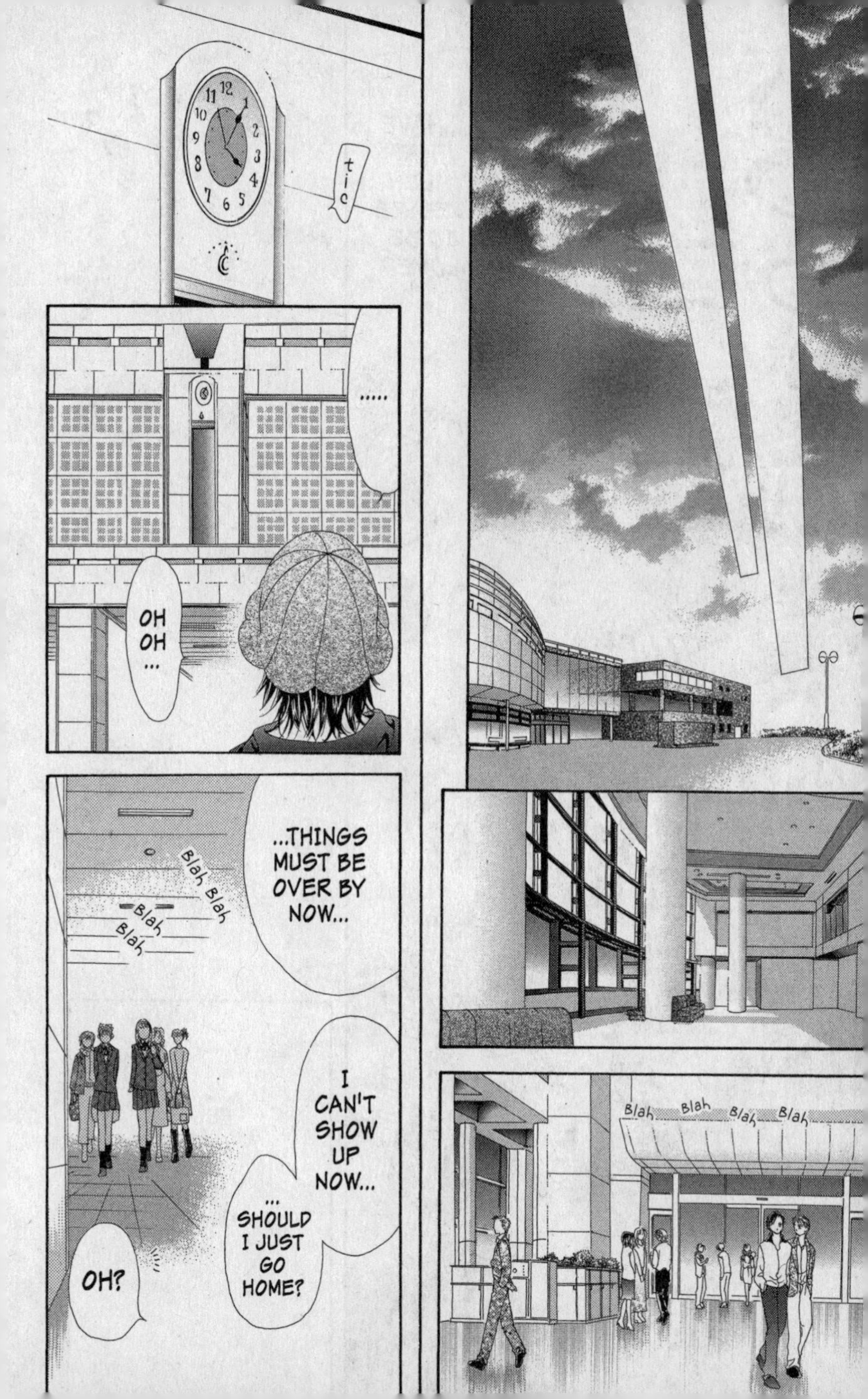
Blah Blah Blah Blah
tic
.....
OH OH ...
...THINGS MUST BE OVER BY NOW...
Blah Blah Blah Blah
I CAN'T SHOW UP NOW...
... SHOULD I JUST GO HOME?
OH?

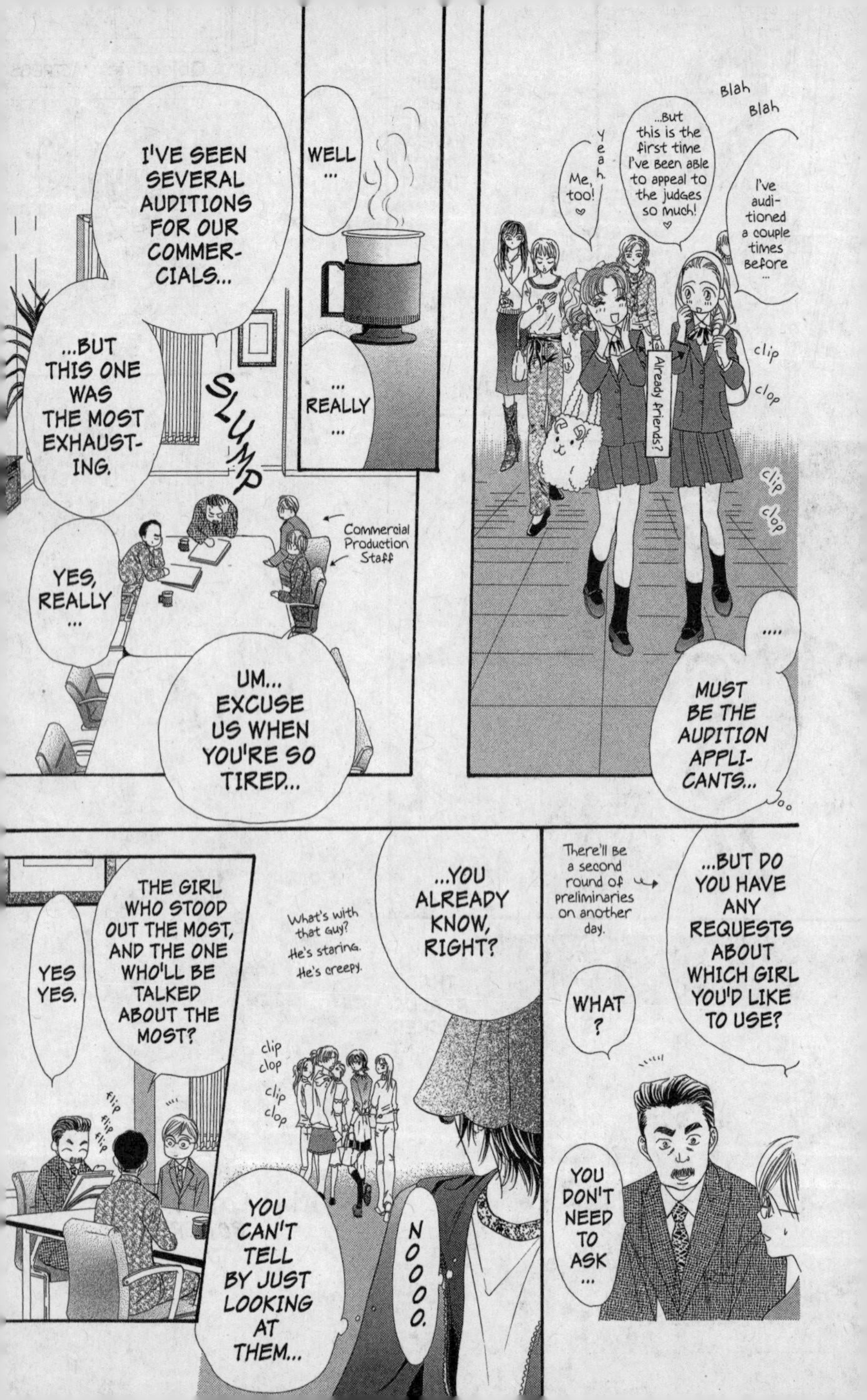
Blah Blah
I've auditioned a couple times before...
...But this is the first time I've been able to appeal to the judges so much! ♡
Yeah.
Me, too! ♡
Already friends?
clip clop
clip clop
....
MUST BE THE AUDITION APPLICANTS...
WELL...
...REALLY...
I'VE SEEN SEVERAL AUDITIONS FOR OUR COMMERCIALS...
...BUT THIS ONE WAS THE MOST EXHAUSTING.
SLUMP
Commercial Production Staff
YES, REALLY...
UM... EXCUSE US WHEN YOU'RE SO TIRED...
There'll be a second round of preliminaries on another day.
...BUT DO YOU HAVE ANY REQUESTS ABOUT WHICH GIRL YOU'D LIKE TO USE?
WHAT?
YOU DON'T NEED TO ASK...
...YOU ALREADY KNOW, RIGHT?
What's with that guy?
He's staring.
He's creepy.
clip clop
clip clop
YOU CAN'T TELL BY JUST LOOKING AT THEM...
NOOOO.
THE GIRL WHO STOOD OUT THE MOST, AND THE ONE WHO'LL BE TALKED ABOUT THE MOST?
YES YES.
flip flip flip

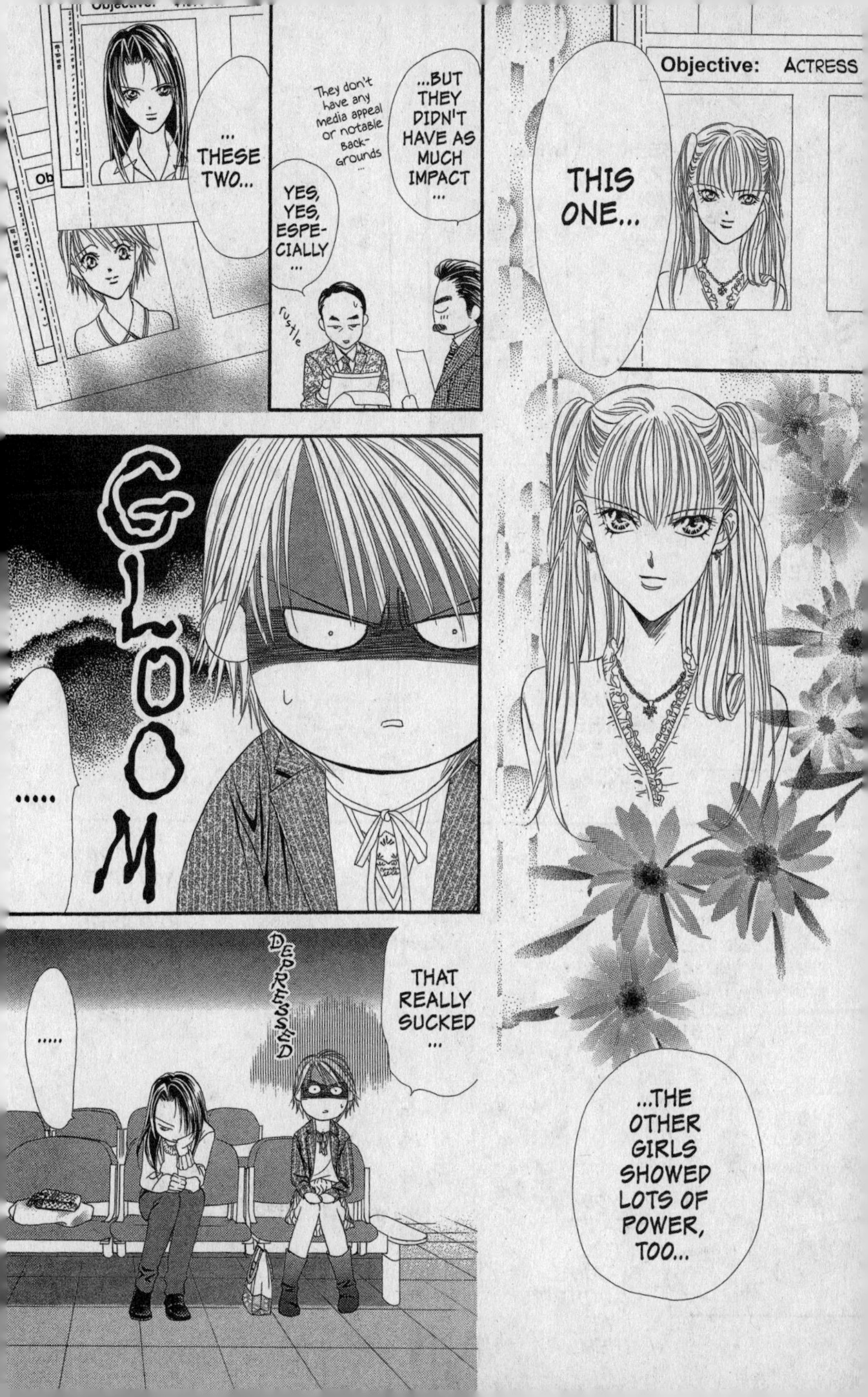

Objective: ACTRESS
THIS ONE...
...THE OTHER GIRLS SHOWED LOTS OF POWER, TOO...
...BUT THEY DIDN'T HAVE AS MUCH IMPACT...
They don't have any media appeal or notable back-grounds...
YES, YES, ESPE-CIALLY...
rustle
...THESE TWO...
Ob
GLOOM
.....
DEPRESSED
THAT REALLY SUCKED...
.....

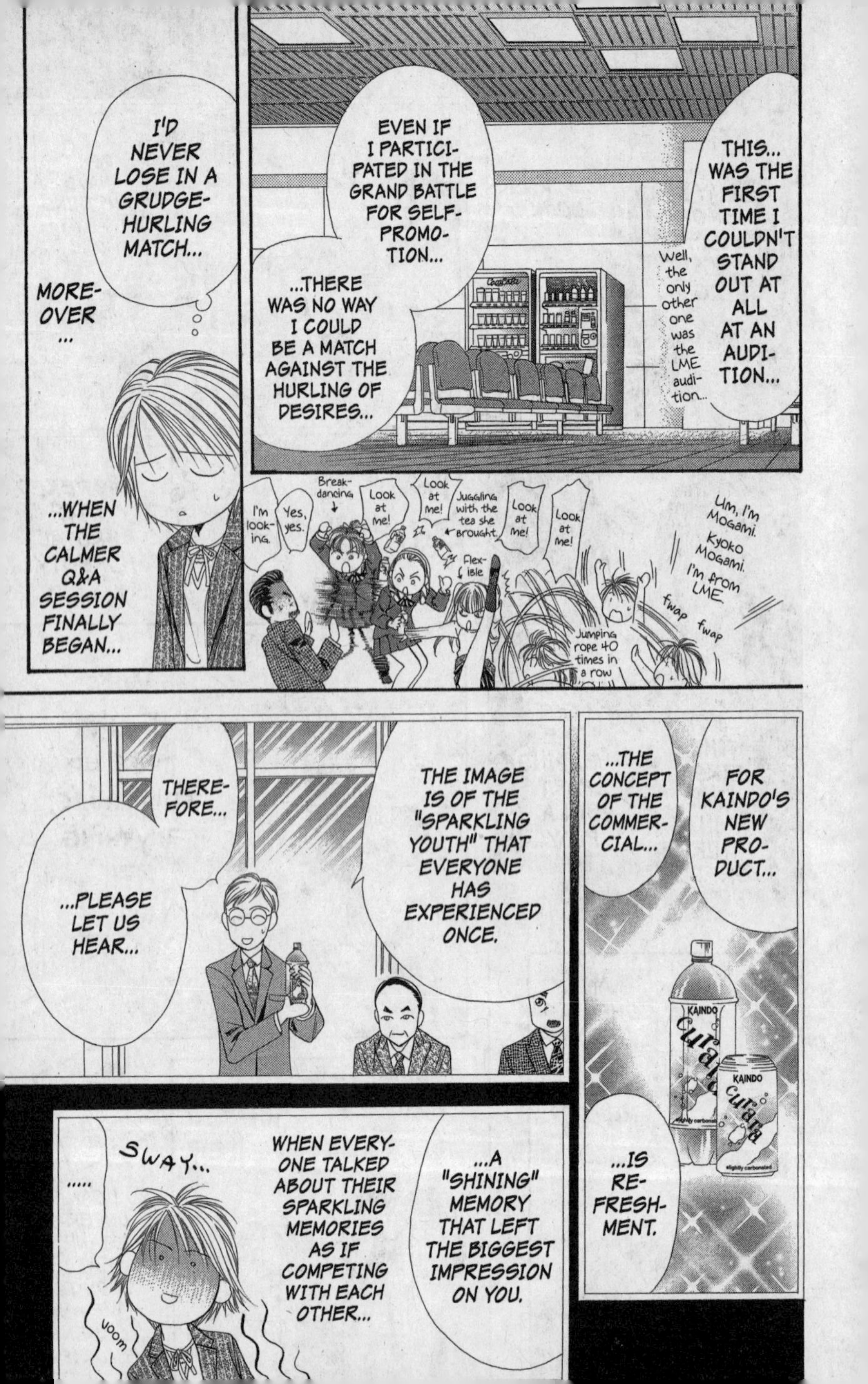

THIS... WAS THE FIRST TIME I COULDN'T STAND OUT AT ALL AT AN AUDITION...
Well, the only other one was the LME audition...
EVEN IF I PARTICIPATED IN THE GRAND BATTLE FOR SELF-PROMOTION...
...THERE WAS NO WAY I COULD BE A MATCH AGAINST THE HURLING OF DESIRES...
Um, I'm Mogami. Kyoko Mogami. I'm from LME.
fwap fwap
Jumping rope 40 times in a row
Look at me!
Flex-ible
Look at me!
Juggling with the tea she brought
Look at me!
Look at me!
Break-dancing
Yes, yes.
I'm look-ing.
I'D NEVER LOSE IN A GRUDGE-HURLING MATCH...
MORE-OVER...
...WHEN THE CALMER Q&A SESSION FINALLY BEGAN...
FOR KAINDO'S NEW PRODUCT...
...THE CONCEPT OF THE COMMERCIAL...
KAINDO curara slightly carbonated
KAINDO curara slightly carbonated
...IS REFRESHMENT.
THE IMAGE IS OF THE "SPARKLING YOUTH" THAT EVERYONE HAS EXPERIENCED ONCE.
THEREFORE...
...PLEASE LET US HEAR...
...A "SHINING" MEMORY THAT LEFT THE BIGGEST IMPRESSION ON YOU.
WHEN EVERYONE TALKED ABOUT THEIR SPARKLING MEMORIES AS IF COMPETING WITH EACH OTHER...
.....
SWAY...
voom

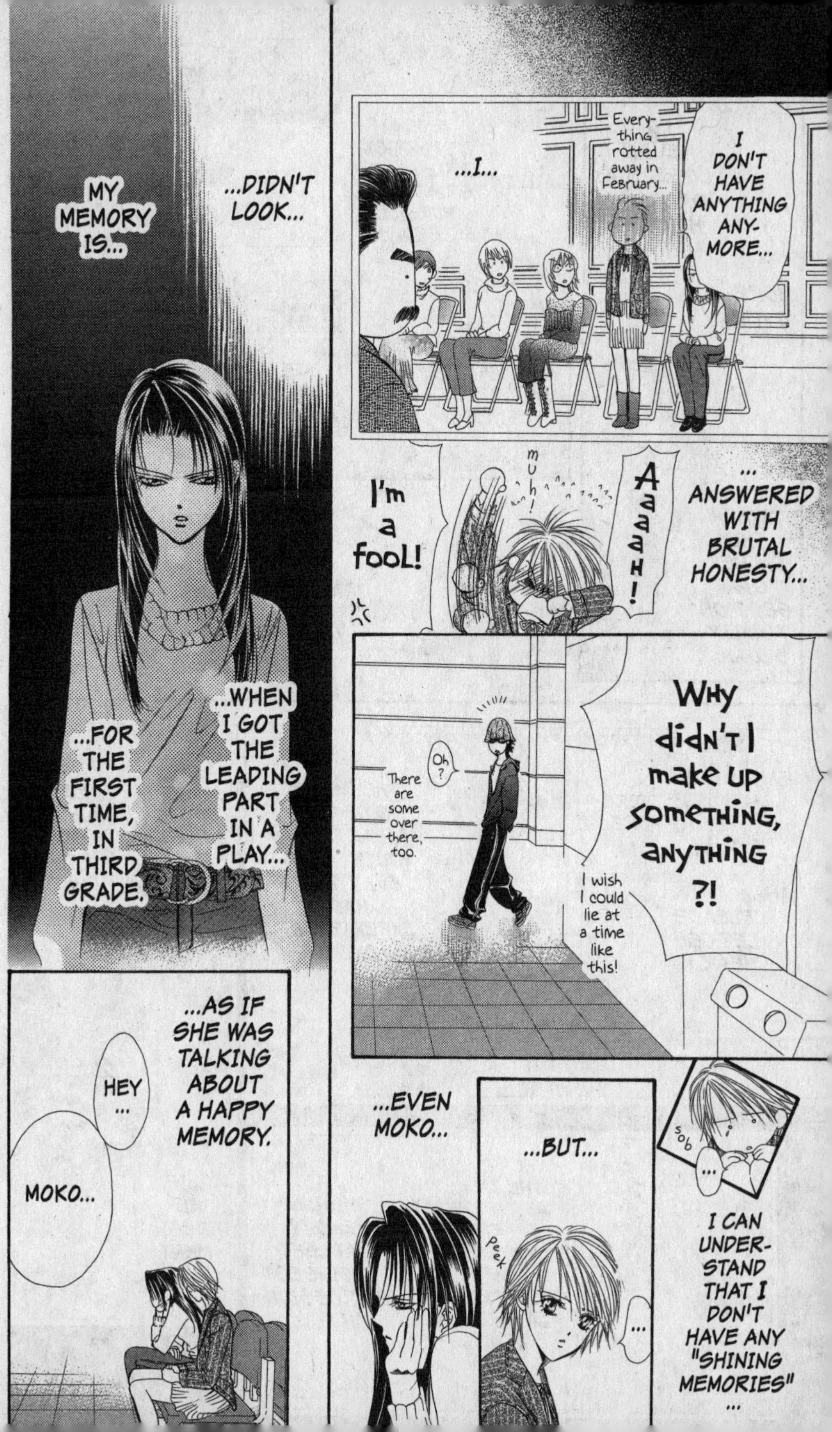

I DON'T HAVE ANYTHING ANYMORE...
Everything rotted away in February...
...I...
...ANSWERED WITH BRUTAL HONESTY...
Aaaaah!
muh!
I'm a fool!
Why didn't I make up something, anything?!
I wish I could lie at a time like this!
Oh?
There are some over there, too.
sob
...
I CAN UNDERSTAND THAT I DON'T HAVE ANY "SHINING MEMORIES"...
...BUT...
Peek
...
...EVEN MOKO...
...DIDN'T LOOK...
MY MEMORY IS...
...WHEN I GOT THE LEADING PART IN A PLAY...
...FOR THE FIRST TIME, IN THIRD GRADE.
...AS IF SHE WAS TALKING ABOUT A HAPPY MEMORY.
HEY...
MOKO...

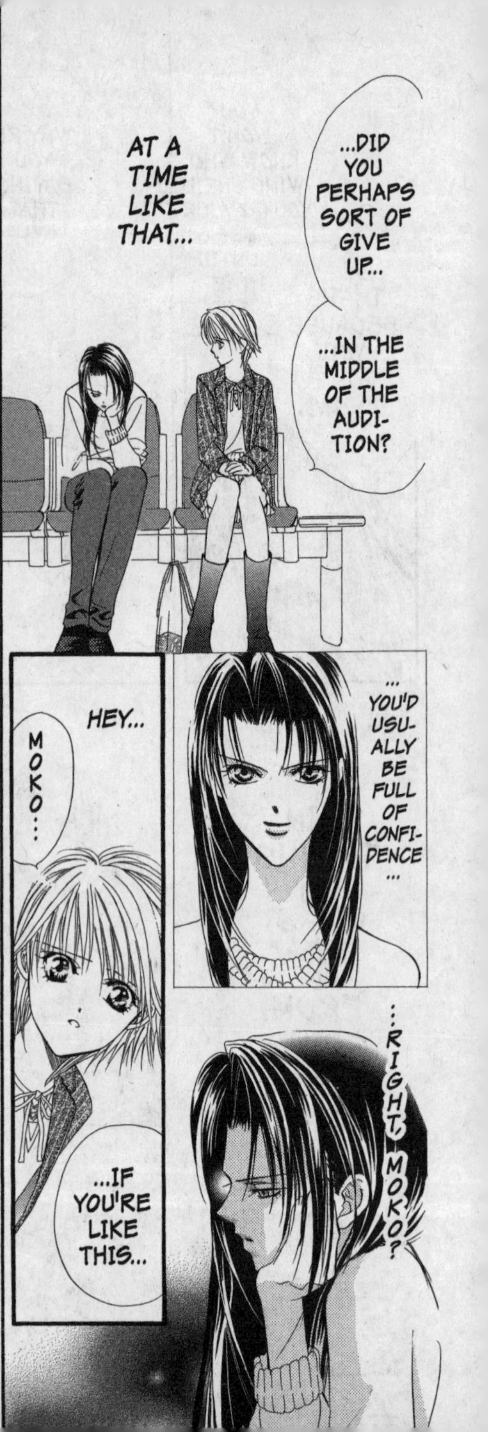
...DID YOU PERHAPS SORT OF GIVE UP...
...IN THE MIDDLE OF THE AUDITION?
AT A TIME LIKE THAT...
...YOU'D USUALLY BE FULL OF CONFIDENCE...
...RIGHT, MOKO?
HEY...
MOKO...
...IF YOU'RE LIKE THIS...
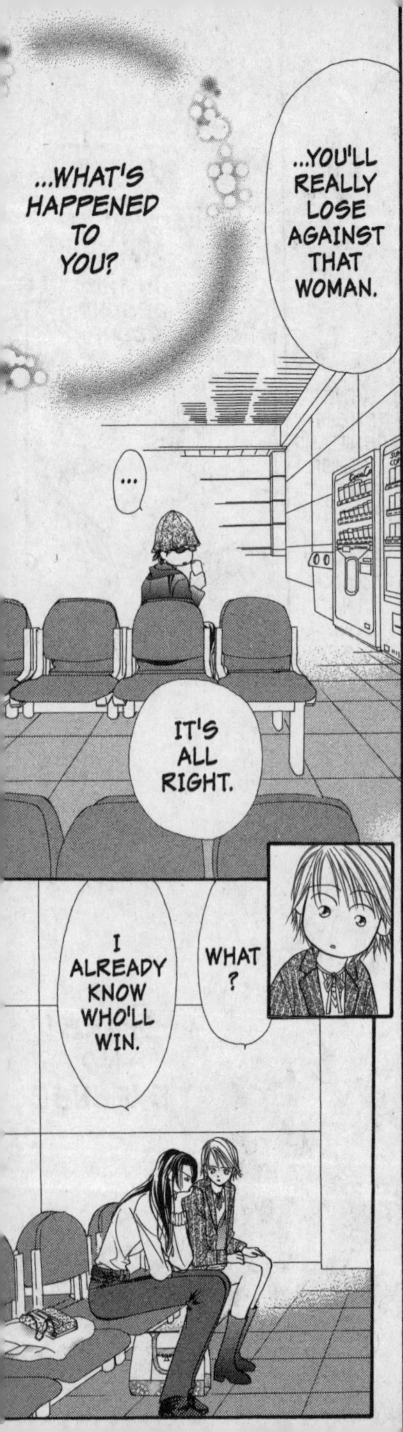
...YOU'LL REALLY LOSE AGAINST THAT WOMAN.
...WHAT'S HAPPENED TO YOU?
...
IT'S ALL RIGHT.
WHAT?
I ALREADY KNOW WHO'LL WIN.

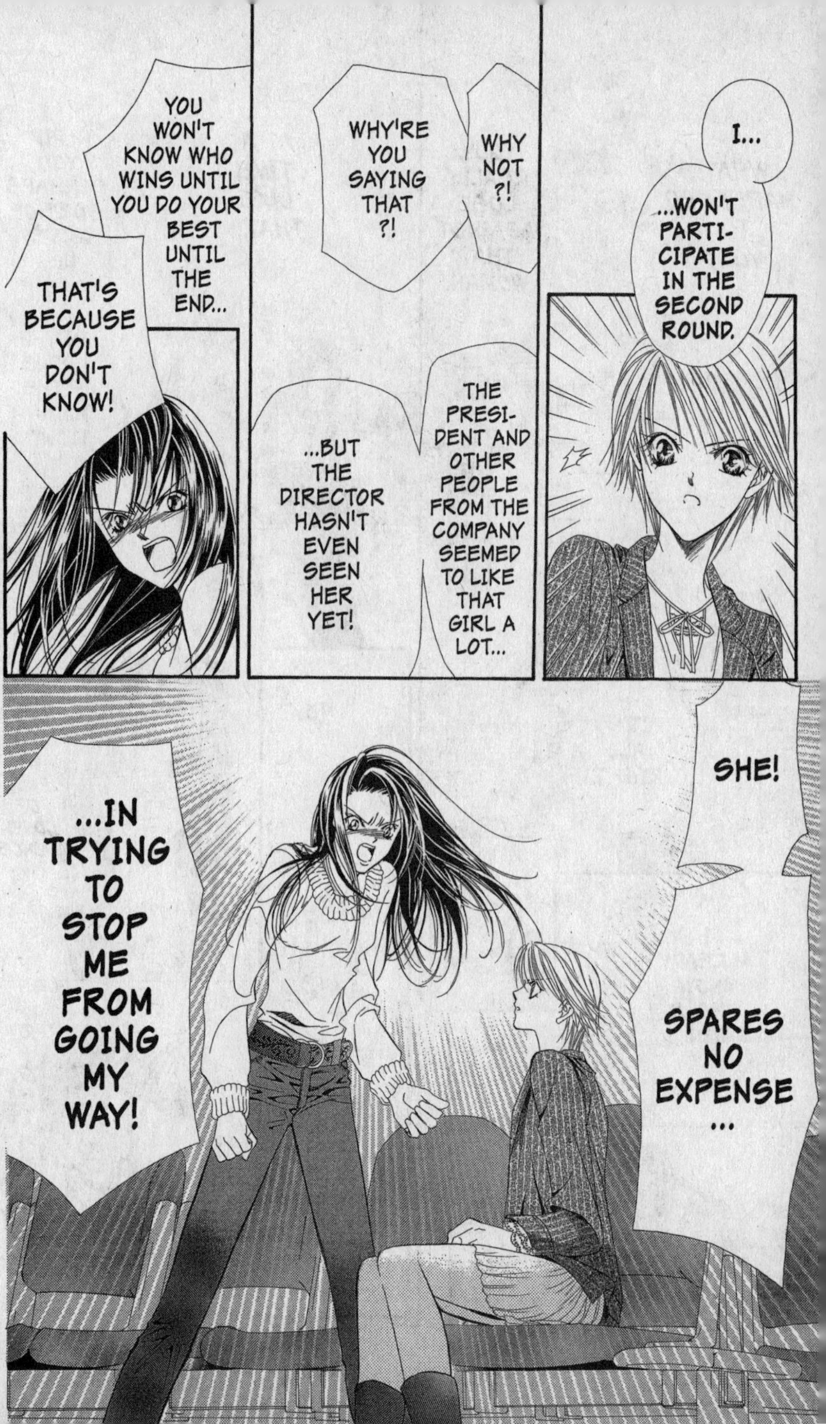
I...
...WON'T PARTICIPATE IN THE SECOND ROUND.
WHY NOT ?!
WHY'RE YOU SAYING THAT ?!
THE PRESIDENT AND OTHER PEOPLE FROM THE COMPANY SEEMED TO LIKE THAT GIRL A LOT...
...BUT THE DIRECTOR HASN'T EVEN SEEN HER YET!
YOU WON'T KNOW WHO WINS UNTIL YOU DO YOUR BEST UNTIL THE END...
THAT'S BECAUSE YOU DON'T KNOW!
SHE!
SPARES NO EXPENSE ...
...IN TRYING TO STOP ME FROM GOING MY WAY!

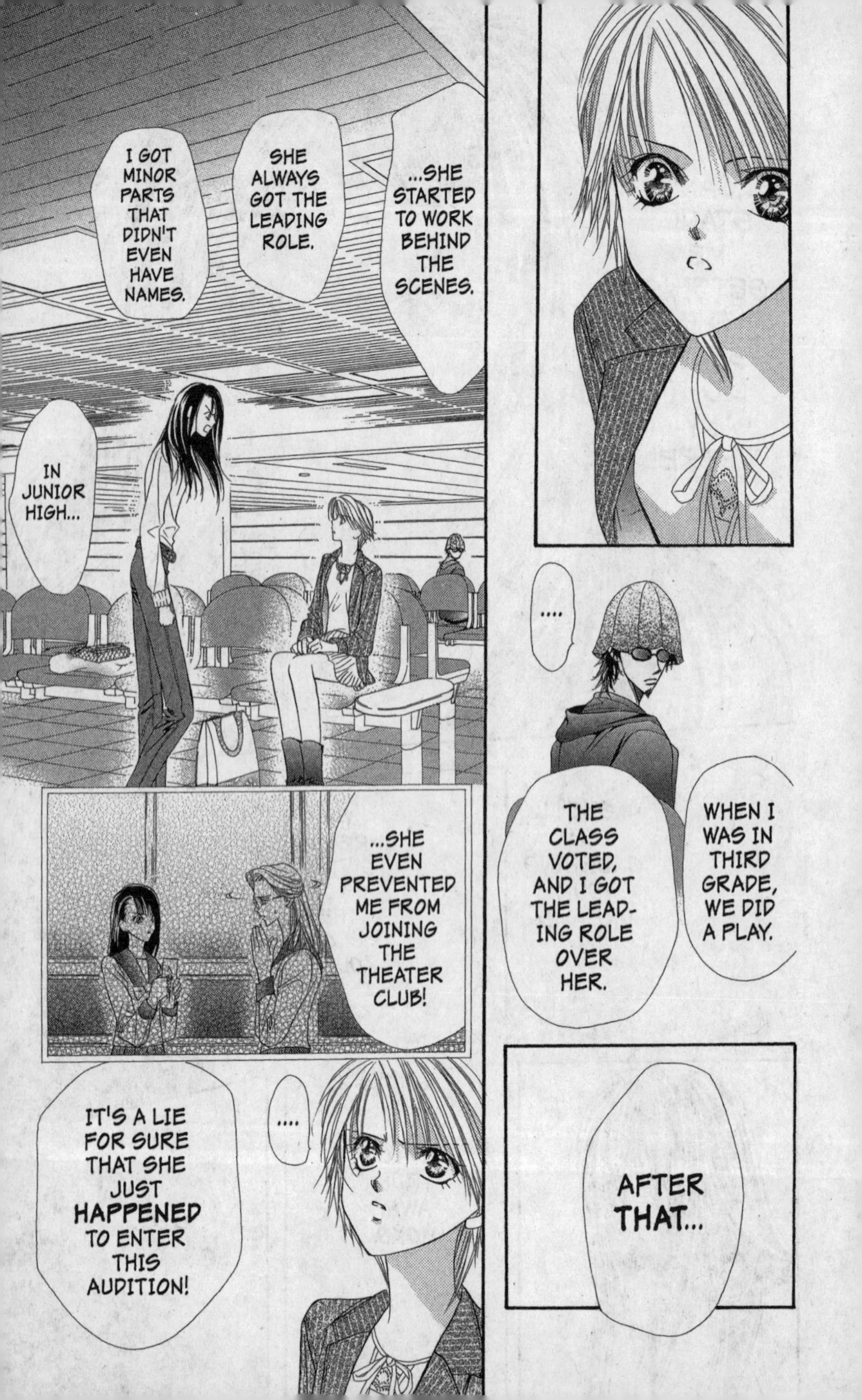
....
WHEN I WAS IN THIRD GRADE, WE DID A PLAY.
THE CLASS VOTED, AND I GOT THE LEAD-ING ROLE OVER HER.
AFTER THAT...
...SHE STARTED TO WORK BEHIND THE SCENES.
SHE ALWAYS GOT THE LEADING ROLE.
I GOT MINOR PARTS THAT DIDN'T EVEN HAVE NAMES.
IN JUNIOR HIGH...
...SHE EVEN PREVENTED ME FROM JOINING THE THEATER CLUB!
....
IT'S A LIE FOR SURE THAT SHE JUST HAPPENED TO ENTER THIS AUDITION!

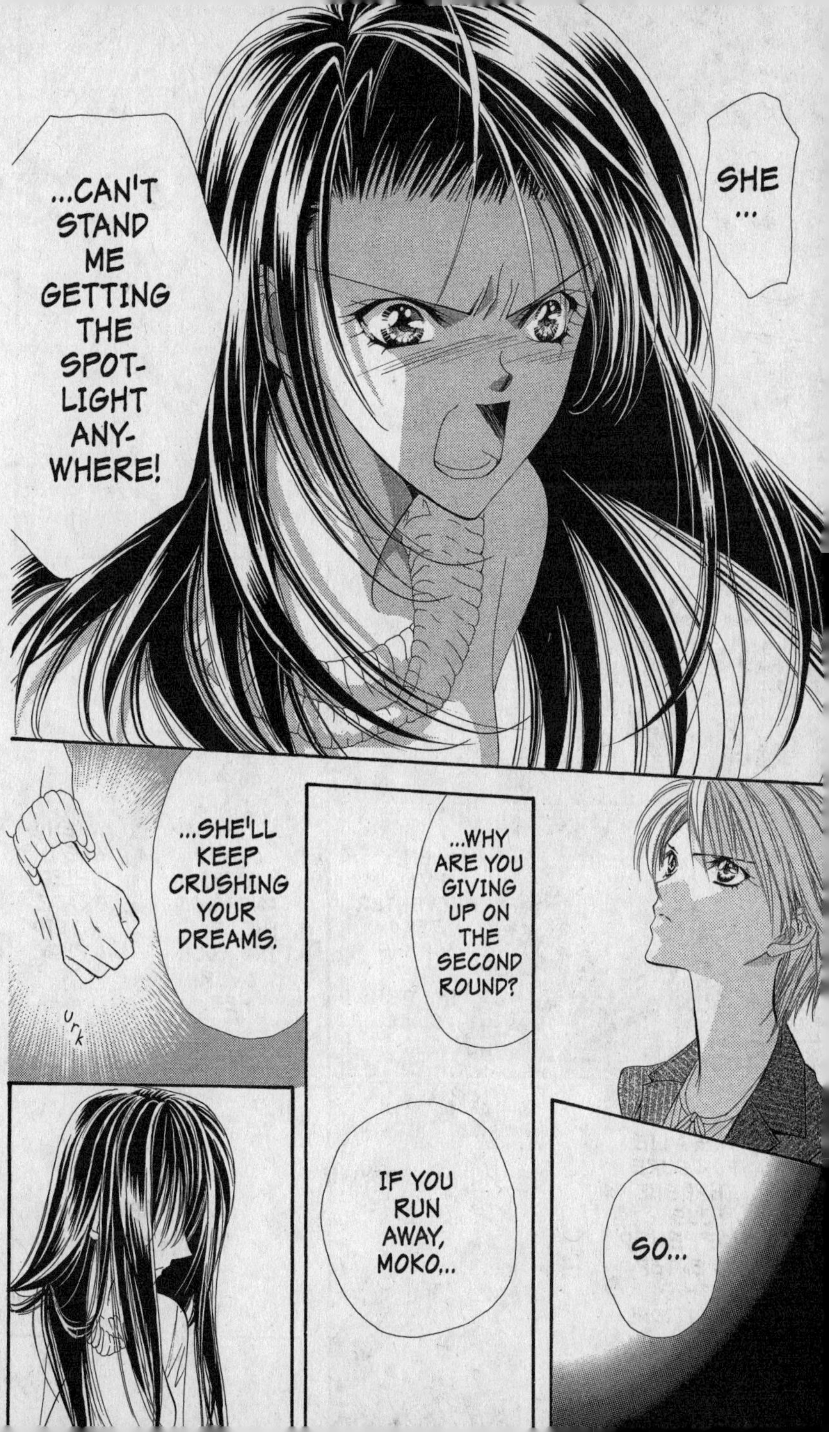
SHE...
...CAN'T STAND ME GETTING THE SPOT-LIGHT ANY-WHERE!
...WHY ARE YOU GIVING UP ON THE SECOND ROUND?
SO...
IF YOU RUN AWAY, MOKO...
...SHE'LL KEEP CRUSHING YOUR DREAMS.
urk

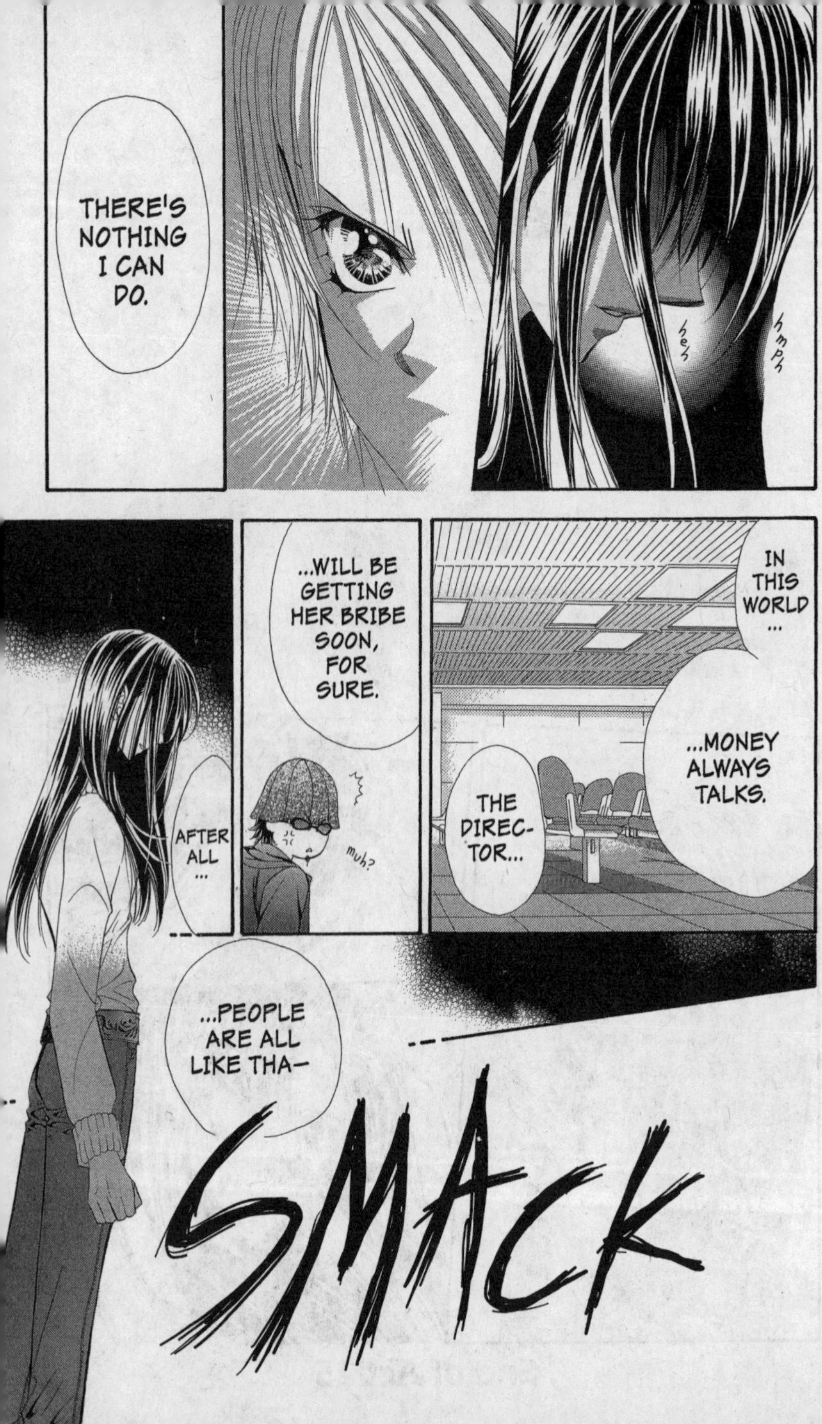
hmph
heh
THERE'S NOTHING I CAN DO.
IN THIS WORLD ...
...MONEY ALWAYS TALKS.
THE DIREC-TOR...
...WILL BE GETTING HER BRIBE SOON, FOR SURE.
muh?
AFTER ALL ...
...PEOPLE ARE ALL LIKE THA—
SMACK

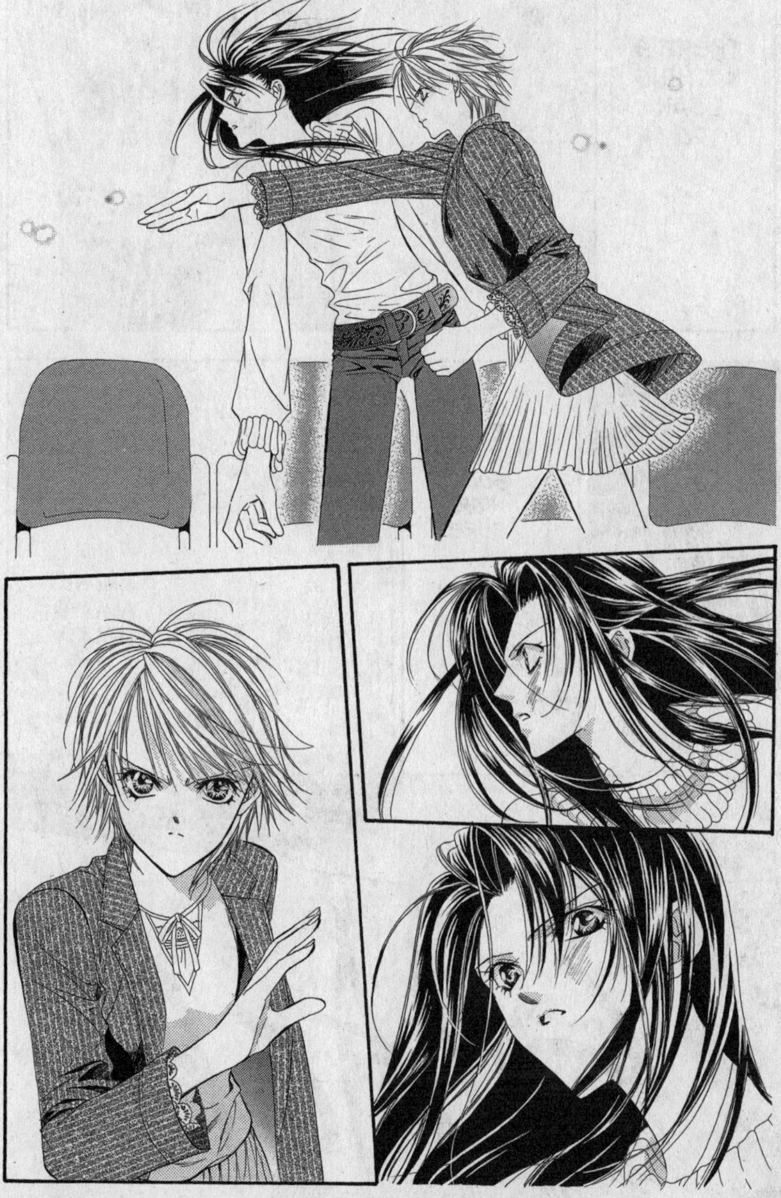

End of Act 25

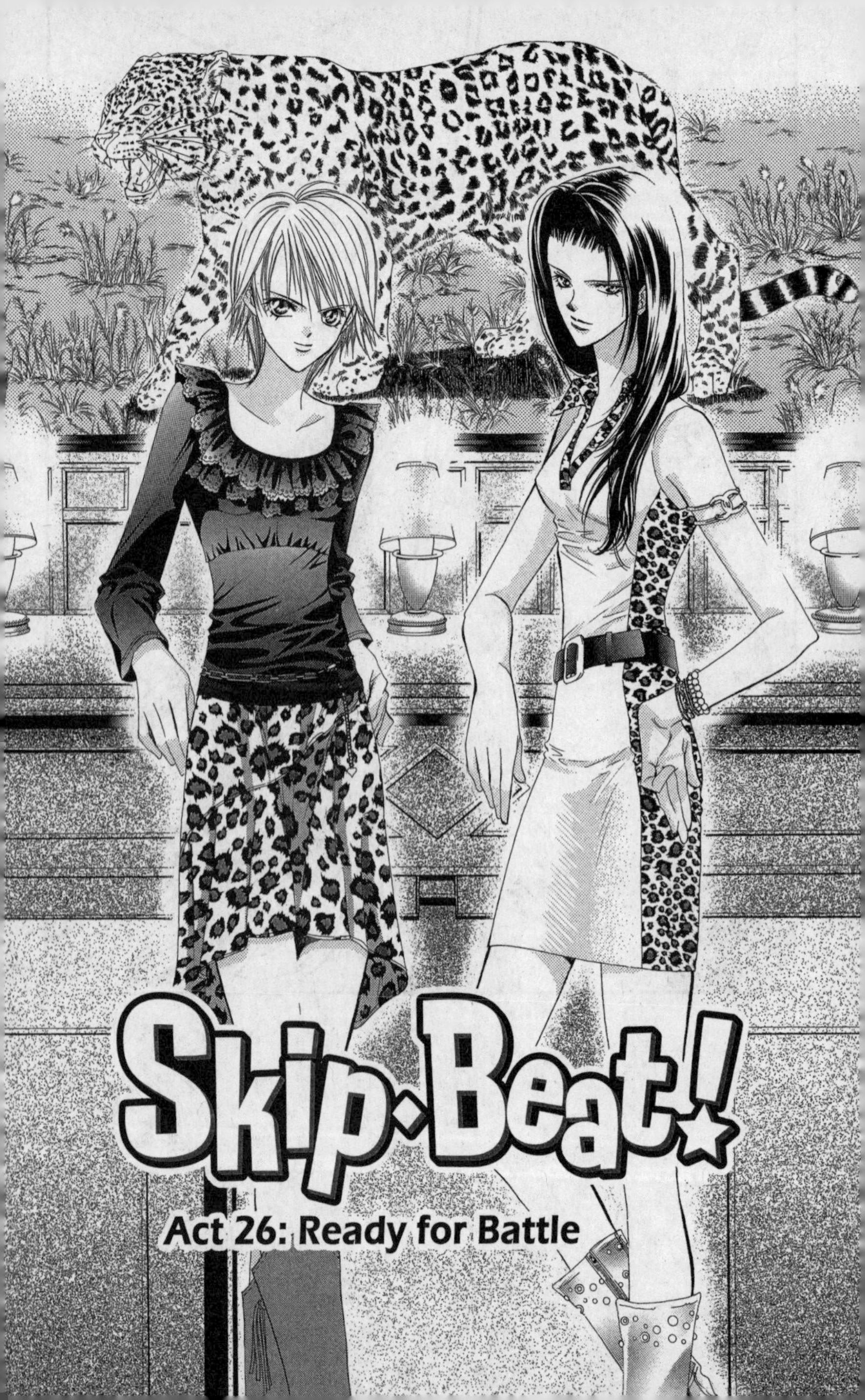
Skip·Beat!
Act 26: Ready for Battle

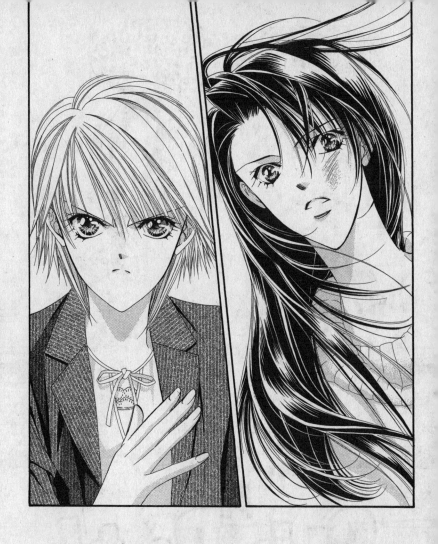

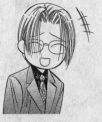

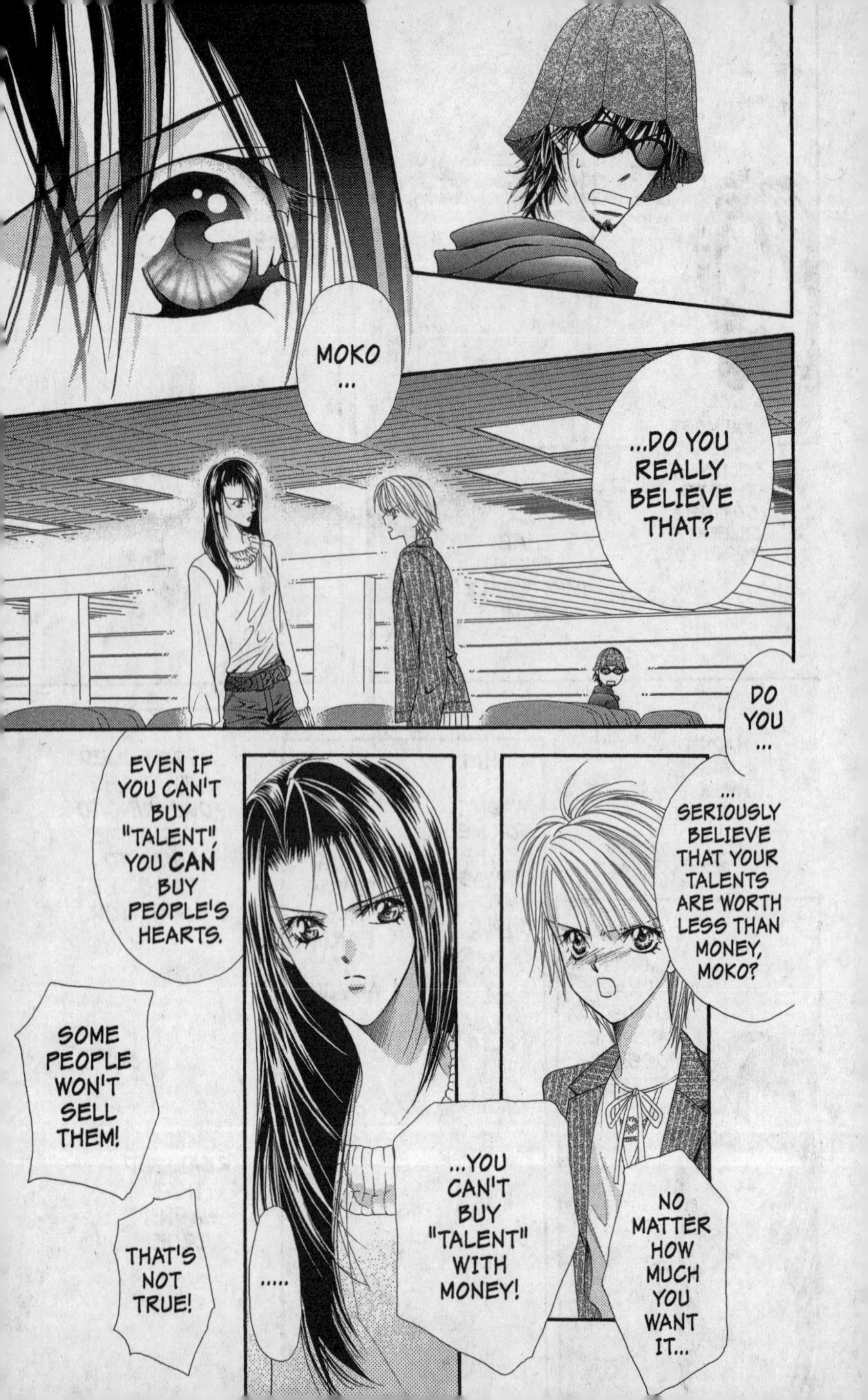
MOKO ...
...DO YOU REALLY BELIEVE THAT?
DO YOU ...
... SERIOUSLY BELIEVE THAT YOUR TALENTS ARE WORTH LESS THAN MONEY, MOKO?
EVEN IF YOU CAN'T BUY "TALENT", YOU CAN BUY PEOPLE'S HEARTS.
NO MATTER HOW MUCH YOU WANT IT...
...YOU CAN'T BUY "TALENT" WITH MONEY!
.....
SOME PEOPLE WON'T SELL THEM!
THAT'S NOT TRUE!

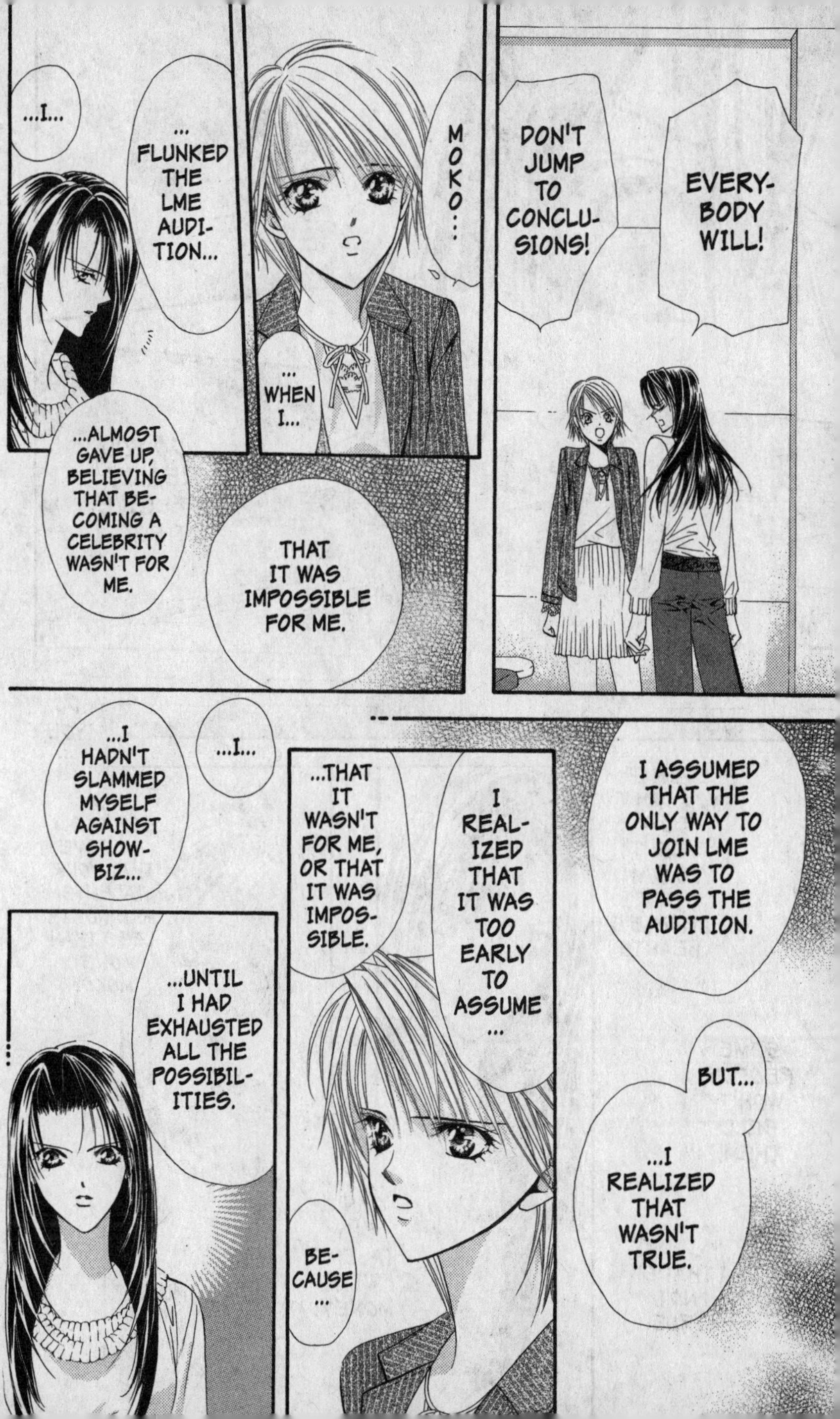
EVERYBODY WILL!
DON'T JUMP TO CONCLUSIONS!
MOKO...
...WHEN I...
...FLUNKED THE LME AUDITION...
...I...
...ALMOST GAVE UP, BELIEVING THAT BECOMING A CELEBRITY WASN'T FOR ME.
THAT IT WAS IMPOSSIBLE FOR ME.
I ASSUMED THAT THE ONLY WAY TO JOIN LME WAS TO PASS THE AUDITION.
BUT...
...I REALIZED THAT WASN'T TRUE.
I REALIZED THAT IT WAS TOO EARLY TO ASSUME...
...THAT IT WASN'T FOR ME, OR THAT IT WAS IMPOSSIBLE.
BECAUSE...
...I...
...I HADN'T SLAMMED MYSELF AGAINST SHOWBIZ...
...UNTIL I HAD EXHAUSTED ALL THE POSSIBILITIES.

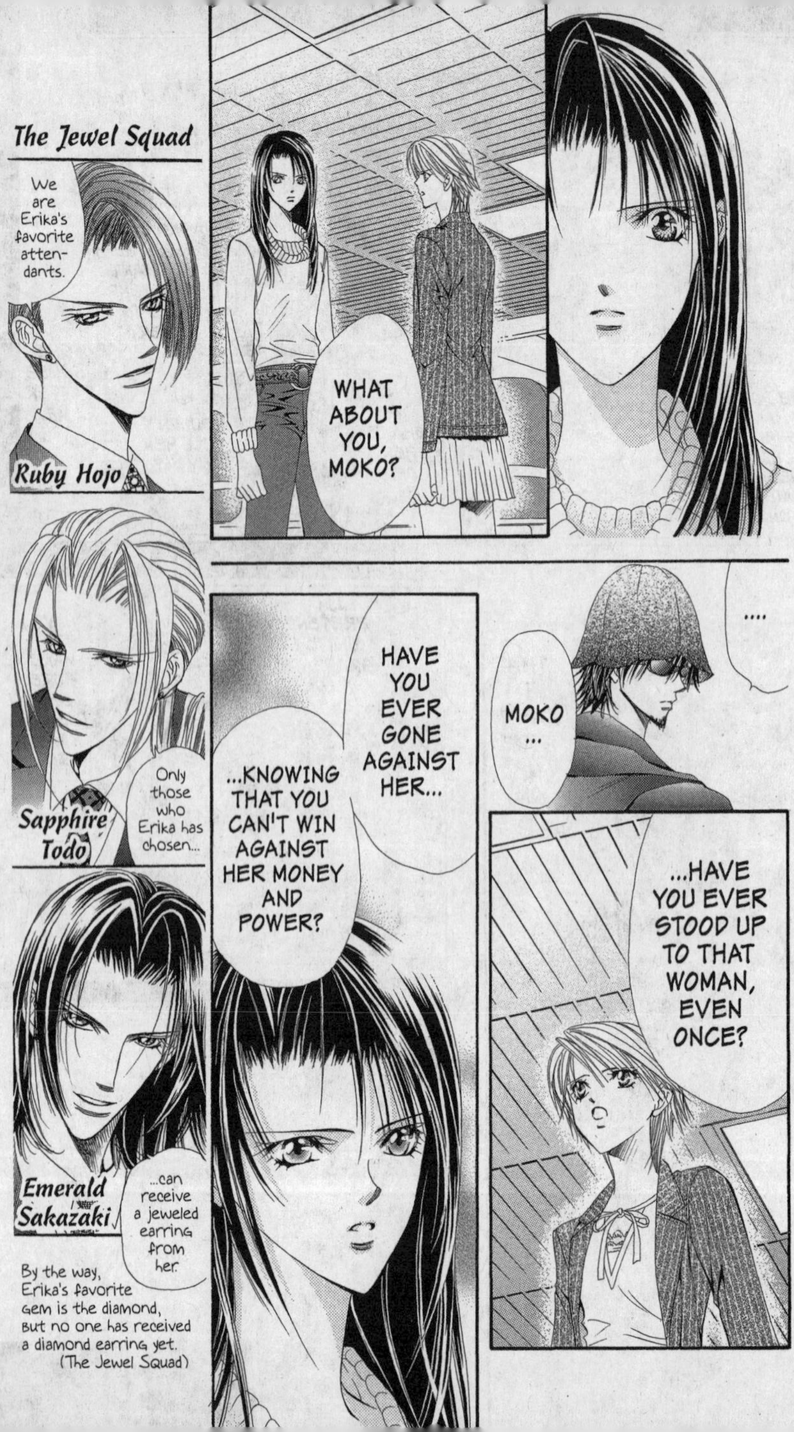

WHAT ABOUT YOU, MOKO?
....
MOKO ...
HAVE YOU EVER GONE AGAINST HER...
...KNOWING THAT YOU CAN'T WIN AGAINST HER MONEY AND POWER?
...HAVE YOU EVER STOOD UP TO THAT WOMAN, EVEN ONCE?
The Jewel Squad
We are Erika's favorite attendants.
Ruby Hojo
Only those who Erika has chosen...
Sapphire Todo
...can receive a jeweled earring from her.
Emerald Sakazaki
By the way, Erika's favorite gem is the diamond, but no one has received a diamond earring yet. (The Jewel Squad)

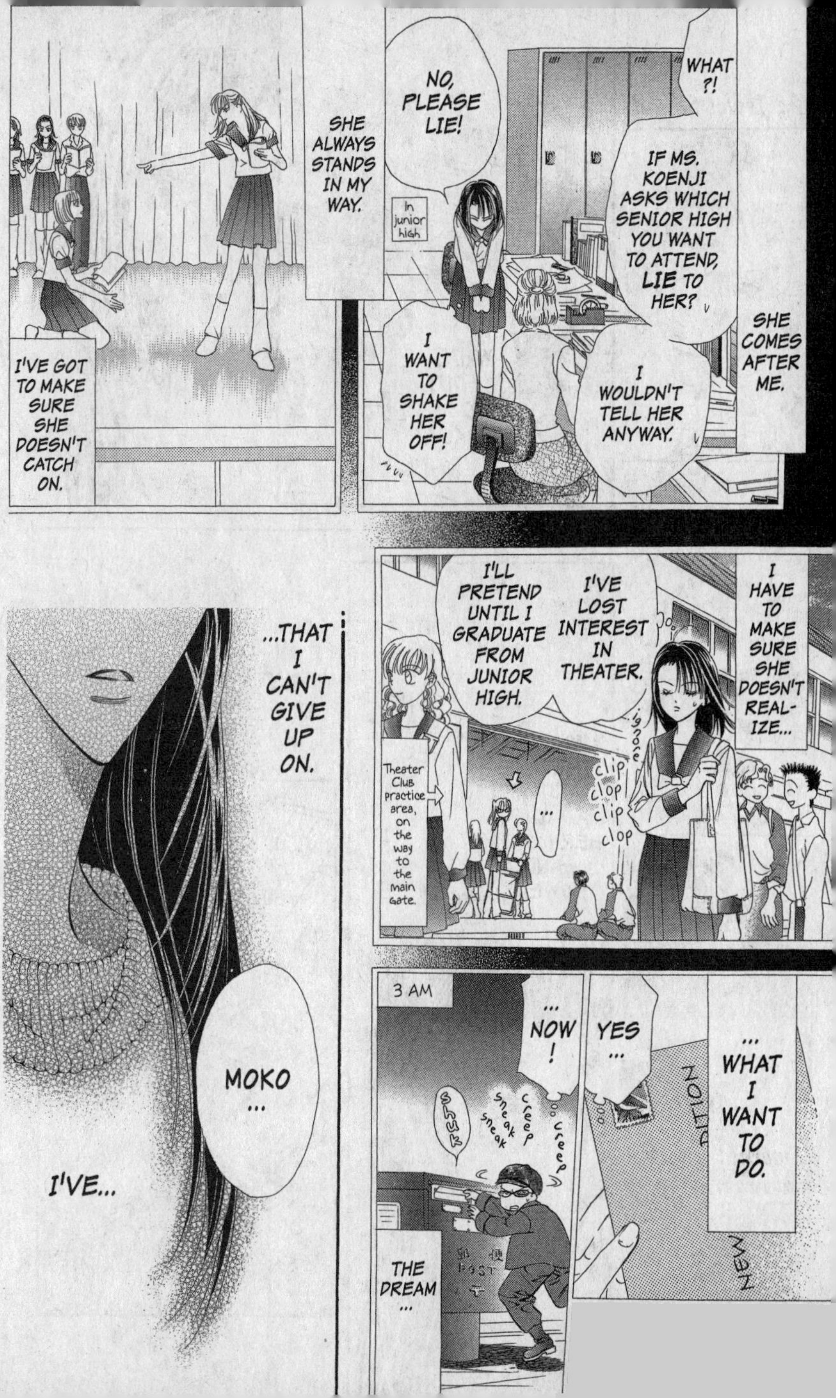
WHAT?!
IF MS. KOENJI ASKS WHICH SENIOR HIGH YOU WANT TO ATTEND, LIE TO HER?
SHE COMES AFTER ME.
I WOULDN'T TELL HER ANYWAY.
NO, PLEASE LIE!
In junior high
I WANT TO SHAKE HER OFF!
SHE ALWAYS STANDS IN MY WAY.
I'VE GOT TO MAKE SURE SHE DOESN'T CATCH ON.
I HAVE TO MAKE SURE SHE DOESN'T REALIZE...
I'VE LOST INTEREST IN THEATER.
I'LL PRETEND UNTIL I GRADUATE FROM JUNIOR HIGH.
ignore
clip clop clip clop
...
Theater Club practice area, on the way to the main gate.
...WHAT I WANT TO DO.
YES...
...NOW!
3 AM
creep creep
sneak sneak
shuk
NEW
THE DREAM...
...THAT I CAN'T GIVE UP ON.
MOKO...
I'VE...

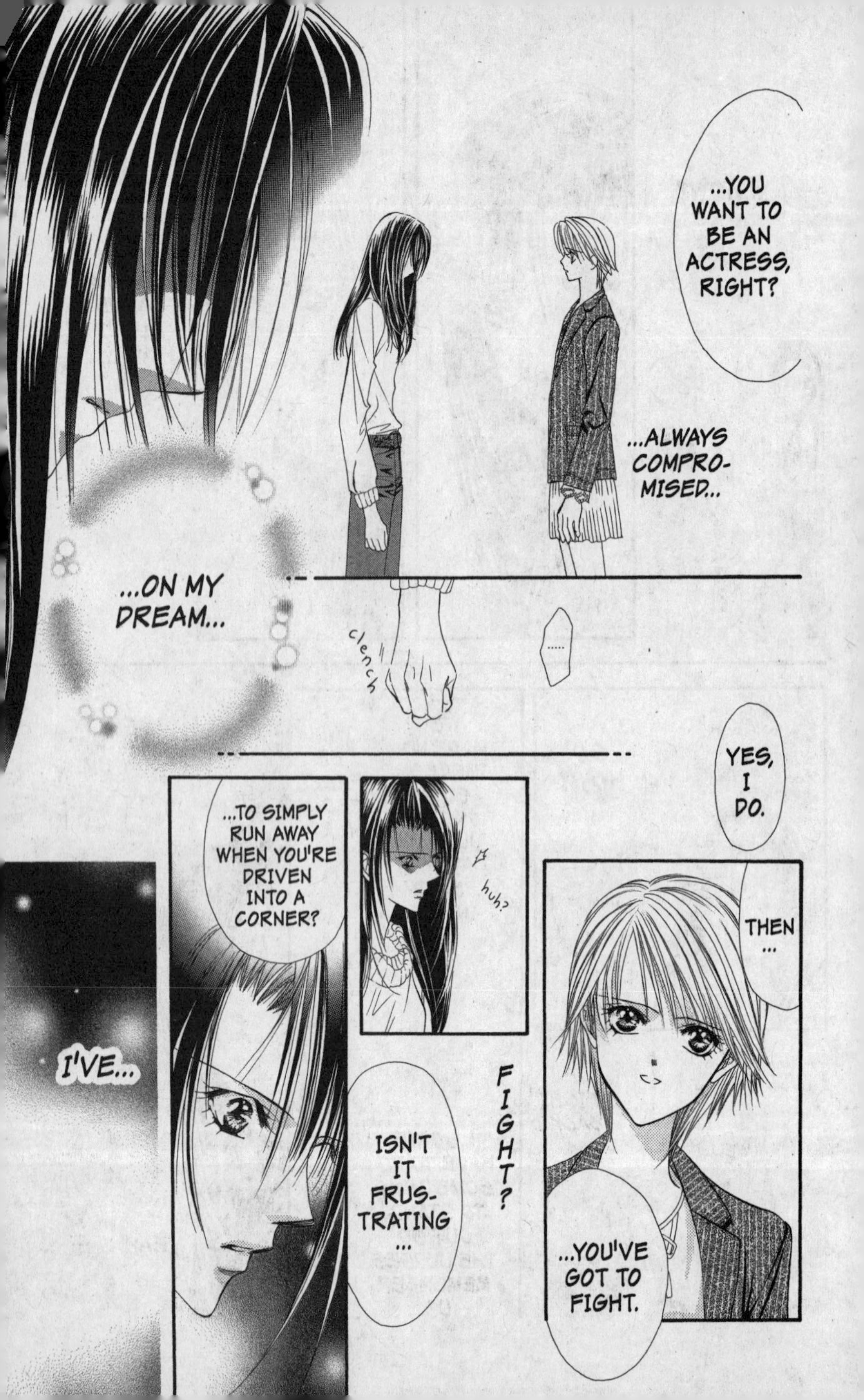
...YOU WANT TO BE AN ACTRESS, RIGHT?
...ALWAYS COMPROMISED...
......
clench
...ON MY DREAM...
YES, I DO.
THEN...
...YOU'VE GOT TO FIGHT.
huh?
FIGHT?
...TO SIMPLY RUN AWAY WHEN YOU'RE DRIVEN INTO A CORNER?
ISN'T IT FRUSTRATING...
I'VE...

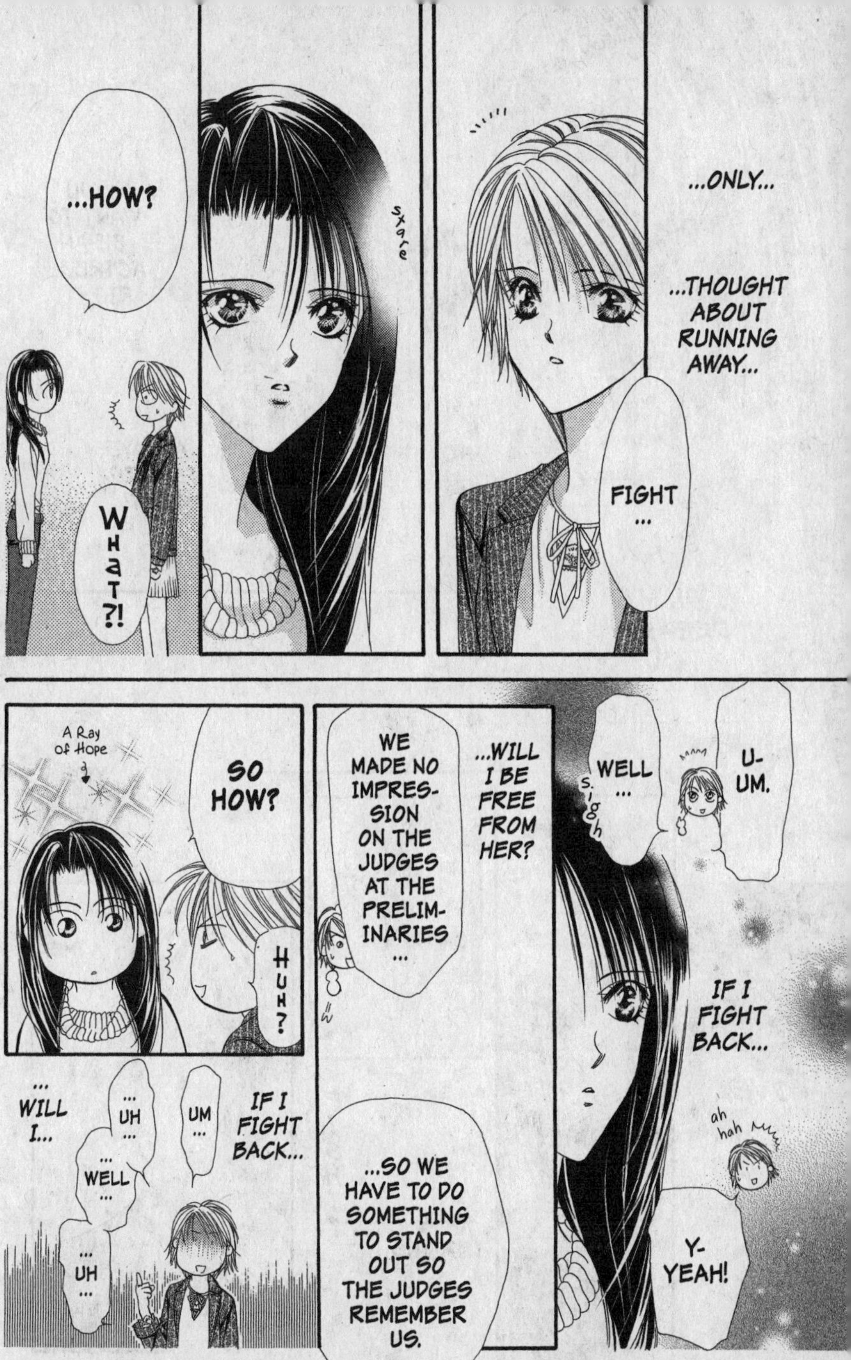
...ONLY...
...THOUGHT ABOUT RUNNING AWAY...
FIGHT ...
stare
...HOW?
WHAT?!
U-UM.
WELL ...
sigh
IF I FIGHT BACK...
ah hah
Y-YEAH!
...WILL I BE FREE FROM HER?
WE MADE NO IMPRESSION ON THE JUDGES AT THE PRELIMINARIES ...
...SO WE HAVE TO DO SOMETHING TO STAND OUT SO THE JUDGES REMEMBER US.
SO HOW?
A Ray of Hope
HUH?
IF I FIGHT BACK...
UM ...
... UH ...
... WILL I...
... WELL ...
... UH ...

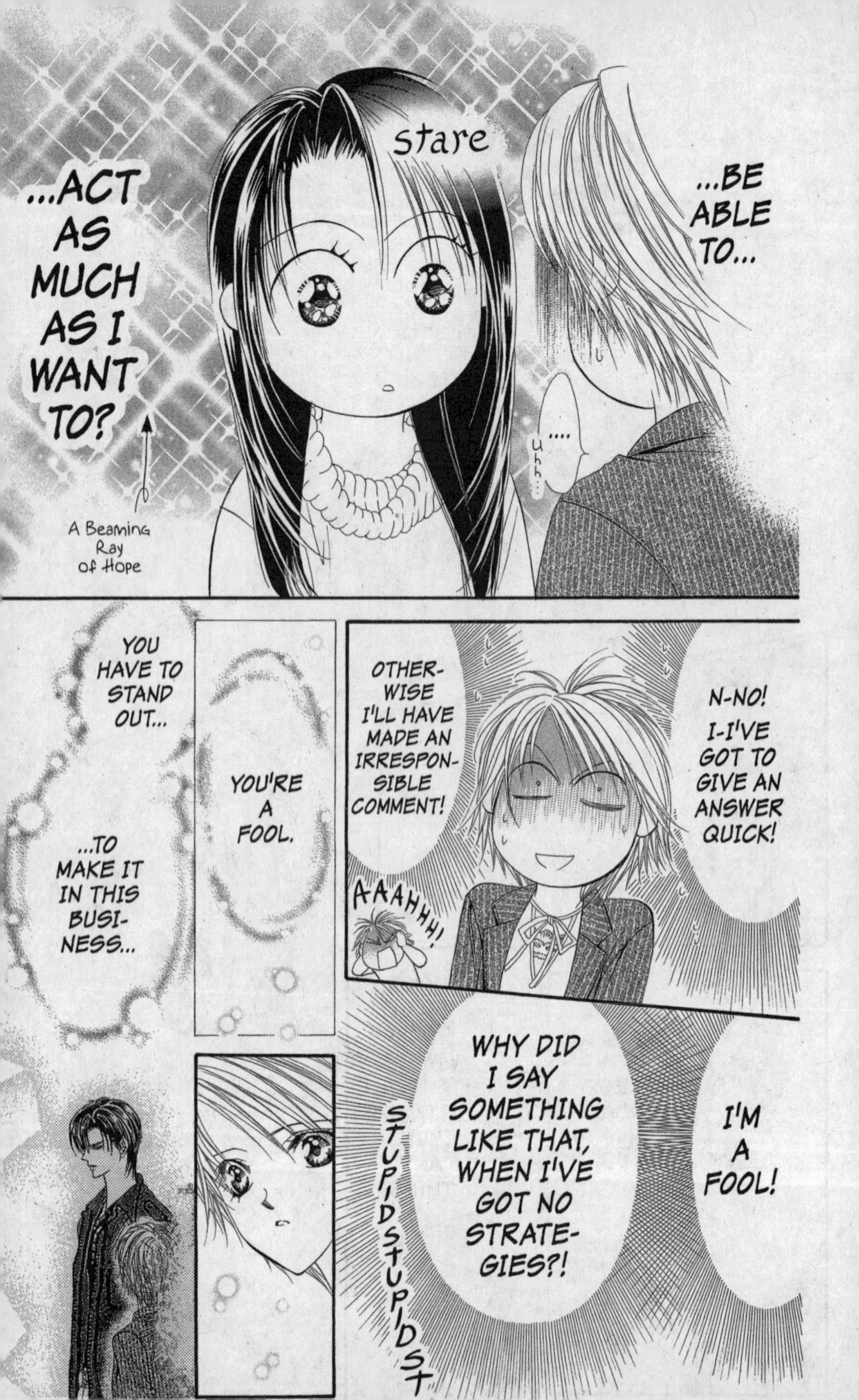
...BE ABLE TO...
Stare
...ACT AS MUCH AS I WANT TO?
....
Uhh...
A Beaming Ray of Hope
N-NO! I-I'VE GOT TO GIVE AN ANSWER QUICK!
OTHERWISE I'LL HAVE MADE AN IRRESPONSIBLE COMMENT!
AAAHHH!
YOU'RE A FOOL.
YOU HAVE TO STAND OUT...
...TO MAKE IT IN THIS BUSINESS...
I'M A FOOL!
WHY DID I SAY SOMETHING LIKE THAT, WHEN I'VE GOT NO STRATEGIES?!
STUPIDSTUPIDST

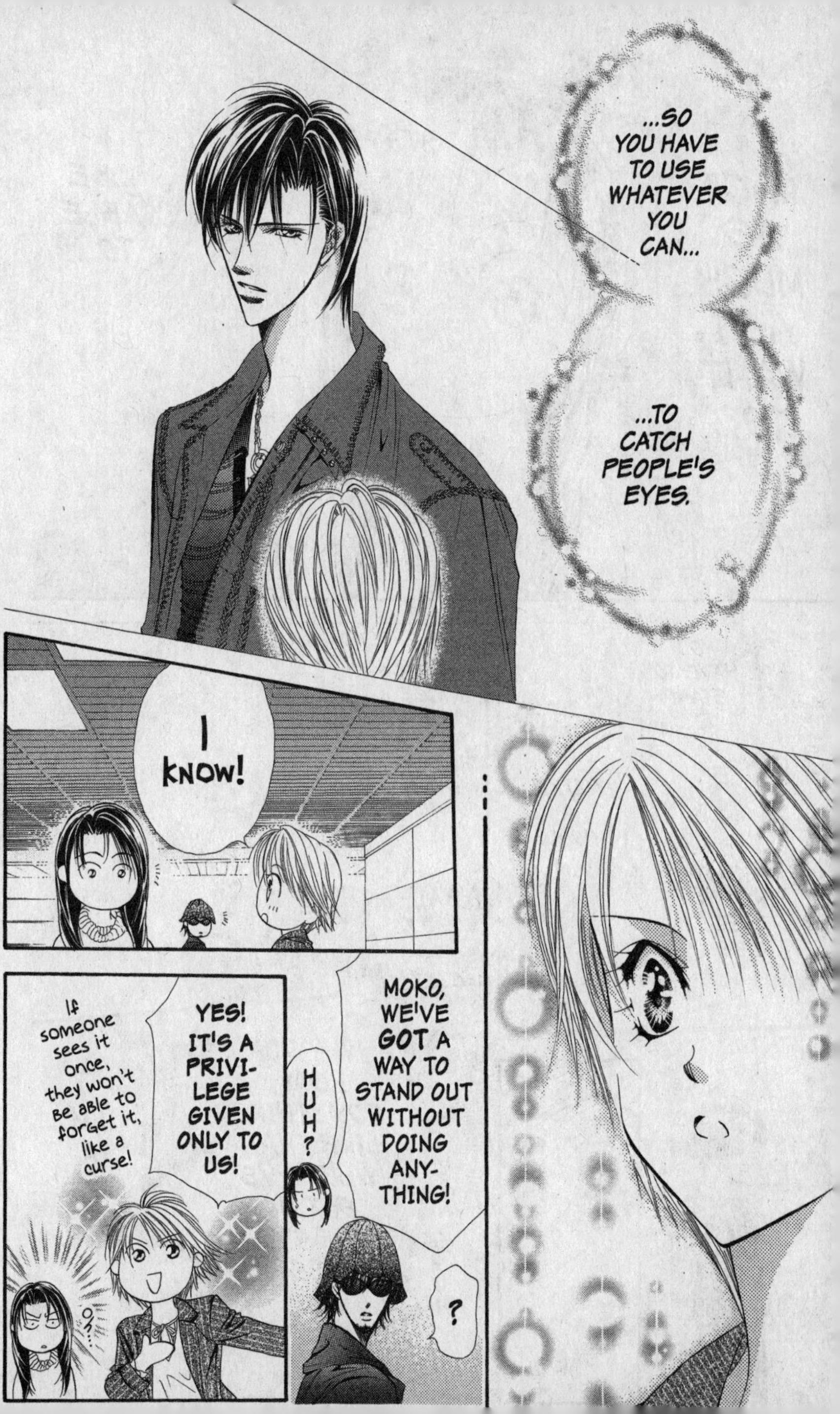
...SO YOU HAVE TO USE WHATEVER YOU CAN...
...TO CATCH PEOPLE'S EYES.
I KNOW!
MOKO, WE'VE GOT A WAY TO STAND OUT WITHOUT DOING ANYTHING!
?
HUH?
YES! IT'S A PRIVILEGE GIVEN ONLY TO US!
If someone sees it once, they won't be able to forget it, like a curse!

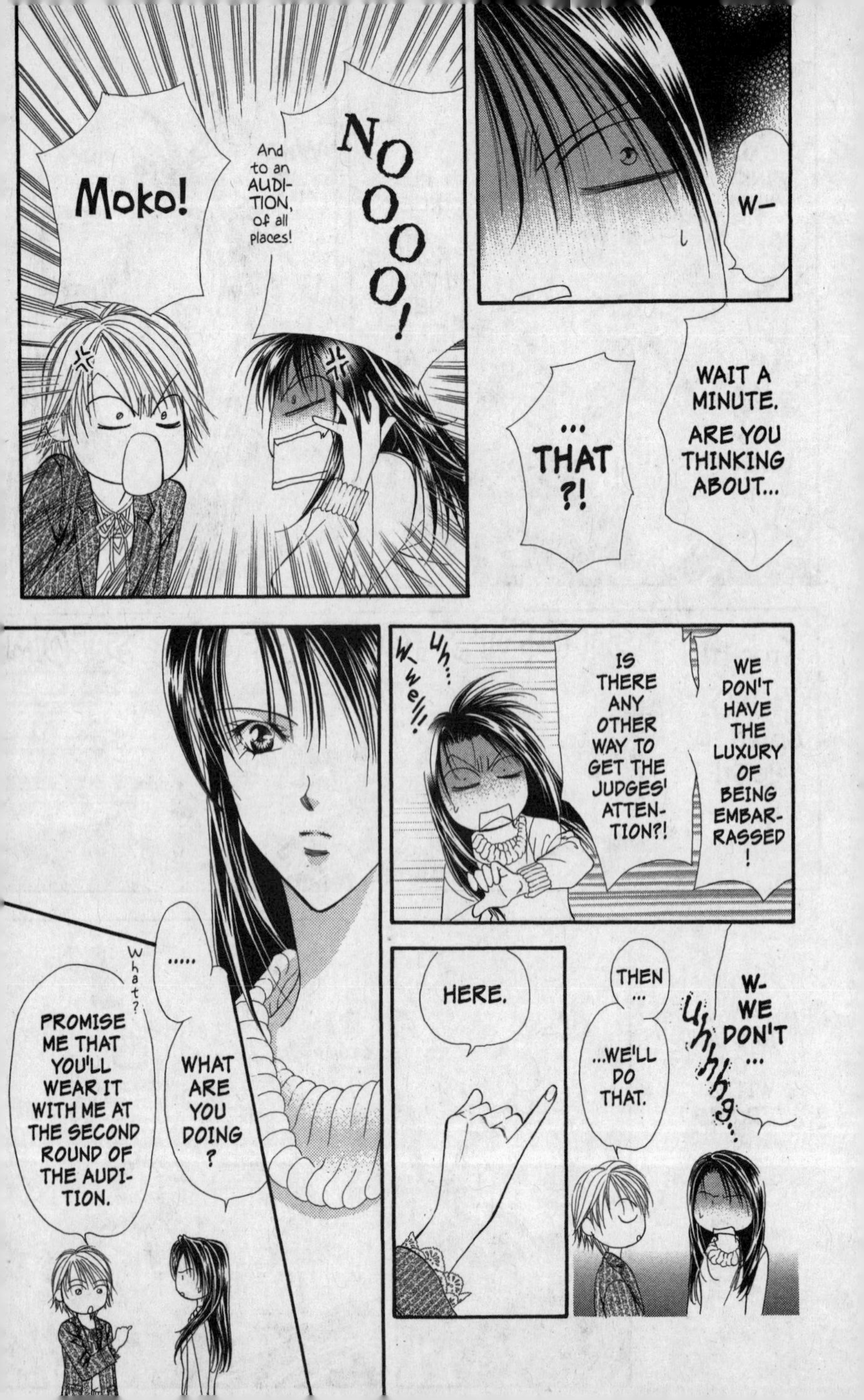
W-
WAIT A MINUTE. ARE YOU THINKING ABOUT...
...THAT?!
NOOOO!
And to an AUDITION, of all places!
Moko!
WE DON'T HAVE THE LUXURY OF BEING EMBARRASSED!
IS THERE ANY OTHER WAY TO GET THE JUDGES' ATTENTION?!
Uh... W-well!!
W-WE DON'T...
Uhhhg...
THEN...
...WE'LL DO THAT.
HERE.
.....
What?
WHAT ARE YOU DOING?
PROMISE ME THAT YOU'LL WEAR IT WITH ME AT THE SECOND ROUND OF THE AUDITION.

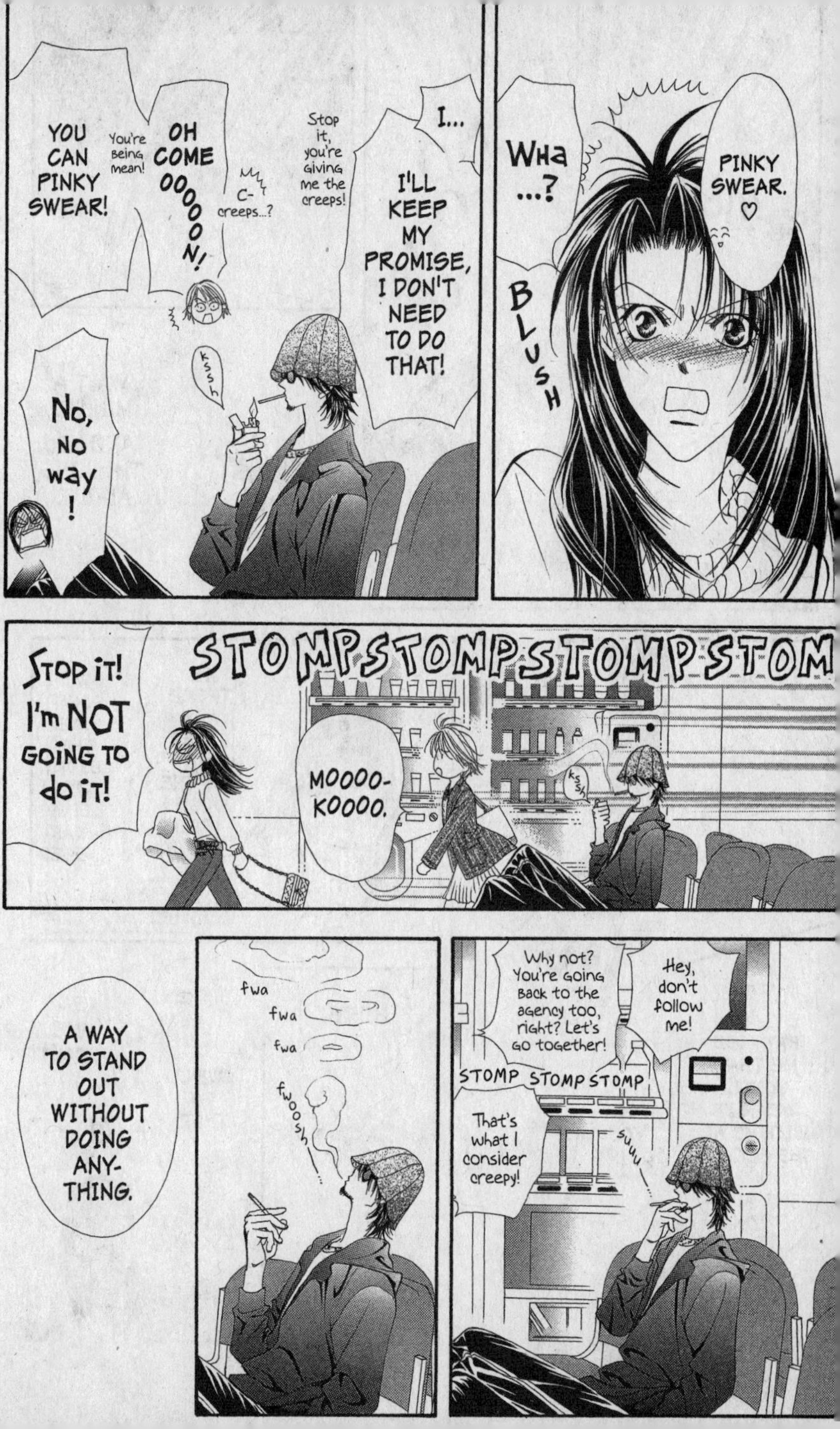
PINKY SWEAR. ♡
Wha...?
BLUSH
I...
I'LL KEEP MY PROMISE, I DON'T NEED TO DO THAT!
Stop it, you're giving me the creeps!
C-creeps...?
OH COME OOOOOON!
You're being mean!
YOU CAN PINKY SWEAR!
kssh
No, no way!
STOMPSTOMPSTOMPSTOM
kssh
MOOOO-KOOOO.
Stop it! I'm NOT going to do it!
Hey, don't follow me!
Why not? You're going back to the agency too, right? Let's go together!
STOMP STOMP STOMP
That's what I consider creepy!
suuu
fwa
fwa
fwa
fwoosh
A WAY TO STAND OUT WITHOUT DOING ANYTHING.

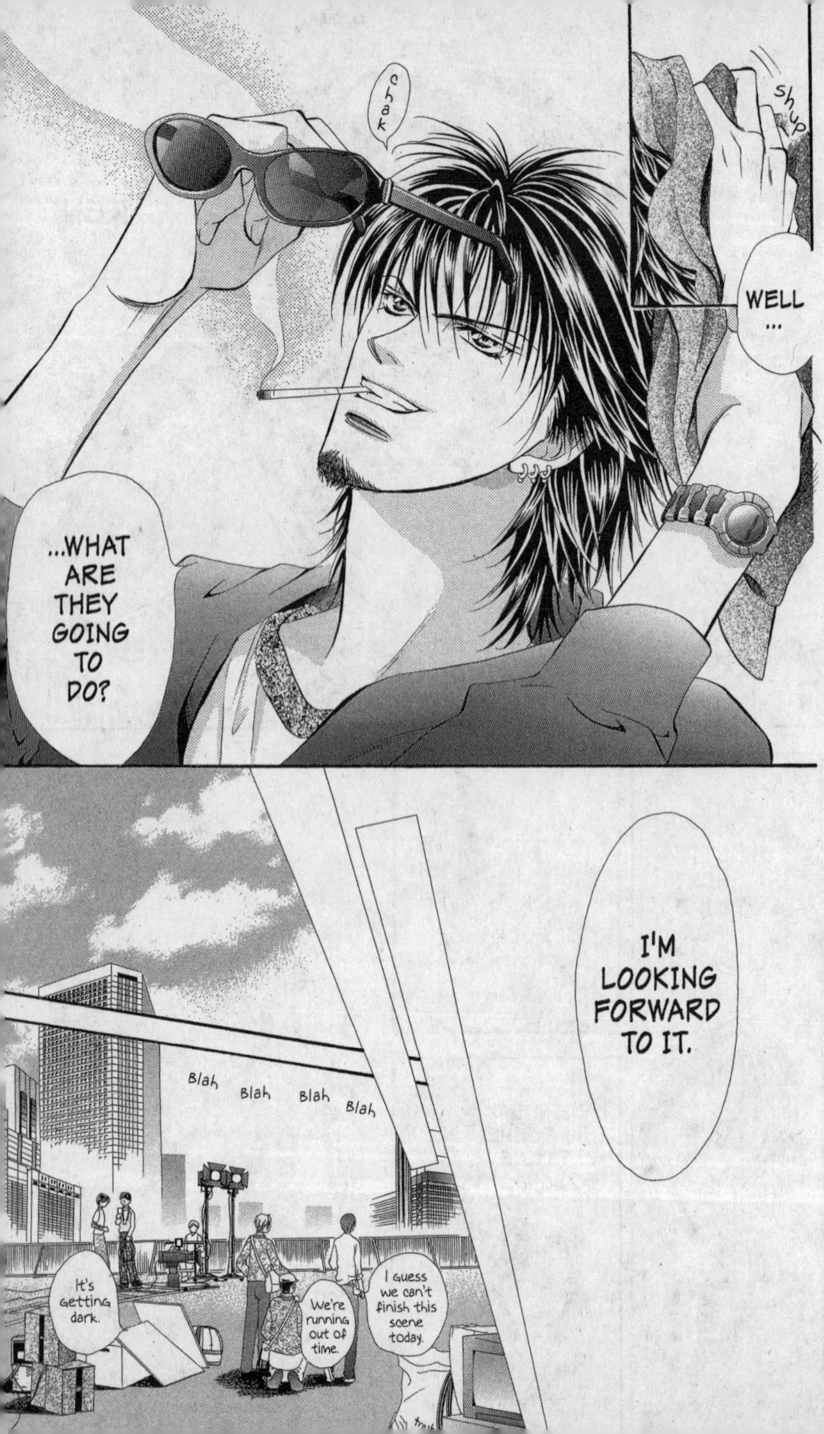
shup
WELL ...
chak
...WHAT ARE THEY GOING TO DO?
I'M LOOKING FORWARD TO IT.
Blah Blah Blah Blah
I guess we can't finish this scene today.
We're running out of time.
It's getting dark.

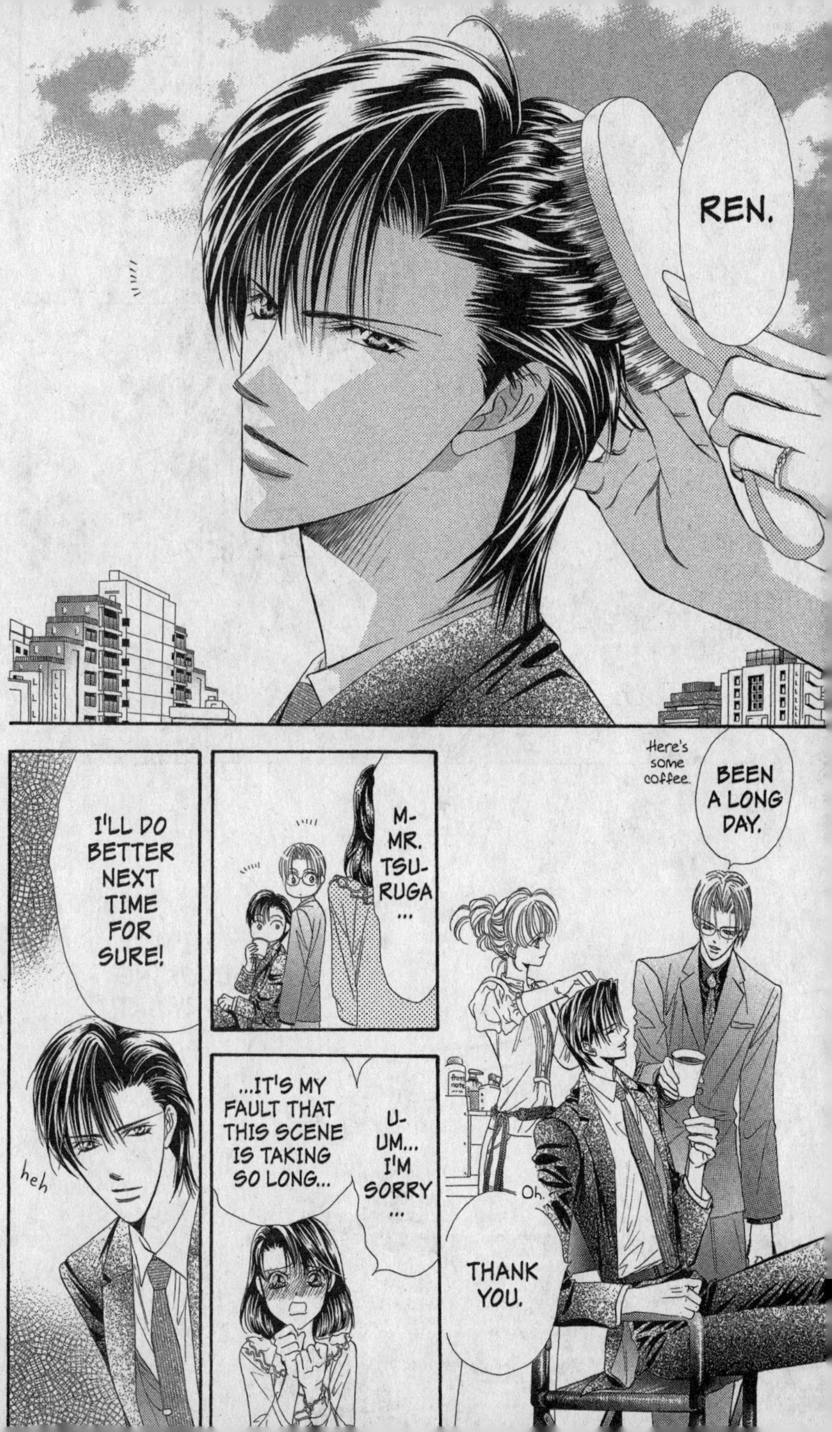
REN.
Here's some coffee.
BEEN A LONG DAY.
Oh.
THANK YOU.
M-MR. TSURUGA...
U-UM... I'M SORRY...
...IT'S MY FAULT THAT THIS SCENE IS TAKING SO LONG...
I'LL DO BETTER NEXT TIME FOR SURE!
heh

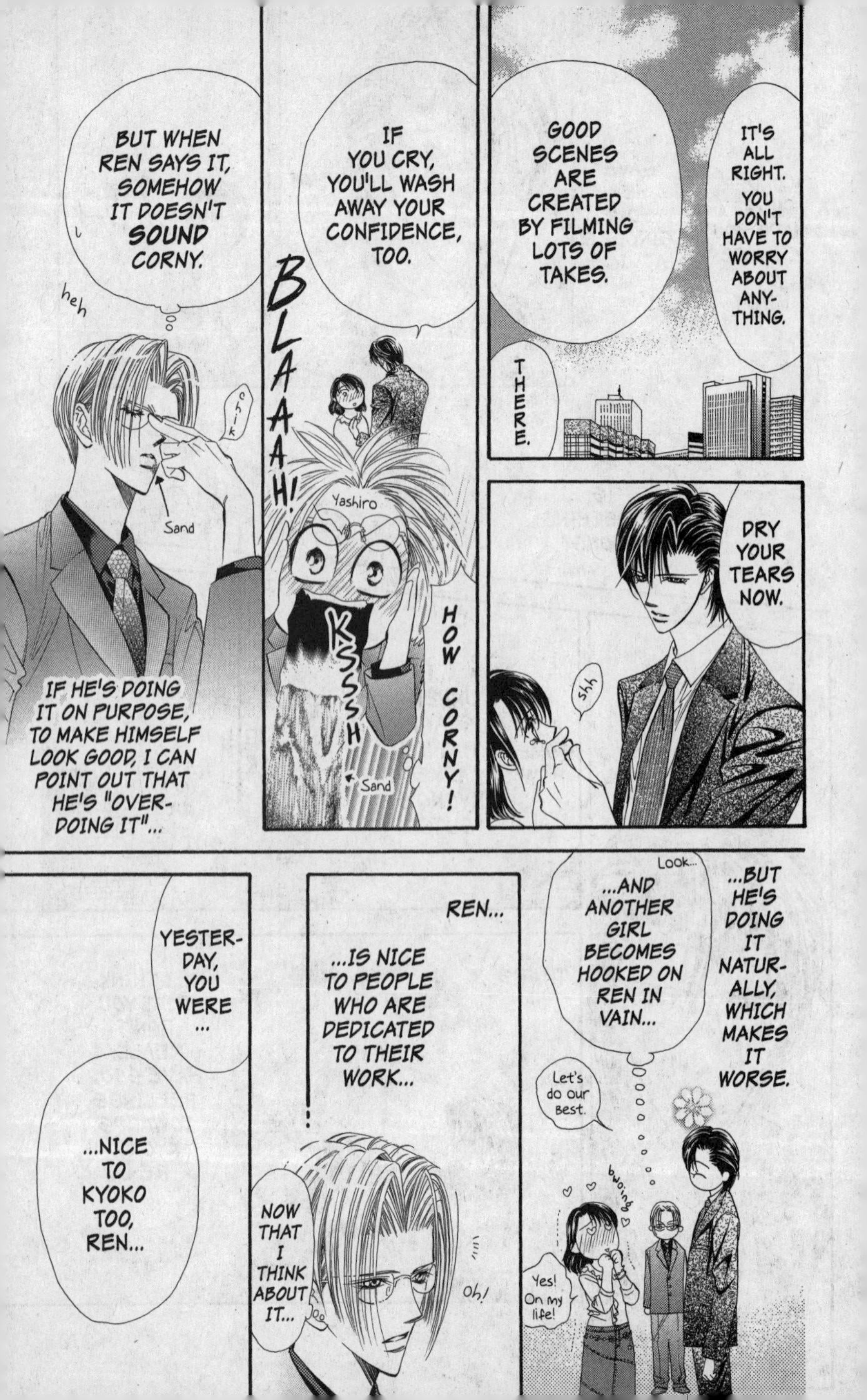
IT'S ALL RIGHT. YOU DON'T HAVE TO WORRY ABOUT ANY-THING.
GOOD SCENES ARE CREATED BY FILMING LOTS OF TAKES.
THERE.
DRY YOUR TEARS NOW.
shh
IF YOU CRY, YOU'LL WASH AWAY YOUR CONFIDENCE, TOO.
BLAAAAH!
Yashiro
HOW CORNY!
KSSSH
Sand
BUT WHEN REN SAYS IT, SOMEHOW IT DOESN'T SOUND CORNY.
heh
chik
Sand
IF HE'S DOING IT ON PURPOSE, TO MAKE HIMSELF LOOK GOOD, I CAN POINT OUT THAT HE'S "OVER-DOING IT"...
...BUT HE'S DOING IT NATUR-ALLY, WHICH MAKES IT WORSE.
Look...
...AND ANOTHER GIRL BECOMES HOOKED ON REN IN VAIN...
Let's do our best.
bwoing
Yes! On my life!
REN...
...IS NICE TO PEOPLE WHO ARE DEDICATED TO THEIR WORK...
Oh!
NOW THAT I THINK ABOUT IT...
YESTER-DAY, YOU WERE ...
...NICE TO KYOKO TOO, REN...

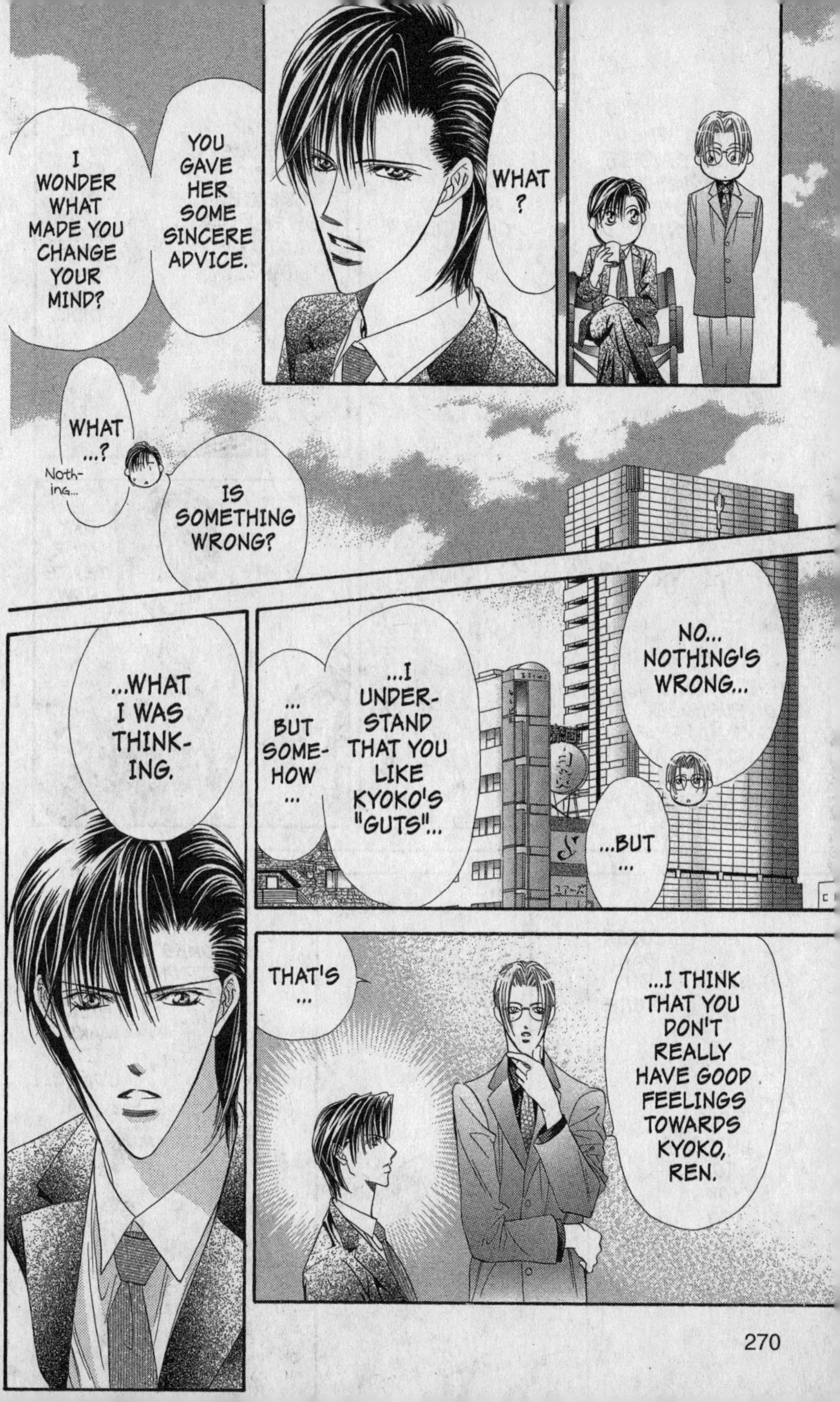
WHAT ?
YOU GAVE HER SOME SINCERE ADVICE.
I WONDER WHAT MADE YOU CHANGE YOUR MIND?
IS SOMETHING WRONG?
WHAT ...?
Nothing...
NO... NOTHING'S WRONG...
...BUT ...
...I UNDERSTAND THAT YOU LIKE KYOKO'S "GUTS"...
... BUT SOMEHOW ...
...I THINK THAT YOU DON'T REALLY HAVE GOOD FEELINGS TOWARDS KYOKO, REN.
THAT'S ...
...WHAT I WAS THINKING.

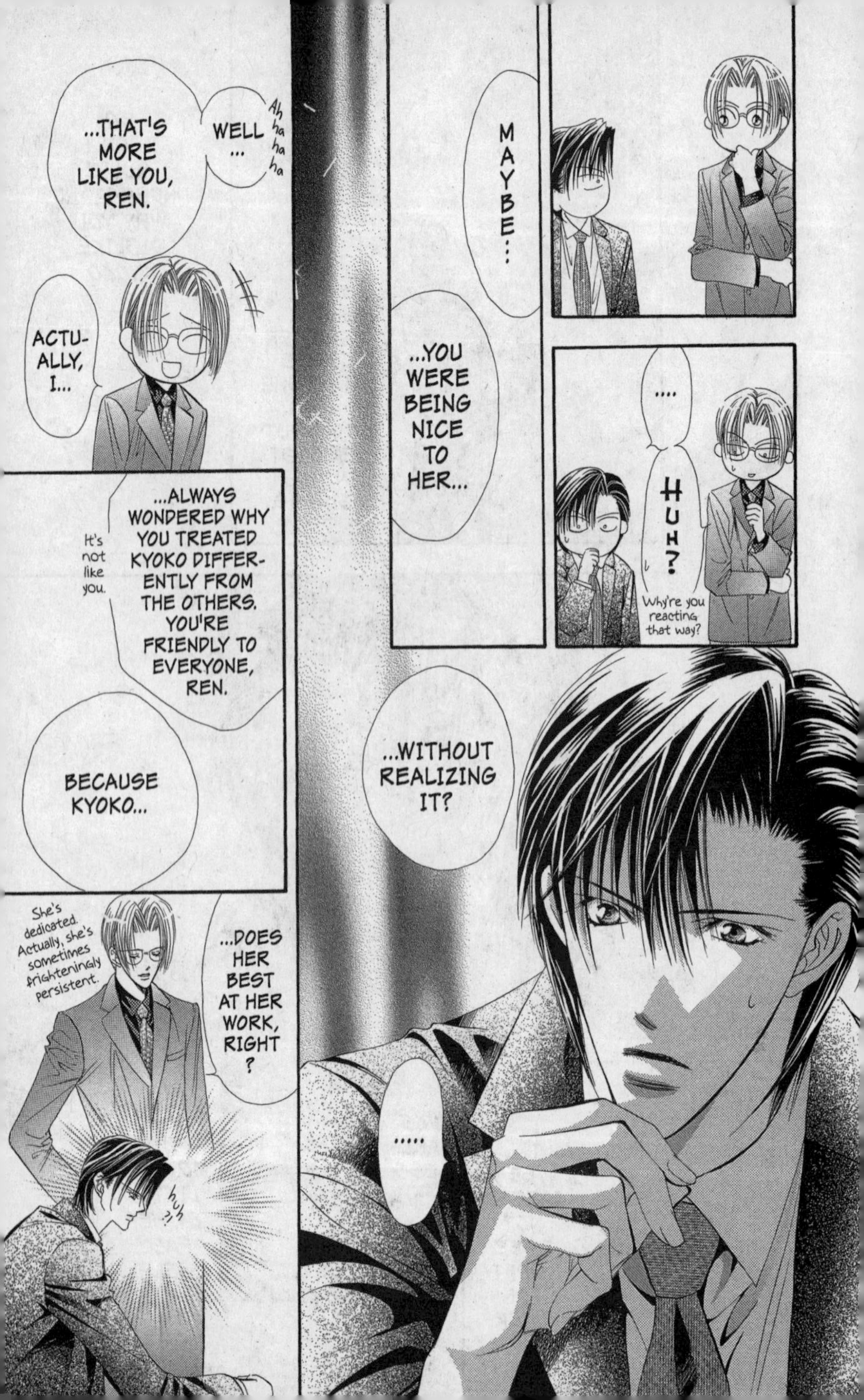
WELL ...
Ah ha ha ha
...THAT'S MORE LIKE YOU, REN.
ACTU-ALLY, I...
...ALWAYS WONDERED WHY YOU TREATED KYOKO DIFFER-ENTLY FROM THE OTHERS. YOU'RE FRIENDLY TO EVERYONE, REN.
It's not like you.
BECAUSE KYOKO...
...DOES HER BEST AT HER WORK, RIGHT?
She's dedicated. Actually, she's sometimes frighteningly persistent.
huh ?!
MAYBE...
...YOU WERE BEING NICE TO HER...
....
HUH?
Why're you reacting that way?
...WITHOUT REALIZING IT?
.....

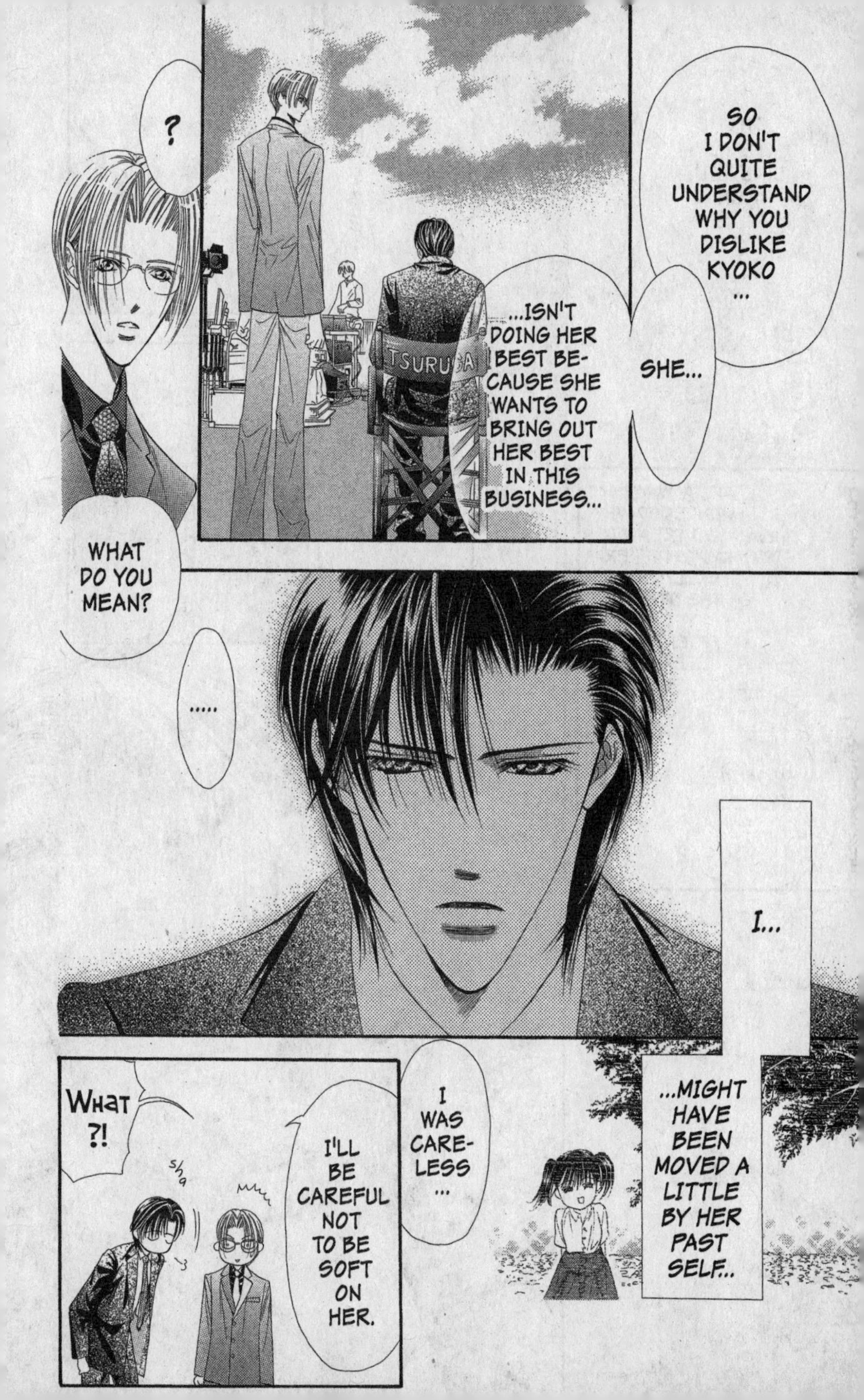
SO I DON'T QUITE UNDERSTAND WHY YOU DISLIKE KYOKO ...
SHE...
...ISN'T DOING HER BEST BE- CAUSE SHE WANTS TO BRING OUT HER BEST IN THIS BUSINESS...
TSURUGA
?
WHAT DO YOU MEAN?
I...
.....
...MIGHT HAVE BEEN MOVED A LITTLE BY HER PAST SELF..
I WAS CARE- LESS ...
I'LL BE CAREFUL NOT TO BE SOFT ON HER.
WHAT ?!
sha

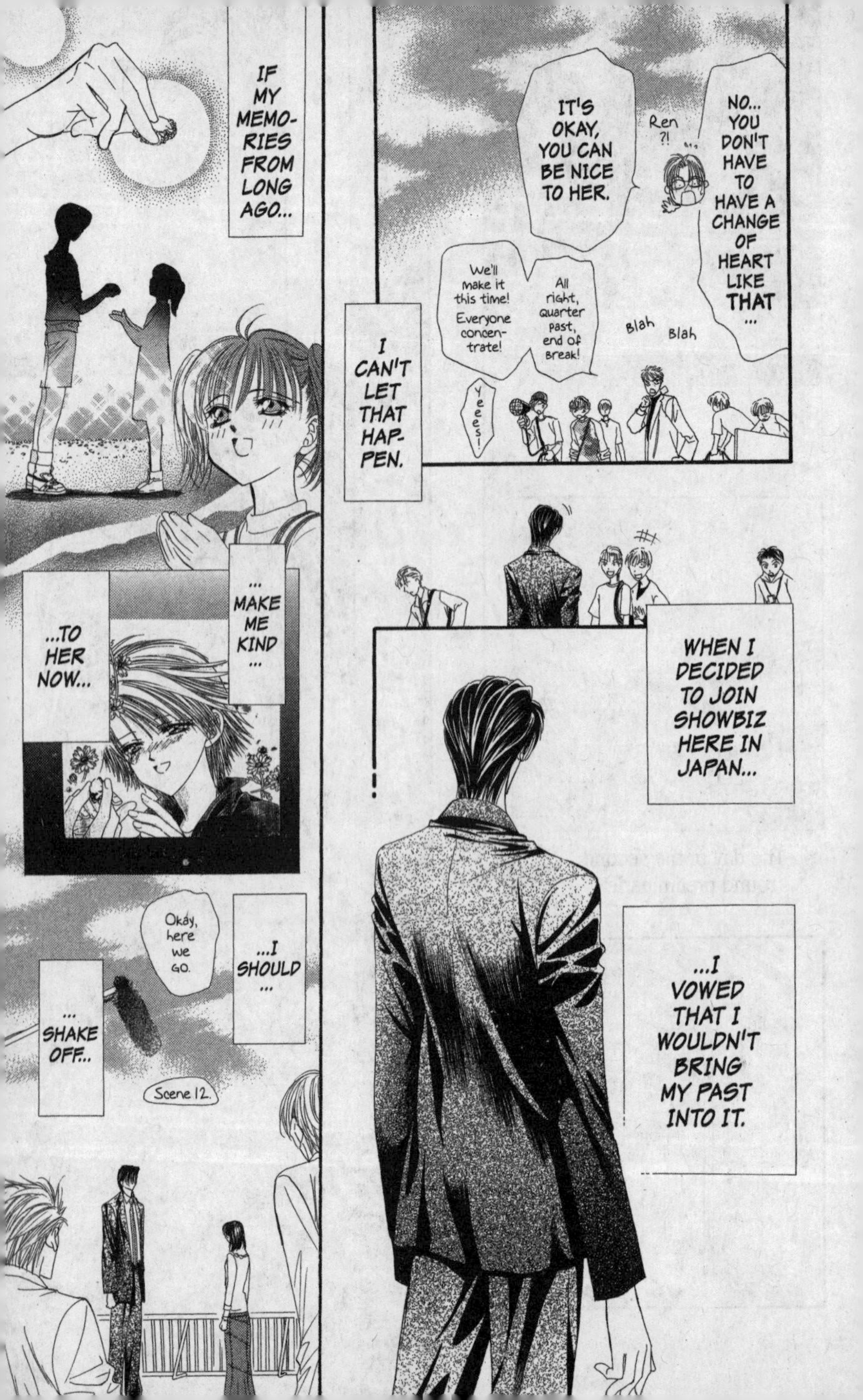
NO... YOU DON'T HAVE TO HAVE A CHANGE OF HEART LIKE THAT...
Ren ?!
IT'S OKAY, YOU CAN BE NICE TO HER.
Blah Blah
All right, quarter past, end of break!
We'll make it this time! Everyone concentrate!
Yeees!
I CAN'T LET THAT HAPPEN.
!
WHEN I DECIDED TO JOIN SHOWBIZ HERE IN JAPAN...
...I VOWED THAT I WOULDN'T BRING MY PAST INTO IT.
IF MY MEMORIES FROM LONG AGO...
...MAKE ME KIND...
...TO HER NOW...
...I SHOULD...
Okay, here we go.
...SHAKE OFF...
Scene 12.

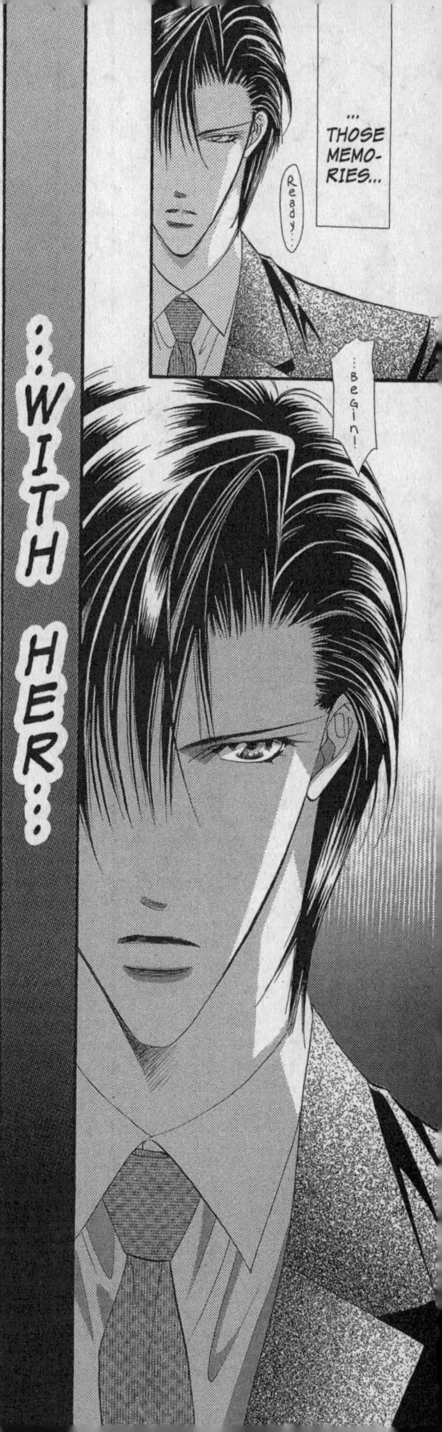

... THOSE MEMORIES...
Ready...
...Begin!
..WITH HER..

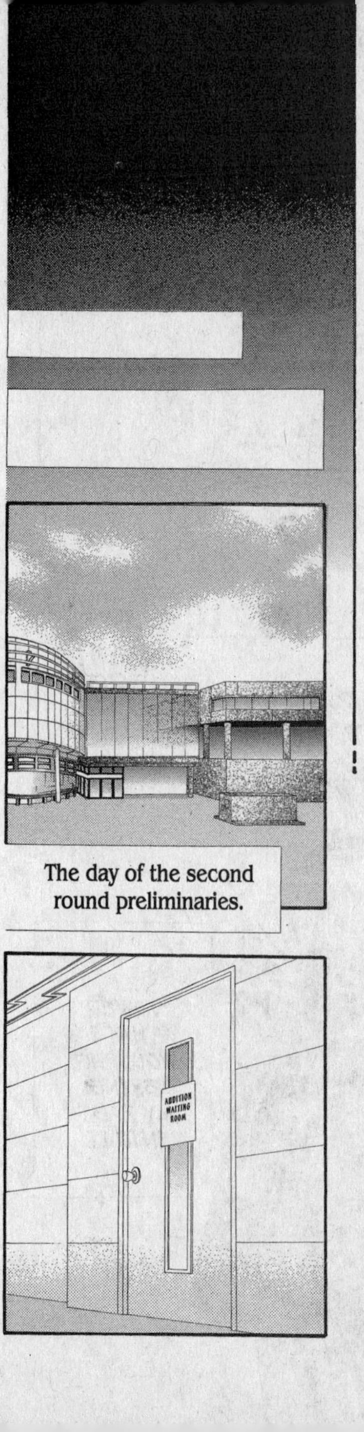

The day of the second round preliminaries.
AUDITION WAITING ROOM

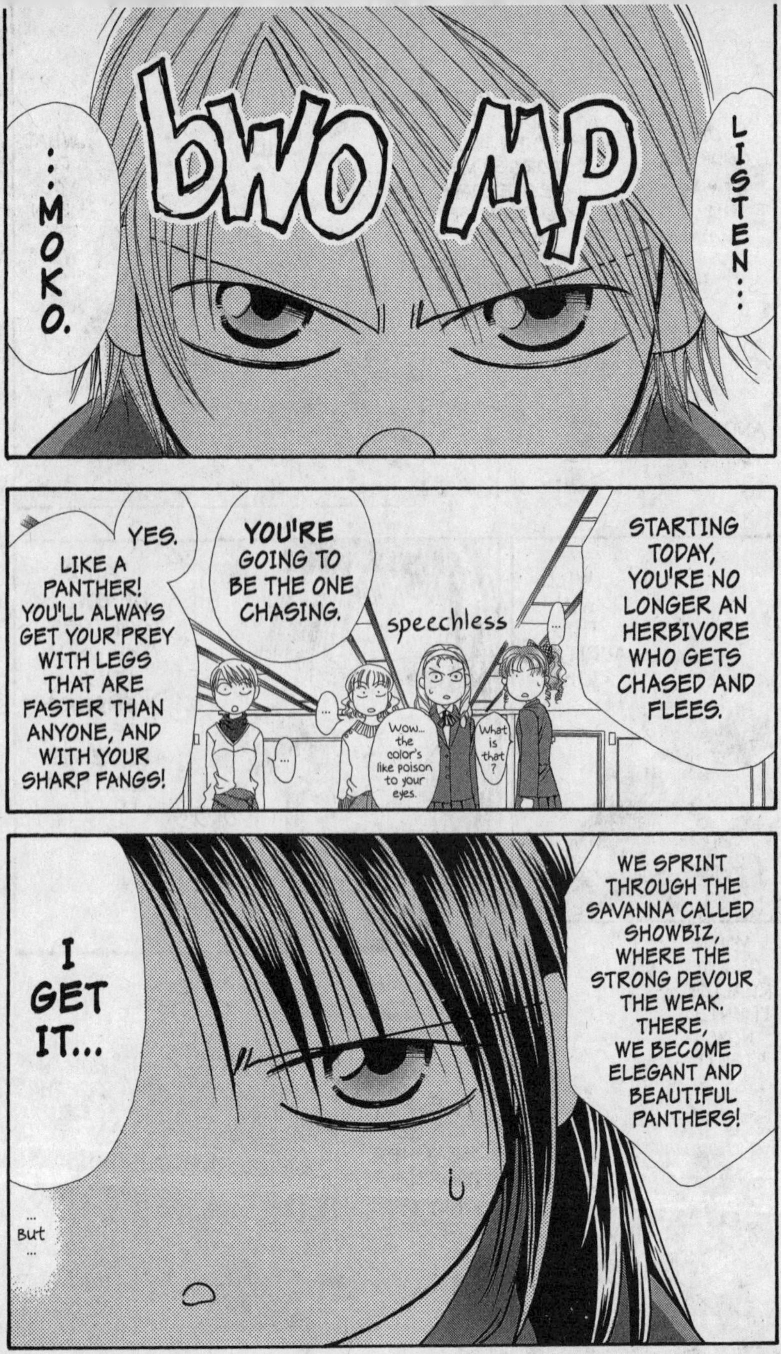
BWOMP
LISTEN...
...MOKO.
STARTING TODAY, YOU'RE NO LONGER AN HERBIVORE WHO GETS CHASED AND FLEES.
YOU'RE GOING TO BE THE ONE CHASING.
YES. LIKE A PANTHER! YOU'LL ALWAYS GET YOUR PREY WITH LEGS THAT ARE FASTER THAN ANYONE, AND WITH YOUR SHARP FANGS!
...
speechless
What is that?
Wow... the color's like poison to your eyes.
...
...
WE SPRINT THROUGH THE SAVANNA CALLED SHOWBIZ, WHERE THE STRONG DEVOUR THE WEAK. THERE, WE BECOME ELEGANT AND BEAUTIFUL PANTHERS!
I GET IT...
...But...

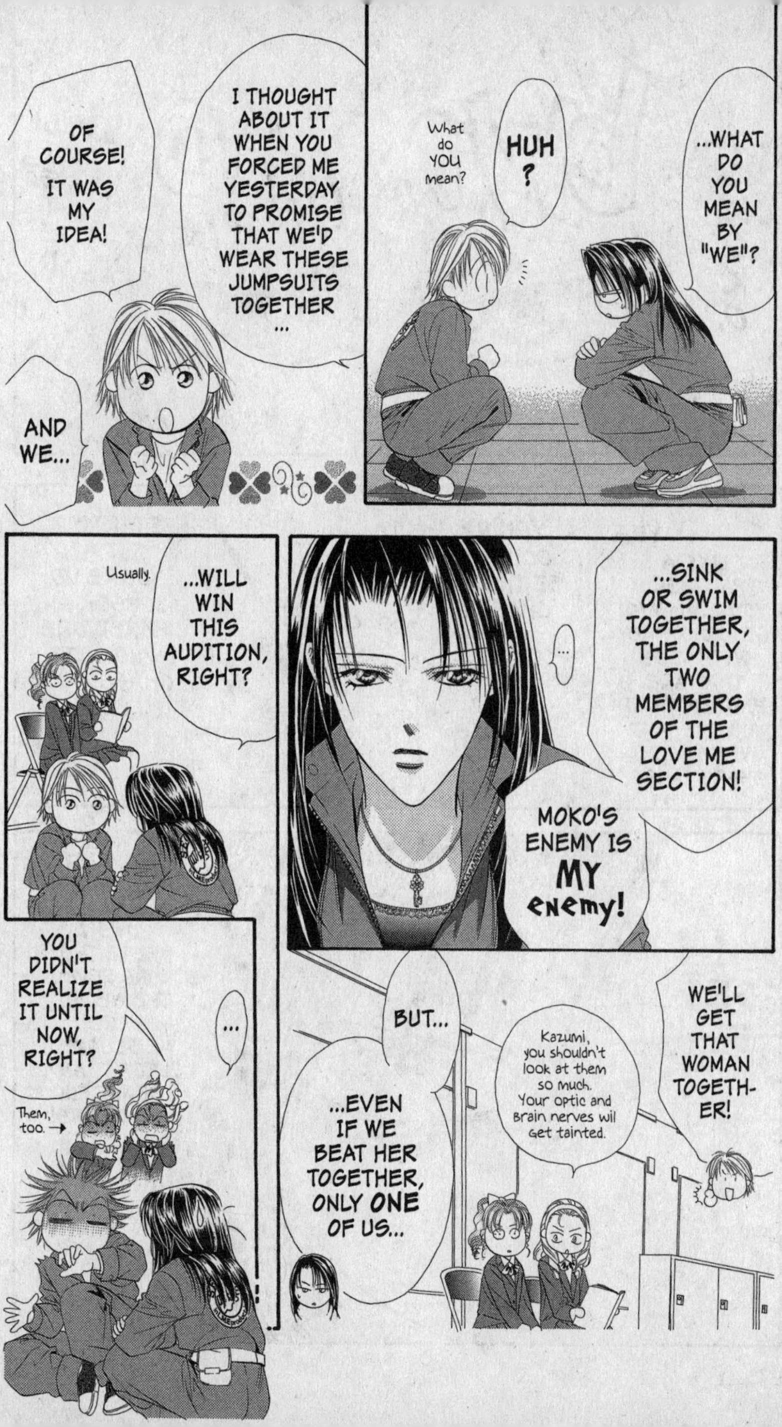
...WHAT DO YOU MEAN BY "WE"?
HUH?
What do YOU mean?
I THOUGHT ABOUT IT WHEN YOU FORCED ME YESTERDAY TO PROMISE THAT WE'D WEAR THESE JUMPSUITS TOGETHER ...
OF COURSE! IT WAS MY IDEA!
AND WE...
...SINK OR SWIM TOGETHER, THE ONLY TWO MEMBERS OF THE LOVE ME SECTION!
...
MOKO'S ENEMY IS MY enemy!
...WILL WIN THIS AUDITION, RIGHT?
Usually.
WE'LL GET THAT WOMAN TOGETHER!
Kazumi, you shouldn't look at them so much. Your optic and brain nerves wil get tainted.
BUT...
...EVEN IF WE BEAT HER TOGETHER, ONLY ONE OF US...
YOU DIDN'T REALIZE IT UNTIL NOW, RIGHT?
...
Them, too. →

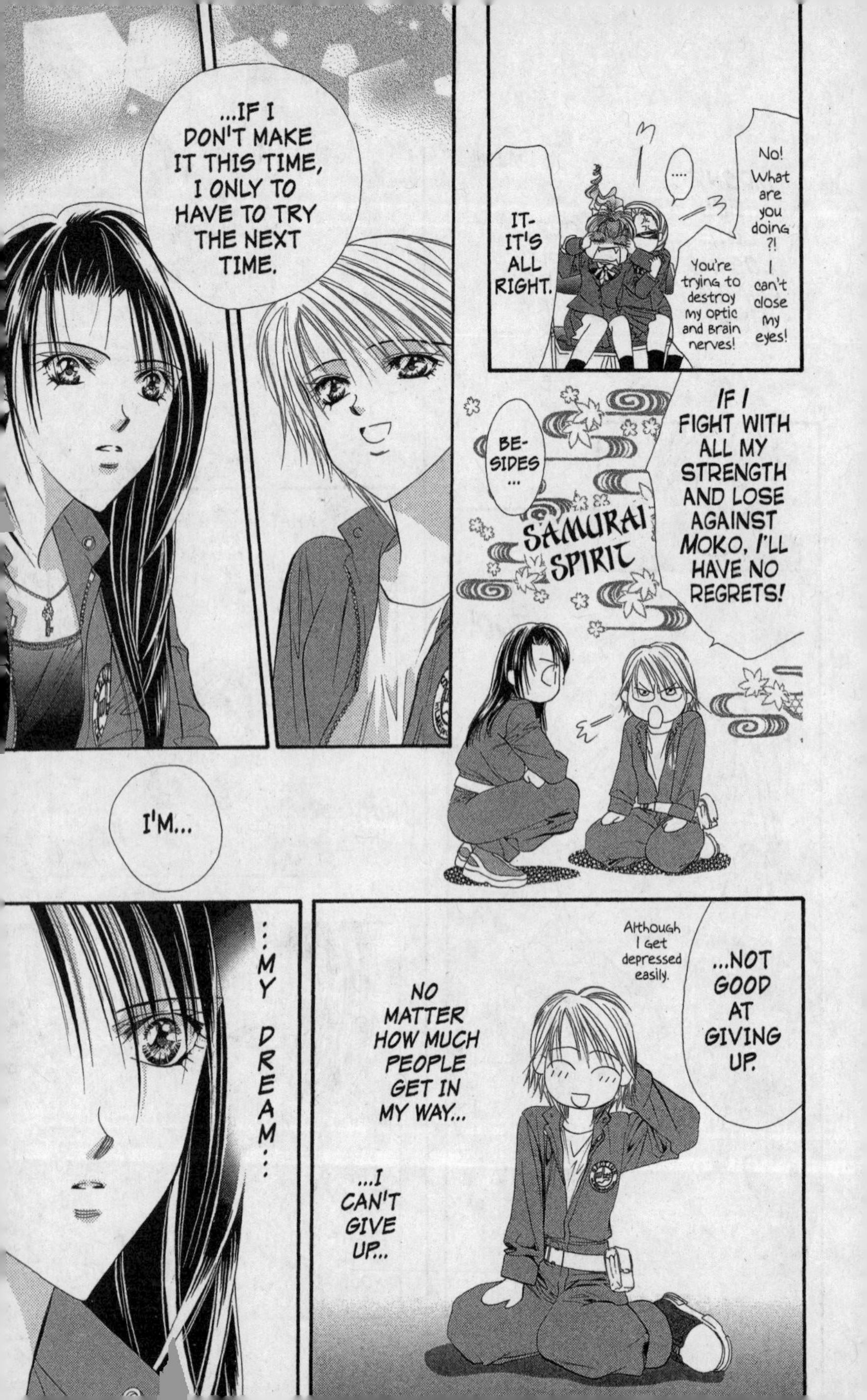

No! What are you doing?! I can't close my eyes!
You're trying to destroy my optic and brain nerves!
....
IT-IT'S ALL RIGHT.
...IF I DON'T MAKE IT THIS TIME, I ONLY TO HAVE TO TRY THE NEXT TIME.
BE-SIDES...
IF I FIGHT WITH ALL MY STRENGTH AND LOSE AGAINST MOKO, I'LL HAVE NO REGRETS!
SAMURAI SPIRIT
I'M...
...NOT GOOD AT GIVING UP.
Although I get depressed easily.
NO MATTER HOW MUCH PEOPLE GET IN MY WAY...
...I CAN'T GIVE UP...
...MY DREAM...

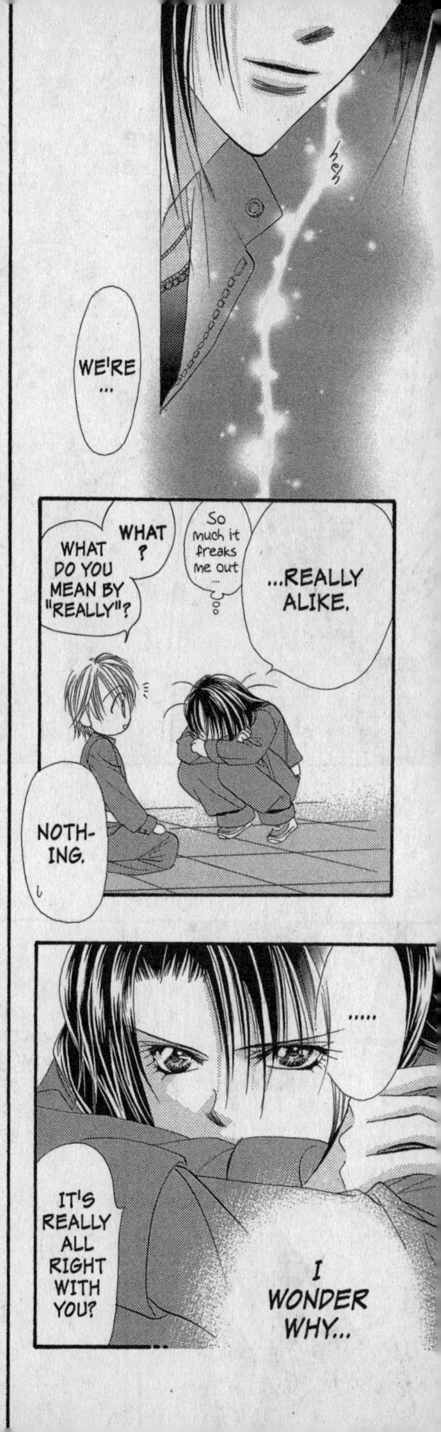
heh
WE'RE ...
...REALLY ALIKE.
So much it freaks me out ...
WHAT ?
WHAT DO YOU MEAN BY "REALLY"?
NOTH-ING.
.....
IT'S REALLY ALL RIGHT WITH YOU?
I WONDER WHY...
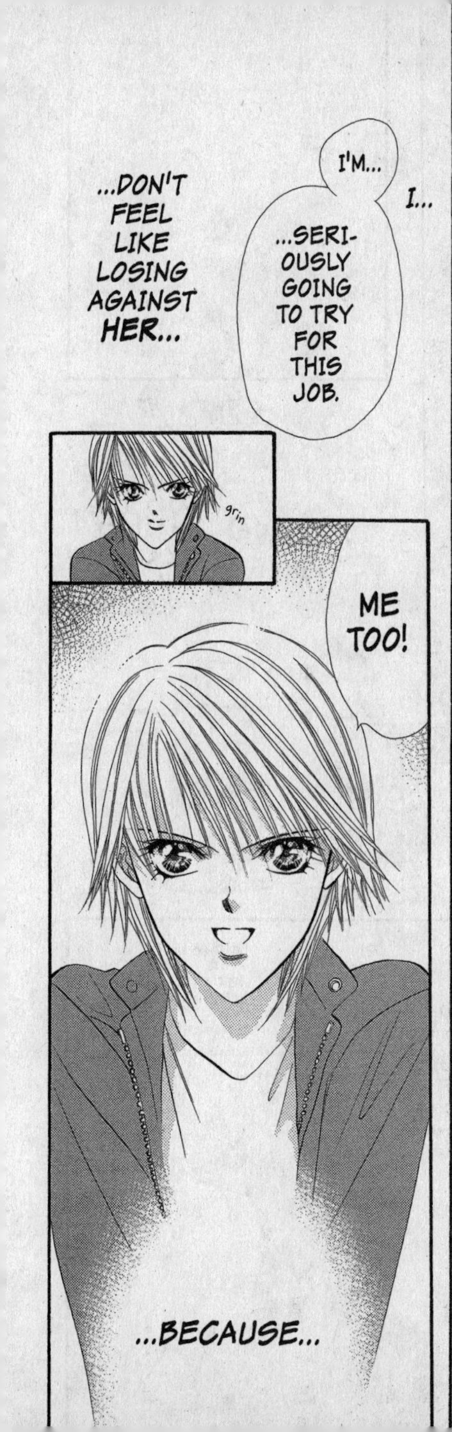
I...
I'M...
...SERI-OUSLY GOING TO TRY FOR THIS JOB.
...DON'T FEEL LIKE LOSING AGAINST HER...
grin
ME TOO!
...BECAUSE...

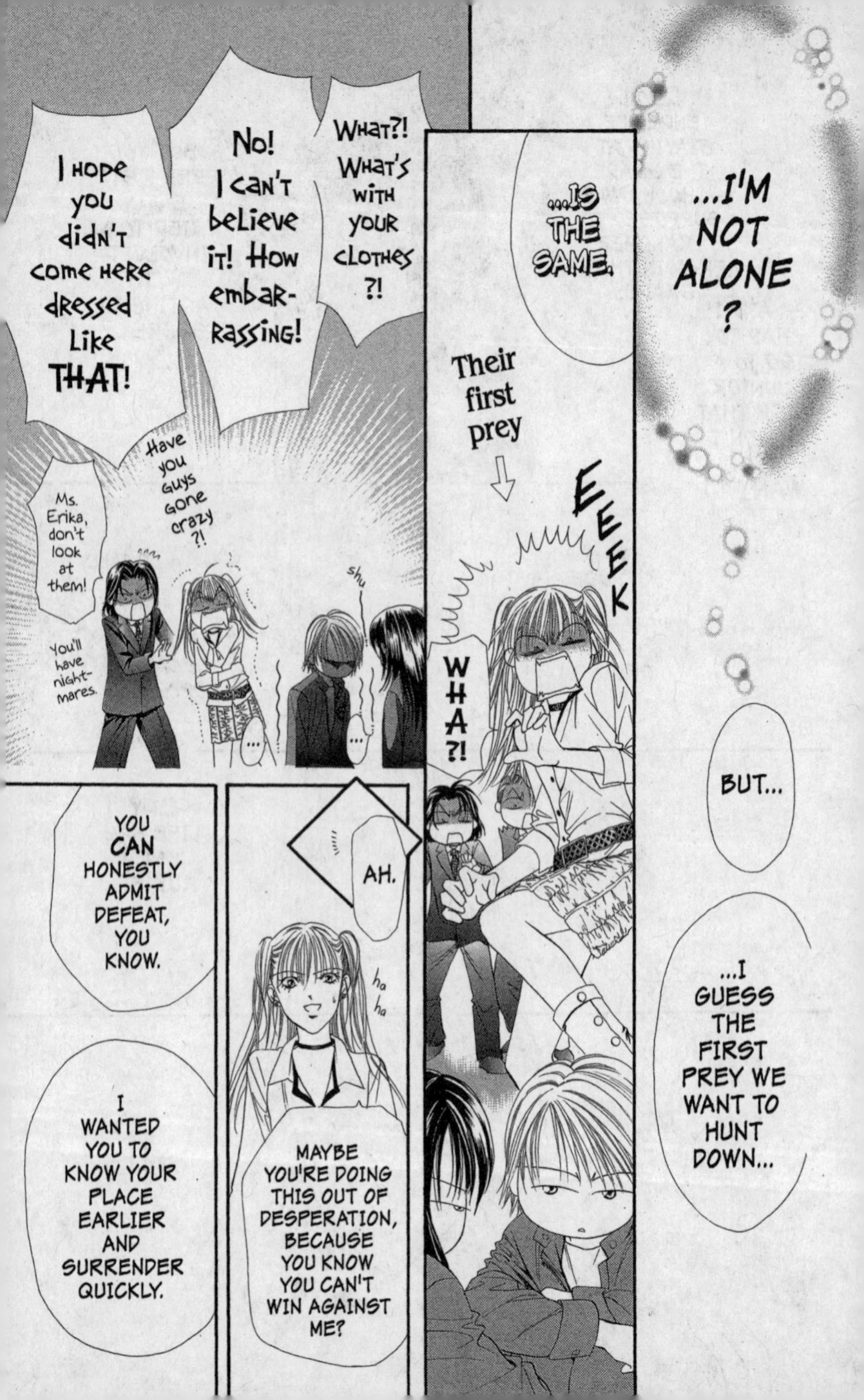

...I'M NOT ALONE?
BUT...
...I GUESS THE FIRST PREY WE WANT TO HUNT DOWN...
...IS THE SAME.
Their first prey
EEEK
WHA?!
WHAT?! WHAT'S WITH YOUR CLOTHES?!
No! I can't believe it! How embarrassing!
I hope you didn't come here dressed like THAT!
Have you guys gone crazy?!
Ms. Erika, don't look at them!
You'll have nightmares.
shu
...
...
AH.
ha ha
MAYBE YOU'RE DOING THIS OUT OF DESPERATION, BECAUSE YOU KNOW YOU CAN'T WIN AGAINST ME?
YOU CAN HONESTLY ADMIT DEFEAT, YOU KNOW.
I WANTED YOU TO KNOW YOUR PLACE EARLIER AND SURRENDER QUICKLY.

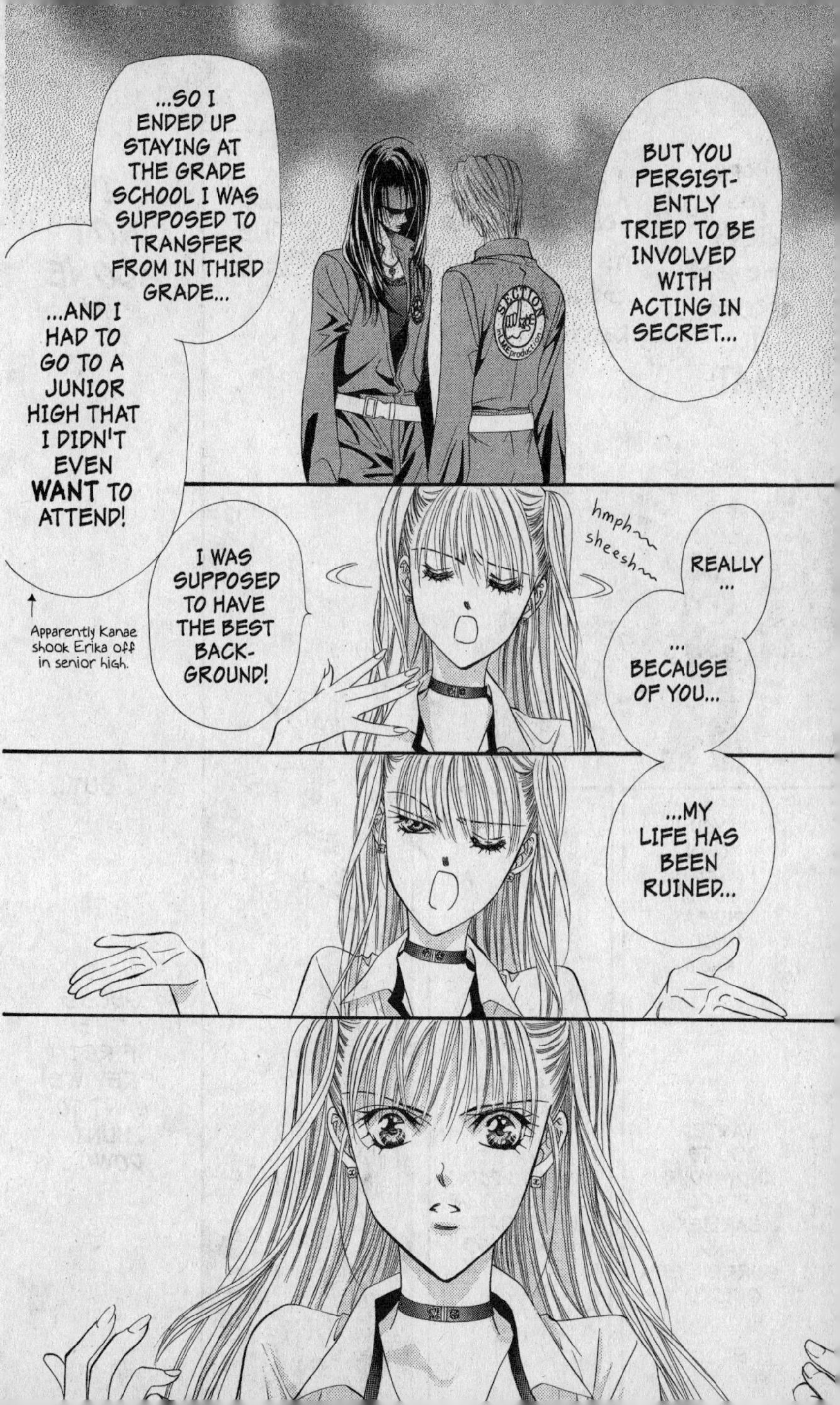
BUT YOU PERSISTENTLY TRIED TO BE INVOLVED WITH ACTING IN SECRET...
...SO I ENDED UP STAYING AT THE GRADE SCHOOL I WAS SUPPOSED TO TRANSFER FROM IN THIRD GRADE...
...AND I HAD TO GO TO A JUNIOR HIGH THAT I DIDN'T EVEN WANT TO ATTEND!
Apparently Kanae shook Erika off in senior high.
hmph~
sheesh~
I WAS SUPPOSED TO HAVE THE BEST BACKGROUND!
REALLY...
...BECAUSE OF YOU...
...MY LIFE HAS BEEN RUINED...

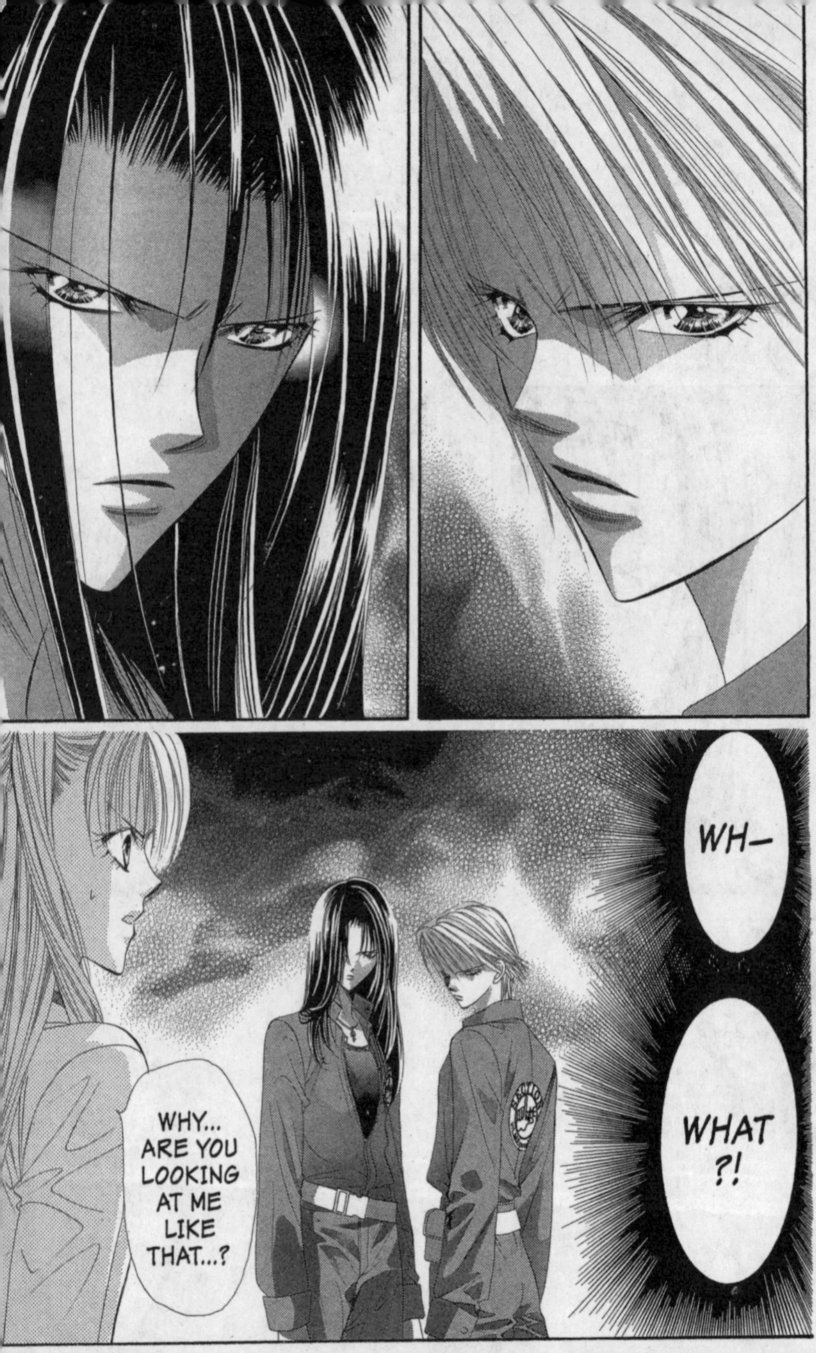
WH—
WHAT ?!
WHY... ARE YOU LOOKING AT ME LIKE THAT...?

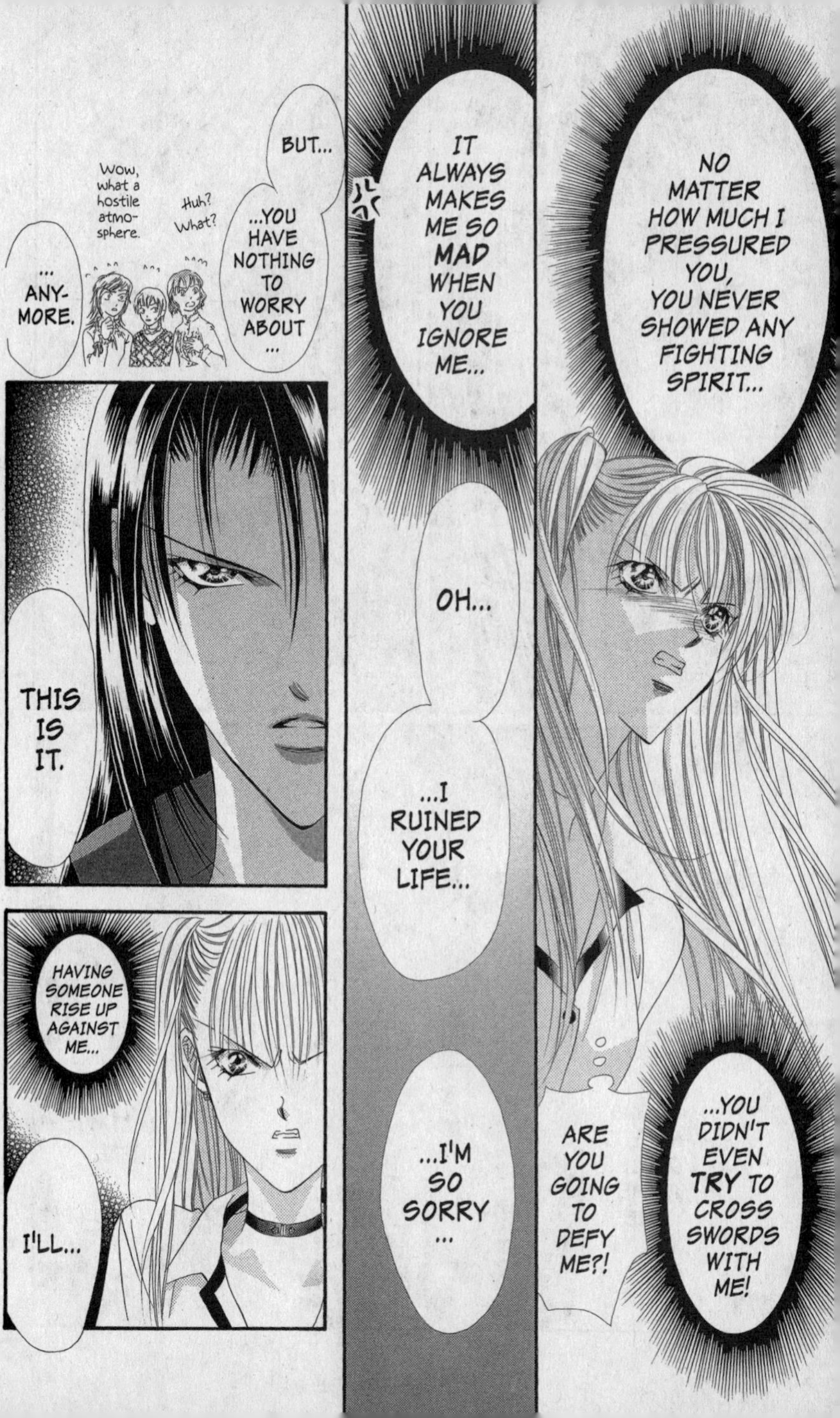
NO MATTER HOW MUCH I PRESSURED YOU, YOU NEVER SHOWED ANY FIGHTING SPIRIT...
...YOU DIDN'T EVEN TRY TO CROSS SWORDS WITH ME!
ARE YOU GOING TO DEFY ME?!
IT ALWAYS MAKES ME SO MAD WHEN YOU IGNORE ME...
OH...
...I RUINED YOUR LIFE...
...I'M SO SORRY ...
BUT...
...YOU HAVE NOTHING TO WORRY ABOUT ...
Huh? What?
Wow, what a hostile atmosphere.
... ANYMORE.
THIS IS IT.
HAVING SOMEONE RISE UP AGAINST ME...
I'LL...

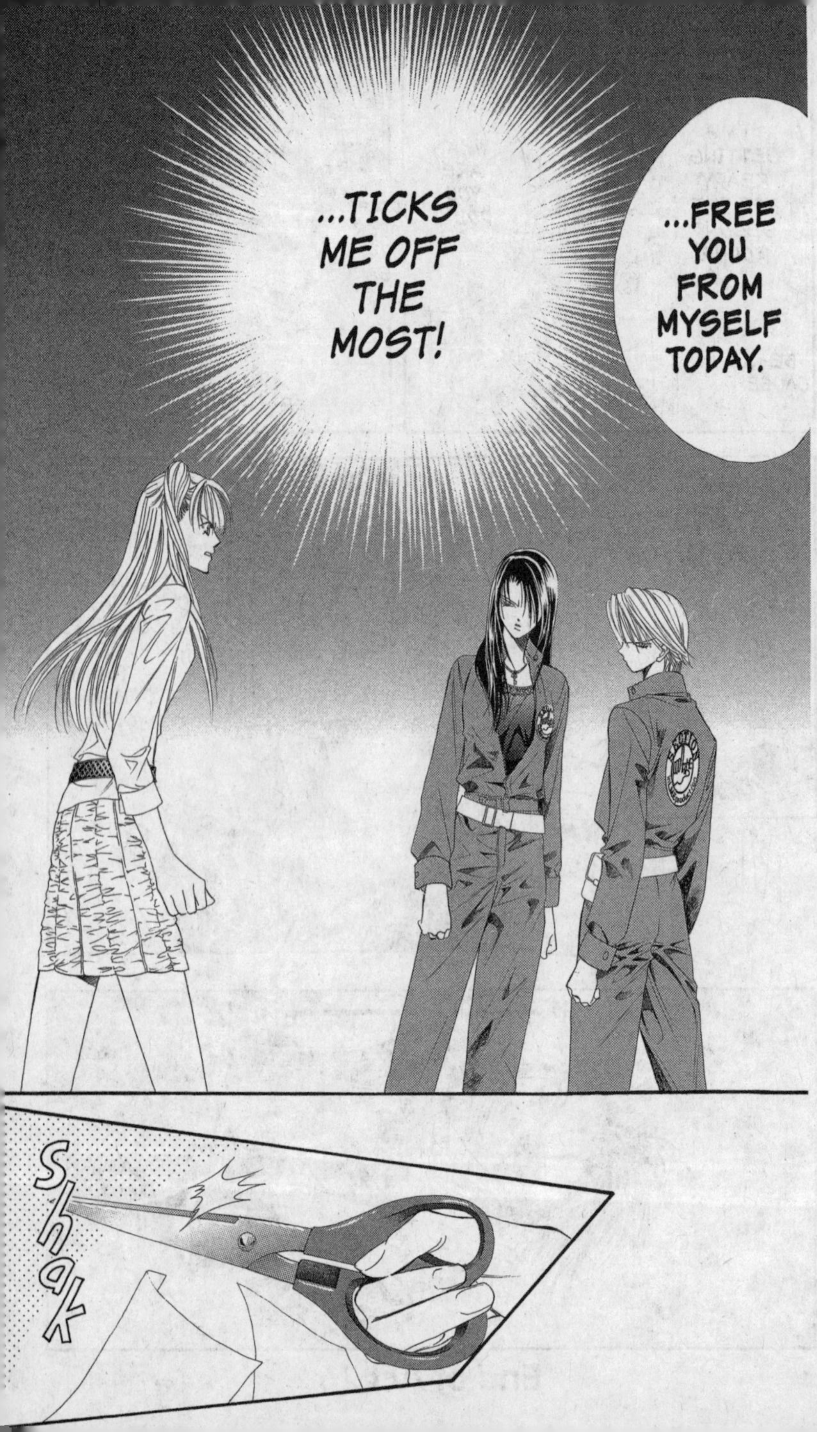
...FREE YOU FROM MYSELF TODAY.
...TICKS ME OFF THE MOST!
Shak

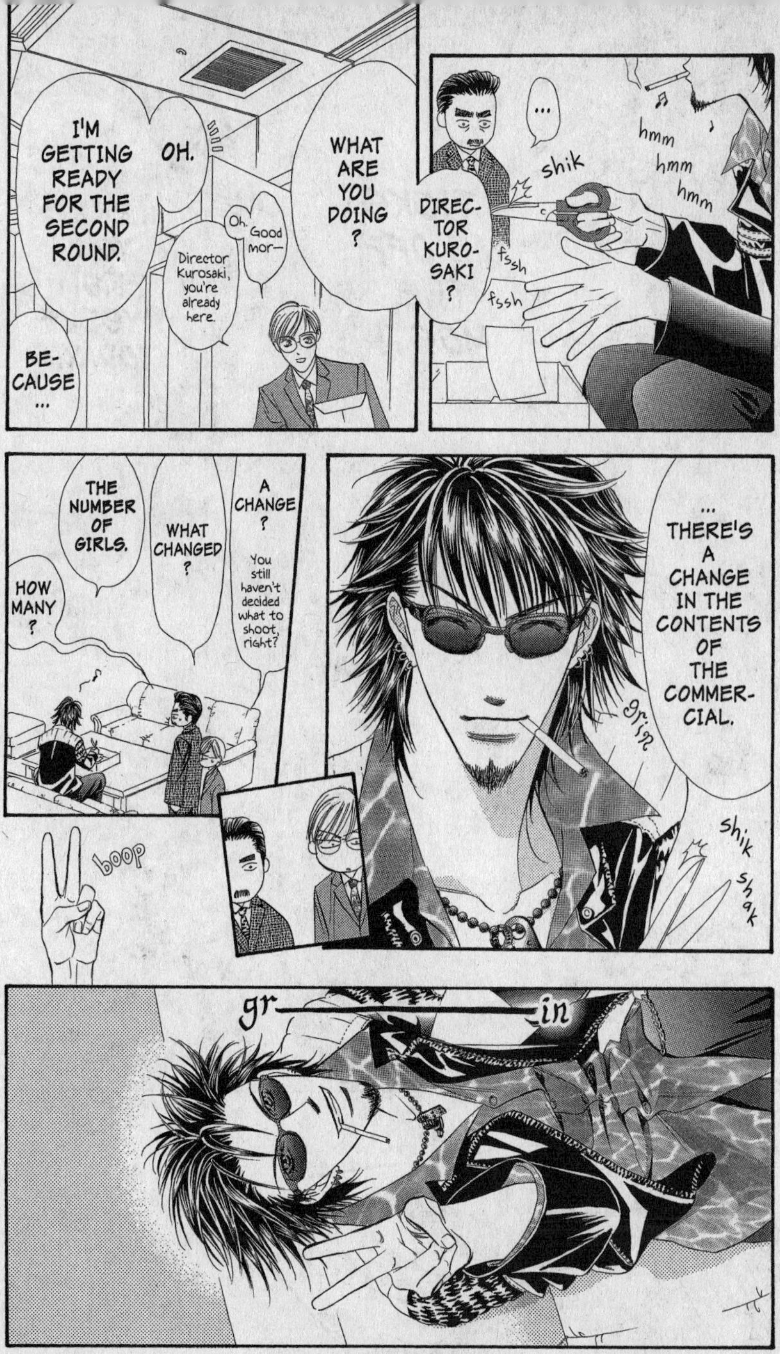
hmm
hmm
hmm
...
shik
DIREC-TOR KURO-SAKI?
fssh
fssh
WHAT ARE YOU DOING?
Oh. Good mor—
Director Kurosaki, you're already here.
OH.
I'M GETTING READY FOR THE SECOND ROUND.
BE-CAUSE...
...THERE'S A CHANGE IN THE CONTENTS OF THE COMMER-CIAL.
grin
shik
shak
A CHANGE?
You still haven't decided what to shoot, right?
WHAT CHANGED?
THE NUMBER OF GIRLS.
HOW MANY?
boop
gr——in

End of Act 26

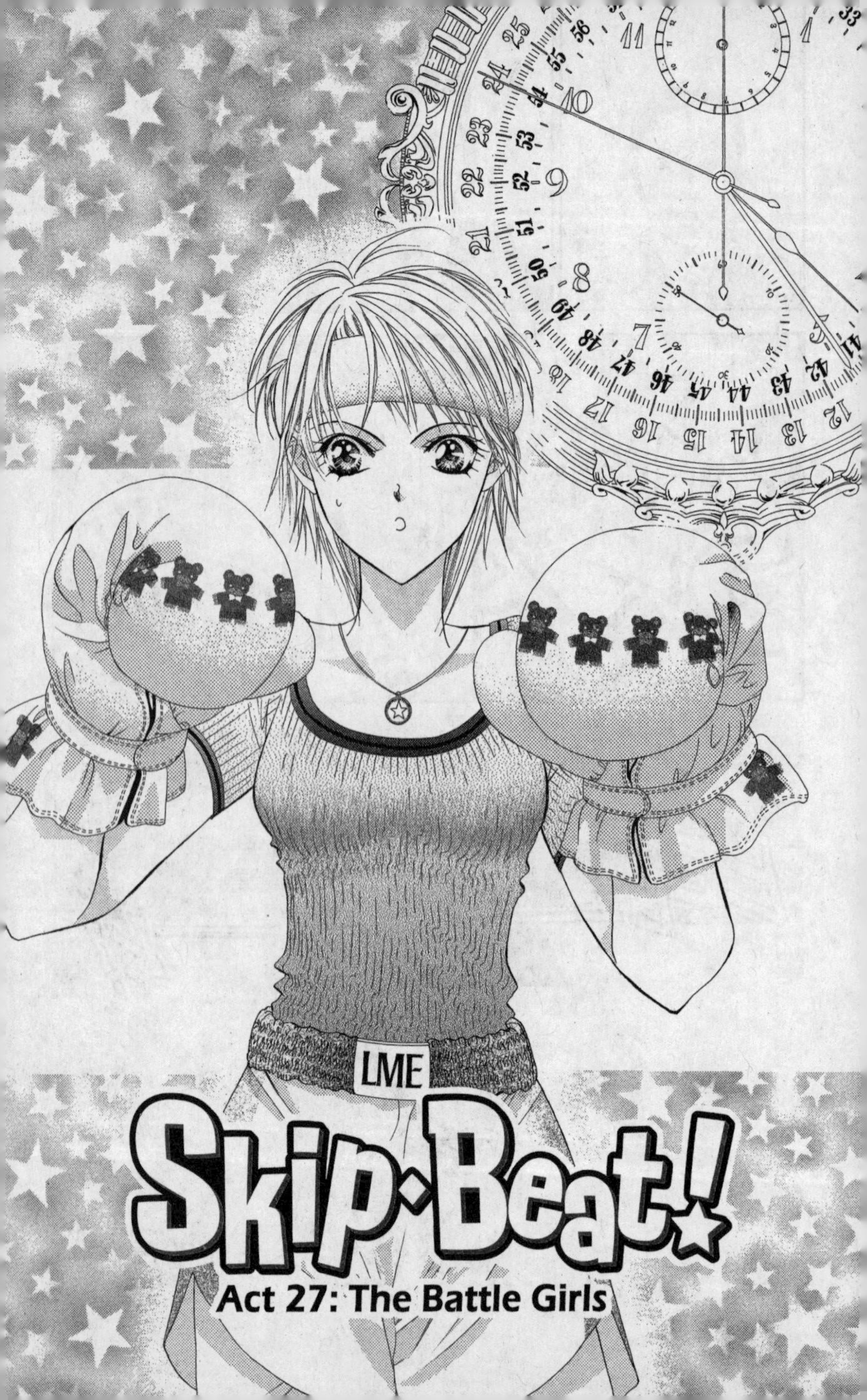
LME
Skip·Beat!
Act 27: The Battle Girls

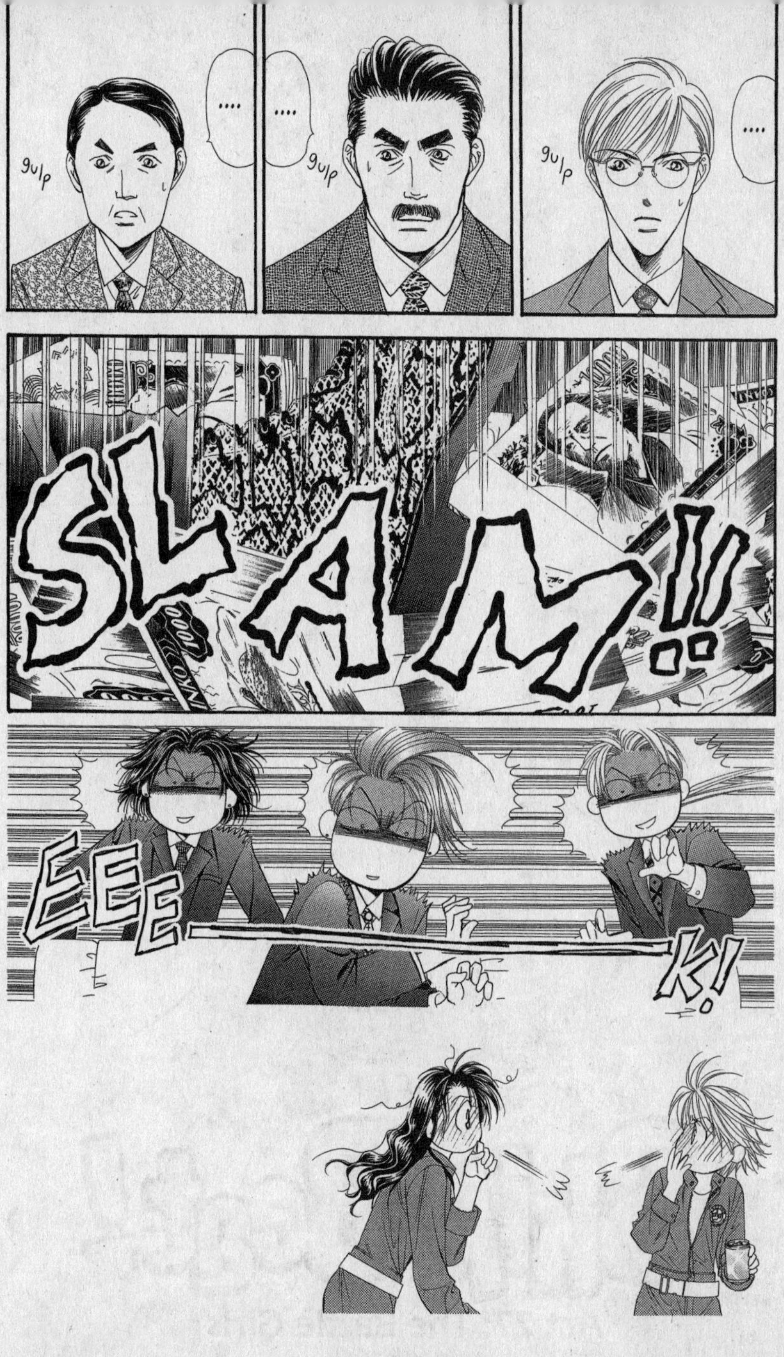
....
gulp
....
gulp
....
gulp
SLAM!!
EEE—K!

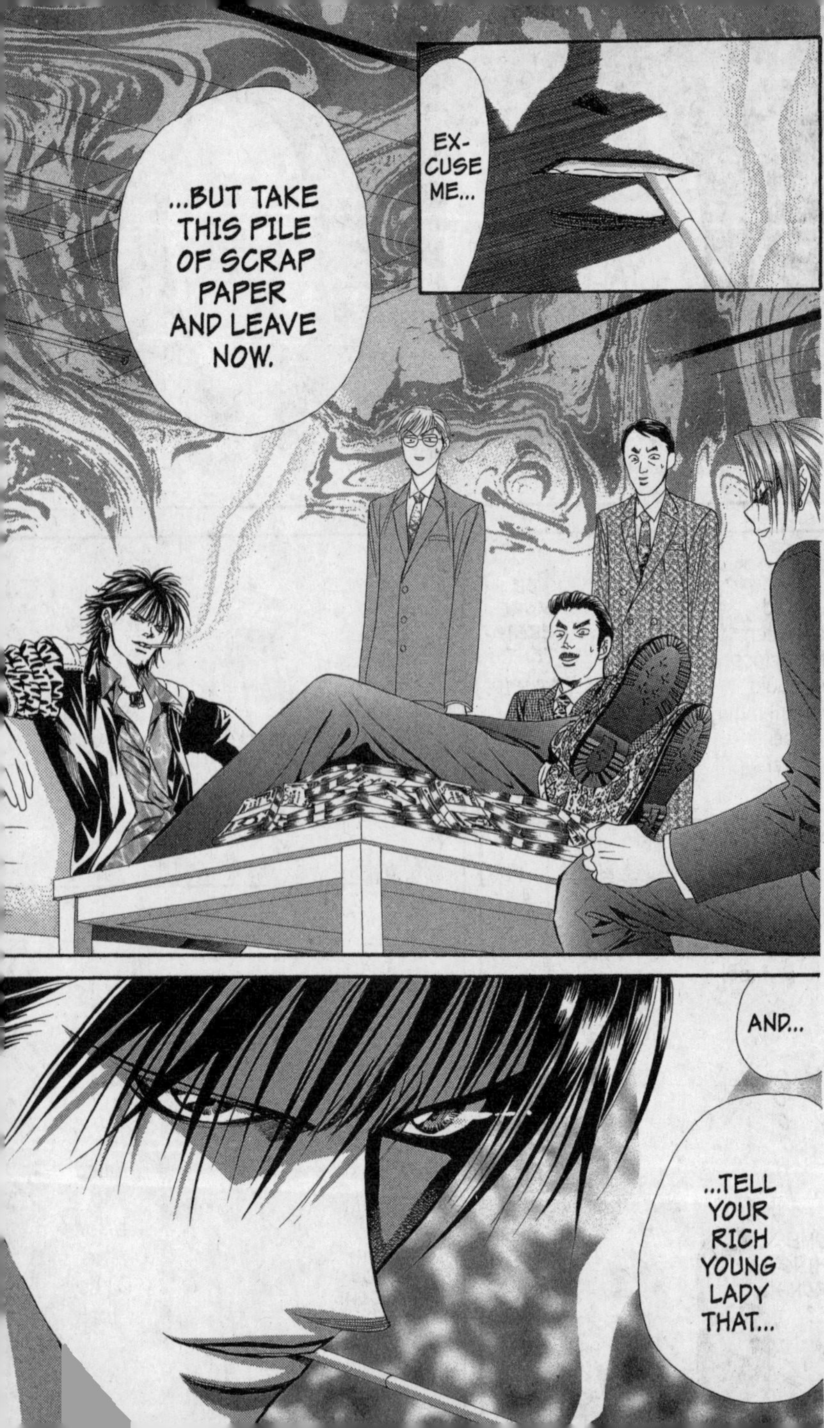
EX-CUSE ME...
...BUT TAKE THIS PILE OF SCRAP PAPER AND LEAVE NOW.
AND...
...TELL YOUR RICH YOUNG LADY THAT...

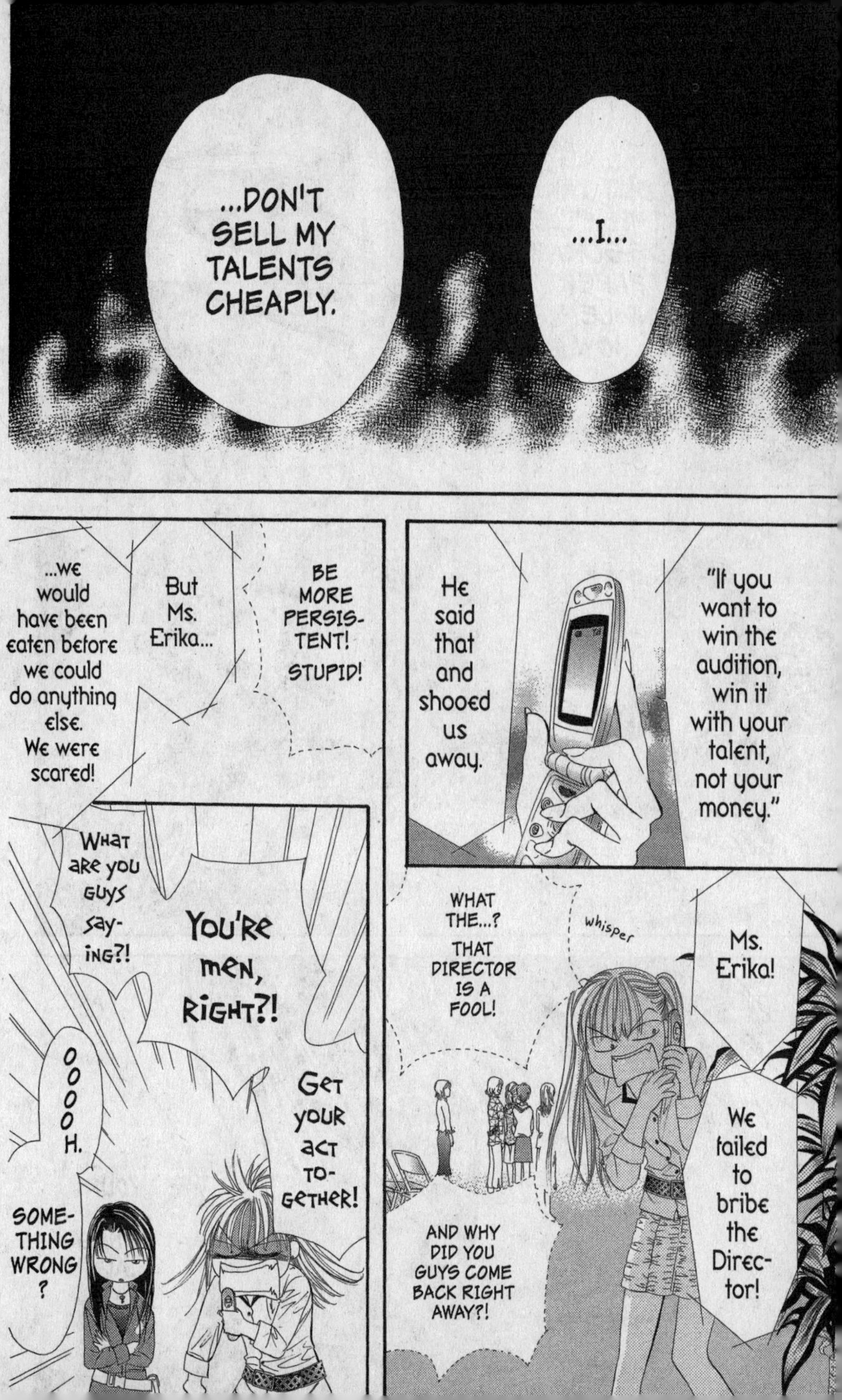

...I...
...DON'T SELL MY TALENTS CHEAPLY.
"If you want to win the audition, win it with your talent, not your money."
He said that and shooed us away.
Ms. Erika!
We failed to bribe the Director!
whisper
WHAT THE...? THAT DIRECTOR IS A FOOL!
AND WHY DID YOU GUYS COME BACK RIGHT AWAY?!
BE MORE PERSIS-TENT! STUPID!
But Ms. Erika...
...we would have been eaten before we could do anything else. We were scared!
You're men, RIGHT?!
What are you guys say-ing?!
Get your act to-gether!
OOOOOH.
SOME-THING WRONG?

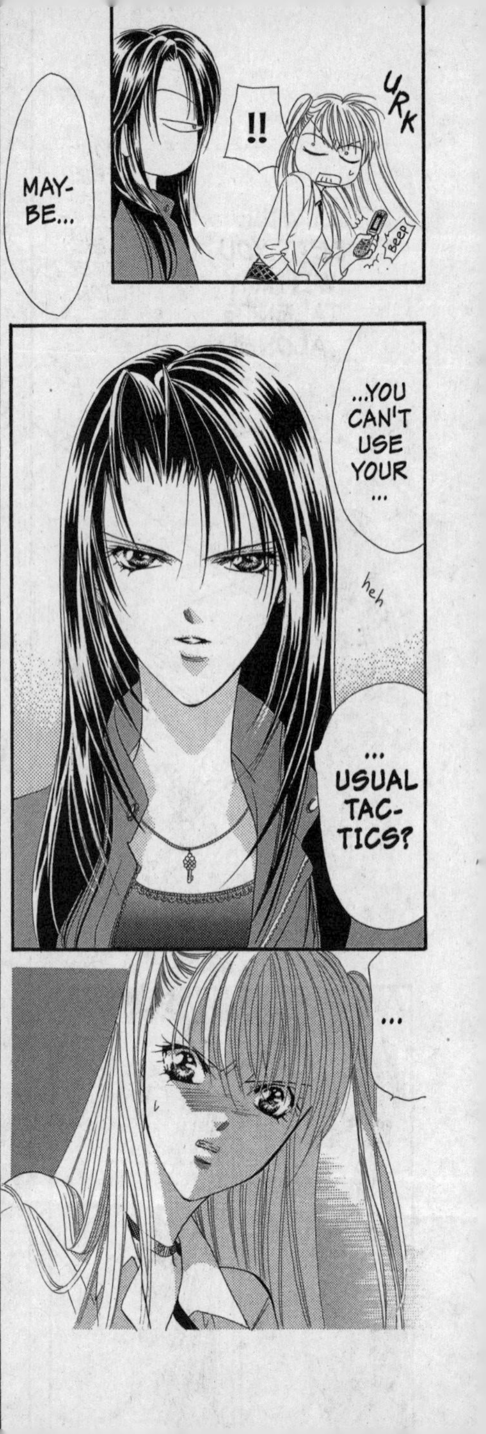
URK
!!
Beep
MAY-BE...
...YOU CAN'T USE YOUR ...
heh
... USUAL TAC-TICS?
...

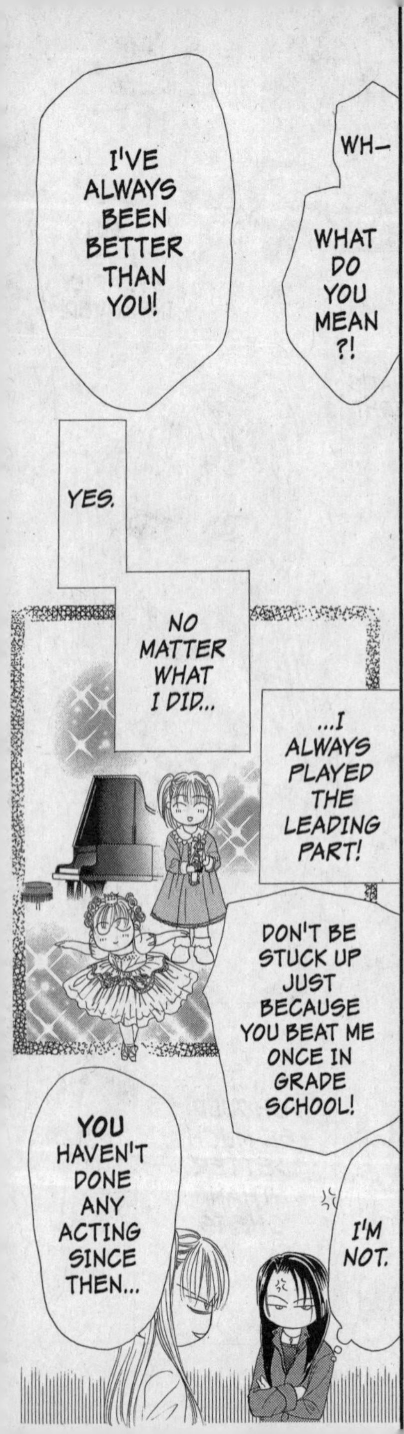
WH—
WHAT DO YOU MEAN ?!
I'VE ALWAYS BEEN BETTER THAN YOU!
YES.
NO MATTER WHAT I DID...
...I ALWAYS PLAYED THE LEADING PART!
DON'T BE STUCK UP JUST BECAUSE YOU BEAT ME ONCE IN GRADE SCHOOL!
I'M NOT.
YOU HAVEN'T DONE ANY ACTING SINCE THEN...

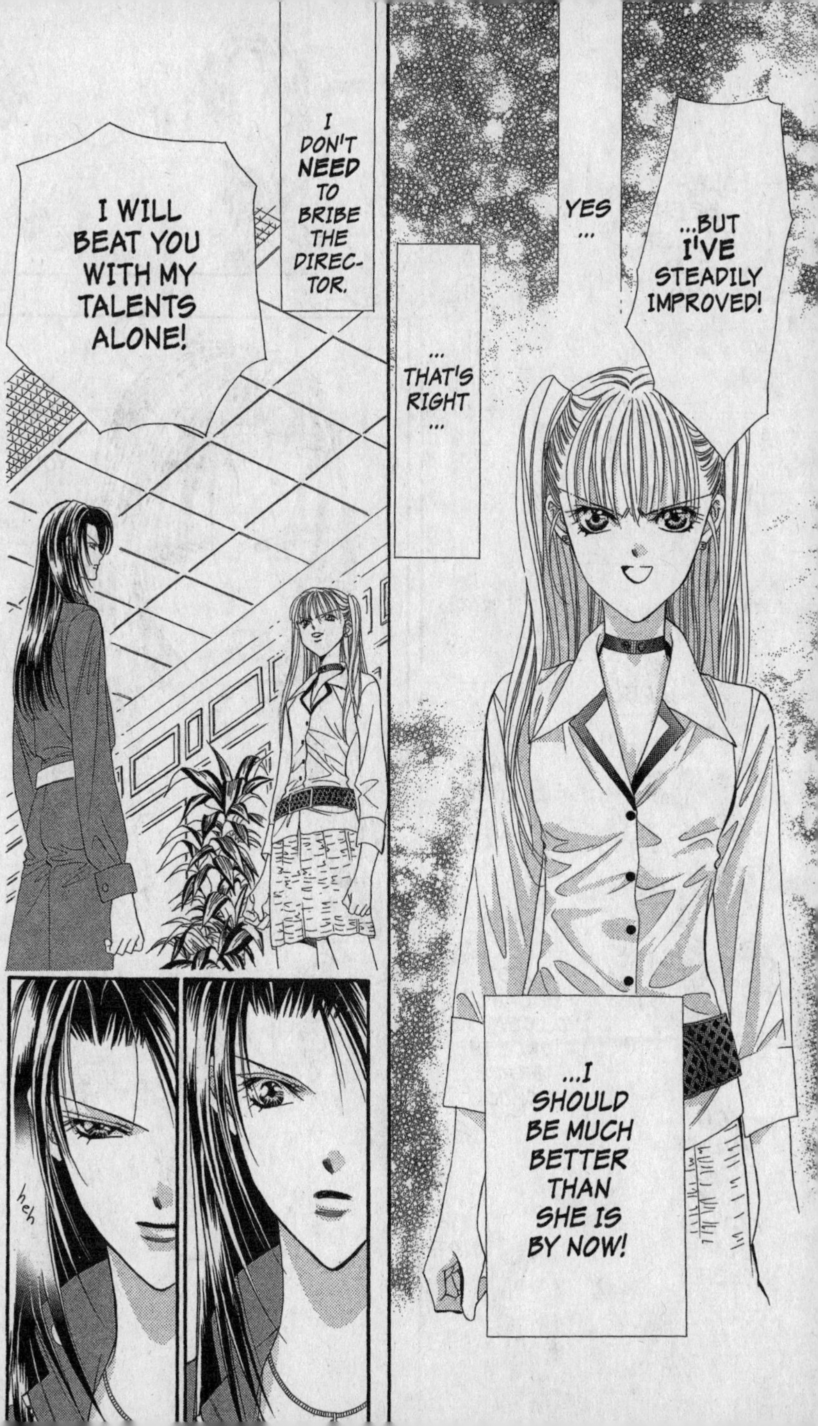
...BUT I'VE STEADILY IMPROVED!
YES ...
... THAT'S RIGHT ...
...I SHOULD BE MUCH BETTER THAN SHE IS BY NOW!
I DON'T NEED TO BRIBE THE DIRECTOR.
I WILL BEAT YOU WITH MY TALENTS ALONE!
heh

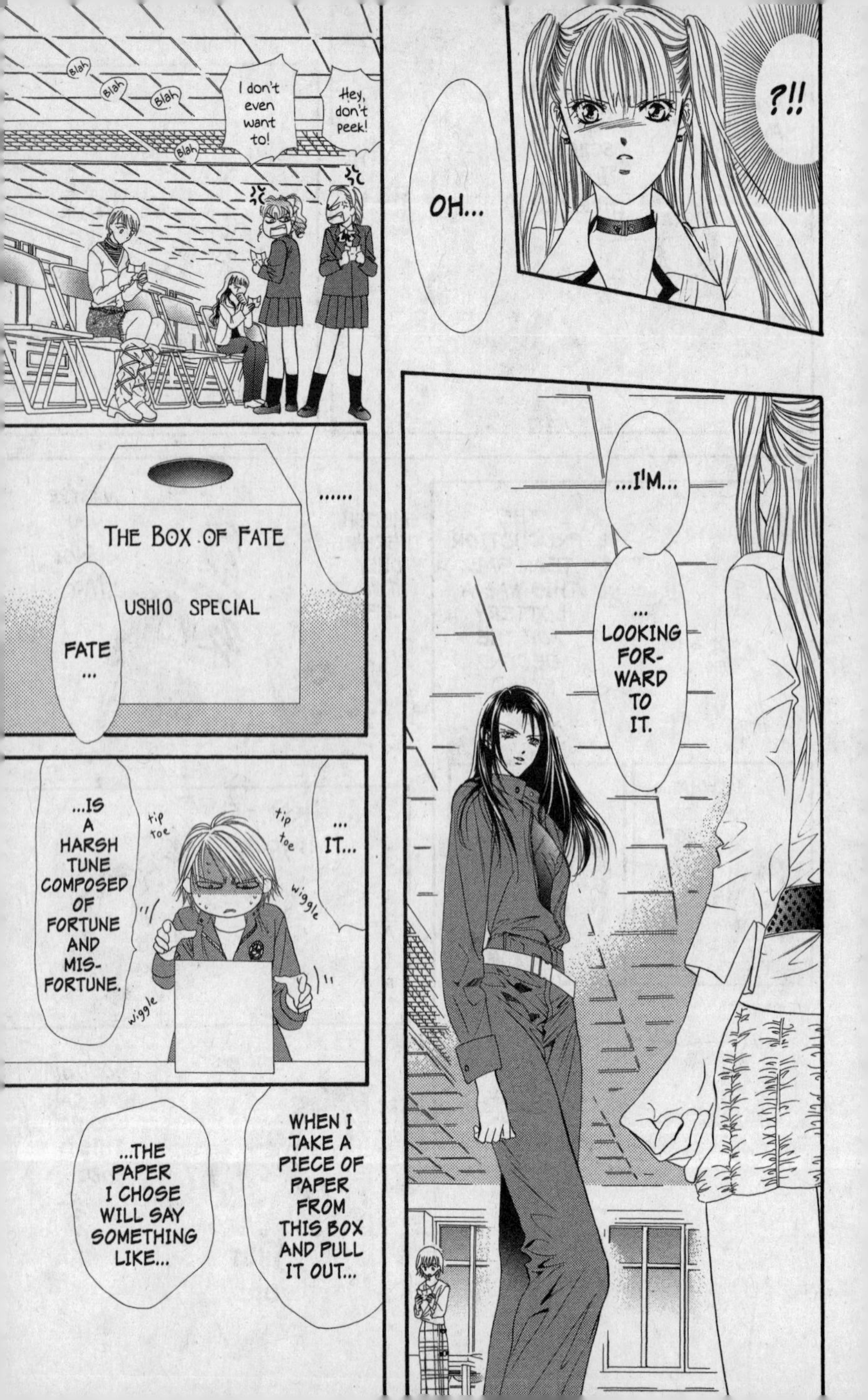
?!!
OH...
...I'M...
...LOOKING FOR-WARD TO IT.
Hey, don't peek!
I don't even want to!
Blah
Blah
Blah
Blah
......
THE BOX OF FATE
USHIO SPECIAL
FATE...
... IT...
tip toe
tip toe
...IS A HARSH TUNE COMPOSED OF FORTUNE AND MIS-FORTUNE.
wiggle
wiggle
WHEN I TAKE A PIECE OF PAPER FROM THIS BOX AND PULL IT OUT...
...THE PAPER I CHOSE WILL SAY SOMETHING LIKE...

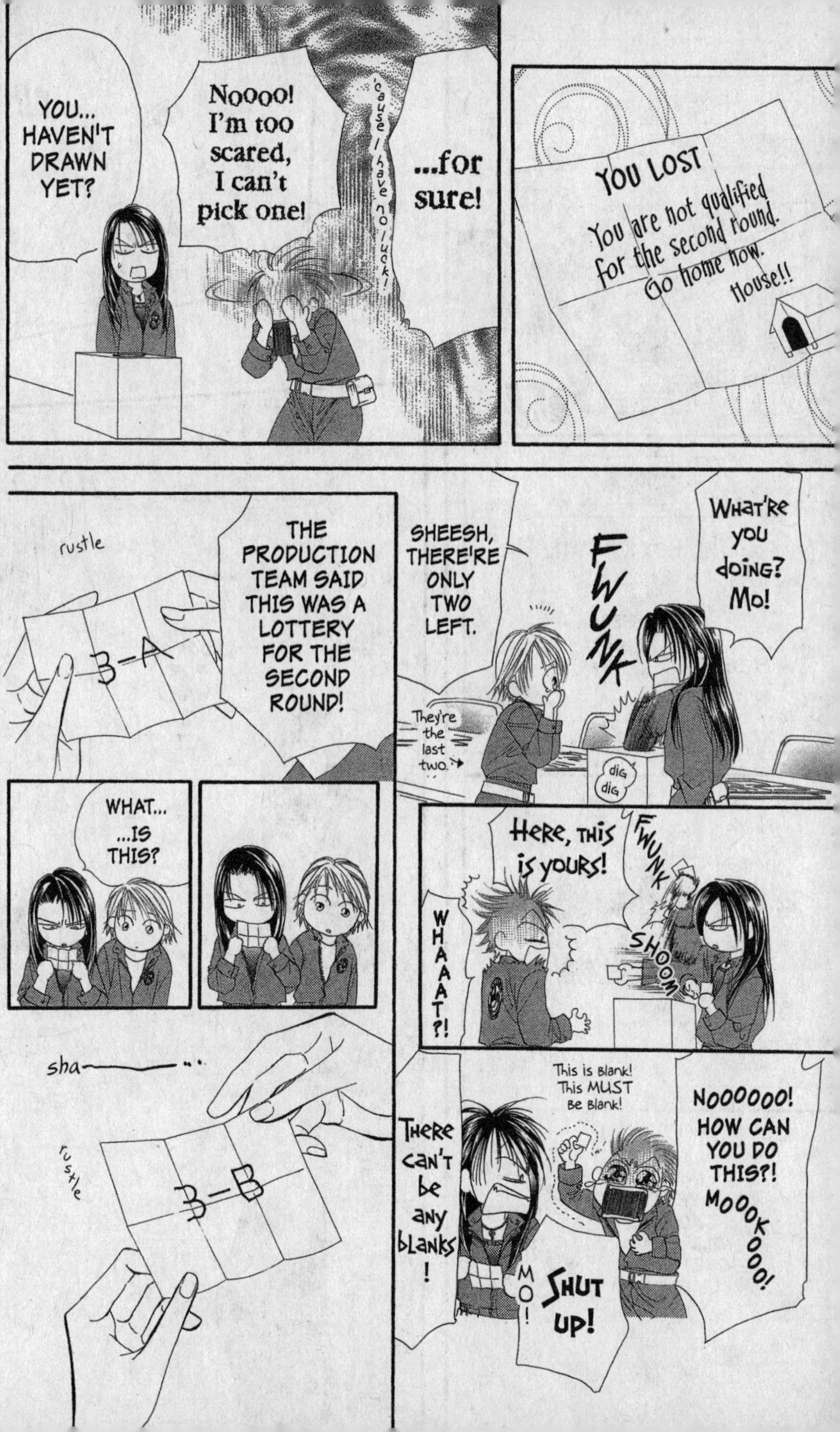
YOU LOST
You are not qualified for the second round. Go home now.
House!!
...for sure!
'cause I have no luck!
Noooo! I'm too scared, I can't pick one!
YOU... HAVEN'T DRAWN YET?
WHAT're you doing? Mo!
FWUNK
SHEESH, THERE'RE ONLY TWO LEFT.
They're the last two.
dig dig
THE PRODUCTION TEAM SAID THIS WAS A LOTTERY FOR THE SECOND ROUND!
rustle
3-A
FWUNK
Here, THIS is YOURS!
WHAAAAT?!
SHOOM
NOOOOOO! HOW CAN YOU DO THIS?! MOOOKOOO!
This is Blank! This MUST Be Blank!
There can't be any blanks!
SHUT UP!
MO!
WHAT... ...IS THIS?
sha——
rustle
3-B

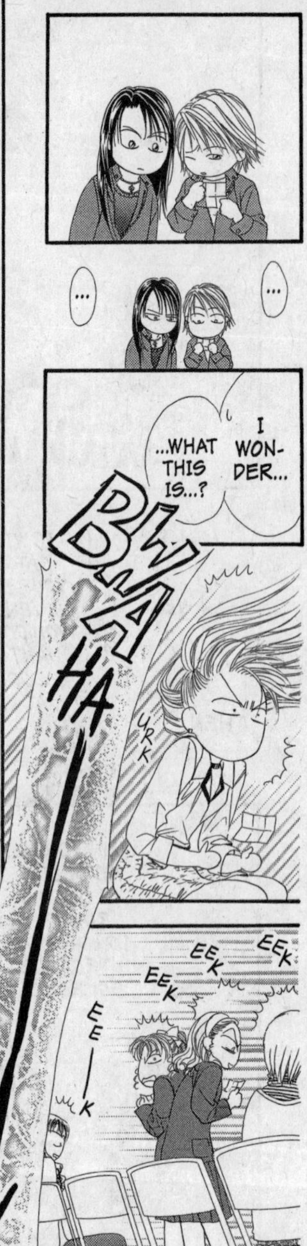
...
...
I WONDER...
...WHAT THIS IS...?
BWAHAHA!!
URK
EEK
EEK
EEK
EEE-K

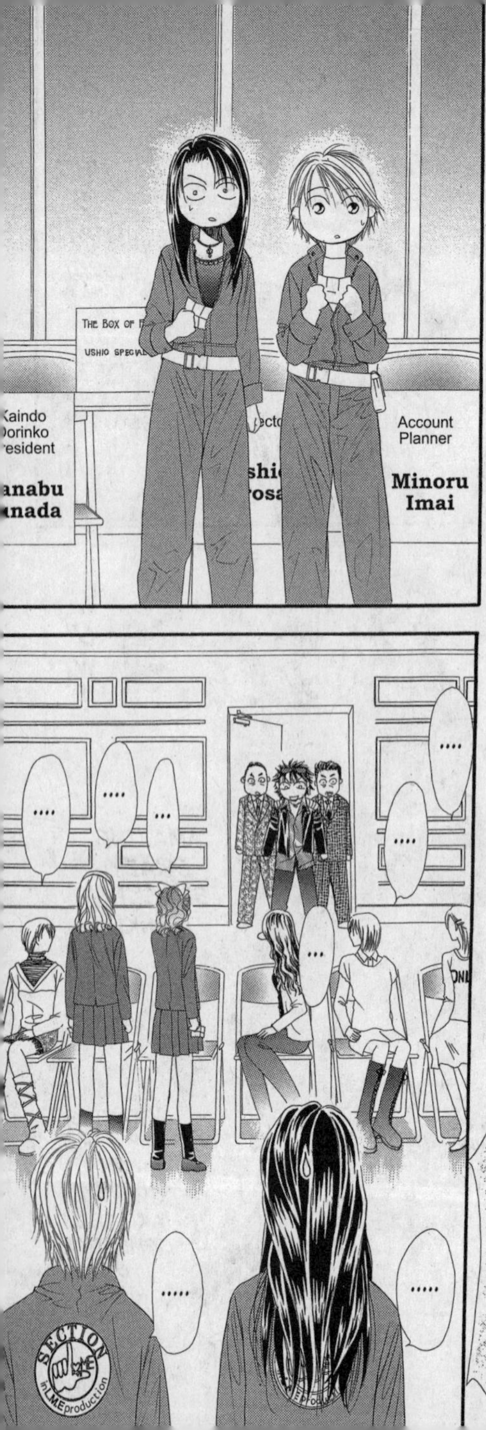
THE BOX OF
Account Planner
Minoru Imai
....
....
....
...
....
...
......
.....
SECTION
LME
in LME production

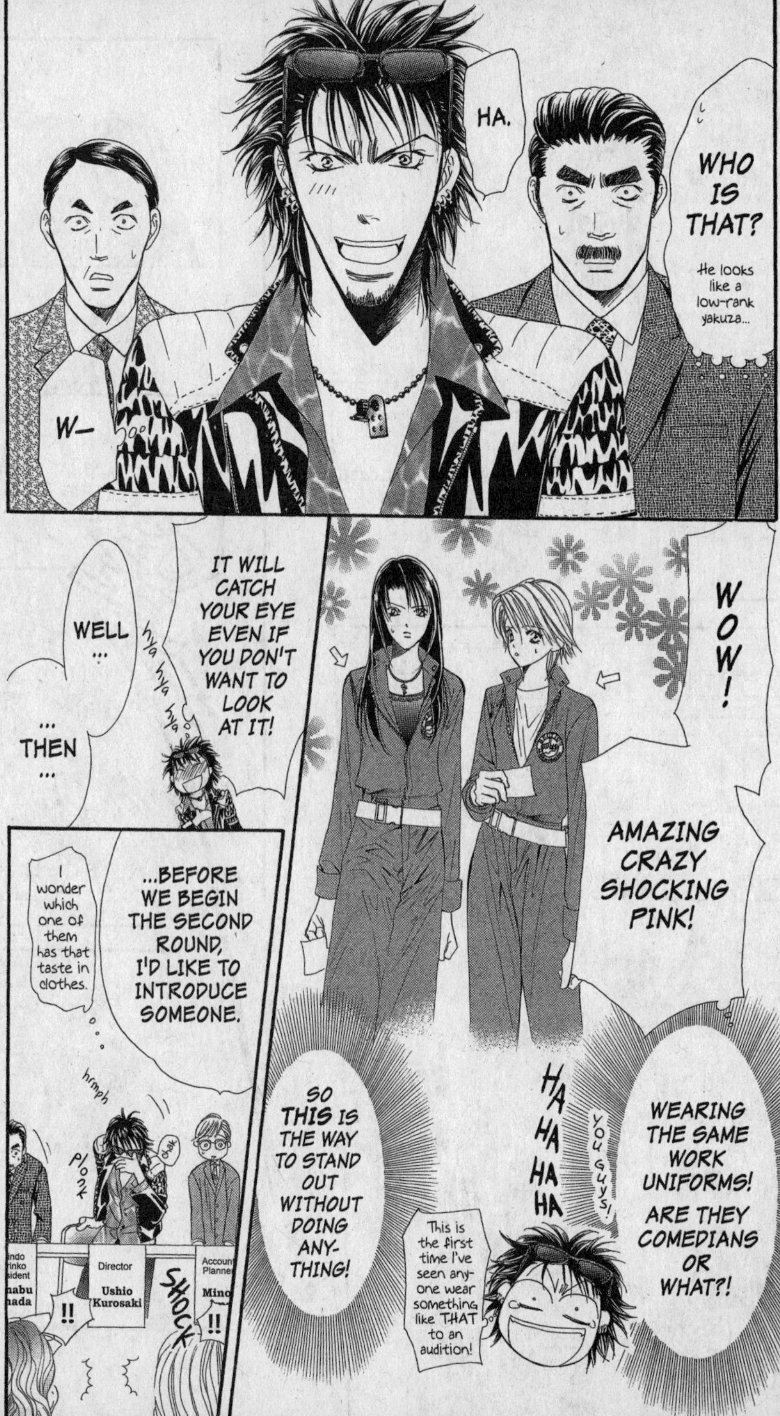
WHO IS THAT?
He looks like a low-rank yakuza...
HA.
W—
WOW!
AMAZING CRAZY SHOCKING PINK!
WEARING THE SAME WORK UNIFORMS! ARE THEY COMEDIANS OR WHAT?!
YOU GUYS!
HA HA HA HA HA
SO THIS IS THE WAY TO STAND OUT WITHOUT DOING ANY-THING!
This is the first time I've seen any-one wear something like THAT to an audition!
IT WILL CATCH YOUR EYE EVEN IF YOU DON'T WANT TO LOOK AT IT!
hya hya hya
WELL...
...THEN...
...BEFORE WE BEGIN THE SECOND ROUND, I'D LIKE TO INTRODUCE SOMEONE.
I wonder which one of them has that taste in clothes.
hrmph
chak
plonk
Director
Ushio Kurosaki
SHOCK
!!
!!

Ushio Kurosaki

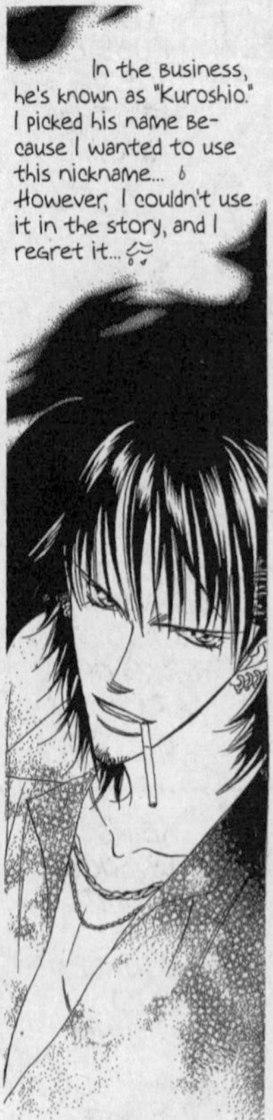

In the business, he's known as "Kuroshio." I picked his name because I wanted to use this nickname... However, I couldn't use it in the story, and I regret it...

Personally, I wanted to make him more like a hardcore low-rank yakuza...a wild man who cuts you like a knife if you touch him (Ah...I love that type of guy...( ) He didn't turn out perfectly. Maybe he'd have looked more yakuza-like if his hair went straight back and his bangs were hanging lazily...But...a guy who obviously looks like a yakuza... My editor has...gently forbidden yakuza... My editor knows well that I go berserk... Ho ho ho...

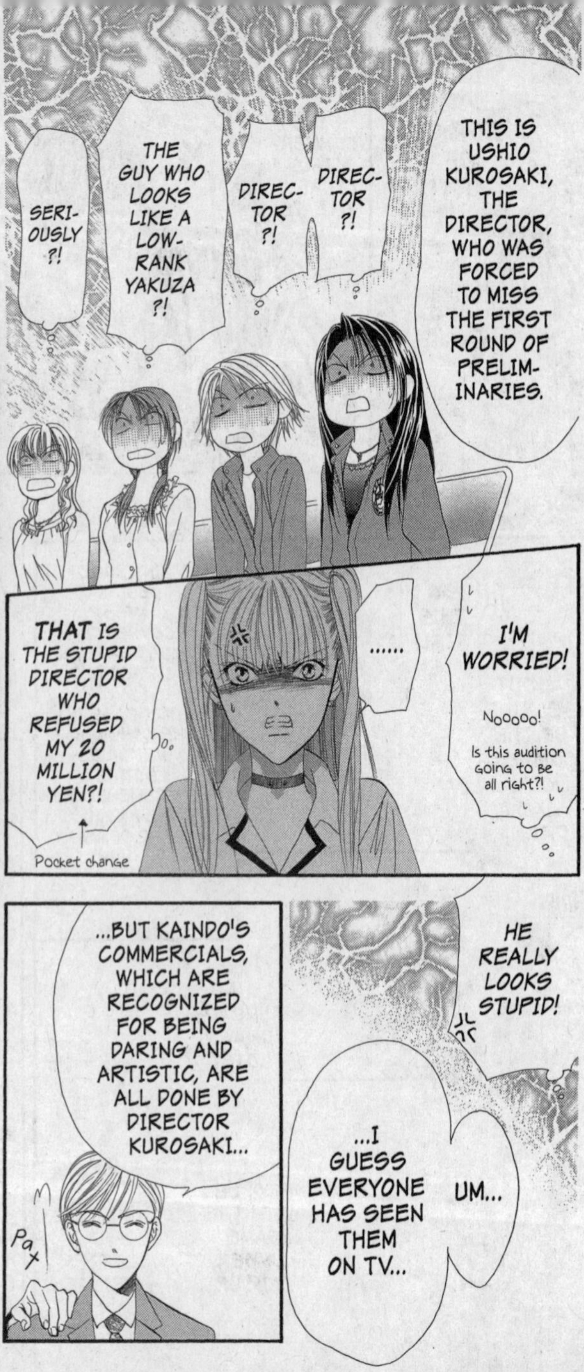
THIS IS USHIO KUROSAKI, THE DIRECTOR, WHO WAS FORCED TO MISS THE FIRST ROUND OF PRELIMINARIES.
DIRECTOR?!
DIRECTOR?!
THE GUY WHO LOOKS LIKE A LOW-RANK YAKUZA?!
SERIOUSLY?!
I'M WORRIED!
Noooo! Is this audition going to be all right?!
......
THAT IS THE STUPID DIRECTOR WHO REFUSED MY 20 MILLION YEN?!
Pocket change
HE REALLY LOOKS STUPID!
...BUT KAINDO'S COMMERCIALS, WHICH ARE RECOGNIZED FOR BEING DARING AND ARTISTIC, ARE ALL DONE BY DIRECTOR KUROSAKI...
Pax
UM...
...I GUESS EVERYONE HAS SEEN THEM ON TV...

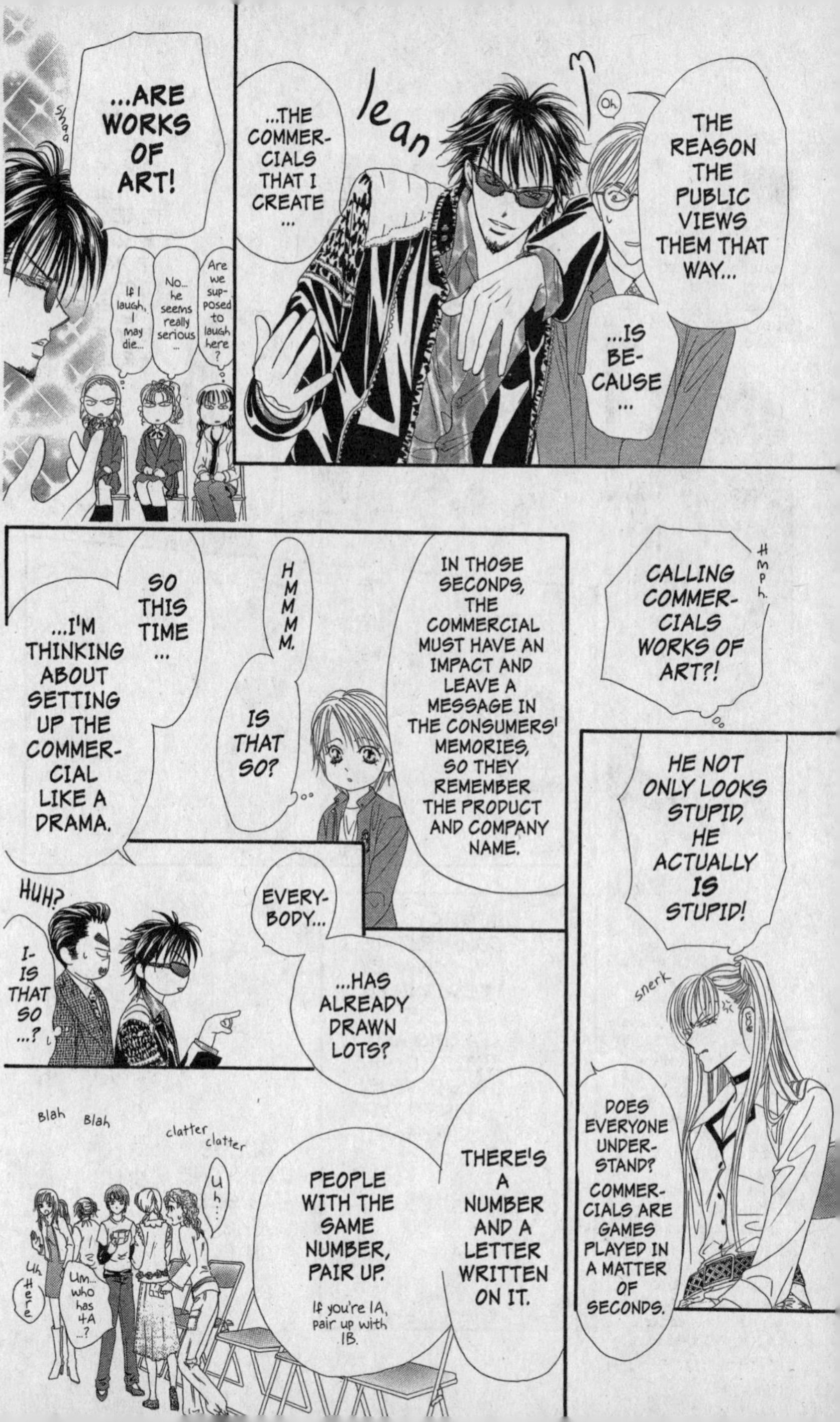
THE REASON THE PUBLIC VIEWS THEM THAT WAY...
Oh
...IS BE-CAUSE...
lean
...THE COMMER-CIALS THAT I CREATE...
...ARE WORKS OF ART!
shaa
Are we sup-posed to laugh here?
No... he seems really serious...
If I laugh, I may die...
CALLING COMMER-CIALS WORKS OF ART?!
Hmph.
HE NOT ONLY LOOKS STUPID, HE ACTUALLY IS STUPID!
snerk
DOES EVERYONE UNDER-STAND? COMMER-CIALS ARE GAMES PLAYED IN A MATTER OF SECONDS.
IN THOSE SECONDS, THE COMMERCIAL MUST HAVE AN IMPACT AND LEAVE A MESSAGE IN THE CONSUMERS' MEMORIES, SO THEY REMEMBER THE PRODUCT AND COMPANY NAME.
HMMMM.
IS THAT SO?
SO THIS TIME...
...I'M THINKING ABOUT SETTING UP THE COMMER-CIAL LIKE A DRAMA.
EVERY-BODY...
...HAS ALREADY DRAWN LOTS?
HUH?
I-IS THAT SO...?
THERE'S A NUMBER AND A LETTER WRITTEN ON IT.
PEOPLE WITH THE SAME NUMBER, PAIR UP.
If you're 1A, pair up with 1B.
clatter clatter
Uh...
Blah Blah
Um... who has 4A...?
Uh here

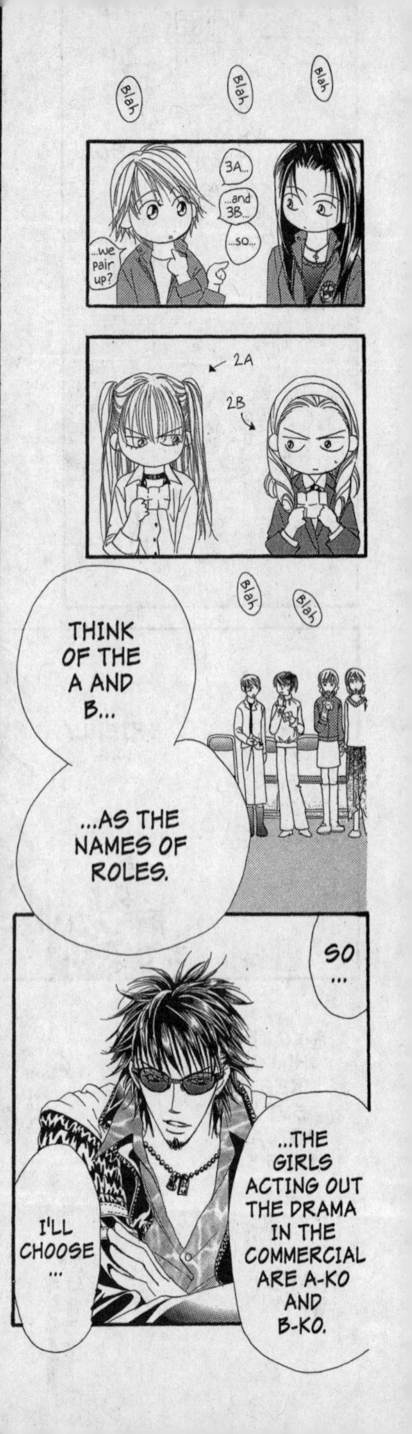
Blah
Blah
Blah
3A...
...and 3B...
...so...
...we pair up?
2A
2B
Blah
Blah
THINK OF THE A AND B...
...AS THE NAMES OF ROLES.
SO ...
...THE GIRLS ACTING OUT THE DRAMA IN THE COMMERCIAL ARE A-KO AND B-KO.
I'LL CHOOSE ...
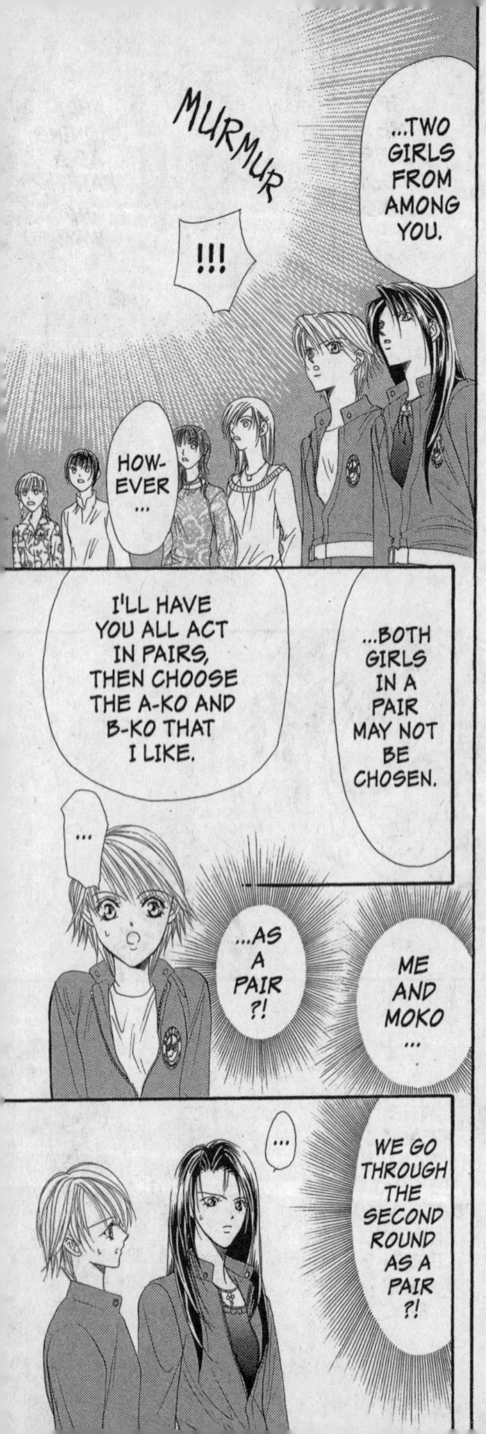
...TWO GIRLS FROM AMONG YOU.
MURMUR
!!!
HOW-EVER ...
...BOTH GIRLS IN A PAIR MAY NOT BE CHOSEN.
I'LL HAVE YOU ALL ACT IN PAIRS, THEN CHOOSE THE A-KO AND B-KO THAT I LIKE.
ME AND MOKO ...
...AS A PAIR ?!
...
WE GO THROUGH THE SECOND ROUND AS A PAIR ?!
...

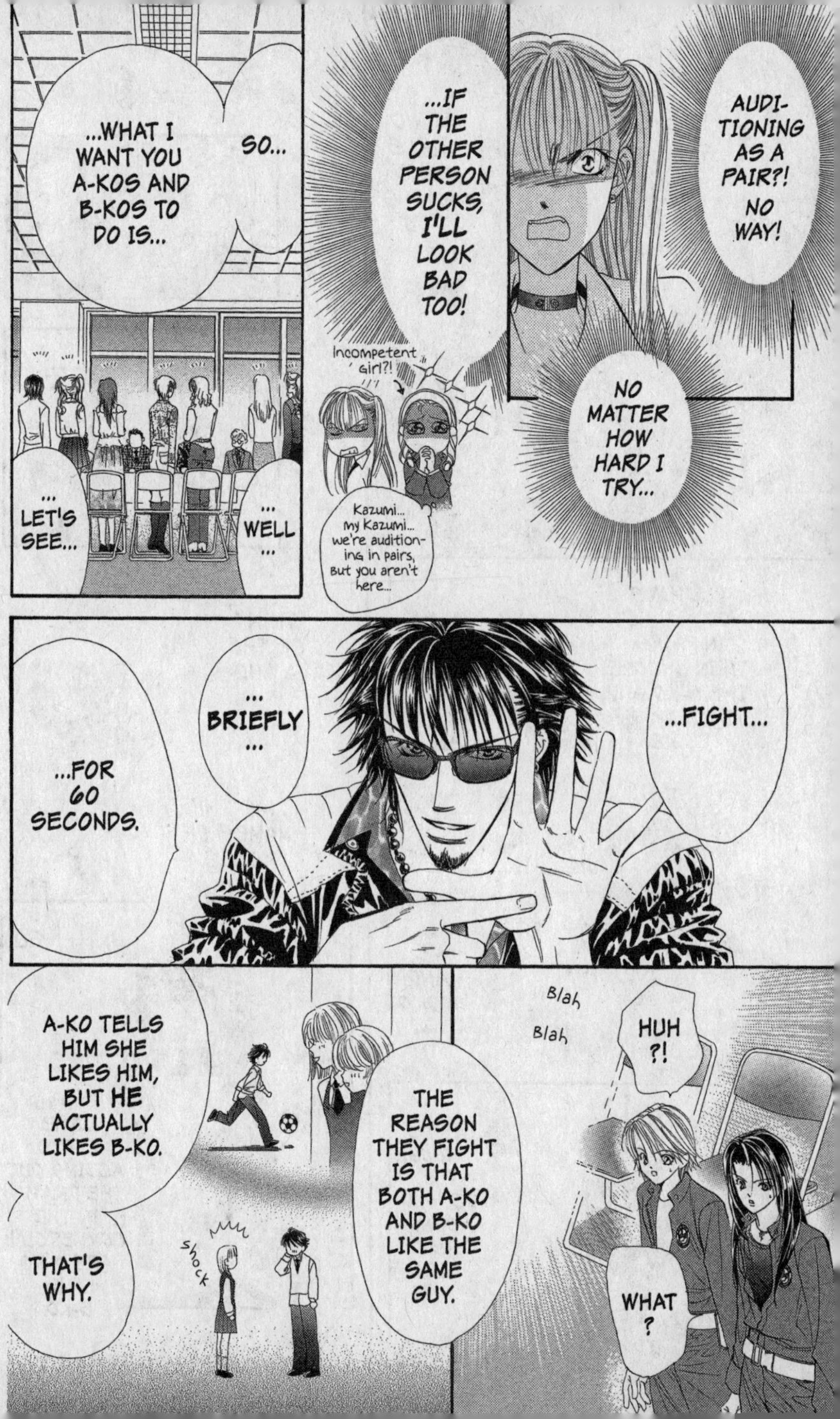
AUDI-TIONING AS A PAIR?! NO WAY!
...IF THE OTHER PERSON SUCKS, I'LL LOOK BAD TOO!
NO MATTER HOW HARD I TRY...
Incompetent girl?!
Kazumi... my Kazumi... we're audition-ing in pairs, but you aren't here...
SO...
...WHAT I WANT YOU A-KOS AND B-KOS TO DO IS...
...WELL...
...LET'S SEE...
...FIGHT...
...BRIEFLY...
...FOR 60 SECONDS.
Blah
Blah
HUH?!
WHAT?
THE REASON THEY FIGHT IS THAT BOTH A-KO AND B-KO LIKE THE SAME GUY.
A-KO TELLS HIM SHE LIKES HIM, BUT HE ACTUALLY LIKES B-KO.
shock
THAT'S WHY.

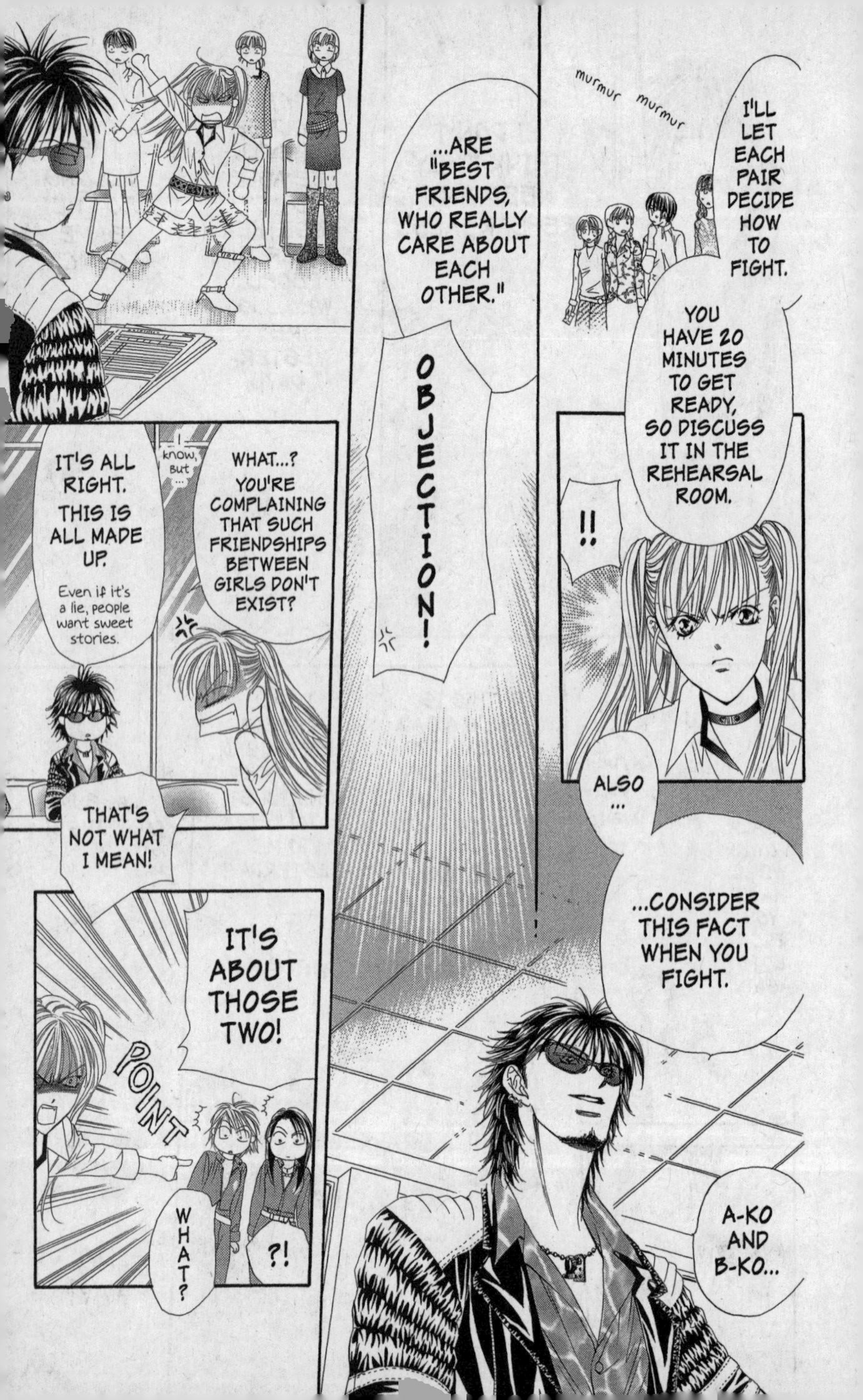
murmur murmur
I'LL LET EACH PAIR DECIDE HOW TO FIGHT.
YOU HAVE 20 MINUTES TO GET READY, SO DISCUSS IT IN THE REHEARSAL ROOM.
!!
ALSO...
...CONSIDER THIS FACT WHEN YOU FIGHT.
A-KO AND B-KO...
...ARE "BEST FRIENDS, WHO REALLY CARE ABOUT EACH OTHER."
OBJECTION!
WHAT...? YOU'RE COMPLAINING THAT SUCH FRIENDSHIPS BETWEEN GIRLS DON'T EXIST?
I know, but...
IT'S ALL RIGHT. THIS IS ALL MADE UP.
Even if it's a lie, people want sweet stories.
THAT'S NOT WHAT I MEAN!
IT'S ABOUT THOSE TWO!
POINT
?!
WHAT?

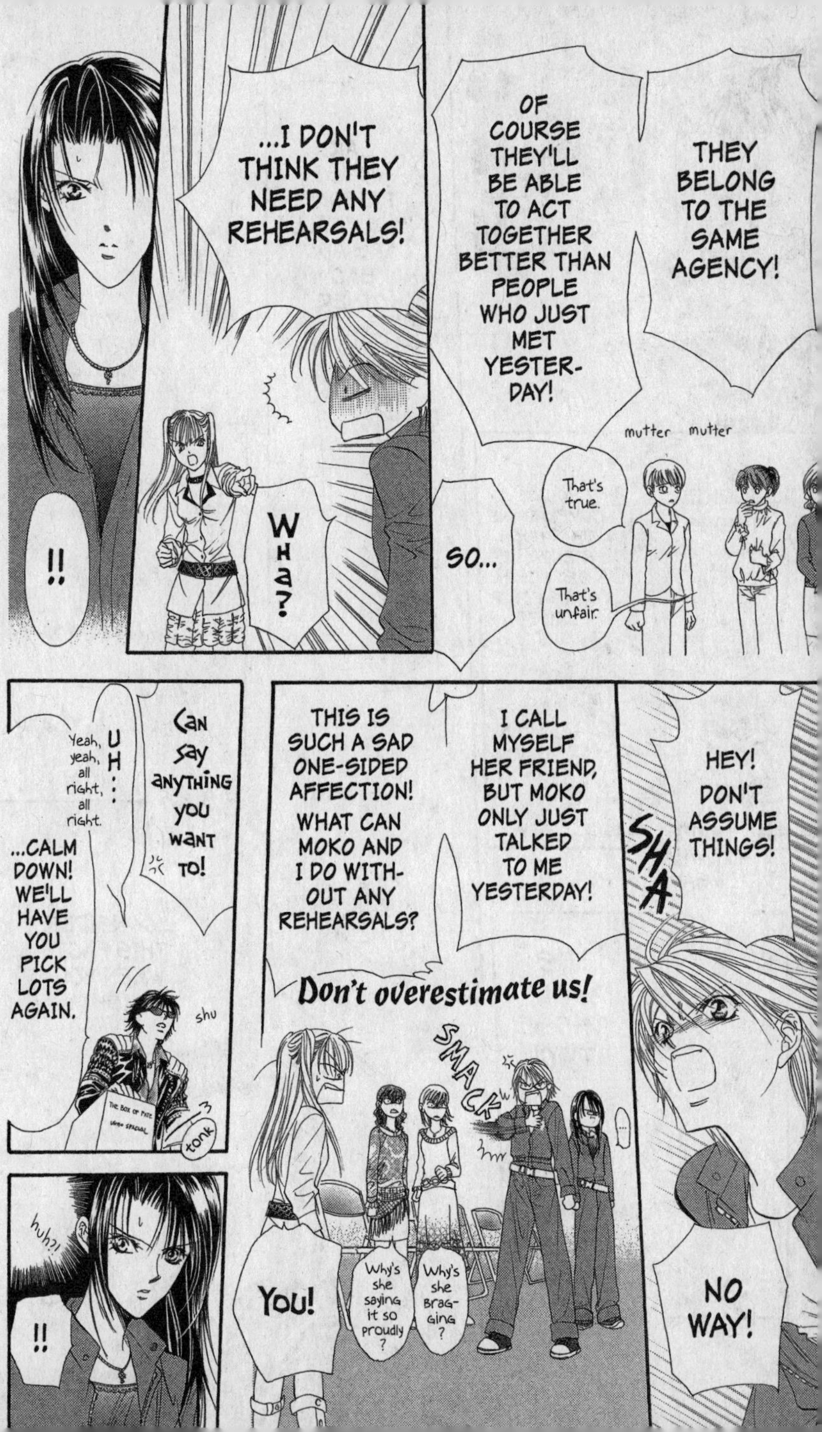
THEY BELONG TO THE SAME AGENCY!
OF COURSE THEY'LL BE ABLE TO ACT TOGETHER BETTER THAN PEOPLE WHO JUST MET YESTER-DAY!
mutter mutter
That's true.
That's unfair.
SO...
...I DON'T THINK THEY NEED ANY REHEARSALS!
Wha?
!!
HEY! DON'T ASSUME THINGS!
SHA
NO WAY!
I CALL MYSELF HER FRIEND, BUT MOKO ONLY JUST TALKED TO ME YESTERDAY!
THIS IS SUCH A SAD ONE-SIDED AFFECTION! WHAT CAN MOKO AND I DO WITH-OUT ANY REHEARSALS?
Don't overestimate us!
SMACK
...
You!
Why's she brag-ging?
Why's she saying it so proudly?
Can say anything you want to!
UH...
Yeah, yeah, all right, all right.
...CALM DOWN! WE'LL HAVE YOU PICK LOTS AGAIN.
shu
THE BOX OF FATE
tonk
huh?!
!!

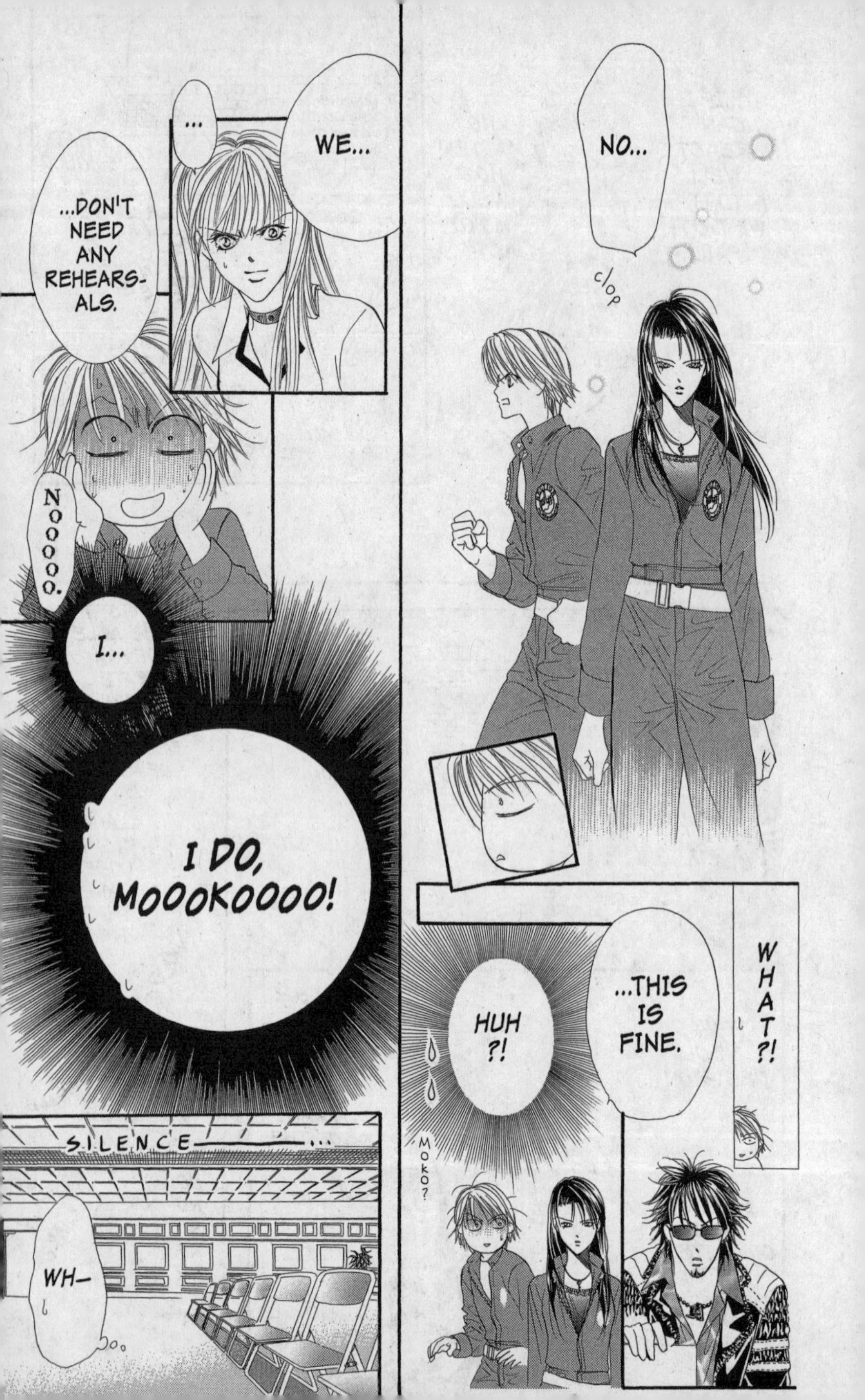
NO...
clop
WHAT?!
...THIS IS FINE.
HUH?!
MOKO?
WE...
...
...DON'T NEED ANY REHEARS-ALS.
NOOOOOO.
I...
I DO, MOOOKOOOO!
SILENCE—...
WH—

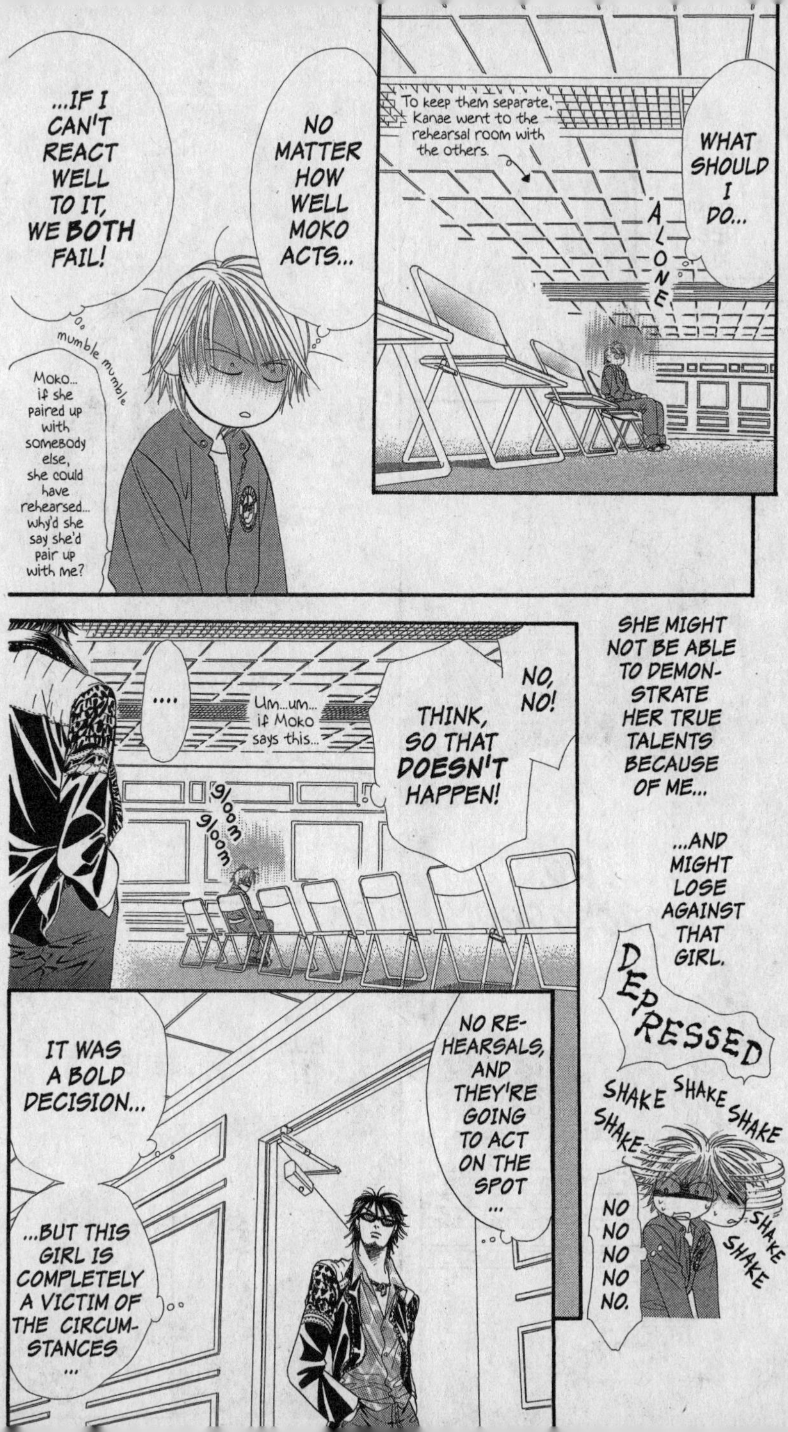
WHAT SHOULD I DO...
To keep them separate, Kanae went to the rehearsal room with the others.
ALONE
NO MATTER HOW WELL MOKO ACTS...
...IF I CAN'T REACT WELL TO IT, WE BOTH FAIL!
mumble mumble
Moko... if she paired up with somebody else, she could have rehearsed... why'd she say she'd pair up with me?
SHE MIGHT NOT BE ABLE TO DEMONSTRATE HER TRUE TALENTS BECAUSE OF ME...
...AND MIGHT LOSE AGAINST THAT GIRL.
DEPRESSED
SHAKE SHAKE SHAKE SHAKE SHAKE SHAKE
NO NO NO NO NO.
NO, NO!
THINK, SO THAT DOESN'T HAPPEN!
Um...um... if Moko says this...
gloom gloom
....
NO REHEARSALS, AND THEY'RE GOING TO ACT ON THE SPOT...
IT WAS A BOLD DECISION...
...BUT THIS GIRL IS COMPLETELY A VICTIM OF THE CIRCUMSTANCES...

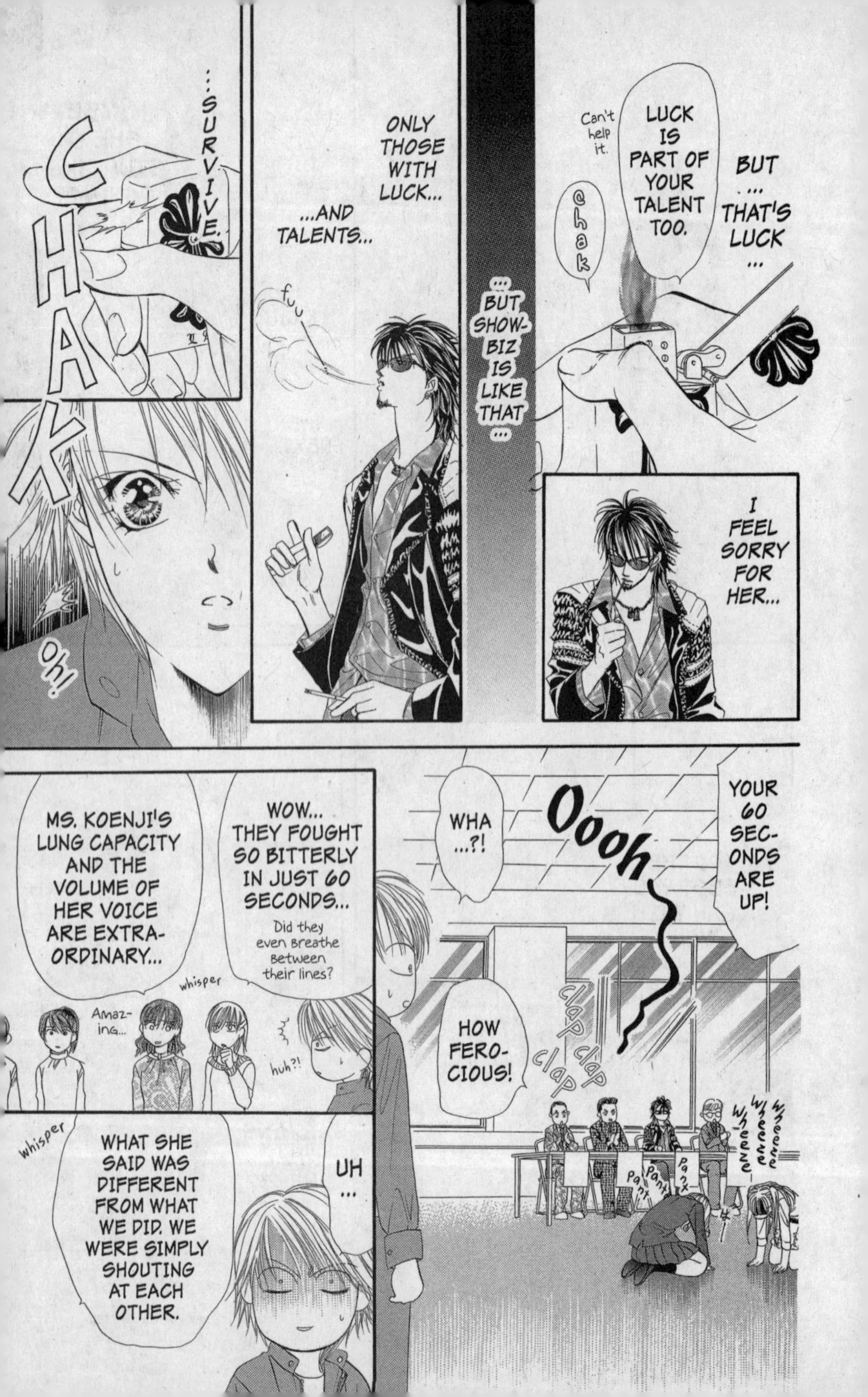
BUT ... THAT'S LUCK ...
LUCK IS PART OF YOUR TALENT TOO.
Can't help it.
Chak
I FEEL SORRY FOR HER...
...BUT SHOW-BIZ IS LIKE THAT...
ONLY THOSE WITH LUCK...
...AND TALENTS...
fuu
...SURVIVE.
CHAK
Oh!
YOUR 60 SECONDS ARE UP!
Oooh
WHA ...?!
HOW FEROCIOUS!
clap clap clap
Wheeze wheeze wheeze
Pant pant pant
WOW... THEY FOUGHT SO BITTERLY IN JUST 60 SECONDS...
Did they even breathe between their lines?
MS. KOENJI'S LUNG CAPACITY AND THE VOLUME OF HER VOICE ARE EXTRA-ORDINARY...
whisper
Amaz-ing...
huh?!
UH ...
WHAT SHE SAID WAS DIFFERENT FROM WHAT WE DID. WE WERE SIMPLY SHOUTING AT EACH OTHER.
whisper

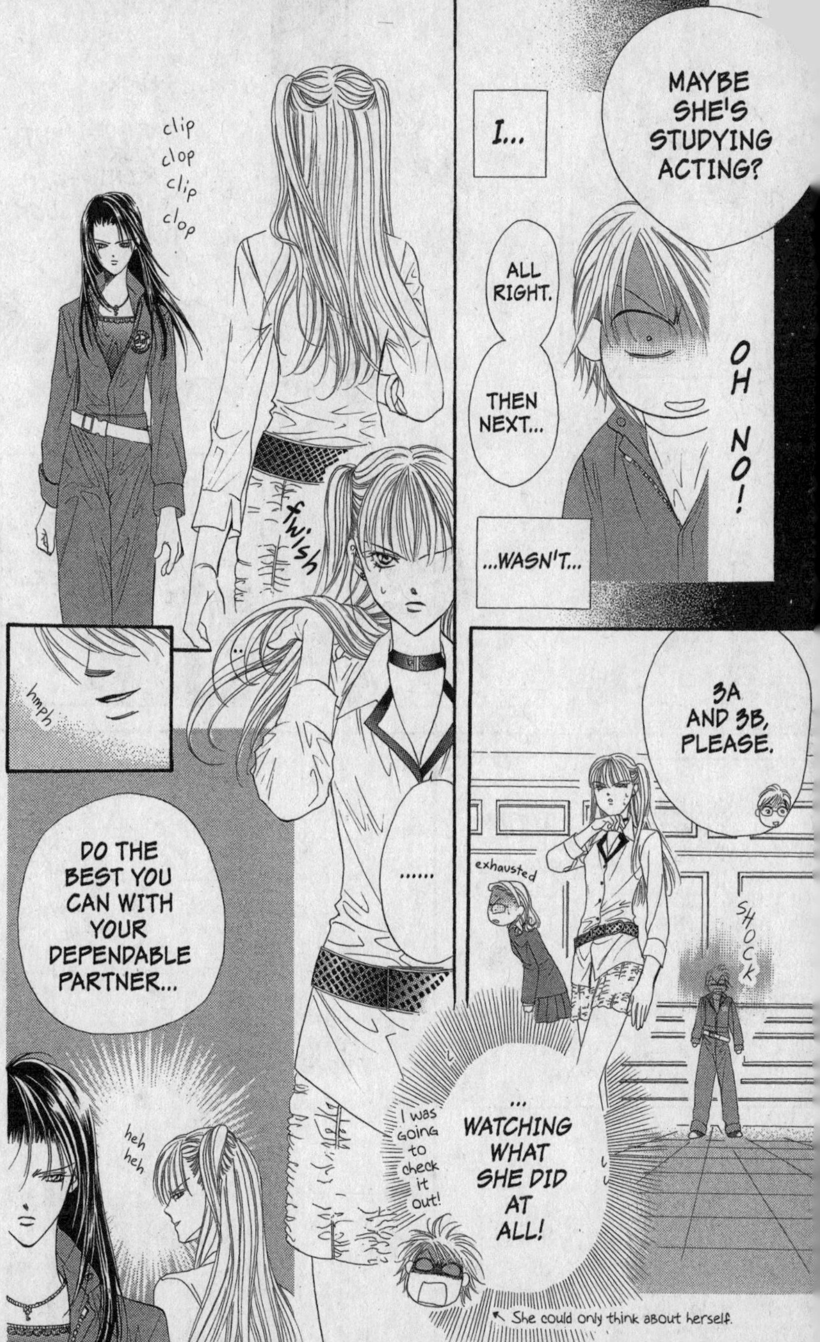
MAYBE SHE'S STUDYING ACTING?
I...
OH NO!
ALL RIGHT.
THEN NEXT...
...WASN'T...
3A AND 3B, PLEASE.
SHOCK
exhausted
... WATCHING WHAT SHE DID AT ALL!
I was going to check it out!
She could only think about herself.
clip clop clip clop
twish
...
......
hmph
DO THE BEST YOU CAN WITH YOUR DEPENDABLE PARTNER...
heh heh

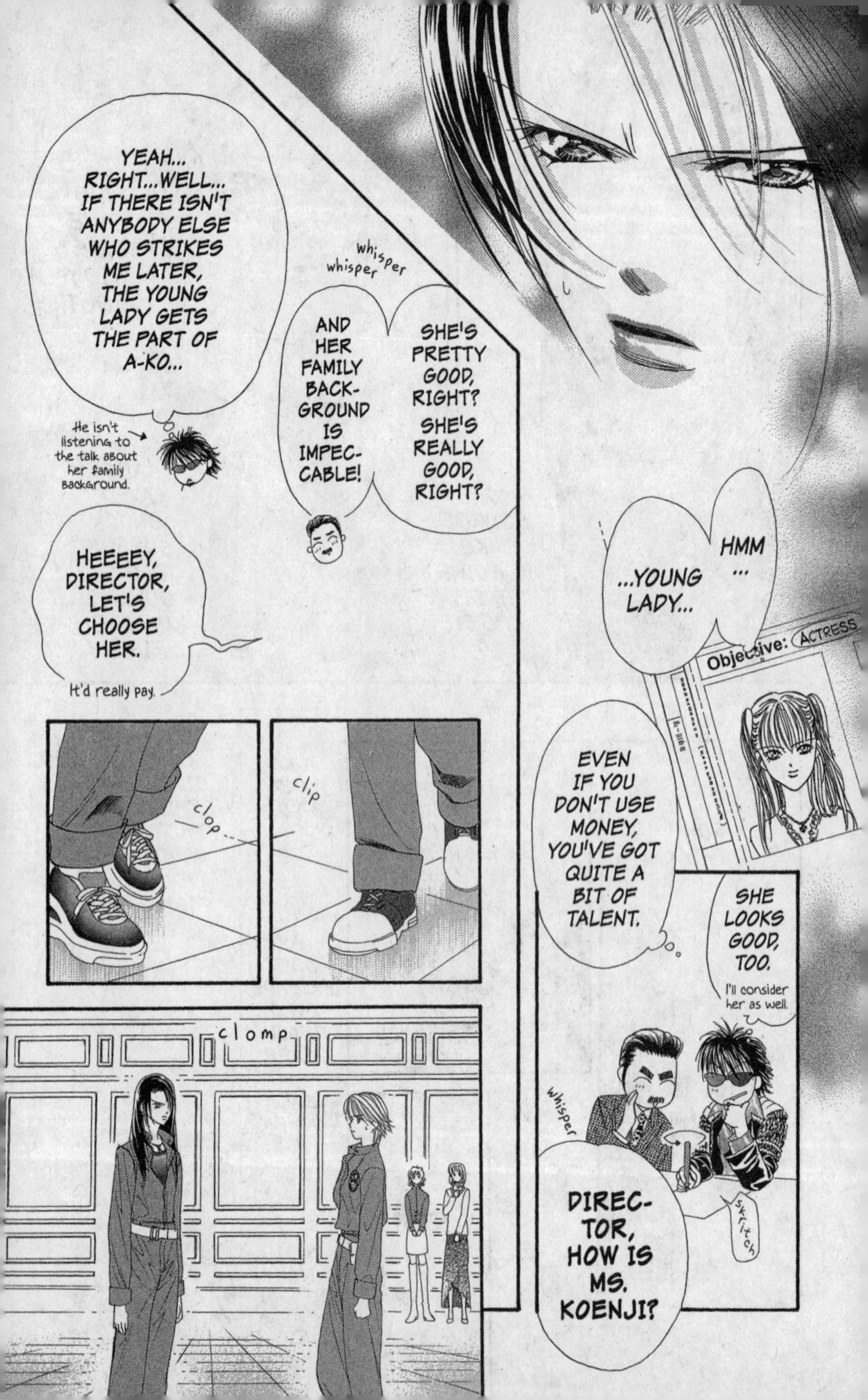
HMM ...
...YOUNG LADY...
Objective: ACTRESS
EVEN IF YOU DON'T USE MONEY, YOU'VE GOT QUITE A BIT OF TALENT.
SHE LOOKS GOOD, TOO.
I'll consider her as well.
whisper
DIREC-TOR, HOW IS MS. KOENJI?
skritch
whisper whisper
SHE'S PRETTY GOOD, RIGHT? SHE'S REALLY GOOD, RIGHT?
AND HER FAMILY BACK-GROUND IS IMPEC-CABLE!
YEAH... RIGHT...WELL... IF THERE ISN'T ANYBODY ELSE WHO STRIKES ME LATER, THE YOUNG LADY GETS THE PART OF A-KO...
He isn't listening to the talk about her family background.
HEEEEY, DIRECTOR, LET'S CHOOSE HER.
It'd really pay.
clip
clop
clomp

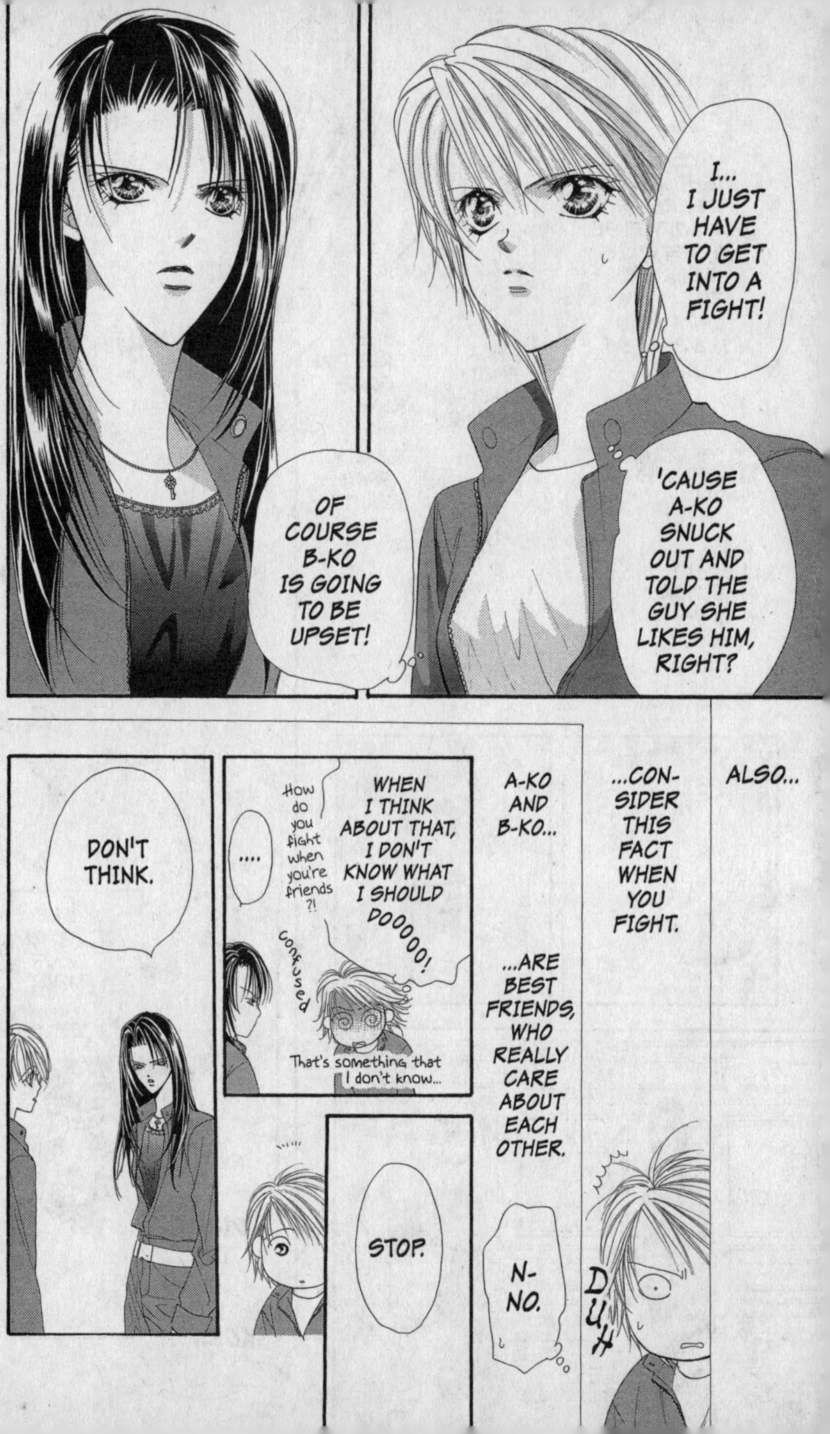

I... I JUST HAVE TO GET INTO A FIGHT!
'CAUSE A-KO SNUCK OUT AND TOLD THE GUY SHE LIKES HIM, RIGHT?
OF COURSE B-KO IS GOING TO BE UPSET!
ALSO...
...CON-SIDER THIS FACT WHEN YOU FIGHT.
A-KO AND B-KO...
...ARE BEST FRIENDS, WHO REALLY CARE ABOUT EACH OTHER.
DUH
N-NO.
WHEN I THINK ABOUT THAT, I DON'T KNOW WHAT I SHOULD DOOOOO!
How do you fight when you're friends?!
....
confused
That's something that I don't know...
STOP.
DON'T THINK.

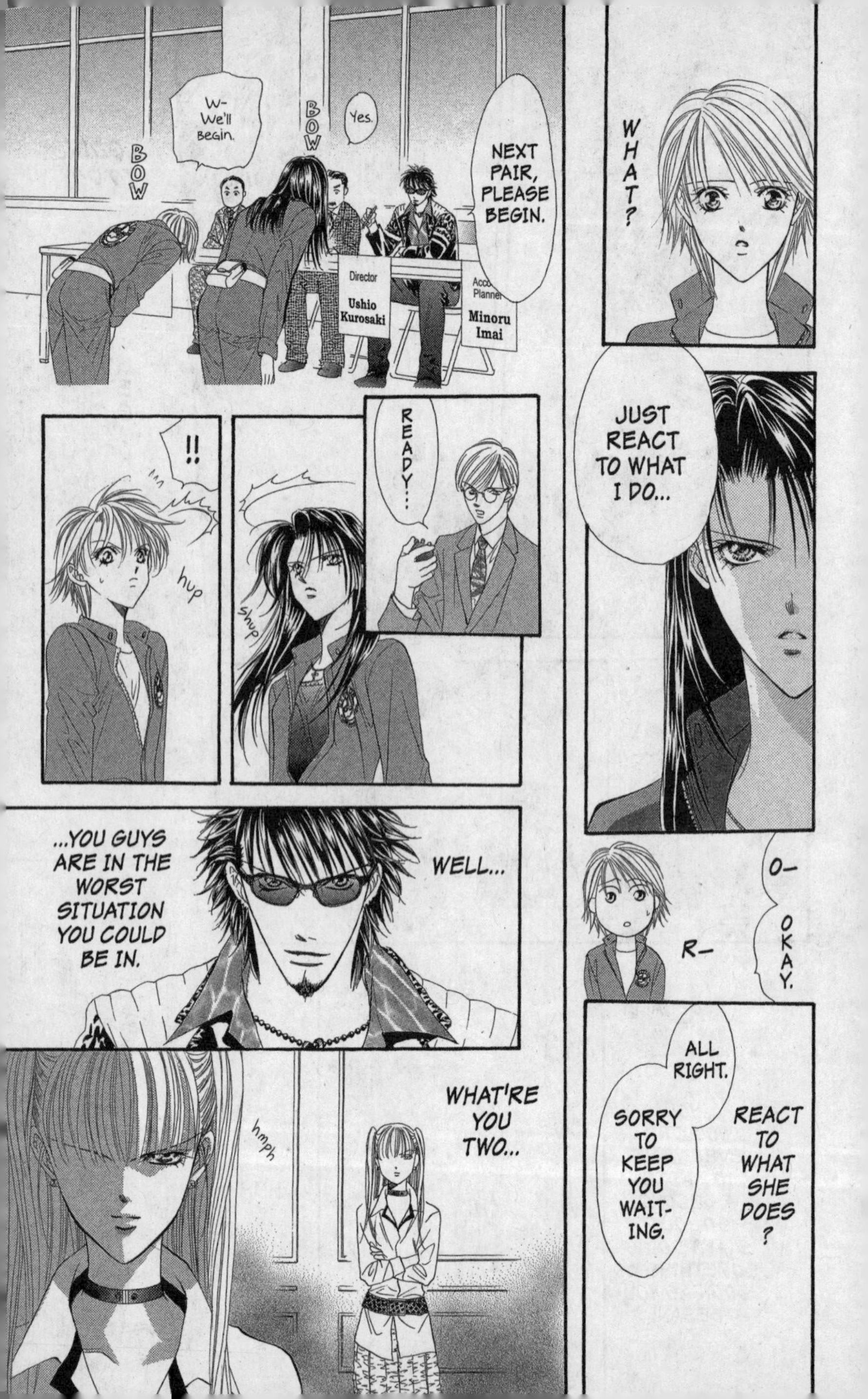
WHAT?
JUST REACT TO WHAT I DO...
O-OKAY.
R-
REACT TO WHAT SHE DOES?
ALL RIGHT.
SORRY TO KEEP YOU WAIT-ING.
NEXT PAIR, PLEASE BEGIN.
Yes.
BOW
W-We'll begin.
BOW
Director
Ushio Kurosaki
Acco
Planner
Minoru Imai
READY...
shup
hup
!!
WELL...
...YOU GUYS ARE IN THE WORST SITUATION YOU COULD BE IN.
WHAT'RE YOU TWO...
hmph

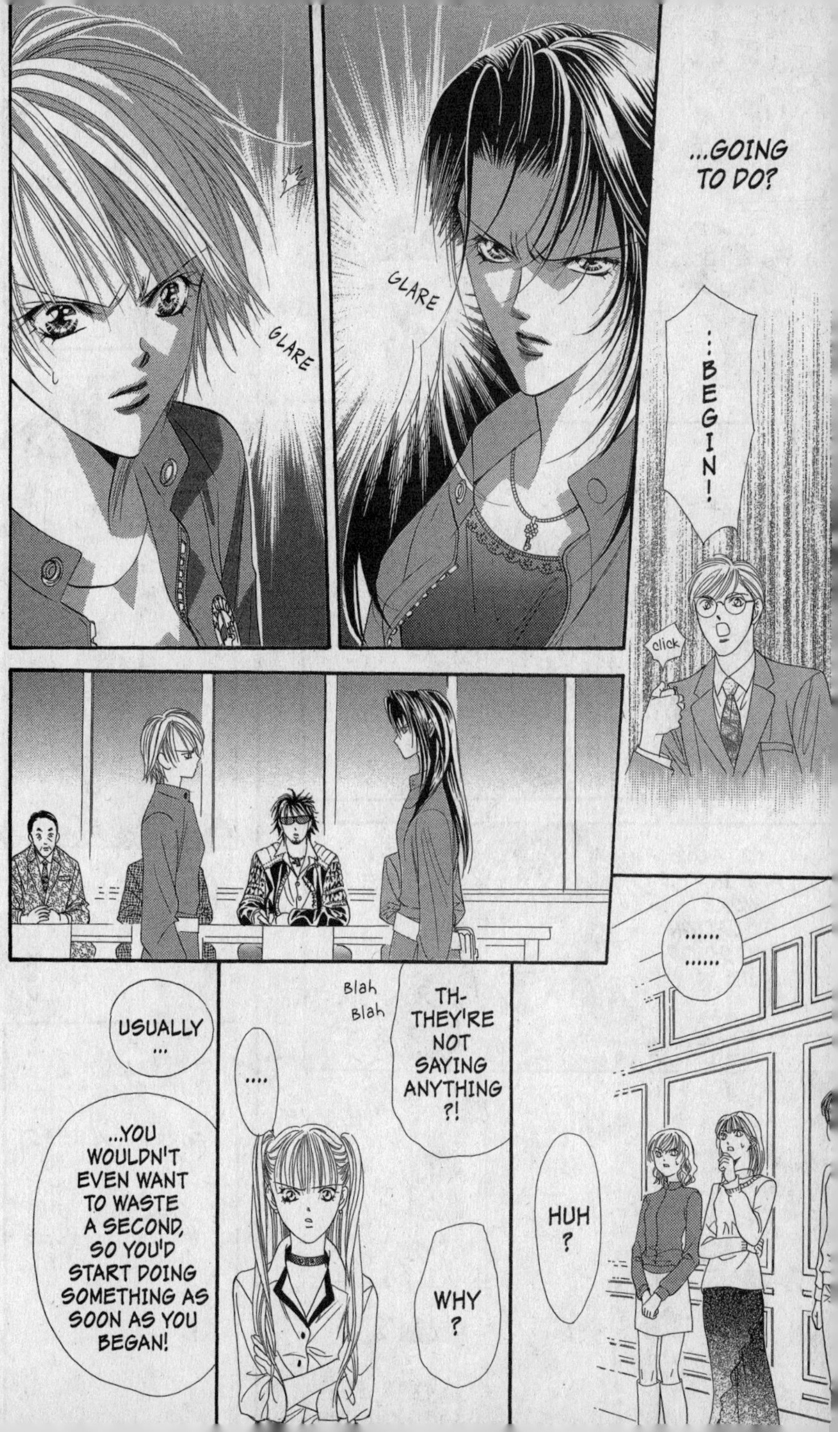

...GOING TO DO?
...BEGIN!
click
GLARE
GLARE
......
......
HUH?
TH-THEY'RE NOT SAYING ANYTHING?!
Blah Blah
....
WHY?
USUALLY...
...YOU WOULDN'T EVEN WANT TO WASTE A SECOND, SO YOU'D START DOING SOMETHING AS SOON AS YOU BEGAN!

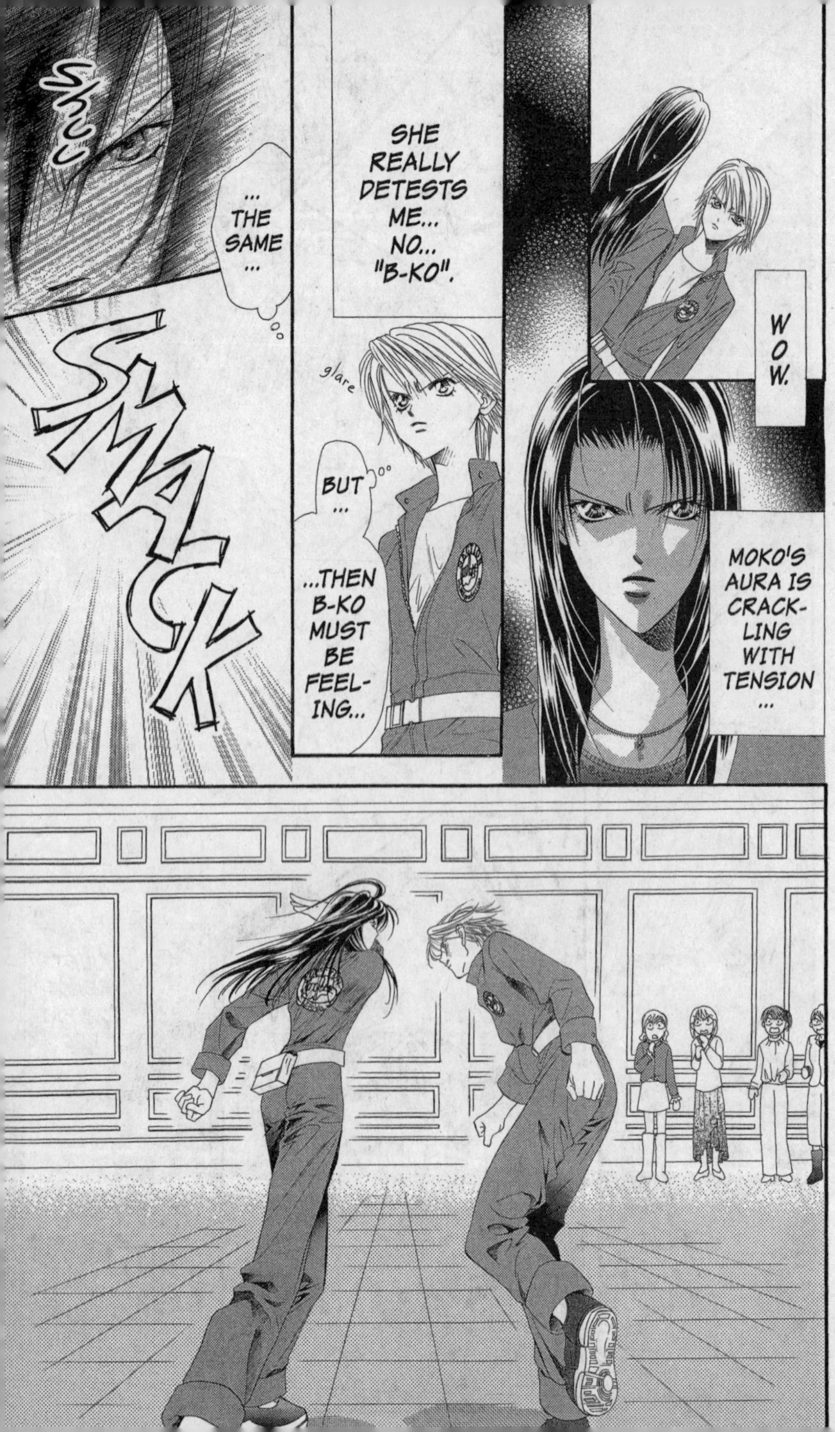
WOW.
MOKO'S AURA IS CRACKLING WITH TENSION ...
SHE REALLY DETESTS ME... NO... "B-KO".
glare
BUT ...
...THEN B-KO MUST BE FEELING...
... THE SAME ...
SHUU
SMACK

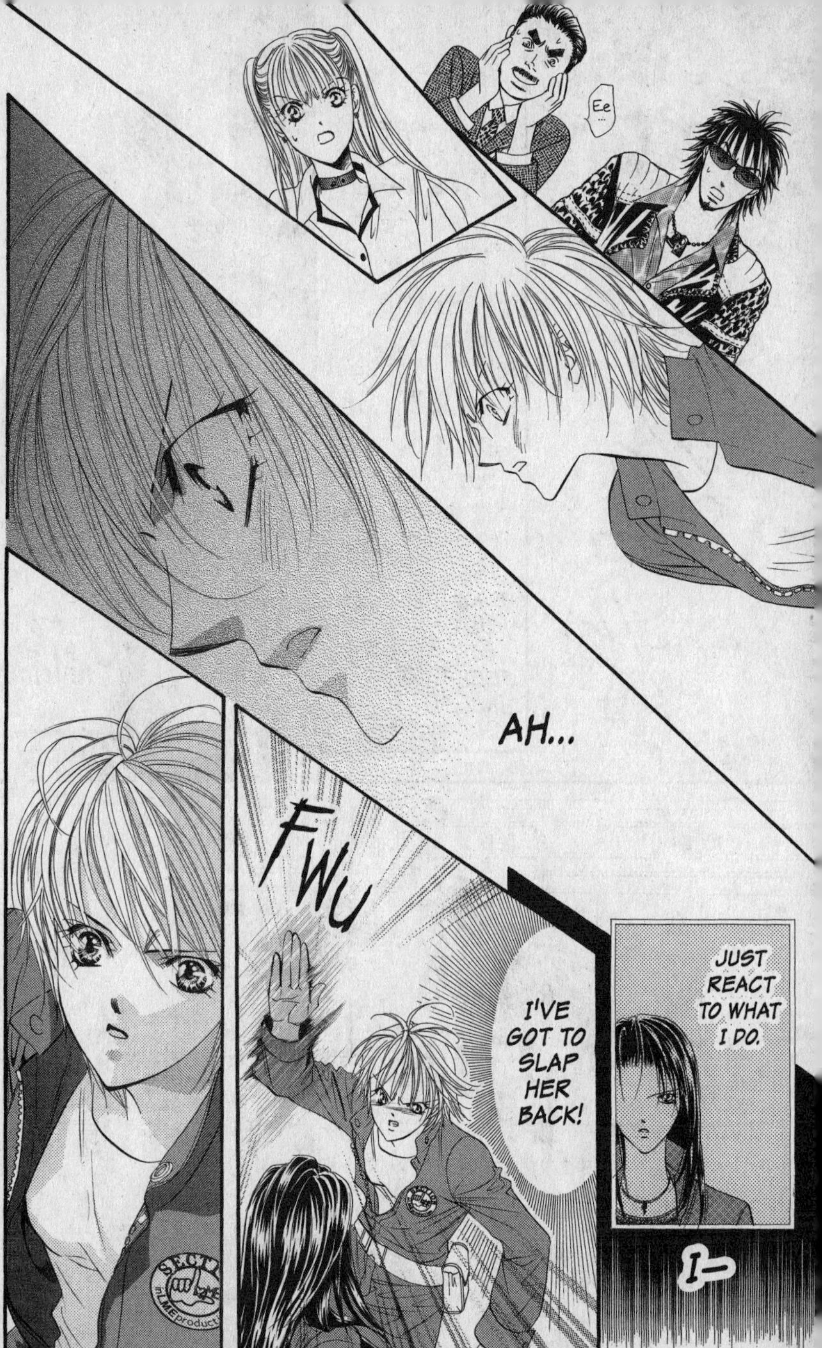
Ee ...
AH...
JUST REACT TO WHAT I DO.
I—
I'VE GOT TO SLAP HER BACK!
FWU

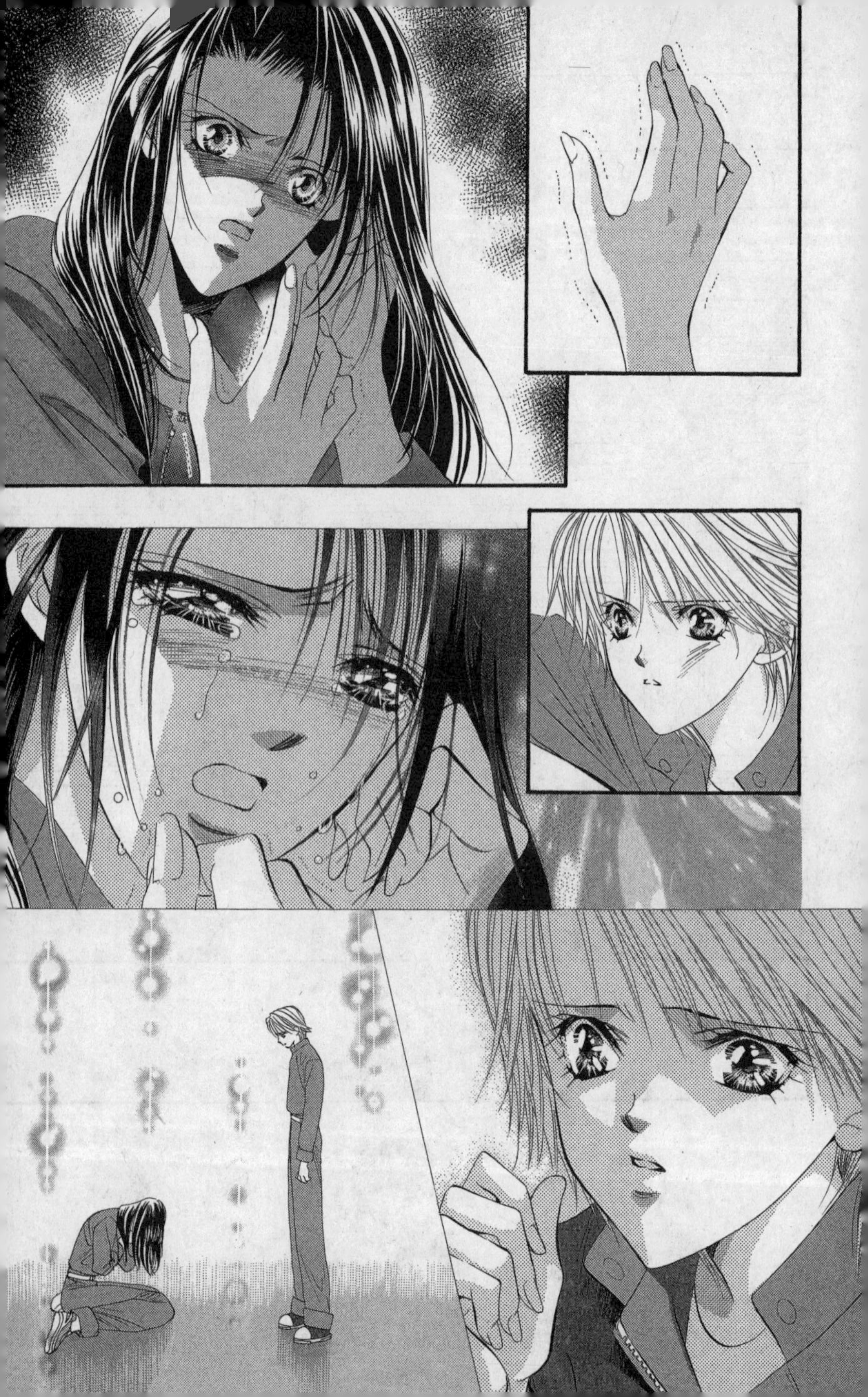

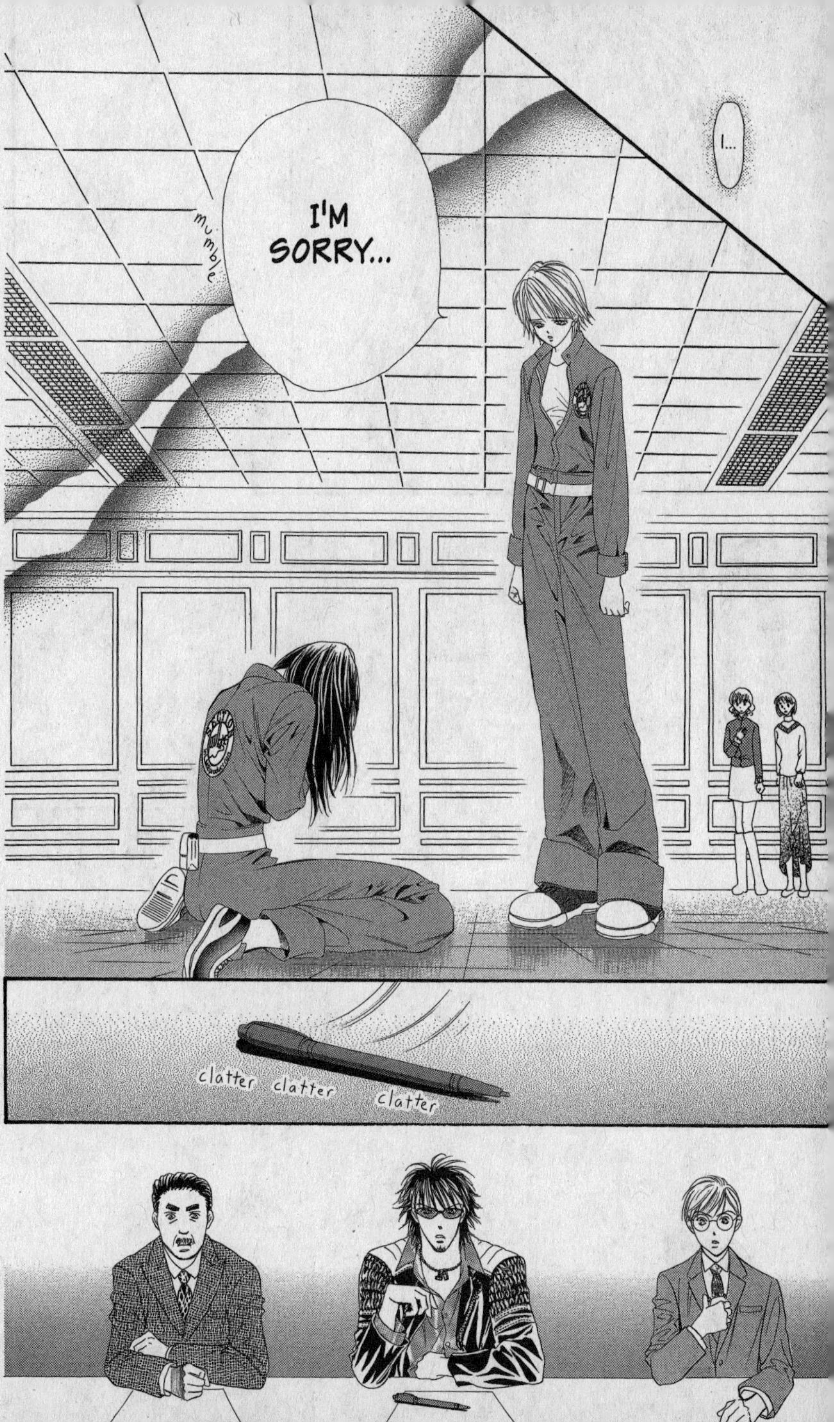
I...
mumble
I'M SORRY...
clatter clatter clatter

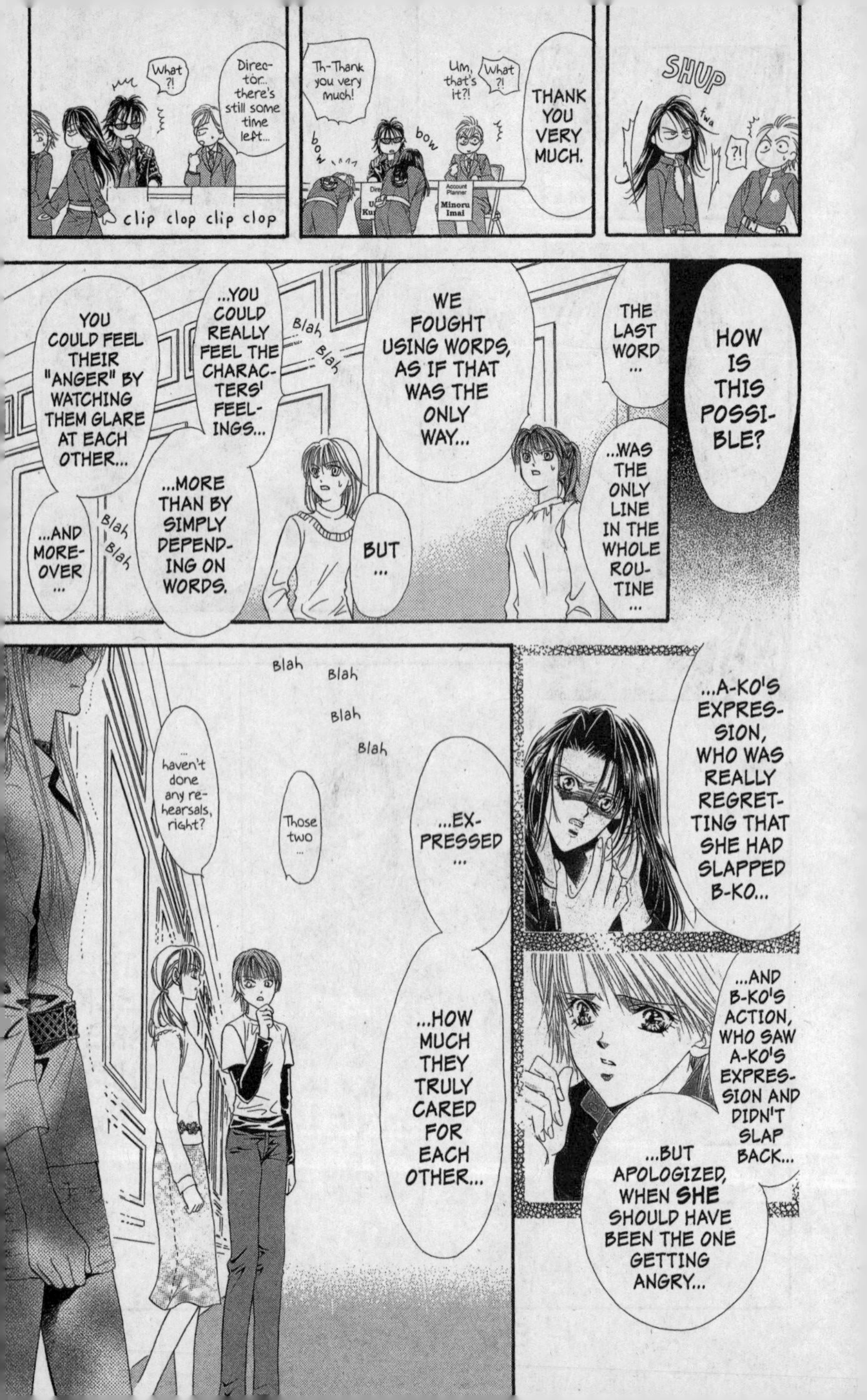
SHUP
fwa
?!
THANK YOU VERY MUCH.
Um, that's it?!
What ?!
Th-Thank you very much!
bow
bow
Account Planner Minoru Imai
Director... there's still some time left...
What ?!
clip clop clip clop
HOW IS THIS POSSIBLE?
THE LAST WORD...
...WAS THE ONLY LINE IN THE WHOLE ROUTINE...
WE FOUGHT USING WORDS, AS IF THAT WAS THE ONLY WAY...
BUT...
Blah Blah
...YOU COULD REALLY FEEL THE CHARACTERS' FEELINGS...
...MORE THAN BY SIMPLY DEPENDING ON WORDS.
YOU COULD FEEL THEIR "ANGER" BY WATCHING THEM GLARE AT EACH OTHER...
...AND MOREOVER...
Blah Blah
...A-KO'S EXPRESSION, WHO WAS REALLY REGRETTING THAT SHE HAD SLAPPED B-KO...
...AND B-KO'S ACTION, WHO SAW A-KO'S EXPRESSION AND DIDN'T SLAP BACK...
...BUT APOLOGIZED, WHEN SHE SHOULD HAVE BEEN THE ONE GETTING ANGRY...
Blah Blah Blah Blah
...EXPRESSED...
...HOW MUCH THEY TRULY CARED FOR EACH OTHER...
Those two...
...haven't done any rehearsals, right?

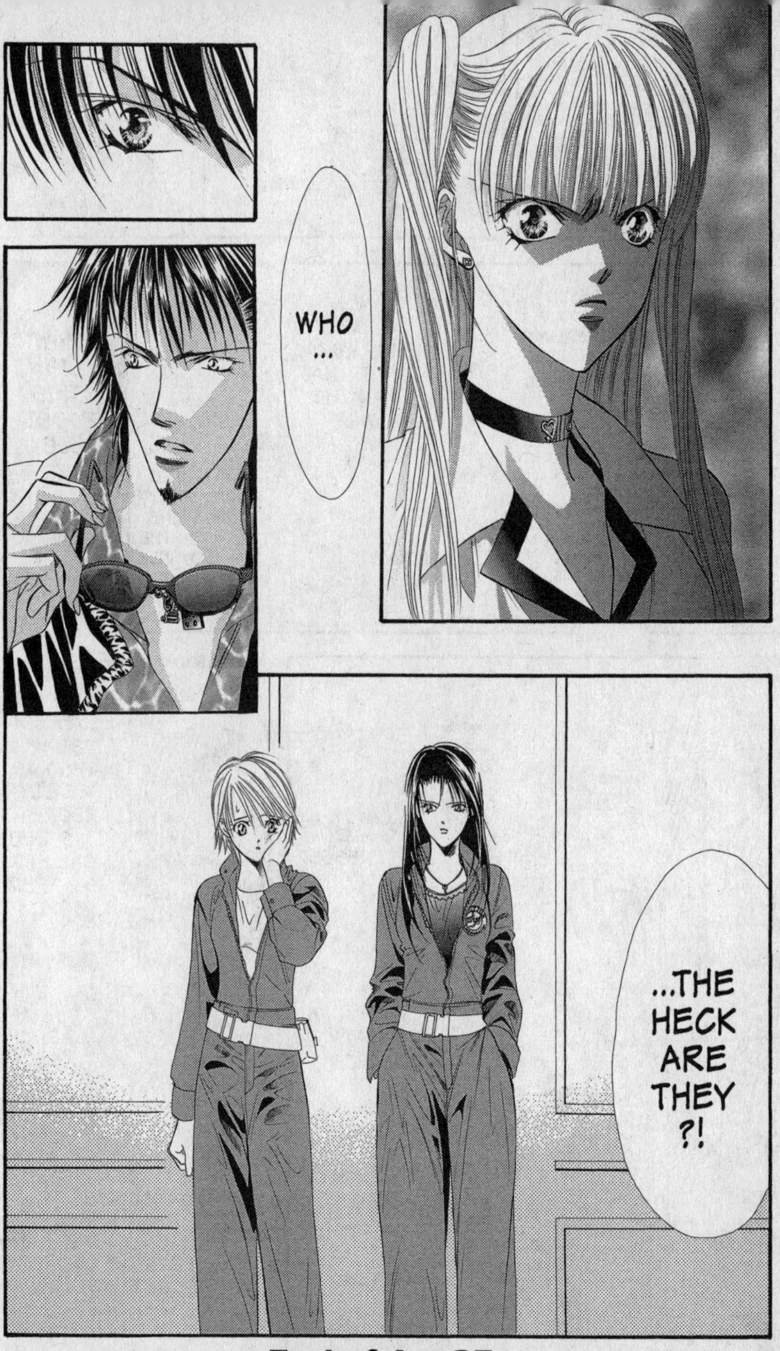
WHO ...
...THE HECK ARE THEY ?!

End of Act 27

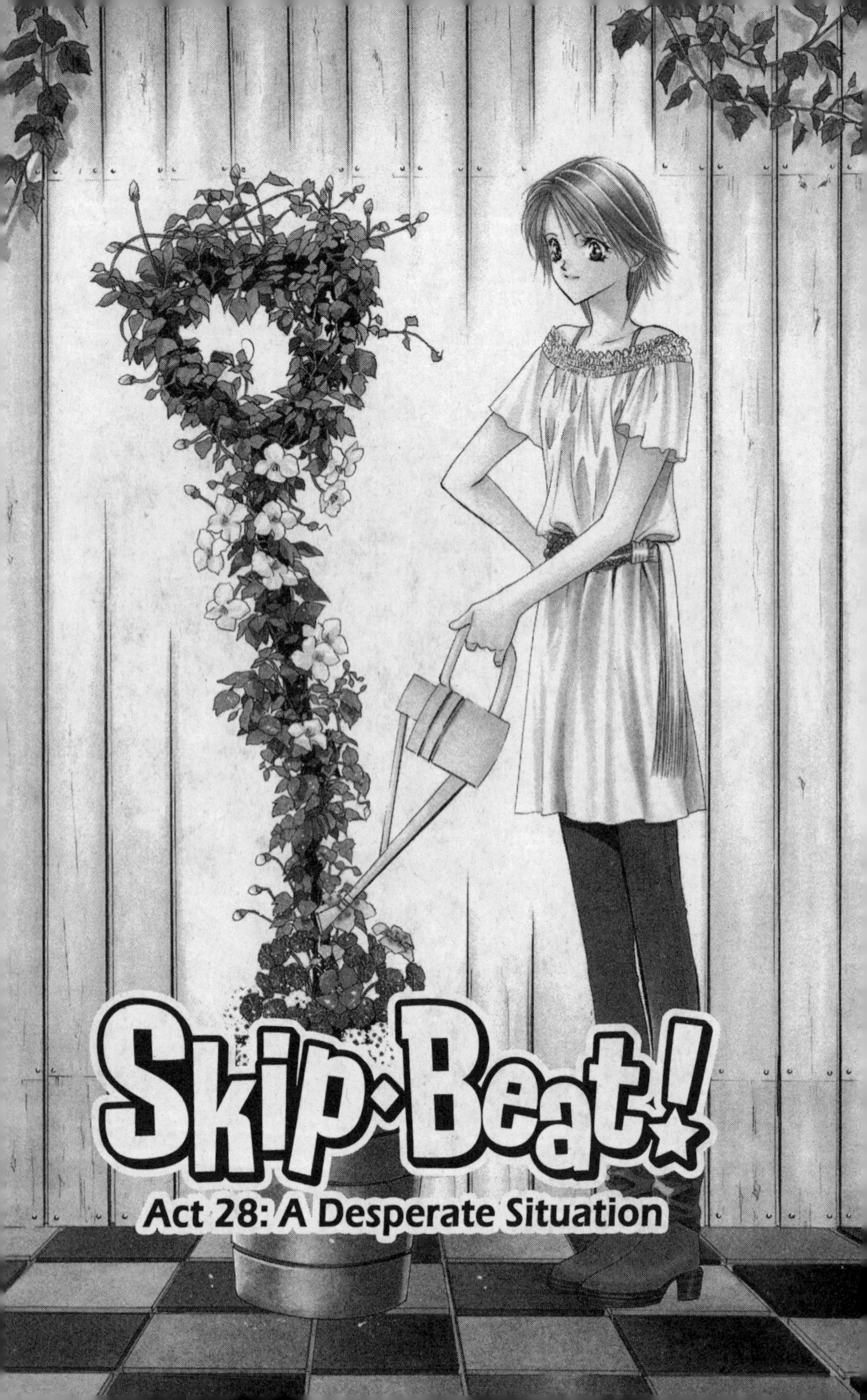
Skip·Beat!
Act 28: A Desperate Situation

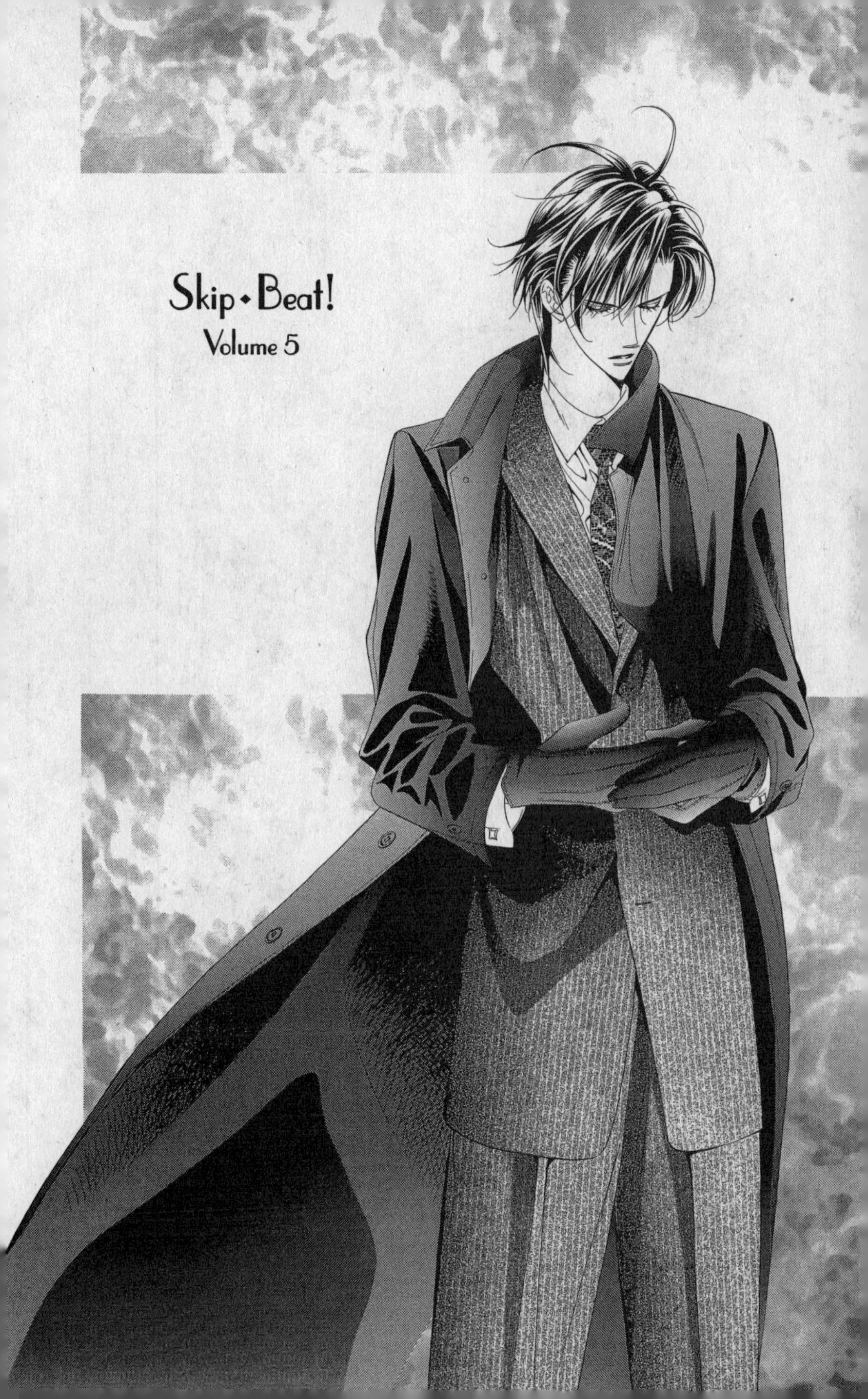
Skip•Beat!
Volume 5

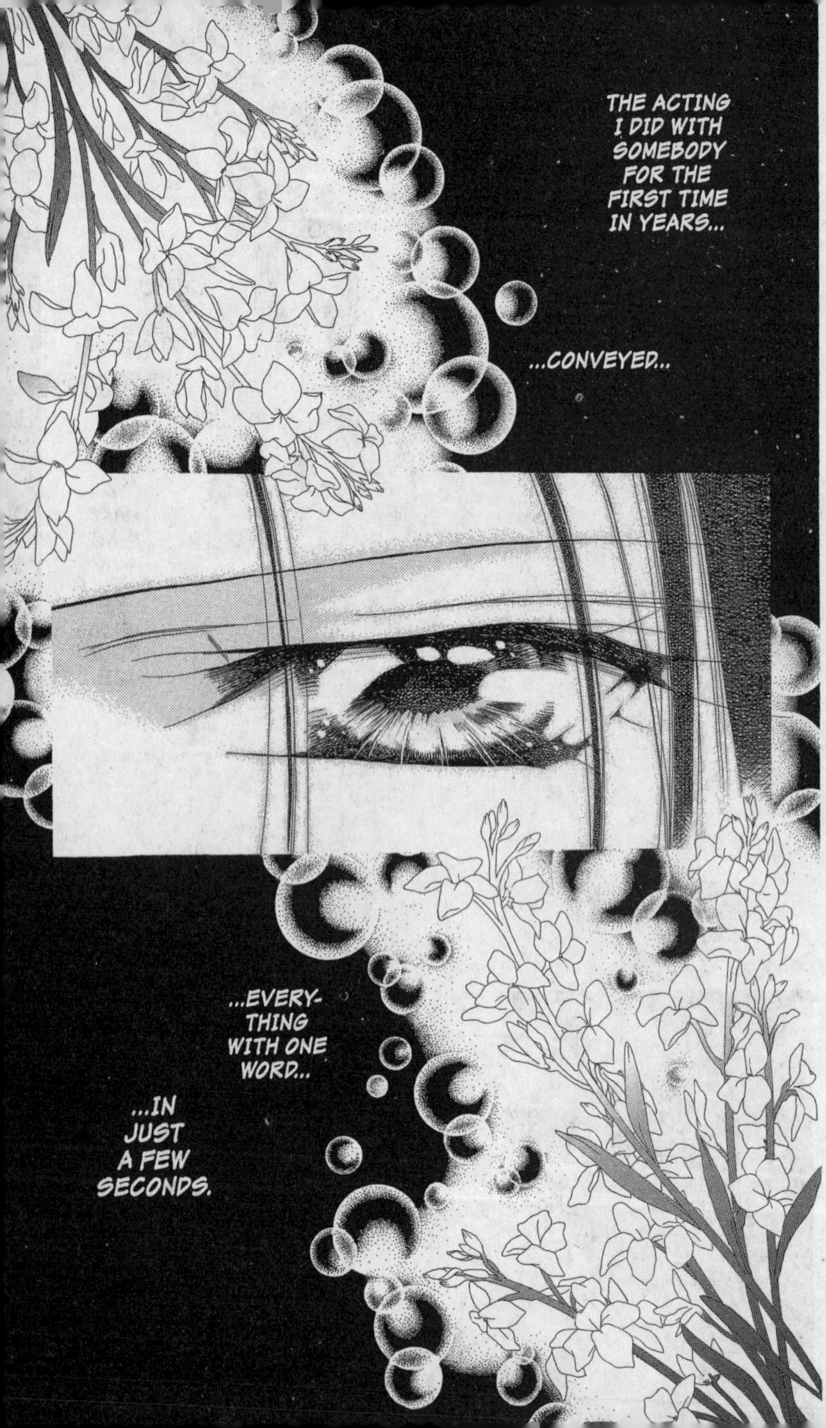
THE ACTING I DID WITH SOMEBODY FOR THE FIRST TIME IN YEARS...
...CONVEYED...
...EVERY-THING WITH ONE WORD...
...IN JUST A FEW SECONDS.

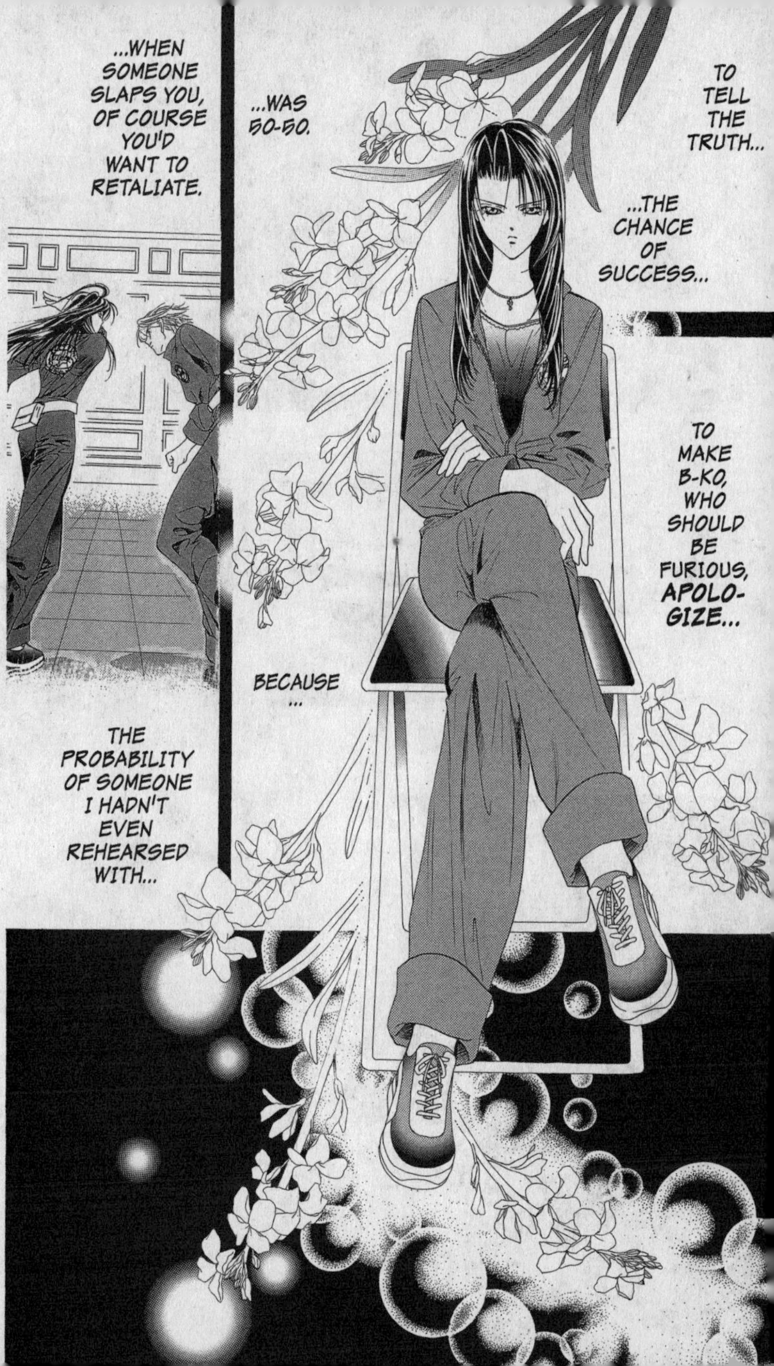
TO TELL THE TRUTH...
...THE CHANCE OF SUCCESS...
...WAS 50-50.
TO MAKE B-KO, WHO SHOULD BE FURIOUS, APOLOGIZE...
BECAUSE ...
THE PROBABILITY OF SOMEONE I HADN'T EVEN REHEARSED WITH...
...WHEN SOMEONE SLAPS YOU, OF COURSE YOU'D WANT TO RETALIATE.

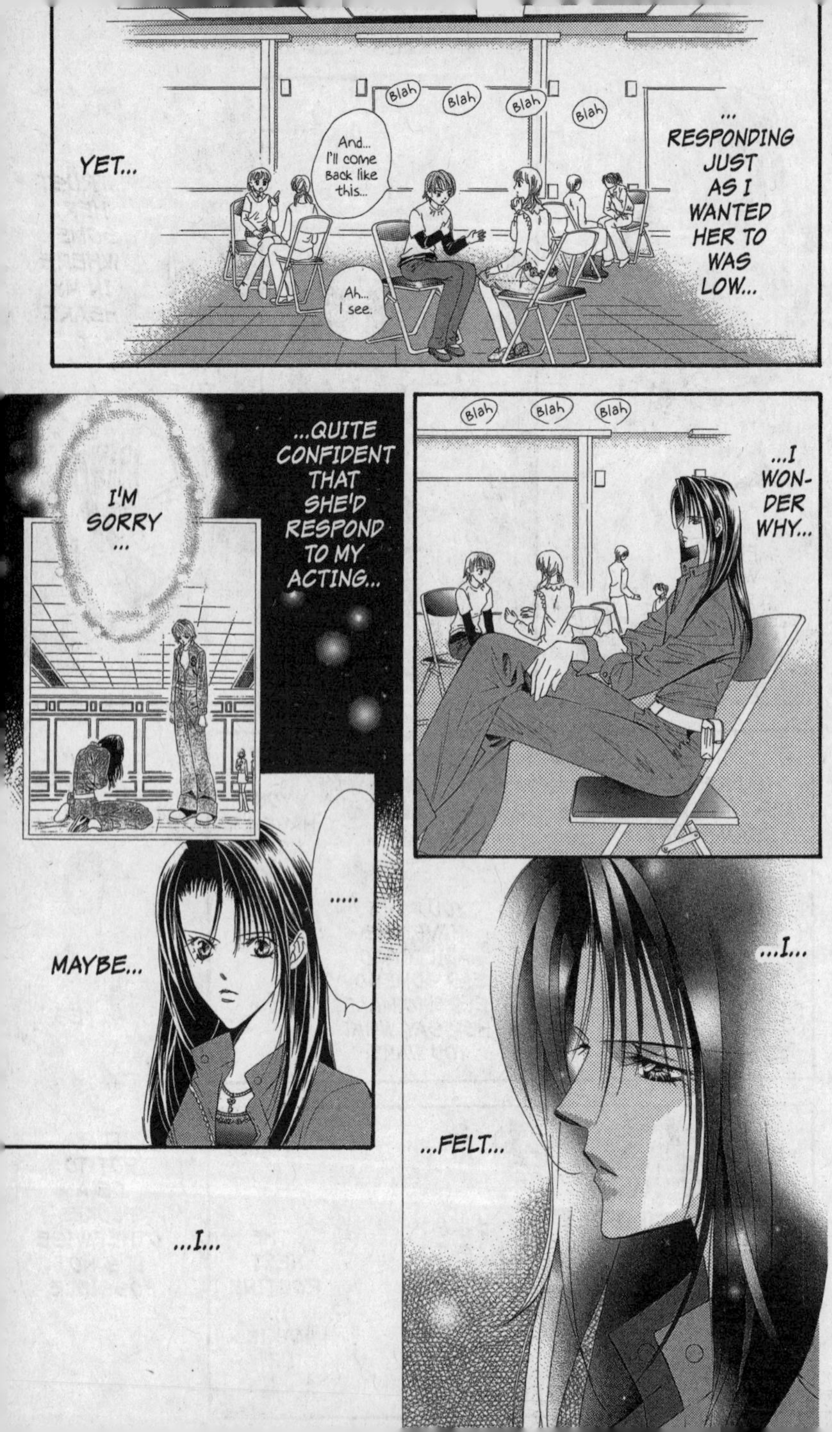
...RESPONDING JUST AS I WANTED HER TO WAS LOW...
Blah
Blah
Blah
Blah
And... I'll come back like this...
Ah... I see.
YET...
Blah
Blah
Blah
...I WONDER WHY...
...QUITE CONFIDENT THAT SHE'D RESPOND TO MY ACTING...
I'M SORRY ...
.....
MAYBE...
...I...
...FELT...
...I...

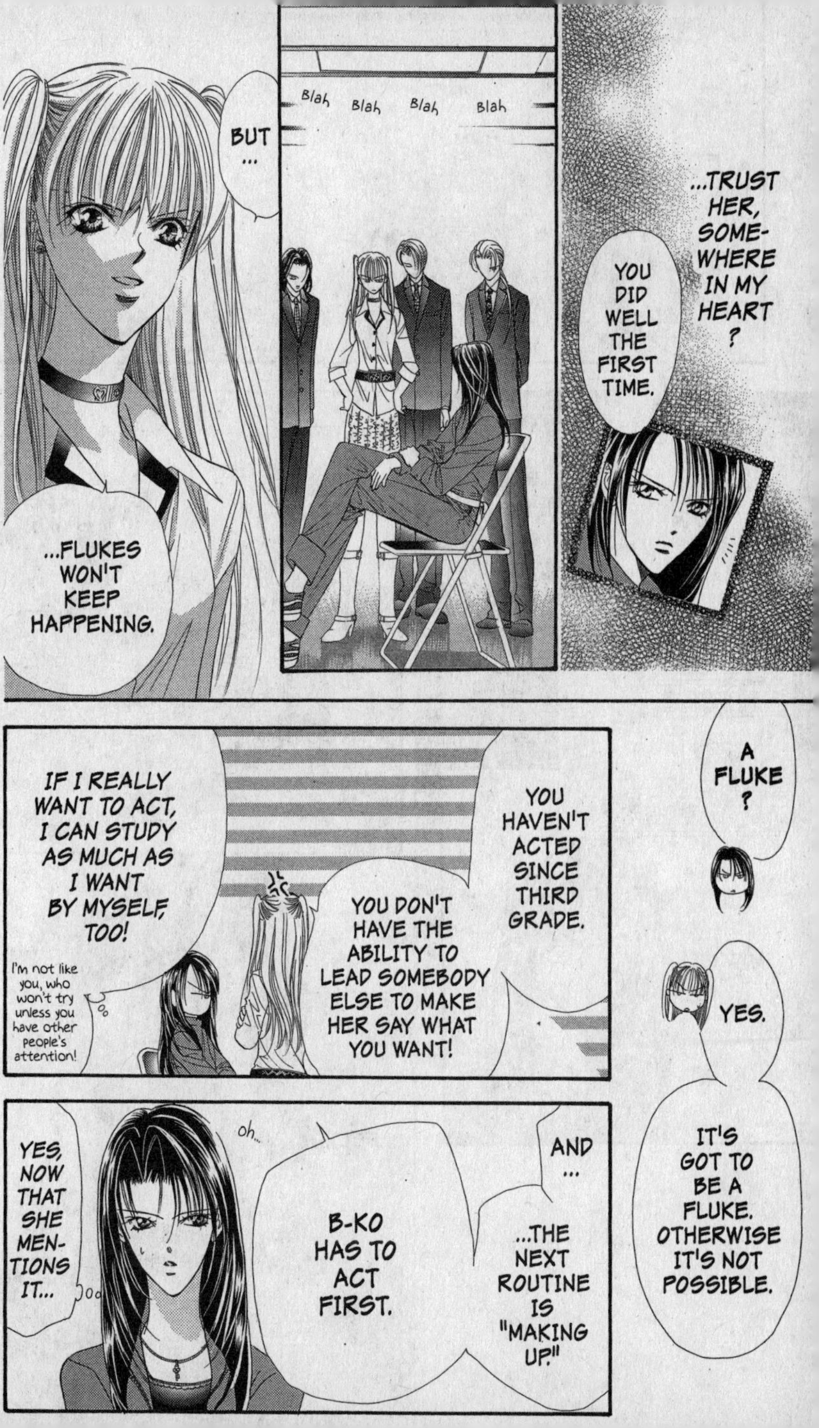
...TRUST HER, SOMEWHERE IN MY HEART?
YOU DID WELL THE FIRST TIME.
Blah Blah Blah Blah
BUT...
...FLUKES WON'T KEEP HAPPENING.
A FLUKE?
YES.
IT'S GOT TO BE A FLUKE. OTHERWISE IT'S NOT POSSIBLE.
YOU HAVEN'T ACTED SINCE THIRD GRADE.
YOU DON'T HAVE THE ABILITY TO LEAD SOMEBODY ELSE TO MAKE HER SAY WHAT YOU WANT!
IF I REALLY WANT TO ACT, I CAN STUDY AS MUCH AS I WANT BY MYSELF, TOO!
I'm not like you, who won't try unless you have other people's attention!
AND...
...THE NEXT ROUTINE IS "MAKING UP."
B-KO HAS TO ACT FIRST.
oh...
YES, NOW THAT SHE MENTIONS IT...

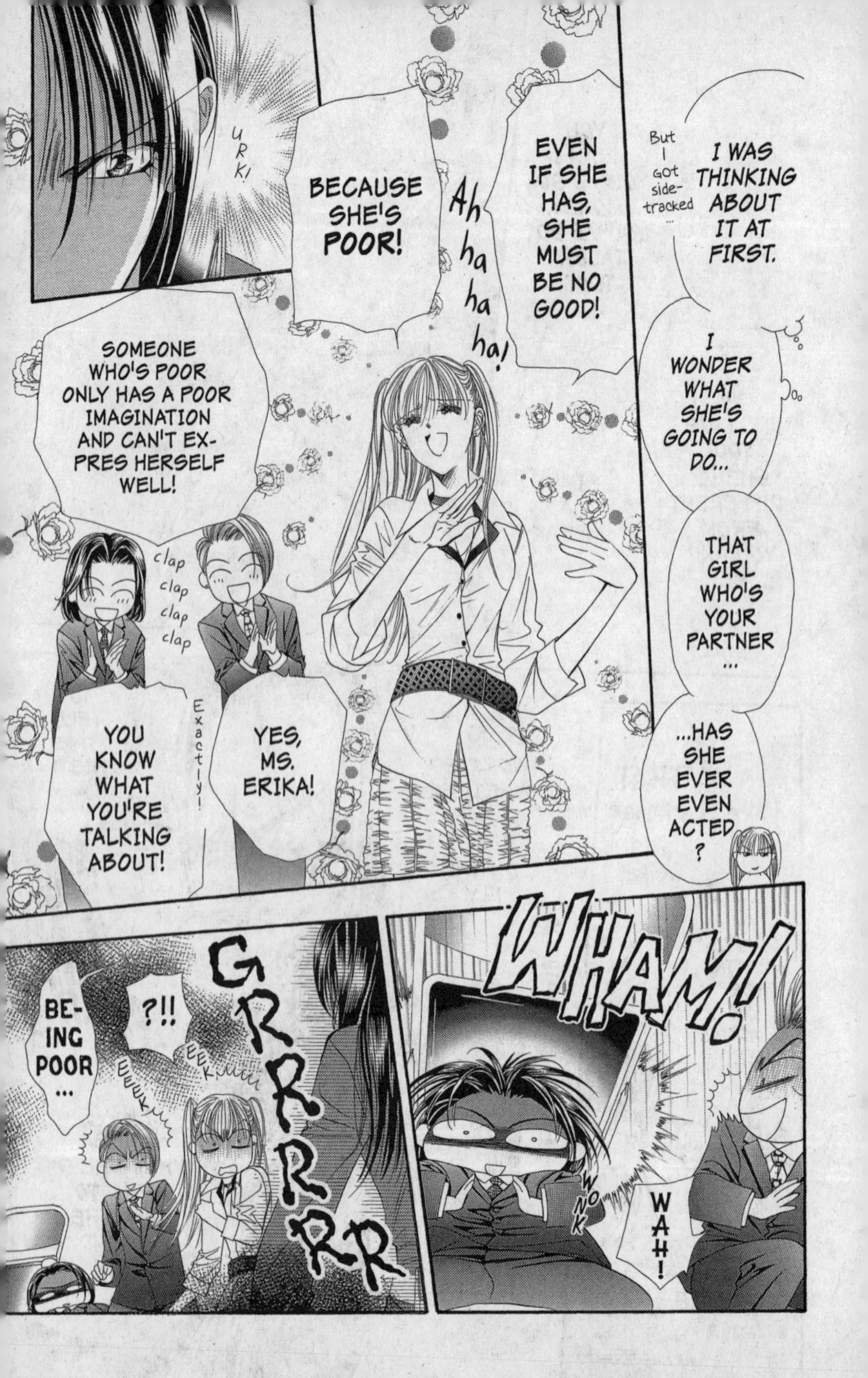
I WAS THINKING ABOUT IT AT FIRST.
But I got side-tracked...
I WONDER WHAT SHE'S GOING TO DO...
THAT GIRL WHO'S YOUR PARTNER...
...HAS SHE EVER EVEN ACTED?
EVEN IF SHE HAS, SHE MUST BE NO GOOD!
BECAUSE SHE'S POOR!
URK!
Ah ha ha ha!
SOMEONE WHO'S POOR ONLY HAS A POOR IMAGINATION AND CAN'T EX-PRES HERSELF WELL!
clap clap clap clap
YES, MS. ERIKA!
Exactly!
YOU KNOW WHAT YOU'RE TALKING ABOUT!
WHAM!
WAH!
WONK
GRRRRRR
?!!
BE-ING POOR...
EEEK
EEEK

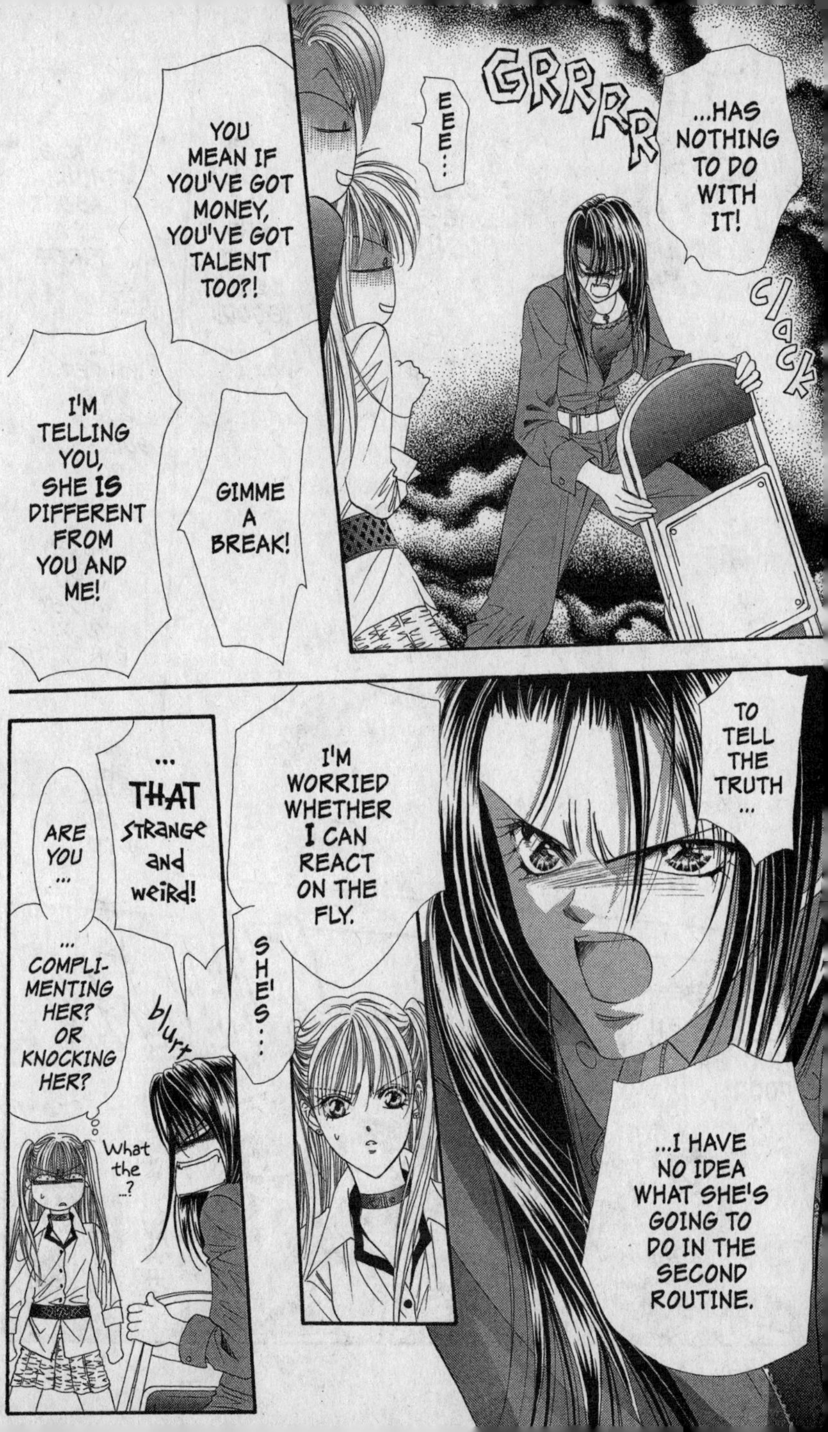
GRRRR
...HAS NOTHING TO DO WITH IT!
clack
EEE...
YOU MEAN IF YOU'VE GOT MONEY, YOU'VE GOT TALENT TOO?!
GIMME A BREAK!
I'M TELLING YOU, SHE IS DIFFERENT FROM YOU AND ME!
TO TELL THE TRUTH...
...I HAVE NO IDEA WHAT SHE'S GOING TO DO IN THE SECOND ROUTINE.
I'M WORRIED WHETHER I CAN REACT ON THE FLY.
SHE'S...
...THAT strange and weird!
blurt
What the ...?
ARE YOU ...
... COMPLIMENTING HER? OR KNOCKING HER?

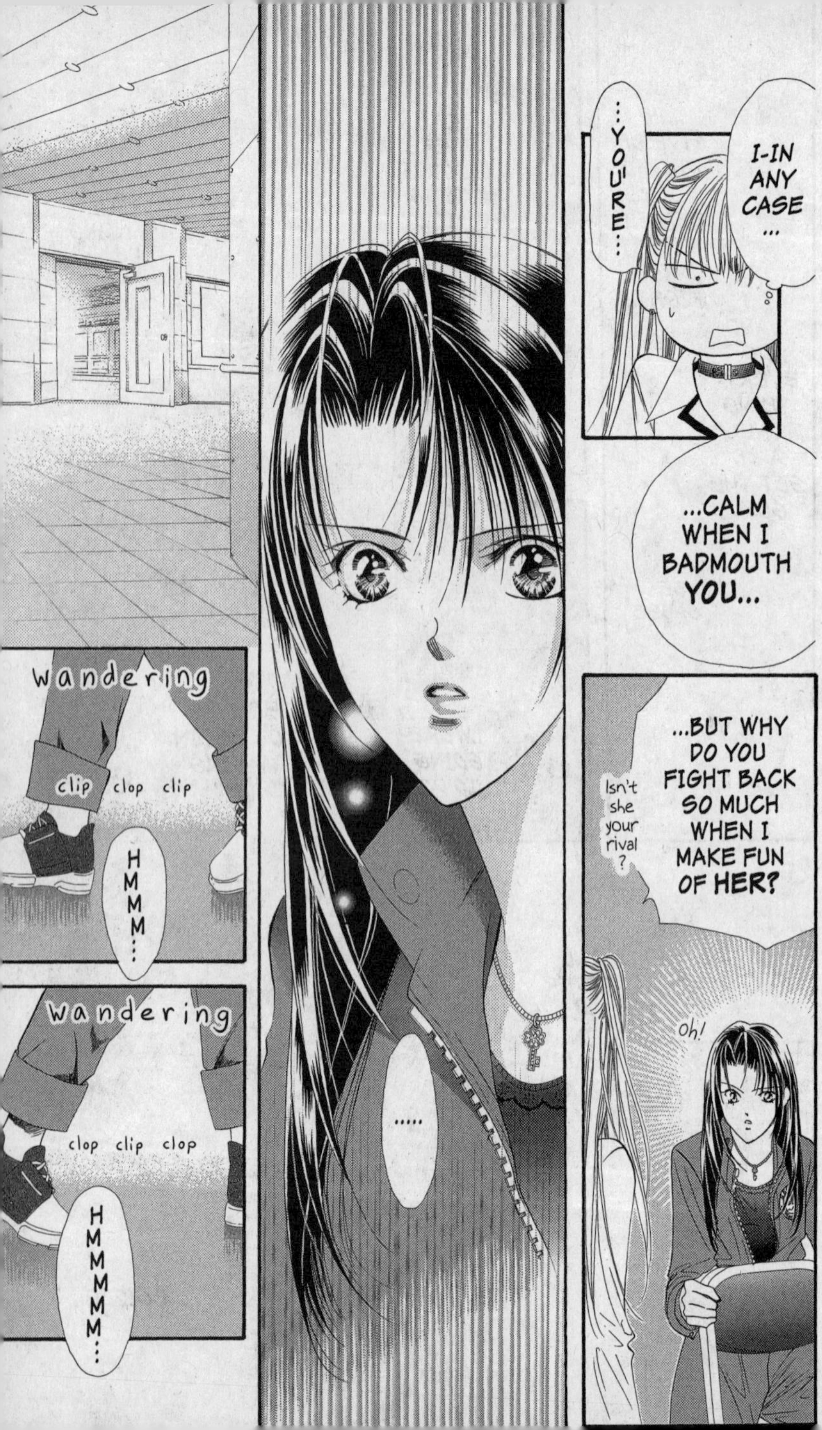
I-IN ANY CASE...
...YOU'RE...
...CALM WHEN I BADMOUTH YOU...
...BUT WHY DO YOU FIGHT BACK SO MUCH WHEN I MAKE FUN OF HER?
Isn't she your rival?
Oh!
.....
wandering
clip clop clip
HMMM...
wandering
clop clip clop
HMMMMM...

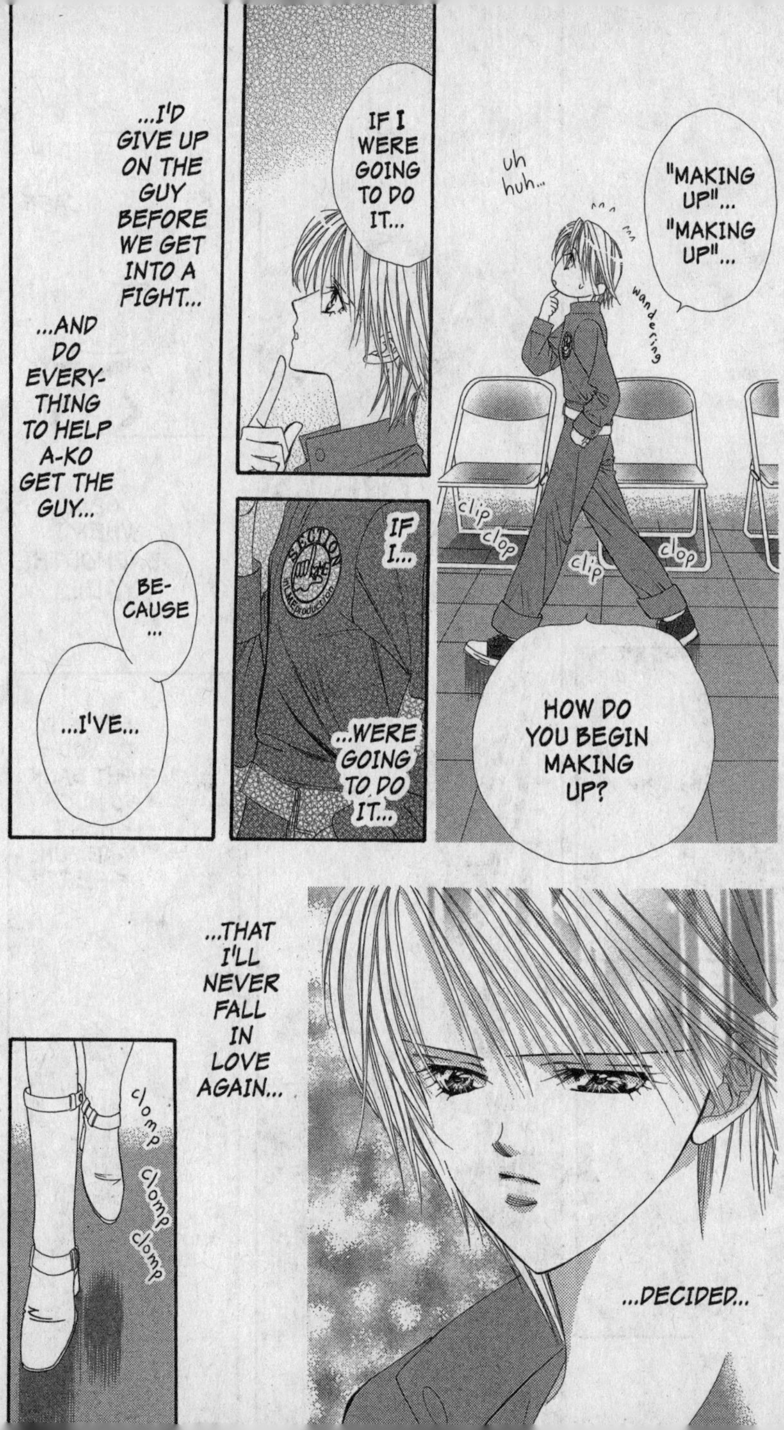
uh huh...
"MAKING UP"... "MAKING UP"...
wandering
clip clop clip clop
HOW DO YOU BEGIN MAKING UP?
IF I WERE GOING TO DO IT...
IF I...
...WERE GOING TO DO IT...
...I'D GIVE UP ON THE GUY BEFORE WE GET INTO A FIGHT...
...AND DO EVERY-THING TO HELP A-KO GET THE GUY...
BE-CAUSE...
...I'VE...
...DECIDED...
...THAT I'LL NEVER FALL IN LOVE AGAIN...
clomp clomp clomp

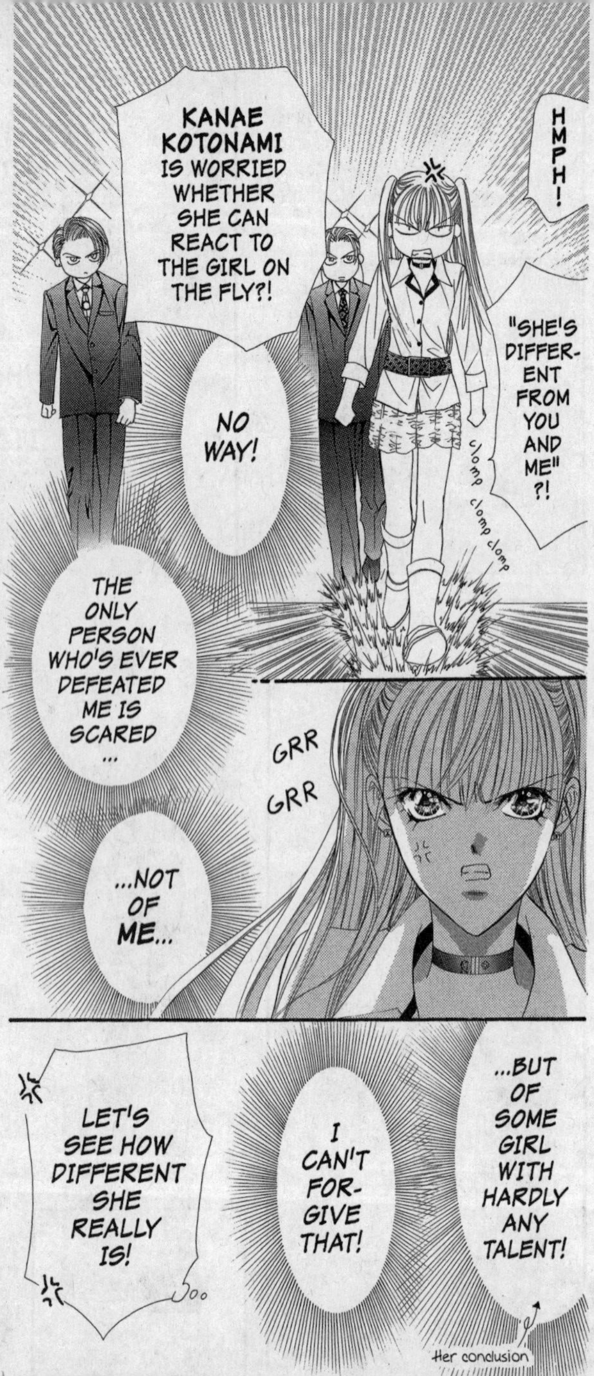
HMPH!
KANAE KOTONAMI IS WORRIED WHETHER SHE CAN REACT TO THE GIRL ON THE FLY?!
"SHE'S DIFFERENT FROM YOU AND ME"?!
NO WAY!
clomp clomp clomp clomp
THE ONLY PERSON WHO'S EVER DEFEATED ME IS SCARED ...
GRR
GRR
...NOT OF ME...
...BUT OF SOME GIRL WITH HARDLY ANY TALENT!
I CAN'T FORGIVE THAT!
LET'S SEE HOW DIFFERENT SHE REALLY IS!
Her conclusion

Curara

I don't drink soda much, so I don't know much about them...I didn't even know that plastic bottles containing soda and non-soda drinks are shaped differently...(the body and the bottom of the bottle are different) In the story, when Kyoko realizes that Curara is a soda, my assistant noticed "What, Curara was a soda?!"

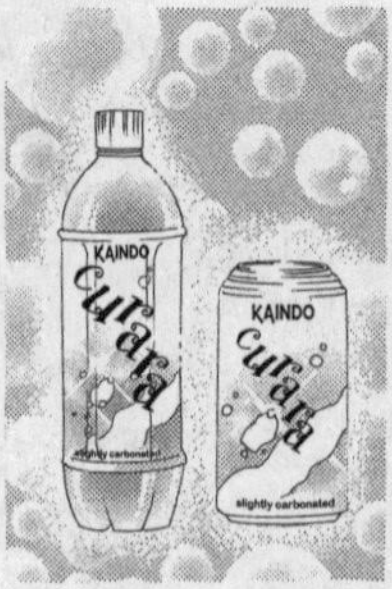
KAINDO
Curara
slightly carbonated
KAINDO
Curara
slightly carbonated

and told me about the difference in the bottom of the container eh heh heh. So the Curara that first appeared in the magazine is not a soda container...Because I really didn't know... And I thought "soft drinks" were soda... Because the dictionary said they were cold drinks containing carbonic acid for example...I thought they were called cooling drinks because you feel refreshed after you drink them... I was really convinced... But on sodas, it says "carbonated drink" and drinks labeled "soft drinks" are...

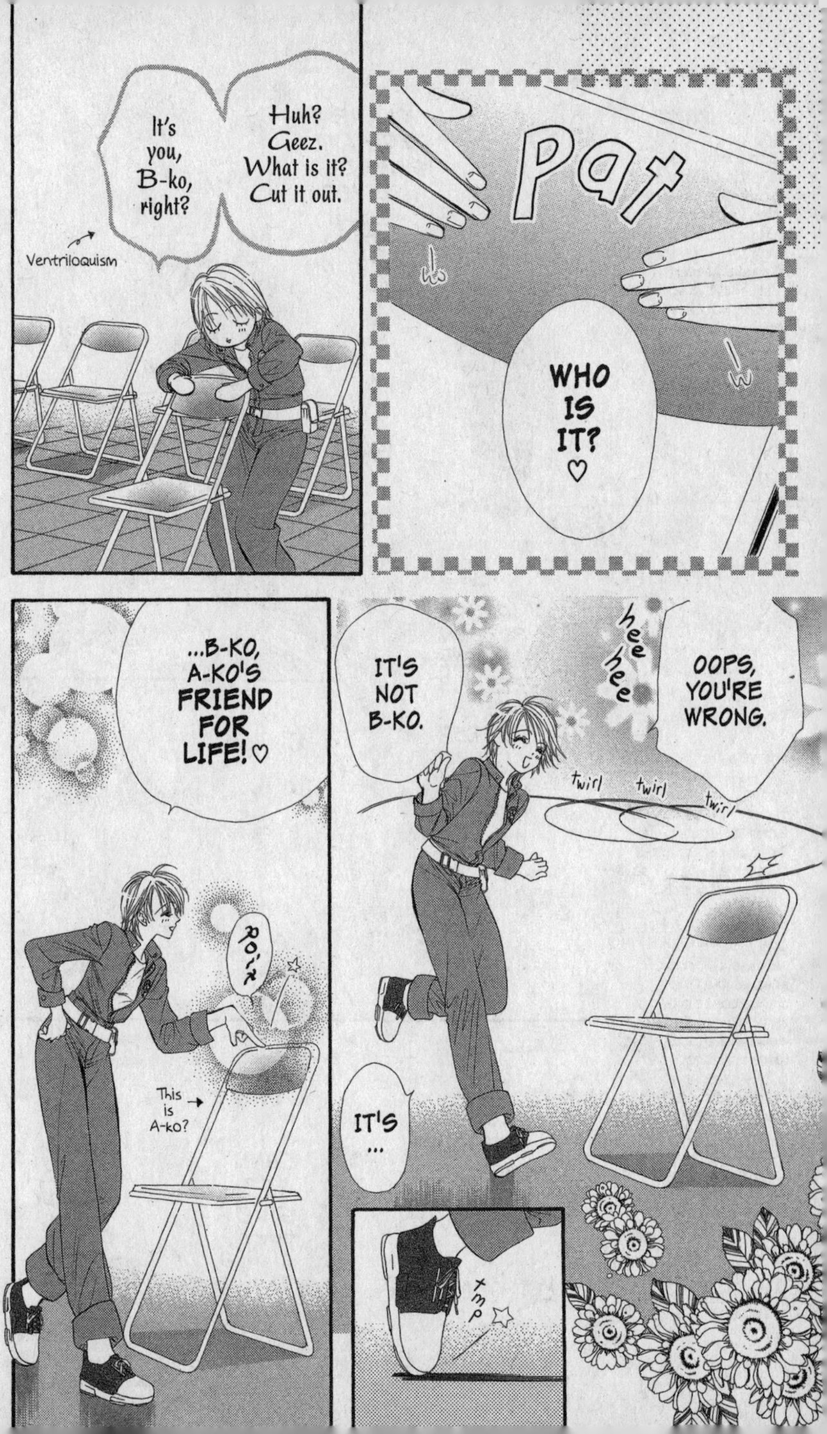

Pat
WHO IS IT? ♡
Huh? Geez. What is it? Cut it out.
It's you, B-ko, right?
Ventriloquism
hee hee
OOPS, YOU'RE WRONG.
IT'S NOT B-KO.
twirl twirl twirl
IT'S ...
tmp
...B-KO, A-KO'S FRIEND FOR LIFE! ♡
This is A-ko?

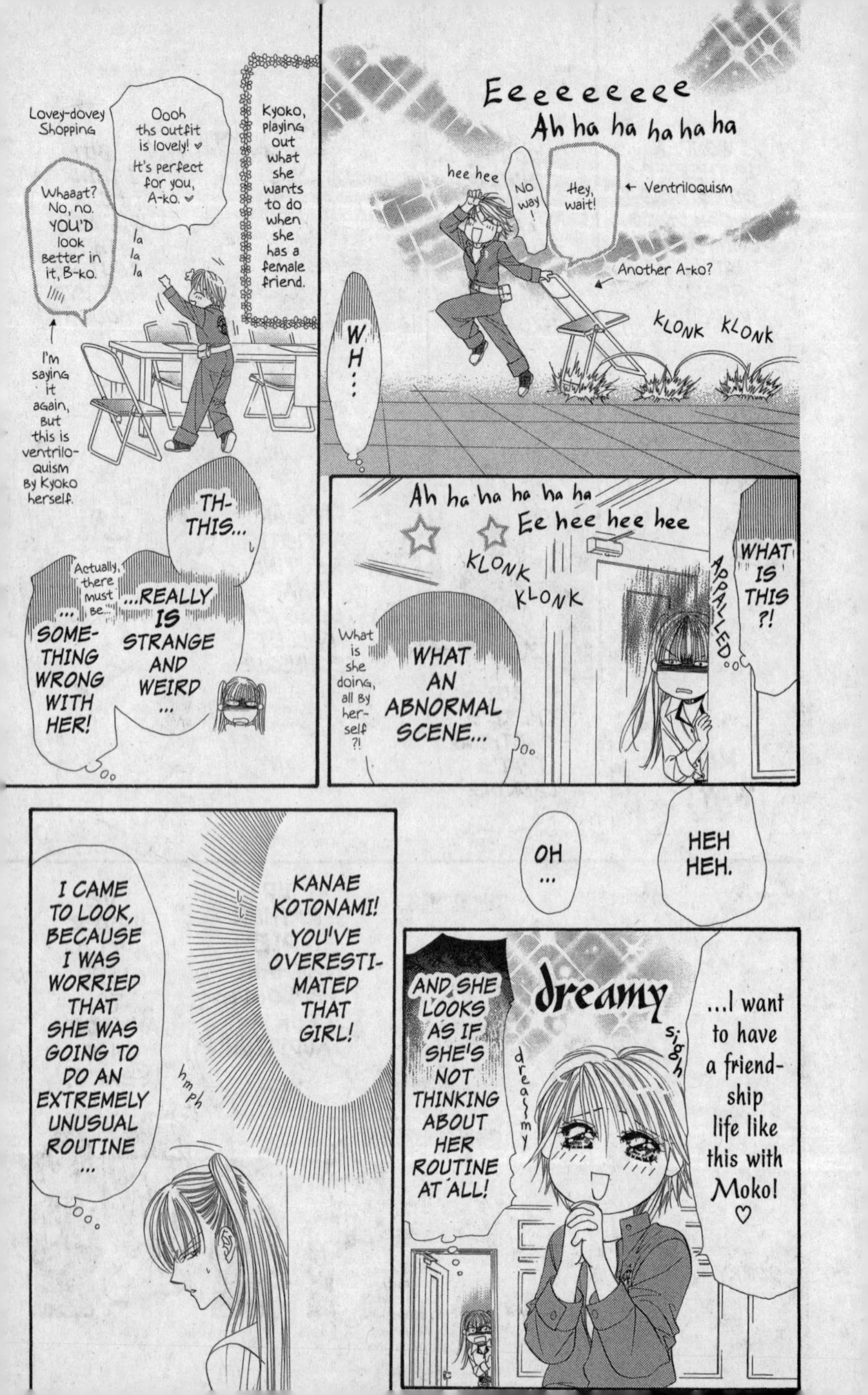

Eeeeeeee
Ah ha ha ha ha ha
Hey, wait!
← Ventriloquism
No way!
hee hee
Another A-ko?
KLONK KLONK
WH...
Ah ha ha ha ha ha
Ee hee hee hee
KLONK KLONK
WHAT IS THIS?!
APPALLED
What is she doing, all by her-self?!
WHAT AN ABNORMAL SCENE...
Kyoko, playing out what she wants to do when she has a female friend.
Oooh ths outfit is lovely! ♥
It's perfect for you, A-ko. ♥
Lovey-dovey Shopping
la la la
Whaaat? No, no. YOU'D look better in it, B-ko.
I'm saying it again, but this is ventrilo-quism by Kyoko herself.
TH-THIS...
...REALLY IS STRANGE AND WEIRD...
Actually, there must be...
...SOME-THING WRONG WITH HER!
HEH HEH.
OH...
...I want to have a friend-ship life like this with Moko! ♡
sigh
dreamy
dreamy
AND SHE LOOKS AS IF SHE'S NOT THINKING ABOUT HER ROUTINE AT ALL!
KANAE KOTONAMI! YOU'VE OVERESTI-MATED THAT GIRL!
I CAME TO LOOK, BECAUSE I WAS WORRIED THAT SHE WAS GOING TO DO AN EXTREMELY UNUSUAL ROUTINE...
hmph

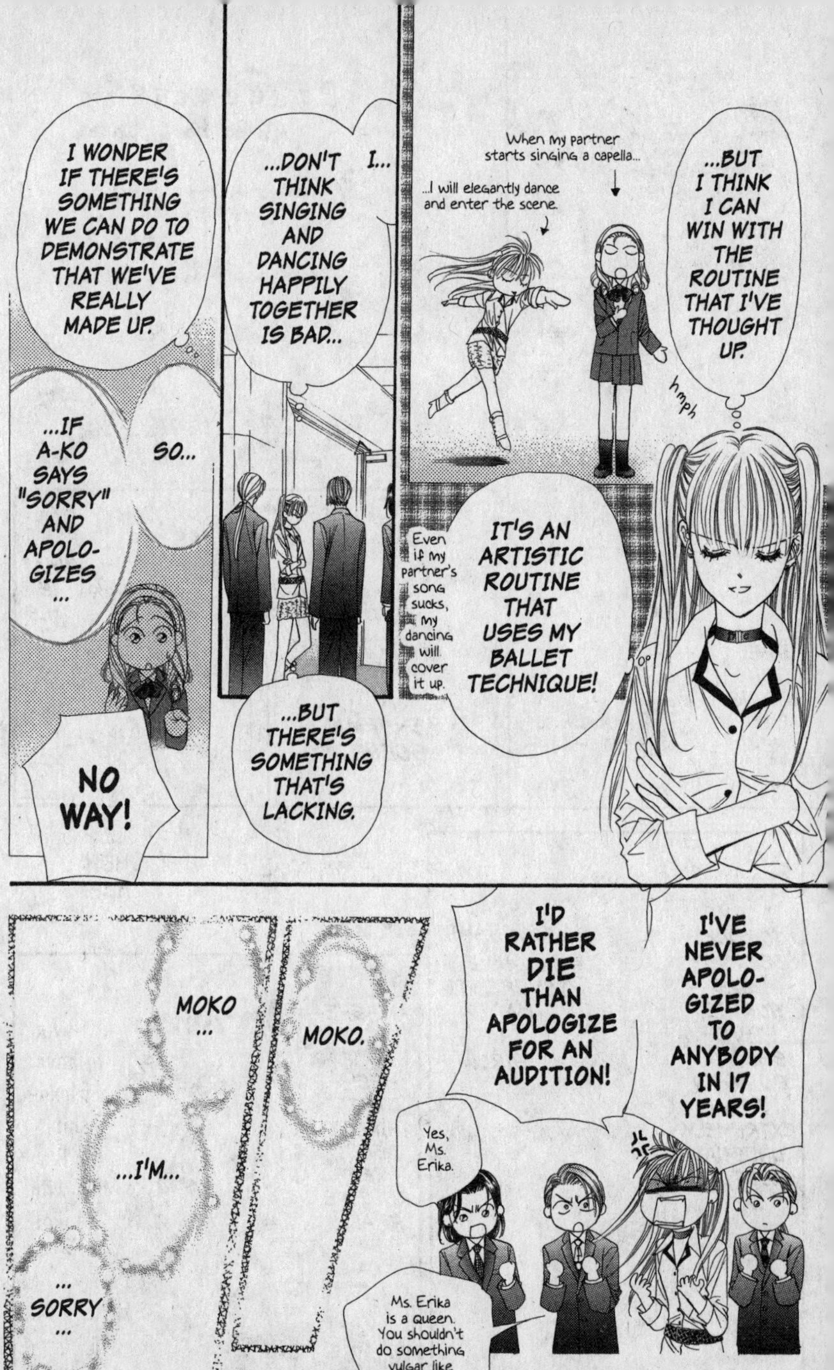

...BUT I THINK I CAN WIN WITH THE ROUTINE THAT I'VE THOUGHT UP.
When my partner starts singing a capella...
...I will elegantly dance and enter the scene.
hmph
IT'S AN ARTISTIC ROUTINE THAT USES MY BALLET TECHNIQUE!
Even if my partner's song sucks, my dancing will cover it up.
I...
...DON'T THINK SINGING AND DANCING HAPPILY TOGETHER IS BAD...
...BUT THERE'S SOMETHING THAT'S LACKING.
I WONDER IF THERE'S SOMETHING WE CAN DO TO DEMONSTRATE THAT WE'VE REALLY MADE UP.
SO...
...IF A-KO SAYS "SORRY" AND APOLOGIZES...
NO WAY!
I'VE NEVER APOLOGIZED TO ANYBODY IN 17 YEARS!
I'D RATHER DIE THAN APOLOGIZE FOR AN AUDITION!
Yes, Ms. Erika.
Ms. Erika is a Queen. You shouldn't do something vulgar like apologizing!
MOKO.
MOKO...
...I'M...
...SORRY...

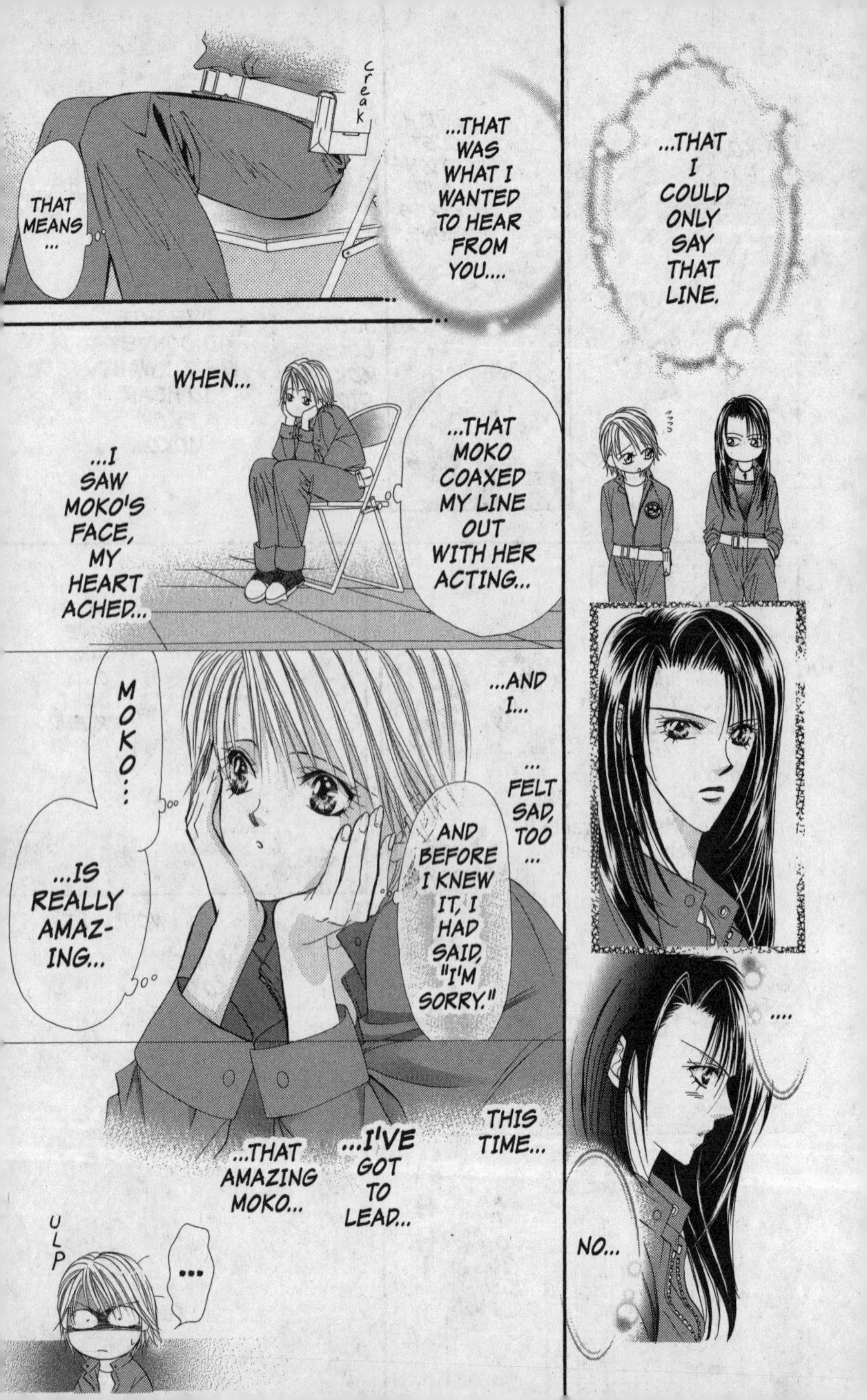
...THAT I COULD ONLY SAY THAT LINE.
....
NO...
...THAT WAS WHAT I WANTED TO HEAR FROM YOU....
Creak
THAT MEANS...
...THAT MOKO COAXED MY LINE OUT WITH HER ACTING...
WHEN...
...I SAW MOKO'S FACE, MY HEART ACHED...
...AND I...
...FELT SAD, TOO...
AND BEFORE I KNEW IT, I HAD SAID, "I'M SORRY."
MOKO...
...IS REALLY AMAZING...
THIS TIME...
...I'VE GOT TO LEAD...
...THAT AMAZING MOKO...
...
ULP

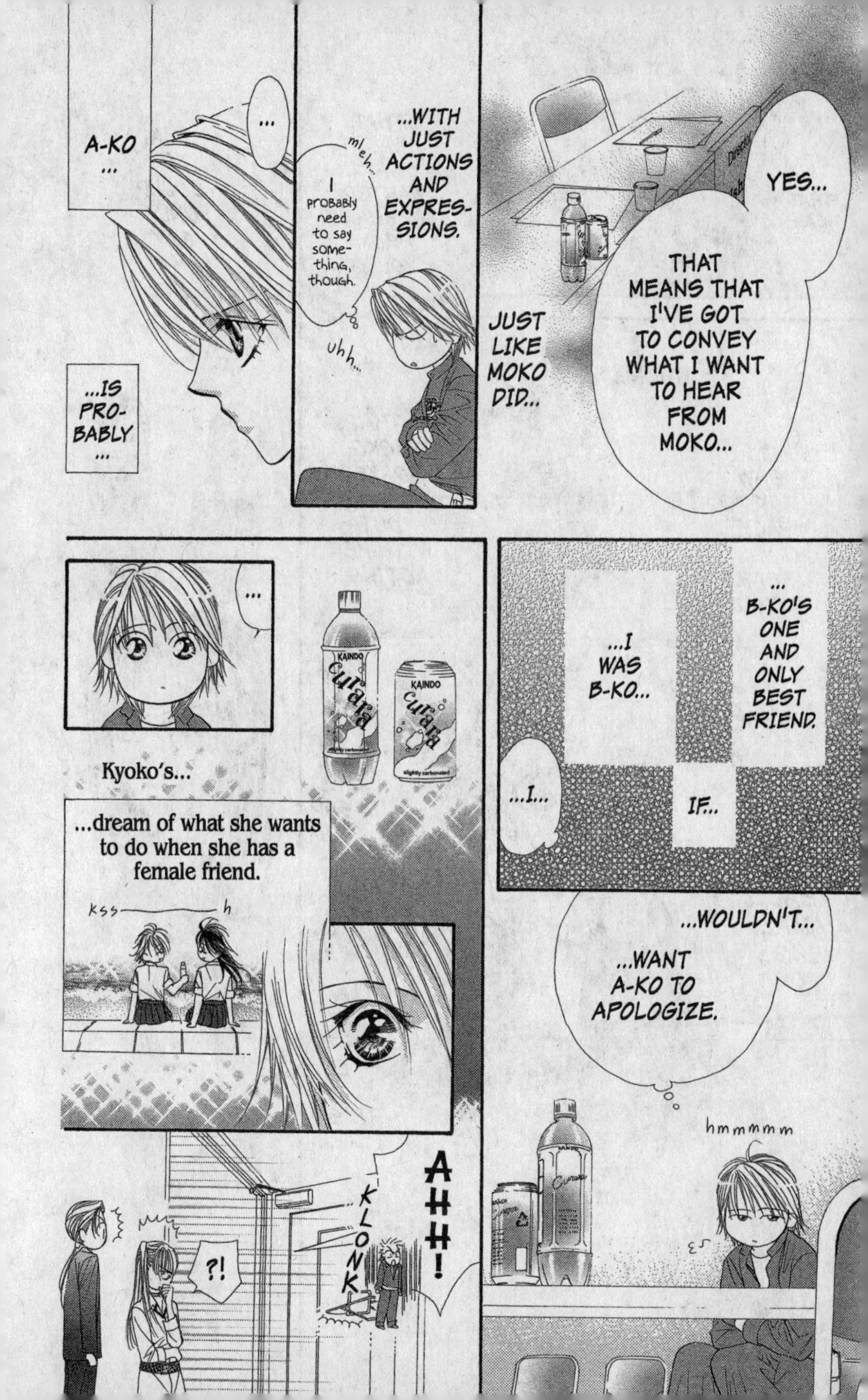
YES...
THAT MEANS THAT I'VE GOT TO CONVEY WHAT I WANT TO HEAR FROM MOKO...
JUST LIKE MOKO DID...
...WITH JUST ACTIONS AND EXPRESSIONS.
mleh...
I probably need to say something, though.
uhh...
...
A-KO ...
...IS PROBABLY ...
... B-KO'S ONE AND ONLY BEST FRIEND.
...I WAS B-KO...
IF..
...I...
...
KAINDO
Curara
slightly carbonated
Kyoko's...
...dream of what she wants to do when she has a female friend.
kss——h
...WOULDN'T...
...WANT A-KO TO APOLOGIZE.
hmmmmm
AHH!
KLONK
?!

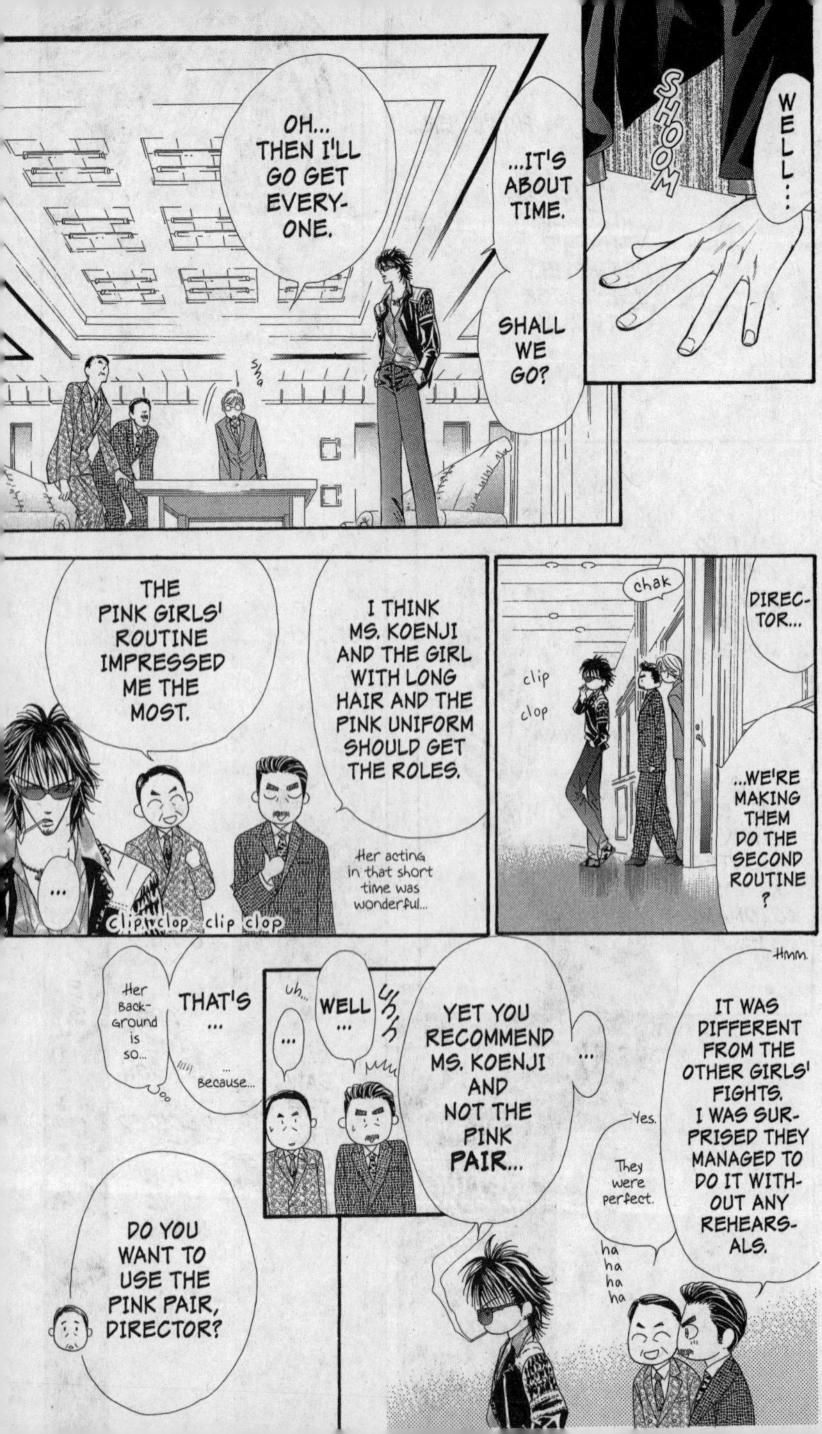
WELL...
SHOOM
...IT'S ABOUT TIME.
SHALL WE GO?
OH... THEN I'LL GO GET EVERYONE.
sha
chak
DIRECTOR...
...WE'RE MAKING THEM DO THE SECOND ROUTINE?
clip clop
I THINK MS. KOENJI AND THE GIRL WITH LONG HAIR AND THE PINK UNIFORM SHOULD GET THE ROLES.
Her acting in that short time was wonderful...
THE PINK GIRLS' ROUTINE IMPRESSED ME THE MOST.
...
clip clop clip clop
Hmm.
IT WAS DIFFERENT FROM THE OTHER GIRLS' FIGHTS. I WAS SURPRISED THEY MANAGED TO DO IT WITHOUT ANY REHEARSALS.
Yes.
They were perfect.
ha ha ha ha
YET YOU RECOMMEND MS. KOENJI AND NOT THE PINK PAIR...
...
WELL...
uhh
uh...
...
THAT'S...
... Because...
Her Back-Ground is so...
DO YOU WANT TO USE THE PINK PAIR, DIRECTOR?

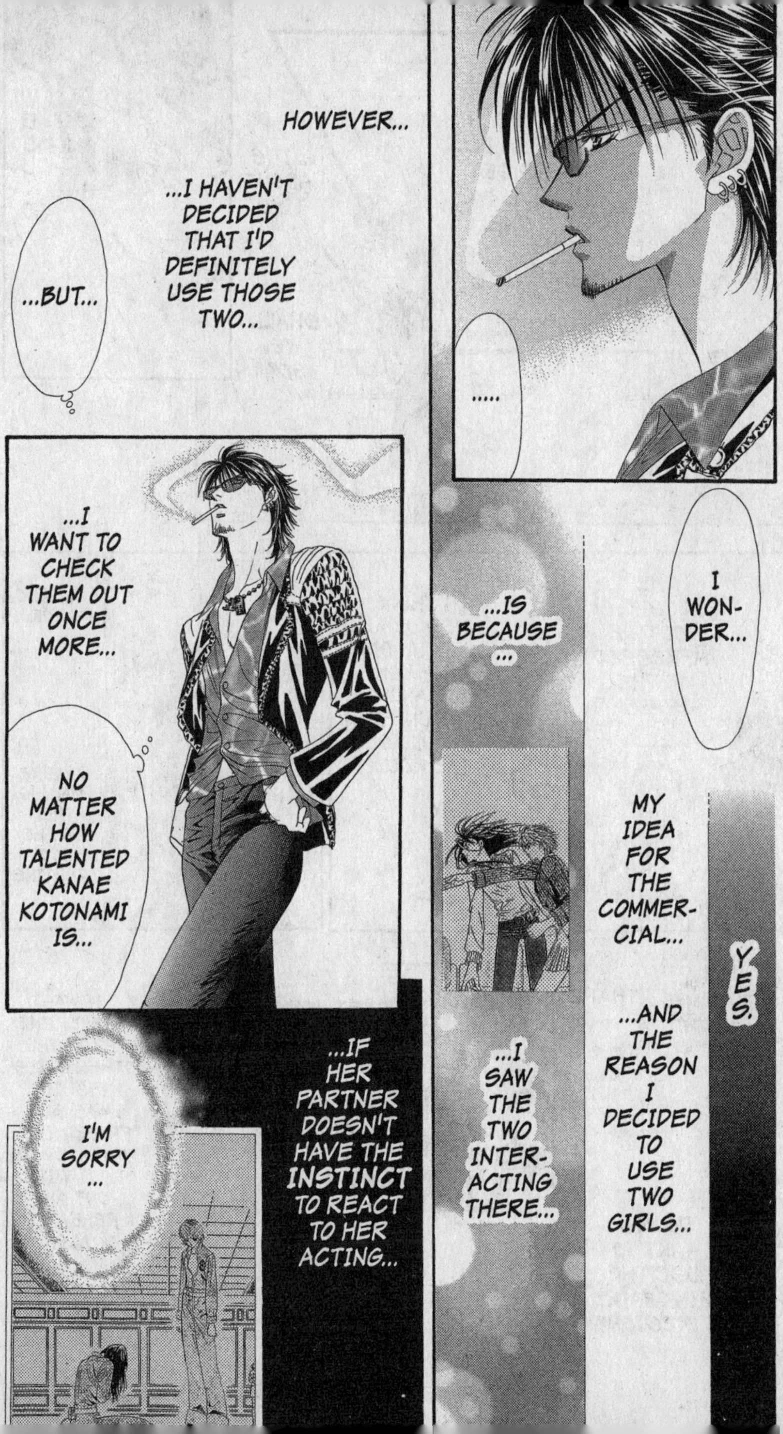
.....
HOWEVER...
...I HAVEN'T DECIDED THAT I'D DEFINITELY USE THOSE TWO...
...BUT...
I WONDER...
MY IDEA FOR THE COMMERCIAL...
YES.
...AND THE REASON I DECIDED TO USE TWO GIRLS...
...IS BECAUSE...
...I SAW THE TWO INTERACTING THERE...
...I WANT TO CHECK THEM OUT ONCE MORE...
NO MATTER HOW TALENTED KANAE KOTONAMI IS...
...IF HER PARTNER DOESN'T HAVE THE INSTINCT TO REACT TO HER ACTING...
I'M SORRY...

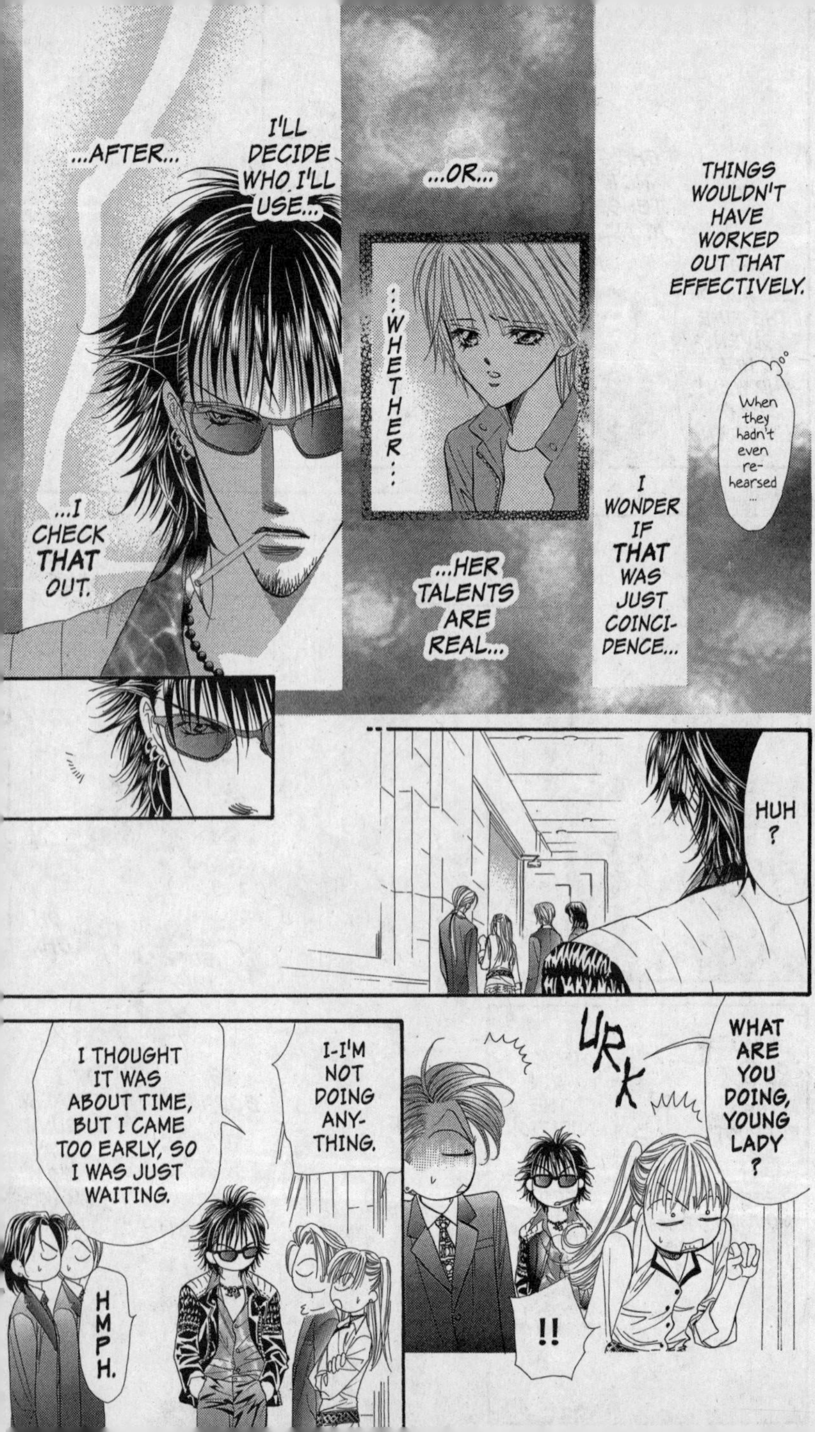
THINGS WOULDN'T HAVE WORKED OUT THAT EFFECTIVELY.
When they hadn't even re-hearsed ...
I WONDER IF THAT WAS JUST COINCIDENCE...
...OR...
...WHETHER...
...HER TALENTS ARE REAL...
I'LL DECIDE WHO I'LL USE...
...AFTER...
...I CHECK THAT OUT.
HUH?
WHAT ARE YOU DOING, YOUNG LADY?
URK
!!
I-I'M NOT DOING ANYTHING.
I THOUGHT IT WAS ABOUT TIME, BUT I CAME TOO EARLY, SO I WAS JUST WAITING.
HMPH.

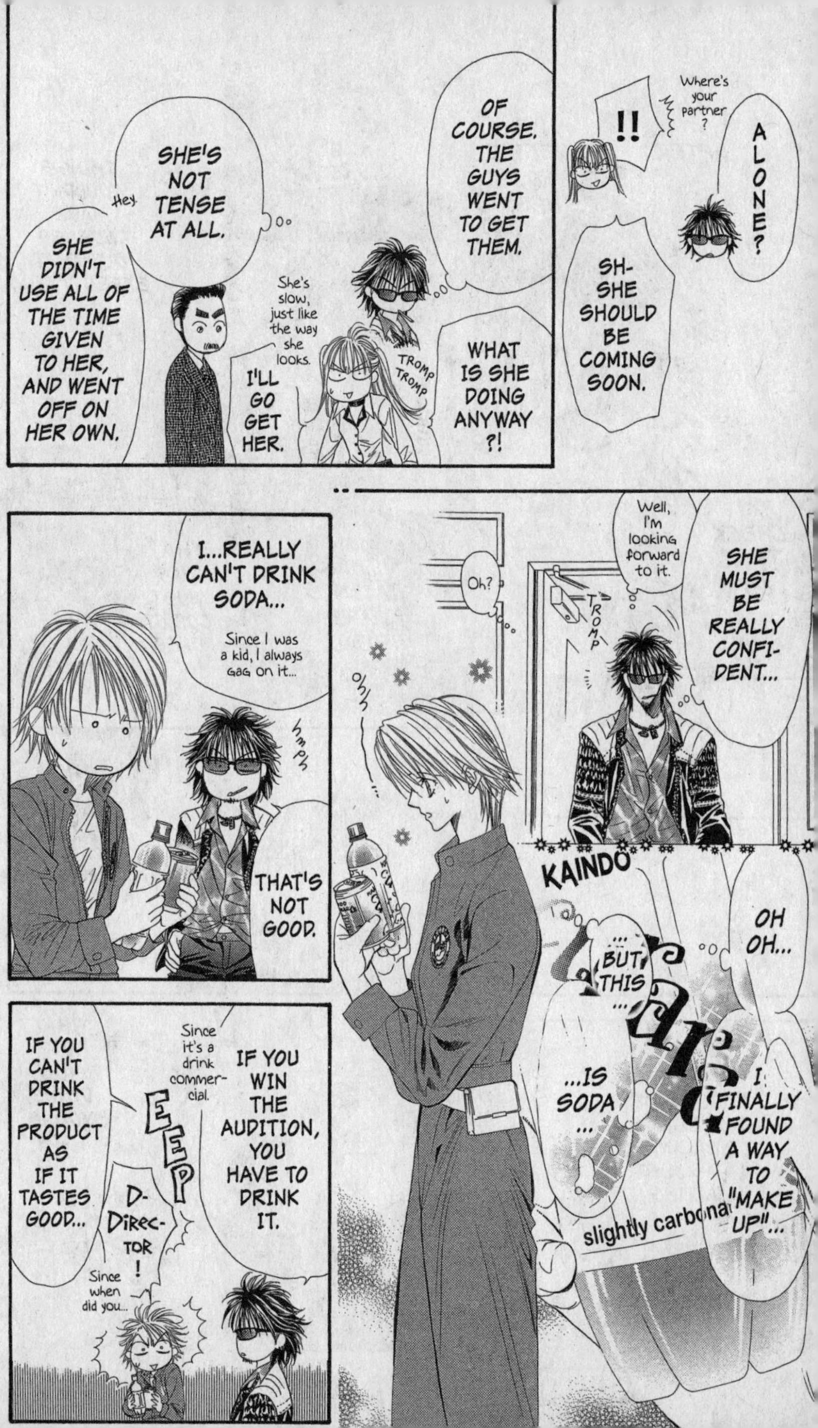
Where's your partner?
ALONE?
!!
SH-SHE SHOULD BE COMING SOON.
OF COURSE. THE GUYS WENT TO GET THEM.
WHAT IS SHE DOING ANYWAY?!
TROMP TROMP
She's slow, just like the way she looks.
I'LL GO GET HER.
SHE'S NOT TENSE AT ALL.
Hey.
SHE DIDN'T USE ALL OF THE TIME GIVEN TO HER, AND WENT OFF ON HER OWN.
SHE MUST BE REALLY CONFIDENT...
Well, I'm looking forward to it.
TROMP
Oh?
ohh
OH OH...
I FINALLY FOUND A WAY TO "MAKE UP"...
KAINDO
...BUT THIS...
...IS SODA...
slightly carbona
I...REALLY CAN'T DRINK SODA...
Since I was a kid, I always gag on it...
hmph
THAT'S NOT GOOD.
IF YOU WIN THE AUDITION, YOU HAVE TO DRINK IT.
Since it's a drink commercial.
EEP
D-DIRECTOR!
IF YOU CAN'T DRINK THE PRODUCT AS IF IT TASTES GOOD...
Since when did you...

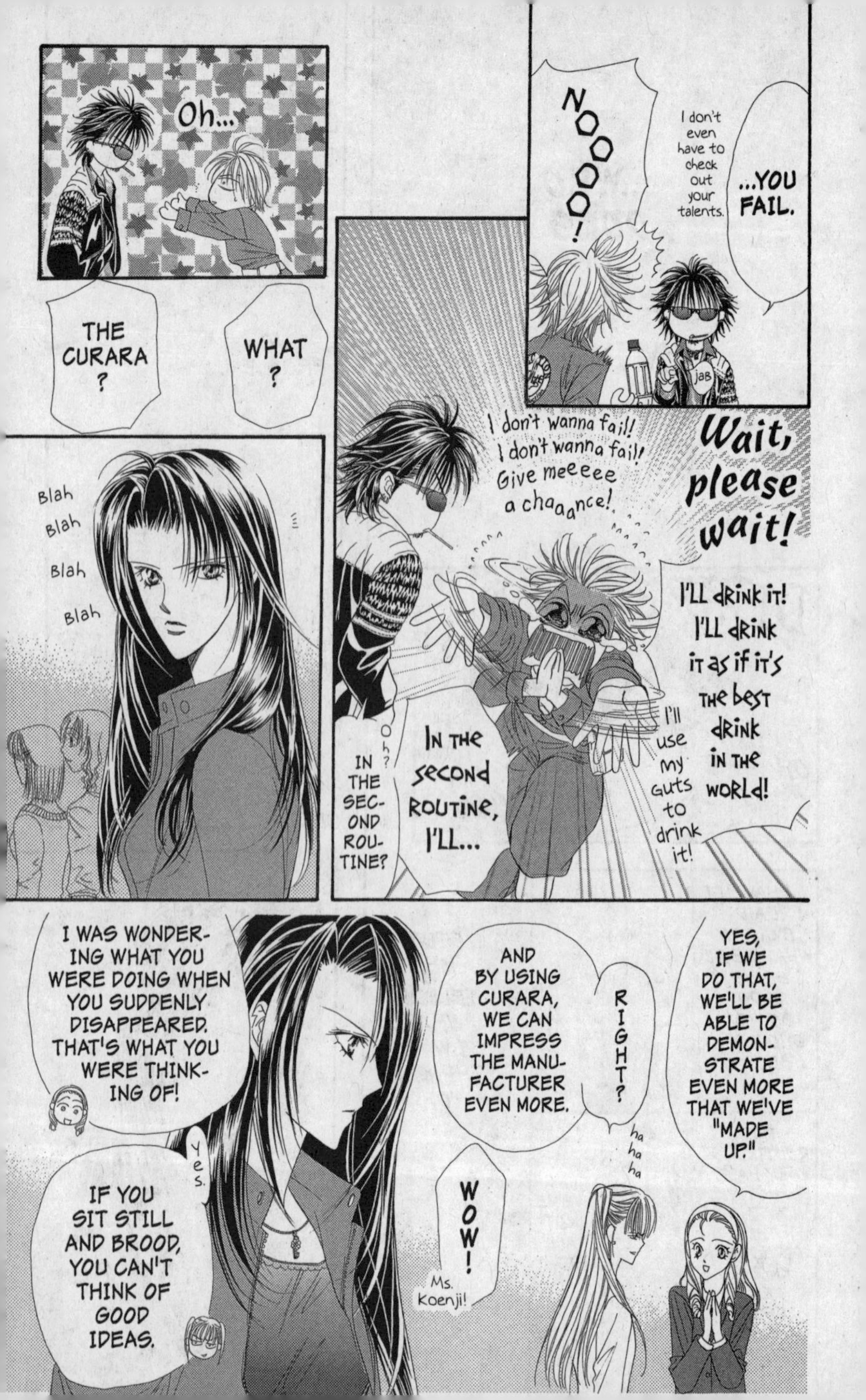
I don't even have to check out your talents.
...YOU FAIL.
NOOOO!
jab
Wait, please wait!
I'LL drink it! I'LL drink it as if it's the best drink in the world!
I don't wanna fail! I don't wanna fail! Give meeeee a chaaaance!
I'll use my guts to drink it!
In the second routine, I'll...
Oh?
IN THE SEC-OND ROU-TINE?
Oh...
WHAT?
THE CURARA?
Blah
Blah
Blah
Blah
YES, IF WE DO THAT, WE'LL BE ABLE TO DEMON-STRATE EVEN MORE THAT WE'VE "MADE UP."
RIGHT?
AND BY USING CURARA, WE CAN IMPRESS THE MANU-FACTURER EVEN MORE.
ha ha ha
WOW!
Ms. Koenji!
I WAS WONDER-ING WHAT YOU WERE DOING WHEN YOU SUDDENLY DISAPPEARED. THAT'S WHAT YOU WERE THINK-ING OF!
Yes.
IF YOU SIT STILL AND BROOD, YOU CAN'T THINK OF GOOD IDEAS.

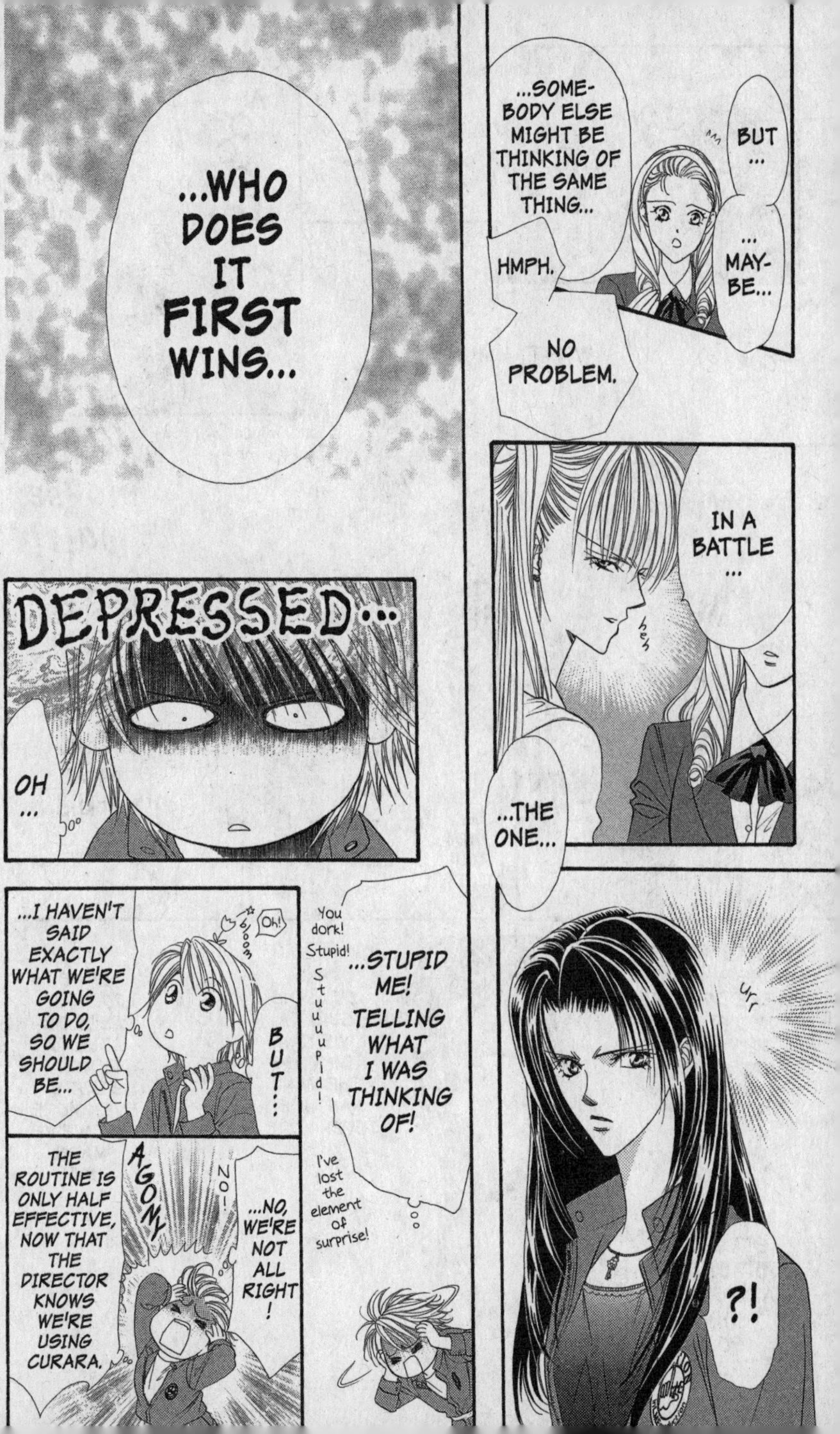
BUT ...
... MAY-BE...
...SOME-BODY ELSE MIGHT BE THINKING OF THE SAME THING...
HMPH.
NO PROBLEM.
IN A BATTLE ...
heh
...THE ONE...
...WHO DOES IT FIRST WINS...
urr
?!
DEPRESSED...
OH ...
Oh!
bloom
...I HAVEN'T SAID EXACTLY WHAT WE'RE GOING TO DO, SO WE SHOULD BE...
BUT...
AGONY
NO!
...NO, WE'RE NOT ALL RIGHT!
THE ROUTINE IS ONLY HALF EFFECTIVE, NOW THAT THE DIRECTOR KNOWS WE'RE USING CURARA.
...STUPID ME! TELLING WHAT I WAS THINKING OF!
You dork!
Stupid!
Stuuuupid!
I've lost the element of surprise!

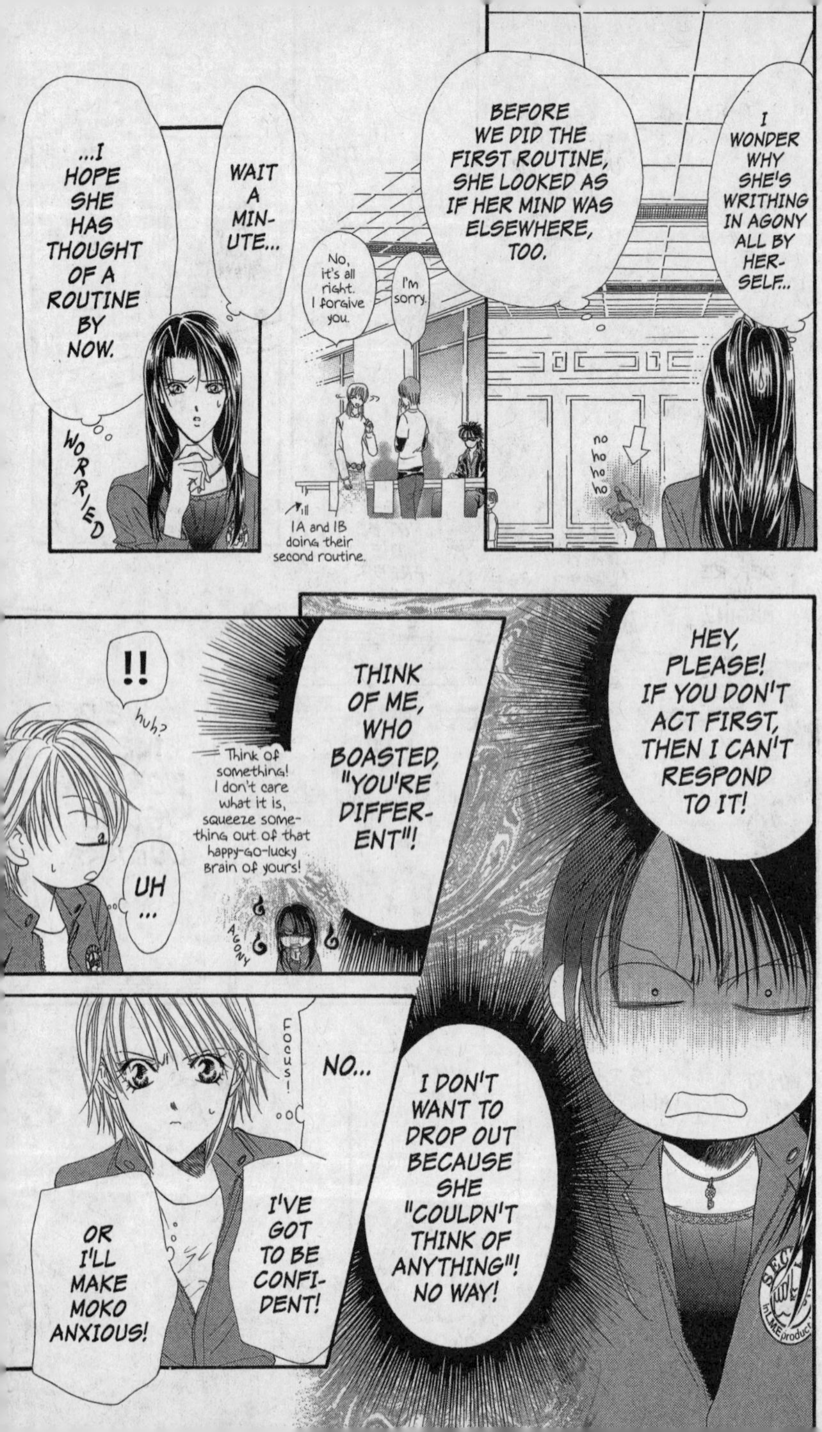
I WONDER WHY SHE'S WRITHING IN AGONY ALL BY HER-SELF...
BEFORE WE DID THE FIRST ROUTINE, SHE LOOKED AS IF HER MIND WAS ELSEWHERE, TOO.
no ho ho ho
I'm sorry.
No, it's all right. I forgive you.
ill
1A and 1B doing their second routine.
WAIT A MIN-UTE...
...I HOPE SHE HAS THOUGHT OF A ROUTINE BY NOW.
WORRIED
HEY, PLEASE! IF YOU DON'T ACT FIRST, THEN I CAN'T RESPOND TO IT!
I DON'T WANT TO DROP OUT BECAUSE SHE "COULDN'T THINK OF ANYTHING"! NO WAY!
THINK OF ME, WHO BOASTED, "YOU'RE DIFFER-ENT"!
Think of something! I don't care what it is, squeeze some-thing out of that happy-go-lucky brain of yours!
AGONY
!!
huh?
UH ...
NO...
Focus!
I'VE GOT TO BE CONFI-DENT!
OR I'LL MAKE MOKO ANXIOUS!

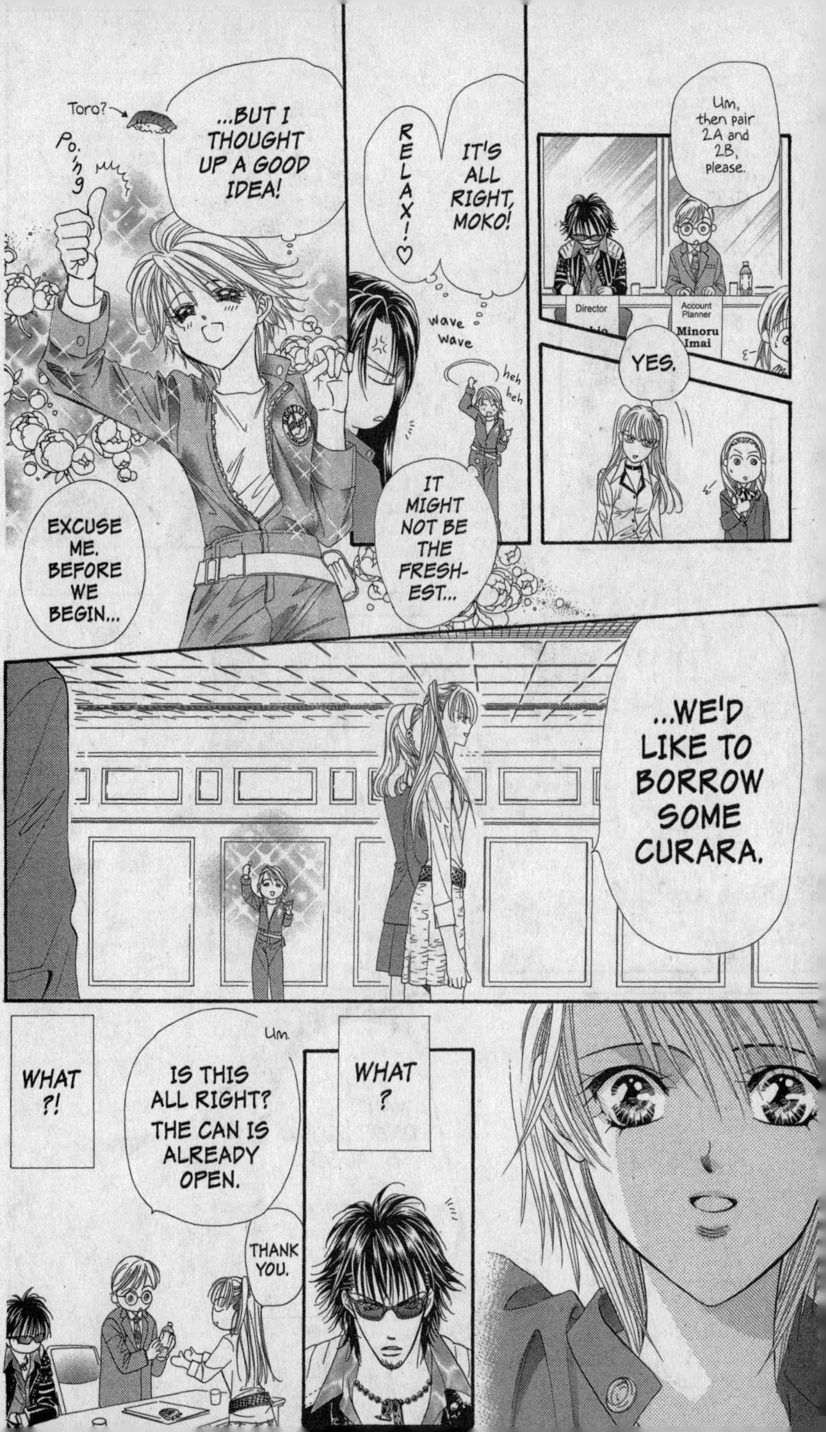
Um, then pair 2A and 2B, please.
Director
Account Planner
Minoru Imai
YES.
IT'S ALL RIGHT, MOKO!
RELAX! ♡
wave wave
heh heh
IT MIGHT NOT BE THE FRESHEST...
...BUT I THOUGHT UP A GOOD IDEA!
Toro?
Poing
EXCUSE ME. BEFORE WE BEGIN...
...WE'D LIKE TO BORROW SOME CURARA.
WHAT ?
WHAT ?!
Um.
IS THIS ALL RIGHT? THE CAN IS ALREADY OPEN.
THANK YOU.

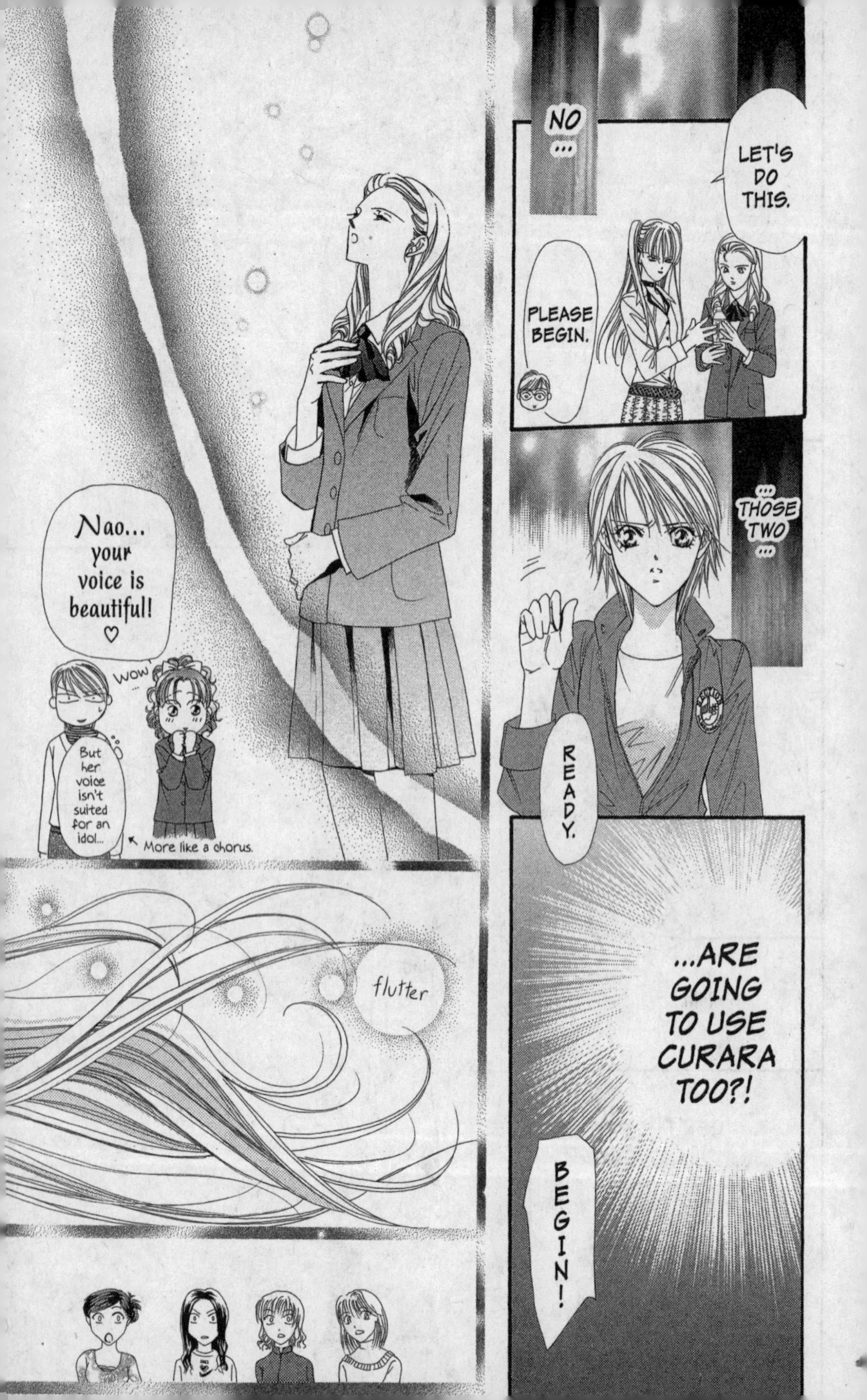
LET'S DO THIS.
NO...
PLEASE BEGIN.
...THOSE TWO...
READY.
...ARE GOING TO USE CURARA TOO?!
BEGIN!
Nao... your voice is beautiful! ♡
Wow...
But her voice isn't suited for an idol...
More like a chorus.
flutter

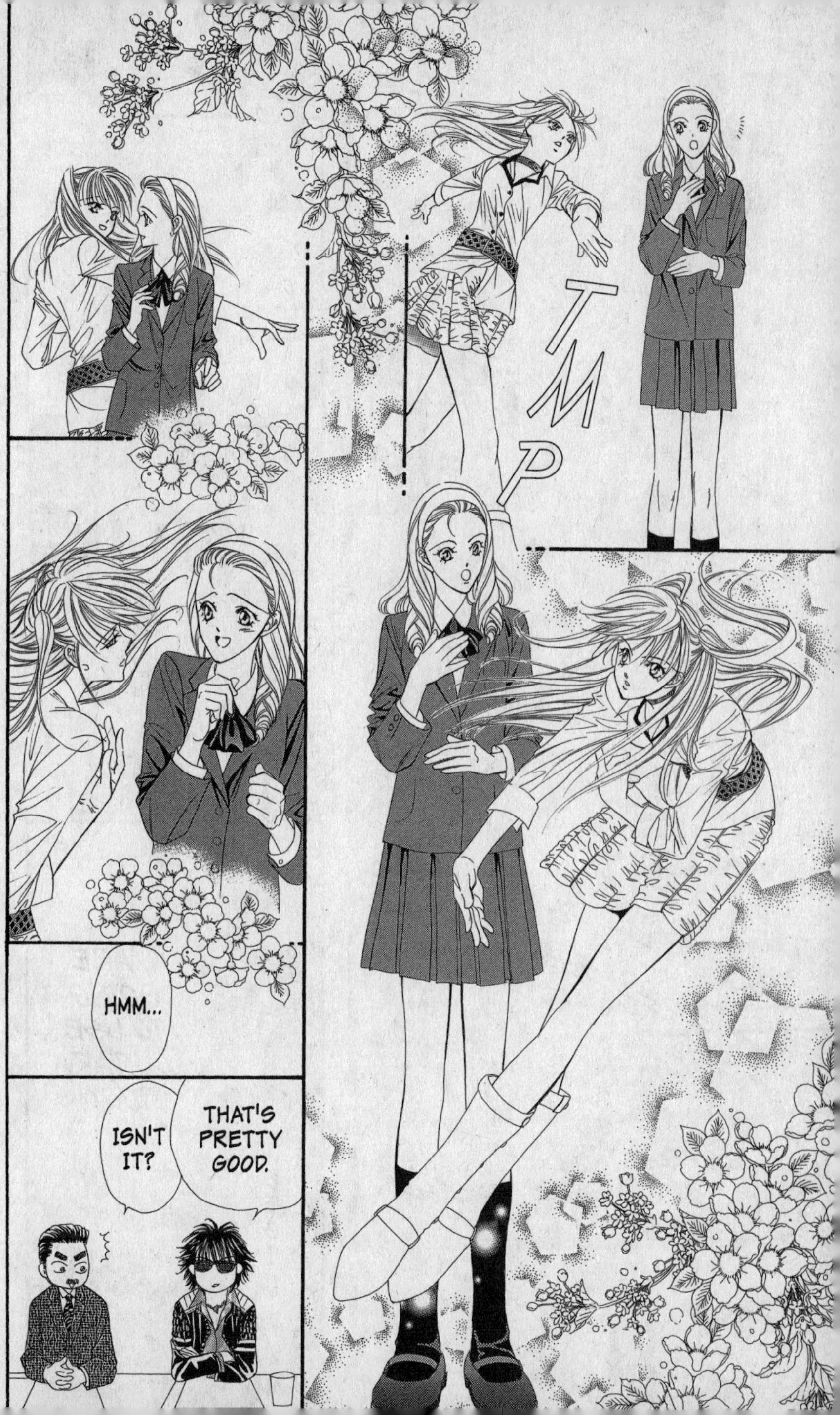
TMP
HMM...
THAT'S PRETTY GOOD.
ISN'T IT?

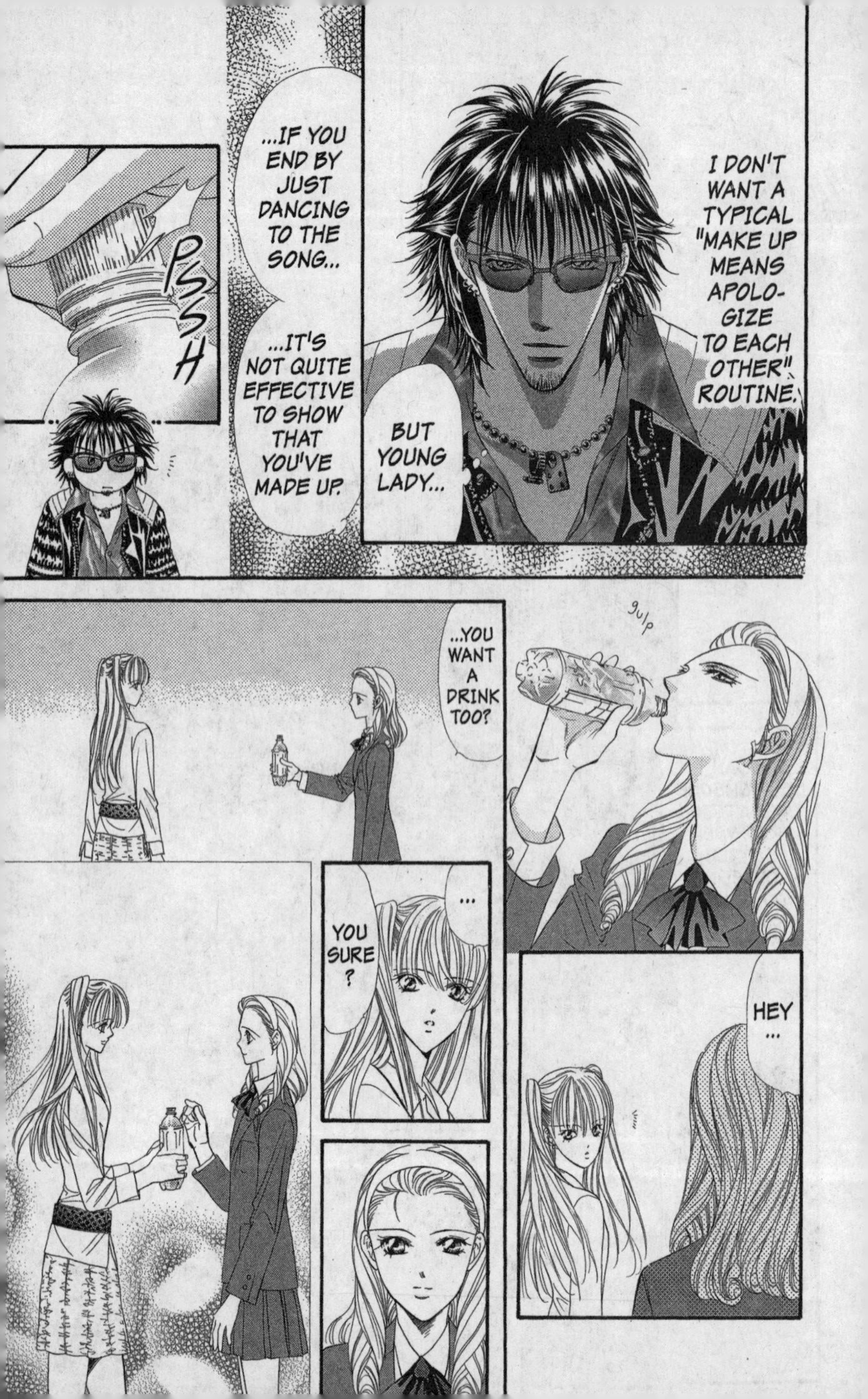
I DON'T WANT A TYPICAL "MAKE UP MEANS APOLOGIZE TO EACH OTHER" ROUTINE.
BUT YOUNG LADY...
...IF YOU END BY JUST DANCING TO THE SONG...
...IT'S NOT QUITE EFFECTIVE TO SHOW THAT YOU'VE MADE UP.
PSSH
gulp
...YOU WANT A DRINK TOO?
HEY ...
...
YOU SURE?

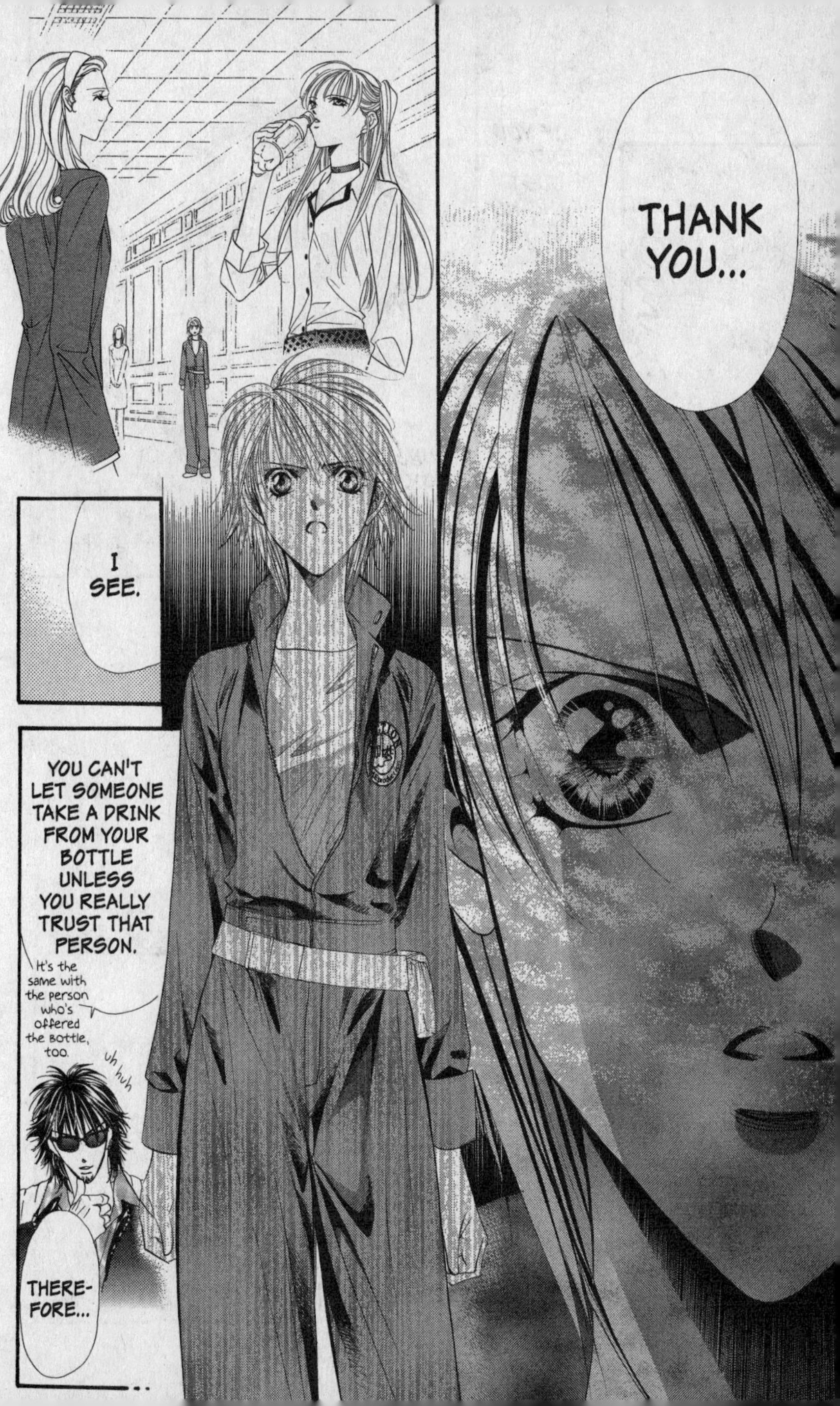
THANK YOU...
I SEE.
YOU CAN'T LET SOMEONE TAKE A DRINK FROM YOUR BOTTLE UNLESS YOU REALLY TRUST THAT PERSON.
It's the same with the person who's offered the bottle, too.
uh huh
THERE-FORE...

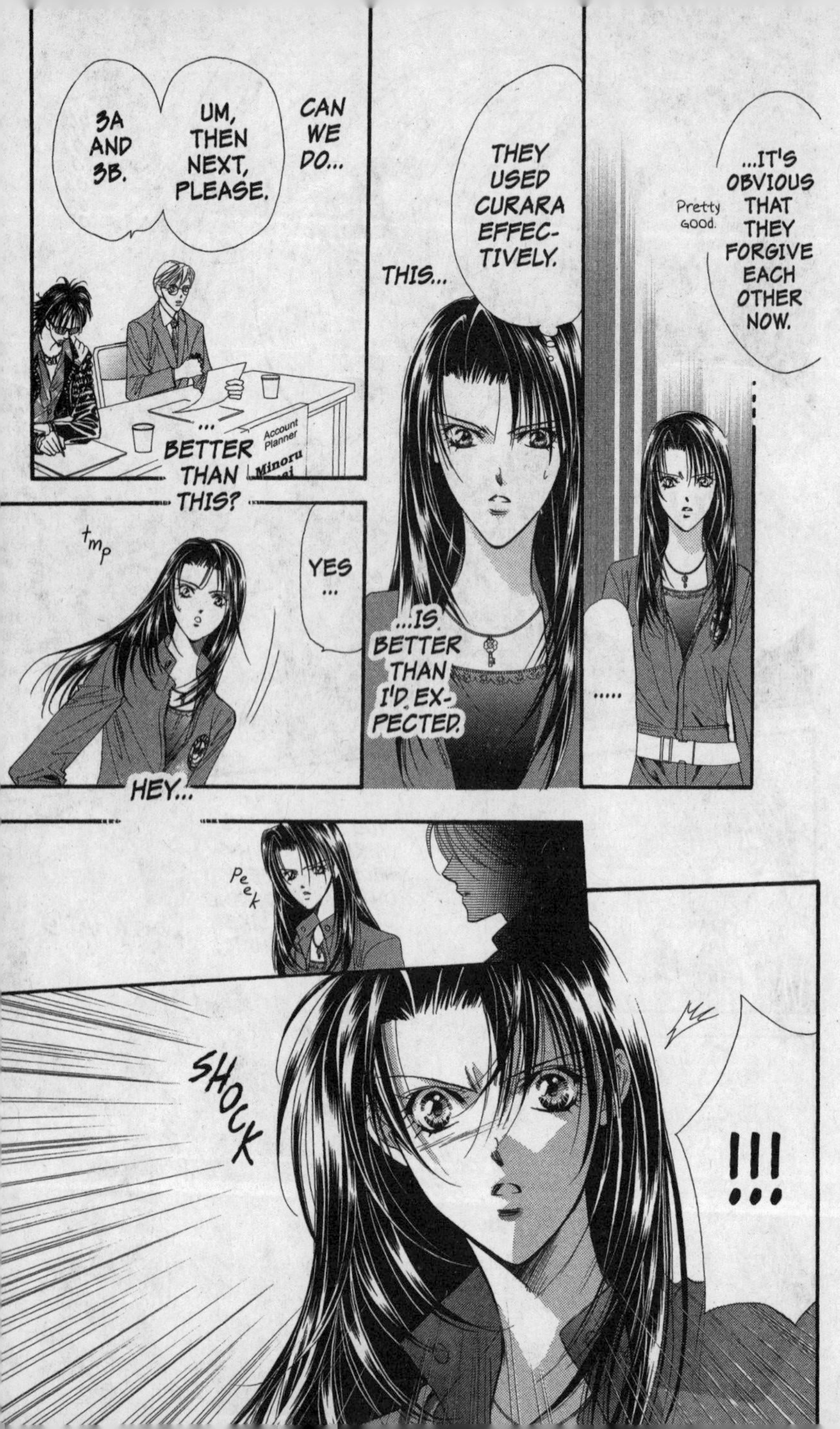
...IT'S OBVIOUS THAT THEY FORGIVE EACH OTHER NOW.
Pretty GOOD.
.....
THEY USED CURARA EFFECTIVELY.
THIS...
...IS BETTER THAN I'D EXPECTED.
CAN WE DO...
UM, THEN NEXT, PLEASE.
3A AND 3B.
Account Planner
...BETTER THAN THIS?
YES...
tmp
HEY...
Peek
!!!
SHOCK

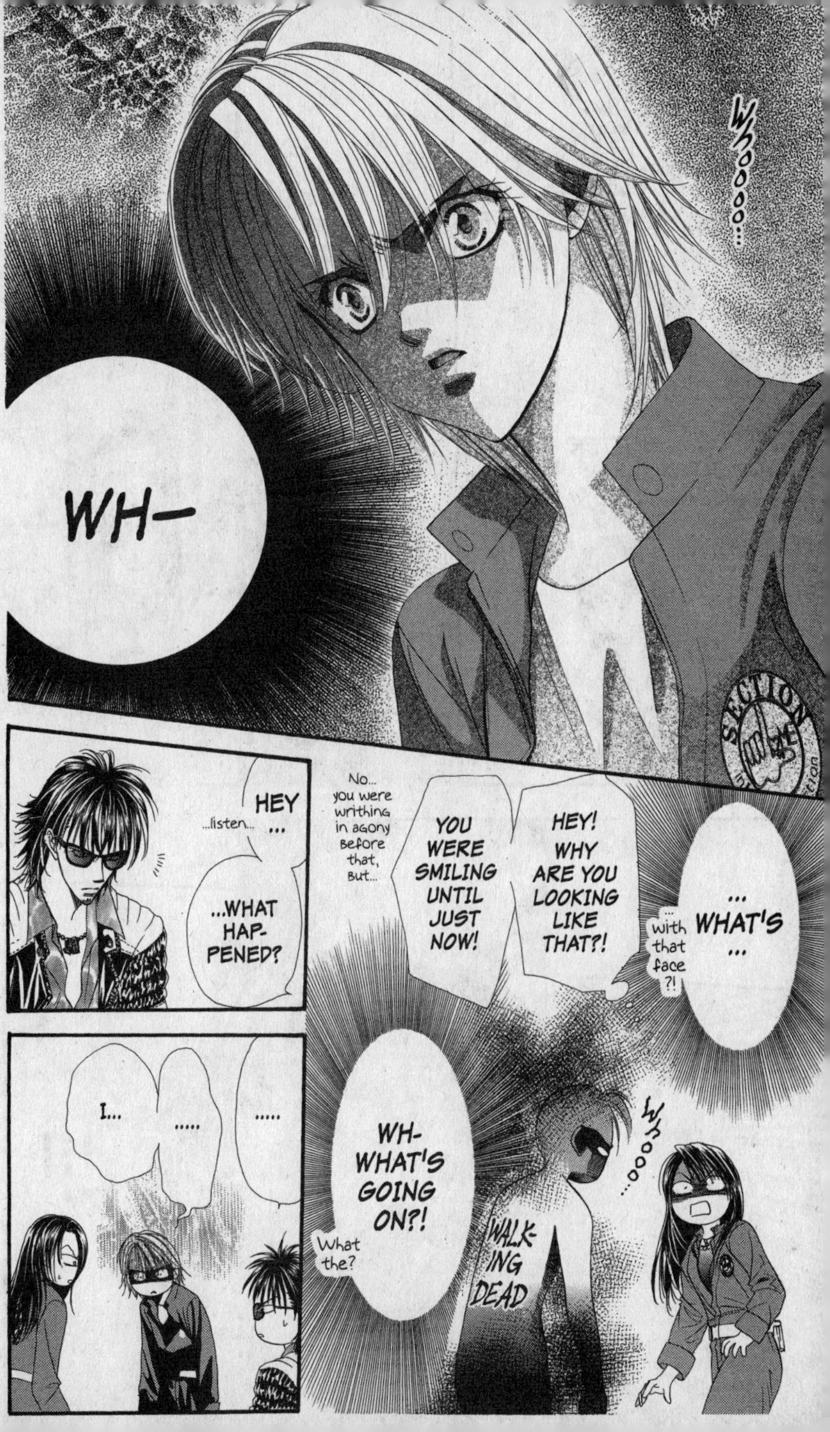
Whoooooo...
WH-
... WHAT'S ...
... with that face ?!
HEY! WHY ARE YOU LOOKING LIKE THAT?!
YOU WERE SMILING UNTIL JUST NOW!
No... you were writhing in agony before that, but...
Whoooo...
WH- WHAT'S GOING ON?!
What the?
WALK-ING DEAD
HEY ...
...listen...
...WHAT HAP-PENED?
.....
.....
I...

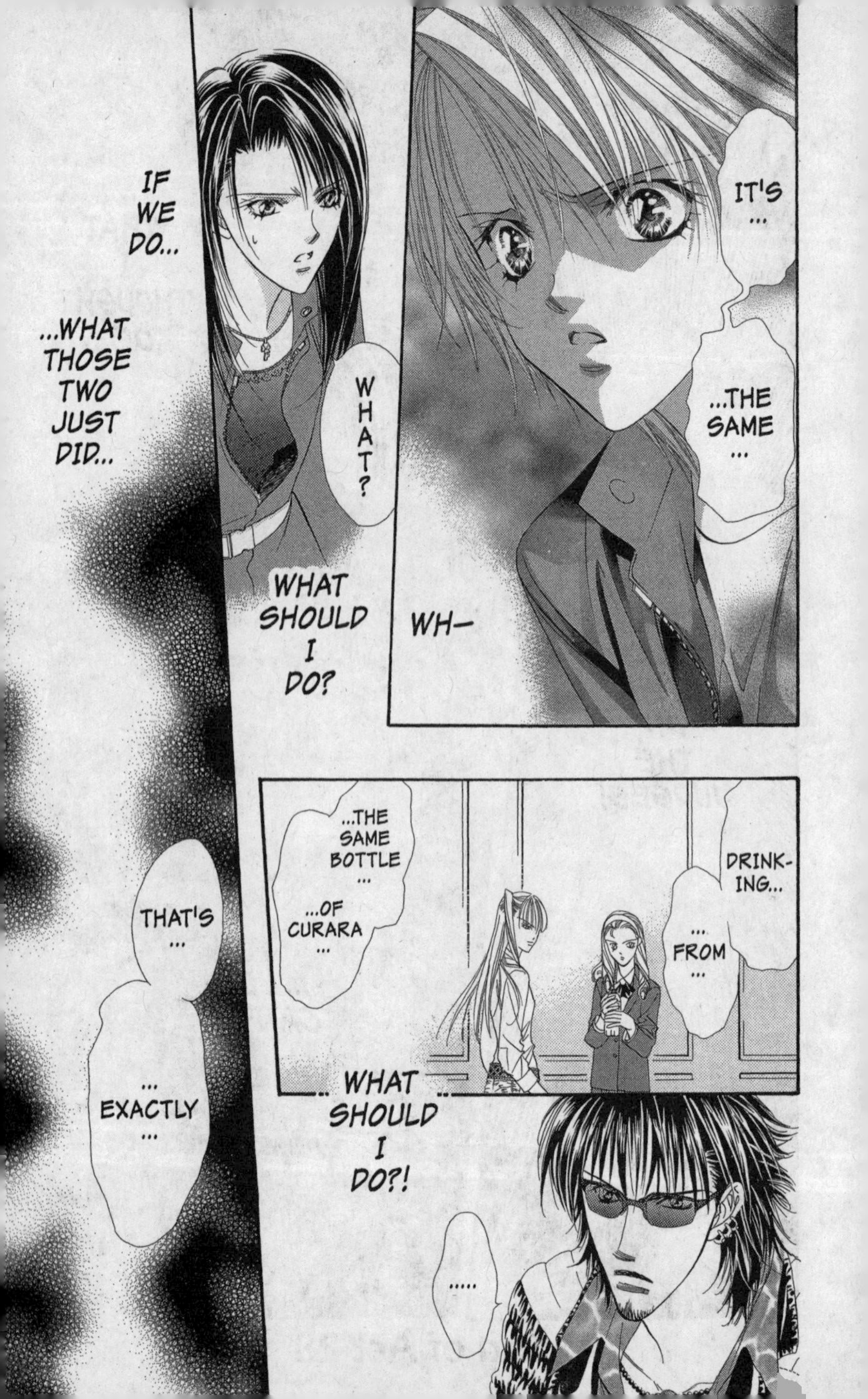
IT'S ...
...THE SAME ...
WH—
DRINKING... ... FROM ...
...THE SAME BOTTLE ... ...OF CURARA ...
...WHAT SHOULD I DO?!
.....
WHAT?
WHAT SHOULD I DO?
IF WE DO...
...WHAT THOSE TWO JUST DID...
THAT'S ...
... EXACTLY ...

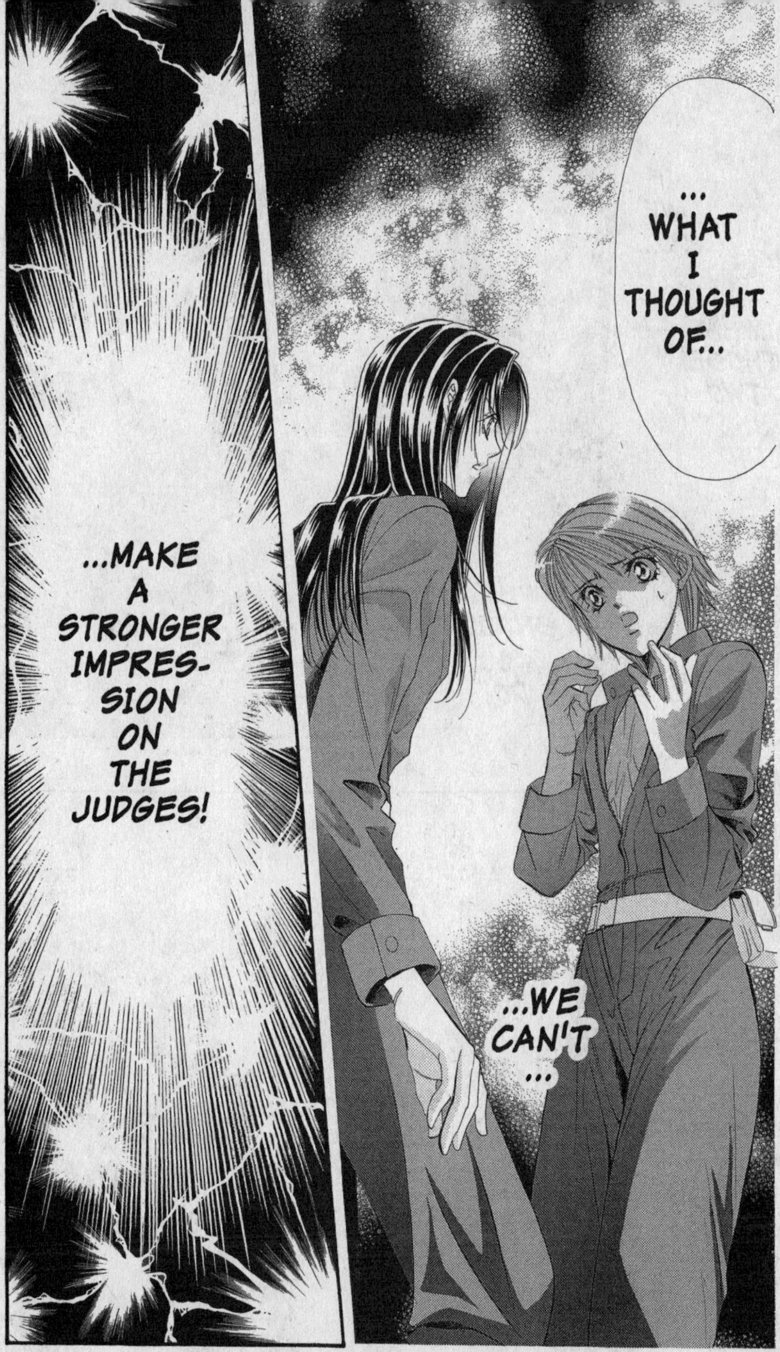
...WHAT I THOUGHT OF...
...WE CAN'T ...
...MAKE A STRONGER IMPRES-SION ON THE JUDGES!

End of Act 28

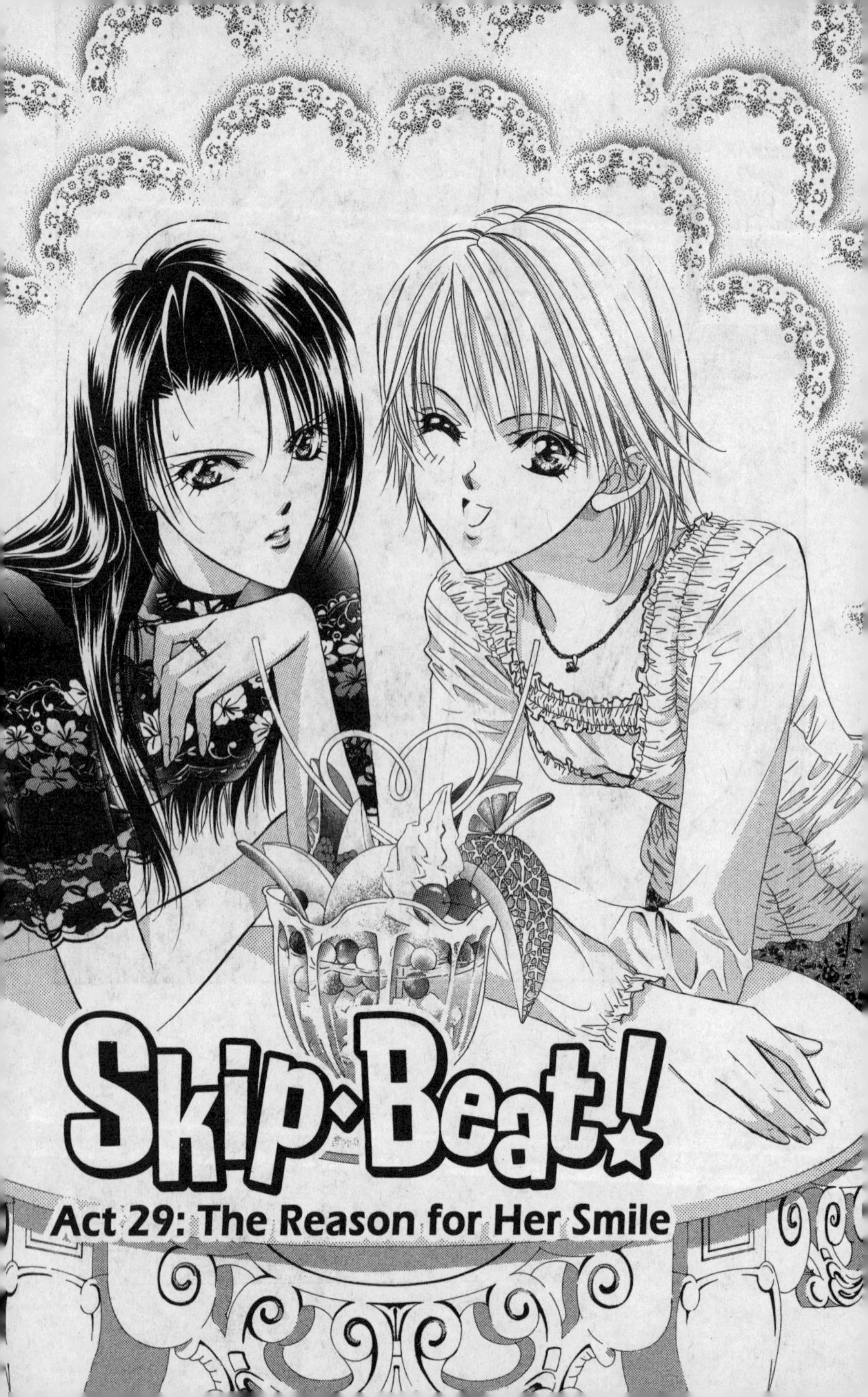
Skip·Beat!
Act 29: The Reason for Her Smile

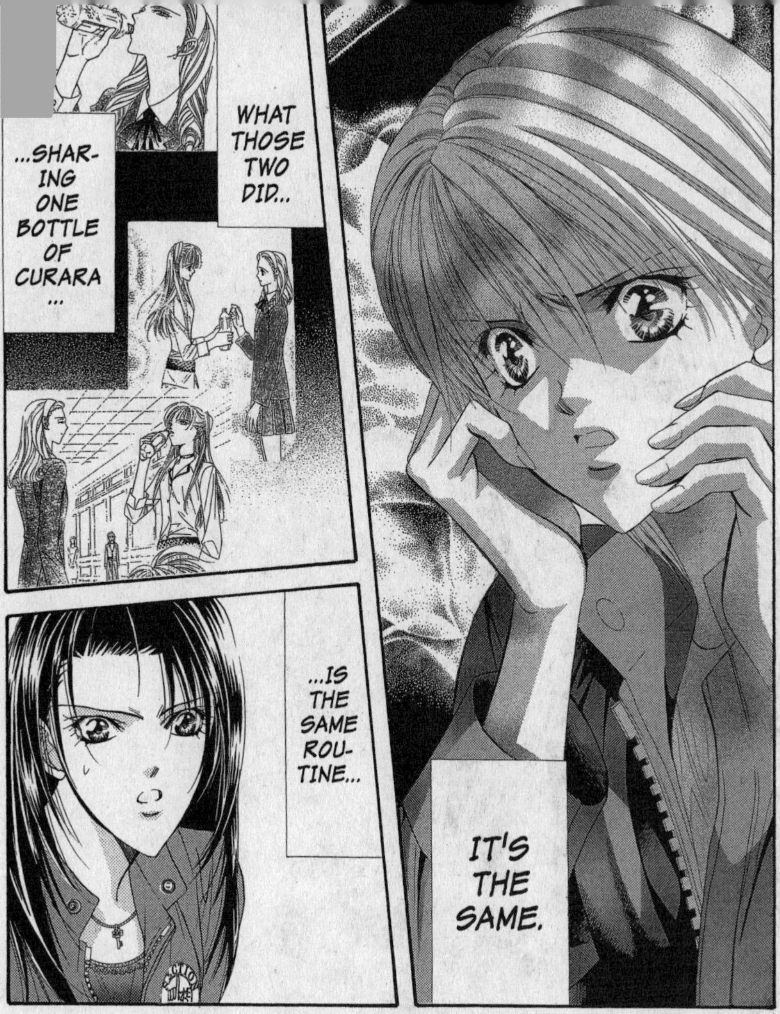
IT'S THE SAME.
WHAT THOSE TWO DID...
...SHARING ONE BOTTLE OF CURARA...
...IS THE SAME ROUTINE...

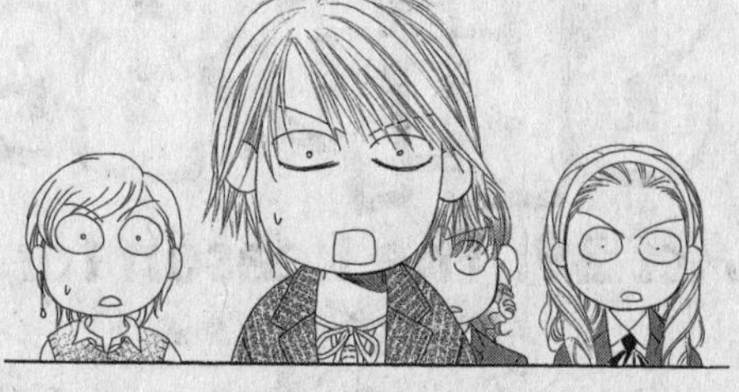

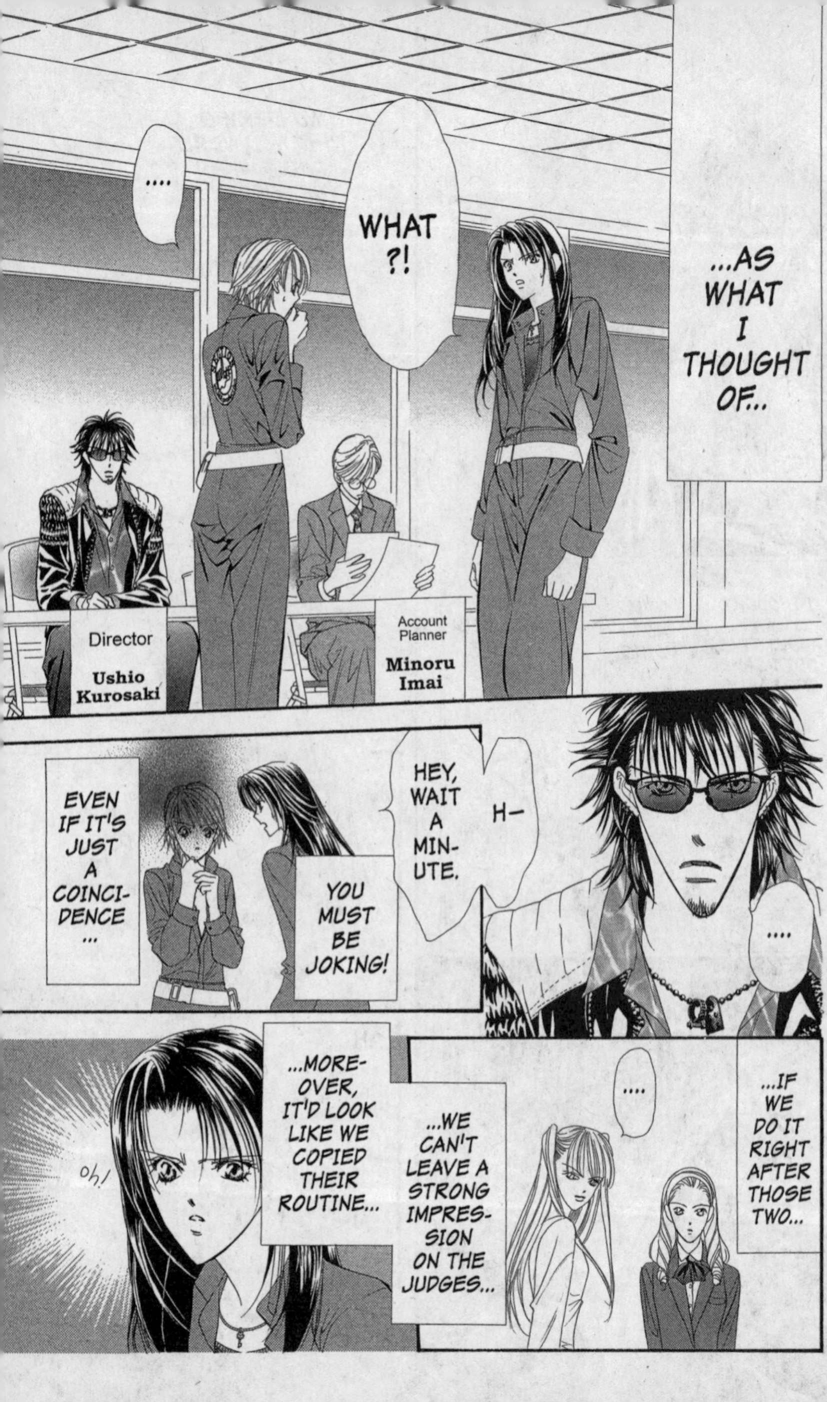
...AS WHAT I THOUGHT OF...
WHAT ?!
....
Director
Ushio Kurosaki
Account Planner
Minoru Imai
H–
....
HEY, WAIT A MINUTE.
YOU MUST BE JOKING!
EVEN IF IT'S JUST A COINCIDENCE...
...IF WE DO IT RIGHT AFTER THOSE TWO...
....
...WE CAN'T LEAVE A STRONG IMPRESSION ON THE JUDGES...
...MOREOVER, IT'D LOOK LIKE WE COPIED THEIR ROUTINE...
oh!

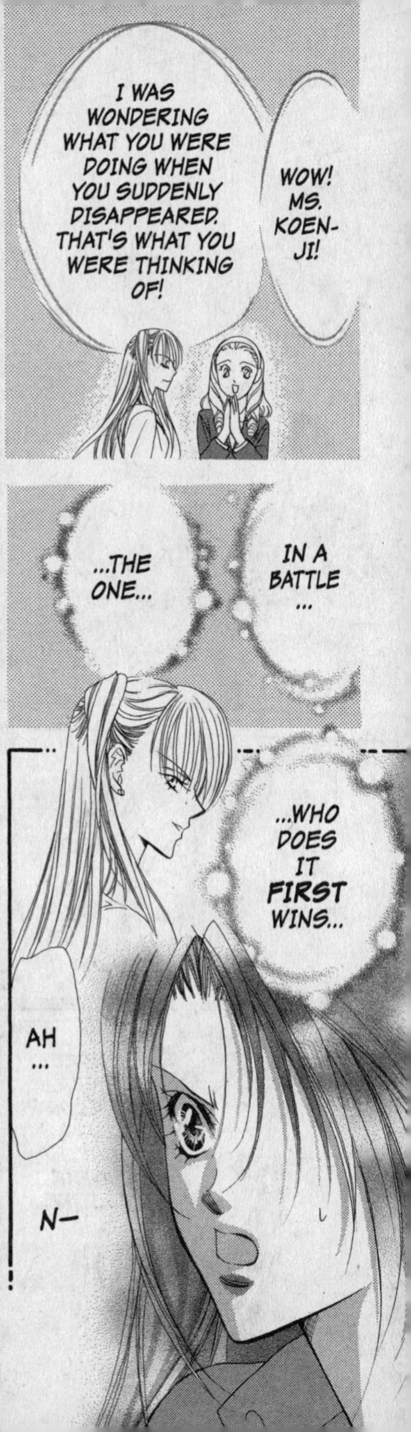
WOW! MS. KOEN-JI!
I WAS WONDERING WHAT YOU WERE DOING WHEN YOU SUDDENLY DISAPPEARED. THAT'S WHAT YOU WERE THINKING OF!
IN A BATTLE ...
...THE ONE...
...WHO DOES IT FIRST WINS...
AH ...
N—
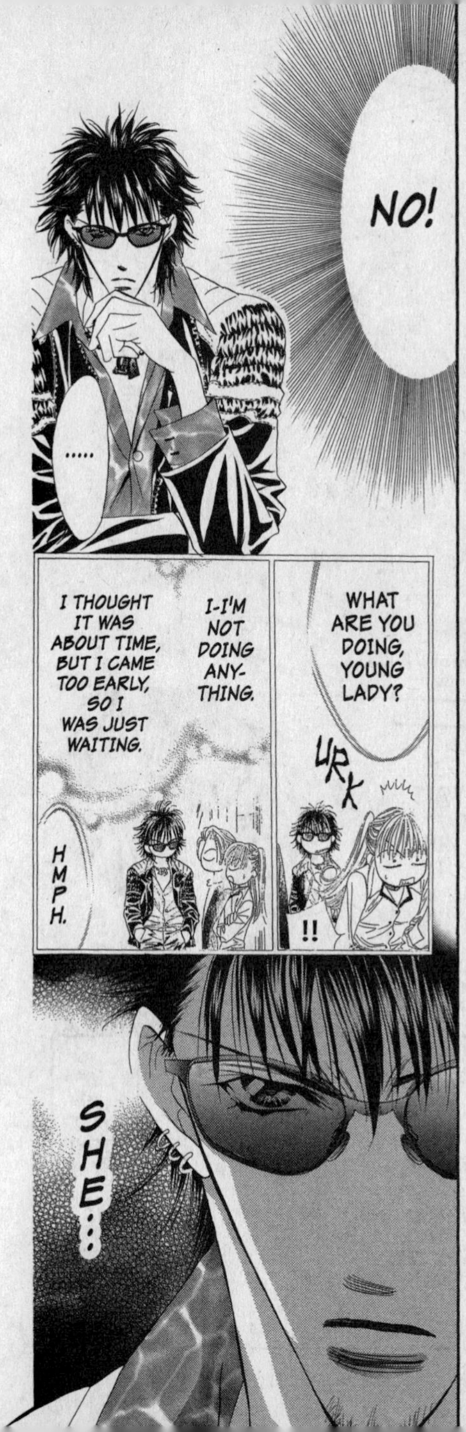
NO!
.....
WHAT ARE YOU DOING, YOUNG LADY?
URK
!!
I-I'M NOT DOING ANY-THING.
I THOUGHT IT WAS ABOUT TIME, BUT I CAME TOO EARLY, SO I WAS JUST WAITING.
HMPH.
SHE...

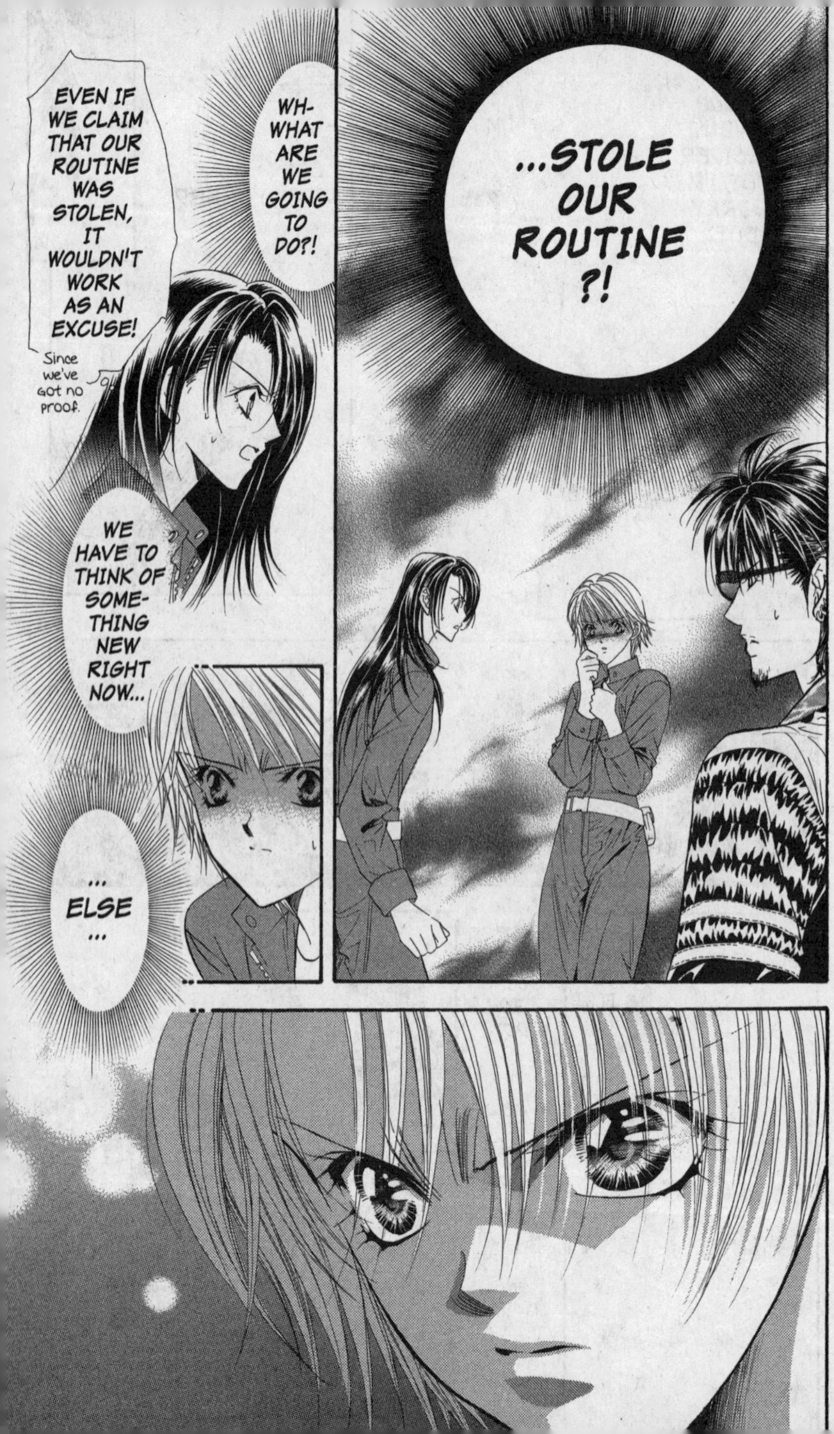
...STOLE OUR ROUTINE?!
WH-WHAT ARE WE GOING TO DO?!
EVEN IF WE CLAIM THAT OUR ROUTINE WAS STOLEN, IT WOULDN'T WORK AS AN EXCUSE!
Since we've got no proof.
WE HAVE TO THINK OF SOME-THING NEW RIGHT NOW...
...ELSE...

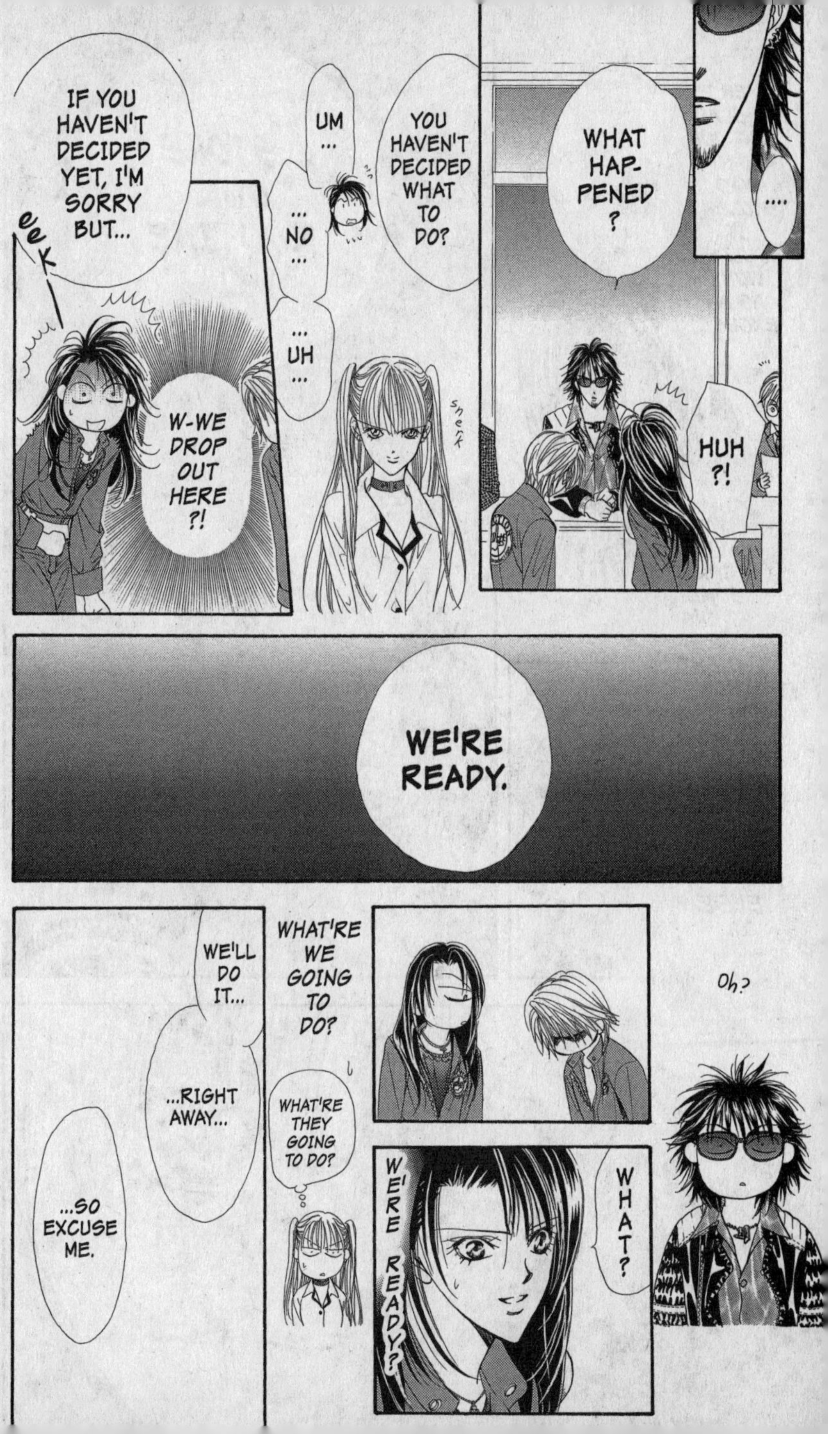
....
WHAT HAP-PENED?
HUH?!
YOU HAVEN'T DECIDED WHAT TO DO?
UM...
...NO...
...UH...
snerk
IF YOU HAVEN'T DECIDED YET, I'M SORRY BUT...
eek
W-WE DROP OUT HERE?!
WE'RE READY.
Oh?
WHAT'RE WE GOING TO DO?
WHAT?
WE'RE READY?
WHAT'RE THEY GOING TO DO?
WE'LL DO IT...
...RIGHT AWAY...
...SO EXCUSE ME.

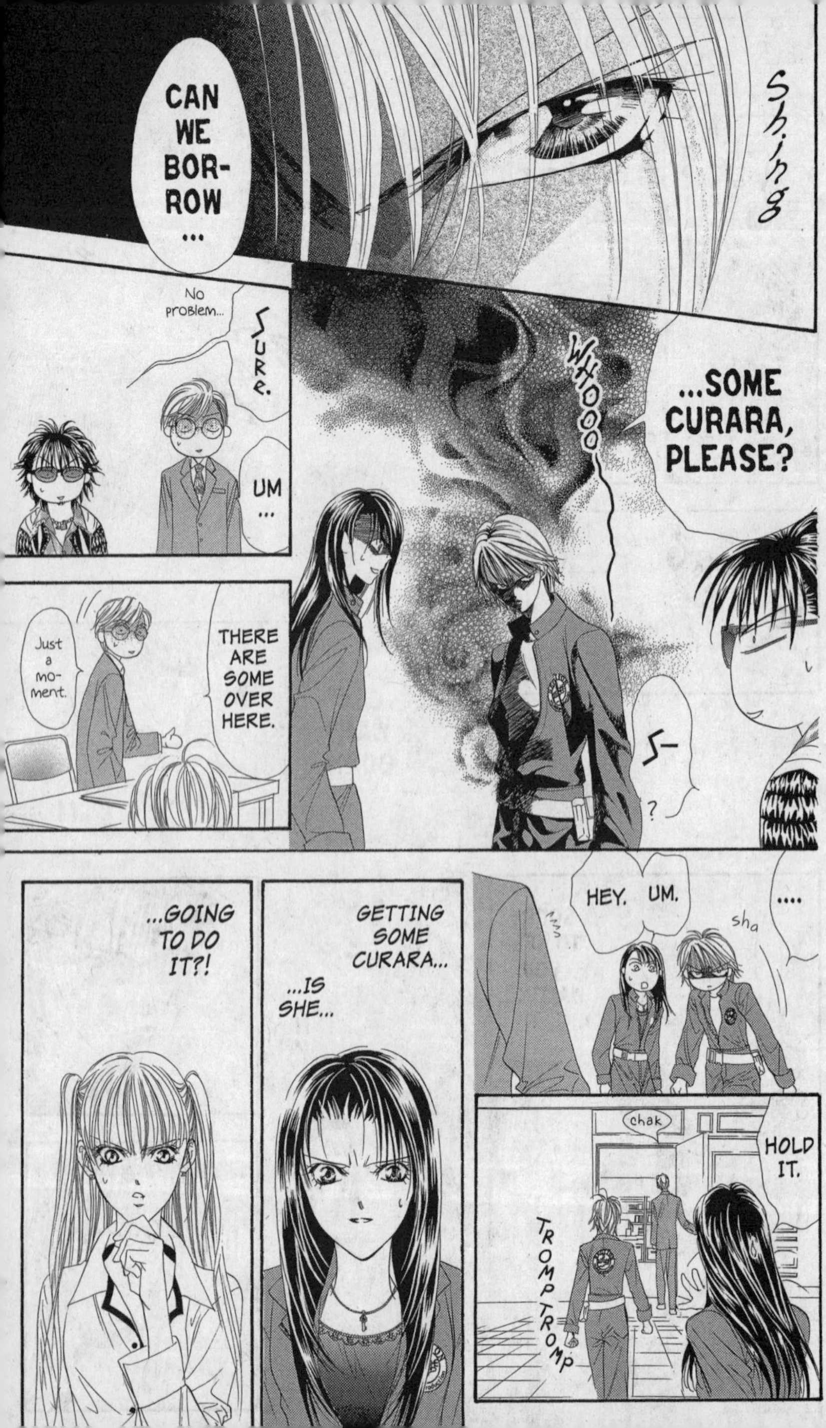
Shing
CAN WE BORROW...
...SOME CURARA, PLEASE?
WHOOO
S—
?
UM...
Sure.
No problem...
THERE ARE SOME OVER HERE.
Just a moment.
....
HEY. UM.
sha
HOLD IT.
chak
TROMP TROMP
GETTING SOME CURARA...
...IS SHE...
...GOING TO DO IT?!

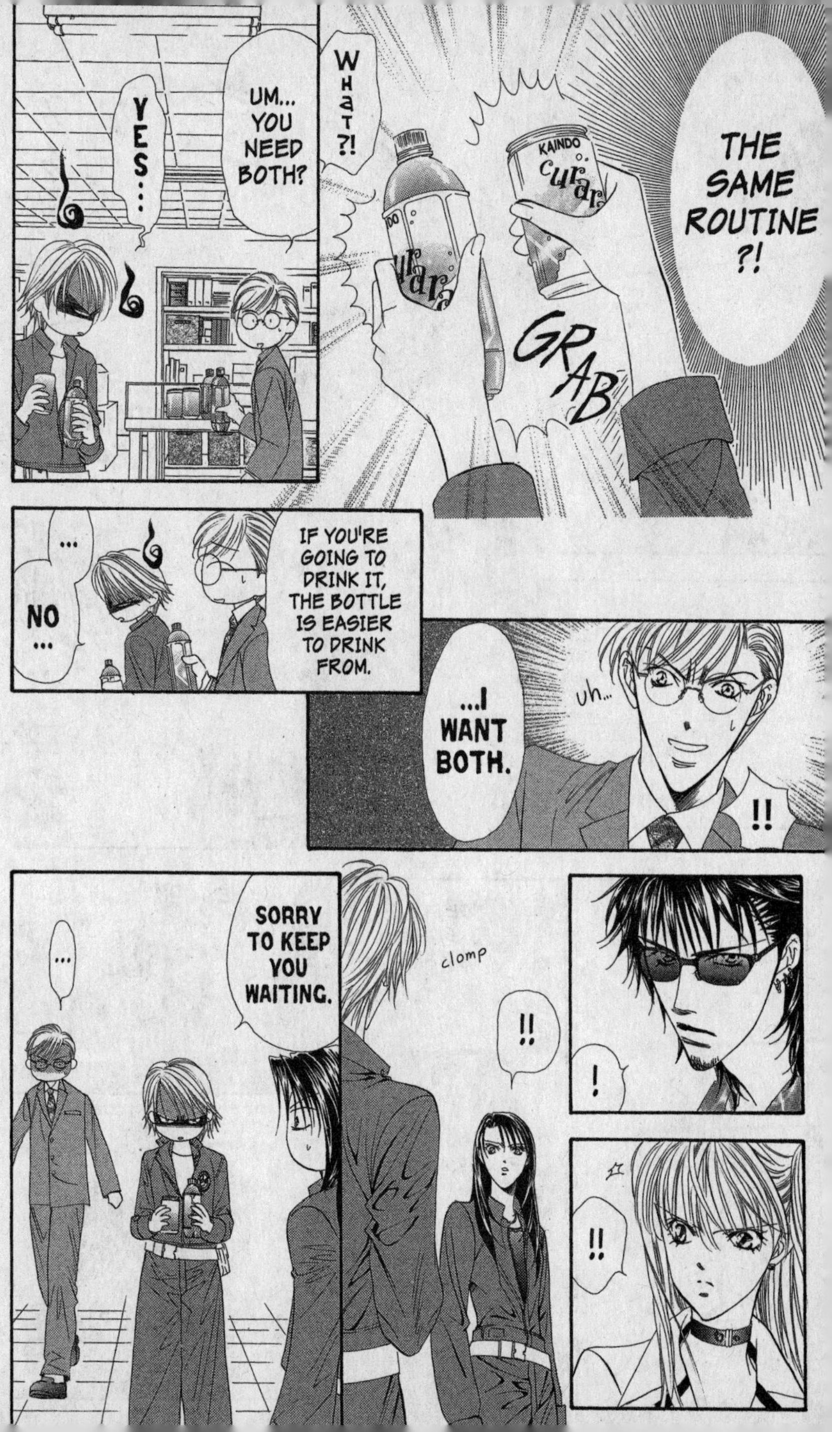
THE SAME ROUTINE ?!
KAINDO curara
curara
GRAB
WHAT?!
UM... YOU NEED BOTH?
YES...
IF YOU'RE GOING TO DRINK IT, THE BOTTLE IS EASIER TO DRINK FROM.
... NO ...
...I WANT BOTH.
uh...
!!
!
!!
SORRY TO KEEP YOU WAITING.
clomp
!!
...

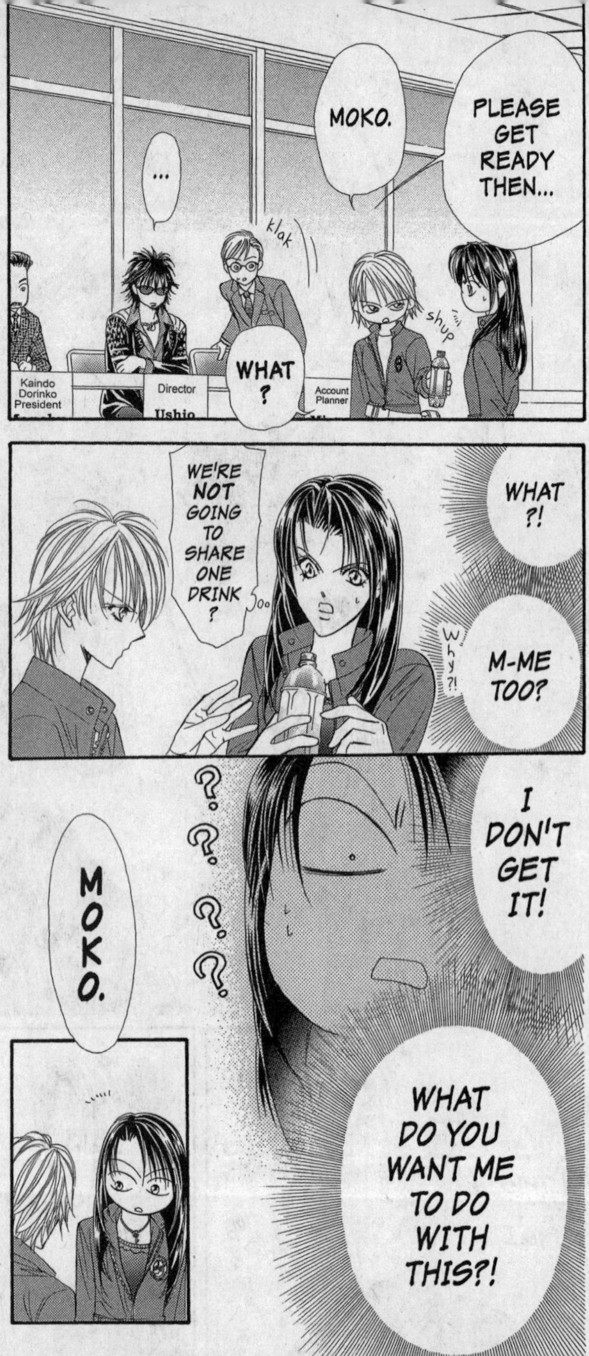
PLEASE GET READY THEN...
MOKO.
...
klak
shup
WHAT?
Account Planner
Director
Ushio
Kaindo Dorinko President
WHAT?!
M-ME TOO?
Why?!
WE'RE NOT GOING TO SHARE ONE DRINK?
I DON'T GET IT!
WHAT DO YOU WANT ME TO DO WITH THIS?!
MOKO.

...drinks like tea and sports drinks...And like Kanae, I thought that soda that comes in plastic bottles spurts out like canned soda...at work, we bought cans and plastic bottles (slightly carbonated) and all the staff tested how the liquid spurts out... well, well...so we were bustling about while working on the commercial audition arc. I never really have sufficient time to do my work... It's probably because I take twice as much time as other people to do the storyboards... I won't say that's the only reason, but I really haven't studied enough about showbiz. I gathered materials since I was going to draw a showbiz story, but there are too many things that I don't understand yet...so those of you who know the ins and outs of showbiz...please give me information!! Please, please.

APOLOGY

About Kyoko's lines in Act 26 about panthers. It might seem that cheetahs are more appropriate, but I chose panthers because it sounded better, and when I was working on the storyboard, I wanted to make the subtitle "The Pink Panthers' Counterattack" so I used panthers... But the subtitle wasn't used in the end...well, it wasn't much of a counterattack, so...

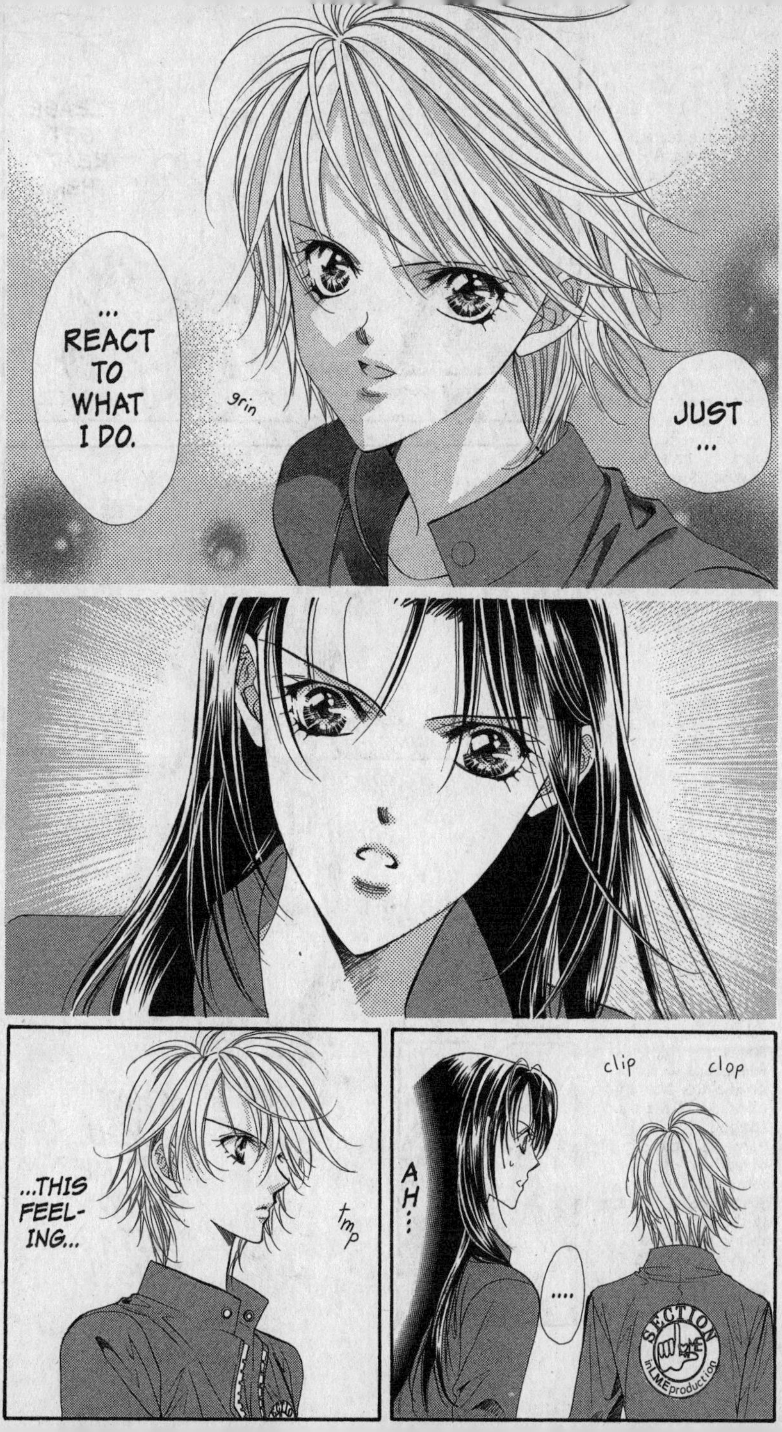
JUST ...
grin
... REACT TO WHAT I DO.
clop
clip
AH...
....
...THIS FEEL-ING...
tmp

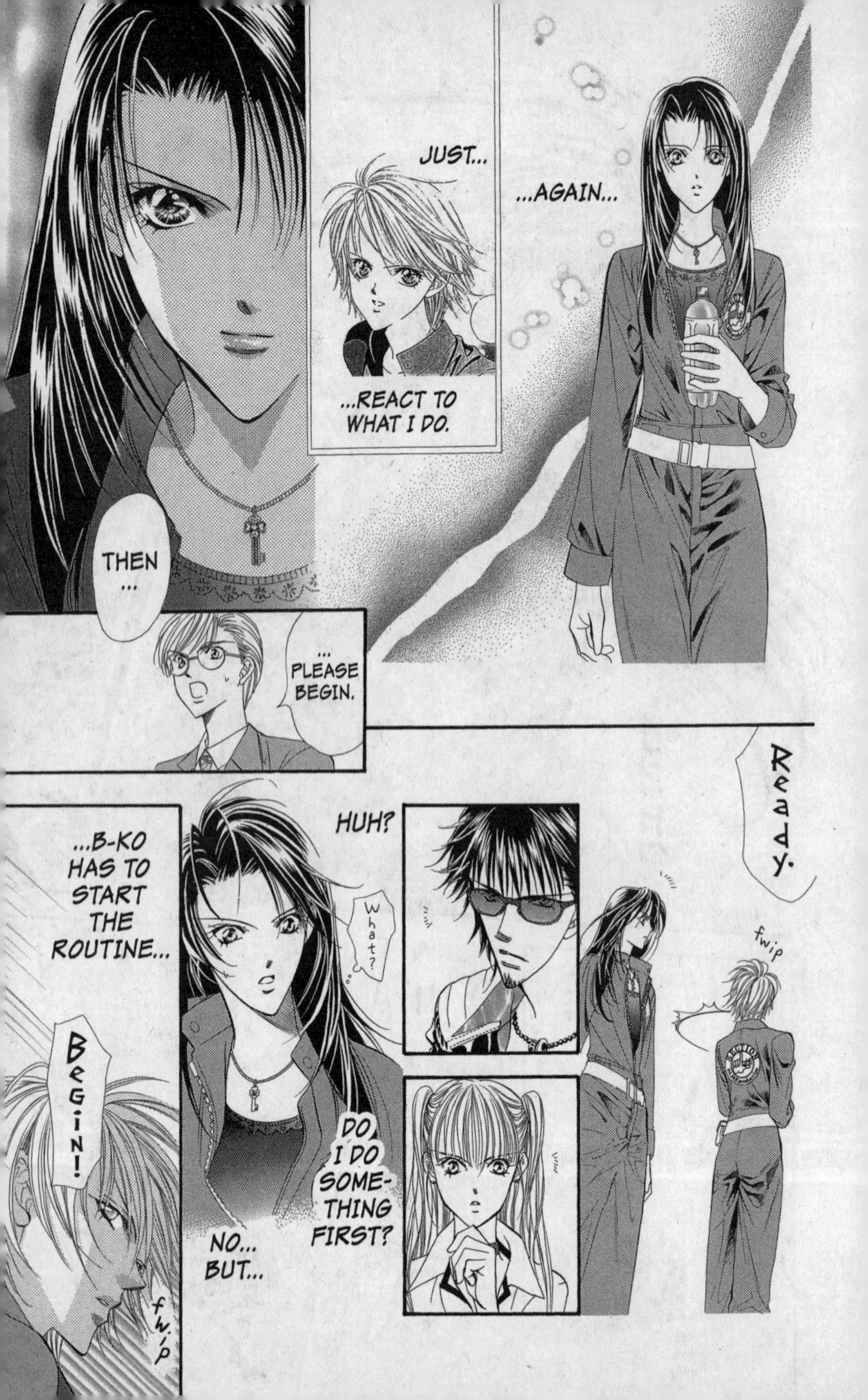
...AGAIN...
JUST...
...REACT TO WHAT I DO.
THEN ...
... PLEASE BEGIN.
Ready.
fwip
HUH?
What?
DO I DO SOME-THING FIRST?
NO... BUT...
...B-KO HAS TO START THE ROUTINE...
Begin!
fwip

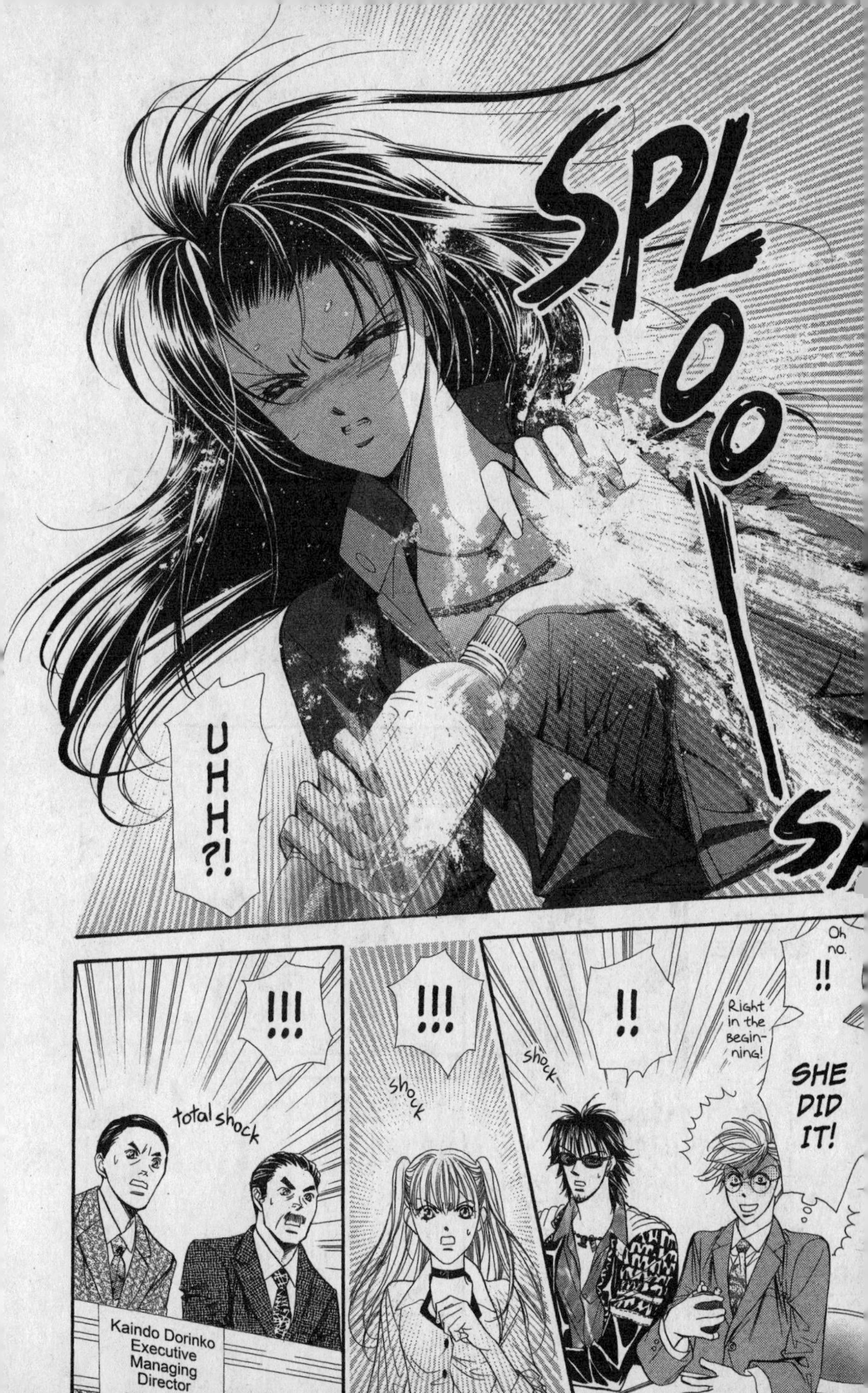
SPLOO
SP
UHH?!
Oh no.
!!
Right in the begin-ning!
SHE DID IT!
!!
shock
!!!
shock
!!!
total shock
Kaindo Dorinko Executive Managing Director

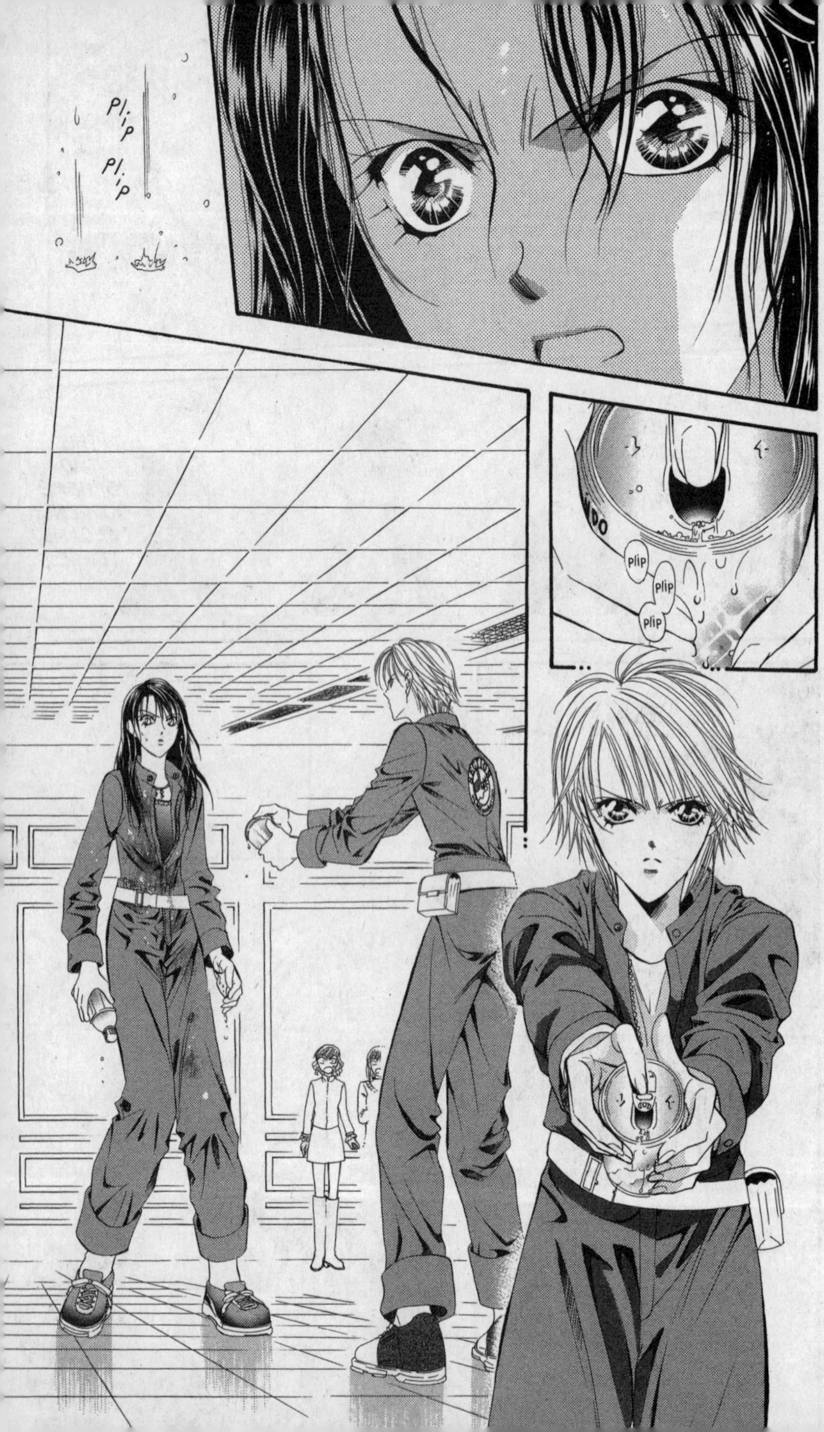
Plip
Plip
plip
plip
plip

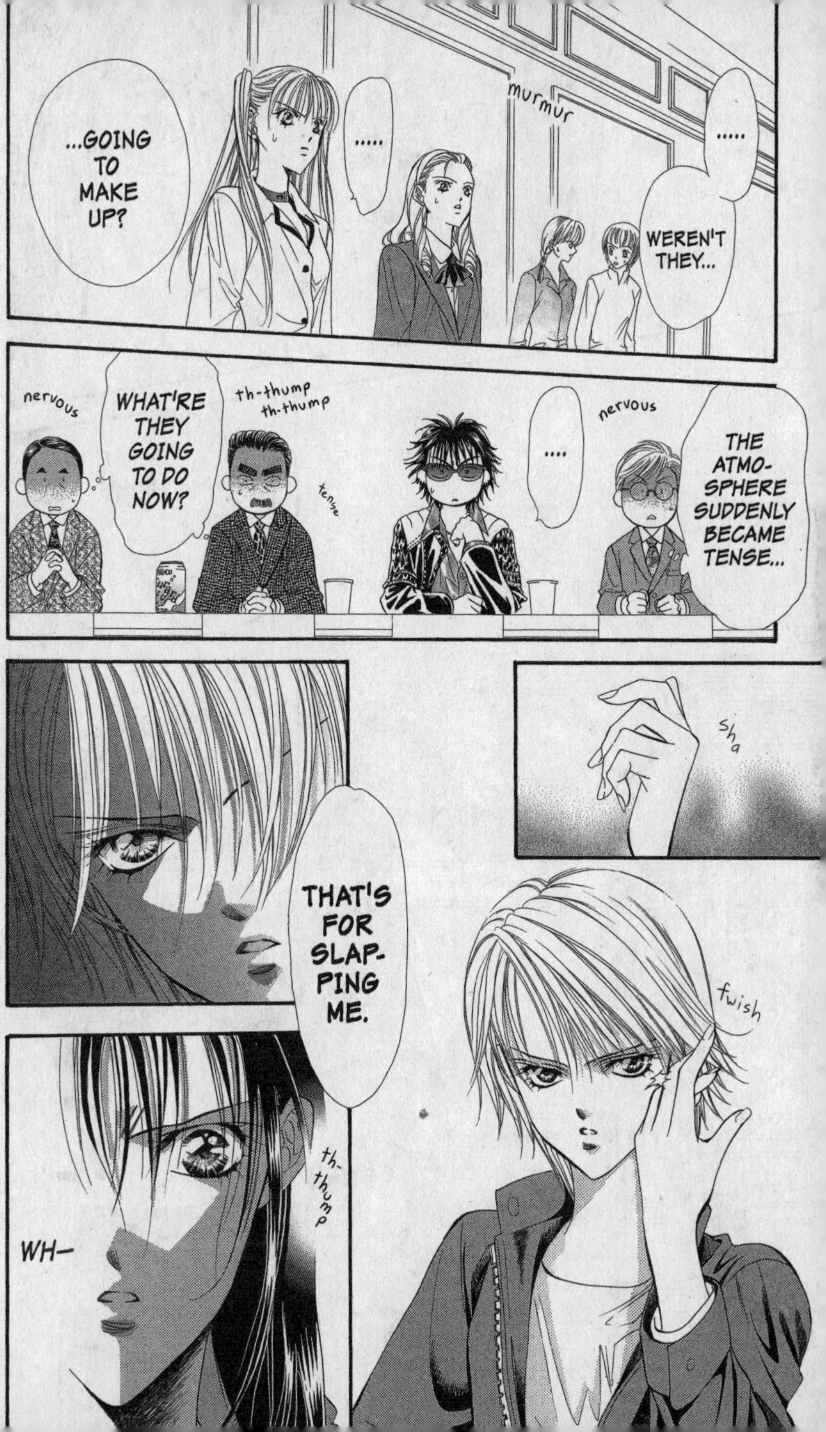
.....
WEREN'T THEY...
murmur
.....
...GOING TO MAKE UP?
THE ATMOSPHERE SUDDENLY BECAME TENSE...
nervous
....
tense
th-thump th-thump
WHAT'RE THEY GOING TO DO NOW?
nervous
sha
fwish
THAT'S FOR SLAPPING ME.
th-thump
WH-

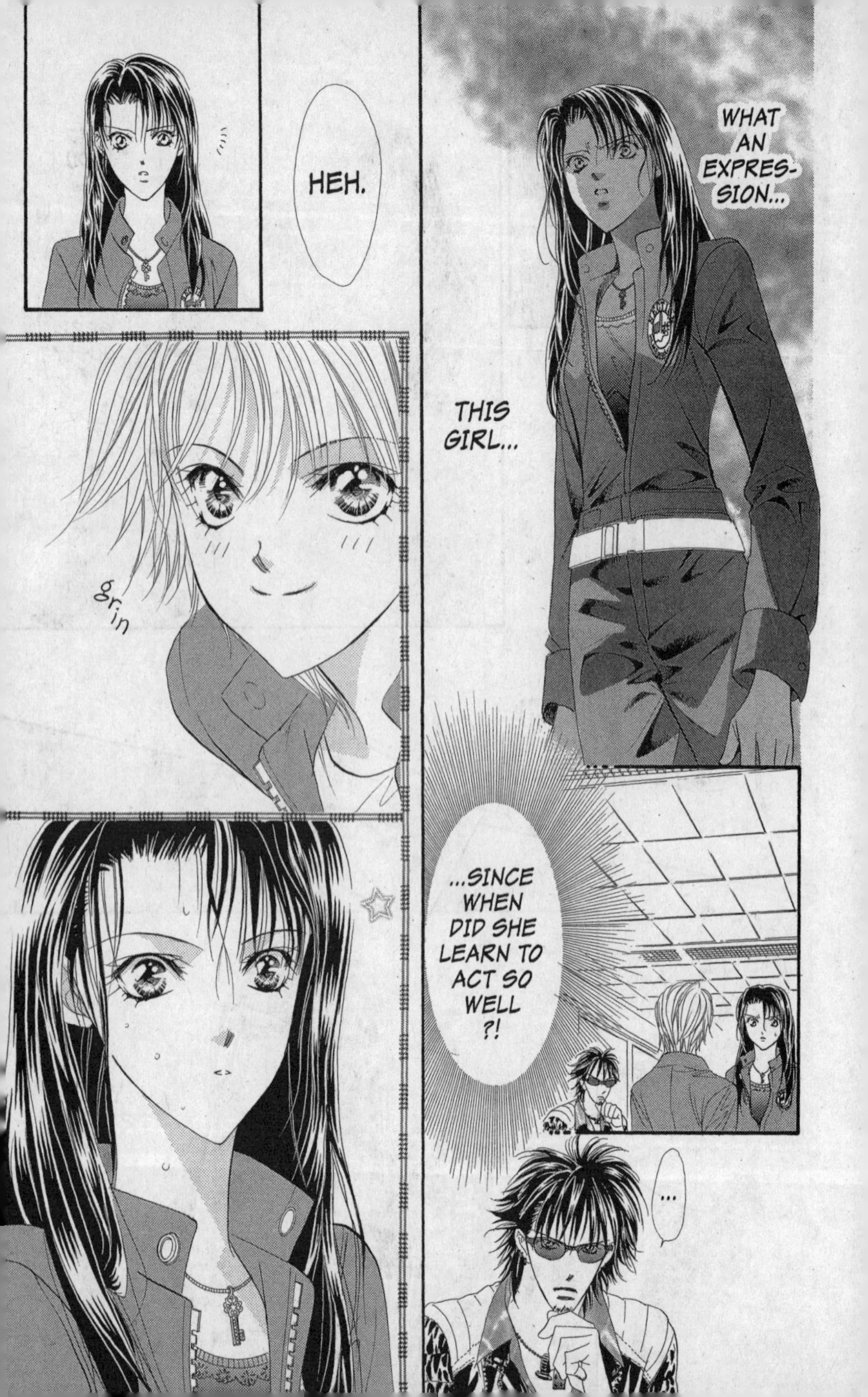
WHAT AN EXPRES-SION...
THIS GIRL...
...SINCE WHEN DID SHE LEARN TO ACT SO WELL ?!
...
HEH.
grin

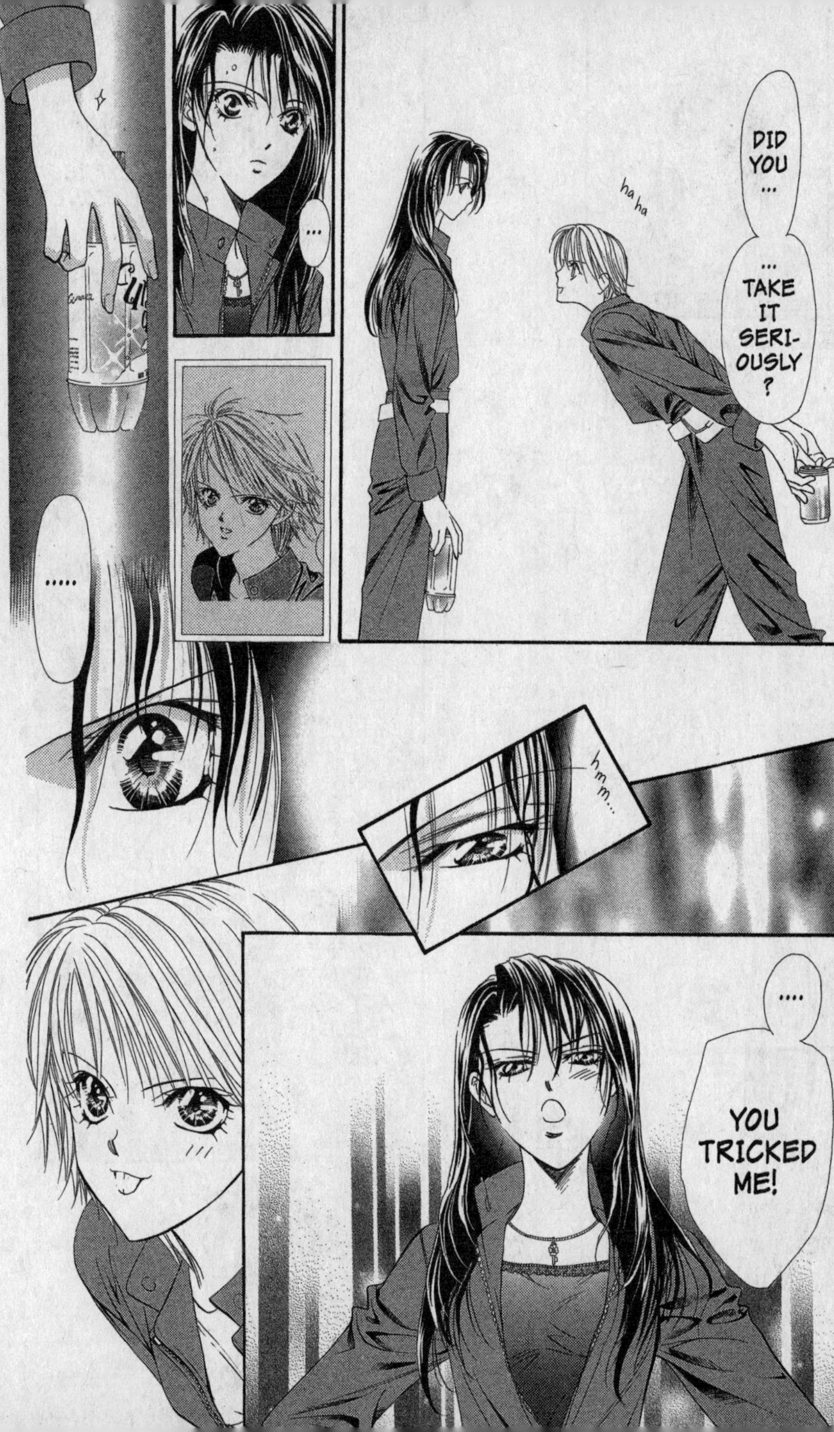
ha ha
DID YOU ...
... TAKE IT SERI-OUSLY ?
....
.....
hmm...
....
YOU TRICKED ME!

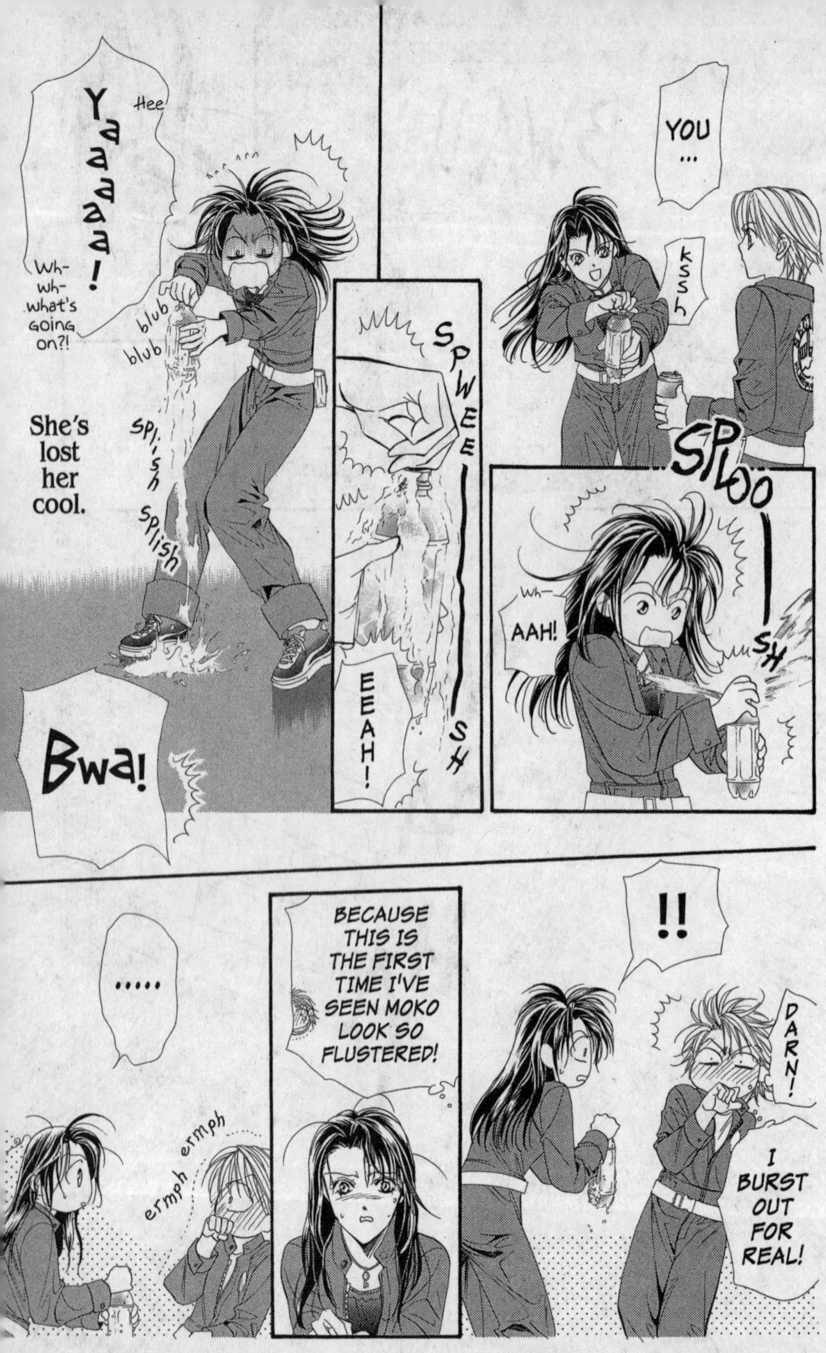
YOU ...
kssh
SPLOO-SH
Wh-
AAH!
SPWEE-SH
EEAH!
Yaaaaa!
Hee
Wh-wh-what's going on?!
blub blub
splish splish
She's lost her cool.
Bwa!
!!
DARN!
I BURST OUT FOR REAL!
BECAUSE THIS IS THE FIRST TIME I'VE SEEN MOKO LOOK SO FLUSTERED!
ermph ermph
.....

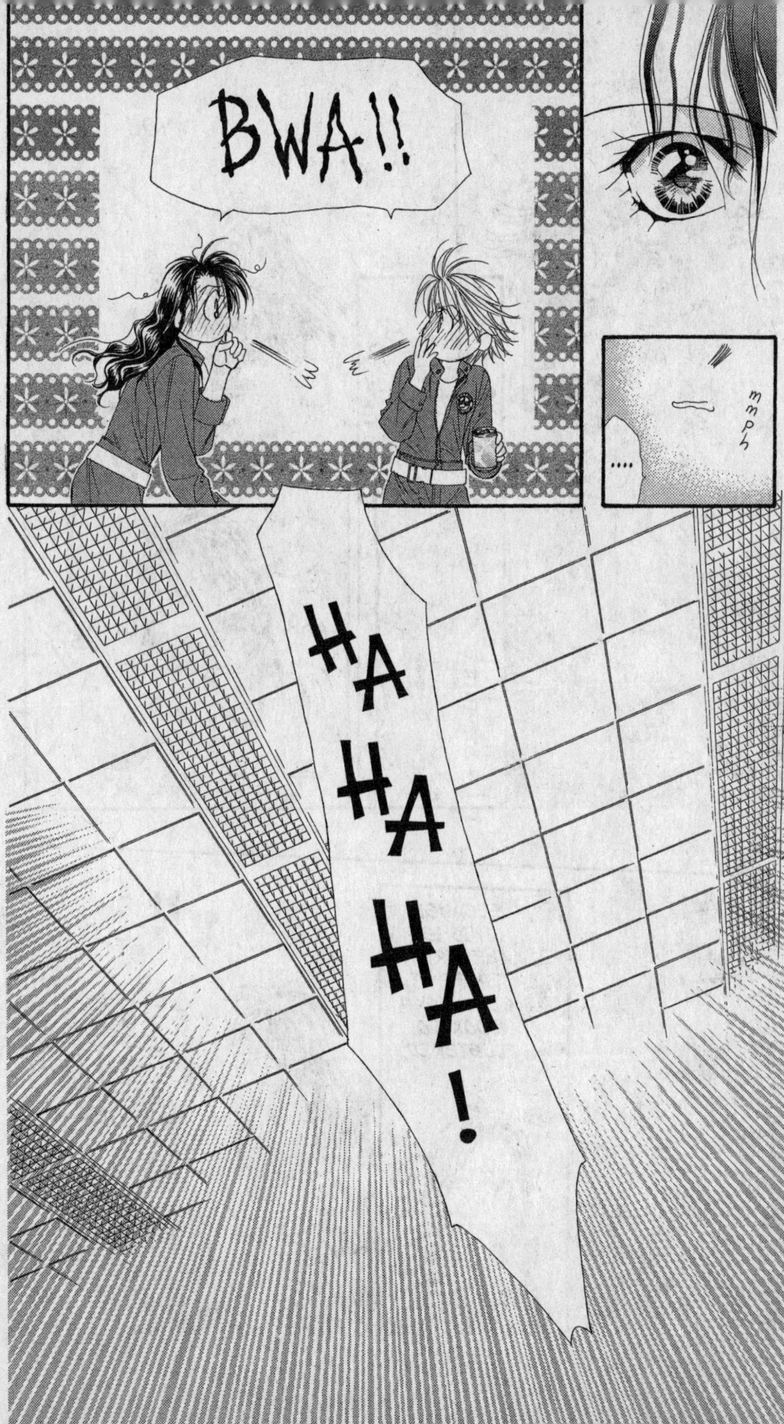
mmph
....
BWA!!
HA HA HA!

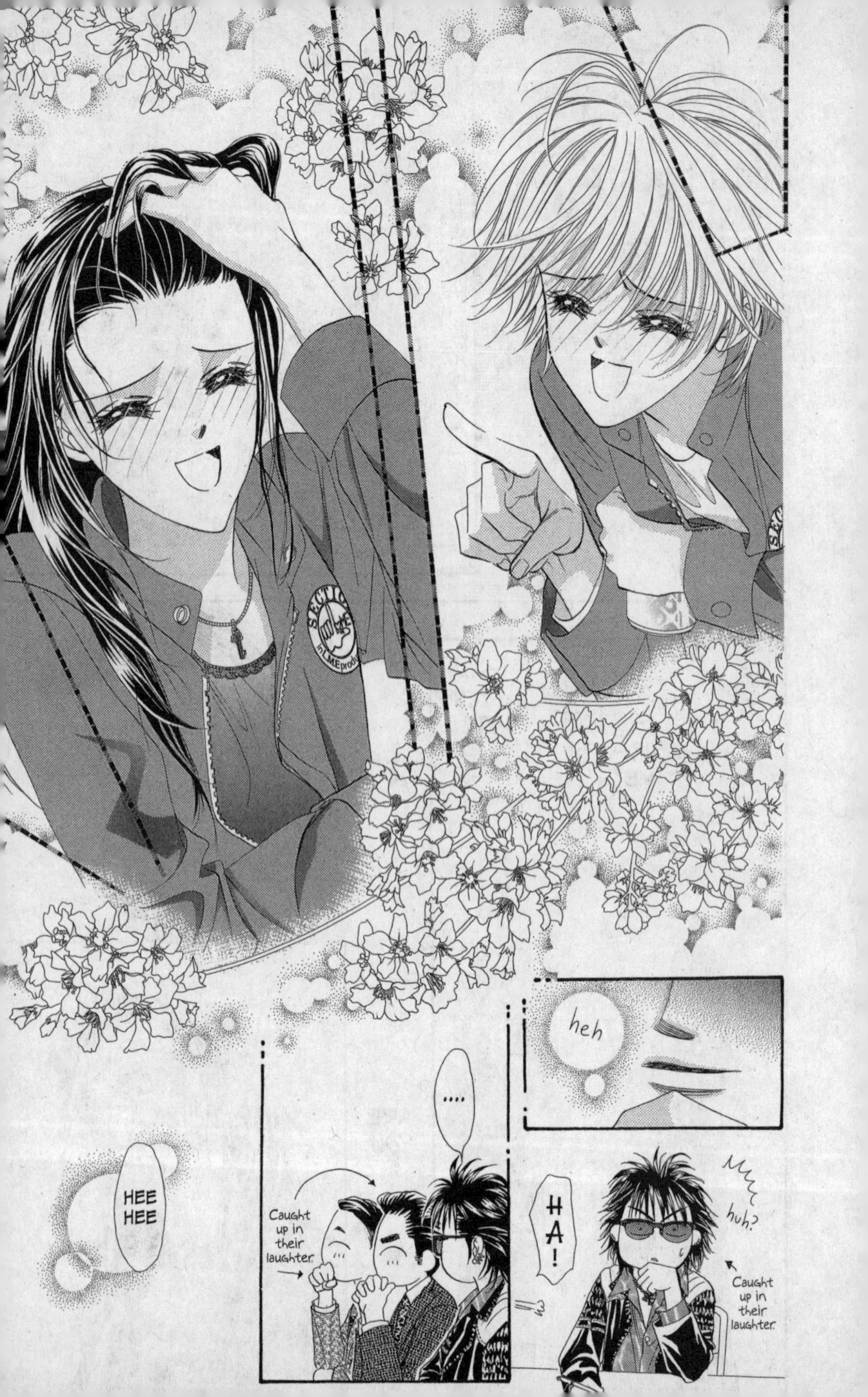
heh
huh?
Caught up in their laughter.
HA!
....
Caught up in their laughter.
HEE HEE

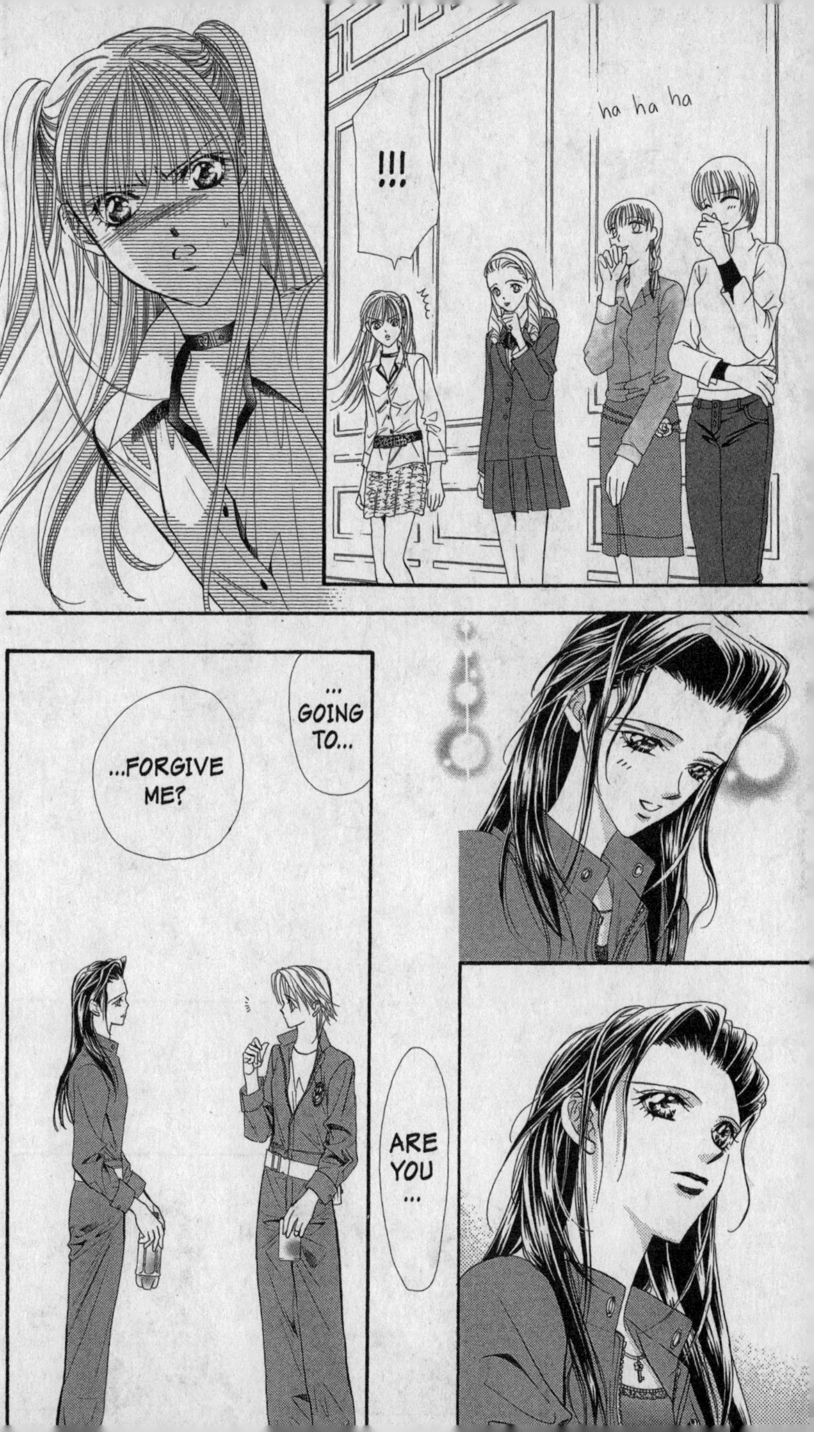
ha ha ha
!!!
ARE YOU ...
... GOING TO...
...FORGIVE ME?

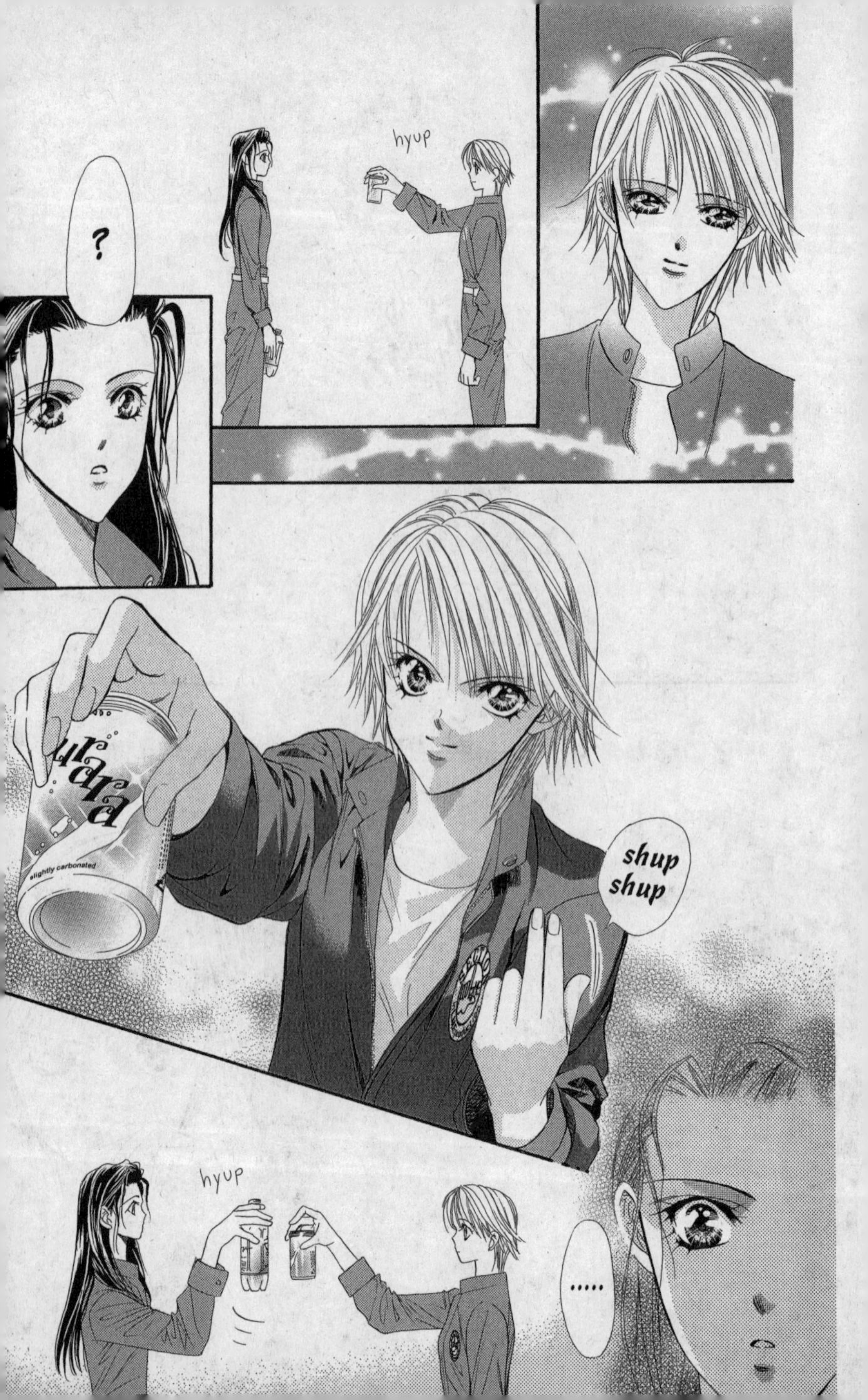
hyup
?
urara
slightly carbonated
shup shup
......
hyup

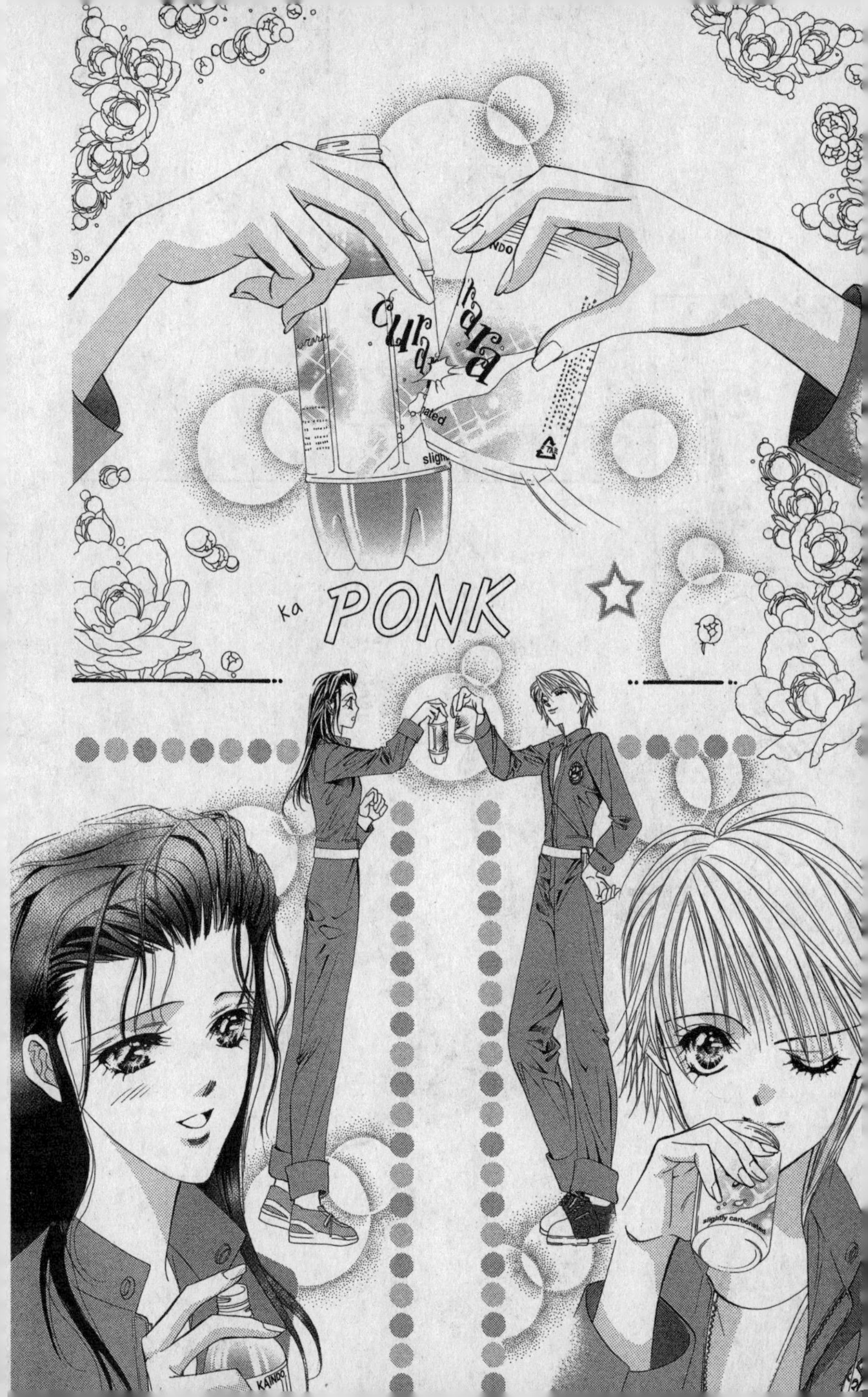
ka PONK
slightly carbonated
KAINDO

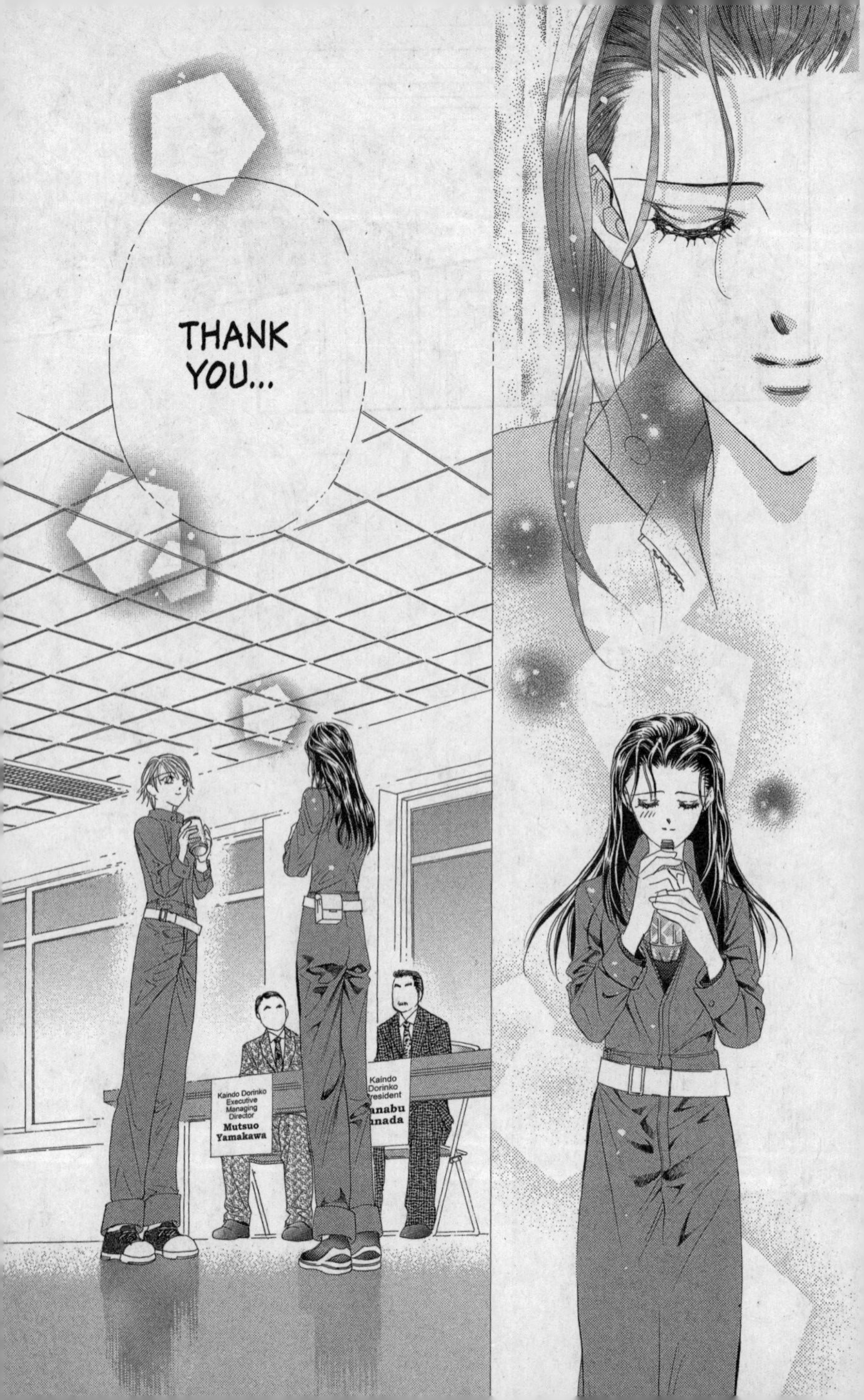
THANK YOU...
Kaindo Dorinko Executive Managing Director
Mutsuo Yamakawa
Kaindo Dorinko

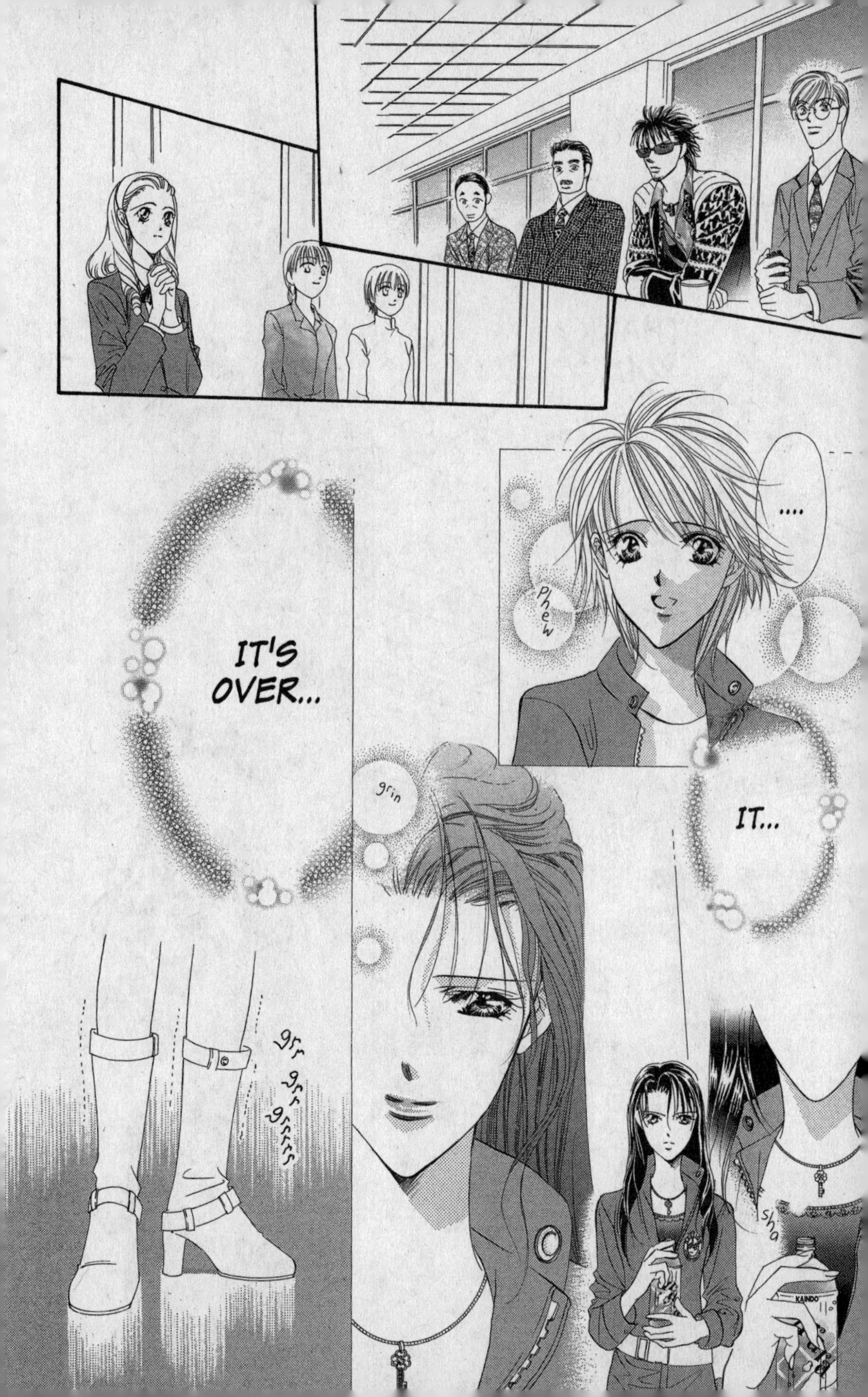
....
Phew
IT...
IT'S OVER...
grin
sha
KAINDO
grr grr grrrrs

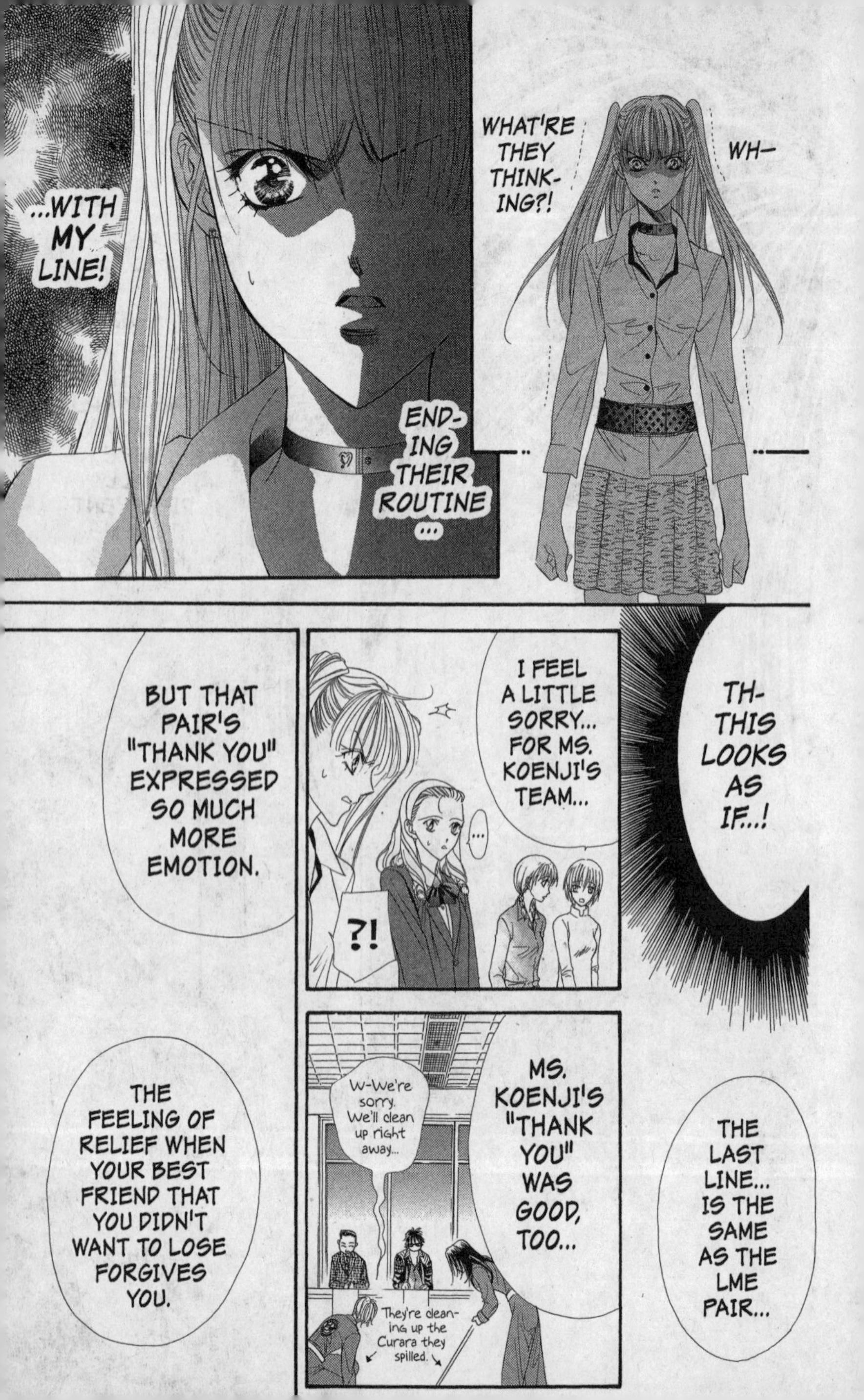
WH-
WHAT'RE THEY THINKING?!
END-ING THEIR ROUTINE...
...WITH MY LINE!
TH-THIS LOOKS AS IF...!
I FEEL A LITTLE SORRY... FOR MS. KOENJI'S TEAM...
...
?!
THE LAST LINE... IS THE SAME AS THE LME PAIR...
MS. KOENJI'S "THANK YOU" WAS GOOD, TOO...
W-We're sorry. We'll clean up right away...
They're clean-ing up the Curara they spilled.
BUT THAT PAIR'S "THANK YOU" EXPRESSED SO MUCH MORE EMOTION.
THE FEELING OF RELIEF WHEN YOUR BEST FRIEND THAT YOU DIDN'T WANT TO LOSE FORGIVES YOU.

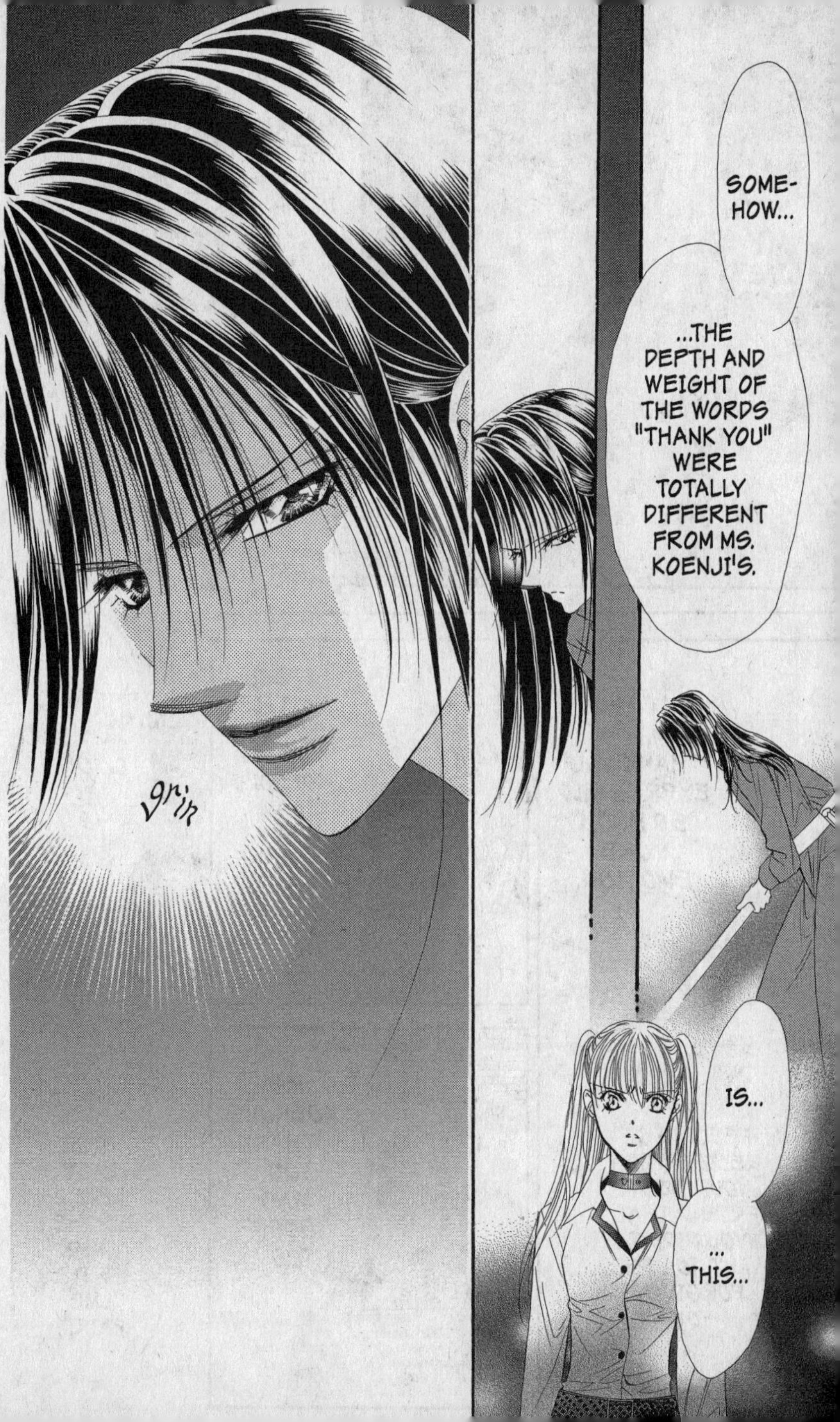
SOME-HOW...
...THE DEPTH AND WEIGHT OF THE WORDS "THANK YOU" WERE TOTALLY DIFFERENT FROM MS. KOENJI'S.
IS...
... THIS...
grin

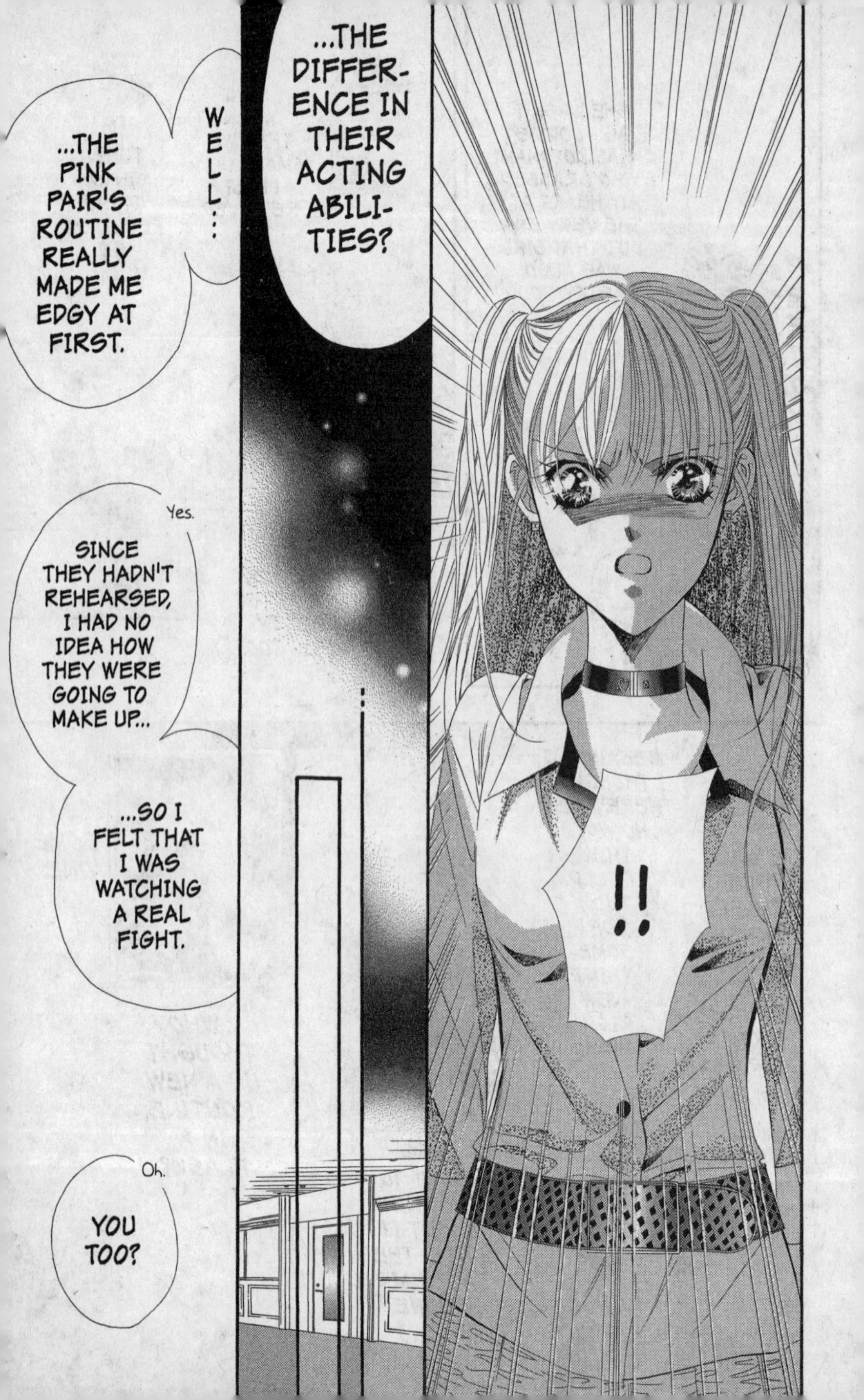
!!
...THE DIFFERENCE IN THEIR ACTING ABILITIES?
WELL...
...THE PINK PAIR'S ROUTINE REALLY MADE ME EDGY AT FIRST.
Yes.
SINCE THEY HADN'T REHEARSED, I HAD NO IDEA HOW THEY WERE GOING TO MAKE UP...
...SO I FELT THAT I WAS WATCHING A REAL FIGHT.
Oh.
YOU TOO?

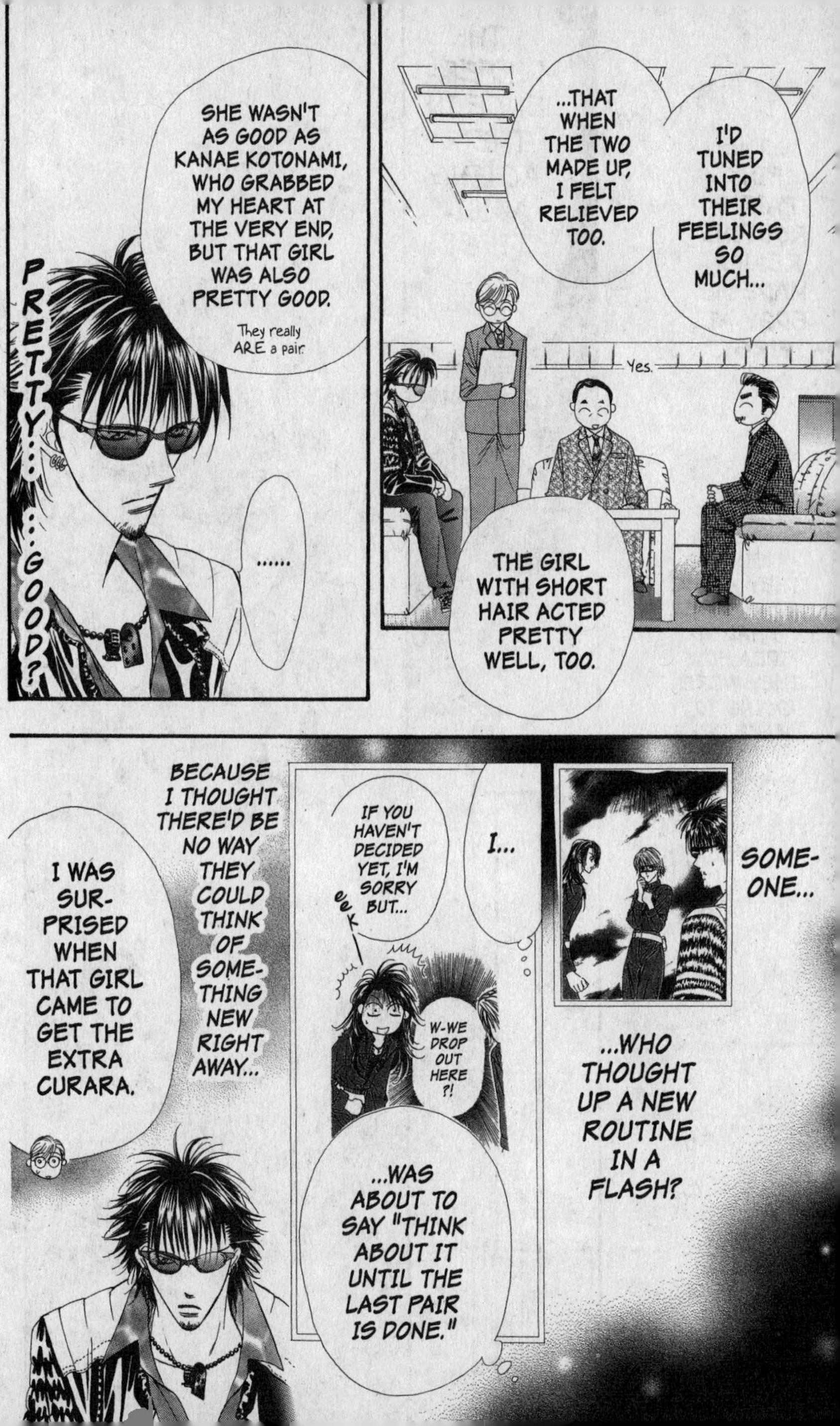
I'D TUNED INTO THEIR FEELINGS SO MUCH...
...THAT WHEN THE TWO MADE UP, I FELT RELIEVED TOO.
Yes.
THE GIRL WITH SHORT HAIR ACTED PRETTY WELL, TOO.
SHE WASN'T AS GOOD AS KANAE KOTONAMI, WHO GRABBED MY HEART AT THE VERY END, BUT THAT GIRL WAS ALSO PRETTY GOOD.
They really ARE a pair.
......
PRETTY... ...GOOD?
SOME-ONE...
...WHO THOUGHT UP A NEW ROUTINE IN A FLASH?
I...
IF YOU HAVEN'T DECIDED YET, I'M SORRY BUT...
eek
W-WE DROP OUT HERE ?!
...WAS ABOUT TO SAY "THINK ABOUT IT UNTIL THE LAST PAIR IS DONE."
BECAUSE I THOUGHT THERE'D BE NO WAY THEY COULD THINK OF SOME-THING NEW RIGHT AWAY...
I WAS SUR-PRISED WHEN THAT GIRL CAME TO GET THE EXTRA CURARA.

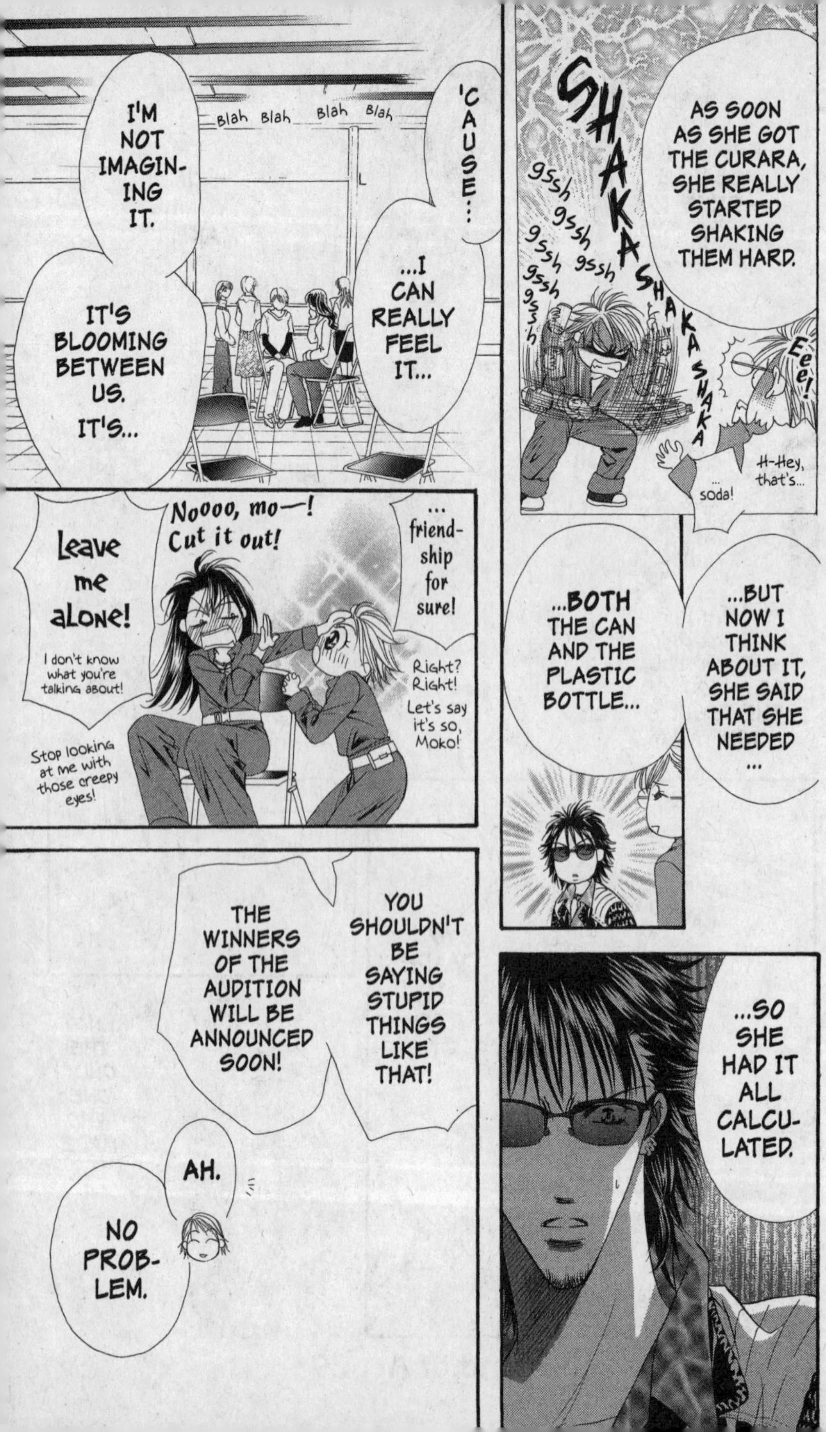
AS SOON AS SHE GOT THE CURARA, SHE REALLY STARTED SHAKING THEM HARD.
SHAKA SHAKA SHAKA SHAKA
gssh gssh gssh gssh gssh gssh
Eee!
H-Hey, that's...
... soda!
'CAUSE...
I'M NOT IMAGINING IT.
Blah Blah Blah Blah
...I CAN REALLY FEEL IT...
IT'S BLOOMING BETWEEN US. IT'S...
...BUT NOW I THINK ABOUT IT, SHE SAID THAT SHE NEEDED ...
...BOTH THE CAN AND THE PLASTIC BOTTLE...
... friendship for sure!
Noooo, mo—! Cut it out!
Leave me alone!
I don't know what you're talking about!
Right? Right! Let's say it's so, Moko!
Stop looking at me with those creepy eyes!
...SO SHE HAD IT ALL CALCULATED.
YOU SHOULDN'T BE SAYING STUPID THINGS LIKE THAT!
THE WINNERS OF THE AUDITION WILL BE ANNOUNCED SOON!
AH.
NO PROBLEM.

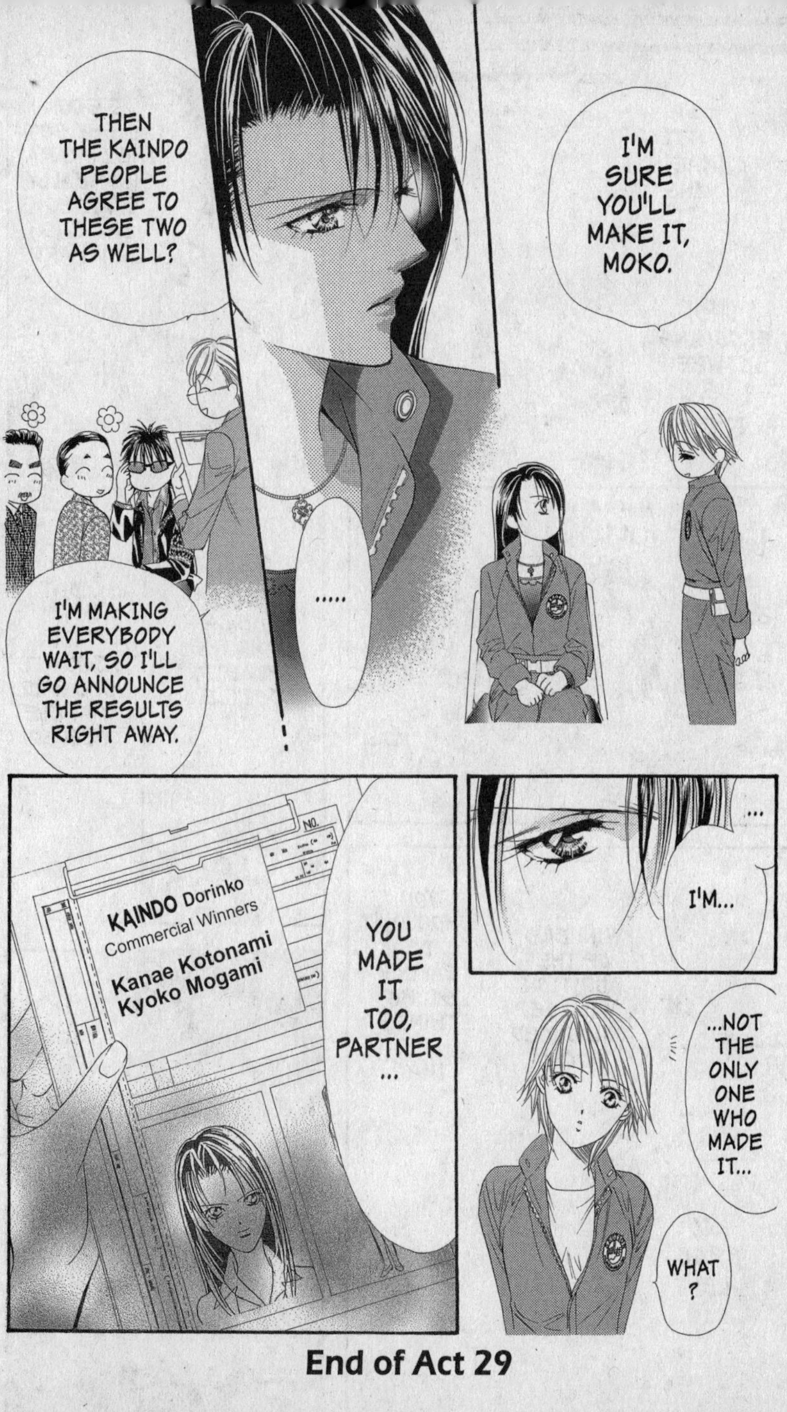
I'M SURE YOU'LL MAKE IT, MOKO.
THEN THE KAINDO PEOPLE AGREE TO THESE TWO AS WELL?
.....
I'M MAKING EVERYBODY WAIT, SO I'LL GO ANNOUNCE THE RESULTS RIGHT AWAY.
... I'M...
...NOT THE ONLY ONE WHO MADE IT...
WHAT?
KAINDO Dorinko
Commercial Winners
Kanae Kotonami
Kyoko Mogami
YOU MADE IT TOO, PARTNER...

End of Act 29

Skip·Beat! End Notes
Everyone knows how to be a fan, but sometimes cool things
from other cultures need a little help crossing the language barrier.

Page 195, panel 5: Comedian and straight man
In the Kansai region of Japan, comedy teams are called *manzai*. The comedian is the *boke* and the straight man is the *tsukkomi*.

Page 198, panel 4: Amulet
Gokaku kigan, a type of amulet used for good luck in passing exams.

Page 269, panel 3: Ksssssh
This is the sound of Ren's manager vomiting sand in reaction to Ren's sappy lines. In Japan, the saying goes, "That's so corny, I want to vomit sand."

Page 295, sidebar: Kuroshio
In Japan, nicknames are often formed by combining the first parts of the last and first name. Ushio Kurosaki's nickname is also the name of the Japanese Current, an ocean current similar to the Gulf Stream. Literally, it means "black stream."

Page 297, panel 5: A-ko and B-ko
Ko means "child", and is a common ending for girls' names. A-ko and B-ko are the same as Girl A and Girl B, but sound more like real names.

Page 338, panel 4: Toro?
A pun on the word *neta*, which can mean either "idea" or "the fish on sushi." *Toro* is fatty tuna, and a popular type of sushi.

Shojo Beat

Skip·Beat!

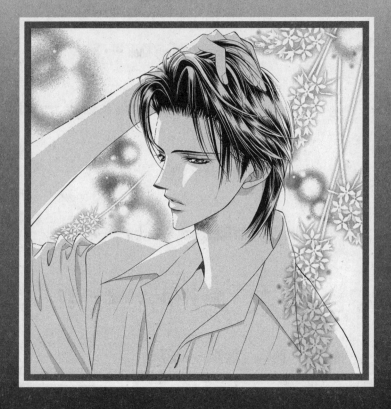

6

Story & Art by Yoshiki Nakamura

Skip·Beat!
Volume 6

CONTENTS

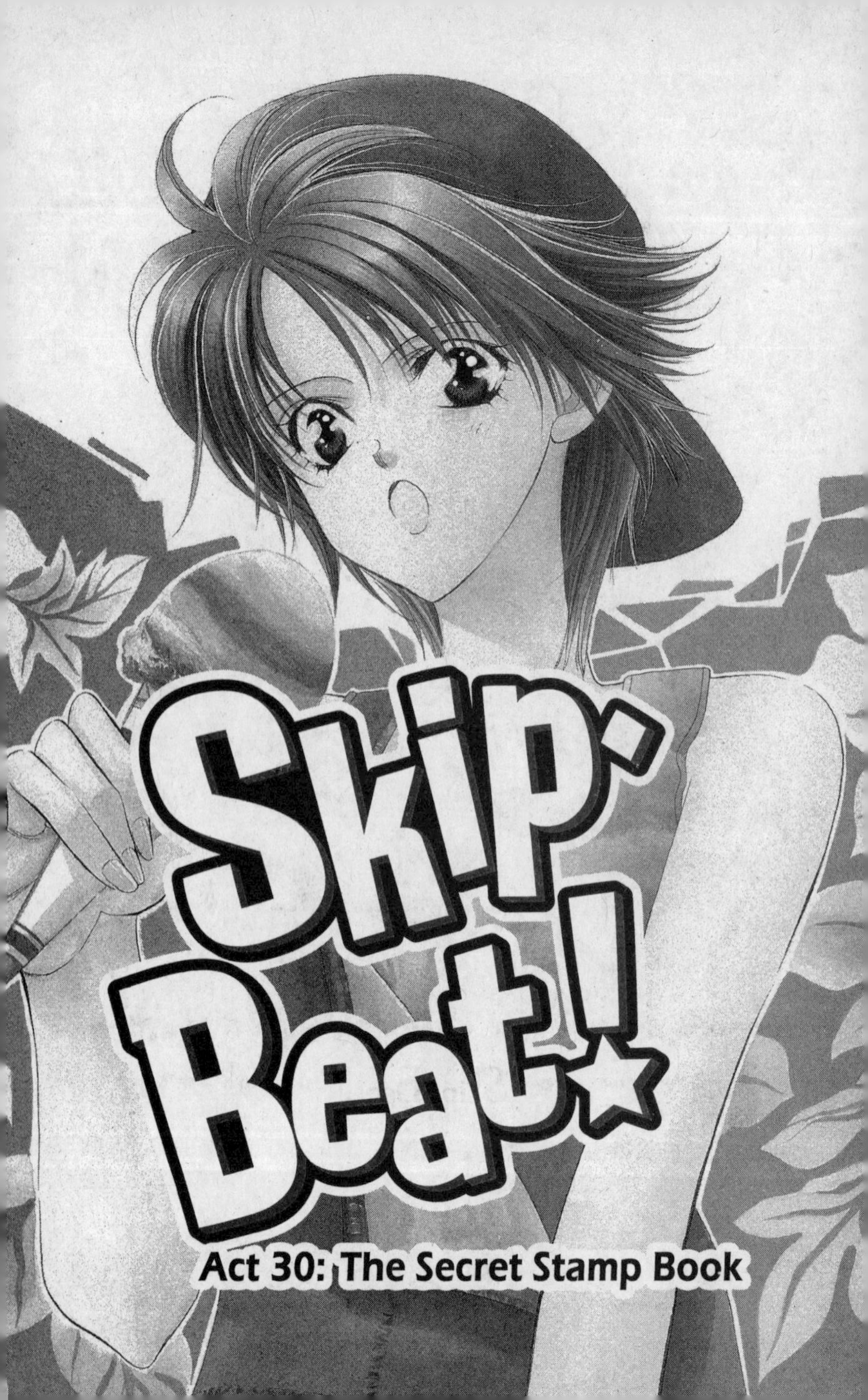

Skip·Beat!
Act 30: The Secret Stamp Book

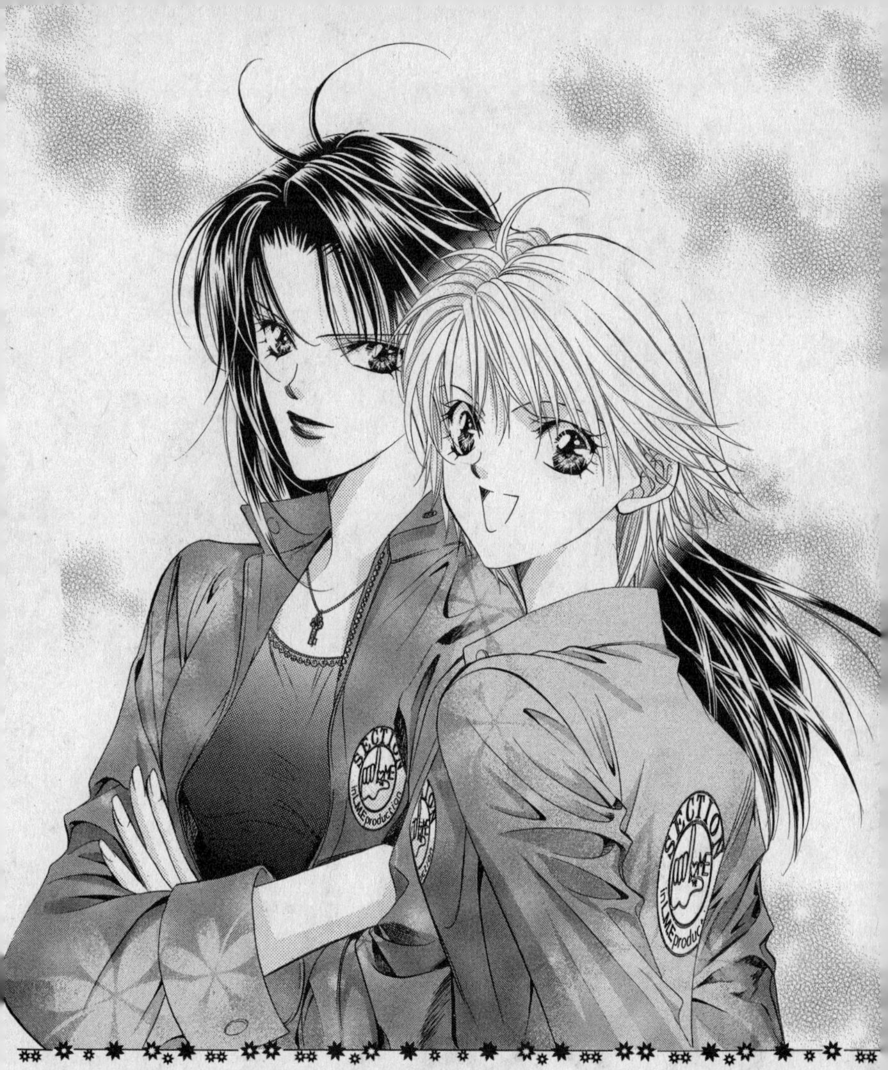
SECTION

Skip・Beat!

6

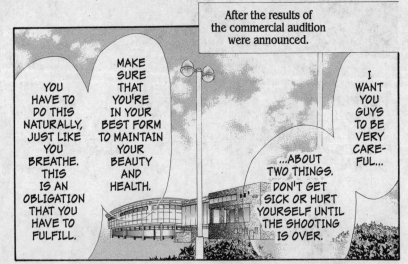

After the results of the commercial audition were announced.
I WANT YOU GUYS TO BE VERY CAREFUL...
...ABOUT TWO THINGS. DON'T GET SICK OR HURT YOURSELF UNTIL THE SHOOTING IS OVER.
MAKE SURE THAT YOU'RE IN YOUR BEST FORM TO MAINTAIN YOUR BEAUTY AND HEALTH.
YOU HAVE TO DO THIS NATURALLY, JUST LIKE YOU BREATHE. THIS IS AN OBLIGATION THAT YOU HAVE TO FULFILL.
THAT'S BECAUSE...
...EVEN IF YOU ARE A NEWCOMER, OR A NO-NAME, ONCE YOU'RE GETTING PAID TO DO WORK, YOU'RE A PROFESSIONAL.
Your body doesn't only belong to you anymore.
YOUR BODY IS YOUR TOOL FOR THIS BUSINESS...
...AND ANYBODY WHO CAN'T MAINTAIN THAT LACKS PROFESSIONALISM.

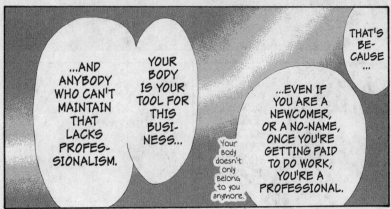

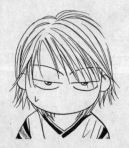

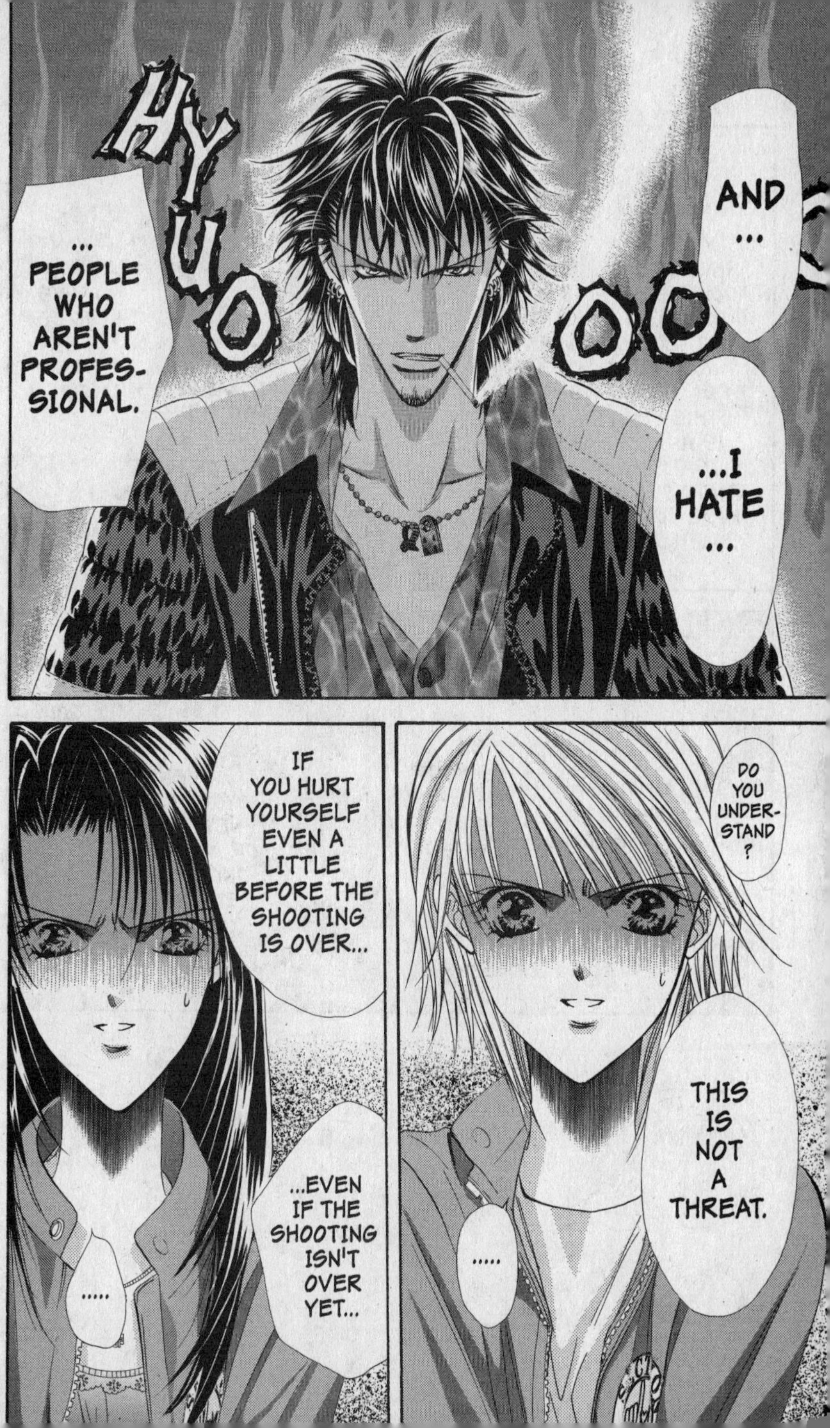
AND ...
HYUOOO
...I HATE ...
... PEOPLE WHO AREN'T PROFES-SIONAL.
DO YOU UNDER-STAND?
THIS IS NOT A THREAT.
.....
IF YOU HURT YOURSELF EVEN A LITTLE BEFORE THE SHOOTING IS OVER...
...EVEN IF THE SHOOTING ISN'T OVER YET...
.....

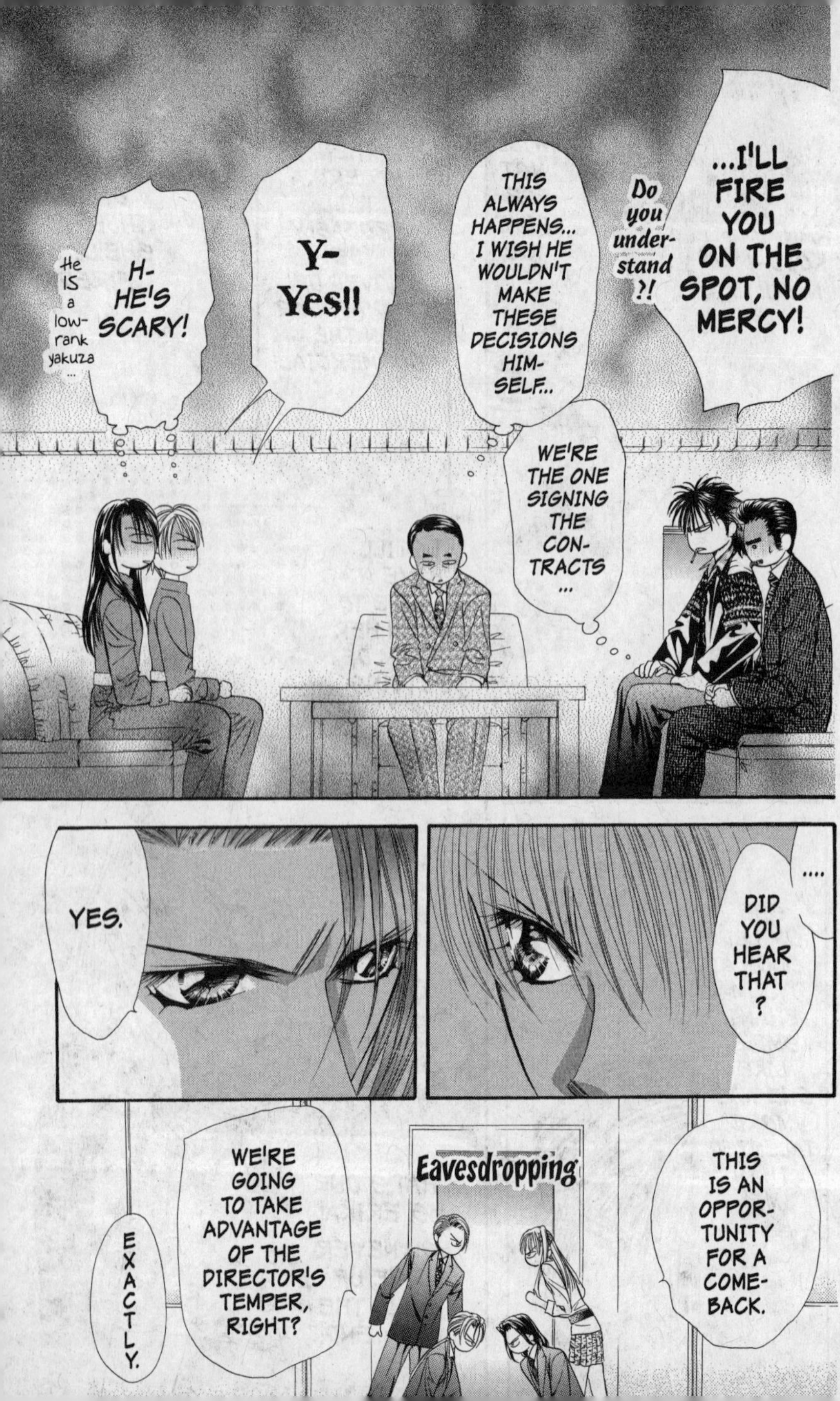
...I'LL FIRE YOU ON THE SPOT, NO MERCY!
Do you under-stand?!
THIS ALWAYS HAPPENS... I WISH HE WOULDN'T MAKE THESE DECISIONS HIM-SELF...
WE'RE THE ONE SIGNING THE CON-TRACTS...
Y-Yes!!
H-HE'S SCARY!
He IS a low-rank yakuza...
....
DID YOU HEAR THAT?
YES.
THIS IS AN OPPOR-TUNITY FOR A COME-BACK.
Eavesdropping
WE'RE GOING TO TAKE ADVANTAGE OF THE DIRECTOR'S TEMPER, RIGHT?
EXACTLY.

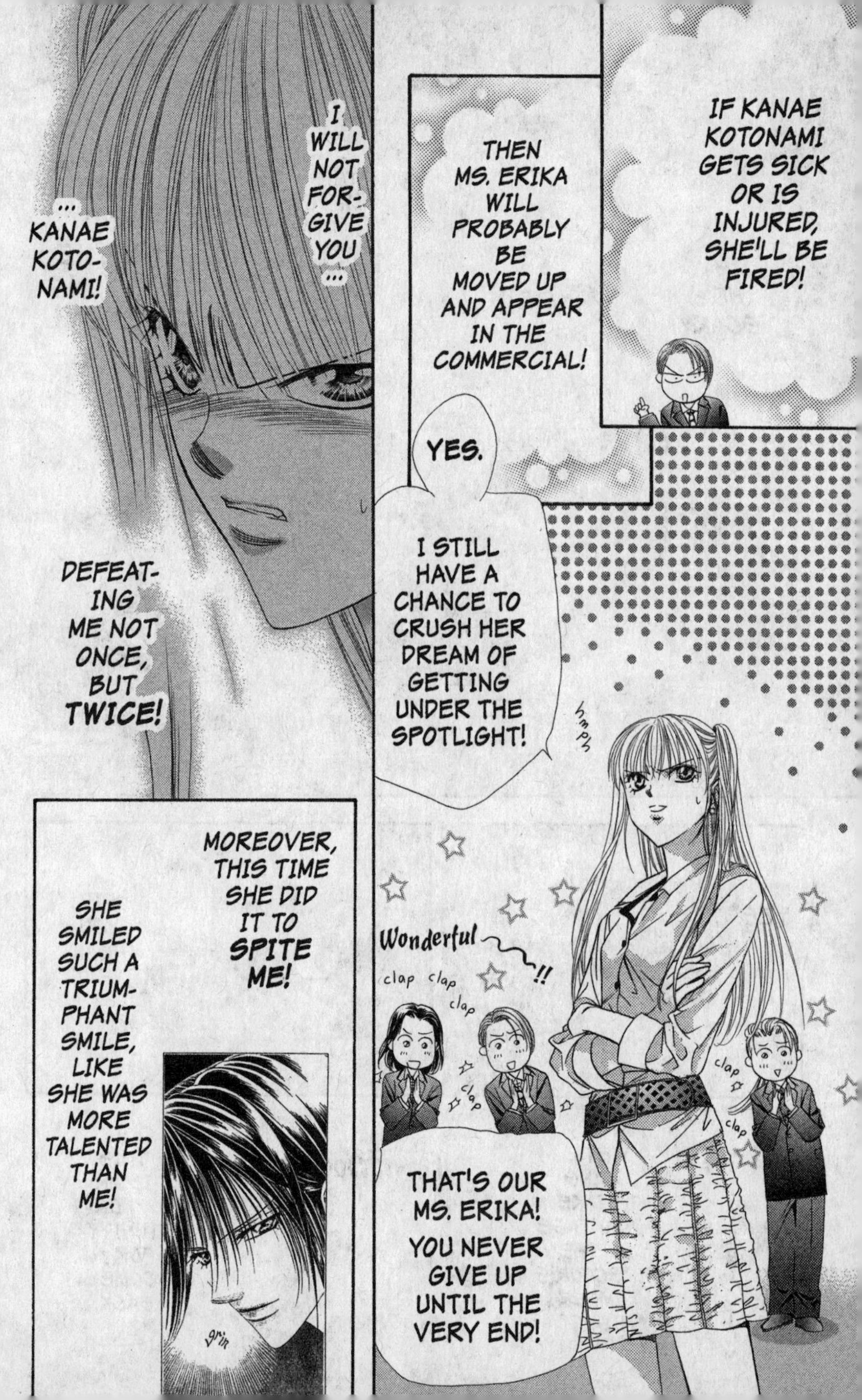
IF KANAE KOTONAMI GETS SICK OR IS INJURED, SHE'LL BE FIRED!
THEN MS. ERIKA WILL PROBABLY BE MOVED UP AND APPEAR IN THE COMMERCIAL!
YES.
I STILL HAVE A CHANCE TO CRUSH HER DREAM OF GETTING UNDER THE SPOTLIGHT!
hmph
Wonderful!!
clap clap clap
clap clap clap
THAT'S OUR MS. ERIKA! YOU NEVER GIVE UP UNTIL THE VERY END!
I WILL NOT FORGIVE YOU...
...KANAE KOTONAMI!
DEFEATING ME NOT ONCE, BUT TWICE!
MOREOVER, THIS TIME SHE DID IT TO SPITE ME!
SHE SMILED SUCH A TRIUMPHANT SMILE, LIKE SHE WAS MORE TALENTED THAN ME!
grin

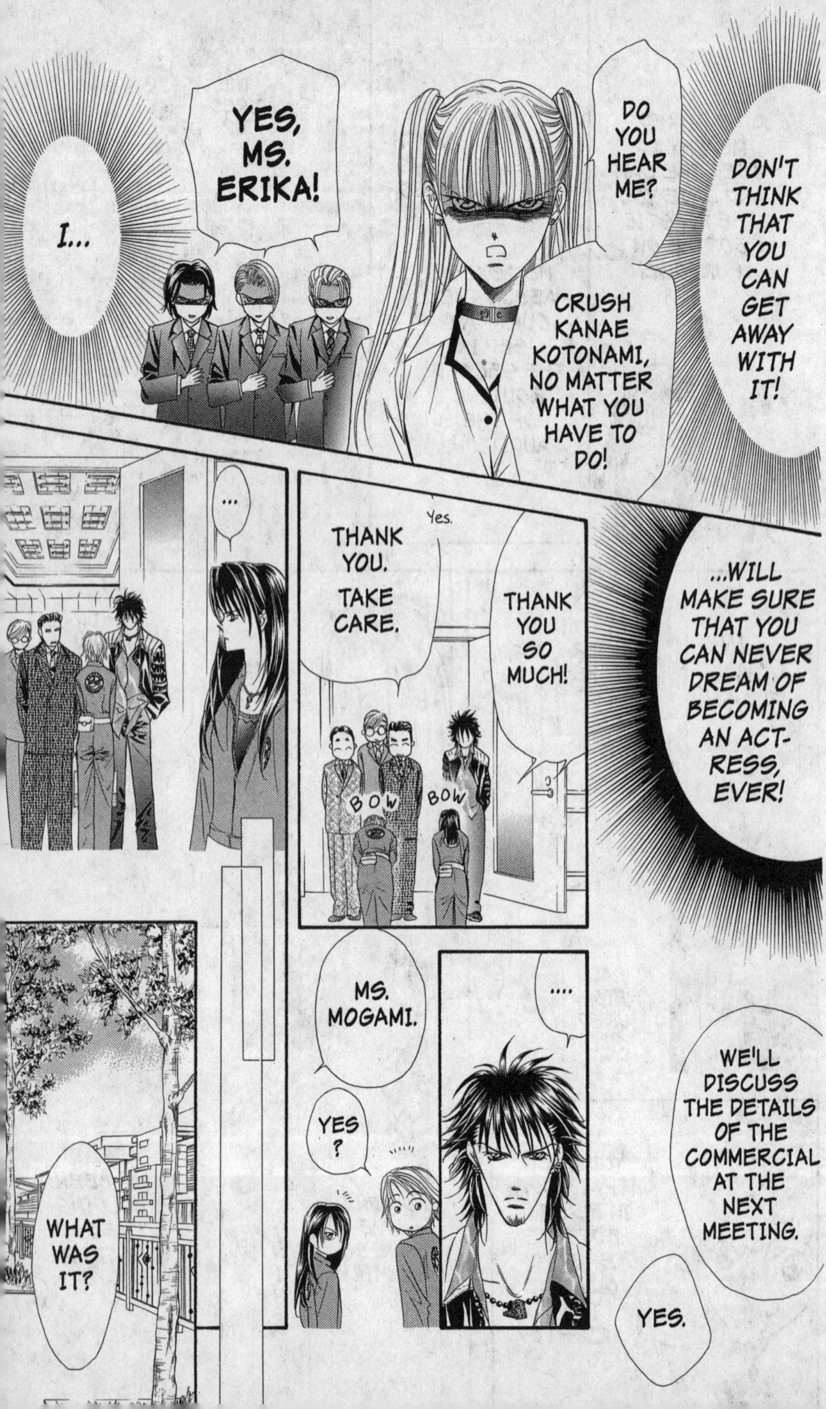
DON'T THINK THAT YOU CAN GET AWAY WITH IT!
DO YOU HEAR ME?
CRUSH KANAE KOTONAMI, NO MATTER WHAT YOU HAVE TO DO!
YES, MS. ERIKA!
I...
...WILL MAKE SURE THAT YOU CAN NEVER DREAM OF BECOMING AN ACT-RESS, EVER!
THANK YOU SO MUCH!
Yes.
THANK YOU. TAKE CARE.
BOW
BOW
...
WE'LL DISCUSS THE DETAILS OF THE COMMERCIAL AT THE NEXT MEETING.
YES.
....
MS. MOGAMI.
YES?
WHAT WAS IT?

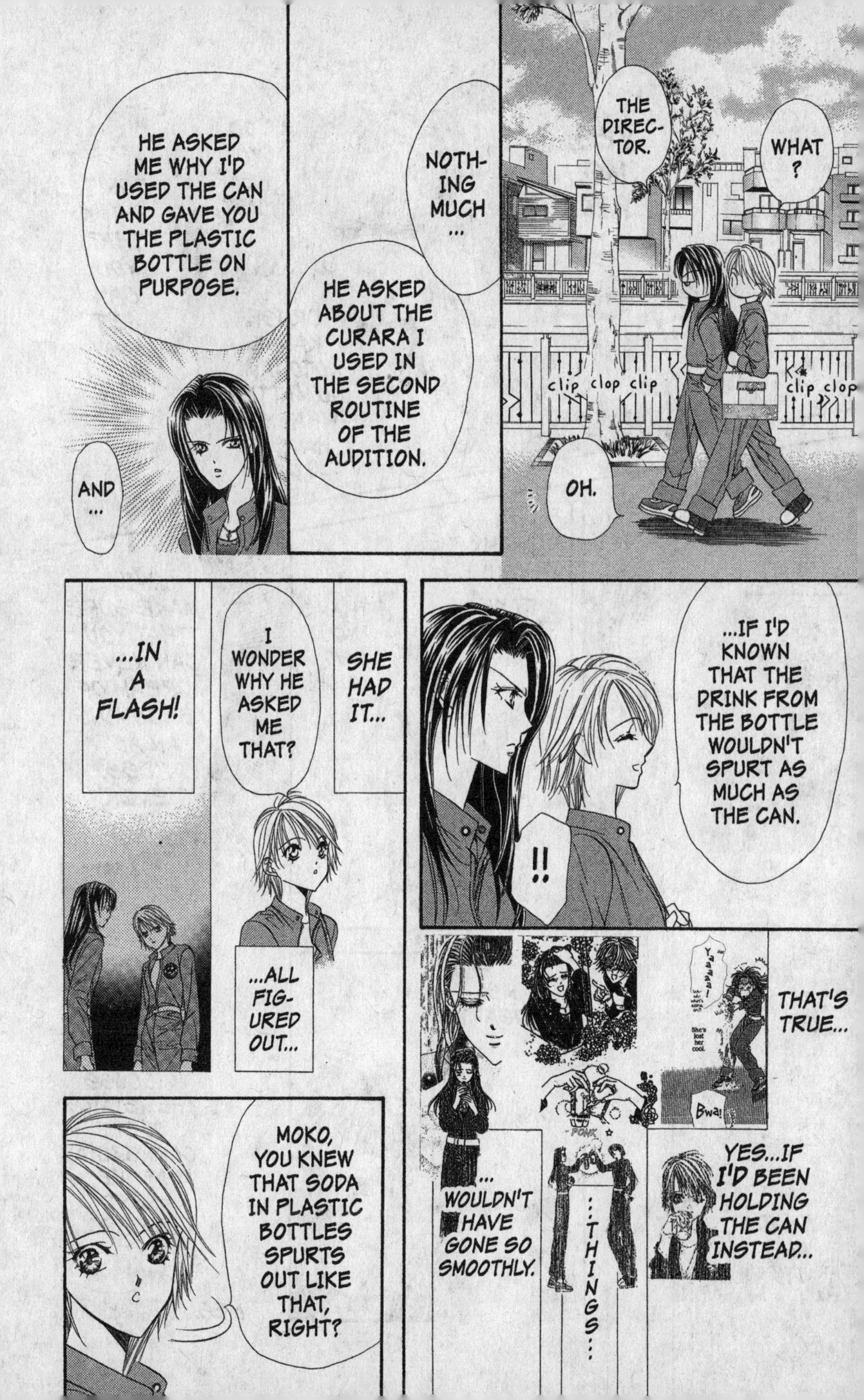
WHAT?
THE DIREC-TOR.
clip clop
clip clop clip
OH.
NOTH-ING MUCH...
HE ASKED ABOUT THE CURARA I USED IN THE SECOND ROUTINE OF THE AUDITION.
HE ASKED ME WHY I'D USED THE CAN AND GAVE YOU THE PLASTIC BOTTLE ON PURPOSE.
AND...
...IF I'D KNOWN THAT THE DRINK FROM THE BOTTLE WOULDN'T SPURT AS MUCH AS THE CAN.
!!
THAT'S TRUE...
Yaaa!
She's lost her cool.
Bwa!
PONK
YES...IF I'D BEEN HOLDING THE CAN INSTEAD...
...THINGS...
...WOULDN'T HAVE GONE SO SMOOTHLY.
SHE HAD IT...
I WONDER WHY HE ASKED ME THAT?
...IN A FLASH!
...ALL FIG-URED OUT...
MOKO, YOU KNEW THAT SODA IN PLASTIC BOTTLES SPURTS OUT LIKE THAT, RIGHT?

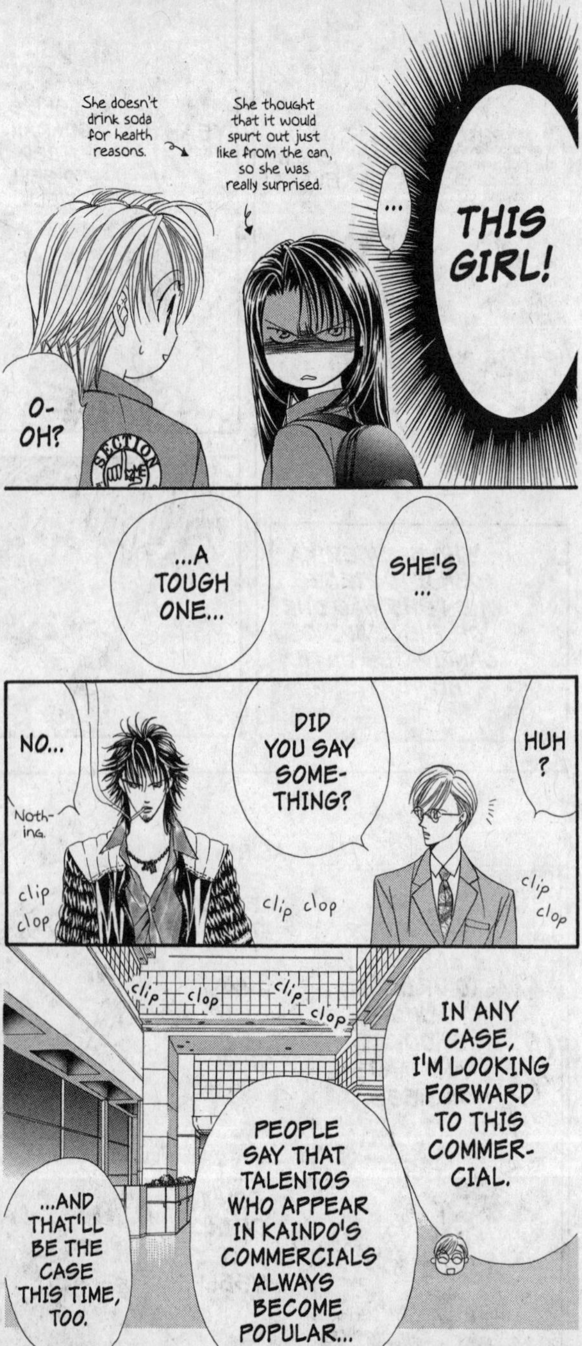
THIS GIRL!
...
She thought that it would spurt out just like from the can, so she was really surprised.
She doesn't drink soda for health reasons.
O-OH?
SECTION
SHE'S ...
...A TOUGH ONE...
HUH?
DID YOU SAY SOMETHING?
NO...
Nothing.
clip clop
clip clop
clip clop
IN ANY CASE, I'M LOOKING FORWARD TO THIS COMMERCIAL.
clip clop
clip clop
PEOPLE SAY THAT TALENTOS WHO APPEAR IN KAINDO'S COMMERCIALS ALWAYS BECOME POPULAR...
...AND THAT'LL BE THE CASE THIS TIME, TOO.

Digression

I liked Ruby's idea of Yanki fashion quite a bit when it was first printed in the magazine. But not as much as drawing it in the sidebar now...

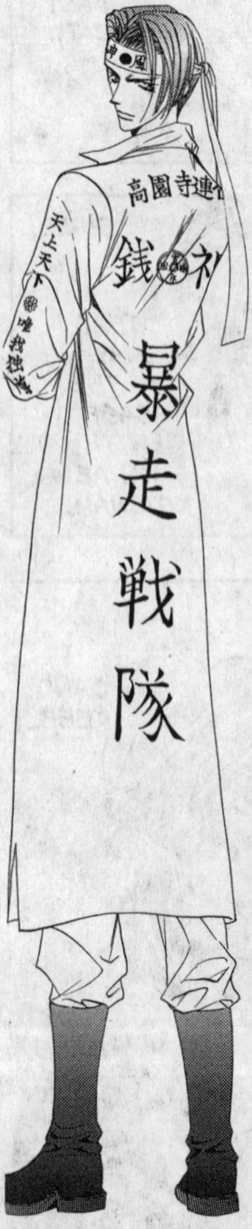

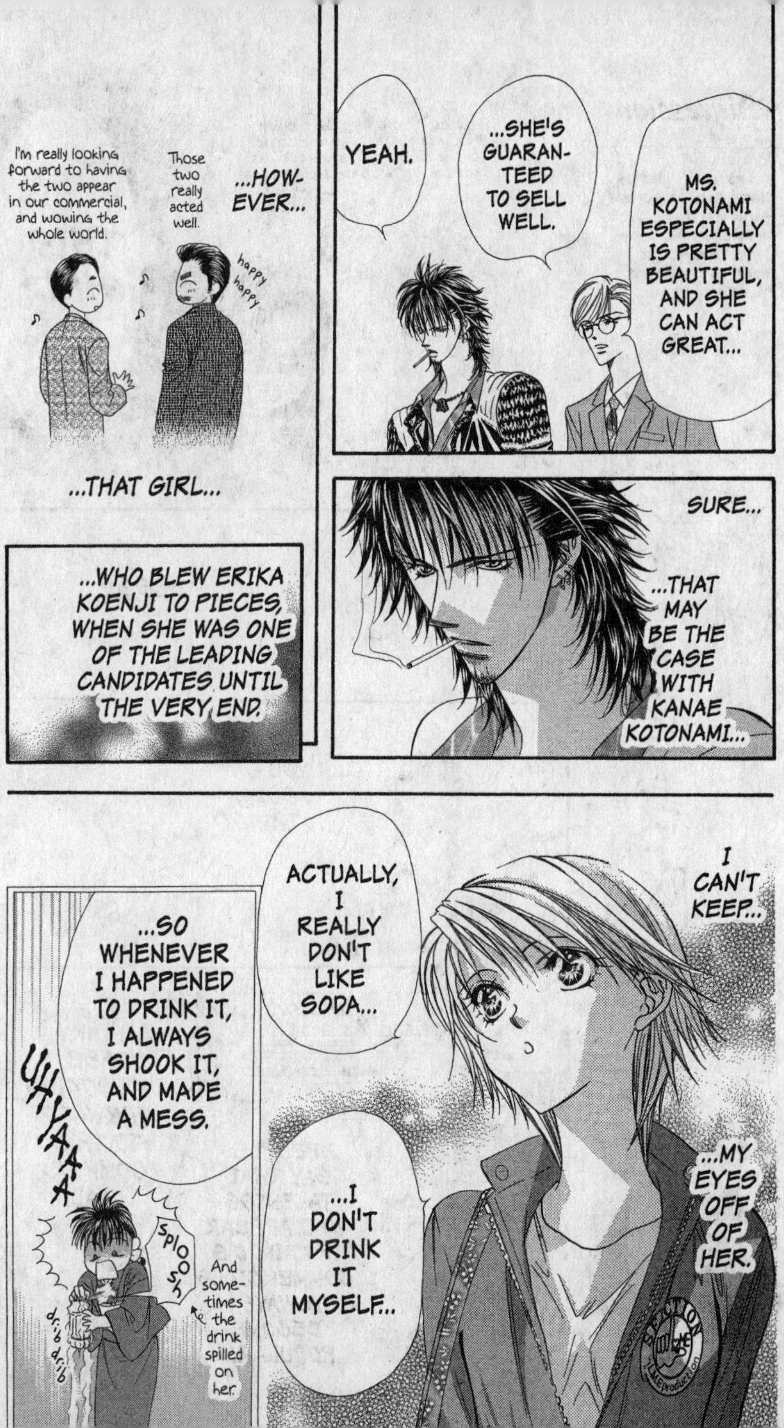
MS. KOTONAMI ESPECIALLY IS PRETTY BEAUTIFUL, AND SHE CAN ACT GREAT...
...SHE'S GUARAN-TEED TO SELL WELL.
YEAH.
SURE...
...THAT MAY BE THE CASE WITH KANAE KOTONAMI...
...HOW-EVER...
happy happy
Those two really acted well.
I'm really looking forward to having the two appear in our commercial, and wowing the whole world.
...THAT GIRL...
...WHO BLEW ERIKA KOENJI TO PIECES, WHEN SHE WAS ONE OF THE LEADING CANDIDATES UNTIL THE VERY END.
I CAN'T KEEP...
ACTUALLY, I REALLY DON'T LIKE SODA...
...MY EYES OFF OF HER.
...I DON'T DRINK IT MYSELF...
...SO WHENEVER I HAPPENED TO DRINK IT, I ALWAYS SHOOK IT, AND MADE A MESS.
UHYAAAA
splooosh
And sometimes the drink spilled on her.
drib drib

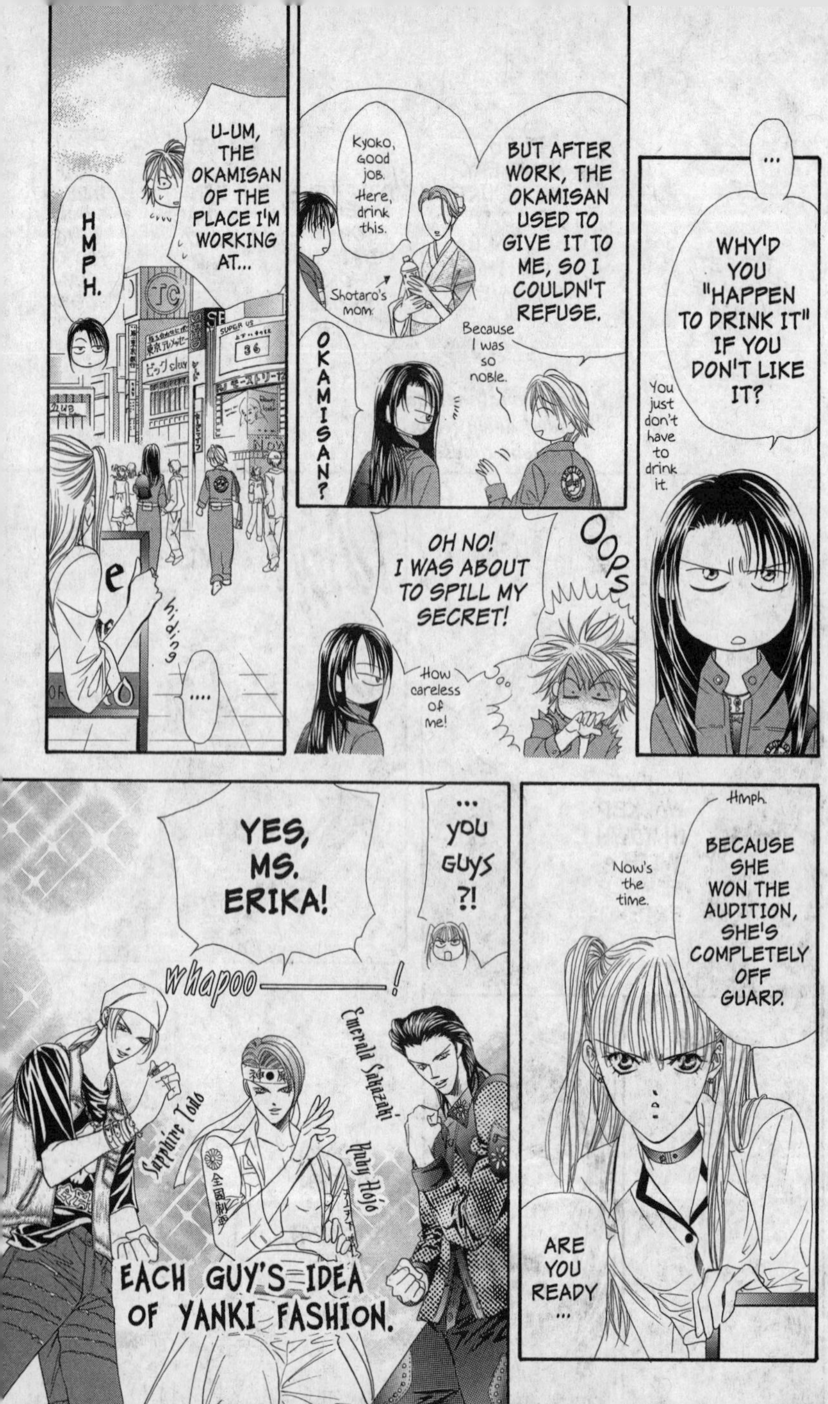
...
WHY'D YOU "HAPPEN TO DRINK IT" IF YOU DON'T LIKE IT?
You just don't have to drink it.
BUT AFTER WORK, THE OKAMISAN USED TO GIVE IT TO ME, SO I COULDN'T REFUSE.
Kyoko, good job. Here, drink this.
Shotaro's mom
OKAMISAN?
Because I was so noble.
OOPS
OH NO! I WAS ABOUT TO SPILL MY SECRET!
How careless of me!
U-UM, THE OKAMISAN OF THE PLACE I'M WORKING AT...
HMPH.
hiding
....
Hmph.
BECAUSE SHE WON THE AUDITION, SHE'S COMPLETELY OFF GUARD.
Now's the time.
ARE YOU READY ...
... YOU GUYS ?!
YES, MS. ERIKA!
whapoo———!
Emerald Sakazaki
Ruby Hojo
Sapphire Todo
EACH GUY'S IDEA OF YANKI FASHION.

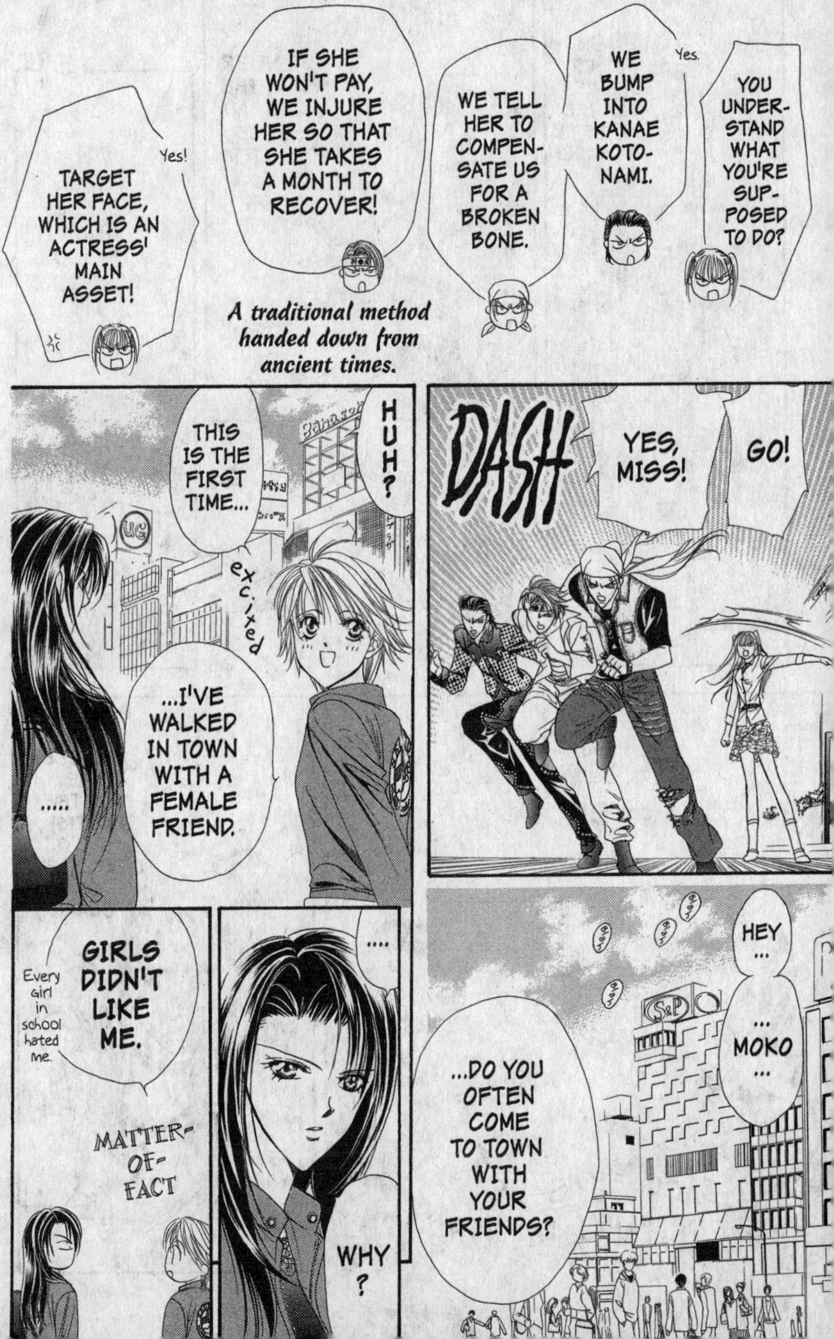
YOU UNDERSTAND WHAT YOU'RE SUPPOSED TO DO?
Yes.
WE BUMP INTO KANAE KOTONAMI.
WE TELL HER TO COMPENSATE US FOR A BROKEN BONE.
IF SHE WON'T PAY, WE INJURE HER SO THAT SHE TAKES A MONTH TO RECOVER!
Yes!
TARGET HER FACE, WHICH IS AN ACTRESS' MAIN ASSET!
A traditional method handed down from ancient times.
GO!
YES, MISS!
DASH
HUH?
THIS IS THE FIRST TIME...
excited
...I'VE WALKED IN TOWN WITH A FEMALE FRIEND.
.....
HEY... ...MOKO...
...DO YOU OFTEN COME TO TOWN WITH YOUR FRIENDS?
....
WHY?
GIRLS DIDN'T LIKE ME.
Every girl in school hated me.
MATTER-OF-FACT

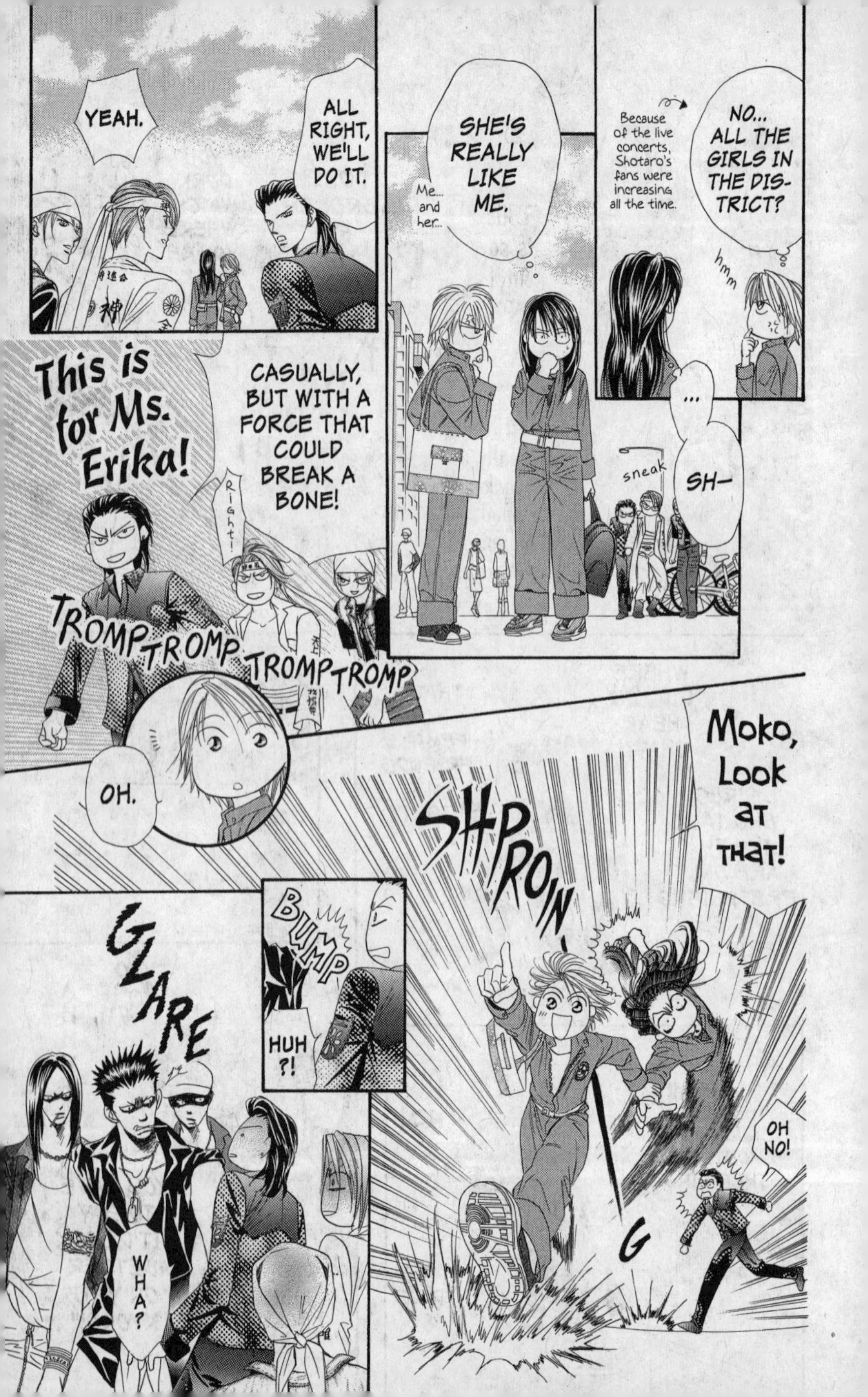
NO... ALL THE GIRLS IN THE DIS-TRICT?
Because of the live concerts, Shotaro's fans were increasing all the time.
hmm
SHE'S REALLY LIKE ME.
Me... and her...
...
SH—
sneak
ALL RIGHT, WE'LL DO IT.
YEAH.
This is for Ms. Erika!
CASUALLY, BUT WITH A FORCE THAT COULD BREAK A BONE!
Right!
TROMP TROMP TROMP TROMP
Moko, Look at that!
SHPROIN
OH.
OH NO!
G
BUMP
HUH?!
GLARE
WHA?

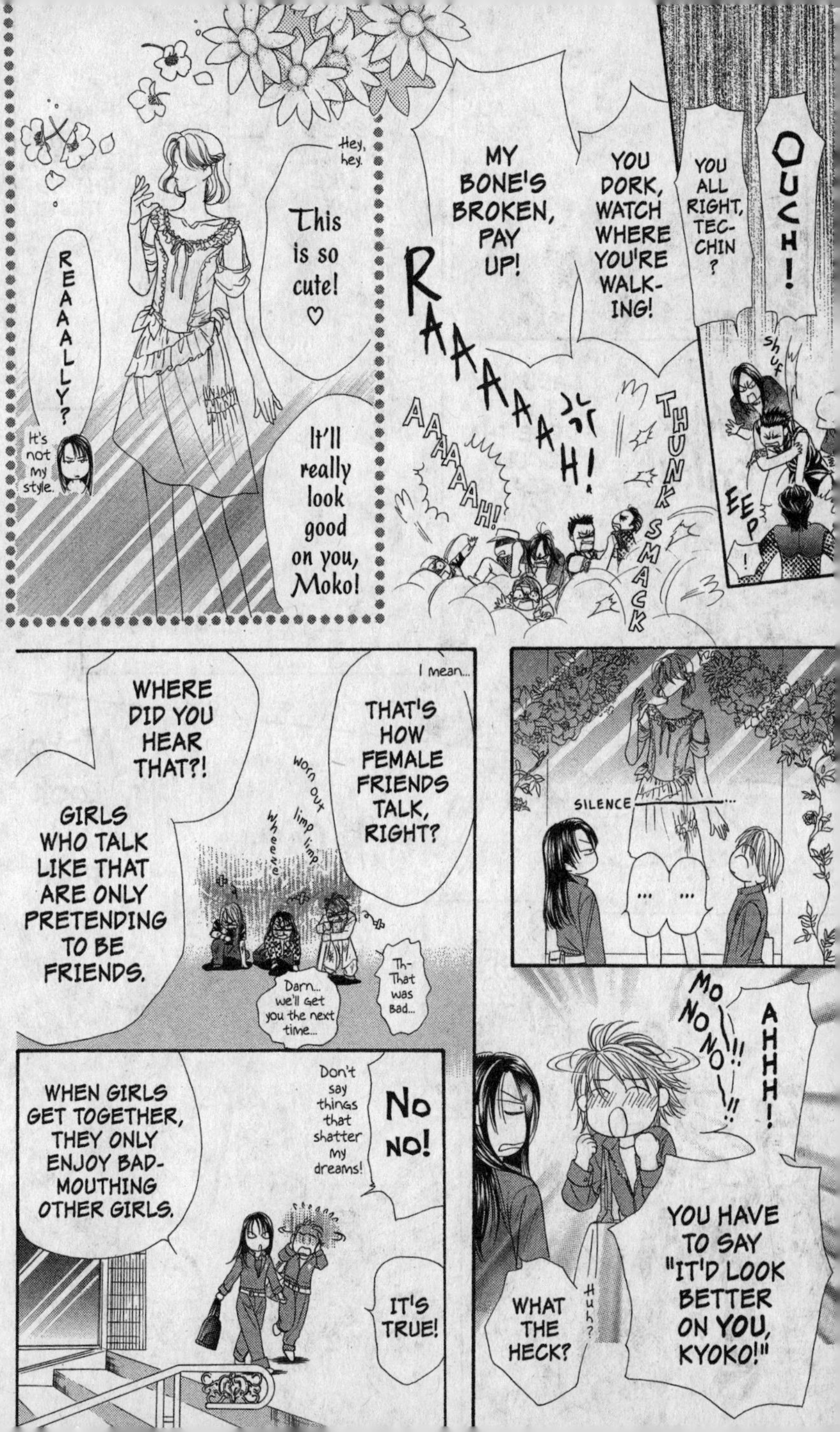
OUCH!
YOU ALL RIGHT, TEC-CHIN?
shuf
EEP!
YOU DORK, WATCH WHERE YOU'RE WALKING!
MY BONE'S BROKEN, PAY UP!
RAAAAAAH!
AAAAAAAH!
THUNK
SMACK
Hey, hey.
This is so cute! ♡
It'll really look good on you, Moko!
REAAAALLY?
It's not my style.
SILENCE
... ...
I mean...
THAT'S HOW FEMALE FRIENDS TALK, RIGHT?
WHERE DID YOU HEAR THAT?!
GIRLS WHO TALK LIKE THAT ARE ONLY PRETENDING TO BE FRIENDS.
worn out
limp limp
wheeze
Th-That was bad...
Darn... we'll get you the next time...
AHHH!
MO NO NO!!
YOU HAVE TO SAY "IT'D LOOK BETTER ON YOU, KYOKO!"
Huh?
WHAT THE HECK?
No NO!
Don't say things that shatter my dreams!
WHEN GIRLS GET TOGETHER, THEY ONLY ENJOY BAD-MOUTHING OTHER GIRLS.
IT'S TRUE!

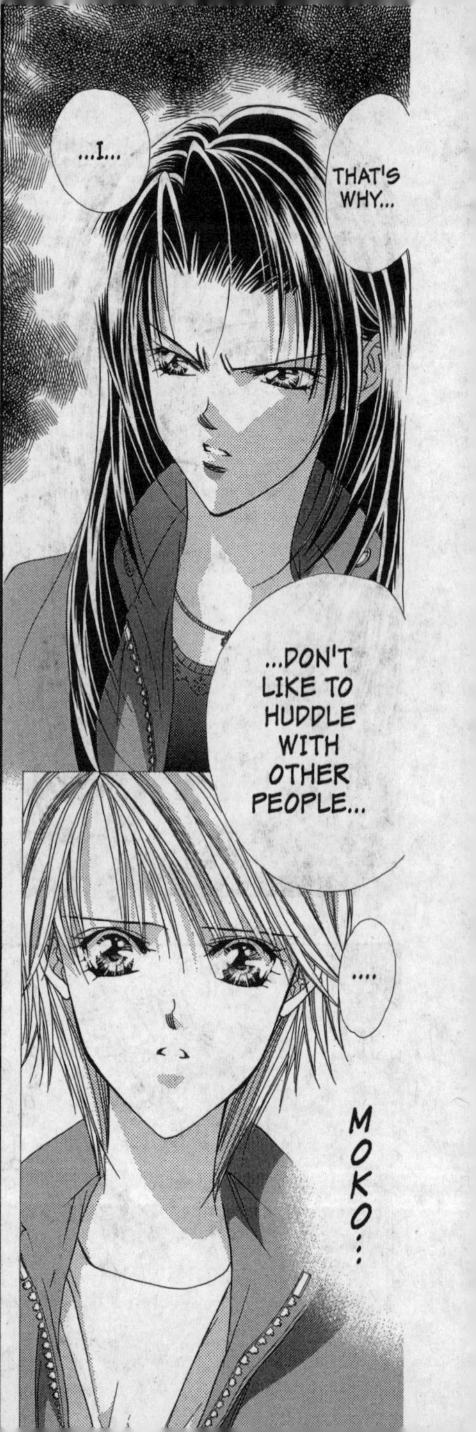
THAT'S WHY...
...I...
...DON'T LIKE TO HUDDLE WITH OTHER PEOPLE...
....
MOKO...
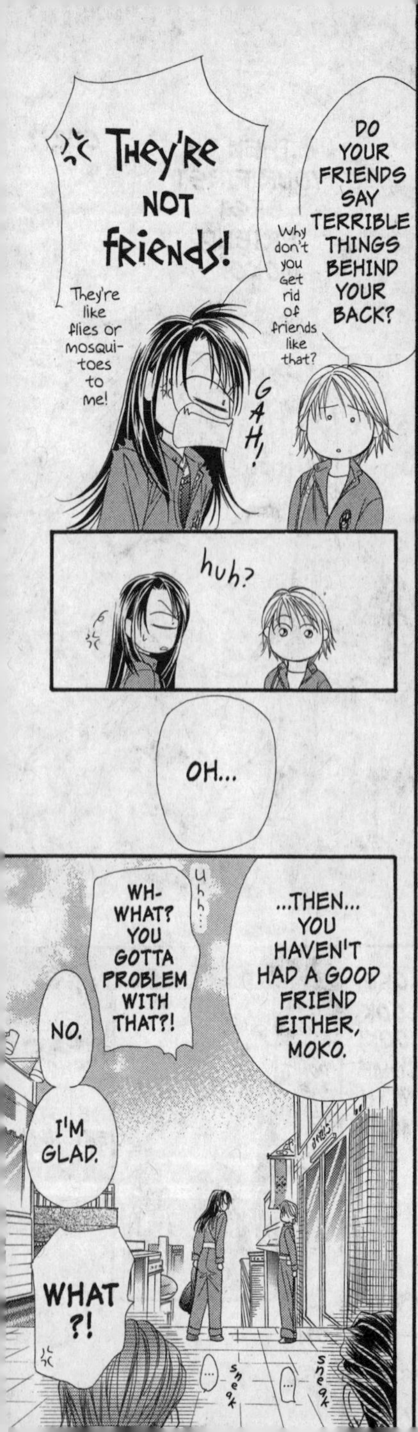
DO YOUR FRIENDS SAY TERRIBLE THINGS BEHIND YOUR BACK?
Why don't you get rid of friends like that?
They're NOT friends!
They're like flies or mosqui-toes to me!
GAH!
huh?
OH...
...THEN... YOU HAVEN'T HAD A GOOD FRIEND EITHER, MOKO.
Uhh...
WH-WHAT? YOU GOTTA PROBLEM WITH THAT?!
NO.
I'M GLAD.
WHAT?!
...
sneak
...
sneak

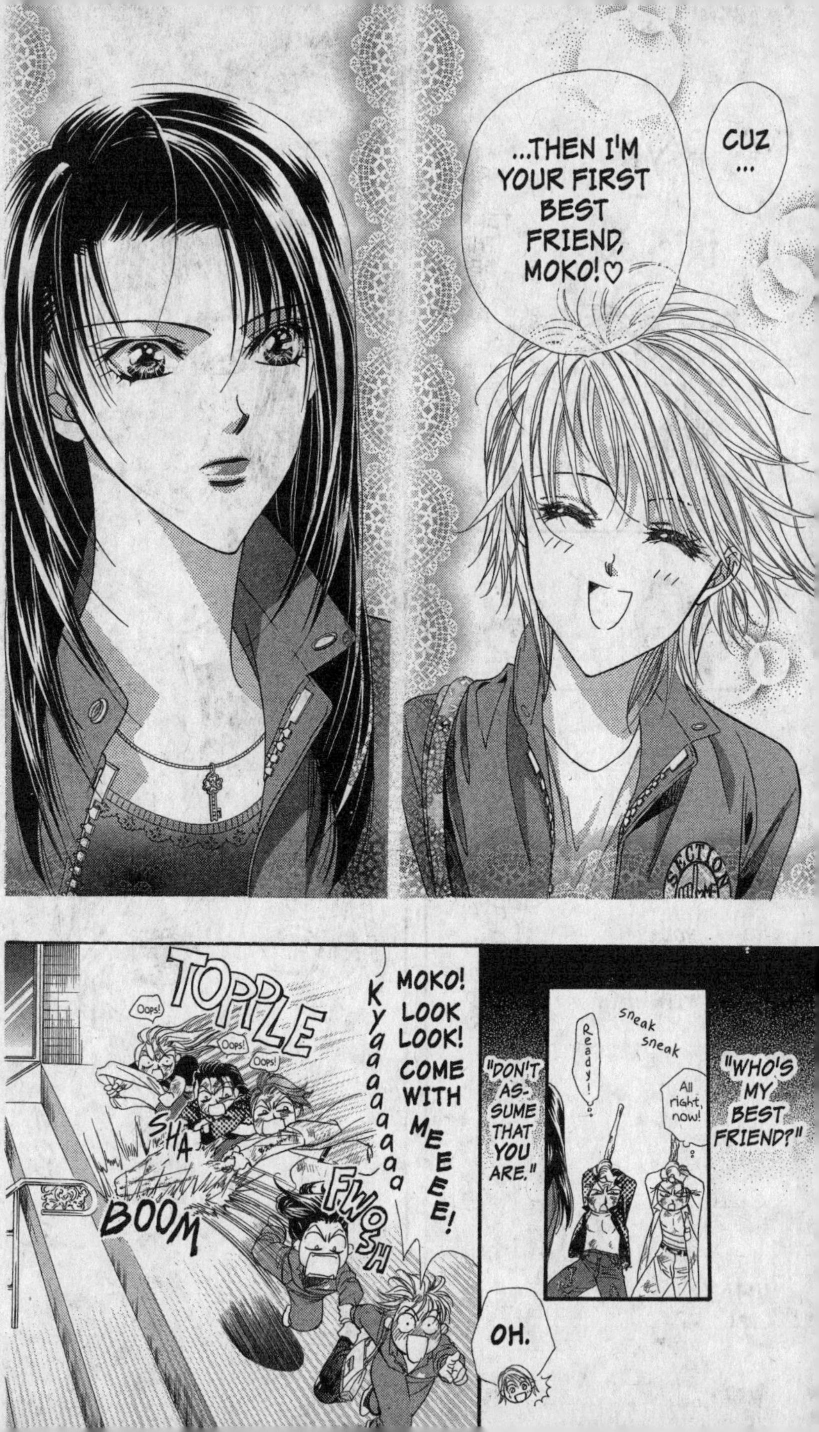
CUZ ...
...THEN I'M YOUR FIRST BEST FRIEND, MOKO!♡
"WHO'S MY BEST FRIEND?"
All right, now!
Ready!
sneak sneak
"DON'T AS-SUME THAT YOU ARE."
OH.
MOKO! LOOK LOOK! COME WITH MEEEE!
Kyaaaaaaaaaa
FWOSH
TOPPLE
Oops!
Oops!
Oops!
SHA
BOOM

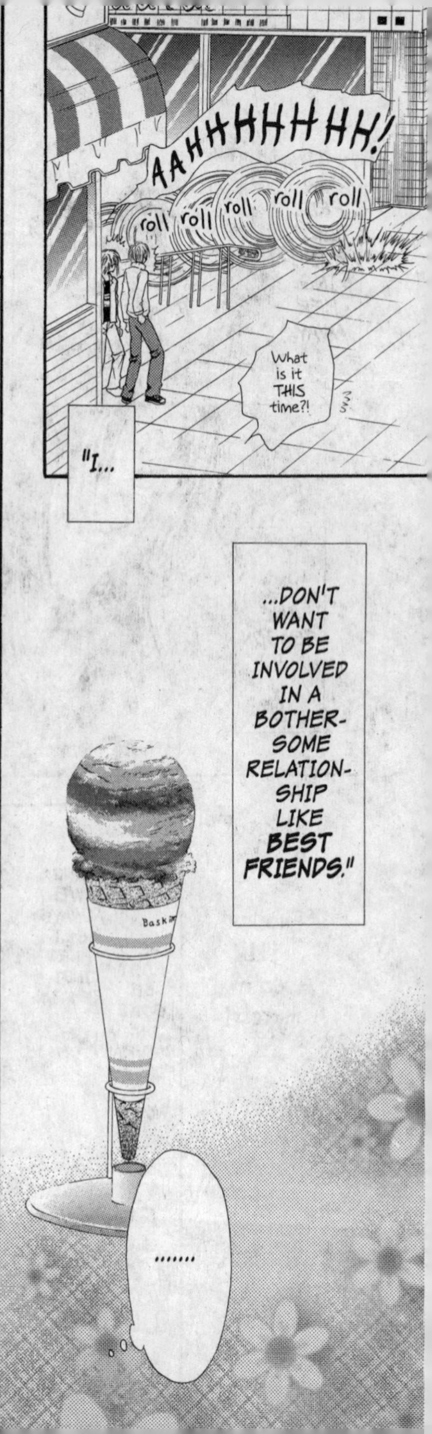
AAHHHHHHHH!
roll roll roll roll roll
What is it THIS time?!
"I...
...DON'T WANT TO BE INVOLVED IN A BOTHERSOME RELATIONSHIP LIKE BEST FRIENDS."
Bask
....

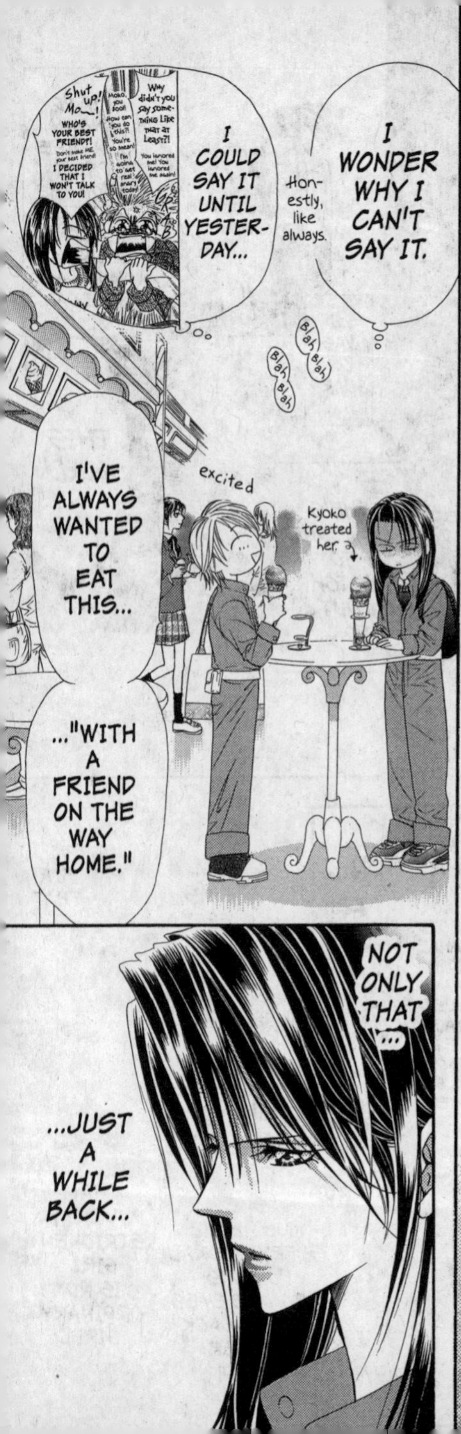
I WONDER WHY I CAN'T SAY IT.
Honestly, like always.
I COULD SAY IT UNTIL YESTERDAY...
Why didn't you say something like that at least?!
You ignored me! You ignored me again!
Moko, you fool! How can you do this?! You're so mean! I'm going to get real angry today!
Shut up! Mo~!
WHO'S YOUR BEST FRIEND?!
Don't make ME your best friend!
I DECIDED THAT I WON'T TALK TO YOU!
Blah Blah Blah Blah
I'VE ALWAYS WANTED TO EAT THIS...
..."WITH A FRIEND ON THE WAY HOME."
Kyoko treated her.
excited
NOT ONLY THAT...
...JUST A WHILE BACK...

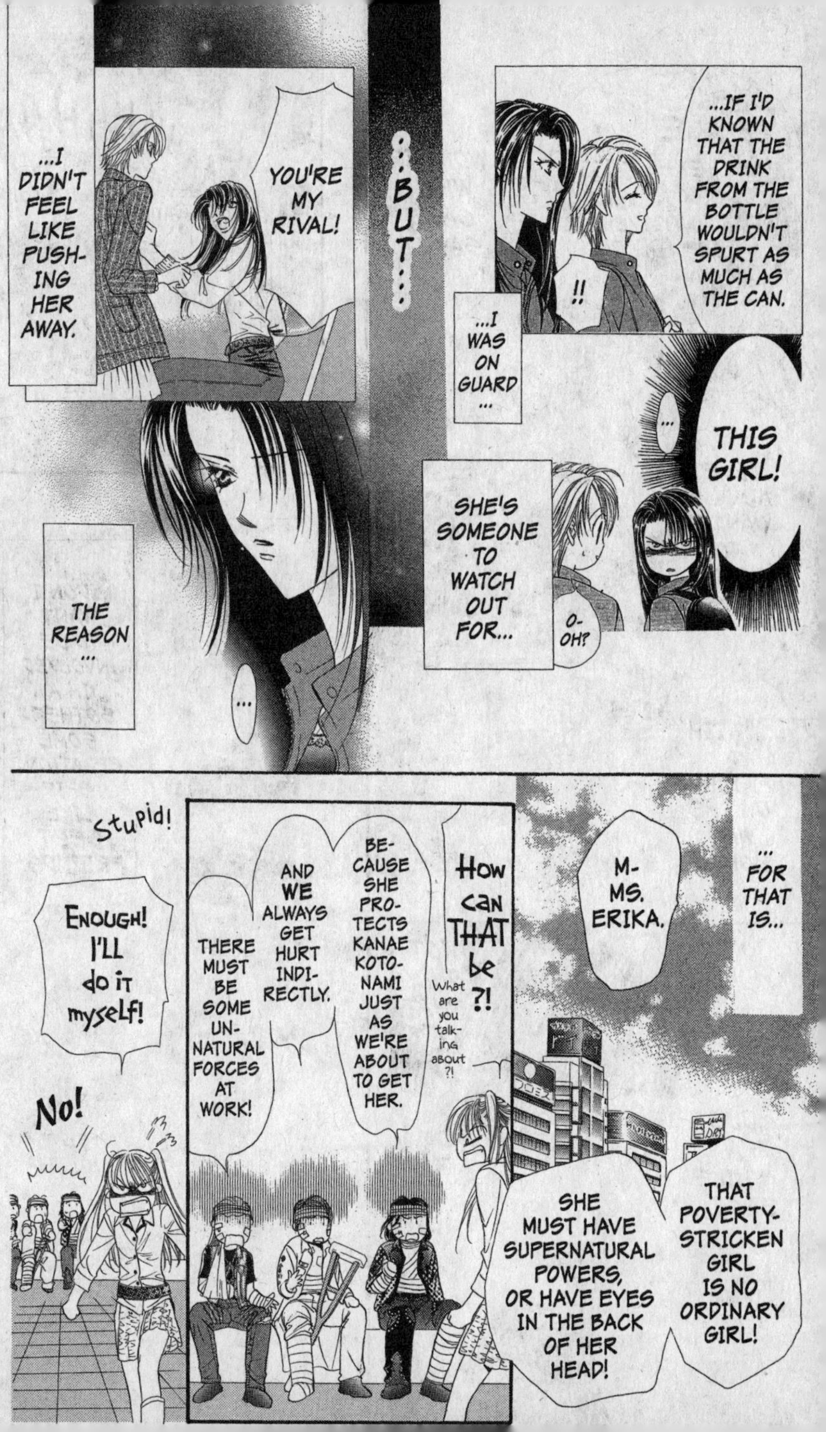
...IF I'D KNOWN THAT THE DRINK FROM THE BOTTLE WOULDN'T SPURT AS MUCH AS THE CAN.
!!
...I WAS ON GUARD ...
THIS GIRL!
...
SHE'S SOMEONE TO WATCH OUT FOR...
O-OH?
...BUT...
YOU'RE MY RIVAL!
...I DIDN'T FEEL LIKE PUSHING HER AWAY.
THE REASON ...
...
... FOR THAT IS...
M-MS. ERIKA.
THAT POVERTY-STRICKEN GIRL IS NO ORDINARY GIRL!
SHE MUST HAVE SUPERNATURAL POWERS, OR HAVE EYES IN THE BACK OF HER HEAD!
How can THAT be?!
What are you talking about?!
BECAUSE SHE PROTECTS KANAE KOTONAMI JUST AS WE'RE ABOUT TO GET HER.
AND WE ALWAYS GET HURT INDIRECTLY.
THERE MUST BE SOME UNNATURAL FORCES AT WORK!
Stupid!
ENOUGH! I'LL do it myself!
No!

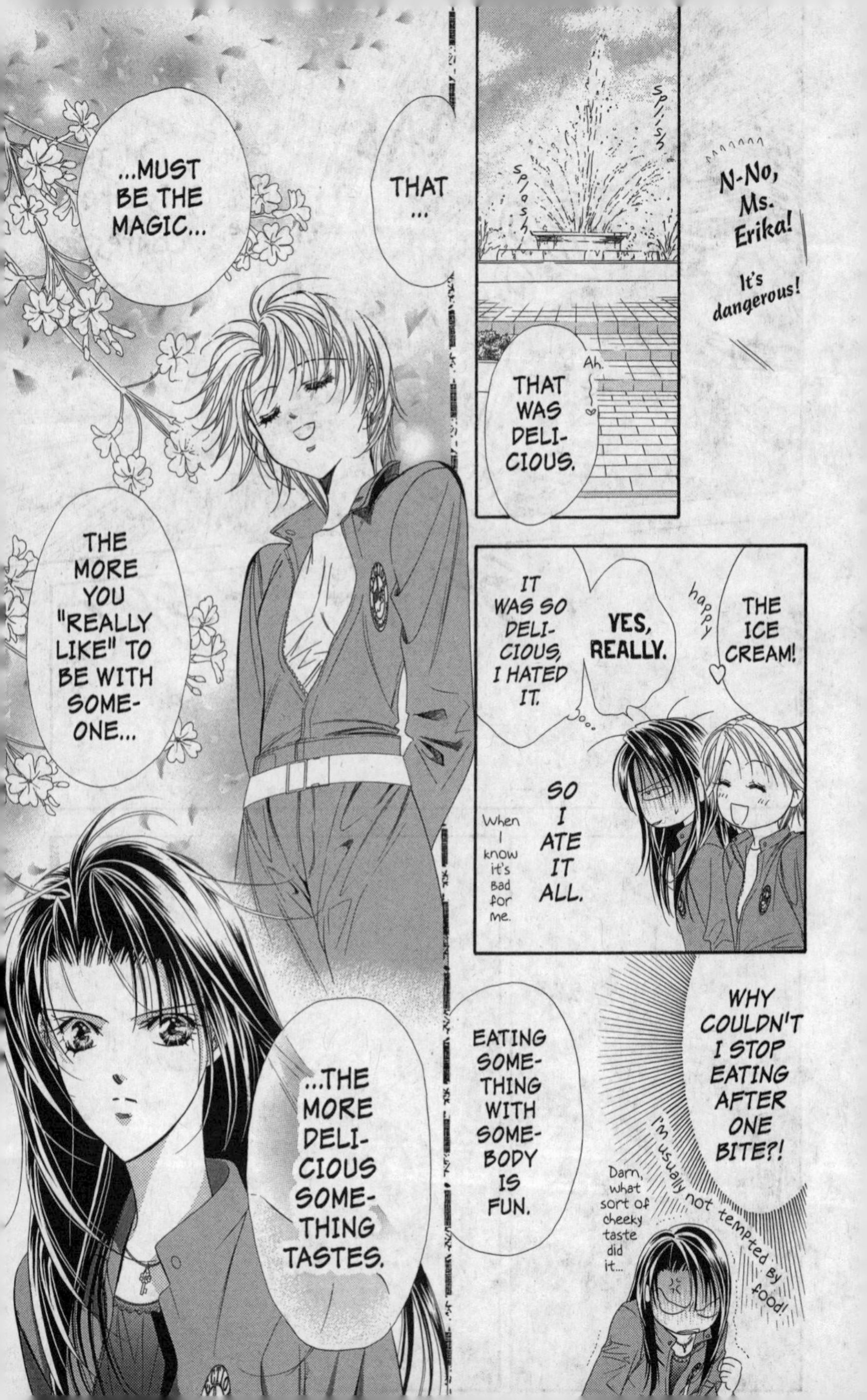
N-No, Ms. Erika!
It's dangerous!
splish
splosh
Ah.
THAT WAS DELICIOUS.
THE ICE CREAM!
happy
YES, REALLY.
IT WAS SO DELICIOUS, I HATED IT.
SO I ATE IT ALL.
When I know it's bad for me.
WHY COULDN'T I STOP EATING AFTER ONE BITE?!
I'm usually not tempted by food!
Darn, what sort of cheeky taste did it...
EATING SOMETHING WITH SOMEBODY IS FUN.
THAT...
...MUST BE THE MAGIC...
THE MORE YOU "REALLY LIKE" TO BE WITH SOMEONE...
...THE MORE DELICIOUS SOMETHING TASTES.

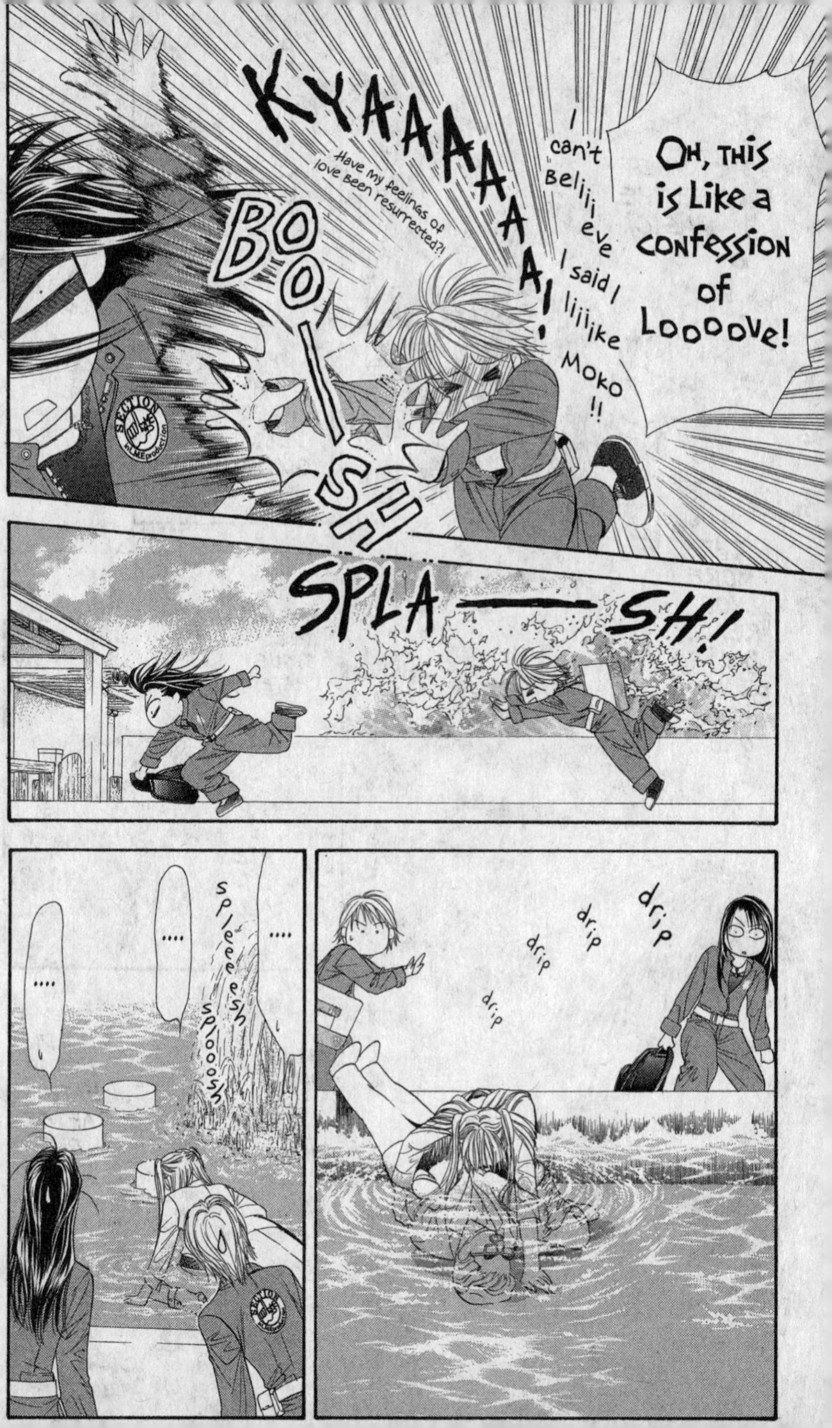

OH, THIS IS LIKE A CONFESSION OF LOOOOVE!
I can't Beliiiieve I said I liiiiike Moko!!
KYAAAAAAAA!
Have my feelings of love been resurrected?!
BOOOSH
SPLA——SH!
drip
drip
drip
drip
....
....
spleeeesh
splooosh
....

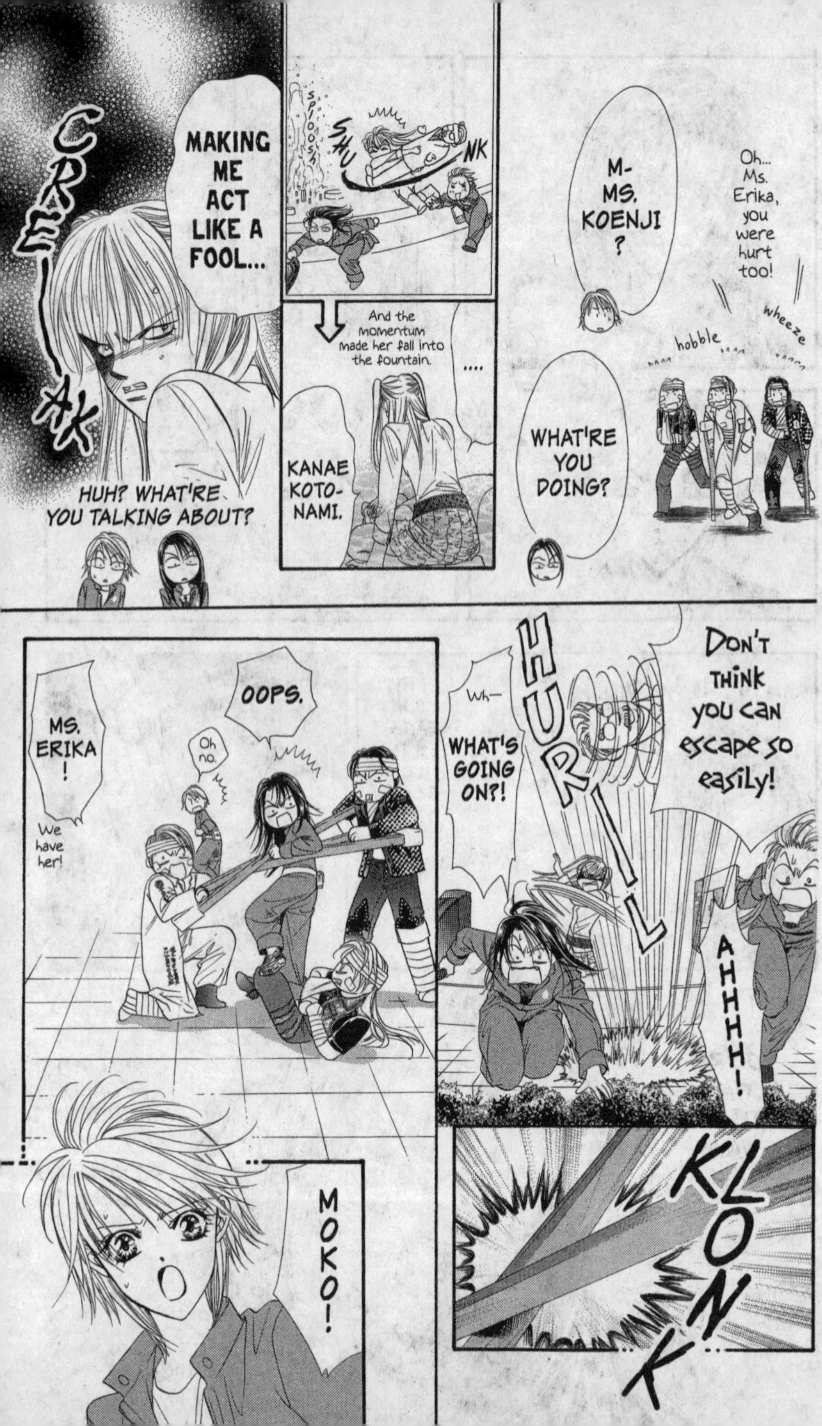
Oh... Ms. Erika, you were hurt too!
M-MS. KOENJI?
wheeze
hobble
WHAT'RE YOU DOING?
SPLOOSH
SHUNK
And the momentum made her fall into the fountain.
....
KANAE KOTONAMI.
CREAK
MAKING ME ACT LIKE A FOOL...
HUH? WHAT'RE YOU TALKING ABOUT?
DON'T THINK YOU CAN ESCAPE SO EASILY!
HURL
Wh—
WHAT'S GOING ON?!
AHHHH!
OOPS.
MS. ERIKA!
We have her!
Oh no.
KLONK
MOKO!

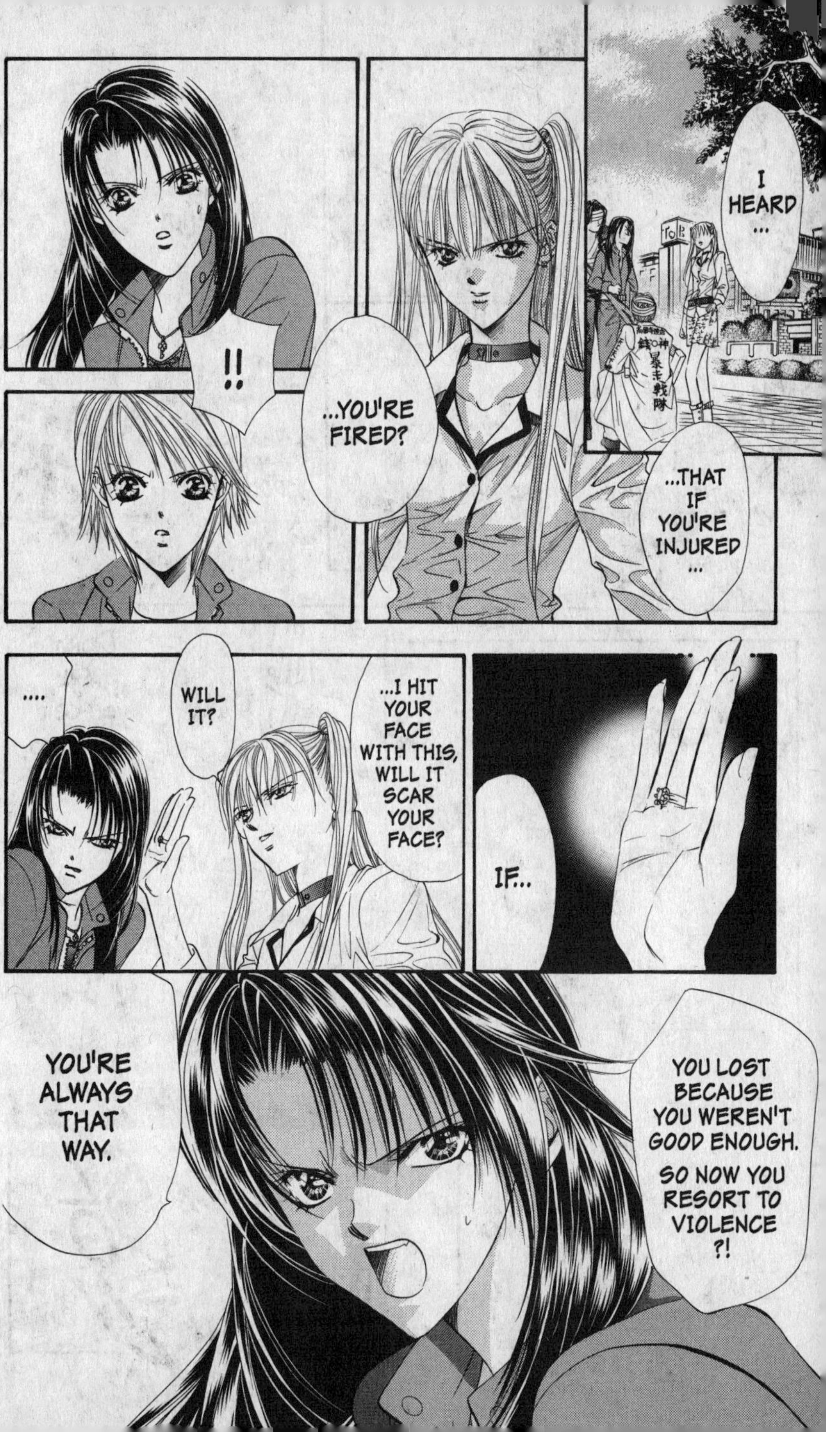
I HEARD ...
...THAT IF YOU'RE INJURED ...
...YOU'RE FIRED?
!!
IF...
...I HIT YOUR FACE WITH THIS, WILL IT SCAR YOUR FACE?
WILL IT?
....
YOU LOST BECAUSE YOU WEREN'T GOOD ENOUGH.
SO NOW YOU RESORT TO VIOLENCE ?!
YOU'RE ALWAYS THAT WAY.

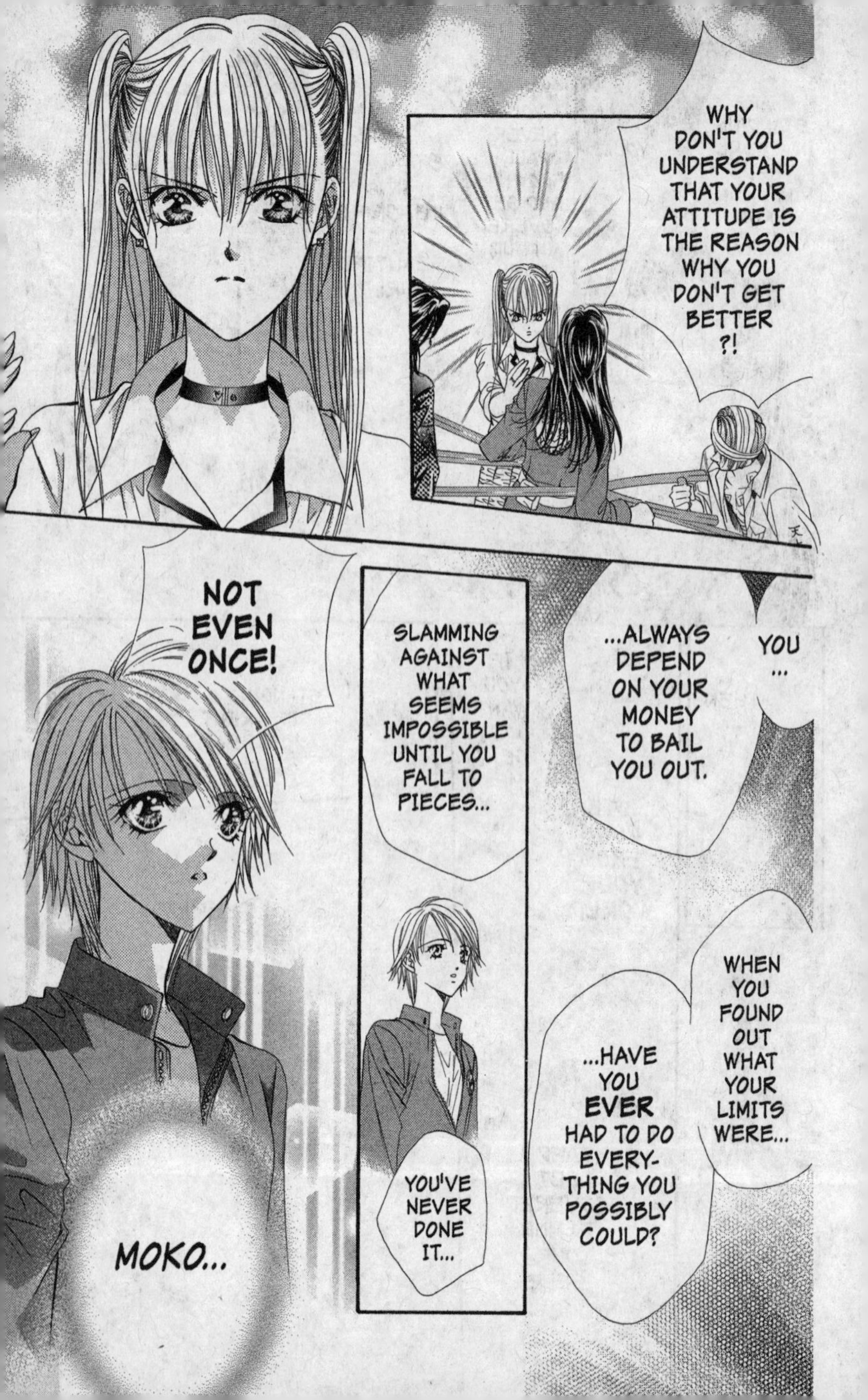

WHY DON'T YOU UNDERSTAND THAT YOUR ATTITUDE IS THE REASON WHY YOU DON'T GET BETTER ?!
YOU ...
...ALWAYS DEPEND ON YOUR MONEY TO BAIL YOU OUT.
WHEN YOU FOUND OUT WHAT YOUR LIMITS WERE...
...HAVE YOU **EVER** HAD TO DO EVERY-THING YOU POSSIBLY COULD?
SLAMMING AGAINST WHAT SEEMS IMPOSSIBLE UNTIL YOU FALL TO PIECES...
YOU'VE NEVER DONE IT...
NOT EVEN ONCE!
MOKO...

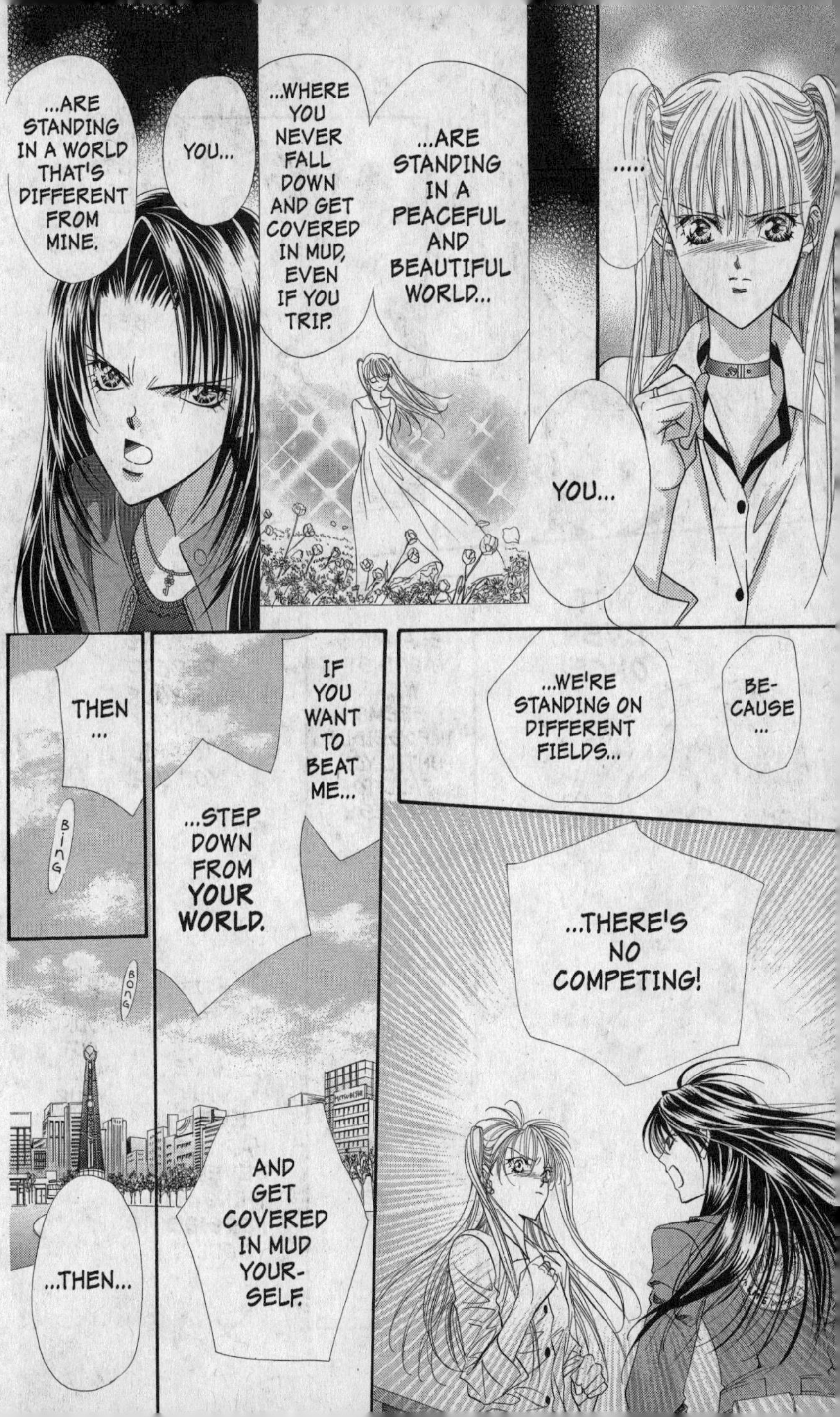
.....
YOU...
...ARE STANDING IN A PEACEFUL AND BEAUTIFUL WORLD...
...WHERE YOU NEVER FALL DOWN AND GET COVERED IN MUD, EVEN IF YOU TRIP.
YOU...
...ARE STANDING IN A WORLD THAT'S DIFFERENT FROM MINE.
BE-CAUSE...
...WE'RE STANDING ON DIFFERENT FIELDS...
...THERE'S NO COMPETING!
IF YOU WANT TO BEAT ME...
...STEP DOWN FROM YOUR WORLD.
AND GET COVERED IN MUD YOUR-SELF.
THEN...
BING
BONG
...THEN...

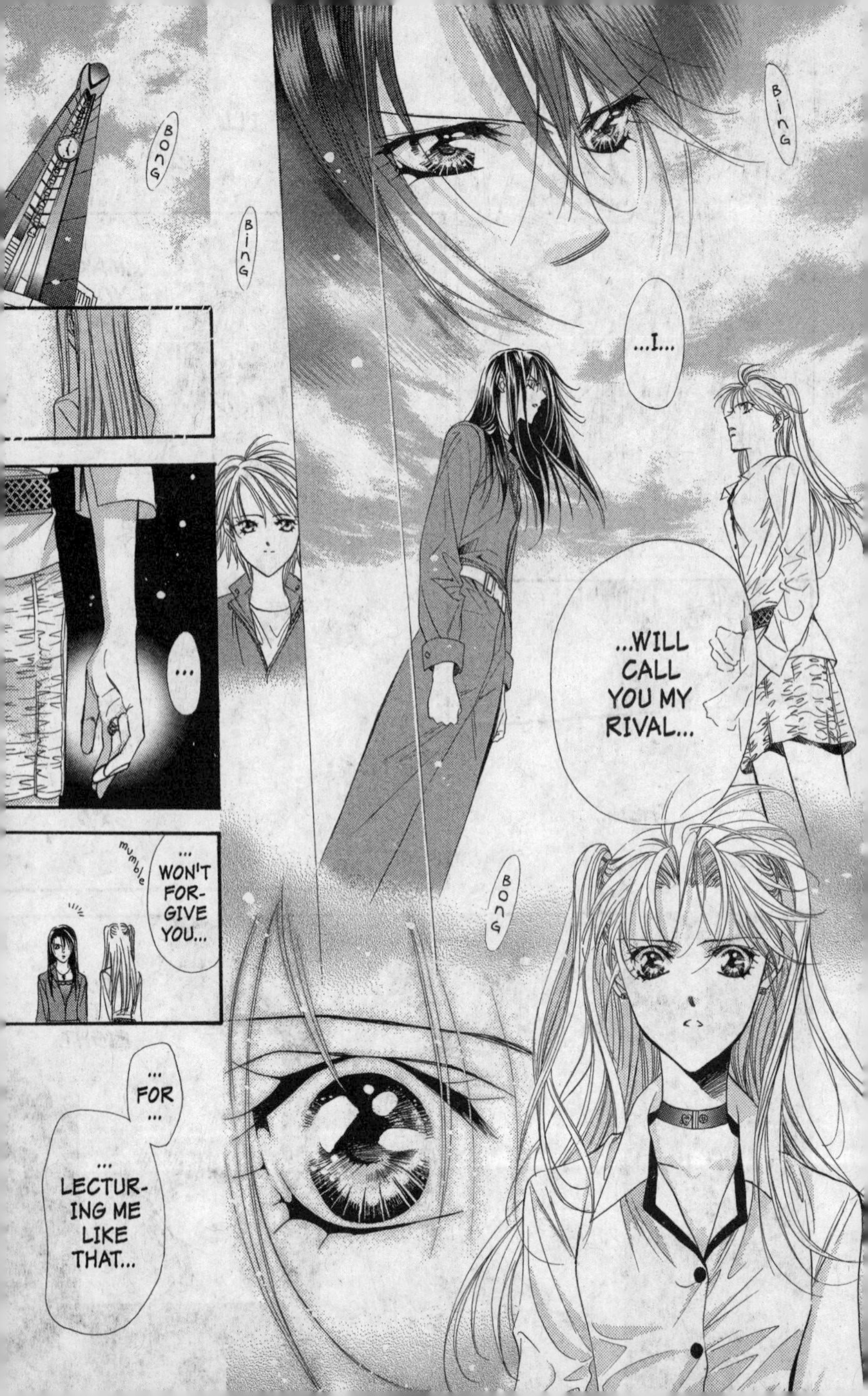
BING
...I...
...WILL CALL YOU MY RIVAL...
BONG
BONG
BING
...
mumble
...WON'T FORGIVE YOU...
...FOR...
...LECTURING ME LIKE THAT...

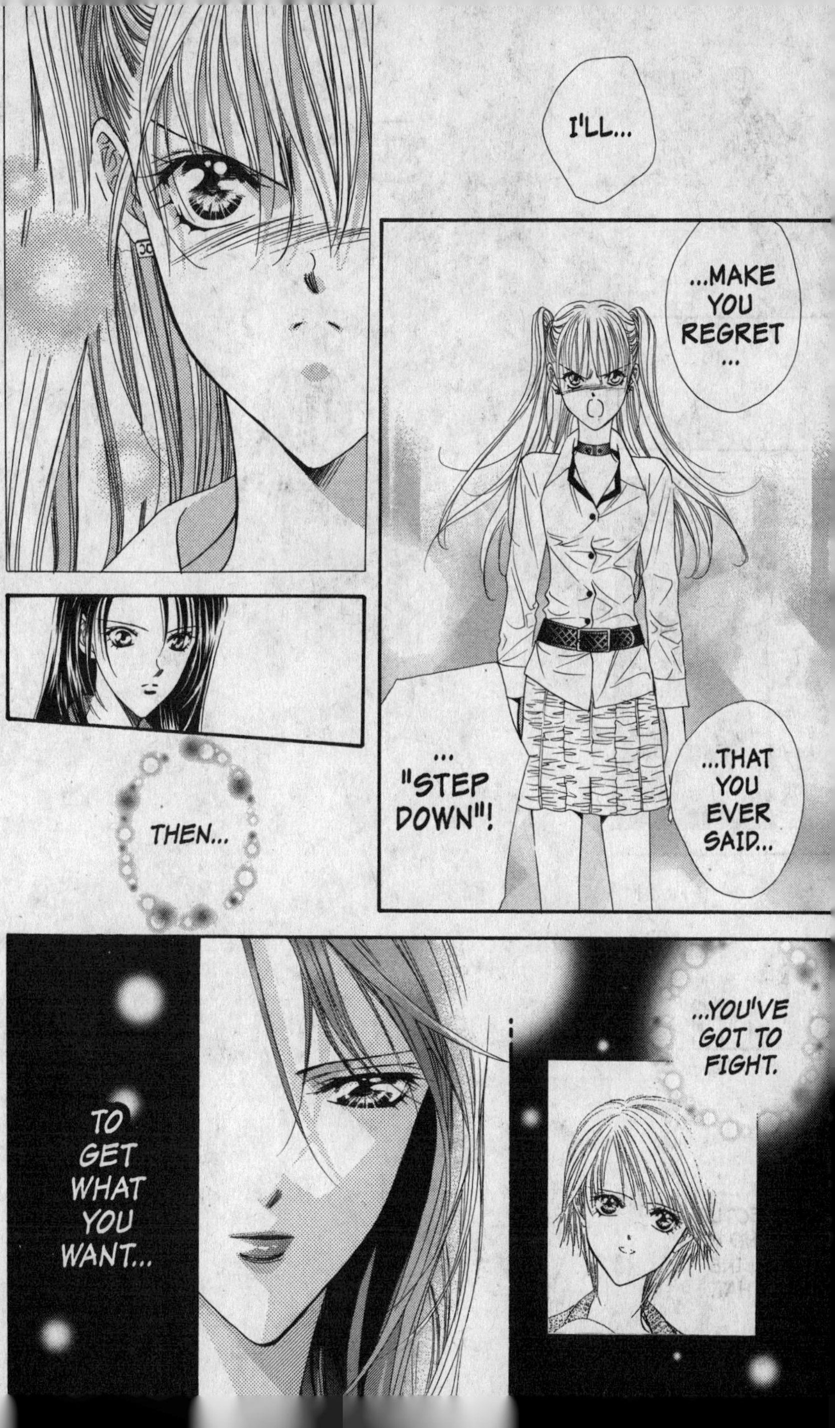
I'LL...
...MAKE YOU REGRET ...
...THAT YOU EVER SAID...
... "STEP DOWN"!
THEN...
...YOU'VE GOT TO FIGHT.
TO GET WHAT YOU WANT...

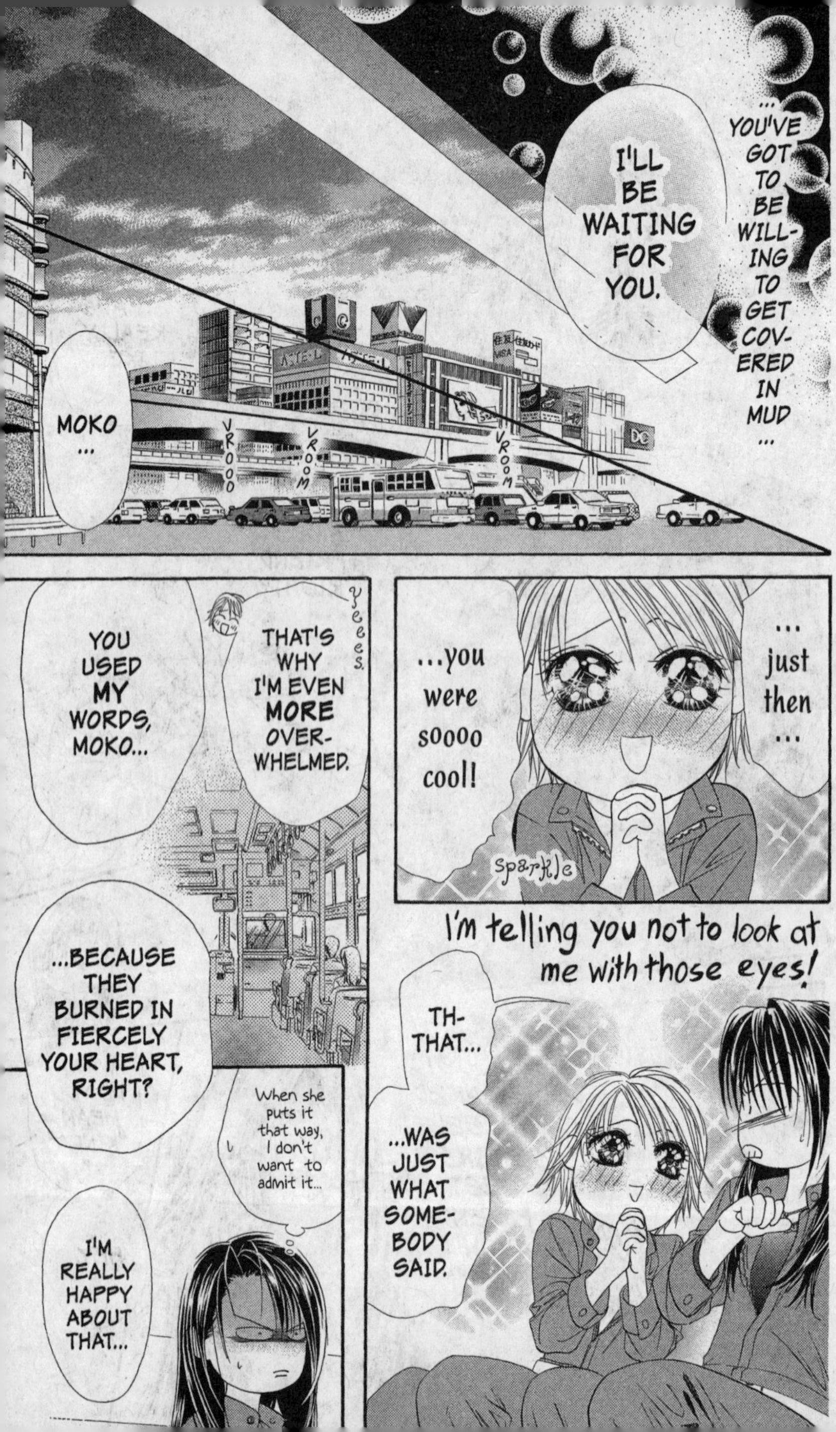
...YOU'VE GOT TO BE WILLING TO GET COVERED IN MUD...
I'LL BE WAITING FOR YOU.
VROOOM
VROOM
VROOOM
MOKO...
...just then...
...you were soooo cool!
sparkle
I'm telling you not to look at me with those eyes!
TH-THAT...
...WAS JUST WHAT SOMEBODY SAID.
YOU USED MY WORDS, MOKO...
Yeeees.
THAT'S WHY I'M EVEN MORE OVERWHELMED.
...BECAUSE THEY BURNED IN FIERCELY YOUR HEART, RIGHT?
When she puts it that way, I don't want to admit it...
I'M REALLY HAPPY ABOUT THAT...

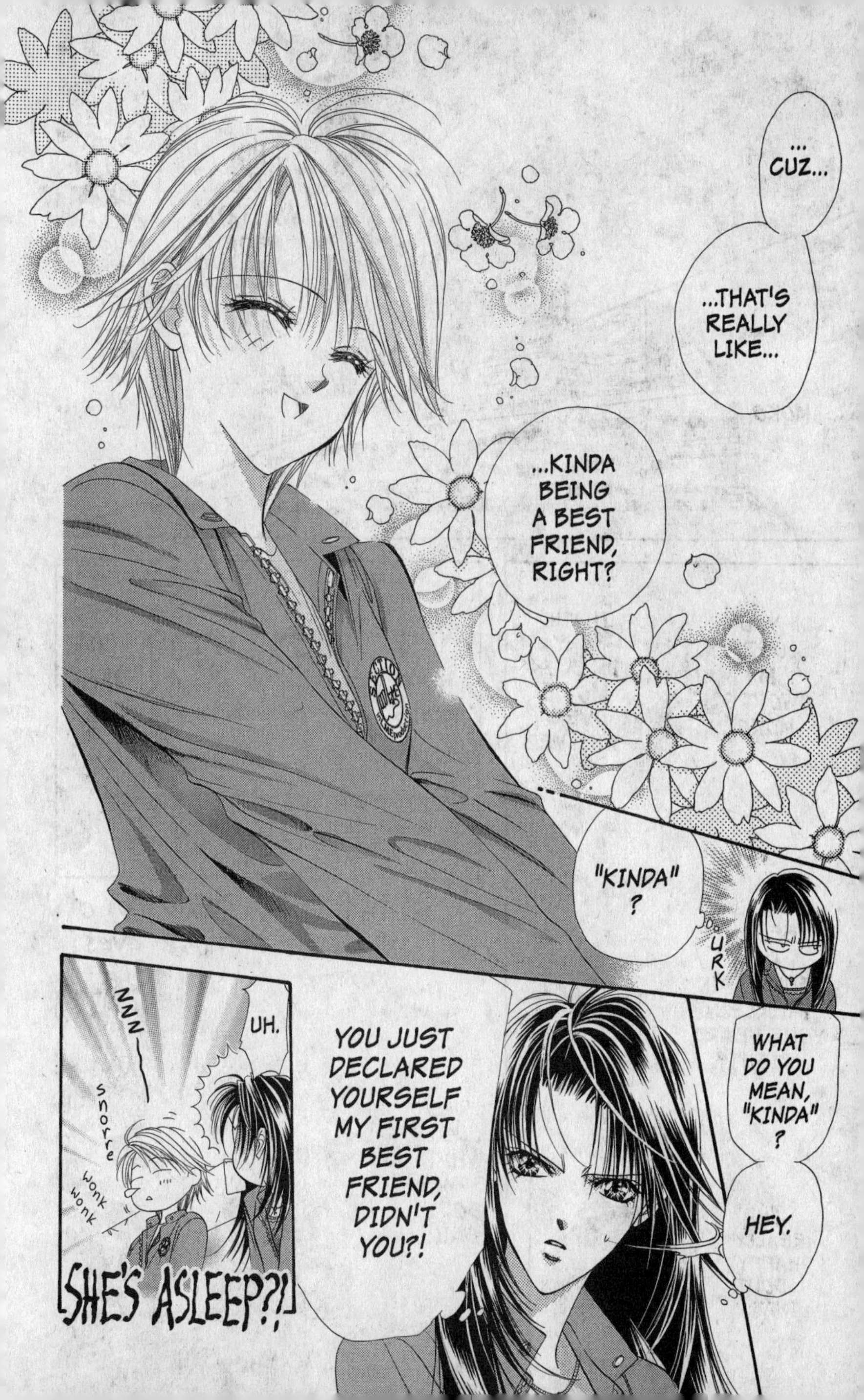
...CUZ...
...THAT'S REALLY LIKE...
...KINDA BEING A BEST FRIEND, RIGHT?
"KINDA"?
URK
WHAT DO YOU MEAN, "KINDA"?
HEY.
YOU JUST DECLARED YOURSELF MY FIRST BEST FRIEND, DIDN'T YOU?!
UH.
ZZZ—
snorre
wonk wonk
SHE'S ASLEEP?!

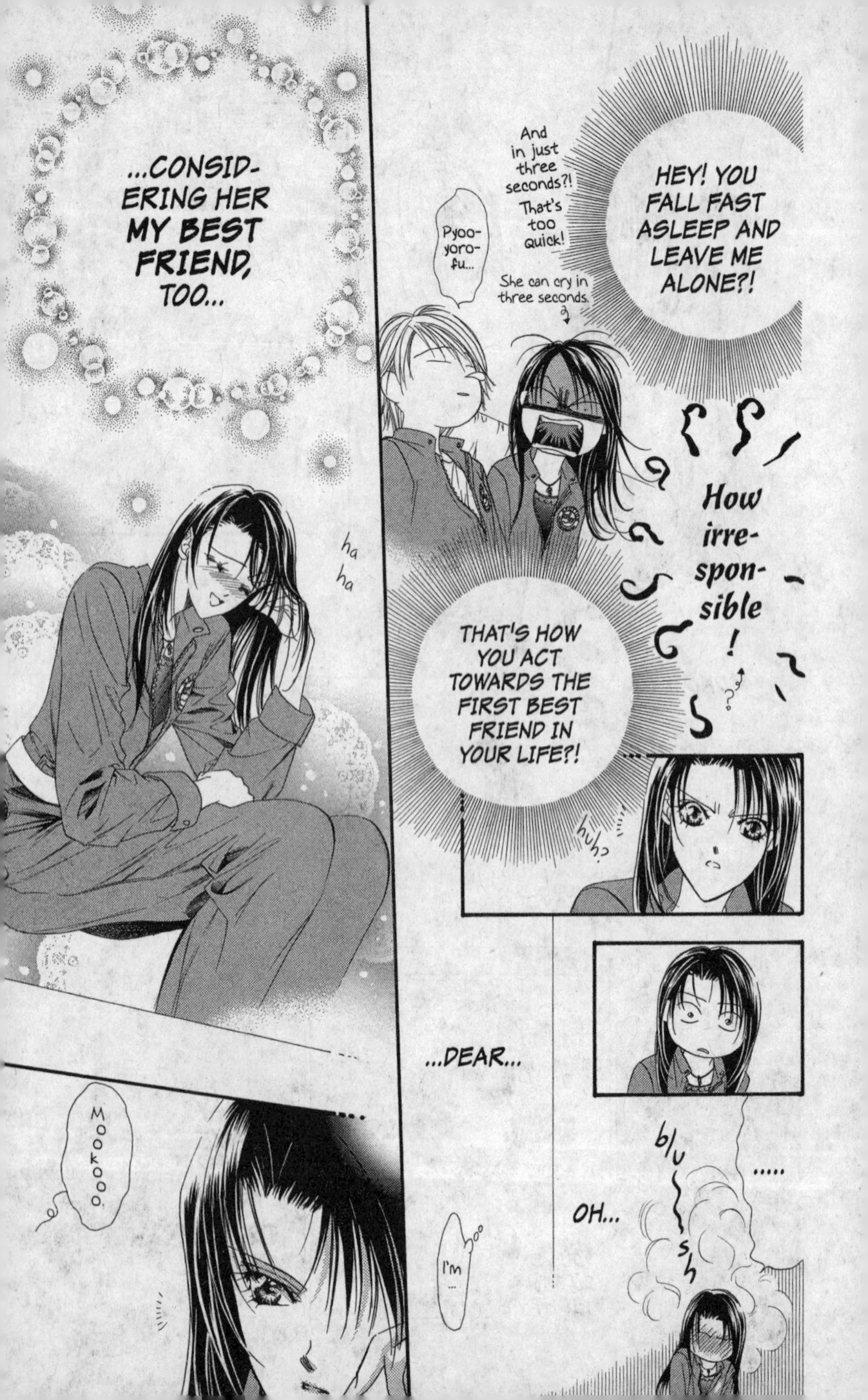
HEY! YOU FALL FAST ASLEEP AND LEAVE ME ALONE?!
And in just three seconds?! That's too quick!
Pyoo-yoro-fu...
She can cry in three seconds.
How irre-spon-sible!
THAT'S HOW YOU ACT TOWARDS THE FIRST BEST FRIEND IN YOUR LIFE?!
huh?
...DEAR...
.....
blu~sh
OH...
I'm ...
...CONSID-ERING HER MY BEST FRIEND, TOO...
ha ha
MOOKOOO.

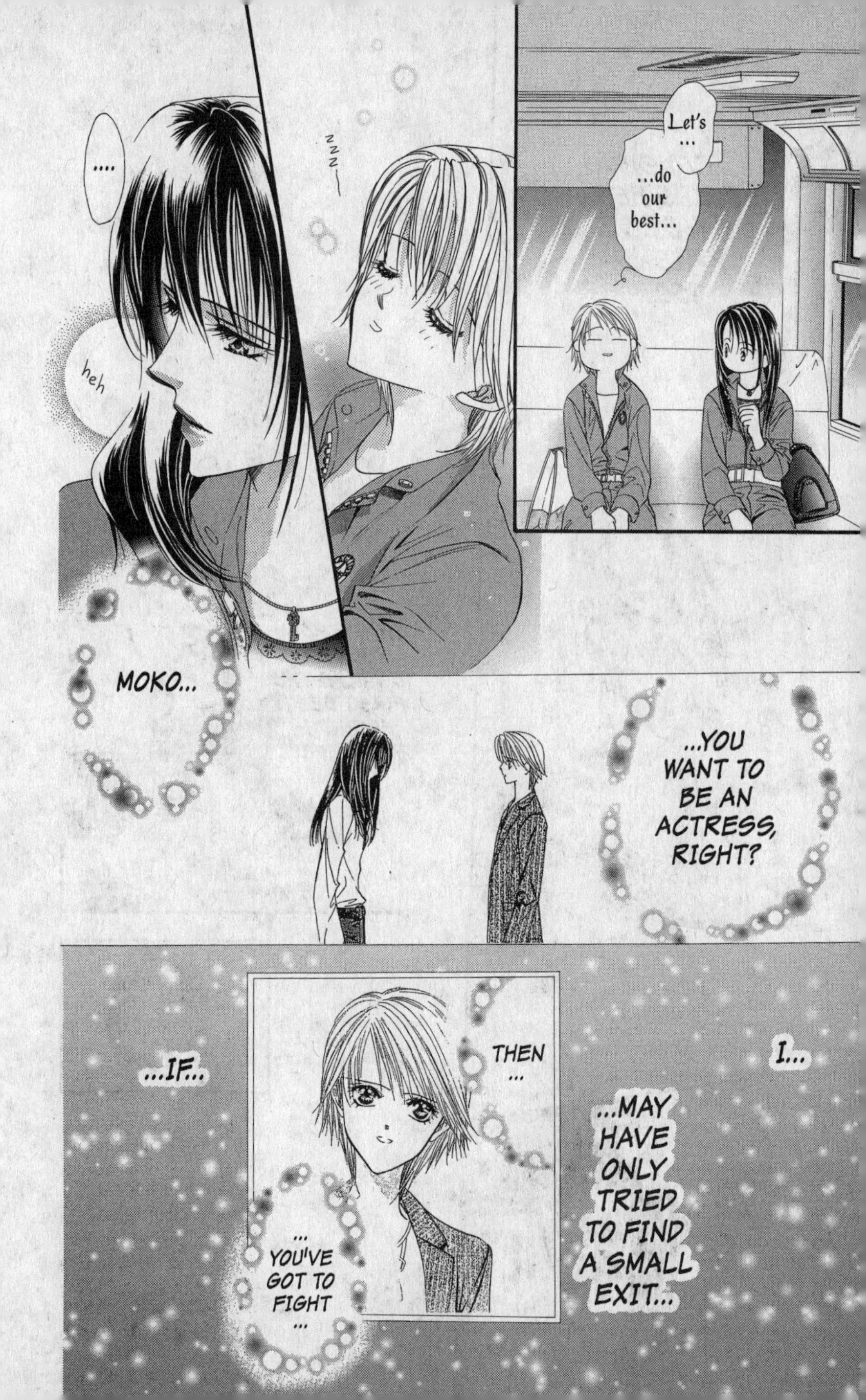

Let's ... ...do our best...
ZZZ
....
heh
MOKO...
...YOU WANT TO BE AN ACTRESS, RIGHT?
I...
...MAY HAVE ONLY TRIED TO FIND A SMALL EXIT...
THEN ...
... YOU'VE GOT TO FIGHT ...
...IF...

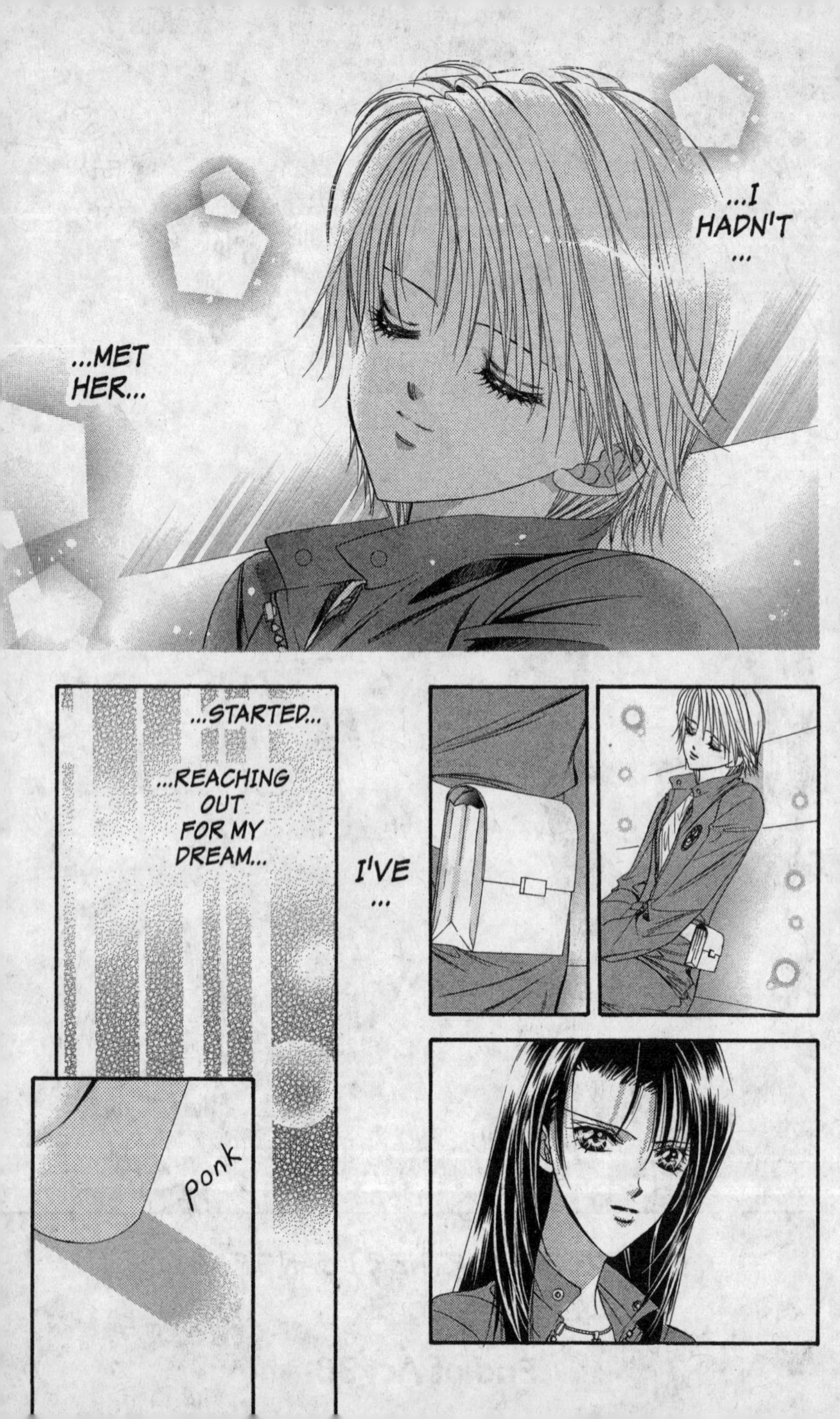
...I HADN'T ...
...MET HER...
I'VE ...
...STARTED...
...REACHING OUT FOR MY DREAM...
ponk

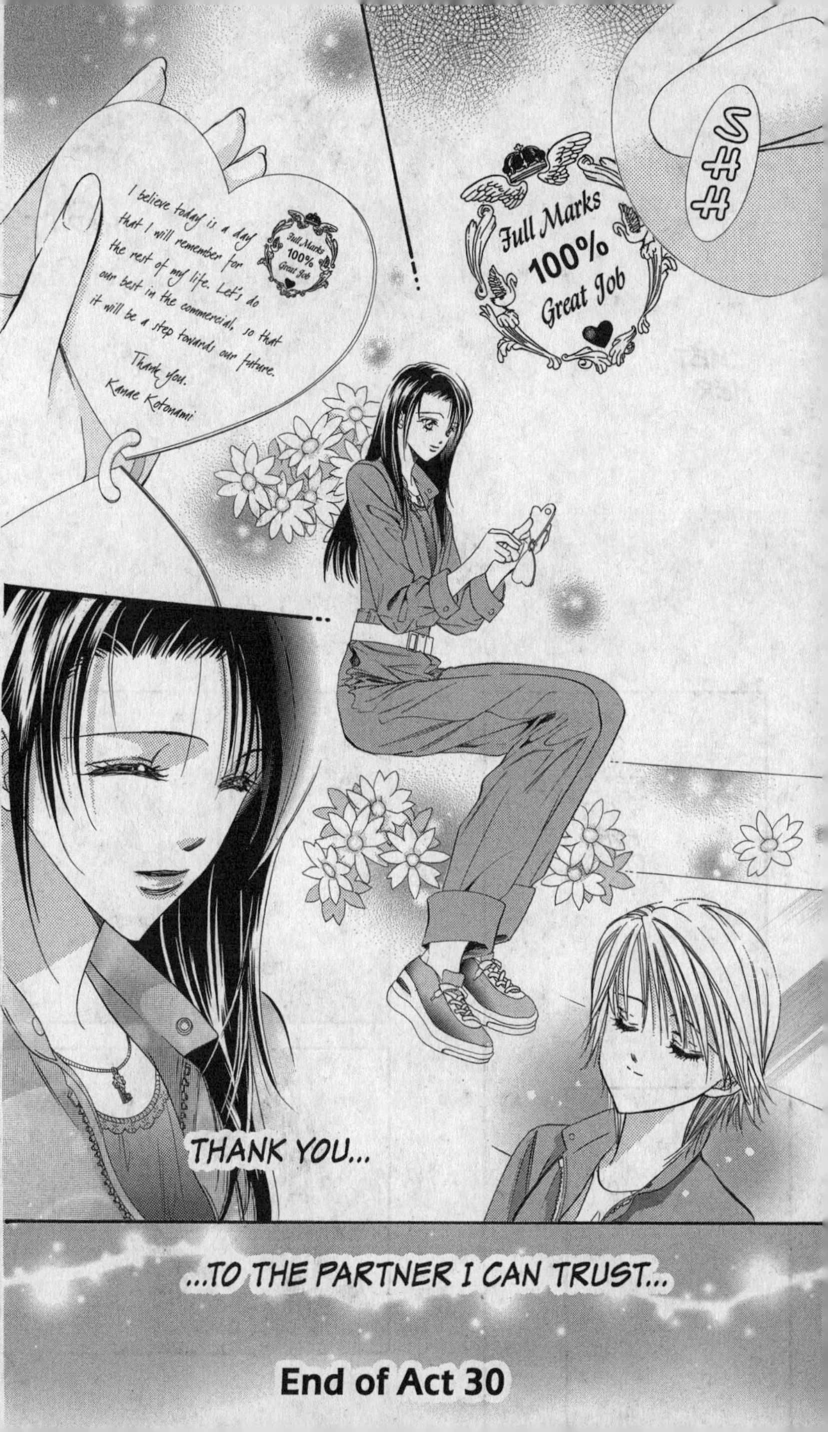
S
Full Marks
100%
Great Job
I believe today is a day that I will remember for the rest of my life. Let's do our best in the commercial, so that it will be a step towards our future.
Thank you.
Kanae Kotonami
Full Marks
100%
Great Job
THANK YOU...
...TO THE PARTNER I CAN TRUST...
End of Act 30

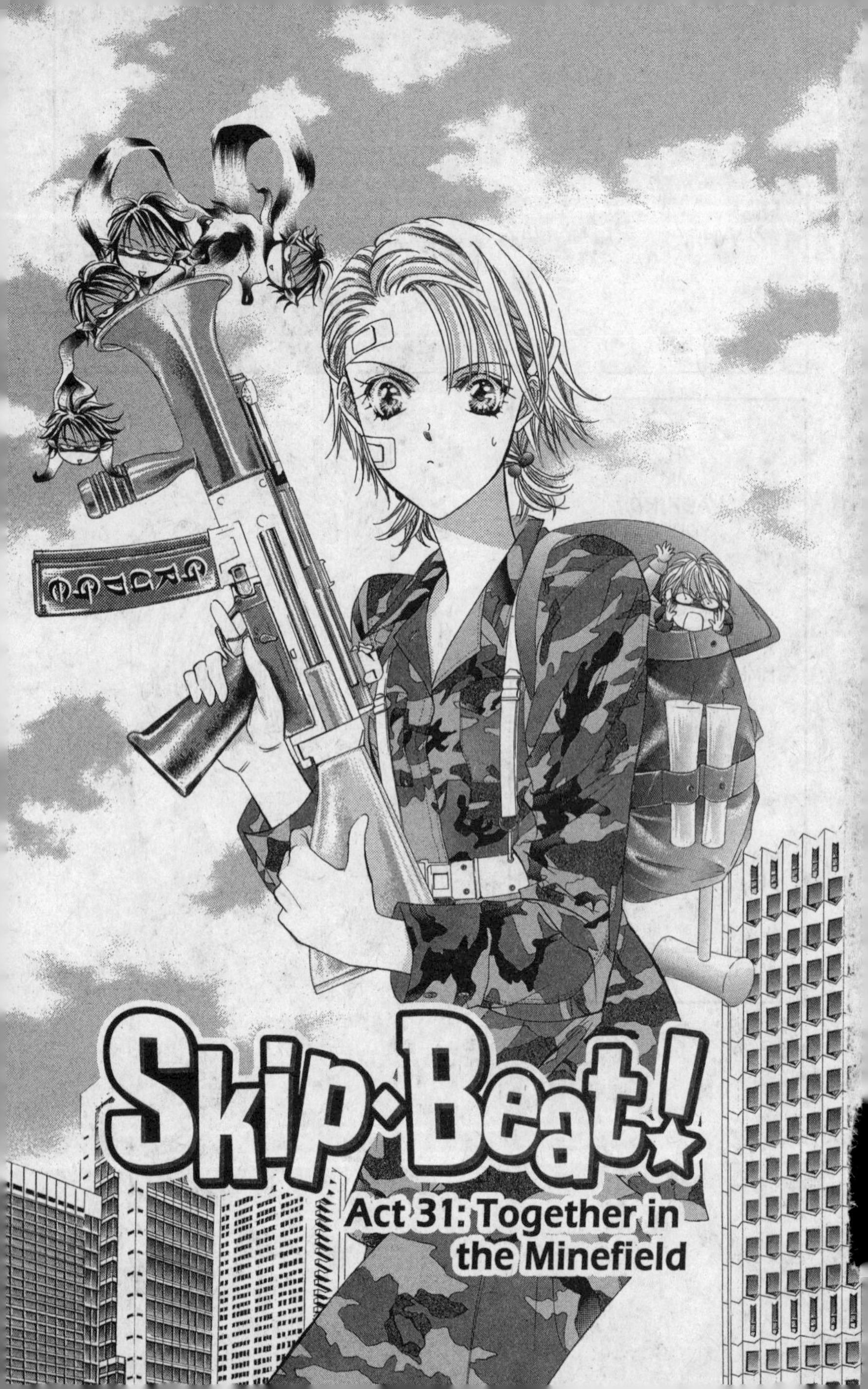
Skip·Beat!
Act 31: Together in the Minefield

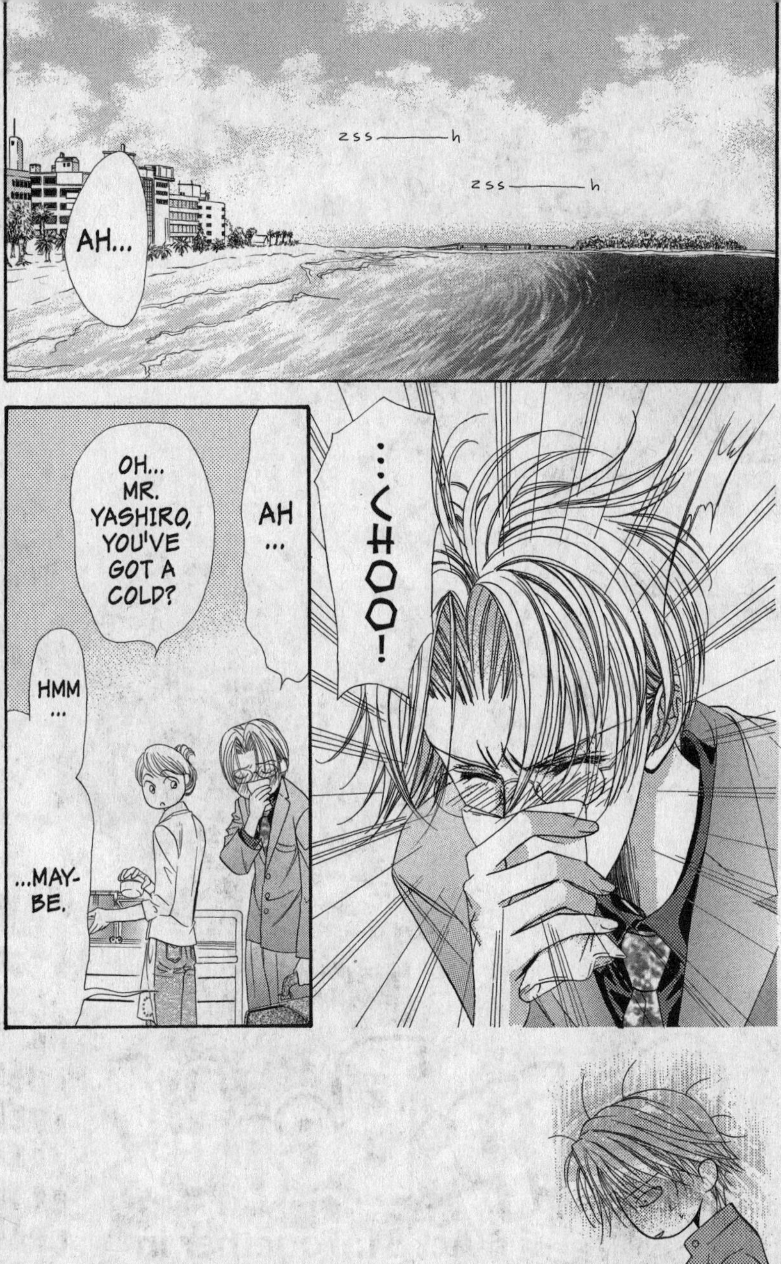
zss———h
zss———h
AH...
...CHOO!
AH ...
OH... MR. YASHIRO, YOU'VE GOT A COLD?
HMM ...
...MAY-BE.

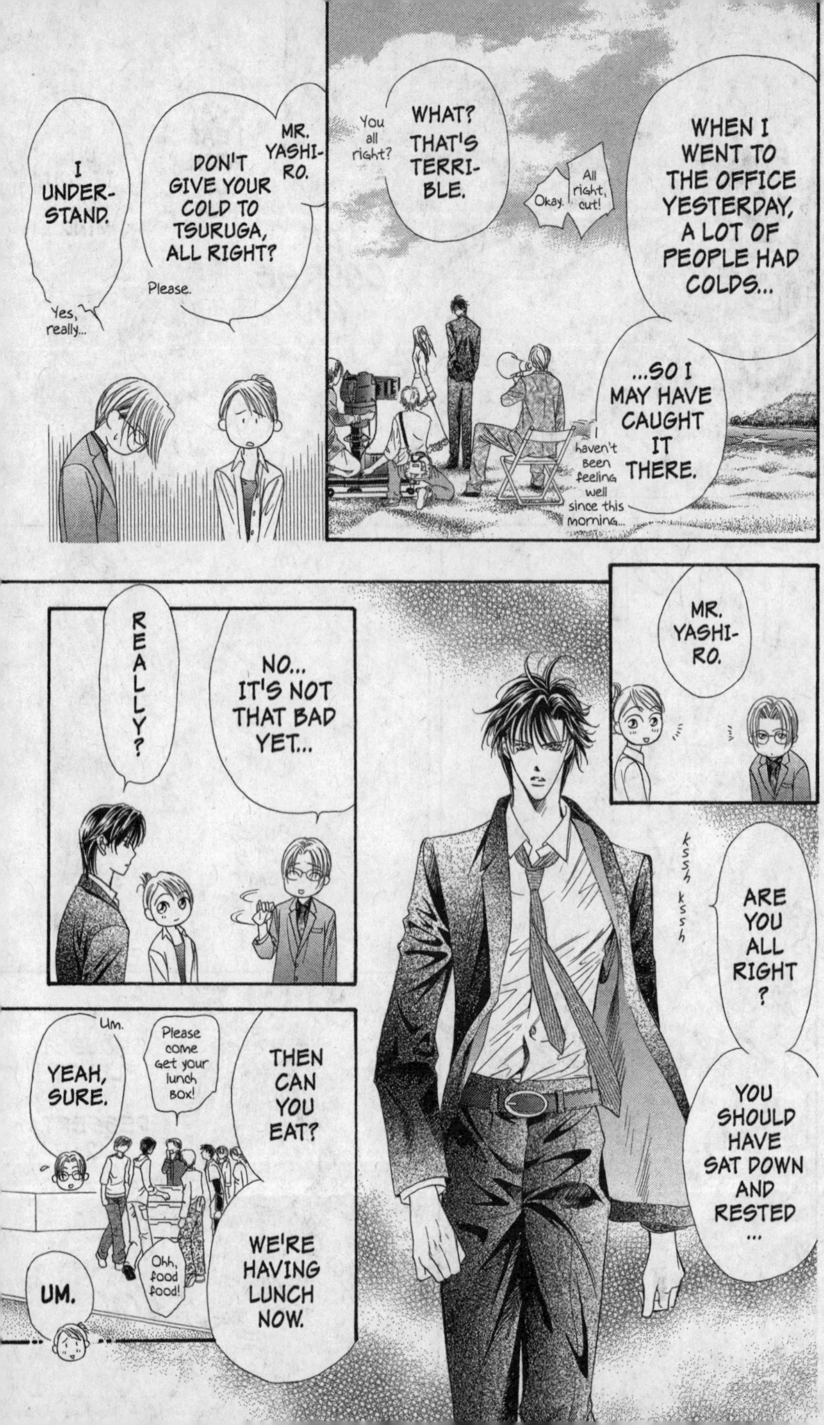
WHEN I WENT TO THE OFFICE YESTERDAY, A LOT OF PEOPLE HAD COLDS...
All right, cut!
Okay.
WHAT? THAT'S TERRIBLE.
You all right?
...SO I MAY HAVE CAUGHT IT THERE.
I haven't been feeling well since this morning...
MR. YASHIRO.
DON'T GIVE YOUR COLD TO TSURUGA, ALL RIGHT?
Please.
I UNDERSTAND.
Yes, really...
MR. YASHIRO.
ARE YOU ALL RIGHT?
kssh kssh
YOU SHOULD HAVE SAT DOWN AND RESTED...
NO... IT'S NOT THAT BAD YET...
REALLY?
THEN CAN YOU EAT?
Please come get your lunch box!
YEAH, SURE.
Um.
WE'RE HAVING LUNCH NOW.
Ohh, food food!
UM.

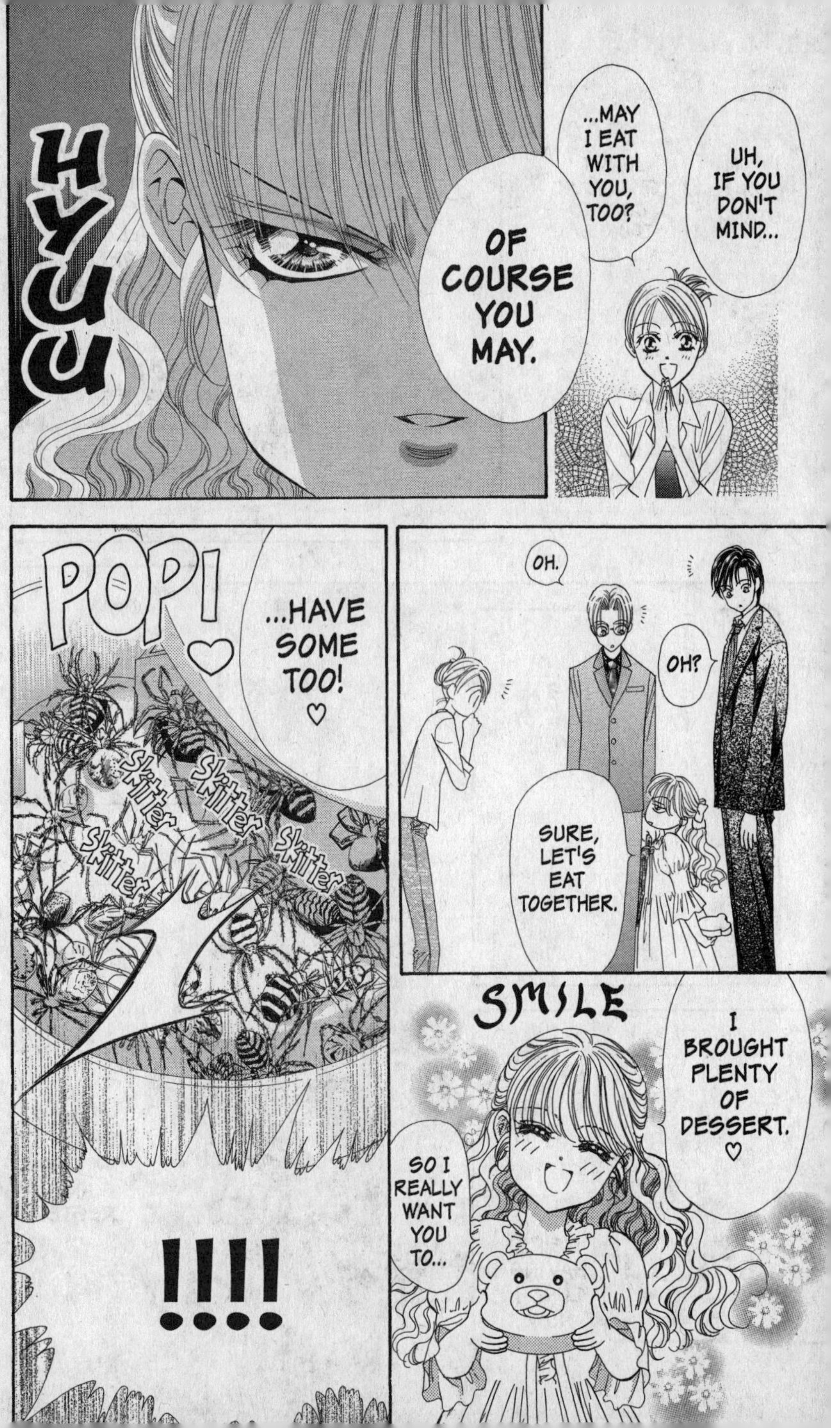
UH, IF YOU DON'T MIND...
...MAY I EAT WITH YOU, TOO?
OF COURSE YOU MAY.
HYUU
OH.
OH?
SURE, LET'S EAT TOGETHER.
SMILE
I BROUGHT PLENTY OF DESSERT. ♡
SO I REALLY WANT YOU TO...
POP! ♡
...HAVE SOME TOO! ♡
Skitter
Skitter
Skitter
Skitter
!!!!

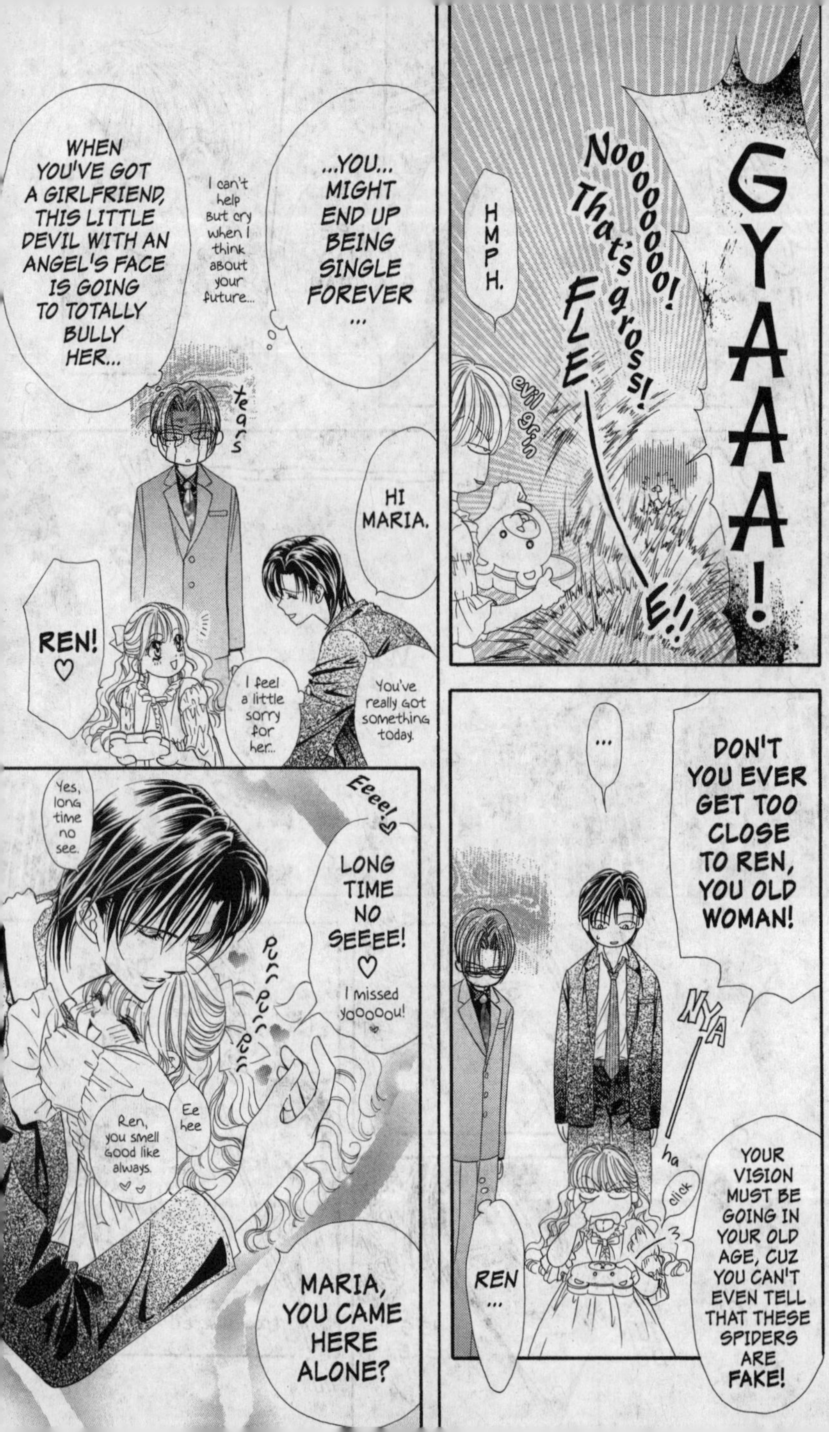
WHEN YOU'VE GOT A GIRLFRIEND, THIS LITTLE DEVIL WITH AN ANGEL'S FACE IS GOING TO TOTALLY BULLY HER...
I can't help but cry when I think about your future...
...YOU... MIGHT END UP BEING SINGLE FOREVER ...
tears
REN! ♡
HI MARIA.
I feel a little sorry for her...
You've really got something today.
Yes, long time no see.
Eeeee!♡
LONG TIME NO SEEEEE! ♡
I missed yoooooou!
Purr Purr Purr
Ren, you smell good like always. ♡♡
Ee hee
MARIA, YOU CAME HERE ALONE?
HMPH.
evil grin
Noooooooo!
That's gross!
FLE—E!!
GYAAA!
REN ...
...
DON'T YOU EVER GET TOO CLOSE TO REN, YOU OLD WOMAN!
NYA
ha
click
YOUR VISION MUST BE GOING IN YOUR OLD AGE, CUZ YOU CAN'T EVEN TELL THAT THESE SPIDERS ARE FAKE!

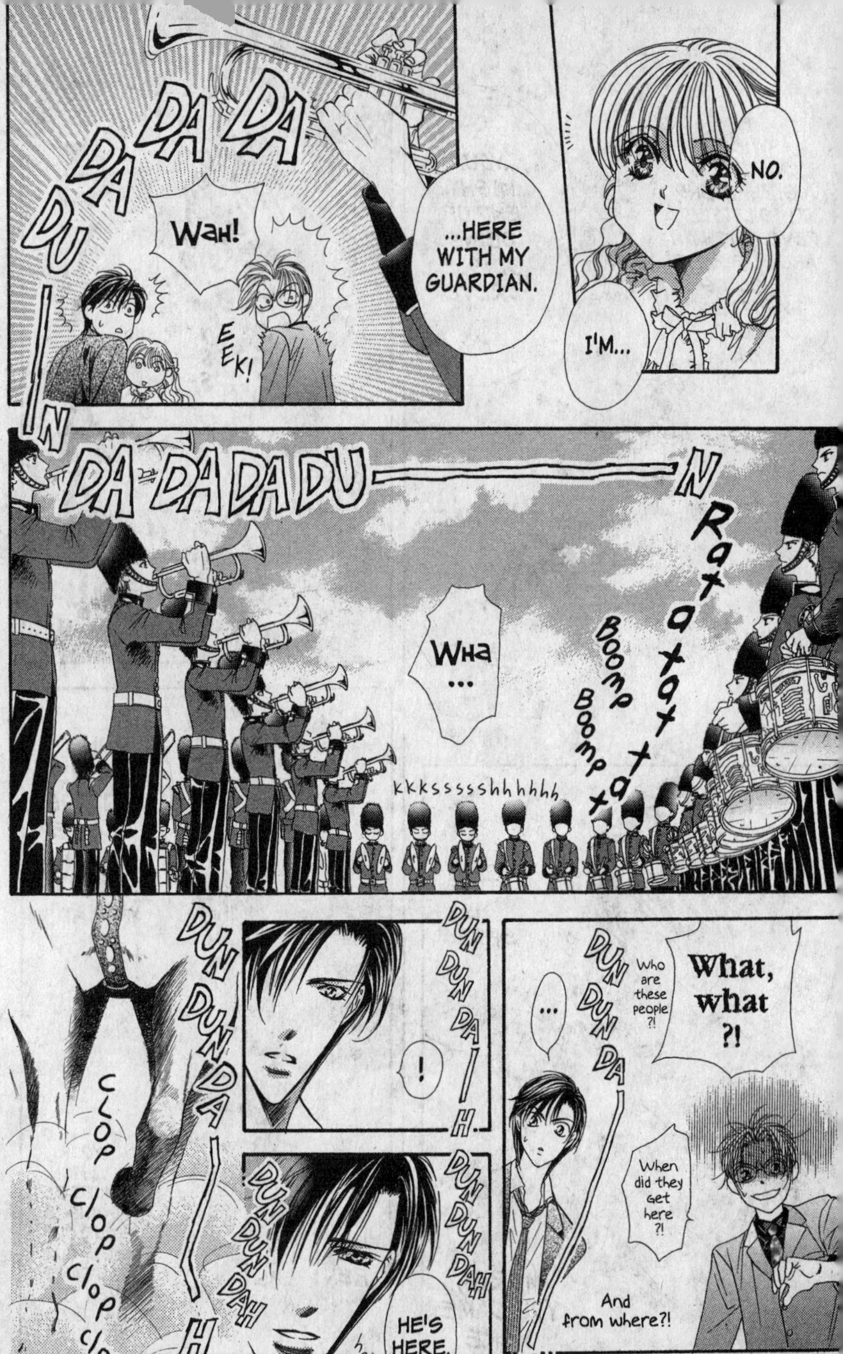
NO.
I'M...
...HERE WITH MY GUARDIAN.
DADA DA DA DA DU——N
WAH!
EEK!
DA DA DA DA DU——N
Ratatat tat
Boomp Boomp
Wha...
kkksssssshhhhhh
What, what?!
Who are these people?!
DUN DUN DUN DA——H
...
When did they get here?!
And from where?!
DUN DUN DUN DA——H
!
DUN DUN DUN DAH
HE'S HERE.
heh
DUN DUN DUN DAH
DUN DUN DUN DA——H
clop clop clop clop

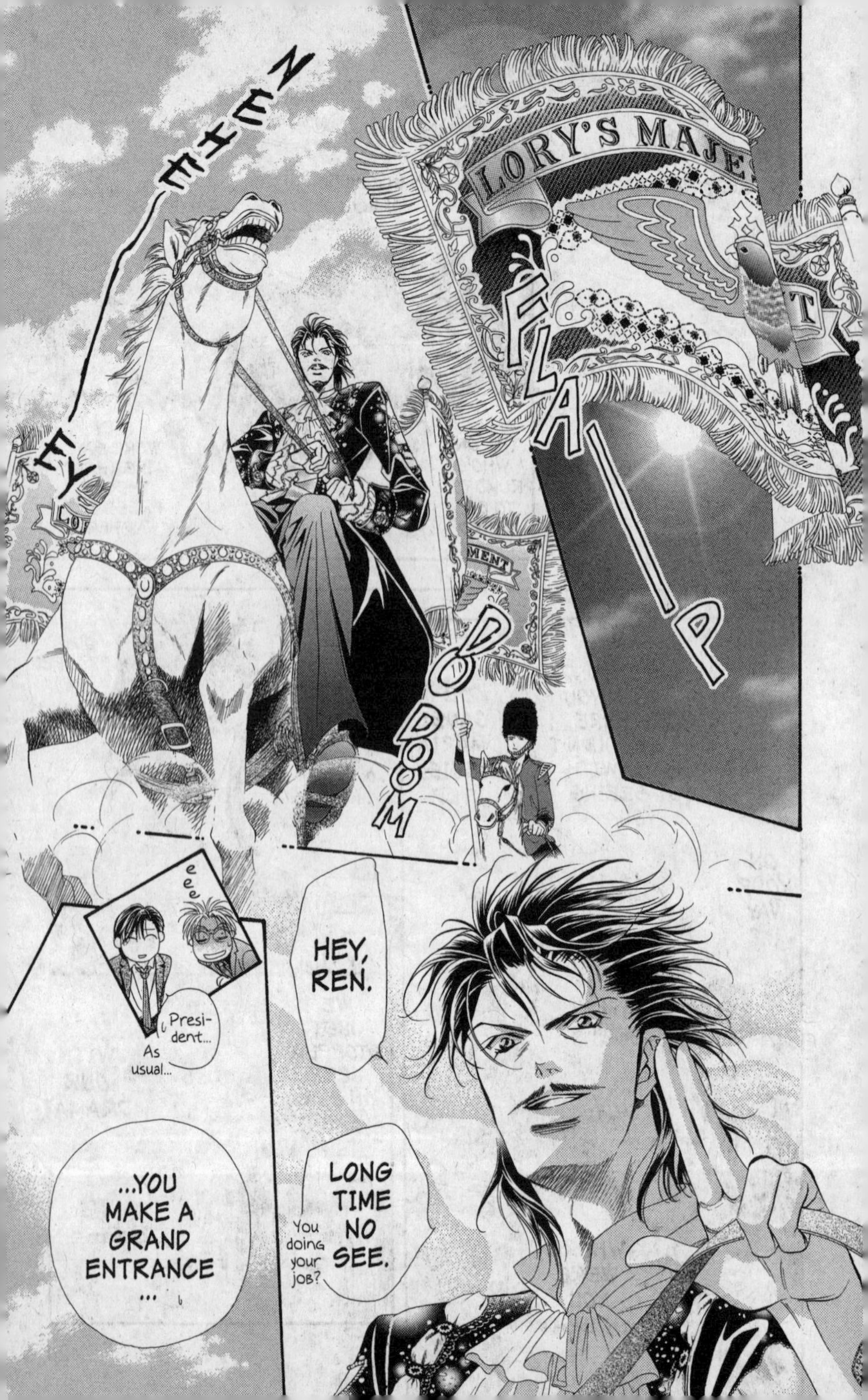

LORY'S MAJE
FLAIIP
NEHEHE
EY
DODOOM
HEY, REN.
LONG TIME NO SEE.
You doing your job?
eee
President...
As usual...
...YOU MAKE A GRAND ENTRANCE...

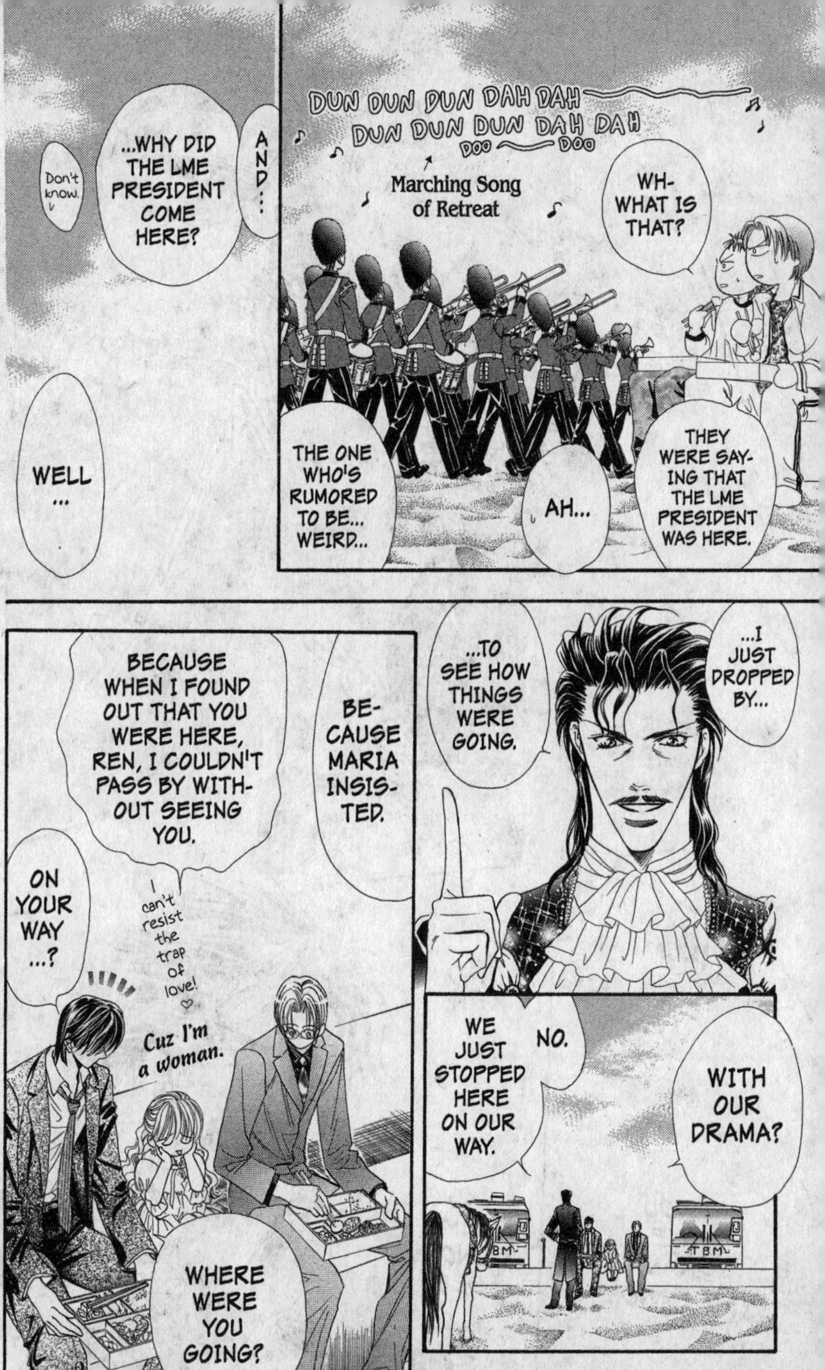
DUN DUN DUN DAH DAH~
DUN DUN DUN DAH DAH
DOO~DOO
Marching Song of Retreat
WH- WHAT IS THAT?
THEY WERE SAYING THAT THE LME PRESIDENT WAS HERE.
AH...
THE ONE WHO'S RUMORED TO BE... WEIRD...
AND...
...WHY DID THE LME PRESIDENT COME HERE?
Don't know.
WELL...
...I JUST DROPPED BY...
...TO SEE HOW THINGS WERE GOING.
WITH OUR DRAMA?
NO.
WE JUST STOPPED HERE ON OUR WAY.
BE-CAUSE MARIA INSIS-TED.
BECAUSE WHEN I FOUND OUT THAT YOU WERE HERE, REN, I COULDN'T PASS BY WITH-OUT SEEING YOU.
I can't resist the trap of love!
ON YOUR WAY ...?
Cuz I'm a woman.
WHERE WERE YOU GOING?

Lory's Name

I wrote before that there is a reason why Lory's name is spelled in Japanese with a small "i" at the end instead of with a dash. The reason is this.

Lory Bird

This is a name that only we call it by.

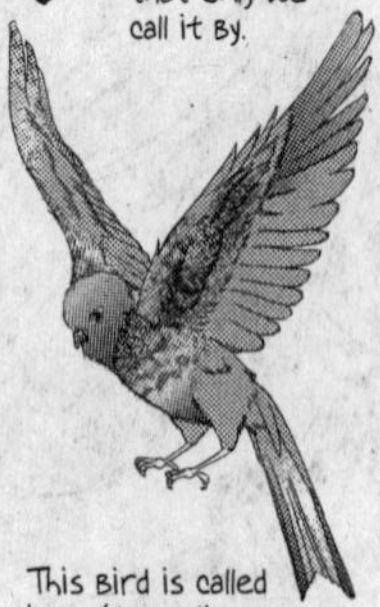

This bird is called Lory (depending on the type of bird, there seem to be names like Swainson's Lories and Rainbow Lory...)...anyway this Lory bird (called Rainbow above) is tropically colorful...so much...that you're greedy for using so many colors just by yourself... ♪ ...the one I used as a model was about five colors... ♪ ...So Lory Takarada's name comes from the Lory bird. The reason Lory's costumes always make my assistants cry is also because the Lory bird is a colorful, showy bird.

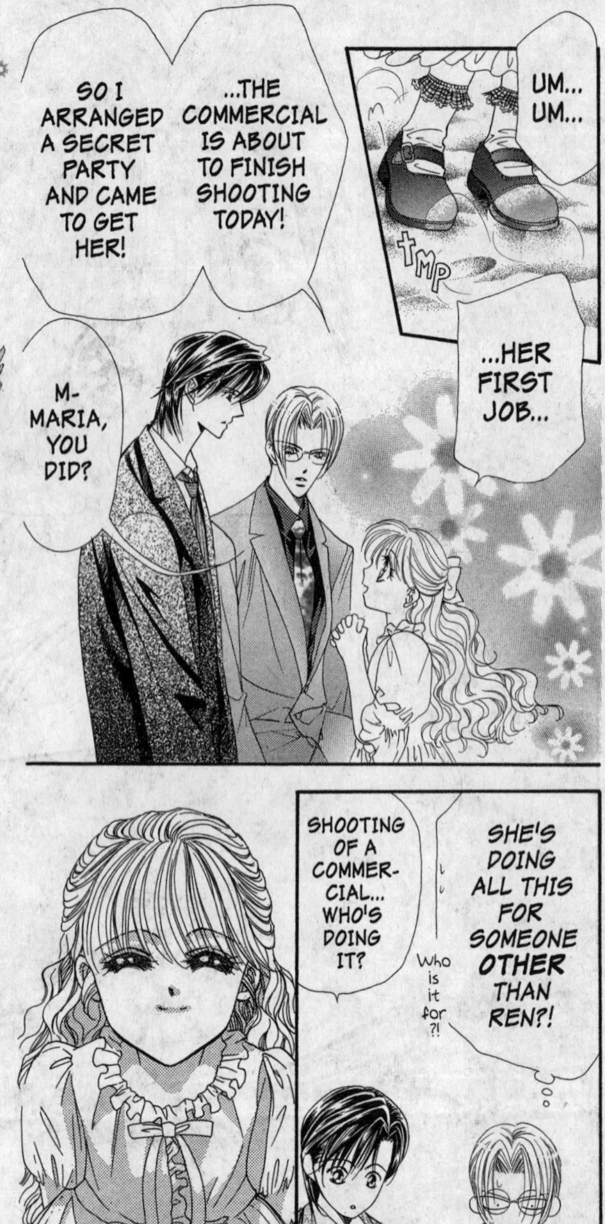
UM... UM...
tmp
...HER FIRST JOB...
...THE COMMERCIAL IS ABOUT TO FINISH SHOOTING TODAY!
SO I ARRANGED A SECRET PARTY AND CAME TO GET HER!
M-MARIA, YOU DID?
SHE'S DOING ALL THIS FOR SOMEONE OTHER THAN REN?!
Who is it for ?!
SHOOTING OF A COMMERCIAL... WHO'S DOING IT?

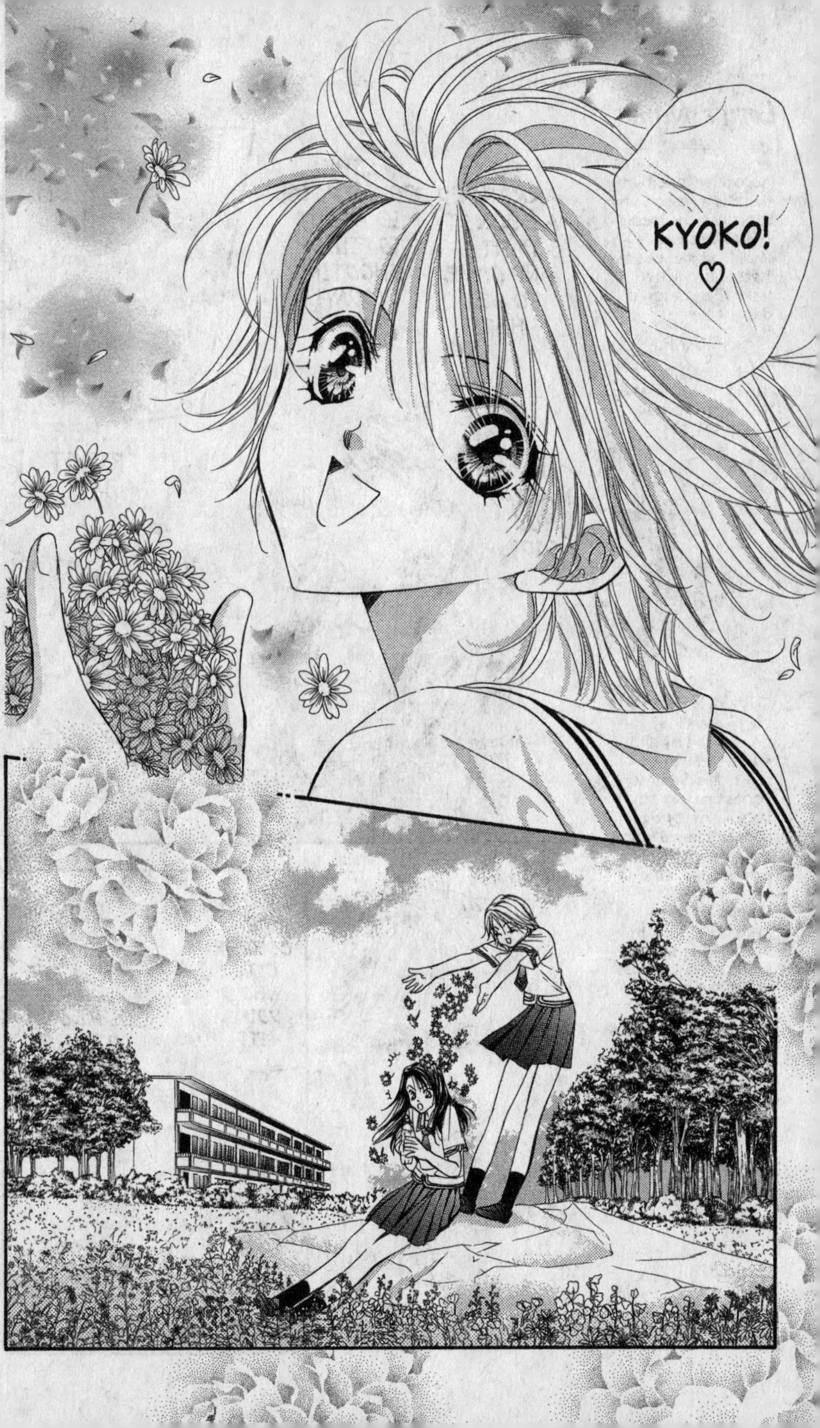
KYOKO! ♡

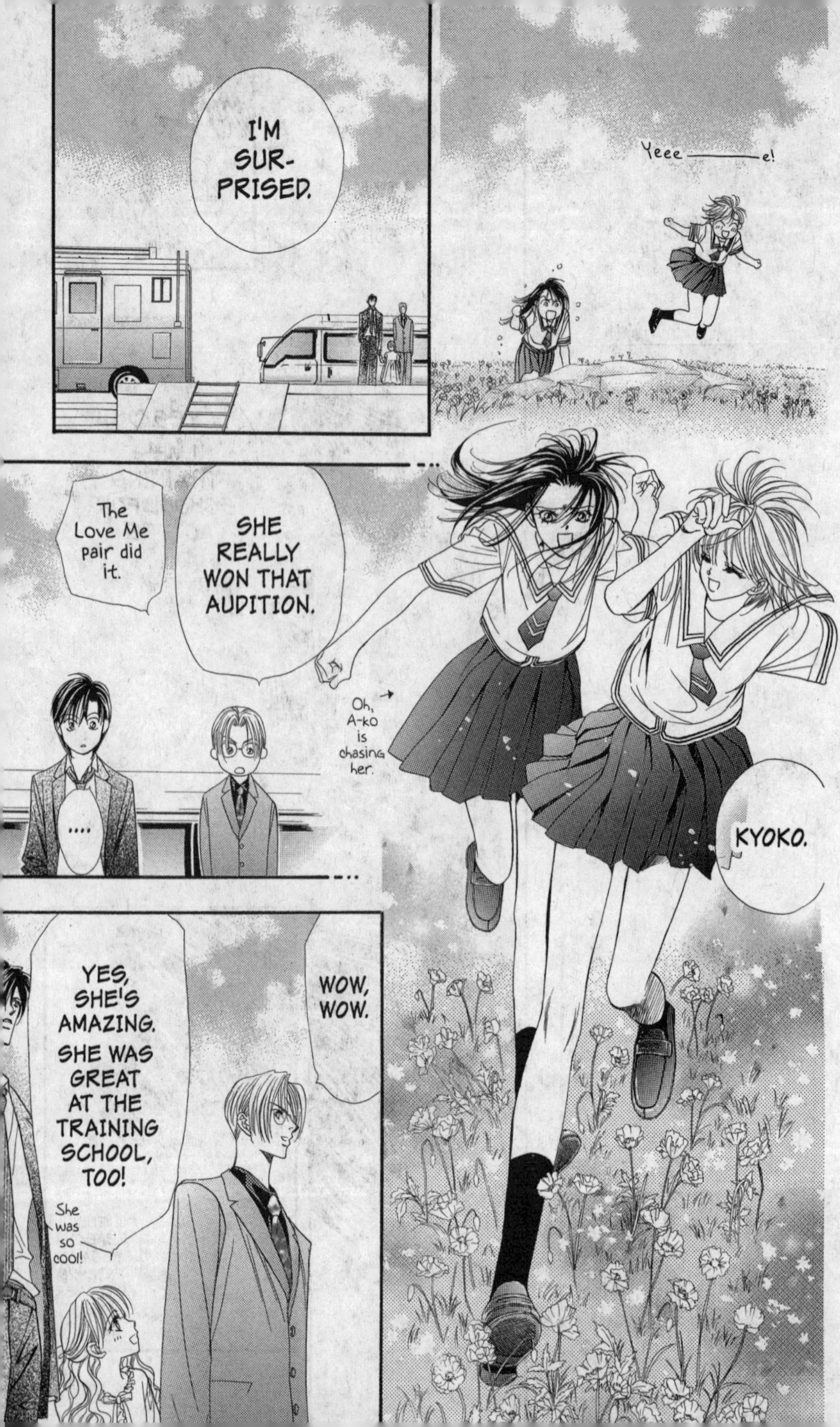

Yeee———e!
Oh, A-ko is chasing her.
KYOKO.
I'M SURPRISED.
SHE REALLY WON THAT AUDITION.
The Love Me pair did it.
....
WOW, WOW.
YES, SHE'S AMAZING. SHE WAS GREAT AT THE TRAINING SCHOOL, TOO!
She was so cool!

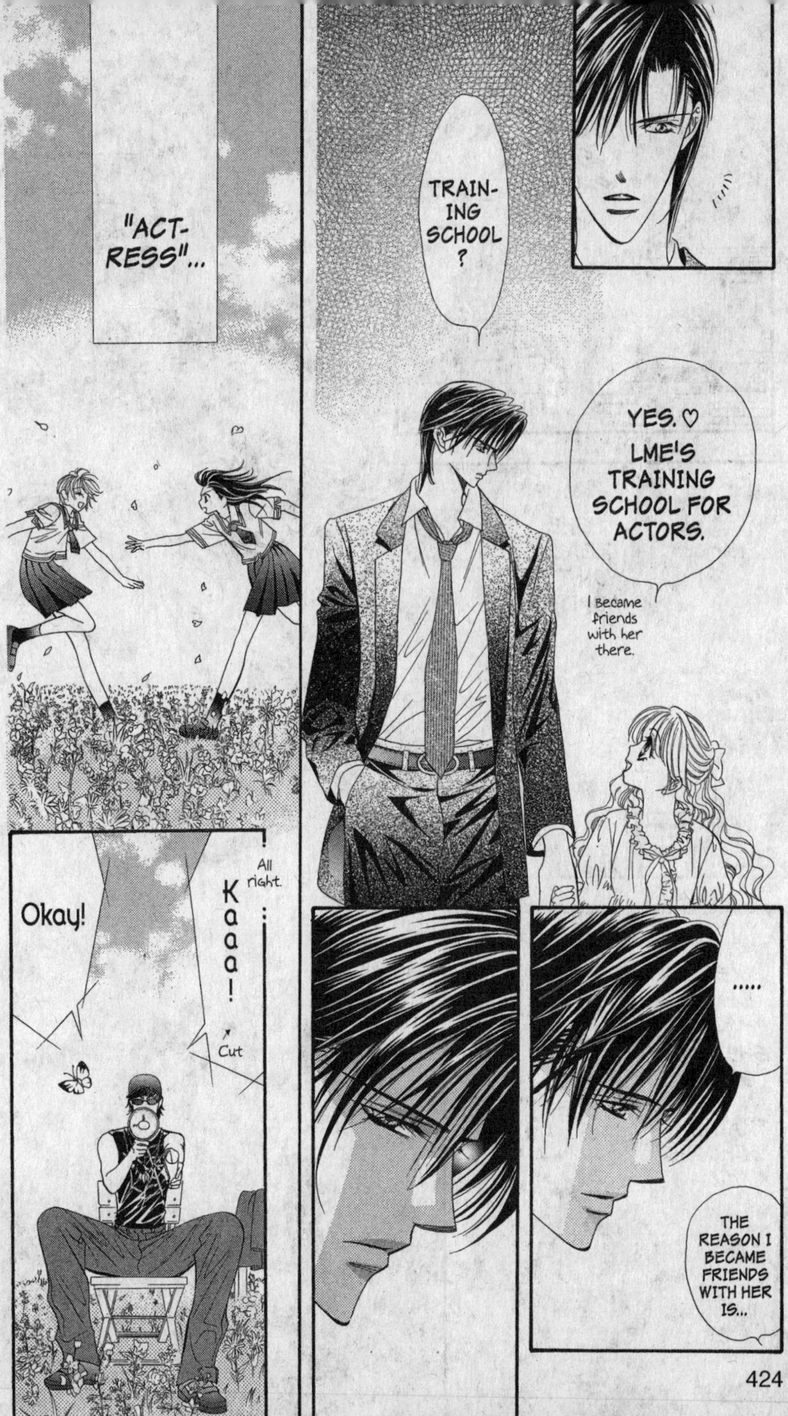
TRAIN-ING SCHOOL?
YES. ♡ LME'S TRAINING SCHOOL FOR ACTORS.
I became friends with her there.
.....
THE REASON I BECAME FRIENDS WITH HER IS...
"ACT-RESS"...
All right.
Kaaa!
Cut
Okay!

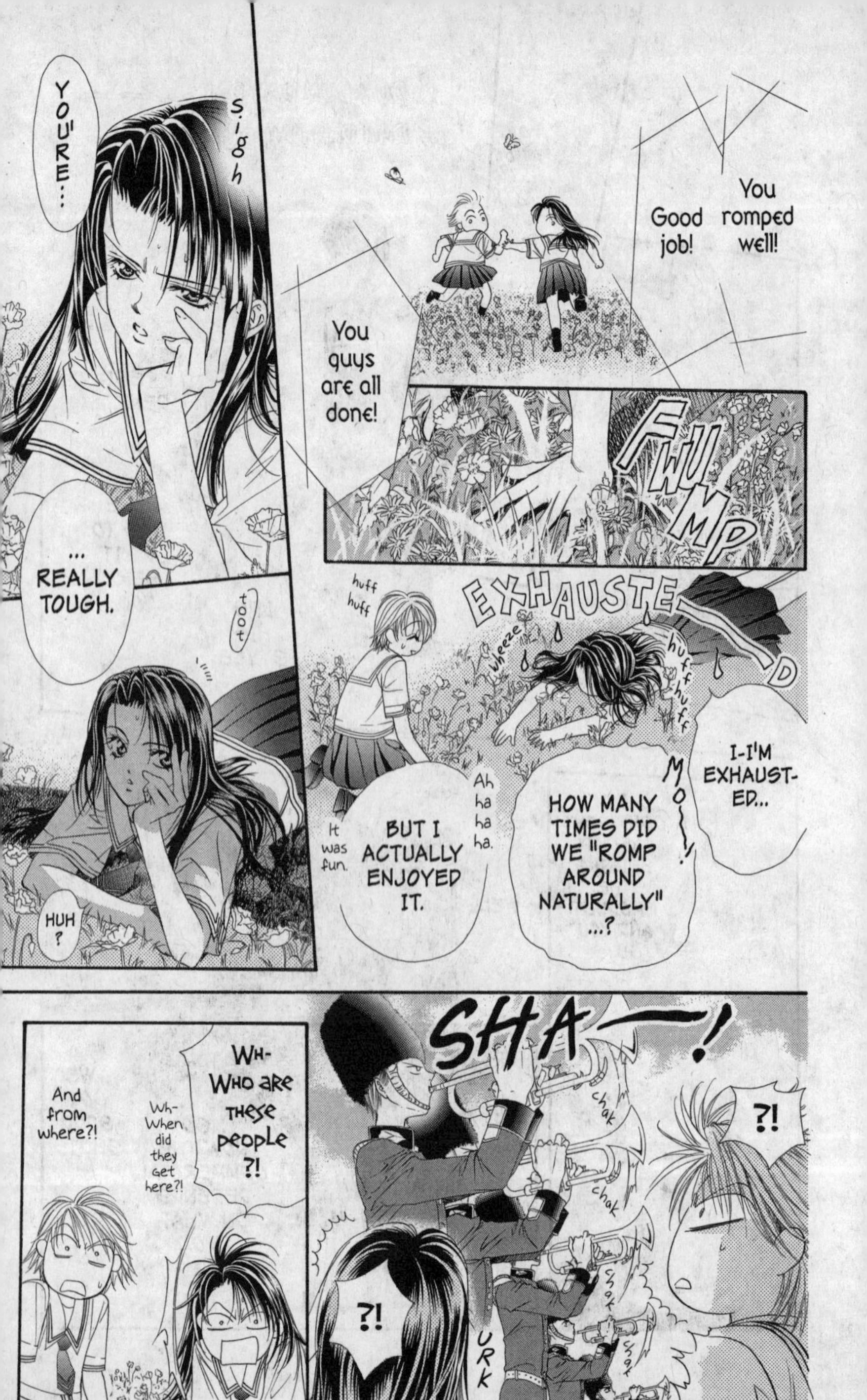
You romped well!
Good job!
You guys are all done!
FWUMP
EXHAUSTED
huff huff
I-I'M EXHAUSTED...
MO—!
HOW MANY TIMES DID WE "ROMP AROUND NATURALLY" ...?
wheeze
huff huff
Ah ha ha ha.
BUT I ACTUALLY ENJOYED IT.
It was fun.
YOU'RE...
sigh
... REALLY TOUGH.
toot
HUH?
SHA—!
?!
chak
chak
chak
chak
?!
URK
WH-WHO ARE THESE PEOPLE?!
Wh-When did they get here?!
And from where?!

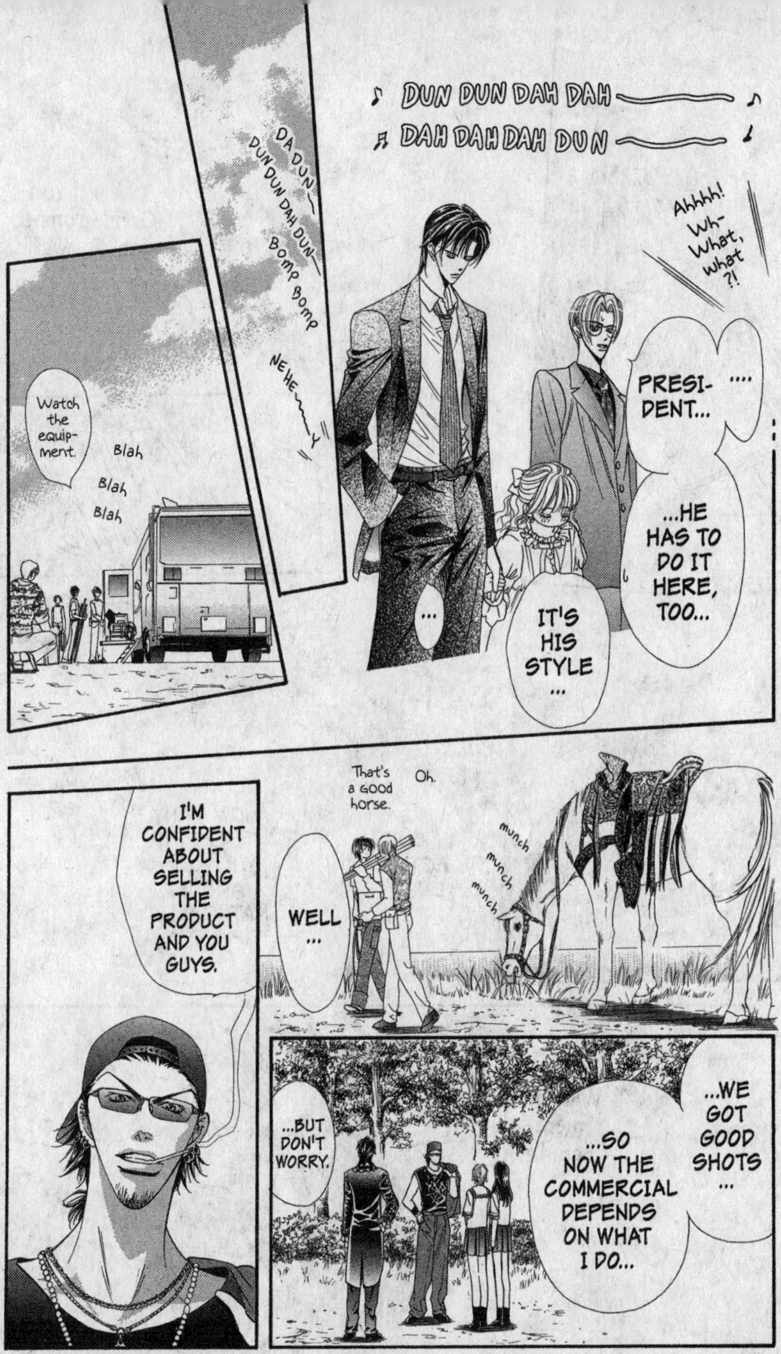
DUN DUN DAH DAH
DAH DAH DAH DUN
Ahhhh! Wh-What, what?!
PRESIDENT...
....
...HE HAS TO DO IT HERE, TOO...
IT'S HIS STYLE...
...
DA DUN~ DUN DUN DAH DUN~
Bomp Bomp
NEHE~Y
Watch the equipment.
Blah
Blah
Blah
Oh.
That's a good horse.
munch
munch
munch
WELL...
...WE GOT GOOD SHOTS...
...SO NOW THE COMMERCIAL DEPENDS ON WHAT I DO...
...BUT DON'T WORRY.
I'M CONFIDENT ABOUT SELLING THE PRODUCT AND YOU GUYS.

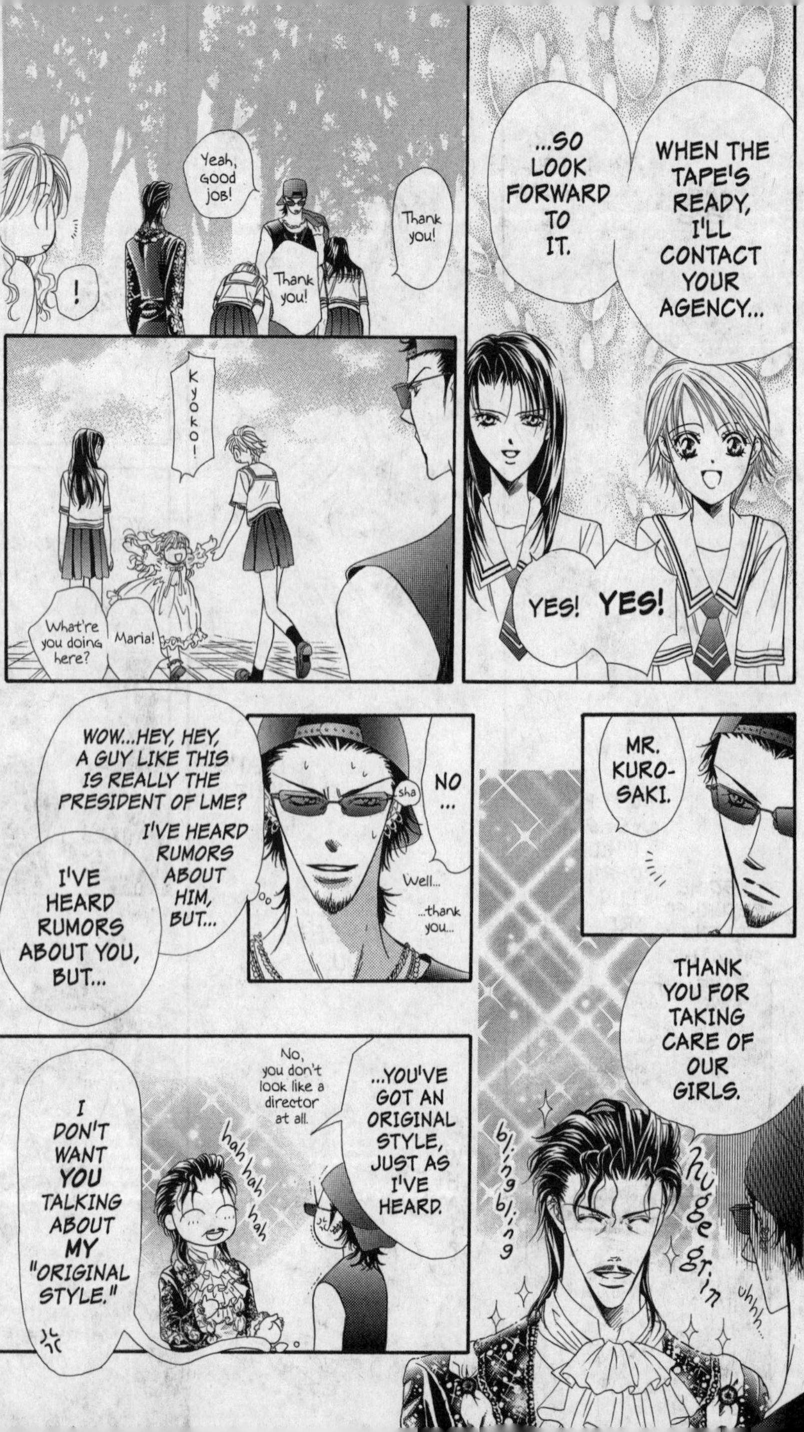
WHEN THE TAPE'S READY, I'LL CONTACT YOUR AGENCY...
...SO LOOK FORWARD TO IT.
YES!
YES!
Thank you!
Thank you!
Yeah, Good job!
!
K y o k o !
Maria!
What're you doing here?
MR. KURO-SAKI.
THANK YOU FOR TAKING CARE OF OUR GIRLS.
huge grin
uhhh...
bling bling
NO ...
sha
Well... ...thank you...
WOW...HEY, HEY, A GUY LIKE THIS IS REALLY THE PRESIDENT OF LME?
I'VE HEARD RUMORS ABOUT HIM, BUT...
I'VE HEARD RUMORS ABOUT YOU, BUT...
...YOU'VE GOT AN ORIGINAL STYLE, JUST AS I'VE HEARD.
No, you don't look like a director at all.
hah hah hah
I DON'T WANT YOU TALKING ABOUT MY "ORIGINAL STYLE."

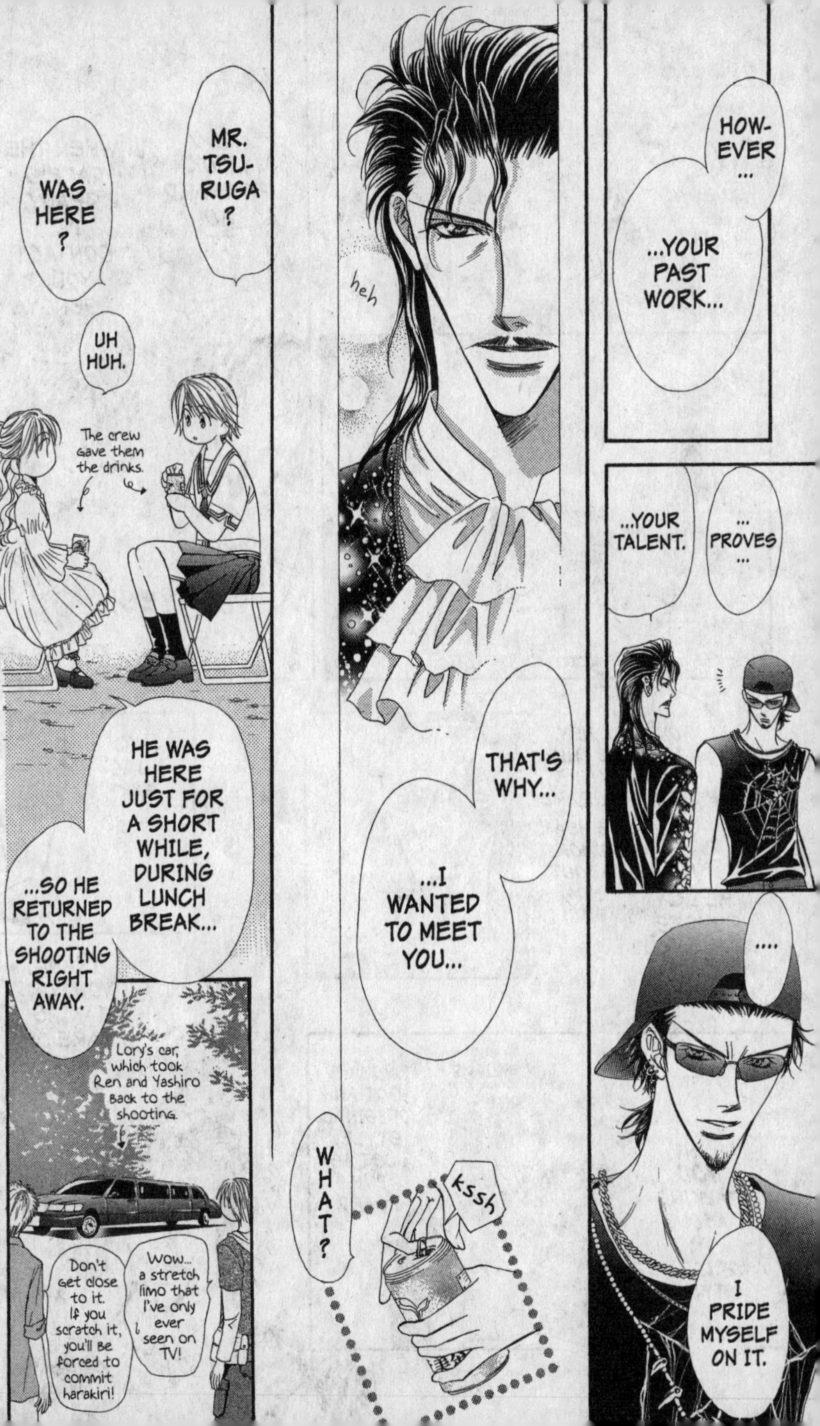
HOW-EVER...
...YOUR PAST WORK...
...PROVES...
...YOUR TALENT.
....
I PRIDE MYSELF ON IT.
heh
THAT'S WHY...
...I WANTED TO MEET YOU...
kssh
WHAT?
MR. TSURUGA?
WAS HERE?
UH HUH.
The crew gave them the drinks.
HE WAS HERE JUST FOR A SHORT WHILE, DURING LUNCH BREAK...
...SO HE RETURNED TO THE SHOOTING RIGHT AWAY.
Lory's car, which took Ren and Yashiro back to the shooting.
Wow... a stretch limo that I've only ever seen on TV!
Don't get close to it. If you scratch it, you'll be forced to commit harakiri!

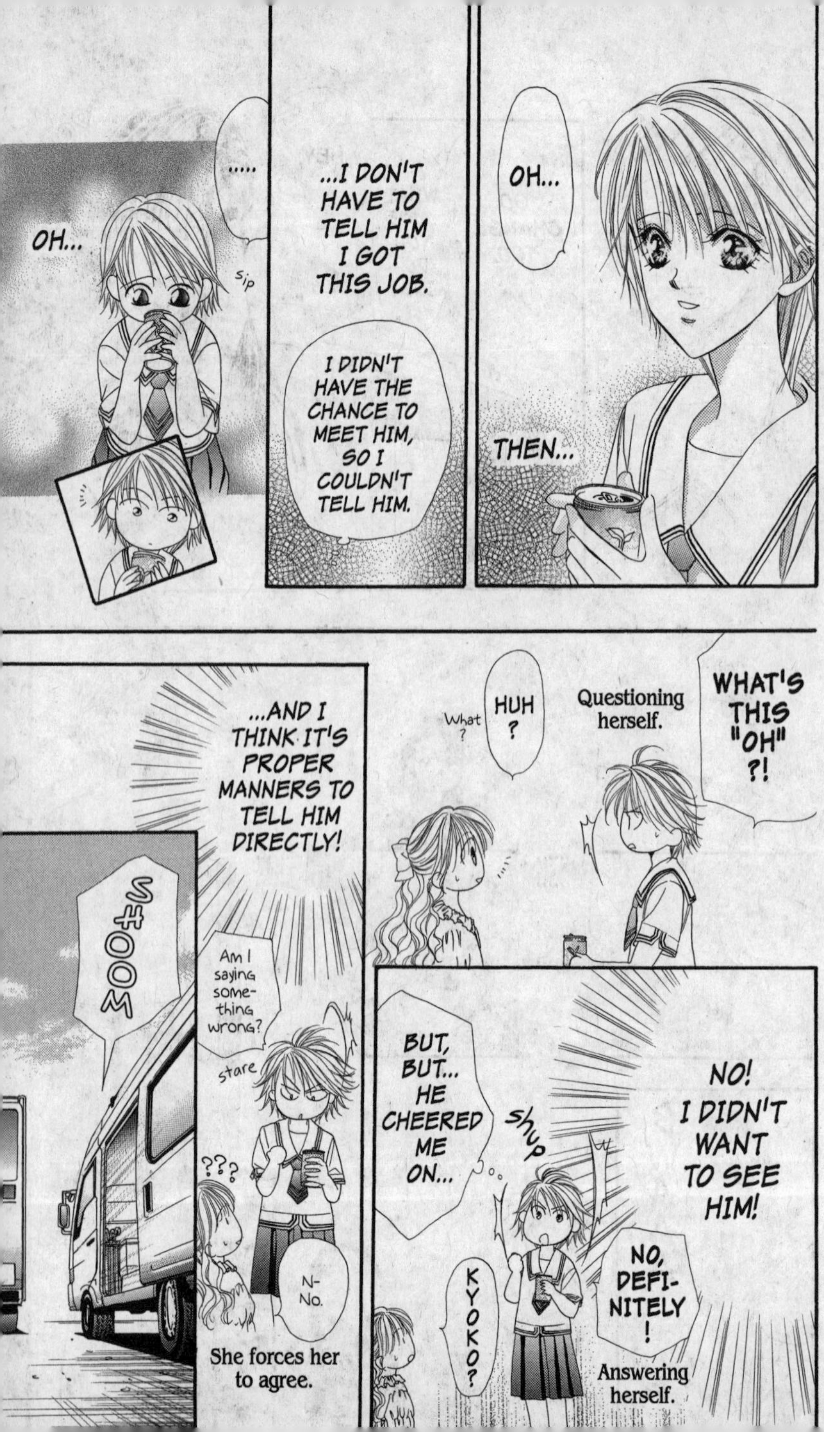

OH...
THEN...
...I DON'T HAVE TO TELL HIM I GOT THIS JOB.
I DIDN'T HAVE THE CHANCE TO MEET HIM, SO I COULDN'T TELL HIM.
.....
OH...
sip
WHAT'S THIS "OH"?!
Questioning herself.
HUH?
What?
...AND I THINK IT'S PROPER MANNERS TO TELL HIM DIRECTLY!
NO! I DIDN'T WANT TO SEE HIM!
BUT, BUT... HE CHEERED ME ON...
shup
NO, DEFINITELY!
KYOKO?
Answering herself.
Am I saying something wrong?
stare
???
N-No.
She forces her to agree.
WOOSH

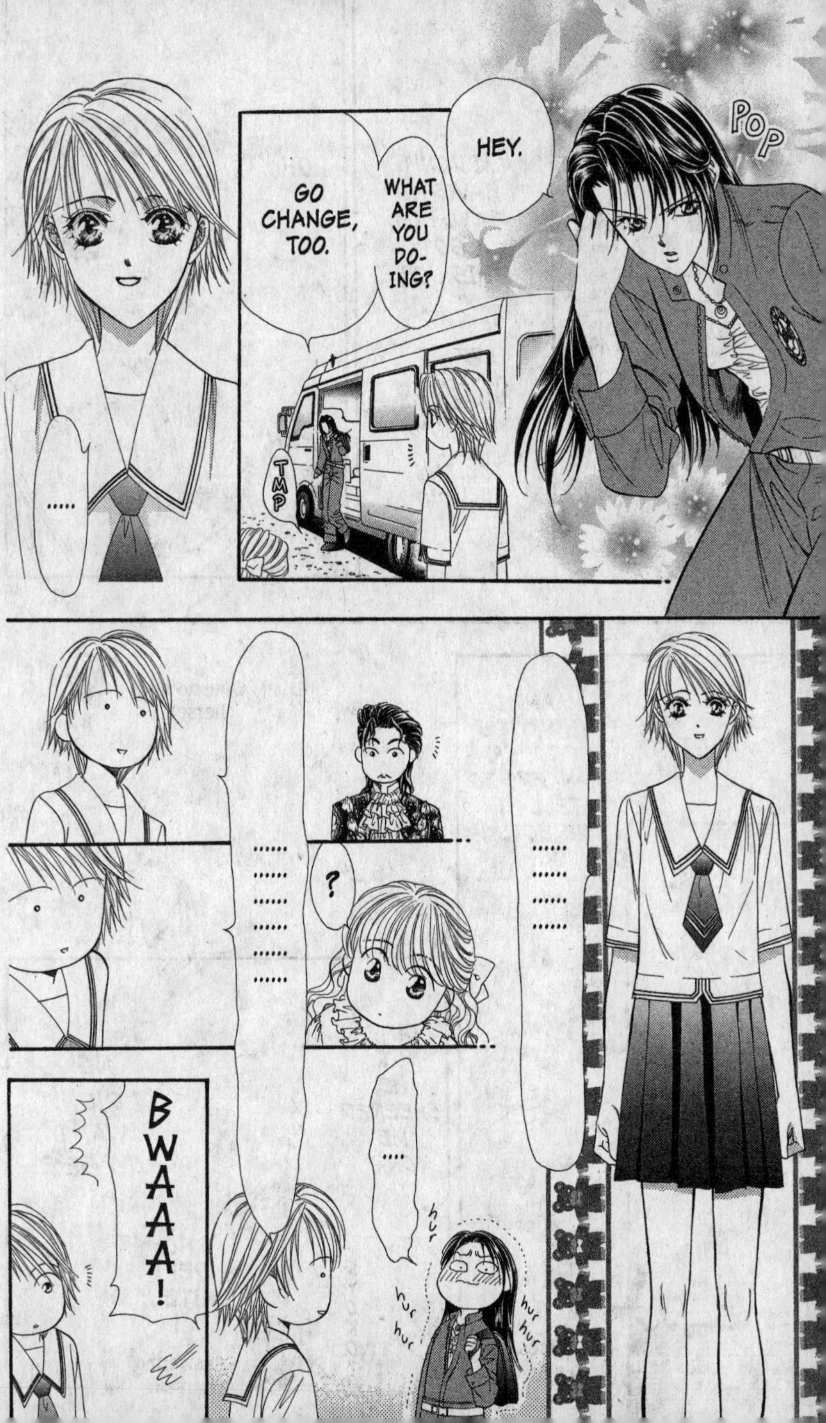
POP
HEY.
WHAT ARE YOU DO-ING?
GO CHANGE, TOO.
TMP
.....
......
......
......
......
......
......
......
......
......
......
?
....
hur hur hur hur hur hur
BWAAAA!

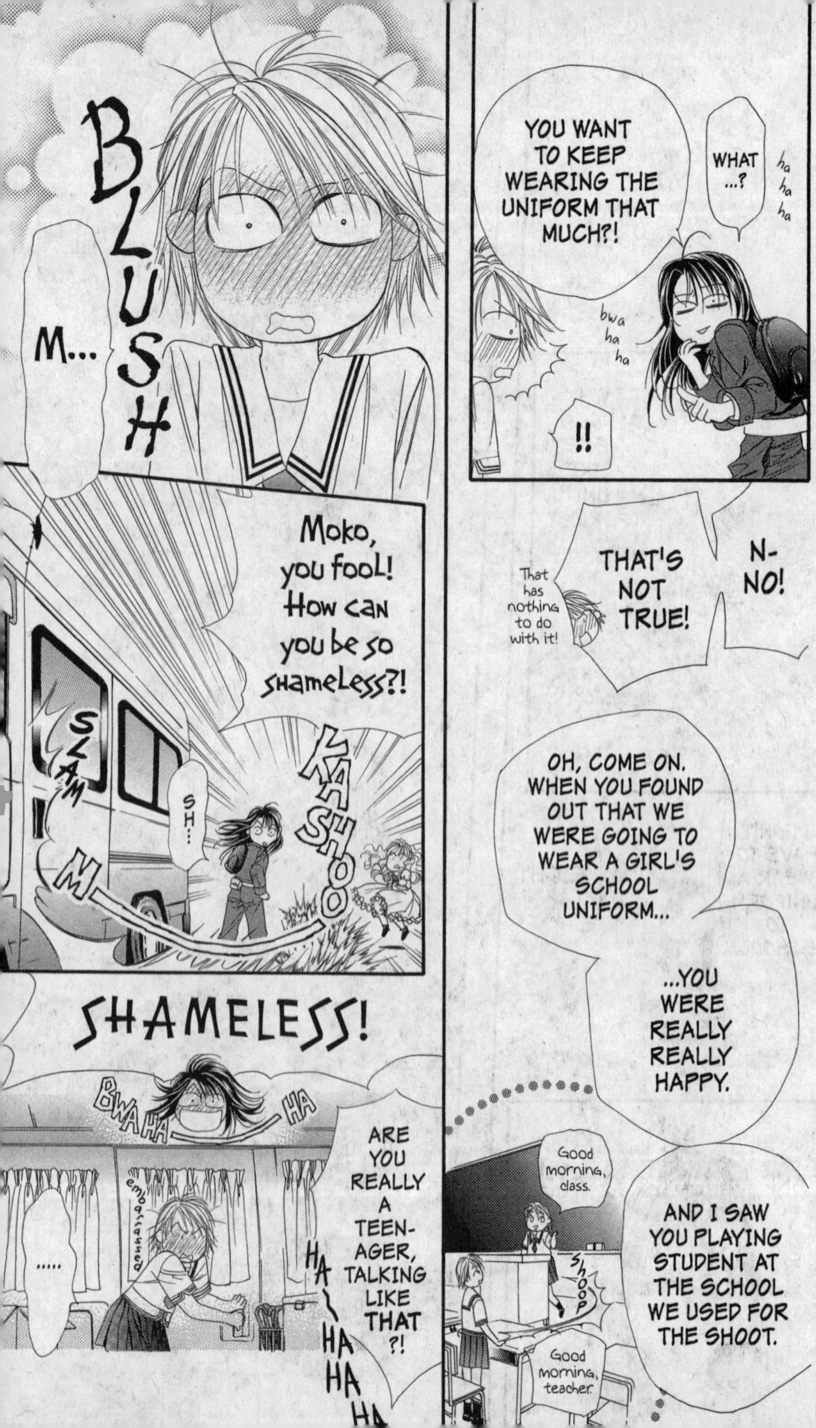
ha ha ha
WHAT ...?
YOU WANT TO KEEP WEARING THE UNIFORM THAT MUCH?!
bwa ha ha
!!
N-NO!
THAT'S NOT TRUE!
That has nothing to do with it!
OH, COME ON. WHEN YOU FOUND OUT THAT WE WERE GOING TO WEAR A GIRL'S SCHOOL UNIFORM...
...YOU WERE REALLY REALLY HAPPY.
AND I SAW YOU PLAYING STUDENT AT THE SCHOOL WE USED FOR THE SHOOT.
Good morning, class.
SHOOP
Good morning, teacher.
BLUSH
M...
Moko, you fool! How can you be so shameless?!
KASHOO
SH...
SLAM
SHAMELESS!
BWAHAHA HA
ARE YOU REALLY A TEEN-AGER, TALKING LIKE THAT?!
HA HA HA HA
embarrassed
.....

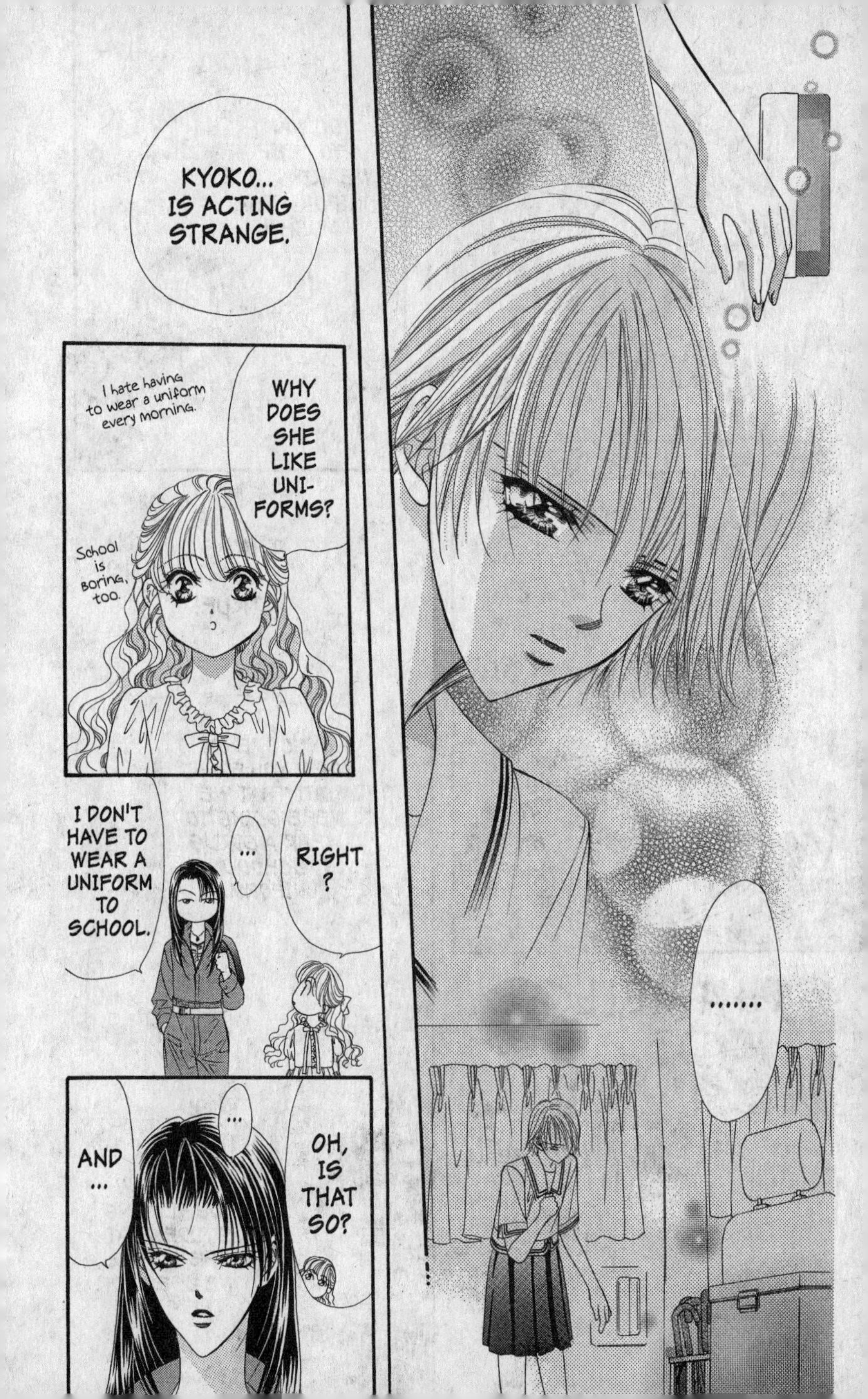
....
KYOKO... IS ACTING STRANGE.
WHY DOES SHE LIKE UNI-FORMS?
I hate having to wear a uniform every morning.
School is boring, too.
RIGHT?
...
I DON'T HAVE TO WEAR A UNIFORM TO SCHOOL.
OH, IS THAT SO?
...
AND ...

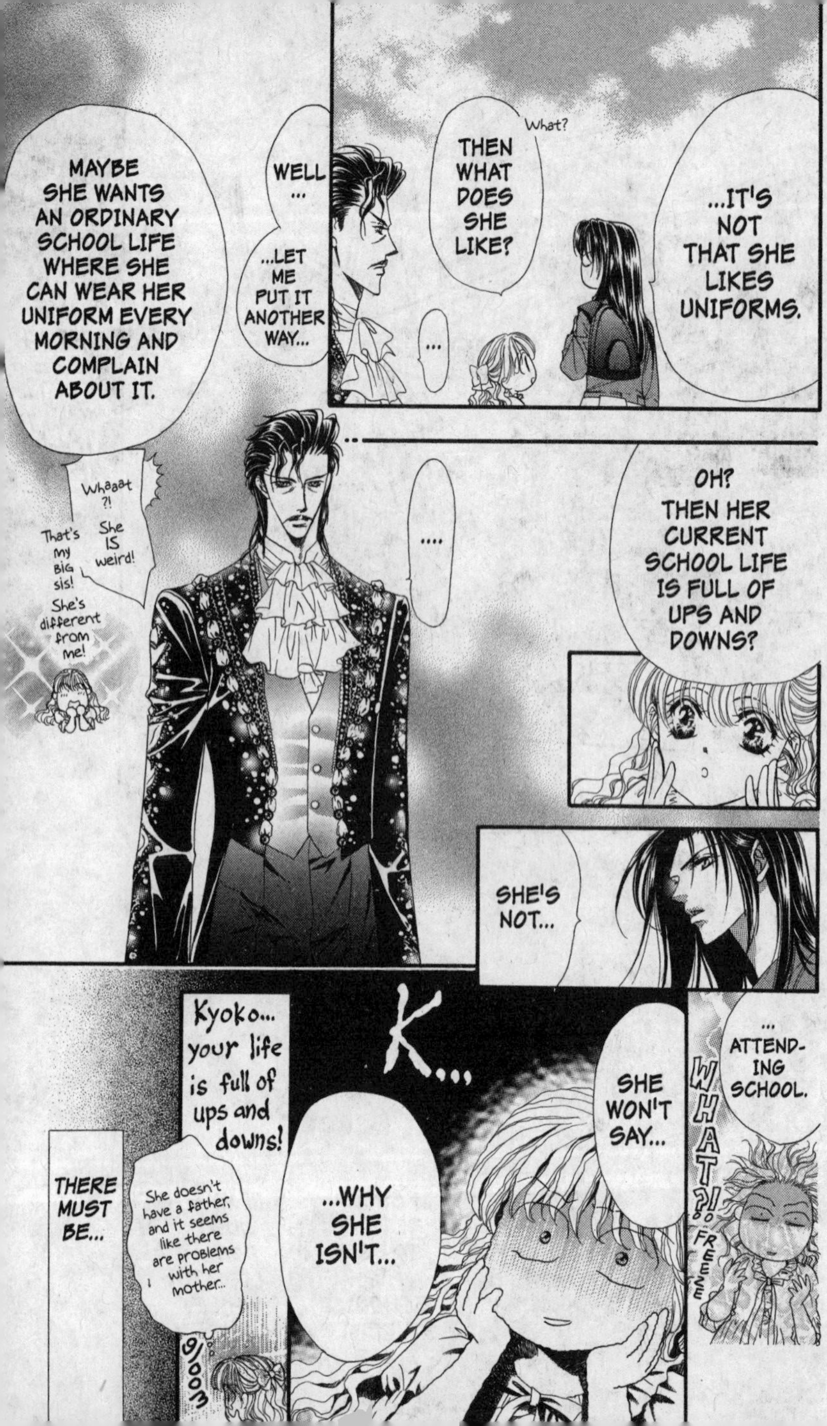
...IT'S NOT THAT SHE LIKES UNIFORMS.
What?
THEN WHAT DOES SHE LIKE?
...
WELL ...
...LET ME PUT IT ANOTHER WAY...
MAYBE SHE WANTS AN ORDINARY SCHOOL LIFE WHERE SHE CAN WEAR HER UNIFORM EVERY MORNING AND COMPLAIN ABOUT IT.
Whaaat?!
She IS weird!
That's my BIG sis!
She's different from me!
....
OH? THEN HER CURRENT SCHOOL LIFE IS FULL OF UPS AND DOWNS?
SHE'S NOT...
... ATTENDING SCHOOL.
WHAT?!
FREEZE
SHE WON'T SAY...
...WHY SHE ISN'T...
K...,
Kyoko... your life is full of ups and downs!
THERE MUST BE...
She doesn't have a father, and it seems like there are problems with her mother...
gloom

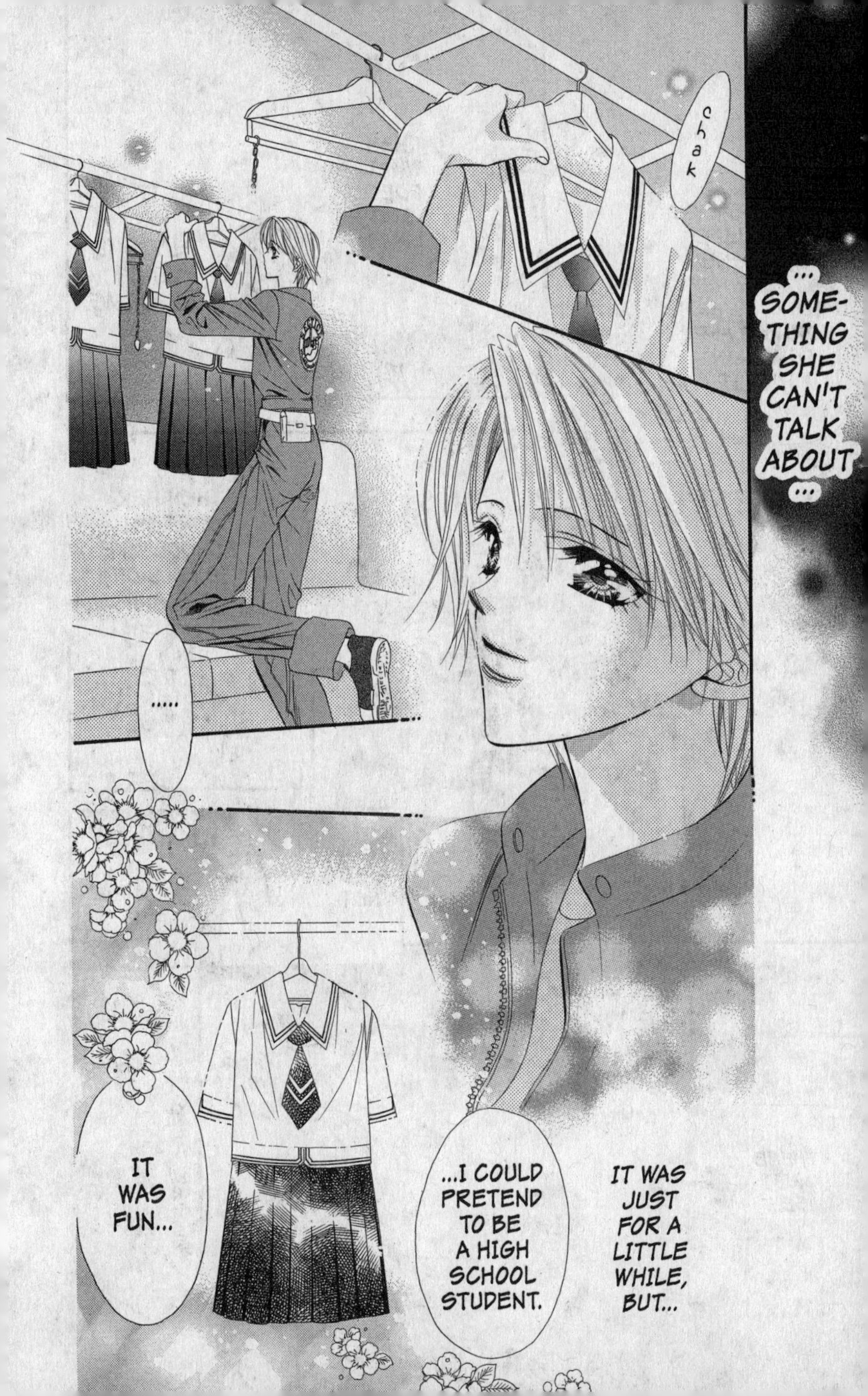
chak
... SOMETHING SHE CAN'T TALK ABOUT ...
.....
IT WAS JUST FOR A LITTLE WHILE, BUT...
...I COULD PRETEND TO BE A HIGH SCHOOL STUDENT.
IT WAS FUN...

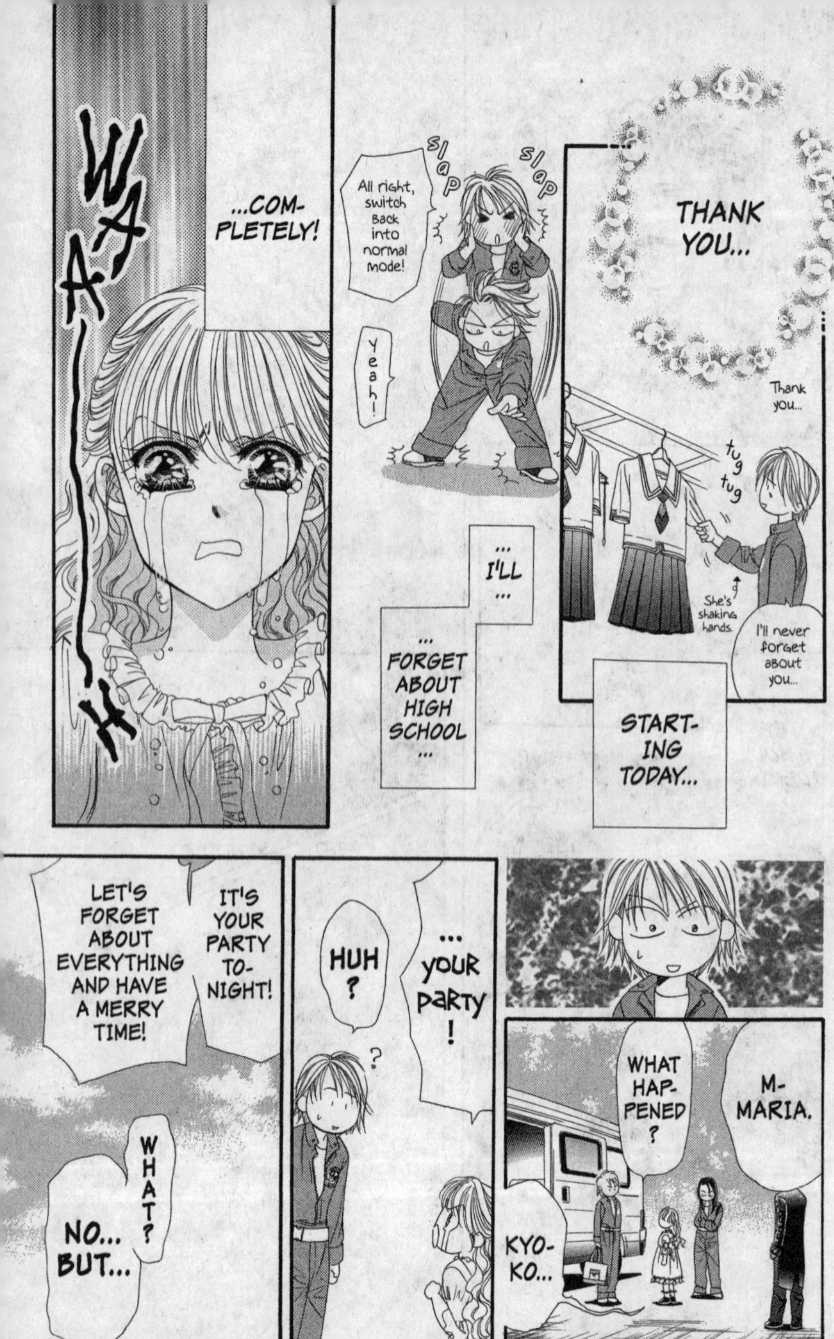
THANK YOU...
Thank you...
tug tug
She's shaking hands.
I'll never forget about you...
STARTING TODAY...
slap slap
All right, switch back into normal mode!
Yeah!
...I'LL...
...FORGET ABOUT HIGH SCHOOL...
...COMPLETELY!
WAAAH
M-MARIA.
WHAT HAPPENED?
KYOKO...
...YOUR PARTY!
HUH?
?
IT'S YOUR PARTY TONIGHT!
LET'S FORGET ABOUT EVERYTHING AND HAVE A MERRY TIME!
WHAT?
NO... BUT...

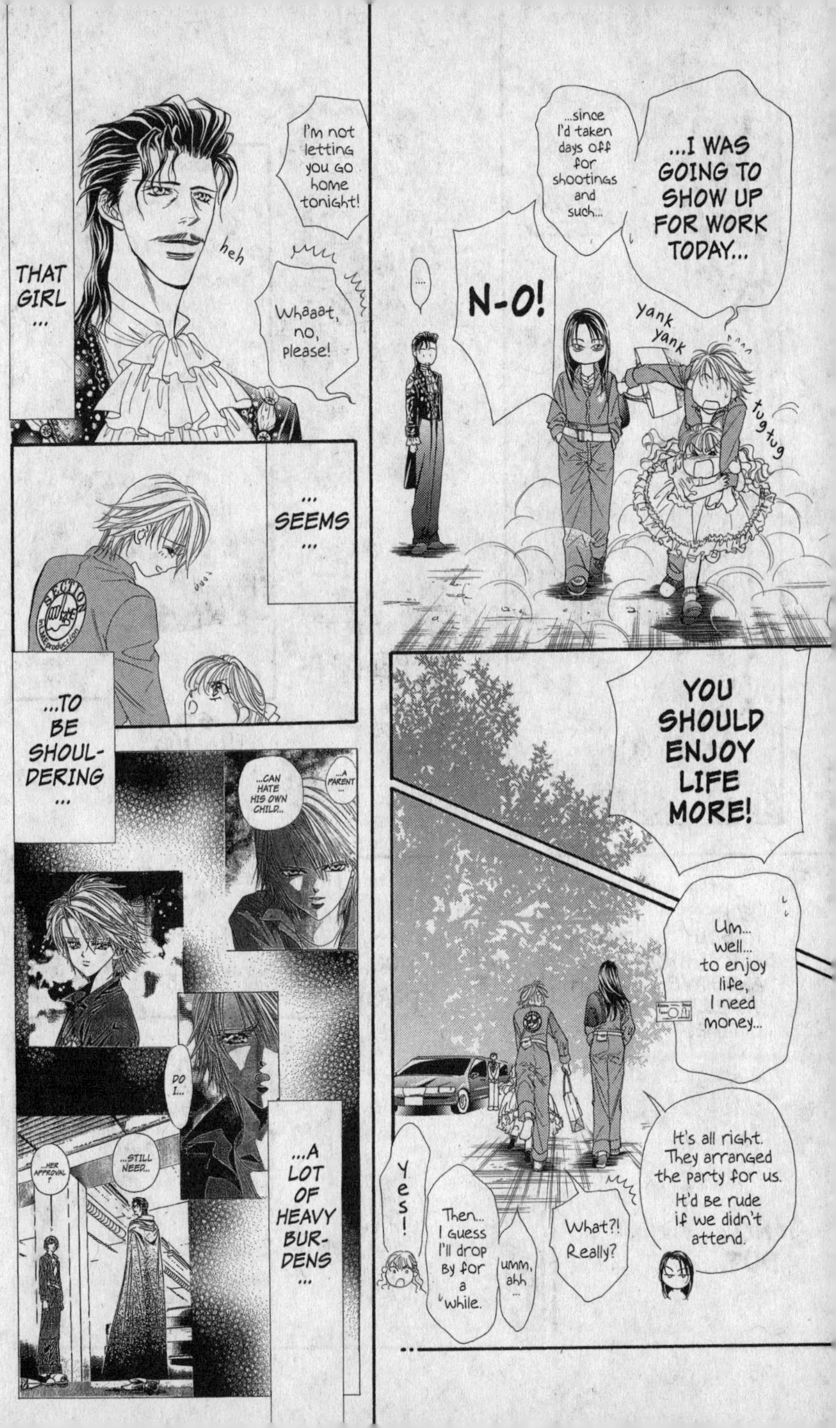
...I WAS GOING TO SHOW UP FOR WORK TODAY...
...since I'd taken days off for shootings and such...
N-O!
....
yank yank
tugtug
YOU SHOULD ENJOY LIFE MORE!
Um... well... to enjoy life, I need money...
It's all right. They arranged the party for us. It'd be rude if we didn't attend.
What?! Really?
umm, ahh ...
Then... I guess I'll drop by for a while.
Yes!
I'm not letting you go home tonight!
heh
Whaaat, no, please!
THAT GIRL ...
... SEEMS ...
...TO BE SHOULDERING ...
...A PARENT ...
...CAN HATE HIS OWN CHILD...
DO I...
...STILL NEED...
...HER APPROVAL?
...A LOT OF HEAVY BURDENS ...

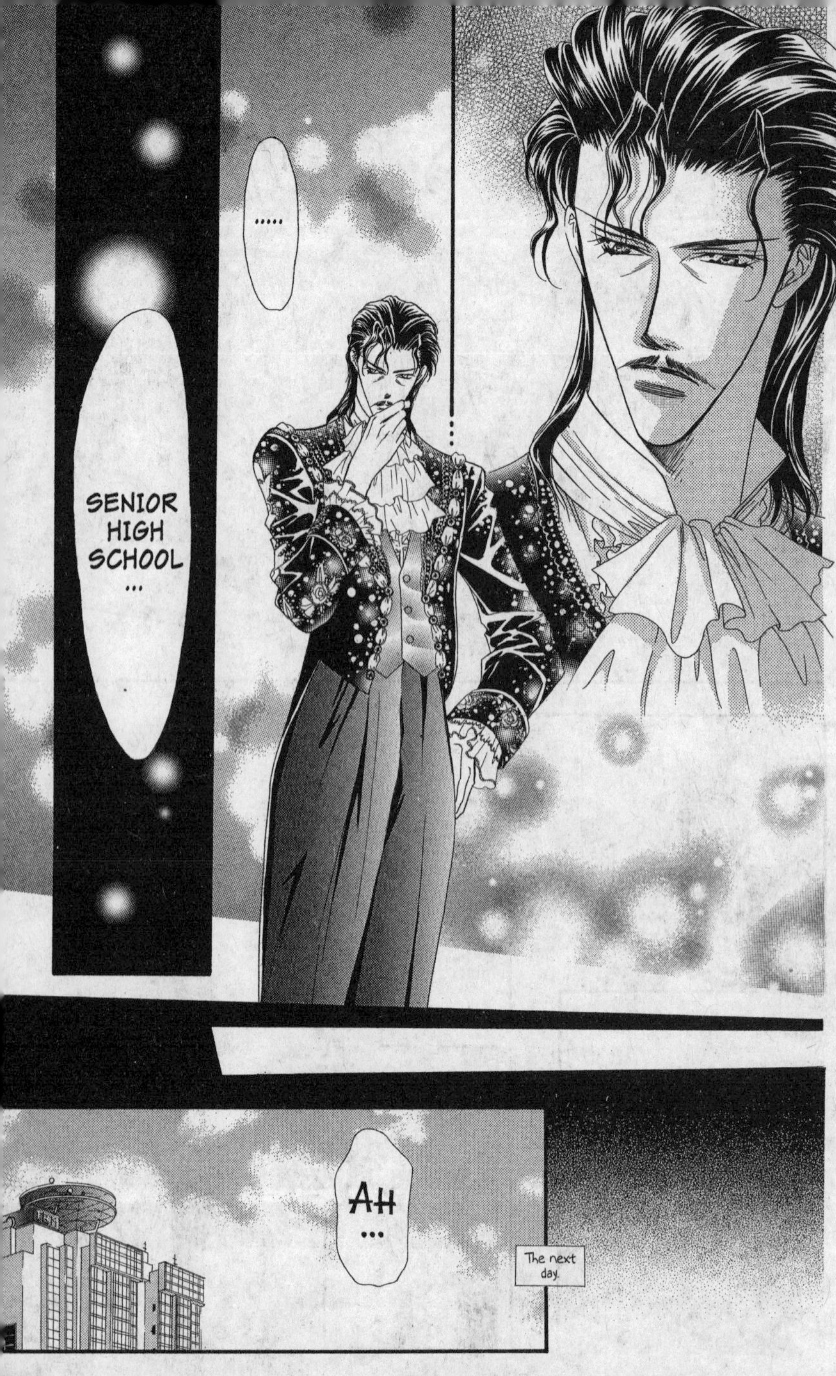
......
SENIOR HIGH SCHOOL ...
The next day.
AH ...

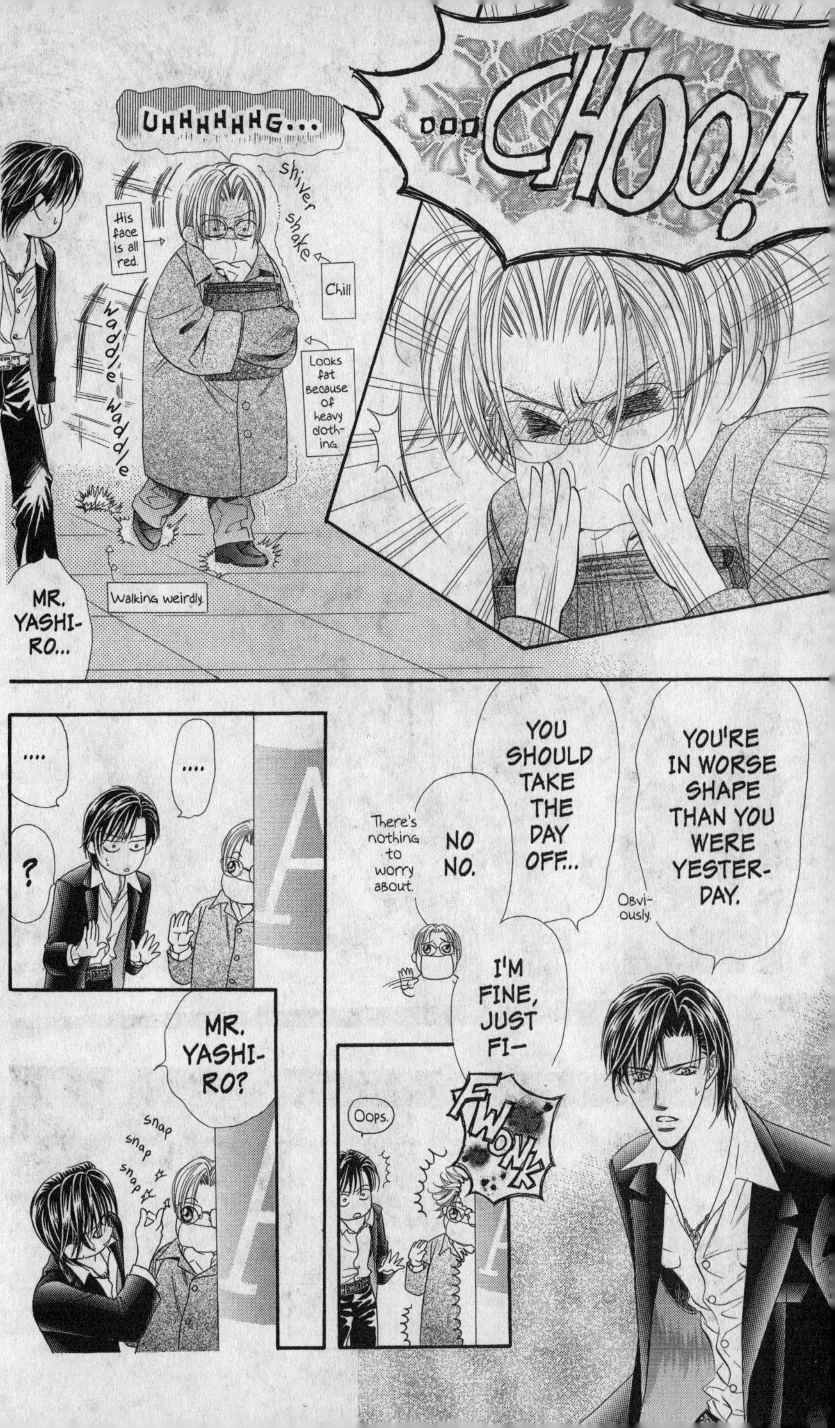
...CHOO!
UHHHHHHG...
shiver shake
Chill
Looks fat because of heavy clothing.
His face is all red.
waddle waddle
Walking weirdly.
MR. YASHIRO...
YOU'RE IN WORSE SHAPE THAN YOU WERE YESTERDAY.
Obviously.
YOU SHOULD TAKE THE DAY OFF...
NO NO.
There's nothing to worry about.
I'M FINE, JUST FI—
....
....
?
MR. YASHIRO?
snap snap snap
FWONK
Oops.

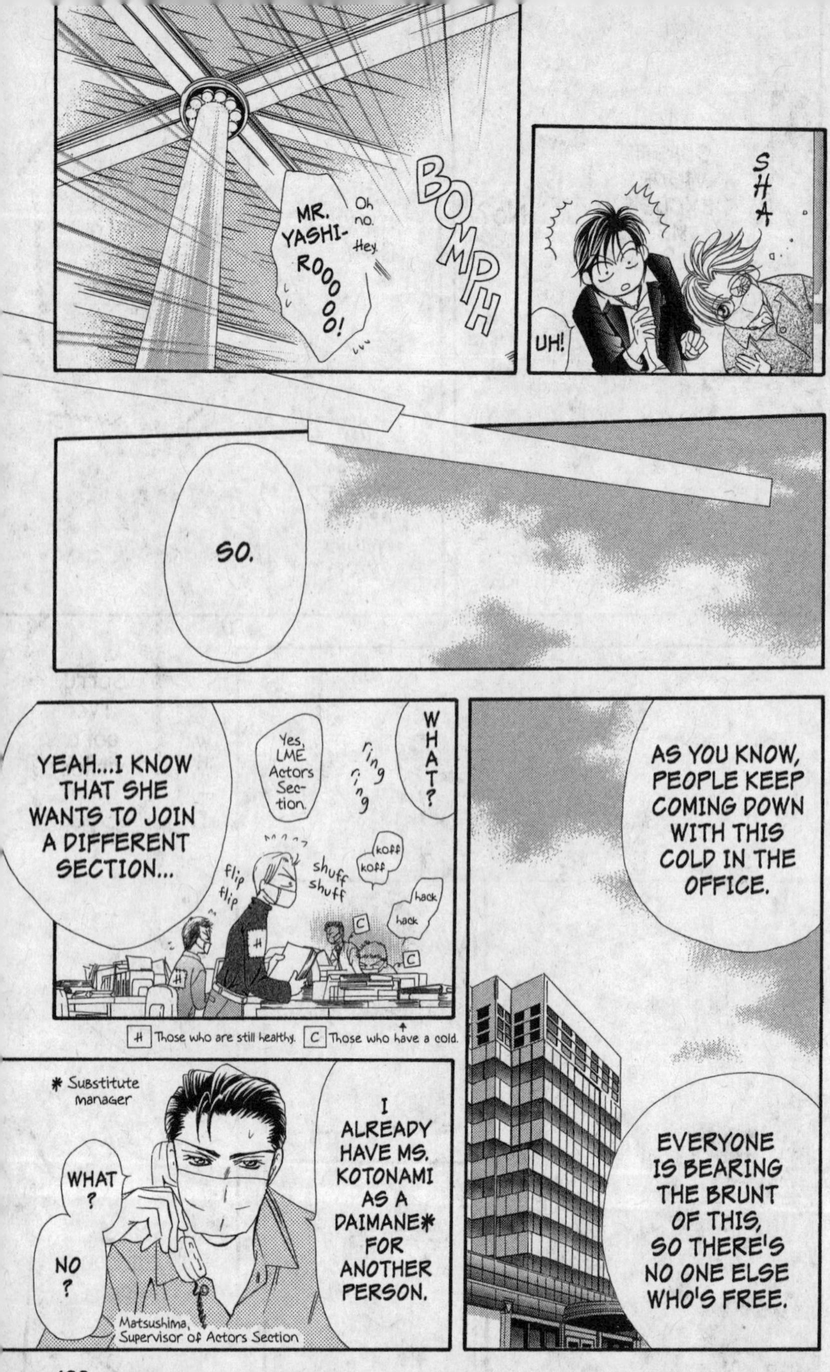
SHA
UH!
BOMPH
MR. YASHIROOOOOO!
Oh no.
Hey.
SO.
AS YOU KNOW, PEOPLE KEEP COMING DOWN WITH THIS COLD IN THE OFFICE.
EVERYONE IS BEARING THE BRUNT OF THIS, SO THERE'S NO ONE ELSE WHO'S FREE.
WHAT?
ring ring
Yes, LME Actors Section.
koff koff
hack hack
shuff shuff
flip flip
YEAH...I KNOW THAT SHE WANTS TO JOIN A DIFFERENT SECTION...
H Those who are still healthy.
C Those who have a cold.
I ALREADY HAVE MS. KOTONAMI AS A DAIMANE* FOR ANOTHER PERSON.
WHAT?
NO?
* Substitute manager
Matsushima, Supervisor of Actors Section

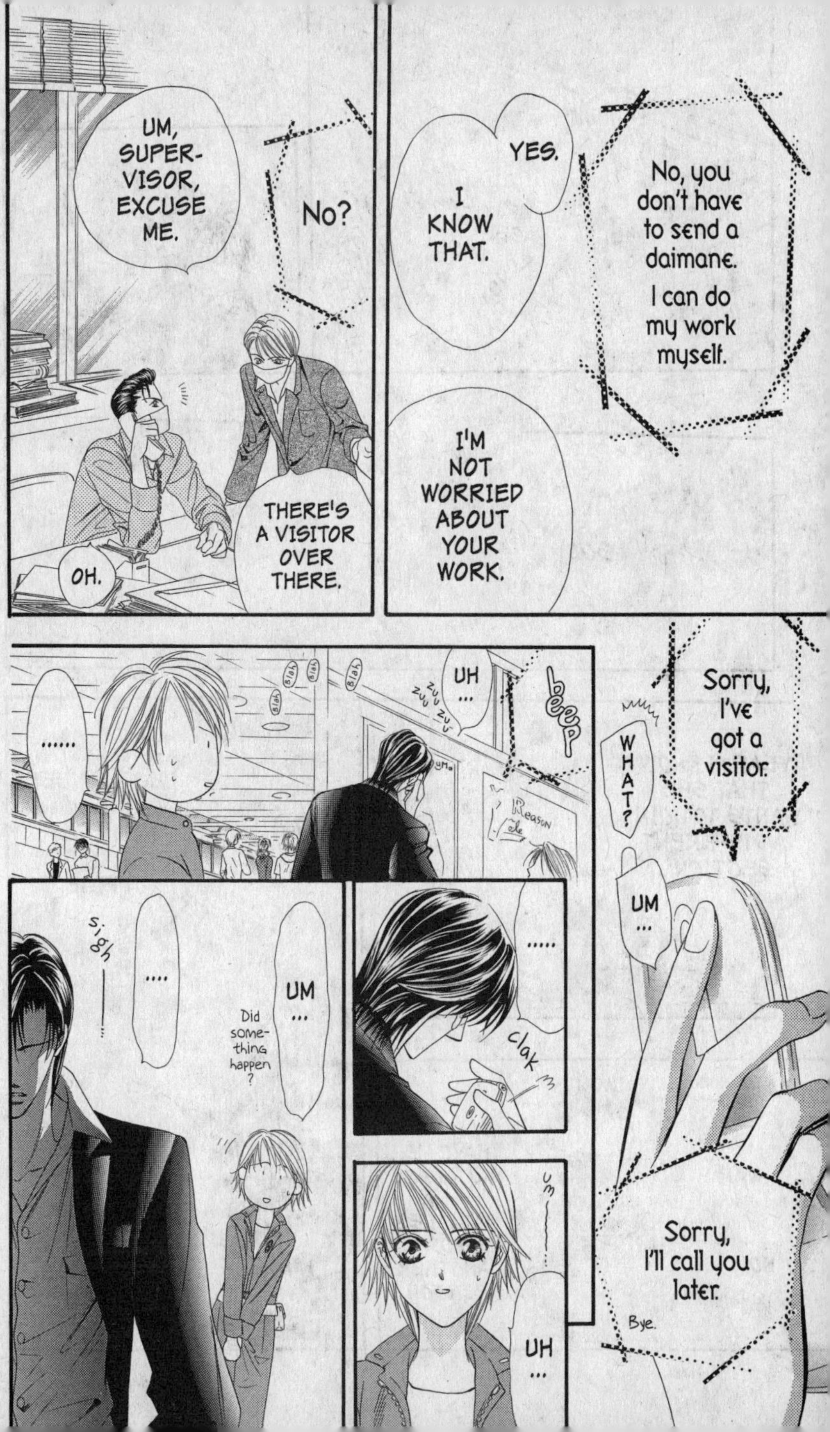

No, you don't have to send a daimane. I can do my work myself.
YES. I KNOW THAT.
I'M NOT WORRIED ABOUT YOUR WORK.
No?
UM, SUPER-VISOR, EXCUSE ME.
THERE'S A VISITOR OVER THERE.
OH.
Sorry, I've got a visitor.
WHAT?
UM ...
Sorry, I'll call you later.
Bye.
beep
UH ...
zuzuzuzu
blah blah blah blah
......
.....
clak
um——
UH ...
UM ...
Did some-thing happen?
....
sigh——

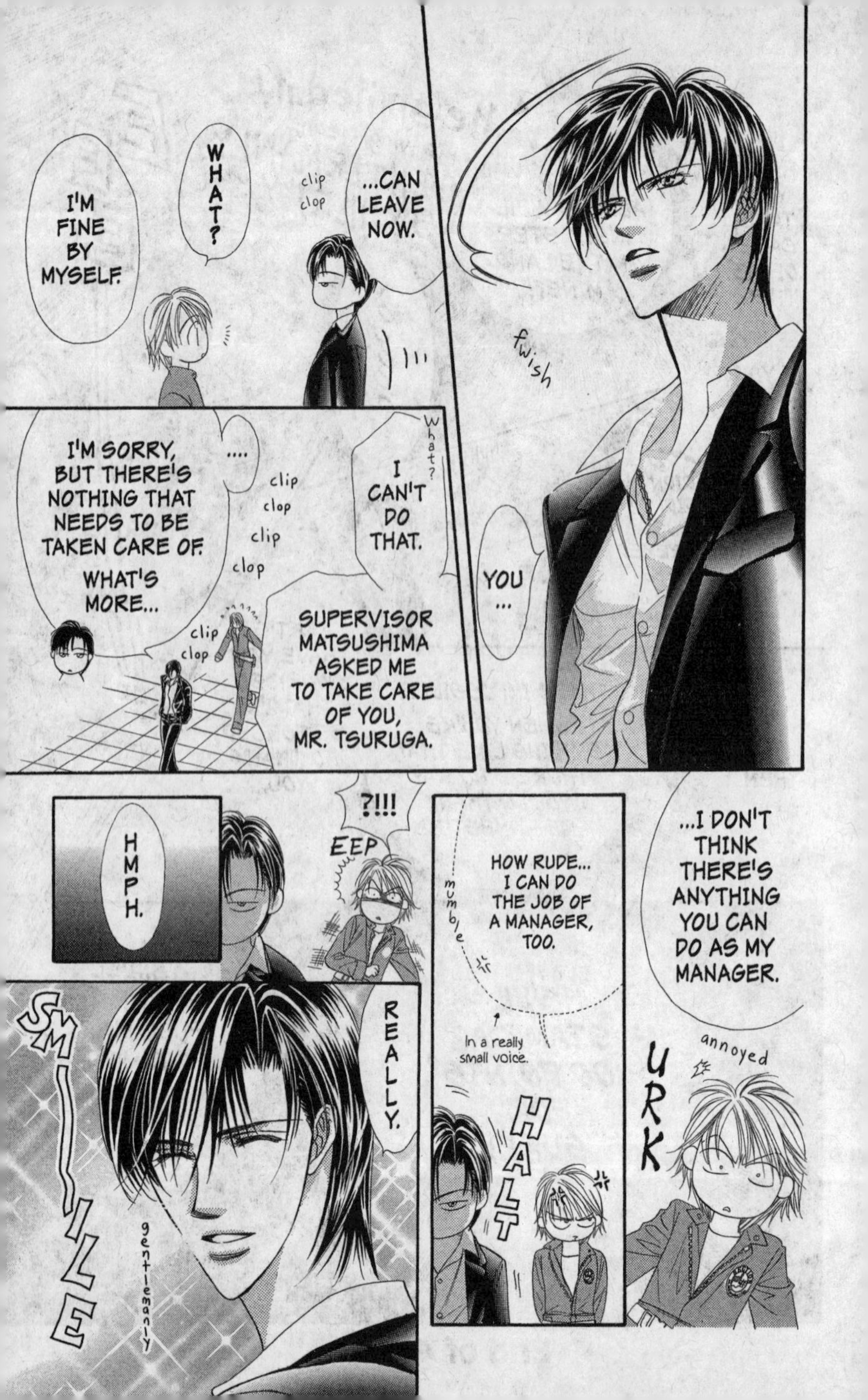
fwish
YOU...
...CAN LEAVE NOW.
clip clop
WHAT?
I'M FINE BY MYSELF.
What?
I CAN'T DO THAT.
SUPERVISOR MATSUSHIMA ASKED ME TO TAKE CARE OF YOU, MR. TSURUGA.
....
clip clop clip clop
I'M SORRY, BUT THERE'S NOTHING THAT NEEDS TO BE TAKEN CARE OF.
WHAT'S MORE...
clip clop
...I DON'T THINK THERE'S ANYTHING YOU CAN DO AS MY MANAGER.
annoyed
URK
HOW RUDE... I CAN DO THE JOB OF A MANAGER, TOO.
mumble
In a really small voice.
HALT
?!!!
EEP
HMPH.
REALLY.
SMIIILE
gentlemanly

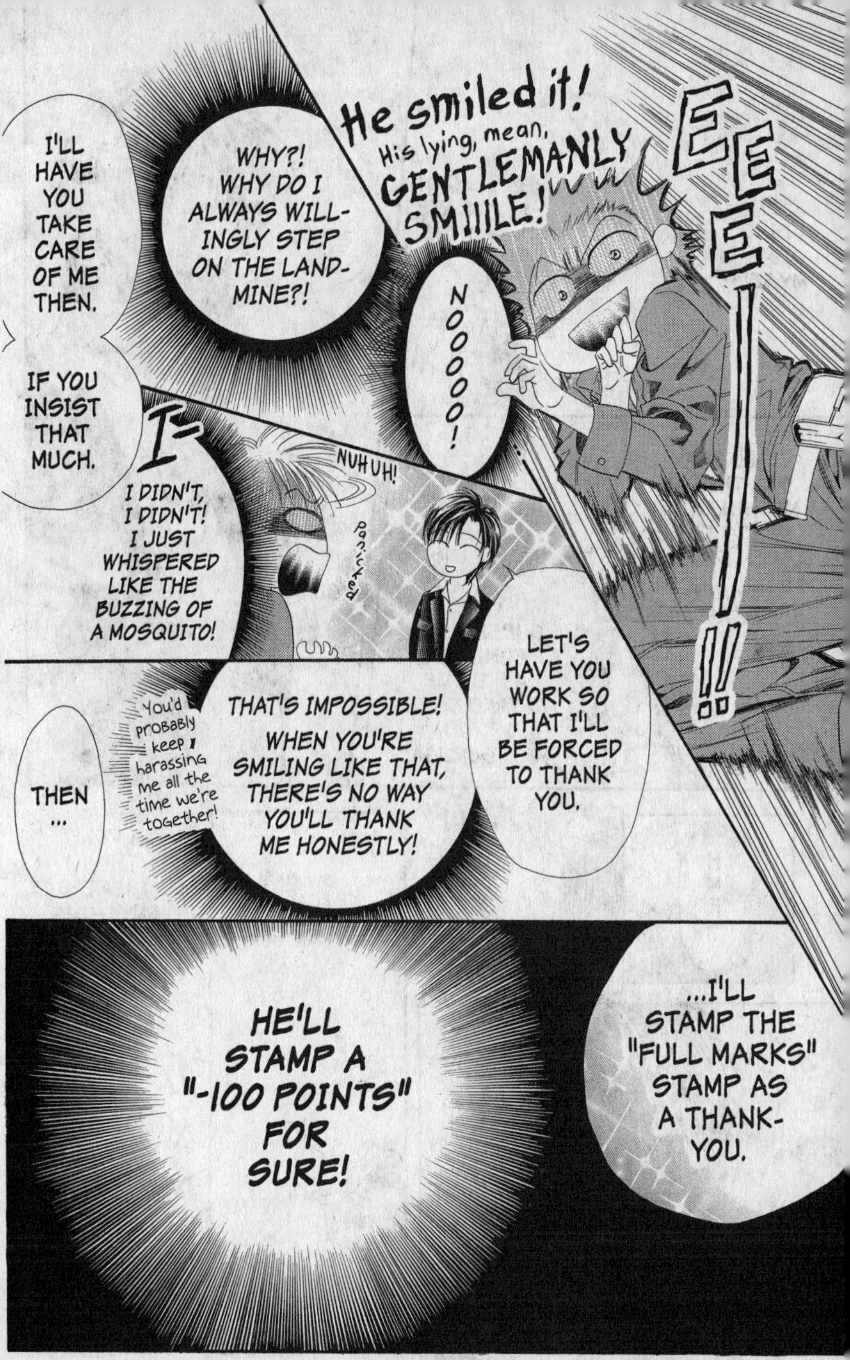
EEEE!!!!
He smiled it!
His lying, mean, GENTLEMANLY SMIIIILE!
NOOOOOO!
WHY?! WHY DO I ALWAYS WILL-INGLY STEP ON THE LAND-MINE?!
I'LL HAVE YOU TAKE CARE OF ME THEN.
IF YOU INSIST THAT MUCH.
NUH UH!
I-
I DIDN'T, I DIDN'T! I JUST WHISPERED LIKE THE BUZZING OF A MOSQUITO!
panicked
LET'S HAVE YOU WORK SO THAT I'LL BE FORCED TO THANK YOU.
THAT'S IMPOSSIBLE!
WHEN YOU'RE SMILING LIKE THAT, THERE'S NO WAY YOU'LL THANK ME HONESTLY!
You'd probably keep harassing me all the time we're together!
THEN ...
...I'LL STAMP THE "FULL MARKS" STAMP AS A THANK-YOU.
HE'LL STAMP A "-100 POINTS" FOR SURE!

End of Act 31

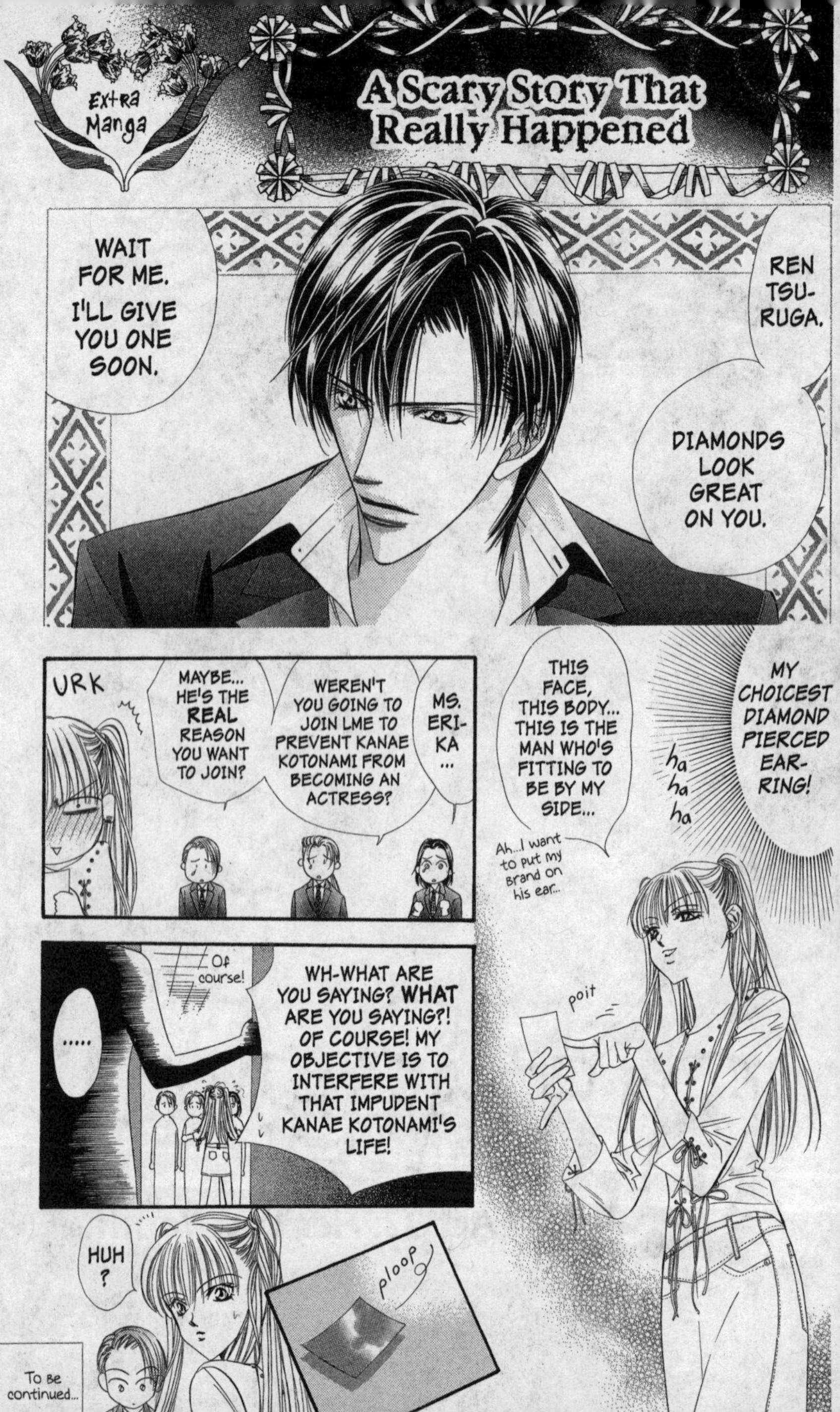

A Scary Story That Really Happened
Extra Manga
REN TSURUGA.
DIAMONDS LOOK GREAT ON YOU.
WAIT FOR ME. I'LL GIVE YOU ONE SOON.
MY CHOICEST DIAMOND PIERCED EARRING!
ha ha ha
THIS FACE, THIS BODY... THIS IS THE MAN WHO'S FITTING TO BE BY MY SIDE...
Ah...I want to put my brand on his ear...
poit
MS. ERIKA...
WEREN'T YOU GOING TO JOIN LME TO PREVENT KANAE KOTONAMI FROM BECOMING AN ACTRESS?
MAYBE... HE'S THE REAL REASON YOU WANT TO JOIN?
URK
WH-WHAT ARE YOU SAYING? WHAT ARE YOU SAYING?! OF COURSE! MY OBJECTIVE IS TO INTERFERE WITH THAT IMPUDENT KANAE KOTONAMI'S LIFE!
Of course!
.....
ploop
HUH?
To be continued...

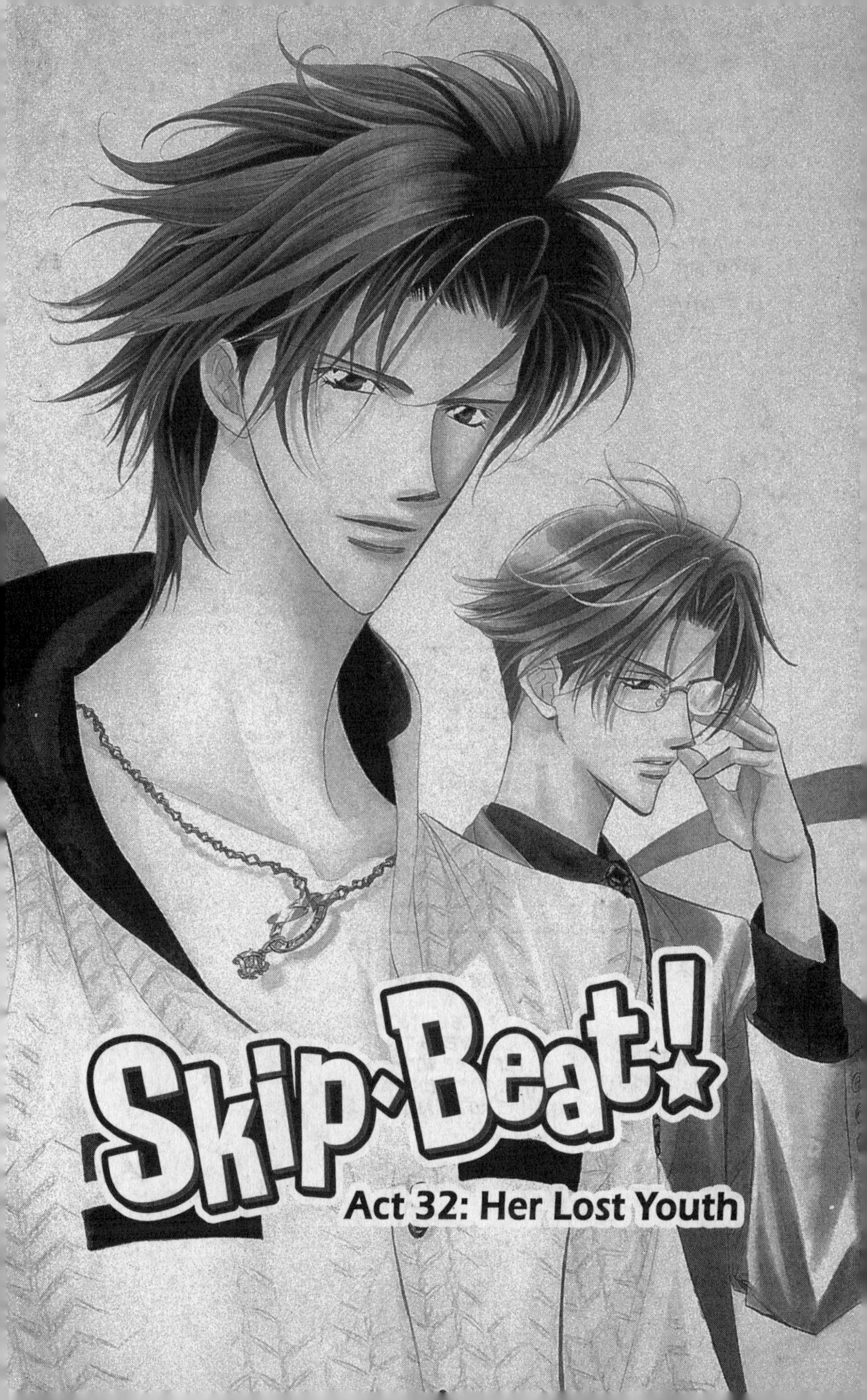
Skip·Beat!
Act 32: Her Lost Youth

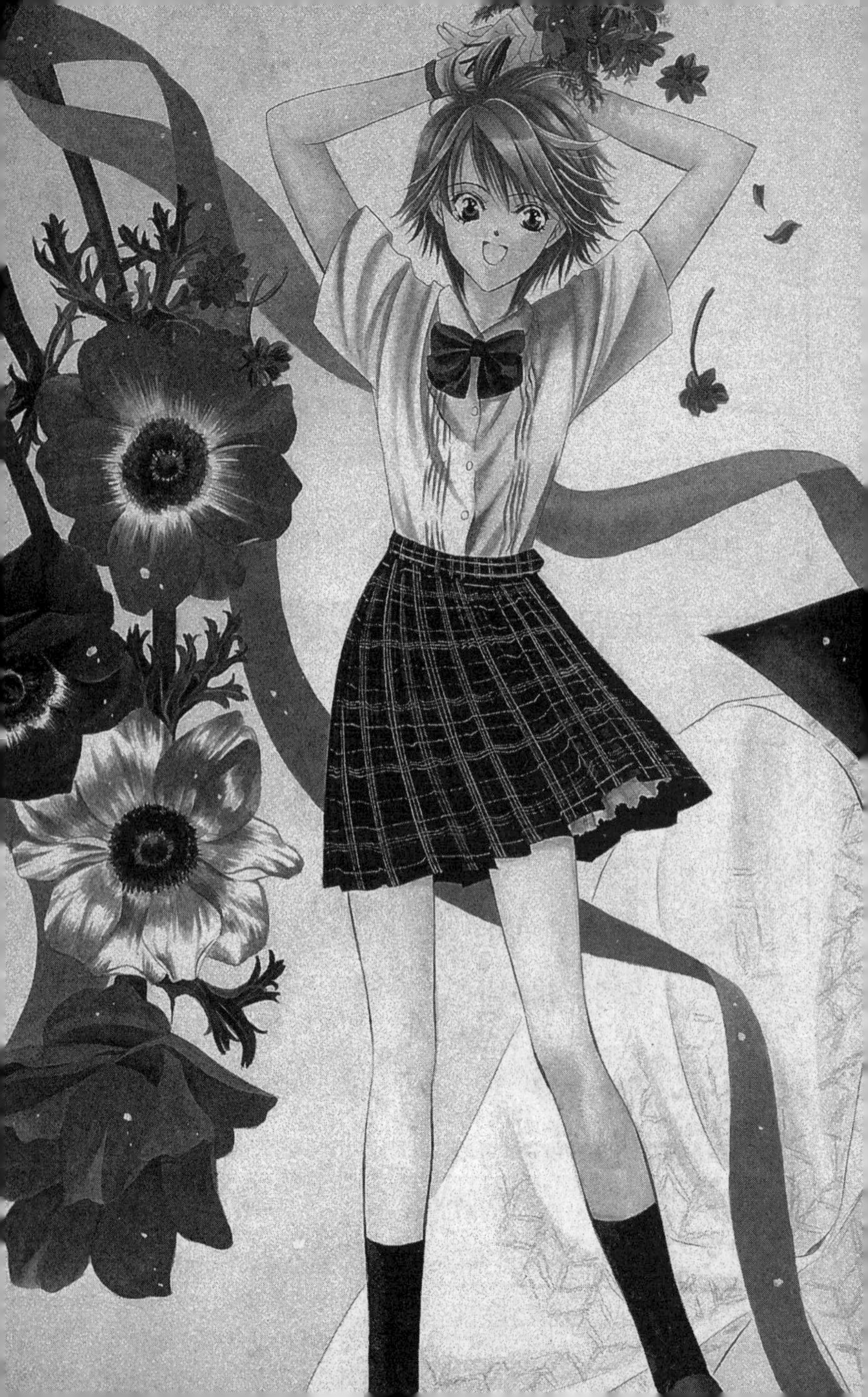

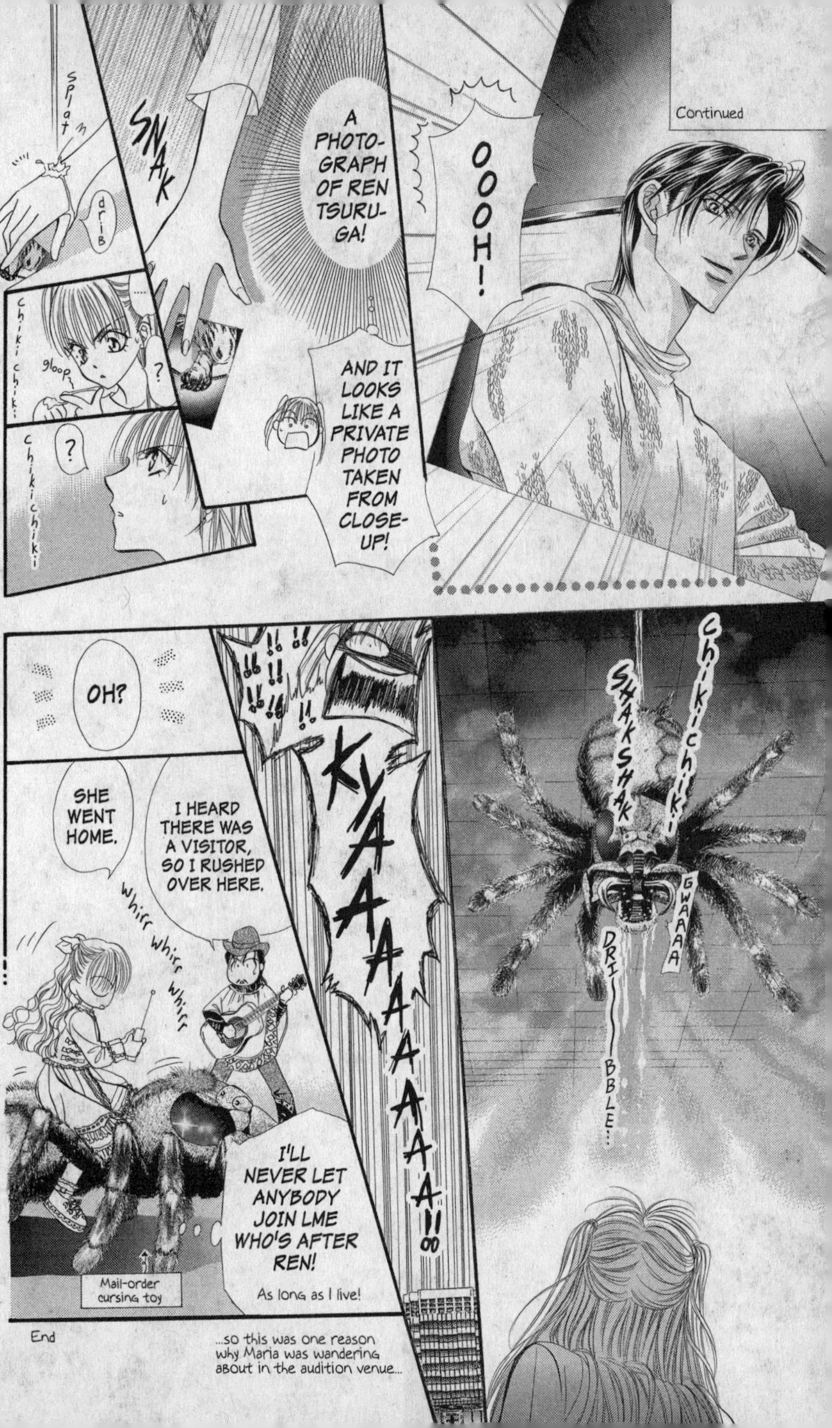
Continued
OOOOH!
A PHOTOGRAPH OF REN TSURUGA!
AND IT LOOKS LIKE A PRIVATE PHOTO TAKEN FROM CLOSE-UP!
SNAK
splat
drib
?
chikichiki
gloop
?
chikichiki
chikichiki
SHAKSHAK
GWAAAA
DRIBBLE...
!!
KYAAAAAAAAA!!
OH?
I HEARD THERE WAS A VISITOR, SO I RUSHED OVER HERE.
SHE WENT HOME.
whirr whirr whirr
I'LL NEVER LET ANYBODY JOIN LME WHO'S AFTER REN!
As long as I live!
Mail-order cursing toy
End
...so this was one reason why Maria was wandering about in the audition venue...

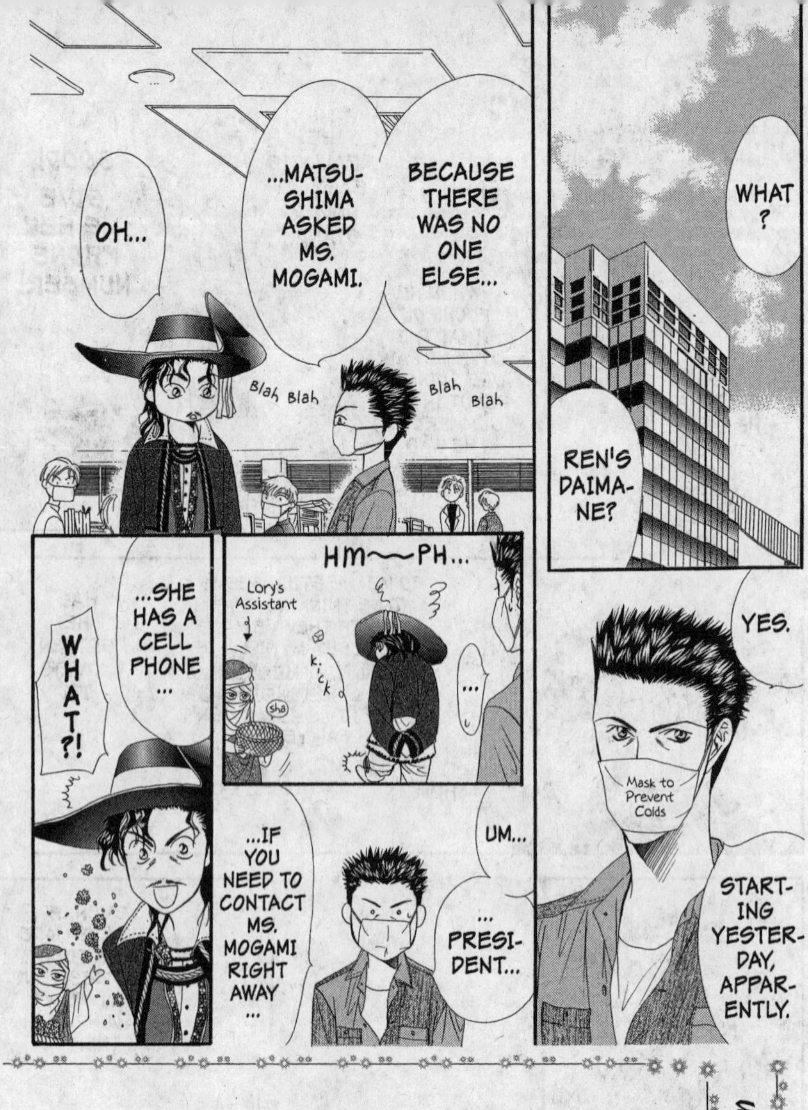
WHAT?
REN'S DAIMANE?
BECAUSE THERE WAS NO ONE ELSE...
...MATSUSHIMA ASKED MS. MOGAMI.
OH...
Blah Blah
Blah Blah
YES.
Mask to Prevent Colds
STARTING YESTERDAY, APPARENTLY.
HM~~PH...
...
Lory's Assistant
kick
sha
UM...
...PRESIDENT...
...IF YOU NEED TO CONTACT MS. MOGAMI RIGHT AWAY...
...SHE HAS A CELL PHONE...
WHAT?!

What LME Stands For

When *Skip•Beat!* began, there were three people who set up LME, and LME stood for the initials of those three. Well...but I had only decided on "L" for Lory at that time... The name LME came to me first, so even if I hadn't decided on the other two people's names, it was LME. LME came from...there are probably people who have guessed it...LOVE ME...? I'd decided on LME, and was going to think up of the three founders' names. But...I couldn't develop the story to make the other two appear...actually...even if they appeared...

—To Be Continued—

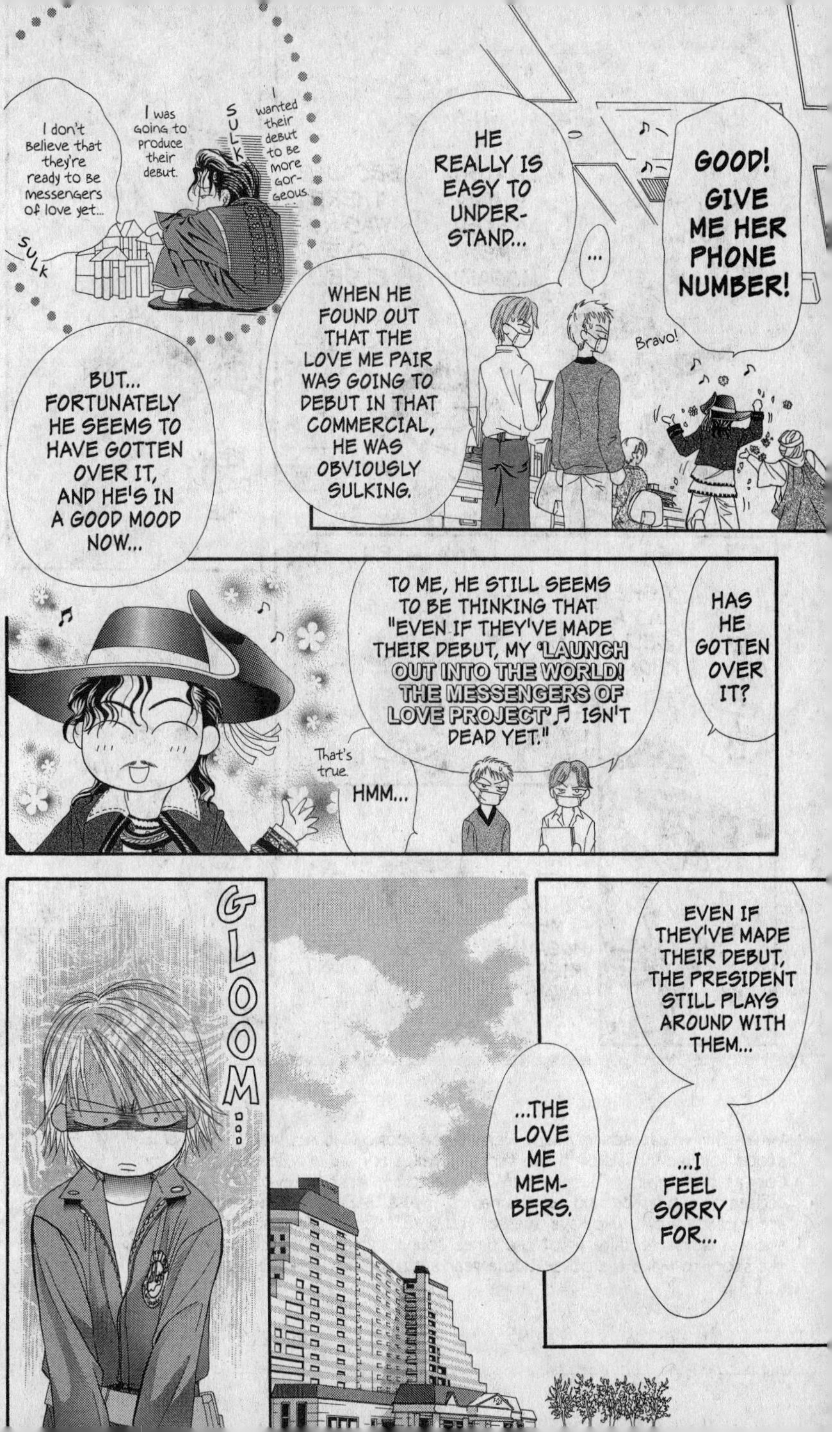
GOOD! GIVE ME HER PHONE NUMBER!
Bravo!
...
HE REALLY IS EASY TO UNDERSTAND...
WHEN HE FOUND OUT THAT THE LOVE ME PAIR WAS GOING TO DEBUT IN THAT COMMERCIAL, HE WAS OBVIOUSLY SULKING.
I wanted their debut to be more gorgeous.
SULK
I was going to produce their debut.
I don't believe that they're ready to be messengers of love yet...
SULK
BUT... FORTUNATELY HE SEEMS TO HAVE GOTTEN OVER IT, AND HE'S IN A GOOD MOOD NOW...
HAS HE GOTTEN OVER IT?
TO ME, HE STILL SEEMS TO BE THINKING THAT "EVEN IF THEY'VE MADE THEIR DEBUT, MY 'LAUNCH OUT INTO THE WORLD! THE MESSENGERS OF LOVE PROJECT'♬ ISN'T DEAD YET."
HMM...
That's true.
EVEN IF THEY'VE MADE THEIR DEBUT, THE PRESIDENT STILL PLAYS AROUND WITH THEM...
...I FEEL SORRY FOR...
...THE LOVE ME MEMBERS.
GLOOM...

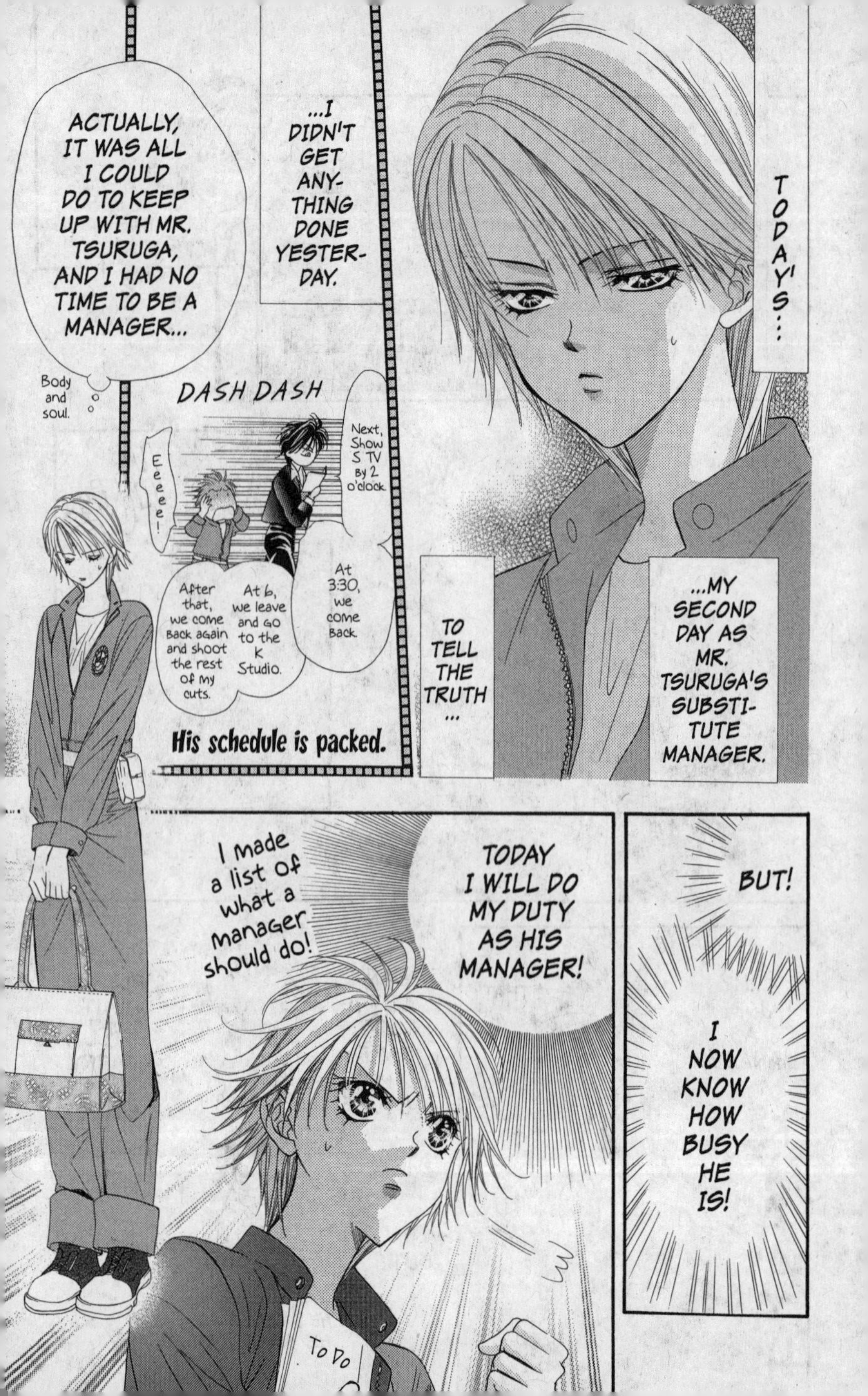
TODAY'S...
...MY SECOND DAY AS MR. TSURUGA'S SUBSTITUTE MANAGER.
TO TELL THE TRUTH...
...I DIDN'T GET ANYTHING DONE YESTERDAY.
Next, Show S TV By 2 o'clock.
At 3:30, we come Back
At 6, we leave and GO to the K Studio.
After that, we come Back again and shoot the rest of my cuts.
Eeeee!
DASH DASH
His schedule is packed.
ACTUALLY, IT WAS ALL I COULD DO TO KEEP UP WITH MR. TSURUGA, AND I HAD NO TIME TO BE A MANAGER...
Body and soul.
BUT!
I NOW KNOW HOW BUSY HE IS!
TODAY I WILL DO MY DUTY AS HIS MANAGER!
I made a list of what a manager should do!
To Do

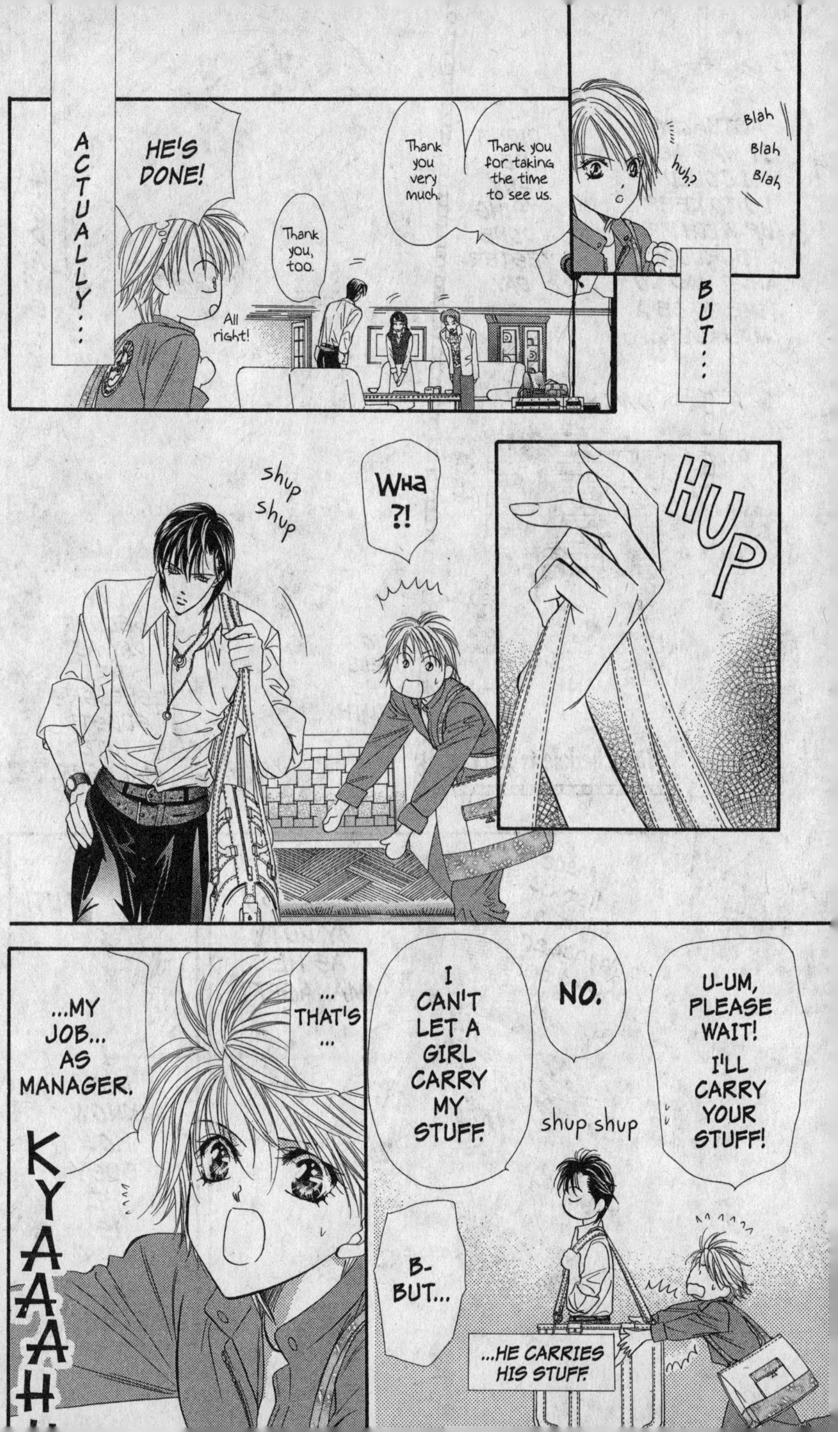
Blah
Blah
Blah
huh?
BUT...
Thank you for taking the time to see us.
Thank you very much.
Thank you, too.
HE'S DONE!
ACTUALLY...
All right!
HUP
WHA ?!
shup shup
U-UM, PLEASE WAIT! I'LL CARRY YOUR STUFF!
NO.
shup shup
I CAN'T LET A GIRL CARRY MY STUFF.
B-BUT...
...HE CARRIES HIS STUFF.
...THAT'S...
...MY JOB... AS MANAGER.
KYAAAH

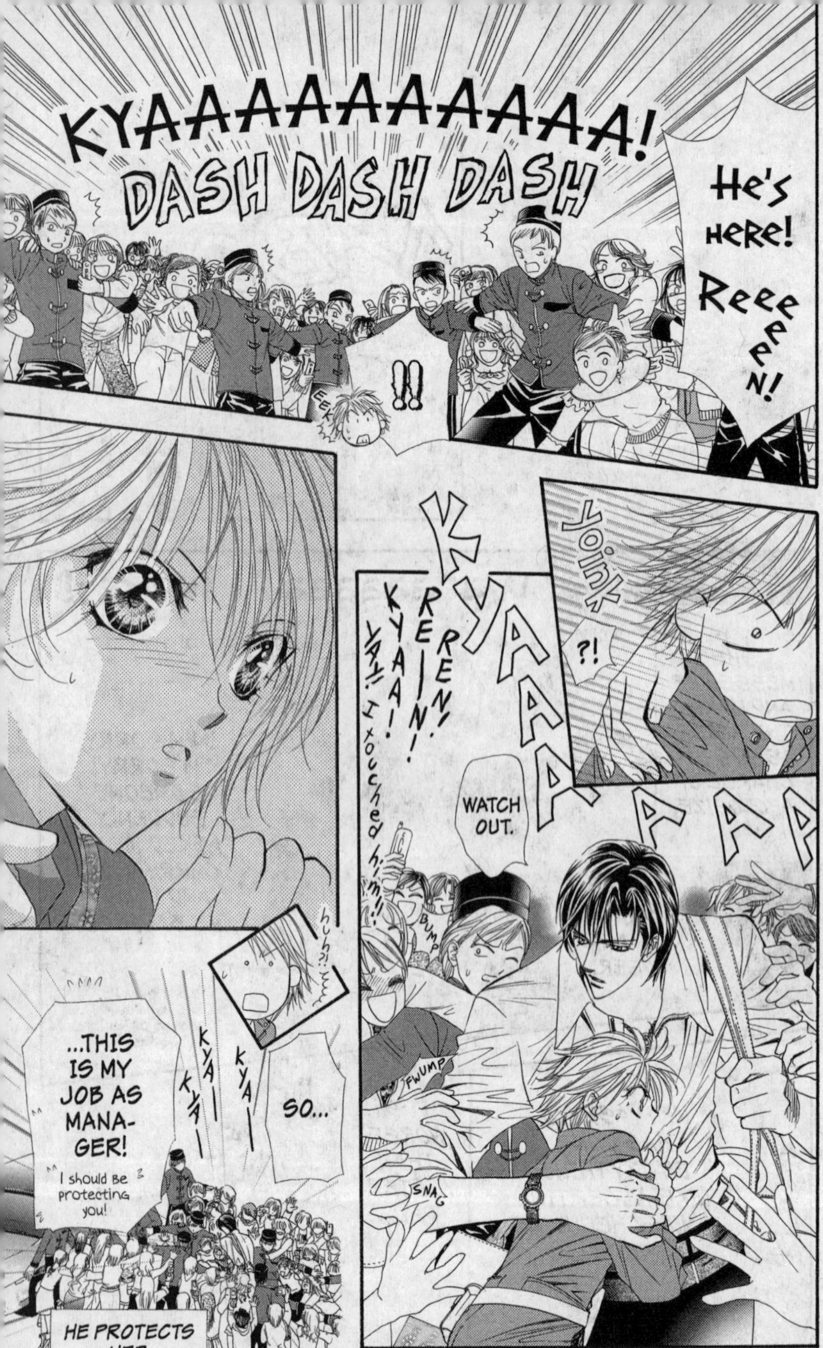
He's here! Reeeeen!
KYAAAAAAAAAAA!
DASH DASH DASH
!!
EEK
Yoink
?!
KYAAAAAA
REN! REN!
KYAA! YAY! I touched him!!
WATCH OUT.
BUMP
FWUMP
SNAG
huh?!
SO...
KYA KYA KYA
...THIS IS MY JOB AS MANAGER!
I should be protecting you!
HE PROTECTS HER.

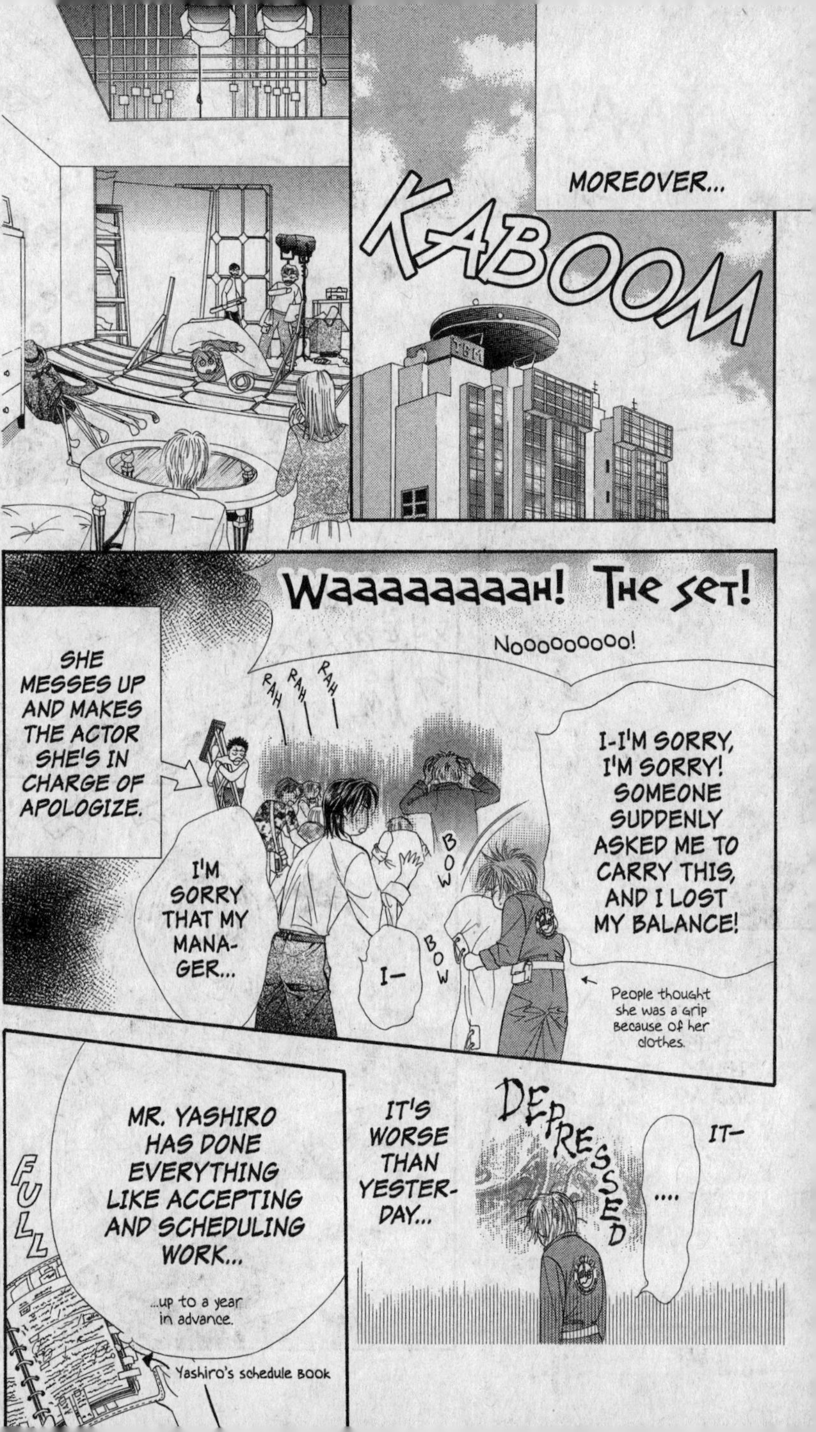
MOREOVER...
KABOOM
Waaaaaaaaah! The set!
Noooooooo!
I-I'M SORRY, I'M SORRY! SOMEONE SUDDENLY ASKED ME TO CARRY THIS, AND I LOST MY BALANCE!
People thought she was a grip because of her clothes.
BOW
BOW
I—
I'M SORRY THAT MY MANA-GER...
RAH
RAH
RAH
SHE MESSES UP AND MAKES THE ACTOR SHE'S IN CHARGE OF APOLOGIZE.
IT—
....
DEPRESSED
IT'S WORSE THAN YESTER-DAY...
MR. YASHIRO HAS DONE EVERYTHING LIKE ACCEPTING AND SCHEDULING WORK...
...up to a year in advance.
FULL
Yashiro's schedule book

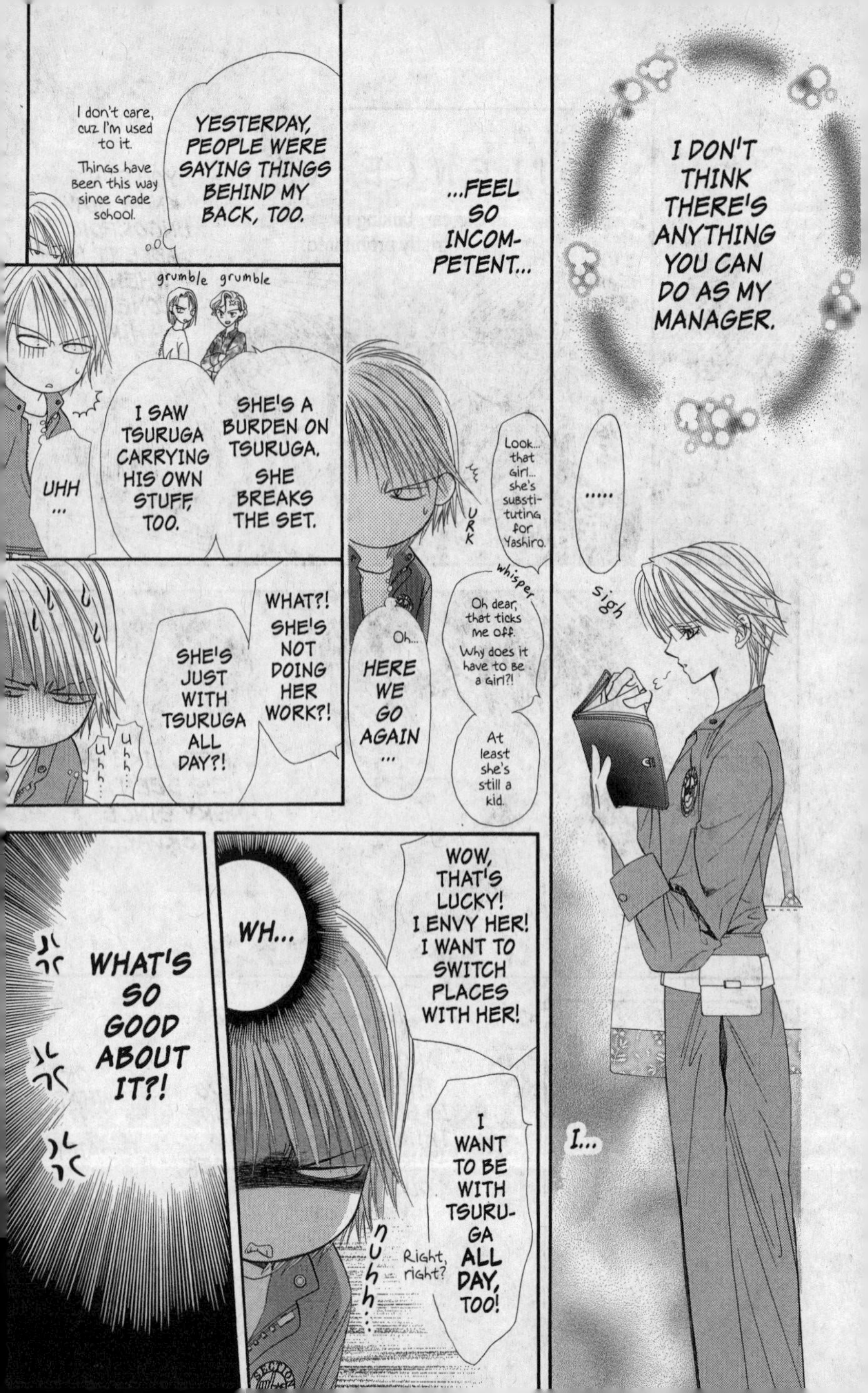
I DON'T THINK THERE'S ANYTHING YOU CAN DO AS MY MANAGER.
.....
sigh
I...
...FEEL SO INCOMPETENT...
Look... that girl... she's substituting for Yashiro.
URK
whisper
Oh dear, that ticks me off. Why does it have to be a girl?!
At least she's still a kid.
Oh... HERE WE GO AGAIN...
YESTERDAY, PEOPLE WERE SAYING THINGS BEHIND MY BACK, TOO.
I don't care, cuz I'm used to it.
Things have been this way since grade school.
grumble grumble
SHE'S A BURDEN ON TSURUGA. SHE BREAKS THE SET.
I SAW TSURUGA CARRYING HIS OWN STUFF, TOO.
UHH...
WHAT?! SHE'S NOT DOING HER WORK?!
SHE'S JUST WITH TSURUGA ALL DAY?!
Uhh... Uhh...
WOW, THAT'S LUCKY! I ENVY HER! I WANT TO SWITCH PLACES WITH HER!
I WANT TO BE WITH TSURUGA ALL DAY, TOO!
Right, right?
WH...
nuhh...
WHAT'S SO GOOD ABOUT IT?!

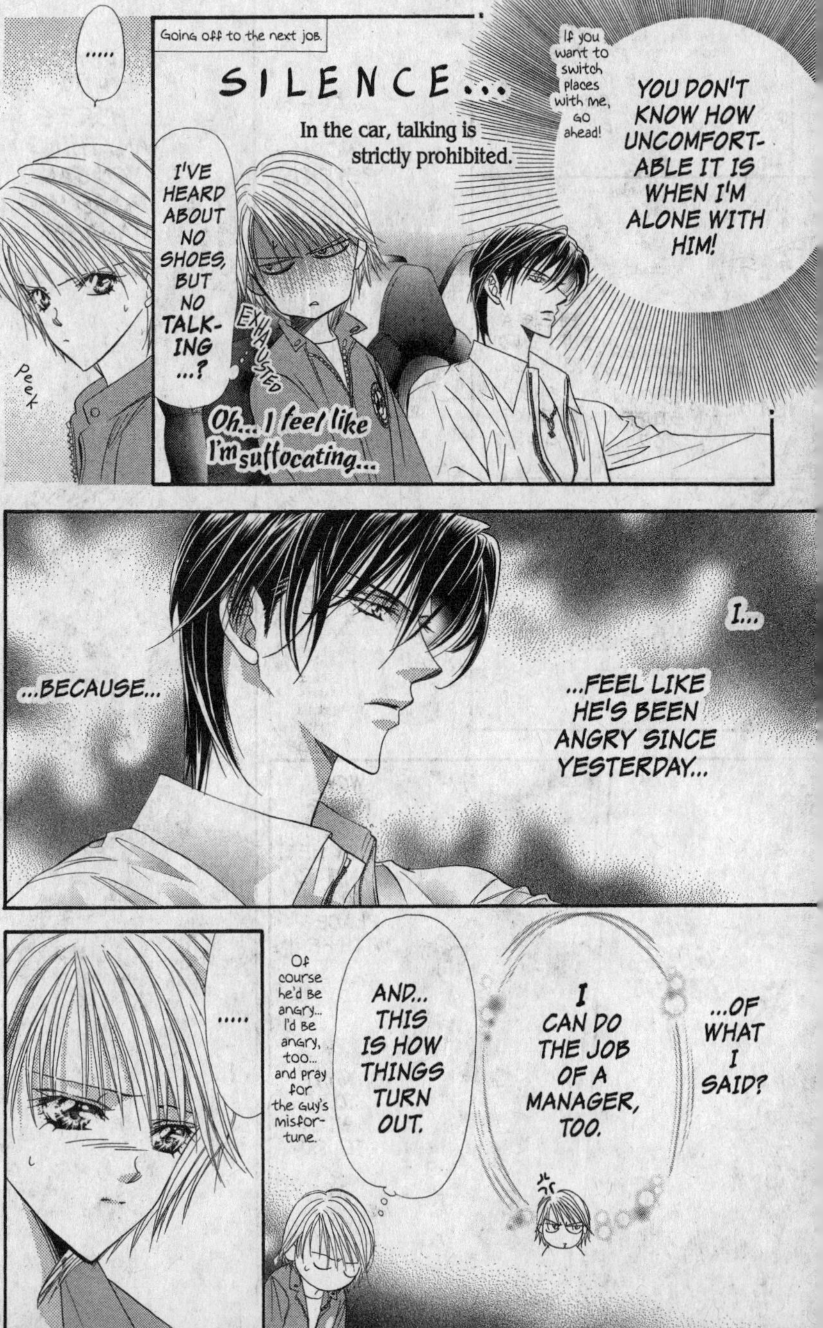
YOU DON'T KNOW HOW UNCOMFORT-ABLE IT IS WHEN I'M ALONE WITH HIM!
If you want to switch places with me, GO ahead!
Going off to the next job.
SILENCE...
In the car, talking is strictly prohibited.
I'VE HEARD ABOUT NO SHOES, BUT NO TALK-ING ...?
EXHAUSTED
Oh... I feel like I'm suffocating...
.....
Peek
I...
...FEEL LIKE HE'S BEEN ANGRY SINCE YESTERDAY...
...BECAUSE...
...OF WHAT I SAID?
I CAN DO THE JOB OF A MANAGER, TOO.
AND... THIS IS HOW THINGS TURN OUT.
Of course he'd be angry... I'd be angry, too... and pray for the guy's misfor-tune.
.....

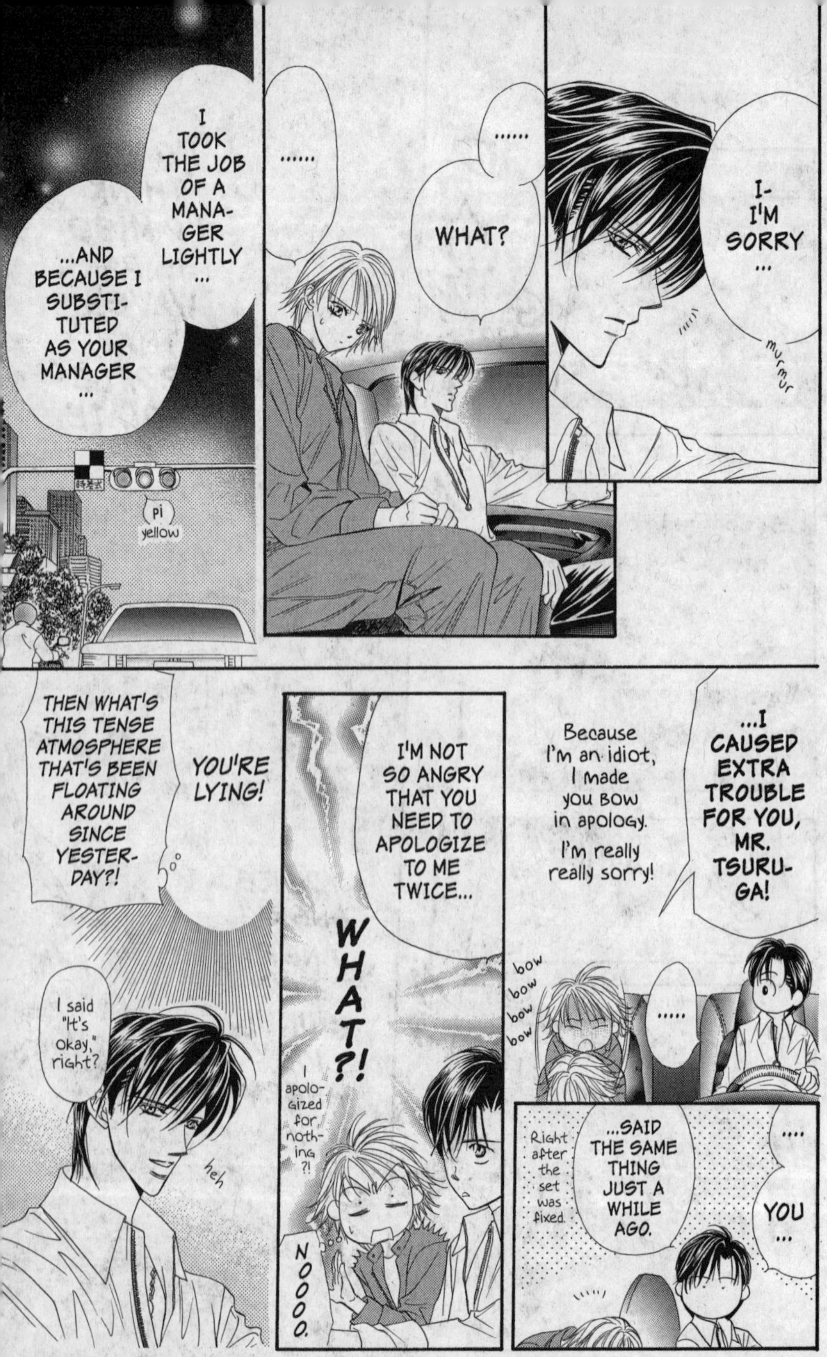
I- I'M SORRY...
murmur
......
WHAT?
......
I TOOK THE JOB OF A MANAGER LIGHTLY...
...AND BECAUSE I SUBSTITUTED AS YOUR MANAGER...
pi
yellow
...I CAUSED EXTRA TROUBLE FOR YOU, MR. TSURUGA!
Because I'm an idiot, I made you bow in apology. I'm really really sorry!
bow bow bow bow
.....
....YOU...
...SAID THE SAME THING JUST A WHILE AGO.
Right after the set was fixed.
I'M NOT SO ANGRY THAT YOU NEED TO APOLOGIZE TO ME TWICE...
WHAT?!
I apologized for nothing?!
NOOOO.
THEN WHAT'S THIS TENSE ATMOSPHERE THAT'S BEEN FLOATING AROUND SINCE YESTERDAY?!
YOU'RE LYING!
I said "It's okay," right?
heh

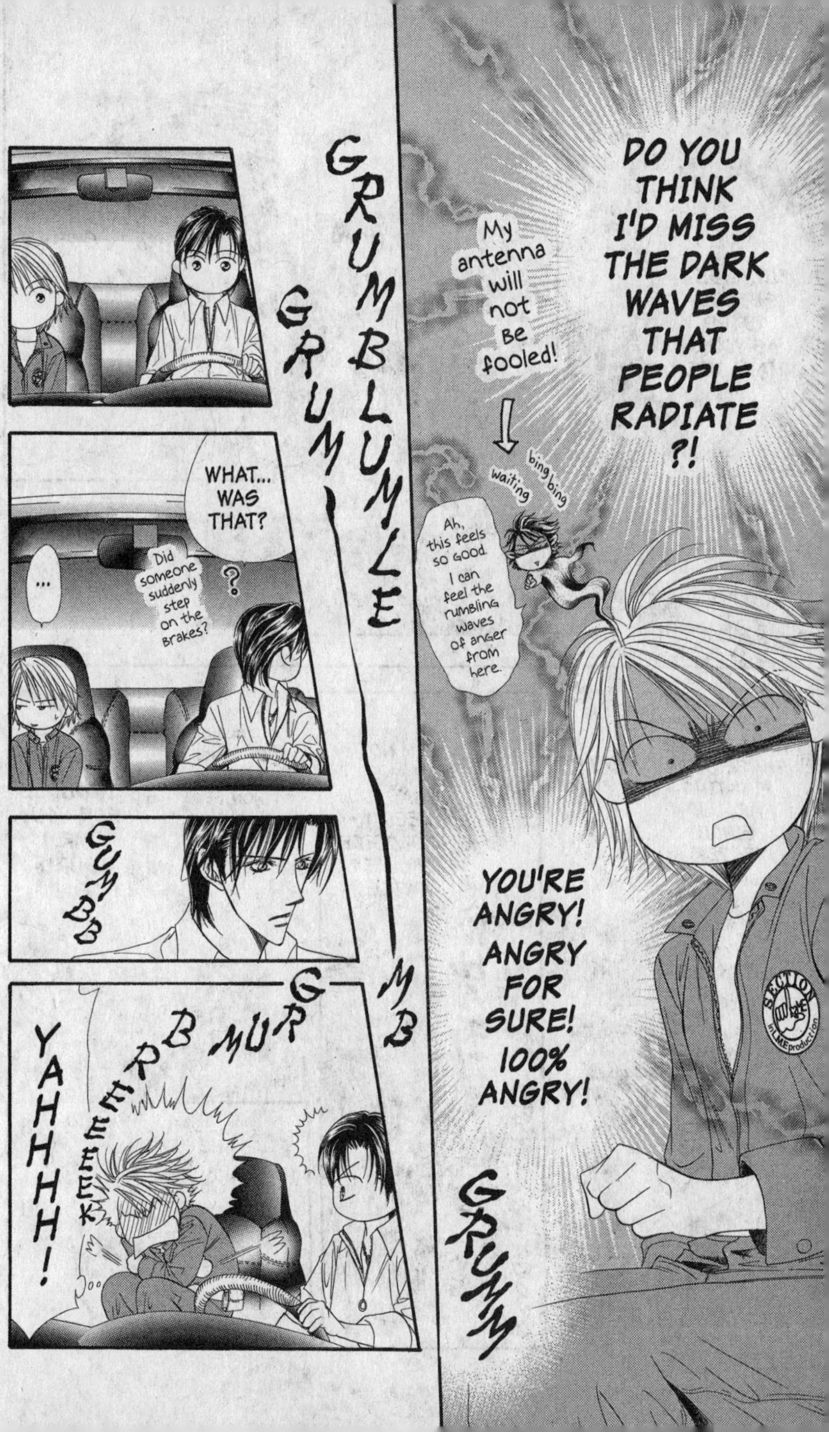
DO YOU THINK I'D MISS THE DARK WAVES THAT PEOPLE RADIATE?!
My antenna will not be fooled!
bing bing
waiting
Ah, this feels so good. I can feel the rumbling waves of anger from here.
YOU'RE ANGRY! ANGRY FOR SURE! 100% ANGRY!
GRUMM
GRUMBLUMLE
GRUM
WHAT... WAS THAT?
Did someone suddenly step on the brakes?
?
...
GUMBB
MB
GRUMB MURB
YAHHHHH!
REEEEEK

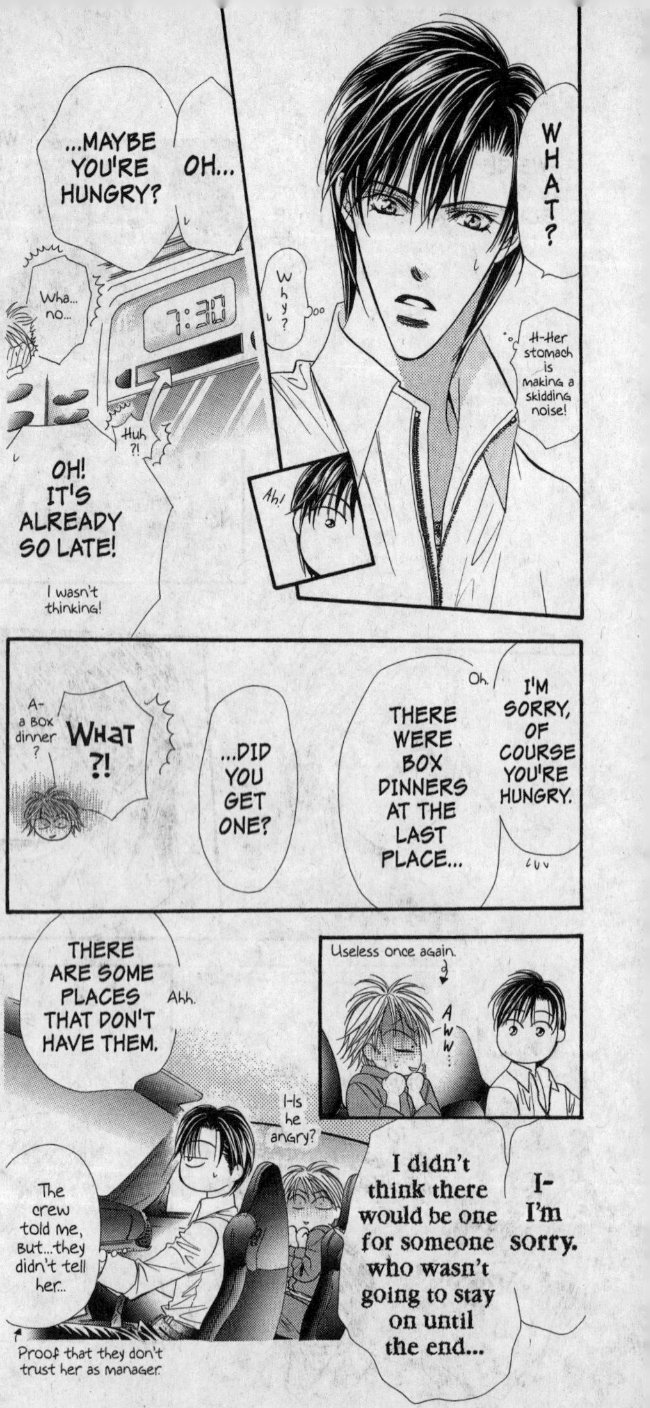
WHAT?
H-Her stomach is making a skidding noise!
Why?
Ah!
OH...
...MAYBE YOU'RE HUNGRY?
Wha... no...
7:30
Huh ?!
OH! IT'S ALREADY SO LATE!
I wasn't thinking!
I'M SORRY, OF COURSE YOU'RE HUNGRY.
Oh.
THERE WERE BOX DINNERS AT THE LAST PLACE...
...DID YOU GET ONE?
WHAT ?!
A- a box dinner ?
Useless once again.
AWW...
THERE ARE SOME PLACES THAT DON'T HAVE THEM.
Ahh.
I- I'm sorry.
I didn't think there would be one for someone who wasn't going to stay on until the end...
I-Is he angry?
The crew told me, but...they didn't tell her...
Proof that they don't trust her as manager.

I Was Surprised, Too

When I think about it, the first time the script "The Forest of Spirals" appeared was in the chapter when Ren was having problems with "tentekomai"...To tell the truth, I created that script on the spot just for the line using "tentekomai." So I had only a vague image of the contents and Ren's role, and I thought that the script would never appear...

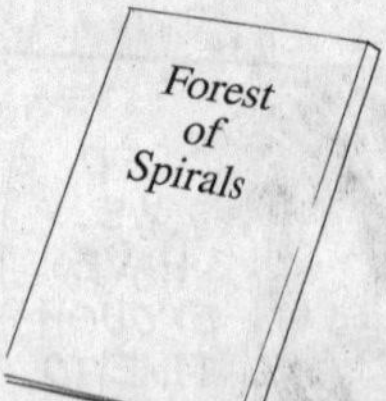
Forest of Spirals

...But it appeared... Again...
I don't watch many dramas, but I thought about whether it was possible to appear in another drama at the same time (there were actors who were...) and there were other things I was pondering about... I wondered how true it was to the way dramas are shot nowadays...But I used "The Forest of..." anyway.

—To Be Continued—

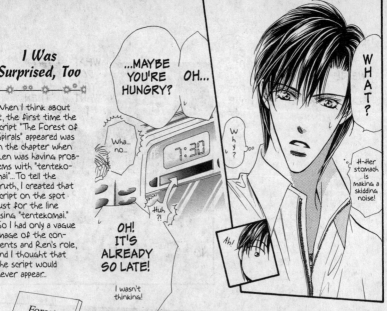

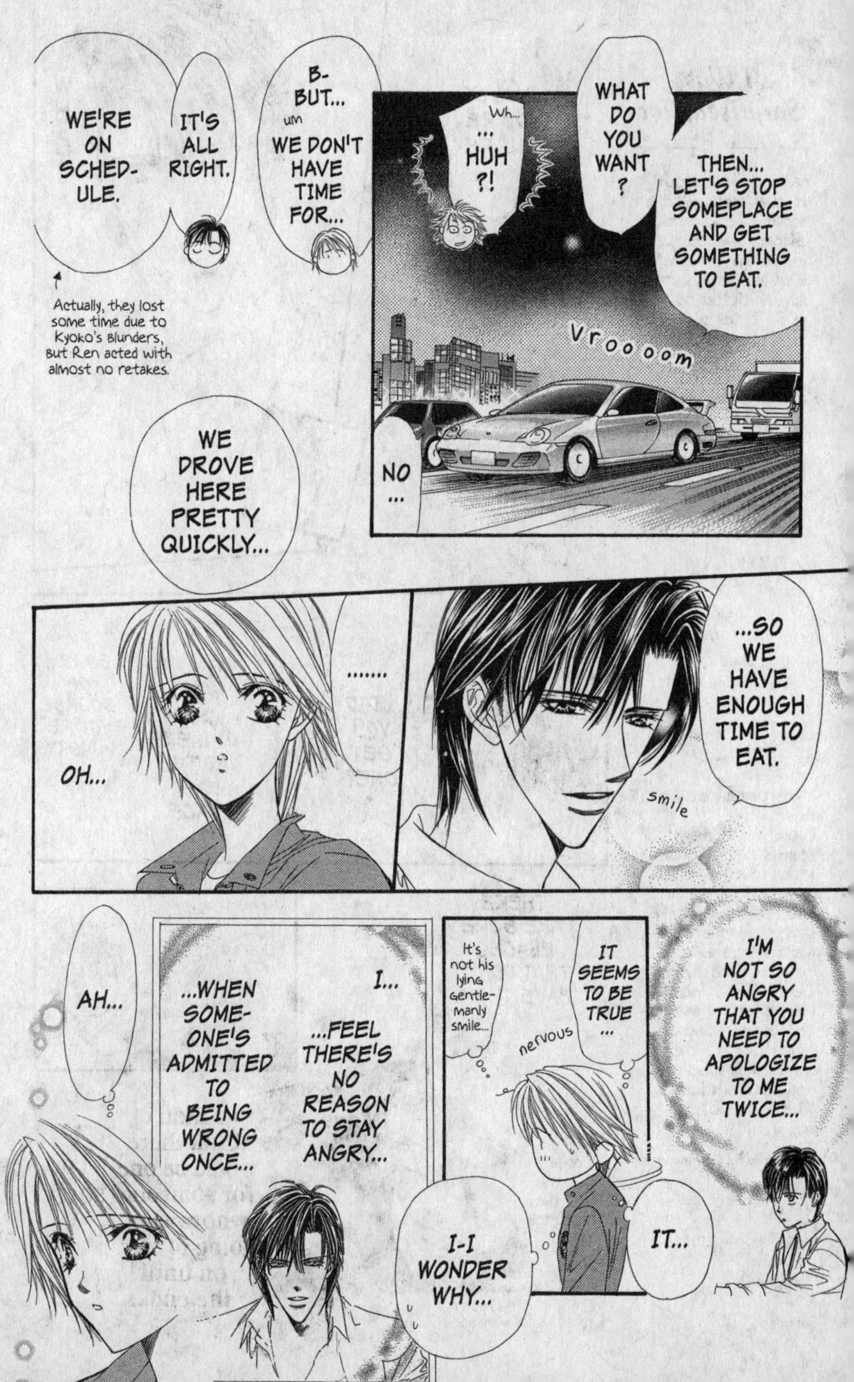
THEN... LET'S STOP SOMEPLACE AND GET SOMETHING TO EAT.
WHAT DO YOU WANT?
Wh...
...HUH?!
Vroooom
NO...
B-BUT...
um
WE DON'T HAVE TIME FOR...
IT'S ALL RIGHT.
WE'RE ON SCHEDULE.
Actually, they lost some time due to Kyoko's blunders, but Ren acted with almost no retakes.
WE DROVE HERE PRETTY QUICKLY...
...SO WE HAVE ENOUGH TIME TO EAT.
smile
....
OH...
I'M NOT SO ANGRY THAT YOU NEED TO APOLOGIZE TO ME TWICE...
IT SEEMS TO BE TRUE...
It's not his lying gentlemanly smile...
nervous
IT...
I-I WONDER WHY...
I...
...FEEL THERE'S NO REASON TO STAY ANGRY...
...WHEN SOMEONE'S ADMITTED TO BEING WRONG ONCE...
AH...

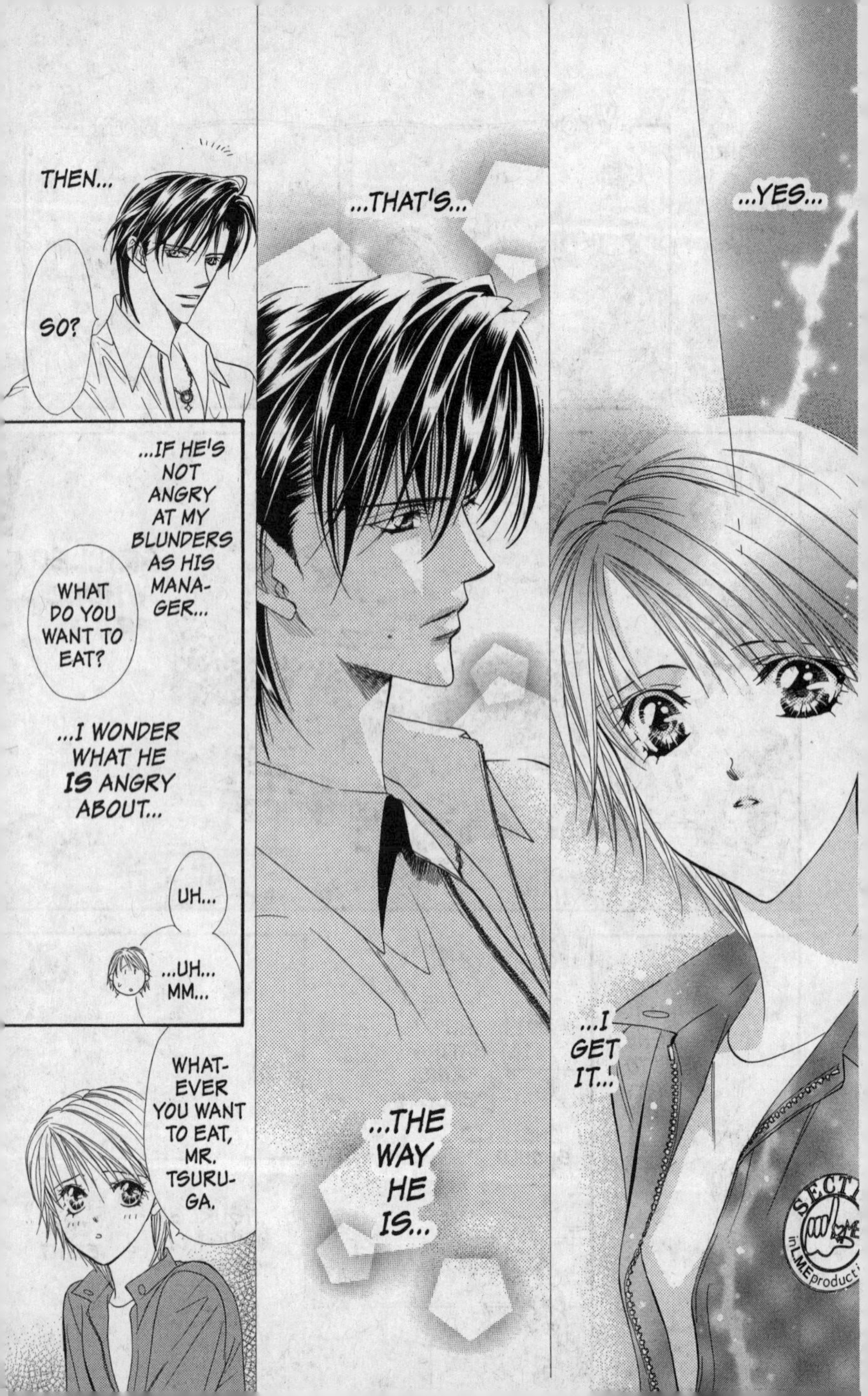
...YES...
...I GET IT...
...THAT'S...
...THE WAY HE IS...
THEN...
SO?
...IF HE'S NOT ANGRY AT MY BLUNDERS AS HIS MANAGER...
WHAT DO YOU WANT TO EAT?
...I WONDER WHAT HE **IS** ANGRY ABOUT...
UH...
...UH... MM...
WHATEVER YOU WANT TO EAT, MR. TSURUGA.

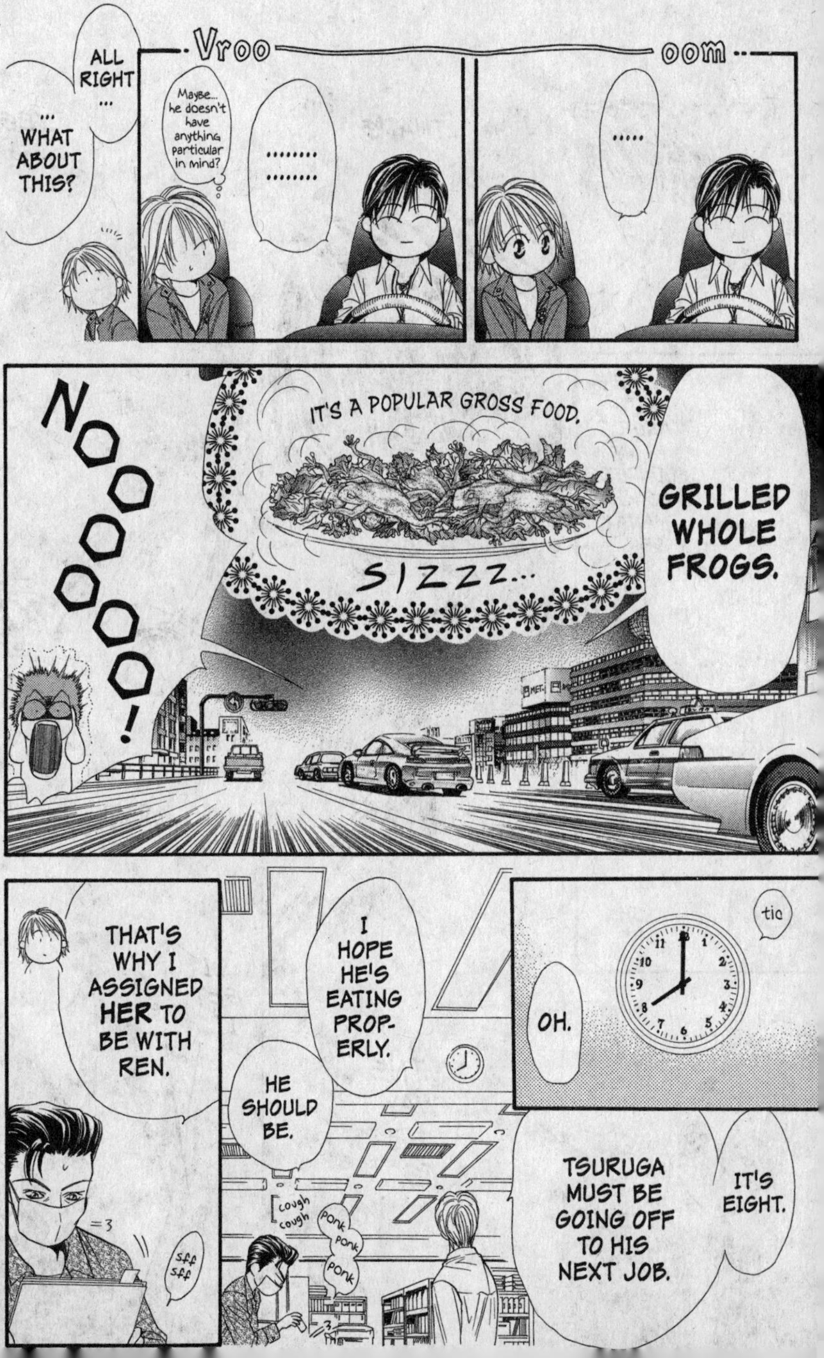
Vroo——oom
.....
....
....
Maybe... he doesn't have anything particular in mind?
ALL RIGHT ...
... WHAT ABOUT THIS?
GRILLED WHOLE FROGS.
IT'S A POPULAR GROSS FOOD.
SIZZZ...
NOOOOOOO!
tic
OH.
IT'S EIGHT.
TSURUGA MUST BE GOING OFF TO HIS NEXT JOB.
I HOPE HE'S EATING PROP-ERLY.
HE SHOULD BE.
cough cough
PONK PONK PONK
sff sff
THAT'S WHY I ASSIGNED HER TO BE WITH REN.

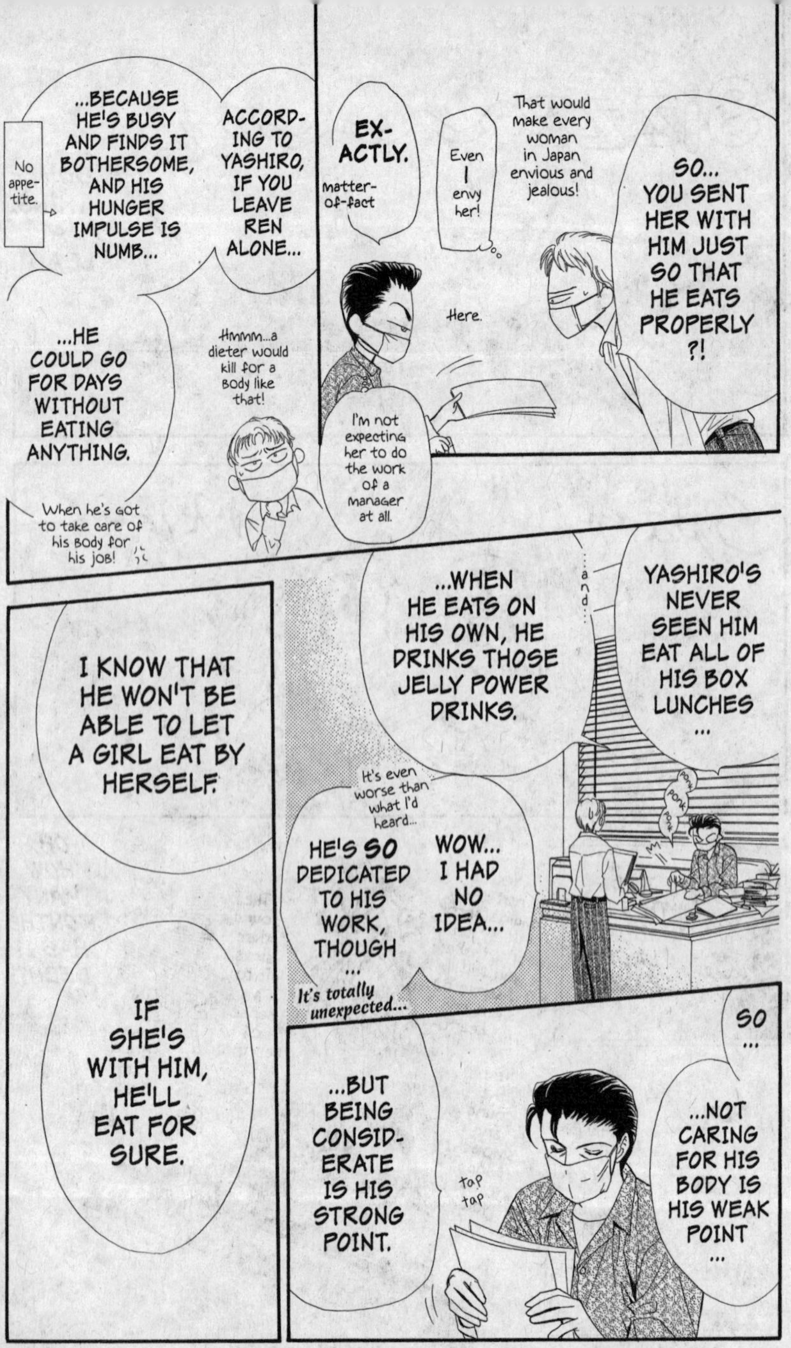
SO... YOU SENT HER WITH HIM JUST SO THAT HE EATS PROPERLY?!
That would make every woman in Japan envious and jealous!
Even I envy her!
EX-ACTLY.
matter-of-fact
Here.
I'm not expecting her to do the work of a manager at all.
ACCORD-ING TO YASHIRO, IF YOU LEAVE REN ALONE...
...BECAUSE HE'S BUSY AND FINDS IT BOTHERSOME, AND HIS HUNGER IMPULSE IS NUMB...
No appe-tite.
...HE COULD GO FOR DAYS WITHOUT EATING ANYTHING.
Hmmm...a dieter would kill for a body like that!
When he's got to take care of his body for his job!
YASHIRO'S NEVER SEEN HIM EAT ALL OF HIS BOX LUNCHES...
...and...
...WHEN HE EATS ON HIS OWN, HE DRINKS THOSE JELLY POWER DRINKS.
PONK PONK PONK
WOW... I HAD NO IDEA...
It's even worse than what I'd heard...
HE'S SO DEDICATED TO HIS WORK, THOUGH...
It's totally unexpected...
SO...
...NOT CARING FOR HIS BODY IS HIS WEAK POINT...
tap tap
...BUT BEING CONSID-ERATE IS HIS STRONG POINT.
I KNOW THAT HE WON'T BE ABLE TO LET A GIRL EAT BY HERSELF.
IF SHE'S WITH HIM, HE'LL EAT FOR SURE.

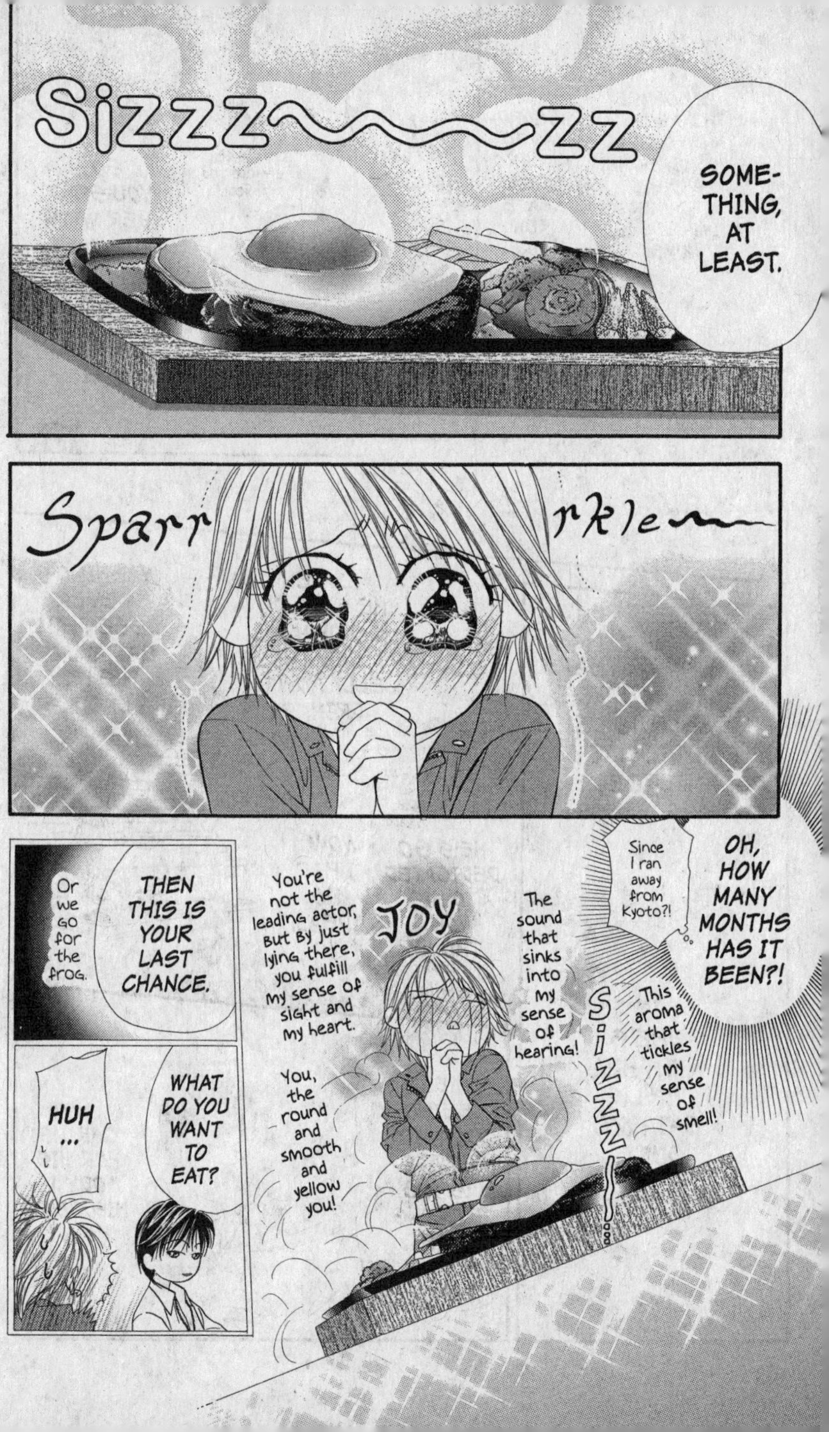
SOMETHING, AT LEAST.
Sizzz~~~zz
Sparrrkle~~
OH, HOW MANY MONTHS HAS IT BEEN?!
Since I ran away from Kyoto?!
This aroma that tickles my sense of smell!
The sound that sinks into my sense of hearing!
SIZZZ...
JOY
You're not the leading actor, but by just lying there, you fulfill my sense of sight and my heart.
You, the round and smooth and yellow you!
THEN THIS IS YOUR LAST CHANCE.
Or we go for the frog.
WHAT DO YOU WANT TO EAT?
HUH...

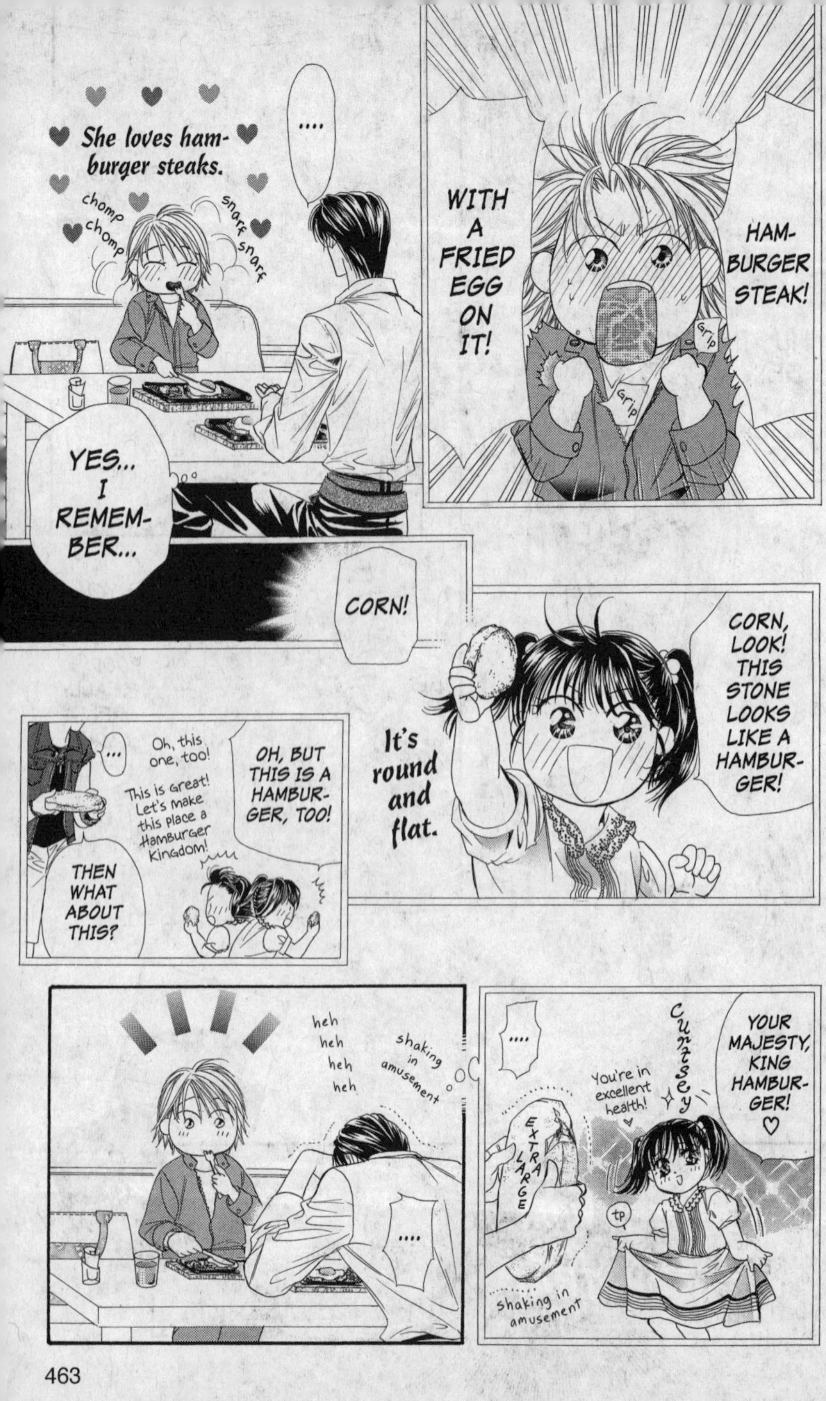
HAMBURGER STEAK!
WITH A FRIED EGG ON IT!
Grip
Grip
....
She loves hamburger steaks.
snarf snarf
chomp chomp
YES... I REMEMBER...
CORN!
CORN, LOOK! THIS STONE LOOKS LIKE A HAMBURGER!
It's round and flat.
OH, BUT THIS IS A HAMBURGER, TOO!
Oh, this one, too!
This is Great! Let's make this place a Hamburger Kingdom!
...
THEN WHAT ABOUT THIS?
YOUR MAJESTY, KING HAMBURGER! ♡
Curtsey
You're in excellent health! ♥
....
EXTRA LARGE
tp
shaking in amusement
heh heh heh heh
shaking in amusement
....
....

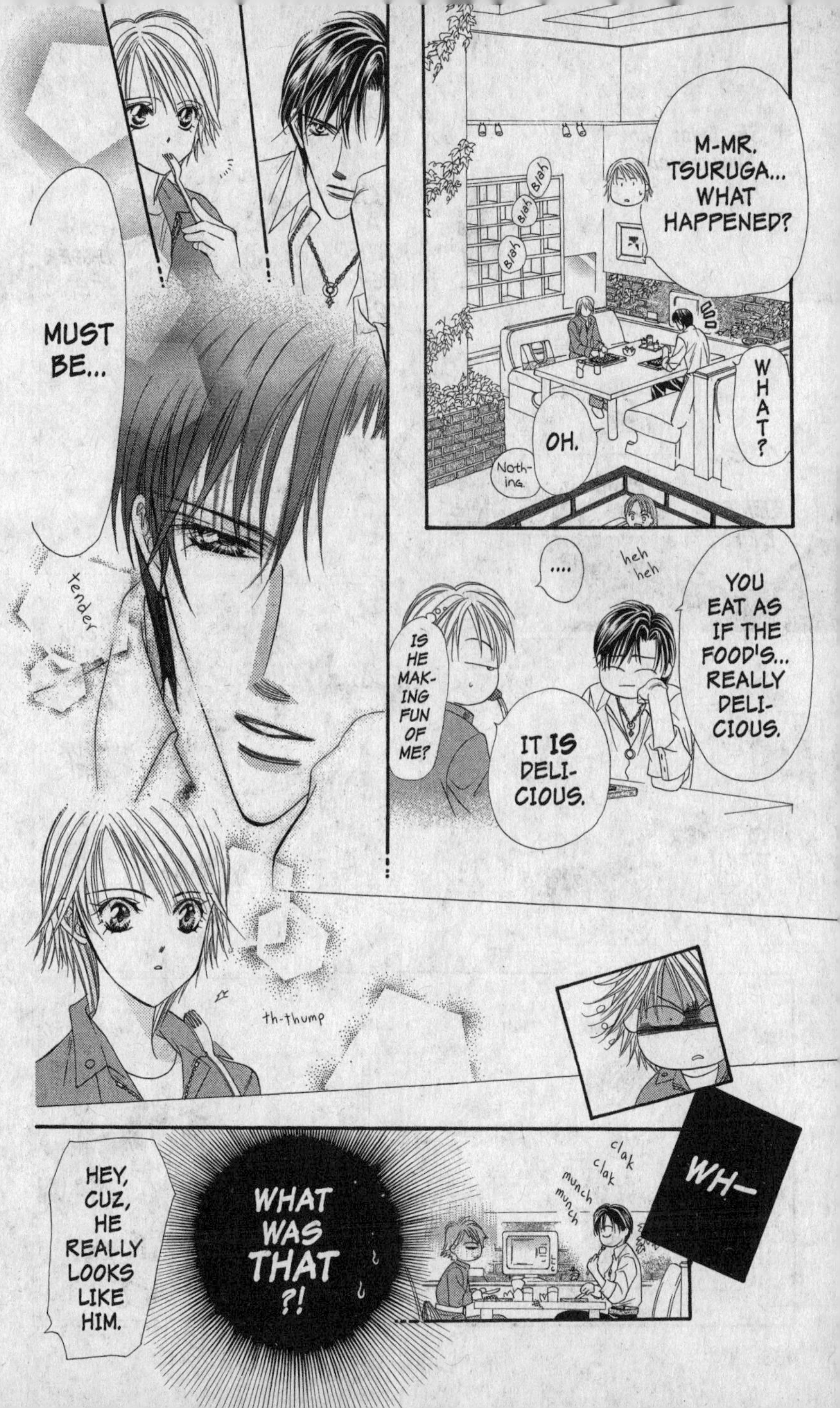
M-MR. TSURUGA... WHAT HAPPENED?
Blah Blah Blah Blah
WHAT?
OH.
Noth-ing.
YOU EAT AS IF THE FOOD'S... REALLY DELICIOUS.
heh heh
....
IS HE MAKING FUN OF ME?
IT IS DELICIOUS.
MUST BE...
tender
th-thump
WH-
clak clak
munch munch
WHAT WAS THAT?!
HEY, CUZ, HE REALLY LOOKS LIKE HIM.

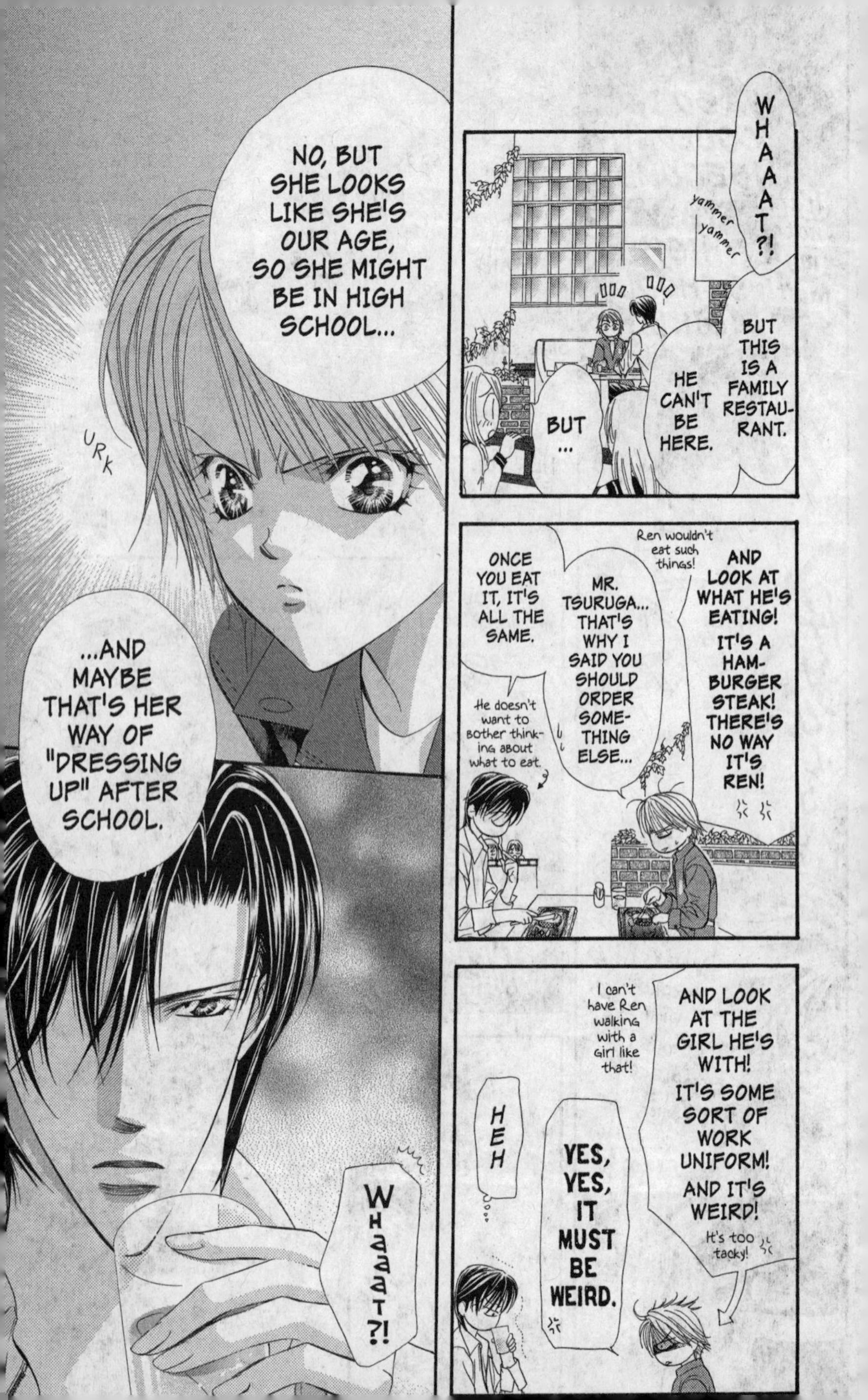
WHAAAT?!
yammer yammer
BUT THIS IS A FAMILY RESTAURANT.
HE CAN'T BE HERE.
BUT...
AND LOOK AT WHAT HE'S EATING! IT'S A HAMBURGER STEAK! THERE'S NO WAY IT'S REN!
Ren wouldn't eat such things!
MR. TSURUGA... THAT'S WHY I SAID YOU SHOULD ORDER SOMETHING ELSE...
ONCE YOU EAT IT, IT'S ALL THE SAME.
He doesn't want to bother thinking about what to eat.
AND LOOK AT THE GIRL HE'S WITH! IT'S SOME SORT OF WORK UNIFORM! AND IT'S WEIRD!
It's too tacky!
I can't have Ren walking with a girl like that!
YES, YES, IT MUST BE WEIRD.
HEH
NO, BUT SHE LOOKS LIKE SHE'S OUR AGE, SO SHE MIGHT BE IN HIGH SCHOOL...
URK
...AND MAYBE THAT'S HER WAY OF "DRESSING UP" AFTER SCHOOL.
WHaaaT?!

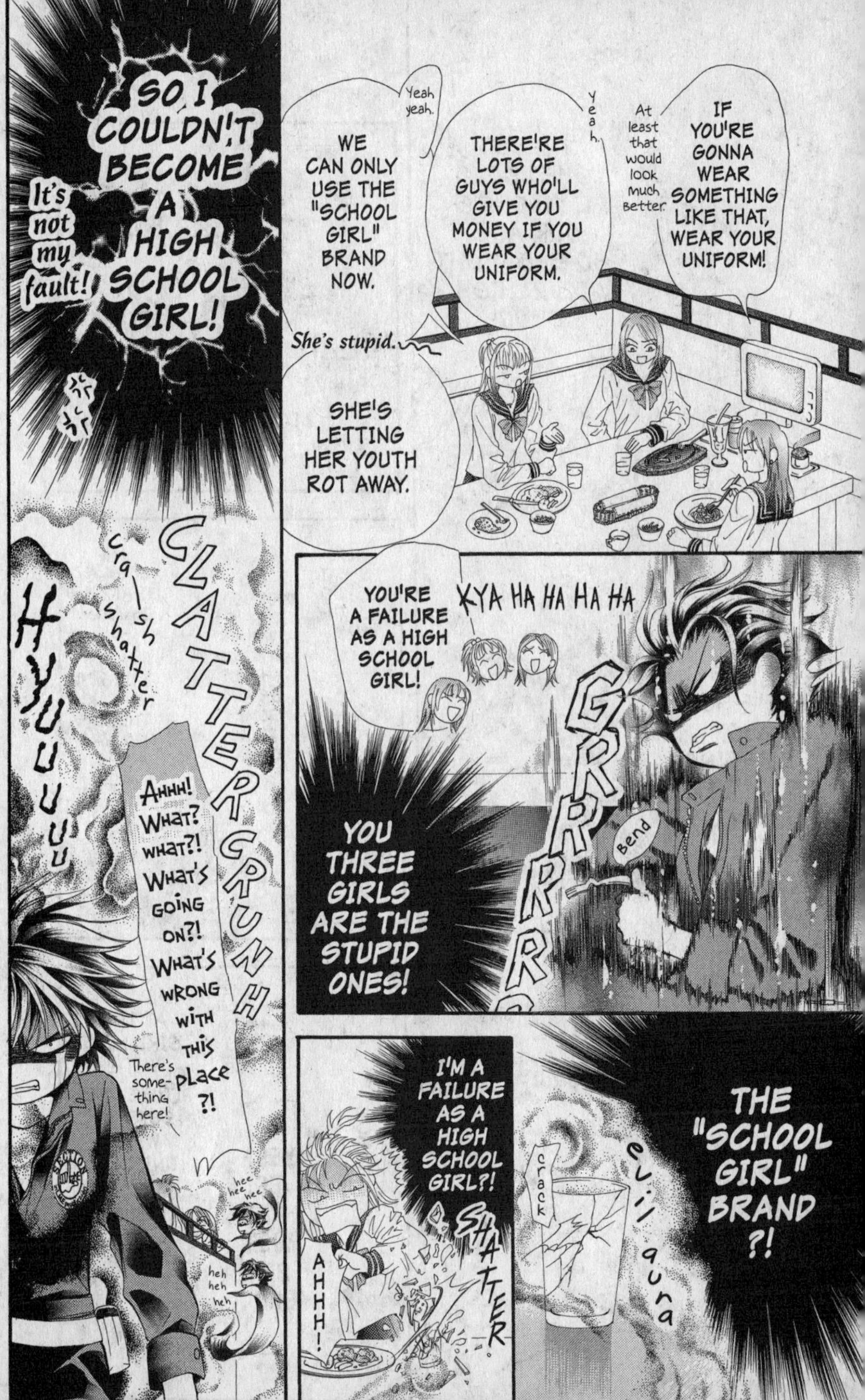
IF YOU'RE GONNA WEAR SOMETHING LIKE THAT, WEAR YOUR UNIFORM!
At least that would look much better.
Yeah.
THERE'RE LOTS OF GUYS WHO'LL GIVE YOU MONEY IF YOU WEAR YOUR UNIFORM.
Yeah yeah.
WE CAN ONLY USE THE "SCHOOL GIRL" BRAND NOW.
She's stupid.
SHE'S LETTING HER YOUTH ROT AWAY.
GRRRR
Bend
KYA HA HA HA HA
YOU'RE A FAILURE AS A HIGH SCHOOL GIRL!
YOU THREE GIRLS ARE THE STUPID ONES!
THE "SCHOOL GIRL" BRAND?!
evil aura
crack
I'M A FAILURE AS A HIGH SCHOOL GIRL?!
SHATTER
AHHH!
SO I COULDN'T BECOME A HIGH SCHOOL GIRL!
It's not my fault!
CLATTER CRUNCH
crash shatter
HYUUUUUU
Ahhh! What? what?! What's going on?! What's wrong with this place?!
There's something here!
hee hee hee
heh heh heh

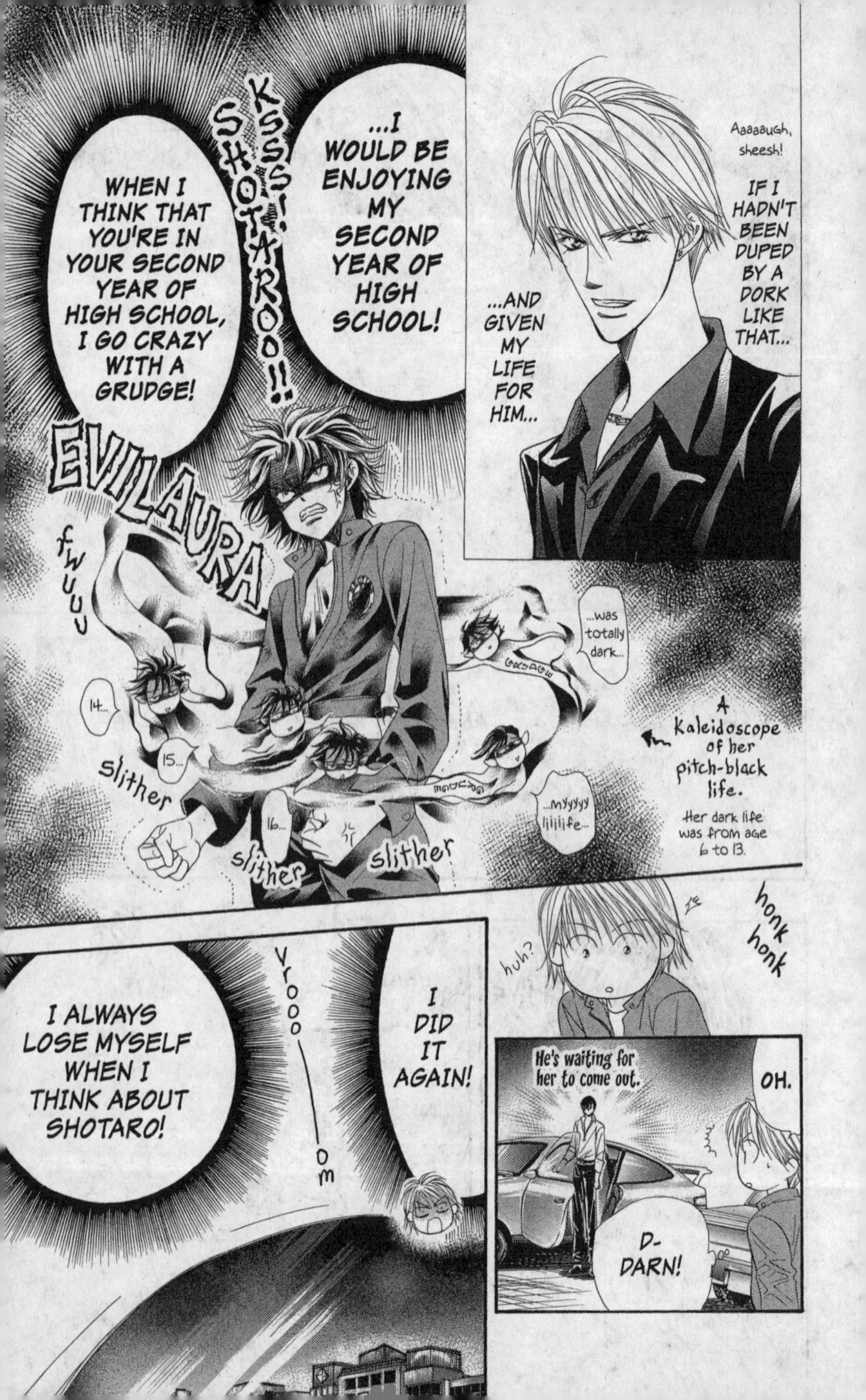
Aaaaaugh, sheesh!
IF I HADN'T BEEN DUPED BY A DORK LIKE THAT...
...AND GIVEN MY LIFE FOR HIM...
...I WOULD BE ENJOYING MY SECOND YEAR OF HIGH SCHOOL!
KSSS!
SHOTARO!!
WHEN I THINK THAT YOU'RE IN YOUR SECOND YEAR OF HIGH SCHOOL, I GO CRAZY WITH A GRUDGE!
EVIL AURA
fwuuu
...was totally dark...
A kaleidoscope of her pitch-black life.
Her dark life was from age 6 to 13.
...myyyy liiiiife...
14...
15...
16...
slither
slither
slither
honk honk
huh?
OH.
He's waiting for her to come out.
D-DARN!
I DID IT AGAIN!
Vrooo—om
I ALWAYS LOSE MYSELF WHEN I THINK ABOUT SHOTARO!

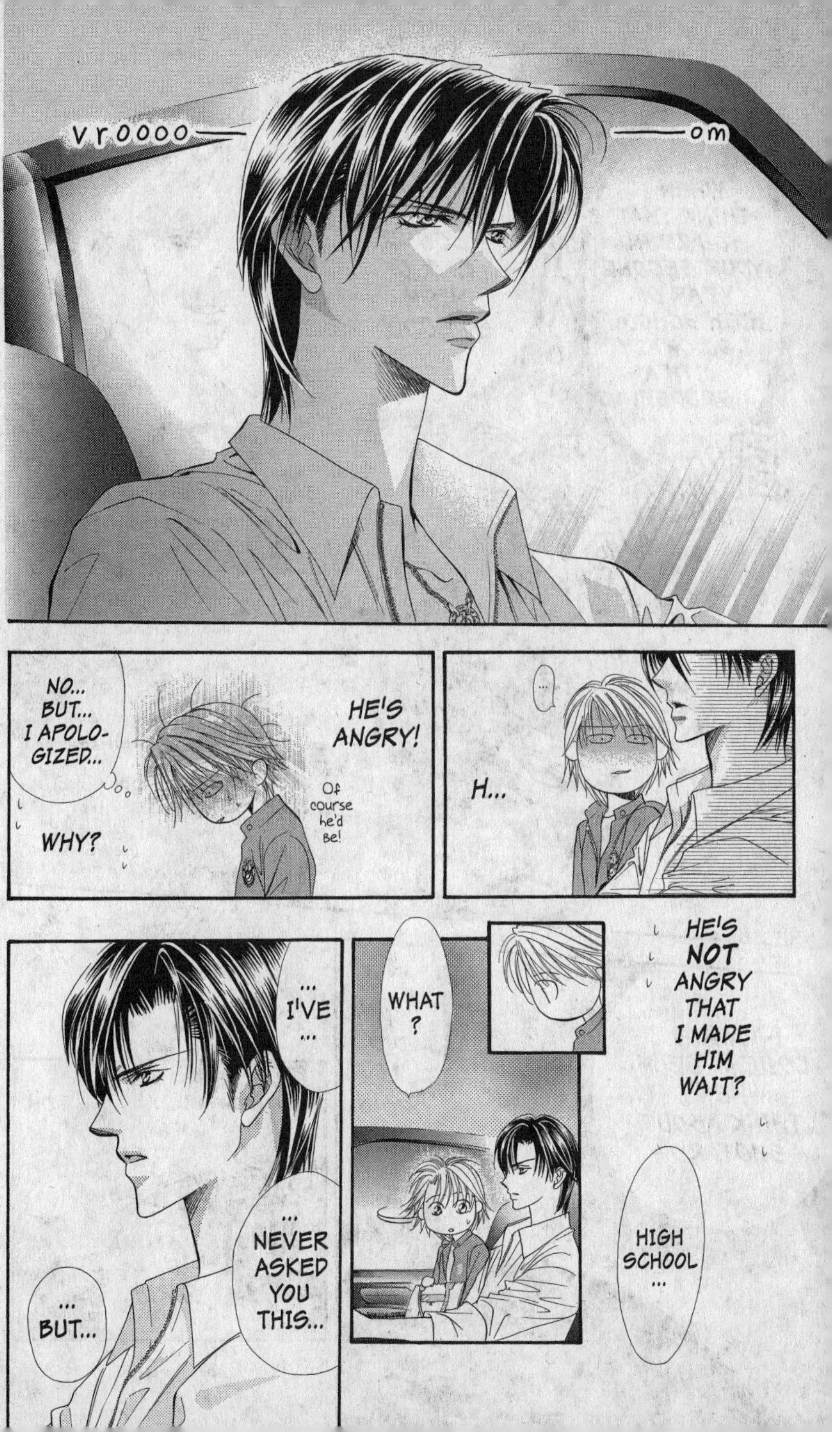
vroooo——om
...
H...
HE'S ANGRY!
NO... BUT... I APOLOGIZED...
Of course he'd be!
WHY?
HE'S NOT ANGRY THAT I MADE HIM WAIT?
HIGH SCHOOL...
WHAT?
... I'VE ...
... NEVER ASKED YOU THIS...
... BUT...

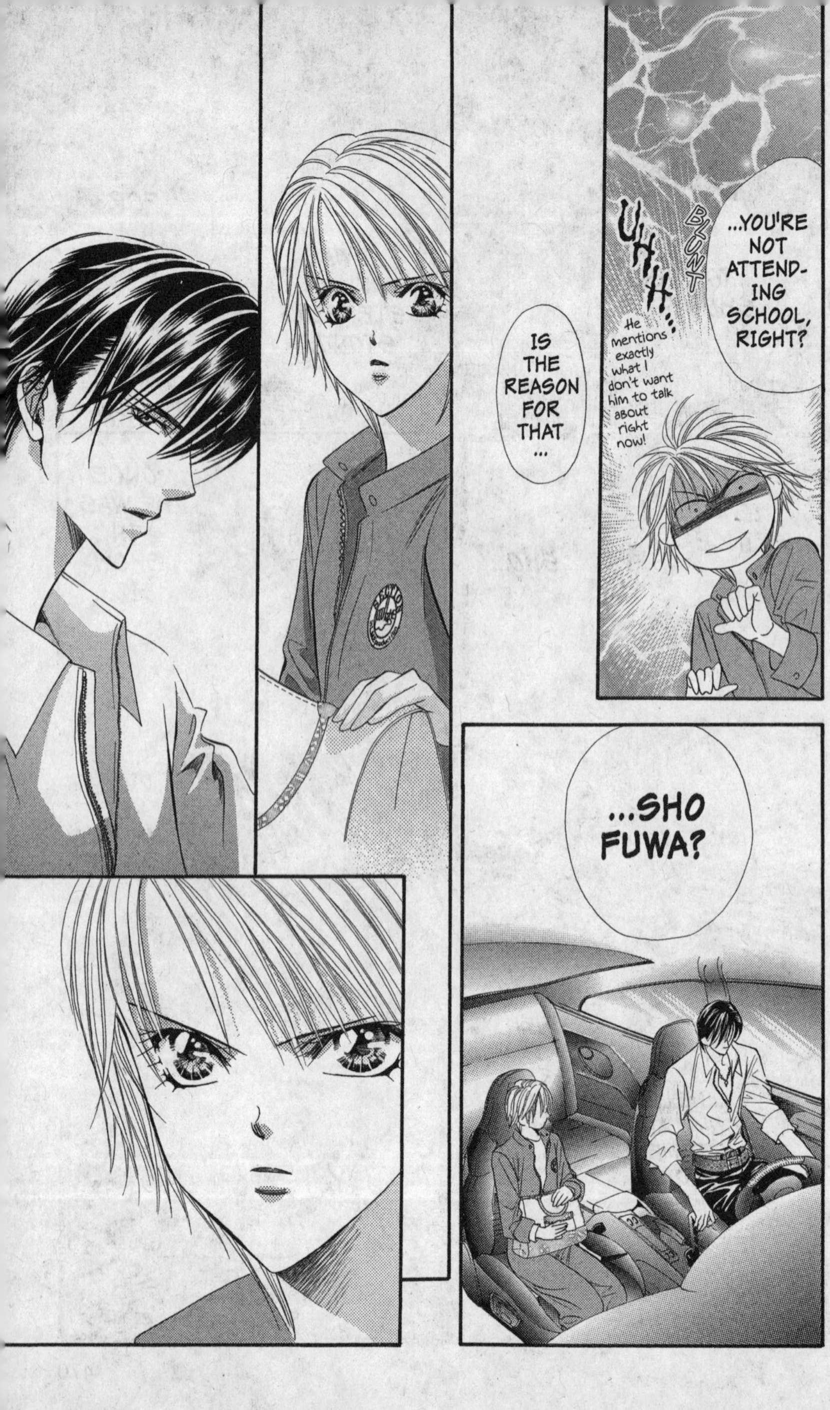

...YOU'RE NOT ATTENDING SCHOOL, RIGHT?
BLUNT
UHH...
He mentions exactly what I don't want him to talk about right now!
IS THE REASON FOR THAT ...
...SHO FUWA?

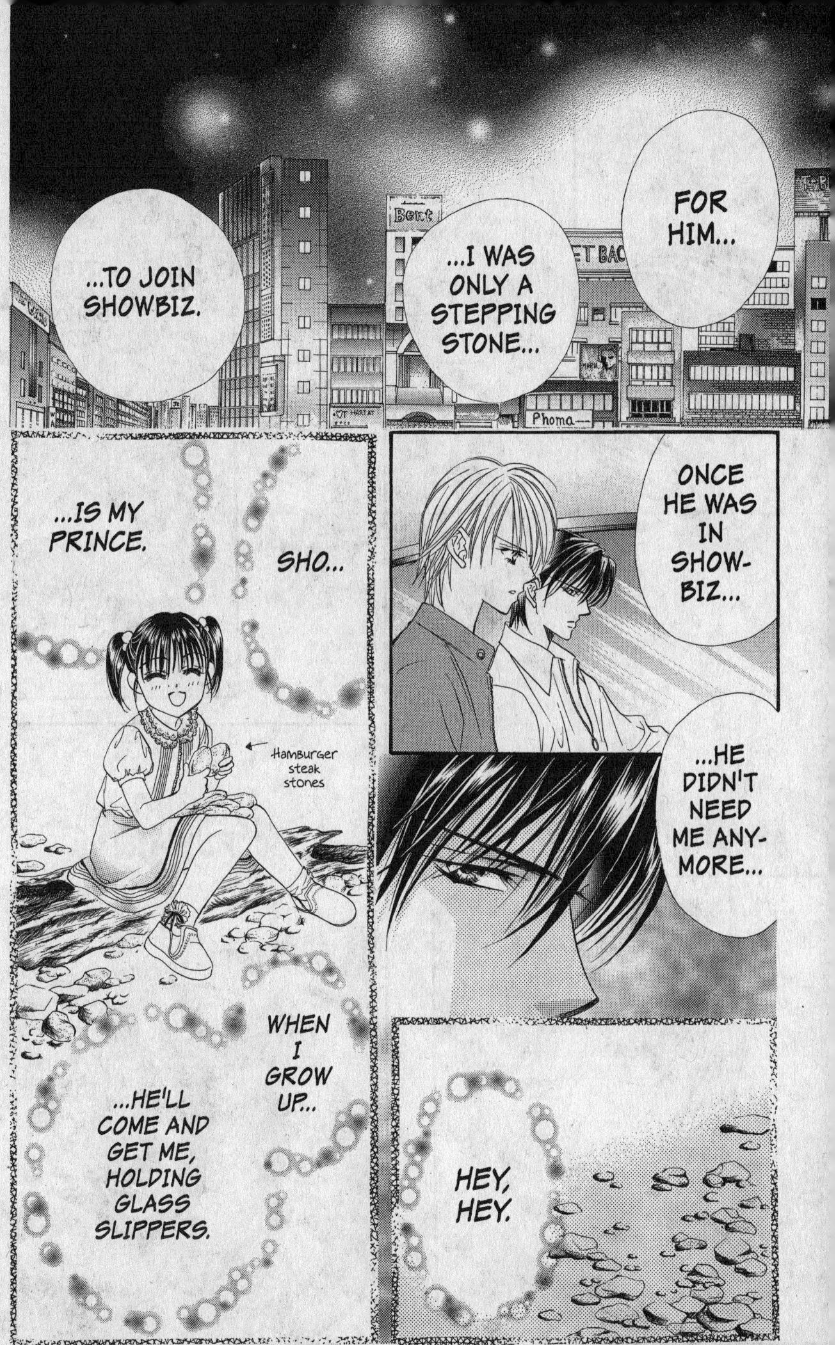
FOR HIM...
...I WAS ONLY A STEPPING STONE...
...TO JOIN SHOWBIZ.
ONCE HE WAS IN SHOW-BIZ...
...HE DIDN'T NEED ME ANY-MORE...
HEY, HEY.
SHO...
...IS MY PRINCE.
Hamburger steak stones
WHEN I GROW UP...
...HE'LL COME AND GET ME, HOLDING GLASS SLIPPERS.

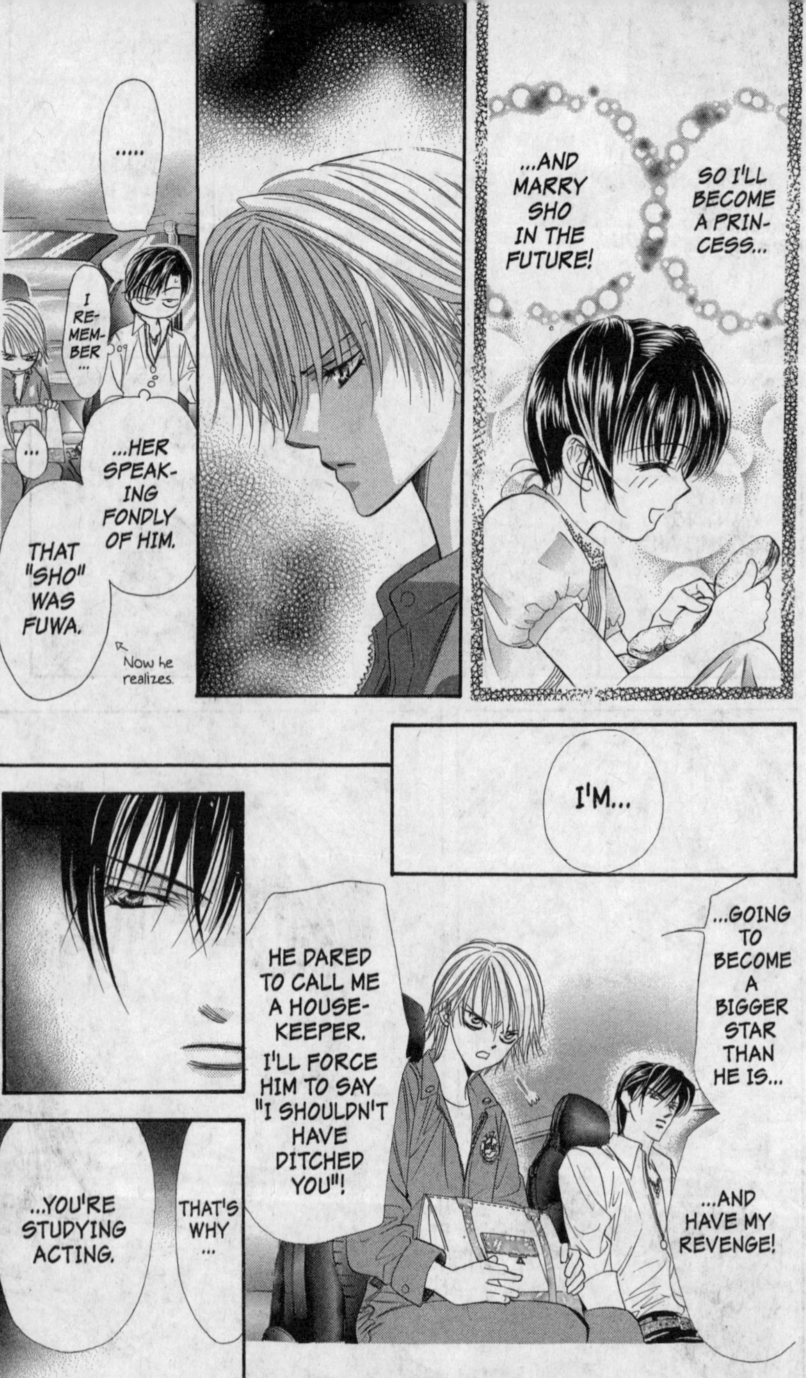
SO I'LL BECOME A PRINCESS...
...AND MARRY SHO IN THE FUTURE!
.....
I REMEMBER...
...HER SPEAKING FONDLY OF HIM.
...
THAT "SHO" WAS FUWA.
Now he realizes.
I'M...
...GOING TO BECOME A BIGGER STAR THAN HE IS...
...AND HAVE MY REVENGE!
HE DARED TO CALL ME A HOUSEKEEPER.
I'LL FORCE HIM TO SAY "I SHOULDN'T HAVE DITCHED YOU"!
THAT'S WHY...
...YOU'RE STUDYING ACTING.

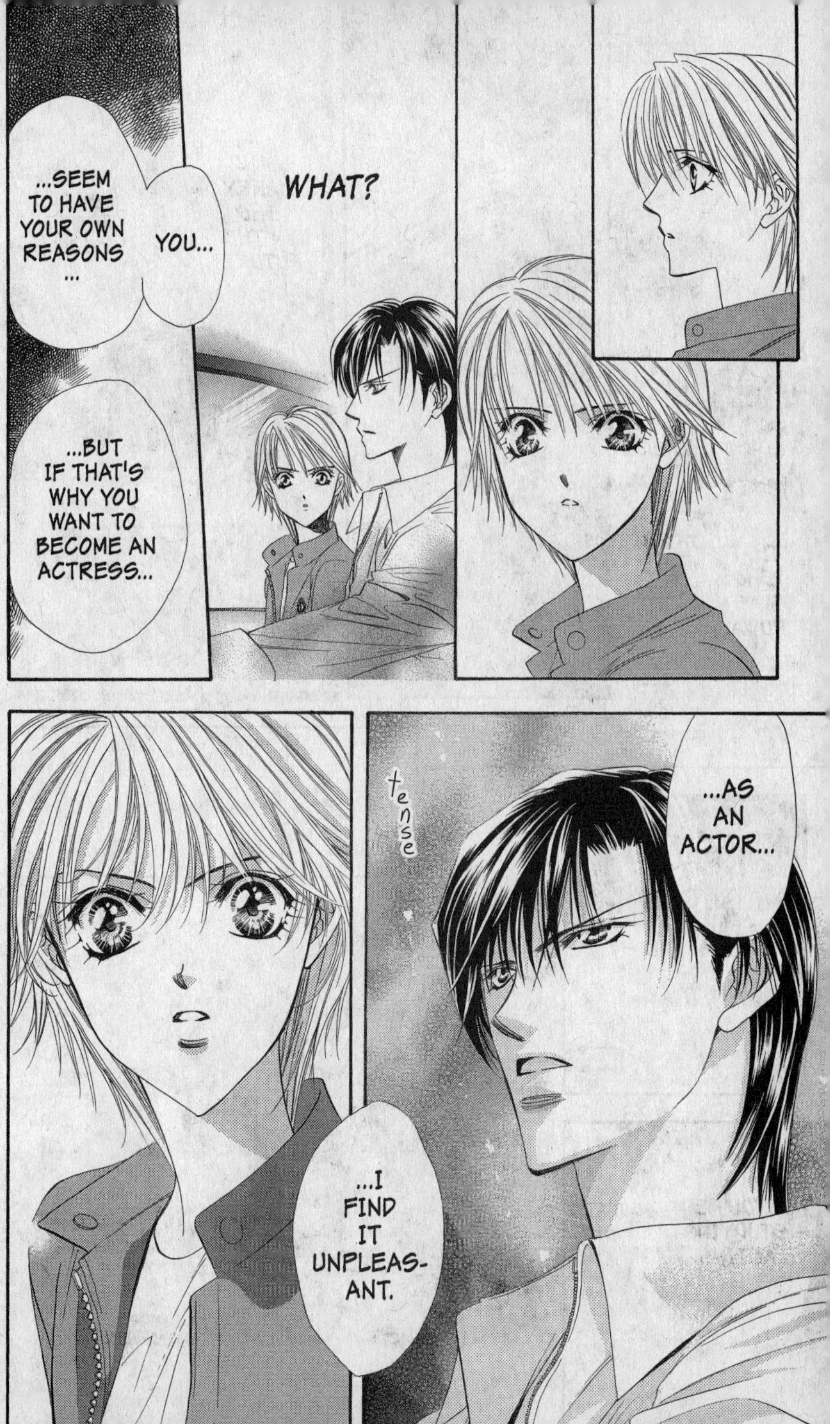
WHAT?
YOU...
...SEEM TO HAVE YOUR OWN REASONS...
...BUT IF THAT'S WHY YOU WANT TO BECOME AN ACTRESS...
...AS AN ACTOR...
tense
...I FIND IT UNPLEAS-ANT.

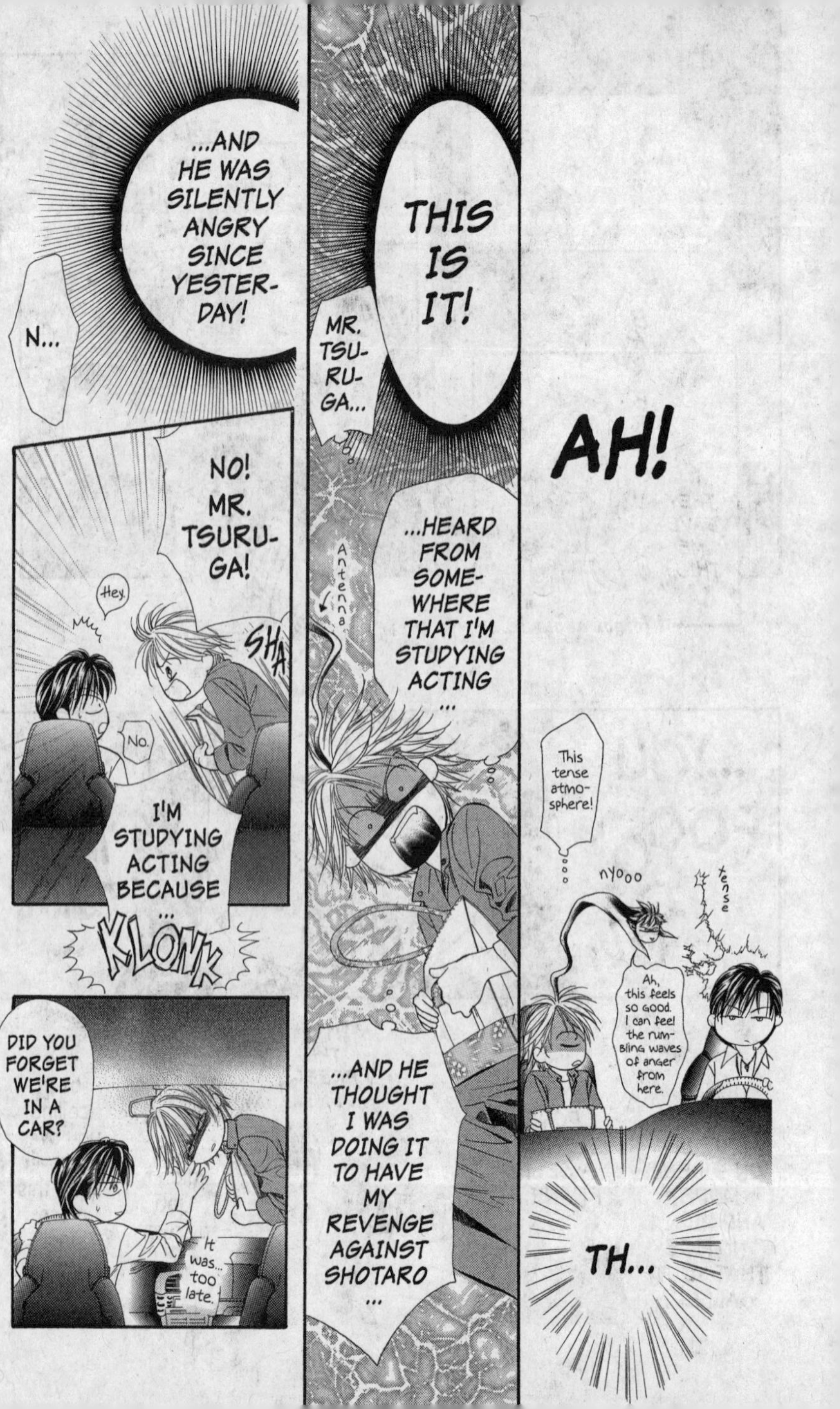
AH!
This tense atmosphere!
nyooo
tense
Ah, this feels so good. I can feel the rumbling waves of anger from here.
TH...
THIS IS IT!
MR. TSURUGA...
...HEARD FROM SOMEWHERE THAT I'M STUDYING ACTING...
Antenna
...AND HE THOUGHT I WAS DOING IT TO HAVE MY REVENGE AGAINST SHOTARO...
...AND HE WAS SILENTLY ANGRY SINCE YESTERDAY!
N...
NO! MR. TSURUGA!
Hey.
SHA
No.
I'M STUDYING ACTING BECAUSE...
KLONK
DID YOU FORGET WE'RE IN A CAR?
It was... too late.

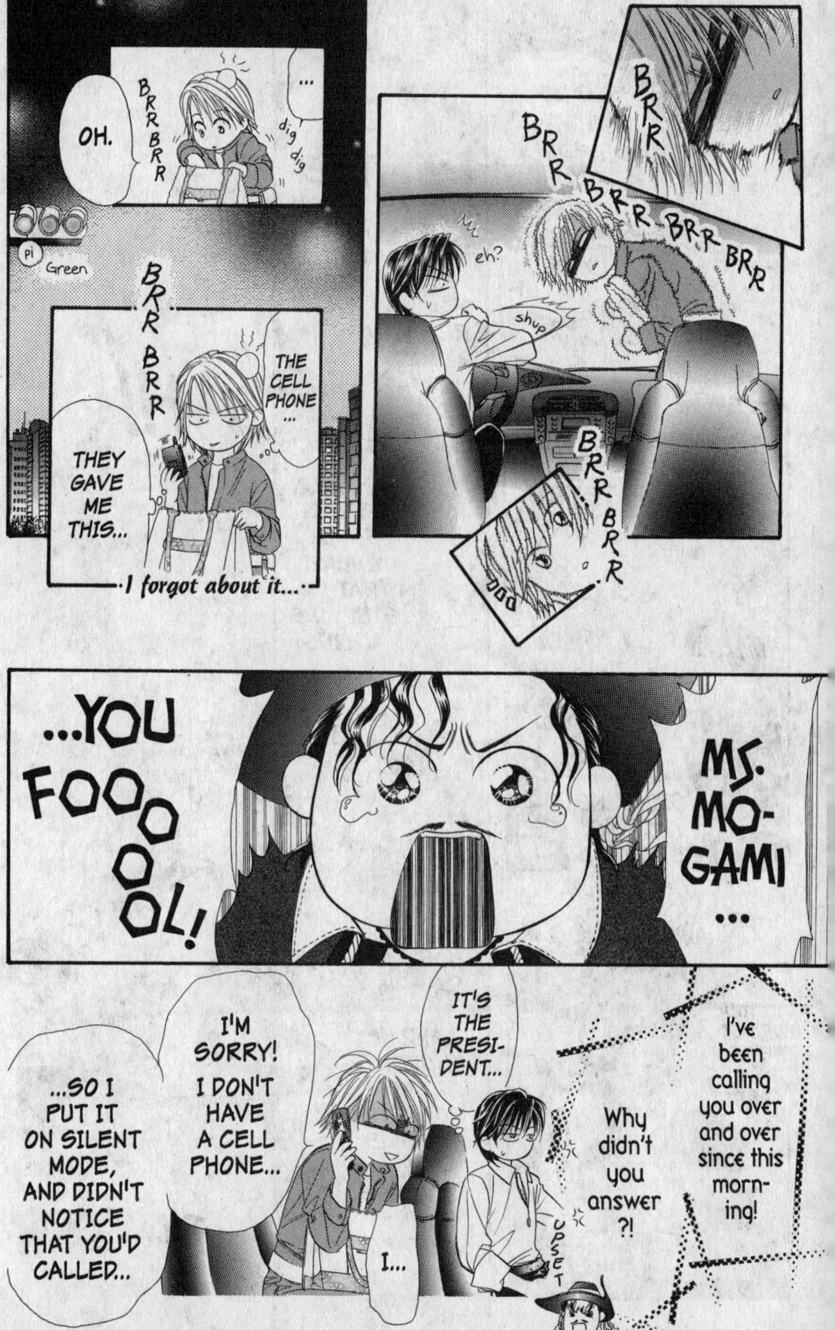
BRR
BRR BRR BRR BRR
eh?
shup
BRR BRR
DOC
...
OH.
BRR BRR BRR
dig dig
pi
Green
BRR BRR BRR
THE CELL PHONE...
THEY GAVE ME THIS...
I forgot about it...
MS. MO-GAMI...
...YOU FOOOOOOL!
I've been calling you over and over since this morn-ing!
Why didn't you answer?!
UPSET
IT'S THE PRESI-DENT...
I'M SORRY! I DON'T HAVE A CELL PHONE...
I...
...SO I PUT IT ON SILENT MODE, AND DIDN'T NOTICE THAT YOU'D CALLED...

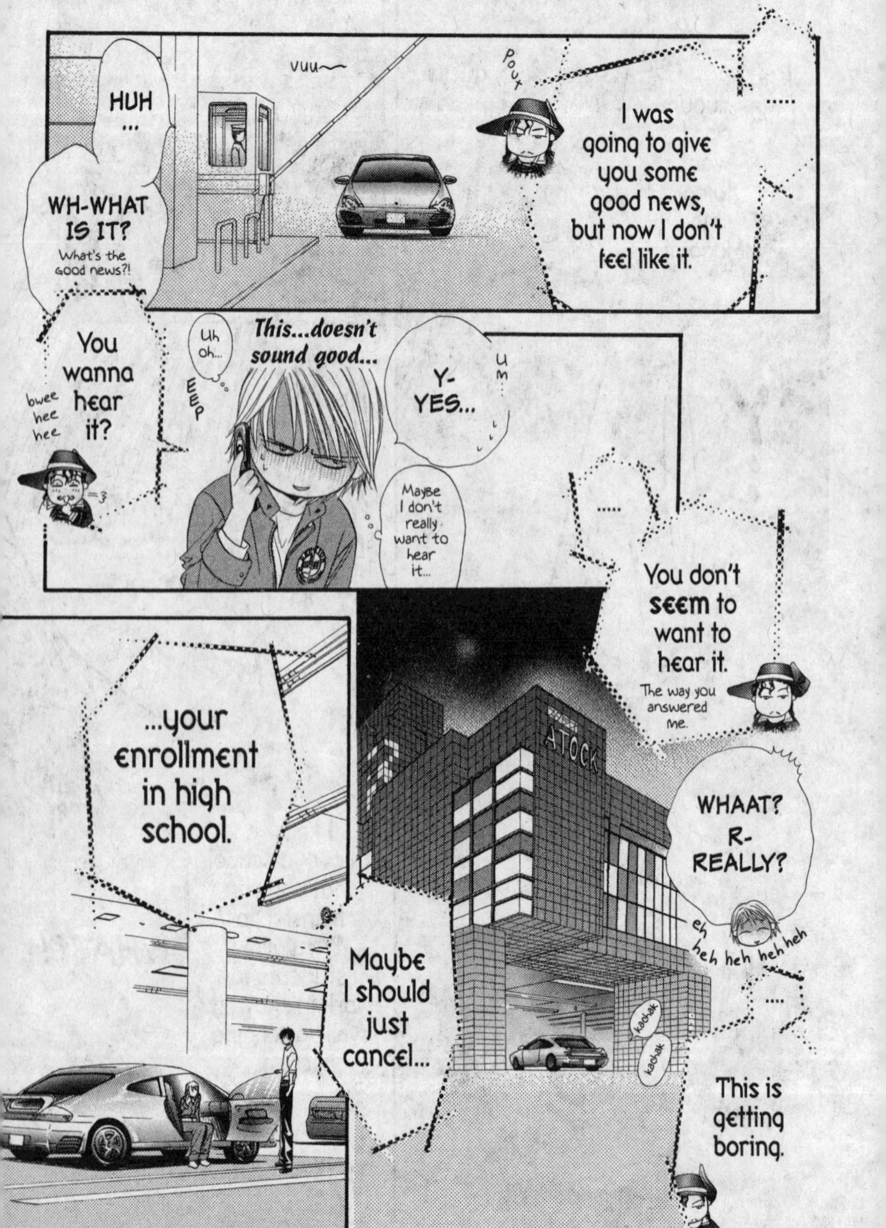
Pout
....
I was going to give you some good news, but now I don't feel like it.
vuu~~
HUH ...
WH-WHAT IS IT?
What's the good news?!
....
Um...
Y-YES...
Maybe I don't really want to hear it...
This...doesn't sound good...
Uh oh...
EEP
You wanna hear it?
bwee hee hee
You don't seem to want to hear it.
The way you answered me.
Maybe I should just cancel...
...your enrollment in high school.
WHAAT? R-REALLY?
eh heh heh heh heh
kachak
kachak
....
This is getting boring.

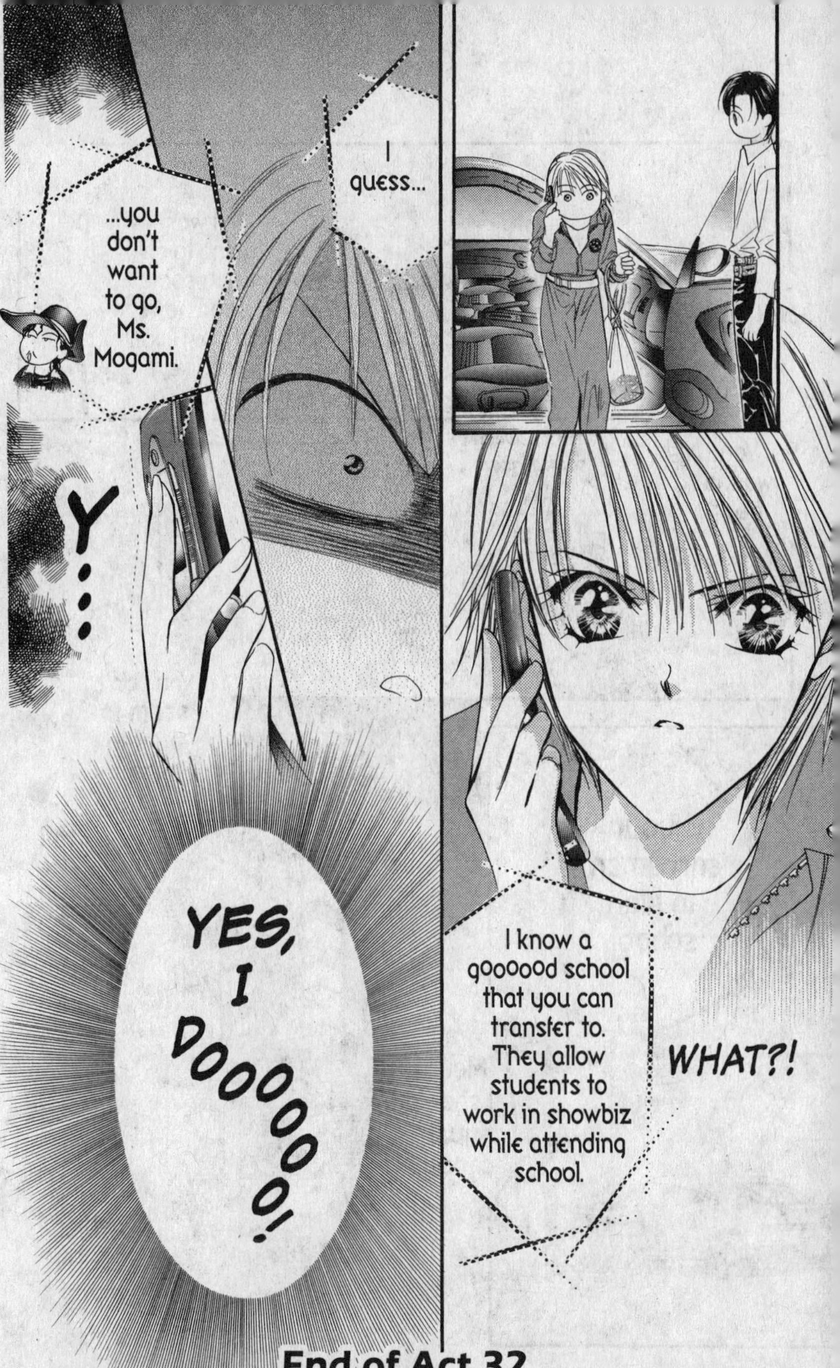
I know a gooooood school that you can transfer to. They allow students to work in showbiz while attending school.
WHAT?!
I guess...
...you don't want to go, Ms. Mogami.
Y...
YES, I DOOOOOOO!

End of Act 32

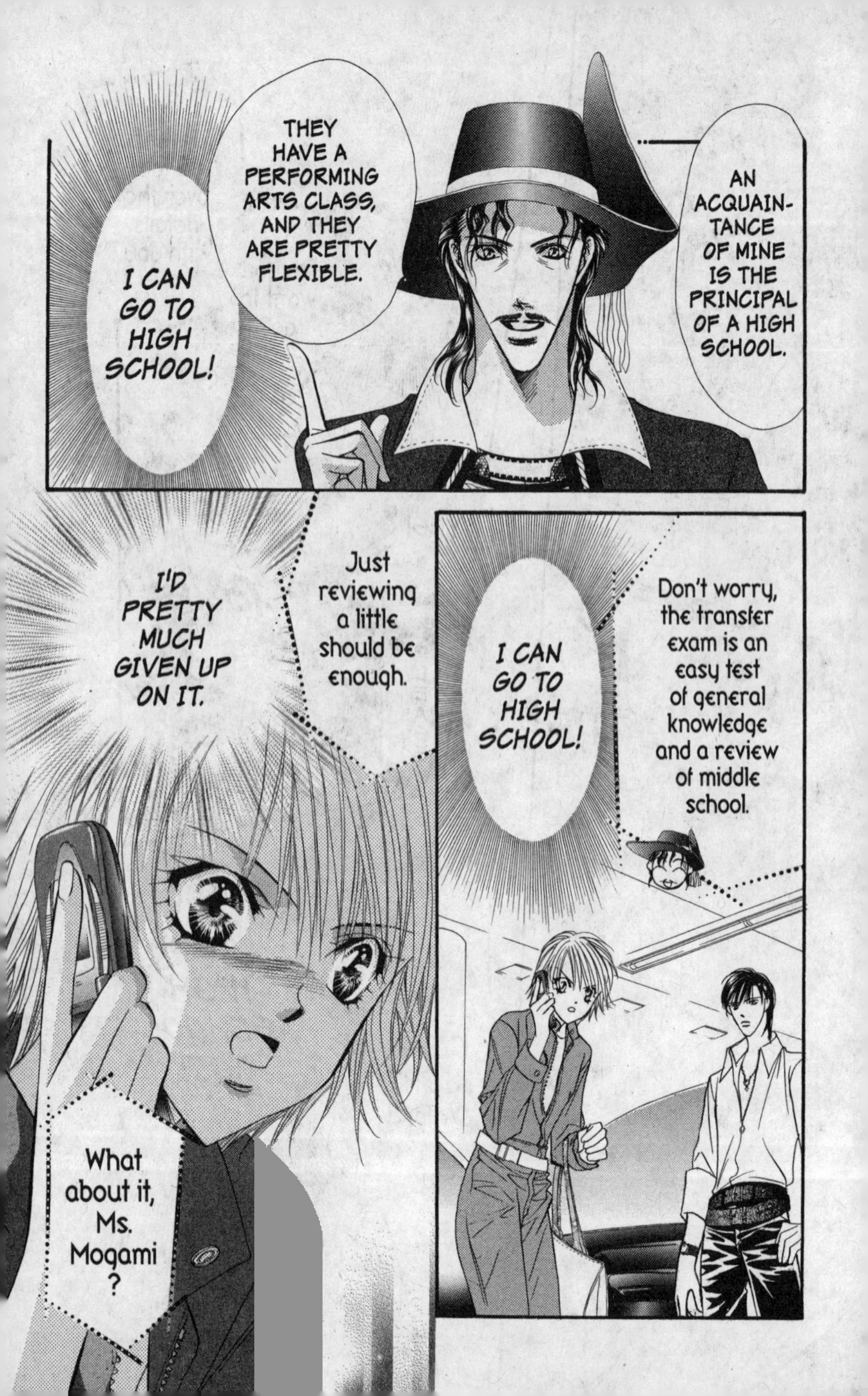
AN ACQUAINTANCE OF MINE IS THE PRINCIPAL OF A HIGH SCHOOL.
THEY HAVE A PERFORMING ARTS CLASS, AND THEY ARE PRETTY FLEXIBLE.
I CAN GO TO HIGH SCHOOL!
Don't worry, the transfer exam is an easy test of general knowledge and a review of middle school.
I CAN GO TO HIGH SCHOOL!
Just reviewing a little should be enough.
I'D PRETTY MUCH GIVEN UP ON IT.
What about it, Ms. Mogami?

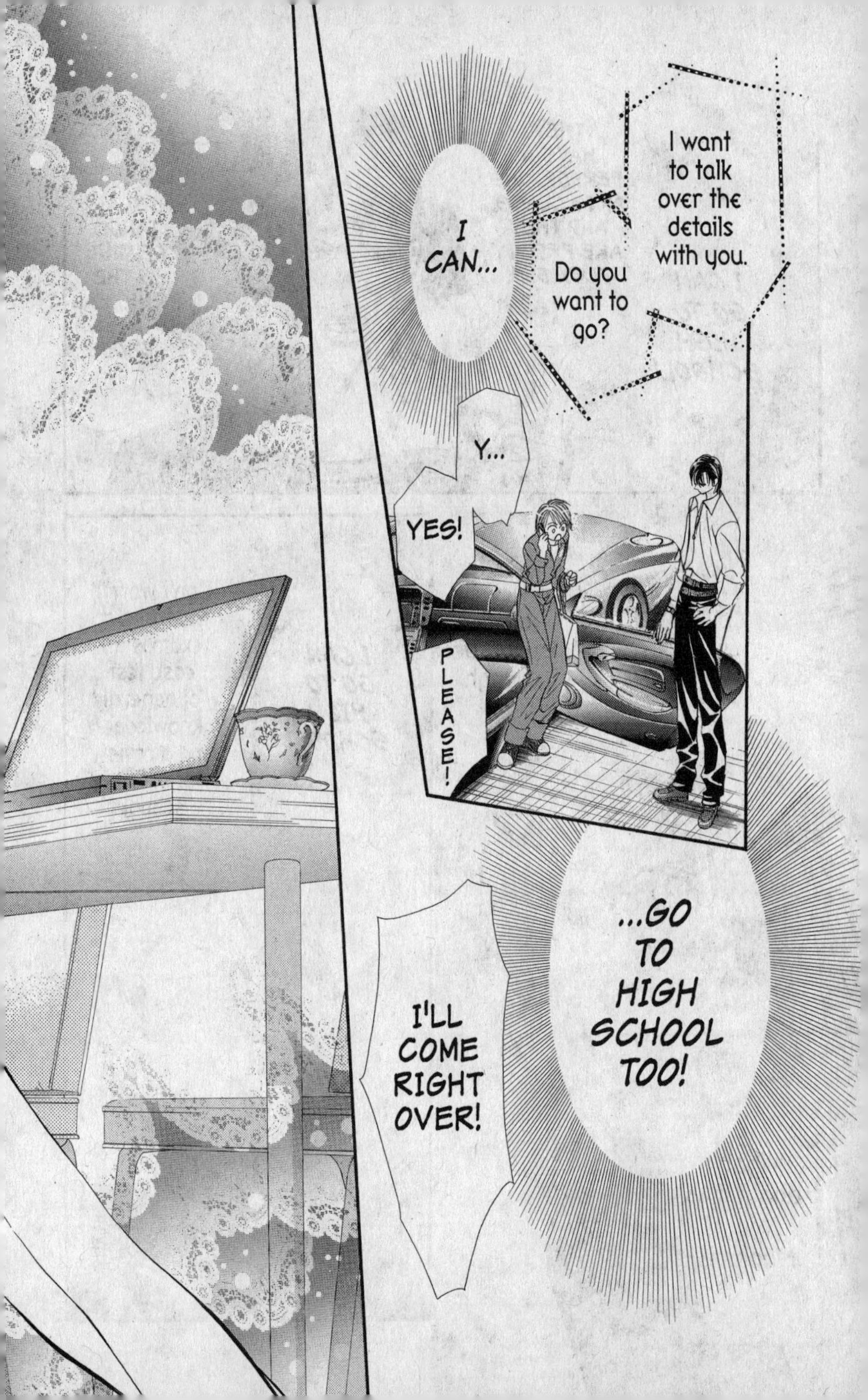
I want to talk over the details with you.
Do you want to go?
I CAN...
Y...
YES!
PLEASE!
...GO TO HIGH SCHOOL TOO!
I'LL COME RIGHT OVER!

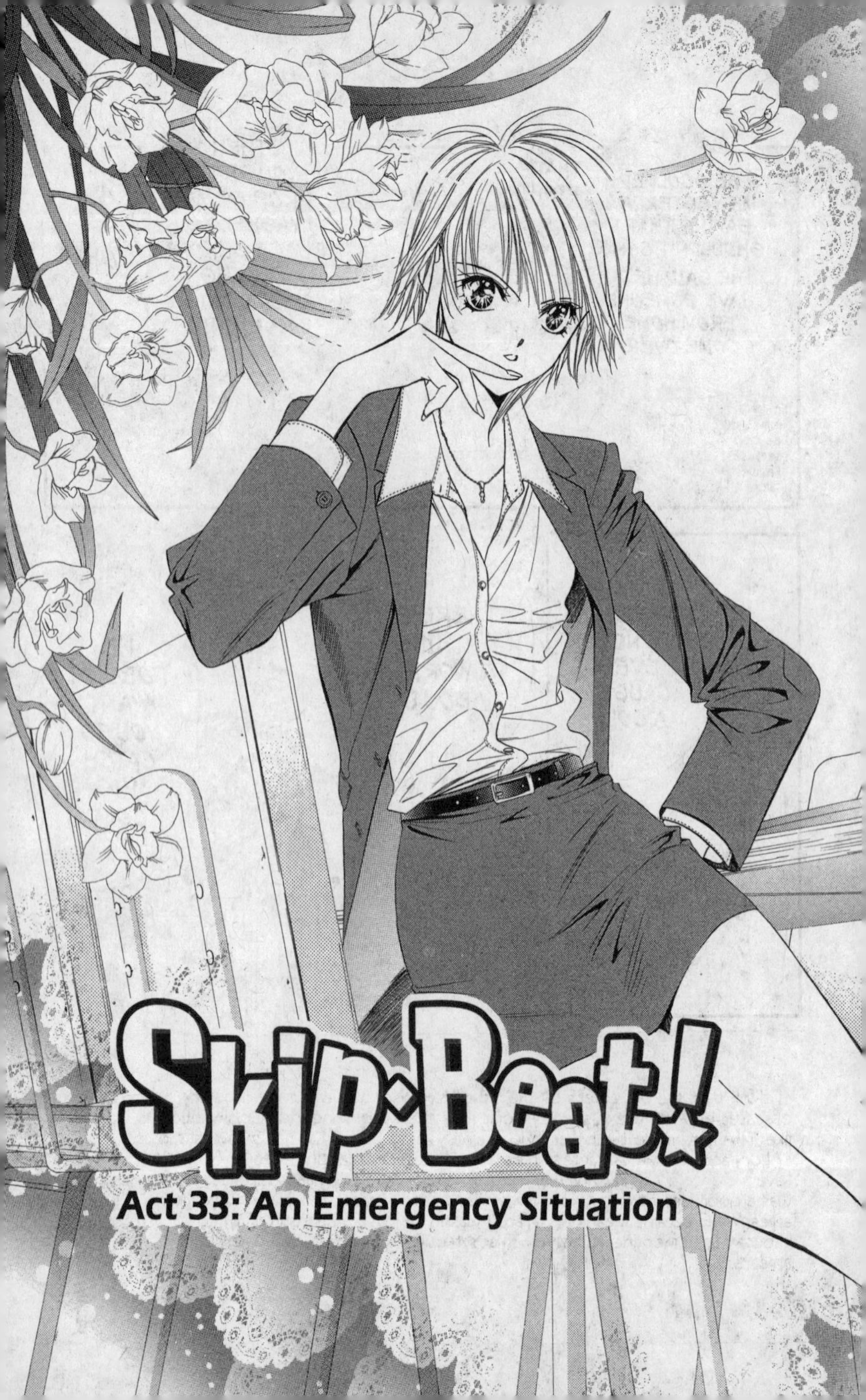
Skip·Beat!
Act 33: An Emergency Situation

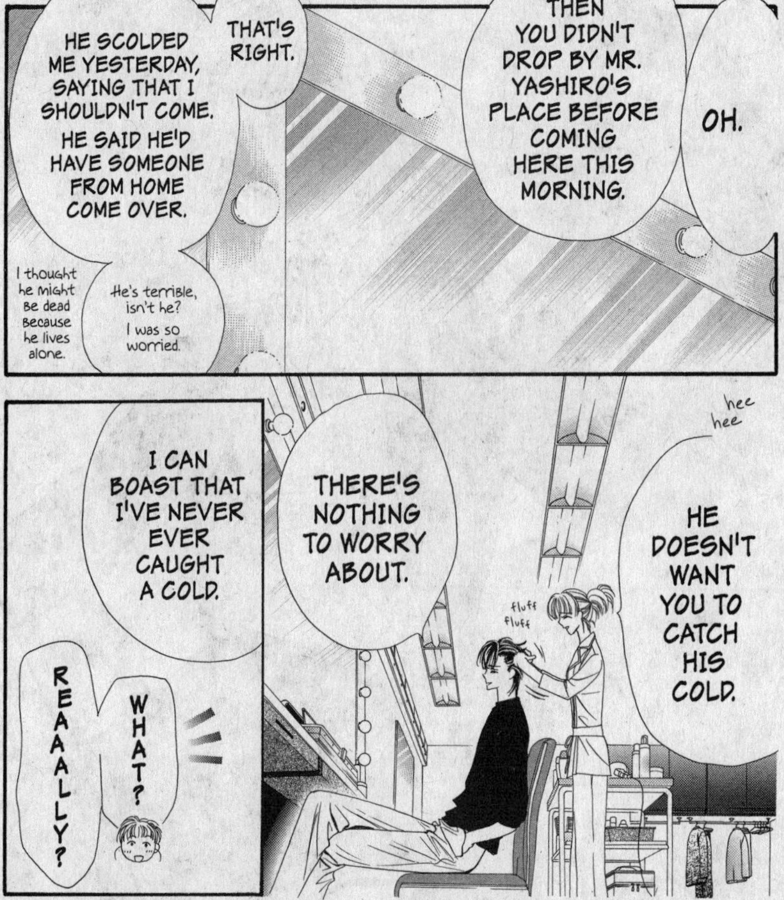
OH.
THEN YOU DIDN'T DROP BY MR. YASHIRO'S PLACE BEFORE COMING HERE THIS MORNING.
THAT'S RIGHT.
HE SCOLDED ME YESTERDAY, SAYING THAT I SHOULDN'T COME.
HE SAID HE'D HAVE SOMEONE FROM HOME COME OVER.
He's terrible, isn't he?
I was so worried.
I thought he might be dead because he lives alone.
hee hee
HE DOESN'T WANT YOU TO CATCH HIS COLD.
fluff fluff
THERE'S NOTHING TO WORRY ABOUT.
I CAN BOAST THAT I'VE NEVER EVER CAUGHT A COLD.
WHAT?
REAAAALLY?

What LME Stands For (continued)

...I think that the characters of the other two might have become like Lory, obsessed with ♥♥ love ♥, so they would have been very annoying. Or since Lory is like THAT, if I made the other two ordinary people, they'd have been overshadowed by Lory and become characters that weren't really needed...in reality, M&E didn't have a chance to appear and weren't born, but now I think about it, I believe it was a good idea not to have them appear ◊ ...and because the other two didn't appear, M&E became meaningless, and I was in a bind...So I consulted my editor and thought up something for M&E. That's the THING that appears when Lory appears.

—Continued—

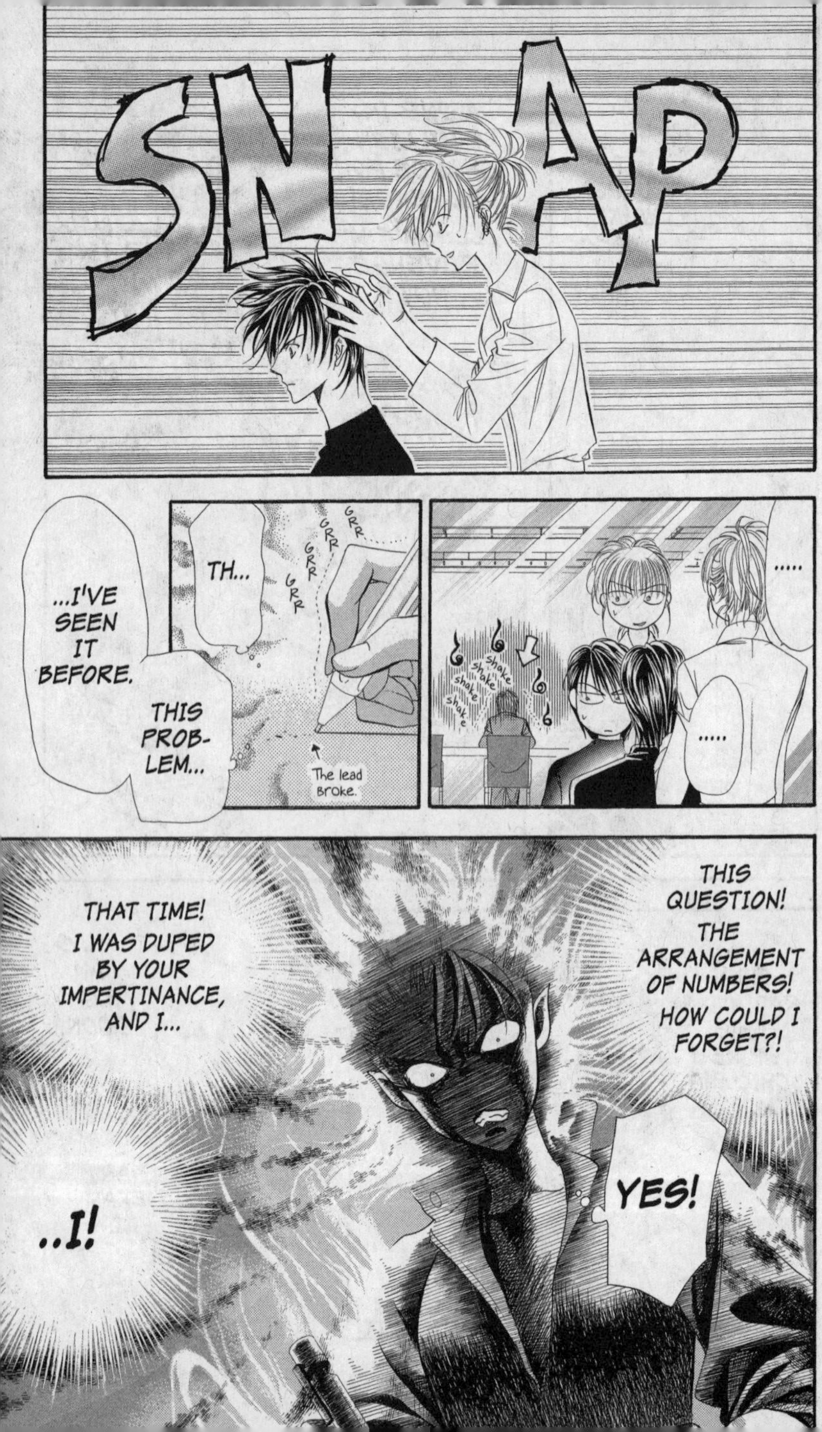
SNAP
.....
shake shake shake shake
.....
GRR GRR GRR GRR
TH...
The lead broke.
...I'VE SEEN IT BEFORE.
THIS PROBLEM...
THIS QUESTION! THE ARRANGEMENT OF NUMBERS! HOW COULD I FORGET?!
THAT TIME! I WAS DUPED BY YOUR IMPERTINANCE, AND I...
YES!
..I!

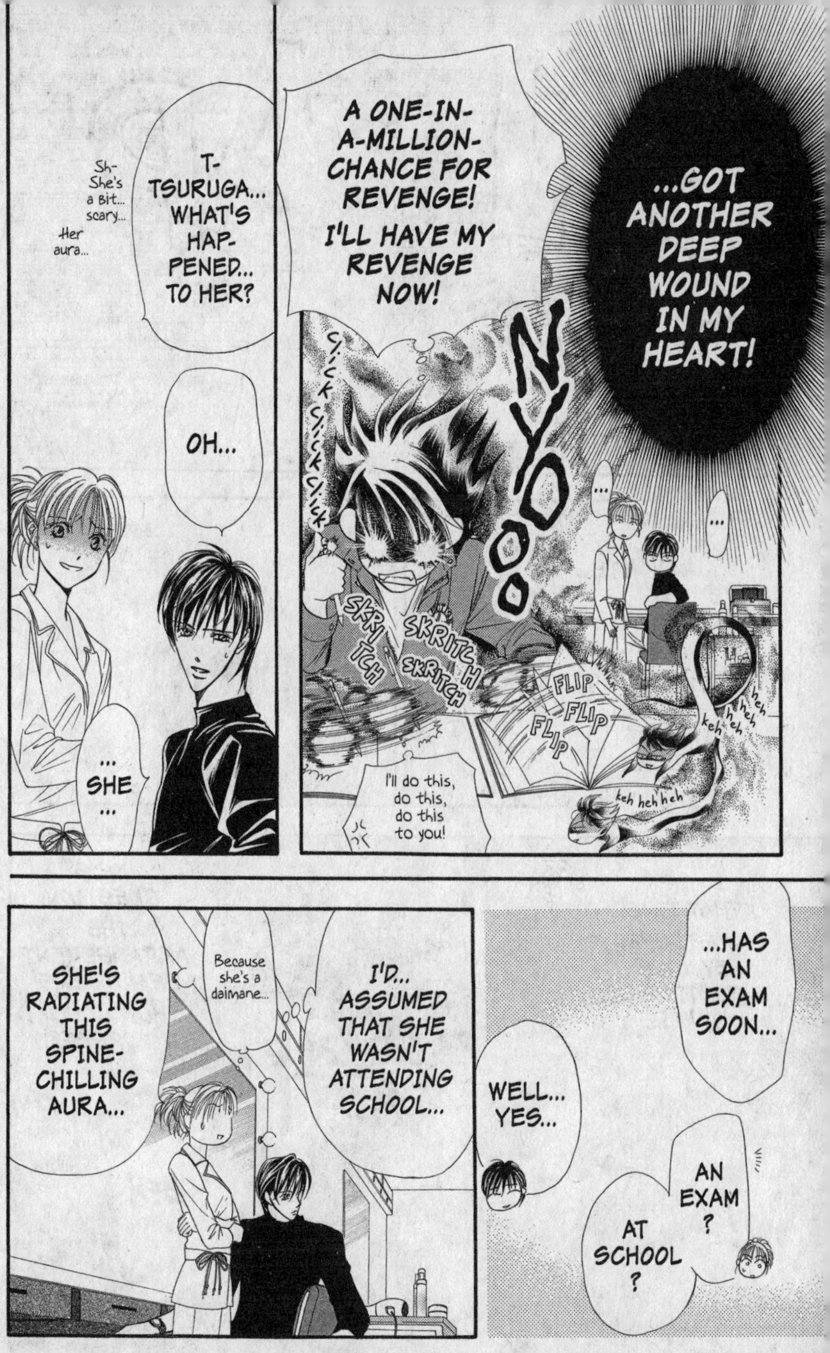

...GOT ANOTHER DEEP WOUND IN MY HEART!
A ONE-IN-A-MILLION-CHANCE FOR REVENGE! I'LL HAVE MY REVENGE NOW!
NYOOO
...
...
click click click click
SKRITCH SKRITCH SKRITCH
FLIP FLIP FLIP
heh heh heh keh
keh heh heh heh
I'll do this, do this, do this to you!
T-TSURUGA... WHAT'S HAPPENED... TO HER?
Sh-She's a bit... scary... Her aura...
OH...
...SHE...
...HAS AN EXAM SOON...
AN EXAM?
AT SCHOOL?
WELL... YES...
I'D... ASSUMED THAT SHE WASN'T ATTENDING SCHOOL...
Because she's a daimane...
SHE'S RADIATING THIS SPINE-CHILLING AURA...

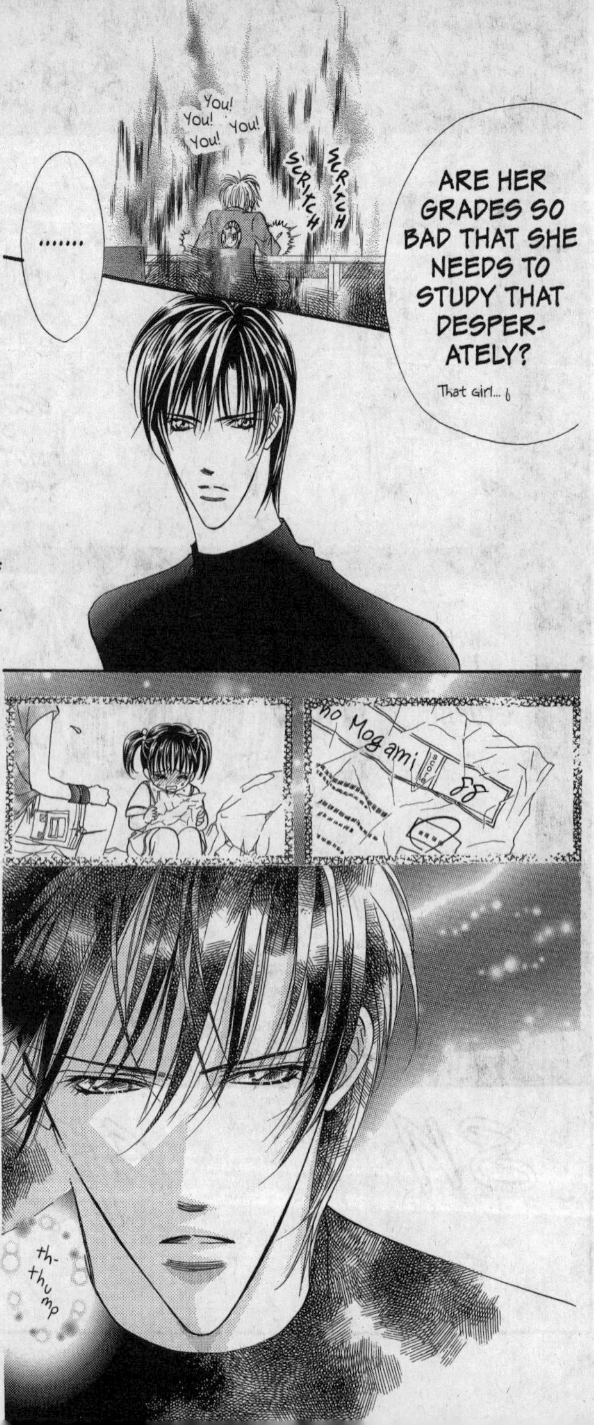
ARE HER GRADES SO BAD THAT SHE NEEDS TO STUDY THAT DESPERATELY?
That girl...
SCRITCH SCRITCH
You! You! You! You!
....
no Mogami
th-thump

...But...even if nothing concrete was decided in the beginning, I didn't think "The Forest of..." would turn into a detective drama... When Ren was struggling with "tentekomai" he was dressed up as...a gigolo?)"... At that time, according to me, "The Forest of..." was a slightly mysterious drama with the night business as the setting...

The Messiah for Colds

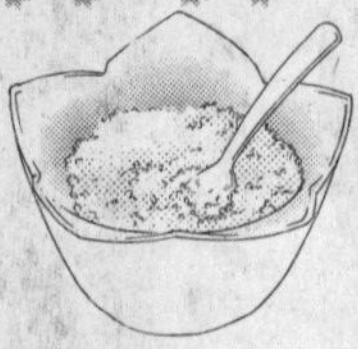

My mother often makes this for me when I have a cold and a sore throat. (But the daikon is cut into cubes.) When I eat this (which has been chilled in the fridge) when I've got a high fever, I feel refreshed. The daikon juice is just sweet enough with the honey, and soothes my sore throat...that's what I feel...yes. Anyway, even if I don't have an appetite, I can eat this...I can...I'll say it many times, because I think there are readers who think, "That must taste bad". It doesn't taste bad... I don't think so.

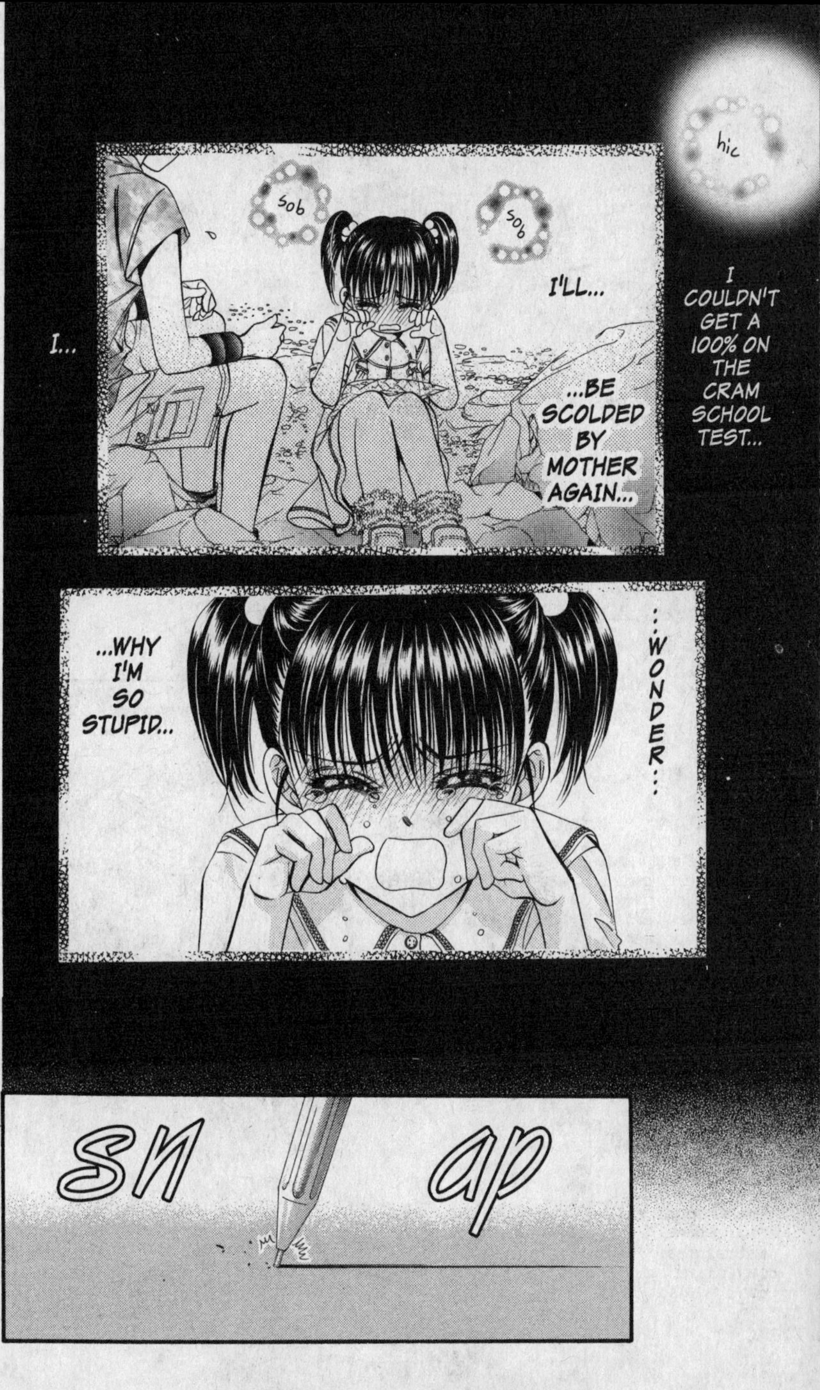
hic
I COULDN'T GET A 100% ON THE CRAM SCHOOL TEST...
sob
sob
I'LL...
...BE SCOLDED BY MOTHER AGAIN...
I...
...WONDER...
...WHY I'M SO STUPID...
SN
AP

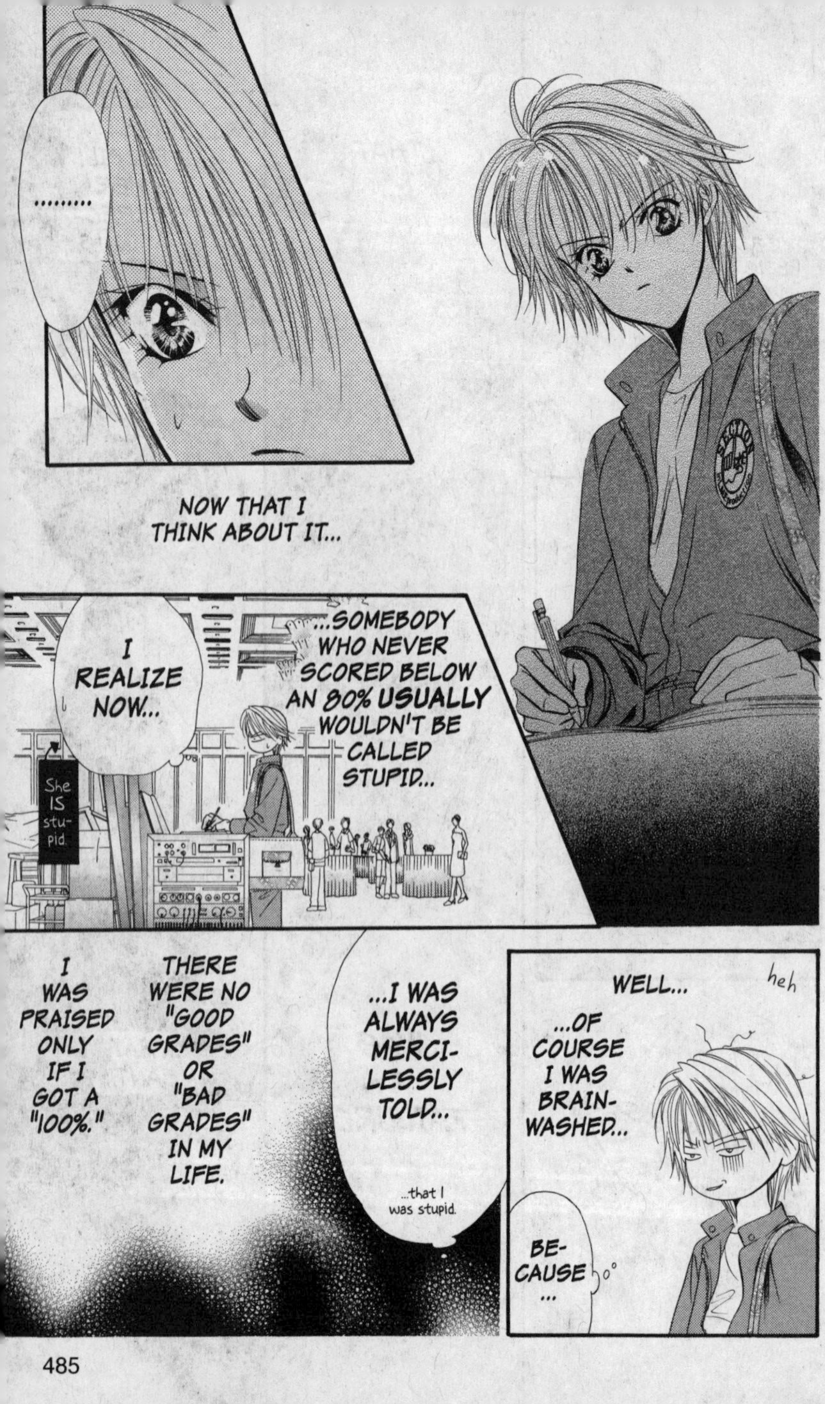

....
NOW THAT I THINK ABOUT IT...
...SOMEBODY WHO NEVER SCORED BELOW AN 80% USUALLY WOULDN'T BE CALLED STUPID...
I REALIZE NOW...
She IS stupid.
heh
WELL...
...OF COURSE I WAS BRAIN-WASHED...
BE-CAUSE...
...I WAS ALWAYS MERCI-LESSLY TOLD...
...that I was stupid.
THERE WERE NO "GOOD GRADES" OR "BAD GRADES" IN MY LIFE.
I WAS PRAISED ONLY IF I GOT A "100%."

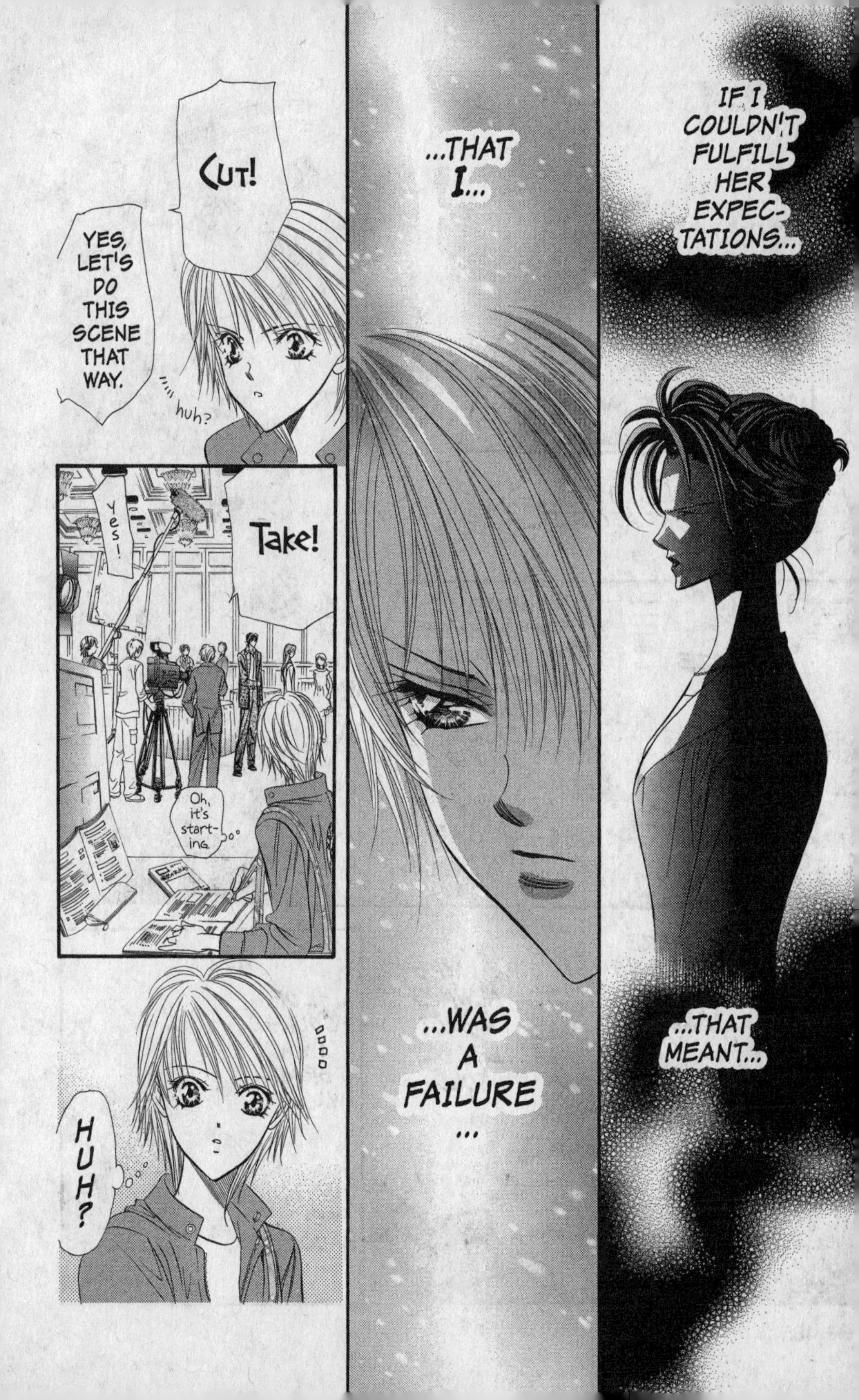
IF I COULDN'T FULFILL HER EXPECTATIONS...
...THAT MEANT...
...THAT I...
...WAS A FAILURE...
CUT!
YES, LET'S DO THIS SCENE THAT WAY.
huh?
Take!
Yes!
Oh, it's start-ing.
HUH?

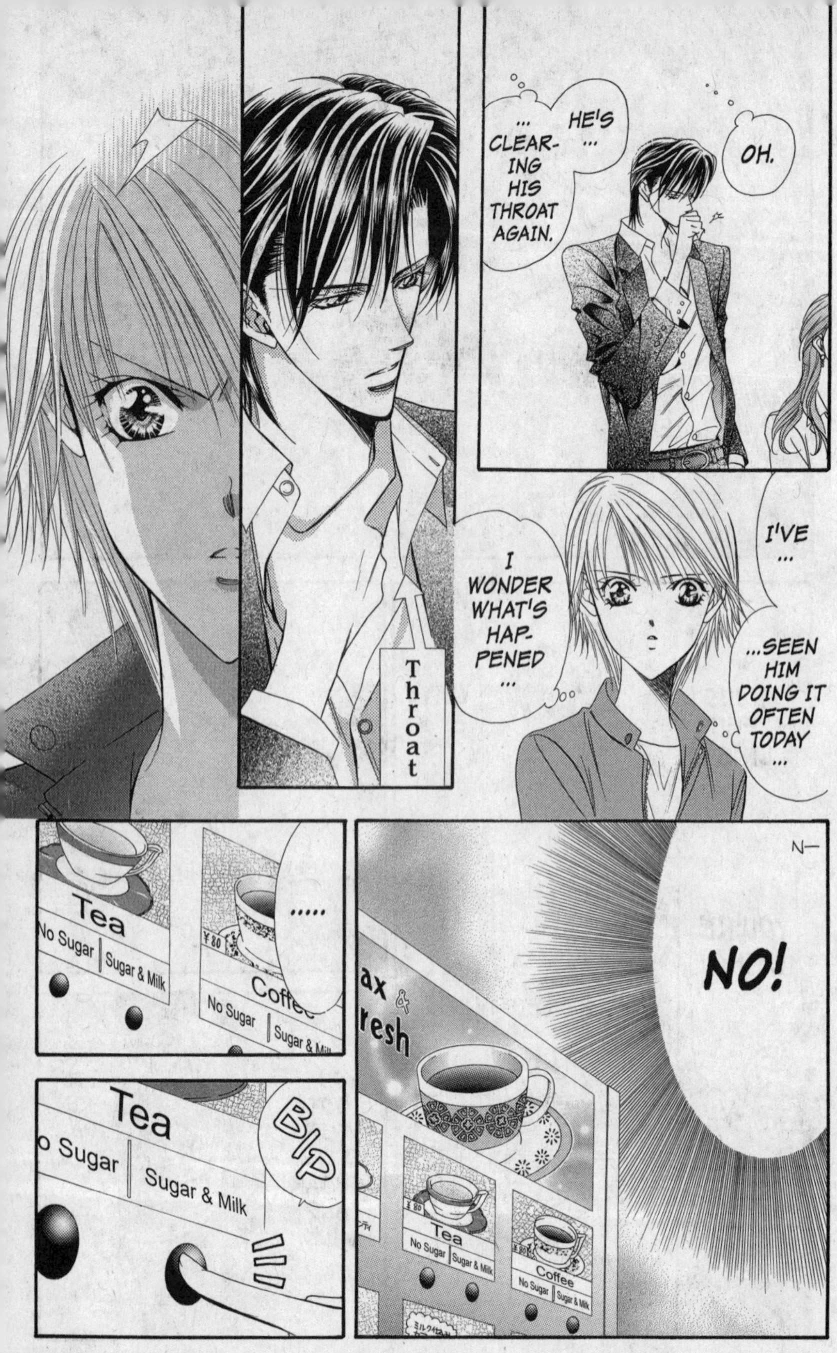

OH.
... HE'S ... CLEARING- ING HIS THROAT AGAIN.
I'VE ...
...SEEN HIM DOING IT OFTEN TODAY ...
I WONDER WHAT'S HAP- PENED ...
Throat
N—
NO!
ax & resh
Tea
No Sugar
Sugar & Milk
Coffee
No Sugar
Sugar & Milk
.....
Tea
No Sugar
Sugar & Milk
Coffee
No Sugar
Sugar & Milk
B/P
Tea
o Sugar
Sugar & Milk

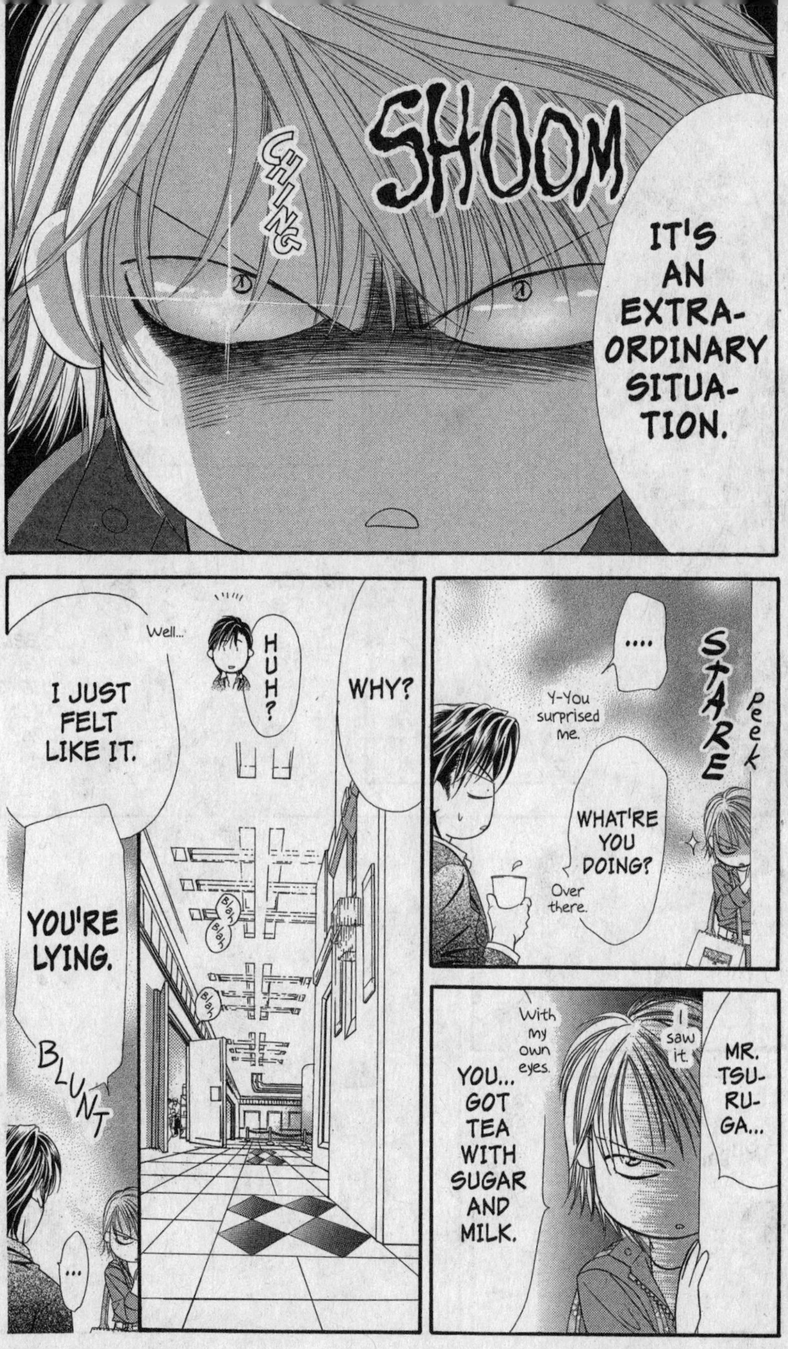
IT'S AN EXTRA-ORDINARY SITUATION.
SHOOM
CHING
STARE
Peek
....
Y-You surprised me.
WHAT'RE YOU DOING?
Over there.
MR. TSURUGA...
I saw it.
With my own eyes.
YOU... GOT TEA WITH SUGAR AND MILK.
WHY?
HUH?
Well...
I JUST FELT LIKE IT.
Blah
Blah
Blah
YOU'RE LYING.
BLUNT
...

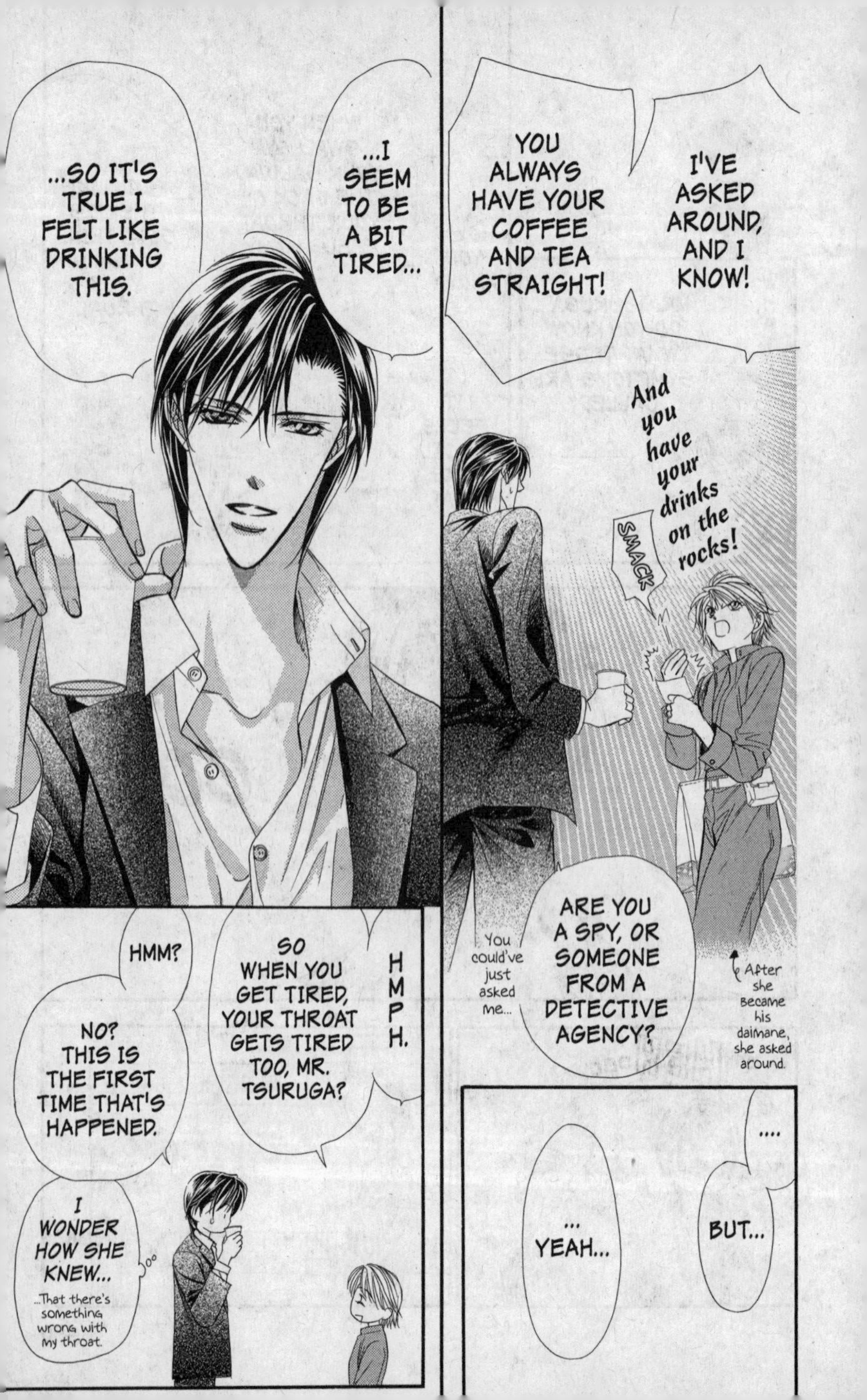

I'VE ASKED AROUND, AND I KNOW!
YOU ALWAYS HAVE YOUR COFFEE AND TEA STRAIGHT!
And you have your drinks on the rocks!
SMACK
After she became his daimane, she asked around.
ARE YOU A SPY, OR SOMEONE FROM A DETECTIVE AGENCY?
You could've just asked me...
....
BUT...
... YEAH...
...I SEEM TO BE A BIT TIRED...
...SO IT'S TRUE I FELT LIKE DRINKING THIS.
HMPH.
SO WHEN YOU GET TIRED, YOUR THROAT GETS TIRED TOO, MR. TSURUGA?
HMM?
NO? THIS IS THE FIRST TIME THAT'S HAPPENED.
I WONDER HOW SHE KNEW...
...That there's something wrong with my throat.

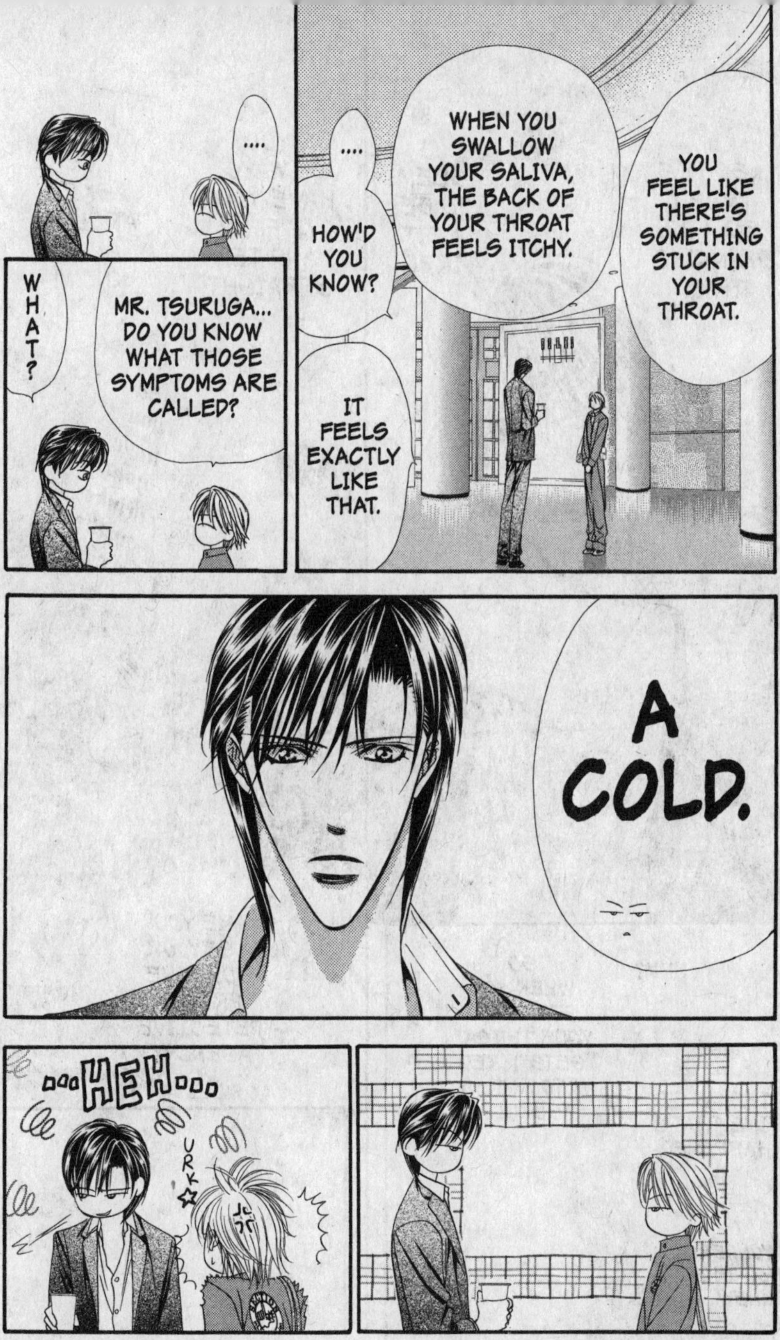

YOU FEEL LIKE THERE'S SOMETHING STUCK IN YOUR THROAT.
WHEN YOU SWALLOW YOUR SALIVA, THE BACK OF YOUR THROAT FEELS ITCHY.
....
HOW'D YOU KNOW?
IT FEELS EXACTLY LIKE THAT.
....
MR. TSURUGA... DO YOU KNOW WHAT THOSE SYMPTOMS ARE CALLED?
WHAT?
A COLD.
...HEH...
URK

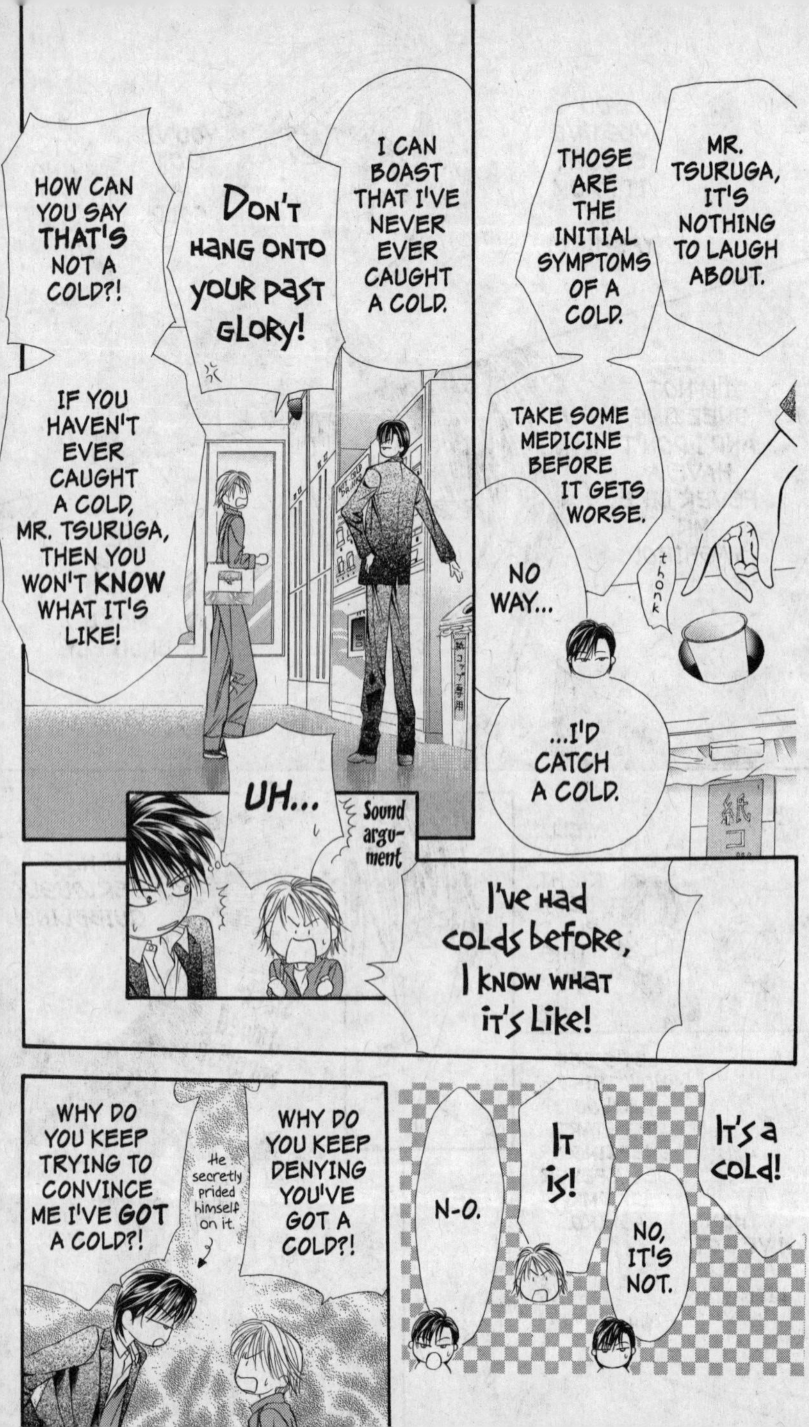
MR. TSURUGA, IT'S NOTHING TO LAUGH ABOUT.
THOSE ARE THE INITIAL SYMPTOMS OF A COLD.
TAKE SOME MEDICINE BEFORE IT GETS WORSE.
thonk
NO WAY...
...I'D CATCH A COLD.
I CAN BOAST THAT I'VE NEVER EVER CAUGHT A COLD.
Don't hang onto your past glory!
HOW CAN YOU SAY THAT'S NOT A COLD?!
IF YOU HAVEN'T EVER CAUGHT A COLD, MR. TSURUGA, THEN YOU WON'T KNOW WHAT IT'S LIKE!
I've had colds before, I know what it's like!
UH...
Sound argument
It's a cold!
NO, IT'S NOT.
It is!
N-O.
WHY DO YOU KEEP DENYING YOU'VE GOT A COLD?!
He secretly prided himself on it.
WHY DO YOU KEEP TRYING TO CONVINCE ME I'VE GOT A COLD?!

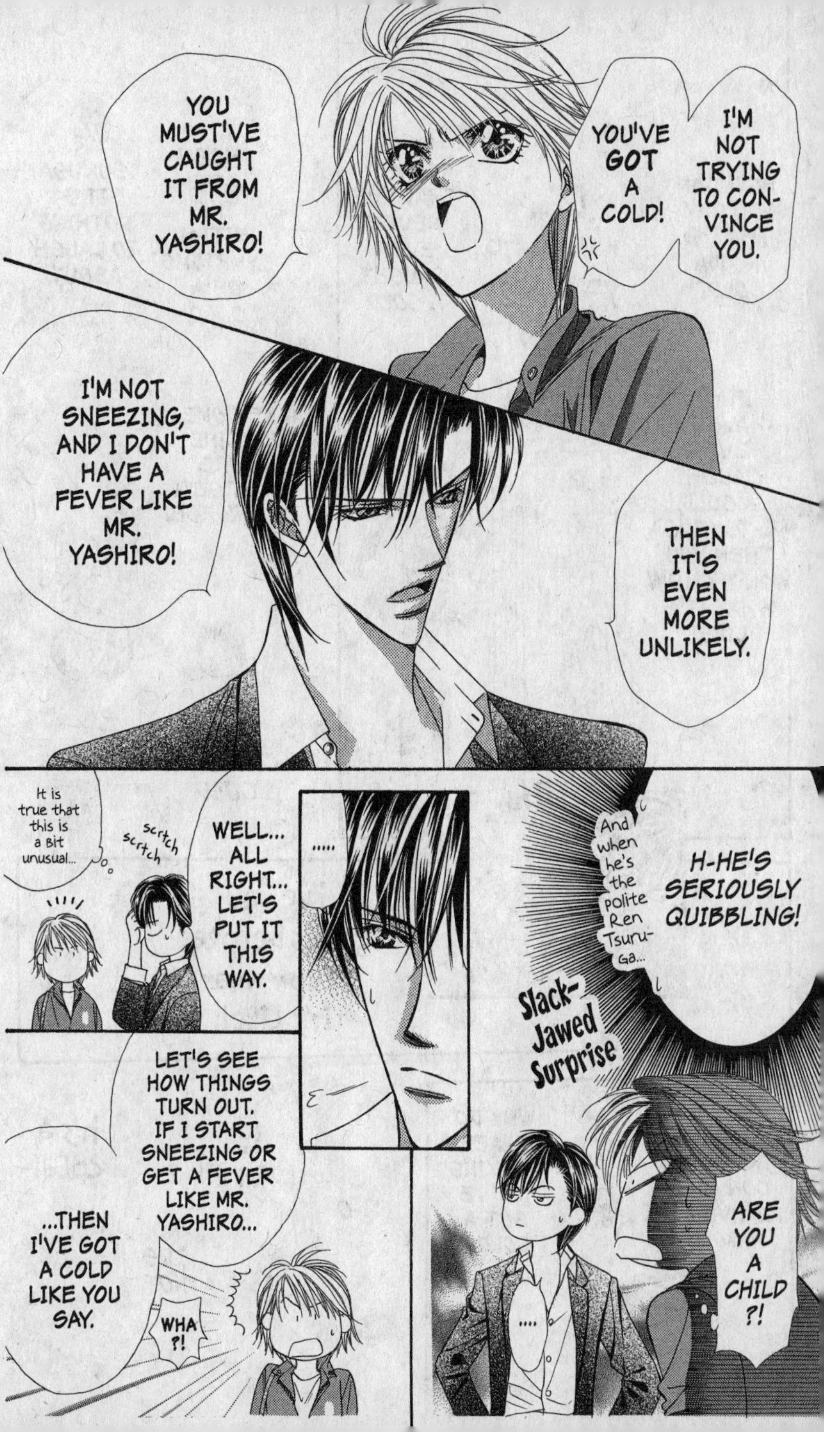
I'M NOT TRYING TO CON-VINCE YOU.
YOU'VE GOT A COLD!
YOU MUST'VE CAUGHT IT FROM MR. YASHIRO!
THEN IT'S EVEN MORE UNLIKELY.
I'M NOT SNEEZING, AND I DON'T HAVE A FEVER LIKE MR. YASHIRO!
H-HE'S SERIOUSLY QUIBBLING!
And when he's the polite Ren Tsuru-Ga...
Slack-Jawed Surprise
ARE YOU A CHILD ?!
....
.....
WELL... ALL RIGHT... LET'S PUT IT THIS WAY.
scrtch scrtch
It is true that this is a bit unusual...
LET'S SEE HOW THINGS TURN OUT. IF I START SNEEZING OR GET A FEVER LIKE MR. YASHIRO...
...THEN I'VE GOT A COLD LIKE YOU SAY.
WHA ?!

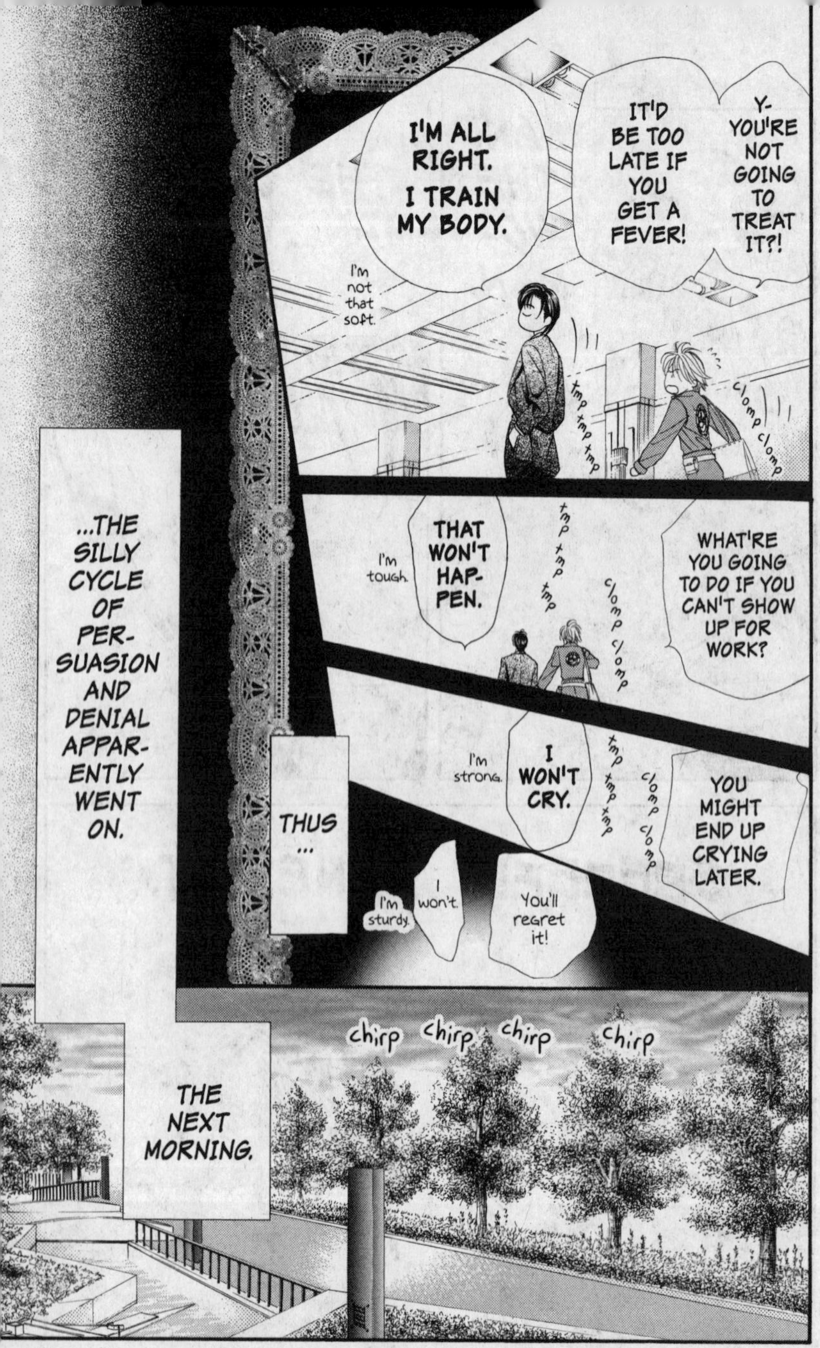
Y- YOU'RE NOT GOING TO TREAT IT?!
IT'D BE TOO LATE IF YOU GET A FEVER!
I'M ALL RIGHT. I TRAIN MY BODY.
I'm not that soft.
clomp clomp
tmp tmp tmp
WHAT'RE YOU GOING TO DO IF YOU CAN'T SHOW UP FOR WORK?
clomp clomp
tmp tmp tmp
THAT WON'T HAP-PEN.
I'm tough.
YOU MIGHT END UP CRYING LATER.
clomp clomp
tmp tmp tmp
I WON'T CRY.
I'm strong.
You'll regret it!
I won't.
I'm sturdy.
THUS ...
...THE SILLY CYCLE OF PER-SUASION AND DENIAL APPAR-ENTLY WENT ON.
chirp chirp chirp chirp
THE NEXT MORNING.

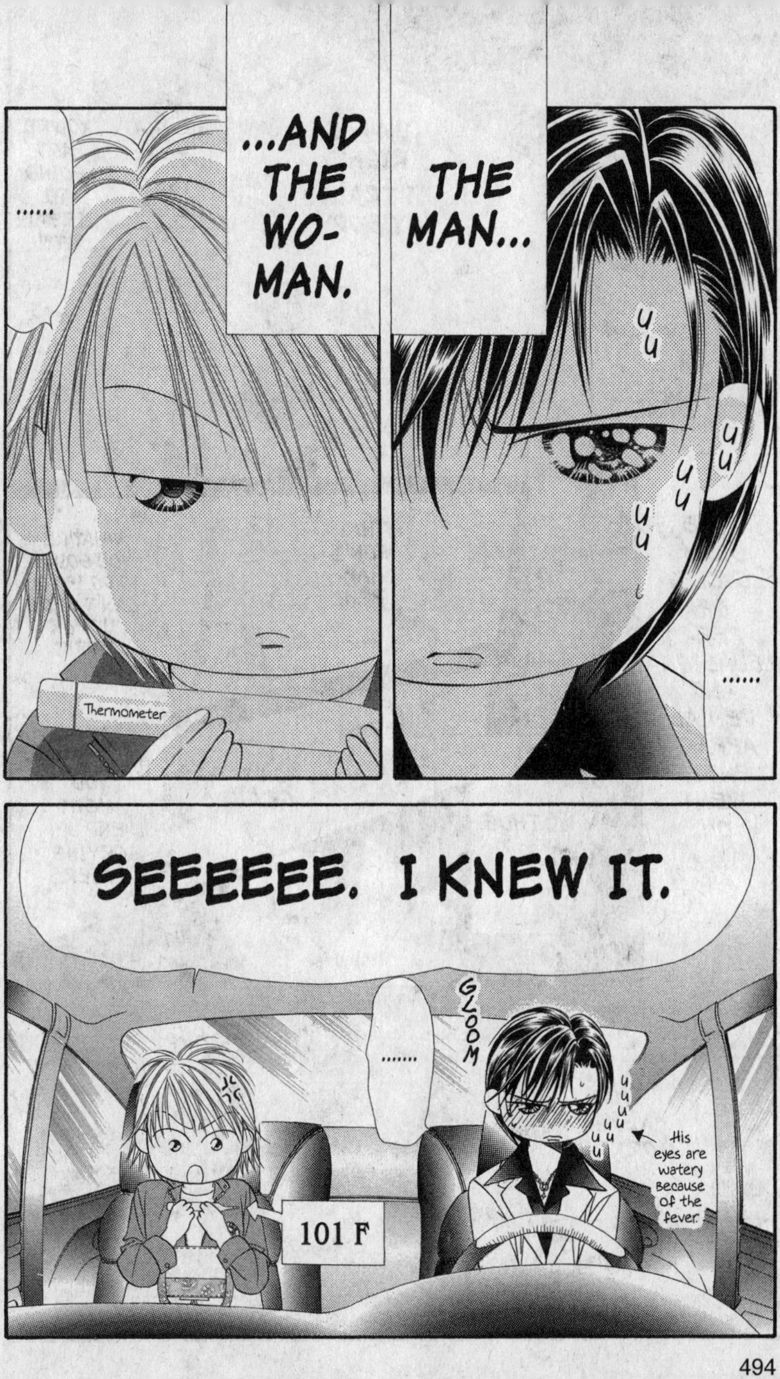
THE MAN...
uu uu uu uu
......
...AND THE WO-MAN.
......
Thermometer
SEEEEEE. I KNEW IT.
GLOOM
uu uu uu
His eyes are watery because of the fever.
......
101 F

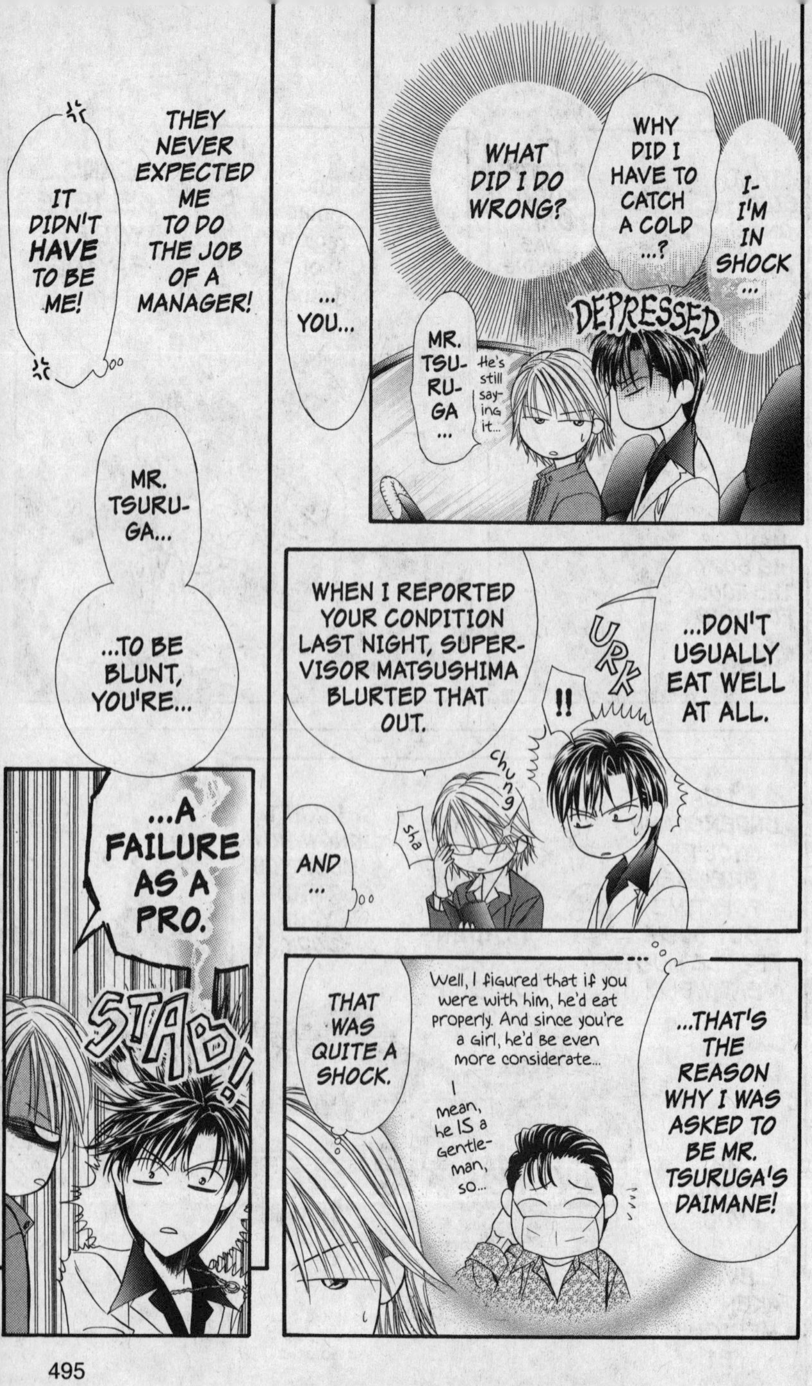
I- I'M IN SHOCK...
WHY DID I HAVE TO CATCH A COLD...?
WHAT DID I DO WRONG?
DEPRESSED
MR. TSURUGA...
He's still saying it...
...YOU...
...DON'T USUALLY EAT WELL AT ALL.
URK
!!
WHEN I REPORTED YOUR CONDITION LAST NIGHT, SUPERVISOR MATSUSHIMA BLURTED THAT OUT.
chung
sha
AND...
...THAT'S THE REASON WHY I WAS ASKED TO BE MR. TSURUGA'S DAIMANE!
...
Well, I figured that if you were with him, he'd eat properly. And since you're a girl, he'd be even more considerate...
I mean, he IS a gentleman, so...
THAT WAS QUITE A SHOCK.
THEY NEVER EXPECTED ME TO DO THE JOB OF A MANAGER!
IT DIDN'T HAVE TO BE ME!
MR. TSURUGA...
...TO BE BLUNT, YOU'RE...
...A FAILURE AS A PRO.
STAB!

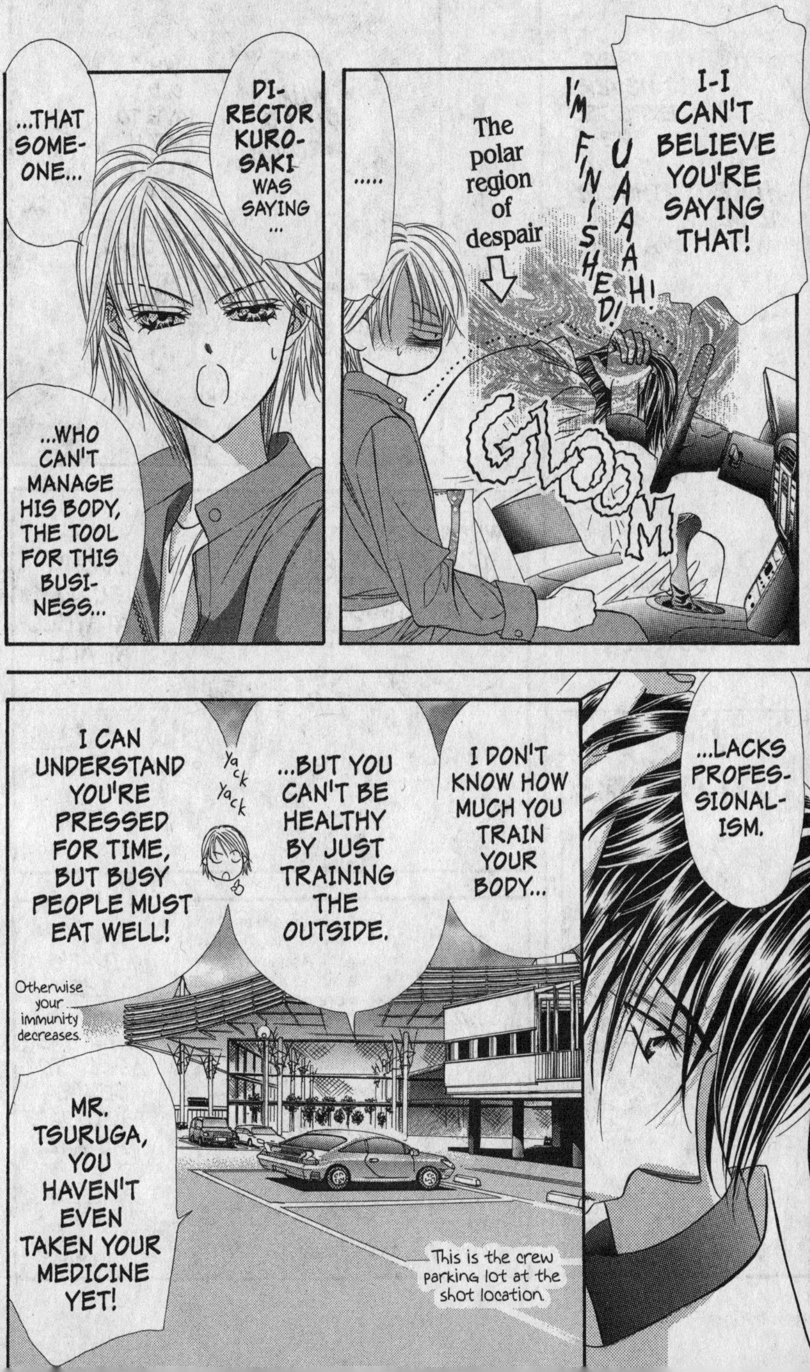
I-I CAN'T BELIEVE YOU'RE SAYING THAT!
UAAAAH!
I'M FINISHED!
The polar region of despair
.....
GLOOM
DIRECTOR KUROSAKI WAS SAYING...
...THAT SOMEONE...
...WHO CAN'T MANAGE HIS BODY, THE TOOL FOR THIS BUSINESS...
...LACKS PROFESSIONALISM.
I DON'T KNOW HOW MUCH YOU TRAIN YOUR BODY...
...BUT YOU CAN'T BE HEALTHY BY JUST TRAINING THE OUTSIDE.
Yack Yack
I CAN UNDERSTAND YOU'RE PRESSED FOR TIME, BUT BUSY PEOPLE MUST EAT WELL!
Otherwise your immunity decreases.
This is the crew parking lot at the shot location.
MR. TSURUGA, YOU HAVEN'T EVEN TAKEN YOUR MEDICINE YET!

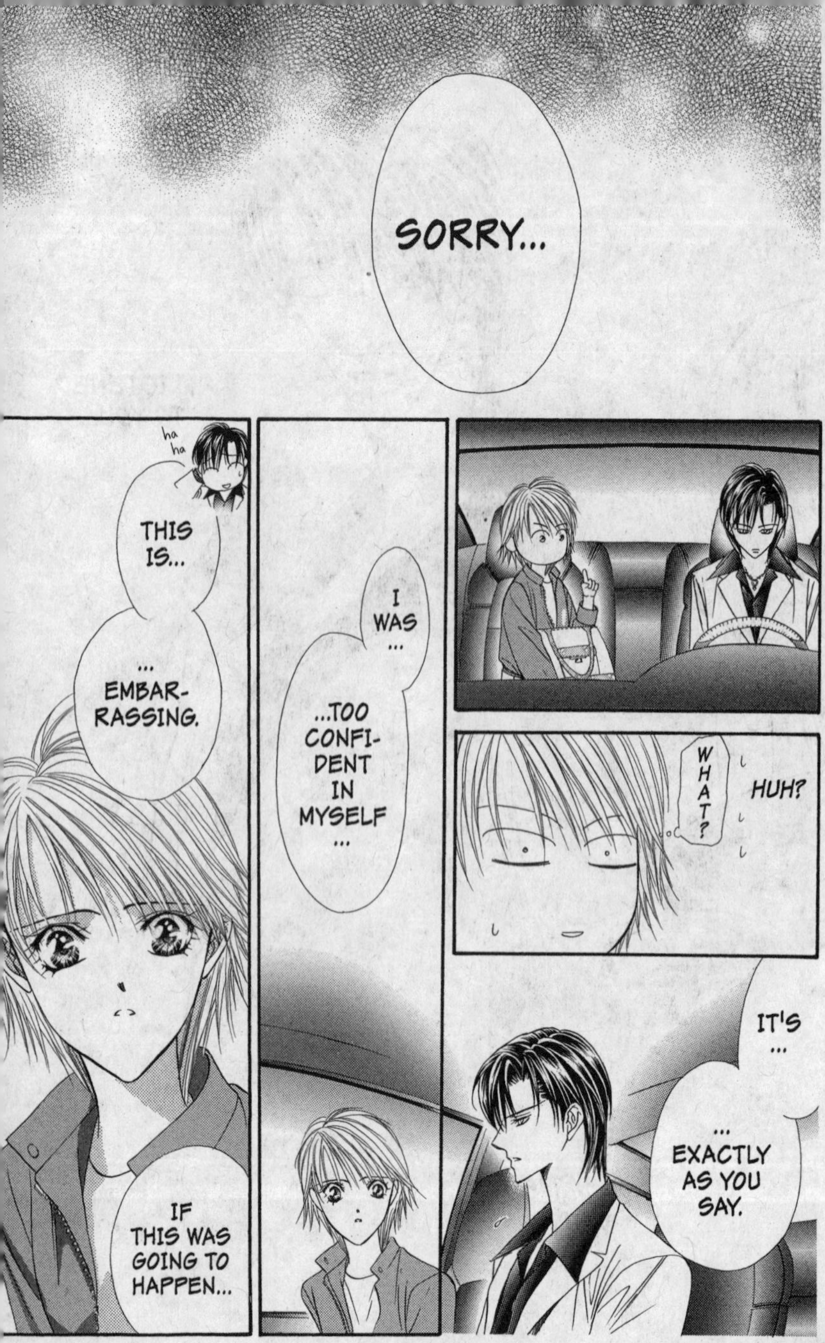
SORRY...
HUH?
WHAT?
I WAS...
...TOO CONFIDENT IN MYSELF...
IT'S...
...EXACTLY AS YOU SAY.
ha ha
THIS IS...
...EMBARRASSING.
IF THIS WAS GOING TO HAPPEN...

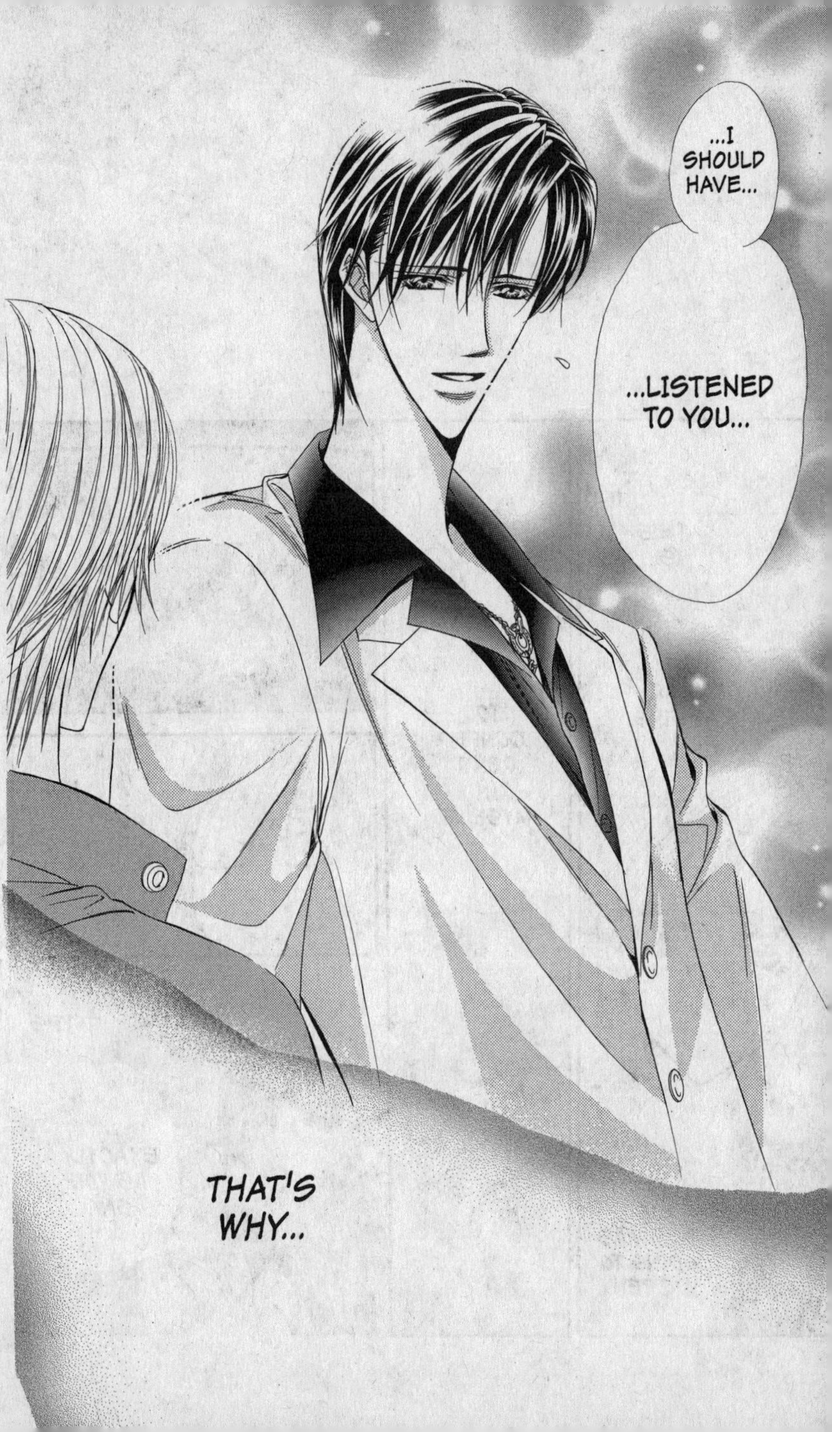
...I SHOULD HAVE...
...LISTENED TO YOU...
THAT'S WHY...

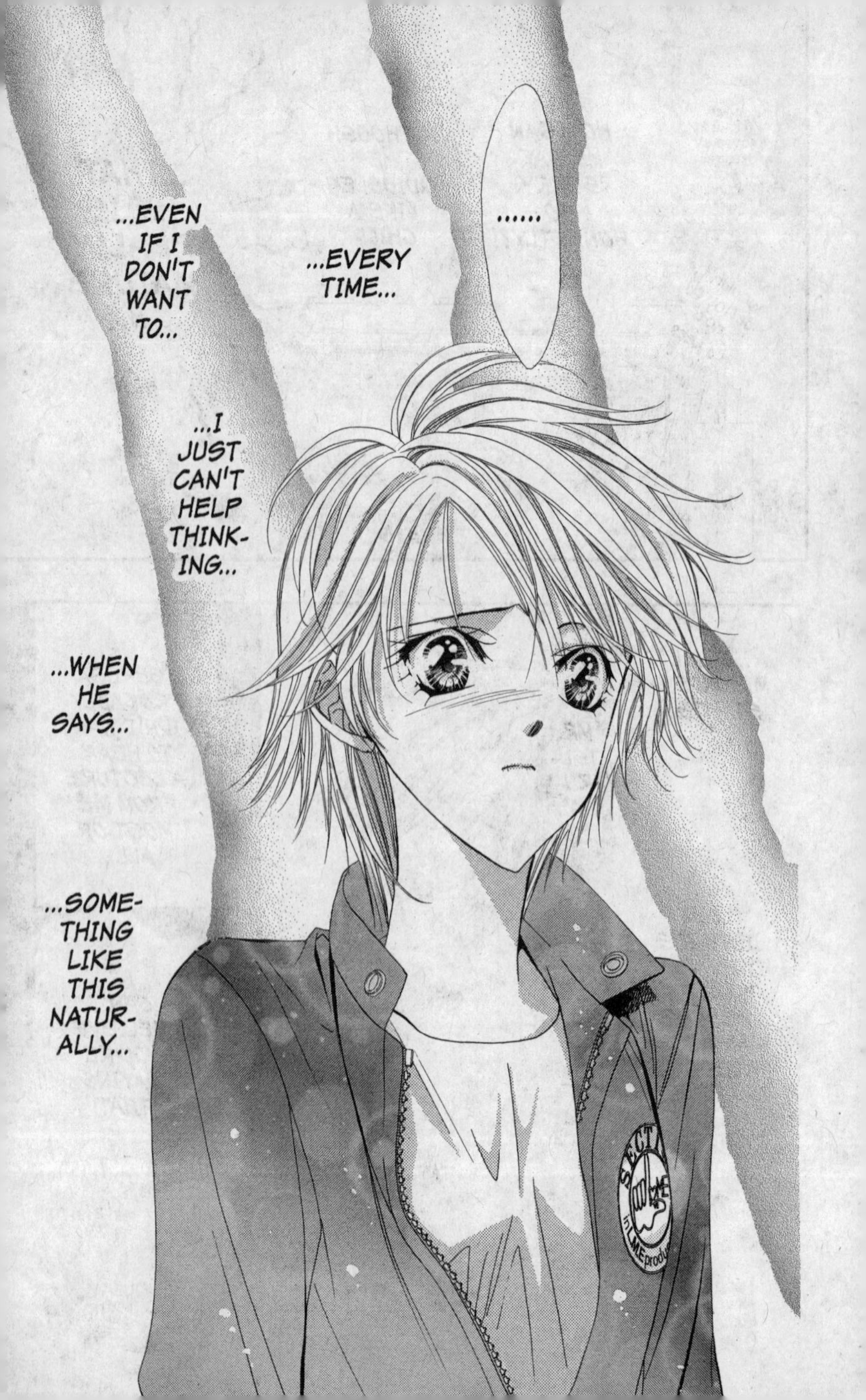
......
...EVERY TIME...
...EVEN IF I DON'T WANT TO...
...I JUST CAN'T HELP THINKING...
...WHEN HE SAYS...
...SOMETHING LIKE THIS NATURALLY...

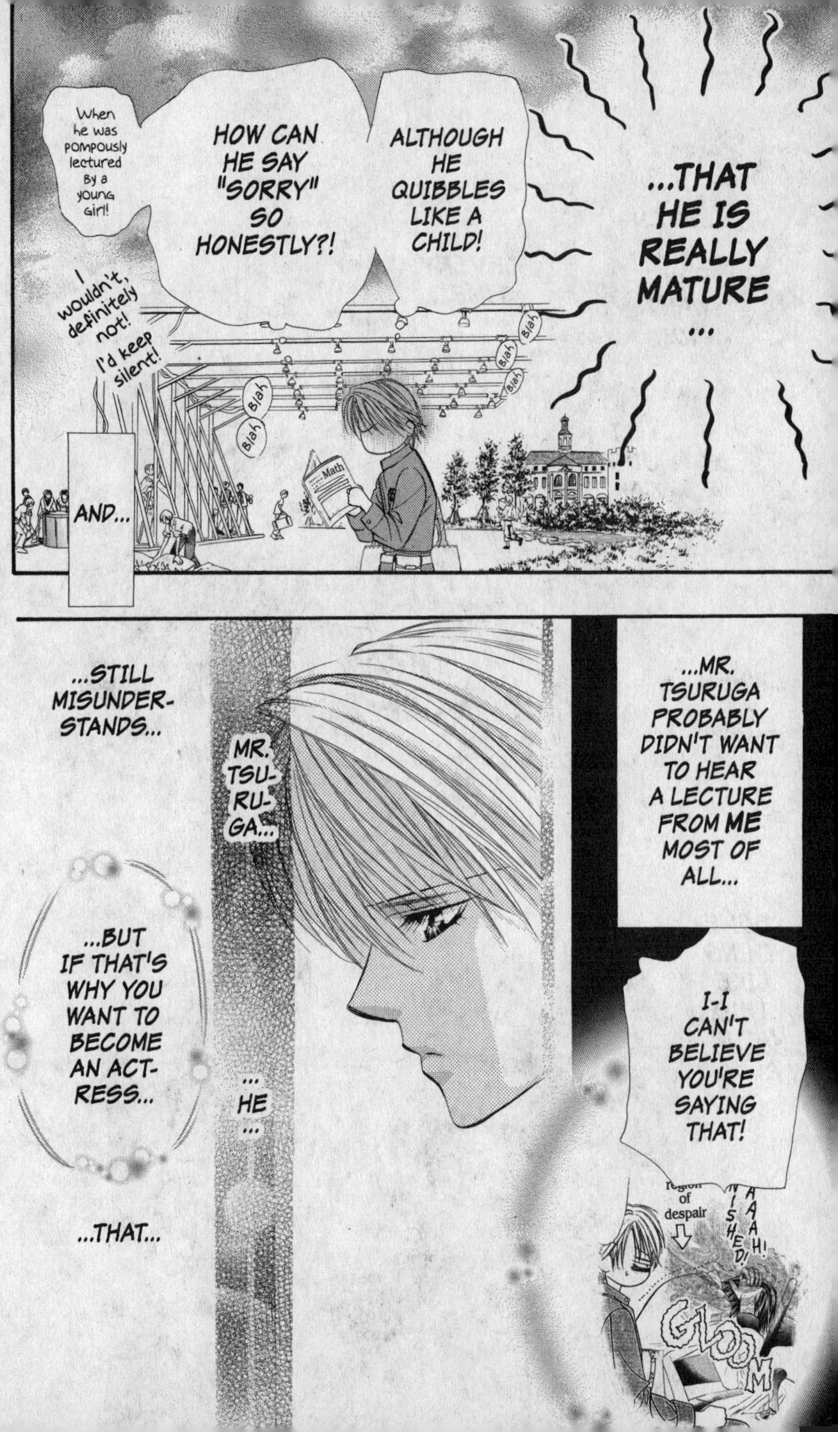
...THAT HE IS REALLY MATURE...
ALTHOUGH HE QUIBBLES LIKE A CHILD!
HOW CAN HE SAY "SORRY" SO HONESTLY?!
When he was pompously lectured By a young Girl!
I wouldn't, definitely not! I'd keep silent!
Blah Blah
Blah Blah
Blah Blah
AND...
...MR. TSURUGA PROBABLY DIDN'T WANT TO HEAR A LECTURE FROM ME MOST OF ALL...
I-I CAN'T BELIEVE YOU'RE SAYING THAT!
AAAAH!
NISHED!
region of despair
GLOOM
MR. TSU-RU-GA...
...HE...
...STILL MISUNDER-STANDS...
...BUT IF THAT'S WHY YOU WANT TO BECOME AN ACT-RESS...
...THAT...

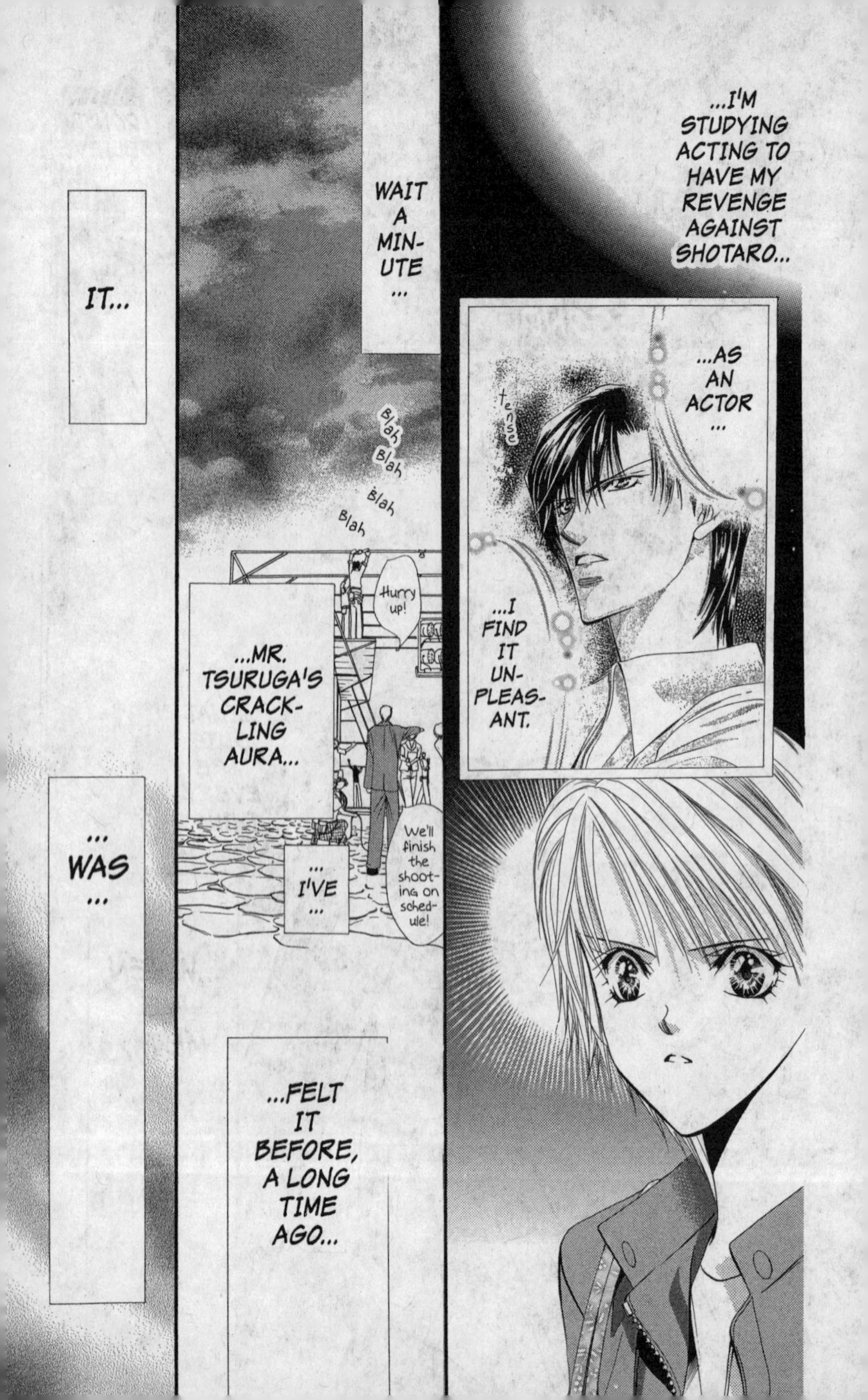
...I'M STUDYING ACTING TO HAVE MY REVENGE AGAINST SHOTARO...
...AS AN ACTOR...
tense
...I FIND IT UNPLEASANT.
WAIT A MINUTE...
Blah Blah Blah Blah
Hurry up!
...MR. TSURUGA'S CRACKLING AURA...
We'll finish the shooting on schedule!
...I'VE...
...FELT IT BEFORE, A LONG TIME AGO...
IT...
...WAS...

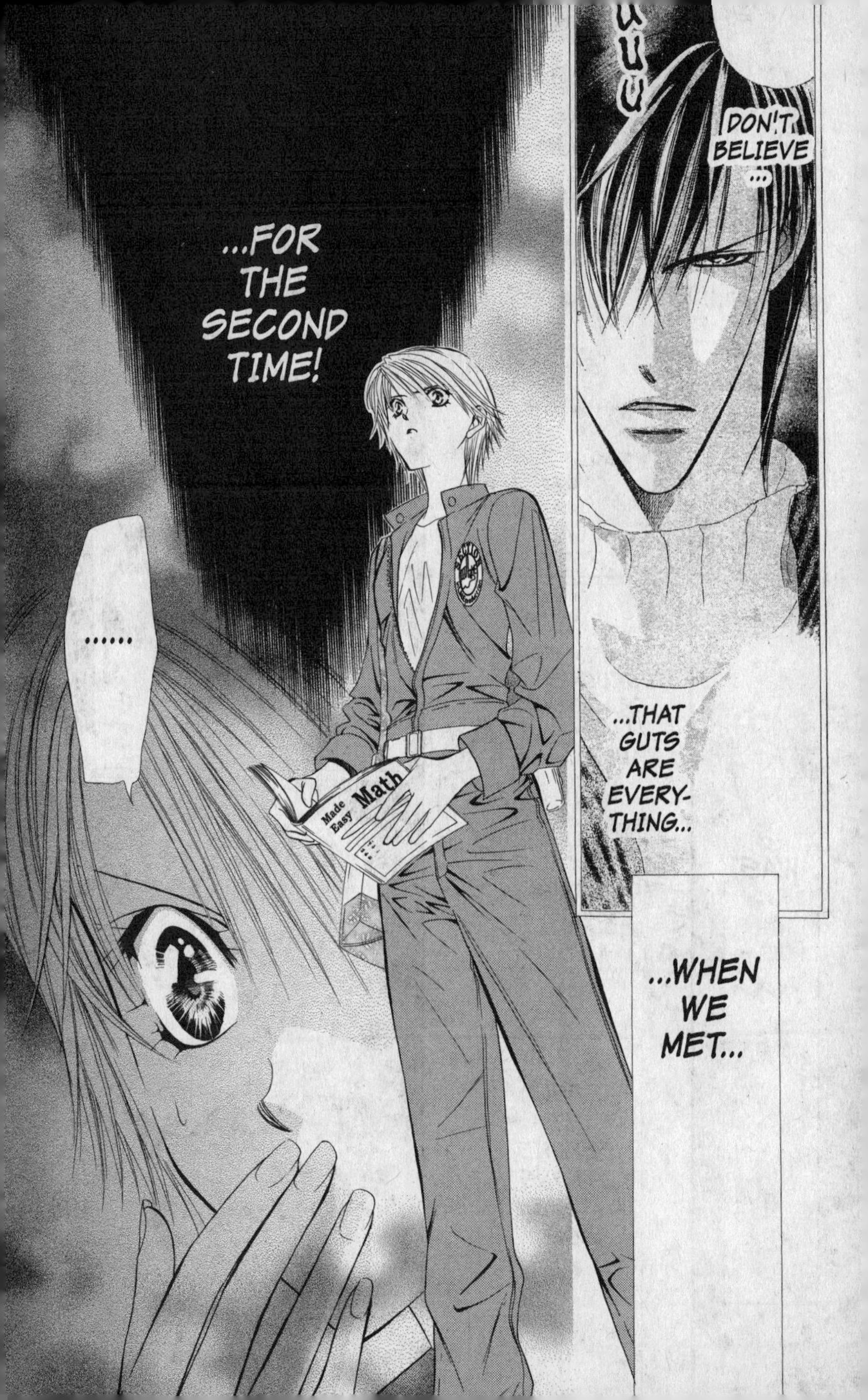
DON'T BELIEVE ...
...THAT GUTS ARE EVERYTHING...
...WHEN WE MET...
...FOR THE SECOND TIME!
......

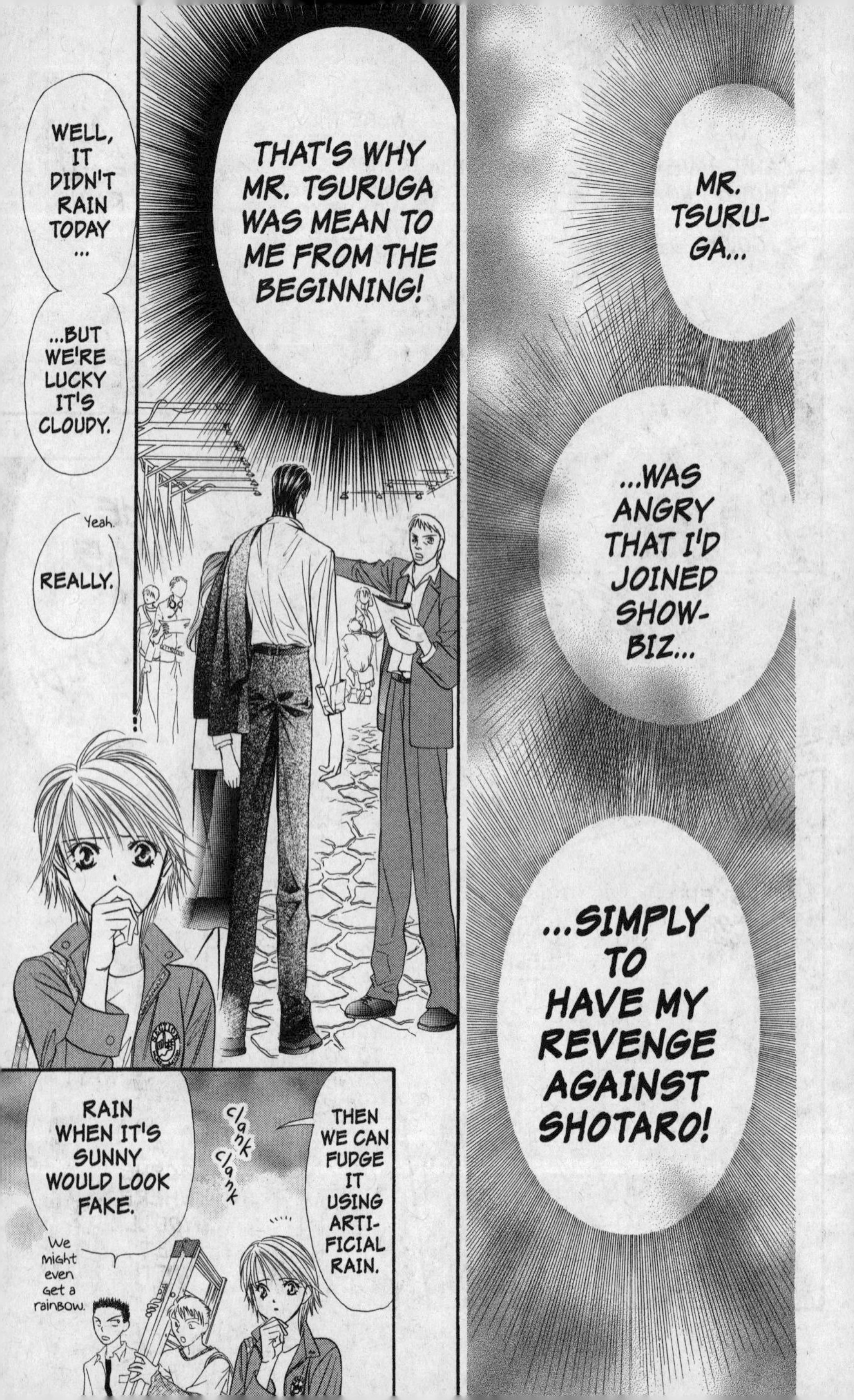
MR. TSURU-GA...
...WAS ANGRY THAT I'D JOINED SHOW-BIZ...
...SIMPLY TO HAVE MY REVENGE AGAINST SHOTARO!
THAT'S WHY MR. TSURUGA WAS MEAN TO ME FROM THE BEGINNING!
WELL, IT DIDN'T RAIN TODAY...
...BUT WE'RE LUCKY IT'S CLOUDY.
Yeah.
REALLY.
THEN WE CAN FUDGE IT USING ARTI-FICIAL RAIN.
clank clank
RAIN WHEN IT'S SUNNY WOULD LOOK FAKE.
We might even get a rainbow.

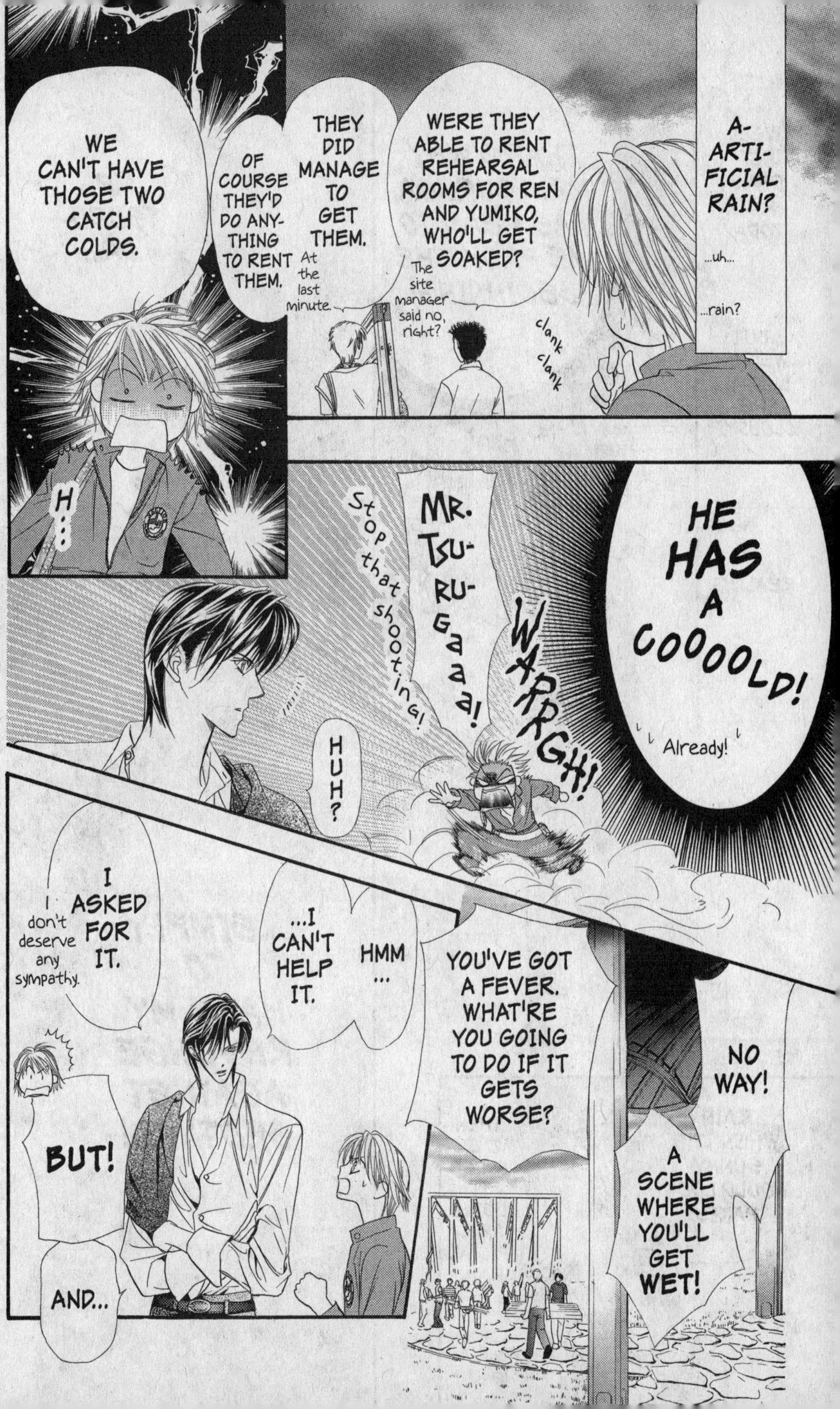
A-ARTIFICIAL RAIN?
...uh...
...rain?
WERE THEY ABLE TO RENT REHEARSAL ROOMS FOR REN AND YUMIKO, WHO'LL GET SOAKED?
The site manager said no, right?
clank clank
THEY DID MANAGE TO GET THEM.
At the last minute.
OF COURSE THEY'D DO ANYTHING TO RENT THEM.
WE CAN'T HAVE THOSE TWO CATCH COLDS.
H...
HE HAS A COOOOOLD!
Already!
WARRGH!
MR. TSURUGaaaa!
Stop that shooting!
HUH?
NO WAY!
A SCENE WHERE YOU'LL GET WET!
YOU'VE GOT A FEVER. WHAT'RE YOU GOING TO DO IF IT GETS WORSE?
HMM...
...I CAN'T HELP IT.
I ASKED FOR IT.
I don't deserve any sympathy.
BUT!
AND...

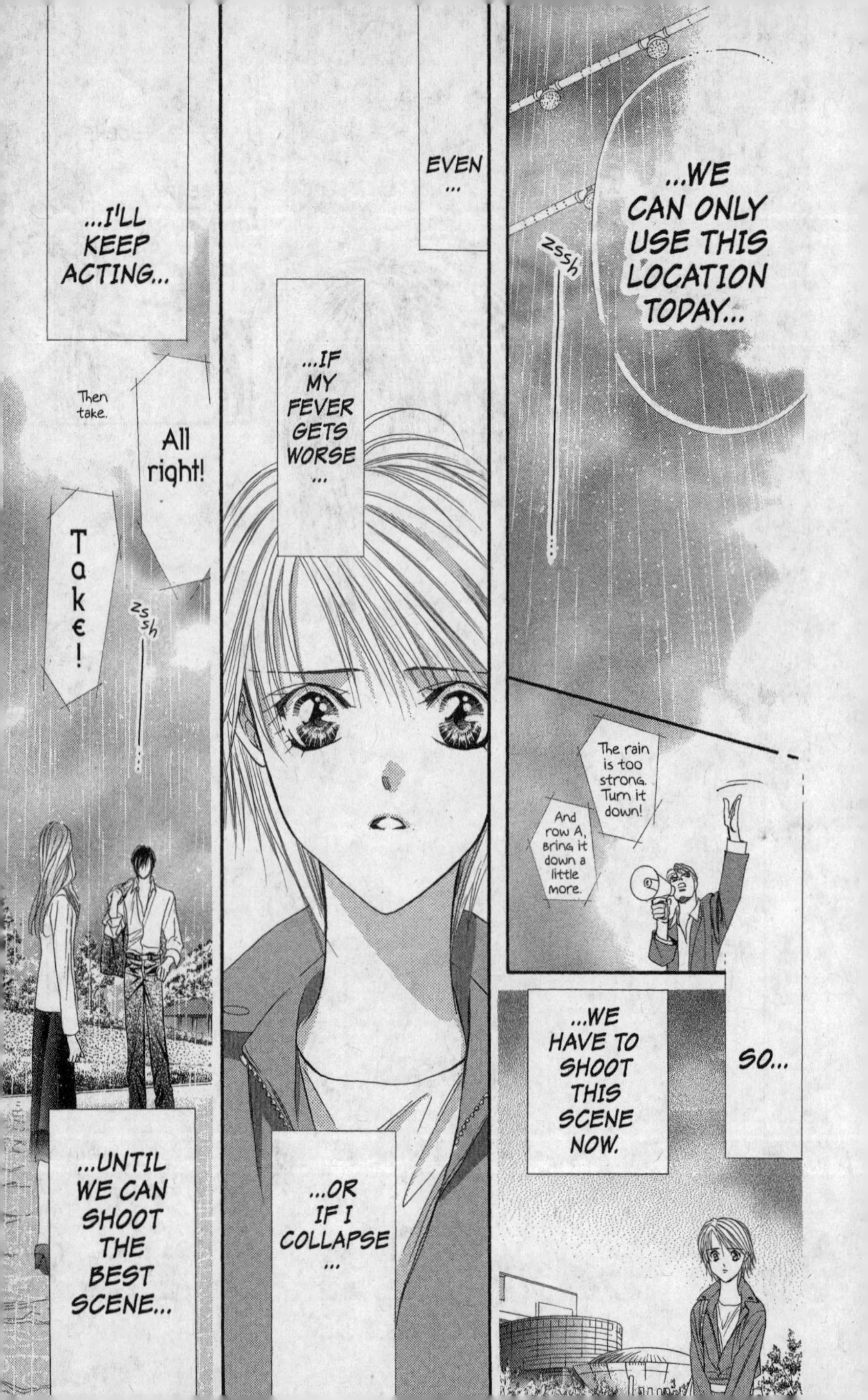
...WE CAN ONLY USE THIS LOCATION TODAY...
zssh
The rain is too strong. Turn it down!
And row A, bring it down a little more.
SO...
...WE HAVE TO SHOOT THIS SCENE NOW.
EVEN ...
...IF MY FEVER GETS WORSE ...
...OR IF I COLLAPSE ...
...I'LL KEEP ACTING...
All right!
Then take.
Take!
zssh
...UNTIL WE CAN SHOOT THE BEST SCENE...

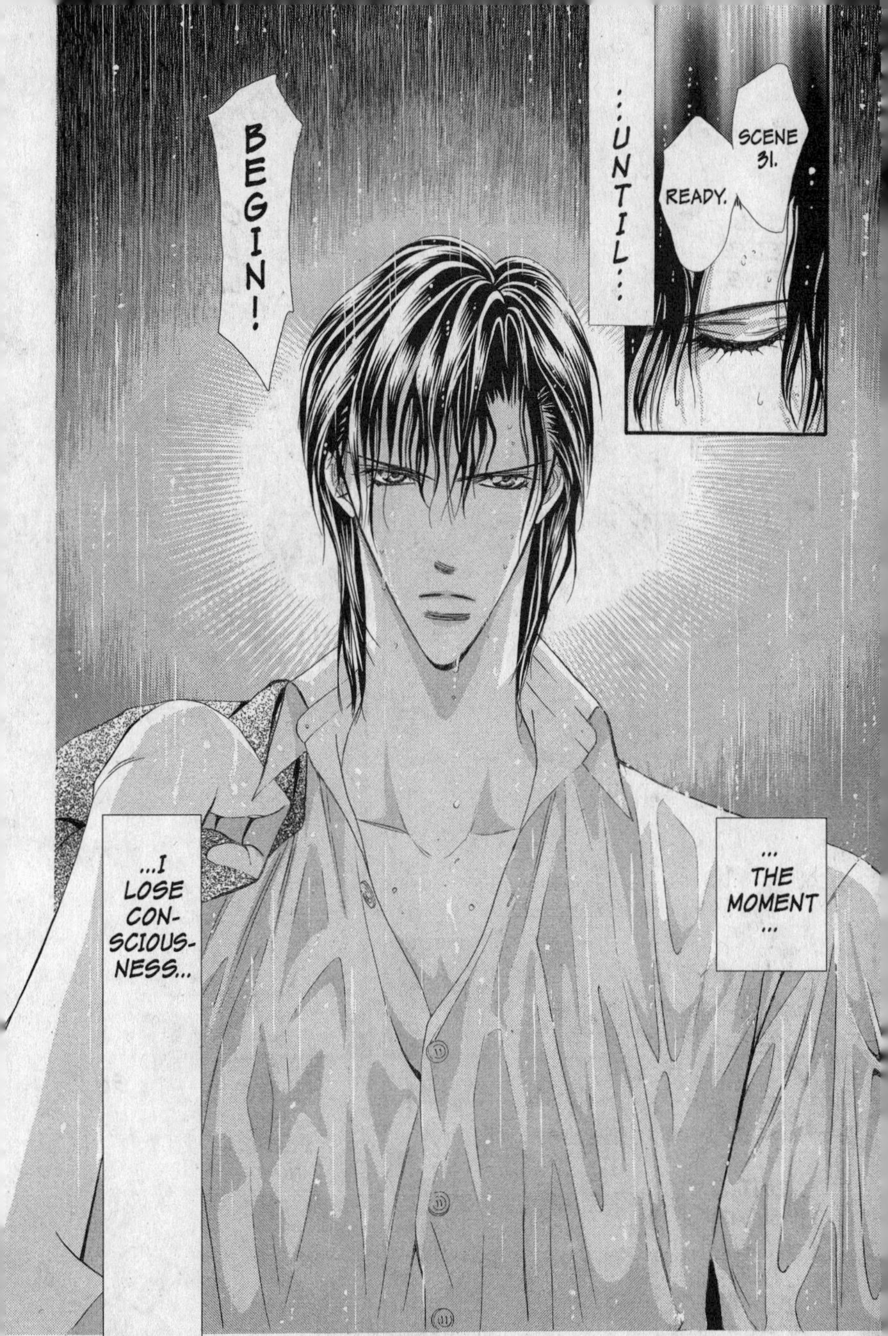
SCENE 31.
READY.
...UNTIL...
BEGIN!
... THE MOMENT ...
...I LOSE CON-SCIOUS-NESS...

End of Act 33

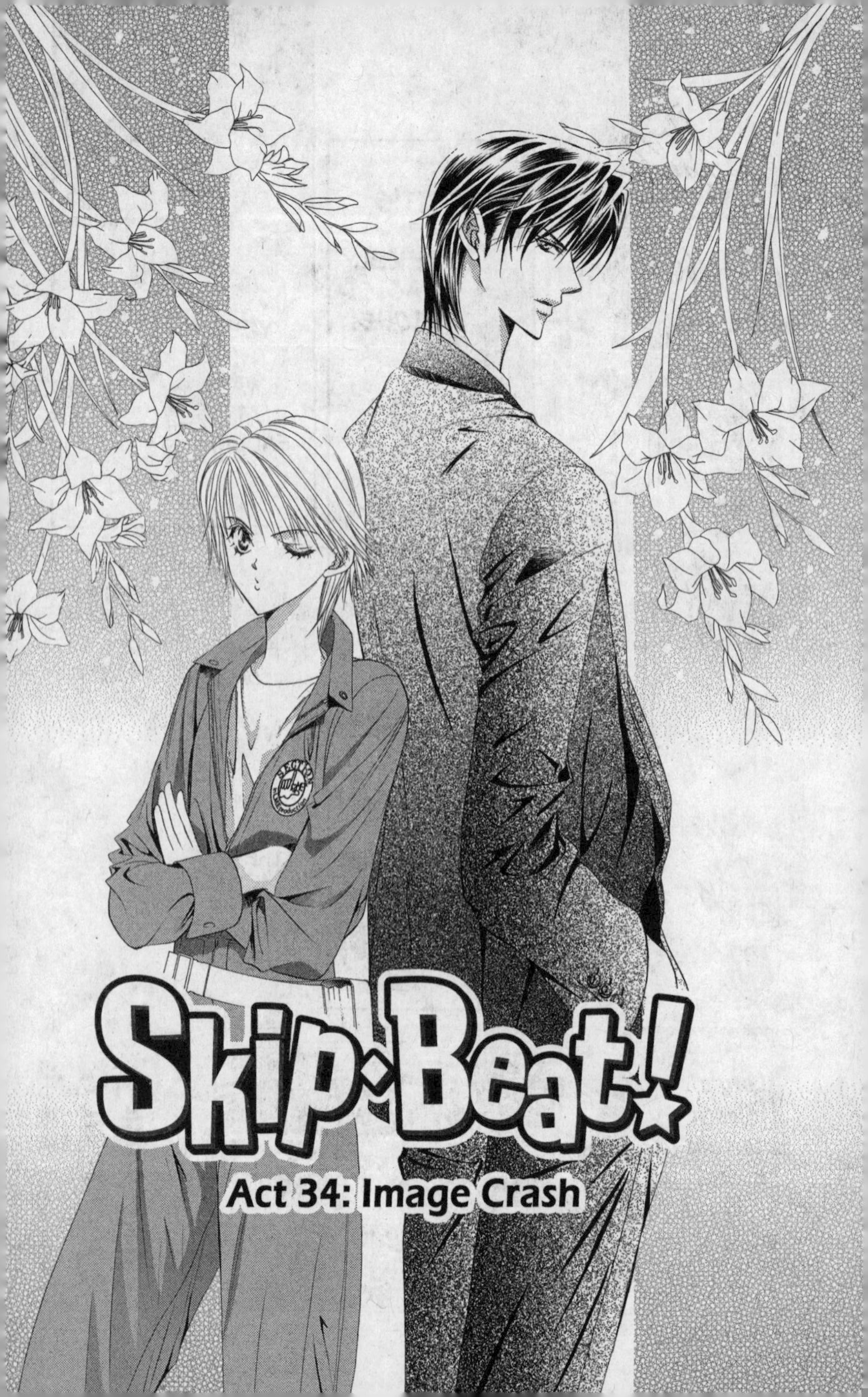
Skip·Beat!
Act 34: Image Crash

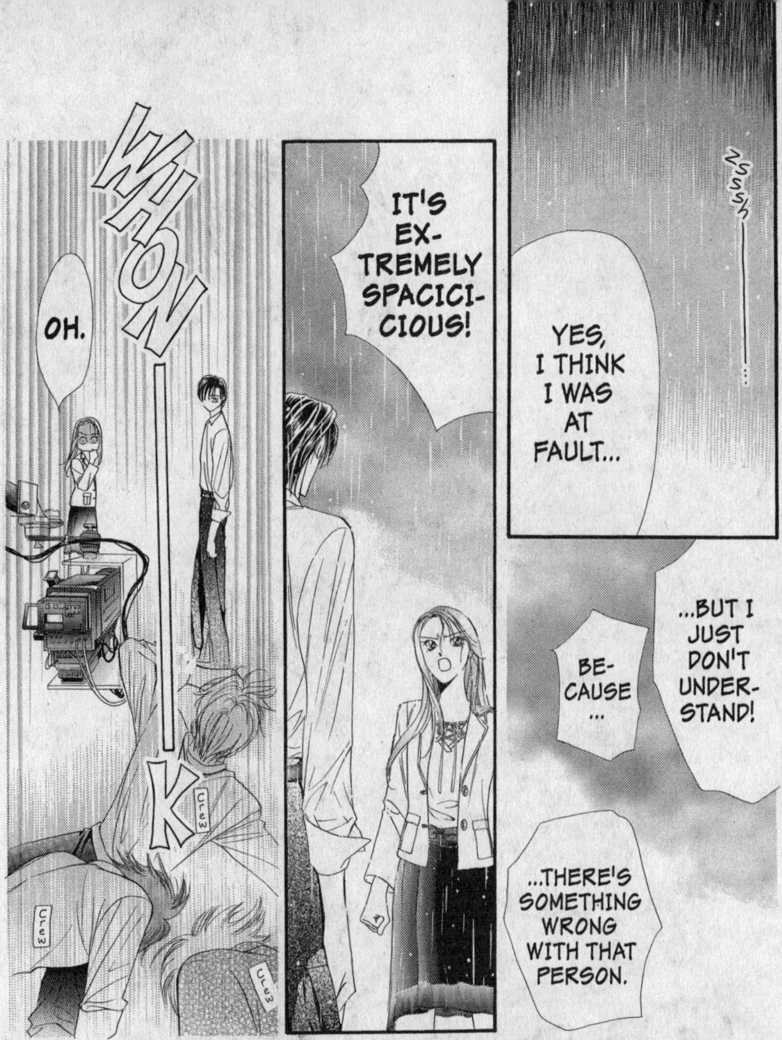
ZSSSH——...
YES, I THINK I WAS AT FAULT...
...BUT I JUST DON'T UNDERSTAND!
BE-CAUSE...
...THERE'S SOMETHING WRONG WITH THAT PERSON.
IT'S EX-TREMELY SPACICI-CIOUS!
WHON—K
OH.
Crew
Crew
Crew

This is LME's Formal Name

This...!! ↙

LORY'S MAJESTIC ENTERTAINMENT

Lory's Majestic Entertain-ment.

Please remember it, everybody.

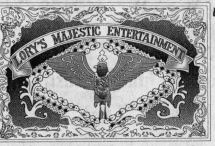

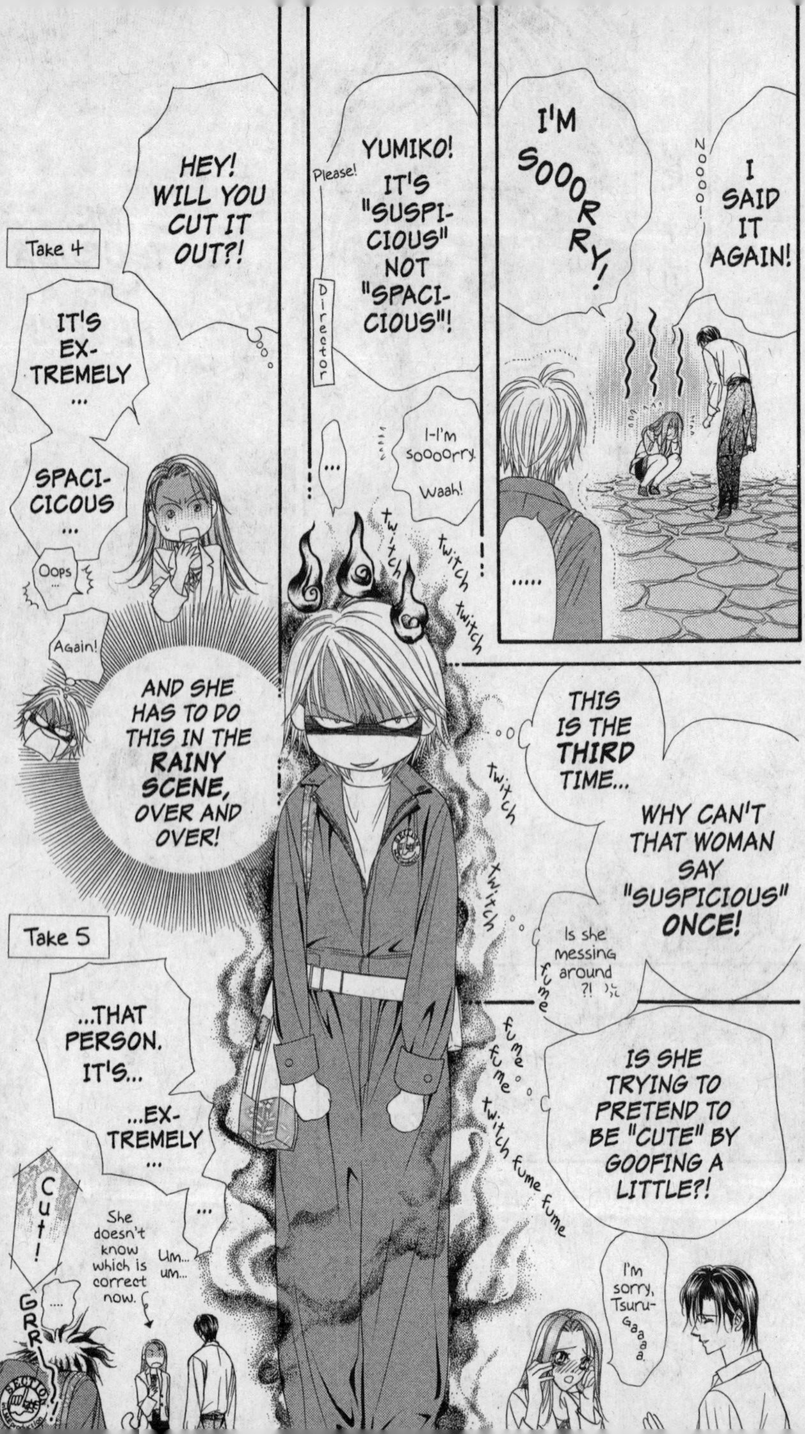
I SAID IT AGAIN!
NOOOO!
I'M SOOORRY!
.....
YUMIKO! IT'S "SUSPICIOUS" NOT "SPACICIOUS"!
Please!
Director
...
I-I'm soooorry.
Waah!
twitch
twitch
twitch
THIS IS THE THIRD TIME...
WHY CAN'T THAT WOMAN SAY "SUSPICIOUS" ONCE!
Is she messing around?!
twitch
twitch
fume
IS SHE TRYING TO PRETEND TO BE "CUTE" BY GOOFING A LITTLE?!
fume fume
twitch fume fume
I'm sorry, Tsuru-Gaaaa.
Take 4
HEY! WILL YOU CUT IT OUT?!
IT'S EX-TREMELY ...
SPACI-CICOUS ...
Oops ...
Again!
AND SHE HAS TO DO THIS IN THE RAINY SCENE, OVER AND OVER!
Take 5
...THAT PERSON. IT'S...
...EX-TREMELY ...
...
Um... um...
She doesn't know which is correct now.
Cut!
....
GRR!

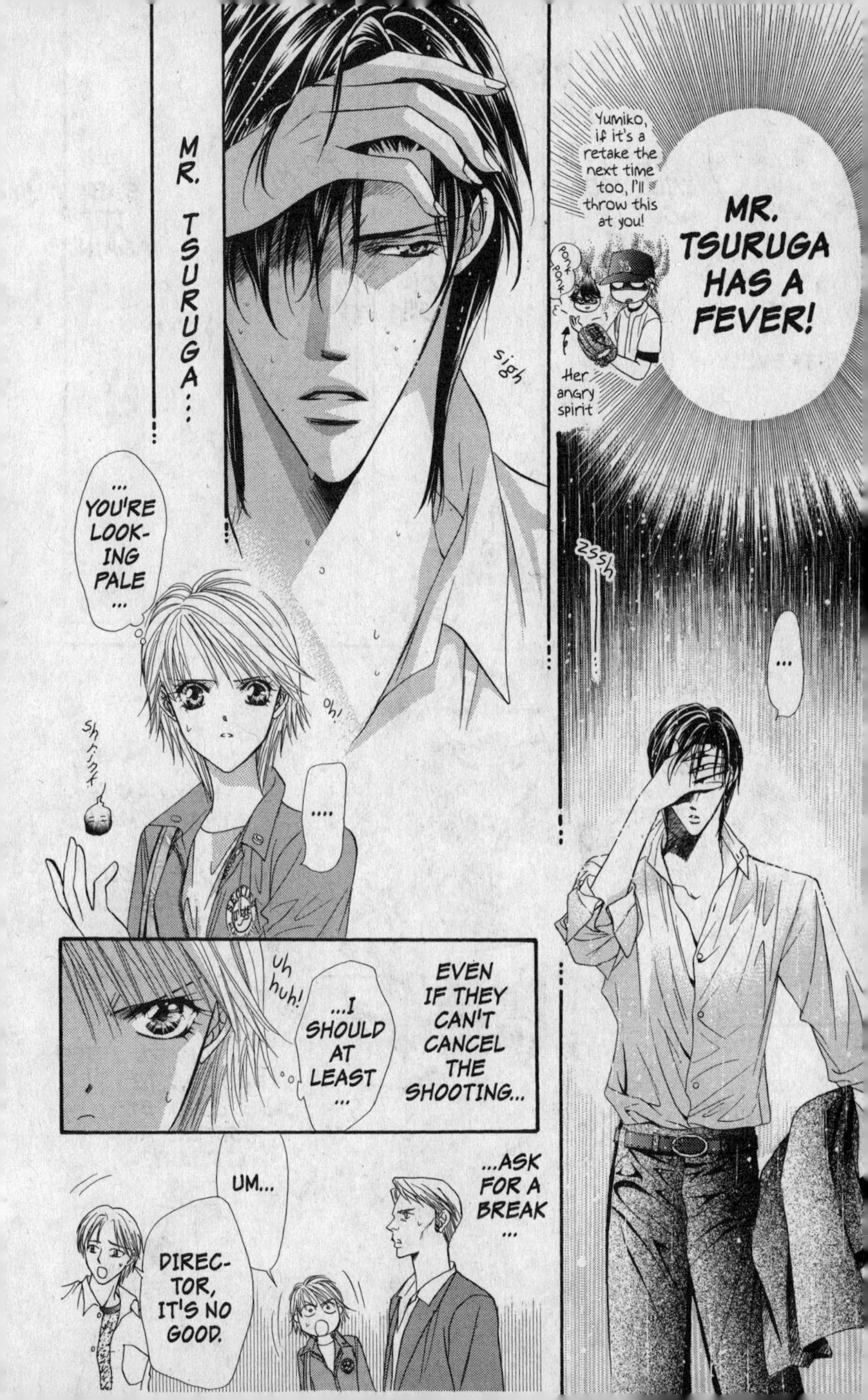
MR. TSURUGA HAS A FEVER!
Yumiko, if it's a retake the next time too, I'll throw this at you!
pont pont
Her angry spirit
zssh
...
MR. TSURUGA...
sigh
...YOU'RE LOOKING PALE...
oh!
shrink
....
EVEN IF THEY CAN'T CANCEL THE SHOOTING...
...I SHOULD AT LEAST...
uh huh!
...ASK FOR A BREAK...
UM...
DIRECTOR, IT'S NO GOOD.

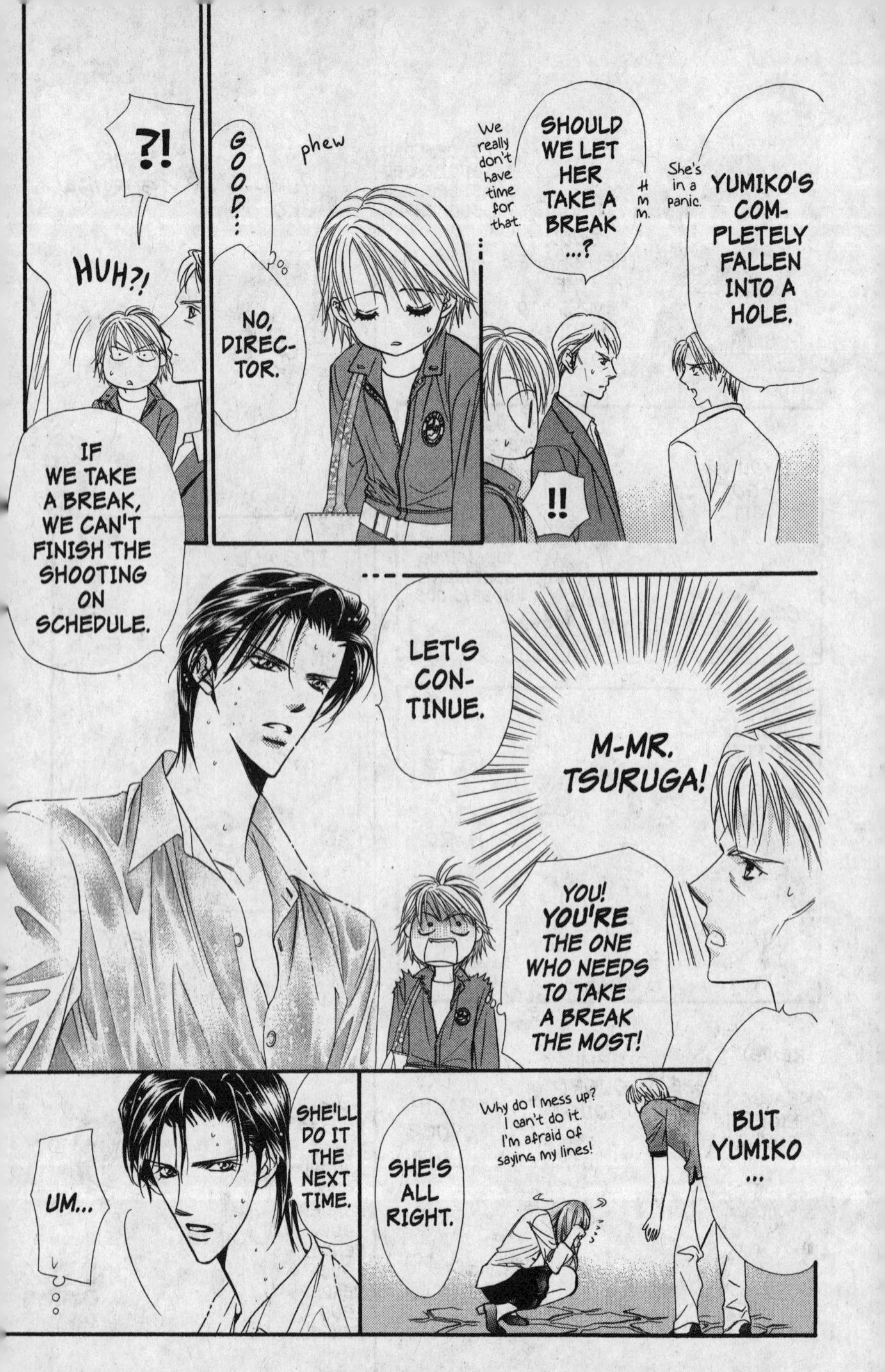
YUMIKO'S COMPLETELY FALLEN INTO A HOLE.
She's in a panic.
Hmm.
SHOULD WE LET HER TAKE A BREAK ...?
We really don't have time for that.
!!
phew
GOOD...
NO, DIRECTOR.
?!
HUH?!
IF WE TAKE A BREAK, WE CAN'T FINISH THE SHOOTING ON SCHEDULE.
LET'S CONTINUE.
M-MR. TSURUGA!
YOU! YOU'RE THE ONE WHO NEEDS TO TAKE A BREAK THE MOST!
BUT YUMIKO ...
Why do I mess up? I can't do it. I'm afraid of saying my lines!
SHE'S ALL RIGHT.
SHE'LL DO IT THE NEXT TIME.
UM...

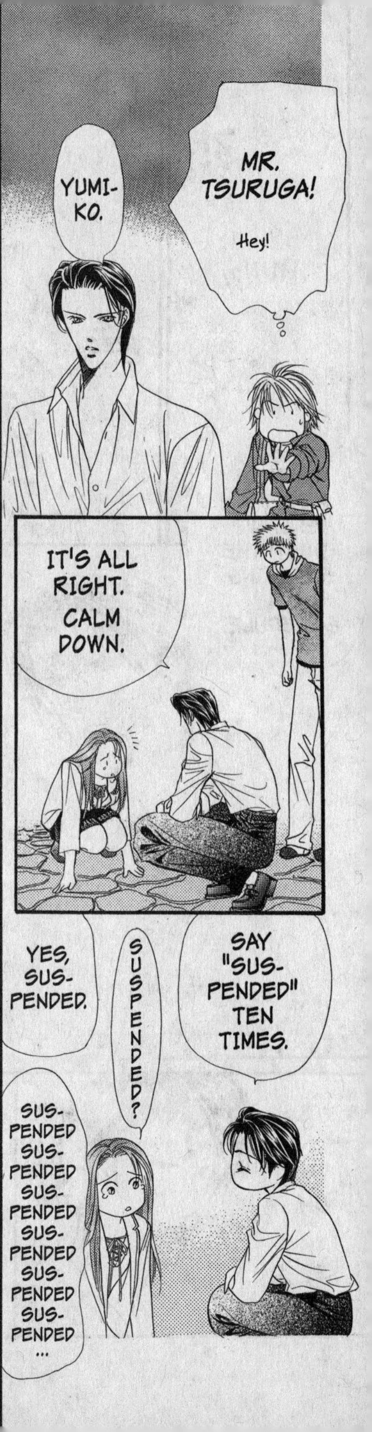
MR. TSURUGA!
Hey!
YUMI-KO.
IT'S ALL RIGHT. CALM DOWN.
SAY "SUS-PENDED" TEN TIMES.
SUSPENDED?
YES, SUS-PENDED.
SUS-PENDED SUS-PENDED SUS-PENDED SUS-PENDED SUS-PENDED SUS-PENDED ...
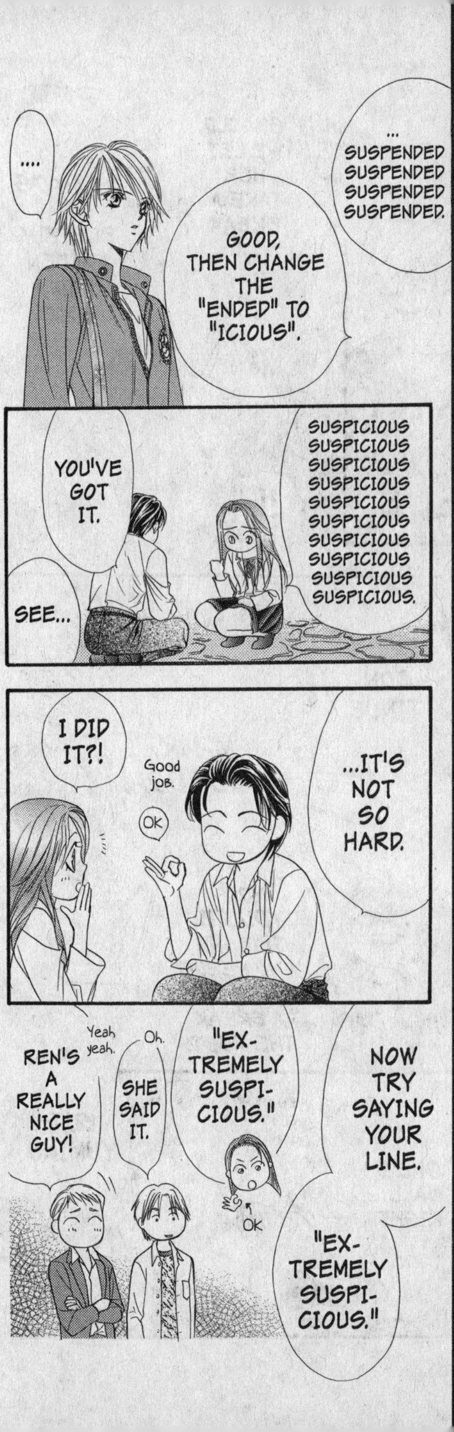
... SUSPENDED SUSPENDED SUSPENDED SUSPENDED.
GOOD, THEN CHANGE THE "ENDED" TO "ICIOUS".
....
SUSPICIOUS SUSPICIOUS SUSPICIOUS SUSPICIOUS SUSPICIOUS SUSPICIOUS SUSPICIOUS SUSPICIOUS SUSPICIOUS SUSPICIOUS.
YOU'VE GOT IT.
SEE...
...IT'S NOT SO HARD.
OK
Good job.
I DID IT?!
NOW TRY SAYING YOUR LINE.
"EX-TREMELY SUSPI-CIOUS."
OK
"EX-TREMELY SUSPI-CIOUS."
Oh.
SHE SAID IT.
Yeah yeah.
REN'S A REALLY NICE GUY!

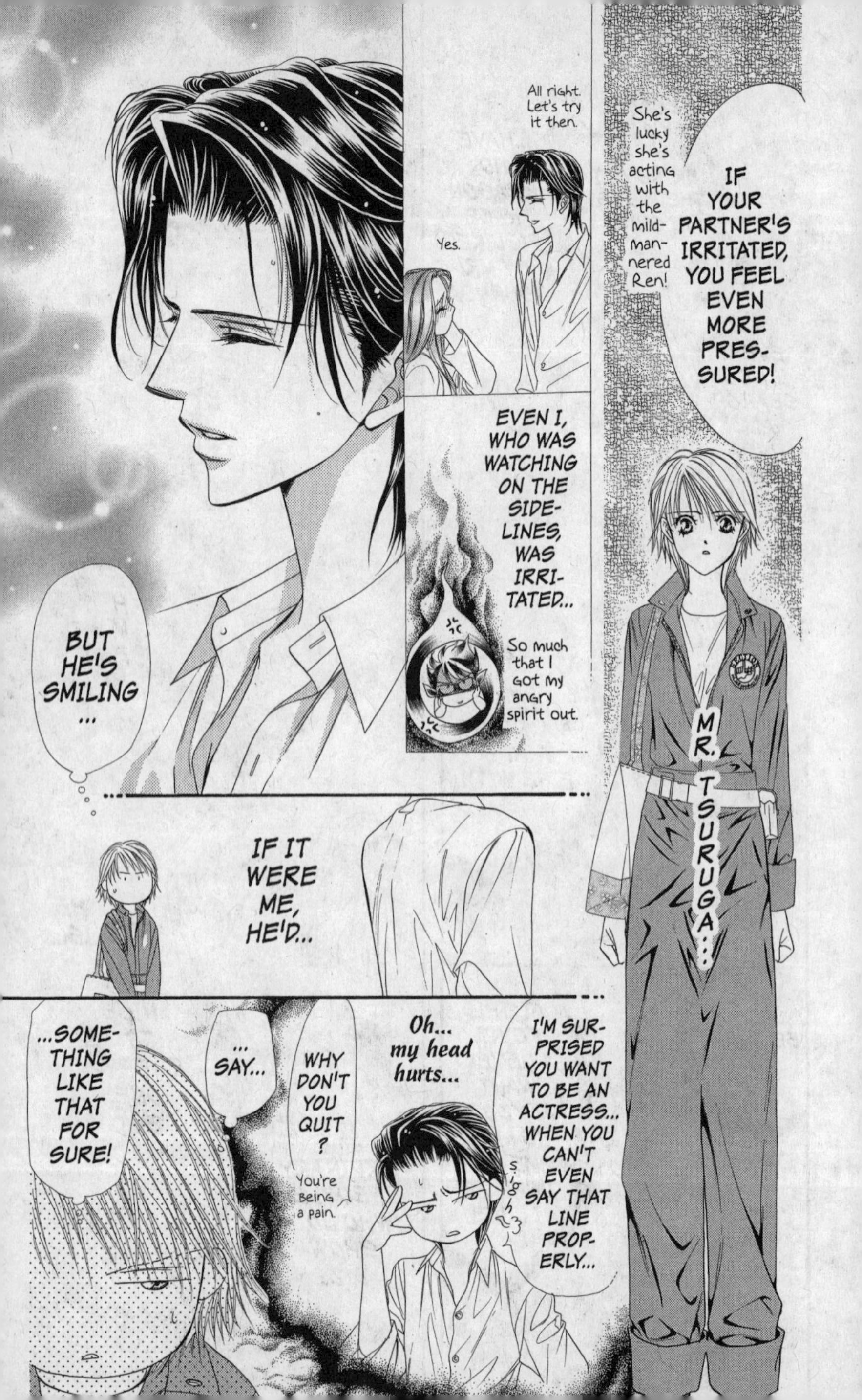
IF YOUR PARTNER'S IRRITATED, YOU FEEL EVEN MORE PRES-SURED!
She's lucky she's acting with the mild-mannered Ren!
MR. TSURUGA...
All right. Let's try it then.
Yes.
EVEN I, WHO WAS WATCHING ON THE SIDE-LINES, WAS IRRITATED...
So much that I got my angry spirit out.
BUT HE'S SMILING...
IF IT WERE ME, HE'D...
I'M SURPRISED YOU WANT TO BE AN ACTRESS... WHEN YOU CAN'T EVEN SAY THAT LINE PROPERLY...
sigh
Oh... my head hurts...
WHY DON'T YOU QUIT?
You're being a pain.
...SAY...
...SOMETHING LIKE THAT FOR SURE!

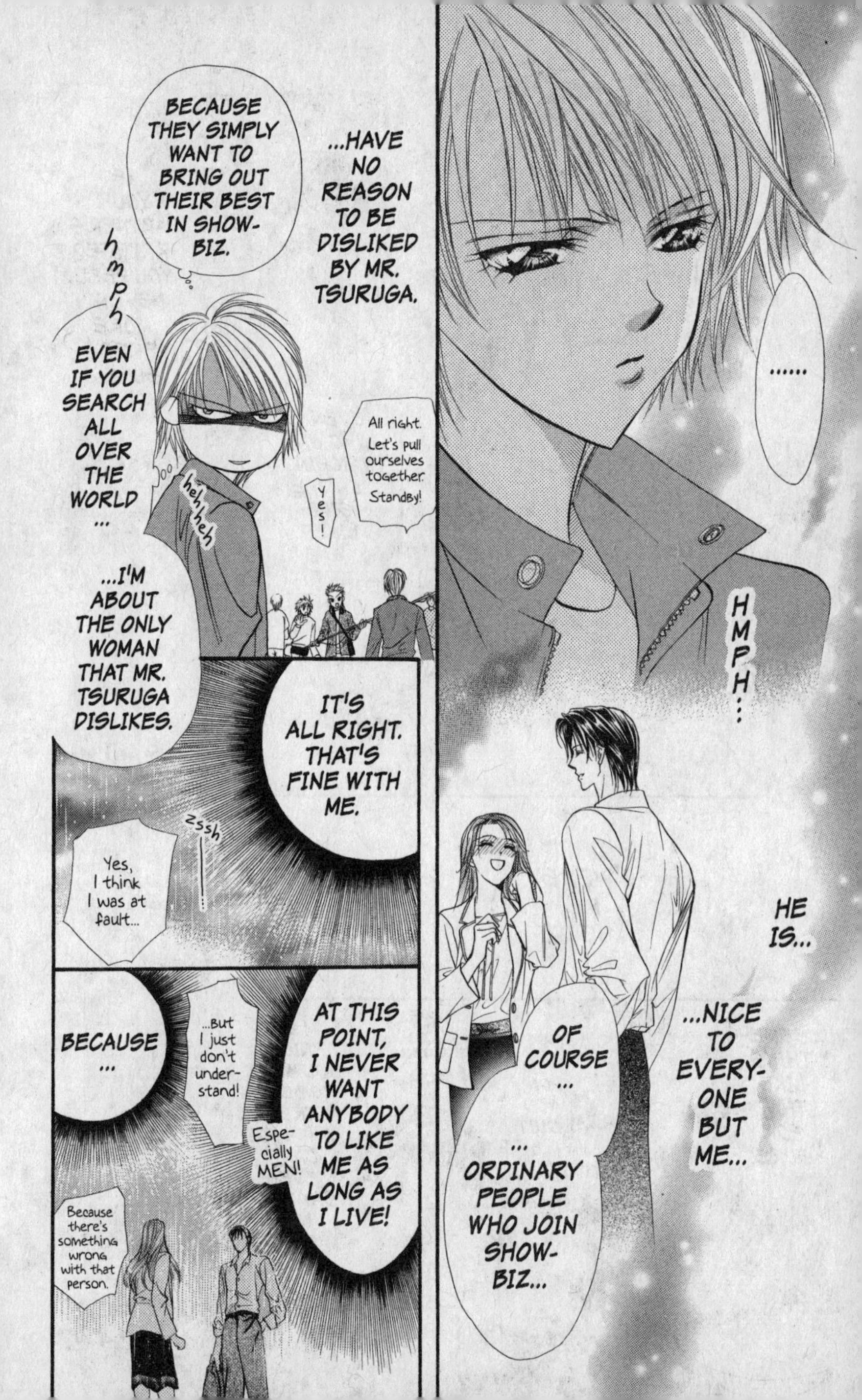

......
HMPH...
HE IS...
...NICE TO EVERYONE BUT ME...
OF COURSE...
...ORDINARY PEOPLE WHO JOIN SHOW-BIZ...
...HAVE NO REASON TO BE DISLIKED BY MR. TSURUGA.
BECAUSE THEY SIMPLY WANT TO BRING OUT THEIR BEST IN SHOW-BIZ.
hmph
All right. Let's pull ourselves together. Standby!
Yes!
heh heh heh
EVEN IF YOU SEARCH ALL OVER THE WORLD...
...I'M ABOUT THE ONLY WOMAN THAT MR. TSURUGA DISLIKES.
IT'S ALL RIGHT. THAT'S FINE WITH ME.
zssh
Yes, I think I was at fault...
AT THIS POINT, I NEVER WANT ANYBODY TO LIKE ME AS LONG AS I LIVE!
Especially MEN!
...But I just don't understand!
BECAUSE...
Because there's something wrong with that person.

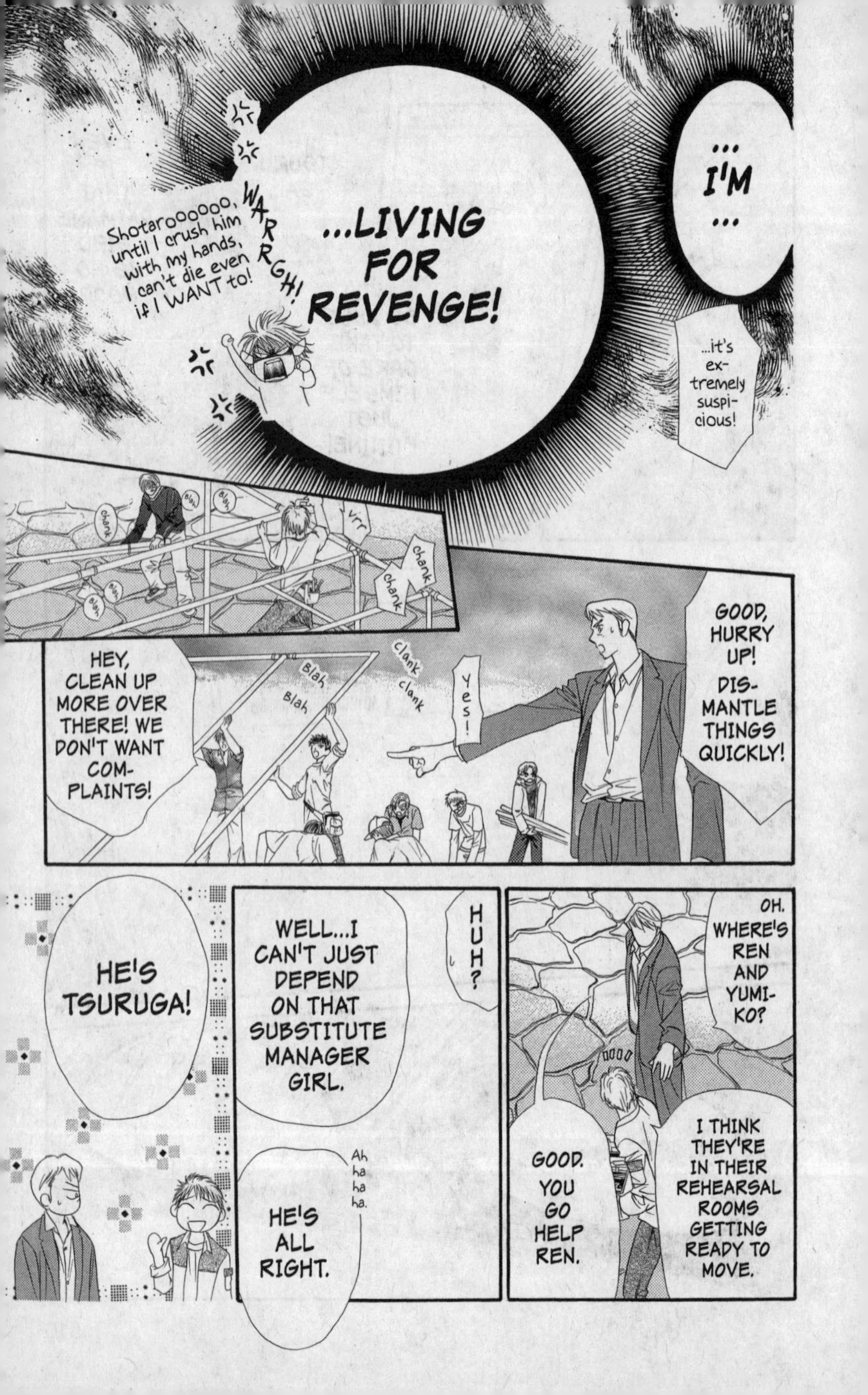
... I'M ...
...LIVING FOR REVENGE!
...it's extremely suspicious!
WARRGH!
Shotarooooooo, until I crush him with my hands, I can't die even if I WANT to!
blah
blah
chank
vrr
chank
chank
blah
blah
GOOD, HURRY UP! DIS-MANTLE THINGS QUICKLY!
Yes!
clank clank
Blah Blah
HEY, CLEAN UP MORE OVER THERE! WE DON'T WANT COM-PLAINTS!
OH. WHERE'S REN AND YUMI-KO?
I THINK THEY'RE IN THEIR REHEARSAL ROOMS GETTING READY TO MOVE.
GOOD. YOU GO HELP REN.
HUH?
WELL...I CAN'T JUST DEPEND ON THAT SUBSTITUTE MANAGER GIRL.
Ah ha ha ha.
HE'S ALL RIGHT.
HE'S TSURUGA!

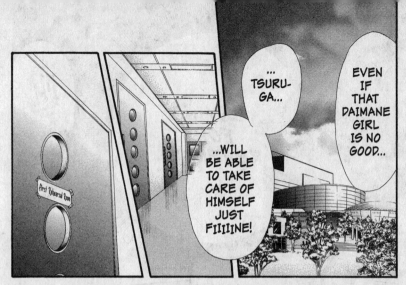

...
TSURU-
GA...

EVEN IF THAT DAIMANE GIRL IS NO GOOD...

...WILL BE ABLE TO TAKE CARE OF HIMSELF JUST FIIIIINE!

First Rehearsal Room

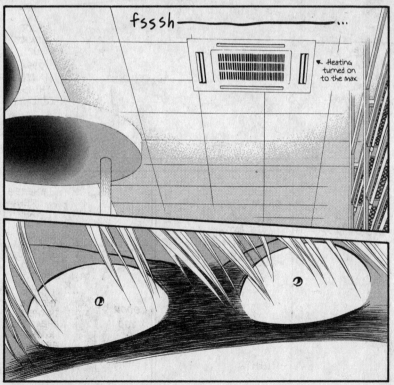

fsssh——...

Heating turned on to the max

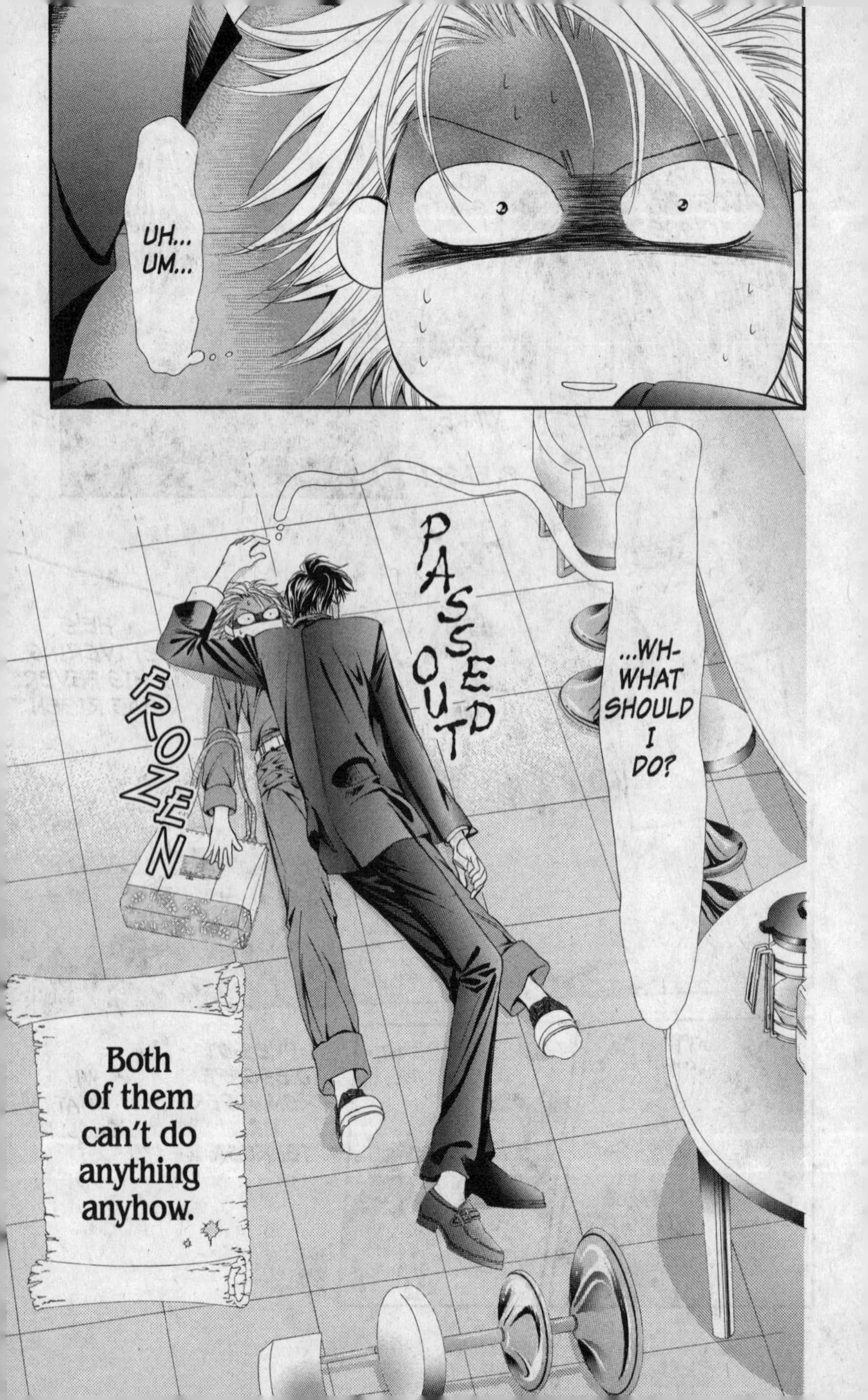
UH... UM...
...WH-WHAT SHOULD I DO?
PASSED OUT
FROZEN
Both of them can't do anything anyhow.

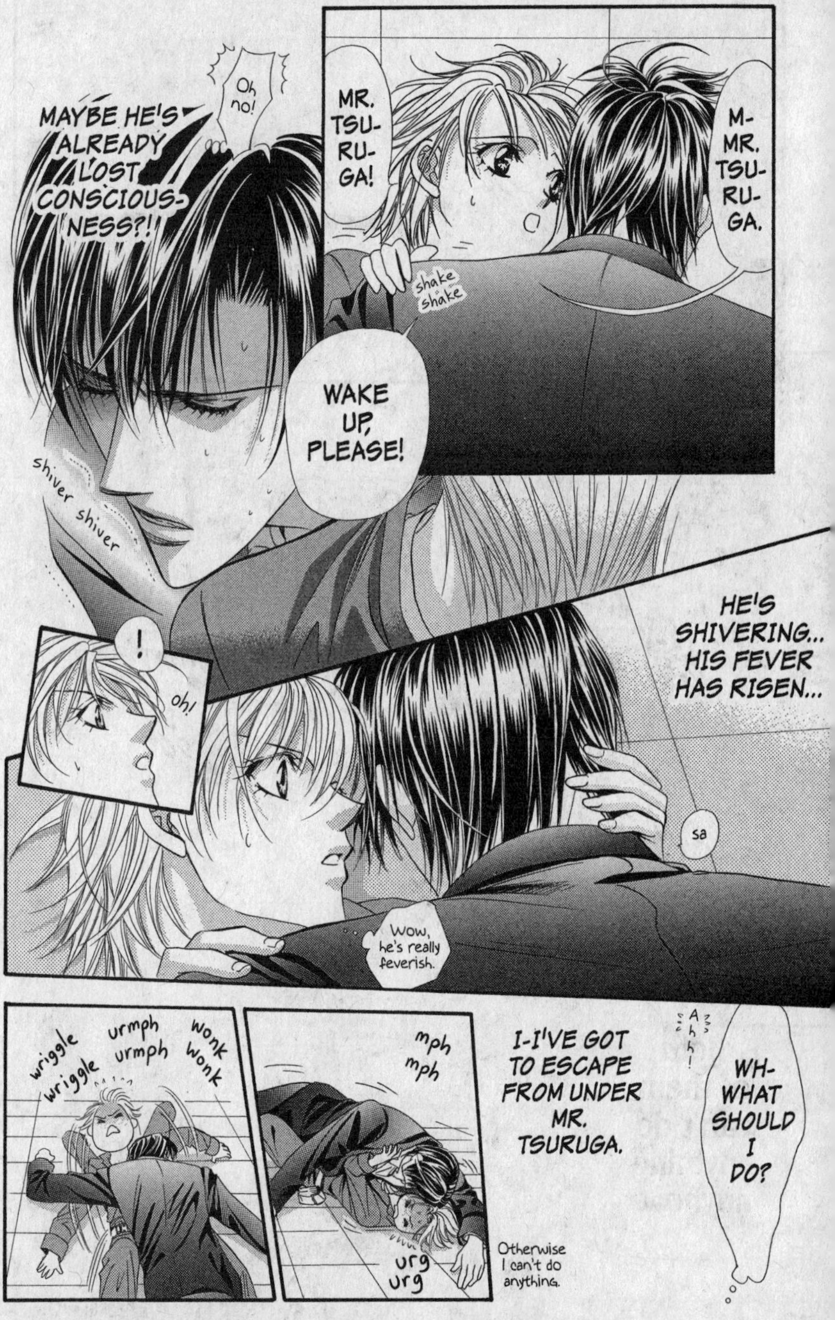
M-MR. TSURUGA.
MR. TSURUGA!
shake shake
WAKE UP, PLEASE!
Oh no!
MAYBE HE'S ALREADY LOST CONSCIOUSNESS?!
shiver shiver
HE'S SHIVERING... HIS FEVER HAS RISEN...
sa
!
oh!
Wow, he's really feverish.
Ahh!
WH-WHAT SHOULD I DO?
I-I'VE GOT TO ESCAPE FROM UNDER MR. TSURUGA.
Otherwise I can't do anything.
mph mph
urg urg
wonk wonk
urmph urmph
wriggle wriggle

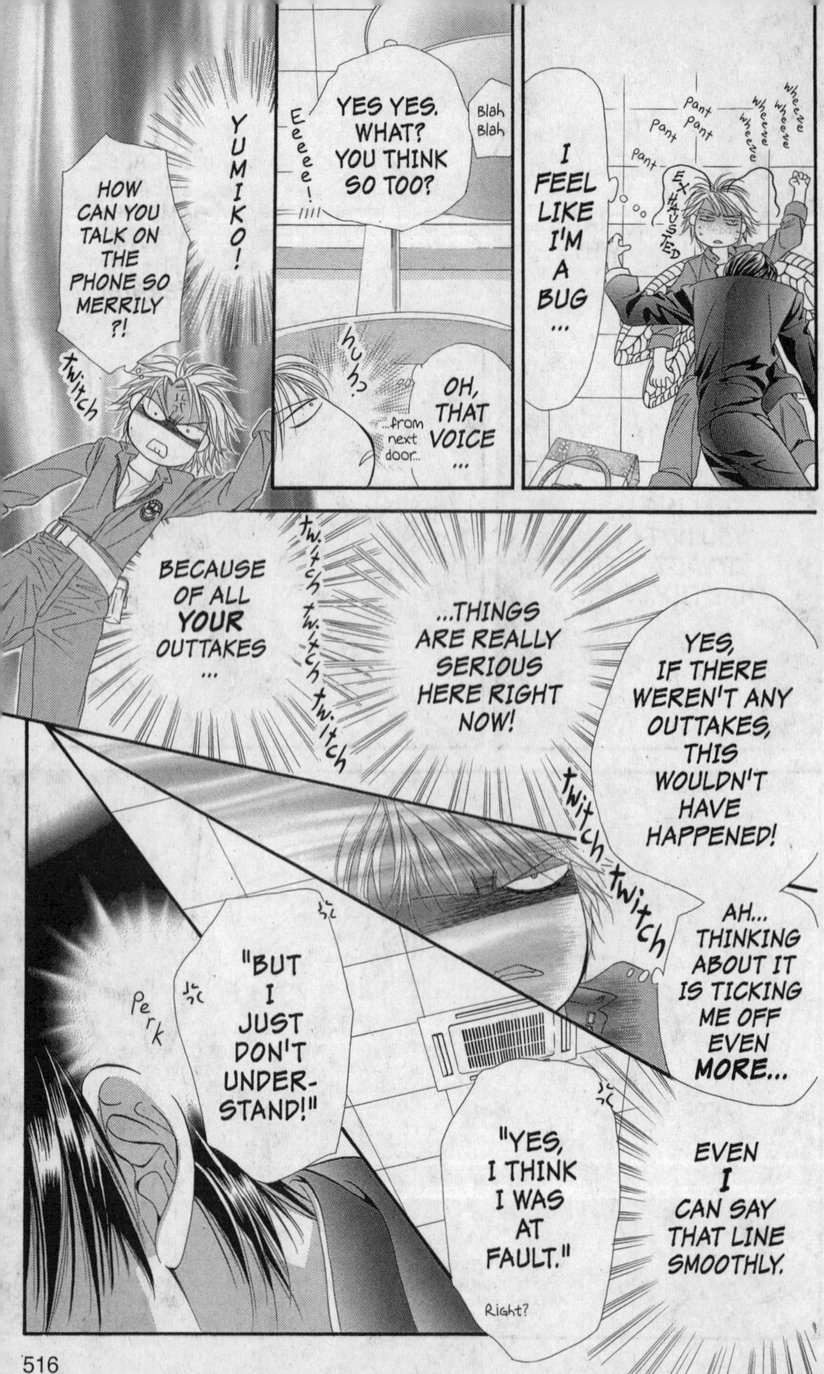
wheeze wheeze
wheeze wheeze
pant pant
pant
pant
EXHAUSTED
I FEEL LIKE I'M A BUG ...
Blah Blah
YES YES. WHAT? YOU THINK SO TOO?
Eeeee!
huh?
OH, THAT VOICE ...
...from next door...
YUMIKO!
HOW CAN YOU TALK ON THE PHONE SO MERRILY ?!
twitch
BECAUSE OF ALL **YOUR** OUTTAKES ...
twitch twitch twitch
...THINGS ARE REALLY SERIOUS HERE RIGHT NOW!
YES, IF THERE WEREN'T ANY OUTTAKES, THIS WOULDN'T HAVE HAPPENED!
AH... THINKING ABOUT IT IS TICKING ME OFF EVEN **MORE**...
twitch twitch
EVEN **I** CAN SAY THAT LINE SMOOTHLY.
"YES, I THINK I WAS AT FAULT."
Right?
"BUT I JUST DON'T UNDER-STAND!"
Perk

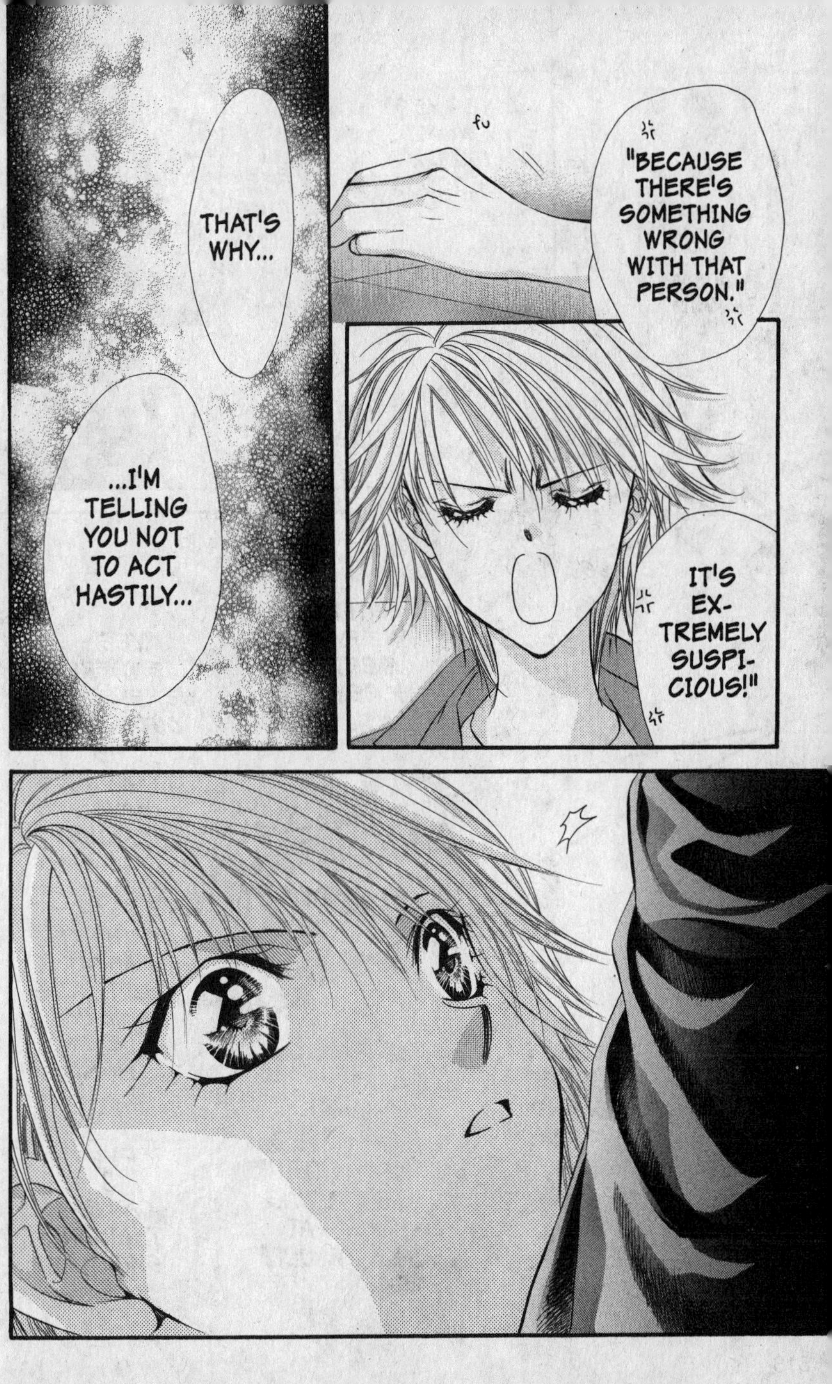
"BECAUSE THERE'S SOMETHING WRONG WITH THAT PERSON."
fu
IT'S EX-TREMELY SUSPI-CIOUS!"
THAT'S WHY...
...I'M TELLING YOU NOT TO ACT HASTILY...

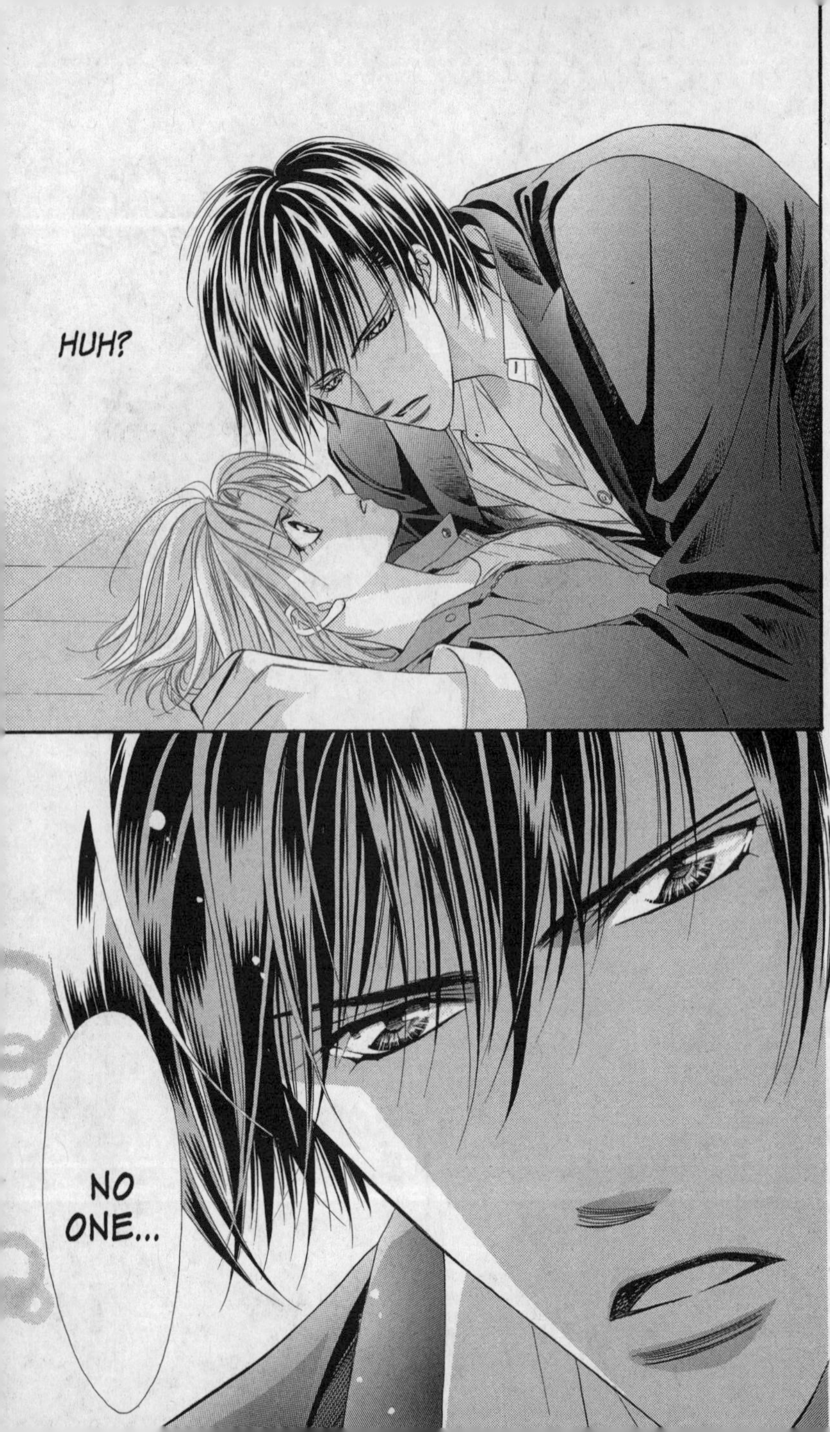
HUH?
NO ONE...

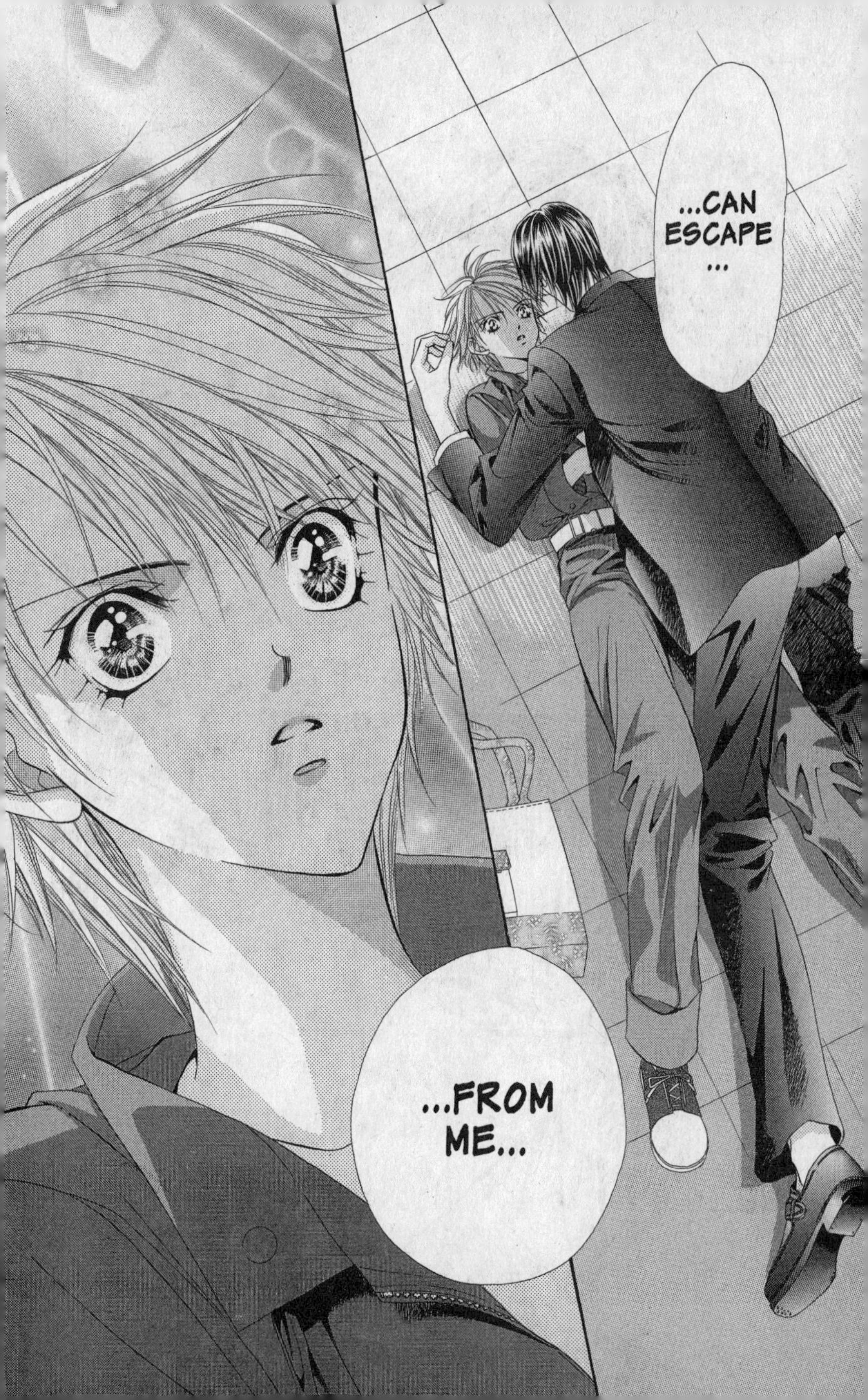
...CAN ESCAPE ...
...FROM ME...

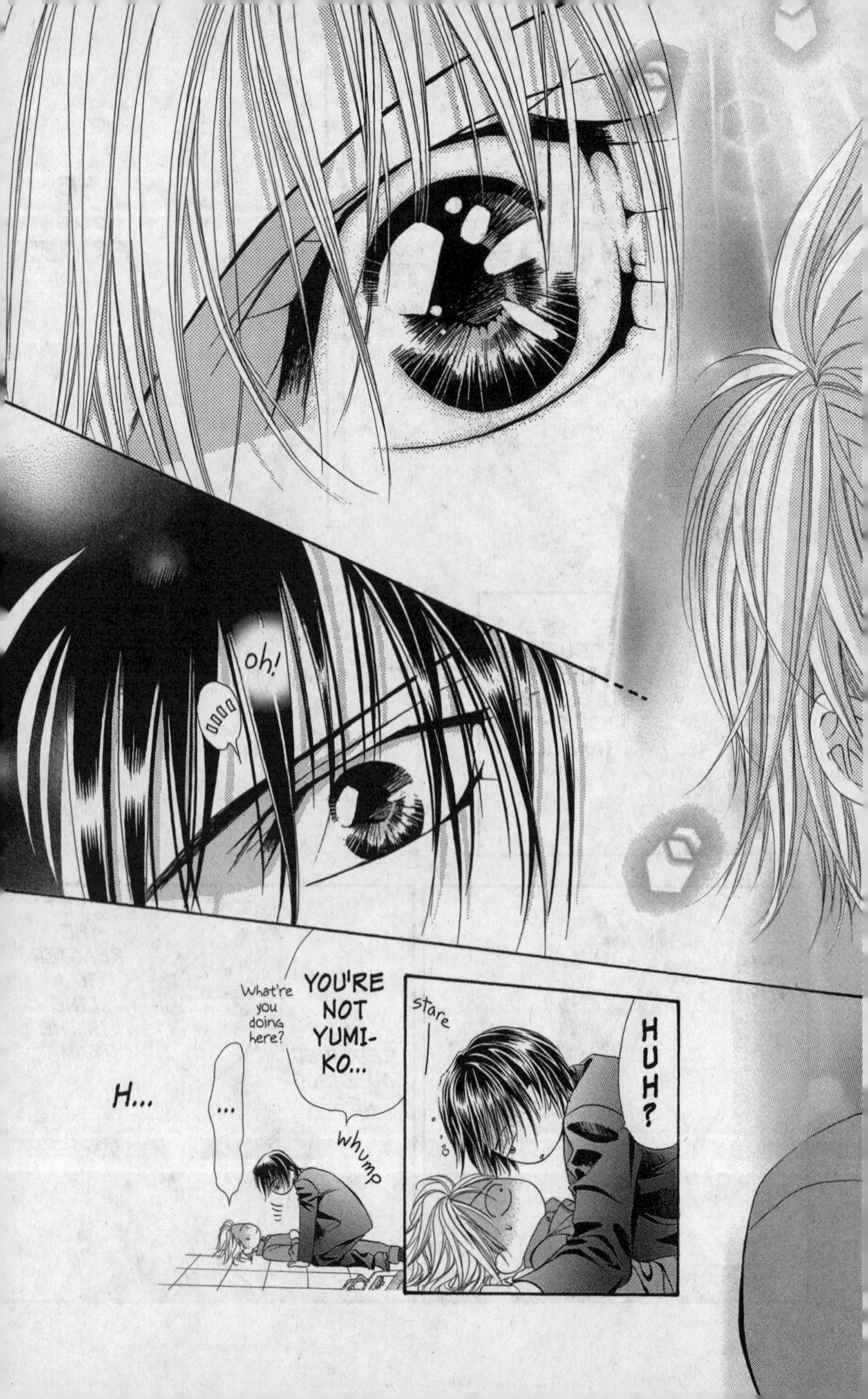
oh!
HUH?
stare
YOU'RE NOT YUMI-KO...
What're you doing here?
whump
...
H...

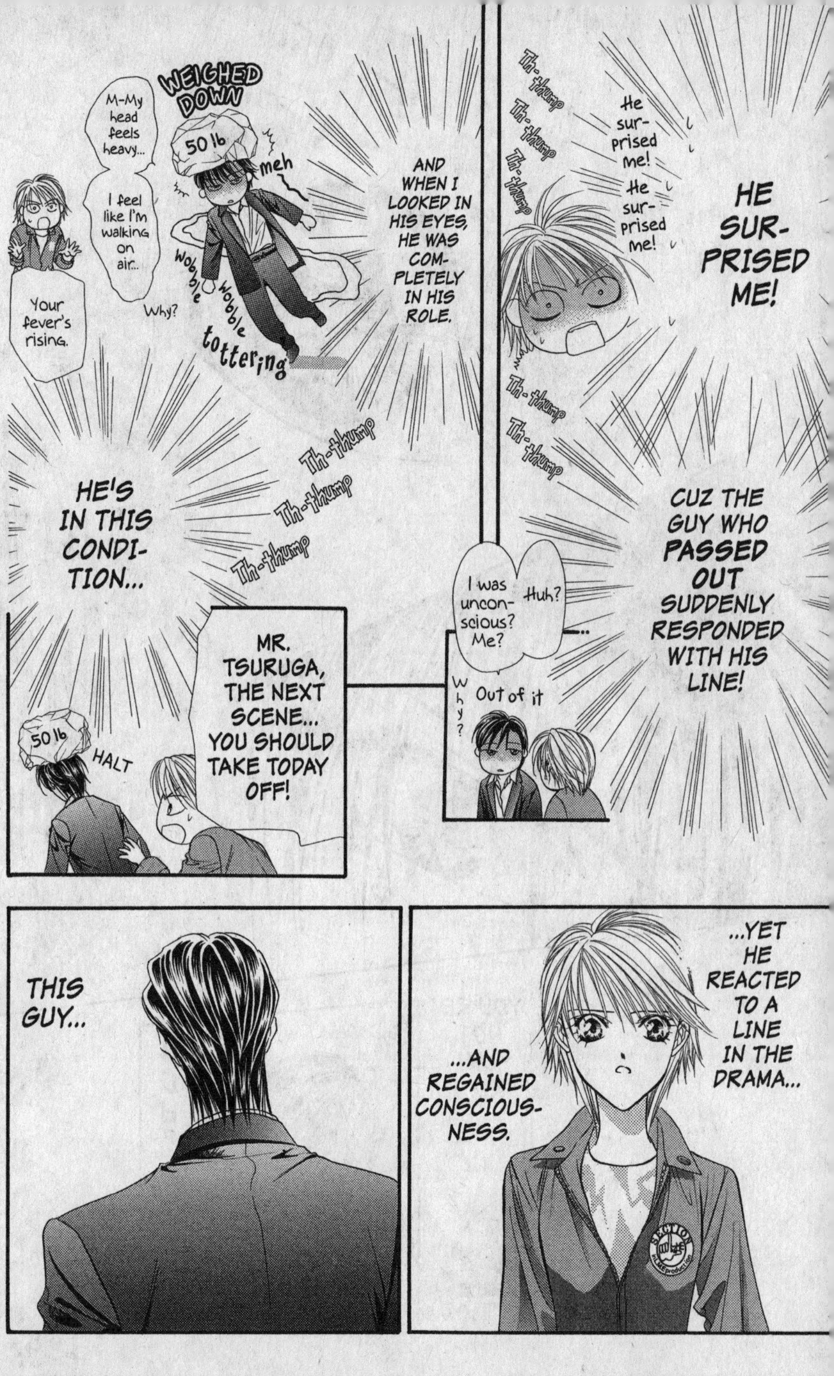

Th-thump
Th-thump
Th-thump
He surprised me!
He surprised me!
HE SURPRISED ME!
Th-thump
Th-thump
CUZ THE GUY WHO PASSED OUT SUDDENLY RESPONDED WITH HIS LINE!
Huh?
I was unconscious? Me?
Why?
Out of it
AND WHEN I LOOKED IN HIS EYES, HE WAS COMPLETELY IN HIS ROLE.
WEIGHED DOWN
50 lb
meh
M-My head feels heavy...
I feel like I'm walking on air...
wobble wobble
tottering
Why?
Your fever's rising.
Th-thump
Th-thump
Th-thump
HE'S IN THIS CONDITION...
MR. TSURUGA, THE NEXT SCENE... YOU SHOULD TAKE TODAY OFF!
50 lb
HALT
...YET HE REACTED TO A LINE IN THE DRAMA...
...AND REGAINED CONSCIOUSNESS.
SECTION LME production
THIS GUY...

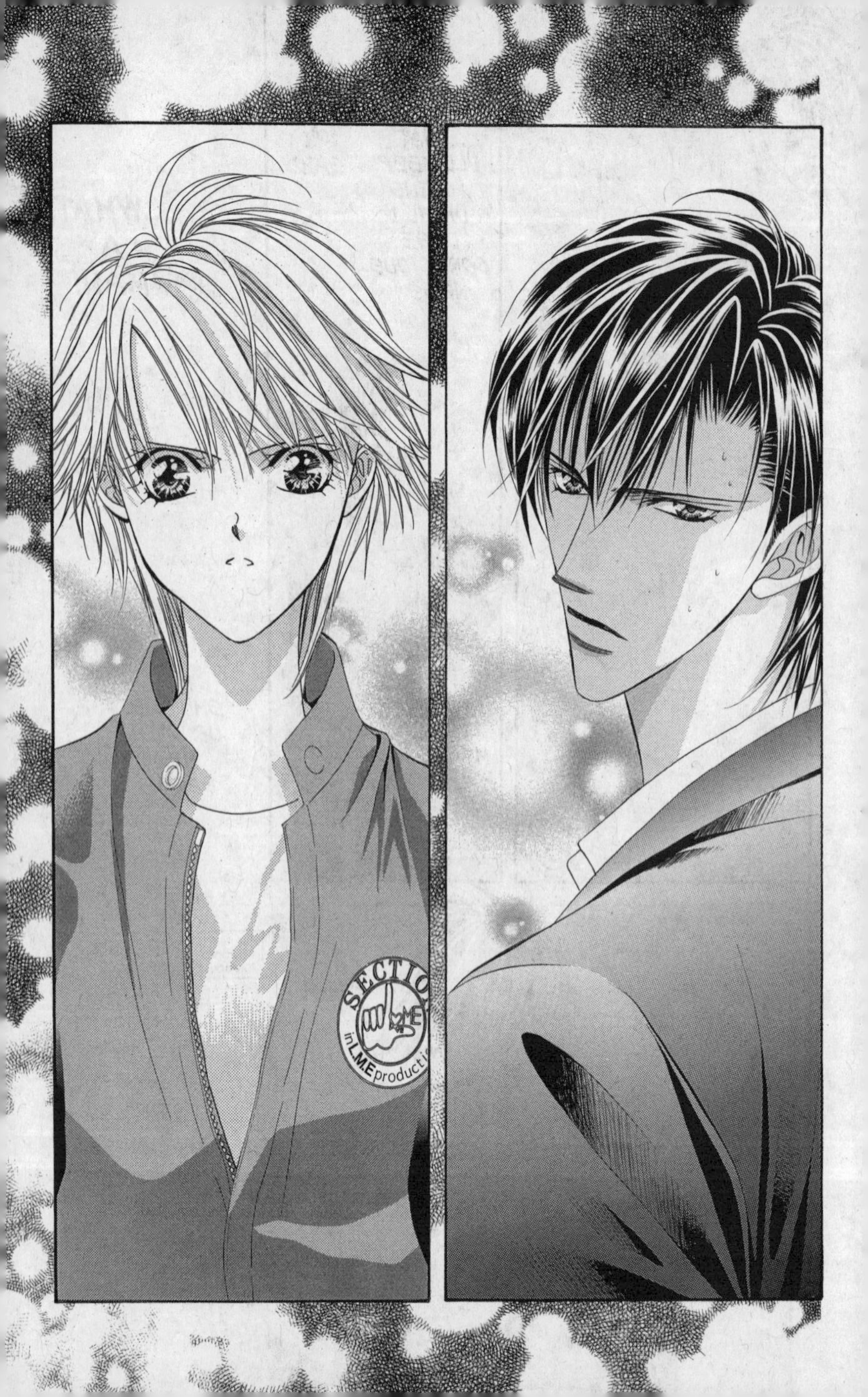

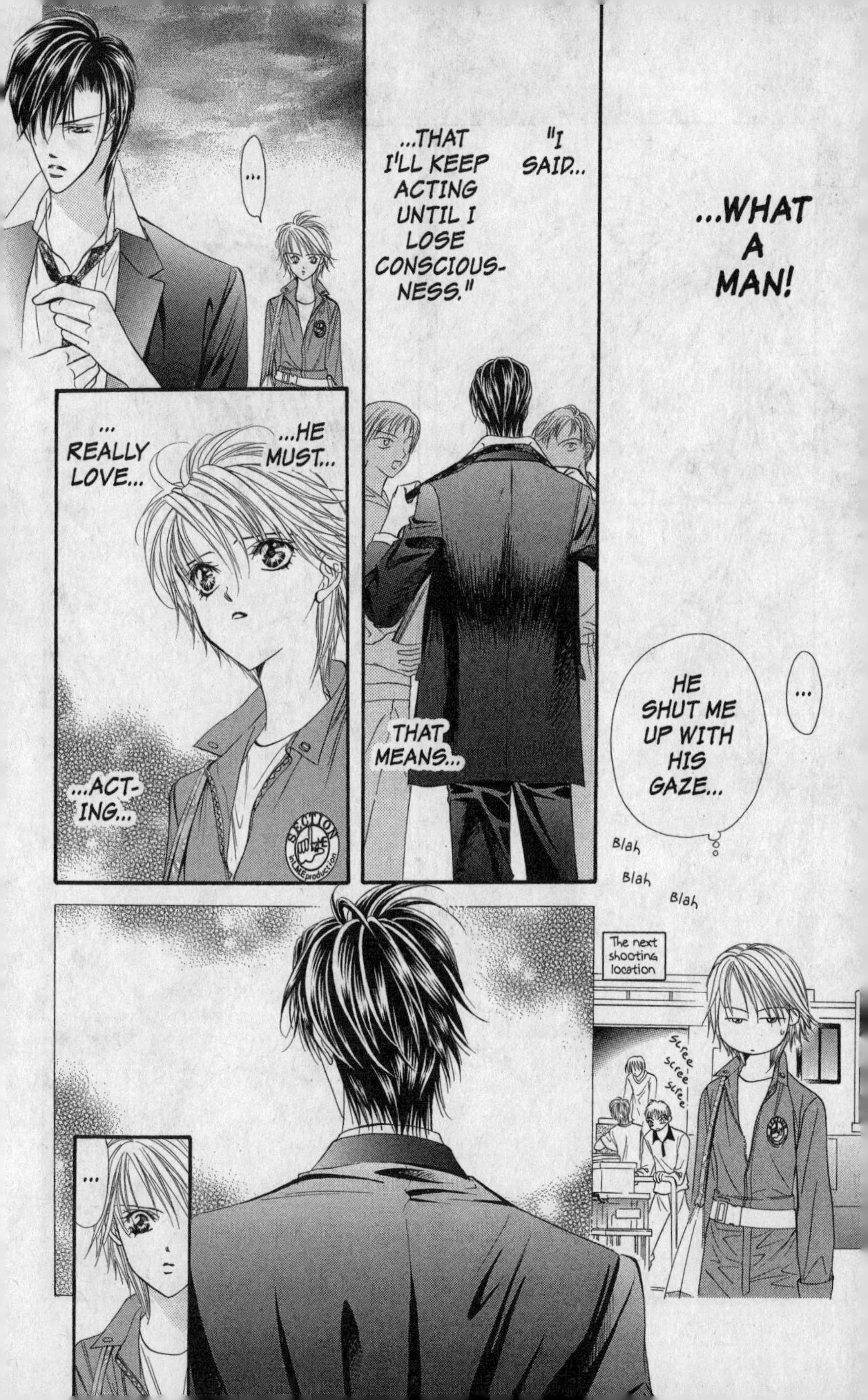
...WHAT A MAN!
"I SAID...
...THAT I'LL KEEP ACTING UNTIL I LOSE CONSCIOUS-NESS."
...
...
HE SHUT ME UP WITH HIS GAZE...
Blah
Blah
Blah
THAT MEANS...
...HE MUST...
...REALLY LOVE...
...ACT-ING...
The next shooting location
scree
scree
scree
...

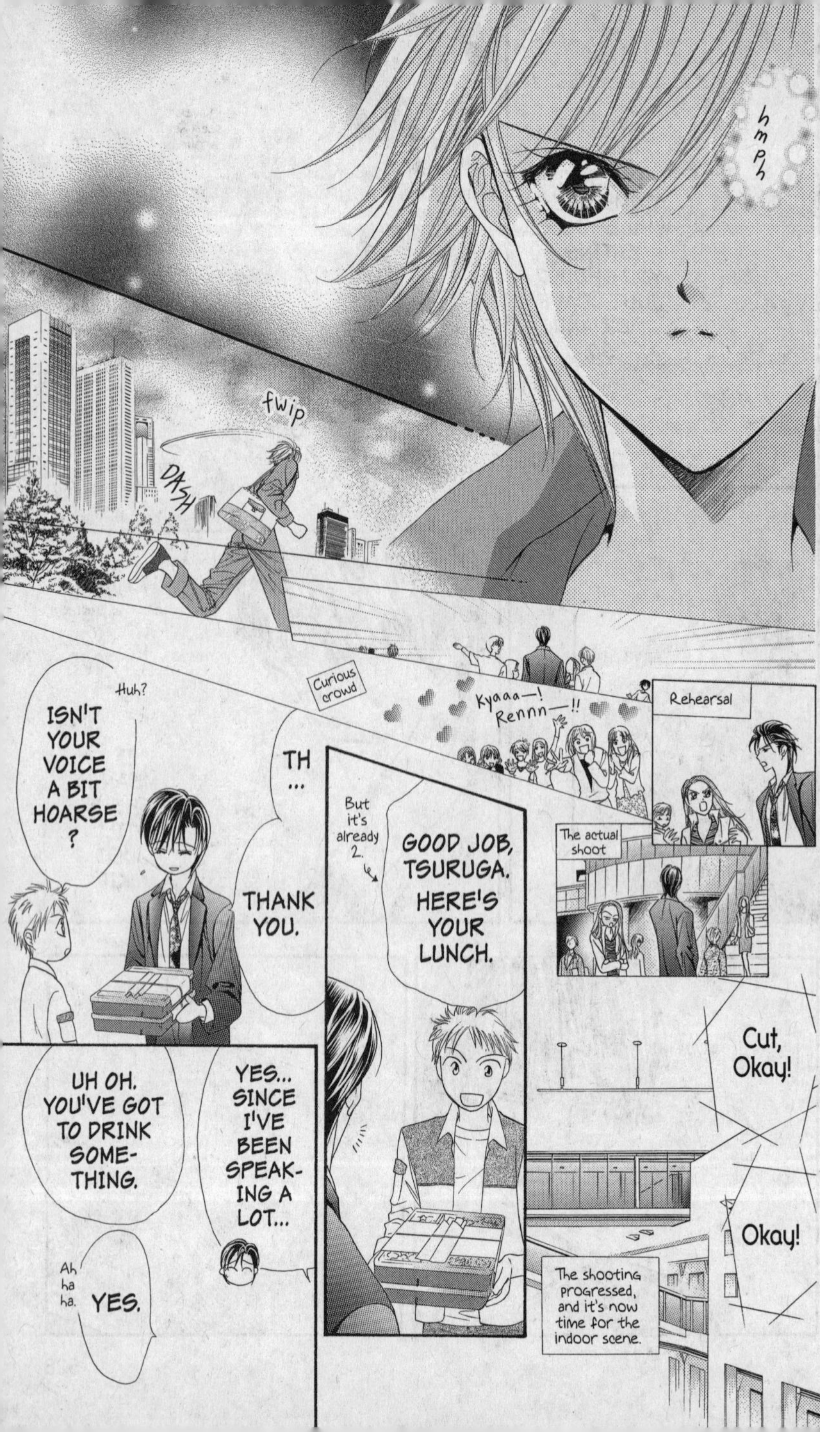
hmph
fwip
DASH
Rehearsal
Curious crowd
Kyaaa—! Rennn—!!
The actual shoot
Cut, Okay!
Okay!
The shooting progressed, and it's now time for the indoor scene.
GOOD JOB, TSURUGA. HERE'S YOUR LUNCH.
But it's already 2.
TH ...
THANK YOU.
Huh?
ISN'T YOUR VOICE A BIT HOARSE?
YES... SINCE I'VE BEEN SPEAKING A LOT...
UH OH. YOU'VE GOT TO DRINK SOMETHING.
Ah ha ha.
YES.

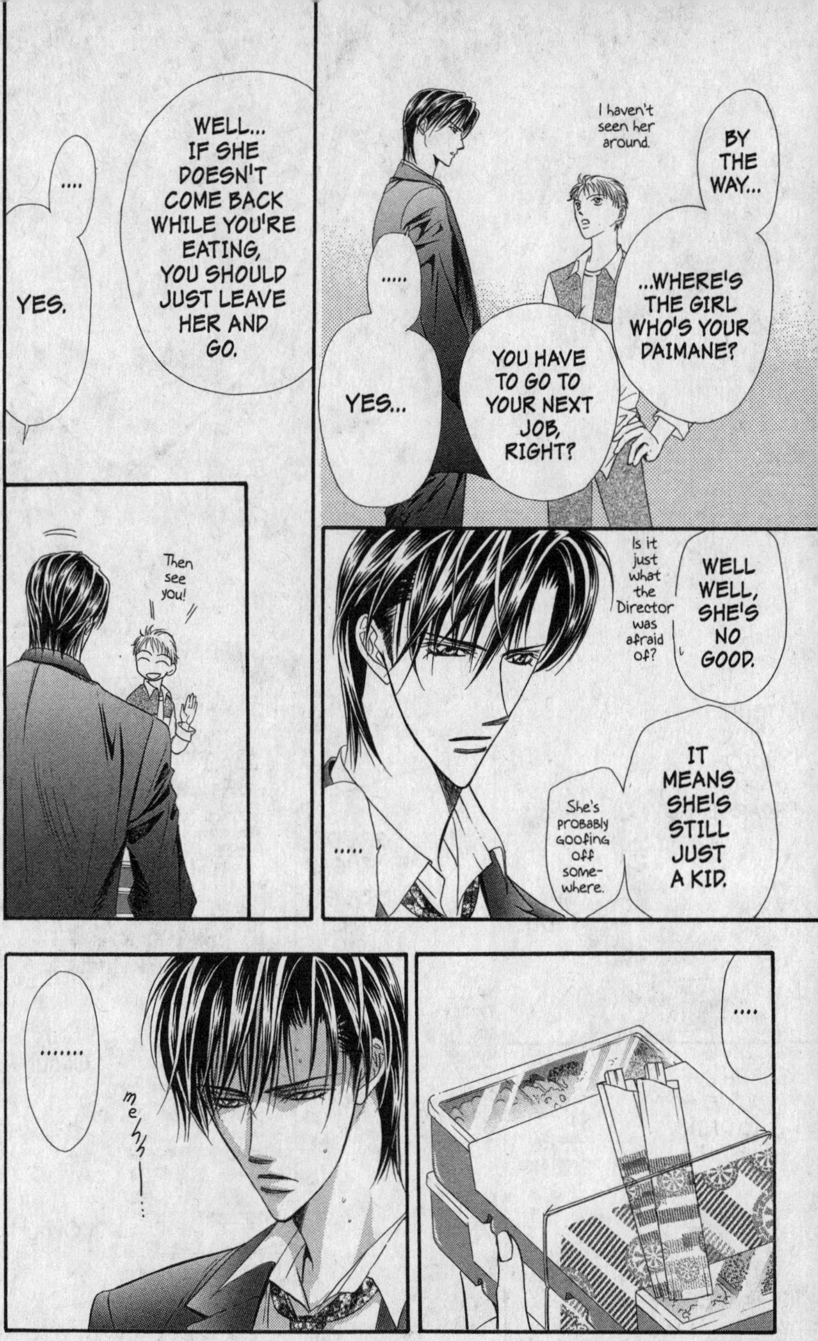

BY THE WAY...
I haven't seen her around.
...WHERE'S THE GIRL WHO'S YOUR DAIMANE?
YOU HAVE TO GO TO YOUR NEXT JOB, RIGHT?
.....
YES...
WELL... IF SHE DOESN'T COME BACK WHILE YOU'RE EATING, YOU SHOULD JUST LEAVE HER AND GO.
....
YES.
WELL WELL, SHE'S NO GOOD.
Is it just what the Director was afraid of?
IT MEANS SHE'S STILL JUST A KID.
She's probably goofing off some-where.
.....
Then see you!
....
....
mehh—...

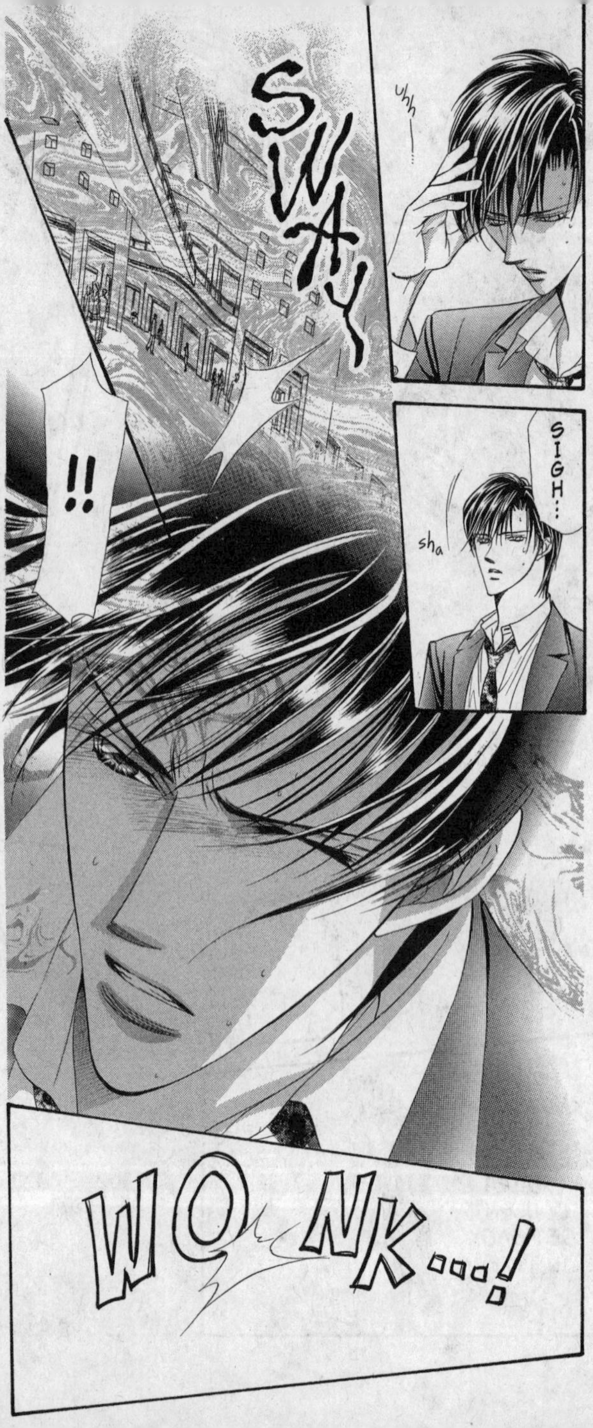
uhh...
SIGH...
sha
SWAY
!!
WONK...!

The Reason for Giving Up

When Kyoko took care of Ren, one thing I was at a loss about was the ice bag. Nowadays, when you have a fever, the Hiepita does the job. The ice bag I know was the old model that Ren uses in the story. However, right before I got to work, I found out that there is a newer model. I bought it, thinking "I want to use it for sure!"...I did...buy it...but the ice bag I so looked forward to, when it's used...

...turns into...

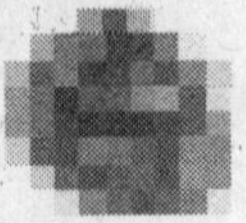

...a shape like this...

I hesitated putting the old model on Ren's forehead, so I leapt at the newest model... ♪ the latest ice bag has multiple functions and is wonderful!!... B-But...with that on his forehead, Ren's smile and his lines are ruined (I...I apologize to the manufacturer!!) A-Anyway, it was fatal picture-wise (maybe it's not that bad...? ♪)

—To Be Continued—

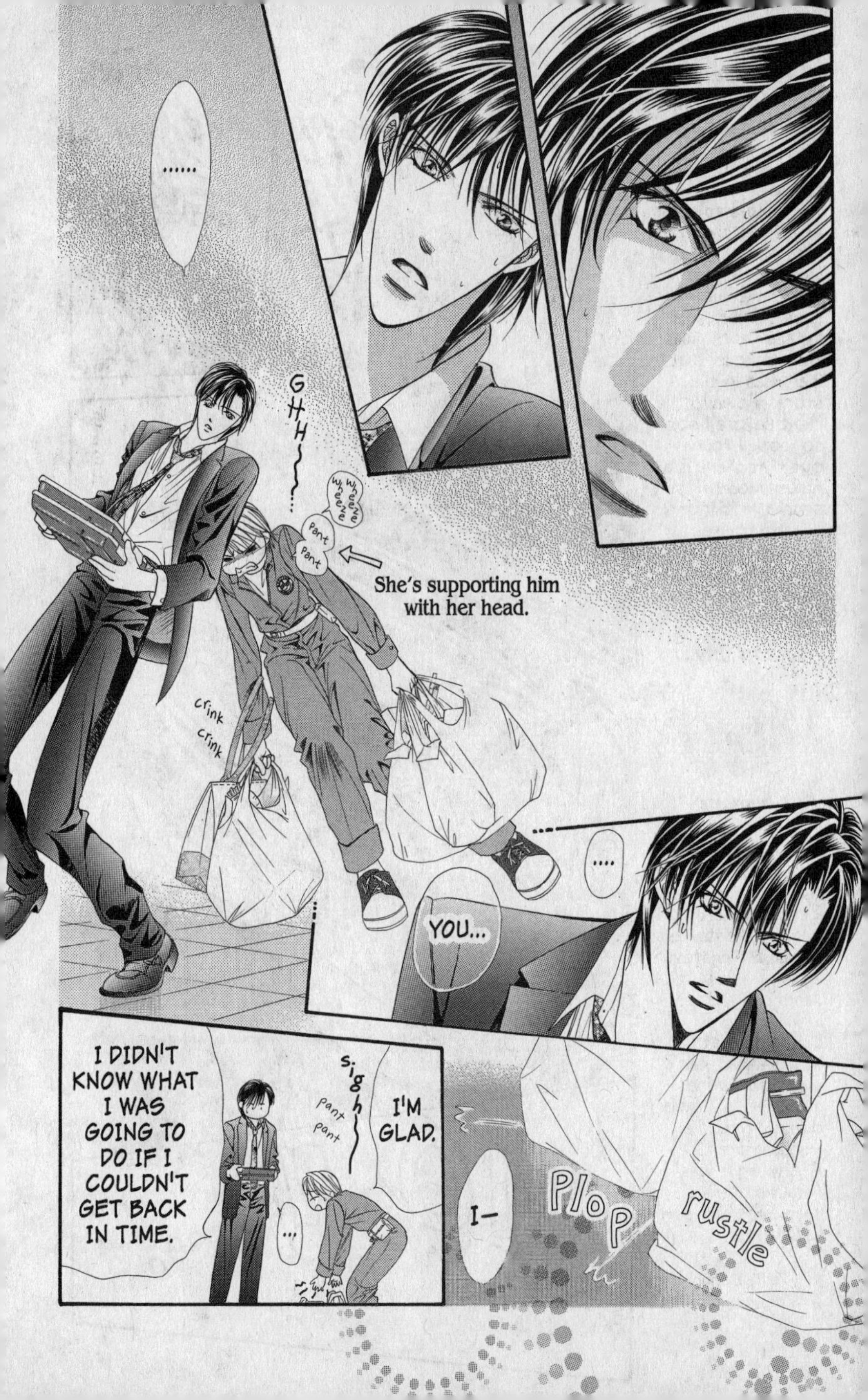
......
GHH~...
wheeze wheeze
Pant Pant
She's supporting him with her head.
crink crink
....
YOU...
I—
Plop
rustle
I'M GLAD.
sigh~
pant pant
I DIDN'T KNOW WHAT I WAS GOING TO DO IF I COULDN'T GET BACK IN TIME.
...

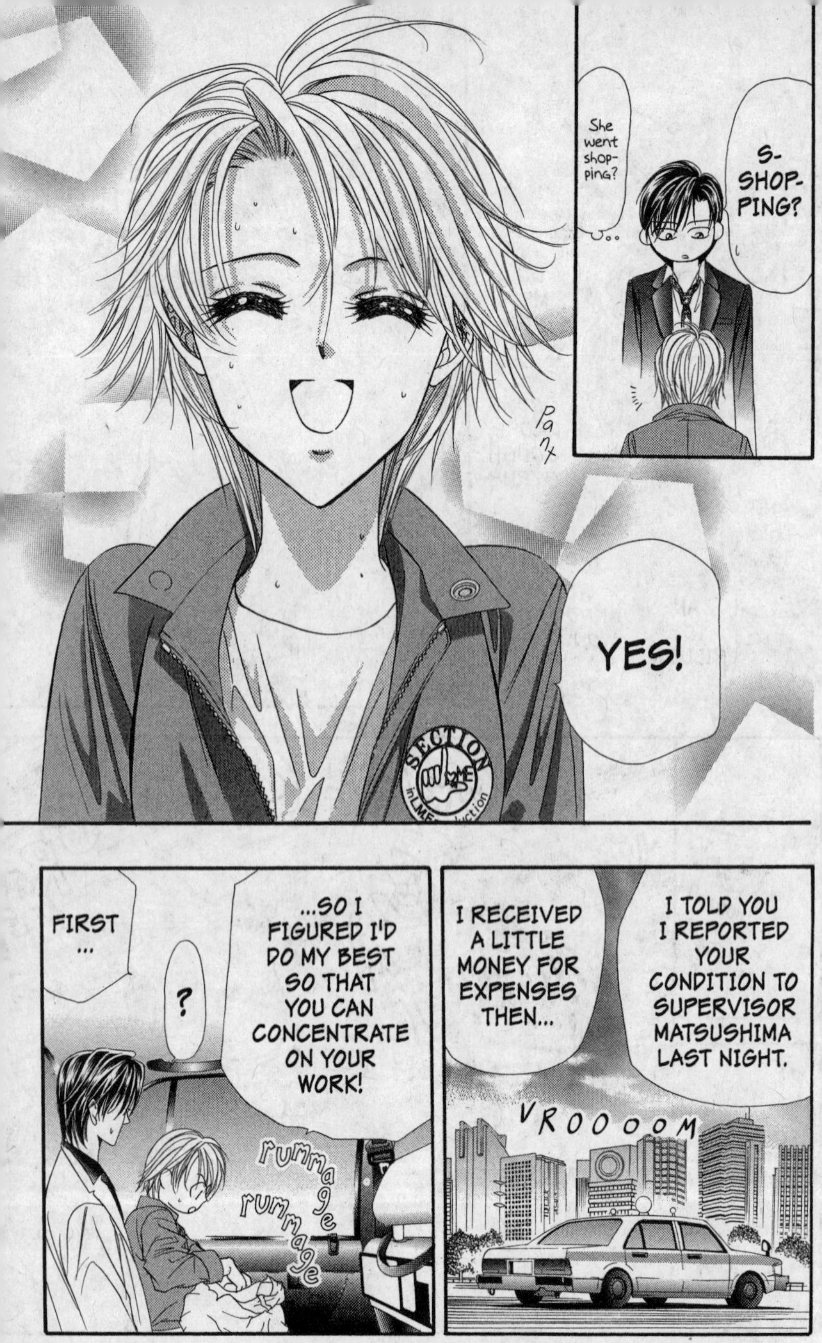
S-SHOPPING?
She went shopping?
Pant
YES!
I TOLD YOU I REPORTED YOUR CONDITION TO SUPERVISOR MATSUSHIMA LAST NIGHT.
I RECEIVED A LITTLE MONEY FOR EXPENSES THEN...
VROOOOM
...SO I FIGURED I'D DO MY BEST SO THAT YOU CAN CONCENTRATE ON YOUR WORK!
?
FIRST ...
rummage
rummage

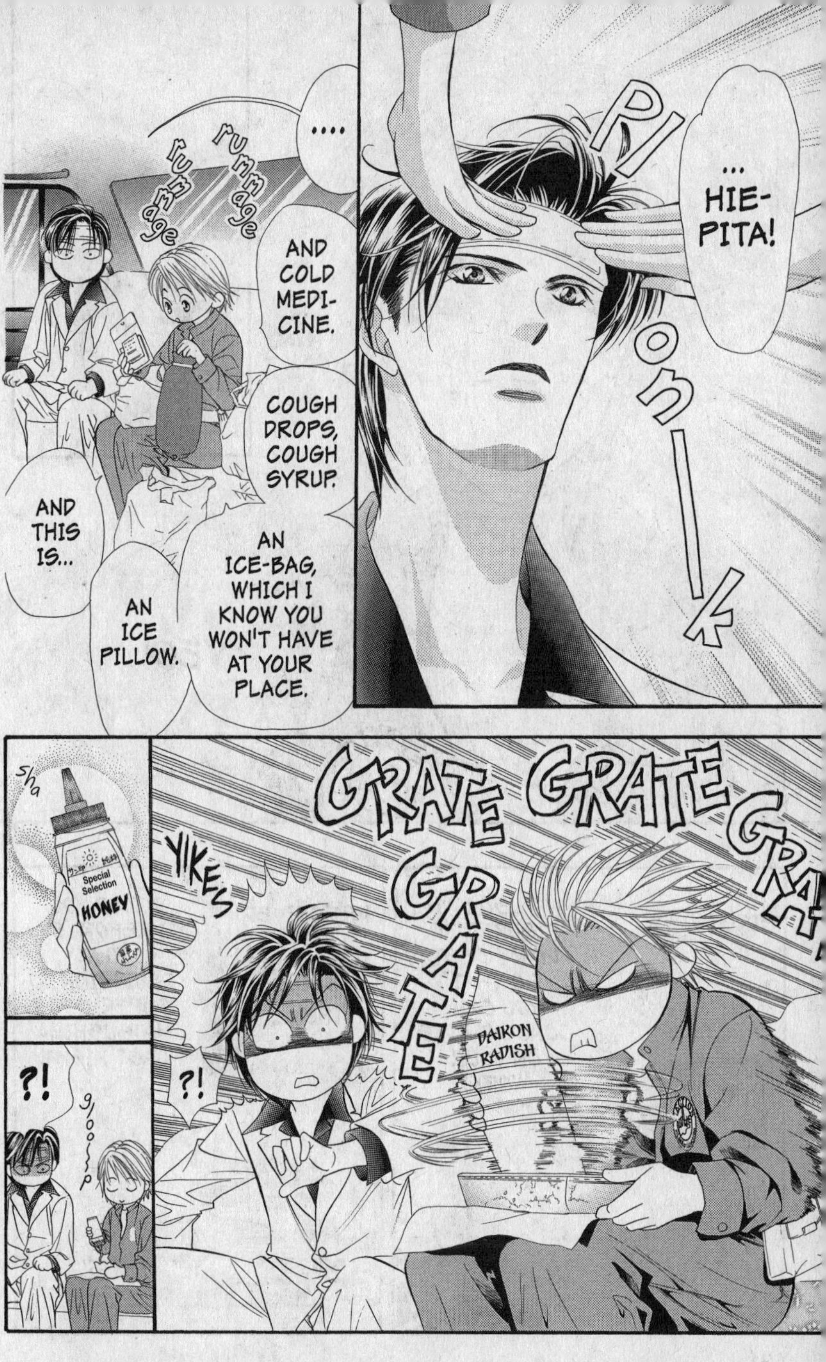
PI
...
HIE-
PITA!
on---k
rummage rummage
....
AND COLD MEDI-CINE.
COUGH DROPS, COUGH SYRUP.
AN ICE-BAG, WHICH I KNOW YOU WON'T HAVE AT YOUR PLACE.
AND THIS IS...
AN ICE PILLOW.
GRATE GRATE GRA
GRATE
GRATE
YIKES
?!
DAIKON RADISH
sha
Special Selection
HONEY
?!
glooo---p

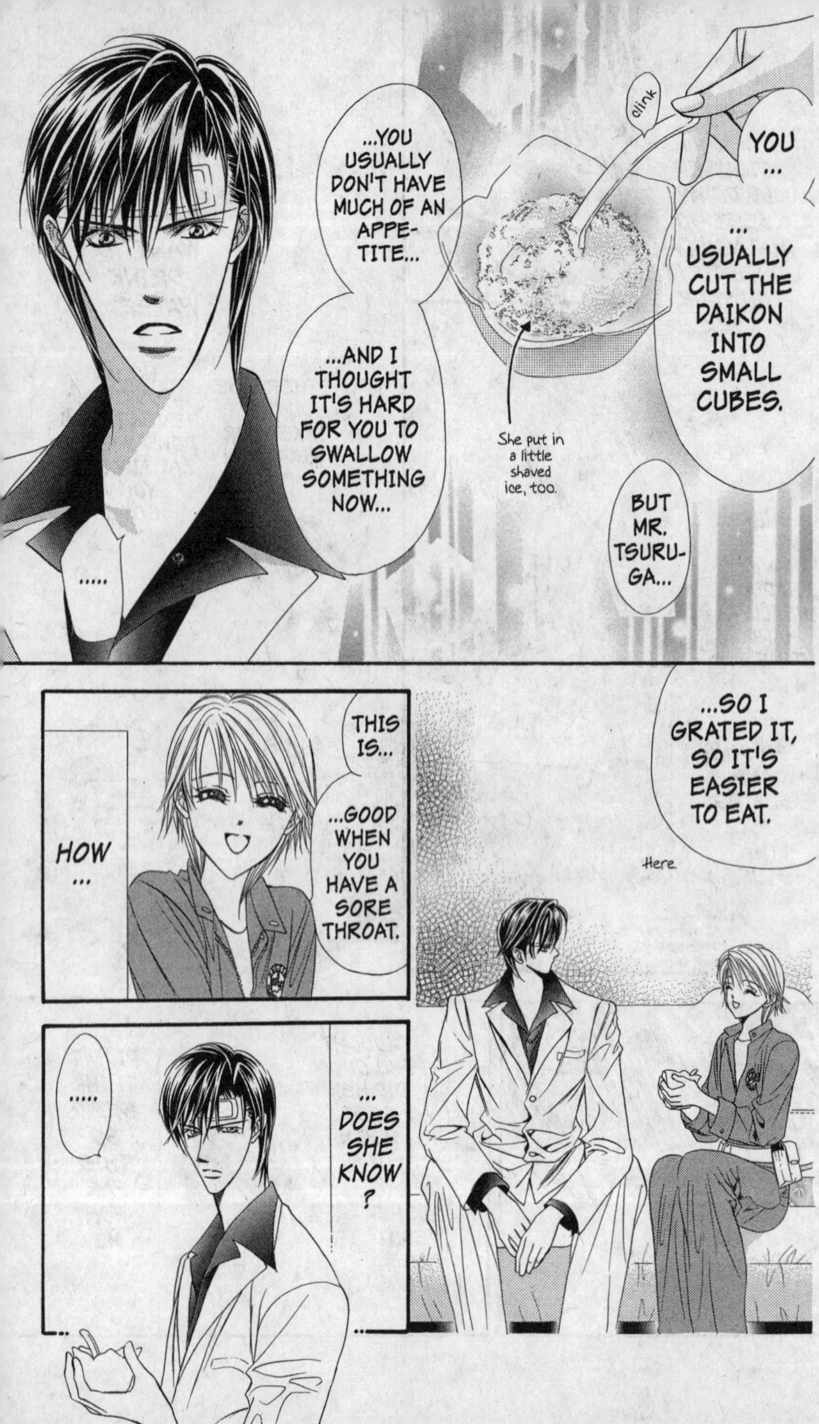

clink
YOU ...
... USUALLY CUT THE DAIKON INTO SMALL CUBES.
BUT MR. TSURUGA...
She put in a little shaved ice, too.
...YOU USUALLY DON'T HAVE MUCH OF AN APPETITE...
...AND I THOUGHT IT'S HARD FOR YOU TO SWALLOW SOMETHING NOW...
.....
...SO I GRATED IT, SO IT'S EASIER TO EAT.
Here.
THIS IS...
...GOOD WHEN YOU HAVE A SORE THROAT.
HOW ...
... DOES SHE KNOW ?
.....

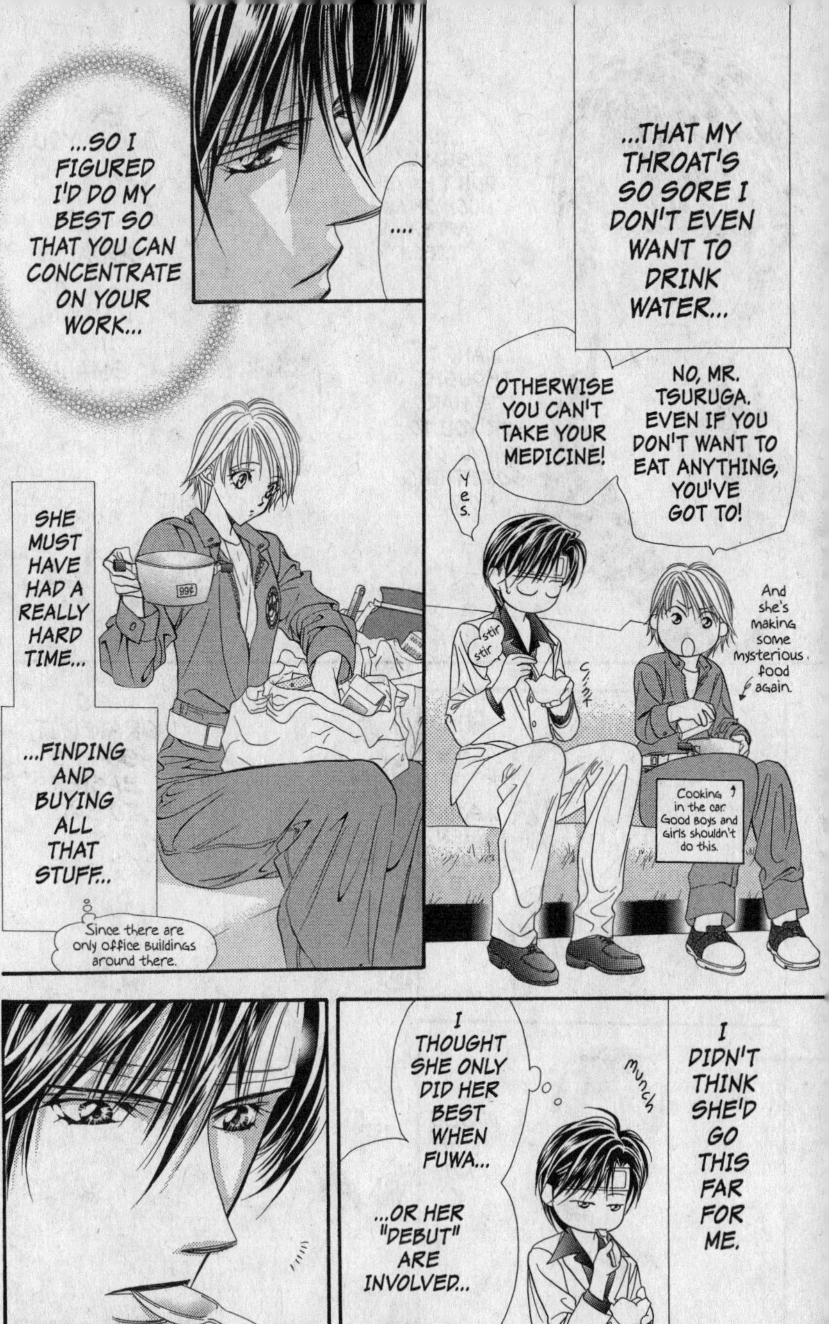
...THAT MY THROAT'S SO SORE I DON'T EVEN WANT TO DRINK WATER...
NO, MR. TSURUGA. EVEN IF YOU DON'T WANT TO EAT ANYTHING, YOU'VE GOT TO!
OTHERWISE YOU CAN'T TAKE YOUR MEDICINE!
Yes.
And she's making some mysterious food again.
stir stir
Cooking in the car. Good boys and girls shouldn't do this.
....
...SO I FIGURED I'D DO MY BEST SO THAT YOU CAN CONCENTRATE ON YOUR WORK...
SHE MUST HAVE HAD A REALLY HARD TIME...
...FINDING AND BUYING ALL THAT STUFF...
Since there are only office buildings around there.
I DIDN'T THINK SHE'D GO THIS FAR FOR ME.
I THOUGHT SHE ONLY DID HER BEST WHEN FUWA...
...OR HER "DEBUT" ARE INVOLVED...
munch

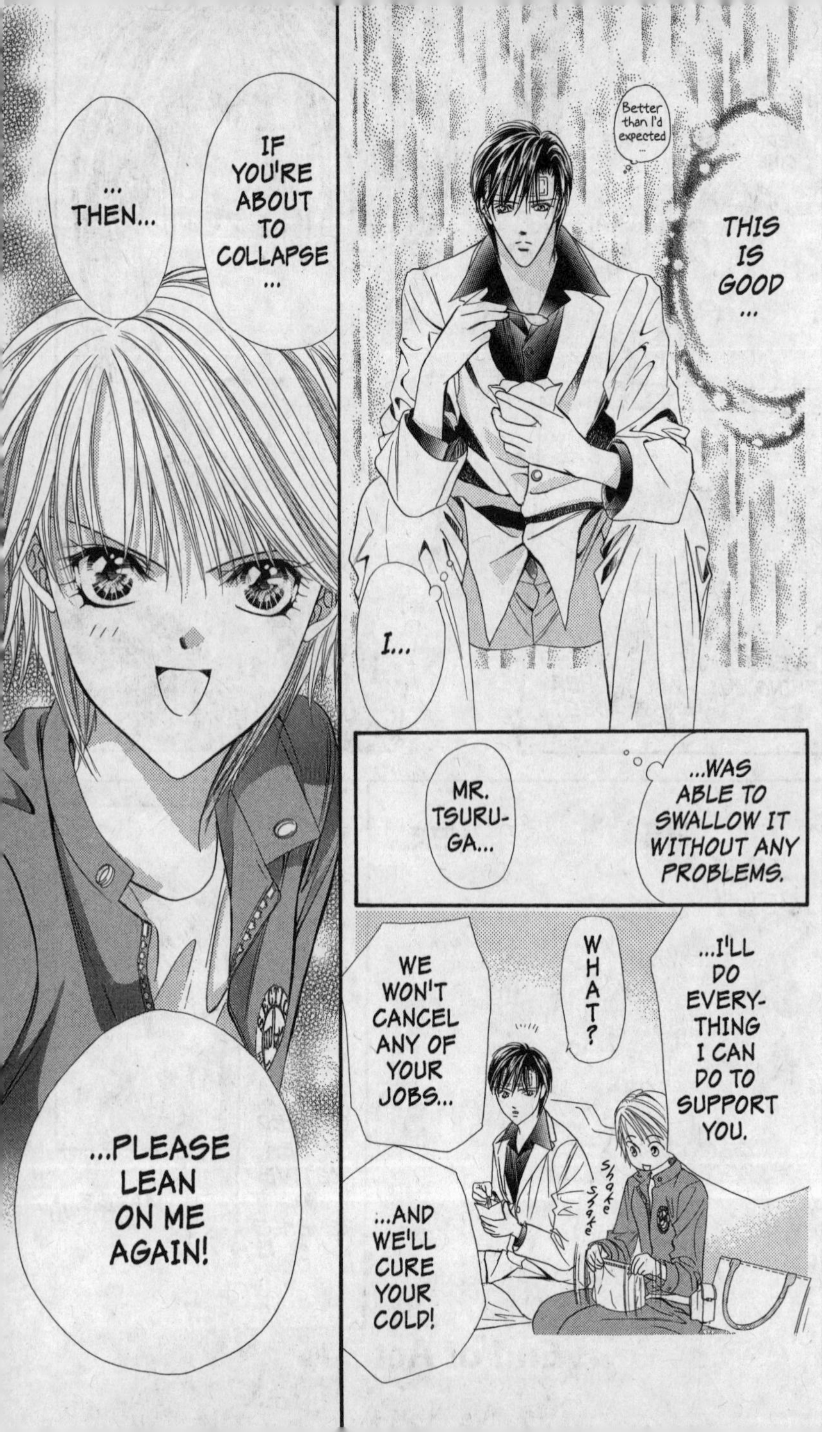
THIS IS GOOD...
Better than I'd expected...
I...
...WAS ABLE TO SWALLOW IT WITHOUT ANY PROBLEMS.
MR. TSURUGA...
...I'LL DO EVERYTHING I CAN DO TO SUPPORT YOU.
WHAT?
WE WON'T CANCEL ANY OF YOUR JOBS...
Shake Shake
...AND WE'LL CURE YOUR COLD!
IF YOU'RE ABOUT TO COLLAPSE...
...THEN...
...PLEASE LEAN ON ME AGAIN!

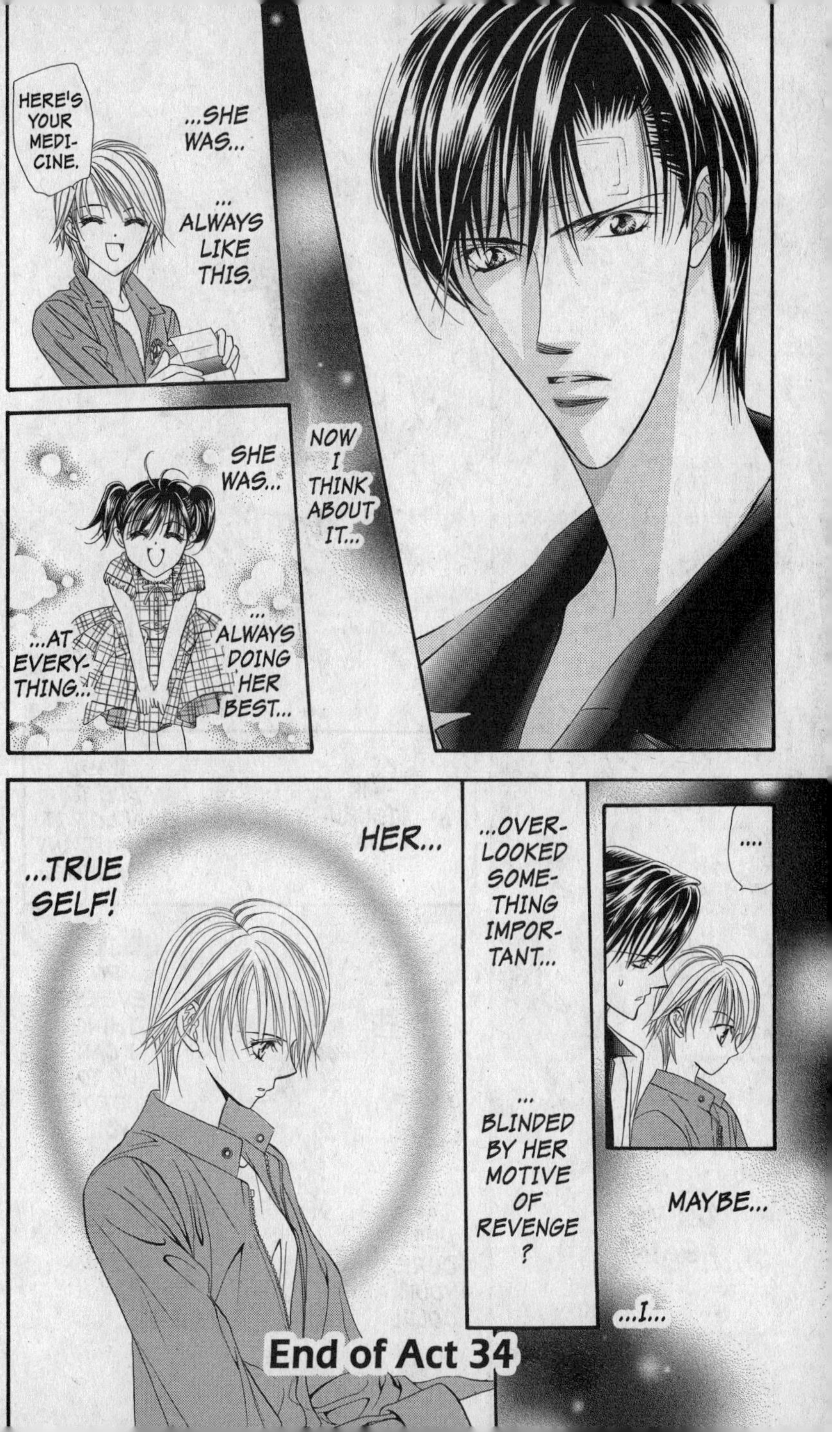
NOW I THINK ABOUT IT...
HERE'S YOUR MEDI-CINE.
...SHE WAS...
...ALWAYS LIKE THIS.
SHE WAS...
...ALWAYS DOING HER BEST...
...AT EVERY-THING...
....
MAYBE...
...I...
...OVER-LOOKED SOME-THING IMPOR-TANT...
...BLINDED BY HER MOTIVE OF REVENGE?
HER...
...TRUE SELF!
End of Act 34

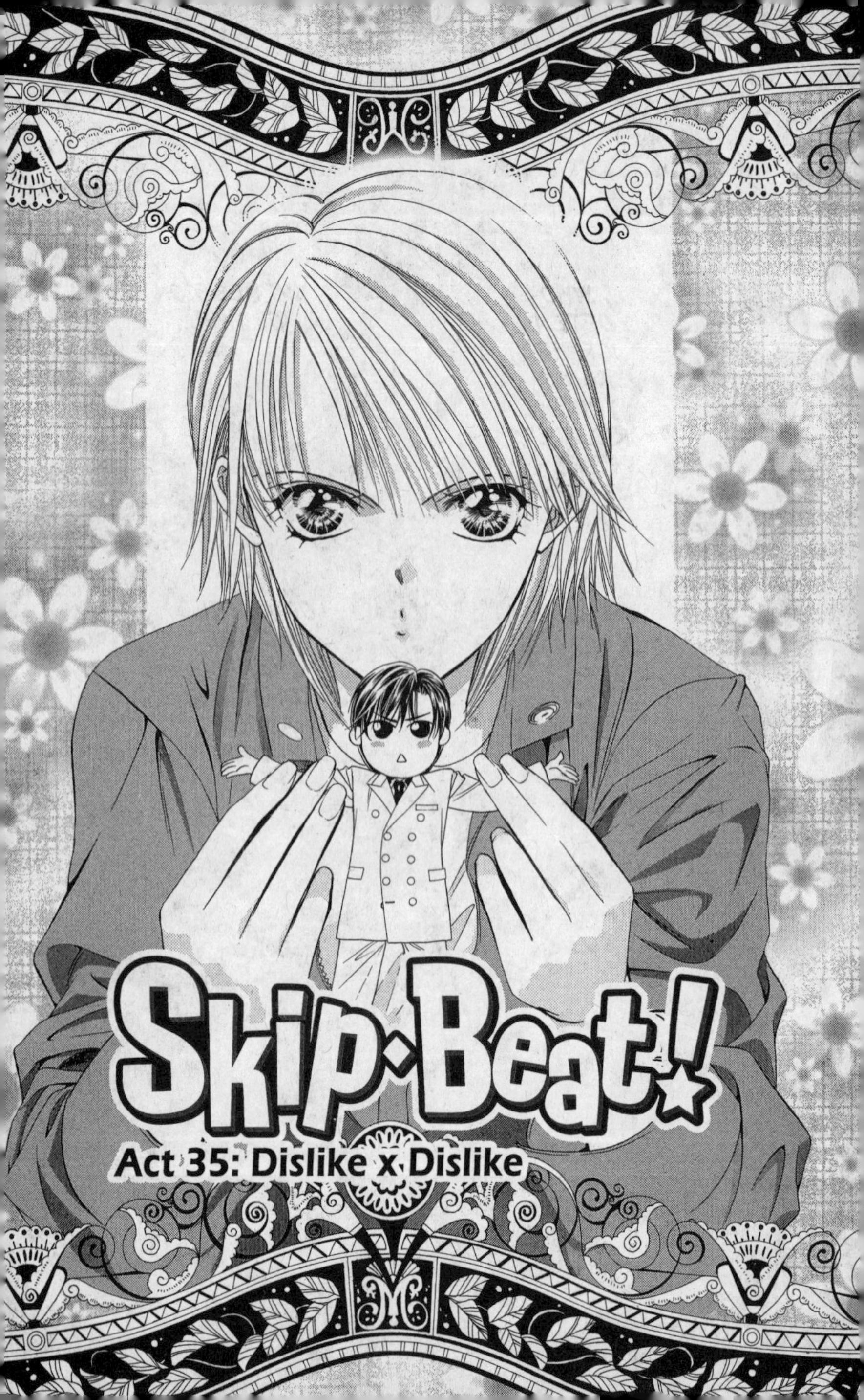
Skip·Beat!
Act 35: Dislike x Dislike

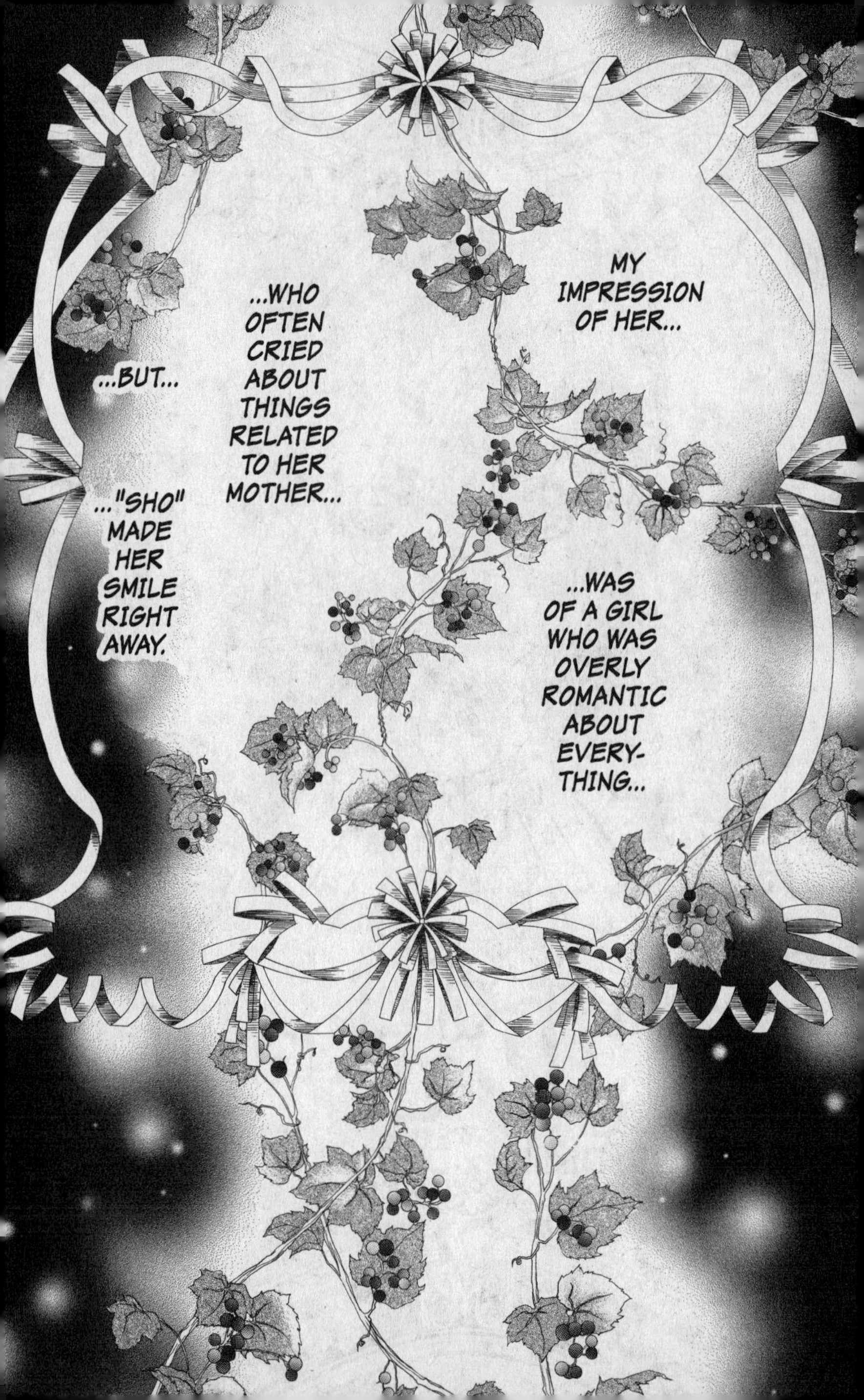
MY IMPRESSION OF HER...
...WAS OF A GIRL WHO WAS OVERLY ROMANTIC ABOUT EVERY-THING...
...WHO OFTEN CRIED ABOUT THINGS RELATED TO HER MOTHER...
...BUT...
..."SHO" MADE HER SMILE RIGHT AWAY.

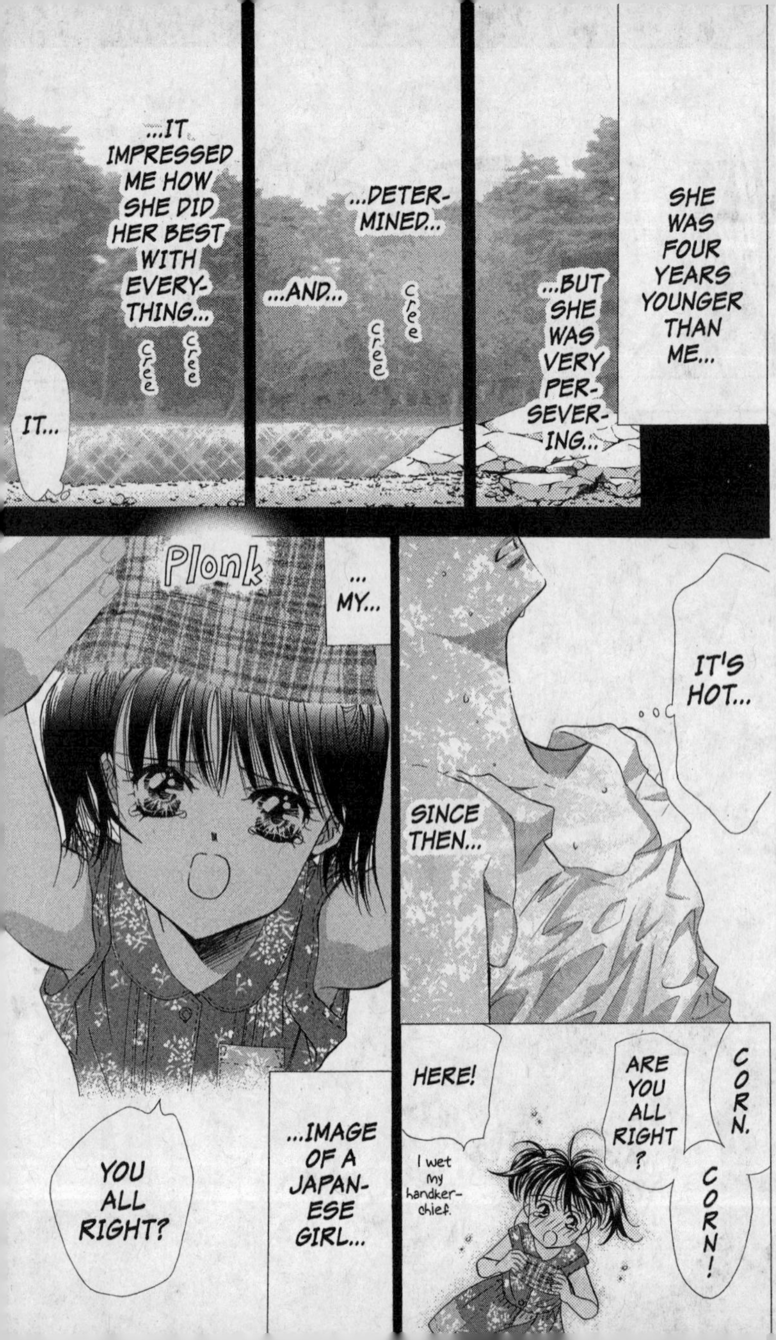
SHE WAS FOUR YEARS YOUNGER THAN ME...
...BUT SHE WAS VERY PER-SEVER-ING...
...DETER-MINED...
cree
cree
...AND...
...IT IMPRESSED ME HOW SHE DID HER BEST WITH EVERY-THING...
cree
cree
IT...
IT'S HOT...
SINCE THEN...
CORN.
CORN!
ARE YOU ALL RIGHT?
HERE!
I wet my handker-chief.
... MY...
Plonk
...IMAGE OF A JAPAN-ESE GIRL...
YOU ALL RIGHT?

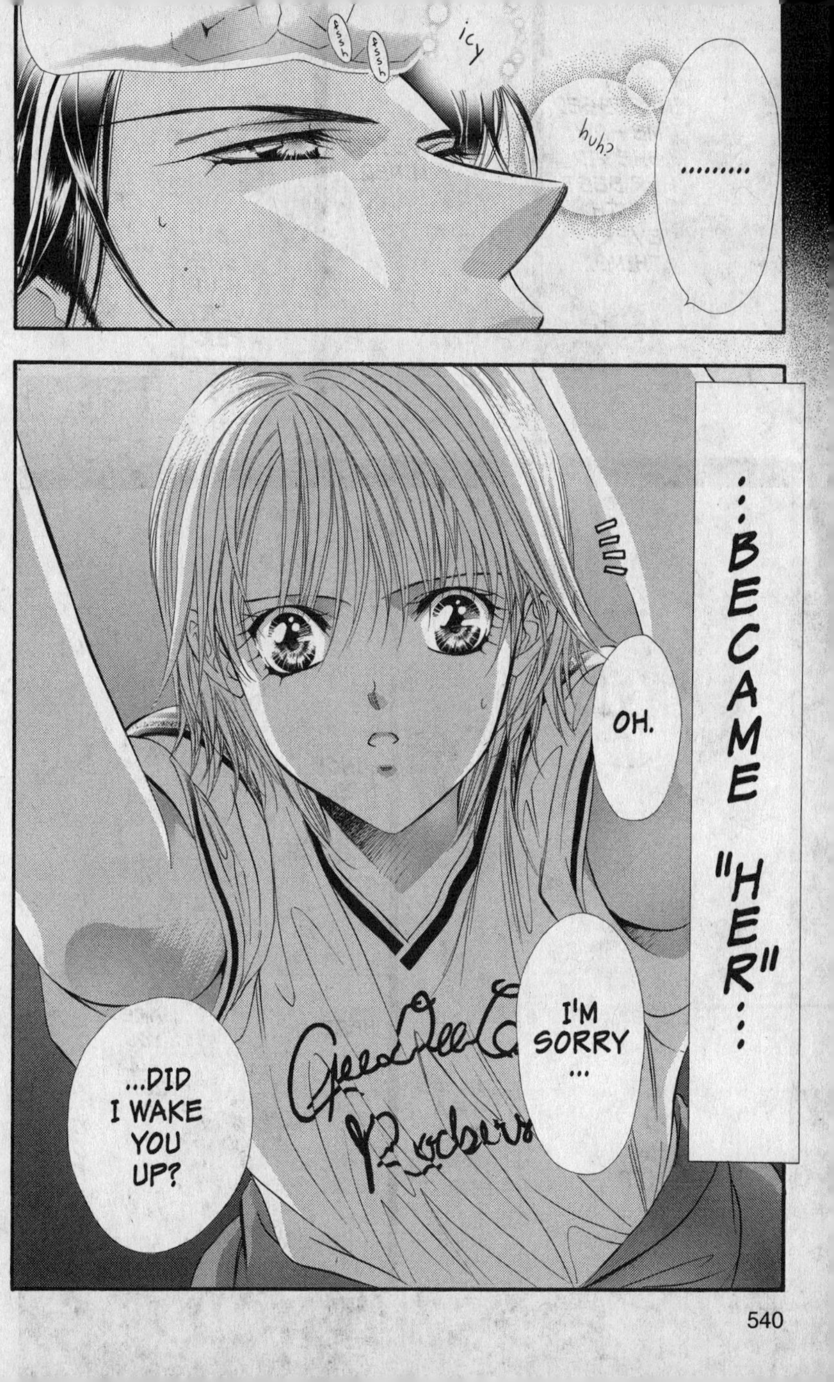
fssh
fssh
icy
....
huh?
...BECAME "HER"...
OH.
I'M SORRY ...
...DID I WAKE YOU UP?

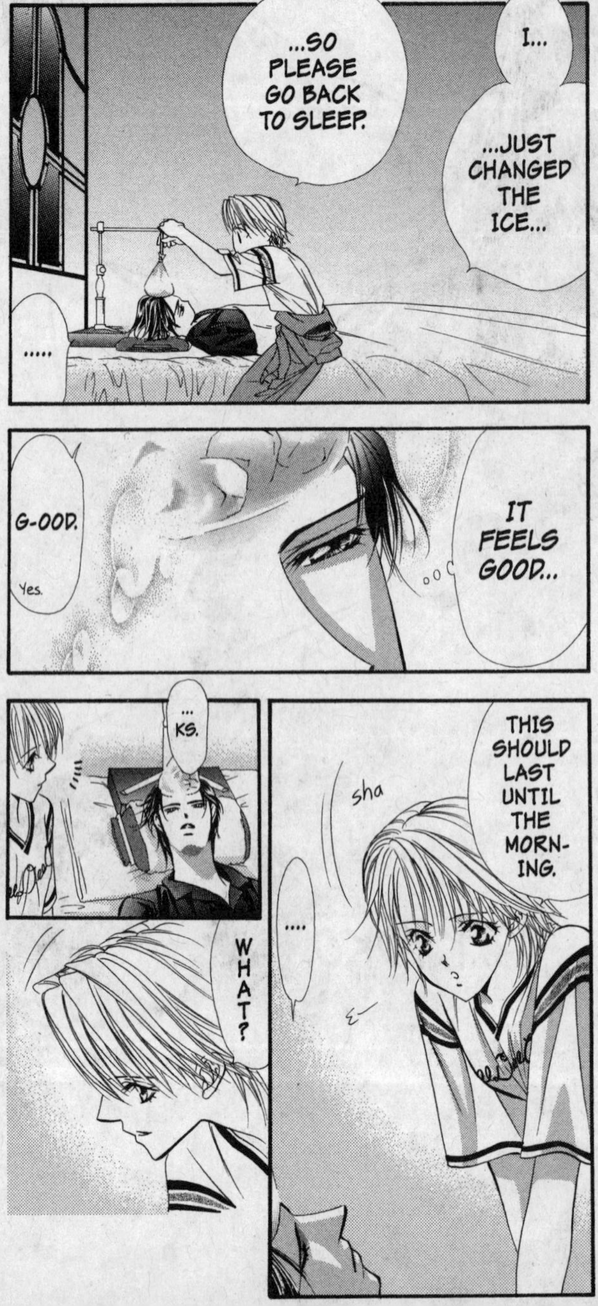
I...
...JUST CHANGED THE ICE...
...SO PLEASE GO BACK TO SLEEP.
.....
IT FEELS GOOD...
G-OOD.
Yes.
THIS SHOULD LAST UNTIL THE MORN-ING.
sha
....
... KS.
WHAT?

Continued

...But it makes you laugh more than the old model... no... that's what I think... But...s-so I intended to write what shape the latest ice bag is like, and what sort of joke I made the moment I saw it, but I don't want the readers to laugh every time they see that scene (Because I don't want people to laugh at the scene.) So I won't write about it...I-I'm sorry... In the magazine, I said I might write the reason why...

...By the way, when I was drawing, I felt that you wouldn't use ice bags nowadays. But, using a Hiepita would have been dull...and she wouldn't have stayed up all night taking care of Ren...that's why I used the ice bag, but now that I think about it, I'd forgotten the easy method of wetting a towel with ice water... That would have been even more like taking care of Ren without any sleep!!...why didn't I think of it...it pains me...

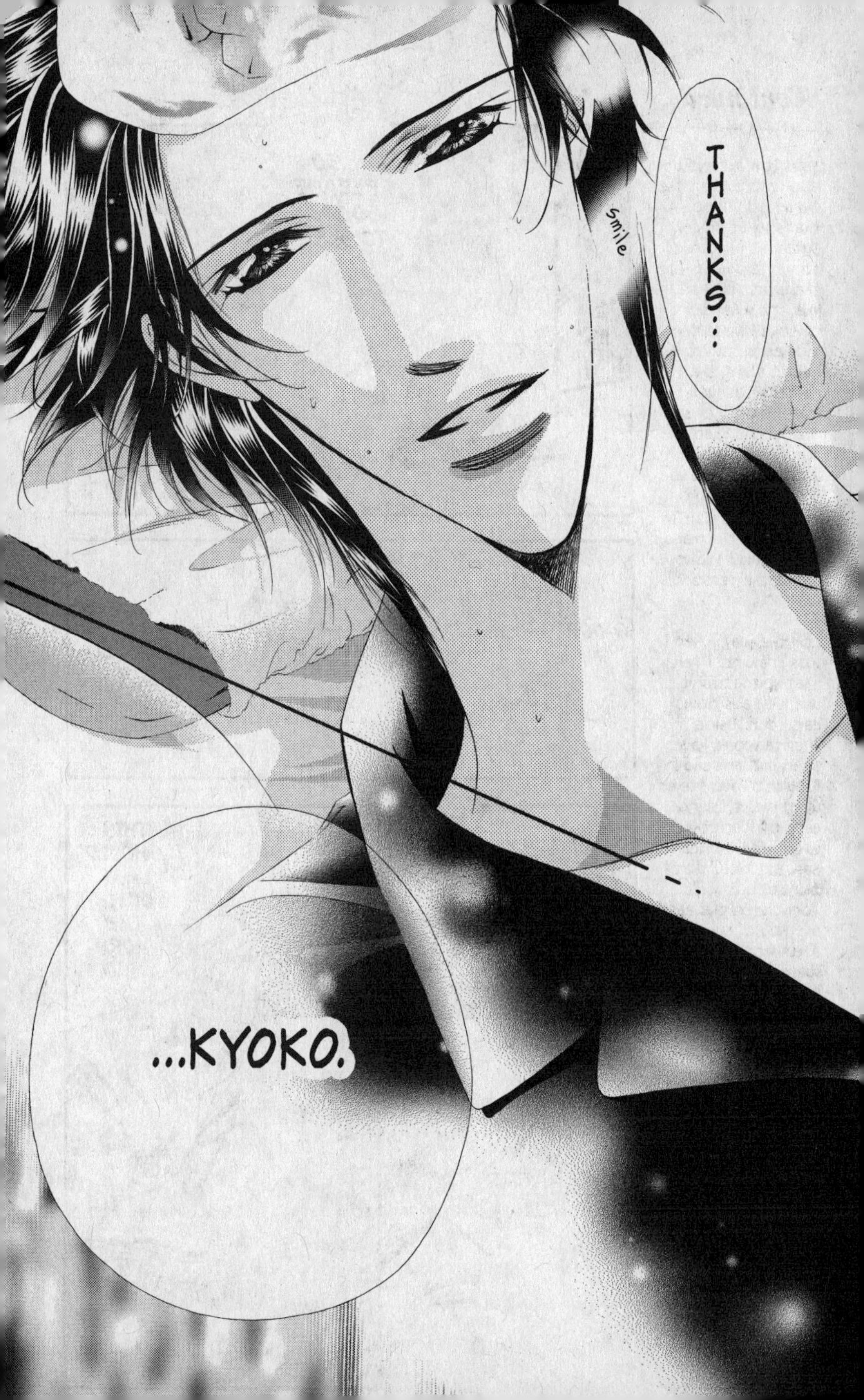
THANKS...
smile
...KYOKO.

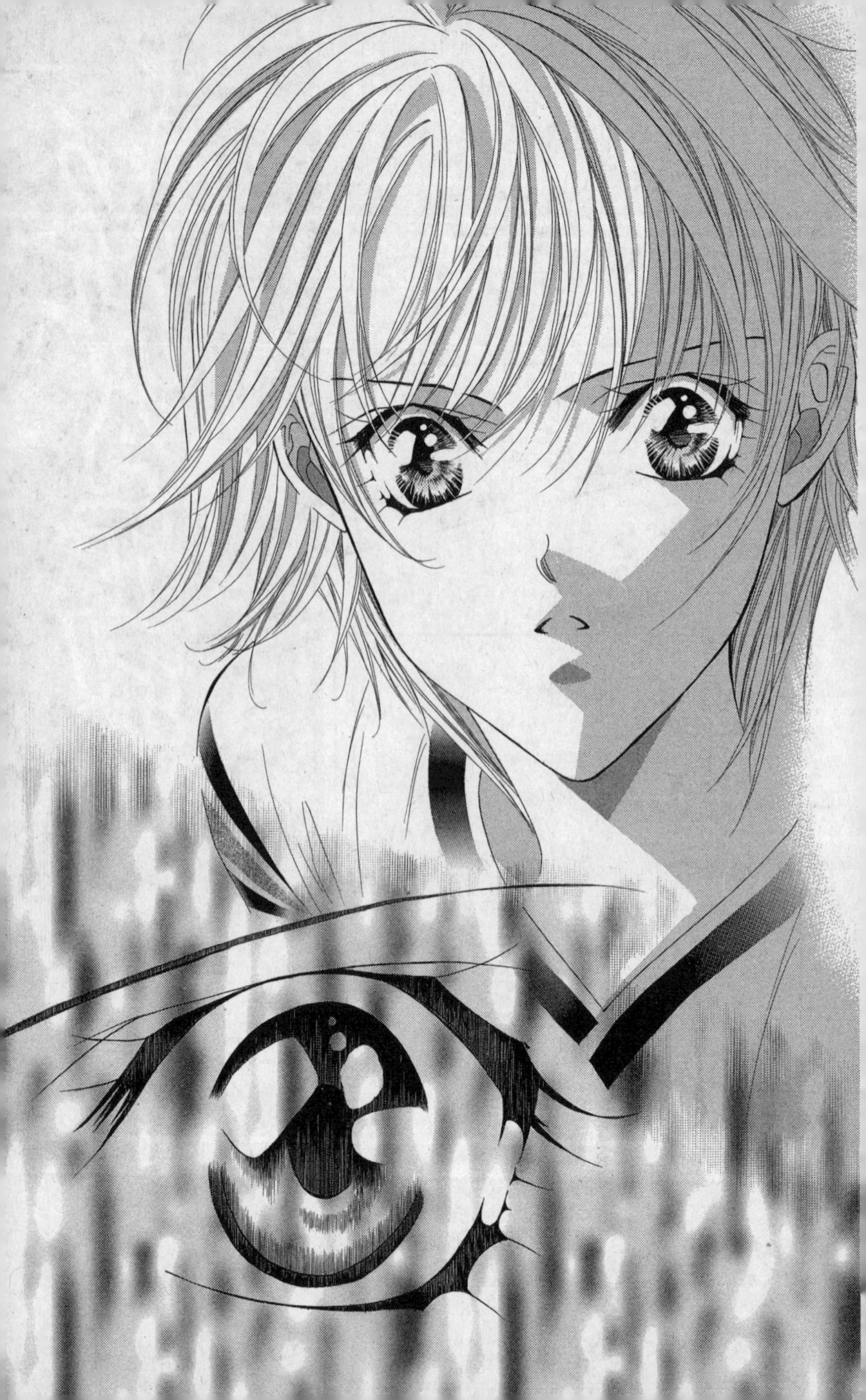

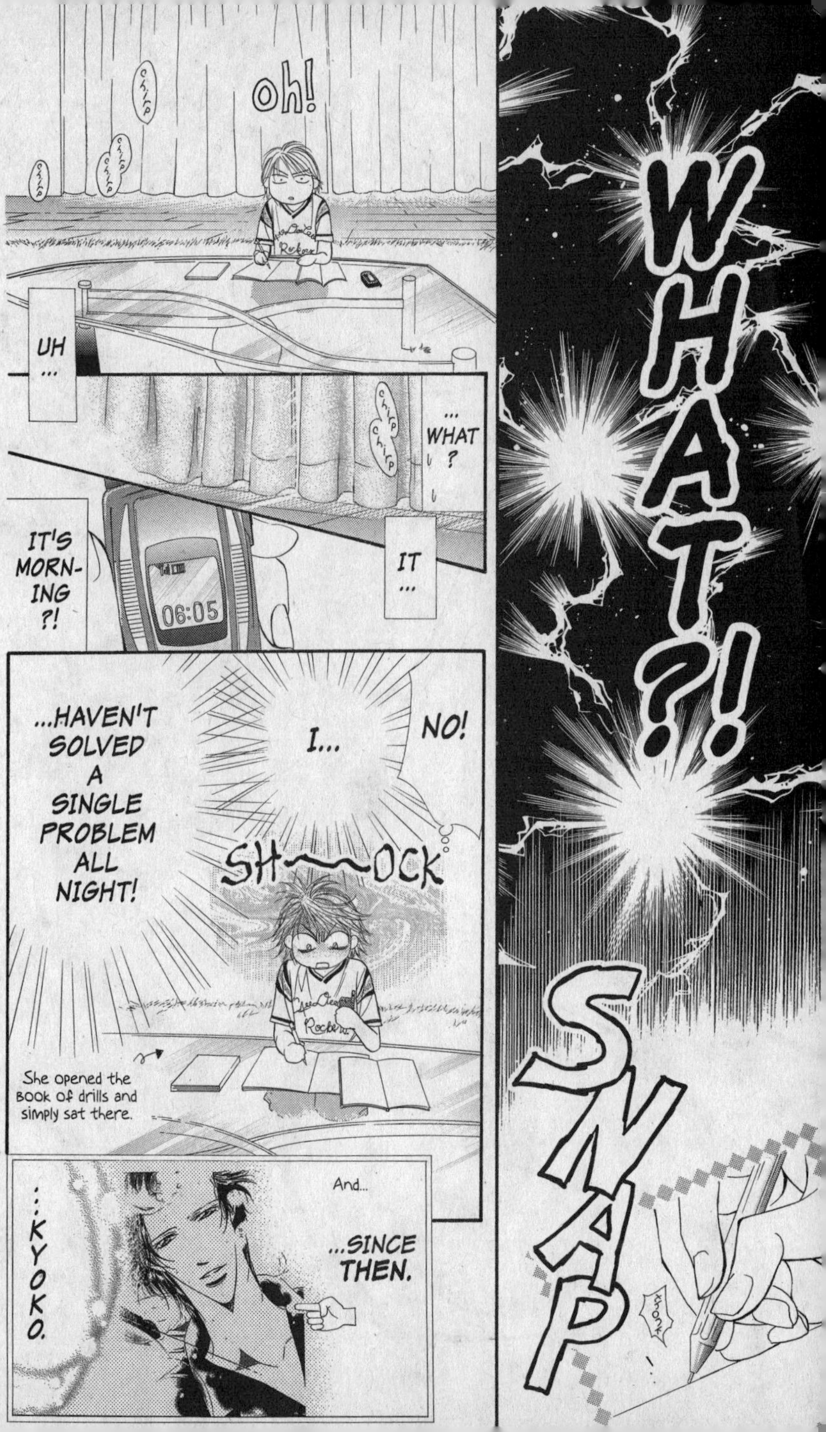
WHAT?!
SNAP
thonk
chirp
chirp chirp
chirp
oh!
UH ...
chirp chirp
... WHAT ?
IT ...
IT'S MORNING-ING ?!
06:05
NO!
I...
...HAVEN'T SOLVED A SINGLE PROBLEM ALL NIGHT!
SH—OCK
She opened the book of drills and simply sat there.
And...
...SINCE THEN.
...KYOKO.

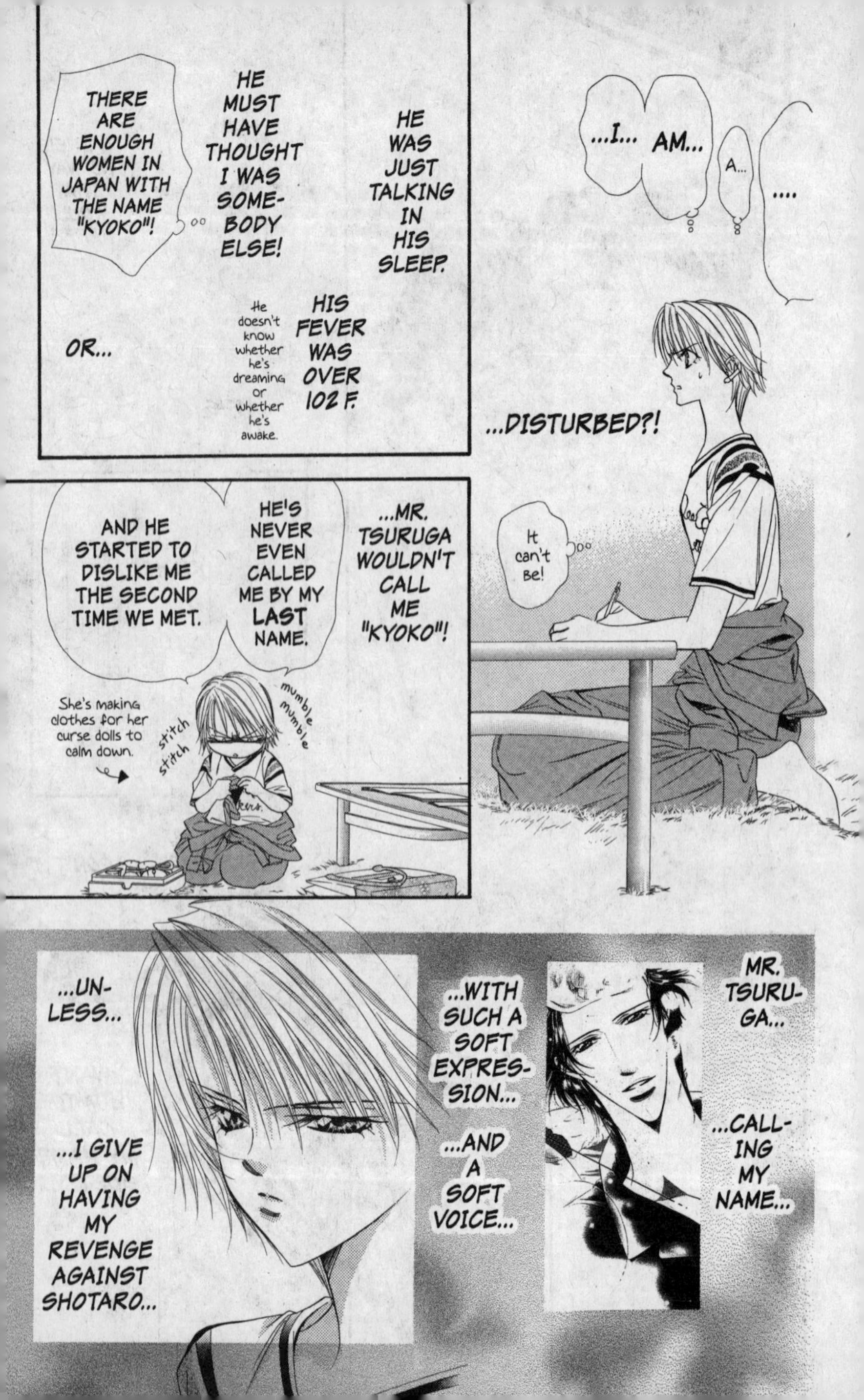
...I... AM...
A...
....
...DISTURBED?!
It can't be!
HE WAS JUST TALKING IN HIS SLEEP.
HE MUST HAVE THOUGHT I WAS SOME-BODY ELSE!
THERE ARE ENOUGH WOMEN IN JAPAN WITH THE NAME "KYOKO"!
HIS FEVER WAS OVER 102 F.
He doesn't know whether he's dreaming or whether he's awake.
OR...
...MR. TSURUGA WOULDN'T CALL ME "KYOKO"!
HE'S NEVER EVEN CALLED ME BY MY LAST NAME.
AND HE STARTED TO DISLIKE ME THE SECOND TIME WE MET.
mumble mumble
stitch stitch
She's making clothes for her curse dolls to calm down.
MR. TSURU-GA...
...CALL-ING MY NAME...
...WITH SUCH A SOFT EXPRES-SION...
...AND A SOFT VOICE...
...UN-LESS...
...I GIVE UP ON HAVING MY REVENGE AGAINST SHOTARO...

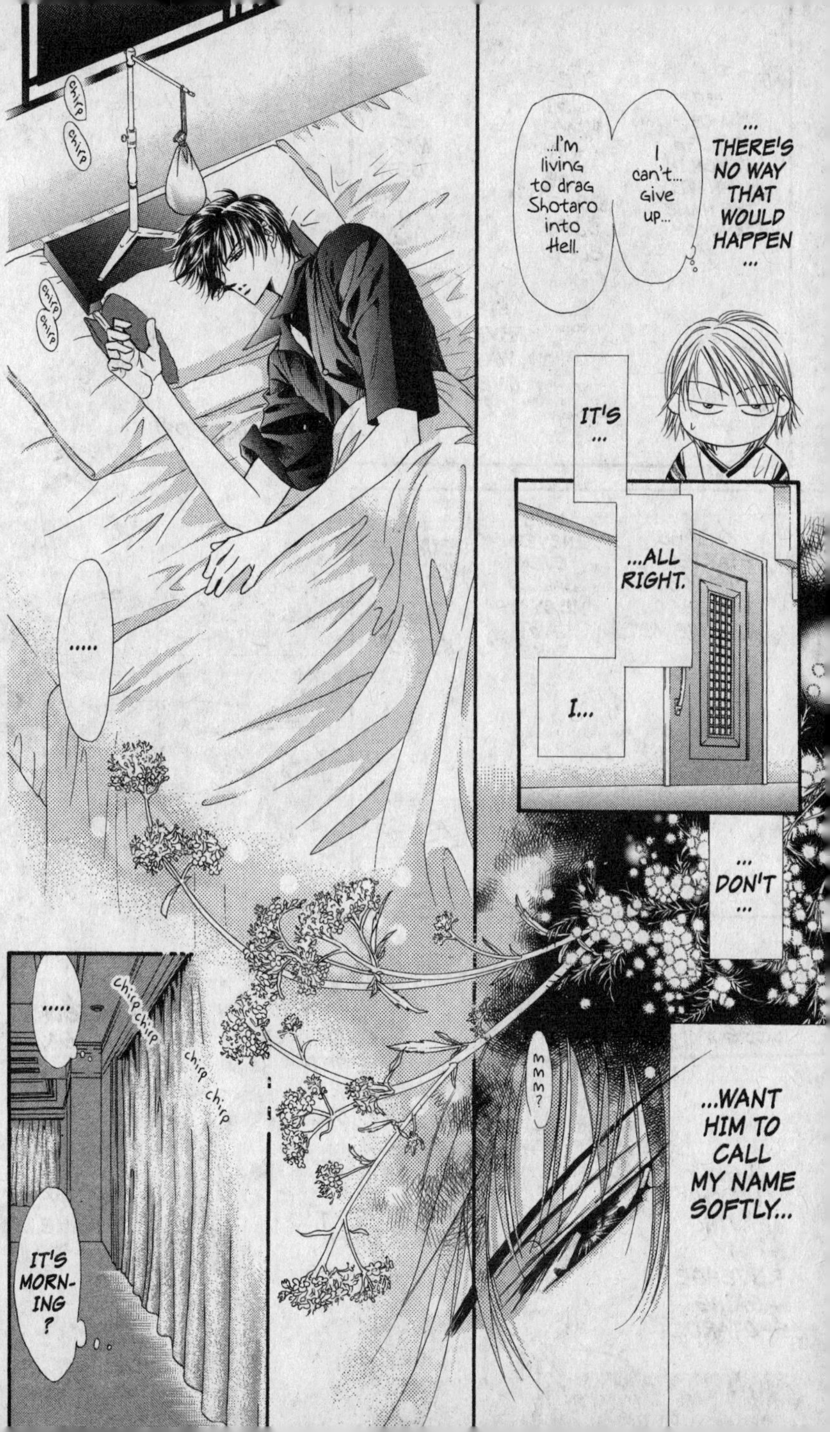
...THERE'S NO WAY THAT WOULD HAPPEN...
I can't... give up...
...I'm living to drag Shotaro into Hell.
IT'S...
...ALL RIGHT.
I...
...DON'T...
...WANT HIM TO CALL MY NAME SOFTLY...
MMM?
chirp
chirp
chirp
chirp
.....
chirp chirp
chirp chirp
.....
IT'S MORNING?

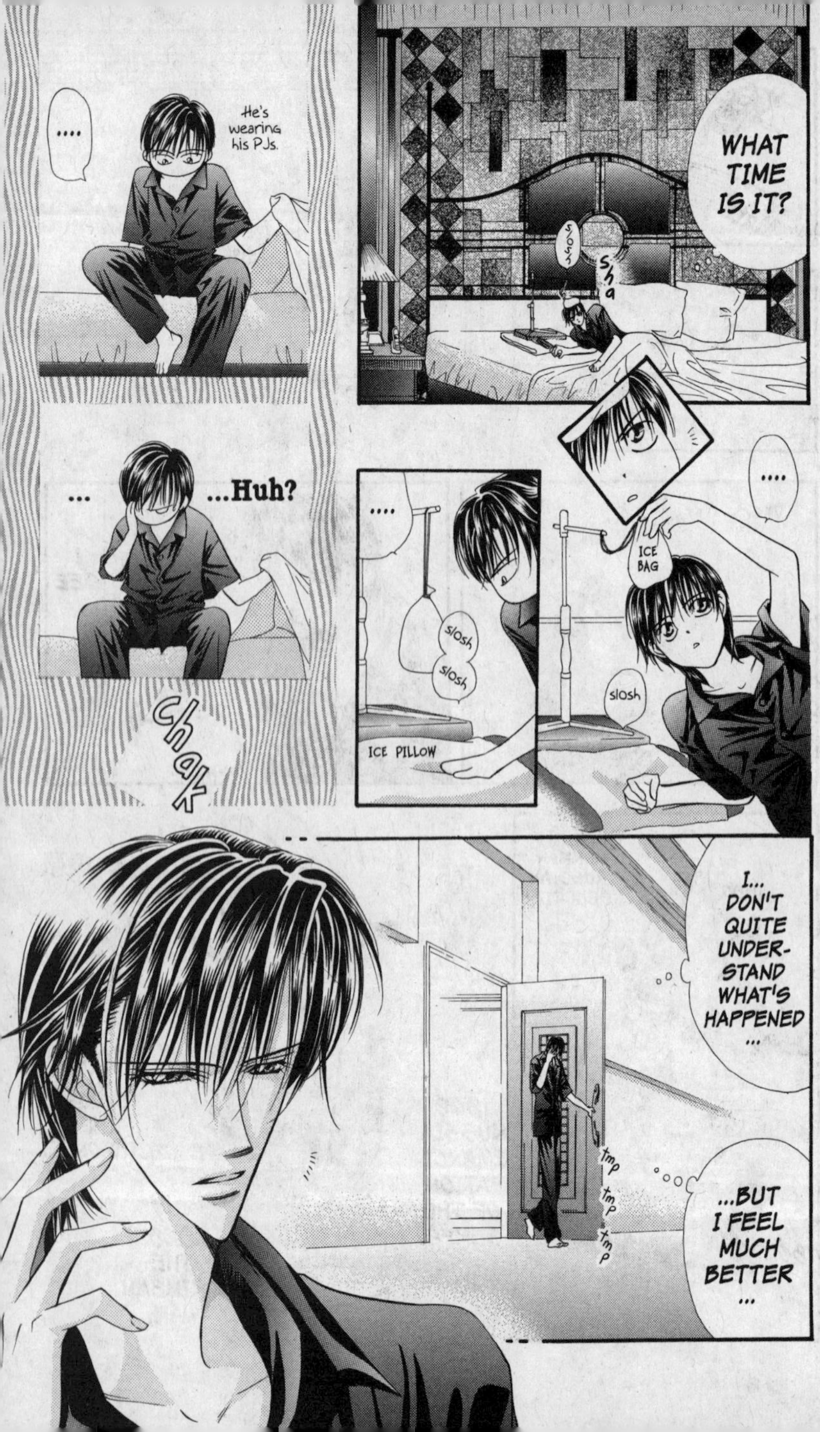
WHAT TIME IS IT?
slosh
Sha
....
He's wearing his PJs.
....
ICE BAG
slosh
....
slosh
slosh
ICE PILLOW
...
...Huh?
Chak
I... DON'T QUITE UNDER-STAND WHAT'S HAPPENED...
...BUT I FEEL MUCH BETTER...
tmp
tmp
tmp

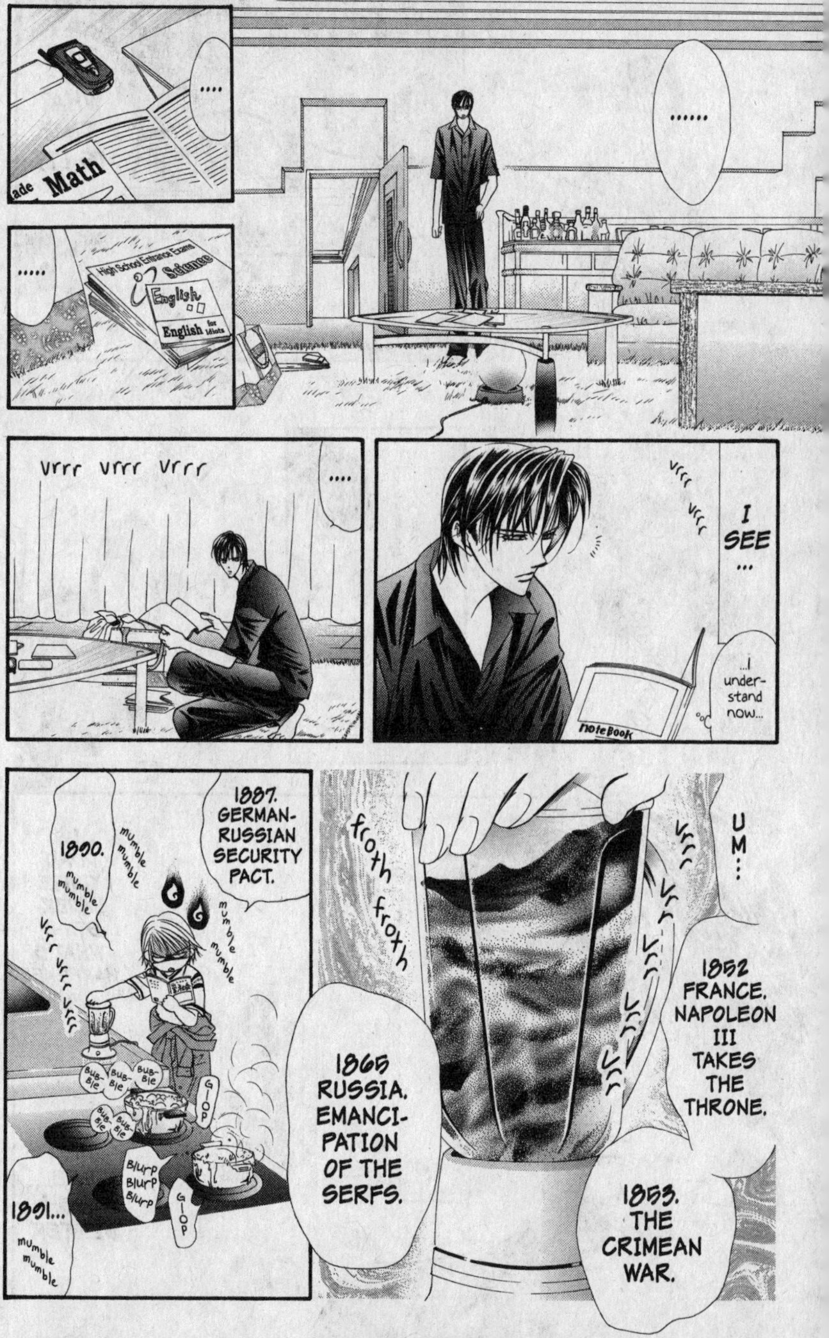

......
Math
....
High School Entrance Exams
Science
English
English for Idiots
......
Vrrr vrrr
I SEE...
...I understand now...
NoteBook
Vrrr vrrr vrrr
....
UM...
froth froth
Vrrr Vrr Vrr Vrr Vrr
1852 FRANCE. NAPOLEON III TAKES THE THRONE.
1853. THE CRIMEAN WAR.
1865 RUSSIA. EMANCIPATION OF THE SERFS.
1887. GERMAN-RUSSIAN SECURITY PACT.
mumble mumble
1890.
mumble mumble
mumble mumble
Vrrr vrrr vrrr vrrr
GIOP
Bub-ble Bub-ble Bub-ble Bub-ble Bub-ble
GIOP
Blurp Blurp Blurp
1891...
mumble mumble

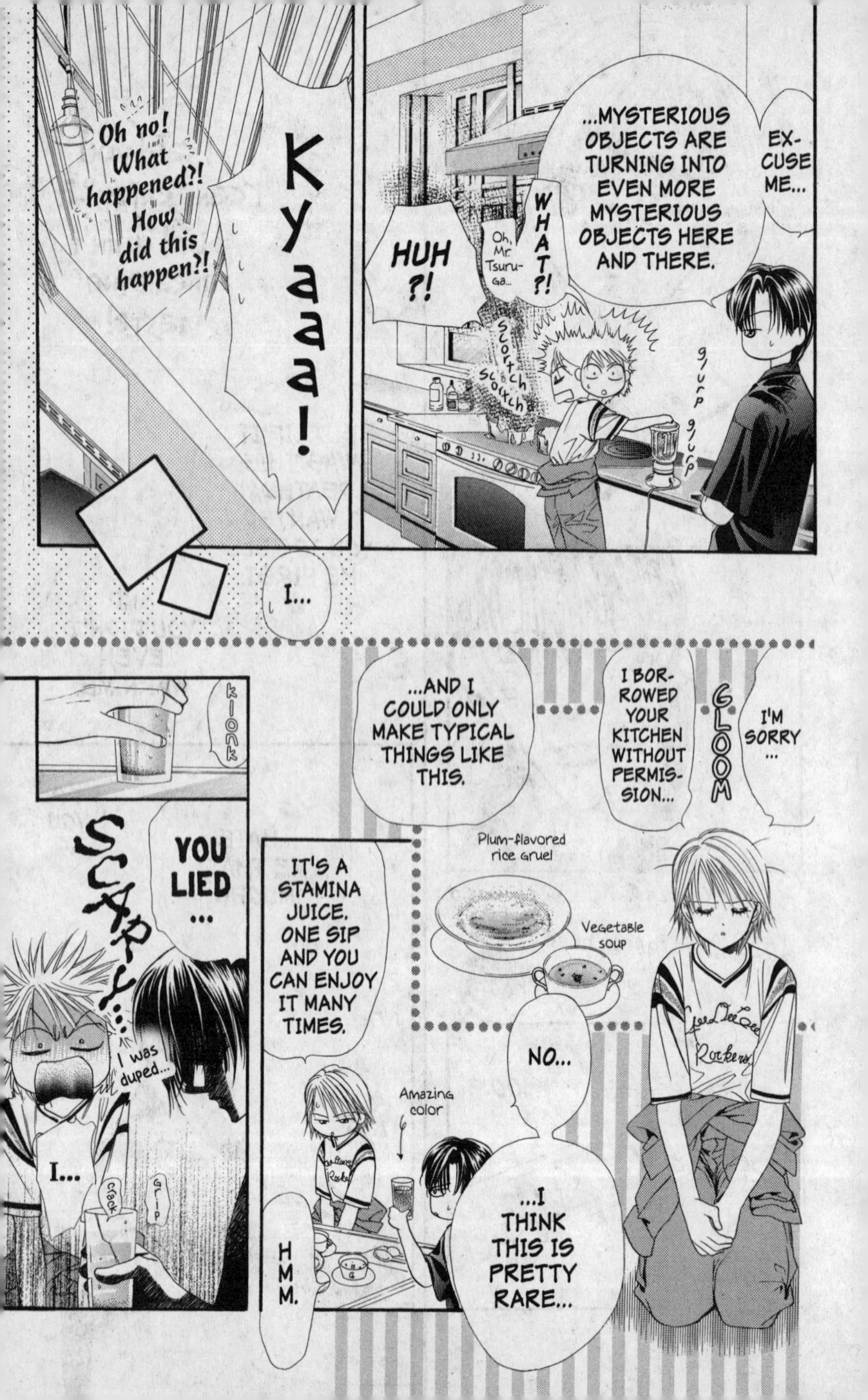
EX-CUSE ME...
...MYSTERIOUS OBJECTS ARE TURNING INTO EVEN MORE MYSTERIOUS OBJECTS HERE AND THERE.
WHAT?!
Oh, Mr. Tsuru-ga...
HUH?!
scortch scortch
glurp glurp
Kyaaa!
Oh no! What happened?! How did this happen?!
I...
I'M SORRY...
GLOOM
I BOR-ROWED YOUR KITCHEN WITHOUT PERMIS-SION...
...AND I COULD ONLY MAKE TYPICAL THINGS LIKE THIS.
Plum-flavored rice gruel
Vegetable soup
NO...
...I THINK THIS IS PRETTY RARE...
IT'S A STAMINA JUICE. ONE SIP AND YOU CAN ENJOY IT MANY TIMES.
Amazing color
HMM.
klonk
YOU LIED...
SCARY...
I was duped...
I...
crack
grip

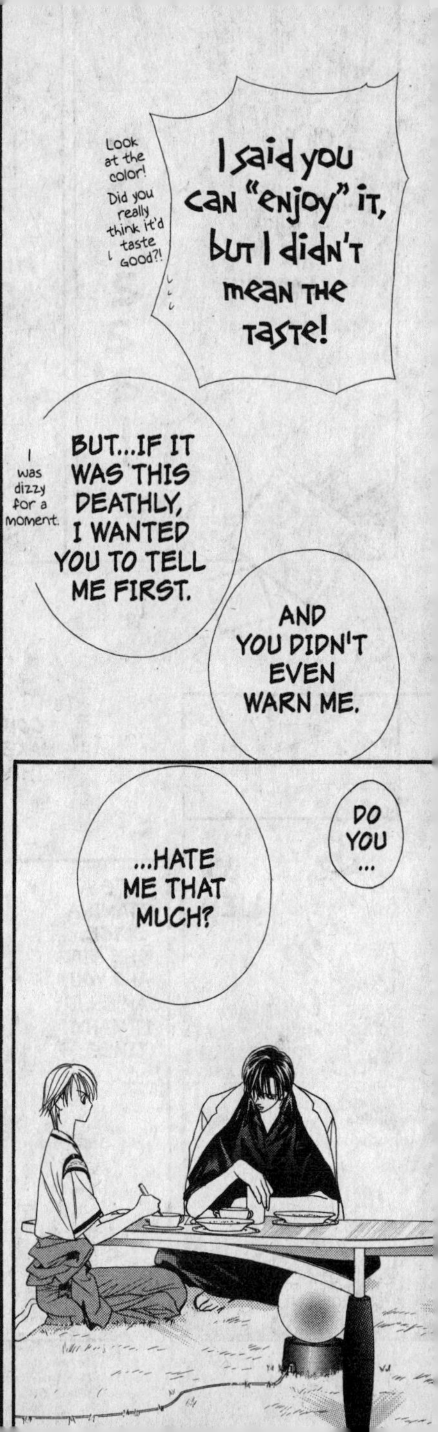
I said you can "enjoy" it, but I didn't mean the taste!
Look at the color! Did you really think it'd taste good?!
BUT...IF IT WAS THIS DEATHLY, I WANTED YOU TO TELL ME FIRST.
AND YOU DIDN'T EVEN WARN ME.
I was dizzy for a moment.
DO YOU...
...HATE ME THAT MUCH?
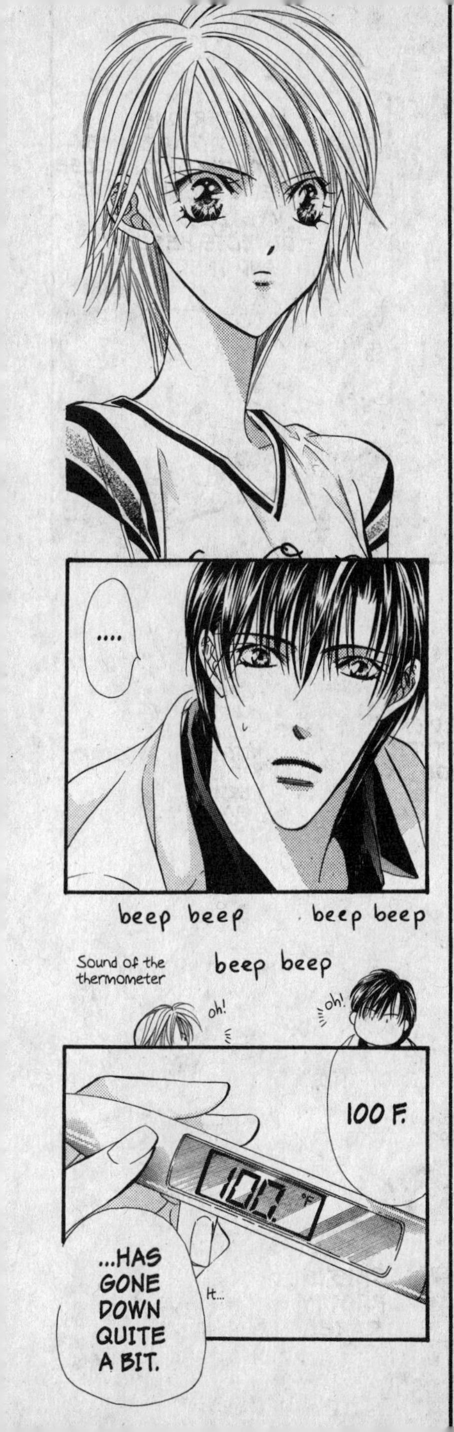
....
beep beep
beep beep
beep beep
Sound of the thermometer
oh!
oh!
100 F.
It...
...HAS GONE DOWN QUITE A BIT.

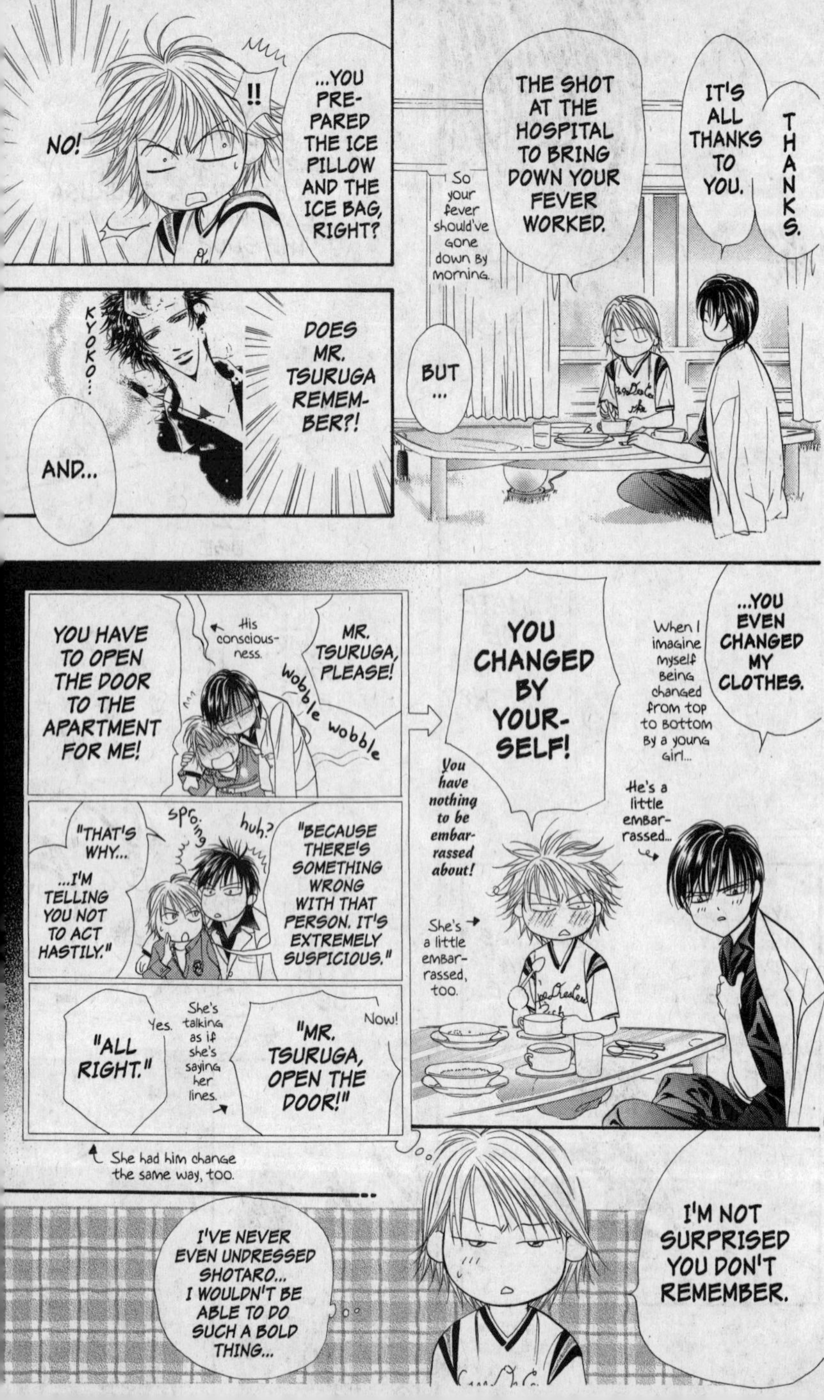
THANKS.
IT'S ALL THANKS TO YOU.
THE SHOT AT THE HOSPITAL TO BRING DOWN YOUR FEVER WORKED.
So your fever should've gone down by morning.
BUT ...
...YOU PRE-PARED THE ICE PILLOW AND THE ICE BAG, RIGHT?
!!
NO!
DOES MR. TSURUGA REMEM-BER?!
KYOKO...
AND...
...YOU EVEN CHANGED MY CLOTHES.
When I imagine myself being changed from top to bottom by a young girl...
YOU CHANGED BY YOUR-SELF!
You have nothing to be embar-rassed about!
He's a little embar-rassed...
She's a little embar-rassed, too.
MR. TSURUGA, PLEASE!
His conscious-ness.
wobble wobble
YOU HAVE TO OPEN THE DOOR TO THE APARTMENT FOR ME!
"BECAUSE THERE'S SOMETHING WRONG WITH THAT PERSON. IT'S EXTREMELY SUSPICIOUS."
huh?
sproing
"THAT'S WHY...
...I'M TELLING YOU NOT TO ACT HASTILY."
Now!
"MR. TSURUGA, OPEN THE DOOR!"
She's talking as if she's saying her lines.
Yes.
"ALL RIGHT."
She had him change the same way, too.
I'M NOT SURPRISED YOU DON'T REMEMBER.
I'VE NEVER EVEN UNDRESSED SHOTARO... I WOULDN'T BE ABLE TO DO SUCH A BOLD THING...

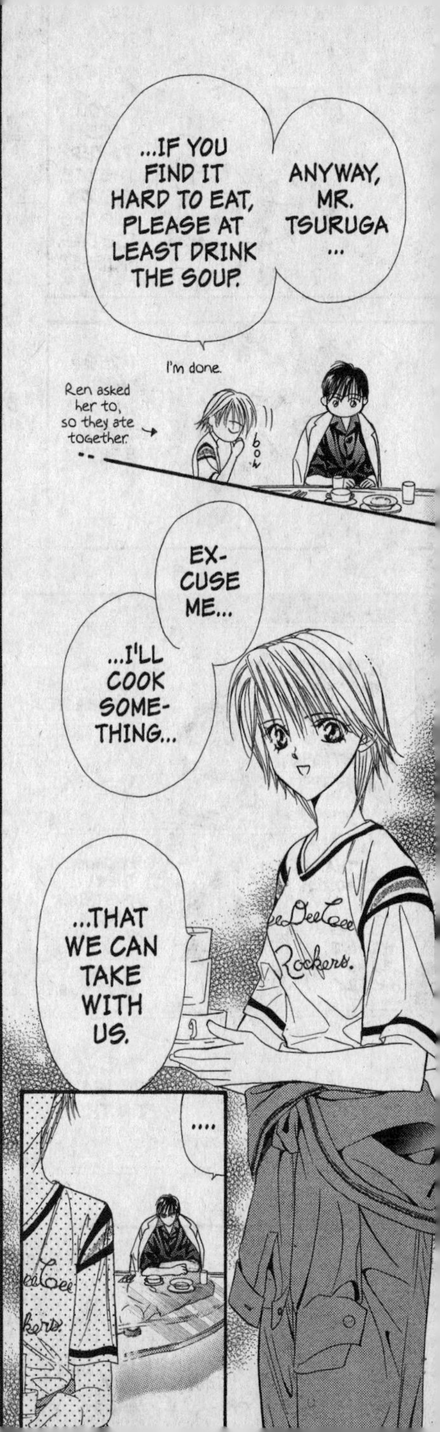
ANYWAY, MR. TSURUGA ...
...IF YOU FIND IT HARD TO EAT, PLEASE AT LEAST DRINK THE SOUP.
I'm done.
bow
Ren asked her to, so they ate together.
EX-CUSE ME...
...I'LL COOK SOME-THING...
...THAT WE CAN TAKE WITH US.
....
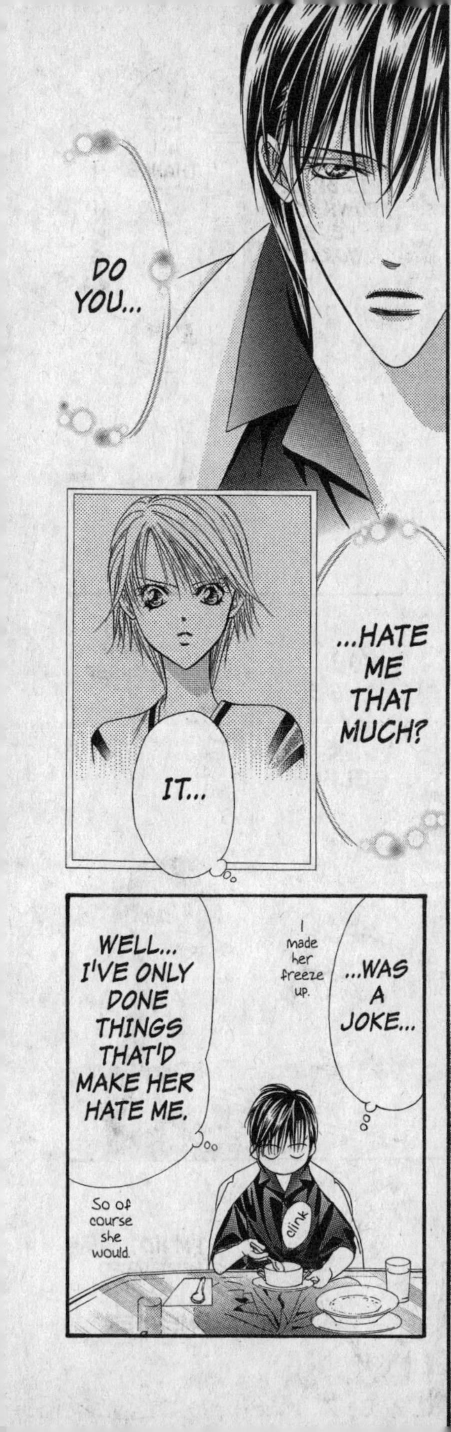
DO YOU...
...HATE ME THAT MUCH?
IT...
...WAS A JOKE...
I made her freeze up.
WELL... I'VE ONLY DONE THINGS THAT'D MAKE HER HATE ME.
clink
So of course she would.

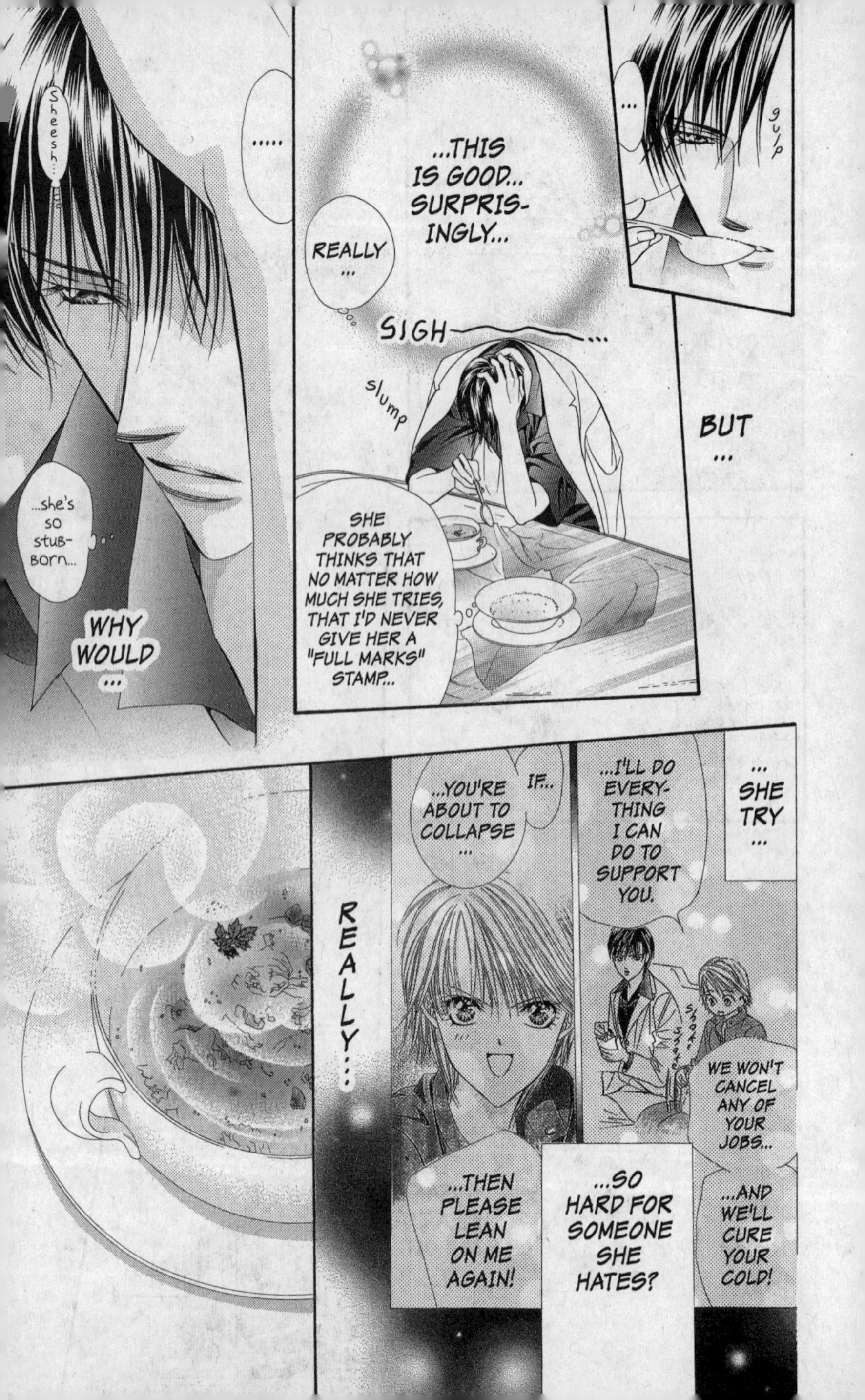
...
gulp
BUT ...
...THIS IS GOOD... SURPRISINGLY...
REALLY ...
SIGH...
slump
SHE PROBABLY THINKS THAT NO MATTER HOW MUCH SHE TRIES, THAT I'D NEVER GIVE HER A "FULL MARKS" STAMP...
.....
Sheesh...
...she's so stubborn...
WHY WOULD ...
... SHE TRY ...
...I'LL DO EVERYTHING I CAN DO TO SUPPORT YOU.
WE WON'T CANCEL ANY OF YOUR JOBS...
...AND WE'LL CURE YOUR COLD!
...SO HARD FOR SOMEONE SHE HATES?
IF...
...YOU'RE ABOUT TO COLLAPSE ...
...THEN PLEASE LEAN ON ME AGAIN!
REALLY...

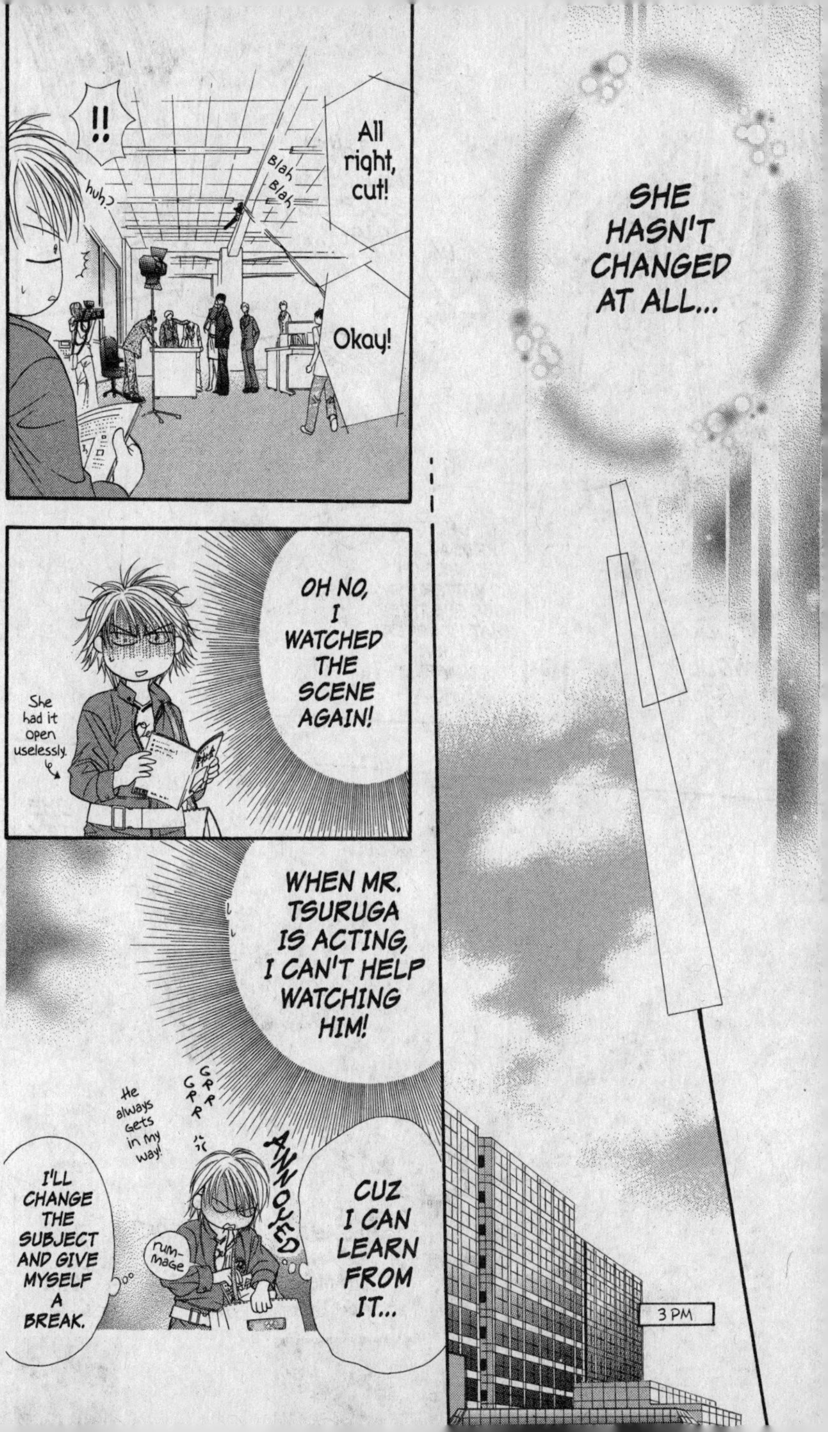
SHE HASN'T CHANGED AT ALL...
3 PM
All right, cut!
Blah Blah
!!
huh?
Okay!
OH NO, I WATCHED THE SCENE AGAIN!
She had it open uselessly.
WHEN MR. TSURUGA IS ACTING, I CAN'T HELP WATCHING HIM!
CUZ I CAN LEARN FROM IT...
ANNOYED
GRR GRR
He always gets in my way!
rum-mage
I'LL CHANGE THE SUBJECT AND GIVE MYSELF A BREAK.

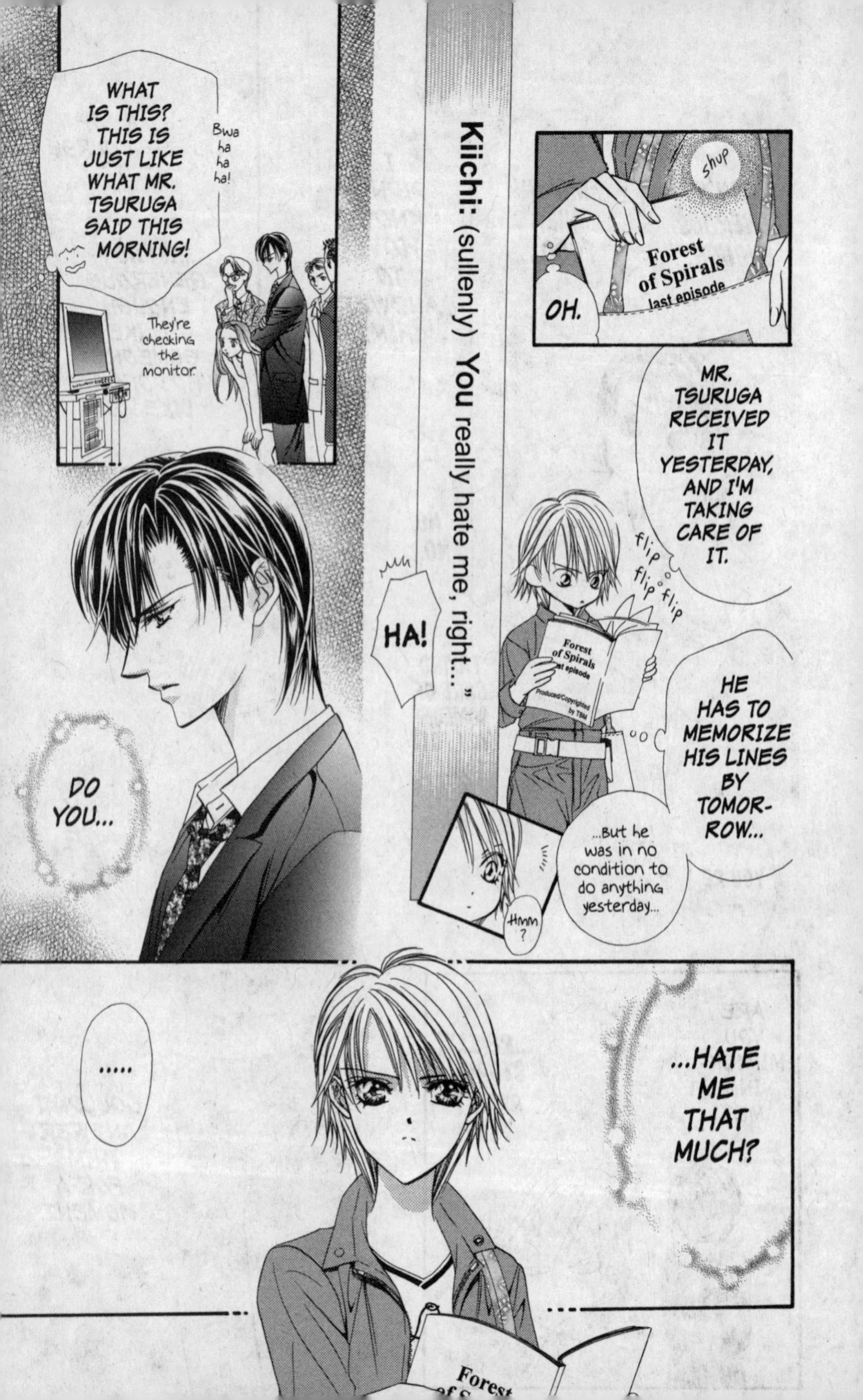
shup
OH.
Forest of Spirals last episode
MR. TSURUGA RECEIVED IT YESTERDAY, AND I'M TAKING CARE OF IT.
flip flip flip
Forest of Spirals last episode Produced/Copyrighted by TBM
HE HAS TO MEMORIZE HIS LINES BY TOMOR-ROW...
...But he was in no condition to do anything yesterday...
Hmm?
Kiichi: (sullenly) You really hate me, right..."
HA!
WHAT IS THIS? THIS IS JUST LIKE WHAT MR. TSURUGA SAID THIS MORNING!
Bwa ha ha ha!
They're checking the monitor.
DO YOU...
...HATE ME THAT MUCH?
.....
Forest

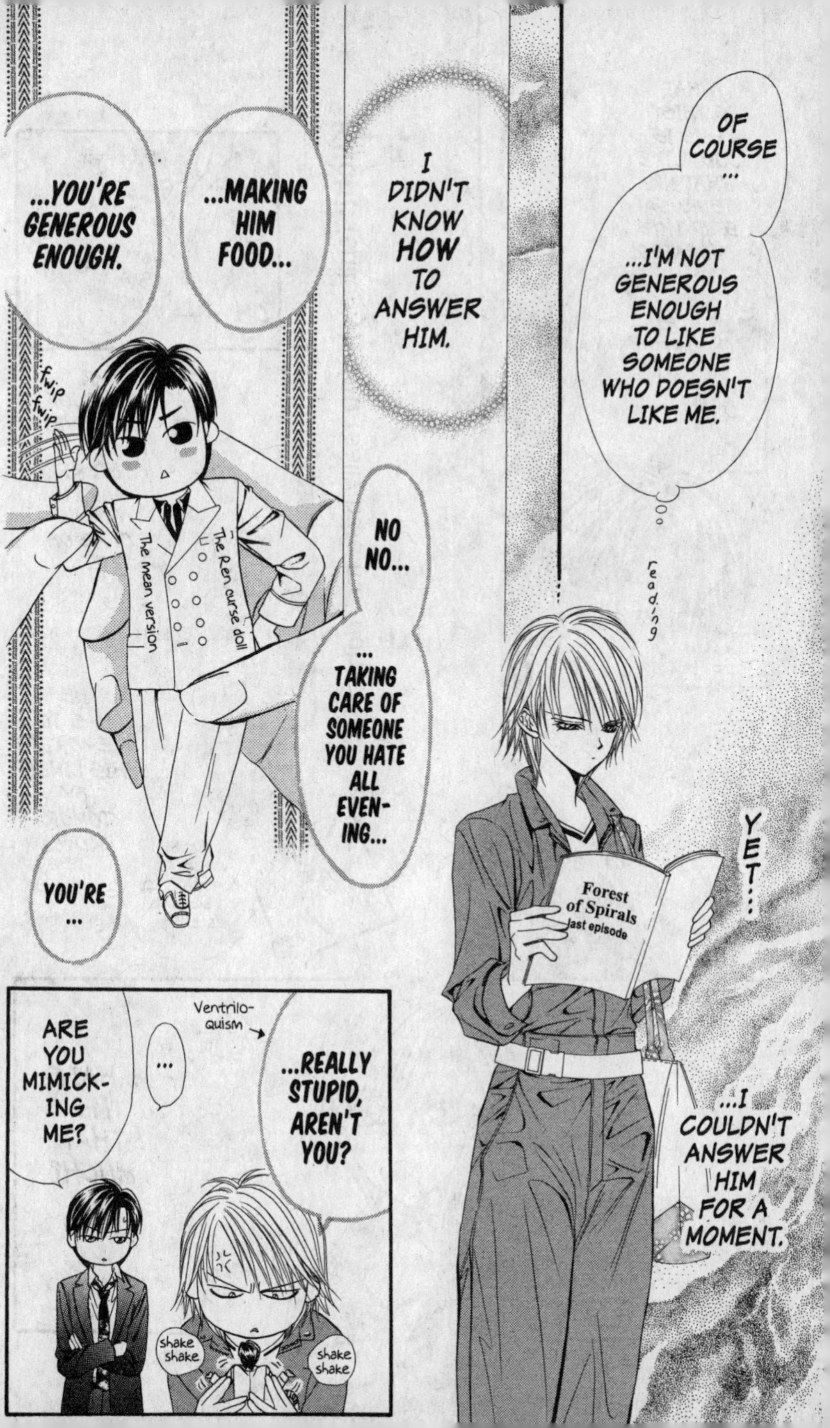
OF COURSE ...
...I'M NOT GENEROUS ENOUGH TO LIKE SOMEONE WHO DOESN'T LIKE ME.
reading
Forest of Spirals last episode
YET...
...I COULDN'T ANSWER HIM FOR A MOMENT.
I DIDN'T KNOW HOW TO ANSWER HIM.
NO NO...
...TAKING CARE OF SOMEONE YOU HATE ALL EVENING...
...MAKING HIM FOOD...
...YOU'RE GENEROUS ENOUGH.
fwip fwip
The Ren curse doll
The mean version
YOU'RE ...
Ventriloquism
...REALLY STUPID, AREN'T YOU?
...
ARE YOU MIMICKING ME?
shake shake
shake shake

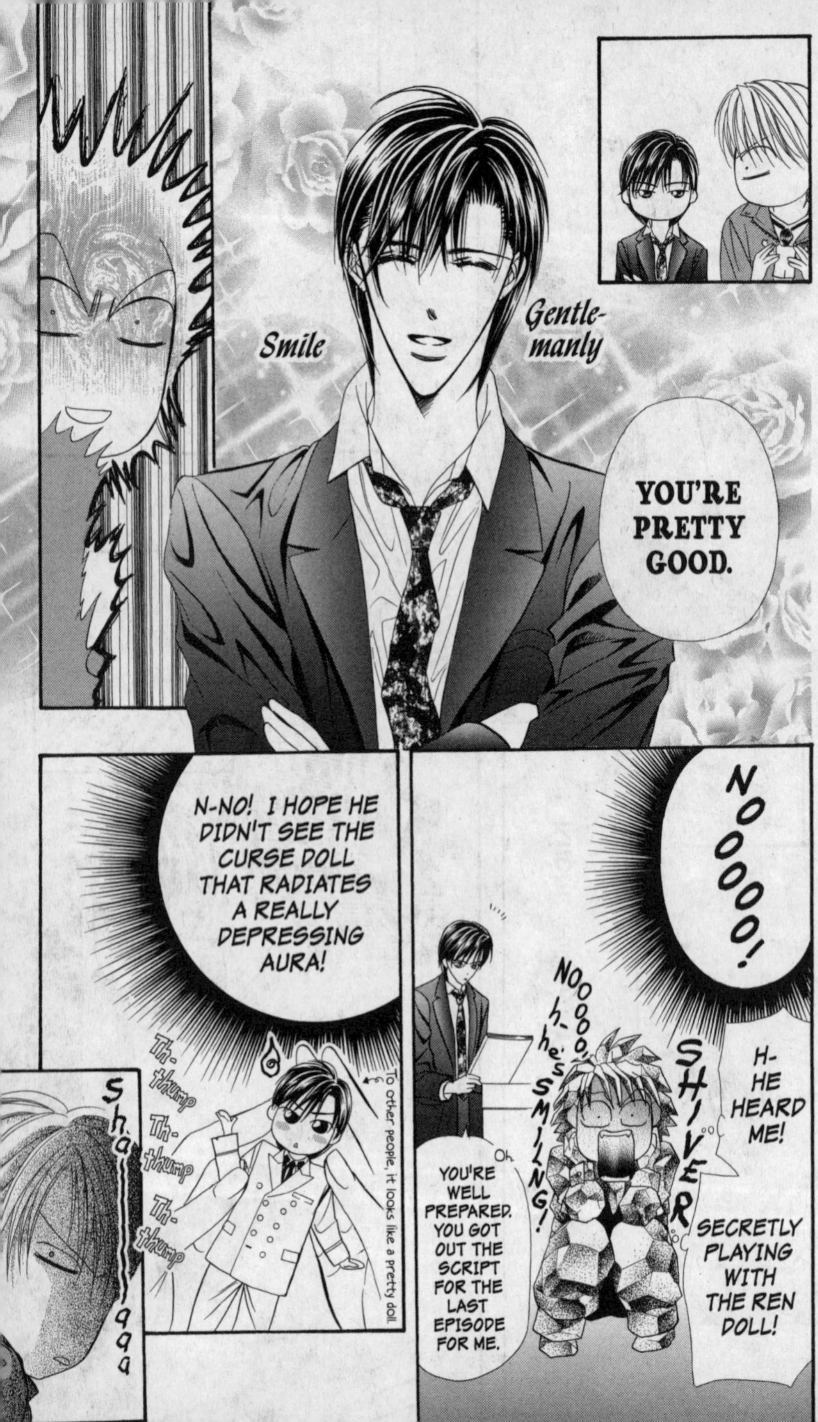
Gentle-manly
Smile
YOU'RE PRETTY GOOD.
NOOOOOO!
H-HE HEARD ME!
SHIVER
NOOOOO... h-he's SMILING!
SECRETLY PLAYING WITH THE REN DOLL!
Oh.
YOU'RE WELL PREPARED. YOU GOT OUT THE SCRIPT FOR THE LAST EPISODE FOR ME.
N-NO! I HOPE HE DIDN'T SEE THE CURSE DOLL THAT RADIATES A REALLY DEPRESSING AURA!
To other people, it looks like a pretty doll.
Th-thump
Th-thump
Th-thump
Shaaaa

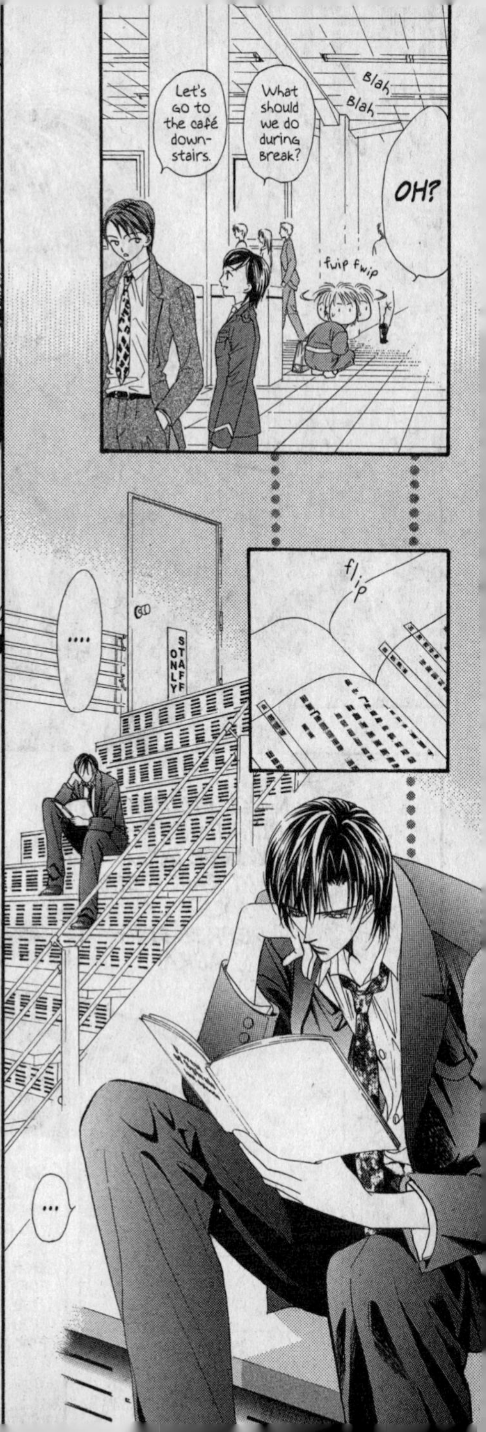
OH?
Blah Blah
What should we do during break?
Let's go to the café downstairs.
fwip fwip
flip
....
STAFF ONLY
...

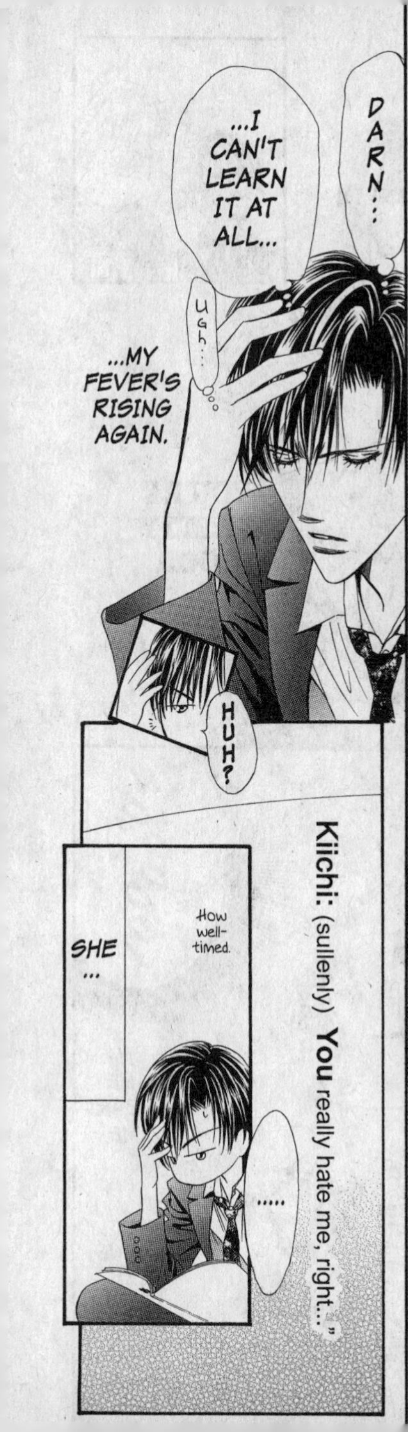
DARN...
...I CAN'T LEARN IT AT ALL...
Ugh...
...MY FEVER'S RISING AGAIN.
HUH?
Kiichi: (sullenly) You really hate me, right..."
SHE ...
How well-timed.
.....

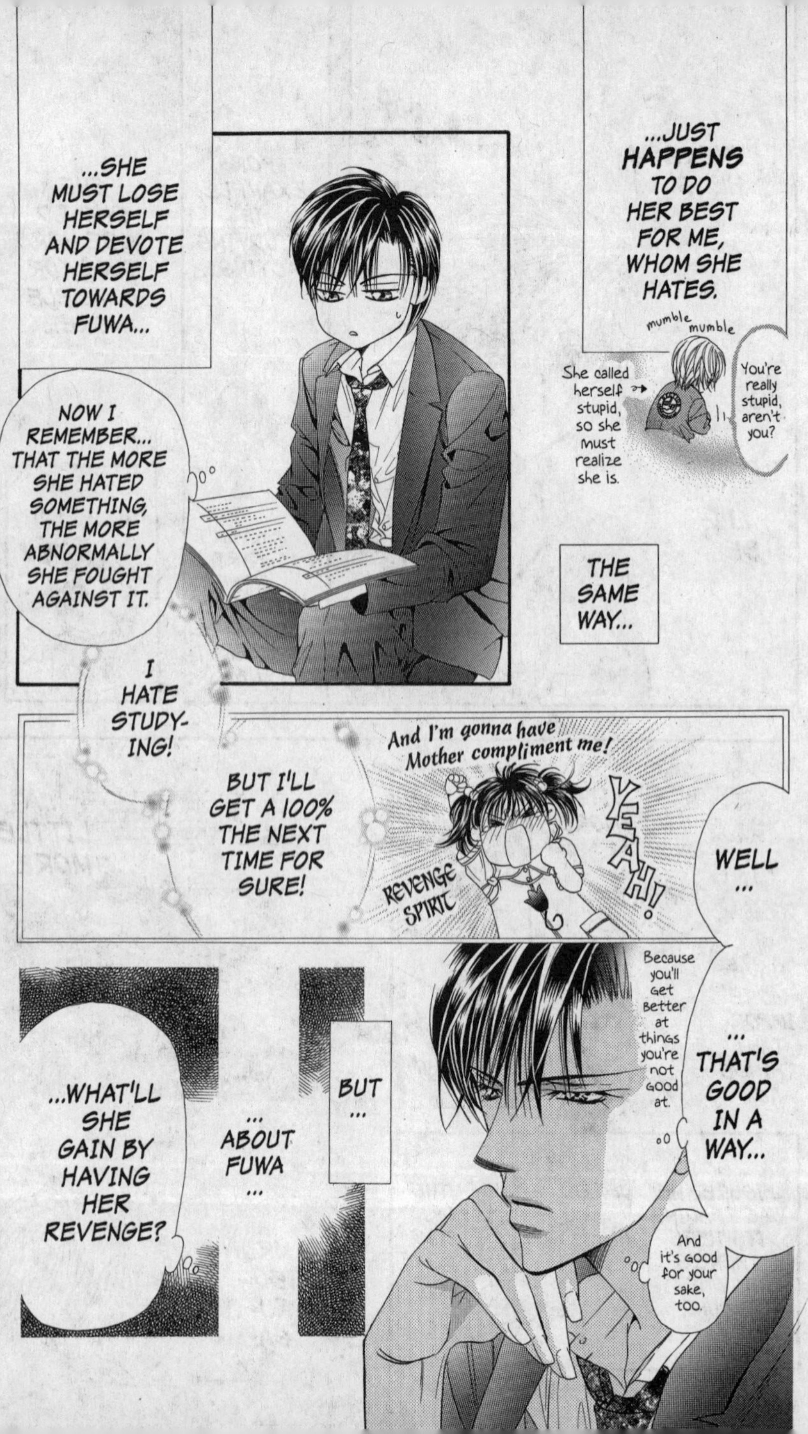
...JUST HAPPENS TO DO HER BEST FOR ME, WHOM SHE HATES.
mumble mumble
You're really stupid, aren't you?
She called herself stupid, so she must realize she is.
THE SAME WAY...
...SHE MUST LOSE HERSELF AND DEVOTE HERSELF TOWARDS FUWA...
NOW I REMEMBER... THAT THE MORE SHE HATED SOMETHING, THE MORE ABNORMALLY SHE FOUGHT AGAINST IT.
I HATE STUDYING!
BUT I'LL GET A 100% THE NEXT TIME FOR SURE!
And I'm gonna have Mother compliment me!
YEAH!
REVENGE SPIRIT
WELL ...
... THAT'S GOOD IN A WAY...
Because you'll get better at things you're not good at.
And it's good for your sake, too.
BUT ...
... ABOUT FUWA ...
...WHAT'LL SHE GAIN BY HAVING HER REVENGE?

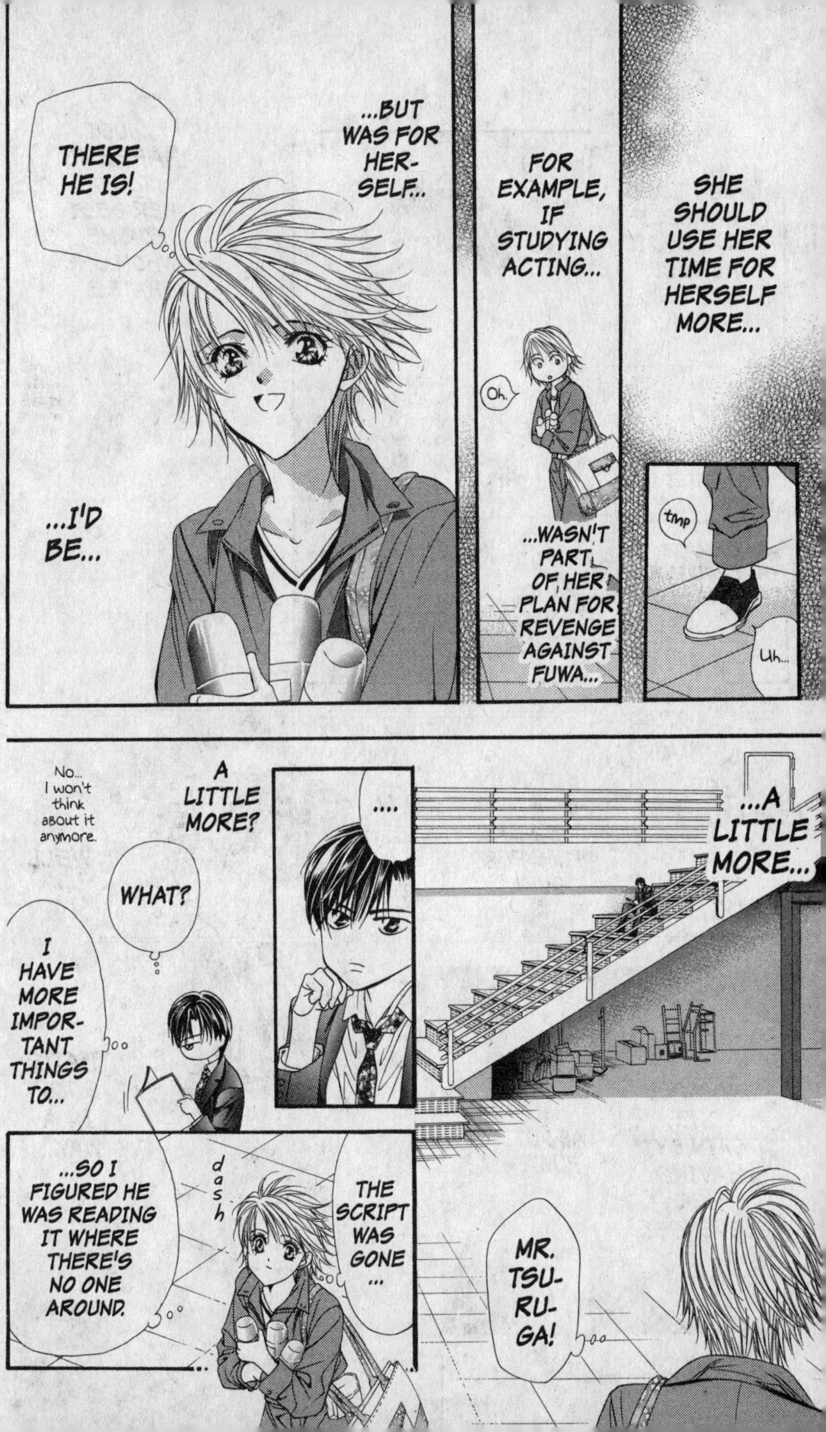
SHE SHOULD USE HER TIME FOR HERSELF MORE...
tmp
Uh...
FOR EXAMPLE, IF STUDYING ACTING...
Oh.
...WASN'T PART OF HER PLAN FOR REVENGE AGAINST FUWA...
...BUT WAS FOR HER-SELF...
THERE HE IS!
...I'D BE...
...A LITTLE MORE...
....
A LITTLE MORE?
WHAT?
No... I won't think about it anymore.
I HAVE MORE IMPOR-TANT THINGS TO...
MR. TSU-RU-GA!
THE SCRIPT WAS GONE...
dash
...SO I FIGURED HE WAS READING IT WHERE THERE'S NO ONE AROUND.

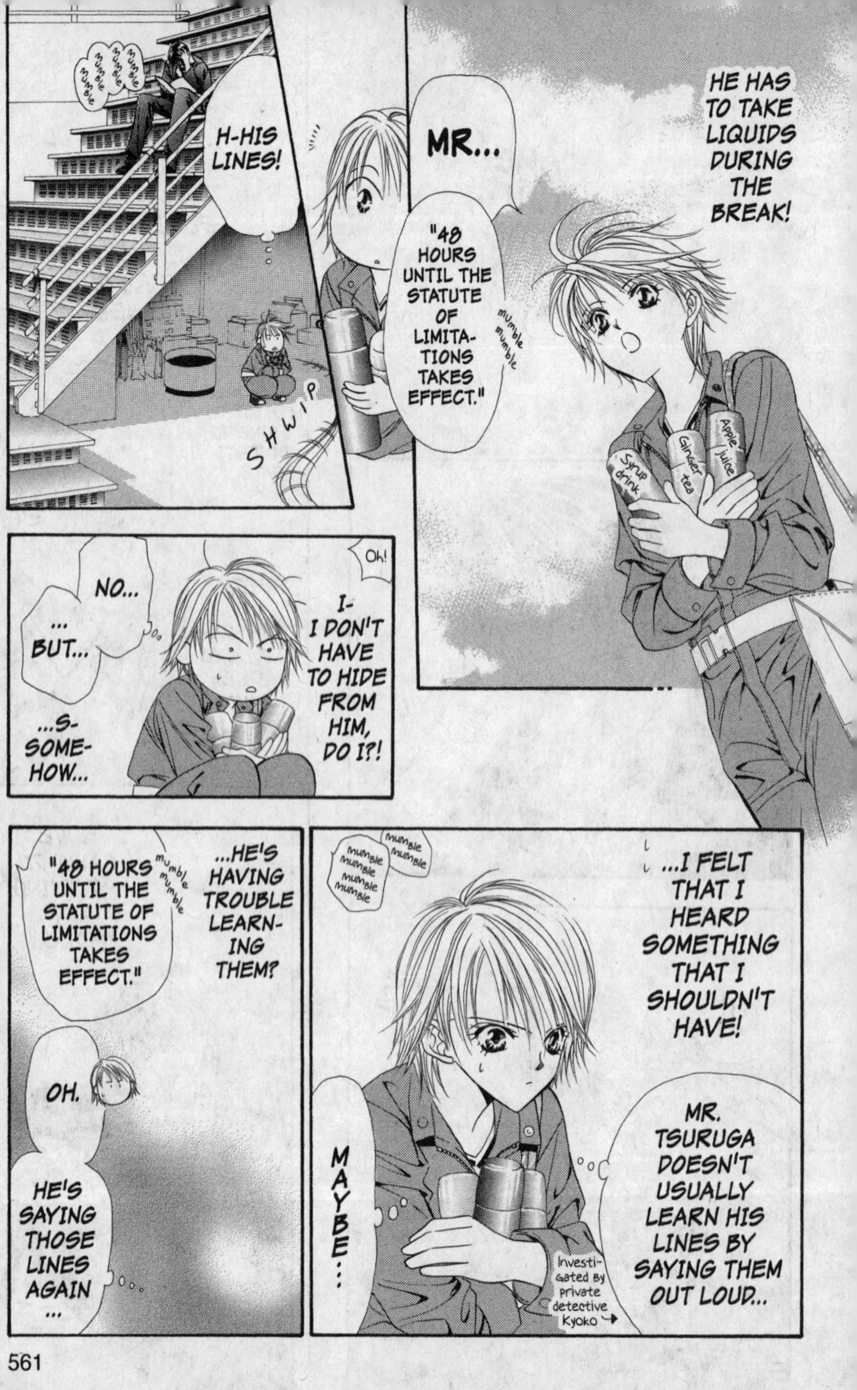

HE HAS TO TAKE LIQUIDS DURING THE BREAK!
Apple juice
Ginger tea
Syrup drink
MR...
"48 HOURS UNTIL THE STATUTE OF LIMITATIONS TAKES EFFECT."
mumble mumble
mumble mumble mumble mumble
H-HIS LINES!
SHWIP
Oh!
I- I DON'T HAVE TO HIDE FROM HIM, DO I?!
NO...
...BUT...
...S-SOMEHOW...
mumble mumble
mumble mumble mumble mumble
...I FELT THAT I HEARD SOMETHING THAT I SHOULDN'T HAVE!
MR. TSURUGA DOESN'T USUALLY LEARN HIS LINES BY SAYING THEM OUT LOUD...
MAYBE...
Investigated by private detective Kyoko
"48 HOURS UNTIL THE STATUTE OF LIMITATIONS TAKES EFFECT."
mumble mumble
...HE'S HAVING TROUBLE LEARNING THEM?
OH.
HE'S SAYING THOSE LINES AGAIN...

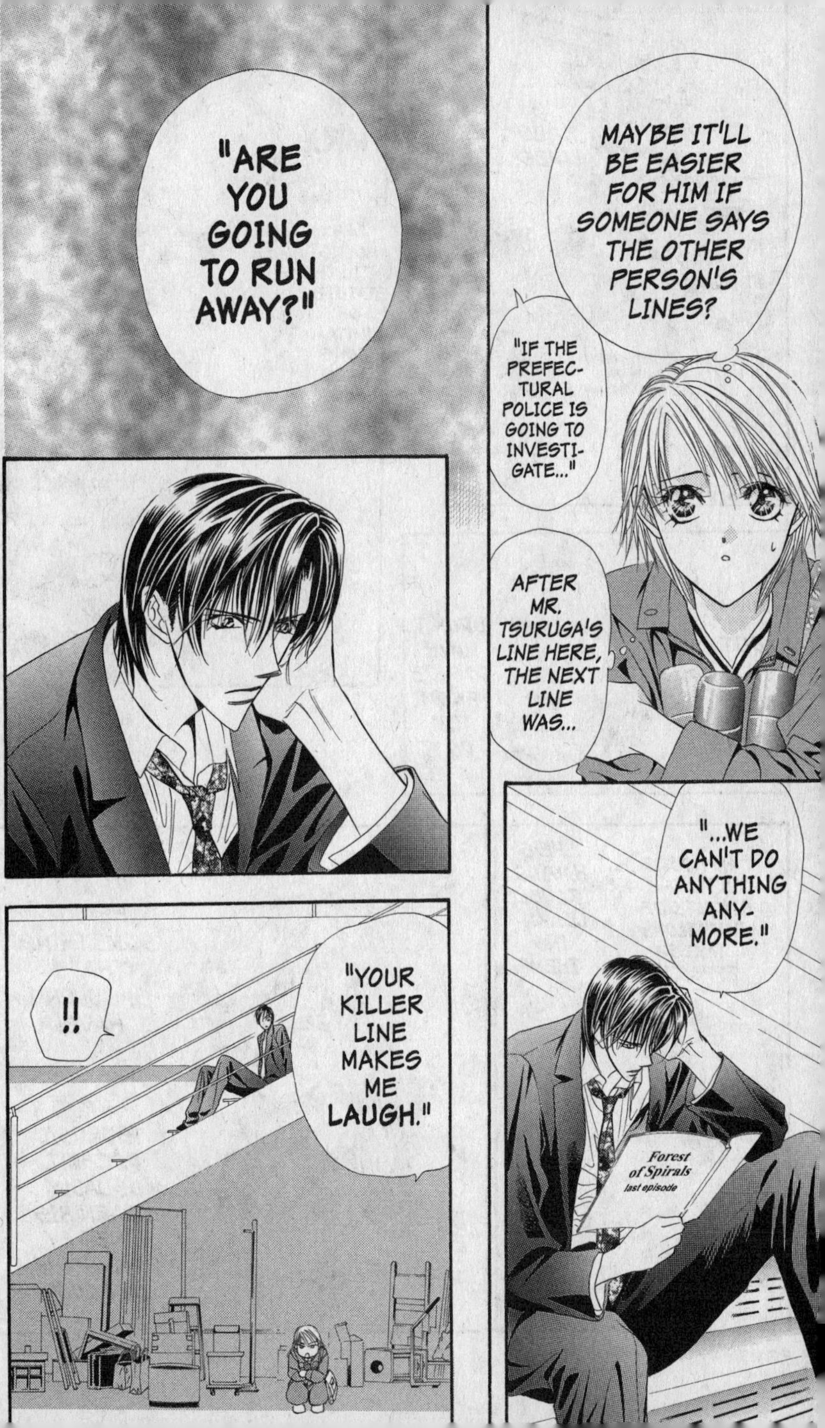
MAYBE IT'LL BE EASIER FOR HIM IF SOMEONE SAYS THE OTHER PERSON'S LINES?
"IF THE PREFECTURAL POLICE IS GOING TO INVESTIGATE..."
AFTER MR. TSURUGA'S LINE HERE, THE NEXT LINE WAS...
"...WE CAN'T DO ANYTHING ANYMORE."
Forest of Spirals
last episode
"ARE YOU GOING TO RUN AWAY?"
"YOUR KILLER LINE MAKES ME LAUGH."
!!

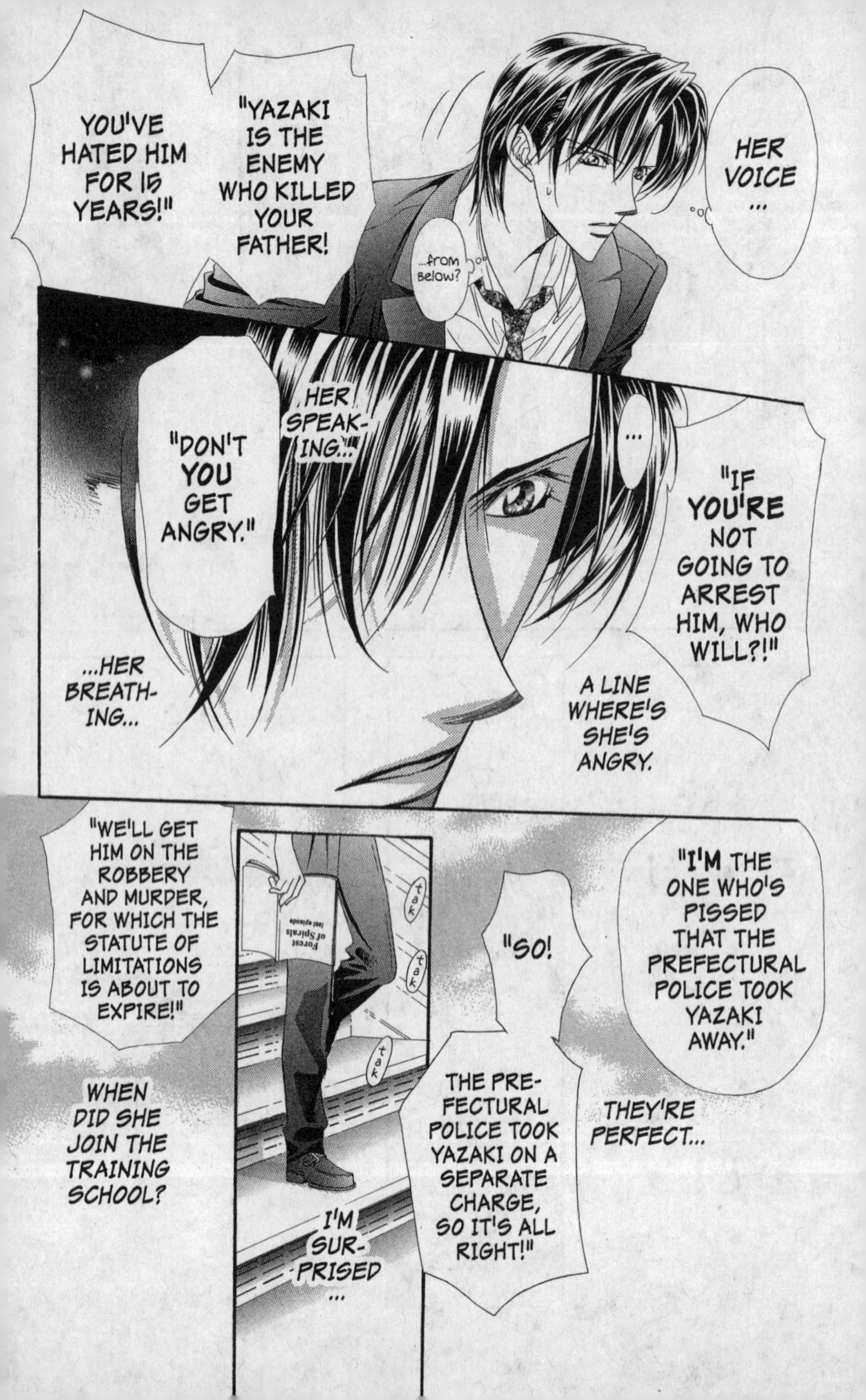
HER VOICE ...
...from below?
"YAZAKI IS THE ENEMY WHO KILLED YOUR FATHER!
YOU'VE HATED HIM FOR 15 YEARS!"
...
"IF YOU'RE NOT GOING TO ARREST HIM, WHO WILL?!"
A LINE WHERE'S SHE'S ANGRY.
HER SPEAKING...
"DON'T YOU GET ANGRY."
...HER BREATHING...
"I'M THE ONE WHO'S PISSED THAT THE PREFECTURAL POLICE TOOK YAZAKI AWAY."
"SO!
THEY'RE PERFECT...
THE PREFECTURAL POLICE TOOK YAZAKI ON A SEPARATE CHARGE, SO IT'S ALL RIGHT!"
I'M SURPRISED ...
tak
tak
tak
Forest of Spirals last episode
"WE'LL GET HIM ON THE ROBBERY AND MURDER, FOR WHICH THE STATUTE OF LIMITATIONS IS ABOUT TO EXPIRE!"
WHEN DID SHE JOIN THE TRAINING SCHOOL?

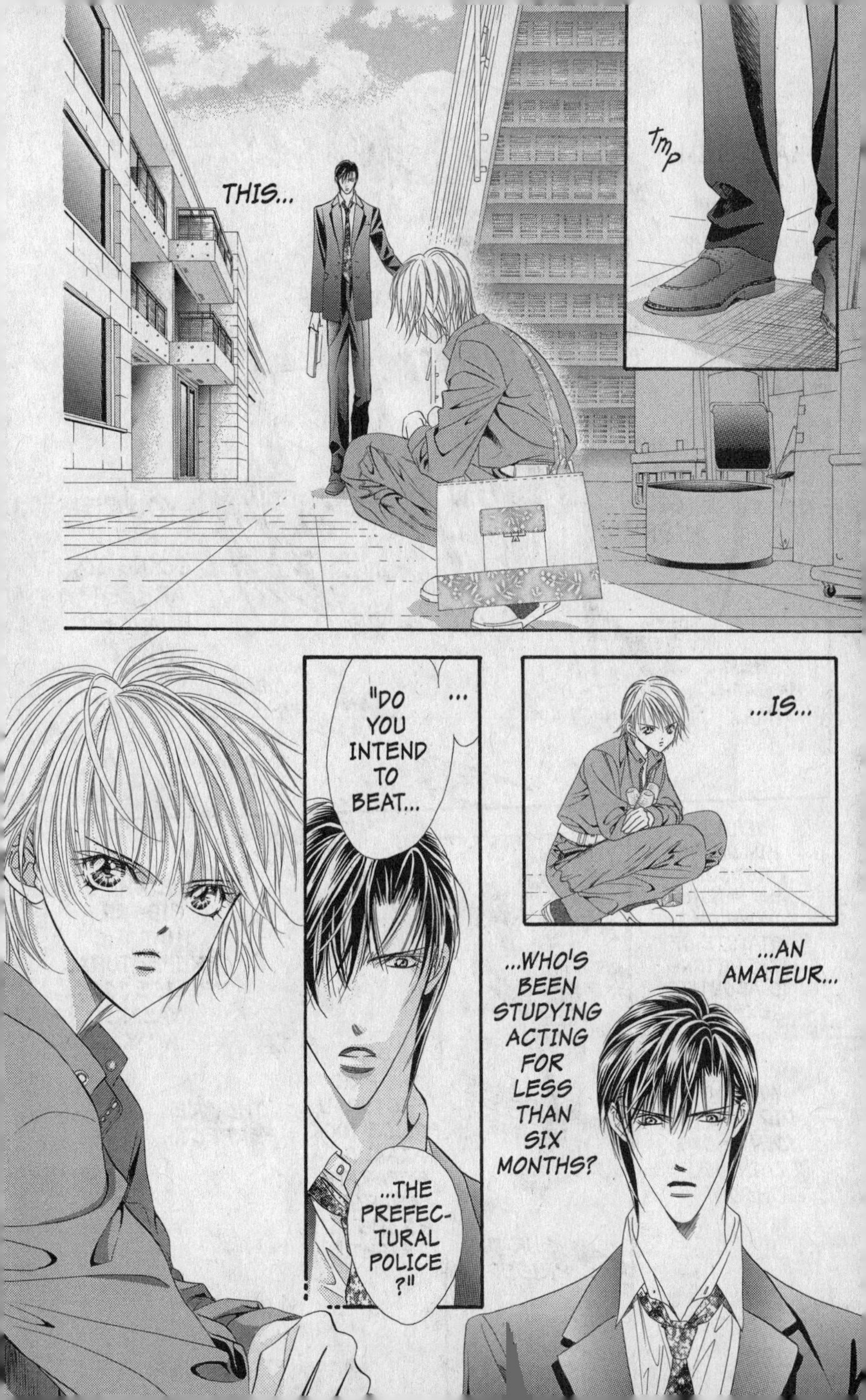
tmp
THIS...
...IS...
...AN AMATEUR...
...WHO'S BEEN STUDYING ACTING FOR LESS THAN SIX MONTHS?
...
"DO YOU INTEND TO BEAT...
...THE PREFECTURAL POLICE?"

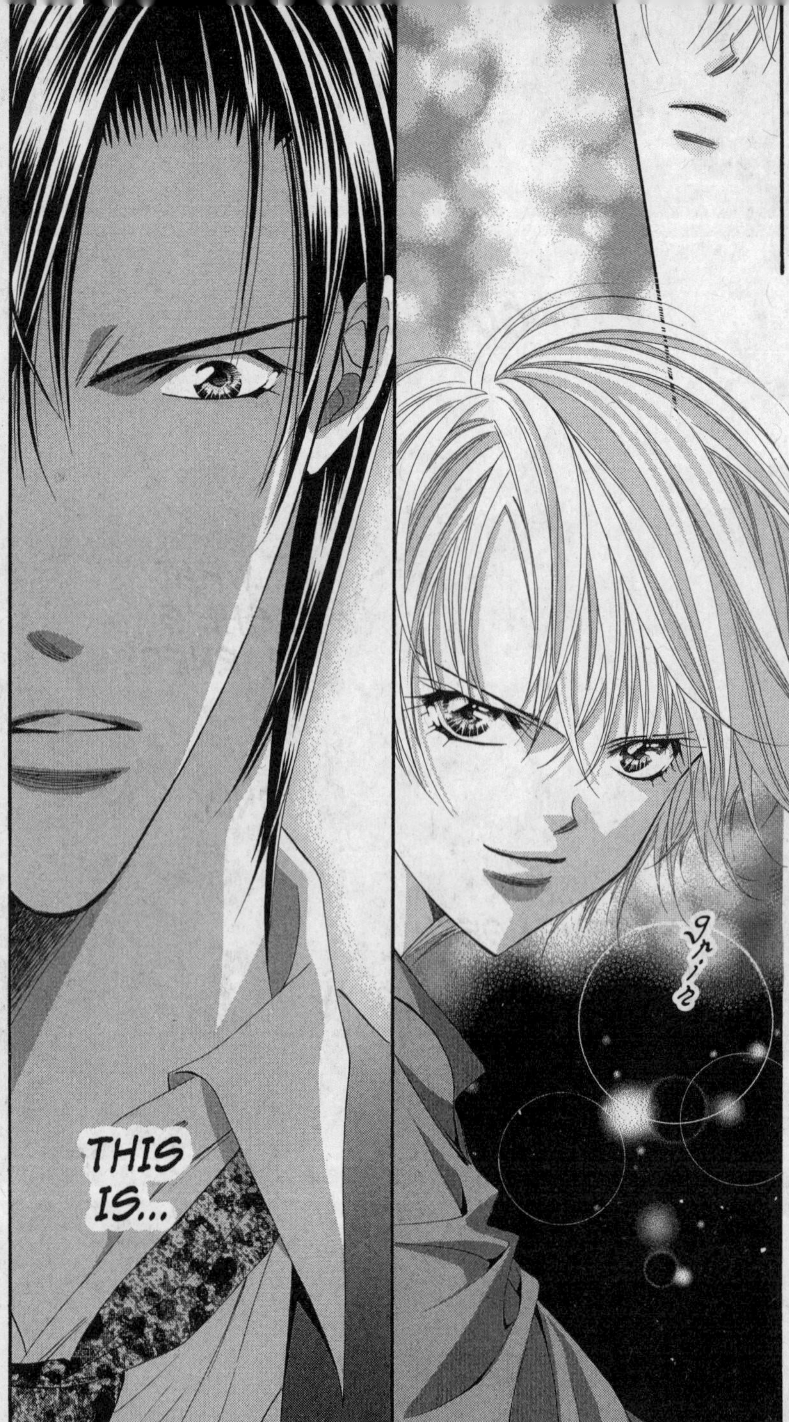
grin
THIS IS...

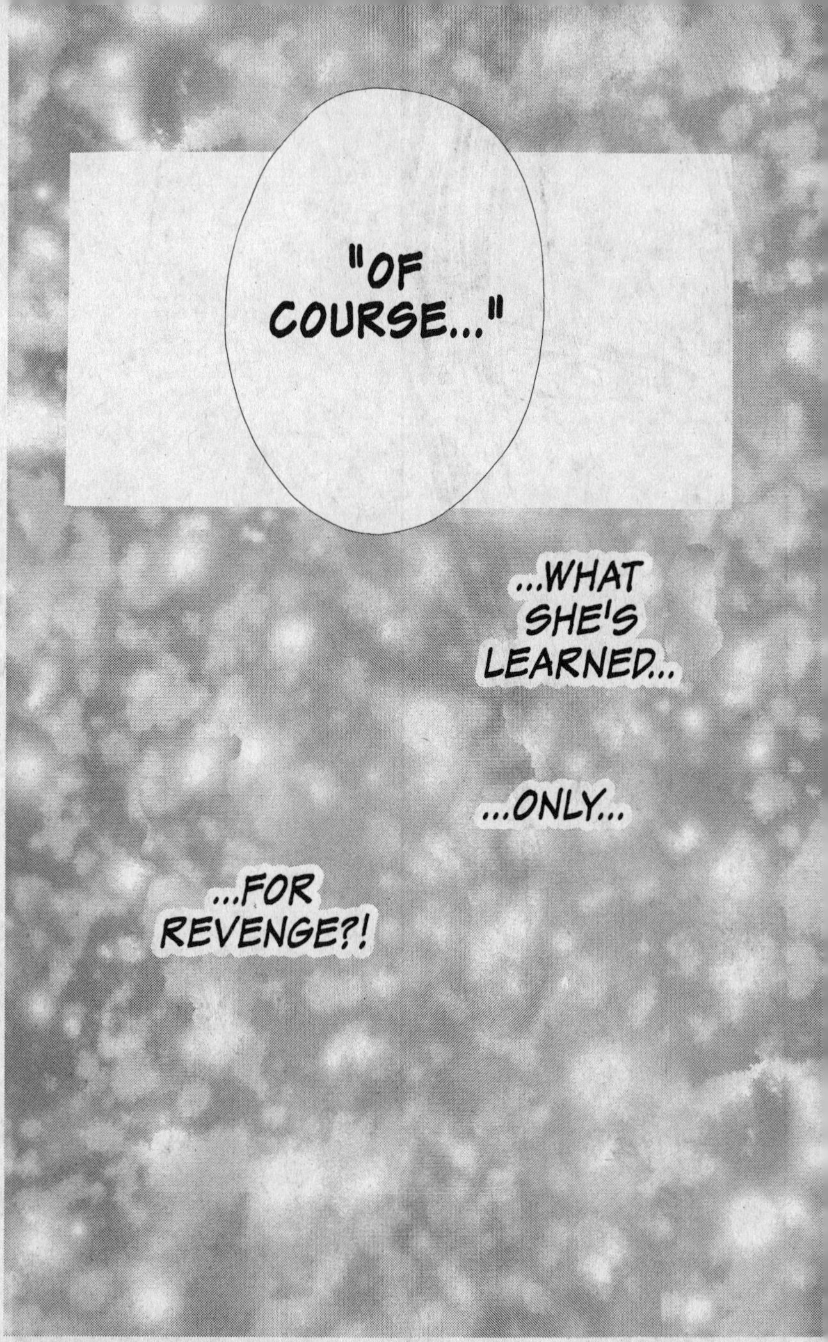

End of Act 35

Skip-Beat! End Notes
Everyone knows how to be a fan, but sometimes cool things
from other cultures need a little help crossing the language barrier.

Page 389, sidebar: Yanki
A slang term for teen gangs of delinquents, bikers and dropouts. The word
probably originates from the American "Yankee" GIs, who brought their
love of rock 'n' roll and rebellion to Japan.

Page 433, panel 3-4: Not attending school
Unlike in the U.S., compulsory education in Japan stops at middle school.
Students are not required to go to high school, although it is still socially
encouraged.

Page 439, panel 6: Daimane
Short for *dairi manager*, or substitute manager.

Page 463, panel 1: Hamburger steak
Japanese hamburgers are closer to Salisbury steak or meatloaf than the
hamburgers Americans are used to. The ground meat is mixed with bread
crumbs, egg, sautéed onions and soy sauce and served on a plate rather
than a bun. Sometimes the hamburger is topped with a fried egg.

Page 467, panel 2: My life was totally dark
This is probably a parody of the hit song by Keiko Fuji (mother of pop
singer Hikaru Utada), which goes "When I was 15, 16, 17 my life was
gloomy."

Page 508, panel 3: Spacicicious
The original Japanese phrase is *Fushin kiwaramai naiwa*, which means "It
is extremely suspicious." Yumiko pronounces it *Fushin kimawari naiwa* in
Japanese.

Page 529, sidebar: Hiepita
A cooling gel pack used to reduce the effects of a fever.

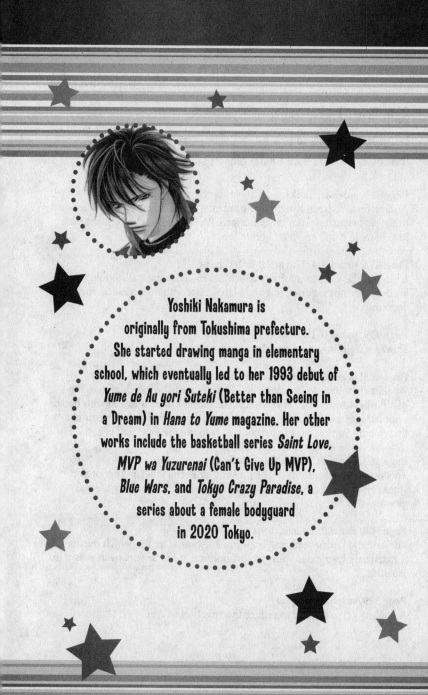

Yoshiki Nakamura is
originally from Tokushima prefecture.
She started drawing manga in elementary
school, which eventually led to her 1993 debut of
Yume de Au yori Suteki (Better than Seeing in
a Dream) in *Hana to Yume* magazine. Her other
works include the basketball series *Saint Love,
MVP wa Yuzurenai* (Can't Give Up MVP),
Blue Wars, and *Tokyo Crazy Paradise,* a
series about a female bodyguard
in 2020 Tokyo.

SKIP·BEAT!

3-in-1 Edition

Vol. 2

A compilation of graphic novel volumes 4-6

STORY AND ART BY YOSHIKI NAKAMURA

English Translation & Adaptation/Tomo Kimura
Touch-up Art & Lettering/Sabrina Heep
Design/Yukiko Whitley
Editor/Pancha Diaz

Printed in the U.S.A.

Published by VIZ Media, LLC
P.O. Box 77010
San Francisco, CA 94107

www.viz.com
www.shojobeat.com

10 9 8 7 6 5
3-in-1 edition first printing, May 2012
Fifth printing, April 2017

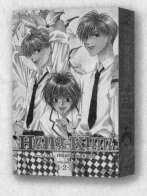 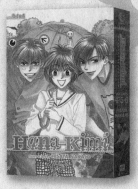 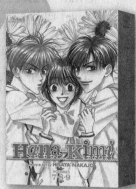

Don't Hide What's *Inside*

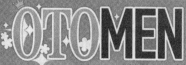
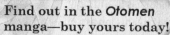
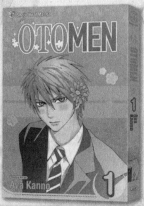
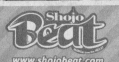

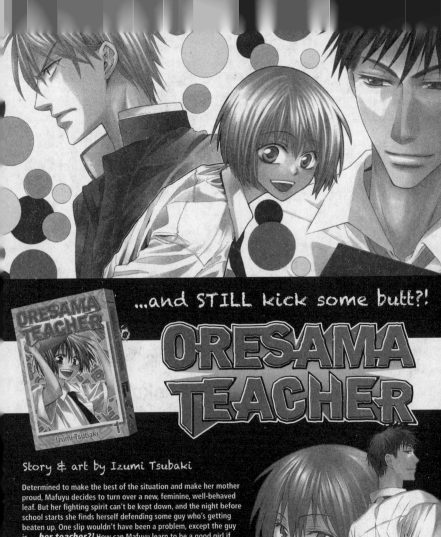

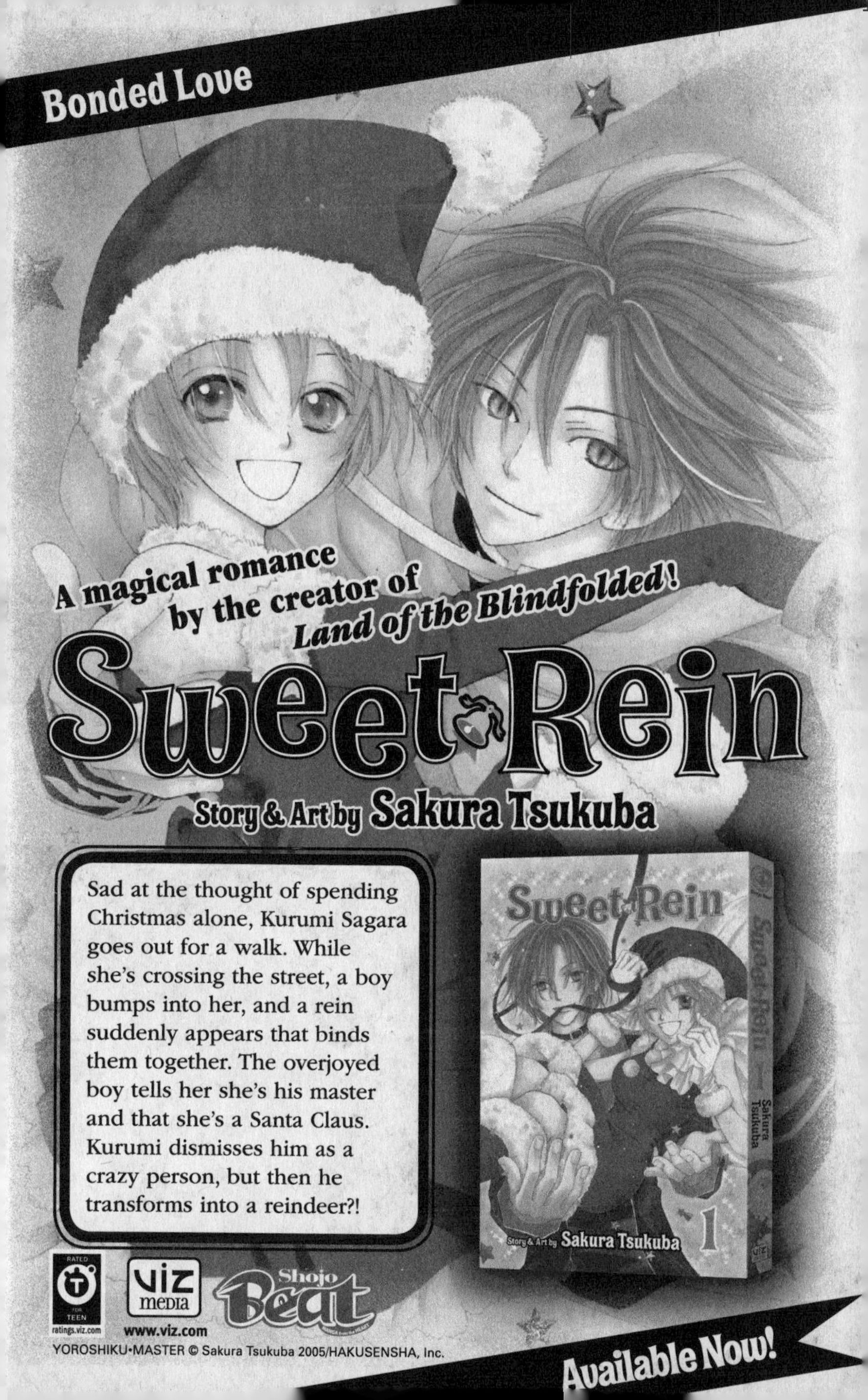

Bonded Love
A magical romance by the creator of Land of the Blindfolded!
Sweet Rein
Story & Art by Sakura Tsukuba
Sad at the thought of spending Christmas alone, Kurumi Sagara goes out for a walk. While she's crossing the street, a boy bumps into her, and a rein suddenly appears that binds them together. The overjoyed boy tells her she's his master and that she's a Santa Claus. Kurumi dismisses him as a crazy person, but then he transforms into a reindeer?!
Sweet Rein
Story & Art by Sakura Tsukuba
1
RATED T FOR TEEN
ratings.viz.com
VIZ media
Shojo Beat
www.viz.com
YOROSHIKU•MASTER © Sakura Tsukuba 2005/HAKUSENSHA, Inc.
Available Now!

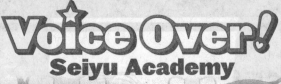

SURPRISE!

You may be reading the wrong way!

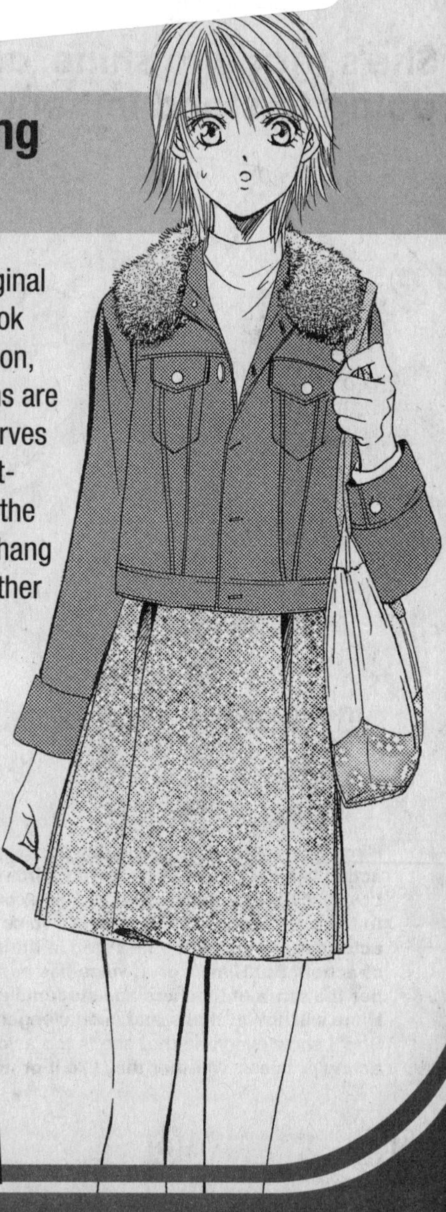

It's true: In keeping with the original Japanese comic format, this book reads from right to left—so action, sound effects, and word balloons are completely reversed. This preserves the orientation of the original artwork—plus, it's fun! Check out the diagram shown here to get the hang of things, and then turn to the other side of the book to get started!

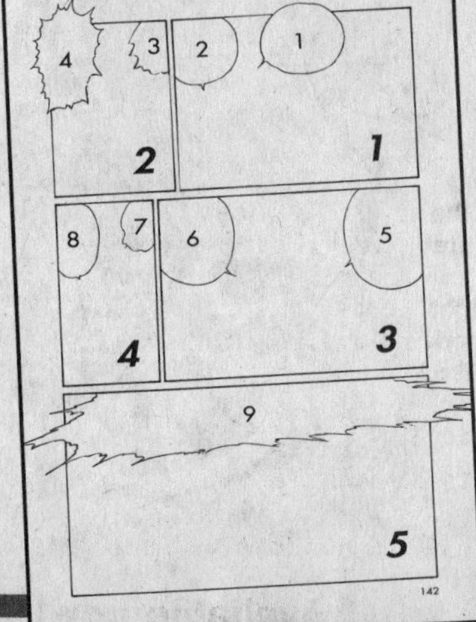
1
2
1
3
4
2
5
6
3
7
8
4
9
5
142